Lecture Notes in Computer Science

Lecture Notes in Artificial Intelligence 16949

Founding Editor

Jörg Siekmann

The series Lecture Notes in Artificial Intelligence (LNAI) was established in 1988 as a topical subseries of LNCS devoted to artificial intelligence.

The series publishes state-of-the-art research results at a high level. As with the LNCS mother series, the mission of the series is to serve the international R & D community by providing an invaluable service, mainly focused on the publication of conference and workshop proceedings and postproceedings.

Mitra Baratchi · Francesco Bonchi ·
Riccardo Guidotti · Francesco Gullo ·
Peter Flach · Giuseppe Manco ·
Myra Spiliopoulou · Elio Masciari
Editors

Machine Learning and Knowledge Discovery in Databases

Applied Data Science Track

European Conference, ECML PKDD 2026
Naples, Italy, September 7–11, 2026
Proceedings, Part IX

Springer

Editors
Mitra Baratchi
Leiden University
Leiden, The Netherlands

Francesco Bonchi
Intesa Sanpaolo AI Research
Turin, Italy

Riccardo Guidotti
University of Pisa
Pisa, Italy

Francesco Gullo
University of L'Aquila
L'Aquila, Italy

Peter Flach
University of Bristol
Bristol, UK

Giuseppe Manco
ICAR-CNR
Rende, Italy

Myra Spiliopoulou
Otto von Guericke University Magdeburg
Magdeburg, Germany

Elio Masciari
University of Naples Federico II
Naples, Italy

ISSN 0302-9743 ISSN 1611-3349 (electronic)
Lecture Notes in Artificial Intelligence
ISBN 978-3-032-37681-7 ISBN 978-3-032-37682-4 (eBook)
https://doi.org/10.1007/978-3-032-37682-4

LNCS Sublibrary: SL7 – Artificial Intelligence

This Springer imprint is published by the registered company Springer Nature Switzerland AG
The registered company address is: Gewerbestrasse 11, 6330 Cham, Switzerland

Preface

The 2026 edition of the European Conference on Machine Learning and Principles and Practice of Knowledge Discovery in Databases (ECML PKDD 2026) was held in Naples, Italy from September 7 to 11, 2026.

The annual ECML PKDD conference is a premier worldwide platform dedicated to showcasing the latest advancements and fostering insightful discussions in the fields of machine learning and knowledge discovery in databases. Held jointly since 2001, ECML PKDD has firmly established its reputation as the leading European conference in these disciplines. It provides researchers and practitioners with an unparalleled opportunity to exchange knowledge, share innovative ideas, and explore the latest technical advancements. The conference particularly values the synergy between foundational theoretical advances and groundbreaking practical data science applications, actively encouraging contributions that demonstrate how Machine Learning and Data Mining are being effectively employed to address complex real-world challenges. Over the years, technologies evolve, and the needs of the individuals, society and the world change. ECML PKDD remains committed to the presentation of cutting-edge research that reflects this evolution.

The Naples edition of ECML PKDD was a truly special one, marked both by an exceptionally high number of scientific contributions and by an outstanding level of participation from the industrial community. The remarkable response from researchers, practitioners, and companies reflects the growing relevance of machine learning, data mining, and artificial intelligence across both academic and industrial domains. In particular, the significant engagement of leading companies and technology stakeholders further strengthened the dialogue between research and real-world applications, making this edition a vibrant meeting point for scientific excellence, innovation, and industrial impact.

The Conference Tracks

The three middle days of the conference were organized in the following tracks:

- The **Research Track** received the impressive number of 1,150 full paper submissions, going for the first time above the 1,000 submissions mark, and an absolute increase of more than 200 submissions over the previous edition, which also had a substantial increase in submissions; of these submissions, 280 were accepted, demonstrating a highly competitive acceptance rate of 24.3%. The review process was double blind, and submissions received three reviews each on average.

- The **Applied Data Science Track** received 381 submissions, of which 90 were accepted. This resulted in a similar acceptance rate of 23.6%. The review process was double blind, and submissions received 3.9 reviews each on average.
- The **Journal Track** received 213 submissions, of which 34 papers were accepted in the Machine Learning Journal and 24 in the Data Mining and Knowledge Discovery Journal, while 7 papers are still under review.
- The **Nectar Track** solicited submissions of summaries of recently published, impactful scientific papers presenting advances at the forefront of machine learning and data mining, as well as their applications in other disciplines. This track received 26 submissions.
- The **Demo Track** solicited submissions that showcase practical applications and prototypes; it received 38 submissions, with 27 accepted demo papers. The review process was single blind, and submissions received two reviews each on average.
- The **Industrial Track** received a record of 42 submissions, 21 of which were accepted for presentation at the conference. The review process was single blind, and submissions received three reviews each on average.

The Keynotes

ECML PKDD 2026 featured five keynote talks by internationally leading experts, one on each day of the conference in this order:

- **Mihaela van der Schaar** (University of Cambridge) spoke on *Rethinking the Role of Scientific Discovery in the Era of AI*. She presented a framework that rethinks discovery as an agentic process, in which networks of interacting AI agents and human experts jointly explore, critique, and refine hypotheses under shared norms of evaluation.
- **Stefanie Jegelka** (Technical University of Munich) explored the link between *Neural Networks and Algorithms*. She argued that an algorithmic view can help understand not only the capabilities of deep learning models, such as self-correction or the ability to solve certain optimization problems, but also how to design and train models to better solve challenging tasks, from optimization problems to reasoning.
- **Sihem Amer-Yahia** (CNRS and Laboratoire d'Informatique de Grenoble) gave a keynote entitled *From Dialogue to Decision: Orchestrating Agents for Conversational Data Exploration and Multi-Objective Optimization* in which she investigated the intersection of conversational data exploration, an incremental process where agents help users articulate needs through data interaction, and multi-objective sequential decision making.
- **Francesca Rossi** (Thomas J. Watson IBM Research Center) spoke on key issues around *AI ethics and governance* and how they have evolved with the dramatically increased AI capabilities of today. She also discussed instrumental and value-based approaches which make investing in AI ethics and governance worthwhile.

- **Gianni Riotta** (Luiss University) presented his perspective under the title *The AI Ghosts and Us: Machine Writing as a Spectral Culture*. He advocated a radically new philosophical reading of AI-generated text as a "Ghost" inhabiting contemporary human discourse, and argued that machine writing constitutes a spectral hybrid: neither fully human nor purely artificial, but a liminal presence emerging from the archive of human language.

Scholarships

We awarded 10 scholarship grants of 1,000 EUR each to students and early-career researchers.

Acknowledgements

We want to thank the authors, organizing committee, workshop and tutorial organizers, and participants whose scientific contributions made this such an exciting event.

We are greatly indebted to the reviewers and senior reviewers: their dedication, vigilance, and enormous time investment made it possible to manage the large number of submissions, ensure the high quality for which ECML PKDD is known, and put together an outstanding conference program. A special thanks goes to the emergency reviewers who finished the last missing reviews at short notice.

This large event would not have run smoothly without the many volunteers and sessions chairs. Finally, we want to express our heartfelt gratitude to all the local organizers – they dealt with all the little details that were needed to make the conference a memorable event.

We want to cordially thank our sponsors for their generous financial support. We also want to thank Springer for their continuous support and Microsoft for allowing us to use their CMT software for conference management and for providing help throughout. We very much appreciate the advice and guidance provided by the ECML PKDD Steering Committee from the moment the organization of the 2026 edition started.

September 2026

Elio Masciari
Peter Flach
Giuseppe Manco
Myra Spiliopoulou
General Chairs

Michelangelo Ceci
Dragi Kocev
Anna Monreale
Celine Vens
Research Track Chairs

Mitra Baratchi
Francesco Bonchi
Riccardo Guidotti
Francesco Gullo
Applied Data Science Track Chairs

Paolo Mignone
Mouzhi Ge
Vincenzo Moscato
Demo Track Chairs

Chiara Celsi
Ruggero G. Pensa
Fabrizio Silvestri
Industrial Track Chairs

Organization

General Chairs

Peter Flach	University of Bristol, UK
Giuseppe Manco	ICAR-CNR, Italy
Elio Masciari	University of Naples Federico II, Italy
Myra Spiliopoulou	Otto von Guericke University Magdeburg, Germany

Research Track Chairs

Michelangelo Ceci	University of Bari Aldo Moro, Italy
Dragi Kocev	Jožef Stefan Institute, Slovenia
Anna Monreale	University of Pisa, Italy
Celine Vens	KU Leuven, Belgium

Applied Data Science Track Chairs

Mitra Baratchi	Leiden University, Netherlands
Francesco Bonchi	Intesa Sanpaolo AI Research, Italy
Riccardo Guidotti	University of Pisa, Italy
Francesco Gullo	University of L'Aquila, Italy

Journal Track Chairs

Zahraa S. Abdallah	University of Bristol, UK
Annalisa Appice	University of Bari Aldo Moro, Italy
Przemysław Biecek	Warsaw University of Technology, Poland
Andrea Tagarelli	University of Calabria, Italy

Industrial Track Chairs

Chiara Celsi — Deloitte Italy, Italy
Ruggero G. Pensa — University of Turin, Italy
Fabrizio Silvestri — Sapienza University of Rome, Italy

Workshop Chairs

Dino Ienco — INRAE, Inria, UMR TETIS, University of Montpellier, France
Gianvito Pio — University of Bari Aldo Moro, Italy

Tutorial Chairs

Antonio Maria Rinaldi — University of Naples Federico II, Italy
Cristiano Russo — University of Naples Federico II, Italy

Nectar Track Chairs

Aniello Murano — University of Naples Federico II, Italy
Chiara Renso — ISTI-CNR, Italy
Salvo Rinzivillo — ISTI-CNR, Italy

PhD Forum Chairs

Giuseppina Andresini — University of Bari Aldo Moro, Italy
Silvia Rossi — University of Naples Federico II, Italy

Awards Committee Chairs

Sergio Di Martino — University of Naples Federico II, Italy
Donato Malerba — University of Bari Aldo Moro, Italy
Carlo Sansone — University of Naples Federico II, Italy

Proceedings Chairs

Irena Koprinska	University of Sydney, Australia
Angelica Liguori	ICAR-CNR, Italy
Eliana Pastor	Politecnico di Torino, Italy

Diversity and Inclusion Chairs

Esma Aimeur	Université de Montréal, Canada
Flora Amato	University of Naples Federico II, Italy
Christine Markarian	University of Dubai, United Arab Emirates
Rosa Meo	University of Turin, Italy

Demo Chairs

Paolo Mignone	Università Pegaso, Italy
Mouzhi Ge	Deggendorf Institute of Technology, Germany
Vincenzo Moscato	University of Naples Federico II, Italy

Discovery Challenge Chairs

Mark Cotè	King's College London, UK
Stefano Marrone	University of Naples Federico II, Italy
Roberto Trasarti	ISTI-CNR, Italy

Panel Chairs

Massimo Bernaschi	IAC-CNR, Italy
Luca Caviglione	IMATI-CNR, Italy

Publicity Chairs

Roberto Interdonato	Cirad, Inria, UMR TETIS, Montpellier, France
Enea Vincenzo Napolitano	University of Naples Federico II, Italy
Vincenzo Pasquadibisceglie	University of Bari Aldo Moro, Italy

Senior Sponsors Chairs

Mariam Barry	BNP Paribas, France
Robert Jan van Wijk	ASML, Netherlands

Local Sponsors Chairs

Antonino Ferraro	Pegaso University, Italy
Simona Fioretto	University of Naples Federico II, Italy
Cristian Tommasino	University of Naples Federico II, Italy

Web, Social Media and Conference App Chairs

Michela Gravina	University of Naples Federico II, Italy
Simone Mungari	ICAR-CNR, Revelis s.r.l., Italy
Franca Rocco di Torrepadula	University of Naples Federico II, Italy

CMT Chairs

Antonio Galli	University of Naples Federico II, Italy
Giancarlo Sperlì	University of Naples Federico II, Italy

Whova App and Slides Chair

Giuseppe Papuzzo	ICAR-CNR, Italy

Steering Committee

Tijl De Bie	Ghent University, Belgium
Albert Bifet	University of Waikato, New Zealand - Télécom Paris, France
Francesco Bonchi	Intesa Sanpaolo AI Research, Italy
Ilaria Bordino	UniCredit, Italy
Saso Dzeroski	Jožef Stefan Institute, Slovenia
Ioanna Miliou	Stockholm University, Sweden
Siegfried Nijssen	KU Leuven, Belgium

Andrea Passerini	University of Trento, Italy
Robert Jan van Wijk	ASML, the Netherlands
Wenbin Zhang	Florida International University, USA
Albrecht Zimmermann	Université de Caen Normandie, France
Elena Baralis	Politecnico di Torino, Italy
Claudia Plant	Universität Wien, Austria
Manuel Gomez Rodriguez	Max Planck Institute for Software Systems, Germany
Jesse Davis	KU Leuven, Belgium
Tomas Krilavičius	Vytautas Magnus University, Lithuania
Panagiotis Papapetrou	Stockholm University, Sweden
Myra Spiliopoulou	Otto-von-Guericke University Magdeburg, Germany
Pedro Henriques Abreu	University of Coimbra, CISUC, Portugal
João Gama	University of Porto, INESC-TEC, Portugal
Sepideh Pashami	Halmstad University, Sweden
Rita P. Ribeiro	University of Porto, INESC TEC, Portugal

Program Committee

Area Chairs, Applied Data Science Track

Pedro Henriques Abreu	CISUC, Portugal
Tiago Almeida	Federal University of São Carlos, Brazil
Annalisa Appice	University of Bari Aldo Moro, Italy
Anthony Bagnall	University of Southampton, UK
Gustavo Batista	University of New South Wales, Australia
Jessa Bekker	KU Leuven, Belgium
Bettina Berendt	TU Berlin, Germany
Concha Bielza	Universidad Politécnica de Madrid, Spain
Albert Bifet	University of Waikato, New Zealand
Hendrik Blockeel	KU Leuven, Belgium
Henrik Boström	KTH Royal Institute of Technology, Sweden
Zied Bouraoui	CRIL CNRS & University of Artois, France
Ulf Brefeld	Leuphana University of Lüneburg, Germany
Toon Calders	University of Antwerp, Belgium
Jesús Cerquides	IIIA-CSIC, Spain
Sara Colantonio	Institute of Information Science and Technologies of the National Research Council of Italy, Italy
Roberto Corizzo	American University, USA
Fabrizio Costa	University of Exeter, UK

Jesse Davis	KU Leuven, Belgium
Tom Diethe	AstraZeneca/University of Bristol, UK
Wouter Duivesteijn	Eindhoven University of Technology, Netherlands
Tome Eftimov	Jožef Stefan Institute, Slovenia
Sophie Fellenz	RPTU Kaiserslautern-Landau, Germany
Stefano Ferilli	University of Bari Aldo Moro, Italy
Cèsar Ferri	Universitat Politècnica de València, Spain
Eibe Frank	University of Waikato, New Zealand
Elisa Fromont	Université Rennes, IRISA/Inria, France
Johannes Fürnkranz	Johannes Kepler University Linz, Austria
Esther Galbrun	University of Eastern Finland, Finland
Pierre Geurts	University of Liège, Belgium
Aristides Gionis	KTH Royal Institute of Technology, Sweden
Chen Gong	Nanjing University of Science and Technology, China
Barbara Hammer	Bielefeld University, Germany
Jose Hernandez-Orallo	Universitat Politècnica de València/University of Cambridge, Spain/UK
Sibylle Hess	Eindhoven University of Technology, Netherlands
Georgiana Ifrim	University College Dublin, Ireland
Manfred Jaeger	Aalborg University, Denmark
Nathalie Japkowicz	American University, USA
Szymon Jaroszewicz	Polish Academy of Sciences, Poland
Adam Jatowt	University of Innsbruck, Austria
Ioannis Katakis	University of Nicosia, Cyprus
Megha Khosla	TU Delft, Netherlands
Marius Kloft	RPTU Kaiserslautern-Landau, Germany
Arno Knobbe	Leiden University, Netherlands
Danai Koutra	University of Michigan, USA
Petra Kralj Novak	Central European University, Austria
Niels Landwehr	University of Hildesheim, Germany
Pedro Larranaga	Universidad Politécnica de Madrid, Spain
Mark Last	Ben-Gurion University of the Negev, Israel
Jefrey Lijffijt	Ghent University, Belgium
Jessica Lin	George Mason University, USA
Ana Carolina Lorena	Instituto Tecnológico de Aeronáutica, Brazil
Jörg Lücke	Universität Innsbruck, Austria
Xiao Luo	University of Wisconsin–Madison, USA
Michael Madden	University of Galway, Ireland
Donato Malerba	University of Bari Aldo Moro, Italy
Fragkiskos Malliaros	CentraleSupélec, France
Ernestina Menasalvas	Universidad Politécnica de Madrid, Spain

Jilles Vreeken	CISPA Helmholtz Center for Information Security, Germany
Willem Waegeman	Ghent University, Belgium
Jörg Wicker	University of Auckland, New Zealand
Wei Ye	Tongji University, China
Wenbin Zhang	Florida International University, USA
Indre Zliobaite	University of Helsinki, Finland

Program Committee, Applied Data Science Track

Kamil Adamczewski	Max Planck Institute for Intelligent Systems, Germany
Timilehin Aderinola	Insight Research Ireland Centre for Data Analytics, University College Dublin, Ireland
Linara Adilova	RC Trust, Germany
Stergos Afantenos	Université de Toulouse, France
Juba Agoun	Université Lumière Lyon 2, France
Azim Ahmadzadeh	University of Missouri - St. Louis, USA
Deepak Ajwani	University College Dublin, Ireland
Reza Akbarinia	Inria, France
Esra Akbas	Georgia State University, USA
Cuneyt Akcora	University of Central Florida, USA
Youhei Akimoto	University of Tsukuba/RIKEN AIP, Japan
Ozge Alacam	Ludwig-Maximilians-Universität München, Germany
Tahani Aladwani	University of Glasgow, UK
Dima Alberg	SCE Shamoon College of Engineering, Israel
Fayad Ali Banna	Laboratoire Hubert Curien, France
Benjamin Allaert	IMT Nord Europe, France
Simeon Allmendinger	University of Bayreuth, Germany
Sarra Alqahtani	Wake Forest University, USA
Jose Alvarez	Santander AI Lab, Spain
Ehsan Aminian	INESC TEC, Portugal
Christos Anagnostopoulos	University of Glasgow, UK
Giuseppina Andresini	University of Bari Aldo Moro, Italy
Piotr Andruszkiewicz	Warsaw University of Technology, Poland
Ekaterina Antonenko	Mines Paris - PSL, France
Alessandro Antonucci	IDSIA, Switzerland
Nelson Antunes	University of Algarve and University of Lisbon, Portugal
Edward Apeh	Bournemouth University, UK
Pasquale Ardimento	University of Bari Aldo Moro, Italy

Benedikt Blumenstiel	IBM Research, USA
Martin Bobak	Institute of Informatics, Slovak Academy of Sciences, Slovakia
Tyler Bonnet	Imperial College London, UK
Ludovico Boratto	University of Cagliari, Italy
Manuel Borja	Ghent University, Belgium
Stefano Bortoli	Microblink, Italy
Annelot Bosman	Leiden University, Netherlands
Lydia Boudjeloud-Assala	Université de Lorraine, CNRS, LORIA, France
Sara Bouguelia	Université Lumière Lyon 2, France
Veranika Boukun	Carl von Ossietzky Universität Oldenburg, Germany
Louenas Bounia	LIPN - Université Sorbonne Paris Nord, France
Antoine Boutet	INSA-Lyon, Inria, France
Mohamed-el-Amine Brahmia	CESI LINEACT, France
Susana Brás	IEETA, Portugal
Murat Bronz	ENAC, France
Dariusz Brzezinski	Poznań University of Technology, Poland
Maria Sofia Bucarelli	CNRS, Inria, I3S, France
Florian Büttner	DKFZ, Germany
Davide Buscaldi	Université Sorbonne Paris Nord, France
Sebastian Buschjäger	Lamarr Institute for ML and AI, Germany
Veronica Buttaro	University of Bari Aldo Moro, Italy
Guénaël Cabanes	Université de Lorraine, France
Paul Caillon	LAMSADE Université Paris Dauphine - PSL, France
Erik Calcina	Jožef Stefan Institute, Slovenia
Ricardo Campello	University of Southern Denmark, Denmark
Giuseppe Casalicchio	Ludwig-Maximilians-Universität München, Germany
Elena Casiraghi	University of Milan, Italy
Giovanna Castellano	University of Bari Aldo Moro, Italy
Remzi Celebi	Maastricht University, Netherlands
Andrea Ceni	University of Pisa, Italy
Vitor Cerqueira	University of Porto, Portugal
Mattia Cerrato	JGU Mainz, Germany
Aman Chadha	Stanford University/Amazon Inc., USA
Faïcel Chamroukhi	IRT SystemX, France
Joydeep Chandra	Indian Institute of Technology Patna, India
Victor Charpenay	Mines Saint-Étienne, France
Arthur Charpentier	Université du Québec à Montréal, Canada
Vaggos Chatziafratis	Stanford University, USA

Sotirios Chatzis	Cyprus University of Technology, Cyprus
Chunchun Chen	Tongji University, China
Defang Chen	Zhejiang University, China
Hongyang Chen	Zhejiang Lab, China
Huaming Chen	University of Sydney, Australia
Huiping Chen	University of Birmingham, UK
Jiawei Chen	Tianjin University, China
Lingwei Chen	Rochester Institute of Technology, USA
Minyu Chen	Shenzhen Technology University, China
Tianyi Chen	Boston University, USA
Wei-Peng Chen	Fujitsu, Japan
Xuefeng Chen	Chongqing University, China
Zhong Chen	Southern Illinois University Carbondale, USA
Ziheng Chen	Walmart, USA
Cheng Cheng	Carnegie Mellon University, USA
Mao Cheng	University of California, Berkeley, USA
Xi Cheng	Cornell University, USA
Belkacem Chikhaoui	Université TÉLUQ, Canada
Stephane Chretien	Université Lumière Lyon 2, France
Hua Chu	Xidian University, China
Ferdinando Cicalese	University of Verona, Italy
Gaetano Cimino	University of Salerno, Italy
Martina Cinquini	University of Pisa, Italy
Gabriele Ciravegna	Intesa Sanpaolo Innovation Center, Italy
Stefano Cirillo	University of Salerno, Italy
Paul Clarke	University of Agder, Norway
Johanne Cohen	LISN-CNRS, France
Erica Coppolillo	University of Calabria, Italy
Denis Coquenet	IRISA, France
Luca Corbucci	University of Pisa, Italy
Barbara Toniella Corradini	Italian Institute of Technology, Italy
Andrea Cossu	University of Pisa, Italy
Ivor Cribben	University of Alberta, Canada
Bertrand Cuissart	University of Caen Normandie, France
Alfredo Cuzzocrea	University of Calabria, Italy
Sebastian Cygert	NASK, Poland
Annunziata D'Aversa	University of Bari Aldo Moro, Italy
Rajjat Dadwal	University of Bonn, Germany
Thi-Bich-Hanh Dao	University of Orléans, France
Paul Davidsson	Malmö University, Sweden
Athanasios Davvetas	NCSR Demokritos, Greece
Johan de Aguas	University of Oslo, Norway

Andre de Carvalho	University of São Paulo, Brazil
Marcilio de Souto	LIFOUniversity of Orléans, France
Gaetan De Waele	University of Antwerp, Belgium
Jochen De Weerdt	KU Leuven, Belgium
Kamil Deja	Warsaw University of Technology, Poland
Julien Delaunay	Inria, France
Elena Demidova	University of Bonn and Lamarr Institute, Germany
Angus Dempster	Monash University, Australia
Cheng Deng	University of Edinburgh, UK
Mariachiara Di Cosmo	Università degli Studi “G. d’Annunzio”, Italy
Andrea Giuseppe Di Francesco	Sapienza University of Rome, Italy
Luca Di Stefano	TU Wien, Austria
Lamine Diop	EPITA, France
Christos Diou	Harokopio University of Athens, Greece
Jasminka Dobša	University of Zagreb, Croatia
Vlastislav Dohnal	Masaryk University, Czech Republic
Ruihai Dong	University College Dublin, Ireland
Emilio Dorigatti	Boehringer Ingelheim GmbH, Germany
Moises Dos Santos	University of Porto, Portugal
Gaoyuan Du	University of Tennessee, Knoxville, USA
Haizhou Du	Shanghai University of Electric Power, China
Liang Du	Shanxi University, China
Qihan Du	Renmin University of China, China
Xin Du	University of Edinburgh, UK
Jamie Duell	Sheffield Hallam University, UK
Inês Dutra	University of Porto, Portugal
Elod Egyed-Zsigmond	LIRIS/INSA Lyon, France
Moshe Eliasof	University of Cambridge, UK
Mohamed Elmahallawy	Washington State University, USA
Rémi Emonet	Laboratoire Hubert Curien/Université Jean Monnet, France
Davide Evangelista	University of Bologna, Italy
Bojan Evkoski	Central European University, Austria
Kamil Faber	AGH University of Science and Technology, Poland
Ronan Fablet	IMT Atlantique, France
Issam Falih	Université Clermont Auvergne, CNRS, LIMOS, France
Ruiyi Fang	Western University, Canada
Catherine Faron	Université Côte d’Azur, CNRS, Inria, France
Marco Favier	University of Antwerp, Belgium

Faramarz Fekri	Georgia Institute of Technology, USA
Yuanjun Feng	University of Lausanne, Switzerland
Raphael Feraud	Orange, France
Amine Ferdjaoui	Sogeti - Centre Borelli, France
Daniel Fernández-Sánchez	Aalto University, Finland
Luca Ferragina	University of Calabria, Italy
Pedro Ferreira	University of Porto, Portugal
Yousra Fettach	Ghent University, Belgium
Álvaro Figueira	University of Porto, Portugal
Katarzyna Filus	Institute of Theoretical and Applied Informatics Polish Academy of Sciences, Poland
Raphael Fischer	TU Dortmund University, Germany
Michele Fontana	University of Pisa, Italy
Teodor-Florin Fortis	West University of Timisoara, Romania
Raphael Fournier-S'niehotta	CNAM, France
Giulia Fracastoro	Politecnico di Torino, Italy
Kary Framling	Umeå University, Sweden
Benoît Frénay	University of Namur, Belgium
Christian Frey	University of Technology Nuremberg, Germany
Holger Fröning	University of Heidelberg, Germany
Fabio Fumarola	Prometeia, Italy
Mikel Galar	Universidad Pública de Navarra, Spain
Luis Galárraga	Inria, France
Jose Gamez	Universidad de Castilla-La Mancha, Spain
Shengxiang Gao	Kunming University of Science and Technology, China
Yifeng Gao	University of Texas Rio Grande Valley, USA
Jade Garcia Bourrée	EPFL, Switzerland
Dario Garigliotti	University of Bergen, Norway
Moncef Garouani	Toulouse Capitole University, France
Jean-Gabriel Gaudreault	University of Ottawa, Canada
Dominique Gay	Université de La Réunion, France
Luise Ge	Washington University in St Louis, USA
Michaela Geierhos	University of the Bundeswehr Munich, Germany
Petia Georgieva	University of Aveiro, Portugal
Kushankur Ghosh	University of Alberta, Canada
Luca Giamattei	University of Naples Federico II, Italy
Giorgos Giannopoulos	National Observatory of Athens, Greece
Nikos Gkorgkolis	University of Crete, Greece
Vanessa Gómez-Verdejo	Universidad Carlos III de Madrid, Spain
Sónia Gouveia	University of Aveiro, Portugal
Brandon Gower-Winter	Utrecht University, Netherlands

Michael Granitzer	University of Passau, Germany
Alban Grastien	CEA-List, France
Magda Gregorova	Technical University of Applied Sciences Würzburg-Schweinfurt, Germany
Bram Grooten	Eindhoven University of Technology, Netherlands
Gerrit Grossmann	DFKI, Germany
Sergei Grudinin	LJK CNRS, Université Grenoble Alpes, France
Luciano Gualà	University of Rome Tor Vergata, Italy
Xinyu Guan	Xi'an Jiaotong University, China
Massimo Guarascio	ICAR-CNR, Italy
Bertha Guijarro-Berdiñas	University of A Coruña, Spain
Ce Guo	Imperial College London, UK
Muhao Guo	Arizona State University, USA
Shanqing Guo	Shandong University, China
Yuhong Guo	Carleton University, Canada
Phuong Hoai Ha	UiT The Arctic University of Norway, Norway
Piotr Habas	Amazon, USA
Christian Hakert	TU Dortmund University, Germany
Anaïs Halftermeyer	Laboratoire d'Informatique Fondamentale d'Orléans, France
Maria Halkidi	University of Pireaus, Greece
Benjamin Halstead	University of Auckland, New Zealand
Donghong Han	Northeastern University, China
Marcus Handte	University of Duisburg-Essen, Germany
Tom Hanika	University of Hildesheim, Germany
Sébastien Harispe	IMT Mines Alès, France
Claudio Hartmann	TU Dresden, Germany
Marwan Hassani	Eindhoven University of Technology, Netherlands
Zirui He	New Jersey Institute of Technology, USA
Stefan Heindorf	Paderborn University, Germany
Tobias Hille	University of Kassel, Germany
Martin Holena	Institute of Computer Science, Czech Republic
Mike Holenderski	Eindhoven University of Technology, Netherlands
Vasant Honavar	Pennsylvania State University, USA
Paul Honeine	LITIS Lab, Université de Rouen Normandie, France
Shifu Hou	Case Western Reserve University, USA
Miao Hu	Queen's University Belfast, UK
Xin Hu	University of Michigan, USA
Yizheng Huang	York University, Canada
Charmayne Hughes	Technische Universität Berlin, Germany
Yasutoshi Ida	NTT, Japan

Dino Ienco	INRAE, France
Abdelhak Imoussaten	IMT Mines Alès, France
Angelo Impedovo	NSA Italia s.r.l., Italy
Alessandro Incremona	Catholic University of the Sacred Heart, Italy
Wissem Inoubli	CRIL, University of Artois, France
Vasileios Iosifidis	SCHUFA Holding AG, Germany
Ali Ismail-Fawaz	IRIMAS, Université de Haute-Alsace, France
Nevo Itzhak	Ben-Gurion University of the Negev, Israel
Mirjana Ivanovic	University of Novi Sad, Serbia
Said Jabbour	CRIL CNRS, France
Tobias Jacobs	NEC Laboratories Europe GmbH, Germany
Johannes Jakubik	IBM Research, USA
Henri Jamet	University of Lausanne, Switzerland
Waqas Jamil	Bournemouth University, UK
Kuk Jin Jang	Hongik University, South Korea
Arkadiusz Janz	Wrocław University of Science and Technology, Poland
Hui Ji	University of Pittsburgh, USA
Yuheng Jia	Southeast University, China
Weiwei Jiang	Beijing University of Posts and Telecommunications, China
Xi Jiang	Southern University of Science and Technology, China
Sebastian Jimenez	Ghent University, Belgium
Guangyin Jin	National University of Defense Technology, China
Jiahui Jin	Southeast University, China
Mira Jürgens	Ghent University, Belgium
Tomasz Kajdanowicz	Wrocław University of Science and Technology, Poland
Jan Kalina	Czech Academy of Sciences, Institute of Computer Science, Czech Republic
Sevvandi Kandanaarachchi	CSIRO, Australia
Bo Kang	Ghent University, Belgium
Jurgita Kapočiūtė-Dzikienė	Tilde SIA, University of Latvia, Tilde IT, Vytautas Magnus University, Latvia/Lithuania
Athresh Karanam	University of Texas at Dallas, USA
Jacek Karolczak	Poznań University of Technology, Poland
Peter Karsmakers	KU Leuven, Belgium
Gjergji Kasneci	Technical University of Munich, Germany
Branko Kavsek	University of Primorska, Slovenia
Daniyal Kazempour	Christian-Albrechts-Universität zu Kiel, Germany
Mark Keane	University College Dublin, Ireland

Stefan Kesselheim	Forschungszentrum Jülich, Germany
Rabindra Khadka	University of Oslo, Norway
Asma Kharrat	Liris, France
Mohamadsadegh Khosravani	University of Regina, Canada
Adem Kikaj	KU Leuven, Belgium
Hyunju Kim	King's College London, UK
Sofoklis Kitharidis	LIACS, Netherlands
Frank Klawonn	Ostfalia University, Germany
Tomas Kliegr	University of Economics Prague, Czech Republic
Jakub Klikowski	Wrocław University of Science and Technology, Poland
Marek Klonowski	Wrocław University of Science and Technology, Poland
Boshko Koloski	Jožef Stefan Institute, Slovenia
Joanna Komorniczak	Wrocław University of Science and Technology, Poland
Aritra Konar	KU Leuven, Belgium
Frederic Koriche	Université d'Artois, CRIL CNRS UMR 8188, France
Grazina Korvel	Vilnius University, Lithuania
N'Dah Jean Kouagou	Paderborn University, Germany
Emmanouil Krasanakis	CERTH, Greece
Chethan Krishnamurthy Ramanaik	University of the Bundeswehr Munich, Germany
Amer Krivosija	TU Dortmund University, Germany
Oleg Kudryavtsev	Southern Federal University, Russia
Sebastian Kula	Kempelen Institute of Intelligent Technologies, Slovakia
Pawan Kumar	IIIT, Hyderabad, India
Vivek Kumar	Trinity College Dublin, Ireland
Olga Kurasova	Vilnius University, Lithuania
Semih Kurt	Ghent University, Belgium
Tomasz Kuśmierczyk	Jagiellonian University, Poland
Valerio La Gatta	Northwestern University, USA
Antti Laaksonen	University of Helsinki, Finland
Charlotte Laclau	Polytechnique Institute, Télécom Paris, France
Jean-Marie Lagniez	CRIL CNRS, France
Aonghus Lawlor	University College Dublin, Ireland
Duc Le	University of Twente, Netherlands
Tuan Le	New Mexico State University, USA
Hoel Le Capitaine	University of Nantes, France
Erwan Le Merrer	Inria, France
Tai Le Quy	University of Koblenz, Germany

Marcos M. Raimundo	University of Campinas, Brazil
Kira Maag	Heinrich Heine University Düsseldorf, Germany
Rakesh Chowdary Machineni	Rockwell Automation, USA
Henryk Maciejewski	Wrocław University of Science and Technology, Poland
Michael Madden	University of Galway, Ireland
Sindri Magnusson	Stockholm University, Sweden
Yasir Mahmood	Paderborn University, Germany
Cristina Maier	Boston College, USA
Akshay Malhotra	Interdigital, USA
Hua Mao	Northumbria University, UK
Antonio Marceddu	Politecnico di Torino, Italy
Virginijus Marcinkevičius	Vilnius University, Lithuania
Gabriel Marques Tavares	Ludwig-Maximilians-Universität München, Germany
Christophe Marsala	LIP6, Sorbonne Université, France
Jorge Martinez-Gil	Software Competence Center Hagenberg GmbH, Austria
Fernando Martínez-Plumed	Universitat Politècnica de València, Spain
Ana Martins	University of Aveiro, Portugal
Koji Maruhashi	Fujitsu, Japan
Marc Masana	Graz University of Technology, Austria
Rytis Maskeliūnas	Polsl, Poland
Carlo Masone	Politecnico di Torino, Italy
Michael Mathioudakis	University of Helsinki, Finland
Stan Matwin	Dalhouise University, Canada
Nicolas Maudet	Sorbonne Université, France
Tom Maye-Lasserre	Télécom Paris, IP Paris, France
Giacomo Medda	University of Cagliari, Italy
Nida Meddouri	LRE-EPITA, France
Behzad Mehrbakhsh	Universitat Politècnica de València, Spain
Wagner Meira Jr.	Federal University of Minas Gerais, Brazil
Marco Mellia	Politecnico di Torino, Italy
Joao Mendes-Moreira	University of Porto, Portugal
Rui Meng	Beijing Normal-Hong Kong Baptist University, China
Vlado Menkovski	Eindhoven University of Technology, Netherlands
Engelbert Mephu Nguifo	Université Clermont Auvergne, CNRS, LIMOS, France
Paolo Merialdo	Università degli Studi Roma Tre, Italy
Sebastian Mežnar	Jožef Stefan Institute, Slovenia
Bojan Mihaljevic	Universidad Politécnica de Madrid, Spain

Matej Mihelčić	University of Zagreb, Croatia
Miloud Mihoubi	University of Téluq, Canada
Tsunenori Mine	Kyushu University, Japan
Valentina Minnetti	Italian National Institute of Statistics, Italy
Jelena Mitrović	University of Passau, Germany
Pierre Monnin	Université Côte d'Azur, Inria, CNRS, I3S, France
Eduardo Montesuma	Université Paris-Saclay, France
Raha Moraffah	Worcester Polytechnic Institute, USA
Pierre Moreau	Ekimetrics, France
Jose Moreira	University of Aveiro, Portugal
Paulina Morillo	Universitat Politècnica de València, Spain
Yael Moros-Daval	Universitat Politècnica de València, Spain
Thomas Mortier	Ghent University, Belgium
Roman Mouček	University of West Bohemia, Czech Republic
Elena Maria Muià	Sapienza University of Rome, Italy
Koyel Mukherjee	Adobe Research, India
Ian Nabney	University of Bristol, UK
Mohamed Nadif	Centre Borelli UMR9010-Université Paris Cité, France
Mohamed Nafea	Missouri University of Science and Technology, USA
Felipe Kenji Nakano	KU Leuven, Belgium
Géraldin Nanfack	Concordia University, Canada
Mirco Nanni	CNR-ISTI Pisa, Italy, Italy
Apurva Narayan	University of Western Ontario, Canada
Francesca Naretto	University of Pisa, Italy
Fateme Nateghi Haredasht	Stanford University, USA
Claire Nédellec	INRAE, MaIAGE, France
Dang Nguyen	Deakin University, Australia
Kien Nguyen	University of Delaware, USA
Minh Nguyen	University of Texas at Austin, USA
Nikolaos Nikolaou	University College London, UK
Simona Nisticò	University of Calabria, Italy
Navid Nobani	University of Milano-Bicocca, Italy
Ana Rita Nogueira	INESC TEC, Portugal
Slawomir Nowaczyk	Halmstad University, Sweden
Diana Nurbakova	INSA Lyon - LIRIS UMR 5205 CNRS, France
Iyiola Emmanuel Olatunji	University of Luxembourg, Luxembourg
Arlindo Oliveira	Instituto Superior Técnico, Portugal
Helder Oliveira	University of Porto, Portugal
José Oliveira	University of Porto, Portugal
Makoto Onizuka	Osaka University, Japan

Jose Oramas	University of Antwerp, Belgium
María Óskarsdóttir	University of Southampton, UK
Fannia Pacheco	University of Rouen Normandy, France
Arjun Pakrashi	University College Dublin, Ireland
Egawati Panjei	University of Oklahoma, USA
Apostolos Papadopoulos	Aristotle University of Thessaloniki, Greece
Laurence Park	Western Sydney University, Australia
Emilio Parrado-Hernandez	Universidad Carlos III de Madrid, Spain
Vincenzo Pasquadibisceglie	University of Bari Aldo Moro, Italy
Tatiana Passali	Aristotle University of Thessaloniki, Greece
Eliana Pastor	Politecnico di Torino, Italy
Theodore Patkos	FORTH, Greece
Anand Paul	Louisiana State University HSC, USA
Heiko Paulheim	University of Mannheim, Germany
John Pavlopoulos	Athens University of Economics and Business, Greece
Yulong Pei	Eindhoven University of Technology, Netherlands
Leonardo Pellegrina	University of Padova, Italy
Antonio Pellicani	University of Bari Aldo Moro, Italy
Roberto Pellungrini	University of Pisa, Italy
Frédéric Pennerath	CentraleSupélec - LORIA, France
Francisco Pereira	Technical University of Denmark, Denmark
Lucas Pereira	Interactive Technologies Institute, LARSyS, Técnico Lisboa, Portugal
Franz Pernkopf	Graz University of Technology, Austria
Filipo Perotto	ONERA, France
Linas Petkevicius	Vilnius University, Lithuania
Simone Piaggesi	University of Pisa, Italy
Francesco Piccialli	University of Naples Federico II, Italy
Francesco Pierri	Politecnico di Milano, Italy
Roberto Pietrantuono	University of Naples Federico II, Italy
Martin Pilát	Charles University, Czech Republic
Armando Pinho	University of Aveiro, Portugal
Pedro Pires	Federal University of São Carlos, Brazil
Federico Pirola	University of Milano-Bicocca, Italy
Marc Plantevit	EPITA, France
Marco Podda	University of Pisa, Italy
Marco Polignano	University of Bari Aldo Moro, Italy
Alexander Politowicz	University of Illinois Chicago, USA
Giovanni Ponti	ENEA, Italy
Raluca Portase	Technical University of Cluj Napoca, Romania
Piotr Porwik	University of Silesia in Katowice, Poland

Marco Postiglione	Northwestern University, USA
Andrea Pozzi	University of Pavia, Italy
Steven Prestwich	University College Cork, Ireland
Lucía Prieto-Santamaría	Universidad Politécnica de Madrid, Spain
Chiara Pugliese	IIT - CNR, Italy
Andrea Pugnana	University of Trento, Italy
Satish Puri	Missouri University of Science and Technology, USA
Antonio Purificato	Sapienza University of Rome, Italy
Abdulhakim Qahtan	Utrecht University, Netherlands
Cong Qi	New Jersey Institute of Technology, USA
Xin Qin	California State University, Long Beach, USA
Yijun Quan	University of Warwick, UK
Benjamin Quost	Université de Technologie de Compiègne, France
Dimitrios Rafailidis	University of Thessaly, Greece
Alessio Ragno	EPITA Research Laboratory, France
Muhammad Rajabinasab	University of Southern Denmark, Denmark
Morteza Rakhshaninejad	Ghent University, Belgium
Patrícia Ramos	INESC TEC, Portugal
Md Mashud Rana	Australian Catholic University, Australia
Weixiong Rao	Tongji University, China
Rajeev Rastogi	Amazon, USA
Steffen Rebennack	Karlsruhe Institute of Technology, Germany
Domenico Redavid	University of Bari Aldo Moro, Italy
Michaela Regneri	University of Hamburg, Germany
Wojciech Rejchel	Nicolaus Copernicus University in Toruń, Poland
Francesco Renna	University of Porto, Portugal
Manon Reusens	University of Antwerp, Belgium
Hergys Rexha	Åbo Akademi University, Finland
Ricardo Rios	Federal University of Bahia, Brazil
Tatiane Rios	Federal University of Bahia, Brazil
Guilherme Roberto	University of São Paulo, Brazil
Marko Robnik-Šikonja	University of Ljubljana, Slovenia
Miguel Rocha	University of Minho, Portugal
Christophe Rodrigues	DVRC pôle universitaire Léonard de Vinci, France
Juan Rodriguez	Universidad de Burgos, Spain
Federica Rollo	University of Modena and Reggio Emilia, Italy
Sabin Roman	Jožef Stefan Institute, Slovenia
Nicolas Roque dos Santos	University of California, Riverside, USA
Polina Rozenshtein	Aalto University, Finland
Rimvydas Rubavicius	University of Edinburgh, UK

Krzysztof Rudaś	Institute of Computer Science, Polish Academy of Sciences, Poland
Laura Ruotsalainen	University of Helsinki, Finland
Federico Sabbatini	National Institute for Nuclear Physics - INFN, Italy
Dimitris Sacharidis	Université Libre de Bruxelles, Belgium
Lakhdar Sais	CRIL - CNRS, Artois University, France
Yakoub Salhi	CRIL CNRS, France
Chafik Samir	CNRS-UCA, France
Miriam Santos	University of Porto, Portugal
Ioannis Sarridis	Information Technologies Institute/Centre for Research & Technology, Greece
Roberto Sassi	University of Milan, Italy
Milos Savic	University of Novi Sad, Serbia
Yücel Saygın	Sabancı Universitesi, Turkiye
Katerina Schindlerova	University of Vienna, Austria
Frank-Michael Schleif	Technical University of Applied Sciences Würzburg-Schweinfurt, Germany
Dmitrij Schlesinger	TU Dresden, Germany
Daniel Schlör	University of Würzburg, Germany
Rainer Schlosser	Hasso Plattner Institute, Germany
Melanie Schmidt	Heinrich Heine University Düsseldorf, Germany
Peter Schneider-Kamp	University of Southern Denmark, Denmark
Gesina Schwalbe	Ulm University, Germany
Andreas Schwung	South Westphalia University of Applied Sciences, Germany
Vincenzo Scotti	KASTEL, Karlsruhe Institute of Technology, Germany
Sébastien Destercke	Université de technologie de Compiègne, France
Selpi Selpi	Chalmers University of Technology and Gothenburg University, Sweden
Mattia Setzu	University of Pisa, Italy
Shiv Shankar	University of Massachusetts, USA
Arnab Sharma	Paderborn University, Germany
Shubhranshu Shekhar	Brandeis University, USA
Oleksandr Shekhovtsov	Czech Technical University in Prague, Czech Republic
Hao Shen	fortiss GmbH, Germany
Qiang Sheng	Institute of Computing Technology, Chinese Academy of Sciences, China
John Sheppard	Montana State University, USA
Bin Shi	Xi'an Jiaotong University, China
Jimeng Shi	University of Illinois Urbana-Champaign, USA

Ali Shokoufandeh	Drexel University, USA
Xiao Shou	Baylor University, USA
Md Fahim Sikder	Linköping University, Sweden
Catarina Silva	University of Coimbra, Portugal
Joaquim Silva	NOVA LINCS, Universidade Nova de Lisboa, Portugal
Esther-Lydia Silva-Ramírez	Universidad de Cádiz, Spain
Raivydas Šimėnas	Vilnius University, Lithuania
Giovanni Simonini	University of Modena and Reggio Emilia, Italy
Maneet Singh	Mastercard, India
Andrzej Skowron	University of Warsaw, Poland
Vaclav Smidl	Czech Technical University in Prague, Czech Republic
Marek Smieja	Jagiellonian University, Poland
Filipe Soares	Fraunhofer Portugal AICOS, Portugal
Osvaldo Solarte-Pabon	Universidad del Valle, Colombia
Liyan Song	Harbin Institute of Technology, China
Fabian Spaeh	Celonis, USA
Lorenz Sparrenberg	University of Bonn, Germany
Giancarlo Sperlì	University of Naples Federico II, Italy
Ramya Srinivasan	Fujitsu, Japan
Dimitri Staufer	Technische Universität Berlin, Germany
Marcel Steinmetz	LAAS-CNRS, France
Niklas Strauß	Ludwig-Maximilians-Universität München, Germany
Xuanyu Su	University of Ottawa, Canada
Jérémie Sublime	ISEP, France
Xin Sun	City University of Macau, China
Zhaokai Sun	Tongji University, China
Panagiotis Symeonidis	University of the Aegean, Greece
Tomasz Szandała	Wrocław University of Science and Technology, Poland
Amir Taherkordi	University of Oslo, Norway
Atsuhiro Takasu	National Institute of Informatics, Japan
Nicholas Tan Jerome	Karlsruhe Institute of Technology, Germany
Yufei Tang	Florida Atlantic University, USA
Katerina Taskova	University of Auckland, New Zealand
Olivier Teste	IRIT, University of Toulouse, France
Christoph Tholen	Saarland University of Applied Sciences, Germany
Steffen Thoma	FZI Research Center for Information Technology, Germany

Josephine Thomas	University of Greifswald, Germany
Natan Tourne	Ghent University, Belgium
Panos Trahanias	FORTH, Greece
Alicia Troncoso	Pablo de Olavide University, Spain
Francesco Trovò	Politecnico di Milano, Italy
Giuseppe Trunfio	University of Sassari, Italy
Panayiotis Tsaparas	University of Ioannina, Greece, Greece
Grigorios Tsoumakas	Aristotle University of Thessaloniki, Greece
Jonata Tyska Carvalho	Federal University of Santa Catarina, Brazil
Mihai Udrescu	Politehnica University Timisoara, Romania
Edoardo Urettini	European Central Bank, Germany
Gonzalo Uribarri	Stockholm University, Sweden
Philipp Vaeth	Technical University of Applied Sciences Würzburg-Schweinfurt, University Bielefeld, Germany
Giorgio Valentini	University of Milan, Italy
Diego Vallejo-Huanga	Universitat Politècnica de València, Spain
Jente Van Belle	KU Leuven, Belgium
Peter van der Putten	Leiden University, Netherlands
Lucy Van Kleunen	KU Leuven, Belgium
Fabio Vandin	University of Padova, Italy
Georgios Vardakas	University of Ioannina, Greece
Aparna S. Varde	Montclair State University, USA
Mariana Vargas Vieyra	MostlyAI, Austria
Bruno Veloso	INESC TEC, Portugal
Mathias Verbeke	KU Leuven, Belgium
Wouter Verbeke	KU Leuven, Belgium
Jan Verwaeren	Ghent University, Belgium
Gennaro Vessio	University of Bari Aldo Moro, Italy
Jill-Jênn Vie	Inria, France
Saketh Vishnubhatla	Arizona State University, USA
Marco Viviani	University of Milano-Bicocca, Italy
Maximilian von Zastrow	University of Southern Denmark, Denmark
Tim vor der Brück	Internationale Hochschule, Germany
Ngoc-Son Vu	University of Technology of Troyes, France
Tomasz Walkowiak	Wrocław University of Science and Technology, Poland
Shu Wan	Arizona State University, USA
Ziwen Wan	University of California, Irvine, USA
Deng-Bao Wang	Southeast University, China
Hao Wang	University of Science and Technology of China, China

Jianwu Wang	University of Maryland, Baltimore County, USA
Jing Wang	Amazon, USA
Li Wang	National University of Defense Technology, China
Mengying Wang	Case Western Reserve University, USA
Wendy Hui Wang	Stevens Institute of Technology, USA
Xiaoyang Wang	University of Exeter, UK
Xuemin Wang	Guilin University of Electronic Technology, China
Yanhao Wang	East China Normal University, China
Yongyu Wang	JD Logistics, China
Zhihui Wang	Fudan University, China
Zichong Wang	Florida International University, USA
Pascal Weber	University of Vienna, Austria
Xing Wei	Tongji University, China
Yang Wei	Nanjing University of Science and Technology, China
Tonio Weidler	Maastricht University, Netherlands
Guilherme Weigert Cassales	University of Waikato, New Zealand
Alicja Wieczorkowska	Polish-Japanese Academy of Information Technology, Poland
Szymon Wojciechowski	Wrocław University of Science and Technology, Poland
Michal Wozniak	Wrocław University of Science and Technology, Poland
Bin Wu	Zhengzhou University, China
Boqian Wu	University of Luxembourg, Luxembourg
Nannan Wu	Tianjin University, China
Patrick Wu	American University, USA
Peng Wu	Shanghai Jiao Tong University, China
Wei Wu	Ben Gurion University of the Negev, Israel
Wenjie Xi	George Mason University, USA
Zhiwen Xiao	Southwest Jiaotong University, China
Hong Xie	University of Science and Technology of China, China
Wen-Bo Xie	Southwest Petroleum University, China
Huanlai Xing	Southwest Jiaotong University, China
Xing Xing	Tongji University, China
Duo Xu	Georgia Institute of Technology, USA
Gehui Xu	Imperial College London, UK
Weifeng Xu	University of Baltimore, USA
Qiao Yan	Shenzhen University, China
Yu Yan	Institute of Computing Technology, Chinese Academy of Sciences, China

Jiayi Yang	Tongji University, China
Qian Yang	University of Connecticut, USA
Xin-She Yang	Middlesex University London, UK
Yutong Ye	Beihang University, China
Kalidas Yeturu	Indian Institute of Technology Tirupati, India
Ilkay Yildiz Potter	BioSensics LLC, USA
Zhipeng Yin	Florida International University, USA
Jaemin Yoo	Seoul National University, South Korea
Lei You	Technical University of Denmark, Denmark
Hang Yu	Shanghai University, China
Shuyang Yu	Michigan State University, USA
Wentao Yu	Nanjing University of Science and Technology, China
Jidong Yuan	Beijing Jiaotong University, China
Osmar Zaiane	University of Alberta, Canada
Tetiana Zakharchenko	Ukrainian Catholic University, Ukraine
Obaidullah Zaland	Umeå University, Sweden
Alessio Zanga	University of Milano-Bicocca, Italy
Mario Zanon	IMT School for Advanced Studies Lucca, Italy
Gianluca Zaza	University of Bari Aldo Moro, Italy
Assaad Zeghina	Latmos Lab, France
Akka Zemmari	University of Bordeaux, France
Saber Zerhoudi	University of Passau, Germany
Meriem Zerkouk	Université TÉLUQ, Canada
Chongsheng Zhang	Henan University, China
Hanping Zhang	Carleton University, Canada
Haowen Zhang	Zhejiang Sci-Tech University, China
Pengyu Zhang	University of Amsterdam, Netherlands
Xiaoming Zhang	Beihang University, China
Xinyue Zhang	Kennesaw State University, USA
Xiuzhen Zhang	RMIT University, Australia
Xiyue Zhang	University of Bristol, UK
Yaying Zhang	Tongji University, China
Yin Zhang	University of Electronic Science and Technology of China, China
Zhiwen Zhang	LocationMind Inc., Japan
Zhong Zhang	University of Electronic Science and Technology of China, China
Kaiqi Zhao	Oakland University, USA
Shu Zhao	Anhui University, China
Zhouting Zhao	Trinity College Dublin, Ireland
Yueyuan Zheng	Beihang University, China

Yujia Zheng	Carnegie Mellon University, USA
Yanmin Zhu	Shanghai Jiao Tong University, China
Arthur Zimek	University of Southern Denmark, Denmark
Tommaso Zoppi	University of Florence, Italy
Noé Zufferey	ETH Zurich, Switzerland
Pedro Zuidberg Dos Martires	Örebro University, Sweden
Paweł Zyblewski	Wrocław University of Science and Technology, Poland

Additional Reviewers, Applied Data Science Track

Amgad Abdulmaqsod	Paderborn University, Germany
Aisha Aijaz	Indraprastha Institute of Information Technology, Delhi, India
Moh'd Khier Al Kfari	University of Rostock, Germany
Sokrat Aldarmini	Missouri University of Science and Technology, USA
Konstantinos Alexis	IMSI/Athena Research Center, Greece
Hazrat Ali	University of Stirling, UK
Zafar Ali	Southeast University, China
Hend Amraoui	Higher Institute of Applied Languages and Computer Science of Béja (ISLAI Béja), University of Jendouba, Tunisia
Shin Ando	Tokyo University of Science, Japan
Eugen-Richard Ardelean	Technical University of Cluj-Napoca, Romania
André Artelt	Bielefeld University, Germany
Baran Atalar	Carnegie Mellon University, USA
Kyohei Atarashi	Kyoto University, Japan
Sanket Badhe	Google, USA
Daniel Barley	Heidelberg University, Germany
Ulya Bayram	Canakkale Onsekiz Mart University, Turkey
Ahmad Bdeir	University of Hildesheim, Germany
Jatin Bedi	Thapar Institute of Engineering and Technology, India
Sidahmed Benabderrahmane	New York University, United Arab Emirates
Francesco Benedetti	University of Bari Aldo Moro, Italy
Quentin Bertrand	Inria, France
Aurelie Beynier	Sorbonne Université, France
Martin Binder	LMU Munich, Germany
Valerio Bonsignori	University of Pisa, Italy
Weronika Borek-Marciniec	Wrocław University of Science and Technology, Poland

Onur Boyar	IBM Research, Japan
Maria Sofia Bucarelli	CNRS, Inria, I3S, France
Zhuo Cai	University of Technology Sydney, Australia
Toon Calders	University of Antwerp, Belgium
Lele Cao	Tsinghua University, China
Louis Carpentier	KU Leuven, Belgium
Daniele Castellana	University of Florence, Italy
Mustafa Cavus	Eskisehir Technical University, Turkey
Dong-Kyu Chae	Hanyang University, South Korea
Tanujit Chakraborty	Sorbonne University Abu Dhabi, United Arab Emirates
Anna Chatzipapadopoulou	Athens University of Economics and Business/Archimedes Unit, Athena Research Center, Greece
Lilia Chebbah	Georgia State University, USA
Hao Chen	University of Chinese Academy of Sciences, China
Haopeng Chen	Shanghai Jiao Tong University, China
Sheng-Wei Chen	National Taiwan University, Taiwan
Songcan Chen	Nanjing University of Aeronautics and Astronautics, China
Zhen Chen	University of Science and Technology of China, China
Zhili Chen	East China Normal University, China
Liang Cheng	University of Oslo, Norway
Chak Fong Chong	Macao Polytechnic University, China
Maciej Chrabaszcz	Warsaw University of Technology, NASK National Research Institute, Poland
Michele Craighero	Politecnico di Milano, Italy
Wang-Zhou Dai	China
Uma Damotharan	PES University, USA
Davy Darankoum	Université Grenoble Alpes/SynapCell, France
Mrinal Das	IIT Palakaad, India
Debashis Das Chakladar	Birla Institute of Technology & Science, Hyderabad, India
Arne De Temmerman	KU Leuven, Belgium
Thanh-Dang Diep	Vietnam National University Ho Chi Minh City - University of Technology, Vietnam
Yihao Ding	University of Western Australia, Australia
Jean-François Dollinger	CESI, France
Yingpeng Du	Nanyang Technological University, Singapore
Fabrício Enembreck	Pontifical Catholic University of Paraná, Brazil
A. M. Esfar-E-Alam	University of Oslo, Norway

Fiona Ewald	Ludwig-Maximilians-Universität München, Germany
Ken-ichi Fukui	Kansai University, Japan
Xiaofeng Gao	Shanghai Jiao Tong University, China
Blaise Genest	CNRS, CNRS@CREATE, France
Christos Gkartzios	University of Ioannina, Greece
Filippos Gouidis	ICS/FORTH, Greece
Poonam Goyal	BITS Pilani, India
Shangqi Guo	Tsinghua, China
Yang Guo	Harbin Engineering University, China
Subhash Gurappa	Florida International University, USA
Renda Han	Tianjin University, China
Takahiro Hara	Osaka University, Japan
Ryuichiro Hataya	SB Intuitions & Kyoto University, Japan
Mehdi Hennequin	Omundu, France
Johanna Hillebrand	Heinrich Heine University, Germany
Yi-Te Hong	Academia Sinica, Taiwan
Tanvir Hossain	Georgia State University, USA
Ruijie Hou	Zhejiang University, China
Zhaobo Hu	Institut Polytechnique de Paris, France
Chun Huang	Chongqing University, China
Yu-Shiang Huang	National Taiwan University, Taiwan
Pedro Ilídio	KU Leuven, Belgium
Marek Jeliński	NASK-PIB, Poland
Wanting Ji	Liaoning University, China
Huimin Jiang	University of Science and Technology of China, China
Shu Jiang	Nantong Univerisity, China
Changhong Jin	University College Dublin, Ireland
Yifei Jin	X-Tech (Beijing) Co., Ltd., China
Yue Jin	University of Northampton, UK
Durande Berluskoni Kamga Nguifo	Université Clermont Auvergne, Clermont Auvergne INP, ENSMSE, CNRS, LIMOS, France
Skander Karkar	Mediterranean Institute of Technology, Tunisia
Hisashi Kashima	Kyoto University, Japan
Tsuyoshi Kato	Gunma University, Japan
Ramneek Kaur	IIT Delhi, India
Zulfiqar Ahmad Khan	Umeå University, Sweden
Sejin Kim	Gwangju Institute of Science and Technology, South Korea
YoungBin Kim	Chung-Ang University, South Korea

Zhengquan Luo	Mohamed bin Zayed University of Artificial Intelligence, United Arab Emirates
Giovanni Malaguti	Università di Modena e Reggio Emilia, Italy
Alireza Maleki	Karlsruhe Institute of Technology (KASTEL), Germany
Fragkiskos Malliaros	CentraleSupélec, France
Mohcine Manssouri	Université Lumière Lyon 2, France
Falk Maoro	University of the Bundeswehr Munich, Germany
Nikola Marić	Jožef Stefan Institute, Slovenia
Pierre Marquis	CRIL, University of Artois & CNRS, IUF, France
Patryk Marszałek	Jagiellonian University in Kraków, Poland
Cristian Mascia	University of Naples Federico II, Italy
Sunil Maurya	University of Tokyo, Japan
Bamdev Mishra	Microsoft, India
Rahul Mishra	IIIT Hyderabad, Italy
Yoshihiro Mitsuka	Mitsubishi Electric Corporation, Japan
Nabeel Mohammed	North South University, Bangladesh
Yael Moros-Daval	Universitat Politècnica de València, Spain
Kedian Mu	Peking University, China
Lingyu Mu	Institute of Information Engineering, Chinese Academy of Sciences, China
Shrimon Mukherjee	Indian Association for the Cultivation of Science, India
Anika Murarka	IIT Delhi, India
Dimitrios Myrisiotis	Great Bay University, China
Kiran Mayee Nabigaru	SoFi Technologies, USA
Thin Nguyen	Deakin University, Australia
Bo Ning	Dalian Maritime University, China
Tianzhe Ning	Donghua University, China
Masaaki Nishino	NTT, Japan
Yoshiyuki Norimatsu	Mitsubishi Electric Corporation, Japan
Bastian Oetomo	University of Melbourne, Australia
Gabriel Oliveira	Federal University of Minas Gerais, Brazil
Mounir Ourekouch	Mohammed VI Polytechnic University, Morocco
Satoshi Oyama	Nagoya City University, Japan
Emmanouil Panagiotou	Freie Universität Berlin, Germany
Luca Pepè Sciarria	University of Rome Tor Vergata, Italy
Qiankun Pi	Information Engineering University, China
Sebastiano Piccolo	University of Calabria, Italy
Laura Pollacci	University of Pisa, Italy
Yoann Poupart	LIP6, Sorbonne University, France

Ranjitha Prasad	Indraprastha Institute of Information Technology Delhi, India
Antonio Purificato	Sapienza University of Rome, Italy
Lin Qi	Ocean University of China, China
Tieyun Qian	Wuhan University, China
Weizhu Qian	Soochow University, China
Linbo Qiao	National University of Defense Technology, China
Jintao Qu	University of Southern California, USA
Muhammad Rajabinasab	University of Southern Denmark, Denmark
Gangulie Ranawaka	Informatics Institute of Technology, Sri Lanka
Darshan Rathod	Fujitsu, Japan
Matīss Rikters	National Institute of Advanced Industrial Science and Technology, Japan
Pieter Robberechts	KU Leuven, Belgium
Thibault Roux	ONERA, France
Pablo Ruiz Morales	KU Leuven, Belgium
P. S. Sastry	Indian Institute of Science, India
Aggelos Semoglou	Athens University of Economics & Business & Archimedes Research Unit, Athena Research Center, Greece
Deep Shah	Google LLC, USA
Abdul-Kazeem Shamba	Norwegian University of Science & Technology, Norway
Jie Shao	University of Electronic Science and Technology of China, China
Lifeng Shen	Chongqing University of Posts and Telecommunications, China
Xiaojun Sheng	Guangdong Laboratory of Artificial Intelligence and Digital Economy (SZ), China
Mohamed Sherif	Paderborn University, Germany
Kijung Shin	KAIST, South Korea
Jayakumar Singaram	Independent consultant, India
Atul Kumar Singh	Fujitsu Research of India Pvt. Ltd., India
Damian Sójka	Poznań University of Technology; IDEAS-NCBR, Poland
Youngdoo Son	Dongguk University, South Korea
Andy Song	RMIT University, Australia
Jules Soria	CEA-LIST, Université Paris-Saclay, France
P. K. Srijith	Indian Institute of Technology Hyderabad, India
Gowri Srinivasa	PES University, USA
Sintija Stevanoska	Jožef Stefan Institute, Slovenia

Yutaro Yamaguchi	Osaka University, Japan
Keiichiro Yamamura	ELYZA, Japan
Cheng Yang	Beijing University of Posts and Telecommunications, China
Jiaoyun Yang	Hefei University of Technology, China
Jun Yang	University of Helsinki, Finland
Ruochen Yang	Institute of Information Engineering, Chinese Academy of Sciences, China
Fangli Ying	East China University of Science and Technology, China
Dongjin Yu	Hangzhou Dianzi University, China
Wenjun Yu	Shanghai University of Finance and Economics, China
Yanwei Yu	Ocean University of China, China
Ziyue Yu	Macao Polytechnic University, China
Fangfang Yuan	Institute of Information Engineering, Chinese Academy of Sciences, China
Hang Yuan	Osaka University, Japan
Obaidullah Zaland	Umeå University, Sweden
Lei Zan	Université Grenoble Alpes, CNRS, Grenoble INP, LIG, France
Wojciech Zarzecki	Warsaw University of Technology, Poland
Zheyuan Zhan	Zhejiang University, China
Bolei Zhang	Nanjing University of Posts and Telecommunications, China
Chao Zhang	Beijing Digital Native Digital City Research Center, China
Huan Zhang	Zhengzhou University, China
Jian Zhang	China University of Mining and Technology, China
Kangning Zhang	Shanghai Jiao Tong University, China
Liang Zhang	Shanghai Jiao Tong University, China
Mengxiao Zhang	University of Auckland, New Zealand
Wei Zhang	Singapore Institute of Technology, Singapore
Wenxin Zhang	University of Chinese Academy of Sciences, China
Xuefeng Zhang	Ningbo University, China
Yaqian Zhang	University of Waikato, New Zealand
Yihong Zhang	Osaka University, Japan
Yutong Zhang	Sichuan University, China
Zhongnan Zhang	Xiamen University, China
Qinpei Zhao	Tongji University, China
Weizhong Zhao	Central China Normal University, China

Can Zhou	Imperial College London, UK
Qiaoli Zhou	Shenyang Aerospace University, China
Tianlong Zhou	Tongji University, China
Tongqing Zhou	National University of Defense Technology, China
Yan Zhou	Hohai University, China
Zhengyang Zhou	University of Science and Technology of China, China
Guanghui Zhu	Nanjing University, China
Mengxiao Zhu	North China University of Technology, China

Sponsors

Main

Platinum

Gold

Other Sponsors

Keynotes

Rethinking the Role of Scientific Discovery in the Era of AI

Mihaela van der Schaar

University of Cambridge, UK

Abstract. The growing availability of large-scale scientific datasets creates opportunities for discovery that are no longer driven by narrowly specified research questions. Instead, science increasingly unfolds through sustained exploration of vast, high-dimensional hypothesis spaces, where multiple explanations, mechanisms, and associations may remain plausible. I refer to this mode of inquiry as hypothesis hunting: an open-ended, cumulative search for insight that challenges traditional, pipeline-based models of scientific discovery.

In this talk, I present a framework that rethinks discovery as an agentic process, in which networks of interacting AI agents and human experts jointly explore, critique, and refine hypotheses under shared norms of evaluation. I will discuss how heterogeneous, LLM-based research agents can self-organize into evolving networks that generate, review, and extend findings—trading off novelty, quality, and diversity over time. Drawing on results from biomedical discovery, including cancer cohort analyses, I will argue that such socially structured agent networks can sustain large-scale exploratory discovery, complementing experimental science while reshaping how knowledge is generated, accumulated, and validated in the era of AI.

Neural Networks and Algorithms

Stefanie Jegelka
TU Munich, Germany

Abstract. Deep Learning models are now mastering increasingly complex tasks that consist of many steps of computation or reasoning. This inspires the perspective of viewing neural networks as learning algorithmic procedures. What could we gain from this perspective? This talk will outline examples and directions. First, an algorithmic view can help understand the capabilities of deep learning models, such as self-correction or the ability to solve certain optimization problems. Second, it can help understand how to design and train models to better solve challenging tasks, from optimization problems to reasoning. Yet, while this view has led to many advances, several open questions remain.

From Dialogue to Decision: Orchestrating Agents for Conversational Data Exploration and Multi-objective Optimization

Sihem Amer-Yahia

CNRS, Université Grenoble Alpes, France

Abstract. Modern scientific discovery and decision-making necessitate agents capable of navigating both complex datasets and multifaceted, often conflicting, goal landscapes. This talk explores the intersection of conversational data exploration, an incremental process where agents help users articulate needs through data interaction, and multi-objective sequential decision making. While traditional Reinforcement Learning (RL) has advanced task-specific agent training, we are witnessing a paradigm shift toward zero-shot orchestration. By leveraging a spectrum of techniques, from specialized RL policies to general-purpose Large Language Models (LLMs), we can reuse existing single-objective policies to solve complex multi-objective problems without training from scratch. We will discuss empirical evidence from the field of Education showing that this orchestrated approach can achieve competitive Pareto quality while reducing computational cost. The talk concludes by examining open research questions regarding how LLM context richness and reflective foresight enable agents to bridge the gap between incremental data-driven insights and optimal sequential actions.

AI Ethics and Governance

Francesca Rossi

IBM Research, USA

Abstract. Supported by AI, we will be able to make more grounded decisions and to focus on the main values and goals of a decision process rather than on routine and repetitive tasks. However, such a powerful technology also raises some concerns, related to privacy, fairness, value alignment, explainability, accountability, transparency, misinformation, deep fakes, copyright, and much more. These concerns are among the obstacles that hold AI back or that cause worry for current AI users, adopters, and policy makers. Without concrete answers to these questions, many will not trust AI, and therefore will not fully adopt it nor get its positive impact. In this talk I will present the main issues around AI ethics and safety and how they have evolved over the years, as AI capabilities advanced. I will also discuss the ROI of AI ethics, discussing both instrumental and value-based approaches to investing in AI ethics and governance.

The AI Ghosts and Us: Machine Writing as a Spectral Culture

Gianni Riotta

Luiss University, Italy

Abstract. We need a radically new philosophical reading of AI-generated text as a "Ghost" inhabiting contemporary human discourse. Rather than framing large language models (LLMs) as either tools or autonomous intelligences, we can argue that machine writing constitutes a spectral hybrid—neither fully human nor purely artificial, but a liminal presence emerging from the archive of human language. Drawing on Calvino's reflections on combinatorial literature and the "writing machine," we should revisit the Twentieth-century intuition that narrative could be algorithmically permuted. Calvino saw in literary algorithms both a liberation and a paradox: the machine multiplies possibilities, yet meaning still depends on human interpretation. Today's LLMs operationalize that combinatorial dream at a planetary scale, transforming statistical inference into prose and blurring the boundary between author and reader

Karpathy's notion of neural networks encoding patterns learned from data, rather than an explicit set of rules, reveals how AI systems internalize collective textual memory. The model does not "think" as a subject; it resonates. What appears as originality is a probabilistic echo of cultural sediment. The AI text thus resembles a revenant: language returning to us transformed and detached from any single living author. Revisiting Wiener's cybernetic theory, we could situate LLMs within feedback loops between humans and machines. The literary output of an AI is not an artificial substitute for human creativity, nor a counterfeit consciousness. It is a ghostly hybrid, generated at the intersection of human archives, algorithmic training, and real-time, effective prompts. By conceiving AI text as a cultural ghost, we compose a vocabulary in the age of machine writing. The challenge is not to deny the ghost nor to romanticize it, but to learn how to read and live with its spectral presence in our world.

Contents

Graph Learning and Structured Representation Learning

Competition-Aware CPC Forecasting with Near-Market Coverage 3
Sebastian Frey, Edoardo Beccari, Maximilian Kranz, Nicolò Alberto Pellizzari, Ali Mete Karaman, Qiwei Han, and Maximilian Kaiser

Efficient Attribute-Boosted Diffusion Model for Personalized Sequential Recommendation 19
Dongjing Wang, Shijia Wang, Qiang Xiao, Liwen Xiao, Qimeng Yang, and Chuanjiang Luo

Joint-Centric Dual Contrastive Alignment with Structure-Preserving and Information-Balanced Regularization 38
Habibeh Naderi, Behrouz Haji Soleimani, and Stan Matwin

LeAP: Learnable Adaptive Permutation for Feature Selection in Heterogeneous and Sparse Recommender Systems 56
Yihong Huang, Chen Chu, Fei Chen, Yu Lin, Ruiduan Li, and Zhihao Li

PIANO: Personalized Reranking via Information Aggregation Node for Music Search Optimization 73
Weisheng Li, Chuqiao Huang, Pengcheng Li, Zhengchao Peng, Qiang Xiao, Zhongqian Xie, Qiang Huang, and Chuanjiang Luo

Recovering Business Rules as Cascade Lookups for Enterprise Field Prediction 91
Changxu Duan

Towards Semantic Alignment: Intent-Aware Meta Learning for Urban Fields Recommendation 109
Chunyang Li, Xiuwen Yi, Shumeng Bai, Chengjie Guo, Zheyi Pan, Zhichao Huang, Junbo Zhang, and Yu Zheng

Industrial AI, Monitoring and Digital Twins

A Machine Learning Framework for Turbofan Health Estimation via Inverse Problem Formulation 129
Milad Leyli-Abadi, Lucas Thil, Sébastien Razakarivony, Guillaume Doquet, and Jesse Read

AI-Lite: Adaptive Data Center Cooling Optimization Based on Machine Learning ... 147
Xiaosong Chen, Zizhao Mo, Huanle Xu, Yang Liu, and Wing Cheong Lau

Combining Multiple Dissimilarity Spaces for Industrial Customer Prediction with Multi-matrix Median LVQ ... 164
Lukas Bader, Dietlind Zühlke, and Ina Terwey-Scheulen

From Manual to Real-World: Deep Unfolded Neural Network for Cross-Domain UXO Retrieval ... 181
Gheorghe Marian Craioveanu and Grigore Stamatescu

Geometric Attractor Monitoring: A Robust and Frugal Framework for Multi-modal Industrial Robotic Cycles ... 198
Martin Bonsergent-Brachet, Jesse Read, and Dany Abboud

Interval Estimation in Water Distribution Systems Using Physics-Informed Graph Neural Networks ... 215
Inaam Ashraf, André Artelt, David P. Leins, and Barbara Hammer

Local Intrinsic Dimensionality of Ground Motion for Early Detection of Catastrophic Slope Failure ... 232
Yuansan Liu, James Bailey, and Antoinette Tordesillas

SQC-Guard: A Statistical Quality Control Based Monitoring Framework for NLP Pipelines ... 250
Jaskaran Kawatra, Sanjana Rajamani, Sebin Sabu, Ewart Jonathan Sheldon, Nick James, John Booth, Alex Eze, Daniel Key, Shiren Patel, Alexandros Zenonos, Rebecca Pope, Neil Sebire, and Pavithra Rajendran

Watt's Your Range? An AI-Powered Digital Twin for EV Energy Consumption Estimation ... 268
Lazaros Adaloglou, Markus Englberger, Nikos Avramis, Camiel Beckers, Thanasis Trantas, and Devendra Singh Dhami

Large Language Models, Agents and Reasoning

ARENA: A Cognitive Multi-agent Framework for Modeling Conflict-Driven Multi-party Conversation ... 289
Xu Sun, Lu Zuo, Ziyang Zeng, Trung Hieu Ngo, Kai Liu, Alexis Lechervy, Frédéric Jurie, Julien Hatin, and Emmanuel Bertin

ASDA: Automated Skill Distillation and Adaptation for Financial Reasoning ... 306
Tik Yu Yim, Wenting Tan, Sum Yee Chan, Tak-Wah Lam, and Siu Ming Yiu

Application of LLM Agents for Long-Form Question Answering in Systems Biology ... 324
Charvi Jain, Sahar Vahdati, Pauline Porschitz, Mounir El Hankouri, Nandu Gopan, Ivo F. Sbalzarini, and Jens Lehmann

AutoQA-MAS: An LLM-Based Multi-agent System for Autonomous Website End-to-End Testing ... 342
Adriana-Simona Mihaita and Kai Sor

DynaPitch: A Two-Stage Framework for Dynamic Script Generation in Agent-Assisted Sales Conversations ... 360
Swapnil Parekh, Sonia Sharma, Pooja Voladoddi, Ramakrishnan Sathyavageeswaran, Andrew Mattarella-Micke, and Jiayao Liu

From Semantic Matching to Factual Pattern Mining: Fact-Anchored Iterative Reasoning for Government Hotline Dispatching ... 378
Shun Chen, Xiuwen Yi, Chengjie Guo, Yanyong Huang, Tianrui Li, and Yu Zheng

Game of Phones: Harnessing Game Theory and LLMs in 'Bot Wars' to Counteract Phone Scams ... 395
Nardine Basta, Robin Carpentier, Benjamin Zhao, and Dali Kaafar

LIBER: Lifelong User Behavior Modeling Based on Large Language Models ... 412
Rong Shan, Chenxu Zhu, Shigang Quan, Bo Chen, Jianghao Lin, Xiaoling Cai, Hong Zhu, Xiangyang Li, Yunjia Xi, Weinan Zhang, and Ruiming Tang

Little Brains, Big Feats: Exploring Compact Language Models ... 429
Dari Baturova, Elena Bruches, Ivan Chernov, Roman Derunets, Arsenii Fomin, and Andrey Kostin

MURENA, a MUlti-agent LLM Pipeline for Large-Scale Real Estate MaNAgement ... 446
Marco De Luca , Simone Monaco, Claudiu Tcaciuc, Alice Gorrino, Giovanna De Luca , Daniele Apiletti, and Tania Cerquitelli

NRITYAM: Language Models Meet Art and Heritage of Dance 463
Punit Kumar Singh, Niladri Ghosh, Advait Joshi, Shailee Choudhary, Michael Färber, and Haiqin Yang

Taxonomic and Functional Augmentation of Ecological Networks Using Large Language Models 479
Aleksandra Grzelik, Karol Opara, Aniket Thakur, Jahnavi Persadh, Ursula Scharler, and Ulf Dieckmann

The Illusion of Success: Procedure-Aware Evaluation is Critical for LLM Agents 496
Hongliu Cao, Ilias Driouich, and Eoin Thomas

Natural Language Processing and Information Retrieval

From Clickbait to Answers: Spoiler Generation for Multimodal Chinese News Feeds 515
Haoqian Song, Fuwen Zhao, Haoran Yin, Yiran Du, Xuan Luo, Xindi Ma, and Chaoyuan Zuo

From Rules to Neural Graphs: Scalable Structured Prediction for Patent Prior Art Search 533
Nikolai Zenovkin and Sebastian Björkqvist

From Speech to Subtitles: Evaluating ASR Models in Subtitling Italian Television Programs 550
Alessandro Lucca, Francesco Corso, and Francesco Pierri

Gradient-Scale Collapse in Additive Text-CF Fusion: Early Diagnosis and Minimal Repair 565
Yunan Zhang, Jingjing Fan, and Yanxiao Liu

Offline Metathesaurus Translation for Cross-Lingual Medical Entity Linking 582
Amaury Fierens, Théodore Cousin, François Roucoux, and Sébastien Jodogne

RAPT: Retrieval-Augmented Post-hoc Thresholding for Multi-label Classification 600
Lasal Jayawardena, Nirmalie Wiratunga, Ikechukwu Nkisi-Orji, and Darren Nicol

Remote Sensing, Earth Observation and Environmental Monitoring

A High-Resolution Landscape Dataset for Concept-Based XAI With Application to Species Distribution Models 619
Augustin de la Brosse, Damien Garreau, Thomas Houet, and Thomas Corpetti

Assessing the Benefits of Combining Advanced Deep Learning Techniques for Post-disaster Building Damage Assessment from UAV Imagery 636
Huy Quang Ung, Guillaume Habault, Roberto Legaspi, Hao Niu, Lian Cao, and Masato Taya

Benchmarking Deep Learning for Agricultural Potential Estimation from Multispectral Satellite Time Series 654
Mohammad El Sakka, Lotfi Chaari, and Josiane Mothe

Building a Deep Temporal Emulator of an Ocean Carbon Uptake Model 672
Sweety Mohanty, Daniyal Kazempour, Andrea Göhring, Willi Rath, Lavinia Patara, and Peer Kröger

HADT: A Heterogeneous Multi-agent Differential Transformer for Autonomous Earth Observation Satellite Cluster 690
Mohamad A. Hady, Muhammad Anwar Masum, Siyi Hu, Mahardhika Pratama, Zehong Cao, and Ryszard Kowalczyk

Author Index 707

Graph Learning and Structured Representation Learning

Competition-Aware CPC Forecasting with Near-Market Coverage

Sebastian Frey[1], Edoardo Beccari[1], Maximilian Kranz[1], Nicolò Alberto Pellizzari[1], Ali Mete Karaman[1], Qiwei Han[1](✉), and Maximilian Kaiser[2]

[1] Nova School of Business and Economics, Lisbon, Portugal
{66172,67990,67080,63585,67799,qiwei.han}@novasbe.pt
[2] University of Hamburg, Hamburg, Germany
maximilian.kaiser@uni-hamburg.de

Abstract. Cost-per-click (CPC) in paid search is an auction-generated outcome shaped by a competitive landscape that is only partially observable from any single advertiser's history. From 1.66 billion Google Ads log records for a concentrated car-rental market (2021–2023), we construct a weekly panel of 1,811 keyword series over 127 weeks (218,924 keyword–week observations) and build competition-aware proxies from keyword text, CPC trajectories, and geographic market structure. The design combines (i) semantic neighborhoods and a semantic keyword graph from pretrained transformer-based keyword representations, (ii) behavioral neighborhoods from Dynamic Time Warping (DTW) alignment of CPC trajectories, and (iii) geographic-intent covariates capturing localized demand and marketplace heterogeneity. We evaluate these signals both as exogenous covariates and as relational priors in spatiotemporal graph forecasters, benchmarking them against statistical, neural, and time-series foundation-model baselines. The results reveal a clear horizon crossover. At one week, graph-based models achieve the lowest error, reducing sMAPE by 15.1% relative to the strongest classical/ML baseline; at the six- and twelve-week horizons, covariate-augmented foundation models dominate, reducing sMAPE by 22.5% and 27.6%, respectively. The gains concentrate in the high-CPC, high-volatility keywords where forecasting errors are most costly. A falsification battery supports the competition interpretation at the planning horizon: the semantic competition graph outperforms a confounder-matched non-competitive graph by 4.05 sMAPE points, and matched-neighbour and time-shuffled controls show the six-week gains are competition-specific rather than generic smoothing. Together, the findings establish a horizon-dependent competition-aware forecasting design for auction-driven advertising markets under partial observability.

Keywords: Cost-per-Click Forecasting · Paid Search · Partial Observability · Spatiotemporal Graph Neural Networks · Time-Series Foundation Models

M. Baratchi et al. (Eds.): ECML PKDD 2026, LNAI 16949, pp. 3–18, 2027.
https://doi.org/10.1007/978-3-032-37682-4_1

1 Introduction

Paid search advertising allocates sponsored placements through real-time auctions triggered by user queries, and advertisers typically pay under a cost-per-click (CPC) pricing scheme [6,11,13]. In sponsored search, CPC is not a fixed tariff but an auction-generated outcome shaped by bid-dependent ranking, platform-estimated quality signals, and query-specific auction conditions [7,15,17]. For advertisers, this creates a difficult forecasting problem: CPC determines how much demand a fixed budget can buy, yet the competitive state that generates CPC is only partially observable from any single advertiser's data.

This partial observability is central. Advertisers observe realized CPC, clicks, impressions, and spend, but they do not observe competitor bids, competitor quality signals, or the full auction state underlying price formation [7]. Our objective is therefore not to recover the latent auction state structurally, but to approximate competition through observable proxies. This distinction matters because purely autoregressive approaches are often informative over short horizons, yet become less reliable when regime shifts, localized demand changes, and competitor reallocation increasingly shape CPC dynamics.

To address this limitation, we construct three complementary proxy families from observable data. Semantic similarity captures substitutable intent across keywords; behavioral alignment captures shared exposure to latent demand and auction shocks; and geographic intent captures segmented market context and localized competitive intensity. Operationally, we instantiate these ideas through semantic neighborhoods and a fixed semantic keyword graph, Dynamic Time Warping (DTW)-based behavioral neighborhoods, and hierarchical geographic-intent covariates. These proxy families allow us to study two distinct representation routes: competition-aware covariates for general forecasters, and relational priors for spatiotemporal graph neural networks (STGNNs).

We evaluate this design on large-scale Google Ads logs from the car-rental sector, a setting in which demand is geographically localized, acquisition costs are operationally important, and competition is concentrated among a relatively small set of major advertisers. After preprocessing, the data yield a weekly panel of 1,811 keywords over 127 weeks. This does not imply full market observability. Rather, it creates a setting with sufficiently broad realized-outcome coverage to learn structured competition proxies from repeated interactions while remaining fundamentally partially observed.

Across a broad model universe spanning classical baselines, neural baselines, time-series foundation models (TSFMs), and STGNNs, we find clear horizon dependence in the value of competition-aware forecasting design. Graph-based models perform best at the 1-week horizon, where short-run spillovers are most relevant. At the 6-week and 12-week horizons, covariate-augmented TSFMs become clearly dominant, with coarse geographic structure acting as a particularly strong stabilizing prior. These gains are concentrated in the most operationally consequential part of the market: high-CPC, high-volatility keywords.

The paper makes four contributions. First, it reframes keyword-level CPC forecasting as a problem of partial competition observability, arguing that auction-generated prices can be forecast more effectively when latent competition is approximated through observable proxy structure. Second, it operationalizes this idea at industrial scale by constructing semantic, behavioral, and geographic competition proxies and evaluating them across both covariate-based and graph-based forecasting routes. Third, it shows that the value of competition-aware design is strongly horizon-dependent: semantic relational structure is most useful for short-run spillovers, while coarse geographic context is most useful as a stabilizing prior at medium and longer horizons. Fourth, it stress-tests the competition interpretation with a falsification battery: matched non-competitive, random, and time-shuffled neighbour controls, a confounder-matched non-competitive graph, and per-region segmentation. At the six-week planning horizon the semantic competition graph outperforms the matched non-competitive graph by 4.05 sMAPE points ($p < 10^{-39}$), showing the gains there are competition-specific rather than generic smoothing or feature enrichment, while the same battery delimits precisely the horizons and markets where the effect holds.

2 Related Work

CPC and Paid Search Auctions. In Generalized Second Price (GSP) auctions, ad slots are assigned by ranking advertisers on an effective score that combines bids with platform-estimated quality factors [4,12]. Realized CPC is therefore an endogenous auction outcome shaped by rival bids, click-through-rate predictions, and latent demand shifts [1,8]. A substantial literature explains how CPC is generated in sponsored search and how auction design and ranking affect advertiser outcomes [24]. However, this literature is more informative about price formation than about forecasting under partial competition observability, where the competitive state is not directly observed from one advertiser's history.

Keyword-Level CPC Forecasting. Classical baselines such as ARIMA and Prophet remain common reference points in business forecasting [20], including advertising applications [18], but they often struggle with nonlinear and non-stationary dynamics. More flexible machine-learning and deep-learning approaches can improve performance, yet typically depend on task-specific feature construction and do not directly address the problem that the competitive structure driving CPC is only indirectly observed. The closest adjacent empirical work is [18], which studies keyword-level CPC forecasting with competitive-landscape covariates, but does not evaluate foundation-style forecasters, does not construct text-derived relational structure, and does not compare covariate-based and graph-based competition representations within a unified framework.

Time-Series Foundation Models. Recent time-series foundation models (TSFMs), including TimeGPT [9], Chronos [3], and Moirai [21], have demonstrated strong zero-shot and few-shot performance across diverse forecasting tasks. Their application to advertising-cost forecasting remains limited, and in particular little is known about how these pretrained forecasters interact with competition-aware exogenous covariates in auction-generated settings. This makes CPC forecasting a relevant testbed for understanding whether large pretrained models can absorb proxy-based competition structure without an explicit relational topology.

Graph-Based Forecasting and Latent Interaction Structure. Graph neural networks have become standard tools for spatiotemporal forecasting in traffic, energy, and sensor systems, where graph structure is typically given exogenously by physical topology or network connectivity. CPC forecasting differs in a crucial respect: there is no natural physical graph. Dependence arises from substitutable intent, shared exposure to demand shocks, and localized market overlap rather than from explicit network links [23,24]. In this setting, the central problem is not only forecasting on a graph, but constructing a competition graph and competition covariates when the interaction structure is latent and only indirectly observable.

Research Gap. Three gaps follow. First, sponsored-search research provides rich auction-theoretic intuition but limited guidance for forecasting under partial competition observability. Second, advertising-cost forecasting has not yet systematically incorporated modern TSFMs in a keyword-level CPC setting. Third, existing graph-forecasting work offers limited evidence on how text-derived, behavior-derived, and geography-derived proxy structure should be represented when competition is latent rather than directly observed. Our contribution is therefore not a new universal forecasting architecture, but a competition-aware forecasting design that makes latent market structure usable across heterogeneous model families.

3 Business Context and Data Characteristics

Paid search advertising is one of the most important performance channels in digital marketing, allocating sponsored placements through real-time auctions triggered by user queries [11,13]. In car rental, CPC shocks have direct operational consequences because acquisition costs can compress margins quickly in periods of elevated competition. The sector is a particularly suitable empirical setting because it combines intense competition among a limited set of major rental groups and intermediaries, high online price transparency, and strong geographic concentration around airports and major cities.

We build on a large-scale dataset of keyword-level Google Ads performance logs for the car-rental industry (2021–2023), provided by a European business intelligence company. The raw dataset contains approximately 1.66 billion log-level observations. Each record contains keyword and matched-query text, contextual information such as device category and search type, and core performance metrics including impressions, clicks, and advertising cost.

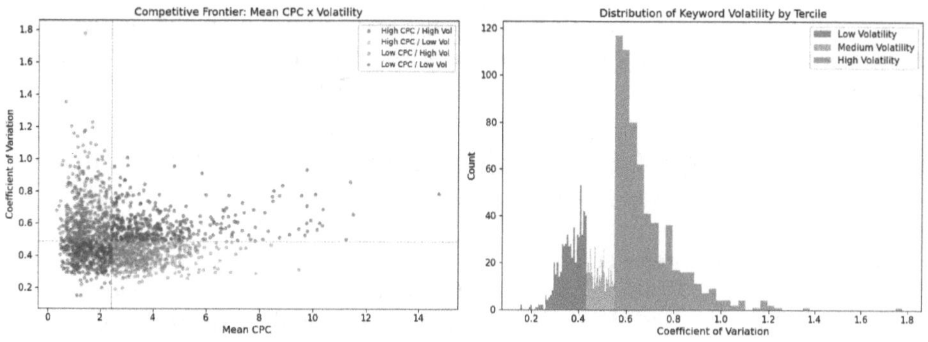

Fig. 1. Competitive frontier segmentation. The scatter plot maps keyword mean CPC against volatility (Coefficient of Variation), with median splits defining four distinct market regimes. The top-right quadrant identifies high-risk, high-value keywords.

To construct a stable forecasting universe, we restrict attention to car-rental intent, normalize keywords to canonical forms, parse landing-page URLs into registrable domains, and apply a domain-quality filter that removes unrelated or extremely low-coverage sites. We then retain keywords observed in at least 110 distinct weeks out of a 127-week window. The final weekly panel contains 1,811 keyword series and 218,924 keyword–week observations.

Weekly CPC is defined as

$$\texttt{cpc\_week}_{k,t} = \frac{\texttt{adcost\_sum}_{k,t}}{\texttt{adclicks\_sum}_{k,t}} \quad \text{for } \texttt{adclicks\_sum}_{k,t} > 0.$$

This weekly aggregation provides a practical compromise between auction-level noise reduction and managerial relevance, as weekly CPC aligns naturally with campaign planning and budget-steering cycles.

The retained domain universe remains concentrated around a relatively small set of continuously active major brands and intermediaries. This does not imply full market observability. Rather, it creates broad realized-outcome coverage and repeated competitive interactions within the focal vertical, making the data dense enough to learn structured competition proxies while preserving the central informational asymmetry of the problem.

The resulting panel exhibits strong right skewness and heavy-tailed behavior typical of paid-search markets. For CPC, the weekly mean is 2.86 while the maximum reaches 80.16, with a pronounced upper tail (p99 = 12.13) and skewness of 3.34. Traffic and spend metrics are substantially more extreme, reflecting a Pareto-like structure in which a small set of highly competitive queries accounts for disproportionate volume [5,16]. This heterogeneity motivates evaluation beyond average forecast error alone.

Figure 1 summarizes this heterogeneity by mapping keyword mean CPC against the coefficient of variation. The resulting four quadrants define distinct market regimes, with the top-right quadrant representing the *competitive frontier*: keywords that are both expensive and volatile. This region is strategically important because forecasting failures there carry disproportionate budget risk. It also provides a natural setting in which to test whether competition-aware proxy design delivers its largest gains where forecasting is hardest.

4 Methodology: Competition-Aware Forecasting Under Partial Observability

Keyword-level CPC forecasting in sponsored search is a prediction problem under partial observability. While advertisers observe realized CPC, impressions, clicks, and spend, they do not observe competitor bids, quality scores, budget constraints, or the full auction state that generates prices. Our objective is therefore not structural recovery of the auction mechanism, but scalable approximation of latent competition through observable proxy structure.

Our contribution lies in competition-proxy design and cross-family evaluation under partial observability, rather than in introducing a new universal forecasting backbone. As illustrated in Fig. 2, we operationalize latent competition through semantic, behavioral, and geographic signals, and study two implementation routes. In the first route, these proxies enter forecasting models as exogenous covariates. In the second, competition is represented relationally and supplied to spatiotemporal graph neural networks through a fixed semantic adjacency matrix. Across both routes, the target is weekly CPC at forecast horizon $h \in \{1, 6, 12\}$.

4.1 Competition Proxy Extraction

We derive three complementary proxy families from observable data. Each proxy is designed to approximate a different aspect of latent competition that is not directly observable from any single advertiser's history.

Semantic Proxy: Substitutable Intent. Keywords with similar user intent often compete for overlapping advertising inventory even when they differ lexically. To capture this intent-level proximity, we encode each keyword k_i using pretrained transformer-based text representations from `all-MiniLM-L6-v2` [19]. The language model is used only as a representational device: it supplies fixed semantic embeddings rather than generative outputs. This yields an embedding $e_i \in \mathbb{R}^{384}$. Pairwise cosine similarity is then used to identify semantically related keywords. These semantic neighborhoods serve two purposes: they generate neighborhood-based competition covariates and they define the topology of a fixed semantic keyword graph.

Behavioral Proxy: Shared Exposure to Latent Shocks. Textual similarity does not exhaust competitive relatedness. Keywords with weak lexical overlap may still exhibit similar CPC dynamics because they are exposed to common demand shocks, campaign timing, or auction reallocation. We therefore construct behavioral neighborhoods using Dynamic Time Warping (DTW), which measures similarity between CPC trajectories while allowing local temporal misalignment [10].

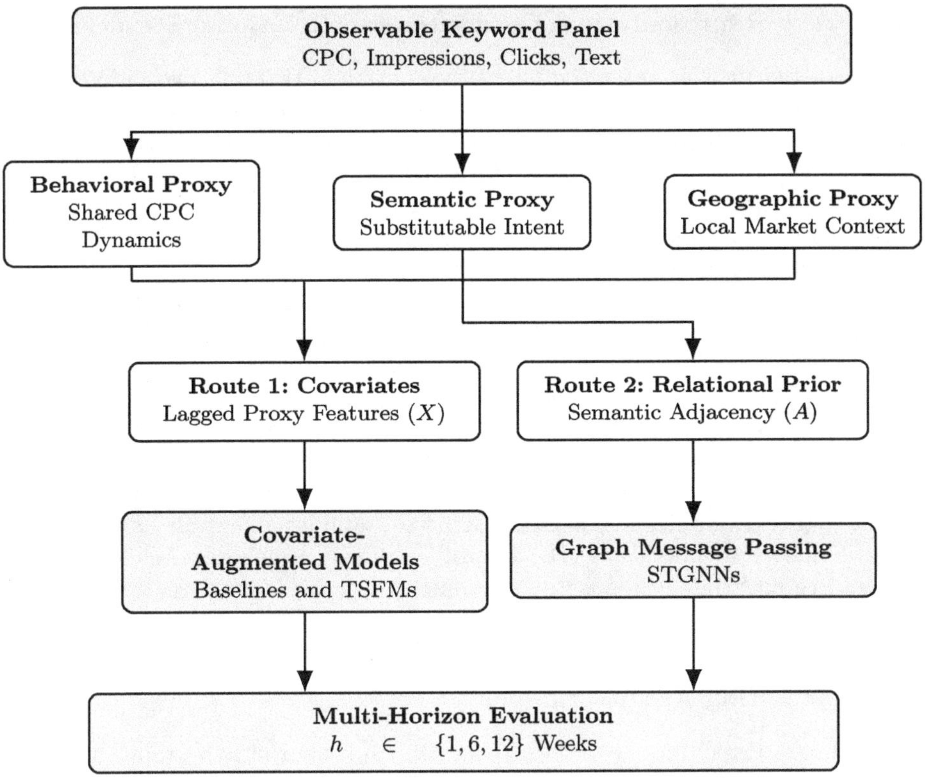

Fig. 2. Competition-aware forecasting design under partial observability. Latent competition is approximated through three proxy families and represented either as exogenous covariates or as a fixed relational prior under a common multi-horizon evaluation protocol.

To avoid pathological alignments, we impose a Sakoe–Chiba band constraint. In the covariate route, these neighbors are summarized into leakage-free behavioral competition features constructed from historical CPC trajectories only.

Geographic Proxy: Segmented Market Context. In the car-rental setting, auction pressure is strongly localized. Queries tied to airports, cities, or countries reflect distinct demand pools and competitive conditions. We extract geographic intent from keyword text, curated gazetteers, and hierarchical geographic mapping. Each keyword is assigned structured location indicators at the continent, country, and city levels. Rather than assuming that finer geography is always better, we retain multiple hierarchical resolutions and evaluate them empirically. These geography-derived variables act as spatial competition proxies by encoding localized demand conditions and marketplace heterogeneity.

4.2 Proxy Representation: Covariates and Relational Structure

The extracted proxies enter the forecasting problem through two different representations. The first route treats competition information as exogenous conditioning variables. These include leakage-free summaries of neighboring CPC histories derived from semantic and DTW neighborhoods, together with structured geographic-intent indicators and core operational controls. This route allows forecasting models to condition on observable approximations to latent competition without imposing an explicit graph topology.

The second route represents competition relationally. Using the keyword embeddings e_i, we construct a fixed semantic graph $A^{sem} \in \mathbb{R}^{N\times N}$ over the keyword universe. For each node, directed edges are assigned to its k nearest semantic neighbors under cosine similarity, with $k = 10$ selected as a stable and competitive graph sparsity level in preliminary experiments. The adjacency matrix is row-normalized before model training.

We restrict the relational route to a fixed semantic graph to isolate the effect of stable text-grounded competition structure and to maintain comparability across STGNN architectures. Behavioral proximity is incorporated instead as leakage-free covariates because its dynamic, trajectory-derived nature makes it less suitable as a fixed *ex ante* adjacency prior.

4.3 Forecasting Architectures

We evaluate three model classes: classical and neural non-graph baselines, covariate-augmented time-series foundation models, and spatiotemporal graph neural networks.

Classical and Neural Baselines. We benchmark a broad suite of traditional forecasting models, including statistical approaches (SARIMAX), tree-based machine learning models (XGBoost, Random Forest, LightGBM), deep neural networks (MLP, LSTM, GRU), and a tabular foundation model (TabPFN). These baselines establish the reference performance attainable from autoregressive and weakly contextual histories.

Covariate-Augmented Foundation Models. We benchmark state-of-the-art TSFMs, including Chronos-2 [2], TimeGPT [9], and Moirai [21], under exogenous conditioning. In this setting, competition proxies are supplied as covariates alongside the historical CPC series and core operational inputs. This route tests whether large pretrained forecasters can absorb competition-aware structure without an explicit relational topology.

Spatiotemporal Graph Neural Networks. To model cross-keyword dependence explicitly, we evaluate STGNNs that consume the fixed semantic graph A^{sem}. The input panel is represented as a spatiotemporal tensor

$$X \in \mathbb{R}^{N\times T\times F},$$

where N is the number of keywords, T the input history length, and F the number of features. The model outputs multi-horizon forecasts $\hat{Y}_{t+h} \in \mathbb{R}^N$.

We focus on three representative STGNN architectures. DCRNN models competition as diffusion over the predefined graph within a recurrent forecasting framework [14]. GConvLSTM integrates graph convolutions directly into LSTM gating, providing a stable convolutional-recurrent formulation. GraphWaveNet combines fixed graph structure with an adaptive component, allowing limited refinement of the exogenous relational prior [22]. All STGNNs are trained globally on the CPC panel using a leakage-free chronological split and optimized with Mean Absolute Error (MAE), which is more robust than squared-error objectives under the heavy-tailed distribution of CPC.

5 Evaluation Procedures and Results

5.1 Experimental Protocol

All models are evaluated on weekly CPC forecasting for 1,811 keyword series under a strict chronological split, with the final 20% of observations reserved for out-of-sample testing to prevent temporal leakage. We study three forecasting horizons, $h \in \{1, 6, 12\}$ weeks, corresponding respectively to short-term bid steering, medium-term tactical planning, and longer-range budget allocation.

We report Symmetric Mean Absolute Percentage Error (sMAPE) as the primary business metric and Root Mean Squared Error (RMSE) as a magnitude-sensitive secondary metric. Because CPC is heavily right-skewed and keyword heterogeneity is substantial, all results are aggregated across the keyword panel and reported as mean $\pm$ standard deviation. Beyond point estimates, we assess whether per-horizon improvements are statistically reliable across the keyword panel using the paired Wilcoxon signed-rank test, a bootstrap 95% confidence interval on the mean sMAPE difference, and the per-keyword win rate. To support reproducibility despite proprietary data restrictions, we release the preprocessing, feature-construction, graph-construction, modelling, and evaluation code together with graph-construction parameters, random seeds, hyperparameter grids, and chronological split definitions.[1]

5.2 Cross-Horizon Family-Level Comparison

Table 1 provides a high-level performance summary using the strongest representative from each model family. The dominant architecture changes systematically across horizons. At the 1-week horizon, STGNNs perform best, indicating that relational structure is especially useful for short-run competitive spillovers. At the 6-week and 12-week horizons, covariate-augmented TSFMs dominate, suggesting that stable contextual priors, especially geographic ones, become more valuable as forecast distance increases. Across all three horizons, competition-aware families outperform classical and non-graph ML baselines. Table 2 reports

[1] https://github.com/Sebastian-Frey/Competition-Aware-GNNs-for-TimeSeriesForecasting.

Table 1. Cross-horizon summary using the strongest representative from each model family. Reported metric is overall sMAPE (%). Lower is better. The strongest representative may differ across horizons.

Model Family Representative	1-Week	6-Week	12-Week
Best Classical/ML Baseline	30.42	35.04	40.23
Best Covariate-Augmented TSFM	26.66	27.14	29.14
Best Spatiotemporal GNN	25.82	30.42	37.46

Table 2. Comprehensive multi-horizon evaluation across all baseline, foundation, and graph-based models. Metrics reflect the best-performing configuration for each model at each horizon. Reported value is mean sMAPE (%).

Model Family	Architecture	1-Week	6-Week	12-Week
Classical & ML Baselines	SARIMAX	43.74	43.93	44.30
	XGBoost	30.71	36.64	40.91
	LightGBM	30.68	36.62	40.89
	RF	31.53	38.25	43.02
	MLP	30.42	38.10	40.23
	LSTM	30.70	36.62	40.39
	GRU	31.00	36.45	40.59
	TabPFN	31.45	35.04	40.79
Covariate-Augmented TSFMs	Moirai	34.22	30.14	34.28
	TimeGPT	26.66	29.29	31.77
	Chronos-2	27.94	27.14	29.14
Spatiotemporal GNNs	GraphWaveNet	25.82	30.57	37.81
	GConvLSTM	26.06	30.69	38.33
	DCRNN	26.06	30.42	37.46
	AGCRN	26.79	30.76	37.77

the full model universe across all three horizons, providing the per-architecture basis for the family-level representatives in Table 1 and confirming the horizon-dependent crossover: STGNNs lead at one week, while covariate-augmented TSFMs lead at six and twelve weeks. The graph-over-classical advantage is also statistically robust at the per-keyword level when comparing the best STGNN against the strongest classical/ML baseline at each horizon (Table 3).

5.3 Main Comparison at the 6-Week Planning Horizon

We focus the main detailed comparison on the 6-week horizon because it is both managerially central and methodologically revealing. Relative to the 1-week horizon, it is less dominated by immediate short-run spillovers. Relative to the 12-week horizon, it is less affected by accumulated long-range drift. It

Table 3. Added value of the best graph model over the best classical/ML baseline at each horizon. The model choices match the per-horizon representatives in Table 1, but the GNN and classical sMAPE columns are re-aggregated over the 1,809 keywords common to both compared models, so Δ equals their difference. Δ is the paired per-keyword mean difference in sMAPE (negative favours the graph model), with a bootstrap 95% confidence interval; all paired differences are significant under a Wilcoxon signed-rank test ($p < 10^{-20}$).

Horizon	Model pair	GNN	Base	Δ	95% CI	Win
1-week	GraphWaveNet vs. MLP	25.77	30.42	−4.65	[−5.13, −4.19]	82%
6-week	DCRNN vs. TabPFN	30.37	35.05	−4.68	[−5.47, −3.91]	65%
12-week	DCRNN vs. MLP	37.38	40.22	−2.84	[−4.34, −1.27]	62%

Table 4. Main comparison of forecasting architectures at the 6-week horizon. Metrics are Mean ± Standard Deviation across 1,811 keywords. Bold values indicate the best result within each model family and globally.

Model Family	Architecture	Best Competition-Aware Setup	sMAPE (%)	RMSE
Statistical & ML Baselines	SARIMAX	Univariate lags	43.93 ± 23.55	1.660 ± 1.759
	XGBoost	Core operational features	36.64 ± 17.51	1.301 ± 1.119
	TabPFN (1-shot)	**Core operational features**	**35.04 ± 17.77**	**1.250 ± 1.133**
Covariate-AugmentedTSFMs	Moirai	Leakage-free lags + calendar stabilization	30.14 ± 18.24	1.000 ± 0.970
	TimeGPT	Calendar conditioning + growth clamp	29.29 ± 17.07	1.002 ± 1.008
	Chronos-2	**Geographic intent covariates**	**27.14 ± 15.04**	**0.841 ± 0.846**
Spatiotemporal GNNs Relational Priors	GraphWaveNet	Semantic graph + search mix	30.57 ± 20.57	1.005 ± 0.941
	GConvLSTM	Semantic graph + continent geography	30.69 ± 20.42	1.001 ± 0.955
	DCRNN	**Semantic graph + geo + semantic CPC**	**30.42 ± 20.42**	**1.000 ± 0.926**

therefore provides the most decision-relevant tactical planning horizon and the clearest separation among model families.

Table 4 reports the strongest configurations within each architecture family at this horizon.

Three patterns emerge. First, isolated or weakly contextual keyword histories reach a clear performance ceiling: the strongest baseline, TabPFN, attains 35.04% sMAPE, while SARIMAX remains substantially worse. Second, competition-aware TSFMs lower the global error floor materially, with Chronos-2 using geographic-intent covariates reaching 27.14% sMAPE, the strongest overall result. This indicates that coarse geographic localization acts as a powerful stabilizing prior for pretrained forecasters. Third, explicit relational modeling remains competitive and clearly improves on the non-graph baseline family: DCRNN, leveraging the semantic keyword graph alongside semantic-neighbor CPC signals, reaches 30.42% sMAPE and provides a structurally distinct route to competition-aware forecasting.

Table 5. Effect of geographic resolution averaged across graph backbones (mean sMAPE; lower is better).

Horizon	Continent (7 dummies)	Country (63 dummies)	City (268 dummies)
1w	26.36	26.72	27.16
6w	30.90	31.51	31.82
12w	37.93	38.70	39.04

Geographic Resolution. Because geographic intent is one of the strongest competition-aware priors, we examine whether finer geographic granularity improves forecasting. The answer is consistently no. As shown in Table 5, continent-level encoding outperforms country- and city-level encodings across all three horizons when averaged across graph backbones, by 0.61 sMAPE points over country and 0.92 over city at the 6-week horizon. The reason is statistical stability rather than semantic richness: coarse geography captures durable regional differences in demand intensity and seasonality without fragmenting the training signal.

5.4 Competitive Frontier Analysis

To assess where competition-aware proxy design matters most, we conduct a structured ablation across the GNN family and segment the keyword panel by CPC intensity and volatility. This segmentation yields well-populated partitions, with the high-CPC/high-volatility *competitive frontier* quadrant containing 402 strategically critical keywords.

The ablation results show that proxy effectiveness depends strongly on both horizon and market regime. At the 6-week horizon, the strongest specification combines geography with semantic-neighbor CPC information (`Core + Geo + Sem CPC`), improving overall sMAPE from 31.61% to 30.71%. More importantly, this combination lowers error in the highly unstable, high-volatility segment by 1.3 percentage points relative to core-only inputs. At 12 weeks, the simpler `Core + Continent` setup becomes the strongest prior, reducing overall error from 38.32% to 37.93%, highlighting that coarse geography serves as a robust anchor against long-term drift.

The results also show that proxy design must be selective. In our setting, indiscriminate feature stacking is consistently counterproductive in noisy auction environments. At the 6-week horizon, naive aggregation of all available proxies produces the weakest performance (34.0% sMAPE, 3.3 points worse than the strongest selective setup); at 12 weeks, this gap widens further. Taken together, these findings provide strong evidence that competition-aware proxy design is especially valuable in the hardest-to-forecast regions of the market, and that structured augmentation is preferable to exhaustive accumulation of all available signals.

5.5 Robustness: Are the Gains Competition-Specific?

A central concern is whether the gains from competition proxies reflect genuine competitive structure or merely generic contextual smoothing and feature enrichment. We address this with a falsification battery applied directly to the graph model: holding the architecture, training protocol, and evaluation fixed, we replace each competition signal with a null control and measure the change in per-keyword sMAPE. We report mean paired differences (real minus control; negative favours the real competition signal) with Wilcoxon signed-rank tests and bootstrap 95% confidence intervals over the 1,811 keywords.[2]

Neighbour and Graph Controls. At the six-week planning horizon, the falsification evidence is strongest for the matched and time-shuffled controls, while the random-neighbour comparison is smaller and should be interpreted as marginal evidence (Table 6). The semantic-neighbour competition covariate outperforms a confounder-matched but non-competitive control by 1.99 sMAPE points ($p < 10^{-16}$), a random-neighbour control by 0.25 ($p < 0.05$), and a time-shuffled version of the same neighbours by 1.69 ($p < 10^{-21}$); removing the covariate entirely costs 0.82 points ($p < 10^{-12}$). The relational route is more nuanced. The matched non-competitive graph is a *hard negative*: it links each keyword to neighbours that match on confounders normally associated with relatedness, such as mean CPC, volatility, and volume, but are semantically dissimilar. Its edges therefore look informative while connecting series that do not co-move, so message passing propagates a *structured, misleading* prior; this degrades accuracy by 4.05 points ($p < 10^{-39}$). A random graph, by contrast, imposes no systematic relationship: its edges carry no consistent signal and average out as noise, leaving it on par with the semantic graph (within 0.6 sMAPE). The contrast indicates that the damage comes from structured but wrong edges rather than from the absence of true competitive edges: an actively misleading prior hurts, a neutral one does not. At this horizon, then, the competition-specific signal resides primarily in the covariate route. This does not contradict the short-horizon result in Table 1; it clarifies the horizon dependence of the graph route: relational priors add value at one week, while medium-horizon gains are driven primarily by structured covariates and contextual stabilization. The advantage over the time-shuffled control further indicates that not only *which* keywords are related but also the *temporal alignment* of their histories carries competitive information.

Horizon Dependence and Scope. The falsification evidence is horizon-specific. At one week, where short-run autoregressive dynamics are strong, the null controls are statistically difficult to separate from the real signal even though graph forecasters perform best overall. At twelve weeks, the relationship reverses within

[2] These robustness experiments are interpreted as within-diagnostic contrasts: each real proxy and its null control are evaluated under the same chronological split, implementation, architecture, and training protocol. The table therefore reports relative paired effects rather than replacing the main benchmark estimates in Table 4.

Table 6. Falsification of competition signals at the six-week horizon. Each entry is the mean paired difference in per-keyword sMAPE (%) between the real competition signal and a null control (negative favours real competition), with a bootstrap 95% confidence interval and Wilcoxon p-value ($n = 1{,}811$).

Control	Δ sMAPE	95% CI	p
Real vs. matched non-competitive neighbours	−1.99	[−2.36, −1.62]	$< 10^{-16}$
Real vs. random neighbours	−0.25	[−0.52, +0.02]	< 0.05
Real vs. time-shuffled neighbours	−1.69	[−2.00, −1.39]	$< 10^{-21}$
Competition covariate on vs. off	−0.82	[−1.08, −0.56]	$< 10^{-12}$
Semantic vs. matched non-competitive graph	−4.05	[−4.57, −3.50]	$< 10^{-39}$

the graph diagnostic: competition covariates and the semantic graph begin to over-condition on noisy long-range competitive signals. Removing the semantic covariate, for instance, improves sMAPE by 2.81 points ($p < 10^{-26}$). This pattern explains why relational priors are most useful for short-run spillovers, while medium- and long-horizon performance is better stabilized by structured covariates, especially coarse geographic priors.

Geographic Heterogeneity. Segmenting the geographic effect by continent shows it is not uniform: continent-level geography significantly helps European keywords (-1.20, $p < 0.01$) and the unlocalised "Global" segment (-0.71, $p < 0.05$), but *hurts* North American keywords ($+0.48$, $p < 0.01$). This heterogeneity is consistent with a market-specific effect rather than a purely generic smoother, and it delimits where geographic conditioning is beneficial.

6 Conclusion

This paper framed CPC forecasting in paid search as a problem of partial competition observability. Advertisers do not observe competitor bids, quality signals, or the full auction state, yet their realized CPC histories carry exploitable traces of competitive structure. Our proxies extract that structure at scale and forecast CPC substantially better than competition-blind baselines: competition-aware foundation-model specifications cut sMAPE by 22.5% and 27.6% at the six- and twelve-week horizons relative to the strongest classical/ML baseline, and our falsification battery confirms the six-week signal is competition-specific rather than generic smoothing.

The main lesson is not that one forecasting architecture uniformly dominates, but that under partial competition observability, different proxy families and representation routes become useful at different forecast horizons. Graph-based models deliver the strongest short-horizon performance, indicating that semantic relational structure is especially useful for capturing short-run competitive spillovers. At medium and longer horizons, covariate-augmented TSFMs become clearly dominant, with coarse geographic context acting as a particularly effective stabilizing prior. These gains are most meaningful in the part of the market where forecasting failures are most costly. Improvements concentrate in high-CPC, high-volatility keywords, where auction pressure is strongest and budget risk is highest. In this sense, competition-aware forecasting does not merely improve average accuracy; it improves robustness in the most operationally consequential segment of the market.

Several limitations remain. The analysis is based on a single vertical with a relatively concentrated competitive landscape, so generalization to broader or less concentrated paid-search categories remains an open question. In addition, the semantic graph is fixed over time and therefore cannot capture evolving keyword relationships, market entry and exit, or shifting competitive regimes. Future work should examine dynamic graph construction, richer competitor-side signals where available, and validation across additional industries and auction settings. Our falsification analysis (Sect. 5.5) further shows that the competition signal is concentrated at the medium horizon and heterogeneous across markets, attenuating, and at the twelve-week horizon reversing, rather than improving uniformly; these are scope conditions of competition-aware design rather than universal guarantees. Finally, all evidence here is offline: because a deployed forecaster can itself influence bidding and hence future CPC—for example, budget reallocation by losing bidders can alter pacing and realized CPC—an online A/B evaluation is an important next step that an observational study cannot provide.

Overall, the findings show that auction-driven advertising markets can be forecast more effectively when competitive structure is modeled explicitly rather than treated as unobserved noise. The contribution is a horizon-dependent competition-aware forecasting design: relational priors are most valuable for short-run spillovers, while structured covariates, especially coarse geographic priors, stabilize medium- and long-horizon forecasts, turning partially observed competition into actionable forecasting signal without requiring bid-level access to the hidden auction state.

Acknowledgements. This work was supported by Fundação para a Ciência e a Tecnologia (UID/00124/2025 and UID/PRR/124/2025; DOI: https://doi.org/10.54499/UID/00124/2025) and by LISBOA2030 (DataLab2030, LISBOA2030-FEDER-01314200).

References

1. Aggarwal, G., Feldman, J., Muthukrishnan, S., Pal, M.: Sponsored search auctions with markovian users. arXiv preprint arXiv:0805.0766 (2008)
2. Amazon Science: Introducing chronos-2: From univariate to universal forecasting (2024). https://www.amazon.science/blog/introducing-chronos-2-from-univariate-to-universal-forecasting. Accessed 10 Jan 2025
3. Ansari, A.F., et al.: Chronos: Learning the Language of Time Series (2024). http://arxiv.org/abs/2403.07815. arXiv:2403.07815

4. Caragiannis, I., et al.: Bounding the inefficiency of outcomes in generalized second price auctions. arXiv preprint arXiv:1201.6429 (2014)
5. Clauset, A., Shalizi, C.R., Newman, M.E.J.: Power-law distributions in empirical data. SIAM Rev. **51**(4), 661–703 (2009)
6. Evans, D.S.: The online advertising industry: economics, evolution, and privacy. J. Econ. Perspect. **23**(3), 37–60 (2009)
7. Feldman, J., Muthukrishnan, S.: Algorithmic methods for sponsored search advertising. In: Performance Modeling and Engineering, pp. 91–122. Springer (2008)
8. Feldman, J., Muthukrishnan, S.: Algorithmic methods for sponsored search advertising. arXiv preprint arXiv:0805.1759 (2008)
9. Garza, A., Challu, C., Mergenthaler-Canseco, M.: TimeGPT-1 (2024). http://arxiv.org/abs/2310.03589. arXiv:2310.03589
10. Herrmann, M., Webb, G.I.: Amercing: an intuitive and effective constraint for dynamic time warping. Pattern Recogn. **137**, 109333 (2023). Open access under CC BY license
11. Jansen, B.J., Liu, Z., Simon, Z.: The effect of ad rank on the performance of keyword advertising campaigns. J. Am. Soc. Inform. Sci. Technol. **64**(10), 2115–2132 (2013)
12. Keerthi, S.S., Tomlin, J.A.: Constructing a maximum utility slate of on-line advertisements. arXiv preprint arXiv:0706.1318 (2007)
13. Laffey, D.: Paid search: the innovation that changed the web. Bus. Horiz. **50**(3), 211–218 (2007)
14. Li, Y., Yu, R., Shahabi, C., Liu, Y.: Diffusion Convolutional Recurrent Neural Network: Data-Driven Traffic Forecasting. arXiv preprint arXiv:1707.01926 (2018)
15. Milgrom, P.: Simplified mechanisms with an application to sponsored-search auctions. Games Econom. Behav. **70**(1), 62–70 (2010)
16. Montgomery, D.C., Runger, G.C.: Applied Statistics and Probability for Engineers, 6th edn. Wiley, Hoboken (2014)
17. Nekipelov, D., Wang, T.: Inference and auction design in online advertising. Commun. ACM **60**(7), 70–79 (2017)
18. Oldenburg, F., Han, Q., Kaiser, M.: Interpretable deep learning for forecasting online advertising costs: insights from the competitive bidding landscape. In: 2024 IEEE 11th International Conference on Data Science and Advanced Analytics (DSAA), pp. 1–10. IEEE (2024)
19. Reimers, N., Gurevych, I.: Sentence-bert: sentence embeddings using siamese bert-networks. arXiv preprint arXiv:1908.10084 (2019)
20. Taylor, S.J., Letham, B.: Forecasting at scale. Am. Stat. **72**(1), 37–45 (2018)
21. Woo, G., Laptev, N., Bessa, A.: Moirai: foundation models for time series forecasting. arXiv preprint arXiv:2402.02592 (2024)
22. Wu, Z., Pan, S., Long, G., Jiang, J., Zhang, C.: Graph wavenet for deep spatial-temporal graph modeling. In: Proceedings of the 28th International Joint Conference on Artificial Intelligence, IJCAI 2019, pp. 1907–1913. AAAI Press (2019)
23. Würfel, M., Han, Q., Kaiser, M.: Online advertising revenue forecasting: an interpretable deep learning approach. In: 2021 IEEE International Conference on Big Data (Big Data), pp. 1980–1989. IEEE (2021)
24. Yang, Y., Zhai, P.: Click-through rate prediction in online advertising: a literature review. Inf. Process. Manag. **59**(2), 102853 (2022)

Efficient Attribute-Boosted Diffusion Model for Personalized Sequential Recommendation

Dongjing Wang[1], Shijia Wang[2], Qiang Xiao[2(✉)], Liwen Xiao[1], Qimeng Yang[1], and Chuanjiang Luo[2]

[1] Hangzhou Dianzi University, Hangzhou 310018, China
{Dongjing.Wang,xiaoliwen,yangqimeng}@hdu.edu.cn
[2] NetEase Cloud Music, Hangzhou 310052, China
{wangshijia1,hzxiaoqiang,luochuanjiang03}@corp.netease.com

Abstract. As an essential stage in sequential recommender systems, the retrieval phase is responsible for generating accurate and diverse candidates based on the user's recent interactions. However, conventional retrieval methods often overlook infrequent user interests, resulting in monotonous and less engaging recommendations. To address this issue, we propose the **E**fficient **A**ttribute-boosted **D**iffusion **M**odel (EADM) for Personalized Sequential Recommendation, which incorporates diffusion models into the sequential recommendation framework to capture diverse and long-tail user interests. Particularly, EADM consists of three key modules: (1) a *transform input layer* to embed items into a continuous latent space, (2) a *noise processing layer* that perturbs both target items and historical sequences to enhance robustness and diversity, and (3) a *cross-attention-based net* (*CA-Net*) to incorporate attribute information while mitigating potential accuracy loss. Furthermore, an acceleration algorithm is designed to ensure scalability and computational efficiency for large-scale deployment. Extensive experiments on real-world datasets demonstrate that EADM consistently outperforms state-of-the-art baselines. Additionally, EADM has been successfully deployed on a music streaming platform, highlighting its strong practical value and industrial applicability. The source code of EADM is publicly available at https://github.com/ZionWong/EADM.

Keywords: Sequential Recommendation · Diffusion Model · Cross Attention · Diversity · Attribute-boosted

1 Introduction

Recommender systems have become essential tools for mitigating information overload in various applications, such as e-commerce and online multimedia services. Generally, large-scale industrial recommender systems consist of two

D. Wang and S. Wang—Equal Contribution.

M. Baratchi et al. (Eds.): ECML PKDD 2026, LNAI 16949, pp. 19–37, 2027.
https://doi.org/10.1007/978-3-032-37682-4_2

phases: retrieval and ranking. The retrieval phase is responsible for identifying candidate items aligned with user interests, thereby narrowing down the search space for the subsequent ranking phase.

With the advent of deep learning, retrieval methods have evolved from traditional collaborative filtering (CF) to representation learning-based sequential recommendation (SR) [26]. These methods typically generate user and item embeddings based on historical behaviors. Most existing methods rely on greedy top-k strategies to retrieve candidates with the highest similarity. However, greedy top-k selection tends to generate homogeneous recommendations, thereby limiting model-level diversity and failing to capture users' long-tail interests. We argue that these limitations stem from two main aspects. (1) **Neglected model-level diversity**: Existing methods primarily focus on modeling similarity, overlooking the need for diversity in the modeling process itself. (2) **Insufficient data-level diversity**: In real-world scenarios, user behaviors are often dominated by a few major interests [20], causing models to overfit these dominant patterns and obscure potential latent preferences. These concerns are supported by existing findings: popularity bias analyses show that point-estimate retrieval concentrates recommendations among head items [3], and coverage studies demonstrate that single-vector user representations systematically underrepresent niche interests [5].

Recently, Diffusion Models (DMs) [8,17] have demonstrated remarkable potential for enhancing diversity via noise injection [21] in CV and NLP. Motivated by this, we explore adapting DMs for the retrieval phase. By leveraging input variability and injecting controlled noise, our approach enables the exploration of diverse regions in the latent space, thereby capturing comprehensive user interests.

However, integrating diffusion models into sequential recommendation poses three critical challenges:

1. **Sequential Dependency**: Unlike standard unconditional generation, DMs in recommendation must be strictly conditioned on complex historical interaction sequences.
2. **Accuracy Degradation**: The stochasticity introduced to enhance diversity inevitably risks compromising recommendation precision.
3. **Efficiency Constraints**: The multi-step generation process of DMs is computationally expensive, making it often infeasible for latency-sensitive industrial systems.

To address these challenges, we propose the **E**fficient **A**ttribute-boosted **D**iffusion **M**odel (EADM). It comprises three key modules designed to tackle the aforementioned issues: (1) The **Transform Input Layer** embeds discrete items into a continuous latent space governed by Multivariate Normal Distributions (MND), capturing fine-grained preferences to facilitate generation (Addressing Challenge 1); (2) The **Noise Processing Layer** injects noise into target items to introduce model-level stochasticity and diversity (Addressing Challenge 1 & 2); (3) **CA-Net** leverages a cross-attention mechanism to incorporate attribute information, constraining the generation process to mitigate accuracy loss (Addressing Challenge 2). Crucially, to ensure practical efficiency (Addressing Challenge 3), we adopt an acceleration strategy based on Denoising Diffusion Implicit Models (DDIM) [17].

Our main contributions are summarized as follows:

- We propose EADM, a novel framework that structurally improves recommendation diversity by addressing both the limitations of the model and the data-level.
- We accelerate diffusion-based generation in recommender systems, thereby improving both efficiency and accuracy.
- We conducted extensive experiments that demonstrate substantial improvements over existing baselines and provide detailed insights into the online deployment of EADM.

2 Related Work

2.1 Sequential Recommendation

Sequential recommendation models user behavior as ordered interactions. Early neural methods use RNNs, e.g., GRU4Rec [7]. Transformer-based models, such as SASRec [9], further capture long- and short-term interests. However, most approaches represent user interests as fixed vectors and select top-scoring items greedily, often producing homogeneous recommendations and failing to reflect diverse intent [5]. To better represent diverse intent, multi-interest models such as MIND [12] extract multiple user vectors via capsule routing. These methods improve coverage but require a pre-set number of interests, which limits adaptability when user intent is highly variable or sparsely observed.

2.2 Diversity and Diffusion-Based Methods

Diversity-aware recommendation has been studied from several angles. Long-tail methods address the imbalance between head and tail items [23], popularity debiasing techniques correct for exposure bias [3], and coverage-oriented approaches optimize objectives beyond accuracy [5]. Within model design, diversity is approached via re-ranking [22], system-level strategies [10], or model-level integration such as balanced loss or heterogeneous preference modeling [25]. Diffusion-based generative methods have recently been explored to enhance diversity, ranging from collaborative filtering models like CODIGEM [19] and DiffRec [21] to sequential variants such as DreamRec [27], and context-aware approaches like CaDiRec [4] and BSARec [16]. These approaches improve diversity and capture complex preference distributions but often incur high computational cost and rely on conventional ranking objectives, limiting fine-grained sequential modeling.

Diffusion offers properties that align with the diversity problem in sequential recommendation. Its stochastic forward–reverse process generates candidates from learned noise, yielding natural exploration rather than greedy top-K

selection. Noise injection lets the model deviate from popularity-biased modes during sampling, and iterative denoising represents preferences as distributions rather than point estimates, capturing multi-modal user intent that single-vector encoders cannot.

EADM differs from prior diffusion-based recommenders in three respects. CODIGEM [19] and DiffRec [21] operate in collaborative filtering settings, whereas EADM targets sequential retrieval where item order and attribute context matter. DreamRec [27] applies diffusion to item generation without attribute guidance; EADM instead introduces a distributional cross-attention module that fuses category information through the 2-Wasserstein distance, addressing the mismatch between item-level noise and attribute-level semantics. Unlike re-ranking diversity methods that act after candidate generation, EADM injects diversity at the model level during retrieval, and the DDIM-based acceleration reduces inference to a single step, making online deployment practical.

3 Problem Formulation

Let $\mathcal{U} = \{u_1, u_2, \ldots, u_{|\mathcal{U}|}\}$, $\mathcal{I} = \{i_1, i_2, \ldots, i_{|\mathcal{I}|}\}$, and $\mathcal{C} = \{c_1, c_2, \ldots, c_{|\mathcal{C}|}\}$ denote the sets of users, items, and categories, respectively. Each item $i \in \mathcal{I}$ is associated with a category $c(i) \in \mathcal{C}$.

For a given user u, we denote the chronologically ordered interaction sequence as $S_u = (s_1, s_2, \ldots, s_n)$ where $s_j \in \mathcal{I}$, and the corresponding category sequence as $C_u = (c(s_1), c(s_2), \ldots, c(s_n))$. The goal of sequential recommendation in the retrieval phase is to predict the next item s_{n+1} that the user is most likely to interact with, and return a ranked set of K candidate items from $\mathcal{I}$.

4 Methodology

To harness the generative power of ***diffusion models***, we propose the **E**fficient **A**ttribute-boosted **D**iffusion **M**odel for Personalized Sequential Recommendation (EADM), introducing stochasticity via noise injection and distributed embeddings to capture diverse user interests. As illustrated in Fig. 1, EADM comprises three main components: ***Transform Input Layer***, ***Noise Processing Layer***, and ***Cross-Attention based Net*** (***CA-Net***).

4.1 Diffusion Model

The diffusion model comprises two processes: the forward and generative (reverse) processes. Below, we detail the integration of these processes within sequential recommendation (SR).

Forward Process. In this phase, the embedding of the target item is perturbed with noise to serve as input for subsequent modeling. Given the original embedding $\mathbf{x}_0$ and the Gaussian noise added in T steps, we can directly obtain $\mathbf{x}_t$

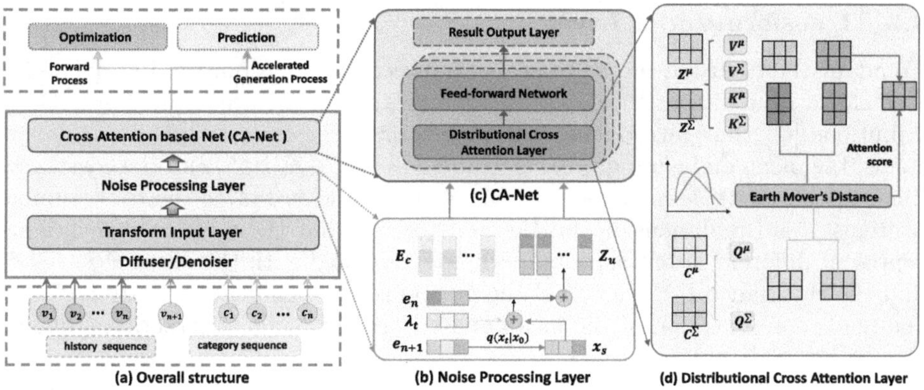

Fig. 1. The overview of EADM, including Transform Input Layer, Noise Processing Layer and CA-Net three key components.

through the Markov chain and the reparameterization trick [11]:

$$\begin{aligned} q(\mathbf{x}_t \mid \mathbf{x}_0) &= \mathcal{N}\left(\mathbf{x}_t; \sqrt{\bar{\alpha}_t}\mathbf{x}_0, (1-\bar{\alpha}_t)\mathbf{I}\right) \\ &= \sqrt{\bar{\alpha}_t}\mathbf{x}_0 + \sqrt{1-\bar{\alpha}_t}\epsilon \end{aligned}, \tag{1}$$

$$\bar{\alpha}_t = \prod_{s=1}^{t} \alpha_s, \quad \alpha_s = 1 - \beta_s, \quad \epsilon \sim \mathcal{N}(0, \mathbf{I}), \tag{2}$$

where $\beta_s \in (0, 1)$ represents the noise added at the s-th diffusion step, which controls how much noise is added into data. $\mathbf{I}$ denotes the identity matrix.

Reverse Process. The reverse process samples $\mathbf{x}'_t \sim \mathcal{N}(0, \mathbf{I})$ and iteratively denoises it to recover $\mathbf{x}'_0$:

$$p(\mathbf{x}_{t-1} \mid \mathbf{x}_t) = \mathcal{N}(\mathbf{x}_{t-1}; \mu_\theta(\mathbf{x}_t, t), \Sigma_\theta(\mathbf{x}_t, t)), \tag{3}$$

where $\mu_\theta(\mathbf{x}_t, t)$ and $\Sigma_\theta(\mathbf{x}_t, t)$ are the mean and variance of the Gaussian distribution parameterized by the θ, which is trained to maximize the Evidence Lower Bound (ELBO). The constant variance can be calculated as $\Sigma_\theta(\mathbf{x}_t, t) = \frac{1-\bar{\alpha}_{s-1}}{1-\bar{\alpha}_s}\beta_s$. Formally, the mean μ_θ can be evaluated with the neural network ϵ_θ as:

$$\mu_\theta(\mathbf{x}_t, t) = \frac{\sqrt{\bar{\alpha}_{t-1}}\beta_t}{1-\bar{\alpha}_t}\epsilon_\theta(\mathbf{x}_t, t) + \frac{\sqrt{\alpha_t}(1-\bar{\alpha}_{t-1})}{1-\bar{\alpha}_t}\mathbf{x}_t. \tag{4}$$

For the sake of simplicity, according to [8], the objective function 3 can also be formulated as:

$$L_{\text{simple}} = \mathbb{E}_{t,\mathbf{x}_0,\epsilon}\left[\left\|\epsilon - \epsilon_\theta\left(\sqrt{\bar{\alpha}_t}\mathbf{x}_0 + \sqrt{1-\bar{\alpha}_t\epsilon}, t\right)\right\|^2\right]. \tag{5}$$

4.2 Transform Input Layer

To adapt the diffusion model to sequential recommendation, we first define the Transform Input Layer to represent discrete items as Multivariate Normal Distributions [6], thus introducing uncertainty into the item embeddings. For all items, the mean embedding table is denoted as $\mathbf{M}_i^{\mu} \in \mathbb{R}^{|\mathcal{I}| \times d}$, and the covariance diagonal vector table is denoted as $\mathbf{M}_i^{\Sigma} \in \mathbb{R}^{|\mathcal{I}| \times d}$, where $|\mathcal{I}|$ is the total number of items, d is the dimension. Furthermore, given that the mean and covariance represent different latent aspects, both are combined with the mean $\mathbf{P}^{\mu} \in \mathbb{R}^{n \times d}$ and the covariance $\mathbf{P}^{\Sigma} \in \mathbb{R}^{n \times d}$ of the positional embedding, respectively. Thus, the final representation of the mean and covariance of the interaction sequence S_u can be obtained:

$$\mathbf{E}_{S_u}^{*} = \left[\mathbf{e}_{s_1}^{*}, \ldots, \mathbf{e}_{s_n}^{*}\right] = \left[\mathbf{m}_{s_1}^{*} + \mathbf{p}_1^{*}, \ldots, \mathbf{m}_{s_n}^{*} + \mathbf{p}_n^{*}\right], \tag{6}$$

where $*$ represent the mean μ and covariance Σ. Similarly, for all categories, the mean embeddings are denoted as $\mathbf{M}_c^{\mu} \in \mathbb{R}^{|\mathcal{C}| \times d}$, and the covariance matrix is denoted as $\mathbf{M}_c^{\Sigma} \in \mathbb{R}^{|\mathcal{C}| \times d}$,where $|\mathcal{C}|$ is the number of categories. And the final representation of the category sequence $\mathbf{E}_{C_u}^{*}$ can be defined in the same way.

In this way, each item in the sequence is represented as a Multivariate Normal Distribution with mean $\mu_{s_i} = \mathbf{e}_{s_i}^{\mu}$ and covariance $\Sigma s_i = diag(\mathbf{e}_{s_i}^{\Sigma}) \in \mathbb{R}^{d \times d}$, denoted as $\mathcal{N}(\mu_{s_i}, \Sigma_{s_i})$. Here, $diag(\cdot)$ refers to the operation of transforming a vector into a diagonal matrix with that vector as its diagonal. In comparison, each category in the sequence is represented as $\mathcal{N}(\mu_{c_i}, \Sigma_{c_i})$.

4.3 Noise Processing Layer

The key intuition of this layer is that injecting calibrated noise into the target item embedding forces the model to reconstruct user intent from a perturbed starting point, effectively widening the exploration cone around dominant preferences and exposing latent long-tail interests that deterministic encoders suppress. In the forward process, s-step noise is added to the target item's mean and covariance embeddings, $\mathbf{e}_{s_{n+1}}^{\mu}$ and $\mathbf{e}_{s_{n+1}}^{\Sigma}$, as

$$\mathbf{x}_s^{*} = \mathcal{N}(\mathbf{x}_s^{*}; \sqrt{\bar{\alpha}_s}\mathbf{e}_{s_{n+1}}^{*}, (1 - \bar{\alpha}_s)\mathrm{I}), \tag{7}$$

with β_s following a truncated linear schedule [13]:

$$\beta_s = \frac{a}{T}s + \frac{b}{s}, \tag{8}$$

where T is the maximum diffusion step, a and b are hyperparameters, If $\beta_s > 1$, then $\beta_s = 0.1\beta_s$. Each historical item embedding $\mathbf{z}_j^{*}$ is updated by fusing information from the noisy target:

$$\mathbf{z}_j^{*} = \mathbf{e}_{s_j}^{*} + \boldsymbol{\lambda}_j \odot (\mathbf{x}_s^{*} + \mathbf{l}_s), \tag{9}$$

where $\mathbf{l}_s$ is a learnable step embedding encoding the current diffusion step s, and $\boldsymbol{\lambda}_j \sim \mathcal{N}(\delta\mathbf{1}, \delta\mathbf{I})$ is a stochastic gating vector with hyperparameter $\delta > 0$ controlling the injection strength.

In the reverse process, the target item is unknown. Thus, we replace $\mathbf{e}^{\mu}_{s_{n+1}}$ and $\mathbf{e}^{\Sigma}_{s_{n+1}}$ with Gaussian noise, combined with historical embeddings, serves as input to CA-Net.

4.4 Cross-Attention Based Net (CA-Net)

While industrial recommender systems commonly fuse item metadata into input embeddings, such concatenation-based approaches treat attributes as static side information and cannot model the *distributional alignment* between noisy item representations and attribute semantics. Our CA-Net addresses this gap: it uses category distributions as queries to attend over item distributions, measuring compatibility via the 2-Wasserstein distance rather than inner products, so that attribute information actively guides denoising toward semantically coherent regions. There are three subcomponents in the CA-Net and the structural diagram of this is illustrated in part (c) of Fig. 1.

Distributional Cross-Attention Layer. When items are represented as MNDs rather than point vectors, the standard dot-product attention score $\mathbf{q}^{\top}\mathbf{k}$ becomes ill-defined—it computes similarity between *samples* rather than between *distributions*, ignoring the rich uncertainty information encoded in the covariance. To address this, we adopt the squared 2-Wasserstein distance W_2^2 as the distributional similarity metric, which satisfies the triangle inequality [2] and naturally captures *collaborative transitivity* [6]: if item a is close to item b, and b is close to c, then a and c should also be reasonably close. The closed-form W_2^2 between two Gaussians is:

$$\mathcal{W}_2^2(m_1, m_2) = \|\mu_{m_1} - \mu_{m_2}\|_2^2 + \text{trace}\left(\Sigma_{m_1} + \Sigma_{m_2} - 2\left(\Sigma_{m_1}^{1/2}\Sigma_{m_2}\Sigma_{m_1}^{1/2}\right)^{1/2}\right), \tag{10}$$

where m follows a distribution with mean μ_m and covariance Σ_m, and trace$(\cdot)$ computes the matrix trace. We use the negative of the squared distance to represent similarity (lower $\mathcal{W}_2^2$ implies higher similarity). For challenge (2), we leverage category information via cross-attention: category sequences serve as queries ($\mathbf{Q}$), and interaction sequences act as keys ($\mathbf{K}$) and values ($\mathbf{V}$). When calculating the attention score A_{pq} (for item i_p to i_q,$(p \leq q)$), we use processed item info (from Sect. 4.2) as m_1 and category info (from Sect. 4.1) as m_2, with their distributions parameterized by:

$$\mu_{i_p} = \mathbf{z}_p^{\mu}\mathbf{W}_K^{\mu}, \Sigma_{i_p} = \text{ELU}(\text{diag}(\mathbf{z}_p^{\Sigma}\mathbf{W}_K^{\Sigma})) + 1, \tag{11}$$

$$\mu_{i_q} = \mathbf{e}_{c_q}^{\mu} W_Q^{\mu}, \Sigma_{i_q} = \text{ELU}(\text{diag}(\mathbf{e}_{c_q}^{\Sigma}\mathbf{W}_Q^{\Sigma})) + 1, \tag{12}$$

where $\mathbf{W}_K^{\mu}, \mathbf{W}_Q^{\mu}, \mathbf{W}_K^{\Sigma}, \mathbf{W}_Q^{\Sigma} \in \mathbb{R}^{d\times d}$ are learnable parameters, diag$(\cdot)$ extracts the main diagonal element, ELU is the exponential linear element activation function.

After normalizing via Softmax to get $\widetilde{\mathbf{A}}_{pq}$, we aggregate the mean and covariance of i_q using cross-attention and Gaussian linear combination properties:

$$\hat{\mathbf{z}}_q^{\mu} = \sum_{p=1}^{q} \widetilde{\mathbf{A}}_{pq} \mathbf{v}_p^{\mu}, \hat{\mathbf{z}}_q^{\Sigma} = \sum_{p=1}^{q} \widetilde{\mathbf{A}}_{pq}^2 \mathbf{v}_p^{\Sigma}, \tag{13}$$

$$\mathbf{v}_p^{\mu} = \mathbf{z}_p^{\mu} \mathbf{W}_V^{\mu}, \mathbf{v}_p^{\Sigma} = \mathrm{diag}(\mathbf{z}_p^{\Sigma}) \mathbf{W}_V^{\Sigma}, \tag{14}$$

where $\mathbf{W}_V^{\mu}$,$\mathbf{W}_V^{\Sigma}$ are learnable parameters, and after aggregation, the new mean and covariance of sequence $\hat{\mathbf{Z}}_u^*$ are obtained.

Feed-Forward Network. To enhance nonlinear modeling and generalization, we apply Layer Normalization (LN) [1] followed by a Feed-Forward Network (FFN) with ELU activation and Dropout on $\hat{\mathbf{z}}_q^{\mu}$ and $\hat{\mathbf{z}}_q^{\Sigma}$.

Result Output Layer. The Distributional Cross Attention Layer and Feed-forward Network form a complete attention block that updates the sequence iteratively. Stacking multiple such blocks yields the final sequence $\hat{\mathbf{Z}}_u^*$. We take the last layer's final element $\hat{\mathbf{z}}_n^*$ as CA-Net's output—this element integrates information from the full sequence. Model training focuses on enhancing CA-Net's reconstruction of $\hat{\mathbf{x}}_0$ to align it with the target item's embedding $\mathbf{e}_{s_{n+1}}^*$.

4.5 Accelerated Generation Process

In the standard reverse process, recovering $\mathbf{x}_0$ from $\mathbf{x}_T$ requires iterating through all T denoising steps, which is prohibitively expensive for online serving. Inspired by DDIM [17], we observe that the denoising trajectory can be made *deterministic* by removing the stochastic term, enabling step-skipping without retraining.

Concretely, given a subsequence of diffusion steps $\tau = (\tau_1, \tau_2, \ldots, \tau_k, 0)$ with $\tau_1 = T$ and $k \ll T$ (e.g., $\tau = [15, 12, 9, 6, 3, 0]$ for $T = 15$), we compute:

$$\mathbf{x}_{\tau_{i+1}}^* = \sqrt{\bar{\alpha}_{\tau_{i+1}}} \tilde{\mathbf{x}}_0^* + \sqrt{1 - \bar{\alpha}_{\tau_{i+1}}} \cdot \frac{\mathbf{x}_{\tau_i}^* - \sqrt{\bar{\alpha}_{\tau_i}} \tilde{\mathbf{x}}_0^*}{\sqrt{1 - \bar{\alpha}_{\tau_i}}}, \tag{15}$$

where $\tilde{\mathbf{x}}_0^*$ is the current CA-Net prediction of the clean target embedding. In practice, we find that setting $k = 1$ (i.e., a single denoising step from T directly to 0) yields the best accuracy–efficiency trade-off, reducing the generation complexity from $O(kn^2 d^3 \log d)$ to $O(n^2 d^3 \log d)$ (Fig. 2).

4.6 Prediction

To generate recommendations, after the accelerated generation process, we use squared 2-Wasserstein distance to compute the probability p_i between the distribution of the predicted item and the candidate items:

$$p_i = \|\hat{\mathbf{x}}_0^{\mu} - \mathbf{e}_i^{\mu}\|_2^2 + \mathrm{trace}(\hat{\mathbf{x}}_0^{\Sigma} + \mathbf{e}_i^{\Sigma} - 2(\hat{\mathbf{x}}_0^{\Sigma^{1/2}} \mathbf{e}_i^{\Sigma^{1/2}} \hat{\mathbf{x}}_0^{\Sigma^{1/2}})^{1/2}), \tag{16}$$

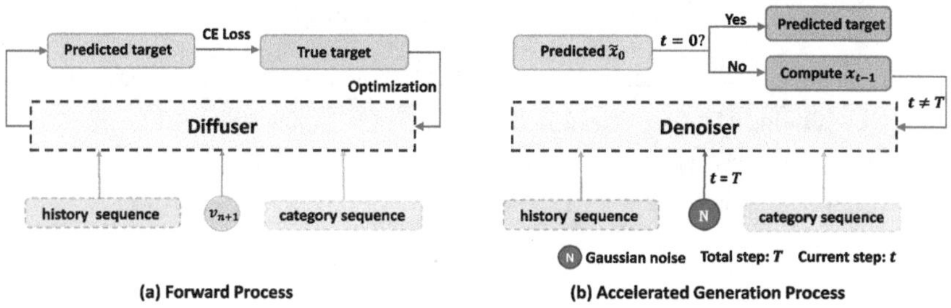

Fig. 2. (a) The process of the forward process, in which the CA-Net is trained. (b) The process of the accelerated generation process to generate target items.

where $\mathbf{e}_i^{\mu}$ and $\mathbf{e}_i^{\Sigma}$ are the mean and covariance of the i-th candidate item. The predicted results of all items are sorted by p_i, and the top items are returned as recommended results.

5 Experiments

In this section, we conduct extensive experiments on two public datasets and one industrial dataset. We analyze experimental results to explore the following research questions:

RQ1: Does the proposed EADM achieve better performance compared with state-of-the-art recommendation methods?

RQ2: How do the hyperparameters (i.e., diffusion steps) affect the performance and efficiency of EADM?

RQ3: How does each key component of EADM affect its performance?

RQ4: How about the diversity of the recommendation results of the EADM?

5.1 Experimental Settings

Datasets. Experiments are conducted on three real-world datasets: **Nowplaying**[1] (music logs from Twitter), **Diginetica**[2](e-commerce sessions), and **Industrial dataset** (industrial dataset of a music streaming platform). All datasets are preprocessed by retaining sequences with at least five interactions and removing infrequent items. Here, *infrequent* items refer to those with only one interaction, which lack sufficient signal for embedding learning; this is distinct from *long-tail* items (those in the lower 50% by frequency), which remain in both the training set and the candidate pool for evaluation. The leave-one-out protocol is adopted for evaluation. Key statistics are summarized in Table 1.

[1] https://zenodo.org/records/2594483.

[2] https://competitions.codalab.org/competitions/11161.

Table 1. Dataset Information

Dataset	# Sequences	# Items	# Categories	Sparsity	Avg.length
Nowplaying	153,549	257,573	37,354	99.99%	8.30
Diginetica	47,212	30,321	817	99.97%	5.73
Industrial	395,802	178,401	42	99.99%	15.72

Baselines. We compare EADM with three representative categories of recommendation methods: (I): Deterministic sequential models (II) Distribution-based embedding models (III) Generative models. For MIND, we set $K = 3$ interest capsules; we verified that $K = 5$ yields comparable results on our datasets, so we report $K = 3$ for efficiency. For SASRec and BERT4Rec, category information is incorporated via feature addition to the input embeddings, ensuring a fair comparison with our attribute-aware model.

- **SASRec (I)** [9] leverages single-direction self-attention mechanisms to capture the sequential patterns and dependencies in user behavior data.
- **BERT4Rec (I)** [18] applies the Bidirectional Encoder Representations from Transformers (BERT) model to sequential recommendation tasks, leveraging its ability to capture contextual information.
- **MIND (I)** [12] incorporates a multi-interest extraction layer based on a capsule routing mechanism, to capture user's diverse interests in the retrieval phase. As a representative multi-interest retrieval model, MIND serves as the primary multi-query baseline in our comparison.
- **BSARec (I)** [16] leverages the Fourier transform to inject an inductive bias and mitigate oversmoothing for sequential recommendation.
- **STOSA (II)** [6] introduces stochastic self-attention mechanism to sequential recommendation, it also model the item representation distributed to inject uncertainty.
- **CDAE (III)** [24] uses the concept of Denoising Autoencoder for top-N recommendations.
- **MultiDAE (III)** [14] is a DAE-based model, which uses a denoising autoencoder and random mask technique to improve the recommendation performance.
- **MultiVAE (III)** [14] is a VAE-based model using a combination of reparameterization techniques and multinomial likelihood for collaborative filtering.
- **DiffRec (III)** [21] applies diffusion to users' interactions to learn the personalized information.
- **DiffuRec (III)** [13]models item representations as distributions to capture user interest diversity based on diffusion model.
- **CaDiRec (III)** [4] employs a context-aware diffusion model to generate more reasonable augmented views.

Table 2. Overall performance comparison. The best and second-best results are bold and underlined, respectively.

Dataset	Metric	BERT4Rec	SASRec	MIND	BSARec	STOSA	DiffRec	DiffuRec	CaDiRec	CDAE	MultiVAE	MultiDAE	**EADM**	Improv.
Nowplaying	HR@5	0.0670	0.0594	0.0736	0.0442	0.0735	0.0540	0.0731	0.0528	0.0777	0.0807	0.0796	**0.0840**	4.09%
	HR@10	0.1057	0.0876	0.1041	0.1035	0.1020	0.0717	0.1009	0.0706	0.1098	0.1132	0.1104	**0.1146**	1.24%
	HR@20	0.1476	0.1258	0.1420	0.1428	0.1347	0.0926	0.1357	0.0889	0.1512	0.1504	**0.1548**	0.1521	-1.74%
	NDCG@5	0.0459	0.0236	0.0524	0.0488	0.0469	0.0366	0.0528	0.0347	0.0572	0.0594	0.0578	**0.0599**	0.84%
	NDCG@10	0.0583	0.0416	0.0622	0.0591	0.0599	0.0421	0.0617	0.0401	0.0677	0.0697	0.0685	**0.0698**	0.14%
	NDCG@20	0.0711	0.0507	0.0718	0.0691	0.0661	0.0474	0.0705	0.0462	0.0785	0.0807	**0.0825**	0.0792	-4.00%
Diginetica	HR@5	0.1232	0.1268	0.1585	0.1349	0.1590	0.1416	0.1401	0.1380	0.1538	0.1571	0.1552	**0.1726**	8.55%
	HR@10	0.1830	0.1787	0.1986	0.1968	0.2064	0.2039	0.2106	0.1993	0.2121	0.2142	0.2030	**0.2364**	10.36%
	HR@20	0.2591	0.2417	0.2861	0.2729	0.2876	0.2805	0.2867	0.2868	0.2690	0.2711	0.2861	**0.3064**	6.54%
	NDCG@5	0.0831	0.0879	0.1105	0.0907	0.1108	0.0972	0.1015	0.0893	0.1005	0.1136	0.1073	**0.1206**	6.12%
	NDCG@10	0.1023	0.1046	0.1118	0.1106	0.1124	0.1074	0.1142	0.1032	0.1043	0.1227	0.1109	**0.1412**	15.08%
	NDCG@20	0.1214	0.1205	0.1530	0.1297	0.1563	0.1368	0.1384	0.1278	0.1292	0.1367	0.1321	**0.1589**	1.66%
Industrial	HR@5	0.0128	0.0142	0.0168	0.0154	0.0126	0.0190	0.0183	0.0181	0.0158	0.0179	0.0161	**0.0203**	6.84%
	HR@10	0.0232	0.0253	0.0276	0.0265	0.0211	0.0305	0.0298	0.0288	0.0258	0.0291	0.0271	**0.0344**	12.79%
	HR@20	0.0412	0.0440	0.0404	0.0424	0.0344	0.0486	0.0476	0.0447	0.0379	0.0445	0.0422	**0.0572**	17.70%
	NDCG@5	0.0078	0.0087	0.0097	0.0091	0.0081	0.0109	0.0116	0.0104	0.0094	0.0105	0.0100	**0.0127**	9.48%
	NDCG@10	0.0111	0.0122	0.0139	0.0132	0.0108	0.0143	0.0158	0.0138	0.0128	0.0137	0.0130	**0.0172**	8.86%
	NDCG@20	0.0156	0.0169	0.0178	0.0178	0.0141	0.0183	0.0197	0.0176	0.0168	0.0171	0.0163	**0.0229**	16.24%

Implementation and Evaluation. The model is implemented with Python 3.8 and PyTorch 1.12, running on an NVIDIA A100 GPU. We employ a 2-layer Transformer encoder with 2 attention heads as the CA-Net. The model is optimized with Adam (learning rate=0.001). The precision of the recommendation is measured by HR@K and NDCG@K (K=5,10,20), while diversity is evaluated using the item coverage (IC) and the GINI coefficient (GINI@K). Specifically, IC measures the proportion of distinct items appearing in top-K lists across all users, and GINI@K quantifies the inequality of item exposure—lower values indicate more uniform coverage. Following [9,18], we report single-run results with a fixed random seed for all methods to ensure fair comparison; we observed consistent convergence across different initializations during development.

5.2 Overall Performance (RQ1)

As shown in the experimental results in Table 2, EADM achieves the best performance on the majority of metrics across all three datasets, with particularly strong gains on Diginetica (up to 15.08% on NDCG@10) and Industrial (up to 17.70% on HR@20). We highlight several key observations:

(1) EADM excels at larger K on complex datasets. On Diginetica and Industrial, the improvement margin *increases* with K (e.g., HR@5 $\rightarrow$ HR@20: 8.55% $\rightarrow$ 6.54% on Diginetica; 6.84% $\rightarrow$ 17.70% on Industrial), suggesting that diffusion-based generation effectively surfaces relevant long-tail items that deterministic methods miss.

(2) Trade-off on short-sequence datasets. On Nowplaying, EADM achieves the best HR@5 and HR@10 but is slightly outperformed by MultiDAE at HR@20 and NDCG@20 (by 1.74% and 4.00%, respectively). We attribute this to the shorter average sequence length (8.30) of Nowplaying: with limited behavioral signals, the distributional embeddings introduce uncertainty that benefits preci-

sion at small K but slightly disperses the candidate set at larger K. This observation also motivates our use of attribute-guided cross-attention to constrain the generation space.

(3) Generative vs. deterministic baselines. Among deterministic models, MIND's multi-interest extraction achieves competitive HR on Diginetica, confirming the value of modeling diverse intents. However, its fixed interest slots lack the continuous flexibility of our distributional approach. Among generative baselines, DiffuRec performs well on Industrial (longer sequences) but falls short on Nowplaying, likely due to its lack of attribute guidance. VAE-based models (MultiVAE, MultiDAE) show strong and stable performance, suggesting that their regularized latent space provides a useful inductive bias; our diffusion-based approach further extends this idea with finer-grained stochastic control.

We note that MultiVAE outperforms DiffRec on Nowplaying and Diginetica, which differs from findings in the original DiffRec paper [21]. This discrepancy arises from differences in the task formulation: DiffRec was evaluated under a collaborative filtering setting with full-ranking metrics, whereas our experiments adopt sequential next-item prediction with sampled negatives and top-K evaluation, where DiffRec's unconditional generation is less effective than the regularized reconstruction of VAE-based methods.

5.3 Hyper-Parameter Analysis (RQ2)

Diffusion Step T. We investigate the impact of diffusion steps T in the forward process by testing T to values in $\{2, 4, 6, 8\}$ on three datasets. Results in Table 3 show that Diginetica and Industrial dataset, being larger and more complex, achieve optimal performance at $T = 6$, while Nowplaying performs best at $T = 4$. Both HR@K and NDCG@K initially improve then decline as T increases, indicating that excessive diffusion steps amplify inherent noise and impair user interest modeling. Notably, further increasing T leads to significant performance degradation, underscoring the need for careful step selection.

Generation Step t. We evaluate the effect of generation steps t in the reverse process on both efficiency and accuracy. As shown in Table 4, setting $t = 1$ achieves the best trade-off: fewer steps reduce noise and the DDIM acceleration cuts cost (see Sect. 4.1).

The Schedule for Noise. In this paper, we calculate the noise added at each step by linear truncated schedule. In this section, we explore the impact of different noise calculation methods on model performance, including *cosine* [8], *linear* [15], and *linear-variance* [8] approaches. We present results for the Nowplaying and Diginetica datasets in Fig. 3.

It is evident that linear-truncated scheduling performs best: it yields smoother noise variation and avoids over-strong perturbation in early training, balancing injection intensity with denoising accuracy.

Table 3. The effect of diffusion steps T in the forward process on the performance of EADM on three datasets.

Dataset	Step	HR@5	HR@10	HR@20	NDCG@5	NDCG@10	NDCG@20
Nowplaying	T = 2	0.0828	0.1139	0.1509	0.0589	0.0587	0.0782
	T = 4	**0.0840**	**0.1146**	**0.1521**	**0.0689**	**0.0688**	**0.0792**
	T = 6	0.0799	0.1134	0.1512	0.0599	0.0568	0.0783
	T = 8	0.0799	0.1105	0.1486	0.0697	0.0666	0.0762
Diginetica	T = 2	0.1715	0.2345	0.3047	0.1197	0.1401	0.1578
	T = 4	0.1718	0.2359	0.3053	0.1200	0.1407	0.1582
	T = 6	**0.1726**	**0.2364**	0.3064	**0.1206**	**0.1412**	0.1589
	T = 8	0.1722	0.2362	**0.3070**	0.1205	0.1411	**0.1590**
Industrial	T = 2	0.0195	0.0342	0.0568	0.0125	0.0165	0.0215
	T = 4	0.0192	0.0341	0.0569	0.0124	0.0153	0.0214
	T = 6	**0.0203**	**0.0344**	**0.0572**	**0.0127**	**0.0172**	**0.0229**
	T = 8	0.0187	0.0332	0.0562	0.0119	0.0158	0.0210

Table 4. The effect of generation steps t in the reverse process on the performance of EADM on Nowplaying and Diginetica datasets, the last column shows the time required to generate a recommended item under different t.

Dataset	Step	HR@5	HR@10	HR@20	NDCG@5	NDCG@10	NDCG@20	time(ms)
Nowplaying	t = 4	0.0789	0.1119	0.1535	0.0552	0.0658	0.0763	2.32
	t = 3	0.0813	0.1124	0.1502	0.058	0.0680	0.0775	2.16
	t = 2	0.0816	0.1122	0.1505	0.0579	0.0678	0.0774	1.97
	t = 1	**0.0899**	**0.1232**	**0.1638**	**0.0646**	**0.0753**	**0.0855**	1.16
Diginetica	t = 6	0.1710	0.2367	**0.3088**	0.1184	0.1396	0.1578	1.63
	t = 4	0.1711	0.2363	0.3067	0.1184	0.1392	0.1573	1.57
	t = 2	**0.1732**	**0.2369**	0.3079	0.1201	0.1407	0.1586	1.46
	t = 1	0.1722	0.2362	0.3070	**0.1205**	**0.1411**	**0.1590**	1.38

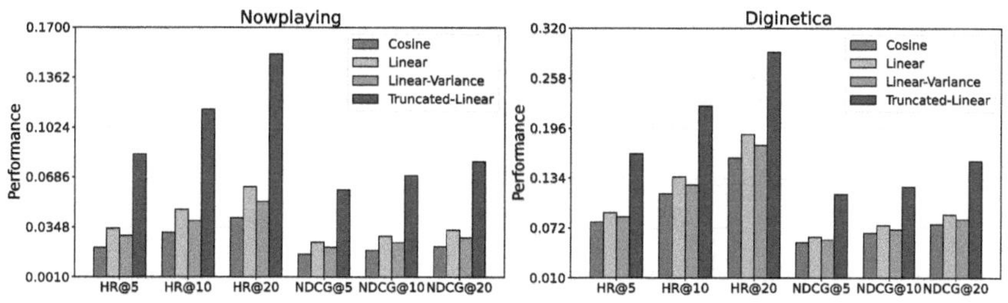

Fig. 3. Results of schedules for noise experiments on Nowplaying and Diginetica datasets.

Table 5. The effect of key parts of EADM on three datasets.

Dataset	Model	HR@5	HR@10	HR@20	NDCG@5	NDCG@10	NDCG@20
Nowplaying	Base	0.0594	0.0876	0.1258	0.0236	0.0416	0.0507
	Base+DM	0.0810	0.1135	0.1538	0.0570	0.0675	0.0776
	Base+DM+MND	0.0820	0.1122	0.1498	0.0583	0.0681	0.0775
	Base+DM+MND+ACC	0.0817	0.1133	0.1525	0.0575	0.0677	0.0776
	Base+DM+CI+ACC	0.0836	0.1138	**0.1543**	0.0586	0.0693	0.0795
	EADM	**0.0840**	**0.1146**	0.1521	**0.0599**	**0.0697**	**0.0792**
Diginetica	Base	0.1268	0.1787	0.2417	0.0879	0.1046	0.1205
	Base+DM	0.1538	0.2179	0.2903	0.1056	0.1263	0.1453
	Base+DM+MND	0.1597	0.2223	0.2914	0.1099	0.1301	0.1475
	Base+DM+MND+ACC	0.1656	0.2333	0.2910	0.1146	0.1328	0.1501
	Base+DM+CI+ACC	0.1666	0.2326	0.2946	0.1149	0.1326	0.1559
	EADM	**0.1726**	**0.2364**	**0.3064**	**0.1206**	**0.1412**	**0.1589**
Industrial	Base	0.0142	0.0253	0.044	0.0087	0.0122	0.0169
	Base+DM	0.0185	0.0320	0.0536	0.0115	0.0159	0.0213
	Base+DM+MND	0.0152	0.0306	0.0514	0.0109	0.0150	0.0203
	Base+DM+MND+ACC	0.0180	0.0312	0.0525	0.0111	0.0154	0.0207
	Base+DM+CI+ACC	0.0190	0.0332	0.0561	0.0119	0.0164	0.0222
	EADM	**0.0203**	**0.0344**	**0.0572**	**0.0127**	**0.0172**	**0.0229**

5.4 Ablation Study (RQ3)

We ablate five variants:

- **Base:** Transformer only, without diffusion, category information, or distributional embeddings.
- **Base+DM:** Adds diffusion, exploring a broader latent space to better capture user preferences.
- **Base+DM+MND:** Uses Multivariate Normal embeddings, enhancing diversity and HR/NDCG on public datasets, with slight accuracy drop on industrial dataset.
- **Base+DM+MND+ACC:** Adds acceleration to reduce generation noise, improving efficiency and stabilizing results.
- **Base+DM+CI+ACC:** Uses fixed embeddings without distributional mapping, highlighting the benefit of category-guided cross-attention.

The results are summarized in Table 5.

5.5 Diversity Analysis (RQ4)

To evaluate the diversity of EADM, we use Item Coverage and Gini coefficient on the Nowplaying and Diginetica datasets (Fig. 4).

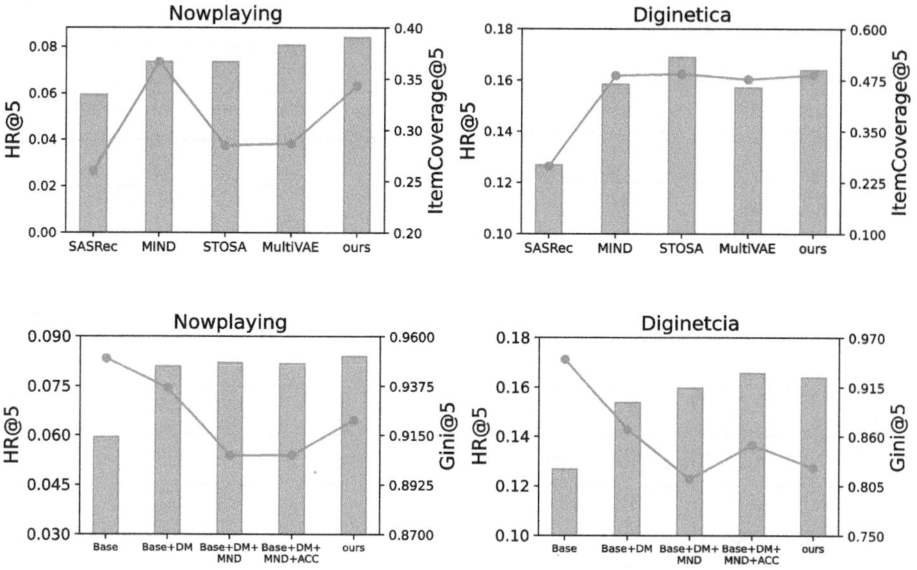

Fig. 4. Comparison of accuracy and diversity on Nowplaying and Diginetica datasets. The HR@5 results are displayed as bar charts with the left y-axis, while ItemCoverage@5 and Gini@5 are presented as line charts on right y-axis.

Representative baselines show that models with distributed embeddings or multiple interest representations (STOSA, MIND) achieve higher Item Coverage than SASRec. STOSA reaches the highest coverage on short-sequence datasets, but for longer sequences, it may fail to fully capture user preferences.

Ablation results indicate that diffusion (Base+DM) improves both accuracy and diversity by exploring a broader latent space. Acceleration and category-guided cross-attention slightly reduce diversity (higher Gini) but improve accuracy, highlighting a trade-off.

The diversity gains stem from how noise injection operates on the distributional item representations. By perturbing the target embedding before denoising, the model reconstructs intent from a neighborhood that includes items outside the user's dominant category, breaking the popularity bias loop. As a result, EADM surfaces minority-interest candidates that deterministic top-K retrieval tends to suppress, achieving the highest Item Coverage while maintaining the lowest Gini coefficient among diffusion-based methods.

6 Deployment

EADM has been deployed as a retrieval branch on a large-scale music streaming platform serving hundreds of millions of daily active users. This section details the production configuration, serving architecture, and practical insights.

6.1 Model Configuration and Training

CA-Net uses a 2-layer Transformer encoder with 2 attention heads and embedding dimension $d = 64$. User behavior sequences are truncated to the most recent 50 interactions, with zero-padding applied for shorter histories. Based on offline evaluation, the diffusion step is set to $T = 6$ and the generation step to $t = 1$ to minimize online latency. The noise schedule follows the truncated linear scheme with $\beta_{\text{min}} = 0.0001$ and $\beta_{\text{max}} = 0.002$. Category information is derived from the platform's genre taxonomy containing 42 leaf-level categories.

The model is trained daily on the past 7 days of user interaction logs (implicit feedback filtered by a minimum listening duration threshold). To counteract the extreme popularity bias in music consumption, we apply stratified sampling to ensure adequate representation of long-tail items in the training distribution. Training is conducted on NVIDIA A100 GPUs, and the trained model is exported to ONNX format for subsequent serving optimization.

6.2 Online Serving

Feature Service. User behavior sequences and category features are maintained in a distributed in-memory key-value store, updated in near-real-time via a streaming pipeline that consumes the platform's user event log.

Inference Optimization. The exported model is optimized via TensorRT with FP16 mixed-precision quantization and operator fusion (multi-head attention, layer normalization, and FFN layers are fused to reduce kernel launch overhead). Incoming requests are grouped via dynamic batching to improve GPU utilization.

Candidate Retrieval. After generating the predicted target distribution $(\hat{\mathbf{x}}_0^\mu, \hat{\mathbf{x}}_0^\Sigma)$, we employ a two-stage retrieval strategy for efficiency: (i) L2 nearest neighbor search on $\hat{\mathbf{x}}_0^\mu$ over a pre-built FAISS index to obtain coarse candidates; (ii) exact W_2^2 re-scoring incorporating covariance on the coarse set to produce the final candidates. This avoids the need for custom distributional ANN indexing while preserving ranking quality.

Fusion and Fault Tolerance. EADM candidates are fused with results from other parallel retrieval branches (collaborative filtering, embedding-based recall, trending, etc.) before entering the downstream ranking stage. A strict timeout of 30 ms is enforced: if EADM fails to respond within the latency budget, the system gracefully degrades by relying on candidates from other branches without affecting user experience.

6.3 Deployment Observations

Compared to the production baseline without the EADM branch, EADM contributes approximately 12% novel candidates that are not covered by existing retrieval branches, demonstrating its complementary value for long-tail content discovery. The end-to-end inference latency is kept below 30 ms, meeting the platform's service-level requirements. The offline latency reported in Table 4 is lower as it excludes network round-trips and feature fetching overhead present in production; TensorRT optimization and dynamic batching bridge this gap. Due to proprietary constraints, detailed online A/B testing metrics cannot be disclosed.

We highlight two practical lessons:

- **Single-step generation is essential.** $t > 1$ caused unacceptable peak-traffic latency; $t = 1$ resolved it with negligible offline degradation, validating DDIM acceleration in production.
- **Stratified sampling is a prerequisite.** Without it, EADM's novel-candidate ratio dropped substantially as the model collapsed toward popular items, confirming that data-level rebalancing is essential to realize diffusion's diversity benefit.

7 Conclusion and Future Work

In this paper, we propose EADM, an Efficient Attribute-boosted Diffusion Model for Personalized Sequential Recommendation, which captures diverse user interests. Discrete items are mapped into a continuous latent space via Multivariate Normal Distributions (Transform Input Layer), while attribute-guided cross-attention (CA-Net) preserves accuracy in long sequences. An acceleration strategy further improves efficiency. Experiments on three datasets demonstrate that EADM effectively balances accuracy and diversity. Future work will explore integrating more attribute types and streamlining the architecture to further enhance performance and reduce inference time. The source code is publicly available at https://github.com/ZionWong/EADM.

Acknowledgements. This research was supported by the Natural Science Foundation of Zhejiang Province under Grant No. LZ25F020010.

Use of Generative AI. Large Language Models were used to assist with writing refinement and content review. The authors take full responsibility for the content.

References

1. Ba, J.L., Kiros, J.R., Hinton, G.E.: Layer normalization. arXiv preprint arXiv:1607.06450 (2016)
2. Bolley, F.: Separability and completeness for the wasserstein distance. In: Séminaire de probabilités XLI, pp. 371–377. Springer (2008)
3. Boratto, L., Fenu, G., Marras, M.: Connecting user and item perspectives in popularity debiasing for collaborative recommendation. Inf. Process. Manag. **58**(1), 102387 (2021)
4. Cui, Z., Wu, H., He, B., Cheng, J., Ma, C.: Context matters: enhancing sequential recommendation with context-aware diffusion-based contrastive learning. In: Proceedings of the 33rd ACM International Conference on Information and Knowledge Management, pp. 404–414 (2024)

5. Du, Y., Ranwez, S., Sutton-Charani, N., Ranwez, V.: Is diversity optimization always suitable? Toward a better understanding of diversity within recommendation approaches. Inf. Process. Manag. **58**(6), 102721 (2021)
6. Fan, Z., et al.: Sequential recommendation via stochastic self-attention. In: Proceedings of the ACM Web Conference 2022, pp. 2036–2047 (2022)
7. Hidasi, B., Karatzoglou, A., Baltrunas, L., Tikk, D.: Session-based recommendations with recurrent neural networks. arXiv preprint arXiv:1511.06939 (2015)
8. Ho, J., Jain, A., Abbeel, P.: Denoising diffusion probabilistic models. Adv. Neural. Inf. Process. Syst. **33**, 6840–6851 (2020)
9. Kang, W.C., McAuley, J.: Self-attentive sequential recommendation. In: 2018 IEEE International Conference on Data Mining (ICDM), pp. 197–206. IEEE (2018)
10. Karakaya, M.Ö., Aytekin, T.: Effective methods for increasing aggregate diversity in recommender systems. Knowl. Inf. Syst. **56**, 355–372 (2018)
11. Kingma, D.P., Welling, M.: Auto-encoding variational bayes. arXiv preprint arXiv:1312.6114 (2013)
12. Li, C., et al.: Multi-interest network with dynamic routing for recommendation at tmall. In: Proceedings of the 28th ACM International Conference on Information and Knowledge Management, pp. 2615–2623 (2019)
13. Li, Z., Sun, A., Li, C.: Diffurec: a diffusion model for sequential recommendation. ACM Trans. Inf. Syst. **42**(3), 1–28 (2023)
14. Liang, D., Krishnan, R.G., Hoffman, M.D., Jebara, T.: Variational autoencoders for collaborative filtering. In: Proceedings of the 2018 World Wide Web Conference, pp. 689–698 (2018)
15. Nichol, A.Q., Dhariwal, P.: Improved denoising diffusion probabilistic models. In: International Conference on Machine Learning, pp. 8162–8171. PMLR (2021)
16. Shin, Y., Choi, J., Wi, H., Park, N.: An attentive inductive bias for sequential recommendation beyond the self-attention. In: Proceedings of the AAAI Conference on Artificial Intelligence, vol. 38, pp. 8984–8992 (2024)
17. Song, J., Meng, C., Ermon, S.: Denoising diffusion implicit models. arXiv preprint arXiv:2010.02502 (2020)
18. Sun, F., et al.: Bert4rec: sequential recommendation with bidirectional encoder representations from transformer. In: Proceedings of the 28th ACM International Conference on Information and Knowledge Management, pp. 1441–1450 (2019)
19. Walker, J., Zhong, T., Zhang, F., Gao, Q., Zhou, F.: Recommendation via collaborative diffusion generative model. In: International Conference on Knowledge Science, Engineering and Management, pp. 593–605. Springer (2022)
20. Wang, S., Zheng, Y., Xiao, Q., Zhao, Y., Yang, Q., Luo, C.: Sparsity-aware personalized pattern extractor network for music multi-task learning. In: Database Systems for Advanced Applications, DASFAA 2024. Lecture Notes in Computer Science, vol. 14856, pp. 352–363. Springer (2024). https://doi.org/10.1007/978-981-97-5575-2_26
21. Wang, W., Xu, Y., Feng, F., Lin, X., He, X., Chua, T.S.: Diffusion recommender model. In: Proceedings of the 46th International ACM SIGIR Conference on Research and Development in Information Retrieval, pp. 832–841 (2023)
22. Wang, Y., et al.: Personalized re-ranking for improving diversity in live recommender systems. arXiv preprint arXiv:2004.06390 (2020)
23. Wei, C., Liang, J., Liu, D., Dai, Z., Li, M., Wang, F.: Meta graph learning for long-tail recommendation. In: Proceedings of the 29th ACM SIGKDD Conference on Knowledge Discovery and Data Mining, pp. 2512–2522 (2023)

24. Wu, Y., DuBois, C., Zheng, A.X., Ester, M.: Collaborative denoising auto-encoders for top-n recommender systems. In: Proceedings of the Ninth ACM International Conference on Web Search and Data Mining, pp. 153–162 (2016)
25. Xie, R., et al.: Improving accuracy and diversity in matching of recommendation with diversified preference network. IEEE Trans. Big Data **8**(4), 955–967 (2021)
26. Yang, Q., et al.: Cascading multimodal feature enhanced contrast learning for music recommendation. In: IEEE International Conference on Data Mining, ICDM 2024, pp. 905–910. IEEE (2024). https://doi.org/10.1109/ICDM59182.2024.00113
27. Yang, Z., Wu, J., Wang, Z., Wang, X., Yuan, Y., He, X.: Generate what you prefer: reshaping sequential recommendation via guided diffusion. Adv. Neural Inf. Process. Syst. **36** (2024)

Joint-Centric Dual Contrastive Alignment with Structure-Preserving and Information-Balanced Regularization

Habibeh Naderi(✉), Behrouz Haji Soleimani, and Stan Matwin

Dalhousie University, Halifax, NS, Canada
{habibeh.naderi,behrouz.hajisoleimani}@dal.ca, stan@cs.dal.ca

Abstract. We propose HILBERT (HIerarchical Long-sequence Balanced Embedding with Reciprocal contrastive Training), a cross-attentive multimodal framework for learning document-level audio-text representations from long sequences in low-resource data settings. HILBERT leverages frozen pre-trained speech and language encoders to extract segment-level features, which are aggregated via cross-modal attention and self-attentive pooling to form modality-specific document representations and a joint cross-attentive embedding. To align modalities while preserving modality-specific structure under severe audio-text dimensional imbalance, we introduce a reciprocal dual contrastive objective that simultaneously aligns audio-to-joint and text-to-joint representations, rather than directly contrasting audio and text alone. Two auxiliary regularizers further stabilize long-sequence fusion: a Centered Kernel Alignment (CKA) loss that preserves structural consistency between each modality and the joint embedding, and a mutual information balancing loss that prevents dominance of a single modality by equalizing information flow from audio and text into the joint space. For downstream prediction, HILBERT employs a Mixture-of-Experts (MoE) classifier over concatenated audio, text, and joint representations to accommodate heterogeneous label regimes. Extensive evaluation across multiple audio-text backbone combinations demonstrates that HILBERT learns semantically meaningful long-sequence representations and achieves superior performance on highly imbalanced multi-class settings.

Keywords: Multimodal Representation Learning · Contrastive Learning · Mixture of Experts · Mental Disorders Prediction

1 Introduction

Multimodal representation learning has emerged as a crucial research area [8,13], leveraging the co-occurrence of observations from interdependent sources, such

---

Supplementary Information The online version contains supplementary material available at https://doi.org/10.1007/978-3-032-37682-4_3.

M. Baratchi et al. (Eds.): ECML PKDD 2026, LNAI 16949, pp. 38–55, 2027.
https://doi.org/10.1007/978-3-032-37682-4_3

as paired audio and text, which act as a form of weak supervision. By integrating information across modalities, multimodal learning outperforms unimodal approaches in feature learning [4,7,9]. However, effectively aligning representations from different modalities while preserving their distinctive characteristics remains a significant challenge [21]. Specifically, in audio-text multimodal learning, a key challenge arises from the high dimensionality of audio representations compared to text, potentially causing imbalanced contributions from each modality.

One of the key approaches for multimodal representation learning is contrastive learning. This method minimizes the distance between semantically related pairs while maximizing the distance between unrelated pairs in the embedded space. Through this objective, contrastive learning produces high-quality multimodal representations that exhibit robustness to distribution shifts and zero-shot transferability. CLIP exemplifies the success of contrastive learning in multimodal domains, playing a key role in advancing text-to-image generation techniques [12].

Simultaneously, sparsely activated Mixture-of-Experts (MoE) models [22] have proven effective for expanding model capacity while maintaining manageable computational costs. By dynamically selecting a subset of parameters for each input, MoE models are particularly well-suited for multimodal learning since expert layers can learn an appropriate partitioning of modalities. These models enhance representation learning, improve multitask performance, and mitigate catastrophic forgetting in continual learning. The sparse MoE architecture provides several advantages: 1) increased model capacity without a proportional increase in computation, as only a subset of experts is typically active for any given input, 2) specialization of experts, where different experts can focus on different aspects of the data or different tasks, and 3) improved handling of heterogeneous data, which is common in multimodal scenarios.

In this work, we introduce HILBERT (HIerarchical Long-sequence Balanced Embedding with Reciprocal contrastive Training), a novel framework for multimodal audio-text representation learning that addresses the challenges of effective cross-modal alignment while preserving modality-specific information, particularly designed for long sequence representation. HILBERT balances modality contributions while preserving both shared and modality-specific features. Our approach leverages frozen pre-trained foundation models for feature extraction, employs a sophisticated dual contrastive learning strategy for cross-modal alignment, and utilizes an MoE architecture for downstream task learning. We design specialized loss functions including Centered Kernel Alignment (CKA) and Mutual Information (MI) losses to ensure balanced and informative joint representations. Our framework effectively handles the inherent imbalance between audio and text modalities, enabling more effective utilization of multimodal information for downstream tasks. HILBERT efficiently learns high-quality multimodal representations ensuring that the learned embeddings preserve semantic richness, effectively capturing both shared and modality-specific features.

The task of multimodal audio-text representation learning aims to map paired audio and text data into a joint representation space where semantically related pairs are placed close together, while unrelated pairs are pushed apart [16,17]. A key challenge is balancing the contributions from different modalities, especially given the disparity in dimensionality and information density between audio and text data [6,15]. Ensuring that the joint representation captures complementary information from both modalities, rather than being dominated by one, is crucial for effective multimodal learning. HILBERT incorporates a dual multimodal contrastive loss, designed to preserve structural alignment between modality-specific and joint representations. Unlike conventional contrastive methods that primarily focus on inter-modality alignment, our approach enforces both inter- and intra-modality consistency, preventing semantically similar representations from being pushed apart in the embedding space. Inspired by prior contrastive learning frameworks such as SimCLR [1] and CrossCLR [21], HILBERT extends contrastive learning principles to multimodal data, improving the quality of learned joint embeddings [10,11].

HILBERT targets a learning regime that is fundamentally distinct from CLAP-style [2] and related cross-modal pretraining frameworks. CLAP variants are designed for large-scale audio-caption corpora and optimized for short audio clips through global embedding alignment, making them ill-suited for long, document-length audio-text inputs. In contrast, HILBERT is explicitly developed for long-sequence, document-level representation learning, leveraging cross-modal self-attention to model segment-level interactions, auxiliary CKA and mutual information losses to balance modality contributions, and an MoE architecture for multi-task prediction. Unlike CLAP's contrastive objective, which operates on pooled audio and text embeddings and does not capture long-range temporal structure, HILBERT directly models cross-modal dependencies across extended sequences. We therefore view CLAP and similar large-scale pretraining methods as complementary, while HILBERT provides a lightweight, backbone-agnostic framework for segment-aware audio-text integration under small-data and constrained training conditions.

By integrating frozen pre-trained models, contrastive objectives, and MoE-based adaptation, HILBERT advances the state-of-the-art in multimodal representation learning for long sequences. Our experiments demonstrate that HILBERT achieves competitive performance in capturing semantically meaningful representations, making it well-suited for a wide range of downstream tasks.

The main contributions of this work are as follows:

- We introduce a dual contrastive learning strategy that simultaneously enforces cross-modal and modality-specific consistency. Unlike conventional contrastive methods that primarily focus on inter-modality alignment, our approach explicitly preserves intra-modality structure, preventing semantically similar instances from being separated in the embedding space.
- We incorporate specialized loss functions including CKA and MI losses to enhance cross-modal alignment while preserving information-theoretic rele-

vance. CKA loss ensures inter-modal and intra-modal alignment while MI loss ensures equitable contribution from both modalities to the joint representation. These specialized loss functions improve the quality of learned representations by ensuring that the joint embedding space remains semantically meaningful and well-structured.

- We develop a multimodal joint encoder architecture that effectively combines frozen pre-trained foundation models with cross-modal self-attention mechanisms to capture complex dependencies between audio and text modalities. This multi-head self-attention mechanism generates high quality document-level representations from segment-level embeddings, capturing complex dependencies among segments.
- We integrate an MoE approach for downstream task learning that adaptively leverages information from different experts based on input features, enabling efficient specialization across heterogeneous data distributions.

2 Proposed Method

In this section, we present our novel framework for multimodal audio-text representation learning, which we call HILBERT (HIerarchical Long-sequence Balanced Embedding with Reciprocal contrastive Training). Our approach leverages pre-trained models for effective representation learning and addresses the challenge of alignment in multimodal learning. The proposed framework extends the principles of multimodal contrastive representation learning and builds on prior state-of-the-art [11,14] while introducing several innovations to enhance representation quality and cross-modal alignment.

The task of multimodal audio-text representation learning aims to learn effective joint representations from paired audio and text data. Let $\mathcal{D} = \{(x_i^a, x_i^t, y_i)\}_{i=1}^N$ denote a dataset containing N audio-text pairs, where x_i^a represents the audio input, x_i^t denotes the corresponding text input, and y_i is the associated label (e.g., emotion, speaker identity, or semantic category). Our objective is to learn a joint representation space where semantically related audio and text pairs are mapped close to each other, while unrelated pairs are pushed apart.

More formally, we aim to train a set of encoders that can map audio inputs x^a and text inputs x^t into a shared latent space, ensuring that the joint representation effectively captures complementary information from both modalities. This embedding space preserves high-quality modality-specific features while also modeling cross-modal interactions, making it well-suited for downstream tasks.

HILBERT Model Architecture: Our HILBERT framework comprises four main components as illustrated in Fig. 1. This architecture is specifically designed to process long sequences, such as large documents and extended audio files. It includes a segmentation step, which can be performed manually or automatically, to break the input into smaller segments before passing them to the model.

1. **Frozen Pre-trained Models and Segment Embedding:** We utilize pre-trained models for audio and text to extract rich feature representations

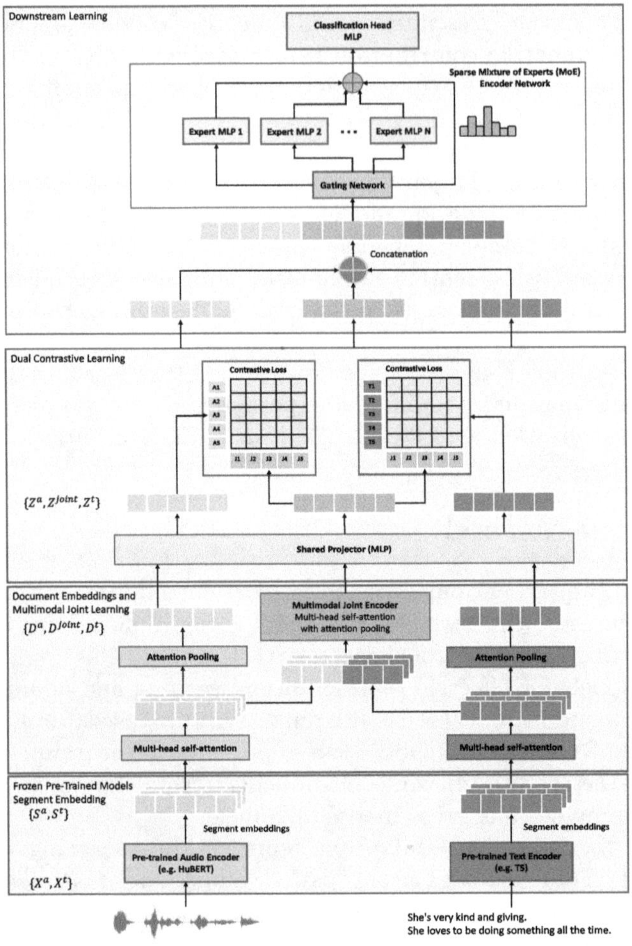

Fig. 1. Our proposed HILBERT model architecture.

from raw inputs. These pre-trained models have been trained on large-scale datasets and can provide high-quality embeddings that capture semantic and structural information.

2. **Document Embeddings and Multimodal Joint Learning:** The segment-level embeddings from the pre-trained models are processed through a multi-head self-attention mechanism to generate document-level representations. A multimodal joint encoder then combines information from both modalities.
3. **Dual Contrastive Learning:** This step consists of a shared encoder that maps inputs into a joint representation. We employ a contrastive learning approach that involves contrasting positive pairs (semantically related audio-text pairs) against negative pairs (unrelated pairs). Our designed contrastive loss

incorporates multimodal knowledge into the each modality embeddings and aligns representations from different modalities through a Centered Kernel Alignment (CKA) loss. To further enhance relevance, we introduce a Mutual Information (MI) loss, ensuring the joint embedding retains meaningful information from each modality.

4. **Downstream Learning with Mixture of Experts (MoE):** For downstream tasks, we utilize an MoE architecture to adaptively leverage information from different experts based on the input.

Our pipeline is hierarchical: long audio and text are segmented, encoded with frozen models, and aggregated via document-level multi-head self-attention with modality-specific pooling and cross-modal fusion. This reduces complexity from frame-level $O(T^2)$ to segment-level $O(L^2)$, with L in the tens. Only the segment-to-document and fusion layers are trained, keeping compute bounded while preserving long-range dependencies. In the following subsections, we elaborate on each component and discuss how they contribute to effective multimodal representation learning.

2.1 Frozen Pre-trained Models and Feature Extraction

For audio encoding, we utilize pre-trained models (e.g., Whisper, HuBERT) that has been trained on large-scale audio data. The pre-trained audio encoder $f_E^a(\cdot)$ extracts rich acoustic and semantic features from the raw audio signal. Given an audio input $\mathbf{X}^a$, the pre-trained encoder processes it to generate segment-level embeddings, $\mathbf{S}^a = f_E^a(\mathbf{X}^a) \in \mathbb{R}^{L \times d_a}$, where L is the number of segments, and d_a is the dimension of the audio embedding space.

Similarly, for text encoding, we employ pre-trained language models (e.g., T5, RoBERTa) that has been trained on large-scale text corpora. The pre-trained text encoder $f_E^t(\cdot)$ processes the text input $\mathbf{X}^t$ to generate segment-level embeddings, $\mathbf{S}^t = f_E^t(\mathbf{X}^t) \in \mathbb{R}^{L \times d_t}$, where L again is the number of segments, and d_t is the dimension of the text embedding space. These segment-level embeddings capture semantic information from the text.

It is important to note that the parameters of these pre-trained models are kept frozen during training to avoid the computational overhead associated with fine-tuning large models and to prevent overfitting on limited data. This approach aligns with the philosophy of leveraging the rich knowledge encoded in pre-trained models while keeping the training process efficient.

2.2 Document Embeddings and Multimodal Joint Learning

Modality-Specific Document Embedding: We first project segment-level embeddings of audio and text (i.e. $\mathbf{S}^a_{d_a}, \mathbf{S}^t_{d_t}$) to the same dimension to obtain $\mathbf{S}^a_d, \mathbf{S}^t_d$. Then to obtain document-level representations for audio and text (i.e. $\mathbf{D}^a$, $\mathbf{D}^t$) from their corresponding segment-level embeddings, we employ multi-head self-attention mechanisms with attention pooling. The multi-head self-attention mechanism allows the model to attend to different parts of the input sequence and capture complex dependencies and relationships among segments.

Multimodal Joint Encoder: The multimodal joint learning module contains a joint encoder $f_E^{joint}(\cdot)$ designed to efficiently fuse the audio-text information. It consists of a cross-modal fusion layer and follows attention-based embedding layers. To achieve this, we take the audio-to-text embedding $\mathbf{S}^{a\to t}$ to show the cross-modal attention:

$$\mathbf{S}^{a\to t} = CM_{a\to t}(\mathbf{S}_d^a, \mathbf{S}_d^t) = \text{softmax}\left(\frac{W_{Q_a}\mathbf{S}_d^a W_{K_t}^T {\mathbf{S}_d^t}^T}{\sqrt{d}}\right) W_{V_t} \tag{1}$$

Similarly, we can get text-to-audio embedding $\mathbf{S}^{t\to a}$. The obtained $\mathbf{S}^{a\to t}$ and $\mathbf{S}^{t\to a}$ will be concatenated together and projected to the latent space as the joint document embedding via a self-attention layer followed by attention pooling:

$$\mathbf{D}^{joint} = f_{AttPool}(\text{SelfAttention}(\mathbf{S}^{a\to t} \oplus \mathbf{S}^{t\to a})) \tag{2}$$

The multimodal joint encoder combines information from both modalities and captures cross-modal interactions. The design of the joint encoder is crucial for effective multimodal representation learning. Unlike simple concatenation or averaging, our joint encoder employs a more sophisticated fusion mechanism that can adaptively weigh the contributions from different modalities based on their informativeness and reliability.

2.3 Contrastive Learning and Cross-Modal Alignment

To enhance the alignment between different modalities and promote effective joint representation learning, we employ a contrastive learning approach. Contrastive learning aims to bring the representations of semantically related samples closer while pushing apart the representations of unrelated samples in the embedding space. This module consists of a shared projector to map all inputs to the same latent space. Given the presence of a joint encoder in our architecture, we employ a dual contrastive learning strategy, which enforces alignment between (i) audio and joint representations and (ii) text and joint representations. Our specialized dual contrastive loss function is composed of three key components: 1) contrastive loss, 2) Centered Kernel Alignment (CKA) loss, and 3) Mutual Information (MI) loss.

Shared Projector: The document-level representations $\mathbf{D}^a$ and $\mathbf{D}^t$ from both modalities as well as the joint document-level embedding $\mathbf{D}^{joint}$ are then fed into a shared projector implemented as a multilayer perceptron (MLP) to map them into a common latent space, $\mathbf{Z}^a = f_{shared}(\mathbf{D}^a) \in \mathbb{R}^{d_{latent}}$, $\mathbf{Z}^t = f_{shared}(\mathbf{D}^t) \in \mathbb{R}^{d_{latent}}$, $\mathbf{Z}^{joint} = f_{shared}(\mathbf{D}^{joint}) \in \mathbb{R}^{d_{latent}}$ where d_{latent} is the dimension of the common latent space and $f_{shared}(\cdot)$ is the shared projection function.

Multimodal Contrastive Loss: We utilize a multimodal contrastive loss to align the joint representation with modality-specific representations. Given a batch of embeddings $B = \{Z_i^a, Z_i^t, Z_i^{joint}\}_{i=1}^{|B|}$, the positive pairs are defined as the joint embedding with its corresponding modality-specific embeddings, i.e., (Z_i^a, Z_i^{joint}) and (Z_i^t, Z_i^{joint}). All other pairing combinations are treated as negative pairs.

Let $\mathrm{c}(x_i, x_j)$ represent the cosine similarity between two embeddings x_i and x_j, and τ be the temperature hyperparameter. The scaled similarity is defined as $\mathrm{sim}(x_i, x_j) = \exp\left(\frac{\mathrm{c}(x_i,x_j)}{\tau}\right)$ and the negative pairs for contrastive learning are defined as:

$$\Omega_i^m = \sum_{j \neq i} \left(\mathrm{sim}(Z_i^m, Z_j^m) + \mathrm{sim}(Z_i^m, Z_j^{joint}) + \mathrm{sim}(Z_i^{joint}, Z_j^{joint}) \right) \tag{3}$$

where $m \in \{a, t\}$ indicates the modality type. The contrastive loss for all data embeddings is then formulated as:

$$L_{con}(B) = -\frac{1}{|B|} \sum_{i=1}^{|B|} \log \left(\frac{\mathrm{sim}(Z_i^a, Z_i^{joint})}{\Omega_i^a} + \frac{\mathrm{sim}(Z_i^t, Z_i^{joint})}{\Omega_i^t} \right) \tag{4}$$

This loss encourages the joint representation to be semantically aligned with both the audio and text representations of the same sample while being distinct from the representations of other samples. Unlike pairwise audio-text, modality-modality, joint-joint schemes, we deliberately avoid audio-text contrast in the objective and instead anchor both modalities to the fused joint space, then enforce covariance alignment and information balance. This reduces modality collapse without over-penalizing intra-modality neighbors, and is tailored to high-dimensional audio versus compact text and to our long-sequence hierarchical fusion.

Centered Kernel Alignment (CKA) Loss: We propose to use Centered Kernel Alignment (CKA) as a measure of similarity between representation spaces. CKA is a powerful tool for measuring the similarity between neural network representations and has been shown to be invariant to orthogonal transformations and isotropic scaling [5]. Given two sets of representations X and Y, the CKA between them is defined as:

$$\mathrm{CKA}(K, L) = \frac{\mathrm{HSIC}(K, L)}{\sqrt{\mathrm{HSIC}(K, K) \cdot \mathrm{HSIC}(L, L)}} \tag{5}$$

where $K = XX^T$ and $L = YY^T$ are the kernel matrices, and HSIC (Hilbert-Schmidt Independence Criterion) [3] is defined as $\mathrm{HSIC}(K, L) = \frac{1}{(n-1)^2}\mathrm{trace}(KHLH)$ where n is the number of samples, $H = I_n - \frac{1}{n}\mathbf{1}_n\mathbf{1}_n^T$ is the centering matrix, I_n is the identity matrix, and $\mathbf{1}_n$ is a vector of ones of length n. Given the centered data matrices $\tilde{X} = HX$ and $\tilde{Y} = HY$, we can express the HSIC in terms of covariance:

$$\mathrm{HSIC}(K, L) = \frac{1}{(n-1)^2}\mathrm{trace}(\tilde{X}\tilde{X}^T\tilde{Y}\tilde{Y}^T) = \|\mathrm{Cov}(\tilde{X}^T, \tilde{Y}^T)\|_F^2 \tag{6}$$

where $\mathrm{Cov}(X, Y)$ is the covariance matrix and $\|\cdot\|_F^2$ is the Frobenius norm of the matrix. With these definitions, the CKA can be formulated as:

$$\mathrm{CKA}(X, Y) = \frac{\|\mathrm{Cov}(X, Y)\|_F^2}{\|\mathrm{Cov}(X, X)\|_F \cdot \|\mathrm{Cov}(Y, Y)\|_F} \tag{7}$$

CKA ranges between 0 and 1, therefore for our multimodal scenario, the CKA loss components become:

$$L^m_{CKA} = 1 - \frac{\|\text{Cov}(Z^{joint}, Z^m)\|_F^2}{\|\text{Cov}(Z^{joint}, Z^{joint})\|_F \cdot \|\text{Cov}(Z^m, Z^m)\|_F} \tag{8}$$

where $m \in \{a, t\}$ is the modality. The total CKA loss remains:

$$L_{CKA} = L^a_{CKA} + L^t_{CKA} \tag{9}$$

This covariance formulation highlights that CKA measures the normalized alignment between the covariance structures of the representations, providing deeper insight into how information is preserved across modalities in the joint representation.

Mutual Information (MI) Loss: To further enhance the informativeness of the joint representation, we introduce an MI loss that maximizes the mutual information between the joint representation and each modality-specific representation. Mutual information measures the amount of information obtained about one random variable through observing another random variable.

Since direct computation of mutual information is challenging, we adopt the InfoNCE estimator, which provides a lower bound on the mutual information:

$$I(Z^{joint}; Z^m) \geq \mathbb{E}\left[\frac{1}{|B|}\sum_{i=1}^{|B|} \log \frac{f(Z_i^{joint}, Z_i^m)}{\frac{1}{|B|}\sum_{j=1}^{|B|} f(Z_i^{joint}, Z_j^m)}\right] = L^m_{MI} \tag{10}$$

where $f(x, y)$ is a scoring function that measures the compatibility between x and y. We use the dot product as the scoring function, $f(x, y) = \exp(x^T y/\gamma)$ where γ is a temperature parameter. The total MI term balances contributions of modalities in the joint embedding and prevents over-emphasis on a single modality:

$$L_{MI} = -(L^a_{MI} + L^t_{MI}) + (L^a_{MI} - L^t_{MI})^2 \tag{11}$$

By minimizing the difference between the mutual information of the joint representation and each modality-specific representation, we ensure that the joint representation captures the essential information from both modalities.

HILBERT uses CKA and MI as mechanisms for modality balancing, not for forcing audio and text to share identical covariance structure. The joint encoder, via cross-attention, naturally integrates both modalities, CKA encourages structural consistency between each modality and the joint embedding, while MI prevents dominance of a single modality. In HILBERT, the modality gap is addressed in three ways: 1) A shared projector maps both modality-specific and joint document embeddings into a common latent space, encouraging a comparable representation scale. 2) CKA between each modality and the joint embedding (not audio↔text directly), ensuring structural information from both inputs is retained without forcing identical covariance. This reduces representational mismatch while preserving modality-specific structure. 3) The MI term explicitly balances the mutual information between the joint embedding and each modality, penalizing dominance of one modality and promoting equitable information flow and stabilizing long-sequence fusion. This is related in spirit to Cacophony's [20] modality-balancing goals but integrated into a long-sequence cross-attentive encoder and MoE classifier.

2.4 Downstream Learning with Mixture of Experts (MoE)

For downstream tasks such as classification, we propose an MoE architecture that can adaptively leverage information from different experts based on the input. The MoE architecture consists of multiple expert networks and a gating network that determines the contribution of each expert to the final output.

Each expert network is implemented as a multilayer perceptron (MLP) that takes the joint representation as input and produces a task-specific output $E_i(Z) = f^i_{MLP}(Z)$ where $Z = [Z^a; Z^{joint}; Z^t]$ represents the concatenation of audio, text, and joint features. The gating network determines the contribution of each expert to the final output. It takes the concatenated features from all modalities as input and outputs a probability distribution over the experts $g = f_{gate}(Z) \in \mathbb{R}^{N_E}$ where N_E is the number of experts, and $f_{gate}(\cdot)$ is implemented as a neural network with softmax activation to ensure that the gating values sum to 1:

$$g_i = \frac{\exp(f^i_{gate}(Z))}{\sum_{j=1}^{N_E} \exp(f^j_{gate}(Z))} \tag{12}$$

The gating network enables the model to dynamically select the most relevant experts based on the input features. This is particularly useful in multimodal scenarios where different experts may specialize in different aspects of the data. The outputs from all experts are combined using the gating values to produce the final representation, $Z_{MoE} = \sum_{i=1}^{N_E} g_i \cdot E_i(Z)$. This weighted combination allows the model to adaptively leverage the strengths of different experts based on the input.

For classification tasks, the MoE output is passed through a final classification head implemented as an MLP, $\hat{y} = f_{sup}(Z_{MoE}) \in \mathbb{R}^C$ where C is the number of classes, and $f_{sup}(\cdot)$ is a multilayer perceptron with softmax activation. For the supervised classification loss, we use the cross-entropy loss:

$$L_{sup} = -\frac{1}{|B|} \sum_{i=1}^{|B|} \sum_{c=1}^{C} y_{i,c} \log(\hat{y}_{i,c}) \tag{13}$$

where $y_{i,c}$ is a binary indicator if class label c is the correct classification for sample i, and $\hat{y}_{i,c}$ is the predicted probability that sample i belongs to class c.

Total Loss Function: The overall loss function for our multimodal representation learning framework combines the supervised classification loss, contrastive loss, CKA loss, and MI loss:

$$L_{total} = L_{sup} + \lambda_{con} L_{con} + \lambda_{CKA} L_{CKA} + \lambda_{MI} L_{MI} \tag{14}$$

where L_{sup} is the supervised classification loss (e.g., cross-entropy loss for classification tasks), and λ_{con}, λ_{CKA}, and λ_{MI} are hyperparameters that control the contribution of each loss term.

3 Dataset

The data used in this work consists of audio speech samples from 369 subjects participating in the Families Overcoming Risks and Building Opportunities for Well-being (FORBOW) research project [18]. Participants are parents, 266 mothers and 103 fathers, in the age range of 28–51 years. In these clinical interviews, parents were asked to talk about their children for five minutes without interruption. Out of these subjects, 149 were diagnosed with Major Depressive Disorder (MDD), 66 were diagnosed with Bipolarity Disorder (BD), 19 were diagnosed with Schizophrenia, and 129 were the control group with no major mood disorders. In addition to the parents' interview files, FORBOW research project started collecting interviews with the children themselves. The audio interviews of children consists of 3 parts: 1) a three minute interview where children talk about themselves, 2) a two minute interview talking about a positive experience they had, and 3) a two minute interview where they talk about a negative experience they had. All three interviews are uninterrupted with a total of 7 min of speech from each child.

We transcribed and broke down each sample into multiple segments based on changes in emotion, sentiment, objectivity/subjectivity, etc. Average word count in a segment is 17 and average audio length for a segment is 6.47 s. Table 1 summarizes the dataset statistics, including the set of prediction tasks at different levels of granularity (segment-level, document-level, and psychological and cognitive tasks), as well as the label distributions and the degree of class imbalance.

Figure 2 illustrates the mood, emotions, and sentiment changes in a random sample from parent interviews. We can also see sample segments shown at the top of the figure which gives an idea of how the segmentation and the labeling is done.

4 Experimental Results

In this section, we provide the experimental results of our proposed contrastive learning framework. We chose six different language models, nliRoBERTa, nliDistilRoBERTa, nliMPNet, paraTinyBERT, sentenceT5XL, and allMiniLM12. We also chose five pre-trained audio models, whisperMedium, wav2vec2LargeFineTune, hubertLargeFineTune, conformerLargeFineTune, and spectrogram. This results in a total of 30 combinations, trained separately on each individual task for both parent and offspring data. Full results using all backbones are reported in the appendix Tables 1 and 2.

For the dimensionality of the shared projector in contrastive embedding we tested 64, 128, and 256 and the quality of predictions was not sensitive to the dimensionality of the contrastive latent space. Therefore, in the following we

Table 1. Dataset information for the parent and offspring data.

Level	Task		Num Samples	Num Classes	Imbalanced (%)	Label 0	Label 1	Label 2	Label 3	Label 4
Parent	Document	affect	484	3	93.18	23	124	337	-	-
Parent	Document	warmth	485	3	39.69	117	194	174	-	-
Parent	Document	overprotection	487	3	85.77	267	182	38	-	-
Parent	Document	cohesion	492	5	92.63	14	14	132	190	142
Parent	Document	criticism	492	4	89.22	232	166	69	25	-
Parent	Document	worry	381	4	93.29	164	147	59	11	-
Parent	Cognitive	spectrum	363	4	87.25	129	149	66	19	-
Parent	Cognitive	introvert	369	2	49.39	245	124	-	-	-
Parent	Cognitive	extrovert	369	2	63.84	271	98	-	-	-
Parent	Cognitive	ADHD	369	2	67.74	279	90	-	-	-
Parent	Cognitive	anxiety	369	2	51.81	249	120	-	-	-
Parent	Cognitive	depression	369	2	89.19	333	36	-	-	-
Offspring	Document	affect	621	4	97.73	16	11	109	485	-
Offspring	Document	coherence	616	5	95.83	11	33	109	264	199
Offspring	Document	richness	614	3	96.70	82	515	17	-	-
Offspring	Cognitive	spectrum	85	4	86.11	36	27	17	5	-
Offspring	Cognitive	introvert	85	2	39.62	53	32	-	-	-
Offspring	Cognitive	extrovert	85	2	53.45	58	27	-	-	-
Offspring	Cognitive	ADHD	85	2	53.45	58	27	-	-	-
Offspring	Cognitive	anxiety	85	2	39.62	53	32	-	-	-
Offspring	Cognitive	depression	85	2	83.56	73	12	-	-	-

only report the results achieved with dimensionality of 128. The expert network consists of 8 experts each of which is a 2 layer MLP with 32 and 32 units. The classification head consists of 3 layer dense network, a 32-unit layer followed by a 16-unit layer followed by a softmax layer with the size corresponding to the classification task. All results in this section are based on a 25-fold cross-validation.

Table 2 reports AUC (%) from 25-fold cross-validation over 6 backbone combinations and 4 architecture configurations on 6 document-level and 7 psychological spectrum tasks using parent data, with methods sorted by average performance across all tasks. Overall, the results demonstrate a clear and consistent

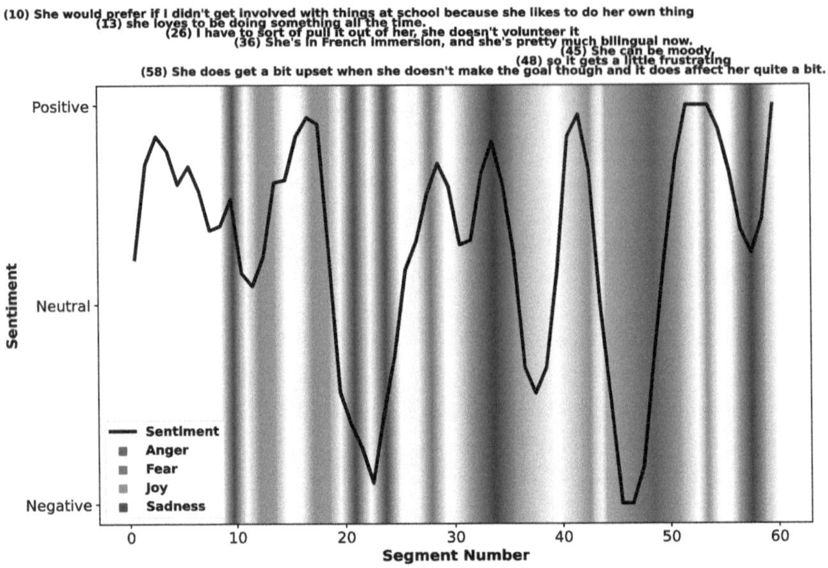

Fig. 2. Emotion and sentiment dynamics for a representative parent interview sample from the FORBOW dataset. The horizontal axis represents time (segmented speech units), and the vertical axis represents normalized sentiment scores. The black curve shows segment-level sentiment trajectories, while colored vertical bands indicate discrete emotion labels (anger, fear, joy, sadness, or neutral) assigned to each segment. Segments are obtained via content-aware partitioning based on changes in affective and linguistic cues. Representative text excerpts are displayed above each plot to illustrate the correspondence between raw speech content, segmentation boundaries, and assigned annotations.

advantage of the full HILBERT (Dual Contrastive + MoE) framework across nearly all backbone combinations. Adding MoE to transfer learning yields modest but systematic improvements, while introducing contrastive learning leads to further gains, particularly on more challenging psychological traits. The complete HILBERT configuration achieves the strongest performance overall, with pronounced improvements on document-level affective tasks and gains of up to 5-10 AUC points over CLAP-based pre-training, highlighting the benefit of task-aware multimodal contrastive learning over generic audio-text alignment.

Across backbones, nMPNet and nRoBERTa combined with hubERT or w2v2 achieve the highest absolute AUCs (e.g., $\sim$ 80 for affect and $\sim$ 70 for cohesion/mood), indicating that stronger text encoders better leverage dual-contrastive supervision. Performance gains are consistent across both task families, suggesting improved generalization rather than task-specific overfitting. Notably, TinyBERT+ConformerLarge (HILBERT) attains the best result on the spectrum task (66.75% AUC), which is the most important task with 4 classes of mental disorders including depression, bipolar, Schizophrenia, and control

Table 2. AUC (%) on a 25-fold cross-validation for document-level and psychological spectrum predictions using parent data.

	Document-level tasks						**Cognitive and Psychological tasks**						
	affect	warmth	overprotect	cohesion	criticism	worry	Spectrum	Introvert	Extrovert	ADHD	Anxiety	Depression	Mood
CLAP-LAION [19]	71.84	56.11	51.73	60.65	56.96	54.86	53.09	55.11	56.18	54.07	57.03	59.86	57.51
TinyBERT+hubLgFT (Baseline: Transfer)	72.88	59.67	57.21	63.93	57.02	59.33	58.53	61.50	56.77	57.11	57.61	59.20	63.60
TinyBERT+hubLgFT (Transfer + MoE)	73.12	59.21	57.49	63.70	58.16	60.88	58.44	61.76	57.59	55.85	58.82	60.24	64.13
TinyBERT+hubLgFT (Contrastive + MoE)	74.68	61.98	58.89	64.91	59.41	61.72	59.47	63.09	59.35	58.88	60.18	61.77	65.61
TinyBERT+hubLgFT (HILBERT: DualC + MoE)	76.30	62.70	57.51	67.67	**61.98**	**63.02**	61.20	**65.38**	59.05	59.87	62.82	61.85	67.63
TinyBERT+confLgFT (Baseline: Transfer)	71.17	60.73	50.65	60.82	55.31	53.75	62.78	55.23	59.67	58.99	58.50	58.17	64.99
TinyBERT+confLgFT (Transfer + MoE)	72.18	61.75	52.44	62.10	56.11	55.00	64.43	55.31	59.94	59.52	59.77	58.76	65.15
TinyBERT+confLgFT (Contrastive + MoE)	74.90	64.31	53.30	63.83	57.26	56.68	66.11	56.26	62.05	61.14	61.84	60.81	67.10
TinyBERT+confLgFT (HILBERT: DualC + MoE)	74.85	66.54	54.91	63.46	60.37	57.41	**66.75**	58.16	65.14	61.52	63.57	63.00	69.62
nRoBERTa+hubLgFT (Baseline: Transfer)	70.31	61.50	54.31	59.33	55.93	59.88	53.80	56.02	58.97	54.92	60.44	59.88	66.05
nRoBERTa+hubLgFT (Transfer + MoE)	71.91	61.32	56.29	59.34	56.76	58.55	55.47	57.53	59.64	55.21	60.98	62.66	67.68
nRoBERTa+hubLgFT (Contrastive + MoE)	73.43	63.40	56.99	61.76	58.61	60.60	56.01	59.07	60.51	58.10	62.47	63.65	69.31
nRoBERTa+hubLgFT (HILBERT: DualC + MoE)	75.30	64.59	57.61	63.52	58.92	58.60	58.21	61.85	59.21	58.49	**64.89**	**67.87**	**70.99**
TinyBERT+w2v2LgFT (Baseline: Transfer)	71.80	60.26	53.54	63.11	55.61	53.30	58.40	58.12	61.34	56.44	56.46	59.85	63.88
TinyBERT+w2v2LgFT (Transfer + MoE)	72.99	59.76	55.03	65.54	56.06	54.62	60.64	60.25	60.57	56.33	58.14	59.01	63.96
TinyBERT+w2v2LgFT (Contrastive + MoE)	73.84	61.87	55.60	65.40	58.05	56.68	61.18	60.69	62.69	58.37	60.07	61.79	66.39
TinyBERT+w2v2LgFT (HILBERT: DualC + MoE)	74.58	63.29	58.97	66.24	58.70	57.73	61.64	62.49	66.37	60.42	61.40	63.08	66.09
nMPNet+hubLgFT (Baseline: Transfer)	74.47	63.98	56.39	63.20	54.30	55.12	55.75	57.19	59.94	57.13	56.29	58.01	60.38
nMPNet+hubLgFT (Transfer + MoE)	74.71	63.38	56.04	63.14	56.71	55.07	56.77	56.74	60.78	58.32	56.78	59.78	60.36
nMPNet+hubLgFT (Contrastive + MoE)	77.21	65.69	57.77	64.65	57.17	57.57	57.68	58.61	62.52	59.48	59.38	61.17	61.93
nMPNet+hubLgFT (HILBERT: DualC + MoE)	79.96	**67.24**	**59.19**	**70.29**	59.19	58.28	58.80	61.70	64.31	59.33	62.18	61.98	65.92
nRoBERTa+w2v2LgFT (Baseline: Transfer)	73.98	59.61	48.47	62.92	58.31	54.19	51.81	57.82	64.94	57.08	55.71	59.89	63.68
nRoBERTa+w2v2LgFT (Transfer + MoE)	73.97	62.21	49.31	61.92	58.87	56.54	52.47	58.41	64.94	57.59	57.16	61.59	63.96
nRoBERTa+w2v2LgFT (Contrastive + MoE)	76.11	63.40	50.85	64.83	59.33	56.80	54.66	60.42	66.41	59.02	58.33	61.68	65.80
nRoBERTa+w2v2LgFT (HILBERT: DualC + MoE)	**80.34**	63.72	52.53	68.25	60.88	59.02	54.98	62.61	**67.83**	**61.90**	61.46	66.57	68.17

group. It is also the most complicated task due to our low resource and highly imbalanced data.

Table 3 presents AUC (%) results from 25-fold cross-validation on offspring data across 3 document-level and 7 psychological spectrum tasks. Similar to the parent setting, the full HILBERT (Dual Contrastive + MoE) framework consistently outperforms transfer-only and partial ablation variants across nearly all backbone combinations. Incorporating MoE yields steady improvements over plain transfer learning, while contrastive learning further enhances performance, particularly on psychological traits. The strongest gains are observed in document-level tasks such as affect, coherence, and richness, where HILBERT achieves substantial margins over CLAP-based pre-training, indicating that task-aware multimodal contrastive learning remains effective despite the increased variability in offspring speech.

Across architectures, TinyBERT+WhisperM, aMiniLM12, and larger text encoders (e.g., sT5-XL, nDRoBERTa) benefit substantially from HILBERT, achieving the highest AUCs on several tasks. Notably, aMiniLM12+spec (HILBERT) attains the best performance on multiple psychological outcomes, including ADHD, Depression, and Mood, while TinyBERT+WhisperM

Table 3. AUC (%) on a 25-fold cross-validation for document-level and psychological spectrum predictions using offspring data.

	Document-level tasks			Cognitive and Psychological tasks						
	affect	coherence	richness	Spectrum	Introvert	Extrovert	ADHD	Anxiety	Depression	Mood
CLAP-LAION [19]	64.23	58.48	60.81	52.67	59.14	55.26	54.35	54.17	61.74	60.56
TinyBERT+whisperM (Baseline: Transfer)	79.99	76.09	73.23	63.84	64.00	56.09	54.15	57.60	63.31	71.90
TinyBERT+whisperM (Transfer + MoE)	80.82	75.98	74.03	64.29	65.18	58.59	52.63	56.39	62.73	73.36
TinyBERT+whisperM (Contrastive + MoE)	81.94	78.61	75.05	64.87	66.61	58.70	55.13	59.31	66.13	73.81
TinyBERT+whisperM (HILBERT: DualC + MoE)	**83.85**	**79.80**	76.96	**67.33**	**68.42**	60.50	55.97	60.20	66.06	77.83
aMiniLM12+spec (Baseline: Transfer)	70.22	59.47	61.66	52.71	57.85	63.47	60.95	69.93	70.70	77.10
aMiniLM12+spec (Transfer + MoE)	71.83	60.44	62.29	54.02	62.20	64.70	62.56	70.90	72.55	79.17
aMiniLM12+spec (Contrastive + MoE)	73.04	62.29	63.84	56.83	61.80	66.38	64.26	72.05	73.92	80.77
aMiniLM12+spec (HILBERT: DualC + MoE)	73.17	63.14	64.66	59.74	63.17	69.75	**65.13**	74.16	**74.58**	**85.31**
sT5XL+whisperM (Baseline: Transfer)	79.52	73.46	75.06	50.12	57.42	67.17	56.38	56.24	63.71	64.32
sT5XL+whisperM (Transfer + MoE)	78.09	74.68	77.29	53.21	59.94	67.21	57.13	56.39	64.90	66.16
sT5XL+whisperM (Contrastive + MoE)	80.60	76.06	77.40	53.80	60.31	69.47	59.82	58.30	66.65	66.98
sT5XL+whisperM (HILBERT: DualC + MoE)	80.81	78.21	**79.97**	56.09	61.82	71.05	61.63	59.86	69.65	71.60
nDRoBERTa+w2v2LgFT (Baseline: Transfer)	72.42	73.18	74.11	48.98	62.58	67.85	51.99	53.95	67.57	62.06
nDRoBERTa+w2v2LgFT (Transfer + MoE)	72.04	73.49	74.58	50.15	61.53	68.06	53.14	56.38	68.21	61.31
nDRoBERTa+w2v2LgFT (Contrastive + MoE)	75.36	73.91	76.52	52.33	64.24	71.35	54.20	58.11	71.17	64.28
nDRoBERTa+w2v2LgFT (HILBERT: DualC + MoE)	76.39	73.88	78.16	57.43	64.95	**75.23**	58.13	59.14	73.66	68.15
nRoBERTa+w2v2LgFT (Baseline: Transfer)	60.50	70.63	66.84	53.24	56.51	59.35	56.13	72.36	63.32	70.63
nRoBERTa+w2v2LgFT (Transfer + MoE)	60.14	72.58	67.31	52.76	58.22	60.35	54.71	71.96	63.40	73.45
nRoBERTa+w2v2LgFT (Contrastive + MoE)	62.24	72.88	69.34	55.91	60.24	62.40	58.94	73.81	65.41	74.62
nRoBERTa+w2v2LgFT (HILBERT: DualC + MoE)	63.50	74.37	70.33	56.34	61.15	62.56	60.73	**74.56**	67.46	74.35
aMiniLM12+whisperM (Baseline: Transfer)	77.68	73.93	73.86	50.51	61.07	55.11	53.81	61.83	60.99	61.41
aMiniLM12+whisperM (Transfer + MoE)	79.65	75.89	74.83	49.56	63.06	54.92	55.18	62.69	61.47	61.00
aMiniLM12+whisperM (Contrastive + MoE)	79.79	76.68	76.87	52.36	62.54	56.67	56.97	64.51	63.09	62.93
aMiniLM12+whisperM (HILBERT: DualC + MoE)	81.97	79.51	76.03	54.60	65.89	56.85	60.89	66.80	63.92	64.61

(HILBERT) achieves the strongest results on affect and coherence. On the 'spectrum' task, HILBERT achieves 67.33% AUC with TinyBERT and Whisper backbone on offspring data. These trends suggest that audio cues play a more prominent role in offspring data, where prosody, intonation, and pauses provide complementary information beyond lexical content. Performance improvements are broad rather than task-specific, suggesting improved generalization under dual-contrastive supervision. Overall, these results confirm that the advantages of HILBERT extend robustly to offspring data, even under noisier acoustic conditions and greater inter-speaker variability.

Ablation Studies of the Auxiliary Loss Functions: Our final objective incorporates three auxiliary losses: contrastive, CKA, and mutual information (MI). We conduct a full brute force ablation over all non-empty combinations of these losses ($\sum_{r=1}^{N}\binom{N}{r} = 2^N - 1$ where $N = 3$) to assess the contribution of each component. The study is performed using the paraTinyBERT and hubert-LargeFineTune configuration, which yields the strongest average performance on parent data. Table 4 reports, for each auxiliary loss, the best validation AUC achieved across combinations that include the loss versus those that exclude it.

Table 4. Across 7 combinations, each row shows the best AUC (%) of all combinations that included the auxiliary loss ✓ vs. those that did not ✗. Validation AUC (%) is the average of 5 folds classification on parent data.

Auxiliary Loss	Validation	
	✗	✓
Contrastive	65.8	66.1
CKA	65.7	65.9
MI	65.7	65.8

All three losses provide consistent gains. The contrastive loss yields the largest improvement in classification performance. The CKA loss substantially enhances multimodal representation alignment. The MI loss further stabilizes training by balancing modality contributions. Based on these observations, we apply distinct weighting coefficients (λ) to appropriately emphasize each auxiliary loss in the final objective.

5 Conclusion

In this work, we introduced HILBERT, a novel framework that effectively addresses the challenges of multimodal audio-text representation learning. Our approach successfully tackles the fundamental problem of aligning cross-modal information while preserving modality-specific characteristics, particularly focusing on the dimensional imbalance between audio and text representations.

The experimental results demonstrate the effectiveness of HILBERT across multiple document-level and psychological spectrum tasks. We achieved an AUC score of 66.75% and 67.33% on the 'spectrum' task using parent and offspring data, respectively. The 'spectrum' task which is the mental disorder prediction is a highly imbalanced multi-class problem and is the most challenging task overall. Interestingly, our findings reveal that the audio component has a more significant impact on offspring data compared to parent data, likely because audio features such as emotions, intonations, and pauses provide additional information beyond spoken words in capturing coherence and mental state in offspring participants.

Several key observations emerge from our experiments. First, the choice of audio and text models significantly influences performance across different tasks, with hubert and whisper showing particular strength in parent and offspring data respectively. Second, smaller language models often outperformed larger models, suggesting that more compact models may be better suited for limited sample sizes in mental health applications.

HILBERT's dual contrastive learning approach, coupled with specialized loss functions and an MoE architecture, offers several advantages over traditional methods. By simultaneously enforcing both inter-modal alignment and intra-modal consistency, our framework creates more balanced and semantically meaningful joint representations. The incorporation of CKA and MI losses ensures that both modalities contribute equitably to the final representation while preserving information-theoretic relevance. Additionally, our multimodal joint encoder effectively captures complex dependencies between modalities through cross-modal self-attention mechanisms, resulting in high-quality document-level representations.

In conclusion, HILBERT advances the state-of-the-art in multimodal representation learning for long sequences, particularly in the context of mental health prediction tasks. Our framework's ability to effectively balance modality contributions while preserving both shared and modality-specific features makes it well-suited for a wide range of downstream applications requiring nuanced understanding of multimodal data.

References

1. Chen, T., Kornblith, S., Norouzi, M., Hinton, G.: A simple framework for contrastive learning of visual representations. In: International Conference on Machine Learning, pp. 1597–1607. PMLR (2020)
2. Elizalde, B., Deshmukh, S., Al Ismail, M., Wang, H.: Clap learning audio concepts from natural language supervision. In: ICASSP, pp. 1–5. IEEE (2023)
3. Gretton, A., Bousquet, O., Smola, A., Schölkopf, B.: Measuring statistical dependence with Hilbert-Schmidt norms. In: International Conference on Algorithmic Learning Theory, pp. 63–77. Springer (2005)
4. Huang, W., Han, A., Chen, Y., Cao, Y., Xu, Z., Suzuki, T.: On the comparison between multi-modal and single-modal contrastive learning. NeurIPS **37**, 81549–81605 (2024)
5. Kornblith, S., Norouzi, M., Lee, H., Hinton, G.: Similarity of neural network representations revisited. In: International Conference on Machine Learning, pp. 3519–3529. PMLR (2019)
6. Naderi, H., Haji Soleimani, B., Matwin, S.: From token imbalance to balanced routing: an elbo-regularized probabilistic framework for contrastive multimodal learning. In: 29th International Conference on Artificial Intelligence and Statistics (AISTATS) (2026)
7. Naderi, H., Soleimani, B.H., Matwin, S.: Manifold learning of overcomplete feature spaces in a multimodal biometric recognition system of iris and palmprint. In: 14th Conference on Computer and Robot Vision (CRV), pp. 191–196. IEEE (2017)
8. Naderi, H., Soleimani, B.H., Matwin, S.: Multimodal deep learning for mental disorders prediction from audio speech samples. arXiv preprint arXiv:1909.01067 (2019)
9. Naderi, H., Soleimani, B.H., Matwin, S.: MAC: multimodal attentive contrastive learning framework. In: Proceedings of the Canadian Conference on Artificial Intelligence (2025). https://caiac.pubpub.org/pub/zpm3p8jv
10. Oord, A.V.D., Li, Y., Vinyals, O.: Representation learning with contrastive predictive coding. arXiv preprint arXiv:1807.03748 (2018)
11. Poklukar, P., Vasco, M., Yin, H., Melo, F.S., Paiva, A., Kragic, D.: Geometric multimodal contrastive representation learning. In: International Conference on Machine Learning, pp. 17782–17800. PMLR (2022)
12. Radford, A., et al.: Learning transferable visual models from natural language supervision. In: ICML, pp. 8748–8763. PMLR (2021)

13. Shi, Y., Paige, B., Torr, P.: Variational mixture-of-experts autoencoders for multimodal deep generative models. Adv. Neural. Inf. Process. Syst. **32** (2019)
14. Shi, Y., Paige, B., Torr, P.H., Siddharth, N.: Relating by contrasting: a data-efficient framework for multimodal generative models. arXiv preprint arXiv:2007.01179 (2020)
15. Soleimani, B.H., Matwin, S.: Dimensionality reduction and visualization by doubly kernelized unit ball embedding. In: Advances in Artificial Intelligence: 31st Canadian Conference on Artificial Intelligence, Canadian AI 2018, Toronto, ON, Canada, 8–11 May 2018, Proceedings 31, pp. 224–230. Springer (2018)
16. Soleimani, B.H., Matwin, S.: Spectral word embedding with negative sampling. In: Proceedings of the AAAI Conference on Artificial Intelligence, vol. 32 (2018)
17. Soleimani, B.H., Matwin, S.: Fast PMI-based word embedding with efficient use of unobserved patterns. In: Proceedings of the AAAI Conference on Artificial Intelligence, vol. 33, pp. 7031–7038 (2019)
18. Uher, R., et al.: A familial risk enriched cohort as a platform for testing early interventions to prevent severe mental illness. BMC Psychiatry **14**(1), 344 (2014)
19. Wu, Y., Chen, K., Zhang, T., Hui, Y., Berg-Kirkpatrick, T., Dubnov, S.: Large-scale contrastive language-audio pretraining with feature fusion and keyword-to-caption augmentation. In: ICASSP, pp. 1–5. IEEE (2023)
20. Zhu, G., Darefsky, J., Duan, Z.: Cacophony: an improved contrastive audio-text model. IEEE/ACM Trans. Audio Speech Lang. Process. (2024)
21. Zolfaghari, M., Zhu, Y., Gehler, P., Brox, T.: Crossclr: cross-modal contrastive learning for multi-modal video representations. In: Proceedings of the IEEE/CVF International Conference on Computer Vision, pp. 1450–1459 (2021)
22. Zoph, B., et al.: ST-MoE: designing stable and transferable sparse expert models. arXiv preprint arXiv:2202.08906 (2022)

LeAP: Learnable Adaptive Permutation for Feature Selection in Heterogeneous and Sparse Recommender Systems

Yihong Huang, Chen Chu(✉), Fei Chen, Yu Lin, Ruiduan Li, and Zhihao Li

Bilibili Inc., Shanghai, China
chuchen.blueblues@gmail.com, {chenfei03,linyu03}@bilibili.com

Abstract. Modern industrial recommender systems rely on thousands of heterogeneous features—ranging from low-dimensional scalars (e.g., statistical value) to high-dimensional embeddings (e.g., user-id embeddings, MLP representations)—to achieve high-precision predictions. Given the immense computational costs associated with training, efficient feature selection is critical. However, existing methods encounter three primary bottlenecks: (1) they typically assume uniform feature dimensions or require costly mapping to a fixed size; (2) they struggle with extreme sparsity, where the majority of features (e.g., 99%+) remain at default values; and (3) traditional permutation-based approaches are computationally prohibitive in large-scale settings.

To address these challenges, we propose LeAP (Learnable Adaptive Permutation), a novel, model-agnostic plug-in module for feature selection. LeAP transforms the inefficient random permutation process into a learnable mechanism, significantly accelerating the evaluation of feature importance. In addition, we introduce an adaptive regularization strategy tailored for heterogeneous dimensions and extreme sparsity, enabling superior feature importance ranking results across asymmetric input spaces. Experiments on four public recommendation datasets demonstrate that LeAP achieves state-of-the-art performance. Furthermore, LeAP has been deployed in a large-scale industrial search ranking model with over a billion daily requests and a 2TB model parameter scale. In this real-world scenario involving 12,000+ total feature dimensions, LeAP successfully identified and removed over 3,600 redundant dimensions without performance degradation, which is 2 to 10 times the ability of compared baseline methods.

Keywords: Feature Selection · Recommendation system · Automated Machine Learning

---

Supplementary Information The online version contains supplementary material available at https://doi.org/10.1007/978-3-032-37682-4_4.

M. Baratchi et al. (Eds.): ECML PKDD 2026, LNAI 16949, pp. 56–72, 2027.
https://doi.org/10.1007/978-3-032-37682-4_4

1 Introduction

In modern industrial search [22], advertising [7], and recommendation systems [9,14], the predictive accuracy of deep learning models heavily relies on massive and complex feature engineering. To accurately capture dynamic user intents and content representations, production models typically process thousands of features. These features exhibit strong **dimensional heterogeneity** and type diversity [6,10]: ranging from 1-dimensional continuous scalars (e.g., real-time statistics, numerical features) to vectors spanning tens to hundreds of dimensions (such as user behavior embeddings [27] or MLP-compressed latent representations). Such complexity in the feature space pushes industrial model sizes to the terabyte (TB) level [28], incurring staggering computational and storage costs for both training and online serving.

Challenge. To alleviate the computational burden and eliminate outdated or redundant information, feature selection [1,26] has become a critical component of model optimization. However, existing feature selection methods encounter significant bottlenecks when deployed in these complex industrial scenarios. First, **most existing approaches are oblivious to the dimensional discrepancy of heterogeneous features.** They often assume homogeneous feature dimensions or enforce mapping all features into a unified dimension space [20]. This not only distorts the original information density but also makes it profoundly difficult to fairly evaluate the true contributions of a 1D feature against a 256D feature under the same metric. Second, **existing methods are highly unfriendly to sparse features.** Because sparse features remain at default states in the vast majority of instances, existing selection mechanisms [5] often misinterpret their "low frequency of activation" as "useless noise," penalizing or discarding them heavily, thereby severely impairing the representation of long-tail personalized signals.

Finally, although methods based on Permutation Feature Importance [8,23] offer high interpretability and model-agnostic capabilities in evaluating true feature contributions, they suffer from **prohibitive computational inefficiency**. Traditional permutation methods require sequentially shuffling each feature in isolation and re-executing the forward pass. For ultra-large-scale models with thousands of features, this one-variable-at-a-time permutation paradigm results in an unbearable computational disaster, making it entirely infeasible to integrate into the daily iterations of industrial models that process billion-level requests.

Method. To break through these dilemmas, we propose **LeAP (Learnable Adaptive Permutation)**, a model-agnostic, plug-in feature selection module explicitly tailored for large-scale industrial models. The core breakthrough of LeAP lies in transforming the traditionally discrete and computationally prohibitive permutation evaluation into an **end-to-end learnable mechanism**. During a single forward pass of model training, LeAP employs a dynamic gating network to learn the fusion weights between the original features and their batch-wise permuted noise counterparts. This design thoroughly circumvents the performance bottleneck of repetitive inference required by traditional permutation methods, drastically reducing the computational complexity from $O(N \times \text{model overhead})$ to $O(1 \times \text{model overhead})$. Consequently, LeAP can be effortlessly embedded into daily training pipelines handling tens of billions of samples.

More crucially, to tackle the notoriously difficult problems of feature heterogeneity and sparsity in industrial settings, LeAP introduces an innovative Adaptive Regularization based on Permutation Divergence. Specifically, LeAP calculates the L_2-norm difference between the original and permuted inputs for each feature in real-time. By applying Exponential Moving Average (EMA) to construct stable statistical bounds, this divergence serves as an adaptive base penalty for the feature's gating weight.

This mechanism exhibits two remarkably elegant desirable properties:

(1) **Dimensionally Adaptive**: For wide features such as 128D or 256D embeddings, the spatial distance before and after permutation is inherently larger than that of 1D scalars. LeAP adaptively imposes a stronger penalty on high-dimensional features, fundamentally offsetting the unfair advantage they often exploit to "hide" from traditional uniform regularization.

(2) **Sparsity-Aware**: For extremely sparse features where 99% of instances hold default values, the permuted values are highly likely to remain defaults. Consequently, their L_2 difference is minimal, and the penalty force shrinks accordingly. This establishes a vital criterion for industrial feature selection: we should not severely penalize a feature simply because it is sparse; it should be discarded only if it is genuinely useless to the predictive objective.

Empowered by this adaptive penalty, LeAP not only outputs highly interpretable feature importance scores (reflecting the model's sensitivity to information loss) but also drives the gating weights to naturally polarize. This polarization implies that redundant features can be directly pruned via straightforward simple thresholding. It eliminates the need for the resource-intensive model retraining typically required by prior methods, allowing for direct online serving with minimal fine-tuning.

Experimental Results. To comprehensively evaluate the effectiveness of LeAP, we conducted extensive experiments on both public datasets and real-world industrial production environments. On four public recommender system datasets, LeAP significantly outperforms existing mainstream and state-of-the-art feature selection methods, consistently achieving SOTA predictive performance across varying feature pruning ratios.

More importantly, LeAP has been successfully deployed in an industrial search ranking model with billions of daily requests. In actual production, the model's heterogeneous input features, spanning over 12,000 dimensions, create a severe CPU-to-GPU memory bandwidth bottleneck. Furthermore, since all existing online features have undergone rigorous business validation, performing secondary pruning among these high-value features poses a tremendous challenge.

Nevertheless, LeAP exhibits remarkable precision and robustness: in the evaluation of feature pruning ROI (Return on Investment), traditional methods suffer significant performance degradation when pruning fewer than 600 dimensions; in contrast, LeAP successfully identifies and eliminates over 30% (3,600+) of the redundant dimensions. It successfully resolves the system bandwidth bottleneck while achieving zero degradation (Zero Diff) in core online business metrics.

In summary, the primary contributions of this paper are as follows:

- **Engineering Architecture Innovation**: We propose LeAP, a model-agnostic feature selection plug-in. It reconstructs the inefficient, discrete feature permutation process into an $O(1)$ end-to-end learnable mechanism, thoroughly breaking the computational bottleneck of traditional permutation-based feature evaluation.
- **Algorithmic Theory Breakthrough**: We design an **Adaptive Regularization based on Permutation Divergence**. This mechanism mathematically overcomes the evaluation biases introduced by heterogeneous dimensions (e.g., 1D vs. 256D) and extremely sparse features, enabling genuinely fair feature selection.
- **Substantial Industrial Deployment Gains**: LeAP not only achieves SOTA results on public datasets but also successfully prunes over 30% of feature dimensions in a 2TB-scale real-world search model with zero loss in business metrics. This provides a highly valuable industrial practice paradigm for feature pruning in ultra-large-scale recommender systems.

Our code is available at https://github.com/goldenNormal/LeAP.

2 Related Work

2.1 Differentiable Mask-Based Feature Selection

Feature selection (FS) is indispensable for mitigating the storage and computational overhead in industrial recommender systems. While traditional statistical and tree-based methods [2,3,13,18] offer interpretability, they are ill-suited for high-dimensional embeddings and cannot be optimized jointly with deep serving models.

Recent paradigms have shifted towards differentiable mask-based methods [11,15,19,20], which integrate learnable gates directly into the model architecture. For instance, AutoField [20] employs Gumbel-Softmax for feature gating, and LPFS [11] utilizes a smoothed L_0 regularization. Despite their success on standard benchmarks, these methods implicitly assume a **homogeneous feature space** (e.g., assuming all fields are embedded into the same dimension D). When applied to heterogeneous industrial input layers—where dense 1D scalars are concatenated with sparse high-dimensional embeddings—these methods typically apply uniform regularization scales. Consequently, high-dimensional representations generate disproportionately larger gradients and variance compared to 1D scalars. This imbalance leads to a biased optimization process where critical low-dimensional signals are heavily penalized and prematurely pruned.

While Dimension Selection (DS) [21,24,25] attempts to assign varying dimensions to different fields, these approaches typically require initializing all fields into a uniform "super-net" embedding space before pruning. Forcing native 1D statistical features into high-dimensional spaces introduces parameter redundancy and information dilution. In contrast, **LeAP operates directly on the native heterogeneous concatenation layer**, ensuring a balanced importance assessment without distorting the original feature representations.

2.2 Permutation-Based Feature Importance

Another prevalent paradigm assesses feature importance via Permutation [8,23]. By measuring the prediction degradation when a specific feature is replaced by random noise across instances, Permutation provides model-agnostic evaluation and clear interpretability.

However, applying permutation-based methods in industrial settings reveals two critical limitations. First, they suffer from **substantial computational overhead**. Standard Permutation and its Taylor-approximated variants, such as SHARK [23], require $O(N)$ repetitive inference passes and iterative "train-prune-train" cycles. Second, **permutation evaluation is inherently biased against extremely sparse features**. For features where the vast majority of instances (e.g., >99%) hold default values, shuffling predominantly exchanges default values with other default values. Consequently, the observed performance drop is minimal, causing standard permutation methods to underestimate the true importance of these features and mistakenly prune critical long-tail signals.

To address the limitations of both aforementioned paradigms, our proposed LeAP serves as a unified plug-in module. It synergizes the $O(1)$ efficiency of differentiable mask-based methods with the interpretability of permutation-based approaches. By shifting from standard discrete permutation evaluation to a learnable permutation divergence mechanism, LeAP effectively avoids the pitfalls of both paradigms. It provides a cohesive solution to the challenges of heterogeneous dimensions and extreme sparsity, requiring minimal modifications to the existing model architecture.

3 Methodology

In this section, we detail the overall architecture and mathematical foundations of **LeAP** (Learnable Adaptive Permutation) module, as shown in Fig. 1. We first introduce the transformation of traditional discrete permutation into an end-to-end learnable gating mechanism in Sect. 3.1. Subsequently, in Sect. 3.2, we elaborate on our core innovation for tackling dimensional heterogeneity and extreme sparsity: Adaptive Regularization via Permutation Divergence. Finally, we provide a theoretical analysis of how this mechanism drives gating polarization (Sect. 3.3) and discuss the deployment paradigm in real-world production environments (Sect. 3.4).

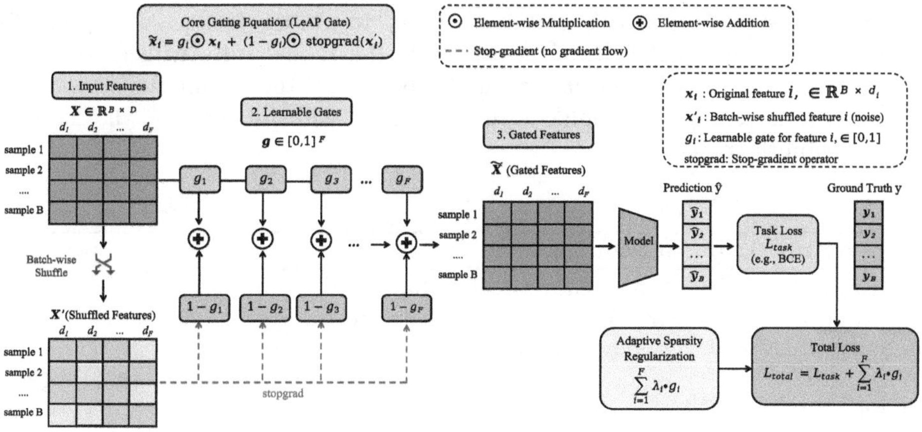

Fig. 1. The overview of LeAP Module.

3.1 Learnable Permutation Module

In deep recommender systems, model inputs typically consist of F feature fields. Due to the diversity of feature types, these features exhibit severe dimensional heterogeneity when mapped into the latent space. Let the representation of the i-th feature be denoted as $\mathbf{x}_i \in \mathbb{R}^{d_i}$, where d_i varies drastically (e.g., $d_i = 1$ for scalar statistical features, whereas $d_i = 256$ for user behavior sequence features).

To evaluate feature importance without requiring multiple forward passes, LeAP introduces a batch-wise learnable permutation mechanism. At each training step, given a mini-batch of size B, we first shuffle the i-th feature $\mathbf{x}_i$ along the batch dimension to obtain its noise counterpart $\mathbf{x}_i'$. This shuffling operation not only breaks the correlation between the feature and the target label but also perfectly preserves the feature's original marginal distribution and sparsity pattern. Algorithm 1 illustrates an implementation.

Next, we introduce a feature-specific learnable gating variable $g_i \in (0, 1)$ to control the information fusion between the original and shuffled features. To ensure end-to-end differentiability, we parameterize it using a temperature-scaled Sigmoid function:

$$g_i = \sigma\left(\frac{\theta_i}{\tau}\right) = \frac{1}{1 + \exp(-\theta_i/\tau)}$$

where $\theta_i \in \mathbb{R}$ is the learnable parameter tied to the i-th feature, and τ is the temperature hyperparameter controlling the smoothness.

The fused output feature $\tilde{\mathbf{x}}_i$ can be expressed as a convex combination of the original and shuffled features $\mathbf{x}_i'$. To ensure the gradients only update the gating weights and do not propagate through the noise to disrupt upstream layers, we apply a stop-gradient operation $\mathrm{sg}(\cdot)$ to the shuffled feature:

$$\tilde{\mathbf{x}}_i = g_i \cdot \mathbf{x}_i + (1 - g_i) \cdot \mathrm{sg}(\mathbf{x}_i')$$

Interpretation: Under this formulation, g_i intuitively reflects the model's reliance on the original feature. As $g_i \to 1$, the model fully utilizes the genuine feature; as $g_i \to 0$, the model tends to rely on the permuted pure noise. If a feature is redundant, replacing it with noise will not degrade the model's predictive performance.

Algorithm 1: Batch Shuffling

Input: $\mathbf{X} \in \mathbb{R}^{B \times D}$: Input tensor within a batch, $D = \sum d_i$
$\mathcal{F} = \{(s_1, e_1), ..., (s_F, e_F)\}$: Feature dimension ranges
Output: $\mathbf{X}' \in \mathbb{R}^{B \times D}$: Shuffled tensor

$\mathbf{X}' \leftarrow \mathbf{0}^{B \times D}$; `// Initialize output tensor`
for $(s_i, e_i) \in \mathcal{F}$ **do**
  $\pi_i \leftarrow \text{RandomPermutation}(B)$
  $\mathbf{X}'_{:, s_i:e_i} \leftarrow \mathbf{X}_{:, s_i:e_i}[\pi_i, :]$; `// Apply shuffling`
end
return $\mathbf{X}'$

3.2 Adaptive Regularization via Permutation Divergence

In standard gated feature selection methods [5,11,16,24], a uniform penalty (e.g., $\lambda \sum g_i$) is typically applied to all gating variables to encourage sparsity. However, when applied directly to the heterogeneous and sparse feature layers in industrial settings, this uniform penalty induces severe evaluation unfairness. High-dimensional features, due to their larger parameter volume, naturally generate greater gradient fluctuations than 1D features. Conversely, extremely sparse features (which are predominantly zero) produce weak gradients, making them highly susceptible to being mistakenly pruned by a uniform regularization term.

To address this critical limitation, LeAP discards the static uniform penalty and innovatively proposes a **data-aware adaptive regularization mechanism**. We argue that the penalization strength on a feature should not be based on its predefined dimensionality, but rather on the magnitude of information perturbation induced by its permutation.

Specifically, within each mini-batch, we calculate the L_2-norm difference (Permutation Divergence) between the original feature $\mathbf{x}_i$ and its shuffled version $\mathbf{x}'_i$:

$$\Delta_i = \frac{1}{B} \sum_{b=1}^{B} \|\mathbf{x}_i^{(b)} - \mathbf{x}_i'^{(b)}\|_2$$

To mitigate data variance across batches and establish a stable statistical bound, we employ an Exponential Moving Average (EMA) to smooth this divergence throughout the training process:

$$\bar{\Delta}_i^{(t)} = \beta \cdot \bar{\Delta}_i^{(t-1)} + (1 - \beta) \cdot \Delta_i^{(t)}$$

where $\beta \in [0, 1)$ is the momentum coefficient, and t denotes the training step. Additionally, to identify constant features, we apply appropriate clipping to $\bar{\Delta}_i$.

Based on this stable permutation divergence, we formulate the adaptive regularization weight λ_i for feature i:

$$\lambda_i = \alpha \cdot \bar{\Delta}_i$$

where α is a global hyperparameter controlling the overall feature sparsity. Finally, the end-to-end optimization objective (Total Loss) of LeAP is defined as the sum of the task loss and the adaptive regularization term:

$$\mathcal{L}_{total} = \mathcal{L}_{task} + \sum_{i=1}^{F} \lambda_i \cdot g_i$$

This highly streamlined mathematical design simultaneously resolves two major industrial pain points:

1. **Inherent Dimensional Normalization**: The L_2 divergence $\bar{\Delta}_i$ of a shuffled 128D embedding is intrinsically much larger than that of a 1D scalar. Consequently, high-dimensional features automatically incur a larger penalty λ_i. This adaptive reweighting fundamentally counteracts the tendency of ineffective parameters in high-dimensional spaces to evade penalization, ensuring fair competition across varying dimensions.
2. **Perfect Tolerance for Sparsity**: For extremely sparse features where 99% of instances hold default values, the shuffling process highly likely swaps default values with other default values. In this scenario, the L_2 divergence $\bar{\Delta}_i \to 0$, resulting in a negligible regularization penalty λ_i. This guarantees that sparse features are not mistakenly pruned simply due to their "low frequency of occurrence"; they are gradually phased out only if they contribute genuinely nothing to the predictive objective $\mathcal{L}_{task}$.

3.3 Theoretical Analysis

Existing gating methods [19,20] often produce ambiguous feature importance scores. In contrast, the core advantage of LeAP lies in its ability to drive gating scores to naturally polarize towards 0 or 1. We provide a theoretical justification for this phenomenon from the perspectives of gradient decoupling and convex optimization.

1. Gradient Decoupling and Scale Alignment. Recall the fusion formulation $\tilde{\mathbf{x}}_i = g_i \cdot \mathbf{x}_i + (1 - g_i) \cdot \mathbf{x}'_i$. The gradient of the expected task loss $J(g_i) = \mathbb{E}[\mathcal{L}_{\text{task}}]$ with respect to the gate g_i can be decoupled via the chain rule:

$$\frac{\partial J(g_i)}{\partial g_i} = \mathbb{E}\left[\underbrace{\left(\frac{\partial \mathcal{L}_{\text{task}}}{\partial \tilde{\mathbf{x}}_i}\right)^T}_{\text{Sensitivity } \mathbf{S}_i} \cdot \underbrace{(\mathbf{x}_i - \mathbf{x}_i')}_{\text{Permutation Divergence}}\right]$$

This equation reveals that the magnitude of the task gradient is naturally proportional to the permutation divergence $\|\mathbf{x}_i - \mathbf{x}_i'\|_2$. Therefore, by setting the adaptive penalty to $\lambda_i = \alpha \cdot \bar{\Delta}_i$, LeAP mathematically achieves an effective scale alignment between the regularization term and the task gradient. This alignment effectively resolves the evaluation bias that high-dimensional and extremely sparse features encounter under uniform penalties.

2. Polarized Gate Guarantee. Based on the aligned total objective function $\mathcal{J}_{\text{total}}(g_i) = J(g_i) + \lambda_i g_i$, the total gradient is given by $\frac{\partial \mathcal{J}_{\text{total}}}{\partial g_i} = \frac{\partial J(g_i)}{\partial g_i} + \lambda_i$. We demonstrate that genuinely useful features are guaranteed to polarize towards 1.

Theorem 1. *Assume the expected task loss $J(g_i)$ is convex. Let $\Delta J = J(0) - J(1)$ denote the loss increment after shuffling the feature (i.e., the signal strength). If $\Delta J > \lambda_i$, the total gradient is negative, and the gate g_i will be driven towards 1.*

Proof. Based on the first-order properties of convex functions, the function curve lies below the chord connecting its endpoints, meaning $J(g_i) \leq g_i J(1) + (1 - g_i)J(0)$. Rearranging this inequality and taking the partial derivative yields an upper bound for the task gradient:

$$\frac{\partial J(g_i)}{\partial g_i} \leq J(1) - J(0) = -\Delta J$$

Substituting this into the total gradient formulation gives:

$$\frac{\partial \mathcal{J}_{\text{total}}}{\partial g_i} \leq -\Delta J + \lambda_i$$

Given the assumption that the valid feature's signal strength satisfies $\Delta J > \lambda_i$, we have $\frac{\partial \mathcal{J}_{\text{total}}}{\partial g_i} < 0$. The optimizer will thus continuously increase g_i until it reaches the upper bound of 1.

Corollary. *Conversely, if a feature is redundant, shuffling it does not impact the prediction, resulting in $\Delta J \approx 0$. The total gradient then degenerates to $\approx \lambda_i > 0$. The regularization term dominates the optimization, rapidly suppressing the gate g_i towards 0.*

3.4 Practical Deployment in Industrial Systems

To meet the stringent iteration and latency requirements of large-scale industrial recommender systems, LeAP adopts a highly decoupled plug-in deployment paradigm. In real-world production environments, the pipeline consists of three streamlined steps:

1. Plug-in & Evaluation. Extract the online model and insert the LeAP module immediately after the feature concatenation layer. The model then iterates normally using the online data stream, accumulating the EMA statistics and updating the gating variables.

2. Hard Pruning via Thresholding. Thanks to the polarization property, the converged gates g_i exhibit strong discriminability. Once the evaluation phase concludes, feature pruning can be executed directly using two strategies:

- **Absolute Thresholding:** Set a fixed threshold (e.g., $\tau = 0.5$) and directly discard all features where $g_i < \tau$.
- **Proportional Ranking:** When facing strict system bandwidth reduction constraints, sort the features in descending order of their g_i scores and retain only the Top-K proportion.

3. Fine-tuning & Serving. After removing the redundant features and the LeAP module itself, the model only requires fine-tuning on the small fraction of training data to convergence.

4 Experiments

In this section, we comprehensively evaluate the effectiveness and engineering value of LeAP through extensive offline evaluations on public datasets and a large-scale industrial deployment. Our experiments are designed to answer the following core research questions:

- **RQ1 (Basic Efficacy):** On homogeneously dimensioned public datasets, can the fundamental mechanism of LeAP outperform existing state-of-the-art (SOTA) feature selection methods?
- **RQ2 (Mechanism Polarization):** Does LeAP genuinely generate highly polarized gating scores with clear physical interpretations, as theoretically proven?
- **RQ3 (Industrial Deployment & Ablation):** In real-world industrial scenarios characterized by extreme dimensional heterogeneity and sparsity, what is the Return on Investment (ROI) of LeAP?

Our code is available at https://github.com/goldenNormal/LeAP.

4.1 Experimental Setup

Datasets:

- **Public Datasets:** We utilize four widely adopted benchmark datasets [12] in the recommender system domain: Avazu[1], Criteo[2], MovieLens-1M (ML-1M)[3], and AliCCP[4]. The feature dimensions of these datasets have been set to a uniform size.

[1] https://www.kaggle.com/competitions/avazu-ctr-prediction.
[2] https://ailab.criteo.com/ressources/.
[3] https://grouplens.org/datasets/movielens/1m/.
[4] https://tianchi.aliyun.com/dataset/408.

- **Industrial Dataset:** This dataset is collected from real-world search, impression, click and interaction logs of a long-video platform with over a billion daily requests. The model incorporates more than 500 validated feature fields, resulting in a concatenated representation exceeding 12,000 dimensions. The feature dimensions vary drastically, ranging from 1D (e.g., statistical features) to 256D (e.g., aggregated behavioral sequence embeddings), and include a substantial number of extremely sparse features (Table 1).

Table 1. Dataset statistics.

Dataset	Avazu	Criteo	ML-1M	AliCCP
Samples	40,428,967	45,850,617	1,000,209	85,316,519
Label	Click	Click	Rating (1-5)	Click
Fields	23	39	9	23

Baselines: We select seven representative feature selection methods as baselines, categorized as follows: (1) **Heuristic:** Lasso [18], Random Forest [2] (RF), XGBoost [3]. (2) **Mask-based:** AutoField [20], LPFS [11], SFS [19]. (3) **Permutation-based:** SHARK [23] (an industry-recognized efficient variant of permutation).

Since the public datasets possess homogeneous feature dimensions, we deploy the base version of LeAP (without adaptive regularization) in Sect. 4.2 to solely validate the superiority of its native learnable permutation mechanism.

Evaluation Metrics: For public datasets, we employ AUC and the cross-dataset aggregated metric, Normalized AUC [17] (S_{AUC}):

$$S_{\text{AUC}}(A) = \frac{1}{|\Gamma|} \sum_{\mathcal{D} \in \Gamma} \frac{\text{AUC}(A, \mathcal{D})}{\max_{A' \in \mathcal{A}} \text{AUC}(A', \mathcal{D})} \tag{1}$$

For offline evaluation in the industrial scenario, we use Group AUC for CTR prediction to reflect core predictive capability. For online deployment, we conduct strict A/B testing to observe core business metrics (e.g., video views, interactions and watch time).

4.2 Offline Evaluation on Public Datasets

Following the standard "Search-Retrain" two-stage evaluation protocol [12], we test all methods using WideDeep [4] as the backbone network. Table 2 presents the retraining performance at target Feature Retention (FR) ratios of 50% and 25%.

1. Overall Dominance: Under both high compression rates of 50% and 25%, LeAP consistently achieves the highest S_{AUC}, which demonstrates its effectiveness in feature selection.

Table 2. Feature Selection and Retrain AUC Results. Best results are highlighted in red. On ML-1M, all top-performing methods converged to the same feature subset, resulting in identical retrained AUC.

Ratio (FR)	Method	Criteo	Avazu	AliCCP	ML-1M	S_{AUC}
50%	*No_Select*	0.8014	0.7882	0.6598	0.7950	0.9954
	Lasso	0.7462	0.7088	0.6054	0.6484	0.8872
	XGBoost	0.7682	0.7412	0.6499	0.8097	0.9710
	RF	0.7921	0.7869	0.6549	0.7924	0.9895
	SHARK	0.7974	0.7870	0.6582	0.8097	0.9977
	LPFS	0.7944	0.7728	0.6554	0.8097	0.9913
	SFS	0.7969	0.7827	0.6579	0.7946	0.9915
	AutoField	0.7974	0.7869	0.6567	0.8077	0.9965
	LeAP (Ours)	**0.7984**	**0.7870**	**0.6583**	**0.8097**	**0.9981**
25%	*No_Select*	0.8014	0.7882	0.6598	0.7950	0.9960
	Lasso	0.7003	0.6016	0.5804	0.5286	0.7928
	XGBoost	0.7157	0.7091	0.5869	0.7338	0.8977
	RF	0.7626	0.7637	0.6032	0.6946	0.9237
	SHARK	0.7717	0.7723	0.6461	0.8078	0.9805
	LPFS	0.7609	0.7714	0.6423	0.8078	0.9754
	SFS	0.7569	0.7685	0.6452	0.8078	0.9733
	AutoField	0.7738	0.7692	0.6485	0.8068	0.9808
	LeAP (Ours)	**0.7841**	**0.7723**	**0.6489**	**0.8078**	**0.9854**

2. Overcoming the "Weight Equals Importance" Assumption (Vs. Mask-based): Methods like AutoField and LPFS operate on the assumption that "smaller gating weights imply less important features." However, in deep non-linear networks, features with small weights can trigger substantial "butterfly effects." LeAP discards weight magnitude in favor of measuring sensitivity to information loss. Consequently, it outperforms all mask-based methods by a significant margin on the complex Criteo and AliCCP datasets.

3. Joint Optimization vs. Greedy Search (Vs. Permutation): While both LeAP and SHARK are sensitivity-based methods, LeAP exhibits slightly superior performance. This is because SHARK employs a greedy, one-by-one feature elimination strategy, which often overlooks feature coupling effects. In contrast, LeAP jointly optimizes all gates during a single forward pass, effectively capturing global feature importance.

4.3 Mechanism Analysis: Polarization

As theoretically analyzed in Sect. 3.3, LeAP's regularization design explicitly drives gating scores to polarize towards 0 or 1. To verify whether this polarization accurately reflects the genuine predictive utility of features, we conduct a stepwise validation on the MovieLens-1M dataset.

As shown in Table 3, we partition the features into a "Retained Zone" ($g_i > 0.5$) and a "Suppressed Zone" ($g_i \approx 0$) based on the converged gating scores g_i. The validation is divided into two phases: first, we incrementally construct the model using features from the Retained Zone (Steps 1–3) to observe performance gains; second, we individually introduce features from the Suppressed Zone into the peak-performance model (Steps 4–9) to assess their redundancy.

Table 3. Stepwise Validation of the LeAP's feature importances (on MovieLens-1M)

Step	Feature Set	Gate Score	Val AUC	Δ AUC	Utility Analysis
Part 1: Constructing with Retained Zone Features (High Gate > 0.5)					
1	[Title]	0.995	0.7336	-	Strong predictive signal
2	+ User_ID	0.941	0.8073	+0.0737	Strong predictive signal
3	+ Genres (Peak Model)	0.757	**0.8105**	**+0.0032**	Weak signal retention
Part 2: Validating Suppressed Zone Features (Base = Peak Model + Single Suppressed Feature)					
4	+ Movie_ID	≈ 0.0	0.8099	−0.0006	Conditional redundancy
5	+ Zip	≈ 0.0	0.8105	0.0000	No significant impact
6	+ Age	≈ 0.0	0.8106	+0.0001	No significant impact
7	+ Occupation	≈ 0.0	0.8106	+0.0001	No significant impact
8	+ Gender	≈ 0.0	0.8107	+0.0002	No significant impact
9	+ Timestamp	≈ 0.0	**0.7938**	**−0.0167**	Harmful noise

Results Analysis:

- **Retention of Weak Signals:** Although the score for *Genres* (0.757) is lower than primary features, its inclusion lifts the AUC by 0.0032. This indicates LeAP effectively identifies and retains weak signals beneficial for generalization, rather than merely filtering out low-weight features.
- **Filtering Conditional Redundancy:** *Movie_ID* is informative when used alone; however, introducing it when *Title* is already known slightly degrades performance (−0.0006). LeAP assigns it a gate score near 0, accurately capturing the co-linearity and redundancy between these features.
- **Noise Suppression:** Features in Steps 5–8 contribute negligibly to performance; retaining them only inflates the model size. Notably, introducing *Timestamp* causes a significant AUC drop (−0.0167). LeAP successfully truncates such noise features that induce overfitting, proving the reliability of the polarization mechanism in streamlining the feature space.

4.4 Industrial Deployment and Ablation Study

In the real-world industrial system, the search ranking model utilizes a concatenated feature representation exceeding 12,000 dimensions. This massive input tensor incurs significant CPU-GPU communication bandwidth overhead during both training and inference. To reduce dimensionality without compromising predictive performance, we compare the Return on Investment (ROI: pruned dimensions vs. GAUC difference) of different baselines.

Experimental Setup: Because the industrial model contains over 500 feature fields, traditional Permutation methods require an equivalent number of independent, full-model inferences. Constrained by computational bottlenecks, we evaluate the Permutation method only on a 1% uniformly sampled subset of the data. In contrast, thanks to their $O(1)$ computational complexity, both LeAP and its ablated version without adaptive regularization (**LeAP-Base**) complete the feature importance search on the full training dataset. Remarkably, the total time for LeAP on the full dataset is even less than that required by the traditional Permutation method to process the 1% sampled subset.

Table 4. Industrial Feature Pruning ROI and Ablation Analysis (Offline CTR GAUC Diff). $\mathbf{10^{-3}}$ is usually considered as a significant difference for our metric.

Pruned Dims	%	Permutation	LeAP-Base (w/o Adaptive Reg.)	LeAP
~500	~4%	- 1×10^{-4}	No Diff	No Diff
~1900	~15%	- $\mathbf{3 \times 10^{-3}}$	- 2×10^{-4}	No Diff
~2500	~20%	N/A	- $\mathbf{1 \times 10^{-3}}$	No Diff
~3600	~30%	N/A	- $\mathbf{2 \times 10^{-2}}$	No Diff
~4300	~35%	N/A	N/A	- 2×10^{-4}
~5100	~40%	N/A	N/A	- 3×10^{-4}
~6400	~50%	N/A	N/A	- $\mathbf{1 \times 10^{-3}}$

Results and Ablation Analysis:

- **Impact of Training Efficiency and Data Scale:** Comparing Permutation with LeAP-Base, the former suffers a performance drop of 3×10^{-3} when pruning 1,900 dimensions due to severe downsampling. Conversely, LeAP-Base, leveraging joint optimization on the full dataset, experiences a negligible drop of only 2×10^{-4} at the same pruning ratio. This highlights the substantial engineering advantage of end-to-end learning mechanisms on massive data scales.
- **Necessity of Adaptive Regularization (Ablation):** Table 4 shows that LeAP-Base (without adaptive regularization) suffers a severe GAUC degradation of 2×10^{-2} when pruning over 3,600 dimensions. This confirms that

uniform regularization heavily over-penalizes high-dimensional and sparse features in heterogeneous spaces. In contrast, the complete **LeAP** maintains consistent performance at the same pruning ratio. Even under an aggressive setting of pruning 50% of the dimensions, the performance drop is strictly bounded to around 1×10^{-3}, demonstrating vastly superior robustness.

Online A/B Testing: Based on the offline ROI evaluation, we deployed the strategy of pruning over 3,600 feature dimensions to the online serving system. After removing the corresponding network structures and performing lightweight fine-tuning, multi-week online A/B testing revealed that LeAP successfully alleviated memory bandwidth pressure while maintaining completely stable (*Neutral*) core business metrics. This validates the tremendous practical utility of LeAP in ultra-large-scale, complex industrial applications.

5 Conclusion

This paper presents LeAP, a plug-in module that transforms the inefficient random permutation process into a learnable mechanism. By introducing Adaptive Regularization based on permutation divergence, LeAP successfully aligns the penalty scale with the task gradient, effectively resolving long-standing evaluation biases in heterogeneous and sparse industrial feature spaces.

Experimental results on four public benchmarks demonstrate that LeAP consistently achieves state-of-the-art performance. Furthermore, its deployment in a billion-requests production system proves its practical efficacy: LeAP successfully pruned over 30% (3,600+) of input dimensions with zero degradation in business metrics. LeAP offers a scalable and interpretable solution for optimizing next-generation, massive-scale recommender systems.

Acknowledgements. Special thanks go to Jiayu Feng for her support and for crafting the schematic diagrams of the LeAP module.

References

1. Bolón-Canedo, V., Sánchez-Maroño, N., Alonso-Betanzos, A.: A review of feature selection methods on synthetic data. Knowl. Inf. Syst. **34**, 483–519 (2013)
2. Breiman, L.: Random forests. Mach. Learn. **45**, 5–32 (2001)
3. Chen, T., Guestrin, C.: Xgboost: a scalable tree boosting system. In: Proceedings of the 22nd ACM SIGKDD International Conference on Knowledge Discovery and Data Mining, pp. 785–794 (2016)
4. Cheng, H.T., et al.: Wide & deep learning for recommender systems. In: Proceedings of the 1st Workshop on Deep Learning for Recommender Systems, DLRS 2016, pp. 7–10. Association for Computing Machinery, New York, NY, USA (2016). https://doi.org/10.1145/2988450.2988454
5. Cherepanova, V., et al.: A performance-driven benchmark for feature selection in tabular deep learning. In: NeurIPS 2023 Second Table Representation Learning Workshop (2023)

6. Covington, P., Adams, J., Sargin, E.: Deep neural networks for youtube recommendations. In: Proceedings of the 10th ACM Conference on Recommender Systems, pp. 191–198 (2016)
7. Du, C., et al.: Exploration in online advertising systems with deep uncertainty-aware learning. In: Proceedings of the 27th ACM SIGKDD Conference on Knowledge Discovery & Data Mining, pp. 2792–2801 (2021)
8. Fisher, A., Rudin, C., Dominici, F.: All models are wrong, but many are useful: learning a variable's importance by studying an entire class of prediction models simultaneously. J. Mach. Learn. Res. JMLR **20** (2019)
9. Gomez-Uribe, C.A., Hunt, N.: The netflix recommender system: algorithms, business value, and innovation. ACM Trans. Manag. Inf. Syst. (TMIS) **6**(4), 1–19 (2015)
10. Gu, Y., Ding, Z., Wang, S., Zou, L., Liu, Y., Yin, D.: Deep multifaceted transformers for multi-objective ranking in large-scale e-commerce recommender systems. In: Proceedings of the 29th ACM International Conference on Information & Knowledge Management, pp. 2493–2500 (2020)
11. Guo, Y., et al.: LPFS: learnable polarizing feature selection for click-through rate prediction. arXiv preprint arXiv:2206.00267 (2022)
12. Jia, P., et al.: Erase: benchmarking feature selection methods for deep recommender systems. In: Proceedings of the 30th ACM SIGKDD Conference on Knowledge Discovery and Data Mining, pp. 5194–5205 (2024)
13. Ke, G., et al.: Lightgbm: a highly efficient gradient boosting decision tree. Adv. Neural. Inf. Process. Syst. **30**, 3146–3154 (2017)
14. Ko, H., Lee, S., Park, Y., Choi, A.: A survey of recommendation systems: recommendation models, techniques, and application fields. Electronics **11**(1), 141 (2022)
15. Lyu, F., Tang, X., Liu, D., Chen, L., He, X., Liu, X.: Optimizing feature set for click-through rate prediction. In: Proceedings of the ACM Web Conference 2023, pp. 3386–3395 (2023)
16. Shi, Y., Miao, J., Wang, Z., Zhang, P., Niu, L.: Feature selection with regularization. IEEE Trans. Neural Netw. Learn. Syst. **29**(10), 4967–4982 (2018)
17. Song, H., Li, P., Liu, H.: Deep clustering based fair outlier detection (2021). https://arxiv.org/abs/2106.05127
18. Tibshirani, R.: Regression shrinkage and selection via the lasso. J. Roy. Stat. Soc.: Ser. B (Methodol.) (1996)
19. Wang, Y., et al.: Single-shot feature selection for multi-task recommendations. In: Proceedings of the 46th International ACM SIGIR Conference on Research and Development in Information Retrieval, pp. 341–351 (2023)
20. Wang, Y., Zhao, X., Xu, T., Wu, X.: Autofield: automating feature selection in deep recommender systems. In: Proceedings of the ACM Web Conference (2022)
21. Yao, Y., et al.: I-razor: a differentiable neural input razor for feature selection and dimension search in DNN-based recommender systems. IEEE Trans. Knowl. Data Eng. **36**(9) (2024). https://doi.org/10.1109/tkde.2023.3332671
22. Yin, D., et al.: Ranking relevance in yahoo search. In: Proceedings of the 22nd ACM SIGKDD International Conference on Knowledge Discovery and Data Mining, pp. 323–332 (2016)
23. Zhang, B., et al.: Shark: a lightweight model compression approach for large-scale recommender systems. In: Proceedings of the 32nd ACM International Conference on Information and Knowledge Management, CIKM 2023 (2023)

24. Zhao, M., et al.: Dimreg: embedding dimension search via regularization for recommender systems. In: Proceedings of the 2024 SIAM International Conference on Data Mining (SDM), pp. 562–570. SIAM (2024)
25. Zhao, X., et al.: Autodim: field-aware embedding dimension searchin recommender systems. In: Proceedings of the Web Conference 2021 (2021)
26. Zheng, R., Qu, L., Cui, B., Shi, Y., Yin, H.: Automl for deep recommender systems: a survey. ACM Trans. Inf. Syst. **41**(4), 1–38 (2023)
27. Zhou, G., et al.: Deep interest network for click-through rate prediction. In: Proceedings of the 24th ACM SIGKDD International Conference on Knowledge Discovery & Data Mining, pp. 1059–1068 (2018)
28. Zhu, J., et al.: Rankmixer: scaling up ranking models in industrial recommenders. In: Proceedings of the 34th ACM International Conference on Information and Knowledge Management, pp. 6309–6316 (2025)

PIANO: Personalized Reranking via Information Aggregation Node for Music Search Optimization

Weisheng Li, Chuqiao Huang, Pengcheng Li, Zhengchao Peng, Qiang Xiao(✉), Zhongqian Xie, Qiang Huang, and Chuanjiang Luo

NetEase Cloud Music, Hangzhou, China
{liweisheng01,huangchuqiao01,lipengcheng06,pengzhengchao,hzxiaoqiang, hzxiezhongqian,huangqiang05,luochuanjiang03}@corp.netease.com

Abstract. Unlike short-video content, music tracks have long lifecycles and lasting value. Effective music search re-ranking must therefore align the user's current query with long-term preferences while jointly optimizing Click-Through Rate (CTR) and Conversion Rate (CVR). However, existing methods suffer from two limitations: (1) sequential methods rely on item-interaction history and therefore cannot use historical search queries to tell which past preferences match the user's current search intent; (2) most listwise models optimize a single objective (e.g., CTR only), and conventional multi-objective methods balance click and conversion at the item level, ignoring how these trade-offs play out across the whole ranked list. To address these limitations, we propose PIANO, a personalized listwise re-ranking framework with two key components: (i) the Query-Driven Interest Refiner (QDIR) uses cross-attention over historical queries to align past intents with the current one; (ii) the Information Aggregation Node (IAN), a learnable [CLS]-style token, aggregates the candidate list and predicts CTR/CVR at the list level. Extensive experiments on public and industrial datasets show consistent gains over strong baselines. In online A/B tests on NetEase Cloud Music, a leading music streaming platform, PIANO achieves statistically significant improvements in CTR (+0.62%) and CVR (+4.45%).

Keywords: Information Aggregation Node · Personalized Re-ranking · Music Search · Multi-objective Optimization

1 Introduction

Music streaming platforms depend heavily on search to link users with specific content. Unlike short-video feeds that prioritize short-term freshness, music tracks typically have long lifecycles and lasting artistic value. This presents a unique challenge for search re-ranking: systems must align users' immediate

W. Li and C. Huang—Equal contribution.

M. Baratchi et al. (Eds.): ECML PKDD 2026, LNAI 16949, pp. 73–90, 2027.
https://doi.org/10.1007/978-3-032-37682-4_5

query intent with long-term listening preferences to ensure sustained satisfaction. Moreover, industrial scenarios require balancing user experience and commercial goals, calling for joint optimization of Click-Through Rate (CTR) and Conversion Rate (CVR).

Despite the critical role of search, current re-ranking frameworks face significant hurdles in this domain. Traditional listwise approaches, such as DLCM [1], PRM [28], and SetRank [27], excel at modeling item interactions within the candidate list but either do not explicitly model user representations (DLCM, SetRank) or rely on a pre-computed user embedding (PRM), leaving historical query semantics underutilized. Meanwhile, two-stage frameworks like PRS [12] improve efficiency but are not designed to capture the semantic evolution of user intent across search queries. This leads to two fundamental gaps in music search scenarios:

First, intent alignment is insufficient. Most sequential models (e.g., DIN [37], SASRec [18]) encode behavior sequences but ignore the rich semantic signals in historical queries. While recent query-aware works [14] exist, they typically rely on static query representations. For example, a user frequently listening to *fast-paced pop* might suddenly search for *calm piano for studying*. Without explicitly modeling the query sequence, the system cannot filter out contextually inconsistent historical preferences, leading to irrelevant recommendations.

Second, effective list-level multi-objective optimization remains challenging. While recent work [5] explores this direction via generative modeling, discriminative frameworks that explicitly use historical search queries to align user intent are still scarce. Existing listwise models are predominantly designed for single-objective tasks (e.g., CTR only) or rely on item-level proxies for multi-objective goals. Conventional multi-objective methods often optimize conflicts (e.g., CTR vs. CVR) at the item level, ignoring how these trade-offs manifest across the entire ranked list. For instance, an item-level multi-objective ranker may push a paid-content song to the top of the list because it has a high CVR score, even though placing it among a list of free indie tracks may hurt the overall click-through rate of the list. Such cross-item trade-offs cannot be captured by item-wise scoring alone. Directly applying these methods to music search thus fails to capture the holistic utility of the slate, resulting in suboptimal balancing of business goals.

To bridge these gaps, we propose **PIANO**, i.e., **P**ersonalized reranking via **I**nformation **A**ggregation **N**ode for music search **O**ptimization—a listwise reranking framework with two key innovations: (1) the Query-Driven Interest Refiner (QDIR) that leverages historical query sequences to dynamically refine long-term preferences via cross-attention; and (2) the Information Aggregation Node (IAN), a learnable `[CLS]`-style token initialized by QDIR to capture global list context for direct multi-objective supervision.

Our main contributions are summarized as follows:

- Query-Aware Interest Modeling: We propose QDIR to dynamically align long-term preferences with short-term query intent using historical query sequences.

- List-Level Multi-Objective Optimization: We design IAN, a `[CLS]`-style token that aggregates list context for direct multi-objective prediction, avoiding item-level proxy optimization.
- Industrial Validation: We validate PIANO through extensive offline experiments on public datasets and online A/B tests on a leading music streaming platform, yielding significant gains in CTR (+0.62%) and CVR (+4.45%).

2 Related Work

Sequential User Interest Modeling. Sequential recommenders capture dynamic user intent from interaction histories. Self-attention models like SASRec [18] model long-range dependencies, while industrial systems like BST [7], DIN [37], and SIM [29] integrate behavior sequences with rich features. Recent works like MIR [34] and RAISE [21] further enrich personalized reranking with multi-level set-to-list interactions and review-based intention modeling, respectively. He et al. [14] incorporate queries into sequential modeling via heterogeneous sequences, but rely on static query representations (e.g., average pooling) without cross-attention against historical queries, which may not fully capture the rapid intent shifts specific to music search re-ranking. Our QDIR employs query-aware cross-attention to dynamically refine long-term preferences based on the current query.

Listwise Re-ranking and Contextual Modeling. Multi-stage recommenders increasingly adopt listwise models to capture cross-item dependencies, crucial for tasks like music search coherence [13]. Existing approaches generally fall into one-stage scoring and two-stage permutation frameworks. **One-stage models** refine candidate scores by encoding the list, evolving from RNNs (DLCM [1], Seq2Slate [2]) to self-attention mechanisms (PRM [28], SetRank [27], RankFormer [4]). **Two-stage frameworks** decouple generation and evaluation to balance efficiency and effectiveness (PRS [12], PIER [31], CLIG [35]). To capture global context, these methods typically rely on `[CLS]`-style tokens or set-to-list attention, yet such nodes are rarely supervised by true list-level outcomes. While RankFormer [4] also augments a listwise Transformer with a `[CLS]` token supervised by a listwide objective, its listwide label is synthesized as the maximum item label rather than a true per-list outcome, and the token itself is a generic learnable parameter; in contrast, IAN is initialized by QDIR's query-conditioned user interest and is directly supervised by real per-list CTR/CVR rates under a multi-objective formulation. Furthermore, regarding user context integration, while works like PEAR [20] incorporate history, they encode user history with item-history alone and lack an explicit query-conditioned alignment of past preferences to the current intent. This is suboptimal for dynamic scenarios like music search. In contrast, our approach introduces an explicitly supervised global node (IAN) and employs query-aware cross-attention to dynamically align intent with preferences.

Multi-objective Re-ranking. Multi-objective re-ranking balances conflicting goals such as CTR and CVR. Item-level multi-task models like ESMM [24], MMoE [23], and PLE [32] jointly predict multiple objectives per item but ignore cross-item dependencies at re-ranking time. Beyond item-level approaches, Nguyen et al. [26] use Kendall tau regularization for multi-stakeholder ranking, and CMR [9] adjusts task weights via hypernetworks. PRECTR [8] couples relevance matching with CTR prediction via conditional probability fusion and a batch-wise listwise consistency regularization, yet its supervision is still defined over per-item click labels rather than per-list outcomes. SORT-Gen [5] pursues list-level multi-objective optimization via autoregressive generation with ordered-regression supervision; in contrast, PIANO adopts a discriminative framework with an explicitly supervised `[CLS]`-style aggregator (IAN) that predicts per-list CTR/CVR rates in a single forward pass, enabling efficient end-to-end joint optimization.

3 Methodology

3.1 Overall Architecture

As illustrated in Fig. 1, PIANO comprises two core components: the Query-Driven Interest Refiner (QDIR) and the Information Aggregation Node (IAN).

Given input signals (query, user history, and candidate items), PIANO first extracts query-conditioned user interests via QDIR, which then initialize the IAN token prepended to the candidate list. Through a Transformer encoder, the model jointly optimizes both item-level and list-level business metrics. In the following subsections, we detail each component and their interactions.

3.2 Problem Definition

A multi-stage search/recommendation pipeline typically comprises matching, ranking, and re-ranking. Denote the result from ranking stages as $I = (i_1, \dots, i_M)$. Let Π_M be the set of all permutations (all possible orderings) of $\{1, \dots, M\}$. For $\pi \in \Pi_M$, write $\pi(I) = (i_{\pi(1)}, \dots, i_{\pi(M)})$. Then the re-ranker selects

$$\pi^* \in \arg\max_{\pi \in \Pi_M} \lambda\, U_{\text{clk}}(\pi(I), C) + (1 - \lambda)\, U_{\text{conv}}(\pi(I), C) \tag{1}$$

where $\lambda \in [0, 1]$ controls the trade-off between the click- and conversion-oriented list-level objectives. In our music search scenario, a *click* denotes a user tapping a song in the returned result list, while a *conversion* refers to a paid membership subscription triggered after such interaction—a key revenue indicator for music streaming platforms. Specifically, $U_{\text{clk}}(\cdot)$ and $U_{\text{conv}}(\cdot)$ denote the *list-wise utility functions.* U_{clk} typically represents the *expected average clicks* over the list, while U_{conv} represents the *expected average conversions.* Both are computed by aggregating item-level predictions across the entire ranked list $\pi(I)$, thereby necessitating a model capable of capturing global list dependencies.

We adopt a weighted-sum scalarization; by varying λ, the system sweeps operating points that approximate the Pareto frontier in practice [15].

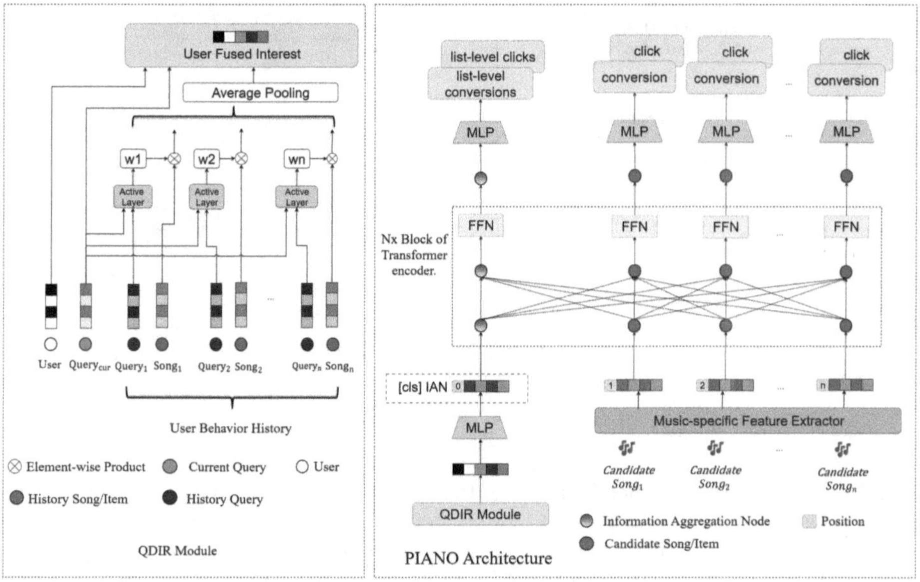

Fig. 1. Overall architecture of PIANO. The QDIR module extracts user interest representations from query-item interaction history. The List-level Information Aggregation Node (IAN) with fixed position encoding is prepended to aggregate global information, which then interacts with candidate items via cross-attention for list-level prediction.

3.3 Music-Specific Representation Model

To capture music-specific semantics, we employ a representation model based on Qwen3-Embedding-0.6B [36], fine-tuned on in-domain query–song pairs with task-specific prompts. The dual-tower design and the training/inference pipeline are illustrated in Fig. 2. Compared to general-purpose encoders, this yields embeddings better tailored to music search and decouples encoder cost from online latency, since song embeddings are pre-computed offline.

3.4 Query-Driven Interest Refiner

As shown in Fig. 1, the **Query-Driven Interest Refiner (QDIR)** aims to align a user's long-term preferences with the short-term intent expressed by the current query. It consists of two components: *Current Intent Representation* and *Historical Query-aware Preference Refinement.*

Current Intent Representation. We first denote the raw current query as q_{cur}. To obtain its semantic representation, we embed the current query using the method demonstrated in Sect. 3.3:

$$q_{\text{cur}}^{\text{emb}} = \phi_{\text{music}}(q_{\text{cur}}) \tag{2}$$

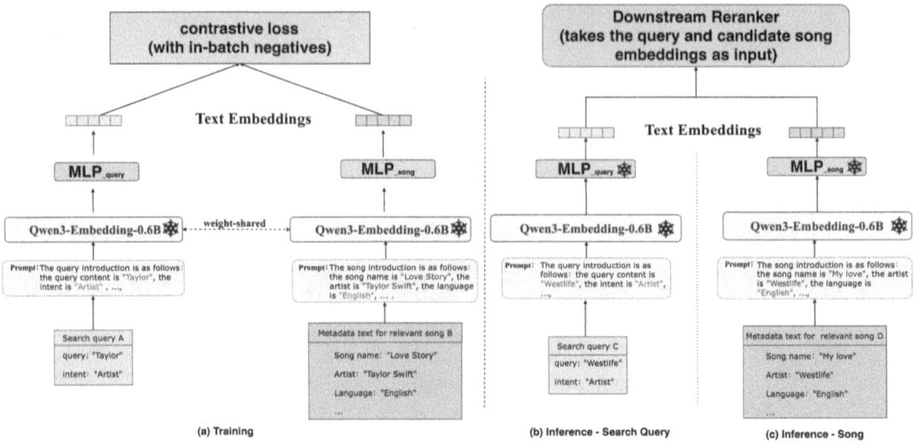

Fig. 2. Pretrained music-specific representation model. (a) **Training**: a frozen Qwen3-Embedding-0.6B encoder is weight-shared between the query and song towers; two tower-specific MLP projection heads (MLP_{query}, MLP_{song}) produce text embeddings, optimized with a contrastive loss using in-batch negatives. (b)(c) **Inference**: both the encoder and the projection heads are frozen. Song embeddings are pre-computed offline, while the query embedding is computed online per search request. Both feed into the downstream re-ranker.

We then form the short-term interest by a learnable linear projection:

$$r_{\text{short}}^{\text{emb}} = W^E q_{\text{cur}}^{\text{emb}} \tag{3}$$

where W^E is a learnable projection initialized to the identity, so that training starts from $r_{\text{short}}^{\text{emb}} = q_{\text{cur}}^{\text{emb}}$ and gradually adapts the current-query embedding into the fusion space used by the cross-attention below.

Historical Query-Aware Preference Refinement. To filter past preferences by the current query, we apply cross-attention [33] with $q_{\text{cur}}^{\text{emb}}$ as the query, the historical query sequence $q_{\text{seq}}^{\text{emb}} = [q_1^{\text{emb}}, \ldots, q_L^{\text{emb}}]$ as keys, and the items interacted under each historical query $s_{\text{seq}}^{\text{emb}} = [s_1^{\text{emb}}, \ldots, s_L^{\text{emb}}]$ as values:

$$r_{\text{long}}^{\text{emb}} = \text{softmax}\left(\frac{QK^\top}{\sqrt{d}}\right) V, \tag{4}$$

where $Q = W^Q q_{\text{cur}}^{\text{emb}}$, $K = W^K q_{\text{seq}}^{\text{emb}}$, $V = W^V s_{\text{seq}}^{\text{emb}}$, and d is the hidden dimension. The attention weights re-weight the historical clicked items by their relevance to the current query.

Fusion of Long- and Short-Term Interests. We integrate the refined long-term preference $r_{\text{long}}^{\text{emb}}$, the short-term intent embedding $r_{\text{short}}^{\text{emb}}$, and the user profile to form a unified, query-conditioned user interest representation:

$$r_{\text{user}}^{\text{emb}} = \text{LayerNormalization}\Big(W_f \cdot \big[\text{concat}(r_{\text{long}}^{\text{emb}}, r_{\text{short}}^{\text{emb}}, r_{\text{user\_profile}})\big] + b\Big), \tag{5}$$

where W_f is a projection matrix mapping to dimension d_{model}, b is a bias, and $r_{\text{user\_profile}}$ denotes the static user profile embedding. This final representation $r_{\text{user}}^{\text{emb}}$ serves as the initialization signal for the IAN token in the subsequent re-ranking stage.

3.5 Information Aggregation Node (IAN)

Motivation and Design. Inspired by [CLS] tokens in BERT [10] and ViT [11], we prepend a learnable [CLS]-style token—the **Information Aggregation Node (IAN)**—to the candidate list (Fig. 1, right). Unlike static pooling (e.g., mean) that ignores item interactions, IAN leverages self-attention to capture list-wise dependencies and to learn a list-level utility that goes beyond a simple sum of item scores.

Initialization and Positional Encoding. The IAN token is initialized using the query-conditioned interest vector from QDIR. Let $g = r_{\text{user}}^{\text{emb}} \in \mathbb{R}^{d_{\text{model}}}$ denote this vector. As shown in Fig. 1, raw candidate songs are first processed by the music-specific representation model (Sect. 3.3) to obtain item representations $h_{1:M} \in \mathbb{R}^{d_{\text{model}}}$. We project g through an MLP to obtain the raw IAN representation:

$$h_0^{\text{raw}} = \text{MLP}_{\text{init}}(g). \tag{6}$$

We then add positional encodings to all positions:

$$\tilde{h}_j = \begin{cases} h_0^{\text{raw}} + \text{PE}(0), & \text{if } j = 0, \\ h_j + \text{PE}(j), & \text{if } j \in \{1, \ldots, M\}, \end{cases} \tag{7}$$

where PE(0) anchors the IAN to a fixed reference position, and PE(j) for $j \geq 1$ retains order sensitivity for item scoring.

3.6 Contextualized Transformer Encoder

Architecture. The positionally-encoded sequence $[\tilde{h}_0, \tilde{h}_1, \ldots, \tilde{h}_M]$ is fed into a stack of $N_x = 2$ pre-norm Transformer encoder blocks [33]:

$$[h'_0, h'_1, \ldots, h'_M] = \text{Transformer}([\tilde{h}_0, \tilde{h}_1, \ldots, \tilde{h}_M]). \tag{8}$$

Each block consists of multi-head self-attention (MHSA) and a position-wise feed-forward network (FFN), both equipped with residual connections and layer normalization.

Prediction Heads. After encoding, the output sequence $[h'_0, h'_1, \ldots, h'_M]$ is utilized by two jointly trained heads for **multi-task prediction** (e.g., click and conversion, as shown in the orange boxes of Fig. 1):

$$\hat{\mathbf{p}}_{\text{list}}^{(t)} = \text{Sigmoid}(\text{MLP}(h'_0)), \tag{9a}$$

$$\mathbf{p}_j^{(t)} = \text{Sigmoid}(\text{MLP}(h'_j)), \tag{9b}$$

where h'_0 acts as a *global list representation* for the list-level classifier (Eq. 9a), and the item heads (Eq. 9b) operate on item representations h'_j for $j \in \{1, \ldots, M\}$. Crucially, the global semantics aggregated by h'_0 are propagated to each item representation h'_j through self-attention, enhancing their contextual awareness.

3.7 Model Prediction and Optimization

We train PIANO by employing two complementary loss functions to jointly optimize list-level and item-level objectives. Note that PIANO uses three weights at different levels: λ (Eq. 1) for click vs. conversion utility; α (Eq. 15) for list- vs. item-level loss; β for click vs. conversion BCE within the item loss.

List-Level Loss. Aligned with Eq. (1), we predict the list-level click rate and conversion rate via two BCE losses on soft labels:

$$L_{\text{list}} = -\frac{1}{N}\sum_{t=1}^{N}\sum_{m\in\{\text{clk},\text{conv}\}}\left[y_m^{(t)}\log\hat{p}_m^{(t)} + (1-y_m^{(t)})\log(1-\hat{p}_m^{(t)})\right] \tag{10}$$

where $\mathbf{y}^{(t)} = (y_{\text{clk}}^{(t)}, y_{\text{conv}}^{(t)}) \in [0,1]^2$ are the per-list rate targets, $\hat{\mathbf{p}}^{(t)} = (\hat{p}_{\text{clk}}^{(t)}, \hat{p}_{\text{conv}}^{(t)})$ are the predicted scores, N is the batch size, and the targets are defined as:

$$y_{\text{clk}}^{(t)} = \frac{\#\text{clicked items in list } t}{\text{length of list } t}, \tag{11}$$

$$y_{\text{conv}}^{(t)} = \frac{\#\text{converted items in list } t}{\text{length of list } t}. \tag{12}$$

Item-Level Loss. For item labels $y_j^{(\text{clk})}, y_j^{(\text{conv})} \in \{0,1\}$, we use binary cross–entropy (BCE) with a conversion weight $\beta \geq 0$:

$$L_{\text{item}} = \frac{1}{N}\sum_{t=1}^{N}\frac{1}{M}\sum_{j=1}^{M}\Big(\ell_{\text{BCE}}\big(y_j^{(\text{clk})}, p_j^{(\text{clk})}\big) + \beta\,\ell_{\text{BCE}}\big(y_j^{(\text{conv})}, p_j^{(\text{conv})}\big)\Big) \tag{13}$$

$$\ell_{\text{BCE}}(y,p) = -y\log p - (1-y)\log(1-p), \tag{14}$$

where β balances the conversion signal relative to click signal. Typically, we set $\beta = 1$.

Joint Objective. The final training objective is a weighted sum:

$$L = \alpha L_{\text{list}} + (1-\alpha)L_{\text{item}}, \tag{15}$$

where $\alpha > 0$ balances list–level supervision and item-level supervision (we study sensitivity to α in Sect. 4.4). Through self-attention, the IAN aggregates global list context into h'_0, which is supervised by L_{list} for holistic utility prediction. Meanwhile, item representations h'_j benefit from this global context via attention, enabling joint optimization aligned with the multi-objective target in Equation (1).

Table 1. Overview of the Datasets

	Yahoo Letor Dataset	Music Search Re-ranking Dataset
#User	-	4,488,871
#Docs/Items	709,877	642,239
#Queries	-	236,191
#Records	29,921	31,336,800

4 Offline Experiments

We evaluate PIANO on the public Yahoo Letor benchmark [6] and our Industrial Music Search Re-ranking Dataset. We first compare against strong baselines, then perform ablations and sensitivity analysis. Specifically, our aim is to address the following research questions.

- **RQ1** Does PIANO outperform strong re-ranking baselines across datasets and metrics?
- **RQ2** Do ablations confirm that **QDIR** and **IAN** each provide measurable gains?
- **RQ3** How does the balancing hyperparameter α affect overall performance?
- **RQ4** How does the length of the historical behavior sequence for QDIR impact ranking effectiveness?
- **RQ5** Does the IAN encode meaningful list-level semantics, as evidenced by diagnostics/visualization?

4.1 Experimental Settings

Datasets. We evaluate on Yahoo! Webscope v2.0 (Yahoo Letor) [6] and the Industrial Music Search Re-ranking Dataset (Table 1).

Yahoo Letor Dataset. Following [2], we binarize relevance grades ($r \geq T_b$) and simulate position bias via $P_{\text{exam}}(i) \propto 1/\text{pos}(i)^{\eta}$.

Music Search Re-ranking Dataset. Constructed from NetEase Cloud Music, a leading music streaming platform, this dataset comprises query contexts, candidate lists, and user feedback. We filter sessions with full first-screen exposure to minimize bias. Features include metadata, behavioral statistics, and textual embeddings (Sect. 3.3). The labels include item-level click and conversion signals, together with their list-wise averages as list-level CTR and CVR targets. We adopt a time-based split to prevent leakage, ensuring all methods share the same candidate pool and features.

Baselines. We compare PIANO with representative learning-to-rank (LTR) and listwise re-ranking baselines [22], covering three dimensions relevant to our contributions: (i) *LTR paradigm* (pointwise/pairwise vs. listwise), (ii) *personalization* (with/without user-side signals), and (iii) *contextual modeling* (independent scoring vs. slate-aware inter-item interaction).

SVMRank [17] is a classic pairwise LTR baseline. As a non-listwise, non-personalized method, it serves as a lower bound to quantify the benefit of inter-item modeling.

LambdaMART [3] is a strong listwise LTR method based on gradient-boosted decision trees, optimizing NDCG through pairwise lambda gradients weighted by list-level metric deltas. We include it as a representative production-grade baseline widely deployed in industrial settings due to its low-latency inference.

DLCM [1] is the seminal listwise re-ranker that encodes the top-n slate with a GRU. As an early sequential listwise model, it serves as a contrast to the self-attention-based re-rankers introduced next.

PRM [28] injects user embeddings into a Transformer self-attention encoder to jointly model user–item and item–item interactions. As the canonical *personalized* self-attention re-ranker, it constitutes the closest non-historical counterpart to PIANO.

SAR [30] is a recent listwise method that captures item–item dependencies through slate-aware contextual modeling. We include it as a contemporary listwise baseline without user-history or query-aware components.

PEAR [20] fuses the initial list and user-history signals via a Transformer for personalized re-ranking. As the most architecturally similar baseline to PIANO, PEAR relies on item-history without query signals; we use it as our key reference point for personalized listwise re-ranking.

Implementation Details

Hyperparameters. For all baselines and for PIANO, we keep critical hyperparameters identical across datasets to ensure fairness. We set the hidden size to $d_{\text{model}} = 128$ for both the Yahoo Letor Dataset and the Industrial Music Search Re-ranking Dataset. All models are trained with Adam [19]. The dropout rate is set to $p_{\text{dropout}} = 0.2$. The mini-batch size is 32 for the Yahoo Letor Dataset and 256 for the Music Search Re-ranking Dataset.

Evaluation Protocol. All experimental results are reported as mean $\pm$ standard deviation over 10 independent runs with different random seeds to ensure statistical reliability.

Feature Alignment Across Datasets. To ensure fair comparison, we align the input representations across datasets while adapting to each dataset's available metadata.

For the Industrial Music Search Re-ranking Dataset, s_i^{emb} is the song embedding produced by the music-specific representation model (Sect. 3.3).

For the Yahoo Letor Dataset, which lacks music metadata, we instead use a trainable ID embedding of the same width d_{model}:

$$s_i^{\text{emb}} = E_{\text{item}}[\text{ID}(i)], \tag{16}$$

where $\text{ID}(\cdot)$ maps each item to its integer index in the item ID set $\mathcal{D}$, and $E_{\text{item}} \in \mathbb{R}^{(|\mathcal{D}|+1)\times d_{\text{model}}}$ is the embedding lookup matrix with an extra `[UNK]` row for unseen items.

In both cases, s_i^{emb} occupies the same d_{model}-dimensional input slot, so all methods receive item representations of identical shape.

Dataset-Specific Adaptations. PEAR requires user behavior sequences unavailable in the Yahoo Letor Dataset, so we evaluate it only on the Industrial Music Search Re-ranking Dataset. For PIANO on the Yahoo Letor Dataset, we disable QDIR's query-sequence component while retaining IAN, ensuring fair comparison under identical feature constraints.

Evaluation Metrics. For offline evaluation, we adopt two standard ranking metrics [16]: **Normalized Discounted Cumulative Gain at k (NDCG@k)**, which weights each position by a logarithmic discount so that relevant items ranked higher contribute more to the score; and **Mean Average Precision (MAP)**, the mean over queries of the average precision computed at the positions of relevant items. Given that our industrial music search scenario displays only the top 5 results, we set $k = 5$ to align with practical deployment.

Table 2. Performance Comparison on Yahoo Letor Dataset

Model	NDCG@5	NDCG@10	MAP
PIANO	**0.6700 ± 0.0008**	**0.7225 ± 0.0006**	**0.6516 ± 0.0005**
PRM	0.6676 ± 0.0008	0.7204 ± 0.0008	0.6494 ± 0.0006
SAR	0.6539 ± 0.0028	0.7107 ± 0.0020	0.6386 ± 0.0023
DLCM	0.6530 ± 0.0019	0.7044 ± 0.0017	0.6353 ± 0.0016
LambdaMART	0.6388 ± 0.0002	0.6992 ± 0.0003	0.6153 ± 0.0001
SVM	0.5943 ± 0.0001	0.6556 ± 0.0002	0.5768 ± 0.0001

4.2 Overall Performance (RQ1)

Tables 2 and 3 report the performance on both datasets. **PIANO** consistently outperforms all baselines across all metrics.

On the Yahoo Letor Dataset, PIANO achieves consistent gains over the strongest neural baseline (PEAR), validating that QDIR and IAN provide measurable benefits even with short candidate lists. The advantages are more pronounced on the Industrial Music Search Re-ranking Dataset, where PIANO

Table 3. Performance Comparison on Industrial Music Search Re-ranking Dataset

Model	NDCG@3	NDCG@5	MAP
PIANO	**0.8296 ± 0.0002**	**0.8606 ± 0.0002**	**0.8100 ± 0.0003**
PEAR	0.8277 ± 0.0001	0.8586 ± 0.0002	0.8081 ± 0.0002
PRM	0.8098 ± 0.0006	0.8433 ± 0.0006	0.7868 ± 0.0008
SAR	0.8062 ± 0.0002	0.8426 ± 0.0001	0.7840 ± 0.0002
DLCM	0.8042 ± 0.0006	0.8398 ± 0.0004	0.7822 ± 0.0006
LambdaMART	0.7767 ± 0.0016	0.8247 ± 0.0017	0.7622 ± 0.0012
SVM	0.7640 ± 0.0014	0.8188 ± 0.0012	0.7542 ± 0.0016

significantly surpasses PEAR and other baselines. These results confirm that fusing query-conditioned interest modeling with explicit list-level multi-objective optimization improves re-ranking quality in real-world scenarios.

4.3 Ablation Study (RQ2)

We conduct ablation studies on the Industrial Music Search Re-ranking Dataset to quantify the contribution of each component (Table 4).

Effect of QDIR. Removing **QDIR** (replaced by query-agnostic pooling) leads to consistent drops in NDCG@k and MAP. This confirms that aligning long-term behavioral signals with the current query is essential for effective personalization, as it filters noise and captures intent shifts.

Effect of IAN. Ablating **IAN** and the list-level head uniformly degrades performance across all metrics. This validates the necessity of list-level multi-objective supervision, which provides global context complementary to item-wise signals.

Table 4. Ablation Study of PIANO on Industrial Music Search Re-ranking Dataset

Model	NDCG@3	NDCG@5	MAP
w/ QDIR, w/ IAN	**0.8296 ± 0.0002**	**0.8606 ± 0.0002**	**0.8100 ± 0.0003**
w/o QDIR, w/ IAN	0.8108 ± 0.0013	0.8442 ± 0.0011	0.7880 ± 0.0015
w/ QDIR, w/o IAN	0.8198 ± 0.0002	0.8507 ± 0.0002	0.8002 ± 0.0003
w/o QDIR, w/o IAN	0.8103 ± 0.0014	0.8437 ± 0.0013	0.7874 ± 0.0018

4.4 Effect of the Balancing Parameter α (RQ3)

We investigate the impact of the balancing parameter α in the joint objective (Eq. 15), which controls the trade-off between list-level and item-level supervision.

As shown in Table 5, performance exhibits a clear inverted-U pattern: $\alpha = 0$ (list-level only) yields suboptimal results due to insufficient item-level guidance, while $\alpha = 0.5$ achieves the best balance, indicating that global list semantics and fine-grained item signals are complementary. Further increasing α to 0.75 leads to diminishing returns, suggesting that over-emphasizing item-level loss may dilute the global aggregation capability of IAN. This validates the necessity of joint optimization and guides our choice of $\alpha = 0.5$ for all subsequent experiments.

Table 5. PIANO performance with different balancing parameter α

α	NDCG@3	NDCG@5	MAP
0.00	0.8199 ± 0.0002	0.8508 ± 0.0002	0.8004 ± 0.0003
0.25	0.8250 ± 0.0003	0.8577 ± 0.0002	0.8052 ± 0.0003
0.50	**0.8296 ± 0.0002**	**0.8606 ± 0.0002**	**0.8100 ± 0.0003**
0.75	0.8262 ± 0.0005	0.8576 ± 0.0004	0.8060 ± 0.0006

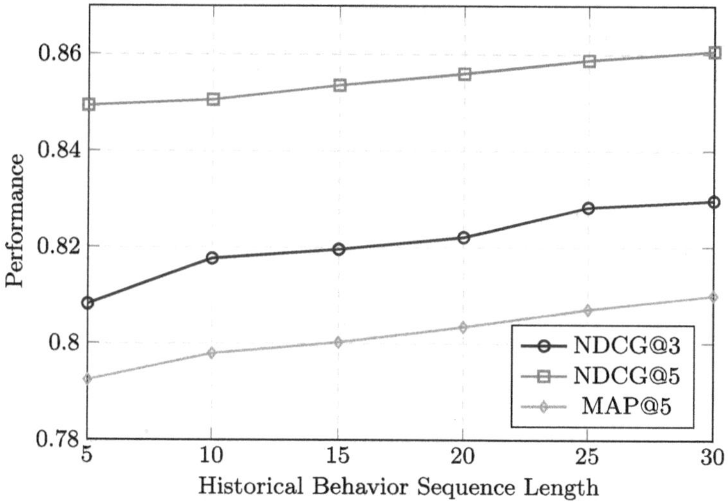

Fig. 3. Impact of historical behavior sequence length on ranking performance.

4.5 Effect of Historical Behavior List Length (RQ4)

Figure 3 reports PIANO's performance under different historical behavior list lengths. A clear monotonic pattern emerges: all metrics consistently improve as the sequence grows from 5 to 30 interactions. These results verify that richer historical behavior sequences provide stronger long-term preference signals for **QDIR**, while its query-driven cross-attention filters out unrelated history, so a longer sequence brings more useful signal without adding noise.

4.6 Visualization of the IAN (RQ5)

To assess whether the **Information Aggregation Node** (IAN) effectively encodes list-level stylistic signals, we extract the post-Transformer IAN embedding h'_0 for a random set of held-out users and project these vectors to two dimensions using t-SNE [25]. We consider eight high-frequency genre tags—*Anime/ACG*, *Children*, *Chinese Traditional*, *Electronic*, *Folk*, *Rock*, *Slow DJ*, and *Soundtrack*—with each point in Fig. 4 colored by the dominant genre of the candidate list.

The visualization reveals clear genre-aligned clustering: *Slow DJ* forms a well-separated cluster on the left, while *Electronic* and *Anime/ACG* occupy distinct regions in the lower-middle and upper-right areas. Other genres exhibit discernible patterns with some overlap reflecting stylistic proximity. This demonstrates that IAN successfully aggregates global candidate list information, producing semantically meaningful representations.

Crucially, this capability directly supports our list-level multi-objective prediction task. Since user engagement varies with list composition (e.g., genre), IAN's ability to cluster stylistically different lists gives the list-level MLP head a useful basis for predicting clicks and conversions. Analogous to BERT's [CLS] token, IAN aggregates item-level features into a list-level summary that simultaneously feeds the list-level head and conditions item-level scoring through self-attention.

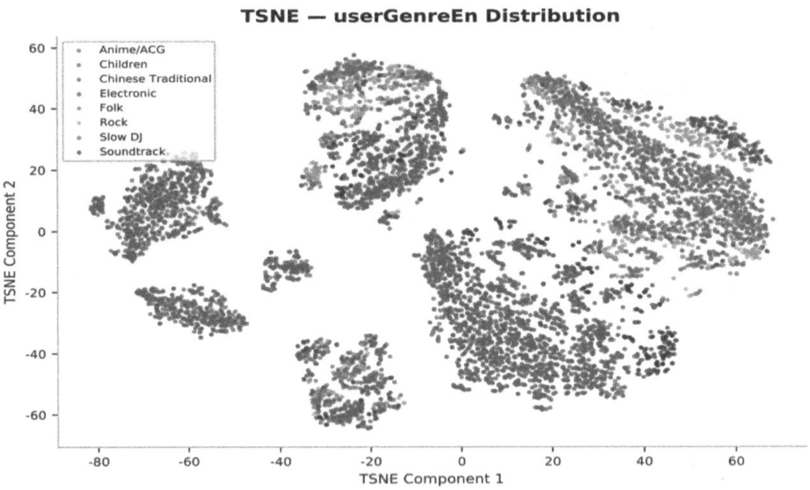

Fig. 4. t-SNE of the Output Embedding of IAN after Transformer Encoder.

5 Online Evaluation and Deployment

5.1 Online A/B Test

We conducted a multi-week online experiment in our industrial music search stack. Users were bucketed by stable identifiers; the treatment used PIANO and the control used the pre-existing re-ranker. The trial showed statistically significant gains of **+0.62%** CTR and **+4.45%** CVR (both with $p < 0.05$, two-sided). The gains were stable across weekdays/weekends and major query categories (Table 6).

Table 6. Online A/B Test Results: Absolute and Relative Changes vs. Control

Week	CTR Abs. (pp)	CTR Rel. (%)	CVR Abs. (pp)	CVR Rel. (%)
Week 1	+0.13* [0.00, 0.26]	+0.46*	+0.006* [0.003, 0.009]	+4.62*
Week 2	+0.18* [0.05, 0.31]	+0.66*	+0.007* [0.004, 0.009]	+4.91*
Week 3	+0.21* [0.05, 0.36]	+0.73*	+0.006* [0.003, 0.011]	+4.02*
Week 4	+0.17* [0.01, 0.33]	+0.61*	+0.007* [0.004, 0.013]	+4.23*
Avg	+0.17	+0.62	+0.005	+4.45

Note: * indicates statistical significance at $p < 0.05$ (two-tailed).

5.2 Online Deployment

We have deployed PIANO for music search at NetEase Cloud Music, a large-scale music streaming platform. The system is integrated as a post-ranking service in the existing *matching→ranking→re-ranking* pipeline: the upstream ranker returns a list I, and PIANO produces the final order π. In steady state, 95% of traffic is served by PIANO (covering millions of daily active users), while a persistent 5% randomized holdout is routed to the baseline for long-horizon KPI tracking. We conduct periodic model refreshes using the latest user interaction logs to adapt to evolving preferences. Since launch, key business metrics have remained consistently above the control group, exhibiting sustained positive uplifts without compromising online latency requirements. This deployment demonstrates that list-aware, query-conditioned re-ranking can be operated reliably at scale in a high-traffic music search system.

6 Conclusion

In this paper, we identified two gaps in music search re-ranking: queries shift faster than item-history alone can capture, and list-level multi-objective signals are usually optimized via item-level proxies. PIANO addresses both with QDIR (query-driven cross-attention over historical queries) and IAN (a `[CLS]`-style token for list-level CTR/CVR prediction). Experiments on public and industrial datasets, together with a multi-week online A/B test on NetEase Cloud Music, a leading music streaming platform, show consistent gains, with +0.62% CTR and +4.45% CVR online. These findings confirm PIANO's robustness and value for deployment in real-world, latency-sensitive information retrieval systems.

Disclosure of Interests. The authors have no competing interests to declare that are relevant to the content of this article.

References

1. Ai, Q., Bi, K., Guo, J., Croft, W.B.: Learning a deep listwise context model for ranking refinement. In: Proceedings of the 41st International ACM SIGIR Conference on Research and Development in Information Retrieval (SIGIR 2018), pp. 135–144 (2018). https://doi.org/10.1145/3209978.3209985
2. Bello, I., Grigsby, S., Sculley, D., Steiner, B.: Seq2slate: re-ranking and slate optimization with RNNs. arXiv preprint arXiv:1810.02019 (2018)
3. Burges, C.J.C.: From ranknet to lambdarank to lambdamart: an overview. Technical report MSR-TR-2010-82, Microsoft Research, Redmond, WA (2010). https://www.microsoft.com/en-us/research/publication/from-ranknet-to-lambdarank-to-lambdamart-an-overview/
4. Buyl, M., Missault, P., Sondag, P.A.: Rankformer: listwise learning-to-rank using listwide labels. In: Proceedings of the 29th ACM SIGKDD Conference on Knowledge Discovery and Data Mining (KDD 2023) (2023). https://doi.org/10.1145/3580305.3599892
5. Cao, Y., Meng, Y., Guo, C., Liu, T., Zheng, B.: A generative re-ranking model for list-level multi-objective optimization at taobao. In: Proceedings of the 48th International ACM SIGIR Conference on Research and Development in Information Retrieval (SIGIR 2025) (2025). https://doi.org/10.1145/3726302.3731935
6. Chapelle, O., Chang, Y.: Yahoo! learning to rank challenge overview. In: Proceedings of the Learning to Rank Challenge, pp. 1–24. PMLR (2011). https://proceedings.mlr.press/v14/chapelle11a.html
7. Chen, Q., Zhao, H., Li, W., Huang, P., Ou, W.: Behavior sequence transformer for e-commerce recommendation in alibaba. In: Proceedings of the 1st International Workshop on Deep Learning Practice for High-Dimensional Sparse Data (DLP-KDD 2019), pp. 1–4 (2019). https://doi.org/10.1145/3326937.3341261
8. Chen, R., Cao, S., He, A., Han, S., Chen, J.: Prectr: a synergistic framework for integrating personalized search relevance matching and ctr prediction. In: Companion Proceedings of the ACM Web Conference 2025 (WWW Companion 2025) (2025). https://doi.org/10.1145/3701716.3715256
9. Chen, S., et al.: Controllable multi-objective re-ranking with policy hypernetworks. In: Proceedings of the 29th ACM SIGKDD Conference on Knowledge Discovery and Data Mining (KDD 2023), pp. 3855–3864 (2023). https://doi.org/10.1145/3580305.3599796
10. Devlin, J., Chang, M.W., Lee, K., Toutanova, K.: Bert: pre-training of deep bidirectional transformers for language understanding. In: Proceedings of the 2019 Conference of the North American Chapter of the Association for Computational Linguistics: Human Language Technologies (NAACL-HLT), pp. 4171–4186 (2019). https://doi.org/10.18653/v1/N19-1423

11. Dosovitskiy, A., et al.: An image is worth 16x16 words: transformers for image recognition at scale. In: International Conference on Learning Representations (ICLR) (2021). https://arxiv.org/abs/2010.11929
12. Feng, Y., Gong, Y., Sun, F., Ge, J., Ou, W.: Revisit recommender system in the permutation prospective. arXiv preprint arXiv:2102.12057 (2021)
13. Gong, B., Kaya, M., Tintarev, N.: Contextual personalized re-ranking of music recommendations through audio features. arXiv preprint arXiv:2009.02782 (2020)
14. He, Z., Zhao, H., Wang, Z., Lin, Z., Kale, A., McAuley, J.: Query-aware sequential recommendation. In: Proceedings of the 31st ACM International Conference on Information and Knowledge Management (CIKM 2022), pp. 4019–4023 (2022). https://doi.org/10.1145/3511808.3557677
15. Jannach, D., Abdollahpouri, H.: A survey on multi-objective recommender systems. Front. Big Data **6**, 1157899 (2023). https://doi.org/10.3389/fdata.2023.1157899
16. Järvelin, K., Kekäläinen, J.: Cumulated gain-based evaluation of IR techniques. ACM Trans. Inf. Syst. (TOIS) **20**(4), 422–446 (2002). https://doi.org/10.1145/582415.582418
17. Joachims, T.: Training linear SVMs in linear time. In: Proceedings of the 12th ACM SIGKDD International Conference on Knowledge Discovery and Data Mining (KDD 2006), pp. 217–226 (2006). https://doi.org/10.1145/1150402.1150429
18. Kang, W.C., McAuley, J.: Self-attentive sequential recommendation. In: 2018 IEEE International Conference on Data Mining (ICDM), pp. 197–206 (2018). https://doi.org/10.1109/ICDM.2018.00035
19. Kingma, D.P., Ba, J.L.: Adam: a method for stochastic optimization. In: International Conference on Learning Representations (ICLR) (2015)
20. Li, Y., et al.: Pear: personalized re-ranking with contextualized transformer for recommendation. In: Companion Proceedings of the Web Conference 2022, pp. 62–66 (2022). https://doi.org/10.1145/3487553.3524208
21. Lin, Z., et al.: Attention over self-attention: intention-aware re-ranking with dynamic transformer encoders for recommendation. arXiv preprint arXiv:2201.05333 (2022)
22. Liu, T.Y.: Learning to rank for information retrieval. Found. Trends Inf. Retr. **3**(3), 225–331 (2009). https://doi.org/10.1561/1500000008
23. Ma, J., Zhao, Z., Yi, X., Chen, J., Hong, L., Chi, E.H.: Modeling task relationships in multi-task learning with multi-gate mixture-of-experts. In: Proceedings of the 24th ACM SIGKDD International Conference on Knowledge Discovery & Data Mining (KDD 2018), pp. 1930–1939 (2018). https://doi.org/10.1145/3219819.3220007
24. Ma, X., et al.: Entire space multi-task model: an effective approach for estimating post-click conversion rate. In: The 41st International ACM SIGIR Conference on Research & Development in Information Retrieval (SIGIR 2018), pp. 1137–1140 (2018). https://doi.org/10.1145/3209978.3210104
25. van der Maaten, L., Hinton, G.: Visualizing high-dimensional data using t-SNE. J. Mach. Learn. Res. **9**, 2579–2605 (2008). https://www.jmlr.org/papers/volume9/vandermaaten08a/vandermaaten08a.pdf
26. Nguyen, P., Dines, J., Krasnodebski, J.: A multi-objective learning to re-rank approach to optimize online marketplaces for multiple stakeholders. arXiv preprint arXiv:1708.00651 (2017)
27. Pang, L., Xu, J., Ai, Q., Lan, Y., Cheng, X., Wen, J.: Setrank: learning a permutation-invariant ranking model for information retrieval. In: Proceedings of

the 43rd International ACM SIGIR Conference on Research and Development in Information Retrieval (SIGIR 2020), pp. 499–508 (2020). https://doi.org/10.1145/3397271.3401104
28. Pei, C., et al.: Personalized re-ranking for recommendation. In: Proceedings of the 13th ACM Conference on Recommender Systems (RecSys 2019), pp. 349–357 (2019). https://doi.org/10.1145/3298689.3347000
29. Pi, Q., et al.: Search-based user interest modeling with lifelong sequential behavior data for click-through rate prediction. In: Proceedings of the 29th ACM International Conference on Information and Knowledge Management (CIKM 2020), pp. 2685–2692 (2020). https://doi.org/10.1145/3340531.3412744
30. Ren, Y., Han, X., Zhao, X., Zhang, S., Zhang, Y.: Slate-aware ranking for recommendation. arXiv preprint arXiv:2302.12427 (2023)
31. Shi, X., et al.: Pier: permutation-level interest-based end-to-end re-ranking framework in e-commerce. In: Proceedings of the 29th ACM SIGKDD Conference on Knowledge Discovery and Data Mining (KDD 2023), pp. 4823–4831 (2023). https://doi.org/10.1145/3580305.3599886
32. Tang, H., Liu, J., Zhao, M., Gong, X.: Progressive layered extraction (PLE): a novel multi-task learning (MTL) model for personalized recommendations. In: Proceedings of the 14th ACM Conference on Recommender Systems (RecSys 2020), pp. 269–278 (2020). https://doi.org/10.1145/3383313.3412236
33. Vaswani, A., et al.: Attention is all you need. In: Advances in Neural Information Processing Systems 30, pp. 5998–6008 (2017)
34. Xi, Y., et al.: Multi-level interaction reranking with user behavior history. In: Proceedings of the 45th International ACM SIGIR Conference on Research and Development in Information Retrieval (SIGIR 2022), pp. 13–23 (2022). https://doi.org/10.1145/3477495.3532026
35. Yang, H., et al.: Comprehensive list generation for multi-generator reranking. In: Proceedings of the 48th International ACM SIGIR Conference on Research and Development in Information Retrieval (SIGIR 2025), pp. 1–11 (2025). https://doi.org/10.1145/3726302.3729933
36. Zhang, Y., et al.: Qwen3 embedding: advancing text embedding and reranking through foundation models. arXiv preprint arXiv:2506.05176 (2025)
37. Zhou, G., et al.: Deep interest network for click-through rate prediction. In: Proceedings of the 24th ACM SIGKDD International Conference on Knowledge Discovery and Data Mining, pp. 1059–1068 (2018). https://doi.org/10.1145/3219819.3219823

Recovering Business Rules as Cascade Lookups for Enterprise Field Prediction

Changxu Duan(✉)

Technische Universität Darmstadt, Darmstadt, Germany
duan@linglit.tu-darmstadt.de

Abstract. Enterprise sales-order systems rely on manually maintained configuration rules to determine fields such as payment terms, shipping points, and sales ownership. When these rules are incomplete or stale, operators must enter values by hand, and downstream errors spread into billing, logistics, and reporting. This paper studies whether missing or outdated rules can be recovered from historical transactions instead of being relearned as opaque statistical patterns. We introduce a knowledge-graph-guided workflow in which an LLM agent proposes candidate business keys, meaning column combinations such as customer and document type, validates them through SQL profiling, and compiles the resulting evidence into deterministic cascade lookups. The LLM is used only during offline rule discovery. At inference time, prediction is a transparent key lookup with no model-serving requirement. Experiments on enterprise sales-order prediction and public relational benchmarks show that cascades are most effective when fields follow stable business rules, while learned graph models remain preferable when prediction depends on temporal or neighborhood patterns. Drift analysis further turns residual errors into diagnostics for configuration maintenance.

Keywords: Enterprise AI · Knowledge Graphs · Relational prediction · ERP systems · LLM agents

1 Introduction

Enterprise Resource Planning (ERP) systems orchestrate business operations, spanning procurement, manufacturing, sales, and finance, by maintaining a unified transactional database across organizational functions. In a sales-order workflow, the system must fill business fields before an order can be billed, shipped, and reported. These fields include payment terms that determine invoice due dates, shipping points that identify the warehouse or dispatch location, Incoterms that allocate shipping cost and risk, and sales ownership fields that assign the responsible sales team. These values are not arbitrary labels. In well-configured ERP systems, they are determined by business rules over customers,

Code and data. https://github.com/Fireblossom/CascadER.

M. Baratchi et al. (Eds.): ECML PKDD 2026, LNAI 16949, pp. 91–108, 2027.
https://doi.org/10.1007/978-3-032-37682-4_6

materials, document types, and organizational units such as sales offices, sales groups, and plants.

SAP, the dominant ERP vendor serving over 400,000 customers worldwide, implements such field-level determination through its Condition Technique, SAP's rule mechanism for assigning default field values from ordered lookup tables called Access Sequences [13,14]. Each table is keyed by a combination of business attributes such as customer, material, and organizational context. However, these Access Sequences must be manually configured and maintained by domain experts. When configurations are incomplete, outdated after system migrations, or invalidated by organizational restructuring, the system either leaves fields blank or applies coarse defaults, forcing sales representatives to select values manually [8].

This configuration gap has tangible business consequences. An incorrect shipping point routes goods from the wrong warehouse and causes fulfillment delays. Mismatched payment terms create billing disputes. Wrong Incoterms misallocate shipping risk between buyer and seller, and inaccurate sales group assignments distort commission calculations. Systematic reviews of enterprise and manufacturing data ecosystems confirm that such data quality defects are a persistent and costly problem [2,19]. Furthermore, these errors are not static because even well-configured rules degrade over time as organizations restructure and customer relationships evolve. On the SALT-KG benchmark [15], which captures 2.3M historical order items from a single SAP S/4HANA ERP system instance, between 17% and 44% of customers changed their most frequently assigned field value within a two-year window, depending on the field (Sect. 4.5). Because each affected customer generates many orders, stale defaults can propagate errors across thousands of transactions before anyone notices.

A prediction system that suggests correct field values during order entry would reduce the need for manual correction, catch configuration drift before it propagates, and provide configuration owners with continuous visibility into which rules are still valid and which have silently broken. Here, configuration drift means that a formerly valid default no longer matches current business assignments because contracts, organizational responsibilities, or logistics settings have changed. We focus on cascade lookups as a practical representation for such suggestions. A cascade lookup is an ordered list of lookup tables, from specific rules to general fallbacks. For example, the system may first try a customer-by-document-type rule, then a customer-only rule, and finally a global default.

Existing approaches treat field prediction as a standard supervised learning problem, but each family of methods encounters a characteristic barrier when applied to rule-governed enterprise data. Gradient-boosted ensembles [1,4,18] perform well on fields with few possible values but struggle on high-cardinality targets whose correct value depends on specific multi-column business rules rather than broad feature correlations. For example, on the SALT-KG benchmark, predicting which internal sales team handles an account (589 possible teams) requires knowing the exact combination of customer and organizational unit that the company's assignment policy prescribes, and the best tree-based model achieves only 51% MRR on this field. Heterogeneous GNNs [7,20] learn relational embeddings by propagating signals along primary-foreign key edges, yet they too fail on fields where the correct value is determined by a specific lookup rule rather than by neighborhood similarity. On SALT-KG, a GNN achieves only 15.8% accuracy on sales team assignment and 37.5% on customer payment terms. KG-enhanced embeddings [15] inject domain metadata as auxiliary features, but yield only modest accuracy gains (<2 percentage points) when limited to field definitions without encoding the determination rules themselves. The common limitation is that these methods model the problem as statistical pattern recognition, while the underlying signal is often configured determinism. By configured determinism, we mean that field values follow explicit lookup rules keyed by specific combinations of customer, document type, material, and organizational unit.

Directly using LLMs at inference time is also impractical. Even with retrieval-augmented approaches, per-order LLM calls introduce latency and cost incompatible with high-throughput transactional systems, and enterprise deployments require that identical inputs always produce identical outputs with full audit trails, a guarantee that stochastic generation cannot provide.

Our key observation is that configured rules, even when missing from the live system, leave recoverable traces in historical transaction data. The challenge is that the space of possible key combinations is combinatorially large, making exhaustive search difficult, while identifying which combinations carry business meaning requires domain knowledge that is not encoded in table schemas alone. We address this by using an LLM agent guided by a Knowledge Graph [15] that provides field-level descriptions and dependency hints derived from SAP's internal ontology. The KG helps prioritize semantically meaningful key combinations, while SQL profiling against the full transaction history validates each candidate rule with coverage and accuracy statistics. The output is a set of deterministic JSON lookup cascades that require no GPU or LLM at inference time, provide built-in interpretability, and can be rebuilt as configurations change.

This paper makes three contributions.

1. A KG-guided rule discovery workflow in which an LLM proposes candidate business keys, profiles them via SQL, and codifies the selected rules as hierarchical cascade lookups, achieving the best results among evaluated baselines on all 8 SALT-KG fields.
2. A generalization study on two public RelBench v2 datasets (rel-arxiv, rel-stack) that characterizes when cascades match or underperform GNNs, showing that the method's advantage is specific to domains with stable, recoverable rules.
3. A drift root-cause analysis linking many residual errors to organizational restructuring and showing how cascade failures can support configuration maintenance.

Application Setting. An SAP sales order consists of a header and one or more line items. The header stores order-wide attributes, while each line item stores product-specific attributes for one ordered product. The 8 target fields in SALT-KG span both levels (Table 1). Our system targets cases where configured Access Sequences fail to resolve a value. The cascade lookup provides an editable suggestion based on statistically recovered rules, with cascade-level provenance visible to the operator.

Table 1. Target field classification. Header-level fields apply to the entire order. Item-level fields are set per product line. Downstream consequence describes the operational impact of an incorrect value.

Field	Level	Downstream consequence of error
CustomerPaymentTerms	Header	Incorrect invoice due dates and early/late payment disputes
SalesGroup	Header	Misattributed revenue reporting and incorrect commission assignment
SalesOffice	Header	Distorted regional sales analytics
HeaderIncoterms	Header	Wrong allocation of shipping risk and cost between buyer and seller
ShippingCondition	Header	Suboptimal carrier selection and delivery delays
ItemIncoterms	Item	Per-line risk allocation inconsistent with contract
ShippingPoint	Item	Goods dispatched from wrong warehouse and fulfillment delay
Plant	Item	Wrong production or sourcing site and inventory discrepancy

2 Related Work

Relational Deep Learning. RelBench [20] established standardized benchmarks for prediction on multi-table relational databases, proposing heterogeneous GNN baselines that construct message-passing graphs from primary and foreign key relationships. RelBench v2 [6] extends this with autocomplete tasks, temporal splits, and stronger GNN/LightGBM baselines. Our method differs fundamentally because instead of learning node embeddings via gradient descent, we generate deterministic lookup tables guided by domain knowledge.

Knowledge Graphs for Structured Prediction. KGs have been used to inject domain semantics into ML pipelines, e.g., as entity embeddings [22], relation-aware features, or constraint layers. Recent visions increasingly emphasize unifying KGs with LLMs to enable synergistic reasoning [16]. In enterprise settings, ontologies can describe business concepts and determination dependencies [14].

Our approach uses the KG as a search guide rather than as an embedding source. The LLM uses KG-provided descriptions to propose SQL profiling candidates, while accepted rules are selected by deterministic validation.

LLM-Based Code Generation for Data Tasks. Recent work applies LLMs as autonomous data analysts, generating SQL queries [5,17], reasoning directly over tabular data [24], writing feature engineering code, and performing iterative data exploration [10]. ReAct [23] demonstrated that interleaving reasoning traces with actions improves task grounding. Our method builds on this paradigm but targets a specific outcome, namely the systematic discovery and codification of deterministic business rules into deployable prediction cascades rather than general-purpose analysis.

Tabular Foundation Models. TabPFN [9] introduced in-context learning for tabular prediction, achieving strong results on small-to-medium datasets without task-specific training. ConTextTab [21] extends this paradigm with semantic embeddings from pretrained language models. However, both architectures face scalability constraints that preclude direct application to enterprise transaction data. TabPFN's in-context mechanism is designed for datasets with up to tens of thousands of samples, while ConTextTab requires 80 GB GPU memory with a context window of 8,192 rows and bagging for larger tables. SALT-KG's 2.3M rows and targets with up to 589 classes fall outside these operating regimes. Our cascade approach sidesteps these limitations. Rule discovery uses an LLM offline, and the resulting JSON lookups require no model serving at inference time.

Enterprise Field Prediction. The SALT benchmark [13] introduced the task of predicting SAP sales order fields with tree-based and GNN baselines. SALT-KG [15] extended it with a metadata Knowledge Graph extracted from SAP's internal ontology via curated SPARQL queries, showing that KG-derived embeddings yield modest MRR improvements. The FMSLT vision [14] argues that enterprise prediction should integrate declarative knowledge, such as ontologies, with procedural knowledge, such as determination procedures. Our approach operationalizes part of the declarative layer through KG-guided SQL profiling, while the drift analysis shows where transaction history alone cannot capture later procedural or organizational changes.

3 Method

3.1 Problem Formulation

We consider a temporal relational autocomplete task. For a target field f, each historical transaction i contains an input tuple x_i, a timestamp t_i, and a target value $y_i \in \mathcal{Y}_f$. Training records satisfy $t_i < T$, and evaluation records satisfy $t_i \geq T$, where T is the temporal cutoff. The task is to predict y_i from the fields available at order-entry time.

A composite key $K = (c_1, \ldots, c_d)$ selects a small set of input columns. For a record i, $x_i[K]$ denotes the corresponding key value. A lookup table for K maps each observed key value k to target values ranked by their empirical frequency among training records with $x_i[K] = k$, subject to a minimum support threshold.

A cascade is an ordered list of lookup tables, from more specific keys to more general fallbacks. At inference time, the system first tries the most specific key. If no matching entry exists, it falls back to the next level, and eventually to the global target distribution. The objective is to choose a short cascade that gives accurate, high-coverage, temporally valid, and auditable predictions.

Figure 1 provides an overview of the end-to-end workflow, from offline rule discovery through runtime deployment.

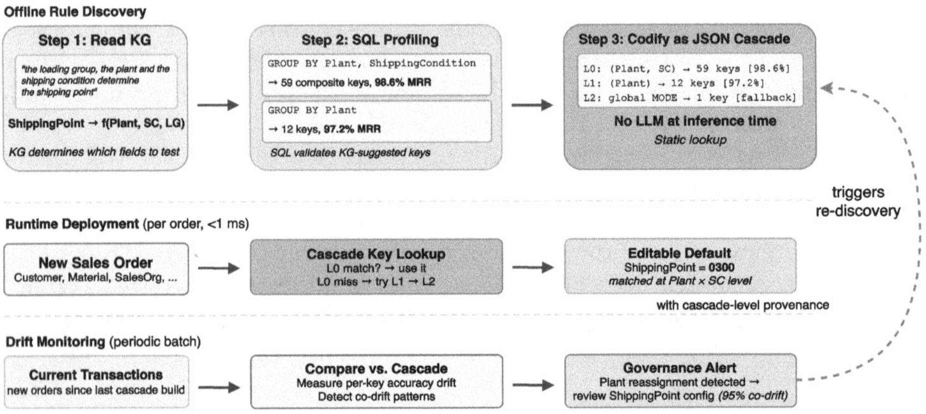

Fig. 1. System overview. The top panel shows offline rule discovery producing JSON cascade files. The middle panel shows runtime key lookup providing editable suggestions during order entry. The bottom panel shows drift monitoring comparing current transactions against cascade mappings and surfacing alerts for governance review.

3.2 Rule Discovery (Explore)

For each target field f, the LLM operates as a rule discovery agent in an iterative propose, profile, score, and refine loop inspired by ReAct [23]. The agent consumes, as a read-only input, the metadata Knowledge Graph published by SALT-KG [15], which was constructed by the SALT-KG authors through curated SPARQL queries against SAP's internal ontology. These queries are used as published and were not authored or modified for this work. At each iteration the agent maintains a state consisting of (i) semantic hints extracted from the KG's natural-language descriptions of f and its related entities, (ii) a set of candidate composite keys under consideration, (iii) SQL profiling evidence such as coverage, purity, and support counts, and (iv) validation accuracy and residual error buckets for the current cascade. SQL profiling refers to grouped aggregate

Algorithm 1: KG-Guided Cascade Discovery

Input: Target field f, KG descriptions $\mathcal{G}_f$, training tables $\mathcal{D}_{\text{train}}$, validation split $\mathcal{D}_{\text{val}}$, improvement threshold ϵ, minimum support m, maximum depth $L_{\max}$
Output: Ordered cascade $(K_1, \ldots, K_L)$
$\mathcal{H} \leftarrow$ extract semantic hints from $\mathcal{G}_f$;
$\mathcal{F} \leftarrow$ initialize candidate frontier from $\mathcal{H}$;
cascade $\leftarrow$ [ ];
repeat
  foreach *candidate key* $K \in \mathcal{F}$ **do**
    mapping$_K \leftarrow$
     `SQL: GROUP BY` K, f`; COUNT(*) and rank` f `by frequency` on $\mathcal{D}_{\text{train}}$ where support $\geq m$;
    $\text{acc}_K, \text{cov}_K \leftarrow$ evaluate mapping$_K$ on $\mathcal{D}_{\text{val}}$;
  $K^* \leftarrow \arg\max_K \text{acc}_K$ among candidates with $\text{cov}_K > 0$;
  if $acc_{K^*} - acc_{current} > \epsilon$ **then**
    Append K^* to cascade;
    Analyze residual errors $\rightarrow$ update $\mathcal{F}$ with error-driven candidates;
until no candidate improves validation accuracy by $> \epsilon$ ***or*** $|cascade| \geq L_{\max}$;
Append global target distribution as final level;
return *cascade*

queries that estimate how often a candidate key is observed and how consistently it maps to a single target value.

The agent's action space consists of four operations. **Propose** adds a new candidate key from KG hints or error analysis. **Profile** evaluates the candidate via SQL aggregation against temporally valid training data. **Score** ranks the candidate by validation accuracy, coverage, and minimum support. **Refine** updates the cascade by appending, reordering, or pruning levels. Throughout this paper, MODE(·) denotes the most frequent value within each group. The key property is that the output of this loop is a deterministic lookup artifact, not a learned model. The LLM is used only during the offline discovery phase and is not needed at prediction time.

Candidate Generation Policy. Candidate keys are drawn from two sources. The first source is entities and attributes explicitly mentioned in the SALT-KG-provided description of field f, such as the KG record that SHIPPINGPOINT depends on plant, shipping condition, and loading group. The second source is error-driven refinements, where the agent inspects which input features distinguish correctly predicted rows from errors and proposes additional key columns accordingly. Candidates are evaluated as single-entity keys, KG-suggested pairwise keys, or higher-order composites. The agent escalates to higher-order keys only when the accuracy gain exceeds a threshold ϵ.

The loop terminates when (i) no candidate improves validation accuracy by more than ϵ, (ii) candidate support falls below m, or (iii) the maximum cascade depth $L_{\max}$ is reached. In practice, cascades converge within 3 to 5 iterations per field.

Example Trace for CustomerPaymentTerms. The SALT-KG-provided description of this field says that the system defaults to the key specified in the customer or vendor master record, which is the central ERP record for a business partner, while users can still enter a key during document entry. The agent interprets this as evidence that (1) the customer identity is the primary determinant, and (2) the document type may override the default. The following compressed trace shows one complete run of Algorithm 1.

1. The KG hint points to defaults from the customer master. The agent queries `GROUP BY SoldToParty`. The result is 80.0% accuracy with 10K keys, so the key is retained as fallback level L_1.
2. The KG hint indicates that document type may override the default. The agent queries `GROUP BY SoldToParty, SalesDocType`. The result is 82.9% accuracy with 69K keys and 95.3% coverage, so the key is promoted to L_0.
3. Error analysis suggests broader organizational keys. The agent queries `GROUP BY SalesOrg, DocType`. The gain is below ϵ, so the key is rejected.
4. The coverage check shows that uncovered rows remain. The agent appends the global target distribution and finalizes the cascade.

Without KG guidance, a minimal entity-level baseline would try only per-customer MODE, achieving 80.0% (see ablation, Sect. 4.3). The KG hint about document-type override directly leads to the composite key that yields +2.9%.

3.3 Cascade Codification (Build)

A finalized cascade for field f is a sequence of levels $(K_1, \ldots, K_L)$, where each K_l is a composite key. For each level we extract an empirical ranked list.

$$\text{mapping}[l][k] = [(y_1, n_1), (y_2, n_2), \ldots], \quad n_1 \geq n_2 \geq \cdots,$$

where n_j is the training support of target value y_j under key value k, and the total support for k must exceed min_support_l. The top-ranked value y_1 is the statistical mode and is used for top-1 accuracy, while the full ranked list is used for MRR. At prediction time, levels are queried in order, and the first match returns the ranked list for that level. This mirrors SAP's Access Sequence mechanism but is derived statistically rather than read from system configuration. For CustomerPaymentTerms, the cascade uses L_0 = (SoldToParty, SalesDocType), then L_1 = (SoldToParty), and finally L_2 = global distribution.

3.4 Inference (Predict)

The output of Phase 2 is a set of JSON lookup files. Prediction requires only key lookup, so no LLM, KG, or model inference is needed at runtime. Cascade sizes range from 88 keys (Plant) to 174K keys (HeaderIncoterms).

Why Cascades Work in Configured Enterprise Data. The method is effective when the target field has low conditional entropy given a small set of business keys. In such cases, historical transactions contain repeated evidence of the same configuration rule. A cascade lookup estimates this conditional distribution directly and preserves exact high-cardinality keys that embedding models may smooth away. The knowledge graph helps reduce the combinatorial search over column subsets by pointing to keys that have business meaning. The LLM does not replace statistical validation. It acts as a controller that translates semantic hints and residual errors into SQL candidates, while every accepted rule is selected by deterministic validation on held-out data.

4 Experiments

4.1 Setup

We evaluate primarily on SALT-KG [15], covering 8 autocomplete tasks across 4 SAP tables with temporal split at 2020-07-01 (train with 1.9M rows and test with 403K rows). For the generalization study (Sect. 4.4), we evaluate on two additional RelBench v2 [6] datasets, namely rel-arxiv for academic papers with 53-class author-category prediction and rel-stack for StackOverflow with 3-class badge-type prediction. We compare against the baselines reported in SALT [13] and SALT-KG [15], and the heterogeneous GraphSAGE GNN from RelBench v2 [6]. All cascade lookups use only temporally valid data before the evaluation split cutoff to prevent data leakage.

Metrics. Accuracy measures whether the top-ranked predicted value equals the held-out target value. MRR measures the reciprocal rank of the true value in the returned candidate list. For cascade methods, each matched lookup table stores target values ranked by their training frequency. The top-ranked value is the statistical mode and is used for accuracy, while the full ranked list is used for MRR. Thus, MODE is not an evaluation metric, but the estimator used to construct lookup entries from temporally valid training data.

Rule Discovery Implementation. The offline rule discovery agent (Sect. 3.2) uses Claude Opus 4.6 with temperature 0. Because every proposed candidate is evaluated deterministically by SQL on temporally valid data, the LLM affects the search process but not the scoring rule. To check sensitivity, we re-ran discovery on two representative fields (CustomerPaymentTerms, Plant) with GPT-5.3-Codex and obtained identical cascade structures and test accuracy. This does not constitute a full LLM-sensitivity study, but it suggests that the accepted rules are primarily constrained by the data and KG evidence.

4.2 SALT-KG Results

Our method outperforms the evaluated GNN baseline on all 8 fields (Tables 2 and 3). The largest gains occur on high-cardinality, semantically complex

Table 2. MRR on rel-salt. Top rows report baselines from SALT [13] without KG. *Best (w/ KG)* is the per-field maximum after adding KG-derived text embeddings [15], computed from published base MRR + ΔMRR at 2-decimal precision. Bottom row reports our cascade method.

Method	PayTrm	Sales Grp.	Hdr Inc.	Item Inc.	ShipCond	ShipPt	Plant	Sales Off.	Avg
Majority Class	0.23	0.05	0.62	0.62	0.41	0.54	0.59	0.99	0.51
XGBoost [1]	0.57	0.51	0.70	0.70	0.68	0.95	0.99	0.99	0.76
LightGBM [11]	0.10	0.02	0.73	0.73	0.51	0.28	0.61	0.99	0.50
CatBoost [18]	0.44	0.16	0.81	0.80	0.71	0.80	0.99	0.99	0.71
CARTE [12]	0.62	0.46	0.77	0.75	0.74	0.97	0.99	0.99	0.79
AutoGluon [4]	0.52	0.34	0.78	0.78	0.74	0.98	0.99	0.99	0.77
GraphSAGE [7]	0.39	0.20	0.59	0.64	0.59	0.97	0.99	0.99	0.67
Best (w/ KG)	0.65	0.51	0.81	0.80	0.78	0.98	0.99	**1.00**	0.815
Ours (cascade)	**0.852**	**0.760**	**0.840**	**0.840**	**0.798**	**0.986**	**0.993**	0.997	**0.883**

Table 3. Accuracy comparison with RelBench v2 baseline. GNN accuracy values are taken directly from the RelBench v2 leaderboard [6] using its default heterogeneous GraphSAGE [7] architecture, hyperparameters, and training protocol. We did not re-train or tune the GNN.

Target Field	Ours (Acc)	GNN (Acc)
CustomerPaymentTerms	**82.86%**	37.47%
SalesGroup	**70.00%**	15.76%
HeaderIncoterms	**77.22%**	62.23%
ItemIncoterms	**77.15%**	69.36%
ShippingCondition	**69.56%**	56.85%
ShippingPoint	**98.65%**	98.39%
Plant	**99.68%**	99.46%
SalesOffice	**99.91%**	99.88%

fields (SalesGroup, CustomerPaymentTerms), where the GNN's message-passing mechanism does not capture well the business logic encoded in SAP's Condition Technique. For near-deterministic organizational mappings (Plant, ShippingPoint, SalesOffice), both methods converge above 98%.

To connect accuracy to operational impact, consider CustomerPaymentTerms. The GNN assigns the correct payment term to only 37.5% of orders, meaning that 62.5% would require manual correction. The cascade achieves 82.9%, reducing the manual correction rate to 17.1%. For SalesGroup (commission-relevant), the GNN's 15.8% accuracy is insufficient for operational use, while the cascade's 70.0% makes it viable as a default suggestion.

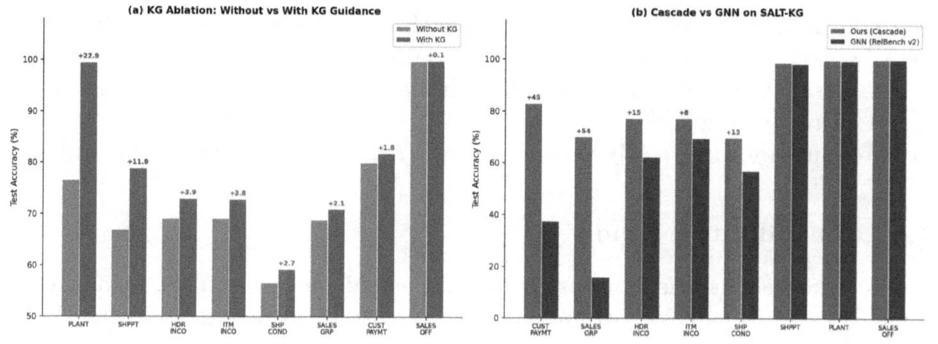

Fig. 2. (a) Semantic key-selection ablation before full error-driven refinement. (b) Final cascade vs. GNN using heterogeneous GraphSAGE from RelBench v2 [6], with per-field test accuracy on SALT-KG. Numbers above bars indicate absolute accuracy difference.

4.3 Semantic Key-Selection Ablation

To quantify the value of semantic key selection, we compare a schema-only entity MODE baseline with a restricted KG-guided cascade that uses the initial KG-suggested keys but not the full error-driven refinement and fallback optimization used in Tables 2 and 3. This ablation is intended to isolate whether KG-provided hints point the search toward more useful keys. It is not an exhaustive comparison against all possible rule-mining methods (Fig. 2, Table 4).

Table 4. Ablation of semantic key selection on SALT-KG test set (accuracy). *Restricted KG* denotes a KG-guided cascade before the full error-driven refinement and fallback optimization used in the main results.

Field	Schema-only	Restricted KG	Δ
PLANT	76.6%	99.5%	**+22.9**
SHIPPINGPOINT	67.0%	78.9%	**+11.9**
HEADERINCOTERMS	69.1%	73.0%	+3.8
ITEMINCOTERMS	69.1%	72.9%	+3.8
SHIPPINGCONDITION	56.6%	59.3%	+2.6
SALESGROUP	68.9%	71.0%	+2.2
CUSTOMERPAYMENTTERMS	80.0%	81.8%	+1.8
SALESOFFICE	99.8%	99.9%	+0.1
Average	**74.1%**	**79.5%**	**+5.4**

The value of semantic key selection varies by field type. Cross-entity fields (PLANT, SHIPPINGPOINT) show the largest gains because the KG points to combinations of plants, shipping conditions, and loading groups, a relationship invisible from table schemas alone. Composite-key fields (HeaderIncoterms, ItemIncoterms, ShippingCondition, SalesGroup) gain between 2% and 4% because KG hints indicate which additional columns may disambiguate the target. Already-simple fields (SalesOffice, CustomerPaymentTerms) gain little because they are nearly determined by a single entity without KG guidance.

4.4 Generalization Study

To test whether cascade lookups generalize beyond enterprise data, we apply the same cascade principle to two public RelBench v2 [6] autocomplete tasks. These datasets do not provide expert enterprise KGs analogous to the SAP ontology, so these experiments use task-specific temporal and entity-level keys rather than the full KG-guided discovery loop. They therefore serve primarily to identify the boundary conditions under which cascades are and are not effective. All aggregation queries are temporally filtered to use only data before the evaluation cutoff, ensuring no label leakage (Table 5).

rel-arxiv/author-category (53-class). For each author, we compute a temporal-weighted MODE(category) from their publications, giving higher weight to recent papers (4×/3×/2×/1× for last 1/2/3/older years). This recency weighting improves test accuracy from 49.7% (uniform MODE) to 50.3%. On the validation set it achieves 52.8%, slightly exceeding GNN (52.6%). Citation- and coauthor-based fallbacks proved inferior to global mode due to topic breadth in cited papers and adjacent subfields among coauthors.

rel-stack/badges-class (3-class, gold/silver/bronze). After RelBench removes the target and metadata columns, badges contain only (Id, UserId, Date). The strongest cascade is per-user MODE(Class). Multi-hop enrichment through user activity (posts, votes, comments) was ineffective because bronze badges dominate the distribution so heavily that MODE returns bronze for every activity level, including the most active users.

Table 5. Generalization study (accuracy on RelBench v2 val and test sets).

Dataset	Task	Classes	Ours (Val)	GNN (Val)	Ours (Test)	GNN (Test)
rel-arxiv	author-cat.	53	52.8%	52.6%	50.3%	50.7%
rel-stack	badges-cls.	3	77.6%	80.0%	79.3%	82.8%

Why Cascades Match But Do Not Surpass GNNs on Non-enterprise Data. Unlike SALT-KG's configured determinism, these tasks lack explicit business rules that cascade lookups can exploit.

1. Cold-start entities dominate. On rel-arxiv, 29% of test authors have no publications before the evaluation cutoff. The cascade can only predict the global mode for these authors (∼2% accuracy). GNNs face the same cold-start problem, explaining why both methods achieve only ∼50% accuracy.
2. MODE(·) is a lossy aggregation. On rel-stack, bronze badges constitute 86% of training data, so MODE(·) returns bronze for every feature combination. GNNs overcome this through learned aggregation functions that amplify minority-class signals, achieving 82.8% vs. our 79.3%.
3. No configured determinism to recover. On rel-arxiv, an author's future category is correlated with past publications, not determined. On rel-stack, badge class is determined by threshold rules such as Great Answer requiring ≥100 upvotes. These rules require per-instance temporal reasoning, not entity-level aggregation.

4.5 Drift Root-Cause Analysis

The temporal split (train < 2020-07-01 < test) exposes concept drift, with per-customer MODE values changing between training and test periods. For each of the 5,576 customers present in both splits, we compute (1) the per-field drift rate, defined as the fraction whose dominant value changed, and (2) the cross-drift correlation, defined as the fraction of customers who drifted in field B among those who drifted in field A. Figure 3 summarizes both analyses.

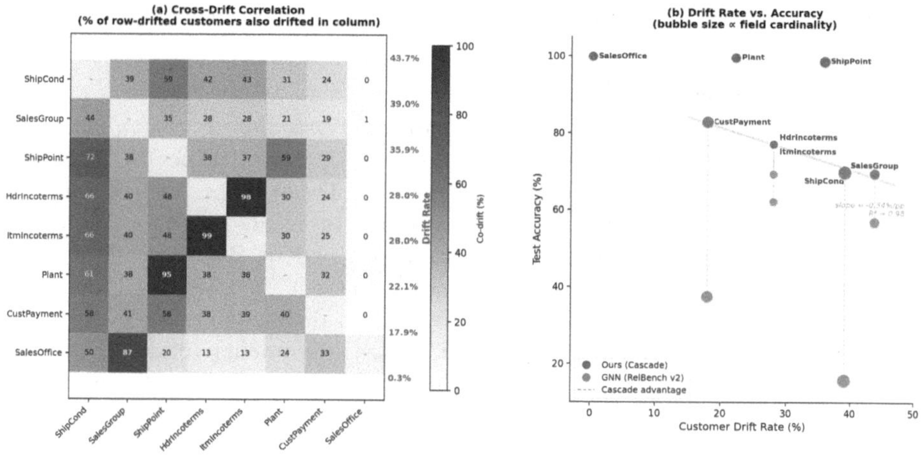

Fig. 3. Drift analysis. (a) Cross-drift conditional correlation matrix, where asymmetric cells show $P(\text{column drifts} \mid \text{row drifts})$. (b) Drift rate vs. test accuracy, with bubble size proportional to field cardinality.

Cross-Drift Structure. Three structural patterns emerge.

1. Coupled pairs move in lockstep. HdrIncoterms↔ItmIncoterms co-drift reaches between 98% and 99%, confirming they are governed by the same business decision. Plant→ShipPoint co-drift reaches 95%, so when the plant changes, the shipping point almost always follows.
2. Upstream-downstream asymmetry reveals causal direction. Plant→ShipPoint is 95%, but ShipPoint→Plant is only 58%, which indicates that shipping point reassignment frequently occurs without changing the plant. Similarly, CustPayment→ShipCond is 57%, but ShipCond→CustPayment is only 23%.
3. Stable fields are nearly drift-free. SalesOffice drifts in only 0.3% of customers (14/5,576).

Drift as a Performance Ceiling. Among the four non-trivial fields (accuracy $< 95\%$), drift rate and test accuracy are consistent with a linear anti-correlation (slope $= -0.54$ pp accuracy per pp drift, $R^2 = 0.98$). Because this fit is based on only four fields, the high R^2 should be interpreted as directionally suggestive rather than statistically conclusive. CustomerPaymentTerms has the lowest drift (17.8%) and highest accuracy (82.9%), while ShippingCondition has the highest drift (43.8%) and lowest accuracy (69.6%). This ceiling is method-agnostic because both cascades and GNNs face the same organizational changes.

For HeaderIncoterms, drifted customers show a directional DDP→DAP transition (495 vs. 89 customers), consistent with documented supply chain risk reallocation during COVID-19 disruptions [3]. For SalesGroup, 76% of drifted customers retained the same Sales Area entirely, confirming that drift is driven by internal team reassignment rather than customer behavior changes.

4.6 Error Analysis and Case Studies

Success Case with Payment Terms Resolved by Customer × Document Type. Consider a customer who places standard orders (document type TA). The cascade's finest level (SoldToParty × SalesDocumentType) maps this combination to payment term 03 (net 30 days), a mapping stable across the entire training period that correctly predicts all test-period orders. The cascade directly encodes the business rule that this customer's contract specifies net-30 for standard orders. Failure cases are structurally tied to drift. As shown in Sect. 4.5, organizational restructuring (e.g., sales team reassignment) renders historical lookup rules obsolete in a way that no method can predict from transaction data alone.

Governance Case with Correlated Drift Revealing Upstream Configuration Dependency. The cross-drift analysis (Fig. 3a) reveals that when a customer's Plant assignment changes, ShippingPoint co-drifts 95% of the time, but the reverse holds only 58%. This asymmetry tells configuration owners that plant reassignment should trigger shipping point review, but not vice versa. Similarly, co-drift between HeaderIncoterms and ItemIncoterms reaches between 98% and 99%, confirming they are governed by the same business decision, a validation that individual field-level audits might miss.

5 Discussion

When to Use Cascades in Practice. The central lesson from our three-domain evaluation is that the quality of available domain knowledge matters more than the sophistication of the model. The differentiator is the alignment between domain knowledge and observable data. Cascades excel when a domain-expert KG provides determination hints that correspond to available data columns, match GNNs when no such expert KG or stable rule structure exists (rel-arxiv with 50.3% vs. 50.7%), and underperform when prediction requires per-instance temporal reasoning that GNNs learn implicitly (rel-stack with 79.3% vs. 82.8%). Practitioners should prefer GNNs when discriminative signal resides in graph neighborhoods or temporal patterns, and use drift analysis as an operational diagnostic regardless of method, since the observed relationship between drift rate and accuracy (Sect. 4.5) enables proactive identification of entities requiring configuration review. In this sense, the method recovers part of the declarative rule structure visible in historical transactions, while procedural configuration changes and organizational restructurings remain outside the observable data.

Practical Advantages. Beyond accuracy, cascades offer interpretability (each prediction traces to a specific composite key), no model-serving cost at inference time (JSON key lookup on CPU, with 12 MB total storage for 8 fields vs. ~200 MB model weights), and rapid updates (rebuild in minutes vs. hours of GPU retraining). We recommend field-specific deployment modes, including editable suggestions for all fields, conservative auto-fill for near-deterministic fields (>99% accuracy), and audit-only logging for high-drift fields.

Prototype-to-Production Path. The current evaluation is offline. A production deployment should first run in shadow mode, where cascade suggestions are logged but not automatically applied. Operational metrics should include suggestion acceptance rate, operator override rate, post-entry correction rate, lookup latency under concurrent load, and the precision of drift alerts as judged by configuration owners. These measurements are required before claiming realized workload reduction in production.

Reproducibility. All code, cascade JSON files, evaluation scripts, and the drift analysis toolkit are publicly released. Experiments are reproducible from the released code and public SALT-KG data [15].

Ethics and Governance. All experiments use pseudonymized keys (integer IDs) without access to personally identifiable information. Cascade mappings should be audited for correlations with protected attributes before deployment. Cascades require periodic rebuilding (e.g., quarterly), with drift alerts flagging customers exceeding historical change rates. Predictions are surfaced as editable suggestions rather than autonomous overwrites, and operators retain full override authority. Each prediction logs the matched cascade level and composite key, supporting post-hoc analysis and regulatory compliance.

Threats to Validity. SALT-KG represents a single SAP S/4HANA ERP system instance. The generalization study partially addresses this, but neither public dataset has comparable configuration richness. The public datasets do not contain expert-curated determination KGs comparable to the enterprise setting, so the generalization study evaluates the cascade principle rather than the full KG-guided workflow. GNN baselines use RelBench v2's default protocol without task-specific tuning. The LLM sensitivity check covers only two representative fields, and weaker models may fail to translate KG hints effectively. The temporal split at 2020-07-01 coincides with COVID-19, and observed drift patterns may reflect pandemic-specific disruptions.

Limitations. (1) Cascades require configured determinism to outperform GNNs. On general relational data they match but do not exceed GNN performance. (2) Cold-start entities fall through to coarse defaults with no viable relational fallback. In deployment, predictions that reach only coarse organizational fallbacks or the global mode should be surfaced as low-confidence suggestions rather than auto-filled values. (3) The system has been validated offline on historical data and has not yet been deployed in a production ERP environment. (4) We did not include classical rule-mining baselines such as association rules, FP-Growth, RuleFit, or decision lists. This limits our ability to separate the benefit of KG-guided key selection from the benefit of symbolic rule extraction in general.

Future Directions. Two extensions are most promising. The first is temporal cascades that perform per-instance temporal-windowed aggregation, enabling rule reconstruction for threshold-based systems like StackOverflow badges. The second is hybrid cascade-GNN architectures that use cascade predictions as features or priors for GNN training, potentially combining interpretability with learned generalization for unseen or recently reorganized entities.

6 Conclusion

The results show that KG-grounded cascade lookups, produced by LLM-guided SQL profiling and deployed as lightweight JSON files, outperform evaluated GNN baselines on all 8 SALT-KG enterprise fields. A generalization study on two public datasets reveals clear boundary conditions. Cascades match GNNs when field values are governed by stable, recoverable rules, but underperform when prediction requires temporal graph reasoning. The drift analysis demonstrates that many residual errors are associated with organizational changes, providing configuration owners with actionable diagnostics. For practitioners, the results suggest that investing in domain knowledge assets can be more valuable than adopting more complex models when the underlying data is governed by recoverable configuration rules.

Acknowledgments. The author was funded by the InsightsNet project (funded by the Federal Ministry of Education and Research (BMBF) under grant no. 01UG2130A).

I gratefully acknowledge the Research group Corpus and Computational Linguistics, Institute of Linguistics and Literary Studies, TU Darmstadt. I gratefully acknowledge support from the hessian.AI Service Center (funded by the Federal Ministry of Research, Technology and Space, BMFTR, grant no. 16IS22091) and the hessian.AI Innovation Lab (funded by the Hessian Ministry for Digital Strategy and Innovation, grant no. S-DIW04/0013/003). I gratefully acknowledge the computing time granted by the Resource Allocation Board and provided on the supercomputer Emmy/Grete at NHR-Nord@Göttingen as part of the NHR infrastructure. The calculations for this research were conducted with computing resources under the project `nhr_he_starter_25563`.

AI Usage. LLMs were used as part of the proposed offline rule-discovery workflow, as described in Sect. 3.2. For manuscript preparation, LLMs were used only for readability and grammar assistance. The author reviewed all content and takes full responsibility.

Disclosure of Interests. The author has no competing interests to declare that are relevant to the content of this article.

References

1. Chen, T., Guestrin, C.: XGBoost: a scalable tree boosting system. In: Proceedings of the 22nd ACM SIGKDD International Conference on Knowledge Discovery and Data Mining, KDD 2016, New York, NY, USA, pp. 785–794. Association for Computing Machinery (2016). https://doi.org/10.1145/2939672.2939785
2. Cui, Y., Kara, S., Chan, K.C.: Manufacturing big data ecosystem: a systematic literature review. Robot. Comput.-Integr. Manuf. **62**, 101861 (2020). https://dx.doi.org/10.1016/j.rcim.2019.101861
3. Davis, J., Vogt, J.: Hidden supply chain risk and incoterms®: analysis and mitigation strategies. J. Risk Financ. Manag. **14**(12), 619 (2021). https://dx.doi.org/10.3390/jrfm14120619
4. Erickson, N., Mueller, J., Shirkov, A., Zhang, H., Larroy, P., Li, M., Smola, A.: AutoGluon-tabular: robust and accurate AutoML for structured data (2020). https://arxiv.org/abs/2003.06505
5. Gao, D., et al.: Text-to-SQL empowered by large language models: a benchmark evaluation. Proc. VLDB Endow. **17**(5), 1132–1145 (2024). https://doi.org/10.14778/3641204.3641221
6. Gu, J., et al.: RelBench v2: a large-scale benchmark and repository for relational data (2026). https://arxiv.org/abs/2602.12606
7. Hamilton, W.L., Ying, R., Leskovec, J.: Inductive representation learning on large graphs. In: Proceedings of the 31st International Conference on Neural Information Processing Systems, NIPS 2017, Red Hook, NY, USA, pp. 1025–1035. Curran Associates Inc. (2017)
8. Haug, A., Stentoft Arlbjørn, J., Pedersen, A.: A classification model of ERP system data quality. Ind. Manag. Data Syst. **109**(8), 1053–1068 (2009). http://dx.doi.org/10.1108/02635570910991292
9. Hollmann, N., Müller, S., Eggensperger, K., Hutter, F.: TabPFN: a transformer that solves small tabular classification problems in a second. In: International Conference on Learning Representations 2023 (2023)

10. Hong, S., et al.: Data interpreter: an LLM agent for data science. In: Che, W., Nabende, J., Shutova, E., Pilehvar, M.T. (eds.) Findings of the Association for Computational Linguistics: ACL 2025, Vienna, Austria, pp. 19796–19821. Association for Computational Linguistics, July 2025. https://doi.org/10.18653/v1/2025.findings-acl.1016
11. Ke, G., et al.: LightGBM: a highly efficient gradient boosting decision tree. In: Proceedings of the 31st International Conference on Neural Information Processing Systems, NIPS 2017, Red Hook, NY, USA, pp. 3149–3157. Curran Associates Inc. (2017)
12. Kim, M.J., Grinsztajn, L., Varoquaux, G.: CARTE: pretraining and transfer for tabular learning. In: Proceedings of the 41st International Conference on Machine Learning, ICML 2024. JMLR.org (2024)
13. Klein, T., Biehl, C., Costa, M., Sres, A., Kolk, J., Hoffart, J.: SALT: sales autocompletion linked business tables dataset. In: NeurIPS 2024 Third Table Representation Learning Workshop (2024). https://openreview.net/forum?id=UZbELpkWIr
14. Klein, T., Hoffart, J.: Position: foundation models for tabular data within systemic contexts need grounding (2026). https://arxiv.org/abs/2505.19825
15. Mulang, I.O., Sasaki, F., Klein, T., Kolk, J., Grechanov, N., Hoffart, J.: SALT-KG: a benchmark for semantics-aware learning on enterprise tables. In: Proceedings of the AI for Tabular Data Workshop at EurIPS 2025 (2025)
16. Pan, S., Luo, L., Wang, Y., Chen, C., Wang, J., Wu, X.: Unifying large language models and knowledge graphs: a roadmap. IEEE Trans. Knowl. Data Eng. **36**(7), 3580–3599 (2024). https://doi.org/10.1109/TKDE.2024.3352100
17. Pourreza, M., Rafiei, D.: DIN-SQL: decomposed in-context learning of text-to-SQL with self-correction. In: Proceedings of the 37th International Conference on Neural Information Processing Systems, NIPS 2023, Red Hook, NY, USA. Curran Associates Inc. (2023)
18. Prokhorenkova, L., Gusev, G., Vorobev, A., Dorogush, A.V., Gulin, A.: CatBoost: unbiased boosting with categorical features. In: Proceedings of the 32nd International Conference on Neural Information Processing Systems, NIPS 2018, Red Hook, NY, USA, pp. 6639–6649. Curran Associates Inc. (2018)
19. Riahi, Y., Saikouk, T., Gunasekaran, A., Badraoui, I.: Artificial intelligence applications in supply chain: a descriptive bibliometric analysis and future research directions. Expert Syst. Appl. **173**, 114702 (2021). http://dx.doi.org/10.1016/j.eswa.2021.114702
20. Robinson, J., et al.: RelBench: a benchmark for deep learning on relational databases. In: The Thirty-Eight Conference on Neural Information Processing Systems Datasets and Benchmarks Track (2024). https://openreview.net/forum?id=WEFxOm3Aez
21. Spinaci, M., Polewczyk, M., Schambach, M., Thelin, S.: ConTextTab: a semantics-aware tabular in-context learner. In: Advances in Neural Information Processing Systems (NeurIPS) (2025)
22. Wang, X., et al.: KEPLER: a unified model for knowledge embedding and pre-trained language representation. Trans. Assoc. Comput. Linguist. **9**, 176–194 (2021). https://aclanthology.org/2021.tacl-1.11/
23. Yao, S., et al.: ReAct: synergizing reasoning and acting in language models. In: The Eleventh International Conference on Learning Representations (2023). https://openreview.net/forum?id=WE_vluYUL-X
24. Zhang, X., et al.: TableLLM: enabling tabular data manipulation by LLMs in real office usage scenarios, pp. 10315–10344, July 2025. https://aclanthology.org/2025.findings-acl.538/

Towards Semantic Alignment: Intent-Aware Meta Learning for Urban Fields Recommendation

Chunyang Li[1], Xiuwen Yi[2(✉)], Shumeng Bai[2], Chengjie Guo[1], Zheyi Pan[3,4], Zhichao Huang[3,4], Junbo Zhang[2,3,4,5], and Yu Zheng[1,2,5]

[1] Xidian University, Xi'an, Shaanxi, China
[2] Southwest Jiaotong University, Chengdu, Sichuan, China
xiuwenyi@swjtu.edu.cn
[3] JD Intelligent Cities Research, Beijing, China
[4] JD iCity, JD Technology, Beijing, China
[5] Beijing Key Laboratory of Traffic Data Mining and Embodied Intelligence, Beijing, China

Abstract. Urban public data collection suffers from severe semantic inconsistencies, i.e., the same real-world concept is often described differently, resulting in persistent data silos. To address this root cause, rather than relying on post-hoc data governance, a more proactive solution is to enforce semantic standardization at the source by incorporating pre-defined fields into form creation. This, however, introduces a unique challenge: how to recommend the most relevant fields from a large standardized library, given the sparse and fragmented form context. Thus, we propose the Adaptive Intent-aware Field Recommendation (IaFR) approach in this paper, which models both global form intents and local field intents. Specifically, our approach 1) introduces Mixed Graph Representation module, which leverages Large Language Models (LLMs) to generate external knowledge and use a graph structure to align data standard with form semantics; 2) presents the Implicit Intent Learning module that disentangles global form intents from local field intents via contrastive learning to model user intent; and 3) proposes the Adaptive Intent Matcher, which incorporates meta-learning to adaptively adjust model parameters, ensuring alignment with specific user intents across different forms. We conducted extensive experiments on two real-world datasets, where the results demonstrate IaFR significantly outperforms nine baselines. Moreover, we have deployed IaFR in the *WidgetForm* system, significantly improving the efficiency of form creation by 55%.

Keywords: Form Field Recommendation · Intent Learning · Data Semantic Alignment · Meta Learning · Urban Computing

1 Introduction

Urban data collection involves vast amounts of public data from multiple sources [5]. Sharing and reusing this data offers immense potential to reduce collection

M. Baratchi et al. (Eds.): ECML PKDD 2026, LNAI 16949, pp. 109–126, 2027.
https://doi.org/10.1007/978-3-032-37682-4_7

costs and enhance operational efficiency. However, the semantics of data fields across different sources are inconsistent. As illustrated in Fig. 1(a), identical real-world attributes are often described differently across domains. For example, "Full Name" and "Employee" both refer to a person's name, but appear as distinct fields in different systems, creating persistent data silos that hinder reuse. This issue is fundamentally rooted in the inherent contradiction between the diversity of natural language expressions and the need for data consistency.

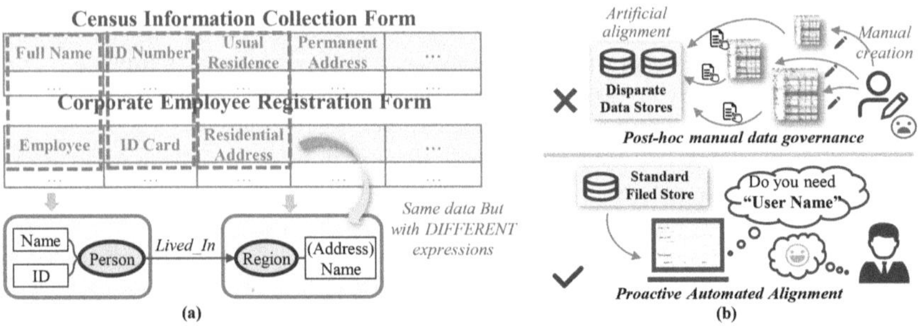

Fig. 1. (a) Identical real-world attributes often exhibit diverse natural language expressions across different domains. (b) Field alignment in two types of business paradigms

To address this, post-hoc manual data governance is typically adopted (Fig. 1(b)). However, this approach is labor-intensive, suffers from time lags and incurs high costs, severely impeding cross-business data sharing. A more proactive solution is to enforce semantic standardization at the source, i.e., constructing data forms directly under a unified standard to achieve preemptive data governance through dynamic human-machine interaction. The Urban Knowledge System (UKS) [14,31] serves as such a standard, providing a comprehensive semantic specification for city-level applications. It distills common entities and relationships from diverse data and constructs standardized field expressions, which have been widely deployed in numerous real-world applications [32,33].

However, the Urban Knowledge System (UKS) defines thousands of fields. Displaying all available fields for users to browse would incur prohibitively high selection costs, where irrelevant information creates visual clutter, increasing configuration difficulty and reducing work efficiency. Consequently, to ensure a smooth user experience, we need a field recommendation method that suggests standardized fields based on form context, allowing users to directly construct standardized forms directly. By analyzing the form theme and configured content, the system infers user intent to recommend and rank suitable fields, minimizing browsing costs and improving both efficiency and user experience.

Existing recommendation methods mainly fall into two categories: user-item recommendation [24] and sequential table learning [2]. User-item recommendation leverages collaborative signals from massive interaction data over large user groups to capture implicit preferences; while sequential table methods rely on rich linear text contexts over flat structures. However, neither approach suits our scenario, as both struggle to model the fragmented, nested structural information inherent in form design, which is a key characteristic that distinguishes our task from traditional recommendation settings.

Specifically, our task faces two unique challenges:

- **Fragmented Context**: The form construction process is progressive, meaning the system observes only a fragmented and incomplete snapshot of the form at any given step. This partial view provides limited semantic information, making it difficult to infer the user's next needed fields.
- **Deterministic Intent**: Unlike user-item recommendations, where user preferences are vague, form creators typically have a blueprint of the final result before they create the form. Consequently, their intent is explicit and deterministic. The recommendation needs to determine exactly what the user has in mind, given the limited existing information. Even minor deviations can disrupt the user's workflow and significantly degrade the usability.

Since the demand for the field selection is naturally determined by the purpose of creating the form, we propose the Intent-aware Field Recommendation (IaFR) framework. IaFR aims to model user intents at both global form and local field levels, bridging the gap between user needs and candidates to improve recommendation accuracy. Specifically, IaFR captures user intent through Mixed Graph Representation and Implicit Intent Learning, and further enhances recommendation quality by employing an Adaptive Intent Matcher to dynamically adjust model parameters to align the model with users.

The key contributions of this work are summarized as follows:

- We propose IaFR[1] a novel framework that models user intent during form creation. By bridging the gap between user intent and field semantics, IaFR significantly enhances recommendation performance for nested form fields.
- We propose the Adaptive Intent Matcher, which leverages meta-learning techniques to innovatively adjust model parameters through the form intent, thereby improving the generalization across diverse user intents.
- Extensive experiments on real-world datasets demonstrate that our IaFR outperforms nine state-of-the-art baselines. Furthermore, we have deployed IaFR in the *WidgetForm* system, improving the efficiency of form creation by 55%.

2 Related Work

2.1 User-Item Recommendation

User-Item Recommendation mainly includes collaborative filtering [20] and content-based recommendation [19]. Collaborative filtering leverages historical behavioral data to compute similarities among users or items, which relies heavily

[1] Code has been published on https://github.com/lichunown/IaFR/.

on abundant interaction data [27], making it ill-suited for form field recommendation. In contrast, content-based algorithms construct high-dimensional profiles for users and items for matching. Some works [3,6,29] rely on fixed node identifiers to construct graphs for information mining, whereas others [13] attempt to extract content features to mitigate cold-start issues. However, these methods mine broad preferences from large-scale interaction data based on implicit interests, whereas form field recommendation deals with clear, specific intents, rendering these methods inapplicable. Given that even minor deviations are unacceptable, this fundamental mismatch renders them unsuitable for our task. Recently, leveraging Large Language Models (LLMs) to mine graph relationships has gained popularity [23]. Yet their high computational cost and slow inference hinder deployment in real-time scenarios requiring high query frequency. Drawing inspiration from these works, IaFR deeply models user intent with an adaptive mechanism. Unlike real-time LLM inference, we employ LLMs strictly for offline knowledge expansion, achieving both high accuracy and fast inference.

2.2 Tabular Data Learning

Current research on tabular data [2,12] primarily focuses on table content understanding [1], classification [7], and content recommendation tasks [30]. However, studies specifically focusing on the semantic learning of form fields remain limited. A notable work is FormLM [18], which assists form design by leveraging language models to recommend questions and block types. However, this approach operates primarily on sequential form structures, failing to consider the hierarchical dependencies inherent in complex forms. While recent works have been proposed to leverage LLMs for tabular learning tasks [21], they have yet to address the specific challenge of nested field recommendation. In contrast to these approaches, IaFR is tailored for form field recommendation, specifically addressing structures characterized by nested relationships.

3 Methodology

3.1 Problem Formulation

In form construction, creators sequentially add fields to a form fragment, termed "focus field". Each focus field permits the expansion of its attributes and linked entity descriptions, resulting in a candidate space determined by $a + e \times r$, where a, e, and r denote the number of attributes, entities, and relations, respectively. The task is to recommend relevant fields associated with the focus field.

- **Definition 1. Form Fragment** represents an intermediate subgraph $\mathcal{G}^{\mathrm{F}} = (\mathcal{V}^{\mathrm{F}}, \mathcal{R}^{\mathrm{F}})$ of a complete form, capturing the creator's partial construction process, where $\mathcal{V}^{\mathrm{F}}$ denotes the set of fields, including their descriptions and UKS associations, and $\mathcal{R}^{F}$ denotes the nested relationships among them.
- **Definition 2. Focus Field** is the operating field $v_{\text{focus}} \in \mathcal{V}^{\mathrm{F}}$ in a form, for which the recommended fields are the relevant nodes of it.

- **Definition 3. Candidate Fields** are pre-defined field node $\mathcal{V}^{\mathrm{U}}$ in UKS. These candidates, along with their pre-defined correlations, constitute a correlation graph $\mathcal{G}^{\mathrm{U}} = (\mathcal{V}^{\mathrm{U}}, \mathcal{R}^{\mathrm{U}})$, where $\mathcal{V}^{\mathrm{U}}$ represents the total available fields and $\mathcal{R}^{\mathrm{U}}$ denotes the pre-defined semantic correlation among them. It is worth noting that the fields in the form fragment are a subset of this, i.e., $\mathcal{V}^{\mathrm{F}} \subseteq \mathcal{V}^{\mathrm{U}}$.
- **Definition 4. Field Recommendation** Given a form fragment $\mathcal{G}^{\mathrm{F}}$ and a focus field v_{focus}, the task is to retrieve the top-k fields from the candidates $v \in \mathcal{V}^{\mathrm{U}}$ that maximize the alignment with the user's latent intent.

3.2 Overview of IaFR

IaFR processes form inputs and cached information to generate relevant scores for candidate fields. By ranking these scores and truncating the list, it selects the top-k most relevant fields for recommendation, as illustrated in Fig. 2. Specifically, IaFR first leverages external knowledge from UKS and LLMs [22] to enhance the form semantics through the Mixed Graph Representation. Then, the Implicit Intent Learning module models user intents into two types: the global *form intent*, which captures the user's form purpose; and the local *field intent*, which reflects the user's purpose at the focus field. Finally, as the distribution of available fields varies with form intents, we propose the Adaptive Intent Matcher, which introduces meta-learning techniques [8] to dynamically adjust model parameters, thereby aligning the model with user needs and enhancing generalization to boost recommendation performance.

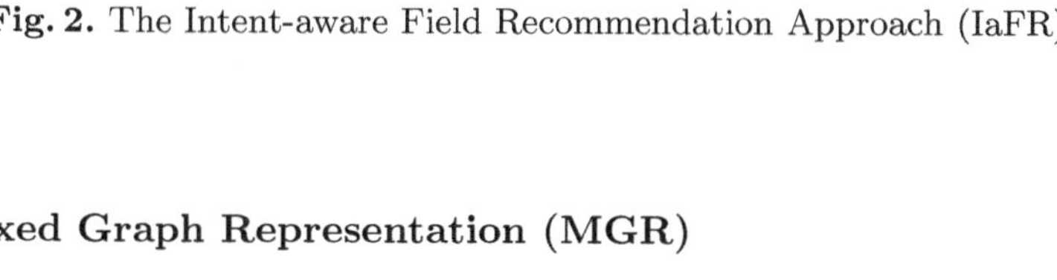

Fig. 2. The Intent-aware Field Recommendation Approach (IaFR)

3.3 Mixed Graph Representation (MGR)

Field textual descriptions are often overly concise, resulting in significant semantic sparsity. Given that form fields, standard UKS expressions, and the relationships within the UKS possess intrinsic structural correlations, we propose the Mixed Graph Representation (MGR) module. This module fuses three hierarchical layers of knowledge: form structure, UKS semantics, and natural language priors, as shown in Fig. 3. Specifically, we first construct a graph from the nested dependencies among the fragmented fields. These fields are then linked to their standardized representations in the UKS, where pre-defined entity relationships form the second layer of knowledge. Finally, to compensate for the concise nature of field descriptions in the UKS, we employ the LLMs to generate rich interpretations and usage contexts, introducing external language priors.

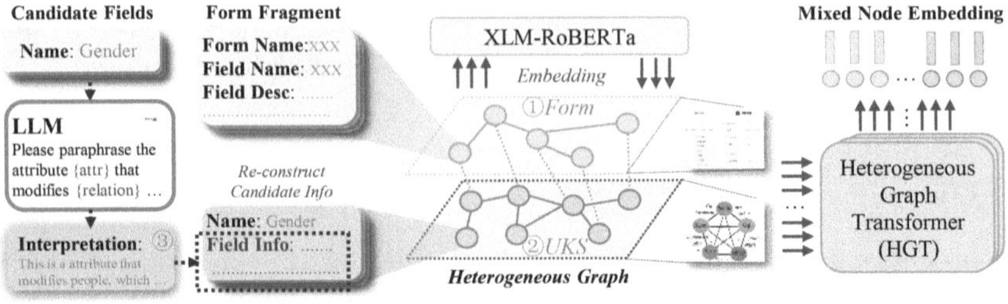

Fig. 3. The Mixed Graph Representation

Subsequently, these multi-layer information sources are organized into a heterogeneous graph $\mathcal{G} = (\mathcal{V}, \mathcal{R})$ based on the structural associations with UKS and forms, where $\mathcal{G} = \mathcal{G}^{\mathrm{F}} \cup \mathcal{G}^{\mathrm{U}}$. To align different semantic spaces and ensure robustness against dynamic field updates, the textual attributes of each node are concatenated and encoded using a pre-trained XLM-RoBERTa model [26]. The generated semantic representation of each node is denoted as $\mathbf{X}_{\mathrm{in}} \in \mathbb{R}^{|\mathcal{V}| \times d}$. Finally, we employ a Heterogeneous Graph Transformer (HGT) [10] to propagate information across the graph, generating the mixed node representations $X = \{\mathbf{X}^{\mathrm{F}}, \mathbf{X}^{\mathrm{U}}\} = f_{\mathrm{HGT}}^{\mathrm{pre}}(\mathbf{X}_{\mathrm{in}})$, where $\mathbf{X}^{\mathrm{F}}, \mathbf{X}^{\mathrm{U}}$ represent the embeddings of form fields and UKS nodes respectively, and f_{HGT} denotes the multi-layer HGT.

3.4 Implicit Intent Learning

The selection of fields is intrinsically governed by the purpose of creating forms and the local field context. Consequently, we decompose user intent into two distinct types: the global **Form Intent**, which represents the creator's overarching purpose for designing the form, and the local **Field Intent**, which reflects the specific requirement within the context of the focus field. As shown in Fig. 4(a), we employ two dedicated modules to learn these intents separately.

For local field intent, we suppose that the intent is encapsulated within the information aggregated to the focus field itself. We leverage HGT to learn the interactive information and extract the representation corresponding to the focus field as the local intent, such that $e_{\mathrm{field}} = f_{\mathrm{HGT}}^{\mathrm{field}}(\mathbf{X})_{i_{\mathrm{focus}}}$. For global form intent, in addition to the form textural information and the mixed node embeddings of fields, we assume that user preferences will still influence the field selection. To this end, we introduce historical field usage statistics as an extra input. Specifically, we first obtain the form representation by mean-pooling all field node embeddings $e_{\text{form}}^{\text{nodes}} = \text{Mean}\left(f_{\text{HGT}}^{\text{form}}(\mathbf{X}_{\text{cat}})_{I^F}\right)$. Then, we calculate the embeddings of the form title and its description $e_{\text{form}}^{\text{txt}}$ through the pre-trained XLM-RoBERTa model [26]. Furthermore, we employ an MLP to learn the user's field preference $e_{\text{form}}^{\text{user}}$ from historical statistics. The final global form intent is generated by fusing these embeddings via a two-layer linear neural network (MLP):

$$e_{\text{form}} = \text{MLP}\left(\text{concat}(e_{\text{form}}^{\text{nodes}}, e_{\text{form}}^{\text{txt}}) + \text{MLP}(\sigma \cdot e_{\text{form}}^{\text{user}})\right),$$

where concat$(\cdot)$ performs direct vector concatenation, and σ is a decay coefficient used to control the influence degree of user preference information.

To further enhance the understanding of intents, we introduce the contrastive learning technique to increase the distance between different intents. Since the creator's global form intent remains consistent throughout the creation process, we assume that subgraphs sampled from the same form correspond to a shared creation objective. Therefore, we treat subgraphs derived from the same form as positive samples and those from different forms as negative samples. Conversely, for local field intent, we posit that fields of the same UKS type within a form are driven by similar local requirements. We select fields of the same type within the form as positive samples, while fields from other forms serve as negative samples. Specifically, we employ the InfoNCE loss [15] to train both form and field intent separately, such that $\mathcal{L}_{\text{form}} = \text{InfoNCE}(e_{\text{form}};:)$, $\mathcal{L}_{\text{field}} = \text{InfoNCE}(e_{\text{field}};:)$. Here, the InfoNCE loss is:

$$\text{InfoNCE}(e; e_{\text{pos}}; e_{\text{neg}}) = -\log \frac{\exp(e \cdot e_{\text{pos}}/\tau)}{\sum_{i=1}^{k} \exp(e \cdot e_i/\tau)}$$

where τ is the temperature hyperparameter that controls the smoothness of the distribution, and $e; e_{\text{pos}}; e_{\text{neg}}$ denotes the intent, positive sample, and negative sample embeddings, respectively. Through sufficient learning of user intents, we can effectively disentangle form-level and field-level user intents, providing discriminative representations for the subsequent matcher.

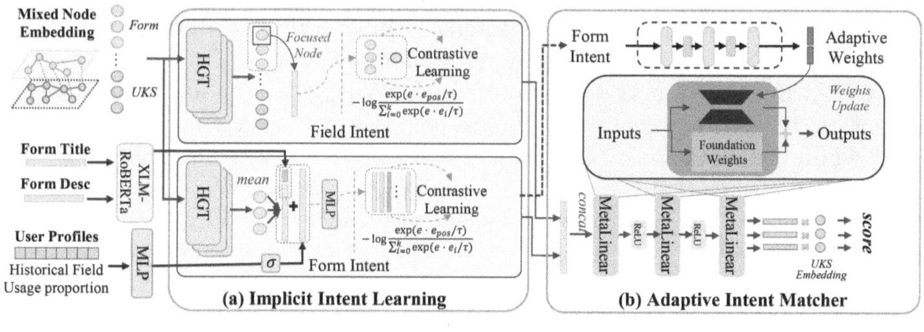

Fig. 4. Architecture of Implicit Intent Learning and Adaptive Intent Matching

3.5 Adaptive Intent Matcher (AIM)

The required fields can vary drastically depending on the form context, even when sharing the same focus. For instance, an "Amount" field in a "Reimbursement Form" implies associated financial rules, whereas in a "Personnel Statistics Form", it relates to population size or distribution. We attribute this to the leading role of global intent, where the need of the specific field can change significantly depending on the form context. Fixed model parameters struggle to capture such context-dependent nuances, leading to generalized yet insufficiently precise recommendations. To this end, we view each form intent as a latent task distribution. Therefore, field recommendations under different intents can be naturally formulated as a meta-learning problem, where the model parameters are adapted according to task-specific intent representations. Building on this formulation, we propose the Adaptive Intent Matcher (AIM) that dynamically adjusts model parameters based on the form intent to improve recommendations.

As shown in Fig. 4(b), AIM primarily consists of sequentially fully connected neural network layers with adaptable parameters, termed *MetaLinear*. The learned field intent and form intent are first concatenated and processed through these MetaLinear layers. Subsequently, the output is concatenated with the candidate field representations learned from the UKS nodes, followed by a cosine similarity calculation. Specifically, the matching score is computed as:

$$s = \text{cosine}\left(f_{\text{AIM}}(\text{concat}(\boldsymbol{e}_{\text{form}}, \boldsymbol{e}_{\text{field}})), \boldsymbol{e}_{\text{UKS}}\right),$$

where $\boldsymbol{e}_{\text{UKS}}$ represents the learned representations of UKS nodes in MGR, and f_{AIM} denotes the function composed of MetaLinear layers and ReLU activation.

Each MetaLinear layer performs like a fully connected linear layer with dynamic parameters, defined as $f_{\text{linear}}(\boldsymbol{x}; \boldsymbol{\Theta}) = \boldsymbol{\Theta}^{\text{T}}\boldsymbol{x} + b$, where $\boldsymbol{x}, b$ denote the inputs, bias of the layer, and $\boldsymbol{\Theta}$ is the model parameters that can be adaptively adjusted based on the global form intent, i.e., $\boldsymbol{\Theta} = g(\boldsymbol{e}_{\text{form}})$.

Directly parameterizing $g(\cdot)$ to output the full parameter matrix [4,16] results in excessive learnable parameters, rendering the model difficult to train. To overcome this, we draw inspiration from the LoRA [9], positing that the adaptive information brought by form intent is inherently low-dimensional. Consequently, we decompose the layer parameters $\boldsymbol{\Theta} \in \mathbb{R}^{d_{\text{in}} \times d_{\text{out}}}$ into a foundation weight matrix $\mathbf{W}$ and a dynamic matrix $\mathbf{W}_{\text{dynamic}}$. The foundation weight $\mathbf{W} \in \mathbb{R}^{d_{\text{in}} \times d_{\text{out}}}$ is directly trained via gradient descent to capture general knowledge, while the dynamic matrix $\mathbf{W}_{\text{dynamic}} \in \mathbb{R}^{d_{\text{in}} \times d_{\text{out}}}$ is dynamically adjusted through the form intent, i.e., $\boldsymbol{\Theta} = \mathbf{W} + \mathbf{W}_{\text{dynamic}}$. Here, $\mathbf{W}_{\text{dynamic}}$ is approximated as the product of two low-rank matrices, such that $\mathbf{W}_{\text{dynamic}} = \mathbf{A} \times \mathbf{B}$, where the $\mathbf{A} \in \mathbb{R}^{d_{\text{in}} \times r}, \mathbf{B} \in \mathbb{R}^{r \times d_{\text{out}}}$ are the decomposed matrices with rank $r \ll d_{\text{in}}, d_{\text{out}}$. Here, we simply employ a three-layer fully connected network to generate the low-rank matrices, expressed as $\mathbf{A}, \mathbf{B} = \text{Reshape}(\text{MLP}(\boldsymbol{e}_{\text{form}}))$, where Reshape is to transform the output parameters into matrix form.

3.6 Training Procedures

The output of IaFR is the scores s for different candidate fields in the UKS. We employ the Binary Cross-Entropy (BCE) loss [34] to train the IaFR, defined as

$$\mathcal{L}_{\text{BCE}} = -\sum_i [y_i \log \delta(s_i) + (1 - y_i) \log(1 - \delta(s_i))],$$

where $y_i \in \{0, 1\}$ denotes the ground truth label and $\delta(s_i)$ represents the sigmoid function. During training procedures, we jointly optimize the model with a contrastive learning loss, resulting in a total loss defined as $\mathcal{L} = \mathcal{L}_{\text{BCE}} + \alpha \cdot (\mathcal{L}_{\text{form}} + \mathcal{L}_{\text{field}})$, where α is the hyperparameter to control the learning objectives.

4 Experiments

4.1 Experiment Settings

We collected business forms from the *WidgetForm* system from August 2024 to February 2025. In total, 3,027 forms were gathered, of which 930 underwent a secondary cleaning process by business experts to correct the associations with UKS. Based on this data, we constructed two datasets: WF-Full and WF-Refined. The detailed statistics are presented in Table 1. We first partition the form data into training, validation, and test datasets in a 6:2:2 ratio. Subsequently, to simulate real-world design scenarios, we independently employ a data augmentation strategy on each split, randomly sampling subgraphs from the form data and selecting focus fields to construct training, validation, and test pairs. These fields are mapped to 4,225 unique expressions in the UKS, comprising 1,034 relational entities and 2,883 attribute expressions.

Table 1. Statistics of Datasets

	Form Num	Total Field Num	Attr Num	Entity/Relation Num
WF-Full	3027	67879	42460	25419
WF-Refined	930	19173	10893	8280

In our experiments, we select the GLM-5 [28] as the LLM backbone to facilitate knowledge expansion in MGR. The hyperparameters are set as $\sigma = 0.001$ and $\tau = 1$. Here we set a lower σ to heavily suppress the user's historical preference $e_{\text{form}}^{\text{user}}$, as form-filling behaviors are highly variable, rendering historical statistics unreliable; thus, the historical preference serves as a minor backup, preventing entirely random guesses during cold-start scenarios when the form context is empty. To prioritize different optimization objectives across training stages, we define α as a decay factor over training steps. In experiments, we adopt $\alpha = \max(0.5^{n_e}, 0.01)$, where n_e denotes the epoch index. Additionally, we set the meta dimension (rank) in the AIM to $r = 8$, which aligns with LoRA.

We compare IaFR against recent graph-based recommendation methods, including GraphRec [6], GraphAug [29], HGT [10], and GFormer [13], as well as LLM-based recommendation approaches such as RLMRec [17] (using the LLM's interpretation in MKR) and FormLM [18] (using XLM-RoBERTa [26] to replace its primary model). These baselines cover both table-based and user-item recommendation tasks. To adapt our tasks for user-item methods, we construct each sample at the field level: we treat the focus field as the "user", the form context as user features, and the UKS field as the "item". Additionally, we evaluate the performance of general-purpose LLMs on this task. Specifically, we concatenate the form structure with the preceding fields into a long prompt and require the LLMs to generate a ranked list of 10 recommended fields. We primarily benchmark against GLM-5 [28], Qwen-3.5 [25], and GPT-4o-mini [11].

To evaluate the recommendation performance, we adopt Recall, Normalized Discounted Cumulative Gain (NDCG), and Area Under the Curve (AUC) as the evaluation metrics. Specifically, Recall measures the proportion of ground-truth items successfully retrieved within the top-k predictions. Given that the system interface typically displays the top-10 recommended fields in two rows (Sect. 5), we prioritize Recall@5 and Recall@10 to assess the model's effectiveness under different exposure scenarios. It is worth noting that for general-purpose LLMs, which generate a list of candidates rather than ranking the entire item corpus, ranking-based metrics like NDCG and AUC are inapplicable. Consequently, we solely report Recall metrics for LLM-based approaches.

4.2 Overall Performance

Table 2. The Overall Performance of Baselines

	WF-Full				WF-Refined				Time(s)
	Recall@5	Recall@10	NDCG	AUC	Recall@5	Recall@10	NDCG	AUC	
GraphRec	0.1525	0.2105	0.6149	0.8912	0.2068	0.2921	0.6013	0.7980	0.0655
HGT	0.2391	0.3902	0.5684	0.7997	0.2375	0.3899	0.4663	0.8022	0.0398
GFormer	0.3333	0.3571	0.6521	0.7773	0.3575	0.3575	0.6288	0.7415	0.0796
GraphAug	0.3077	0.3295	0.6199	0.7631	0.36158	0.3862	0.6355	0.8142	0.0131
RLMRec	0.3741	0.3940	**0.6850**	0.8043	0.3165	0.3344	**0.6357**	0.7644	0.1000
RoBERT	0.3109	0.4281	0.5969	0.5772	0.3187	0.4431	0.5756	0.5510	**0.0075**
GLM5	0.2997	0.3464	-	-	0.3125	0.3640	-	-	84.0609
Qwen-3.5	0.1956	0.2479	-	-	0.2124	0.2717	-	-	32.5054
GPT-4o-mini	0.0553	0.0853	-	-	0.1012	0.1024	-	-	5.2164
IaFR	**0.4224**	**0.4941**	0.6124	**0.9648**	**0.4733**	**0.5555**	0.6248	**0.9557**	0.0478

Table 2 presents the overall comparison among baselines. GraphRec and GraphAug, which rely on node IDs and structural information, fail to capture semantic nuances, resulting in worse performance. Similarly, the text-based

XLM-RoBERTa struggles with complex graph structures, limiting its effectiveness. Although HGT, GFormer, and LLMRec incorporate semantic modeling, they struggle to interpret complex user intents, resulting in suboptimal performance. Specifically, all these models yield moderate NDCG scores, reflecting the difficulty of ranking the complete set of positive fields due to ambiguous user intents. A notable case is RLMRec: while it achieves the highest NDCG, its recall is lower, indicating it tends to rank common generic options at the top but fails to adapt to specific user intents, particularly for secondary requirements affected by long-tail distribution. However, since practical applications focus on top-10 recommendations, recall is more critical for user satisfaction than full-list ranking. Unlike these methods, IaFR explicitly models user intents and explores intent relations in depth via the AIM. By adaptively recognizing specific user intents and providing targeted recommendations based on intent relations, IaFR effectively addresses the aforementioned limitations, thereby achieving a significantly higher recall. Furthermore, for general-purpose LLMs, despite their inherent reasoning capabilities, the zero-shot prediction performance is still poor. Notably, among these LLMs, there is a positive correlation between performance and inference time. However, even the fastest model (GPT-4o-mini) is too slow for real-time use. In contrast, IaFR leverages the LLM solely for offline semantic expansion rather than real-time generation, which significantly accelerates the inference speed and achieves the best performance.

4.3 Ablation Studies

To validate the contribution of different modules to the final results, we define a variant of IaFR that removes all contrastive learning losses and replaces MetaLinear with a standard linear layer as the **Base** model for ablation studies. First, we compare the effects of different input information from MGR: 1) **w/o Graph**: Based on the Base model, removing the relation information from the UKS; 2) **w/o LLM**: Removing the field definitions generated by LLMs. Then, we explore the effects of the intent learning modules: 1) **w** $\mathcal{L}_{field}$: Adding field contrastive loss to the Base model; 2) **w** $\mathcal{L}_{form}$: Adding form contrastive loss to the Base model; 3) **w Meta**: Replacing the vanilla linear layer with MetaLinear; 4) **All**: Training the model with all components integrated.

As shown in Table 3, removing external knowledge sources (w/o Graph and w/o LLM) leads to a significant performance drop compared to the Base model. Notably, the absence of LLM-based semantics (w/o LLM) causes a sharp decline in Recall, highlighting that semantic information is critical for distinguishing field relevance. Furthermore, the integration of intent learning modules yields substantial improvements. Specifically, the field contrastive loss (w Field C) yields significant improvement in Recall, demonstrating its effectiveness in retrieving relevant items. In contrast, the form contrastive loss (w Form C) contributes more to the ranking quality, achieving a higher AUC among the variants. Meanwhile, MetaLinear (w Meta) provides moderate gains over the Base model by adapting to specific intents. Ultimately, the full model (All) achieves the best

Table 3. Ablation Studies of Different Components

Dataset	WF-Full				WF-Refined			
Metrics	Recall@5	Recall@10	NDCG	AUC	Recall@5	Recall@10	NDCG	AUC
w/o Graph	0.2817	0.4103	0.5535	0.7883	0.2981	0.4141	0.4586	0.7994
w/o LLM	0.2391	0.3902	0.5684	0.7997	0.2375	0.3899	0.4663	0.8022
Base	0.3080	0.4120	0.5512	0.8335	0.3011	0.4032	0.4563	0.8460
w Field C	0.4087	0.4903	0.5537	0.9246	0.4618	0.5365	0.5509	0.9505
w Form C	0.3978	0.4932	0.5322	0.9389	0.3855	0.4718	0.5436	0.9433
w Meta	0.3872	0.4862	0.5093	0.9210	0.3895	0.4756	0.5432	0.9463
All	**0.4224**	**0.4941**	**0.6124**	**0.9648**	**0.4733**	**0.5555**	**0.6248**	**0.9557**

performance across all metrics, demonstrating that the synergistic combination of semantic enrichment and intent learning is essential for optimal performance.

4.4 Sensitivity Analysis of Meta Embedding Rank

In the Adaptive Intent Matcher (AIM), we utilize the Form Intent Embedding to generate dynamic parameters $\mathbf{W}_{\text{dynamic}}$ to facilitate precise reasoning of user intents. These parameters are derived from two low-rank matrices, $\mathbf{A}$ and $\mathbf{B}$, where the rank r serves as a critical bottleneck that constrains the model's representational capacity. In this section, we investigate the impact of this rank on model performance, as illustrated in Fig. 5. First, model performance initially improves and then declines across all metrics as the rank increases. This is primarily because a smaller rank limits the representational capacity, preventing the model from capturing complex user intent features. Conversely, an excessively large rank increases the number of parameters and training costs, making it difficult to converge to the optimal solution within a limited number of training iterations. Therefore, we set rank $r = 8$ as the default setting in practice, which aligns with the empirical findings of models like LoRA.

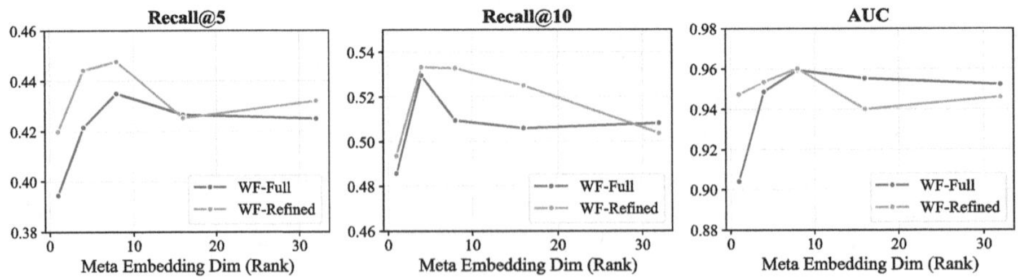

Fig. 5. Impact of Rank r on Model Performance

4.5 Case Study

To investigate the semantic representation properties learned in IaFR, we utilize an LLM [28] to categorize the forms into 13 types (e.g., Education, Public Safety, etc.; detailed categories are displayed in Fig. 8). We extract global form intent representations of randomly sampled data and visualize them via t-SNE, analyzing the distribution patterns from both macro and micro perspectives. As shown in Fig. 6, the left subfigure presents the macro view, where samples from different business types are mixed in the space. This indicates a divergence between the latent intent space learned by the model and human-intuitive business classifications. However, this discrepancy is reasonable as form intent is inherently ambiguous, preventing human-defined labels from fully capturing semantic boundaries, while the model captures deeper functional or structural correlations beyond explicit LLM categorization. The right subfigure presents the micro view, where samples from the same form tightly aggregate into independent clusters, while adjacent clusters often belong to the same business type. This suggests that IaFR could effectively capture fine-grained semantic information, ensuring intent consistency within the same form while mapping semantically similar forms to neighboring spatial regions.

To investigate the impact of the meta-learning module on MetaLinear parameters, we adopt the relative norm ratio to quantify the contribution of dynamic parameters to the final parameters. Specifically, $\textit{Ratio} = ||\mathbf{W}_{\text{dynamic}}||_2/||\mathbf{W}||_2$, where $||\cdot||_2$ denotes the ℓ_2 norm. As AIM employs three layers of MetaLinear, Fig. 7 illustrates the distribution of ratios across these three layers using box plots, where diamonds represent the mean values. It is evident that the contribution of dynamic parameters significantly outweighs that of the base parameters. Notably, this contribution increases progressively as the layers approach the output; the mean relative norm ratios for the three fully connected layers are 0.15, 0.31, and 0.81, respectively. Particularly in the output layer, outliers exhibit relative norms reaching up to 3.34. This trend suggests that IaFR could effectively leverage dynamic parameters to perform sample-specific adaptations, thereby precisely aligning with corresponding form intents. This mechanism is especially beneficial for long-tail forms with limited samples, significantly enhancing the model's flexibility and generalization capability.

We further compared the contribution of dynamic parameters across different form categories. Figure 8 illustrates the relative norms of the second MetaLinear layer across 13 LLM-defined form categories. The relative norms vary significantly across categories, primarily due to differences in fine-grained business characteristics. For instance, the *Urban Planning* category exhibits a relatively high median ratio of 1.2. Since this category encompasses diverse content such as public facility services and demographic statistics, it involves a broad semantic scope, leading to a greater contribution from dynamic parameters. In contrast, the *Complaints* category shows a lower median ratio of 0.6, as it primarily consists of standardized government reporting forms, which require less adaptation from dynamic parameters. This finding echoes the seemingly disordered distri-

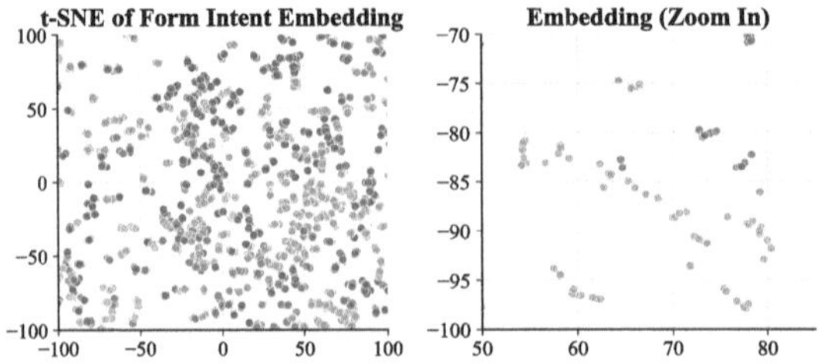

Fig. 6. T-SNE View of the Form Intent Representation. The left is macro view, while the right is micro view

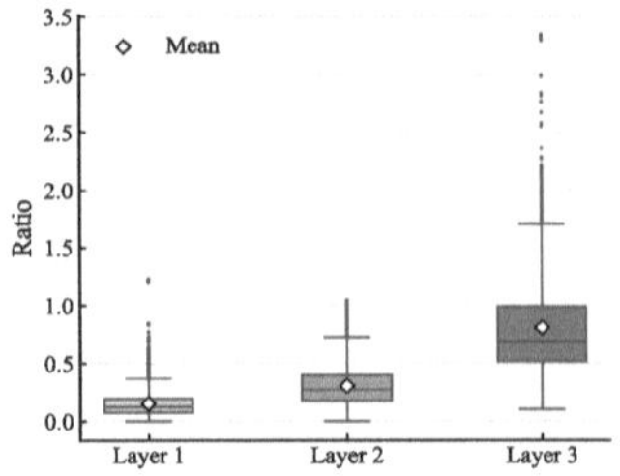

Fig. 7. Relative Norm Ratios across three MetaLinear Layers

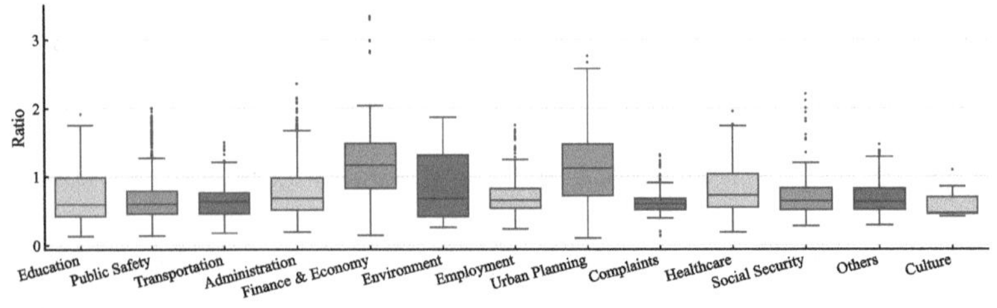

Fig. 8. Relative Norm Ratios across 13 types of Form classifications (Layer 2)

bution observed in the macro view (Fig. 6), highlighting our method's ability to generalize across diverse form types through adaptive parameter adjustment.

5 System

Since January 2025, the IaFR approach has been integrated into the WidgetForm system, a human-computer interactive system for standardized form creation, which has been successfully deployed in real-world applications such as Jingmintong Platform [32]. As shown in Fig. 9(a), the WidgetForm system is built upon the UKS, a city-level data standard that defines entities, relations, and attributes in a graph structure. Similar entities from diverse sources are mapped to unified standard nodes in the UKS (e.g., mapping both "Applicant" and "User" to the "Person"), thereby enabling cross-source semantic alignment. To ensure consistency, form fields in WidgetForm are strictly bound to UKS nodes, preventing arbitrary modifications. However, if a user modifies a field name, the widget becomes a "free field" and decouples from the UKS. During form construction, creators sequentially add fields, termed "focus field". As illustrated in Fig. 9(b), the system recommends all fields associated with the focus field based on the UKS structure. The top 10 relevant fields are presented below the focus field, while users can also proactively search fields to add them.

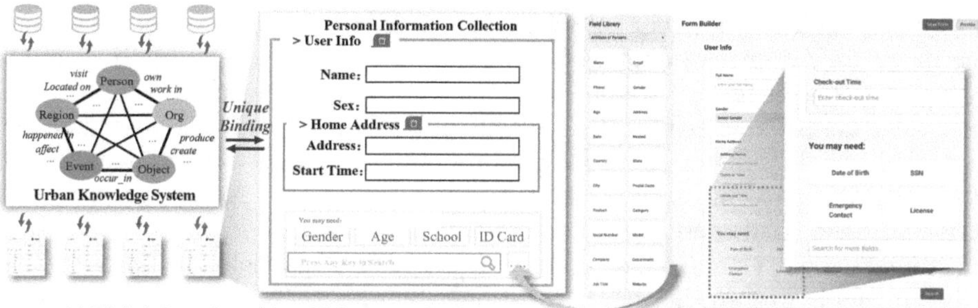

(a) Digital Controls enables efficient cross-business data alignment via unique mappings to the UKS

(b) Snapshot of the Digital Controls interface in real-world business scenarios

Fig. 9. Overview of WidgetForm and its Applications

Since its deployment, the accurate recommendations provided by IaFR have reduced the average form creation time from 10.21 min to 4.54 min. As the recommendation logic is deeply coupled with the core frontend interaction workflow and the feature was updated to all users without any beta transition, a controlled A/B test was infeasible. Therefore, we compare the field association rate with the UKS before and after deployment. The rate improved from $31.2 \pm 41.5\%$ (mean $\pm$ std) pre-deployment to 75.9 ± 9.3 post-deployment. Moreover, in the absence of recommendations, users tend to create free fields that decouple from the UKS. By guiding users toward standardized inputs, the system has raised the field association rate with the UKS from 31.2% to 75.91%, significantly promoting cross-business data alignment. This significant improvement primarily stems from two aspects. First, before deployment, user behavior was highly polarized: experienced users followed standard procedures, while others frequently created free fields that decoupled from the UKS, resulting in extremely high variance. Second, the recommendation system fundamentally altered the interaction paradigm by replacing uncertain manual exploration with deterministic selection. By proactively providing standardized options, it effectively eliminates guesswork and prevents the creation of free fields, thereby ensuring consistent mapping to the UKS. Ultimately, the high accuracy of our recommendation algorithm significantly increases users' adoption of standardized inputs, thereby further substantially enhancing the field association with the UKS.

6 Conclusion

To address semantic inconsistencies in urban public data, we proposed the Intent-aware Field Recommendation (IaFR), which enforces standardization at the source during form creation. Recognizing that field selection is driven by the creator's subjective intent, we introduce an Implicit Intent Learning module that disentangles user intent into global form intent and local field intent. Furthermore, an Adaptive Intent Matcher is employed to adaptively adjust model parameters based on the global intent. This mechanism enables the model to generalize across diverse scenarios, effectively capturing dynamic user demands and significantly enhancing recommendation quality. Experiments demonstrate that IaFR outperforms existing baselines, achieving an average improvement of 20.8% in Recall@10 compared to the strongest baseline. It has been deployed in the *WidgetForm* system, which reduces average form creation time from 10.21 to 4.54 min and increased the standardization rate from 31.2% to 75.91%, validating its practical value in breaking down data silos.

Acknowledgments. This work is supported by the National Natural Science Foundation of China Grant (No. 62502028), the Beijing Natural Science Foundation (No. 4254079), and the Beijing Nova program (20240484515).

References

1. Arik, S.Ö., Pfister, T.: TabNet: attentive interpretable tabular learning. In: Proceedings of the AAAI Conference on Artificial Intelligence, vol. 35 (2021)
2. Borisov, V., Leemann, T., Seßler, K., Haug, J., Pawelczyk, M., Kasneci, G.: Deep neural networks and tabular data: a survey. IEEE Trans. Neural Netw. Learn. Syst. **35**(6), 7499–7519 (2022)
3. Cai, X., Huang, C., Xia, L., Ren, X.: LightGCL: simple yet effective graph contrastive learning for recommendation. arXiv preprint arXiv:2302.08191 (2023)
4. Chen, J., Qiu, X., Liu, P., Huang, X.: Meta multi-task learning for sequence modeling. In: Proceedings of the AAAI Conference on Artificial Intelligence, vol. 32 (2018)
5. Chen, Q., Shi, Q., Cheng, G.: Dataset search over integrated metadata from China's public data open platforms. In: Chen, E., et al. (eds.) BigData 2023. CCIS, vol. 2005, pp. 32–43. Springer, Singapore (2023). https://doi.org/10.1007/978-981-99-8979-9_3
6. Fan, W., et al.: Graph neural networks for social recommendation. In: The World Wide Web Conference, pp. 417–426 (2019)
7. Hegselmann, S., Buendia, A., Lang, H., Agrawal, M., Jiang, X., Sontag, D.: TabLLM: few-shot classification of tabular data with large language models. In: International Conference on Artificial Intelligence and Statistics, pp. 5549–5581. PMLR (2023)
8. Hospedales, T., Antoniou, A., Micaelli, P., Storkey, A.: Meta-learning in neural networks: a survey. IEEE Trans. Pattern Anal. Mach. Intell. **44**(9), 5149–5169 (2021)
9. Hu, E.J., et al.: LoRA: low-rank adaptation of large language models. In: ICLR, vol. 1, no. 2, p. 3 (2022)
10. Hu, Z., Dong, Y., Wang, K., Sun, Y.: Heterogeneous graph transformer. In: Proceedings of the Web Conference 2020, pp. 2704–2710 (2020)
11. Hurst, A., et al.: GPT-4o system card. arXiv preprint arXiv:2410.21276 (2024)
12. Jiang, J.P., Liu, S.Y., Cai, H.R., Zhou, Q.L., Ye, H.J.: Representation learning for tabular data: a comprehensive survey. IEEE Trans. Pattern Anal. Mach. Intell. (2026)

13. Li, C., Xia, L., Ren, X., Ye, Y., Xu, Y., Huang, C.: Graph transformer for recommendation. In: Proceedings of the 46th International ACM SIGIR Conference on Research and Development in Information Retrieval, SIGIR 2023. ACM (2023)
14. Li, C., Sun, Y., Huang, Z., Guo, J.: TermRAG: data resource summarization via term retrieval augmented generation. In: Huang, D.S., Chen, W., Pan, Y., Chen, H. (eds.) Advanced Intelligent Computing Technology and Applications. ICIC 2025. Communications in Computer and Information Science, vol. 2575, pp. 225–237. Springer, Singapore (2025). https://doi.org/10.1007/978-981-95-0017-8_19
15. van den Oord, A., Li, Y., Vinyals, O.: Representation learning with contrastive predictive coding. arXiv preprint arXiv:1807.03748 (2018)
16. Pan, Z., Liang, Y., Wang, W., Yu, Y., Zheng, Y., Zhang, J.: Urban traffic prediction from spatio-temporal data using deep meta learning. In: Proceedings of the 25th ACM SIGKDD International Conference on Knowledge Discovery & Data Mining, KDD 2019, pp. 1720–1730. Association for Computing Machinery (2019)
17. Ren, X., et al.: Representation learning with large language models for recommendation. In: Proceedings of the ACM Web Conference 2024, pp. 3464–3475 (2024)
18. Shao, Y., et al.: FormLM: recommending creation ideas for online forms by modelling semantic and structural information. arXiv preprint arXiv:2211.05284 (2022)
19. Sharma, K., et al.: A survey of graph neural networks for social recommender systems. ACM Comput. Surv. **56**(10), 1–34 (2024)
20. Su, X., Khoshgoftaar, T.M.: A survey of collaborative filtering techniques. Adv. Artif. Intell. **2009**(1), 421425 (2009)
21. Sui, Y., Zhou, M., Zhou, M., Han, S., Zhang, D.: Table meets LLM: can large language models understand structured table data? A benchmark and empirical study. In: Proceedings of the 17th ACM International Conference on Web Search and Data Mining, pp. 645–654 (2024)
22. Thirunavukarasu, A.J., Ting, D.S.J., Elangovan, K., Gutierrez, L., Tan, T.F., Ting, D.S.W.: Large language models in medicine. Nat. Med. **29**(8) (2023)
23. Wang, Y., et al.: LLMRG: improving recommendations through large language model reasoning graphs. In: Proceedings of the AAAI Conference on Artificial Intelligence, vol. 38, pp. 19189–19196 (2024)
24. Wu, L., He, X., Wang, X., Zhang, K., Wang, M.: A survey on accuracy-oriented neural recommendation: from collaborative filtering to information-rich recommendation. IEEE Trans. Knowl. Data Eng. **35**(5) (2022)
25. Yang, A., et al.: Qwen3 technical report. arXiv preprint arXiv:2505.09388 (2025)
26. Youdao, N.: BCEmbedding: bilingual and crosslingual embedding for RAG (2023). https://github.com/netease-youdao/BCEmbedding
27. Yuan, Z., et al.: Where to go next for recommender systems? ID-vs. modality-based recommender models revisited. In: Proceedings of the 46th International ACM SIGIR Conference on Research and Development in Information Retrieval, pp. 2639–2649 (2023)
28. Zeng, A., et al.: GLM-4.5: agentic, reasoning, and coding (ARC) foundation models. arXiv preprint arXiv:2508.06471 (2025)
29. Zhang, Q., Xia, L., Cai, X., Yiu, S.M., Huang, C., Jensen, C.S.: Graph augmentation for recommendation. In: 2024 IEEE 40th International Conference on Data Engineering (ICDE), pp. 557–569. IEEE (2024)
30. Zhang, S., Li, H., Qu, H., Wang, Y.: AdaVis: adaptive and explainable visualization recommendation for tabular data. IEEE Trans. Visual Comput. Graph. **30**(9), 5923–5938 (2023)
31. Zheng, Y.: The knowledge system for intelligent cities. Geomat. Inf. Sci. Wuhan Univ. **48**(01), 1–16 (2023)

32. Zheng, Y.: Building bidirectional digital channels between governments and citizens. Big Data Res. **10**(01), 127–140 (2024)
33. Zheng, Y., Yi, X., Qi, D., Pan, Z.: Elementarisation method for public data based on urban knowledge systems. Big Data Res. **10**(04), 130–148 (2024)
34. Zhou, Z.H.: Machine Learning. Springer, Heidelberg (2021)

Industrial AI, Monitoring and Digital Twins

A Machine Learning Framework for Turbofan Health Estimation via Inverse Problem Formulation

Milad Leyli-Abadi[1(✉)], Lucas Thil[1,2], Sébastien Razakarivony[3], Guillaume Doquet[3], and Jesse Read[2]

[1] Institut de recherche technologique SystemX, Palaiseau, France
milad.leyli-abadi@irt-systemx.fr, thil@lix.polytechnique.fr
[2] École Polytechnique, LIX, Palaiseau, France
[3] Safran Tech, Magny-les-Hameaux, France
sebastien.razakarivony@safrangroup.com

Abstract. Estimating the health state of turbofan engines is a challenging ill-posed inverse problem, hindered by sparse sensing and complex nonlinear thermodynamics. Research in this area remains fragmented, with comparisons limited by the use of unrealistic datasets and insufficient exploration of exploitation of temporal information. This work investigates how to recover component-level health indicators from operational sensor data under realistic degradation and maintenance patterns. To support this study, we introduce a new dataset that incorporates industry-oriented complexities such as maintenance events and usage changes. Using this dataset, we establish an initial benchmark that compares steady-state and nonstationary data-driven models, and Bayesian filters – classic families of methods used to solve this problem. In addition to this benchmark, we introduce self-supervised learning (SSL) approaches that learn latent representations without access to true health labels, a scenario reflective of real-world operational constraints. By comparing the downstream estimation performance of these unsupervised representations against the direct prediction baselines, we establish a practical lower bound on the difficulty to solve this inverse problem. Our results reveal that traditional filters remain strong baselines, while SSL methods reveal the intrinsic complexity of health estimation and highlight the need for more advanced and interpretable inference strategies. For reproducibility, both the generated dataset and the implementation used in this work are made accessible (https://zenodo.org/records/20647259, https://github.com/IRT-SystemX/turbofan-condition-monitoring). The Appendix section is available through the Github repository (https://github.com/IRT-SystemX/turbofan-condition-monitoring/blob/main/paper/Appendix.pdf).

Supplementary Information The online version contains supplementary material available at https://doi.org/10.1007/978-3-032-37682-4_8.

M. Baratchi et al. (Eds.): ECML PKDD 2026, LNAI 16949, pp. 129–146, 2027.
https://doi.org/10.1007/978-3-032-37682-4_8

Keywords: Turbofan engine health monitoring · Realistic simulation data · Time series modeling · Representation learning · State-space models

1 Introduction

Monitoring the health of turbomachines is critical for ensuring reliable aircraft engine monitoring and enabling predictive maintenance. However, modern aircraft operate in mechanical, thermal, and weight constrained environments, which severely limit the number and placement of onboard sensors. As a consequence, available measurements provide only a partial view of the engine's internal state, making health estimation an ill-posed and under-determined problem: several distinct health states may yield nearly identical sensor values.

Engine health is commonly characterized by a thermodynamic model that relates the different measured temperatures and pressures in and out of the engine, depending on the efficiencies and mass flows of each component of the engine (compressors, turbines). Variations in these two quantities serve as *health indicators*, reflecting the level of degradation in each of these components. Health monitoring therefore needs to solve a challenging inverse problem: retrieving the efficiencies and mass flows from a sparse set of measurements.

While the underlying thermodynamics of a turbofan engine are well understood, solving this inverse problem in practice remains challenging. Traditionally, physics-based methods like Gas Path Analysis (GPA) [27] or Kalman filters [15] heavily rely on accurate prior assumptions and can struggle with modeling errors. In contrast, purely data-driven approaches [11] offer flexibility by learning complex representations from data, but often fail to capture domain-specific degradation mechanisms without vast amounts of realistic time-series.

A critical barrier to advancing this field is the lack of a public benchmark that captures the complex degradation patterns found in real-world turbomachinery. Existing datasets often lack the necessary fidelity to validate algorithms, primarily because they do not provide verifiable ground-truth health indicators for the inverse problem. Consequently, it remains difficult to compare different methodological practices and measure progress towards practical, deployable solutions.

Simulated data with more realistic patterns of conditions and degradation processes, coupled with an available open source simulator, is a critical enabler for developing and validating machine learning models before their deployment in real-world settings. Indeed, this framework gives ground-truth latent variables, required for evaluation, and exhibits specific real-world challenges that could not be controlled on real data only.

In this paper, we study the inverse problem of health estimation of turbofan components from sparse sensor data. Our main contributions are:

- **A realistic turbofan dataset:** We release a public dataset reflecting the challenges of real-world engine health monitoring with realistic degradation mechanisms.

- **Comprehensive baseline evaluation:** Conduct a thorough evaluation of established methods applied to the inverse problem of direct estimation the ground health states from sparse measurements.
- **Self-supervised Learning:** We investigate how effectively representations learned on sensor measurement alone can effectively recover the ground truth health states.

The remainder of the article is organized as follows: the related work is presented in Sect. 2. The dataset and the generation process are described in Sect. 3. The methodologies analyzed and experimented in this work are presented in Sect. 4. The experimental settings and results are shown in Sect. 5. In Sect. 6, we conclude the paper giving insights for future works.

2 Related Works

The turbofan engine performance inverse problem (TEP-IP) has been addressed for more than half a century [27], giving rise to several families of methods, from physics-based filtering to machine-learning regression and hybrid formulations. We first review the main approaches and then broaden the scope with a peek on health-state embeddings and datasets of engine health monitoring. For more detailed information, we redirect the readers to recent surveys [24, 29].

2.1 Embedded Model-Based Approaches

The most common works on solving the TEP-IP are the use of Bayesian estimation, and more particularly Kalman Filters (KF). KF models the health state as a latent state evolving through a process model f and observed through an observation model h, using the formalism of the state space model:

$$x_{t+1} = f(x_t) + v, y_t = h(x_t) + w. \tag{1}$$

In our case, x_t represents the component efficiencies and mass flows, while y_t corresponds to sensor measurements. v and w are random variables. The observation model h is usually derived from the thermodynamic simulator, whereas the system-level degradation model f requires assumptions or simplifications, that are not always easy to define (for complete notations, see Appendix A). Many papers using many variants of KF have been published over the years [15, 17, 23], making the Kalman Filter the strongest baseline on this matter. However, these papers do not provide the datasets to reproduce their experiments.

2.2 Machine Learning Approaches

An alternative line of work uses supervised learning to approximate the inverse of the thermodynamic model [9, 16, 30]. These methods use the thermodynamic model by first building a dataset of pairs (x, y) and then learning g such that $x = g(y)$. When the thermodynamic model is not - invertible, the behavior of the estimator strongly depends on architectural choices and regularization strategies. Some more recent works try to adapt estimation strategies, in particular with Reinforcement Learning [22,26], mixing the classic KF and data-driven approaches. However, all of these methods have low explainability.

2.3 Embedding Health States and Self-supervised Learning

Beyond direct inversion, much research targets the prediction of remaining useful life (RUL), but often neglects the explainability of intermediate states. To represent the current condition, others build data-driven health indicators [14]; however, since these are not a core requirement, they lack inherent physical meaning and require post-hoc explanation, limiting diagnostic value. Similarly, some works embed engine states data-drivenly [12,19], but without links to physics-based models, these embeddings also depend on external interpretation and cannot serve as directly meaningful health indicators.

Further works tend to construct features such as reconstruction error or novelty detection to act as a proxy for a health indicator extracted from the output or latent space [10,25], or induce a temporal aspect in the latent representations [13] by computing soft assignment pairs in the observation space. Other methods such as the JEPA architecture focus in predicting directly in the latent [5,8], promising better representation and planning abilities [6].

2.4 Datasets

Most reproducible studies rely on the NASA C-MAPSS dataset [21], which provides run-to-failure trajectories generated from a thermodynamic simulator but assumes a non-realistic and specific degradation pattern. Furthermore, the underlying engine model has some access restrictions. The more recent New-C-MAPSS dataset [4] introduces realistic flight profiles and multiple failure modes, though still with fast degradation dynamics and no maintenance interventions, as any normal engine would encounter in its life. Finally, the PHM2025 challenge dataset [18] provides more accurate degradation, with simulation-based maintenance events. However, it presents only a handful of examples and fixed degradation rates, making it less suited for learning richly parameterized health dynamics.

3 Data and Scenario Design

3.1 Turbomachine Model

Our experiments rely on the OpenDeckSMR simulator [20], a steady-state turbofan performance model designed following industrial engine-simulation practices. This tool solves the thermodynamic balance equations across all engine components to compute temperatures, pressures, power and rotation speeds. Given a set of health parameters—component efficiencies and mass flows—and a specified operating condition (e.g., take-off, climb, cruise), the simulator provides the corresponding sensor measurements. This makes it suitable for generating consistent synthetic data for health-state estimation experiments. The simulator uses ten Health Indicators (HIs), five pairs of (efficiency, mass flow) coefficients of degradation. These input and output variables are summarized in Table 1.

Table 1. Sensor inputs and corresponding engine health indicators. The prefix *PHASE* denotes the flight condition, which can be *Cruise*, *Takeoff*, *Climb1*, or *Climb2*. As such, there are 28 input features and 10 outputs.

Inputs (Sensors)		Outputs (Health Indicators)	
Name	Description	Name	Description
PHASE_HPC_Tout	HPC outlet temperature [K]	deg_CmpBst_s_mapEff_in	Booster compressor efficiency
PHASE_HP_Nmech	HP shaft speed [rpm]	deg_CmpBst_s_mapWc_in	Booster compressor mass flow
PHASE_HPC_Tin	HPC inlet temperature [K]	deg_CmpFan_s_mapEff_in	Fan efficiency
PHASE_LPT_Tin	LPT inlet temperature [K]	deg_CmpFan_s_mapWc_in	Fan mass flow
PHASE_Fuel_flow	Fuel flow [kg/s]	deg_CmpH_s_mapEff_in	HPC efficiency
PHASE_HPC_Pout_st	HPC outlet pressure [Pa]	deg_CmpH_s_mapWc_in	HPC mass flow
PHASE_LP_Nmech	LP shaft speed [rpm]	deg_TrbH_s_mapEff_in	HPT efficiency
		deg_TrbH_s_mapWc_in	HPT mass flow
		deg_TrbL_s_mapEff_in	LPT efficiency
		deg_TrbL_s_mapWc_in	LPT mass flow

3.2 Data Generation

Given a health state at timestep $\boldsymbol{x}_t \in \mathbb{R}^{10}$ and an Operational Condition $\boldsymbol{OC}$, the physical simulator described in the previous section allows to simulate the sensor values $\boldsymbol{y}_t = h(\boldsymbol{x}_t, \boldsymbol{OC})$ at different locations of the engine. This steady-state computation scheme is not adapted to model the real-world problem. Generally, the turbofan engines may degrade gradually over time based on different conditions, usage and maintenance operations performed during their lifetime. The degradation speed may also change with respect to these conditions and regarding the different components in the engine. For example the high pressure compressor (Compressor HP in Fig. 1) degrades faster than the other components, as it is exposed to much higher temperature.

To be representative of realistic problem configuration, in this paper, we design degradation trajectories scenarios taking into account the above mentioned considerations. In this sense, each degradation trajectory S represents a multivariate time series of dimension 10 (number of health indicators corresponding to different components of the engine). Each component of the engine has its own specific degradation pattern and boundaries (minimum and maximum authorized values). Three different degradation speeds (i.e., *slow*, *normal* and *fast*) are considered. The components may degrade following a probability distribution over the three speed values and also to transition from one speed to another with a specific frequency (e.g., every 100 timesteps). The choice of 3 degradation speeds could have been made continuous, but the main feature

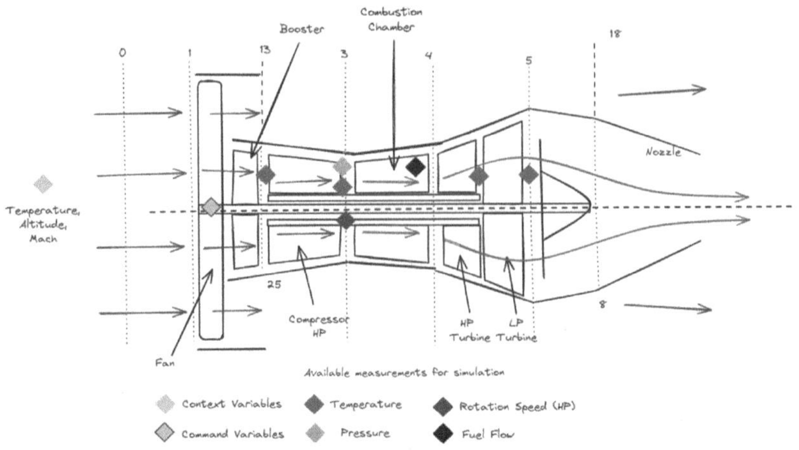

Fig. 1. Turbofan engine; with the courtesy of the team of OpenDeckSMR.

wanted here is multi-modality of the underlying distribution. A multimodal distribution of speed could have been done but without a clear benefit and to the cost of a greater complexity. Maintenance operations could also take place after certain time steps, picking a random value within the interval [200; 500]. The maintenance events allow to partially recover the previous health state, which is controlled by a coefficient selected randomly in the interval [0.6; 0.8]. The generation procedure is summarized in pseudo-code 1 and the generated data can be obtained through this link [3].

For the sake of our experiments and based on the above-mentioned parameters, an ensemble of more than 500 trajectories of health indicators are generated with the maximum length of 2000 time steps, on four operating conditions. An example of a trajectory is shown in Fig. 2. As can be seen, the maintenance events could occur during the lifetime of the engine (the vertical boxes), where we observe that the engine recovers a percentage of its health state from previous operation period. It should be noted that some of the trajectories may have different (shorter) lengths, when one of the health indicators violates the authorized boundary values.

For each trajectory, the sensor measurements are simulated using Turbomachine model and including 4 operational conditions, i.e., *Cruise*, *Takeoff*, *Climb1*, *Climb2*[1]. The measurements for different flight phases are shown in Fig. 3. As can be seen, we added a bounded noise ϵ to each sensor measurement y to approach the real-world condition as follows:

---

[1] It is worth noting that the proposed model relies on a time-scale separation assumption, where health states are assumed to be constant during a flight, while slowly evolving between flights. Indeed, the states for take-off, cruise and climbs are the same. Given that degradation evolves over very long horizons, this simplification is well justified.

Pseudo-code 1. Data generation process

Input: # sequences (N), # timesteps (T), Operational condition (C)
Output: Degradation trajectories (health indicators) $\boldsymbol{X} \in \mathbb{R}^{10}$
  Simulated sensor values (measures) $\boldsymbol{Z} \in \mathbb{R}^7$
Select an operational condition in the set $\{$*Cruise*, *Takeoff*, *Climb1*, *Climb2*$\}$
Initialize the health indicators $\boldsymbol{X}_0 \leftarrow \mathbf{0}$. (Full health state)
repeat
  for each timestep $t = 1..T$ **do**
    for each health indicator x in $\boldsymbol{x}$ **do**
      if t matches a maintenance event **then**
        $x_t \leftarrow$ recover a random fraction $\lambda \in [0.6, 0.8]$ of past degradation and update
      end if
      if speed change frequency reached **then**
        $\mu, \sigma \leftarrow$ resample degradation speed with state-specific probability distribution
      end if
      $m, \epsilon \leftarrow$ Sample slope $\mathcal{N}(\mu, \sigma)$ and a Gaussian noise wrt. the selected speed
      $x_t \leftarrow m + \epsilon$ Update and clip health indicator (using boundary values in Appendix B)
      $z_t \leftarrow \Psi(x_t, C)$ Compute the sensor values using the simulator
      $\tilde{z}_t \leftarrow z_t + \epsilon$ Add a bounded noise into each sensor channel
    end for
  end for
until required number of sequences N
return All trajectory sequence $\boldsymbol{X}$ and corresponding simulated sensor values $\boldsymbol{Z}$

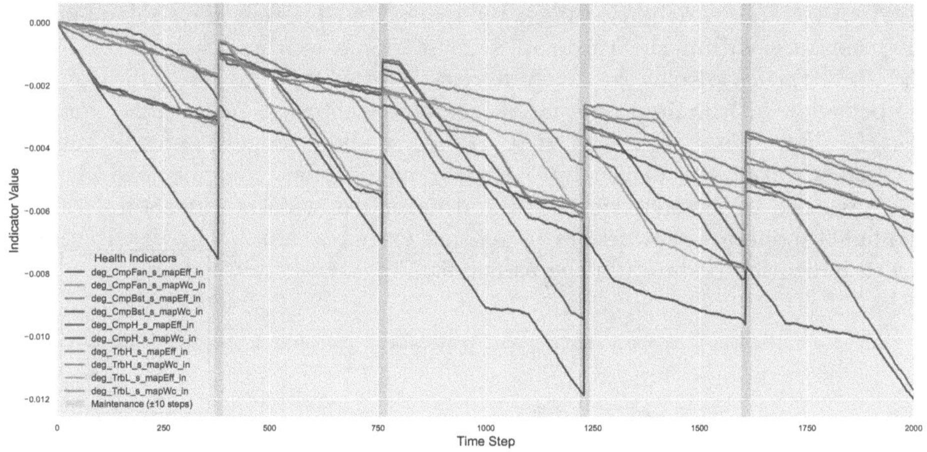

Fig. 2. Generated degradation trajectories for 10 health indicators and 1 engine

$$\Delta = y_{max} - y_{min}; \qquad \tilde{y}(t) = y(t) + \epsilon(t), \qquad \epsilon(t) \sim \mathcal{U}\left(-\gamma\Delta, \gamma\Delta\right), \tag{2}$$

where the $\mathcal{U}$ represents the uniform distribution and gamma controls the noise level which is set to 0.02.

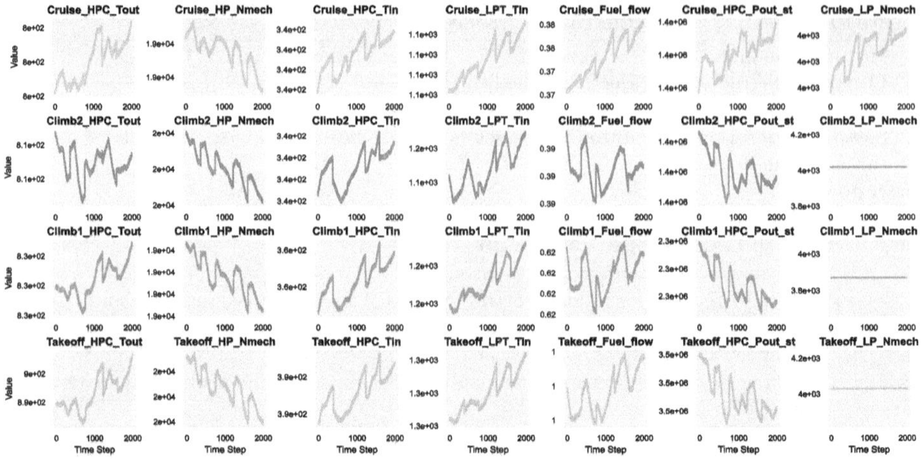

Fig. 3. Simulated sensor values (measurements) for the trajectory in Fig. 2 and corresponding to four flight phases, i.e., *Cruise*, *Takeoff*, *Climb1*, *Climb2*.

The distribution of the seven sensor variables and four operational conditions is shown in Fig. 4. For the sake of comparison, these features are scaled using Min-Max normalization. In this graphic, each sensor exhibits a distinct distribution and variability range, reflecting the different physical quantities they measure within the turbofan system. Some sensors, such as *LPT_Tin* and *HP_Nmech*, display relatively narrow interquartile ranges, indicating stable behavior with limited fluctuation across trajectories. In contrast, variables like *HP_Tout*, *Fuel_flow*, and *HPC_Pout_st* show broader spreads, suggesting higher variability driven by operating conditions or engine load changes. The presence of asymmetric boxes and extended whiskers in several sensors highlights moderate skewness or occasional extreme values. The distribution of health indicators is shown in the Appendix Fig. 1.

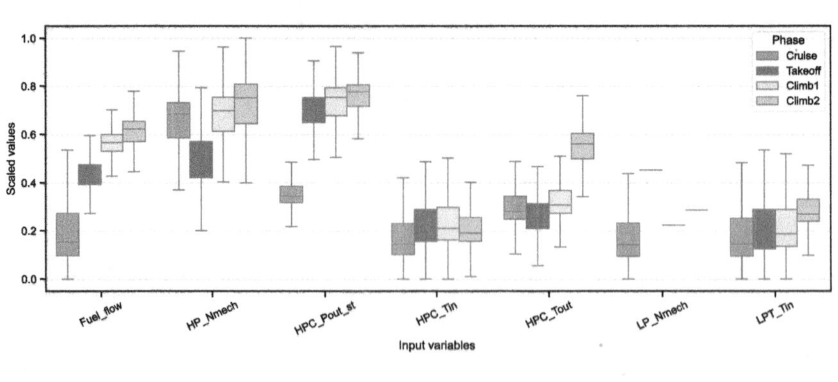

Fig. 4. Sensor variables (measurements) distribution grouped by 4 flight phases.

4 Models

4.1 Baselines

Steady-State Approaches. The steady-state hypothesis considers no temporal dependence between the observations as can be seen in Fig. 5a and each sample is independent and identically distributed (i.i.d). In this configuration, we infer directly the HI state (x_i) from the sensor measurements (y_i). In our experiments, we have considered Gradient Boosting (GB), an ensemble and decision tree-based approach, and also a Multi-Layer Perceptron (MLP) which is a deep neural network-based approach.

Non-stationary Approach. In contrast to the steady-state assumption, temporal-based approaches explicitly model the temporal dependencies between successive observations, thereby adhering to a non-stationary hypothesis. As illustrated in Fig. 5b, these models assume that the current health indicator (HI) state (x_t) cannot be inferred solely from the instantaneous measurement (y_t), but rather depends on the historical sequence of sensor readings ($y_{t-L+1}, \dots, y_t$) and their underlying temporal dynamics. This formulation enables the model to capture trends, degradation patterns, and short or long-term dependencies that are essential in prognostics scenarios where system behavior evolves over time with the presence of maintenance events. To exploit this temporal structure, we consider recurrent or sequence-based architectures capable of processing ordered data. In our experiments, we utilize Gated Recurrent Units (GRU), which is a widely adopted recurrent neural network (RNN) variant designed to mitigate vanishing gradient issues and effectively retain relevant information over long horizons.

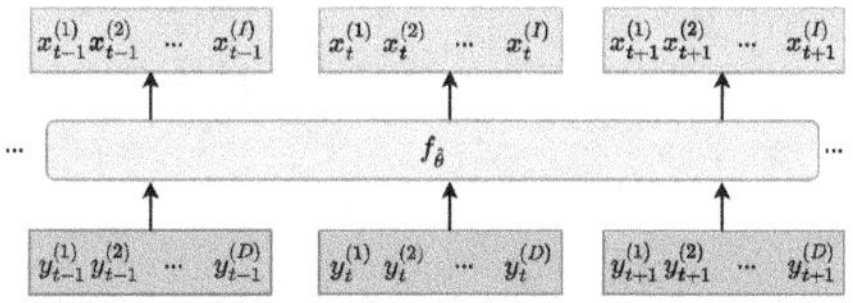
(a) Steady-state hypothesis

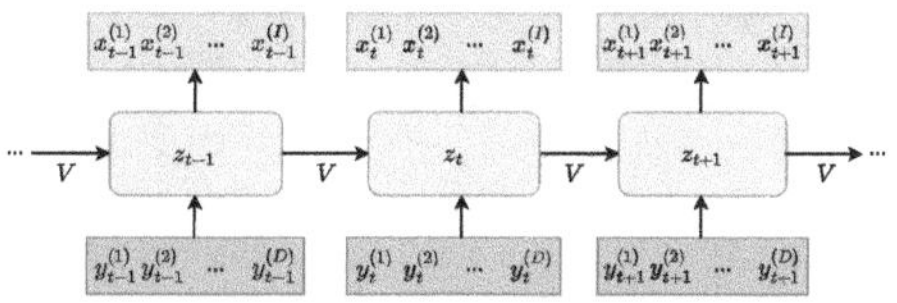
(b) Non-stationary data hypothesis

Fig. 5. Two model categories considering stationary and non-stationary hypotheses. Based on steady-state hypothesis, the model finds a mapping between inputs and outputs. Based on non-stationary hypothesis, the model takes into account the temporal dynamics over time for prediction of outputs.

Bayesian Filtering. In this section, we opt for Kalman Filter method, and more specifically we use an Unscented Kalman Filter (UKF). UKF is a non-linear version of UKF, well suited for our problematic, where the simulator is not linear. We followed the standard formulation and squared-root implementation of [28]. The system is defined as:

$$x_t = g(x_{t-1}) + w_t, \qquad y_t = h(x_t) + v_t, \tag{3}$$

where x_t denotes the engine health state, y_t the observed sensor measurements, and $w_t \sim \mathcal{N}(0, Q)$, $v_t \sim \mathcal{N}(0, R)$. The observation function h corresponds to the OpenDeckSMR simulator, while the state-transition function g is taken as the identity, a common assumption when no explicit degradation dynamics are available. The process noise covariance Q is set to a diagonal matrix with value 10^{-7}, and R is derived from the known sensor noise specifications, divided by 10. These Q and R values where obtained by shallow grid-search. UKF hyperparameters follow the canonical settings typically used for mildly nonlinear systems $((\alpha = 1, \beta = 2, \kappa = 0))$.[2]

4.2 SSL Methods

In many industrial scenarios, access to ground-truth health indicators is unavailable, requiring models to learn representations from sensor data alone. We employ two self-supervised learning approaches: an autoencoder that operates in the observation space (reconstruction) and a JEPA architecture that predicts representations in the latent space. The extracted latents z_t are used for the downstream HI estimation task, as illustrated in Fig. 6.

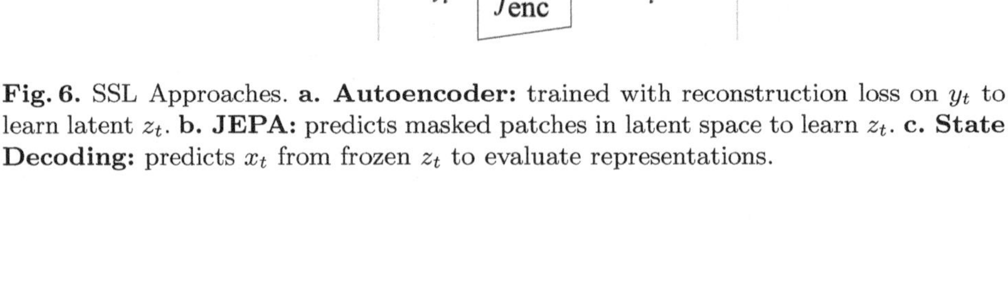

Fig. 6. SSL Approaches. **a. Autoencoder:** trained with reconstruction loss on y_t to learn latent z_t. **b. JEPA:** predicts masked patches in latent space to learn z_t. **c. State Decoding:** predicts x_t from frozen z_t to evaluate representations.

[2] We do not address the simulation-to-reality gap (i.e., inaccuracies in R, Q, or the models g and h). Even in this favorable configuration, our results show that the UKF still leaves room for improvement, making this an interesting direction for future research.

Autoencoder (AE) learns a compressed representation z_t of the input sensor data y_t by training to reconstruct the original input. The encoder f_{enc} maps y_t to a latent representation $z_t = f_{\text{enc}}(y_t)$, and the decoder f_{dec} reconstructs the input as $\hat{y}_t = f_{\text{dec}}(z_t)$. The training objective minimizes the reconstruction error:

$$\mathcal{L}_{\text{AE}} = \|y_t - \hat{y}_t\|_2^2$$

This loss operates entirely in the observation space without requiring ground-truth labels x_t.

Joint Embedding Predictive Architecture (JEPA). While the autoencoder reconstructs in the observation space, JEPA [5] learns by predicting the embeddings of masked patches in a latent space. This approach is well-suited for temporal sensor data, where relationships between time steps can be exploited. We adopt a Video JEPA (VJEPA) variant [6,7] adapted for multivariate time series with multiple sensors and operating contexts.

As shown in Fig. 6, the architecture comprises three components: an online encoder, a target encoder, and a predictor. Input sensor windows are first divided into temporal patches via a 3D convolution. A random masking strategy divides patches into visible context and masked targets. The online encoder processes only visible patches, while the target encoder processes the full sequence to provide stable targets. The predictor attempts to reconstruct the representations of masked patches from the visible context. The training objective minimizes the L1 loss between predicted and target representations for masked positions:

$$\mathcal{L}_{\text{VJEPA}} = \|\text{pred}_{\text{masked}} - \text{target}_{\text{masked}}\|_1$$

Gradients flow only through the online encoder and predictor; the target encoder is updated as an exponential moving average (EMA) of the online encoder to prevent representational collapse. Like the autoencoder, VJEPA is trained without access to ground-truth health indicators x_t. After training, the online encoder extracts latent representations z_t for downstream evaluation through a linear probe evaluated on the underlying states x [2]. Detailed architecture specifications are provided in Appendix D.

5 Experiments

5.1 Experimental Setup

Problem Configuration. For all experiments, the models aim to estimate the health indicator (HI) vector $\boldsymbol{x}_t$ at each time step t using the corresponding sensor measurement vector $\boldsymbol{y}_t$ as the primary source of information. Depending on the model typology, additional historical observations may be incorporated to capture temporal dependencies and long-term system dynamics. For temporal models operating on full sequences, all trajectories are padded with zeros to ensure a uniform sequence length across samples. During training, these padded regions are systematically masked so that they do not contribute to the loss computation or parameter updates, thereby preventing any bias introduced by artificial padding. In addition, all input and output variables are normalized using standard scaling or Min–Max normalization, ensuring stable optimization and comparable feature magnitudes across sensors and HIs. Maintenance effects are implicitly captured through their impact on the observed signals (e.g., abrupt shifts or performance recovery). This approach reflects realistic deployment conditions, where maintenance logs may not always be available in real time. Furthermore, while maintenance events can provide valuable contextual information, incorporating them directly into the model may introduce biases or shortcut learning behaviors, where predictions rely disproportionately on intervention markers rather than on the underlying physical relationships between degradation and measurements. Nevertheless, the impact of obtaining this information is of interest, and could be looked upon in future work.

Datasets. The full set of degradation trajectories S is divided into three disjoint subsets containing 70%, 10%, and 20% of the sequences, which serve respectively as the training, validation, and test datasets. The training set is used to learn the parameters of the models with trainable components, while the validation set is primarily employed for neural network–based approaches to monitor learning behavior and detect potential overfitting. All methods are evaluated on the same test partition to enable a fair and homogeneous comparison. To ensure robustness and reduce performance variability due to dataset partitioning, we perform a 5-fold cross-validation over the sequence set, ensuring that each degradation trajectory acts once as the test sequence. Final performance metrics are reported as the mean and standard deviation computed across the five folds.

Hyperparameter Tuning. To ensure fair and optimized performance across all models, we perform automated hyperparameter search using the Optuna framework [1], a state-of-the-art hyperparameter optimization system based on a define-by-run API and efficient pruning and sampling strategies. Optuna enables the dynamic construction of search spaces and employs advanced algorithms such as Tree-structured Parzen Estimators (TPE) to guide the exploration toward promising regions of the parameter space. During optimization, each model configuration is evaluated using the validation set, and unpromising trials are pruned early to reduce computational cost. The number of trials and search ranges are adapted to the complexity of each model family (e.g., tree-based, feedforward networks, recurrent networks).

Evaluation Criteria. To evaluate and compare the performance of the models, we employ three complementary criteria: the Symmetric Mean Absolute Percentage Error (SMAPE), the Root Mean Squared Error (RMSE), and the Pearson correlation coefficient (P.Corr.) computed between the ground-truth health indicators and the predicted values. These metrics were selected because they capture different and equally important aspects of estimation quality. SMAPE provides a scale-independent measure of relative error, making it suitable for comparing deviations across health indicators with different magnitudes. RMSE emphasizes larger errors due to its quadratic formulation, thereby offering insight into the model's ability to avoid large deviations that may be critical in prognostics applications. Finally, Pearson correlation measures the linear association between predictions and ground truth, reflecting how well the models capture the underlying trends and degradation dynamics. Even if correlation does not capture the value, it allows to see how well a method is performing for trend following, and important use case for health monitoring. Indeed, even with approximate values, the trend of an indicator helps building maintenance strategies.

5.2 Experimental Results

Table 2 reports the performance of tested models for the estimation of the ten HIs from sensor observations. A first observation is that all models achieve good correlation performance across most indicators. This suggests that, despite the underdetermined nature of the treated inverse problem, the simulated sensor signals contain sufficient information to recover the direction of degradation. However, SMAPE show that the overall error is still high, with minimum average value of 14%. It comes from the cumulative errors for the temporal methods, and from the high noise level for stationary ones.

Table 2. Prediction performance for 10 health indicators across model families. Results are reported as mean ± standard deviation over 5-fold cross-validation using SMAPE, RMSE ($\times 10^3$), and Pearson correlation. It should be noted that the mean and std reported in avg column is computed directly on the test sets and is not the average of the 10 columns.

Model	Metric	HI1	HI2	HI3	HI4	HI5	HI6	HI7	HI8	HI9	HI10	Avg
Steady-state												
GB	SMAPE	0.24 ± 0.21	0.19 ± 0.20	0.30 ± 0.26	0.05 ± 0.13	0.09 ± 0.14	0.18 ± 0.21	0.19 ± 0.19	0.16 ± 0.18	0.24 ± 0.22	0.33 ± 0.28	0.20 ± 0.09
	RMSE	2.0 ± 0.10	1.0 ± 0.09	2.0 ± 0.08	0.3 ± 0.02	1.0 ± 0.03	2.0 ± 0.10	1.0 ± 0.07	1.0 ± 0.05	2.0 ± 0.03	3.0 ± 0.10	1.53 ± 0.79
	P.Corr.	0.93 ± 0.00	0.96 ± 0.00	0.88 ± 0.01	1.00 ± 0.00	0.99 ± 0.00	0.97 ± 0.00	0.96 ± 0.00	0.97 ± 0.00	0.93 ± 0.00	0.87 ± 0.01	0.95 ± 0.04
MLP	SMAPE	0.20 ± 0.25	0.15 ± 0.23	0.28 ± 0.25	0.05 ± 0.15	0.07 ± 0.16	0.12 ± 0.21	0.17 ± 0.22	0.12 ± 0.21	0.22 ± 0.24	0.30 ± 0.30	0.17 ± 0.24
	RMSE	1.24 ± 0.05	0.86 ± 0.03	2.07 ± 0.08	0.19 ± 0.01	0.62 ± 0.03	1.24 ± 0.05	1.11 ± 0.06	0.53 ± 0.04	1.59 ± 0.04	2.19 ± 0.11	1.16 ± 0.62
	P.Corr.	0.97 ± 0.01	0.99 ± 0.01	0.91 ± 0.01	1.00 ± 0.01	1.00 ± 0.01	0.99 ± 0.01	0.98 ± 0.01	1.00 ± 0.01	0.96 ± 0.01	0.91 ± 0.01	0.97 ± 0.03
Temporal-based												
GRU	SMAPE	0.12 ± 0.22	0.09 ± 0.19	0.27 ± 0.24	0.04 ± 0.14	0.05 ± 0.16	0.08 ± 0.19	0.16 ± 0.21	0.07 ± 0.19	0.22 ± 0.23	0.28 ± 0.26	0.14 ± 0.22
	RMSE	0.63 ± 0.05	0.48 ± 0.04	2.07 ± 0.07	0.20 ± 0.01	0.39 ± 0.02	0.68 ± 0.03	1.09 ± 0.05	0.31 ± 0.03	1.56 ± 0.03	2.13 ± 0.11	0.95 ± 0.69
	P.Corr.	0.99 ± 0.01	1.00 ± 0.01	0.91 ± 0.01	1.00 ± 0.01	1.00 ± 0.01	1.00 ± 0.01	0.98 ± 0.01	1.00 ± 0.01	0.96 ± 0.01	0.92 ± 0.01	0.97 ± 0.03
State-space models												
K.F.	SMAPE	0.10 ± 0.23	0.08 ± 0.20	0.35 ± 0.37	0.03 ± 0.13	0.04 ± 0.16	0.11 ± 0.28	0.18 ± 0.30	0.07 ± 0.20	0.24 ± 0.27	0.26 ± 0.32	0.15 ± 0.11
	RMSE	0.47 ± 0.01	0.42 ± 0.01	2.14 ± 0.07	0.17 ± 0.00	0.36 ± 0.01	0.89 ± 0.02	0.74 ± 0.02	0.35 ± 0.01	1.44 ± 0.04	1.55 ± 0.05	0.85 ± 0.65
	P.Corr.	1.00 ± 0.00	1.00 ± 0.00	0.91 ± 0.00	1.00 ± 0.00	1.00 ± 0.00	1.00 ± 0.00	0.99 ± 0.00	1.00 ± 0.00	0.96 ± 0.00	0.96 ± 0.00	0.98 ± 0.03
Two-stage SSL representational												
AE	SMAPE	0.25 ± 0.05	0.28 ± 0.05	0.24 ± 0.04	0.23 ± 0.04	0.35 ± 0.12	0.38 ± 0.06	0.28 ± 0.06	0.34 ± 0.09	0.26 ± 0.04	0.32 ± 0.06	0.29 ± 0.05
	RMSE	2.53 ± 0.56	2.88 ± 0.53	2.38 ± 0.36	2.33 ± 0.40	3.35 ± 1.20	3.78 ± 0.67	2.83 ± 0.63	3.40 ± 0.93	2.58 ± 0.33	3.18 ± 0.65	2.92 ± 0.49
	P.Corr.	0.88 ± 0.03	0.88 ± 0.03	0.88 ± 0.03	0.88 ± 0.03	0.88 ± 0.03	0.88 ± 0.03	0.88 ± 0.03	0.88 ± 0.03	0.88 ± 0.03	0.88 ± 0.03	0.88 ± 0.03
VJEPA	SMAPE	0.33 ± 0.01	0.32 ± 0.01	0.33 ± 0.02	0.30 ± 0.03	0.19 ± 0.01	0.21 ± 0.01	0.32 ± 0.03	0.31 ± 0.03	0.31 ± 0.01	0.34 ± 0.01	0.30 ± 0.01
	RMSE	2.38 ± 0.15	2.44 ± 0.17	2.46 ± 0.16	2.11 ± 0.37	2.23 ± 0.08	2.58 ± 0.14	2.32 ± 0.08	2.29 ± 0.37	2.47 ± 0.24	2.60 ± 0.21	2.40 ± 0.11
	P.Corr.	0.89 ± 0.00	0.88 ± 0.02	0.88 ± 0.01	0.91 ± 0.03	0.97 ± 0.00	0.96 ± 0.00	0.90 ± 0.01	0.90 ± 0.02	0.89 ± 0.02	0.87 ± 0.01	0.91 ± 0.01

Another important fact is that performance is consistently worst (across all 3 considered metrics SMAPE, RMSE and correlation) for HI3, HI9 and HI10. This reflects weaker observability of certain degradation factors in the thermodynamic model, and is consistent with prior domain knowledge. Indeed, the Low-Pressure Turbine (HI 9 and 10) is located at the end of the airflow path and integrates the effects of upstream components, resulting in aggregated and highly coupled thermodynamic responses. As a consequence, isolating its specific contribution from measurement data becomes challenging. Similarly, HI3 (booster compressor mass flow) is inherently coupled with fan dynamics, as both components jointly influence mass flow and pressure characteristics. This strong interdependence reduces the identifiability of HI3 from the available measurements alone.

In this work, observability is understood in a practical sense and based on domain knowledge. A health indicator is considered observable if variations in that underlying degradation parameter induce distinct and measurable effects on the available sensor signals. Conversely, a variable is weakly observable when its impact on the measurements is either small (low sensitivity) or difficult to disentangle from other factors (strong coupling). Further theoretical analysis is left for future work.

Overall, this weaker performance on structurally less observable HIs highlights an important limitation of purely data-driven inversion. By contrast, the two-stage SSL approaches interestingly exhibit a much more uniform performance across indicators. This suggests that they learned representations capture global structure in the observations, even if they lack the resolution required for precise component-level attribution.

Concerning temporal information, if Steady-state models achieve interesting performances, the non-stationary models are better. As expected, exploiting the *historical context* of the temporal series can help to disambiguate sensor patterns that pertain to similar instantaneous states. Consequently, incorporating temporal structure appears beneficial even when individual observations are informative by themselves[3].

Unscented Kalman Filter (UKF) provides the best overall performance on several indicators, using also the time information. However, as previously noted in the global statement, the UKF does not perfectly recover all indicators, leaving room for improvements through hybrid approaches or more accurate degradation dynamics modeling. Indeed, its most important problem is the drift of its estimation through time, and difficulty in presence of maintenance pattern, as shown in Fig. 7.

In contrast, the two-stage SSL approaches exhibit significantly higher errors, although they still maintain correlations with the ground-truth health indicators. This gap is expected since these methods do not have access to HI labels during representation learning and must rely solely on the structure of the sensor data. Their performance therefore provides an approximate lower bound on how well the health state can be inferred from sensor observations alone without supervision. In consequence, the results indicate that while SSL representations

[3] As for the model mismatch question, knowledge of the exact degradation distribution is of importance. However, we can see here that even knowing perfectly this distribution is not enough to solve the problem.

capture a meaningful structure in the data, they remain insufficient for precise component-level estimation without task-specific supervision.

Overall, these results highlight three key insights. First, the turbofan inverse problem remains partially non-observable, with certain indicators systematically harder to estimate. Second, temporal information helps to deal with this difficulty, but none of the algorithms completely solve the different challenges. Third, unsupervised representation learning captures global structure but still falls short of supervised inversion for precise health estimation, suggesting that future work should investigate hybrid strategies combining physics-informed modeling with representation learning.

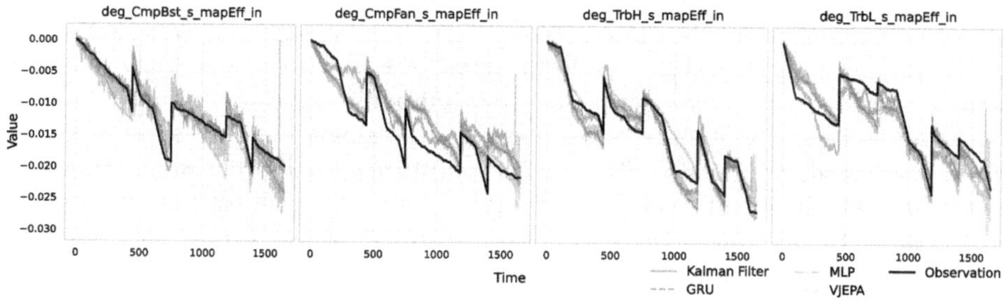

Fig. 7. True health indicators versus predictions made by different models for four HI trajectories with varying levels of prediction difficulty.

To better understand the behavior of the different models in predicting the health indicators, we compare their prediction profiles in Fig. 7. For clarity and conciseness, four representative indicators are selected based on their varying levels of prediction difficulty. Among them, the Booster Compressor indicator (deg_CmpBst) exhibits the simplest dynamics and is generally the easiest for the models to estimate. In contrast, the remaining three indicators associated with the Fan, High-Pressure Turbine, and Low-Pressure Turbine are difficult HIs as previously discussed, and are difficult to estimate for all models. As shown in the figure, the MLP and GRU models exhibit broadly similar behaviors, both capturing the global trend of the health indicator trajectories. However, the GRU produces smoother estimates with noticeably reduced noise, as it considers temporal dependencies. The Kalman Filter adjusts its predictions according to observed variations (such as changes in degradation speed or maintenance events) and performs well in simpler scenarios. Nevertheless, it struggles when confronted with abrupt or highly nonlinear changes in the system. Finally, VJEPA successfully follows the general evolution of the health indicators, but its predictions remain sensitive to noise in the input signals, and show higher variations for prediction of the trajectories.

6 Conclusions and Perspectives

Estimating turbofan component health from sparse sensor measurements is a fundamentally ill-posed inverse problem. In this work, we introduced a benchmark setting designed to study this challenge under more realistic operational conditions, including heterogeneous degradation dynamics, maintenance interventions, and multiple operating regimes, with hundreds of samples spanning more than 1000 time steps. Within this framework, we compared several modeling paradigms ranging from direct supervised regression and temporal sequence models to state-space filtering and self-supervised representation learning.

Our empirical study highlights three structural properties of the problem. First, while supervised approaches can recover a portion of the health state, performance varies substantially across indicators, confirming that ambiguity in the inverse mapping is not uniform across the system. Second, the comparison of modeling strategies suggests that temporal structure can help reduce the non-observability of the system. However, no single method is able to accurately recover all HI. Finally, SSL methods capture global structure in the sensor space but remain insufficient for accurate component-level estimation without supervision. In this sense, these approaches provide a useful reference point for what can be inferred from sensor observations alone, and highlight the gap that task-specific supervision or physics-based constraints must bridge.

Taken together, these results emphasize that turbofan health estimation is a structured inference problem shaped by partial observability, temporal dynamics, and physical constraints. A promising direction for future work is therefore to design hybrid approaches that jointly leverage these three sources of structure. Beyond our methodological comparison, this work also aims to provide the community with a practical experimental framework for studying turbofan health estimation on an industry-oriented dataset.

While the present study demonstrates the effectiveness of the proposed framework on simulated data generated to represent the real-world degradation behavior, the transition toward real-world deployment remains an important next step. The study of the impact between of reality-gap (differences between engine models and real engines) needs further investigation. Future work will focus on a sim-to-real transfer strategy, where the model trained on synthetic data is adapted to operational engine data through domain adaptation, calibration, or transfer learning techniques.

References

1. Akiba, T., Sano, S., Yanase, T., Ohta, T., Koyama, M.: Optuna: a next-generation hyperparameter optimization framework. In: Proceedings of the 25th ACM SIGKDD International Conference on Knowledge Discovery & Data Mining, pp. 2623–2631 (2019)
2. Alain, G., Bengio, Y.: Understanding intermediate layers using linear classifier probes. arXiv preprint arXiv:1610.01644 (2016)

3. Anonymous: Health indicator degradation dataset (2026). https://sandbox.zenodo.org/records/469530, anonymous dataset provided for peer review. Link will be replaced upon publication
4. Arias Chao, M., Kulkarni, C., Goebel, K., Fink, O.: Aircraft engine run-to-failure dataset under real flight conditions for prognostics and diagnostics. Data **6**(1), 5 (2021)
5. Assel, H.V., Ibrahim, M., Biancalani, T., Regev, A., Balestriero, R.: Joint embedding vs reconstruction: provable benefits of latent space prediction for self supervised learning, October 2025. https://doi.org/10.48550/arXiv.2505.12477. arXiv:2505.12477 [cs]
6. Assran, M., Bardes, A., Fan, D., et al.: V-JEPA 2: self-supervised video models enable understanding, prediction and planning, June 2025. https://doi.org/10.48550/arXiv.2506.09985. arXiv:2506.09985 [cs]
7. Bardes, A., et al.: V-JEPA: latent video prediction for visual representation learning (2024)
8. Bordes, F., Garrido, Q., Kao, J.T., Williams, A., Rabbat, M., Dupoux, E.: IntPhys 2: benchmarking intuitive physics understanding in complex synthetic environments, June 2025. https://doi.org/10.48550/arXiv.2506.09849. arXiv:2506.09849 [cs]
9. Castillo, I.G., Loboda, I., Pérez Ruiz, J.L.: Data-driven models for gas turbine online diagnosis. Machines **9**(12), 372 (2021)
10. Costa, N., Sánchez, L.: Variational encoding approach for interpretable assessment of remaining useful life estimation. Reliab. Eng. Syst. Saf. **222**, 108353 (2022). https://doi.org/10.1016/j.ress.2022.108353. https://linkinghub.elsevier.com/retrieve/pii/S0951832022000321
11. De Giorgi, M.G., Strafella, L., Menga, N., Ficarella, A.: Intelligent combined neural network and kernel principal component analysis tool for engine health monitoring purposes. Aerospace **9**(3), 118 (2022)
12. De Pater, I., Mitici, M.: Novel metrics to evaluate probabilistic remaining useful life prognostics with applications to turbofan engines. PHM Soc. Eur. Conf. **7**(1), 96–109 (2022). https://doi.org/10.36001/phme.2022.v7i1.3320. https://papers.phmsociety.org/index.php/phme/article/view/3320
13. Lee, S., Park, T., Lee, K.: Soft contrastive learning for time series, March 2024. https://doi.org/10.48550/arXiv.2312.16424. arXiv:2312.16424 [cs]
14. Liu, D., Zhou, J., Liao, H., Peng, Y., Peng, X.: A health indicator extraction and optimization framework for lithium-ion battery degradation modeling and prognostics. IEEE Trans. Syst. Man Cybern. Syst. **45**(6), 915–928 (2015)
15. Liu, X., Zhu, J., Luo, C., Xiong, L., Pan, Q.: Aero-engine health degradation estimation based on an underdetermined extended Kalman filter and convergence proof. ISA Trans. **125**, 528–538 (2022)
16. Loboda, I., Feldshteyn, Y.: Polynomials and neural networks for gas turbine monitoring: a comparative study (2011)
17. Lu, F., Ju, H., Huang, J.: An improved extended Kalman filter with inequality constraints for gas turbine engine health monitoring. Aerosp. Sci. Technol. **58**, 36–47 (2016)
18. PHM Society: 2025 PHM North America Conference Data Challenge is Now Live! (2025). https://data.phmsociety.org/2025-phm-north-america-conference-data-challenge-is-now-live/
19. Pillai, S., Vadakkepat, P.: Two stage deep learning for prognostics using multi-loss encoder and convolutional composite features. Expert Syst. Appl. **171**, 114569 (2021)

20. Psaropoulos, M., et al.: OpenDeckSMR, November 2025. https://github.com/OpenDeckLab/OpenDeckSMR
21. Saxena, A., Goebel, K., Simon, D., Eklund, N.: Damage propagation modeling for aircraft engine run-to-failure simulation. In: 2008 International Conference on Prognostics and Health Management, pp. 1–9. IEEE (2008)
22. Schirru, R., Vu, D.Q., Razakarivony, S., Thépaut, S., Bauny, A.: Adaptive Kalman filter by reinforcement learning for monitoring aircraft engines' performance against abrupt events. In: Turbo Expo, vol. 88803, p. V004T05A007. American Society of Mechanical Engineers (2025)
23. Simon, D.: A comparison of filtering approaches for aircraft engine health estimation. Aerosp. Sci. Technol. **12**(4), 276–284 (2008)
24. Soleimani, M., Irani, F.N., Yadegar, M., Meskin, N.: Comprehensive review of gas turbine fault diagnostic strategies. Appl. Energy **401**, 126801 (2025)
25. Thil, L., Read, J., Kaddah, R., Doquet, G.: I-GLIDE: input groups for latent health indicators in degradation estimation. In: Ribeiro, R.P., et al. (eds.) Machine Learning and Knowledge Discovery in Databases. Research Track. ECML PKDD 2025. LNCS, vol. 16018, pp. 395–411. Springer, Cham (2026). https://doi.org/10.1007/978-3-032-06106-5_23
26. Tian, Y., Chao, M.A., Kulkarni, C., Goebel, K., Fink, O.: Real-time model calibration with deep reinforcement learning. Mech. Syst. Signal Process. **165**, 108284 (2022)
27. Urban, L.A.: Gas turbine engine parameter interrelationships. Hamilton Standard Division of United Aircraft Corporation (1969)
28. Van Der Merwe, R., Wan, E.A.: The square-root unscented Kalman filter for state and parameter-estimation. In: Proceedings of the IEEE International Conference on Acoustics, Speech, and Signal Processing, vol. 6, pp. 3461–3464. IEEE (2001)
29. Vu, D.Q., Razakarivony, S., Marnissi, Y., Nocture, M.: A comprehensive literature review on the resolution of turbine engine performances' inverse problems. J. Eng. Gas Turbines Power **147**(5), 050801 (2025)
30. Vu, D.Q., Razakarivony, S., Thepaut, S., Doquet, G., Marnissi, Y., Nocture, M.: Aircraft engines performances estimation from multi-point and multi-time operational data via neural networks. Methods **7**, 8 (2024)

AI-Lite: Adaptive Data Center Cooling Optimization Based on Machine Learning

Xiaosong Chen[1], Zizhao Mo[1], Huanle Xu[1(✉)], Yang Liu[2], and Wing Cheong Lau[3]

[1] University of Macau, Macau SAR, China
{yc27909,yc17461,huanlexu}@um.edu.mo
[2] Shanghai University, Shanghai, China
yangliu_cs@shu.edu.cn
[3] The Chinese University of Hong Kong, Hong Kong SAR, China
wclau@ie.cuhk.edu.hk

Abstract. Machine Learning (ML) has become widely prevalent in contemporary data centers (DCs) to optimize cooling energy consumption, a critical factor constituting 40% of the total energy utilized by DCs. Despite the prevalence of ML-based cooling optimization solutions, they are typically customized for one specific DC and cannot be easily adapted to other DCs. In this paper, we introduce AI-Lite, a new cooling system designed for swift adaptation to a variety of modular DCs, irrespective of their size or geographical location. AI-Lite employs effective control schemes through online learning methods. Specifically, AI-Lite integrates bandit approaches with regression models, skillfully narrowing the action space and expediting the convergence process. Our theoretical analysis shows that AI-Lite achieves a sublinear regret bound relative to the optimal policy. Extensive real-world measurements conducted across various physical DCs demonstrate that AI-Lite exhibits rapid convergence from initialization within a few days. Simultaneously, it achieves a noteworthy reduction of up to 30% in cooling energy consumption in practice compared to baseline schemes. Furthermore, AI-Lite has been successfully commercialized and deployed in modular DC products.

Keywords: Data center cooling · Online learning · Multi-armed bandit

1 Introduction

DC has become an indispensable infrastructure in various information technology industries, providing remote computation and data services for business,

X. Chen and Z. Mo—Equal contribution.

Supplementary Information The online version contains supplementary material available at https://doi.org/10.1007/978-3-032-37682-4_9.

M. Baratchi et al. (Eds.): ECML PKDD 2026, LNAI 16949, pp. 147–163, 2027.
https://doi.org/10.1007/978-3-032-37682-4_9

entertainment, and scientific activities [3]. However, owing to their wide-scale server deployment, DCs represent a significant contributor to today's energy consumption. As per a study by Choi et al. [12], DC facilities were responsible for nearly 1% of global energy consumption in 2019, a figure that has seen a twofold increase every four years over the previous decade. A significant proportion of this consumption–approximately 40%–can be attributed to cooling systems [32,35]. Given this landscape, it has become imperative to bolster the energy efficiency of DCs by optimizing the energy consumption of cooling facilities through meticulous controls.

The energy efficiency of DCs is commonly assessed using Power Usage Effectiveness (PUE) [30]. PUE represents the ratio between the total energy consumption in DCs (P_{tps}) and the energy consumption of IT equipment (P_{cs}), expressed as PUE $= P_{tps}/P_{cs}$. Since P_{tps} encompasses the energy consumption of all facilities, a PUE closer to 1 indicates reduced energy usage by the cooling system, signifying higher energy efficiency.

In recent times, ML has emerged as a widespread application for controlling DC cooling systems with the primary goal of optimizing PUE. This marks a departure from traditional cooling control strategies that rely on meticulous and precise modeling of intricate physical systems. ML-based solutions adopt a data-driven approach, negating the necessity for intricate physical modeling. A notable example is Google DeepMind's development of a framework based on Neural Networks to discern the relationship between IT load, control parameters, and PUE [13]. With accurate fitting, this framework can generate optimal controls that minimize PUE under observed IT loads in Google's data centers. In contrast, Google Cloud employs a Reinforcement Learning (RL) approach for the online regulation of temperatures and airflow in large-scale DC cooling systems [21]. While these ML-based solutions surpass traditional PID controllers in terms of PUE, they grapple with fundamental limitations. Firstly, they are customized for specific DCs and lack easy adaptability to others. For instance, Google's fitting framework requires a two-year training phase with collected samples before effective control can be achieved, and when DC size or location changes, this training phase needs repetition. Secondly, these solutions tend to be computationally demanding, necessitating powerful computing resources for training ML agents or finding optimal controls.

Current DCs are typically designed in a modular structure, where each module incorporates diverse components such as IT cabinets, cooling systems, UPS, and environmental sensors for temperature and humidity. Given the variability in geographical location and size of modular DCs, it becomes crucial for the cooling system's control scheme to demonstrate adaptability across all configurations. An ideal solution involves a unified scheme with minimal data collection overhead and swift convergence, addressing the dynamic nature of these installations. Moreover, the control scheme must be responsive to environmental changes and fluctuations in IT load. Striking a balance with cost-efficiency, it is imperative for the scheme to impose only a modest computational overhead, ensuring seamless deployment.

In this paper, we present the design and implementation of AI-Lite, a new ML based cooling control system that can meet all the above requirements for modular DCs. The core principle of AI-Lite lies in the strategic decoupling of the entire control space into discrete and continuous subspaces, a methodology that significantly expedites convergence. For the discrete space, AI-Lite employs a Gaussian-Process-based multi-armed bandit algorithm [1] to intelligently select optimal actions. Each discrete control action is treated as an independent arm, incorporating state information that may evolve over time. The system estimates the mean and variance of the reward associated with each arm using a Gaussian Process model and employs the upper confidence bound (UCB) algorithm [1] for arm selection. In the continuous space, AI-Lite utilizes regression methods to predict the internal state corresponding to each action, subsequently choosing the most effective one. To bridge the two subspaces, the input to the regression models includes decisions made by the UCB algorithm. Furthermore, we establish an analytical framework demonstrating that AI-Lite can achieve a sublinear regret bound with high probability, affirming its rapid convergence from a theoretical perspective.

AI-Lite imposes minimal computational overhead, relying mainly on efficient matrix computations. We conduct comprehensive simulations using our developed simulator to assess AI-Lite. Furthermore, real-world experiments for AI-Lite are executed within multiple physical DCs, encompassing varying numbers of cabinets and locations. The outcomes reveal that AI-Lite consistently achieves a noteworthy reduction of over 20% in PUE and demonstrates the ability to converge from an initial state within a few days. Given its impressive performance across diverse scenarios, AI-Lite has been integrated into modular data center products, facilitating seamless deployment across DCs of various sizes.

2 Background and Related Work

The control of DC cooling systems is complex, often involving various components, such as air cooling units and ventilation. A common method of DC cooling system control is to adjust the set point, which is the target value of different control variables [21]. For example, by carefully setting the temperature control variable at the outlet of each air conditioner (AC), the AC can adjust its internal state to meet the temperature requirements of a DC while consuming the least amount of energy. However, finding the optimal setting is very challenging because the optimization process often requires a deep understanding of the cooling system, ranging from thermodynamics to mechanics [20].

In the literature, diverse strategies have been proposed to enhance the energy efficiency of DC cooling systems. These strategies can be broadly categorized as either hardware-based or software-based. However, hardware-based strategies can only be applied to new DCs or DCs under transformation, and once IT equipment is installed, changes are difficult [2,12].

For software-based approaches, they mainly employ neural networks, model predictive control, and RL. In particular, Google utilizes two years of sample data from large-scale DCs to train a complex neural network regression model, which is used to select the best control action [13]. Li et al. [23] proposed a prediction engine based on deep learning to handle dynamic DC power consumption. One serious limitation of this work is that it cannot adapt to environmental changes. By contrast, AI-Lite takes into account both changes in the environment and fluctuations in IT load.

Zhou et al. [36] adopted a model-predictive-based approach to adaptively control ventilated floor tiles in DCs, with system identification performed via random exploration. This approach designs a two-step optimization method to optimize resource provisioning and distribution for DC cooling. Google Cloud implements model predictive control based on RL to regulate temperature and airflow in large DCs [21]. However, the high complexity behind the control makes it computationally expensive for real-time implementation. Carnerero et al. [6] introduced a management strategy based on model predictive control to decide the number of active servers in a DC with minimum energy consumption. However, the effectiveness of this method highly depends on a careful tuning of hyper-parameters. As a result, the control method may not easily adapt to changes in the location and size of modular DCs.

DC cooling optimization based on RL has attracted significant research attention in recent years [5,11,16,17,25,27,28]. For instance, Luo et al. [25] investigated RL control in multiple commercial HVAC systems and proposed the BCOOLER method. However, BCOOLER requires two months to converge and depends on multi-head neural networks, adding substantial computational overhead. Another approach, LyaSafe, was proposed by Cao et al. [5] as a model-assisted safe deep RL method for DC cooling. While LyaSafe demonstrates the benefits of safe exploration, its deep RL training remains time-consuming. As we show in this paper, deep RL methods generally require long convergence times, making them impractical for modular DCs.

3 System Model

In this section, we present the basic system model for DC cooling control with the goal of optimizing energy efficiency while ensuring that the DC operate under safe conditions.

Air cooling technology is a widely adopted method for DC cooling due to its low maintenance requirements and reasonable operating costs [18]. In this paper, we concentrate on air-cooling and aim to develop an efficient control method for air-cooled DCs. Our approach eliminates the need for manual tuning, ensures fast convergence, and is easy to deploy.

3.1 Problem Formulation

Formally, let $g|(\boldsymbol{e}, \boldsymbol{m}) \rightarrow \mathbb{R}$ define the PUE function for a modular DC of specific size and location. Here, $(\boldsymbol{e}, \boldsymbol{m}) \in \mathcal{E} \times \mathcal{M}$ where $\mathcal{E}$ is the state space and $\mathcal{M}$ is the action space. The space $\mathcal{M}$ encompasses all possible actions we can manipulate, such as the number of ACs turned on and their associated parameters, including AC compressor speed, AC fan speed, and the temperature setting of each AC. Generally, the parameter setting of each AC can take continuous values within a certain range. The space $\mathcal{E}$ comprises the set of all environmental states, with each state encompassing IT load and other relevant environmental parameters like outdoor temperature, outdoor humidity, indoor temperature, and indoor humidity. These environmental states are the events and conditions that we cannot control. In addition to the environmental state, another critical type of state exists—the internal state, which represents the process variable we aim to predict and regulate. This primarily involves the cold-aisle temperature, measured using multiple sensors strategically placed along the server racks in the DC.

When a new environmental state $\boldsymbol{e} \in \mathcal{E}$ is observed, we want to choose an action $\boldsymbol{m} \in \mathcal{M}$ that produces the smallest PUE while guaranteeing that the obtained internal state $T_{(\boldsymbol{e},\boldsymbol{m})}$ is close to the set point T_c to avoid equipment damage caused by running in a high temperature environment. This yields the following optimization problem:

$$\min_{\boldsymbol{m} \in \mathcal{M}} \; g(\boldsymbol{e}, \boldsymbol{m}), \; \text{s.t.,} \quad T_c - W \leq T_{(\boldsymbol{e},\boldsymbol{m})} \leq T_c + W, \tag{1}$$

where W represents the range of allowable fluctuations of the internal state.

It is worth noting that deriving an exact formula for $g(\boldsymbol{e}, \boldsymbol{m})$ and $T_{(\boldsymbol{e},\boldsymbol{m})}$ is challenging, given the intricacy of modeling the entire cooling system. Consequently, traditional optimization methods relying on precise expressions for objectives and constraints are not applicable in our case.

3.2 Reformulation of the Objective

Following a control decision, both the environmental state and internal state may undergo changes due to fluctuations in the IT load or updates in environmental parameters. Consequently, it becomes necessary to select a new control action to accommodate these variations. As the system operates over time, we gain increased confidence in selecting the optimal action for each control based on the accumulated feedback from the system (i.e., PUE). In this context, the entire process can aptly be characterized as a conventional online learning process [4].

Under online learning, one common objective is to maximize the accumulative rewards over a long run. To align more seamlessly with this framework, we introduce a new function $f|(\boldsymbol{e}, \boldsymbol{m}) \to \mathbb{R}$ defined as $f = \frac{1}{g-1}$. In essence, minimizing the PUE function g is equivalent to maximizing the reward function f. Given that PUE is consistently greater than 1, this transformation ensures that f assumes values within the range of $(0, \infty)$. Consequently, the optimization problem can be formulated as follows:

$$\max_{\boldsymbol{m} \in \mathcal{M}} \; f(\boldsymbol{e}, \boldsymbol{m}), \; \text{s.t.}, T_c - W \leq T_{(\boldsymbol{e},\boldsymbol{m})} \leq T_c + W. \tag{2}$$

3.3 Performance Metrics

Concerning the effectiveness of a learning algorithm, we employ a widely-accepted performance metric to characterize theoretical convergence, known as regret [9,19]. Regret is defined as follows:

$$\mathrm{Reg}_T = \sum_{t=1}^{T} r_t = \sum_{t=1}^{T} f(\boldsymbol{e}_t, \boldsymbol{m}_t^*) - f(\boldsymbol{e}_t, \boldsymbol{m}_t). \tag{3}$$

Here, $\boldsymbol{e}_t$ and $\boldsymbol{m}_t$ represent the environmental state and the control decision made by the algorithm in the tth round (i.e., control interval), respectively. T refers to the total number of rounds being examined, while $\boldsymbol{m}_t^*$ signifies the decision made by an optimal solution in the tth round, which is described as follows:

$$\boldsymbol{m}_t^* = \arg\max_{\boldsymbol{m} \in \mathcal{M}} f(\boldsymbol{e}_t, \boldsymbol{m}), \text{ s.t., } T_c - W \leq T_{(\boldsymbol{e}_t, \boldsymbol{m}_t)} \leq T_c + W. \tag{4}$$

The concept of regret can be physically interpreted as follows. On the one hand, a small regret indicates that, over time, the actions chosen by the algorithm closely align with the optimal solutions. On the other hand, a small regret also implies that the algorithm quickly converges to the optimal solution; in other words, after several rounds of exploration, it is capable of making good control decisions in subsequent rounds by effectively leveraging previous controls that yield high rewards. Generally, an algorithm that attains a sublinear regret with respect to T is considered desirable.

4 Design of AI-Lite

4.1 Rationale Behind AI-Lite

Addressing the online optimization problem in Expression 3.2 presents significant challenges. The first hurdle is dealing with noisy estimates of PUE, particularly in scenarios where IT load experiences substantial fluctuations. The second challenge stems from the extensive action space. For example, in a moderately sized DC with six ACs, the control space encompasses over a million actions once all continuous values are discretized. A third challenge emerges from the necessity for the control of the modular DC cooling facility to remain independent of DC size and location.

To tackle the first challenge, AI-Lite applies ML solutions that can avoid modeling complex systems while dealing with uncertainty [13]. To address the second challenge, AI-Lite strategically decouples the entire action space into two subspaces: discrete space and continuous space. For these two subspaces, AI-Lite adopts different schemes to choose an action. This approach mirrors those found in the literature [31], which also address problems that involve the interplay of both continuous and discrete inputs. Such an approach potentially facilitates a more effective utilization of collected data and augments the modeling prowess. However, a distinguishing feature of AI-Lite, in contrast to these works, is its necessity to manage environmental conditions that are not only uncontrollable but also subject to temporal variations. Because of the decoupling, AI-Lite only needs to collect a small number of samples to train the ML model, so it can be easily adapted to DCs of any size and location, thus addressing the last challenge.

4.2 Decoupling the Action Space

For the action space $\mathcal{M}$, AI-Lite decomposes it into $\mathcal{M} = \mathcal{X} \times \mathcal{Z}$. Here, $\mathcal{X}$ denotes the set of discrete actions, with each action corresponding to the activation of a specific number of ACs. Meanwhile, $\mathcal{Z}$ represents the set of continuous actions, where each action delineates the parameter setting (described in Sect. 3.1) for all ACs.

By decoupling the space, each subspace contains a much smaller number of candidate actions than the original space. This can significantly reduce the exploration time of each subspace, thus speeding up the convergence of the whole selection process.

Moreover, discrete actions typically have a greater impact on the overall energy consumption of a cooling system than continuous actions. For example, choosing the correct number of ACs to turn on is critical to energy efficiency because the power consumption of an AC is non-linear with IT load in a DC. Keeping the fewest number of ACs turned on does not necessarily yield the best results. By decoupling the action space, AI-Lite can implement specific algorithms tailored for each space, thus having higher flexibility. For continuous space, AI-Lite uses a regression method that can predict the performance of each action in advance, so as to select the best action.

4.3 Selection Algorithm Design

Overview of AI-Lite. We illustrate the entire selection process for AI-Lite in Fig. 1. When a new environmental state is observed, AI-Lite applies Gaussian-Process Upper Confidence Bound (UCB) method [33] to select a discrete action $\boldsymbol{x} \in \mathcal{X}$. With this action, AI-Lite adopts XGBoost model to predict the internal state $T_{(\boldsymbol{e},\boldsymbol{m})}$ under each candidate action $\boldsymbol{z} \in \mathcal{Z}$ and then selects the action that produces the largest $T_{(\boldsymbol{e},\boldsymbol{m})}$ and satisfies the constraint in (2) for execution. Moreover, Gaussian-Process UCB (GP-UCB) and XGBoost regression use different feedback for online learning and model update.

Gaussian-Process UCB. AI-Lite employs the GP-UCB method for action selection due to its strong ability to address exploration-exploitation tradeoffs in online learning of complex systems [24]. Additionally, this method is able to handle noise [19,29], a necessary feature enabling AI-Lite to cope with the noisy estimation inherent in reward function calculations. Furthermore, the GP-UCB method proves to be sufficiently adaptive to cater to contextual situations where environmental changes may frequently occur [19]. Moreover, the GP-UCB method carries the significant advantage of requiring only efficient matrix computations, resulting in a minimal computational overhead.

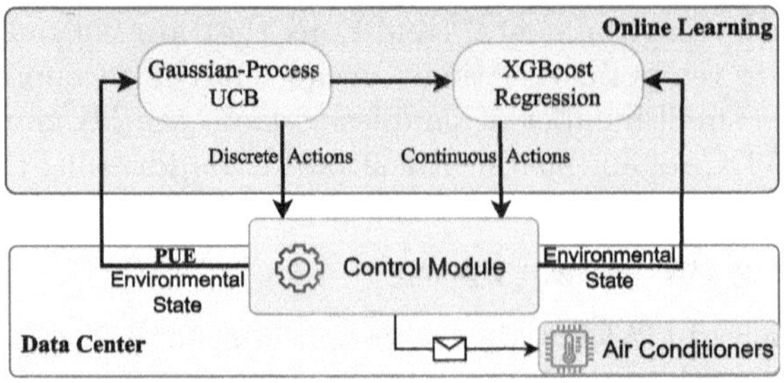

Fig. 1. Framework of AI-Lite.

Under this method, each action in the discrete space is treated as an arm and the reward function $f(\cdot)$ is sampled from a Gaussian process: a collection of dependent random variables for each $\boldsymbol{x} \in \mathcal{X}$, every finite subset of which is multivariate Gaussian distributed consistently [19]. The Gaussian process is specified by its mean function $\mu_t(\cdot)$ and co-variance function $k_t(\cdot,\cdot)$, which are updated iteratively based solely on performance feedback from historical control samples. The co-variance function captures model uncertainty at a given control, and this model is improved iteratively as more controls are sampled.

To be specific, suppose at the beginning of round t, AI-Lite has collected observations $\boldsymbol{y}_{t-1} = \{y_1, y_2, ..., y_{t-1}\}$ at points $\boldsymbol{A}_{t-1} = \{(\boldsymbol{e}_1, \boldsymbol{x}_1), (\boldsymbol{e}_2, \boldsymbol{x}_2), ..., (\boldsymbol{e}_{t-1}, \boldsymbol{x}_{t-1})\}$, where y_i denotes the reward obtained and $\boldsymbol{x}_i$ denotes the control, respectively, corresponding to the environment state $\boldsymbol{e}_i$ of the ith round. As a consequence, the mean and co-variance functions are updated as follows:

$$\begin{aligned}
\mu_{t-1}(\boldsymbol{e},\boldsymbol{x}) &= \boldsymbol{k}_{t-1}((\boldsymbol{e},\boldsymbol{x}))^T(\boldsymbol{K}_{t-1}+\sigma^2\boldsymbol{I})^{-1}\boldsymbol{y}_{t-1}\\
k_{t-1}((\boldsymbol{e},\boldsymbol{x}),(\boldsymbol{e}',\boldsymbol{x}')) &= k((\boldsymbol{e},\boldsymbol{x}),(\boldsymbol{e}',\boldsymbol{x}'))-\\
&\quad \boldsymbol{k}_{t-1}((\boldsymbol{e},\boldsymbol{x}))^T(\boldsymbol{K}_{t-1}+\sigma^2 I)^{-1}\boldsymbol{k}_{t-1}((\boldsymbol{e}',\boldsymbol{x}'))\\
\sigma^2_{t-1}(\boldsymbol{e},\boldsymbol{x}) &= k_{t-1}((\boldsymbol{e},\boldsymbol{x}),(\boldsymbol{e},\boldsymbol{x})),
\end{aligned} \tag{5}$$

where $k((\boldsymbol{e},\boldsymbol{x}),(\boldsymbol{e}',\boldsymbol{x}'))$ is kernel function, $\boldsymbol{k}_{t-1}((\boldsymbol{e},\boldsymbol{x})) = [k((\boldsymbol{e}_1,\boldsymbol{x}_1),(\boldsymbol{e},\boldsymbol{x})); k((\boldsymbol{e}_2,\boldsymbol{x}_2),(\boldsymbol{e},\boldsymbol{x})); \cdots; k((\boldsymbol{e}_{t-1},\boldsymbol{x}_{t-1}),(\boldsymbol{e},\boldsymbol{x}))]$, and $\boldsymbol{K}_{t-1}$ is a positive definite kernel matrix given by: $\boldsymbol{K}_{t-1} = \left[k((\boldsymbol{e},\boldsymbol{x}),(\boldsymbol{e}',\boldsymbol{x}'))\right]_{(\boldsymbol{e},\boldsymbol{x}),(\boldsymbol{e}',\boldsymbol{x}')\in\boldsymbol{A}_{t-1}}$.

There are a series of commonly used kernel functions, such as squared exponential kernel, linear kernel, and Matern kernel. AI-Lite uses city block as it yields the best performance, that is, $k((\boldsymbol{e},\boldsymbol{x}),(\boldsymbol{e}',\boldsymbol{x}')) = \exp\left(-\frac{||(\boldsymbol{e},\boldsymbol{x})-(\boldsymbol{e}',\boldsymbol{x}')||}{2l}\right)$. Based on this, AI-Lite selects the control action for round t as the optimal solution to the following optimization problem:

$$\boldsymbol{x}_t = \arg\max_{\boldsymbol{x}\in\mathcal{X}} \mu_{t-1}(\boldsymbol{e}_t,\boldsymbol{x}) + \beta_{t,x}\cdot\sigma_{t-1}(\boldsymbol{e}_t,\boldsymbol{x}). \tag{6}$$

Here, $\beta_{t,x} = \sqrt{2\log\left(\frac{|\mathcal{X}|\pi^2 t^3}{6\delta n_{t,x}}\right)}$, where $n_{t,x}$ denotes the cumulative number of rounds the arm $\boldsymbol{x}$ was pulled before round t, and δ is a value within the range $(0, 1)$.

Note that AI-Lite decouples the action space, so when employing the GP-UCB method, we assume that AI-Lite has selected an optimal action $\boldsymbol{z}_i^* \in \mathcal{Z}$ associated with $\boldsymbol{x}_i$. While this assumption may not be valid for all rounds, the selection generated by the GP-UCB performs well both theoretically and experimentally.

Algorithm 1. Cooling Optimization Algorithm under AI-Lite

Input: $(\boldsymbol{e}_1, \boldsymbol{x}_1, \boldsymbol{z}_1)$: initial setting
T_c: the target temperature of cold aisles
W: the range of allowable temperature fluctuations of cold aisles
$\mathcal{M}$: search space
Output: the optimal setting $(\boldsymbol{x}_t, \boldsymbol{z}_t)$ corresponding to $\boldsymbol{e}_t$
Use setting $(\boldsymbol{e}_1, \boldsymbol{x}_1, \boldsymbol{z}_1)$ to run the cooling system;
Observe reward y_1 and state $T_{(\boldsymbol{e}_1, \boldsymbol{m}_1)}$;
Add y_1 into $\boldsymbol{y}_1$ and add $(\boldsymbol{e}_1, \boldsymbol{x}_1)$ into $\boldsymbol{A}_1$;
for each $t \in [2, T]$ **do**
  Get the current environment status $\boldsymbol{e}_t$;
  Update $\mu_{t-1}(\boldsymbol{e}, \boldsymbol{x})$ and $\sigma_{t-1}^2(\boldsymbol{e}, \boldsymbol{x})$ based on Eq. (5);
  Select $\boldsymbol{x}_t$ following Eq. (6);
  Select $\boldsymbol{z}_t$ based the XGBoost regression model;
  Observe y_t, $\boldsymbol{z}_t$, and $T_{(\boldsymbol{e}_t, \boldsymbol{x}_t, \boldsymbol{z}_t)}$, and update $\boldsymbol{y}_t$ and $\boldsymbol{A}_t$;
  Retrain the regression model based on the new training sample with feature $(\boldsymbol{e}_t, \boldsymbol{x}_t, \boldsymbol{z}_t)$ and label $T_{(\boldsymbol{e}_t, \boldsymbol{x}_t, \boldsymbol{z}_t)}$;
end for

XGBoost Regression. As shown in Fig. 1, AI-Lite applies regression models to select an action from the continuous space. And the input to the regression model also contains actions selected by the GP-UCB method. Specifically, in round t, for each $\boldsymbol{z} \in \mathcal{Z}$, the regression model takes $(\boldsymbol{e}_t, \boldsymbol{x}_t, \boldsymbol{z})$ as input, and predicts the corresponding internal state, i.e., $T_{(\boldsymbol{e}_t, \boldsymbol{x}_t, \boldsymbol{z})}$. In general, for actions in continuous space, smaller energy consumption usually means larger $T_{(\boldsymbol{e}_t, \boldsymbol{x}_t, \boldsymbol{z})}$. Therefore, AI-Lite selects among all candidates the action that produces the largest $T_{(\boldsymbol{e}_t, \boldsymbol{x}_t, \boldsymbol{z})}$ and satisfies the constraints in (2).

Among all models, AI-Lite adopts XGBoost as it yields the highest prediction accuracy and is also widely used for many problems due to good generalization ability and small overhead [7]. Algorithm 1 exhibits the pseudo-code of the whole selection process.

AI-Lite builds a single regression model to predict in advance the internal state for each control. In contrast, Google's regression method trains two separate models, one for PUE and one for the internal state [21]. Consequently, AI-Lite has much lower training overhead, as the internal state is generally easier to predict accurately than PUE.

4.4 System Implementation

We have implemented AI-Lite in modular DCs. To expedite convergence, AI-Lite initiates the training process of the regression model by randomly generating representative training samples in the initial rounds, typically spanning three days. During this period, it ensures that the temperature of the cold aisle remains below the set point. Additionally, AI-Lite performs a new control action every 60 min to alleviate the impact of noise on PUE observations. If the prediction by the regression model deviates from the true observation by 10%, AI-Lite identifies and collects such samples for incremental training. Furthermore, in instances where the observed cold-aisle temperature surpasses the upper limit of the set point, the temperature setting of each air conditioner is automatically reduced by 1 °C to maintain safety.

AI-Lite has been fully commercialized and packaged for easy deployment in DCs. Its commercial version supports hot-pluggable operation, allowing deployment without disrupting DC operations. AI-Lite can complete the docking process with a DC in under 10 s. More importantly, it is compatible with all types of modular DCs, both new and retrofitted.

4.5 Regret Performance

In this part, we offer an examination of the theoretical performance characteristics of AI-Lite. We demonstrate that, under a set of modest assumptions, the selection algorithm rapidly converges to an optimal solution.

Theorem 1. *Let $\mathcal{X} \subset \mathcal{R}^d$ and $\delta \in (0,1)$, with high probability, the regret achieved by AI-Lite is sublinear with respect to T. Precisely,*

$$\Pr\left\{ Reg_T \leq \mathcal{O}\left(\sqrt{\log\left(|\mathcal{X}|^{\frac{1}{3}}\pi^{\frac{2}{3}}T/\delta^{\frac{1}{3}}\right)\cdot\gamma_T\cdot T}\right)\right\} \geq 1-\delta, \tag{7}$$

where $\gamma_T = \mathcal{O}\big((T\log T)^{\frac{d}{1+d}}\big)$.

When proving Theorem 1, we need to make the following assumptions:

$$\begin{cases} y_t = f(\boldsymbol{e}_t, \boldsymbol{x}_t, \boldsymbol{z}_t) + \epsilon_t, \quad \epsilon_t \sim \mathcal{N}(0, \sigma^2), \\ f(\boldsymbol{e}_t, \boldsymbol{x}_t, \boldsymbol{z}_t) = f(\boldsymbol{e}_t, \boldsymbol{x}_t, \boldsymbol{z}_t^*) + \mathrm{Err}_t, \\ \lim\limits_{t\to\infty} \mathrm{Err}_t \cdot t^\alpha = C, \alpha > 1. \end{cases} \tag{8}$$

The first assumption states that each observation deviates from the true reward due to Gaussian noise with zero mean. The second assumption states that the prediction error caused by the XGBoost regression model asymptotically vanishes at a rate of $1/t^\alpha$, where C is a constant. As the regression model accumulates more training samples over time, this is indeed reasonable, a point we substantiate in the supplemental material [8]. A more detailed explanation, as well as the proof of Theorem 1, can also be found in this additional resource [8].

5 Performance Evaluation

In this section, we comprehensively evaluate AI-Lite's performance. Given the critical role of the cooling system in DC operations [10], we developed an environmental simulator for safety and cost efficiency. We first conducted simulations using this simulator to demonstrate how AI-Lite outperforms state-of-the-art solutions, including numerous ablation studies. We then conducted extensive experiments in diverse real DCs to further examine AI-Lite's adaptability across various IT loads, DC sizes, and geographical locations.

Baseline Schemes: We compared the performance of AI-Lite against RL and AI-Lite SE. RL implements a traditional model-free learning framework that uses deep neural networks [34]. During the tuning process of RL, we conducted multiple rounds of parameter optimization, ensuring comprehensive tuning of all parameters across a vast range. We also explored several learning methodologies including policy gradient, Q-learning, and proximal policy optimization, all in a quest to achieve the most optimal outcome. AI-Lite SE uses a squared exponential kernel, which is widely adopted under GP-UCB [24].

Additionally, we conducted ablation studies by comparing AI-Lite with methods formed by replacing its components. These methods fall into two categories. The first category includes Linear UCB [22]+XGBoost Regression (LinBR), RL [34]+XGBoost Regression (RLR), and Double XGBoost Regression [7] (DR), where the GP-UCB in AI-Lite is replaced. The second category includes GP-UCB+Support Vector Regression [26] (GPSVR), GP-UCB+Random Forest Regression [14] (GPRFR), GP-UCB+Neural Network [15] (GPNN), and Double GP-UCB [24] (DGP), where the XGBoost Regression in AI-Lite is replaced.

5.1 Simulation Results

Our simulator was developed by training a machine learning model using a comprehensive dataset spanning two years. This dataset was collected from a physical DC comprising 200 cabinets. By leveraging this extensive data, our simulator is capable of accurately replicating the real-world environment within the DC. To perform the simulation process, we operated AI-Lite in conjunction with the environmental simulator that we have developed. Specifically, we modulated the

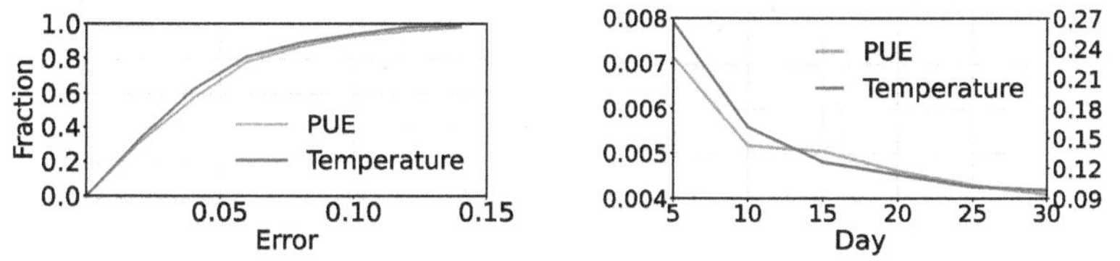

(a) The fidelity of simulator in the 30-day trial.

(b) The average gap in PUE and cold-aisle temperature over time.

Fig. 2. The fidelity of our simulator and the search for optimal value.

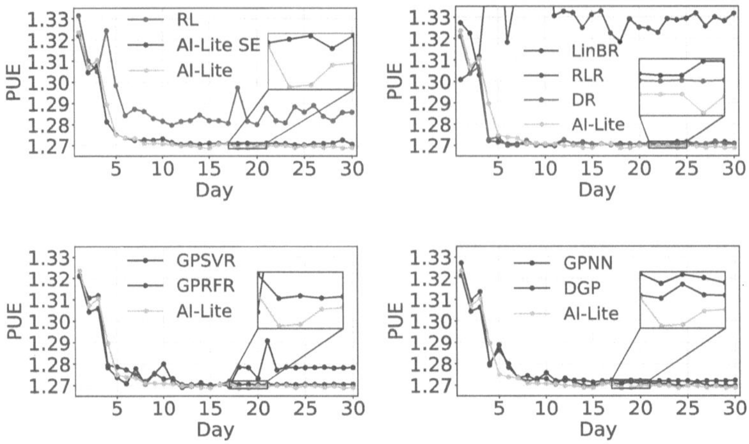

Fig. 3. PUE results from the Environment Simulator under fluctuating IT loads.

IT load of the simulator to oscillate periodically and adjusted the environmental parameters in accordance with shifts in weather conditions.

Simulator Fidelity. It is critical to ensure the fidelity of the simulator, especially for safety-critical systems such as this. The simulator's fidelity was evaluated using the formula: Error $= |\text{True value} - \text{Predictive value}|/\text{True value}$. We measured the fraction of both PUE and cold-aisle temperature over a period of 30 days under various error ranges, as depicted in the Fig. 2a. The results indicated that approximately 95% of errors for both PUE and cold-aisle temperature fell within the interval $(0, 0.10)$.

Optimality of AI-Lite. Given the vast action space, locating the global optimum is virtually unfeasible, even after discretising it. Consequently, we tested a subset including AI-Lite's decisions, generated by offsetting its decision points. The optimal value was found via exhaustive search, and the gap was computed as: Gap $= |\text{Optimal value} - \text{AI-Lite value}|/\text{Optimal value}$. We measured the average gap of both PUE and cold-aisle temperature over time, shown in Fig. 2b. Results indicate that AI-Lite's decoupling can close the gap with the optimum over time, consistent with our theoretical analysis in Sect. 4.5.

As shown in Fig. 3, AI-Lite quickly converges to a better solution within 6 days under fluctuating workloads. The vast majority of methods perform slightly worse than AI-Lite. It should be noted that the convergence of both LinBR and DR is relatively rapid. However, this rapid convergence also leads to insufficient exploration, which, in turn, results in a higher final PUE compared to AI-Lite. In contrast, GPSVR performs relatively poorly and takes 24 days to converge. Additionally, RL and RLR perform significantly worse than other schemes and fail to converge within 20 days. Their cooling energy consumption is 8% and 23% higher than that of AI-Lite, respectively. Notably, we found that under AI-Lite, the selected city block kernel outperforms the squared exponential kernel by 1%.

5.2 Results in Real DCs

In this part, we discuss the performance evaluation of AI-Lite in real DCs. The DC management module samples the control data every five minutes and feeds these data samples to AI-Lite for online learning and model update. In addition, our selection criteria for baselines were based on both cost and time efficiency considerations. RL, a widely-adopted control strategy, was included despite its tendency to converge slowly within the simulator. Our interest was piqued by the potentiality of its performance in real-world scenarios. LinBR was another choice for this comparative study due to its rapid convergence and the fact that its PUE was closely aligned with that of AI-Lite within the simulator. Besides, traditional PID controller was also included in the comparison.

Before initiating the experimental process, we undertook comprehensive testing of the environmental conditions to guarantee their consistency across all experimental groups. Additionally, we endeavored to streamline the testing duration for each algorithm to around half a month. This was done to ensure that all algorithms were assessed within the same seasonal timeframe. Furthermore, our set point for the cold aisle is $T_c = 22\,^\circ\mathrm{C}$, and $W = 2\,^\circ\mathrm{C}$.

Large-Scale Evaluation. We evaluated AI-Lite in real DCs of various sizes located in three different cities during its commercialization phase. As depicted in Table 1, the PUE of AI-Lite is consistently lower across DCs of different sizes. The average cold aisle temperature of AI-Lite is also closer to our set point 22 °C. Notably, compared to PID, the average energy savings achieved by AI-Lite in these three cities were 21.71%, 20.46%, and 7.97%, respectively.

Table 1. Comparison of three different sizes

Cities	Number of IT cabinets	PUE of AI-Lite	Temperature of AI-Lite	PUE of benchmark	Temperature of benchmark	Energy Saving Ratio
City 1	60	1.133	22.36	1.171	23.81	21.71%
City 2	130	1.146	22.34	1.176	23.62	20.46%
City 3	200	1.162	22.34	1.202	23.51	7.97%

Next, we will discuss the evaluation results using the medium-sized DC with 60 IT cabinets and 15 ACs in City 1 as a case study. This case study allows us to provide a more comprehensive understanding of AI-Lite.

Dynamic IT Loads. In this study, we conducted comparative experiments using RL and LinBR as baseline methods. The testing period was divided into two phases. In the first phase, lasting 7 days, the IT load was set to 59 KW to observe whether PUE decreased over time. In the second phase, the IT load was reduced to 45 KW. During the experiments, besides tracking the downward trend of PUE, we also monitored the stability of the cold aisle's average temperature.

We could find that AI-Lite always performs much better than other baselines. As shown in Fig. 4a, after the exploration of three days, AI-Lite is able to reduce

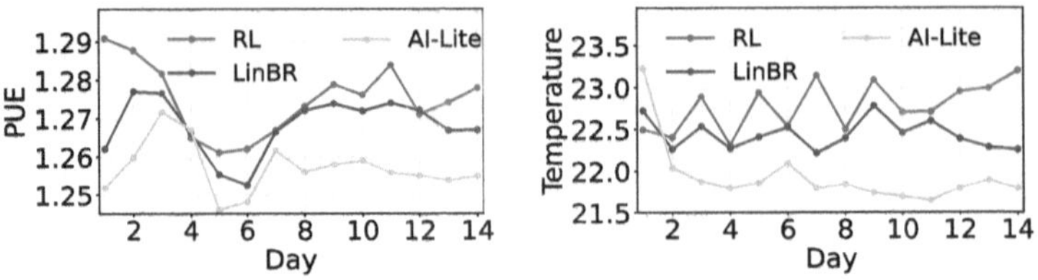

(a) PUE results (b) Cold-aisle temperature

Fig. 4. Results under dynamic IT loads.

the PUE value quickly, i.e., from 1.275 to 1.24. Moreover, the cold-aisle temperature achieved under AI-Lite is also much closer to the set point, as shown in Fig. 4b. Therefore, AI-Lite can better guarantee the security of DCs. On the seventh day when the IT load starts to decrease, we observe an increase in the PUE values for all cooling schemes. This is because smaller IT loads generally result in lower energy efficiency. Still, AI-Lite reduces cooling energy consumption by 10% and 9% compared to RL and LinBR, respectively. Furthermore, AI-Lite only takes several hours to adapt to IT load changes whereas LinBR requires over 6 days to converge and RL even fails to converge.

Fixed IT Load. We also conducted experiments under a fixed IT load of 57 KW to further examine the convergence performance of AI-Lite. Figure 5a shows that the cold-aisle temperature converges to the set point after the forth day. Considering that the first three days were mainly to collect training samples, the convergence speed of AI-Lite is very fast. Figure 5b shows that the number of ACs turned on remains stable after convergence, indicating the GP-UCB method is robust to handling noisy estimations. Moreover, the PUE value drops dramatically from 1.32 to 1.23, implying that the cooling energy consumption has been reduced by 30% after deploying AI-lite.

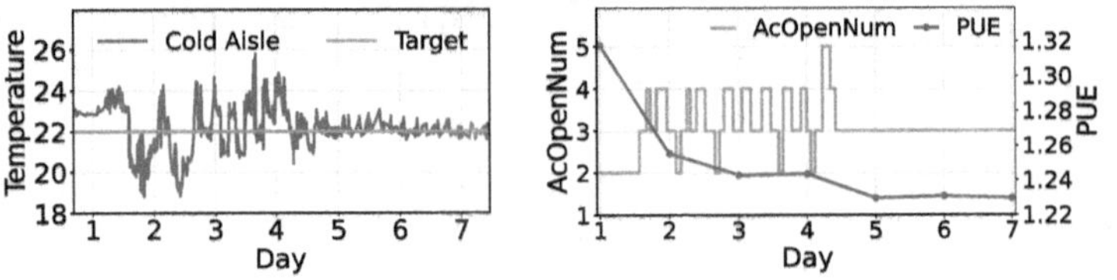

(a) Cold-aisle temperature (b) The number of ACs turned on

Fig. 5. Results under a fixed IT load (57 KW).

Periodical IT Loads. Finally, we describe the experimental results of running AI-Lite in the real DC for another 8 days. In this experiment, we varied the IT load from 44 KW to 64 KW per day following the same pattern to mimic the

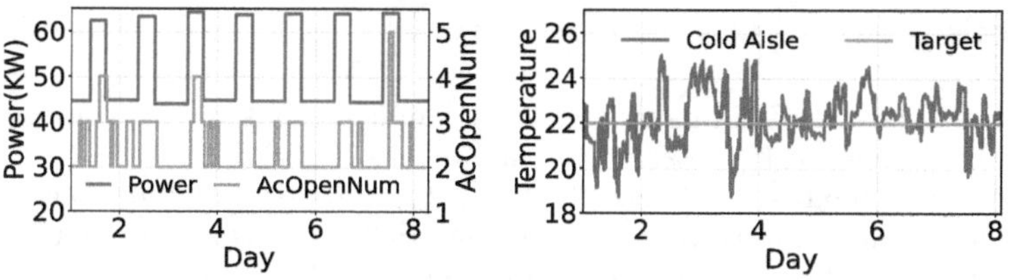

(a) The number of opened ACs (b) The average cold-aisle temperature

Fig. 6. Results under periodical IT loads.

normal behavior of a production DC. As shown in Fig. 6a, the periodic change trend of the number of ACs turned on is consistent with IT load. This indicates that the uncertainty of the learning method decreases gradually with the same parameter setting. Specifically, the percentage of time when the number of ACs turned on was inconsistent decreased from 38% to 7%. As a result, the value stabilizes at less than 8%, suggesting that GP-UCB still retains some exploratory behavior, which is consistent with the strong exploratory nature of GP-UCB.

At the same time, we also analyze the temperature variation of cold aisles. It can be observed from Fig. 6b that the cold-aisle temperature is always close to the set point, and the up and down oscillations weaken over time.

6 Conclusions

This paper presents the design of an efficient cooling system that can accommodate DCs of any size and location. The key idea behind the system is to decouple the whole action space into two separate subspaces, and apply different ML models to select actions from each subspace. By carefully modelling the selection of discrete actions in the context of Gaussian Process Bandit framework and designing the selection algorithms accordingly, the system can quickly converge to an optimal state. Furthermore, the system only needs to collect a small number of training samples and incurs little computational overhead. At the same time, it has been deployed in physical modular DCs, fostering energy conservation and emission reduction, and has been fully commercialized for practical use.

Acknowledgments. We sincerely thank the anonymous reviewers of ECML PKDD 2026 for their valuable feedback. In addition, this work is supported by the Science and Technology Development Fund of Macau (0071/2023/ITP2 and 0041/2025/RIA1), as well as by the Multi-Year Research Grant of University of Macau (MYRG-GRG2024-00255-FST-UMDF and MYRG-GRG2025-00119-FST). This work is also supported in part by the CUHK MobiTeC R&D Fund.

Disclosure of Interests. The authors have no competing interests to declare that are relevant to the content of this article.

References

1. Agrawal, S., Devanur, N.: Linear contextual bandits with knapsacks. In: Advances in Neural Information Processing Systems, vol. 29 (2016)
2. Barroso, L.A., Clidaras, J., Hölzle, U.: The datacenter as a computer: an introduction to the design of warehouse-scale machines. In: Synthesis Lectures on Computer Architecture, vol. 8, pp. 1–154. Morgan & Claypool Publishers (2013)
3. Bilal, K., Malik, S.U.R., Khan, S.U., Zomaya, A.Y.: Trends and challenges in cloud datacenters. IEEE Cloud Comput. **1**, 10–20 (2014)
4. Bubeck, S., Cesa-Bianchi, N.: Regret analysis of stochastic and nonstochastic multi-armed bandit problems. Found. Trends® Mach. Learn. **5**, 1–122 (2012)
5. Cao, Z., Wang, R., Zhou, X., Wen, Y.: Toward model-assisted safe reinforcement learning for data center cooling control: a Lyapunov-based approach. In: Proceedings of the 14th ACM International Conference on Future Energy Systems, pp. 333–346 (2023)
6. Carnerero, A.D., Ramirez, D.R., Alamo, T., Limon, D.: Probabilistically certified management of data centers using predictive control. IEEE Trans. Autom. Sci. Eng. **19**(4), 2849–2861 (2021)
7. Chen, T., Guestrin, C.: XGBoost: a scalable tree boosting system. In: Proceedings of the 22nd ACM SIGKDD International Conference on Knowledge Discovery and Data Mining, pp. 785–794 (2016)
8. Chen, X., Mo, Z., Xu, H., Liu, Y., Lau, W.C.: Supplementary material for AI-Lite (2026). https://doi.org/10.5281/zenodo.20538828
9. Chen, X., Zhuang, H., Liu, Y., Xu, H., Lau, W.C.: Combinatorial multi-armed bandits with fairness constraints: an online convex optimization perspective. J. Artif. Intell. Res. **82**, 1909–1942 (2025)
10. Chervonyi, Y., et al.: Semi-analytical industrial cooling system model for reinforcement learning (2022). arXiv:2207.13131
11. Chi, C., Ji, K., Marahatta, A., Song, P., Zhang, F., Liu, Z.: Jointly optimizing the it and cooling systems for data center energy efficiency based on multi-agent deep reinforcement learning. In: Proceedings of the Eleventh ACM International Conference on Future Energy Systems, pp. 489–495 (2020)
12. Choi, Y.J., Park, B.R., Hyun, J.Y., Moon, J.W.: Development of an adaptive artificial neural network model and optimal control algorithm for a data center cyber-physical system. Build. Environ. **210** (2022)
13. Gao, J.: Machine learning applications for data center optimization (2014)
14. Geurts, P., Ernst, D., Wehenkel, L.: Extremely randomized trees. In: Machine Learning, vol. 63, pp. 3–42. Springer (2006)
15. Glorot, X., Bengio, Y.: Understanding the difficulty of training deep feedforward neural networks. In: Proceedings of the Thirteenth International Conference on Artificial Intelligence and Statistics, pp. 249–256. JMLR Workshop and Conference Proceedings (2010)
16. Hua, T., Wan, J., Jaffry, S., Rasheed, Z., Li, L., Ma, Z.: Comparison of deep reinforcement learning algorithms in data center cooling management: a case study. In: 2021 IEEE International Conference on Systems, Man, and Cybernetics (SMC), pp. 392–397. IEEE (2021)
17. Jeen, S., Abate, A., Cullen, J.M.: Low emission building control with zero-shot reinforcement learning. In: Proceedings of the AAAI Conference on Artificial Intelligence, vol. 37, pp. 14259–14267 (2023)

18. Kheirabadi, A.C., Groulx, D.: Cooling of server electronics: a design review of existing technology. Appl. Thermal Eng. **105** (2016)
19. Krause, A., Ong, C.: Contextual Gaussian process bandit optimization. In: Advances in Neural Information Processing Systems, vol. 24 (2011)
20. Kumar, R., Khatri, S.K., Diván, M.J.: Optimization of power consumption in data centers using machine learning based approaches: a review. In: International Booktitle of Electrical and Computer Engineering, vol. 12, p. 3192. IAES Institute of Advanced Engineering and Science (2022)
21. Lazic, N., et al.: Data center cooling using model-predictive control. In: Advances in Neural Information Processing Systems, vol. 31 (2018)
22. Li, L., Chu, W., Langford, J., Schapire, R.E.: A contextual-bandit approach to personalized news article recommendation. In: Proceedings of the 19th International Conference on World Wide Web, pp. 661–670 (2010)
23. Li, Y., Hu, H., Wen, Y., Zhang, J.: Learning-based power prediction for data centre operations via deep neural networks. In: Proceedings of the 5th International Workshop on Energy Efficient Data Centres, pp. 1–10 (2016)
24. Liu, Y., Xu, H., Lau, W.C.: Accordia: adaptive cloud configuration optimization for recurring data-intensive applications. In: Proceedings of the ACM Symposium on Cloud Computing, p. 479 (2019)
25. Luo, J., et al.: Controlling commercial cooling systems using reinforcement learning. In: Workshop on Advances in Neural Information Processing Systems (2023)
26. Platt, J.: Probabilistic outputs for support vector machines and comparisons to regularized likelihood methods. In: Advances in Large Margin Classifiers, Cambridge, MA, vol. 10, pp. 61–74 (1999)
27. Ran, Y., Hu, H., Wen, Y., Zhou, X.: Optimizing energy efficiency for data center via parameterized deep reinforcement learning. IEEE Trans. Serv. Comput. **16**(2), 1310–1323 (2022)
28. Ran, Y., Zhou, X., Hu, H., Wen, Y.: Optimizing data center energy efficiency via event-driven deep reinforcement learning. IEEE Trans. Serv. Comput. **16**(2), 1296–1309 (2022)
29. Rasmussen, C.E.: Gaussian processes in machine learning. In: Summer School on Machine Learning, pp. 63–71. Springer, Heidelberg (2003)
30. Rasmussen, N.: Electrical efficiency modeling of data centers (2006)
31. Ru, B., Alvi, A., Nguyen, V., Osborne, M.A., Roberts, S.: Bayesian optimisation over multiple continuous and categorical inputs. In: International Conference on Machine Learning, pp. 8276–8285. PMLR (2020)
32. Song, Z., Zhang, X., Eriksson, C.: Data center energy and cost saving evaluation. Energy Procedia **75**, 1255–1260 (2015)
33. Srinivas, N., Krause, A., Kakade, S.M., Seeger, M.: Gaussian process optimization in the bandit setting: no regret and experimental design. In: Proceedings of the International Conference on Machine Learning. PMLR (2010)
34. Wang, Z., Schaul, T., Hessel, M., Hasselt, H., Lanctot, M., Freitas, N.: Dueling network architectures for deep reinforcement learning. In: International Conference on Machine Learning, pp. 1995–2003. PMLR (2016)
35. Yeo, S., Hossain, M.M., Huang, J.C., Lee, H.H.S.: ATAC: ambient temperature-aware capping for power efficient datacenters. In: Proceedings of the ACM Symposium on Cloud Computing, pp. 1–14 (2014)
36. Zhou, R., Bash, C., Wang, Z., McReynolds, A., Christian, T., Cader, T.: Data center cooling efficiency improvement through localized and optimized cooling resources delivery. In: ASME International Mechanical Engineering Congress and Exposition, vol. 45233. American Society of Mechanical Engineers (2012)

Combining Multiple Dissimilarity Spaces for Industrial Customer Prediction with Multi-Matrix Median LVQ

Lukas Bader[1,2(✉)], Dietlind Zühlke[2], and Ina Terwey-Scheulen[1]

[1] August Rüggeberg GmbH, 51709 Marienheide, Germany
lukas.bader@pferd.com

[2] Institut for Data Science, Engineering and Analytics, Technische Hochschule Köln, 51643 Gummersbach, Germany
dietlind.zuehlke@th-koeln.de

Abstract. Predicting customer behavior in industrial applications often relies on heterogeneous information sources describing different aspects of companies. Such data frequently consist of categorical attributes and cannot always be meaningfully represented within a single feature space, resulting in multiple dissimilarity spaces that capture different structural relationships between customers. In this work, we analyze the properties of these dissimilarity spaces with respect to their global geometry, local neighborhood structure, and class separation capabilities. In addition, we investigate the predictive performance of individual dissimilarity representations using Median Generalized Learning Vector Quantization (MGLVQ) as a single-matrix baseline. Our analysis reveals structural differences between the dissimilarity spaces, which are also reflected in their predictive behavior, where different matrices correctly classify different subsets of customers. Together, these observations suggest that the representations contain complementary information and motivate the use of a Multi-Matrix learning approach. Based on this insight, we employ Multi-Matrix Median Generalized Learning Vector Quantization (M^3GLVQ), which adaptively combines multiple dissimilarity matrices by learning their relative importance as weights and aggregating them into a joint representation. Experiments on real-world industrial customer data for purchase prediction show that the joint use of multiple dissimilarity spaces improves predictive performance compared to models based on single dissimilarity matrices, while also providing additional insights into the structural relationships within the data.

Keywords: Dissimilarity Learning · Multi-Matrix Learning · Learning Vector Quantization · Prototype-Based Learning · Customer Behavior Prediction · Heterogeneous Data

---

Supplementary Information The online version contains supplementary material available at https://doi.org/10.1007/978-3-032-37682-4_10.

M. Baratchi et al. (Eds.): ECML PKDD 2026, LNAI 16949, pp. 164–180, 2027.
https://doi.org/10.1007/978-3-032-37682-4_10

1 Introduction

In industrial B2B customer analytics, accurately predicting purchasing behavior is crucial for targeted sales and marketing strategies and activities. A central challenge in modeling customer profiles, particularly in industrial tooling markets, is the strong heterogeneity of the underlying data, which arises from the diversity of the customer base: industrial tools are used across a wide range of industries, for different manufacturing processes, and in highly varying application contexts. In practice, customer profiles consist of highly diversified feature sets that include predominantly categorical data, such as industry sectors (e.g. NAICS codes [17]), applied manufacturing processes, processed materials, and manufactured product types (e.g. represented by HS codes [19]), as well as numerical features such as turnover, number of employees, and geographic location.

However, this heterogeneity does not only mean that there are multiple data sources. Rather, different parts of the customer profile induce different semantic notions of similarity. Two customers may be close with respect to their industry classification, while being dissimilar in terms of manufactured products or manufacturing applications. Collapsing such heterogeneous descriptors into a single feature space or a static dissimilarity therefore risks obscuring structural differences that may be most informative for prediction.

A more adequate representation therefore requires tailored dissimilarity measures for different profiling perspectives, resulting in multiple dissimilarity spaces. Each captures customer relations from a different perspective rather than a redundant variation of the same structure.

For practical deployment in a business context, predictive performance alone is not sufficient. Model decisions must be explainable at the customer level in order to support prioritization, targeting, and expert validation in sales and marketing workflows. Prototype-based classifiers, particularly Median Generalized Learning Vector Quantization (MGLVQ) [12], are highly suitable in this setting. They can process non-vectorial data directly based on pairwise dissimilarities and provide transparent decisions through interpretable representative prototypes.

However, the classical MGLVQ exhibits a critical limitation in this scenario: it is restricted to processing either a single distance matrix or a statically preaggregated one [1]. In scenarios with multiple sources of information, this requires a manual weighting of the matrices prior to training. This approach is not only inflexible but also ignores that the relevance of different dissimilarity views may vary with the prediction task and with the structural regions of the customer population emphasized during learning.

In this work, we hypothesize that the various dissimilarity spaces derived from heterogeneous industrial data exhibit fundamentally different structural properties, which in turn lead to significantly divergent classification behaviors. Consequently, a singular or statically aggregated distance matrix is incapable of fully capturing the complex topology of the customer data.

To address this limitation within an applied data science context, we provide an in-depth evaluation of the recently proposed Multi-Matrix Median Generalized Learning Vector Quantization (M^3GLVQ), a model capable of processing multiple distance matrices simultaneously while dynamically learning the relative importance of each matrix.

The main contributions of this work are threefold. First, we provide a systematic structural analysis of heterogeneous dissimilarity spaces derived from industrial customer profiles. We examine their global geometry, local neighborhood structure, and class separation properties using a set of quantitative metrics.

Second, we investigate how these structural properties translate into predictive behavior by linking pointwise structural measures to classification outcomes obtained from prototype-based models. This analysis reveals that different dissimilarity spaces correctly classify different subsets of customers.

Third, we demonstrate that these complementary structures can be exploited through a Multi-Matrix learning approach. Using M^3GLVQ [1], we show that adaptively combining multiple dissimilarity spaces yields more robust predictions than models relying on single matrices or static aggregations.

The implementation of the proposed approach is available online [2].

2 Related Work

Our work relates to three lines of research: learning from pairwise dissimilarities, prototype-based classification on proximity data, and the combination of multiple heterogeneous representations.

Dissimilarity-based learning provides a general framework for pattern recognition when objects are more naturally compared by pairwise relations than represented in a common vector space [14]. This is particularly relevant for structured, categorical, or set-valued data, where domain-specific similarity notions are often more meaningful than standard feature encodings. Pękalska and Duin established dissimilarity representations as a flexible alternative to conventional vector-space learning and also studied prototype selection in such spaces [14,15]. These ideas are directly relevant to industrial customer profiling, where different feature groups induce different notions of similarity and are more naturally modeled by separate dissimilarity matrices than by a unified representation.

Learning Vector Quantization (LVQ) is a well-established family of prototype-based classifiers with a strong emphasis on interpretability [8,16]. For non-vectorial data, median LVQ extends this paradigm to proximity settings by restricting prototypes to observed samples and operating directly on dissimilarity matrices. Median variants of GLVQ therefore enable discriminative prototype-based learning when only pairwise dissimilarities are available [12,13]. This makes them attractive for industrial applications, where representative prototypes can be interpreted as actual customers and used to explain model decisions.

The combination of multiple representations has been studied in several related areas, including multi-view learning, metric learning, and multiple kernel learning [7,9,20]. Classical multi-view learning emphasizes that different views may provide complementary information [3,20], while multiple kernel learning shows that adaptive combinations of several similarity functions can outperform single-representation models [7]. Closely related ideas have also been explored in LVQ-based settings for heterogeneous data [21]. However, most existing approaches either assume vectorial feature spaces or kernelized representations and therefore do not directly address the joint learning from several dissimilarity matrices within an interpretable median-prototype classifier. A recent step in this direction is Multi-Matrix Median GLVQ, which extends median GLVQ to multiple proximity matrices with adaptive weight learning [1].

Against this background, the present work is not aimed at introducing yet another general framework for heterogeneous representation learning. Its central objective is to understand how structurally different dissimilarity spaces relate to predictive behavior in an applied industrial customer prediction setting, and whether their complementarity can be exploited by adaptive Multi-Matrix learning. To this end, we analyze the induced dissimilarity views at the structural level, relate local structural properties to customer-level prediction behavior, and evaluate how their joint use affects predictive performance within M^3GLVQ.

3 Data and Dissimilarity Views

Our work is motivated by an industrial B2B prediction task in which customers are described by several heterogeneous profiling sources. The application setting is purchase prediction for consumable industrial products, where predictive models are intended to support customer prioritization in sales and marketing. Beyond competitive predictive performance, interpretability is essential in this context, since model decisions must be understandable to domain experts and linked to representative customer profiles.

The dataset comprises 2025 real-world industrial customers from August Rüggeberg GmbH and defines a binary purchase prediction task for a specific product, observation window, and customer selection. The target variable indicates whether a customer made a purchase for this product within the observation period. In total, 1038 customers belong to the positive class and 987 to the negative class, resulting in a nearly balanced class distribution in this scenario.

In this setting, it is particularly important that predictions can be related back to meaningful industrial customer profiles rather than being used as unclear decision rules. This makes representations based on industry, product, and application information valuable, since they reflect operational characteristics that domain experts can interpret directly.

Each customer is represented through three industrial profiling sources describing complementary aspects of its activity: industry classification based on hierarchical NAICS codes, produced products represented as sets of HS codes, and manufacturing applications described by an internal hierarchical engineering classification. The latter is proprietary and therefore not disclosed in detail.

These representations are predominantly categorical, partly hierarchical, and in two cases naturally set-valued.

These characteristics make a single unified vector-space representation unattractive. Standard encodings such as one-hot representations lead to sparse high-dimensional feature spaces and fail to reflect the distinct semantic notions of similarity expressed by the different profiling sources. Consequently, standard vector-space baselines are unsuitable as direct comparators without additional encoding choices. We therefore model each source by its own dissimilarity measure and obtain three complementary dissimilarity matrices, each capturing customer relations from a different perspective.

4 Construction of the Dissimilarity Views

We construct one dissimilarity matrix for each profiling source. For set-valued representations, we use a symmetric k-nearest-neighbor best-match aggregation with $k = 3$, which can be viewed as a k-NN generalization of average-minimum (Chamfer-/modified-Hausdorff-type) set distances [5]. If a set contains fewer than k elements, all available elements are used.

For two sets A_i and A_j, let $\delta(a, b)$ denote a source-specific base dissimilarity between elements $a \in A_i$ and $b \in A_j$. We define the directed set dissimilarity as

$$d_k(A_i, A_j) = \frac{1}{|A_i|} \sum_{a \in A_i} \frac{1}{k_{ij}} \sum_{b \in \mathcal{N}_{k_{ij}}(a; A_j)} \delta(a, b), \qquad k_{ij} = \min(k, |A_j|). \tag{1}$$

where $\mathcal{N}_{k_{ij}}(a; A_j)$ denotes the k_{ij} nearest elements of a in A_j. The final symmetric set dissimilarity is

$$d(A_i, A_j) = \frac{1}{2} \left(d_k(A_i, A_j) + d_k(A_j, A_i) \right). \tag{2}$$

4.1 Industry View (NAICS)

To compare six-digit NAICS codes, we use a gated weighted Hamming-type dissimilarity tailored to the hierarchical structure of NAICS codes. The construction follows the general idea of Hamming-type distances for categorical representations, but adapts it to NAICS by enforcing maximal dissimilarity across different two-digit sectors and by assigning decreasing positional weights to later digits, reflecting the progressively finer hierarchy of the coding system [17]. The gate reflects sector semantics. Let $c_i = (c_{i1}, \dots, c_{iL})$ with $L = 6$. The dissimilarity between companies i and j is

$$d(i, j) = \begin{cases} 1, & \text{if } c_{i1} \neq c_{j1} \vee c_{i2} \neq c_{j2}, \\ \dfrac{\sum_{\ell=3}^{L} w_\ell \, \mathbf{1}[c_{i\ell} \neq c_{j\ell}]}{\sum_{\ell=3}^{L} w_\ell}, & \text{otherwise,} \end{cases} \qquad w_\ell = L - \ell + 1. \tag{3}$$

4.2 Product View (HS)

Produced products are represented as sets of HS codes. To capture hierarchical proximity beyond exact HS6 matches, we combine the set aggregation above with the following Product-based base dissimilarity:

$$\delta_{\mathrm{HS}}(a,b)=\begin{cases}0, & \text{if } a=b,\\ 0.25, & \text{if } \lfloor a/100\rfloor=\lfloor b/100\rfloor \wedge a\neq b,\\ 0.55, & \text{if } \lfloor a/10000\rfloor=\lfloor b/10000\rfloor \wedge \lfloor a/100\rfloor\neq\lfloor b/100\rfloor,\\ 1, & \text{otherwise.}\end{cases} \tag{4}$$

For the customer HS code sets A_i and A_j, the product dissimilarity is given by $d(A_i, A_j)$ using $\delta = \delta_{\mathrm{HS}}$. The HS hierarchy scores were heuristically chosen.

4.3 Application View (AP)

Manufacturing applications are represented as sets of hierarchical codes $x = (A_x, B_x)$ with main category A and subcategory B. Their base dissimilarity is defined as

$$\delta_{\mathrm{app}}(x,y)=\begin{cases}0, & \text{if } A_x=A_y \wedge B_x=B_y,\\ 0.5, & \text{if } A_x=A_y \wedge B_x\neq B_y,\\ 1, & \text{if } A_x\neq A_y.\end{cases} \tag{5}$$

For the application-code sets S_i and S_j of customers i and j, the application dissimilarity is given by $d(S_i, S_j)$ using $\delta = \delta_{\mathrm{app}}$.

4.4 Distance Distribution Summary

Table 1 summarizes the empirical dissimilarity distributions of the three views. The Product and Industry matrices are strongly concentrated toward large dissimilarities and contain a substantial fraction of maximally dissimilar pairs, whereas the Application matrix shows a broader and more graded distribution. This already suggests that the three views induce different global geometries, which we analyze in more detail in the following section.

Table 1. Descriptive statistics of the pairwise dissimilarities in the three views.

Matrix	Mean	Std.	Median	$q_{0.1}$	$q_{0.9}$	Share ($d = 1$)
Industry (NAICS)	0.852	0.208	0.950	0.650	1.000	0.462
Products (HS)	0.914	0.147	1.000	0.677	1.000	0.644
Applications (AP)	0.608	0.273	0.625	0.250	1.000	0.219

5 Structural Analysis of the Dissimilarity Spaces

While the empirical distance distributions already indicated differences in the global geometry of the three representations, this section analyzes their structural properties in greater detail. To characterize the dissimilarity views, we employ a set of complementary structural diagnostics combining class-separation measures, neighborhood-based local structure measures, prototype-based margin analysis, and intrinsic-dimensionality estimation. This choice follows the general perspective of dissimilarity-space analysis and dataset-complexity assessment, where no single metric is sufficient to capture all relevant structural aspects of a representation [10,14]. We first examine each matrix separately with respect to class separation, local neighborhood structure, margin behavior, and intrinsic dimensionality. We then compare the matrices in terms of their global agreement and local neighborhood overlap.

5.1 Single-Matrix Structural Properties

To characterize the individual representations, each dissimilarity matrix is analyzed independently using five structural descriptors: a separation ratio defined as the ratio between mean inter-class and mean intra-class dissimilarity, the mean local kNN purity for $k = 10$, the average pointwise margin $\mu_i = \frac{d_i^- - d_i^+}{d_i^- + d_i^+}$ in the GLVQ sense [16], the fraction of samples with negative margin, and an estimate of intrinsic dimensionality obtained with the Two-Nearest-Neighbors (2NN) estimator [6] (Table 2).

Table 2. Structural characteristics of the individual dissimilarity spaces.

Matrix	Sep. Ratio	kNN Pur.	μ	Neg. μ	Intr. Dim.
Industry (NAICS)	1.0047	0.5704	−0.0311	0.0632	1.2918
Products (HS)	1.0034	0.5260	−0.0207	0.3175	7.6618
Applications (AP)	1.0043	0.5240	−0.0020	0.1536	14.0242

The three views differ more clearly in local than in global structure. Global class separation is weak in all cases, as indicated by separation ratios only slightly above one, meaning that mean inter-class dissimilarities exceed mean intra-class dissimilarities only marginally. This suggests that class information is not primarily reflected in a strong global separation of the customer population. At the local level, however, the Industry view shows the highest kNN purity and the lowest fraction of negative margins, suggesting the most coherent class neighborhoods and the least local overlap between classes. By contrast, the Products and Applications views exhibit lower local purity and substantially higher fractions of negative margins, indicating that samples are more often embedded in locally ambiguous regions. Differences also emerge in intrinsic dimensionality: the Industry view is characterized by a very low estimated dimensionality, whereas the Products and Applications views induce markedly more complex similarity structures. Overall, the results suggest that the three views capture different structural aspects of the customer population rather than redundant variations of the same geometry.

5.2 Comparison Across Views

To compare the three views directly, we analyze their agreement at the global and local level using correlations between vectorized pairwise dissimilarities and overlaps of nearest-neighbor sets.

Table 3. Pearson correlation between vectorized pairwise dissimilarities of the three views.

	Industry (NAICS)	Products (HS)	Applications (AP)
Industry (NAICS)	1.000	0.173	0.127
Products (HS)	0.173	1.000	0.148
Applications (AP)	0.127	0.148	1.000

Pairwise correlations between the dissimilarity matrices are uniformly low, indicating that customer relations differ substantially across views even at the global level. In other words, customer pairs that appear relatively similar in one representation are often not similarly organized in the others. This already suggests that the three views do not provide interchangeable descriptions of the same underlying geometry (Table 3).

Table 4. Mean overlap of k_{NN} neighborhoods between dissimilarity views for $k_{\text{NN}} = 10$.

	Industry (NAICS)	Products (HS)	Applications (AP)
Industry (NAICS)	1.000	0.082	0.011
Products (HS)	0.082	1.000	0.009
Applications (AP)	0.011	0.009	1.000

This difference becomes even more pronounced at the local level. Mean k_{NN} overlap is very small across all view pairs, especially for comparisons involving the Applications view, showing that the nearest-neighbor structure induced by one representation is rarely reproduced by another. The same pattern was observed consistently for $k_{\text{NN}} \in \{5, 10, 25, 50\}$. Taken together, the low matrix correlations indicate weak global agreement, while the minimal neighborhood overlap points to even stronger local complementarity (Table 4). The three dissimilarity views therefore do not merely differ in overall geometry, but organize local customer neighborhoods in substantially different ways, which directly motivates their joint use in the predictive analysis below.

While correlations and neighborhood overlap quantify global and local agreement, they do not yet show whether the views identify the same customer pairs as structurally similar. To further compare the induced similarity structure across views, we analyze whether customer pairs are considered similar or dissimilar in the same way across the matrices. For each view, a pair is treated as similar if its dissimilarity falls below the empirical 10% quantile of that matrix (Table 5).

Table 5. Pairwise agreement of similarity relations between dissimilarity views based on a 10% quantile threshold.

Pair (A-B)	Agree Similar	Agree Dissimilar	A-only Similar	B-only Similar
Products–Applications	0.014	0.814	0.086	0.086
Industry–Applications	0.016	0.800	0.099	0.084
Industry–Products	0.018	0.803	0.097	0.082

The agreement analysis shows that the views rarely identify the same customer pairs as similar. Across all matrix pairs, agreement on similar pairs is extremely small, whereas agreement is much higher for dissimilar pairs. This means that the views are relatively consistent in identifying customer pairs that are clearly far apart, but differ strongly in which local relations they treat as informative similarity. At the same time, the A-only and B-only proportions show that each view identifies its own subset of customer pairs as similar, which are not regarded as similar in the respective other view. This supports the interpretation that the views capture complementary structural information rather than redundant proximity patterns.

6 Single-Matrix Baselines and Structure–Prediction Links

To evaluate the predictive usefulness of the individual dissimilarity views, we first train separate Median Generalized Learning Vector Quantization (MGLVQ) models for each matrix. These models serve as single-view baselines and allow us to analyze how structural properties relate to prediction behavior at the customer level.

For each dissimilarity matrix, the number of prototypes per class K is selected by grid search over

$$K \in \{3, 4, 5, 6, 7, 8, 9, 10\}.$$

The number of training iterations is fixed to $T = 150$. Model selection is performed by stratified cross-validation using balanced accuracy as the primary criterion. For each view, the best configuration is retained and out-of-fold (OOF) predictions are generated for all samples (Table 6).

Table 6. Performance of the single-view MGLVQ baselines based on out-of-fold predictions under the selected hyperparameter configuration.

Matrix	K	Bal. Acc.	Recall	TP	FP	TN	FN
Industry (NAICS)	4	0.554	0.445	462	333	654	576
Products (HS)	5	0.576	0.619	643	461	526	395
Applications (AP)	7	0.542	0.557	578	467	520	460

The three views yield different predictive behavior. In terms of point estimates, the Product view achieves the highest balanced accuracy and recall, whereas the Industry view is more conservative despite its stronger local structural coherence. The Applications view lies between these two extremes. Given the small differences in balanced accuracy, the results should be interpreted carefully. Structural quality and predictive usefulness are related but not identical.

To examine this relationship more directly, we compare local kNN purity values for correctly and incorrectly classified customers in each single-view model. Figure 1 shows that correctly classified samples consistently tend to lie in locally purer neighborhoods.

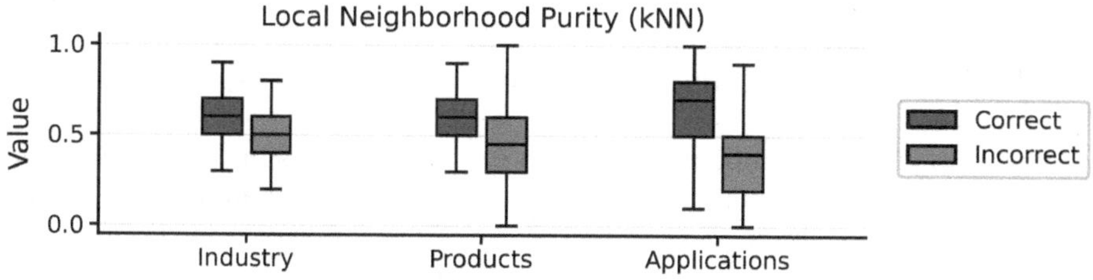

Fig. 1. Distribution of local kNN purity for correctly and incorrectly classified samples in the single-view baseline models.

Across all three views, incorrect predictions are associated with lower local purity, although the strength of this separation differs by representation. This indicates that local neighborhood structure is informative for prediction correctness, but that its predictive role depends on the underlying dissimilarity view.

To further link structure and prediction, we compare for each customer the view with the strongest local structural signal to the view whose single-view model predicts the label correctly. Structural dominance is defined by the highest

Table 7. Customer counts grouped by prediction dominance and structural dominance. Structural dominance denotes the view with the highest local kNN purity. Prediction dominance denotes which single-view MGLVQ models classify a customer correctly.

Prediction dominance	Structural dominance			
	Industry	Products	Application	Mixed
Industry	106	54	20	43
Products	57	38	34	39
Applications	39	14	106	36
Mixed	189	125	228	162
All	130	89	129	115
None	92	73	55	52

local kNN purity per sample, while prediction dominance refers to the view whose model correctly classifies the sample. Table 7 summarizes this relationship.

The table shows partial but not perfect alignment between structural and predictive dominance. For the Industry and Applications views, strong local structure often coincides with correct prediction by the corresponding model. For the Products view, this alignment is weaker, indicating that favorable regions in the product space do not translate into predictive success as consistently.

At the same time, the upper 3×3 block highlights many customers that are correctly classified by exactly one view. These cases show that the predictive signal is not concentrated in a single representation but distributed across the available dissimilarity views. This provides the main motivation for the Multi-Matrix analysis in the next section.

7 Multi-Matrix Learning with M^{3}GLVQ

The preceding analyses indicate that the constructed dissimilarity views differ substantially in their structural properties and predictive behavior. In particular, different single-view models correctly classify different subsets of customers. This motivates a learning approach that combines several dissimilarity views adaptively rather than relying on a single representation.

To this end, we employ M^{3}GLVQ [1], which extends median GLVQ from a single dissimilarity matrix to a set of matrices $\mathcal{D} = \{D^{(1)}, D^{(2)}, \ldots, D^{(V)}\}$. The model forms the weighted combined dissimilarity

$$D^* = \sum_{v=1}^{V} \alpha_v D^{(v)}, \qquad \alpha_v \geq 0, \qquad \sum_{v=1}^{V} \alpha_v = 1. \tag{6}$$

In Eq. (6), coefficients α_v can be interpreted as relative contributions of the views, while prototypes and matrix weights are adapted jointly during training.

7.1 Model Setup and Representative Weight Profiles

Before training, the dissimilarity matrices are normalized to place them on a comparable scale and to avoid trivial weight preferences induced by differences in magnitude. Without this step, matrices with larger numerical ranges could receive lower weights for scale-related rather than predictive reasons. Optimization details follow the original M^3GLVQ formulation in [1]. Hyperparameters were tuned by stratified cross-validation, varying prototype numbers over $K_0, K_1 \in \{3, 4, 5, 6, 7, 8, 9, 10\}$ and the learning rate for matrix-weight adaptation over $\eta \in \{0.003, 0.0075, 0.01, 0.015, 0.025, 0.03, 0.04, 0.05\}$.

Compared to the single-matrix baseline setting, this search space is deliberately broader, because Multi-Matrix learning introduces an additional interaction between prototype allocation and adaptive view weighting. In particular, the matrix-weight learning rate influences whether the model converges to more balanced or more concentrated regimes and therefore affects not only aggregate performance, but also the cross-view interaction realized during training.

To analyze whether strong Multi-Matrix performance is associated with specific weighting regimes, we collected the final weight vectors of all cross-validation runs and retained the top 10% according to balanced accuracy. Rather than focusing on a single best run, this allows us to assess whether competitive performance is tied to one narrowly optimal solution or can emerge under several qualitatively different matrix combinations. The retained solutions were grouped using k-means clustering to obtain representative weight profiles, and we focus on three mixed profiles that reflect different modes of interaction between the available dissimilarity views [11]. This analysis is intended to characterize robust high-performing weighting regimes rather than to overinterpret one possibly dataset-specific parameter setting.

Table 8. Representative mixed weight profiles among the top 10% M^3GLVQ runs with (K_0, K_1) as the cluster-wise mean prototype numbers.

Cluster	α_{NAICS}	α_{HS}	α_{AP}	Bal. Acc.	Recall	(K_0, K_1)
C0	0.546	0.280	0.175	0.5990	0.6485	(5.8, 5.4)
C3	0.376	0.323	0.301	0.5917	0.7062	(5.0, 3.9)
C4	0.815	0.181	0.004	0.5856	0.6064	(4.5, 4.9)

The selected profiles correspond to different weighting regimes. C0 and C4 are more strongly Industry-driven, whereas C3 is the most balanced configuration (Table 8). Although their balanced accuracies are broadly similar, C3 achieves the highest recall, suggesting that different weight profiles induce different trade-offs between conservative and broader predictive behavior.

7.2 Customer-Level Effects Across Prediction-Dominance Groups

Based on these representative profiles, we perform a second evaluation stage with fixed matrix weights. For each selected profile, the corresponding weight vector is kept fixed while the prototypes are optimized under stratified cross-validation, yielding out-of-fold predictions for customer-level analysis.

To relate the selected M^{3}GLVQ variants back to the single-view baseline analysis, we evaluate them across the prediction-dominance groups introduced above. These groups partition the customers according to which of the three single-view MGLVQ models classify them correctly: customers may be correctly classified only by the Industry, Products, or Application model, by more than one but not all models (Mixed), by all three models (All correct), or by none of them (All wrong). This makes it possible to assess which types of single-view predictive signal are preserved, weakened, or recovered under different Multi-Matrix weighting regimes.

Table 9. Number of correctly classified customers for the selected fixed-weight M^{3}GLVQ variants across the prediction-dominance groups obtained from the single-view MGLVQ analysis. The groups indicate whether a customer was correctly classified only by the Industry, Products, or Applications single-view model, by more than one but not all models (Mixed), by all models (All correct), or by none of them (All wrong). For each M^{3}GLVQ profile, the value in parentheses denotes the difference relative to the total number of customers in the respective group.

Single-view group	n	Cluster 0	Cluster 3	Cluster 4
Industry-only	223	109 (−114)	65 (−158)	109 (−114)
Products-only	168	85 (−83)	124 (−44)	84 (−84)
Applications-only	195	45 (−150)	44 (−151)	43 (−152)
Mixed	704	477 (−227)	500 (−204)	444 (−260)
All correct	463	383 (−80)	395 (−68)	392 (−71)
All wrong	272	60 (+60)	51 (+51)	57 (+57)
Total	2025	1159	1179	1129

Table 9 reports, for each group from the single-view analysis, how many customers are correctly classified by the selected fixed-weight M^{3}GLVQ variants. The values in parentheses indicate the difference between this number and the total size of the respective group. Negative values therefore show how many customers from a given single-view group are not recovered by the corresponding Multi-Matrix model, whereas positive values in the All wrong row indicate customers that were missed by all single-view models but become correctly classified under Multi-Matrix learning.

The three profiles differ noticeably in the customer subsets they recover. Cluster 3, the most balanced regime, achieves the highest total number of correct predictions and recovers substantially more Product-dominated cases than the more Industry-focused profiles. Conversely, Clusters 0 and 4 preserve a larger fraction of Industry-specific cases. All three profiles recover only a small fraction of the Application-specific cases, suggesting that predictive signal from the Applications view is difficult to preserve once the views are combined globally.

At the same time, all selected Multi-Matrix variants correctly classify customers in the All wrong group, that is, customers that were missed by all single-view models. This provides direct evidence that jointly combining heterogeneous dissimilarity views can uncover predictive structure that is not accessible from any individual representation alone.

Overall, these results support the main motivation for Multi-Matrix learning: the benefit of M^{3}GLVQ lies not only in aggregate performance, but also in its ability to redistribute predictive strength across customer subsets. Different weight profiles emphasize different structural signals, and more balanced combinations appear particularly promising for exploiting complementary information across the available dissimilarity views.

8 Discussion

The results show that heterogeneous industrial customer profiles give rise to dissimilarity views that are not merely alternative encodings of the same underlying structure. Instead, the three views differ substantially in their global geometry, local neighborhood organization, and predictive behavior. While none of the individual views exhibits strong global class separation, the structural analyses reveal clear differences in local organization, and these differences translate into distinct customer-level prediction patterns.

A central finding is that the views are complementary rather than redundant. The low agreement between the dissimilarity matrices, the minimal neighborhood overlap, and the customer-level analysis of the single-view baselines all indicate that different representations capture different aspects of the customer population. This is particularly important in the present application setting, because it implies that the choice of representation directly affects which customers can be predicted successfully.

At the same time, the relationship between structural quality and predictive performance is not one-dimensional. The Industry view exhibits the most coherent local class structure according to the structural descriptors, yet the Products view yields the strongest single-view predictive performance. This suggests that favorable structural organization alone does not guarantee the strongest task-specific predictive signal. Rather, different views encode different information, some of which is more directly aligned with purchase prediction than others.

A similar picture emerges in the Multi-Matrix setting. Competitive M^{3}GLVQ performance is not tied to one unique weighting profile, but can arise under several qualitatively different combinations of the available views. This indicates that the benefit of Multi-Matrix learning does not stem from a single universally optimal aggregation, but from its ability to redistribute predictive strength across customer subsets depending on which structural signals are emphasized.

At the customer level, this becomes particularly visible. More balanced combinations recover a larger fraction of Product-dominated cases and achieve the strongest overall customer-level performance, whereas more Industry-focused regimes preserve a larger share of industry-specific cases. Moreover, all selected Multi-Matrix variants correctly classify customers missed by all single-view models, providing evidence that joint learning across dissimilarity views can uncover predictive structure that is not accessible from any single representation alone.

The results also point to a limitation of the current formulation. Although global matrix weighting already improves flexibility compared to static aggregation, it does not preserve all single-view-specific strengths equally well. In particular, the predictive signal associated with the Applications view remains difficult to retain consistently in the combined model. This suggests that a single global weight vector may still be too restrictive to reflect local variation in the relevance of the available views across the customer population.

In addition, dense pairwise matrices scale as $\mathcal{O}(VN^2)$ in memory, which may require sparse or prototype-based approximations for larger deployments.

From an application perspective, these findings are relevant beyond the specific industrial use case studied here. In many real-world domains, customer or object profiles are inherently heterogeneous and induce several semantically distinct notions of similarity. The present results indicate that such representations should not be collapsed too early into a single static view. Instead, their structural complementarity should be analyzed explicitly and, where possible, exploited through adaptive multi-view dissimilarity learning.

From this perspective, the main advantage of adaptive Multi-Matrix learning is not merely improved aggregate performance, but a more faithful exploitation of heterogeneous relational structure in the customer population.

9 Conclusion and Future Work

This work studied how multiple heterogeneous dissimilarity views derived from industrial customer profiles can be analyzed and combined for purchase prediction. We showed that the constructed views differ substantially in their structural properties and that these differences translate into distinct customer-level prediction behavior. In particular, single-view models correctly classify different subsets of customers, indicating that the available representations contain complementary predictive information.

Motivated by these findings, we evaluated M^{3}GLVQ as an adaptive approach for combining several dissimilarity views. The results show that Multi-Matrix learning is beneficial not only in terms of aggregate predictive performance, but also in its ability to redistribute predictive strength across customer subsets and to recover cases that are not accessible from any individual representation alone. More generally, the study suggests that heterogeneous industrial customer data should not be collapsed prematurely into a single static representation when structurally distinct dissimilarity views are available, because doing so may hide precisely those complementary relations that are most relevant for prediction.

Taken together, the results support the view that in heterogeneous industrial analytics, the choice and combination of relational representations is itself a central modeling decision rather than a purely technical preprocessing step.

Several directions for future work follow from these results. First, the current model uses a single global weight vector, whereas the customer-level analyses suggest that different local regions of the data may require different combinations of views. Extending the Multi-Matrix median LVQ framework toward localized weighting schemes is therefore a particularly promising direction [4,18]. Second, the present dissimilarity definitions were motivated by the structure of the underlying industrial data but not compared exhaustively against alternative formulations, so a broader study of domain-specific dissimilarity design remains an important next step. Third, beyond binary purchase prediction, richer targets such as purchase intensity, quantity, or multi-product demand patterns could provide an even more informative application setting for heterogeneous dissimilarity learning.

Use of Generative AI. Generative AI tools were used during manuscript preparation for language editing and text refinement. All scientific content, methodological decisions, results, and the final text were reviewed and approved by the authors. The authors take full responsibility for the submitted paper.

Acknowledgments. This contribution has been developed in the project PLan CV. Within the funding program FH-Personal, the project PLan CV (reference number 03FHP109) is funded by the German Federal Ministry of Education and Research (BMBF) and the Joint Science Conference (GWK).

Disclosure of Interests. The authors have no competing interests to declare that are relevant to the content of this article.

References

1. Bader, L., Terwey-Scheulen, I., Zühlke, D.: Implementation of Multi-Matrix median generalized learning vector quantization, pp. 381–386 (2026). https://doi.org/10.14428/esann/2026.ES2026-157
2. Bader, L.: ECML26 (2026). https://github.com/LukasBader31415/ECML26
3. Blum, A., Mitchell, T.: Combining labeled and unlabeled data with co-training. In: Proceedings of the Eleventh Annual Conference on Computational Learning Theory, pp. 92–100. ACM (1998). https://doi.org/10.1145/279943.279962
4. Bunte, K., Hammer, B., Biehl, M.: Nonlinear dimension reduction and visualization of labeled data. In: Jiang, X., Petkov, N. (eds.) CAIP 2009. LNCS, vol. 5702, pp. 1162–1170. Springer, Heidelberg (2009). https://doi.org/10.1007/978-3-642-03767-2_141
5. Dubuisson, M.P., Jain, A.K.: A modified Hausdorff distance for object matching. In: Proceedings of the 12th IAPR International Conference on Pattern Recognition, pp. 566–568 (1994)
6. Facco, E., d'Errico, M., Rodriguez, A., Laio, A.: Estimating the intrinsic dimension of datasets by a minimal neighborhood information. Sci. Rep. **7**, 12140 (2017)

7. Gönen, M., Alpaydın, E.: Multiple kernel learning algorithms. J. Mach. Learn. Res. **12**, 2211–2268 (2011)
8. Kohonen, T.: Self-Organizing Maps. Springer Series in Information Sciences, vol. 30, 3rd edn. Springer, Heidelberg (2001). https://doi.org/10.1007/978-3-642-56927-2
9. Kulis, B.: Metric learning: a survey. Found. Trends Mach. Learn. **5**(4), 287–364 (2012). https://doi.org/10.1561/2200000019
10. Lorena, A.C., et al.: How complex is your classification problem? A survey on measuring classification complexity. ACM Comput. Surv. **52**(5), 107:1–107:34 (2019)
11. MacQueen, J.B.: Some methods for classification and analysis of multivariate observations. In: Proceedings of the Fifth Berkeley Symposium on Mathematical Statistics and Probability, vol. 1, pp. 281–297 (1967)
12. Nebel, D., Hammer, B., Frohberg, K., Villmann, T.: Median variants of learning vector quantization for learning of dissimilarity data. Neurocomputing **169**, 295–305 (2015)
13. Nebel, D., Hammer, B., Villmann, T.: A median variant of generalized learning vector quantization. In: Lee, M., Hirose, A., Hou, Z.-G., Kil, R.M. (eds.) ICONIP 2013. LNCS, vol. 8227, pp. 19–26. Springer, Heidelberg (2013). https://doi.org/10.1007/978-3-642-42042-9_3
14. Pekalska, E., Duin, R.P.: The Dissimilarity Representation for Pattern Recognition. World Scientific, Singapore (2005)
15. Pekalska, E., Duin, R.P., Paclik, P.: Prototype selection for dissimilarity-based classifiers. Pattern Recogn. **39**(2), 189–208 (2006). https://doi.org/10.1016/j.patcog.2005.06.012
16. Sato, A., Yamada, K.: Generalized learning vector quantization. In: Advances in Neural Information Processing Systems, vol. 8, pp. 423–429. MIT Press (1995)
17. U.S. Census Bureau: North American industry classification system (NAICS) (2026). https://www.census.gov/naics. Accessed 12 Mar 2026
18. van Veen, R., Biehl, M., de Vries, G.J.: sklvq: Scikit learning vector quantization. J. Mach. Learn. Res. **22**(231), 1–6 (2021)
19. World Customs Organization: HS Nomenclature 2022 edition (2022). https://www.wcoomd.org/en/topics/nomenclature/instrument-and-tools/hs-nomenclature-2022-edition.aspx. Accessed 12 Mar 2026
20. Xu, C., Tao, D., Xu, C.: A survey on multi-view learning. arXiv preprint arXiv:1304.5634 (2013)
21. Zühlke, D., Schleif, F.M., Geweniger, T., Haase, S., Villmann, T.: Learning vector quantization for heterogeneous structured data. In: Proceedings of ESANN, pp. 271–276. D-Side Publishing (2010)

From Manual to Real-World: Deep Unfolded Neural Network for Cross-Domain UXO Retrieval

Gheorghe Marian Craioveanu and Grigore Stamatescu(✉)

University of Science and Technology Politehnica Bucharest, Bucharest, Romania
{gheorghe.craioveanu,grigore.stamatescu}@upb.ro

Abstract. UneXploded Ordnance (UXO), conventional bombs deployed in past conflicts that failed to detonate, represents a significant challenge for robust deep learning identification in realistic field conditions. This is primarily due to the severe domain shift between noisy field imagery and clean technical manual references. At the same time, UXO mitigation represents a difficult task even for human operators due to stress, fatigue, and the associated risks. Despite major advances in deep learning for binary classification, localisation, and segmentation, practical field identification has remained largely unsolved. This work helps to bridge the gap in smart UXO identification, an application with direct impact on society, by unfolding a parametric shape-fitting procedure into a neural network, thereby embedding domain-specific geometric constraints directly into the learnable architecture. Unlike black-box few-shot encoders, this structured approach preserves the interpretability of classical optimisation while gaining data-driven robustness to occlusions and noise common in operational demining/clearance operations. The learnt unfolded representation ensures the correspondence of munitions in latent space, regardless of whether they originate from field conditions or controlled environments, enabling direct nearest-neighbour retrieval without relying on RGB appearance or class supervision. Experiments on a reference dataset demonstrate that the proposed architecture improves retrieval robustness compared to the baseline methods. In our experimental setup, Recall@1 improves from 53.4% to 62.1%, and Recall@5 improves from 65.4% to 82.1%. These findings show that deep unfolded shape refinement based on UXO characteristics offers a practical, interpretable, and physically grounded approach to identifying unexploded ordnances in real-world conditions.

Keywords: Unexploded Ordnance · Deep Unfolded Network · Cross-Domain Retrieval

1 Introduction

Unexploded Ordnance (UXO), also known as Unexploded Bombs (UXB), poses a serious hazard and an ongoing challenge in contemporary society. According to

M. Baratchi et al. (Eds.): ECML PKDD 2026, LNAI 16949, pp. 181–197, 2027.
https://doi.org/10.1007/978-3-032-37682-4_11

Fig. 1. UXO in the field can be oxidised, partially covered by vegetation/soil, and sometimes even component parts are missing, being difficult to use common retrieval approaches. The illustration is produced by running the Segment Anything Model [24] on the annotated bounding box of a UXO sample from the CTX-UXO dataset [8].

the North Atlantic Treaty Organisation (NATO) [22], UXO represents an explosive object that has been primed, fuzed, armed, or otherwise prepared for use, may have been fired, dropped, launched, or projected, but remains unexploded due to malfunction, design, or any other reason. Based on statistics provided by the United Nations Mine Action Service [17,31], hundreds of millions of explosive remnants of war are present in at least 70 countries around the world. Across Europe, statistical data suggest that this contamination affects all European nations to varying degrees. In Germany, up to 1.6 million tonnes of ammunition are estimated [19] to be located along its coasts or in its waters. In Norway, up to 200,000 tonnes of munitions are believed to remain undiscovered [19]. In Italy, the authorities have estimated [2] that on average up to 60,000 munitions items (including parts of UXOs) are found annually. UXO are also present in other European and non-European countries, but the projected ranges for the total number of explosive items are very broad as they are difficult to quantify. Beyond the risks posed by direct contact, munitions also affect civilian society through soil and water contamination, releasing toxic substances (mainly TNT) that can cause diseases [13,19]. The phenomenon is global in nature and difficult to delimit [31]. It is important to emphasize that unexploded ordnance (UXO) represents a long-standing and continuing hazard, constituting a persistent societal challenge and a major public safety concern that has endured for more than eight decades. We provide a qualitative example with a real-world projectile in Fig. 1.

In this paper, we propose a dual approach, integrating domain-specific Explosive Ordnance Disposal (EOD) expertise with a deep learning architecture, to advance applied research in safety-critical applications represented by UXO. For context, in operational settings UXO identification typically relies on establishing visual correspondence between items observed in the field and reference sources, such as technical documentation and specialised databases. Automating this workflow is non-trivial due to the substantial domain shift between real-world field imagery and the idealised visualisations found in reference materials. The targets may be partially occluded, truncated by image borders, or obscured by environmental clutter (e.g., soil, vegetation) [9]. In contrast, technical manuals provide clear, complete and canonical views of the ordnance.It is important to consult manuals as references in order to replicate the field methodology, since these references typically include technical details (such as calibre, explosive content, origin, and associated risks) that are crucial for the stages that follow identification. This discrepancy results in a domain gap, meaning the statistical characteristics of the field data differ substantially from those of the reference data. As a result, appearance-driven methods, often exhibit suboptimal performance, as they implicitly rely on texture, illumination, and visual context, features which fail to transfer reliably between domains. The main contributions of this work are:

- We introduce a deep unfolded shape refinement network that reformulates an iterative parametric shape fitting process as a learnable neural architecture, yielding a compact and interpretable shape representation that is robust to noise, partial occlusion, and missing shape information;
- We develop a training strategy based solely on field segmentation masks and demonstrate that the learnt unfolded representation enables robust cross-domain retrieval;
- We improve class-level identification under severe domain shift, a necessary step toward fine-grained identification when subtype labels become available. The task is formulated as class-level retrieval inside a common latent space, allowing the method to generalise to UXO types that are previously unseen or that differ substantially in visual appearance;
- We introduce a benchmark that contrasts few-shot methods based on RGB images, traditional shape-matching techniques, and our shape-only refinement neural network. In addition, we conduct an ablation study in Sect. 4 to examine how changes in the number of unfolding steps or in the chosen physically grounded parameters influence performance.

2 Related Work

With the increasing availability of open-source optical images, such as CTX-UXO [8] or CAT-UXO [7], recent works explored the localisation and/or classification of UXO directly from RGB images using convolutional neural networks or transformer architecture configured for UXO image classification and localisation. In this setting, most approaches focus on coarse categorisation [25,34]. Notably, in their dual-domain study [4], the researchers Baur et al. emphasised that deep learning detection models must be easily deployable in portable UAV/UGV systems to facilitate their practical use in the field. Using a drone and a two-stage detection architecture with intermediate region proposals, they achieved results of 71.5% mAP. However, it should be noted that the analysis was conducted in a single class (landmine, binary classification) with only one subtype (butterfly mine, PFM-1). Under favourable conditions, such methods have demonstrated promising performance, mostly when objects are fully visible and imaging conditions are controlled. In a recent preliminary contribution [18], the authors suggested that UXO mitigation should be addressed using an uncertainty-aware framework that relies on Bayesian Networks combined with Monte Carlo Dropout. This work indicates that implementations focusing on architecture-level tailored to the UXO detection problem, while keeping safety measures and explainability, can yield substantial performance gains. However, in the real world, the optical appearance varies significantly between environments, and performance often degrades in realistic field scenarios involving occlusion, clutter, and background variability. This was addressed by introducing contextual representative datasets with real field UXO, such as CTX-UXO [8]. Even if the dataset is representative, it does not include intrinsic metadata, such as calibre or other relevant attributes, meaning that operators are still required to rely on reference materials (databases) [7] augmented with all the metadata necessary for UXO mitigation. Appearance-based methods struggle to infer physically meaningful characteristics, and classification decisions are often driven by texture or contextual cues rather than object geometry. UXO identification has traditionally been addressed using geophysical sensing modalities such as ground penetration radar (GPR) [3] and magnetometry [26]. In these domains, identification is rarely performed through direct classification. Instead, the dominant paradigm relies on interpreting the shape of the measured signal response, such as spatial signatures, temporal waveforms, or polarisation curves, and comparing them against libraries of known responses.

Deep unfolding has emerged as a powerful paradigm for combining the interpretability of iterative algorithms with neural networks [28]. With good results for sparse coding [1] and compressed sensing [36], unfolded networks replace fixed update rules with learnable functions while preserving the algorithmic structure. More recently, shape analysis tasks have been addressed through deep unfolding [35]. Xinyi Wei et al. [35] propose a model-based deep learning framework that incorporates explicit generative priors within a deep unfolding architecture for inverse imaging. They embed a probabilistic flow-based prior directly into the iterative reconstruction, enabling task-adaptive optimisation. Evaluated on denoising, inpainting, and deblurring, and compared with strong ResNet- and U-Net-based proximal baselines, the method delivers competitive or superior results. In deblurring, it reaches 40.55 dB PSNR, outperforming U-Net proximal (38.66 dB) and ResNet-based approaches (35.55 dB). It attains 35.93 dB PSNR for inpainting and 28.24 dB PSNR for denoising, demonstrating robustness across tasks. Our work extends the deep unfolding neural network paradigm to cross-domain UXO shape retrieval, where the unfolding structure enables robust estimation of parametric shape descriptors from noisy observations. We acknowledge that classical shape matching methods, including Iterative Closest

Point (ICP) [37], Procrustes analysis [12], and shape context descriptors [16], provide geometrically grounded representations, but these methods are sensitive to noise and partial observations. ICP iteratively minimises the distance between corresponding point sets through rigid transformations. Procrustes analysis aligns shapes by removing translation, rotation, and scale, allowing direct shape comparison. Statistical shape analysis using Procrustes distances is a core technique in image analysis, as detailed by Dryden et al. [11], and with wide-ranging applications in biology, chemistry, bioinformatics, geography, archaeology, and related disciplines. Principal Component Analysis (PCA) further enhances these methods [11] by reducing noise due to object orientation and rotation and will therefore be applied in the preprocessing stage in this study. For fair benchmarking, Procrustes distance will also serve as a reference measure in the current manuscript. Alternative approaches based on point clouds, such as PointNet [23], were originally designed for 3D point cloud data. Adapting it to the context of our present study would require architectural constraints and modifications, this would constitute a separate line of research in its own right and would considerably broaden the scope of the current manuscript. We further acknowledge a range of recent methods [14,27,29,33], which may prove to be effective. However, these approaches are predicated upon fundamentally divergent paradigms, such that a direct and methodologically transparent comparison cannot, in good faith, be undertaken at present. For this reason, we leave their examination to future work, where they will be explored in a more focused and thorough way.

The current State-Of-The-Art (SoA) enables the localisation of UXO in the field and supports coarse categorisation. However, the precise determination of the exact UXO type remains mostly unresolved for real-world applications, particularly in relation to EOD procedures that rely on cross-referencing technical manuals. It can be observed that challenges highlight the gap between traditional geophysical approaches, which emphasise shape-based signal interpretation, and modern optical methods, which primarily rely on appearance. This observation motivates a return to shape-centric representations, adapted to the optical domain and capable of operating under severe domain mismatch between noisy field imagery and idealised technical references that have the metadata required for post-identification operations.

3 Methods

3.1 Preliminary

We formulate UXO identification as class-level cross-domain retrieval from binary segmentation masks, without relying on RGB appearance, texture, or scale calibration. Let $M \in \{0,1\}^{H \times W}$ denote an instance mask. We extract the foreground coordinates, compute their centroid and covariance matrix, and apply PCA to align the object with its principal axes. If the eigenvalue ratio falls below an isotropy threshold κ, no alignment is performed. The direction of the first principal axis is resolved by a slope-asymmetry criterion, enforcing consistent front–back orientation. In the resulting canonical frame, each foreground point has coordinates (z_i, y_i), with z along the principal axis and y orthogonal. The axial coordinate is normalised to $[0, 1]$ and discretised into N bins, the last bin including the end point to preserve the tip of the object. For each bin, we estimate a radial half-width profile as half the robust width of the orthogonal coordinate distribution, computed by trimming the extreme values to suppress outliers from segmentation noise. Bins with fewer than m points are set to zero and marked as invalid. The maximum calibre $D = 2\max_k r_{\text{raw}}(z_k)$ is used for normalisation to $[0, 1]$. A bin-wise validity vector $\mathbf{v} \in \{0, 1\}^N$ is defined as $v_k = 1$ if the occupancy $n_k \geq m$ and $r_{\text{raw}}(z_k) \geq \alpha \cdot \text{median}\{r_{\text{raw}}(z_j) \mid n_j \geq m\}$, and $v_k = 0$ otherwise. This vector masks unreliable regions during both training and inference.

Additional Notations. Throughout this section: $r_{\text{obs}} \in \mathbb{R}^N$ denotes the raw observed radial profile, $p^{(t)}$ the profile estimate at unfolding iteration t, $\hat{p} := p^{(T)}$ the final unfolded output, and $r_s = \text{SG}(\hat{p})$ the smoothed profile from which derivative-based descriptors are extracted.

3.2 Parametric Shape Representation

We model UXO shapes using a compact parametric vector $\theta \in \mathbb{R}^d$, where d denotes the total number of shape parameters, that captures key geometric features. Given a profile p (either the raw measurement r_{obs} or the unfolded estimate $p^{(T)}$), we generate a smoothed profile $r_s = \text{SG}(p)$ via a Savitzky–Golay filter with window size ω_{SG} and polynomial order d_{SG}, chosen to retain inflection points while attenuating high-frequency quantisation noise. All derivative-based descriptors described below are derived from r_s. Let $\mathcal{I}_f = \{k : z_k \leq \beta\}$ and $\mathcal{I}_b = \{k : z_k \geq 1 - \beta\}$ denote the sets of bins whose centres fall in the frontal and rear portions of the normalised axis, respectively, where $\beta \in (0, 0.5)$ is the consensus coverage threshold. We then introduce end-coverage scores c_f and c_b with the following equations:

$$c_f = \frac{1}{|\mathcal{I}_f|} \sum_{k:\, z_k \in \mathcal{I}_f} v_k \tag{1}$$

$$c_b = \frac{1}{|\mathcal{I}_b|} \sum_{k:\, z_k \in \mathcal{I}_b} v_k \tag{2}$$

In Eq. 1 and Eq. 2, $|\mathcal{I}_f|, |\mathcal{I}_b|$ denote the number of bins with centres in the respective intervals. An end region is considered reliably observed when its coverage score exceeds β; these scores are used to gate the taper-ratio computation (Eq. 3), preventing unreliable slope estimates from corrupting the shape descriptor. Based on domain expertise in ordnance identification, validated by public references [7], and international standards [31], we define five complementary shape parameters. The **length-to-Diameter ratio (L/D)** represents the aspect ratio computed from the *unnormalised* aligned coordinates as L/D, where $L = z_{\max} - z_{\min}$ and $D = 2\max_k r_{\text{raw}}(z_k)$, discriminating elongated projectiles, *teardrop* shaped mortar bombs and grenades. The **profile taper ratio** quantifies the asymmetry between nose and tail using the mean absolute slope of the smoothed profile near each end (central finite differences), defined as:

$$\tau = \frac{\frac{1}{|\mathcal{I}_f|}\sum_{z\in\mathcal{I}_f}|r_s'(z)| + \varepsilon}{\frac{1}{|\mathcal{I}_b|}\sum_{z\in\mathcal{I}_b}|r_s'(z)| + \varepsilon}, \tag{3}$$

The **encoded axial profile** corresponds to the normalised radial profile $p(z)$ sampled at equispaced points N along the principal axis (using $p = r_{\text{obs}}$ before unfolding and $p = p^{(T)}$ after unfolding). **Inflection Point Count** denotes the number of sign changes in the second derivative of $r_s(z)$ (central differences), counted only where $|r_s''(z)| > \gamma$, with γ an adaptive noise floor estimated from the variance of the second derivative on smooth reference shapes. Note that n_{infl} is a discrete, non-differentiable variable that is not involved in gradient-based training and is used only as a manually designed retrieval feature, computed after the fact from $p^{(T)}$. **Fourier Descriptors** are defined as the magnitudes of the first K_F non-zero DFT coefficients of r_s, normalised by the DC component, i.e., $|c_k|/\max(|c_0|, \varepsilon)$ for $k = 1, \dots, K_F$.

We define the deterministic parameter extraction function $h : \mathbb{R}^N \times \mathbb{R}_+ \to \mathbb{R}^d$ that maps a profile p and the raw scale to the complete parameter vector:

$$\theta = \left[\frac{L}{D},\ \tau,\ p(z_1), \dots, p(z_N),\ n_{\text{infl}},\ \frac{|c_1|}{\max(|c_0|, \varepsilon)}, \dots, \frac{|c_{K_F}|}{\max(|c_0|, \varepsilon)}\right]^\top \tag{4}$$

In Eq. 4, $d = 2 + N + 1 + K_F = 75$ parameters for $N = 64$ and $K_F = 8$. Before unfolding, θ is $h(r_{\text{obs}}, L/D)$. After unfolding, the vector is determined by $\hat{\theta} = h(p^{(T)}, L/D)$.

3.3 Datasets and Data Preparation

We used for training and evaluation the Contextual Vision for Unexploded Ordnances (CTX-UXO) dataset [8], which provides labelled UXO images captured under realistic field conditions. In our study, we employ the following classes: Projectile, Mortar Bomb, and Grenade, with a total of 13,789 field instances. We extract the corresponding segmentation mask from the annotations. The masks exhibit realistic degradations that include partial occlusion, boundary truncation, and segmentation noise. The reference database is constructed from CAT-UXO [7], a collection of idealised UXO images sourced from a community EOD Knowledge Hub. Each mask undergoes a sequence of operations: connected component analysis is applied while retaining only the largest foreground region, morphological closing with a disc-shaped structuring element of radius 3 is used to fill small gaps, the orientation is aligned to the principal axis by PCA using an isotropy threshold κ, profiles are obtained through percentile-based radial estimation (p_5, p_{95}) with N bins, and a validation mask is derived from a minimum occupancy threshold m combined with a rejection factor α.

We mention that we used the original train/validation/test split of the datasets, as defined by their authors.

3.4 Unfolded Architecture

At the core of our method lies a deep unfolded network that refines an axial profile from noisy observations. Given an observed profile r_{obs} and the current estimate $p^{(t)}$, each iteration applies a learnable direct mapping:

$$p^{(t+1)} = \Pi_{[0,1]} \left(g_{\phi_t} \left(p^{(t)}, r_{\text{obs}}, v \odot (r_{\text{obs}} - p^{(t)}) \right) \right), \tag{5}$$

In Eq. 5, $\Pi_{[0,1]}$ denotes element-wise clipping to $[0, 1]$, and $g_{\phi_t} : \mathbb{R}^{3N} \to \mathbb{R}^N$ is an MLP whose input is the concatenation of $p^{(t)}$, r_{obs}, and $v \odot (r_{\text{obs}} - p^{(t)})$, each of dimension N (concretely, $\mathbb{R}^{192} \to \mathbb{R}^{64}$), with architecture $192 \to 128 \to 64 \to 32 \to 64$ (ReLU hidden layers, linear output). Each iteration uses its own parameters ϕ_t (unshared weights). In implementation, each linear layer is spectral-normalised and scaled by a spectral bound $s = 0.95$, constraining the Lipschitz constant of each block and thereby limiting the sensitivity of unfolded iterates to input perturbations. The mapping from the latent noise-free profile p^* to the observed profile can be conceptually written as $r_{\text{obs}} = \mathcal{A}(p^*) + \eta$, where $\mathcal{A}$ encapsulates the effects of segmentation and occlusion that lack a tractable closed form. Each step g_{ϕ_t} implicitly approximates the corresponding inverse refinement operator, replacing a fixed gradient or proximal step with a data-driven mapping while retaining the iterative structure as an inductive bias. The initial profile estimate is set to $p^{(0)} = \bar{r}_{\text{train}}$, the mean normalised profile computed over the CTX-UXO training set; the same $p^{(0)}$ is used for both field queries and reference shapes. After the final iteration, we compute the full parameter vector deterministically as $\hat{\theta} = h(p^{(T)}, L/D)$, where h is the parameter extraction function defined in Eq. 4 and L/D is computed directly from the aligned mask. This enforces consistency between scalar descriptors and the reconstructed profile by construction. The validity weighting ensures that updates are driven only by regions where reliable observations exist, preventing error propagation from truncated or occluded portions of the object.

3.5 Training Objectives

The network is trained using only field segmentation masks, without class labels or paired cross-domain examples. The primary objective encourages the predicted profile $\hat{p} = p^{(T)}$ to match observations where valid:

$$\mathcal{L}_{\text{reconstruction}} = \frac{1}{\max(1, \sum_i v_i)} \sum_{i=1}^{N} v_i \cdot \rho_\delta \left(r_{\text{obs}}(z_i) - \hat{p}(z_i) \right), \tag{6}$$

In Eq. 6, ρ_δ denotes the Huber loss, whose parameter δ is chosen as the empirical standard deviation of the residuals $|r_{\text{obs}} - p^{(T)}|$ computed on clean reference shapes. Note that the reconstruction target in training stage is the observed profile itself, rather than a noise-free reference. Denoising arises [6] from three complementary factors: (i) the constrained capacity of the MLP bottleneck (32 dimensions), which compels the network to represent profiles on a low-dimensional manifold of plausible solutions instead of memorising noise; (ii) the validity mask, which excludes unreliable bins from the loss computation; and (iii) the consistency loss (described below), which promotes robustness to perturbations and mitigates overfitting to noise specific to individual observations. To improve robustness to augmentation, we enforce consistency between estimates from augmented views of the same mask:

$$\mathcal{L}_{\text{cons}} = \left\| \hat{\theta}_{\text{prof}}(M) - \hat{\theta}_{\text{prof}}(\mathcal{T}(M)) \right\|_2^2, \tag{7}$$

In Eq. 7, $\hat{\theta}_{\text{prof}}$ represents θ with both the L/D term and the inflection count n_{infl} removed, the L/D term because truncation is not length-invariant, and n_{infl} because it is non-differentiable and thus cannot support gradient backpropagation. Before PCA alignment and profile extraction, $\mathcal{T}$ applies random local perturbations: truncation up to f_{trunc}, erosion/dilation with kernel size $k \in \mathcal{K}$, and Gaussian boundary noise of scale σ_n.

The final training objective is:

$$\mathcal{L} = \mathcal{L}_{\text{reconstruction}} + \mathcal{L}_{\text{cons}} \tag{8}$$

Weights can be assigned to each value of the losses involved depending on the objective of the researchers. At every unfolding step, the update relies on the current profile, the observation, and a residual that reflects its validity, while the output is clipped to the physical interval $[0, 1]$.

3.6 Retrieval Protocol

At inference time, for a query field mask M_q, we first obtain its profile estimate $p^{(T)}(M_q)$, then compute its parameter vector $\hat{\theta}_q = h\left(p^{(T)}(M_q), (L/D)_q\right)$ using the trained unfolded network. CAT-UXO reference shapes are processed identically (connected-component filtering, morphological closing, PCA alignment, profile extraction), then encoded by feeding their observed profiles through the same T-step unfolded network with shared trained weights and the same initialisation $p^{(0)} = \bar{r}_{\text{train}}$, followed by the same deterministic mapping h. Consequently, query and reference embeddings lie in a common latent space.

Retrieval is performed via nearest-neighbour search in a standardised parameter space. Let μ_θ and σ_θ denote the mean and standard deviation of θ calculated in component terms on the CTX-UXO training set. Let $\mathcal{R}$ denote the reference database and define $\bar{\theta}_\ell = (\theta_\ell - \mu_{\theta,\ell})/\sigma_{\theta,\ell}$ for each component ℓ. Retrieval is then carried out according to:

$$\text{match}(M_q) = \arg\min_{j \in \mathcal{R}} \sum_{\ell=1}^{d} \left(\bar{\theta}_{q,\ell} - \bar{\theta}^{\text{ref}}_{j,\ell}\right)^2 \tag{9}$$

4 Experiments

4.1 Evaluation Methodology

We evaluate all methods under a unified retrieval protocol, where embeddings are compared via nearest-neighbour search in the reference database. We used the CTX-UXO [8] test subset for evaluation and CAT-UXO (UXORD-10K) [5,7] as a reference database. For a complete analysis, we compare against several alternative methods (baseline). First, to obtain a non-learnt geometric baseline, we apply Direct Shape Matching [32], which uses classical Procrustes alignment [12] followed by computing point-set distances on contours extracted with marching squares and uniformly resampled at 256 points. Second, we employ Prototypical Networks [30], a popular few-shot learning method, which constructs class prototypes from 5 reference examples per class and classifies CTX-UXO test queries based on the Euclidean distance to these prototypes. The feature extractor is trained on the CTX-UXO training split. Third, we consider a Siamese network [21] using a shared ResNet-50 backbone trained with contrastive loss on CTX-UXO training pairs. Finally, we employ a CNN with cosine-similarity-based retrieval, using a pretrained ResNet-50 with fine-tuning on the CTX-UXO training split. For methods requiring RGB input (Prototypical Networks, Siamese, CNN+Cosine), we use masked RGB crops. In this way, we construct a representative benchmark comprising the principal methods that can be used for retrieval in the context of UXO mitigation. We acknowledge that other methods and models may also be considered in the future, such as those based on Foundation Model architectures (Transformer or Mamba). However, we emphasise that a life-saving solution should not be constrained by computational costs. Moreover, to ensure a fair comparison, we employ different approaches from current State-Of-The-Art (RGB and shape-based) that are feasible for retrieval, specifically in order to highlight the advantages of shape analysis. In the Future Works section, we detail the directions we intend to pursue in our studies.

4.2 Metrics

We report multiple retrieval metrics following standard information retrieval evaluation practices [10,15]. We quantify performance using Recall@K (R@K), which represents the fraction of queries in which at least one correct-class reference appears in the top results K. We report R@1, R@3, and R@5 to capture both precision-critical and recall-orientated scenarios. To assess ranking efficiency, we employ the mean reciprocal rank (MRR), where a higher value indicates that correct matches appear earlier in the ranking, defined as

$$\text{MRR} = \frac{1}{|Q|} \sum_{q \in Q} \frac{1}{\text{rank}(q)}, \tag{10}$$

In Eq. 10, rank is the position of the first correct-class retrieval. Finally, we employ Normalised Discounted Cumulative Gain (NDCG@10), a rank-sensitive metric that assigns higher importance to correct retrievals at top positions, formulated as

$$\text{NDCG@}K = \frac{\text{DCG@}K}{\text{IDCG@}K} \tag{11}$$

For Eq. 11, Discounted Cumulative Gain (DCG) is defined as:

$$\text{DCG@}K = \sum_{i=1}^{K} \frac{\text{rel}_i}{\log_2(i+1)}, \tag{12}$$

In Eq. 12, $\text{rel}_i = 1$ if the i-th retrieved item is of the correct class, and IDCG represents the ideal DCG obtained when all correct items are ranked first. We also report the Domain Shift Score (DSS), defined as the mean Euclidean distance in the standardised parameter space between each query and its nearest correct-class reference. For this metirc (DSS), lower values indicate better cross-domain alignment. All values are expressed as mean ± standard deviation, calculated over 10 independent experimental runs using the same hyperparameters. All hyperparameters are available in the public repository, as described in the Reproducibility section at the end of the paper.

4.3 Results

Figure 2 shows a successful retrieval case and known limitations. Tables 1 and 2 report the cross-domain retrieval performance on the CTX-UXO test set. Our unfolded method attains a Recall@1 of 62.1%, surpassing the strongest Recall@1 baseline (Direct Shape Matching, 53.4±0.4%) by 8.7 percentage points and maintaining the highest scores across all ranking metrics. Notably, even the Direct

Table 1. Cross-domain retrieval recall (%)

Method	R@1	R@3	R@5
Classical Shape Method			
Direct Shape Matching	53.4±0.4	61.2±0.5	65.4±0.4
Few-Shot & Metric Learning			
Prototypical Networks†	20.5±1.4	-	-
Siamese Network	46.9±1.8	72.8±1.5	80.2±1.2
CNN + Cosine	31.1±1.5	42.5±1.4	46.3±1.3
Ours			
Unfolded Shape Network	**62.1±1.2**	**77.3±1.6**	**82.1±1.3**

† Prototypical Networks assigns each query to the nearest class prototype. All top-K retrievals belong to the same predicted class. Prototype-based classification is not well suited for fine-grained cross-domain retrieval, motivating the need for instance-level embedding methods such as the proposed approach.

(a) Qualitative example of when the proposed architecture worked in a difficult case (an oxidised object, partially covered by vegetation). Type of UXO: Mortar Bomb

(b) Limitations: Objects that share closely resembling shapes, typically ones belonging to the same class, are prone to being mistaken for one another. Type of UXO: Grenade

Fig. 2. For each case, on the left is the test instance (CTX-UXO) and on the right is the reference matched instance (CAT-UXO). As a known limitation, the system may partially fail in granular identification when the shapes of UXO subtypes are very similar. For example, an offensive grenade (with grooves) can easily be confused with a defensive grenade (smooth on the surface), as they share a similar ovoid shape.

Table 2. Cross-domain ranking and alignment quality

Method	MRR	NDCG@10	DSS↓
Direct Shape Matching	0.590±0.004	0.529±0.005	1.318±0.008
Prototypical Networks	0.206±0.014	0.205±0.013	1.159±0.015
Siamese Network	0.619±0.016	0.438±0.014	1.162±0.018
CNN + Cosine	0.429±0.013	0.301±0.012	1.463±0.019
Unfolded Shape Network (Ours)	**0.712±0.012**	**0.592±0.010**	**1.112±0.014**

Shape Matching baseline outperforms traditional RGB-based techniques, indicating that munition shape is a more robust cue than appearance for heterogeneous datasets.

4.4 Ablation Study

We conduct ablation experiments to analyse the contribution of each implemented component, namely architecture depth and shape-parameter groups.

Figure 3 shows the effect of varying the number of steps (depth). All three metrics increase up to $T = 5$, after which performance saturates and then gradually declines, suggesting that excessive depth introduces over-refinement. Table 3 evaluates the contribution of each parameter group. The largest drop appears when the L/D ratio is removed, followed by Fourier descriptors. In contrast, removing the axial profile and inflexion count causes only minor changes, suggesting that these features provide complementary information.

Table 3. Ablation on shape parameters

Configuration	R@1	R@3	R@5	MRR
Full model (d=75)	**62.1**±1.2	**77.3**±1.6	**82.1**±1.3	**0.712**±0.012
w/o L/D ratio	55.2±1.4	73.6±1.8	79.8±1.5	0.672±0.014
w/o Taper ratio	59.4±1.3	75.8±1.7	81.0±1.4	0.697±0.013
w/o Fourier desc.	58.1±1.3	74.9±1.7	80.5±1.4	0.689±0.013
w/o Axial profile	61.4±1.2	76.8±1.6	81.7±1.3	0.707±0.012
w/o Inflection count	61.8±1.2	77.0±1.6	81.9±1.3	0.710±0.012

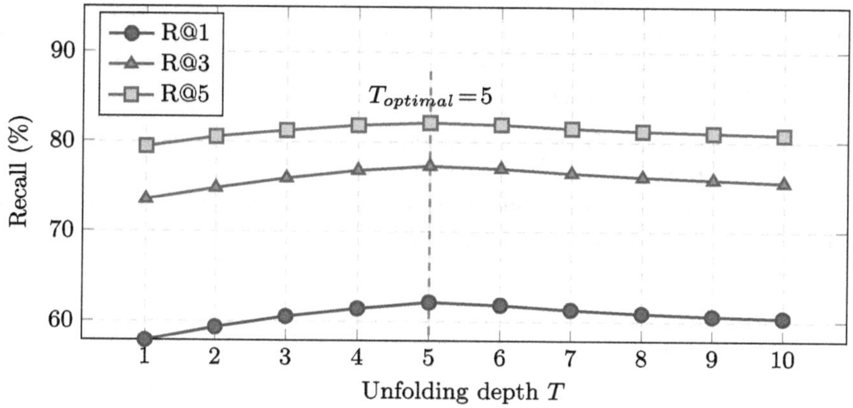

Fig. 3. Impact of unfolding depth T on retrieval recall.

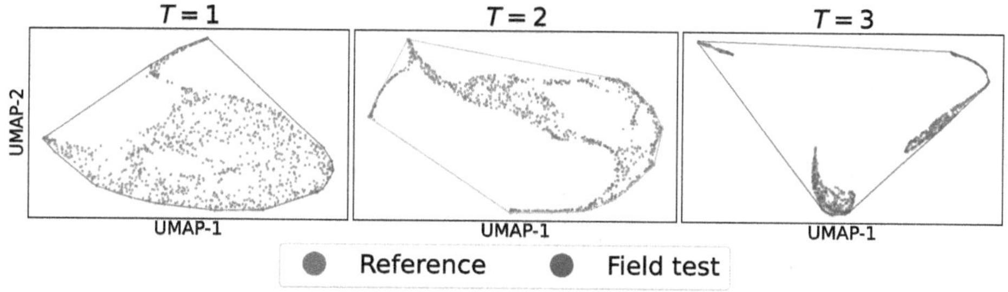

Fig. 4. UMAP visualisation of Grenade embeddings, for different depths (T).

Figure 4 shows UMAP visualisations [20] of the Grenade embeddings for different unfolding depths. Increased depth leads to tighter clustering of field queries around their reference counterparts.

5 Conclusion

We introduced a deep unfolded neural framework for cross-domain UXO retrieval that addresses the fundamental real-world challenge of matching degraded field observations against idealised technical references, with exemplification on UneXPloded Ordnance (UXO). Key insights from applying the architecture to UXO are: (1) shape-based representations yield more reliable cross-domain transfer than fully appearance-based features; (2) the unfolding structure allows for effective processing of incomplete observations; and (3) a compact parametric model is sufficient to distinguish the main ordnance categories. From an operational standpoint, the proposed approach helps humanitarian UXO clearance efforts by offering automated decision support for UXO recognition. Rather than committing to a single label, operators can examine the top-K retrieved references to guide their judgement.

Human in the Loop Recommendation. This system should be deployed as a decision support system (DSS) rather than an autonomous identification system. The retrieval paradigm serves as a vital safeguard when human cognitive performance is compromised by fatigue, high stress environments, or uncertainty in decision making.

Limitations. The dependence on hyperparameters requires careful tuning. However, a sensitivity analysis on the most influential parameters (unfolding depth T) is provided in Sect. 4.4. We acknowledge that only three classes (Projectile, Mortar Bomb, Grenade) currently have sufficient representation in both CTX-UXO and CAT-UXO for cross-domain retrieval. Extending the evaluation to additional types of ordnance requires expanding and consolidating the available reference databases. Additionally, the current pipeline assumes access to reasonably accurate segmentation masks. Limitations in shape-only identification are exemplified in Fig. 2 from Sect. 4.

Future Work. We plan to integrate foundation models in the form of Vision Language Models to derive visual primitives (attributes), such as generic shape descriptors, and to apply neurosymbolic approaches. The unfolding framework can be used on its own, with the main immediate benefit being its reduced computational usage (a checkpoint of only 2.3 MB). We will address all limitations, as well as extend the study to additional architectures, in future work.

Reproducibility

Reproducibility Statement. The notation and initial resources are detailed in Sect. 3.1. The parameter settings are given in Sect. 3.2. The preprocessing procedure is described in Sect. 3.3. Training objectives are described in Sect. 3.5. We elaborate on the retrieval protocol in Sect. 3.6. Evaluation follows standard retrieval methodologies, as discussed in Sect. 4.2. As a life-saving solution should not be restricted, we release the full implementation code, default hyperparameter configurations, model weights, and evaluation scripts in a public (anonymous) repository: https://anonymous.4open.science/r/UXO_DeepUnfolded-8881/. Both datasets are publicly available for research purposes under their respective licences.

Datasets are available at:

- **CTX-UXO**: https://zenodo.org/records/17052675
- **CAT-UXO**: https://m4d.iti.gr/uxord-10k-dataset/ or official website https://cat-uxo.com/

Acknowledgments. We gratefully acknowledge the financial publication support provided by the University of Science and Technology POLITEHNICA of Bucharest through the PubArt program.

Disclosure of Interests. The authors have no competing interests to declare that are relevant to the content of this article.

References

1. Ablin, P., Moreau, T., Massias, M., Gramfort, A.: Learning step sizes for unfolded sparse coding. Adv. Neural. Inf. Process. Syst. **32** (2019)
2. Barone, P.M.: Bombed archaeology: towards a precise identification and a safe management of WWII's dangerous unexploded bombs. Heritage **2**(4), 2704–2711 (2019). https://doi.org/10.3390/heritage2040167. https://www.mdpi.com/2571-9408/2/4/167
3. Baur, J.: Towards Operational UAS-Based Landmine Detection: Vegetation, Validation, and Geophysical Application. Ph.D. thesis, Columbia University (2025)
4. Baur, J., Steinberg, G., Nikulin Ph D, A., Chiu Ph D, K., de Smet Ph D, T.: How to implement drones and machine learning to reduce time, costs, and dangers associated with landmine detection. J. Conventional Weapons Destruction **25**(1), 29 (2021)
5. Begkas, G., et al.: Automatic visual recognition of unexploded ordnances using supervised deep learning. In: Association for Computing Machinery, ICMR 2022, pp. 286–294. New York, NY, USA (2022). https://doi.org/10.1145/3512527.3531383
6. Burger, H.C., Schuler, C.J., Harmeling, S.: Image denoising with multi-layer perceptrons, part 1: comparison with existing algorithms and with bounds. CoRR abs/1211.1544 (2012). http://arxiv.org/abs/1211.1544
7. CAT-UXO: Cat-UXO — collective awareness to exploded ordnance (2026). https://cat-uxo.com/. Accessed 23 Feb 2026
8. Craioveanu, G.M., Stamatescu, G.: CTX-UXO: a comprehensive dataset for detection and identification of unexploded ordnances (2024). https://doi.org/10.21227/cwnm-de53
9. Craioveanu, M.G., Stamatescu, G.: Detection and identification of unexploded ordnance using a two-step deep learning methodology. In: 2024 32nd Mediterranean Conference on Control and Automation (MED), pp. 257–262 (2024). https://doi.org/10.1109/MED61351.2024.10566207

10. Deselaers, T., Keysers, D., Ney, H.: Features for image retrieval: an experimental comparison. Inf. Retrieval **11**(2), 77–107 (2008)
11. Dryden, I.L., Mardia, K.V.: Statistical Shape Analysis: With Applications in R. Wiley (2016)
12. Goodall, C.: Procrustes methods in the statistical analysis of shape. J. Roy. Stat. Soc.: Ser. B (Methodol.) **53**(2), 285–321 (1991)
13. Heiderscheidt, D.: The impact of world war one on the forests and soils of Europe. Ursidae Undergraduate Res. J. Univ. Northern Colorado **7**(3), 3 (2018)
14. Iijima, L., Giakoumoglou, N., Stathaki, T.: A multimodal approach for cross-domain image retrieval. arXiv preprint arXiv:2403.15152 (2024)
15. Jung, D., Kang, D., Kwak, S., Cho, M.: Few-shot metric learning: online adaptation of embedding for retrieval. In: Proceedings of the Asian Conference on Computer Vision, pp. 1875–1891 (2022)
16. Kokkinos, I., Bronstein, M.M., Litman, R., Bronstein, A.M.: Intrinsic shape context descriptors for deformable shapes. In: 2012 IEEE Conference on Computer Vision and Pattern Recognition, pp. 159–166. IEEE (2012)
17. Lacroix, P., Herzog, J., Eriksson, D., Weibel, R.: Methods for visualizing the explosive remnants of war. Appl. Geogr. **41**, 179–194 (2013). https://doi.org/10.1016/j.apgeog.2013.04.007. https://www.sciencedirect.com/science/article/pii/S0143622813001021
18. Lekhak, S., Ientilucci, E.J., Dera, D., Ghosh, S.: Uncertainty quantification in surface landmines and UXO classification using MC dropout. arXiv (2025). https://arxiv.org/abs/2510.06238. arXiv:2510.06238v1
19. Maser, E., Strehse, J.S.: "Don't blast": blast-in-place (BIP) operations of dumped world war munitions in the oceans significantly increase hazards to the environment and the human seafood consumer. Arch. Toxicol. **94**(6), 1941–1953 (2020)
20. McInnes, L., Healy, J., Melville, J.: Umap: uniform manifold approximation and projection for dimension reduction (2020). https://arxiv.org/abs/1802.03426
21. Melekhov, I., Kannala, J., Rahtu, E.: Siamese network features for image matching. In: 2016 23rd International Conference on Pattern Recognition (ICPR), pp. 378–383. IEEE (2016)
22. North Atlantic Treaty Organization: Glossary of Terms and Definitions. NATO Standardization Agency, modified version 02 edn, (2000). updated 07.08
23. Qi, C.R., Su, H., Mo, K., Guibas, L.J.: Pointnet: deep learning on point sets for 3D classification and segmentation. CoRR abs/1612.00593 (2016). http://arxiv.org/abs/1612.00593
24. Ravi, N., et al.: Sam 2: segment anything in images and videos. arXiv preprint arXiv:2408.00714 (2024). https://arxiv.org/abs/2408.00714
25. Samadzadegan, F., Qaderi, F., Haghighi, T.L., Toosi, A., Mousavi, S.M.: Unmanned aerial remote sensing for unexploded ordnance detection: concepts, methods, current status and trends. Sens. Imaging **26**(1), 137 (2025)
26. Ściegienka, P., Blachnik, M.: On the development of a neural network architecture for magnetometer-based UXO classification. Appl. Sci. **15**(15), 8274 (2025)
27. Shakibajahromi, B., Kim, E., Breen, D.E.: Rimeshgnn: a rotation-invariant graph neural network for mesh classification. In: 2024 IEEE/CVF Winter Conference on Applications of Computer Vision (WACV), pp. 3138–3148 (2024)
28. Shlezinger, N., et al.: Deep unfolding: recent developments, theory, and design guidelines. arXiv preprint arXiv:2512.03768 (2025)
29. Siméoni, O., et al.: Dinov3. arXiv preprint arXiv:2508.10104 (2025)
30. Snell, J., Swersky, K., Zemel, R.: Prototypical networks for few-shot learning. In: Advances in Neural Information Processing Systems, p. 30 (2017)

31. United Nations Mine Action Service (UNMAS): United nations mine action service (2026). https://www.unmas.org/. Accessed 23 Feb 2026
32. Veltkamp, R.C., Hagedoorn, M.: State of the art in shape matching. Principles of visual information retrieval, pp. 87–119 (2001)
33. Wang, X., Peng, D., Yan, M., Hu, P.: Correspondence-free domain alignment for unsupervised cross-domain image retrieval. In: Proceedings of the AAAI Conference on Artificial Intelligence, vol. 37, no. 8, pp. 10200–10208 (2023)
34. Ward, C.M., Harguess, J., Hilton, C., Mediavilla, C., Sullivan, K., Watkins, R.: Deep learning for automatic ordnance recognition. In: Geospatial Informatics IX, vol. 10992, pp. 103–112. SPIE (2019)
35. Wei, X., Van Gorp, H., Gonzalez-Carabarin, L., Freedman, D., Eldar, Y.C., van Sloun, R.J.: Deep unfolding with normalizing flow priors for inverse problems. IEEE Trans. Signal Process. **70**, 2962–2971 (2022)
36. Zhang, J., Chen, B., Xiong, R., Zhang, Y.: Physics-inspired compressive sensing: beyond deep unrolling. IEEE Signal Process. Mag. **40**(1), 58–72 (2023)
37. Zhang, J., Yao, Y., Deng, B.: Fast and robust iterative closest point. IEEE Trans. Pattern Anal. Mach. Intell. **44**(7), 3450–3466 (2021)

Geometric Attractor Monitoring: A Robust and Frugal Framework for Multi-modal Industrial Robotic Cycles

Martin Bonsergent-Brachet[1](✉), Jesse Read[1], and Dany Abboud[2]

[1] LIX, École Polytechnique, Institut Polytechnique de Paris, Palaiseau, France
martin.bonsergent-brachet@lix.polytechnique.fr,
jesse.read@polytechnique.edu
[2] Renault, Boulogne-Billancourt, France
dany.abboud@renault.com

Abstract. Monitoring the health of heterogeneous industrial robot fleets is severely challenged by the multi-modal nature of their operational cycles and a persistent scarcity of run-to-failure data. Standard data-driven approaches, particularly deep learning architectures relying on sequential reconstruction, often struggle in this specific setting; they tend to over-smooth complex dynamics, masking early signs of degradation. To address these industrial constraints, we reframe the monitoring problem through a framework based on Phase Space Reconstruction (PSR). Instead of predicting temporal sequences, this framework transforms univariate sensor data into a geometric attractor, explicitly unfolding the mechanical states independently of their temporal occurrence. By evaluating various anomaly scoring techniques within this space, we demonstrate that discrete support estimation provides an effective and computationally frugal Health Indicator (HI). Validated on a real-world dataset of 21 heterogeneous robots over three years and a synthetic Langevin system, our approach outperforms standard deep learning baselines. We show that aligning the algorithmic bias with the geometric properties of the target system yields a pragmatic, traceable and easily deployable approach perfectly tailored to the realities of industrial constraints.

Keywords: Health Indicator · Phase Space Reconstruction · Industrial Time Series · Anomaly Detection

1 Introduction

In the era of Industry 4.0, industrial automation has become the cornerstone of modern manufacturing, particularly in high-throughput sectors like the auto-

Supplementary Information The online version contains supplementary material available at https://doi.org/10.1007/978-3-032-37682-4_12.

M. Baratchi et al. (Eds.): ECML PKDD 2026, LNAI 16949, pp. 198–214, 2027.
https://doi.org/10.1007/978-3-032-37682-4_12

motive industry. Production lines rely on vast fleets of industrial robots operating continuously to meet demanding production targets. In this context, any unplanned downtime due to equipment failure results in significant production losses, increased operational costs, and potential safety hazards for personnel [5]. To mitigate these risks, the paradigm is shifting from traditional preventive maintenance, which is often costly and fails to prevent all failures, towards Prognostics and Health Management (PHM). PHM aims to leverage the large volumes of data from the Industrial Internet of Things (IIoT) to monitor equipment health in real-time and predict failures before they occur.

A central task in PHM is the prediction of Remaining Useful Life (RUL), which estimates the time left before a component or system fails. However, a robust RUL prediction is fundamentally dependent on a preceding step: the construction of a reliable Health Indicator (HI). An HI is a quantitative metric that translates complex sensor data (e.g., temperature, vibration, current) into a simplified, monotonic representation of an asset's degradation state [22,23]. Many researchers argue that decomposing the prognostics problem into two stages; first, constructing a robust HI, and second, predicting RUL from this HI; simplifies the model and enhances the understanding of the degradation behavior compared to "end-to-end" approaches that map raw data directly to RUL [8,23]. This two-step methodology allows for a clearer understanding of the non-linear degradation process and provides a more stable foundation for forecasting. This paper focuses on the first, foundational step: the construction of a HI for an industrial robot fleet.

2 Problem Statement

Despite the recent success of data-driven methods, particularly deep learning models like Autoencoders applied to HI construction [8,13], standard reconstruction-based approaches face critical limitations in real-world industrial settings.

First, industrial robots exhibit highly "multi-modal" behavior. Here, multimodality refers to the multi-modal distribution of a single univariate signal: the torque of one joint visits several disjoint operating regimes. In practice, the generated time series are discontinuous, jumping abruptly between distinct kinematic modes (e.g., waiting, fast movement, high-torque holding). If we observe these dynamics at a macro level, the data points form dense concentrations around specific valid states, separated by sparse transitional values. There is no strict temporal regularity or clear deterministic sequence between these modes, and the signals are subject to frequent temporal phase shifts. Furthermore, these operational modes lack explicit labels, making supervised segregation impossible. Standard regression-based models minimize the Mean Squared Error (MSE) over these sequences [3,10]. Consequently, they tend to over-smooth the complex dynamics, converging towards an average representation of these disjointed modes. These methods are insensitive to mode deviations and therefore to early signs of degradation. They are only sensitive to extreme signal variations, which do not occur in all cases and occur late.

Second, deploying predictive maintenance across a fleet of thousands of robots introduces operational constraints regarding traceability and frugality. The "black-box" nature of deep learning models hinders their adoption by maintenance teams. Engineers require interpretable insights to trust the system's recommendations [16]: when an alarm is triggered, it must be traceable back to a specific kinematic state and physical reality. Moreover, deploying bespoke architectures per asset violates the frugality constraints of large-scale monitoring. An ideal solution should bypass specialized ML hardware (e.g., GPUs) and rely on operations simple enough to run directly within standard existing data architectures.

To address these limitations, we propose a methodological shift from sequential temporal reconstruction to geometric representation learning. The main contributions of this paper are:

- We introduce a geometric HI framework utilizing Phase Space Reconstruction to handle multi-modal industrial dynamics.
- We provide a benchmark comparing discrete support estimation, deep learning models, and classical anomaly detection methods on the exact same phase space input, proving that boundary estimation outperforms reconstruction for degradation tracking in a "multi-modal" setup.
- We validate the proposed methodology on an industrial dataset and a synthetic multi-modal Langevin system to ensure reproducibility.
- We demonstrate that Discrete Support Estimation offers a pragmatic and easily deployable approach perfectly tailored to the realities of industrial constraints

3 Related Work

3.1 Classical Statistical Approaches

Before the advent of Deep Learning, statistical methods such as Change Point Detection (CPD) and Isolation Forests were widely explored for anomaly detection. However, their application to robotic fleets faces intrinsic limitations. Standard CPD algorithms (e.g., CUSUM) rely on stationarity assumptions that are violated by the highly non-stationary, multi-modal nature of robotic cycles, leading to excessive false alarms at every kinematic transition. Similarly, outlier detection methods like Isolation Forests typically isolate anomalies based on data sparsity. Consequently, they often conflate rare but entirely nominal operational modes (e.g., infrequent torque tasks) with mechanical anomalies, leading to a high false positive rate in multi-modal environments.

3.2 Deep Learning for Condition Monitoring

Recent data-driven approaches for HI construction heavily leverage deep learning. Autoencoders (AEs) and their variants are widely used for unsupervised feature learning and anomaly detection, where the reconstruction error often serves as the HI [3,10]. For instance, advanced models like Tensor Autoencoders (TAE) [13] or Spatiotemporal Convolutional Autoencoders (STECAE) [8] have been proposed to better capture complex spatio-temporal dependencies. Variational Autoencoders (VAEs) have also been adapted, sometimes with constraints to enforce degradation trends [14]. Recurrent architectures like LSTMs are also popular, either as part of an autoencoder (LSTM-AE) [21] or for modeling temporal patterns directly.

Furthermore, standard Deep Learning models generally assume that training and test data share the same distribution [7,20]. In a heterogeneous fleet, variations in robot types, payloads, and kinematic tasks induce a significant domain shift between assets. While advanced architectures (e.g., contrastive learning or generative adversarial networks) and Transfer Learning could theoretically bridge this gap or better capture multi-modal distributions [8,13,14], they typically require a massive, representative source domain to learn universal features. More importantly, developing, fine-tuning, and maintaining such complex models for each heterogeneous asset intrinsically violates the computational and frugality constraints of large-scale industrial deployments. In our industrial reality, aggregating data from thousands of robots into such a generalist base is currently prohibitive due to infrastructure maturity and storage costs. With access limited to a small subset of the fleet, relying on large-scale pre-training is not a viable strategy. This creates a strong need for asset-specific methods that self-calibrate without depending on a massive, centralized dataset.

3.3 Prognostics and RUL Estimation

The PHM field often decomposes prognostics into a two-step process: first, constructing a robust HI, and second, predicting the RUL from this HI [22,23]. Many sophisticated methods focus on this two-stage pipeline. For example, some approaches use feature fusion via AEs or MLPs to build an HI, which is then fed into models like LSTMs or Bayesian frameworks for RUL prediction [9,19]. Others use similarity-based methods, comparing a current HI trajectory to a database of run-to-failure curves [4,18].

However, this paradigm still fundamentally relies on the availability of run-to-failure data to either train the RUL predictor or populate the similarity database [2,18]. Many methods also require explicit labels for the start of degradation [2] or are designed for a single failure mode [9], which is unrealistic in complex industrial settings.

3.4 Dynamical Systems in PHM

The analysis of dynamical systems through phase space reconstruction (PSR) is a well-established field for characterizing complex systems from time series data [6,15]. While its application in PHM is less mainstream than deep learning, several studies have successfully used it for fault diagnosis. Early works focused on identifying specific failure modes in rotating machinery by observing changes in the phase portrait's topology. More recently, metrics derived from phase space, such as local prediction errors [11,12], have been used as health features. However, these approaches often focus on diagnosis rather than continuous monitoring, can be sensitive to outliers, or require operational condition labels for normalization. In contrast to these methods that characterize trajectories, our methodology focuses on the continuous monitoring of the attractor's global geometric shape. By explicitly learning the spatial boundaries of the healthy manifold, we track the structural drift of the system over time. This shifts the objective from instantaneous fault classification to the construction of a HI suited for long-term prognostics.

4 The Proposed Framework

4.1 Phase Space Representation

The fundamental assumption of our framework is that the operational cycles of industrial robots are governed by deterministic physical laws, naturally converging toward a low-dimensional attractor. In practice, the full internal state is rarely accessible. We typically rely on univariate observations, such as motor torque, acting as a one-dimensional projection of the underlying dynamics. Following Takens's embedding theorem [15], the topological properties of the original state space can be reconstructed from these partial observations using a delayed embedding. We transform the discrete univariate time-series $\mathcal{X} = \{x_1, x_2, ..., x_N\}$ into a multi-dimensional state vector v_t:

$$v_t = [x_t, x_{t-\tau}, ..., x_{t-(m-1)\tau}]^\top \in \mathbb{R}^m \tag{1}$$

The reconstruction validity depends on the time delay τ and the embedding dimension m. While typically estimated via the Average Mutual Information (AMI) function and the False Nearest Neighbor (FNN) algorithm respectively [1,17], optimal parameters strictly depend on the operational context and the sampling frequency of the monitored system.

4.2 Support Estimation

Once the univariate time-series is successfully embedded into a multi-dimensional phase space, the subsequent step is to systematically characterize the nominal operational dynamics. In dynamical systems terminology, this translates to learning the support of the healthy attractor, representing the specific, bounded region of the phase space densely visited by the state vector v_t during normal operations. Because industrial robotic tasks are multi-modal, this healthy attractor constitutes a complex geometric shape encompassing all valid kinematic states.

To rigorously encapsulate this geometric signature, various estimators can be deployed. Density estimation techniques, such as Gaussian Mixture Models

(GMM), can model the continuous probability distribution across the manifold. Alternatively, boundary-learning algorithms like One-Class Support Vector Machines (OCSVM) or Isolation Forests construct a mathematical envelope around nominal observations. Another effective paradigm is direct, non-parametric estimation through discrete space partitioning, mapping continuous state vectors into a finite grid to form a binary occupancy map.

It is crucial to distinguish this explicit geometric support estimation from the implicit distribution modeling performed by standard deep learning models. By operating directly on the spatial envelope rather than minimizing a sequential reconstruction error, explicit estimators are inherently protected against the temporal phase shifts and amplitude over-smoothing that plague reconstruction-based models in multi-modal environments.

4.3 Health Scoring

The final stage of the proposed framework translates the geometric evaluation of the phase space into a continuous and actionable HI. For any new observation v_t during the monitoring phase, the chosen support estimator outputs an instantaneous anomaly score a_t. Depending on the specific algorithm deployed within the framework, a_t can manifest as a continuous metric or a discrete out-of-distribution flag; its concrete form is made explicit in Eq. 4 for our reference implementation and in Sect. 5 for each baseline.

However, raw point-wise anomaly scores are noisy and sensitive to transient variations: in multi-modal applications, a momentary deviation does not signify irreversible failure. To extract a reliable degradation trend, the instantaneous scores must be temporally aggregated.

We define the continuous Health Indicator, $HI(t)$, as the moving average of the anomaly scores over a sliding observation window of size W:

$$HI(t) = \frac{1}{W} \sum_{k=0}^{W-1} a_{t-k} \tag{2}$$

The selection of the window size W is a critical physical parameter. W must satisfy the ergodic requirement of the monitored system: it must be sufficiently large to encapsulate multiple complete operational cycles. This ensures that the state vector v_t has adequate time to densely and representatively sample the valid regions of the phase space.

4.4 Reference Implementation: Discrete Support Estimation

While the framework accommodates various estimators, we propose (Fig. 1) a non-parametric approach based on discrete space partitioning. This choice is motivated by the non-convex nature of multi-modal robotic attractors, which are naturally captured by a discrete grid. Furthermore, it yields a bounded binary score readily interpretable by domain experts, while guaranteeing strict computational frugality.

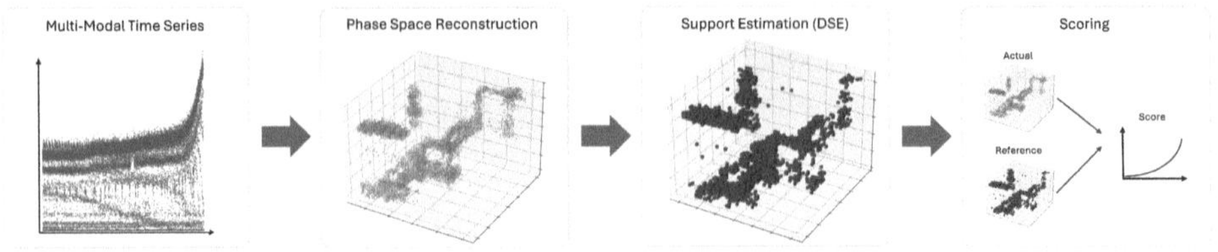

Fig. 1. Overview of the proposed geometric monitoring framework applied to Discrete Support Estimation.

Discretization and Calibration. During the calibration phase, we define the healthy signature using a reference dataset $\mathcal{D}_{ref} = \{v_t\}_{t=1}^{T_{cal}}$ observed during the robot's nominal period. We discretize the m-dimensional phase space into a regular grid with a resolution of B bins per axis. A mapping function $\Phi : \mathbb{R}^m \rightarrow \mathbb{N}^m$ transforms each continuous state vector v_t into discrete coordinates via min-max normalization and integer floor division. The healthy support $\mathcal{S}$ is then defined as the set of all unique cells visited during this period:

$$\mathcal{S} = \{\Phi(v) \mid v \in \mathcal{D}_{ref}\} \tag{3}$$

In practice, $\mathcal{S}$ is implemented as a hash set, enabling $\mathcal{O}(1)$ insertion and lookup operations. The calibration process strictly requires a single pass over $\mathcal{D}_{ref}$, yielding an overall $\mathcal{O}(N)$ time complexity. Since the hash set stores only visited cells, the memory footprint is $\mathcal{O}(|\mathcal{S}|) \leq \mathcal{O}(N)$, never the full B^m grid. Raising m thus costs coverage, not memory: for a fixed calibration budget the support grows sparse, making benign observations fall in unvisited cells (Sect. 6.3).

Anomaly Scoring and Health Indicator. During the monitoring phase, structural degradation is identified when the system's dynamics drift into previously unvisited regions of the phase space. For each new observation v_t, a binary anomaly score a_t is computed in constant time based on its membership in the healthy support:

$$a_t = \begin{cases} 0 & \text{if } \Phi(v_t) \in \mathcal{S} \\ 1 & \text{if } \Phi(v_t) \notin \mathcal{S} \end{cases} \tag{4}$$

The final continuous Health Indicator is then obtained by passing this binary sequence a_t through the ergodic sliding window described in Eq. (2).

We deliberately retain a binary membership test rather than a distance-based score (e.g., a truncated distance transform or an optimal-transport distance). For a non-convex, multi-modal support made of disjoint visited regions, the distance to the healthy set is geometrically ambiguous and, in our experiments, a poor degradation signal: what matters is whether the state has left the visited manifold, not how far one nominal mode lies from another.

5 Experimental Setup

5.1 Industrial Dataset

To validate the proposed framework under real-world constraints, we utilize a proprietary dataset extracted from an automotive manufacturing robot fleet comprising approximately 5000 industrial robots. For this study, a representative subset of 21 robots was selected. The historical data spans a period of up to three years of continuous operation.

The monitored condition variable is the torque disturbance, defined as the residual difference between the controller's reference command and the actual measured torque. Each robot consists of 6 distinct joints, yielding 6 independent and unsynchronized univariate time series per asset. As these joints are mechanically driven by separate gear trains and actuators, we treat each joint as an independent univariate channel: the framework is applied per joint, producing one health indicator per joint rather than a single joint-coupled embedding. This keeps the embedding low-dimensional (Sect. 6.3) and yields a localized indicator that points maintenance directly to the faulty axis.

Within this subset, 16 robots operated nominally without any documented mechanical issues throughout the three-year period. The remaining 5 robots experienced confirmed mechanical failures at known timestamps. For these specific assets, the time series are strictly truncated at the exact date of failure. Crucially, aligning with the unsupervised paradigm of our methodology, the data from these 5 run-to-failure trajectories is used exclusively for the final evaluation of the HI.

5.2 Synthetic Dataset

To replicate the multi-modal nature of industrial robotic cycles, we employ an over-damped, multi-stable Langevin equation. The state x of the synthetic system evolves according to the following equation:

$$dx = (F_{phys}(x, w) + F_{control}(x, t))dt + \sigma dW_t$$

where W_t is a standard Wiener process scaled by a noise magnitude σ. The proportional controller $F_{control}(x, t)$ drives the system toward a discrete cyclic target sequence, forcing continuous multi-modal transitions. The physical environment $F_{phys}(x, w)$ is modeled as a force derived from a non-linear potential field containing five distinct wells, representing the different valid operational modes:

$$F_{phys}(x, w) = \sum_{i=1}^{5} -k_i(w)(x - c_i(w)) \exp\left(-\frac{(x - c_i(w))^2}{0.5}\right)$$

To evaluate the HIs, we introduce a structural degradation parameterized by $w(t) \in [0, 1]$. For the first 40% of the simulation, the system operates nominally. Subsequently, $w(t)$ increases linearly to 1.0. This parameter alters the physical potential by inducing a spatial drift in specific wells (shifting the centers $c_i(w)$). Crucially, to simulate the integral action of a real robotic controller compensating for increased mechanical resistance, the target sequence of the proportional controller is symmetrically shifted.

5.3 General Parameters and Phase Space Configuration

To ensure a fair and rigorous comparative analysis, all evaluated baselines receive the exact same input dimension and are subjected to the same temporal aggregation. For the monitoring phase, all instantaneous anomaly scores are smoothed using an identical sliding window of size $W = 5000$. This specific size guarantees the ergodicity of the evaluation by encompassing multiple operational cycles.

The Phase Space Reconstruction depends on the embedding dimension m and the time delay τ. For the synthetic Langevin system, the Average Mutual Information (AMI) function identifies an optimal delay at $\tau = 58$, and the False Nearest Neighbors (FNN) algorithm confirms that the percentage of false neighbors drops to near zero at $m = 3$. We retain $m = 3$ as it fully unfolds the dynamics while preserving the ability to visually interpret the structural drift of the 3D attractor.

However, for the industrial dataset, AMI and FNN estimations were unstable across different robots. Consequently, we adopt a fixed configuration of $m = 3$ and $\tau = 1$ across the entire fleet. We chose this value for the delay τ because robots time series are already discontinuous. Indeed, the robotic joints are sampled at a low frequency (5 Hz) relative to their movements. The embedding dimension $m = 3$ is chosen because the macroscopic movements of robots are inherently low-dimensional.

To strictly validate this empirical configuration, a sensitivity analysis on the phase space parameters is included in Sect. 6.3. Figure 2 shows the resulting industrial attractor, confirming that the fixed embedding is well-unfolded and

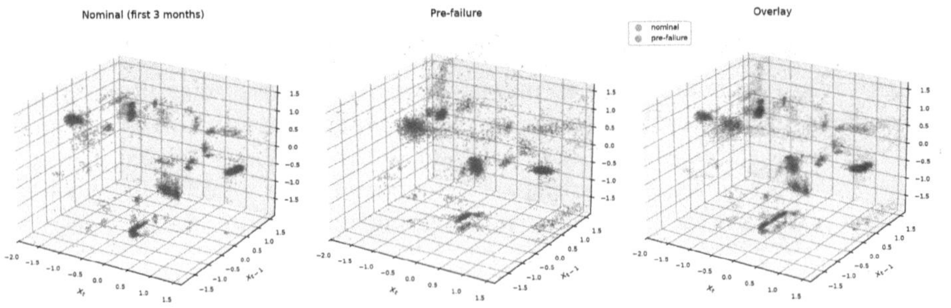

Fig. 2. Reconstructed phase-space attractor ($m = 3$, $\tau = 1$) for one joint of a failed robot. Left: nominal period (first three months); centre: pre-failure period; right: overlay. The fixed embedding yields a well-unfolded, multi-modal attractor, and degradation appears as the state populating cells outside the nominal support.

multi-modal, with degradation appearing as the state drifting outside the nominal support.

5.4 Baselines

We benchmark our Discrete Support Estimation (DSE) against a comprehensive set of anomaly detection models. All baselines in the main experiment are fed the exact same 3D input vector ($v_t \in \mathbb{R}^3$). For full reproducibility, the implementation of all baselines and the synthetic Langevin data generator are publicly available at https://github.com/mart1bb/geometric-attractor-monitoring.

Geometric and Statistical Models. We evaluate several classical anomaly detection algorithms using the scikit-learn library:

- **DSE:** Our reference implementation with a grid resolution fixed to $B = 100$ bins per axis.
- **Gaussian Mixture Model:** Configured with $k = 15$ components. The anomaly score is the negative log-likelihood of the sample.
- **One-Class SVM:** Deployed with a Radial Basis Function (RBF) kernel, scale gamma, and $\nu = 0.01$.
- **Isolation Forest:** Configured with default parameters and an auto-adjusted contamination rate.
- **Centroid:** A baseline computing the Euclidean distance to the 3D center of mass of the healthy state vectors.

Deep Learning Models. We implement standard deep reconstruction and forecasting architectures. All multi-layer perceptron (MLP) based encoders share a harmonized architecture of $[256, 128, 64, 32, d_{latent}]$, with symmetric decoders. All models are trained using the Mean Squared Error (MSE) loss, the Adam optimizer, and a learning rate of 10^{-4}.

- **Autoencoder (AE) and Variational Autoencoder (VAE):** The latent space dimension is strictly constrained to a structural bottleneck of $d_{latent} = 2$. For the VAE, we extract two distinct anomaly scores: the sequential reconstruction error (VAE Rec) and the latent space divergence (VAE latent).
- **LSTM and LSTM-AE:** Recurrent models configured with two stacked hidden layers of 64 units.
- **MLP Predictor:** A feed-forward network forecasting the next coordinate x_{t+1}.

5.5 Evaluation Metrics

To objectively evaluate the performance of the generated HI, we formalize a comprehensive evaluation framework based on standard metrics widely adopted in the PHM literature. Let $\mathbf{h} = (h_1, \ldots, h_K)$ denote the sequence of HI values for a given operational trajectory of length K, and $\mathbf{t} = (1, \ldots, K)$ be the corresponding time vector.

Monotonicity. Monotonicity measures the global irreversibility of the wear process regardless of its non-linear functional form (e.g., exponential degradation). To robustly handle local noise and signal length variations without requiring explicit smoothing, we define Monotonicity as the absolute Spearman rank correlation coefficient between the HI and time:

$$\text{Mon} = \left| \frac{\sum_{t=1}^{K}(\text{rank}(h_t) - \overline{\text{rank}(\mathbf{h})})(\text{rank}(t) - \overline{\text{rank}(\mathbf{t})})}{\sqrt{\sum_{t=1}^{K}(\text{rank}(h_t) - \overline{\text{rank}(\mathbf{h})})^2}\sqrt{\sum_{t=1}^{K}(\text{rank}(t) - \overline{\text{rank}(\mathbf{t})})^2}} \right| \quad (5)$$

Temporal Correlation. While Monotonicity evaluates rank-based irreversibility, Temporal Correlation strictly quantifies the linearity of the degradation rate. This evaluates the HI's suitability for direct linear RUL extrapolation. We compute this using the absolute Pearson correlation coefficient:

$$\text{Corr} = \left| \frac{\sum_{t=1}^{K}(h_t - \bar{h})(t - \bar{t})}{\sqrt{\sum_{t=1}^{K}(h_t - \bar{h})^2}\sqrt{\sum_{t=1}^{K}(t - \bar{t})^2}} \right| \quad (6)$$

Amplitude-Normalized Robustness. Robustness measures the stability of the indicator relative to its own dynamic range. To isolate the macroscopic degradation trend from local residual noise, we extract a perfectly smoothed baseline h_t^{trend} using a Savitzky-Golay filter (polynomial order 2, window length $\approx K/5$). The robustness is then computed by penalizing the residuals normalized by the total degradation amplitude:

$$\text{Rob} = \exp\left(-\frac{1}{K}\sum_{t=1}^{K}\left|\frac{h_t - h_t^{trend}}{\max(\mathbf{h}) - \min(\mathbf{h})}\right|\right) \quad (7)$$

Prognosticability. Prognosticability evaluates the consistency of the final HI value at the moment of failure across multiple assets. A reliable HI should trigger an alarm at a similar threshold regardless of the specific robot. Let $\mathbf{h}_{end}$ be the vector of the final HI values for the broken population, and $\Delta\mathbf{h}$ be the vector of total degradation amplitudes for these assets.

$$\text{Prog} = \exp\left(-\frac{\text{std}(\mathbf{h}_{end})}{\text{mean}(\Delta\mathbf{h})}\right) \quad (8)$$

Discriminability (Signal-to-Noise Proxy). In industrial deployments, minimizing false alarms is a strict constraint. Leveraging our control group of nominal robots, we introduce a Discriminability metric to quantify the separation between true degradation signatures and operational baseline noise.

$$\text{Disc} = \frac{1}{1 + \frac{\bar{\sigma}_{healthy}}{\bar{\Delta}_{broken}}} \quad (9)$$

where $\bar{\sigma}_{healthy}$ is the average standard deviation of the HIs observed on the healthy fleet, and $\bar{\Delta}_{broken}$ is the average degradation amplitude of the failed robots. A score close to 1 indicates that the degradation is distinctively separated from operational variability.

Computational Efficiency. Finally, to validate the frugality constraint of monitoring, we measure the end-to-end execution time.

6 Results and Comparative Analysis

6.1 Overall Monitoring Performance

Table 1 presents the quantitative evaluation of the HIs generated by all baseline models on the industrial dataset evaluated on the exact same low-dimensional phase space input ($v_t \in \mathbb{R}^3$). Figures 3 and 4 illustrate the resulting indicators on two failed robots: DSE exhibits a clear rising trend toward failure, while reconstruction-based baselines remain comparatively flat. As these traces are not strictly monotonic, we rely on the rank-based Monotonicity (Eq. 5), which captures the global degradation trend while tolerating local fluctuations.

While continuous estimators like GMM provide competitive local trend tracking, their high variance across assets reveals a sensitivity to fleet heterogeneity. DSE achieves the highest global score by converting the continuous state into discrete grid boundaries, which immunizes it against the cyclic fluctuations that

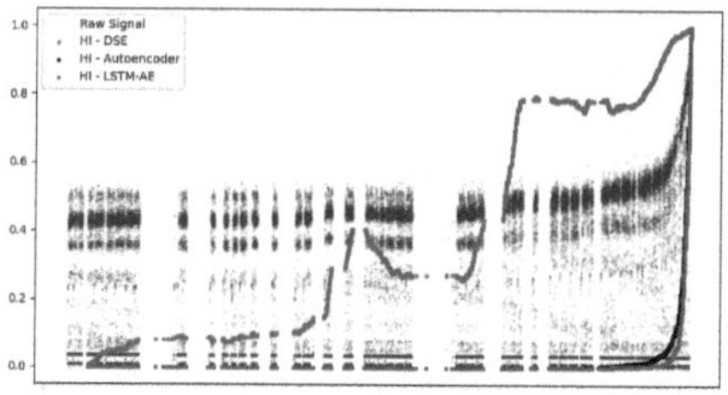

Fig. 3. Comparison of normalized indicators for Robot 1 that had breakdown.

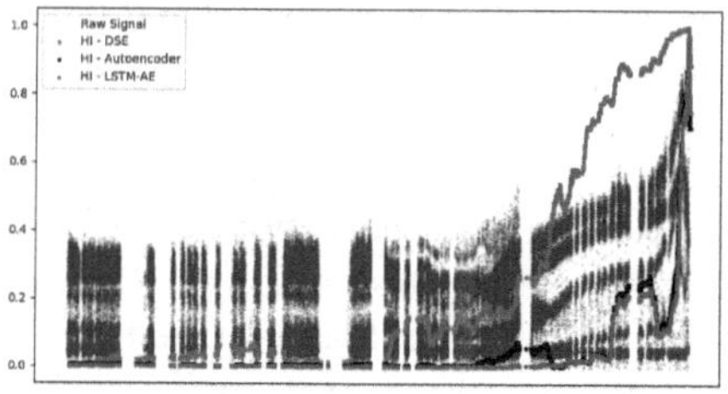

Fig. 4. Comparison of normalized indicators for Robot 2 that had breakdown.

Table 1. Overall monitoring performance on the industrial fleet

Method	Mon.	Time Corr.	Rob.	Prog.	Disc.	Global	Time(s)
DSE	**0.61**±0.20	**0.66**±0.13	0.94±0.02	**0.54**	0.77	**0.70**	0.28±0.34
GMM	0.59±0.15	0.62±0.09	**0.95**±0.02	0.35	0.81	0.66	3.55±5.83
IF	0.50±0.15	0.54±0.11	0.93±0.05	0.45	0.73	0.63	0.60±0.58
OCSVM	0.51±0.08	0.50±0.11	0.93±0.03	0.23	**0.91**	0.62	79.09±244.94
Centroid	0.52±0.08	0.53±0.06	0.93±0.03	0.35	0.67	0.60	**0.01**±0.01
VAE (Rec)	0.52±0.12	0.52±0.12	0.93±0.02	0.32	0.72	0.60	3.04±3.36
LSTM-AE	0.47±0.15	0.45±0.14	0.92±0.03	0.28	0.73	0.57	3.19±3.59
LSTM (Pred)	0.44±0.06	0.50±0.04	0.92±0.03	0.24	0.76	0.57	6.16±7.53
MLP	0.48±0.11	0.48±0.11	0.93±0.02	0.15	0.64	0.54	2.40±2.83
Autoencoder	0.42±0.12	0.45±0.10	0.93±0.03	0.03	0.47	0.46	2.77±3.11
VAE (latent)	0.49±0.14	0.48±0.11	0.93±0.02	0.01	0.11	0.40	3.04±3.36

penalize MSE-based models. This directly translates into higher Prognosticability: the accumulation of strict binary boundary violations keeps the final degradation amplitude consistent across the fleet, whereas unconstrained MSE values vary wildly per asset, resulting in poor prognostic consistency.

While some baselines exhibit higher Discriminability (e.g., OCSVM or AE), this is a common artifact of overly conservative models that output a flat signal across both healthy and broken phases, artificially inflating the signal-to-noise ratio proxy. Their failure to capture the actual degradation renders them unsuitable for predictive maintenance. DSE provides the optimal operational trade-off, successfully tracking the structural drift while maintaining a high rejection rate for false alarms.

We stress that Prognosticability and Discriminability are aggregated over the $N = 5$ run-to-failure assets available in the fleet, so these fleet-level scores carry non-negligible uncertainty. To quantify it, we report bootstrap confidence intervals over the failed population in the supplementary material; DSE retains the highest Prognosticability in 96% of resamples, though the wide intervals confirm that the absolute values should be read as indicative rather than precise.

Beyond diagnostic accuracy, Table 1 shows that DSE processes a complete trajectory with marked computational frugality, allowing the framework to scale across the fleet without specialized hardware acceleration, avoiding the computational overhead of standard deep learning architectures or classical kernel-based methods.

Table 2 presents the monitoring performance on the synthetic Langevin system. These results corroborate the findings from the industrial dataset: geometric and spatial bounding estimators provide a viable alternative to, or even perform better than deep learning baselines in "multi-modal" environment while remaining more computationally efficient. A notable difference with the industrial evaluation is that continuous estimators like Isolation Forest marginally

Table 2. Monitoring performance on the synthetic multi-stable Langevin system

Method	Mon.	Time Corr.	Rob.	Global Score
Isolation Forest	0.996	**0.995**	0.982	**0.991**
DSE	**0.998**	0.983	**0.989**	0.990
GMM	0.998	0.984	0.986	0.989
Centroid	0.991	0.991	0.973	0.985
VAE (latent)	0.990	0.989	0.969	0.983
Autoencoder	0.986	0.986	0.963	0.978
OCSVM	0.965	0.966	0.939	0.957
MLP	0.789	0.794	0.932	0.838
VAE (Rec)	0.724	0.740	0.896	0.787
LSTM-AE	0.716	0.746	0.897	0.786
LSTM (Pred)	0.593	0.627	0.858	0.693

outperform DSE on this synthetic benchmark. This inversion is structurally logical: the injected degradation is a perfectly continuous spatial drift, which continuous estimators accommodate better than a rigid discrete grid. In real-world industrial settings, however, transient noise and non-linear shocks favor the strict spatial boundaries of DSE.

6.2 Long Context Window

To verify if the underperformance of deep learning models stems from an insufficient temporal receptive field, we conducted a study by expanding their context window. The models were provided with an input sequence of $W = 5000$ time steps, perfectly matching the ergodic window, with the exception of the recurrent architectures (LSTM and LSTM-AE) which were restricted to $W = 200$ due to memory constraints. We relaxed the latent bottleneck ($d_{latent} = 20$) and introduced two other sequence-to-sequence architectures: a 1D Convolutional Autoencoder (CNN-AE) and a Transformer.

Table 3. Deep learning models with extended context window

Method	Mon.	Time Corr.	Rob.	Prog.	Disc.	Global	Time(s)
CNN-AE	0.45±0.20	0.53±0.12	0.93±0.02	**0.30**	0.72	**0.59**	170.04±250.97
LSTM-AE	0.42±0.22	0.49±0.13	0.91±0.03	0.23	0.86	0.58	33.17±43.18
LSTM (Pred)	0.42±0.22	0.52±0.14	0.91±0.03	0.24	0.80	0.58	29.07±37.76
Autoencoder	**0.46**±0.19	0.51±0.13	0.93±0.02	0.28	0.72	0.58	**8.10**±9.96
VAE (latent)	0.44±0.23	0.46±0.08	0.93±0.03	0.12	**0.86**	0.56	8.62±10.36
MLP	0.35±0.13	0.50±0.14	0.93±0.02	0.25	0.74	0.55	11.53±12.01
Transformer	0.37±0.15	0.35±0.10	0.91±0.01	0.07	0.55	0.45	274.97±404.19

The results, presented in Table 3, confirm that increasing the context window yields only marginal improvements: the deep architectures consistently fail to match the frugal DSE estimator. This persistent underperformance, despite a receptive field matching the ergodic window, confirms that the bottleneck is the architectural over-smoothing bias discussed in Sect. 2, not an insufficient temporal context.

6.3 Sensitivity Analysis of Phase Space Parameters

To empirically validate the phase space configuration, we conducted a sensitivity analysis on the DSE framework by varying the embedding dimension m and the time delay τ. The experimental results (Fig. 5) demonstrate that the impact of the embedding dimension m is dependent on the chosen time delay τ. For delays $\tau > 5$, increasing m degrades the global performance score. Conversely, for short delays ($\tau \leq 5$), increasing the dimension artificially improves the overall score.

This phenomenon is the curse of dimensionality acting on the discrete support: as m grows, the B^m cells vastly outnumber the fixed calibration budget, so the healthy support becomes sparse and even benign observations fall in unvisited cells. This inflates prognosticability and causes the HI to saturate prematurely into a binary out-of-bounds trigger. Although higher dimensions yield higher quantitative scores at $\tau \leq 5$, we retain the configuration $m = 3$. This specific dimensionality prevents early saturation, yielding a continuous indicator that effectively tracks the physical degradation trend rather than acting as a simple binary out-of-bounds trigger (Fig. 6). Furthermore, maintaining $m = 3$ keeps the healthy support densely sampled and preserves the ability to visually interpret the structural drift of the 3D attractor.

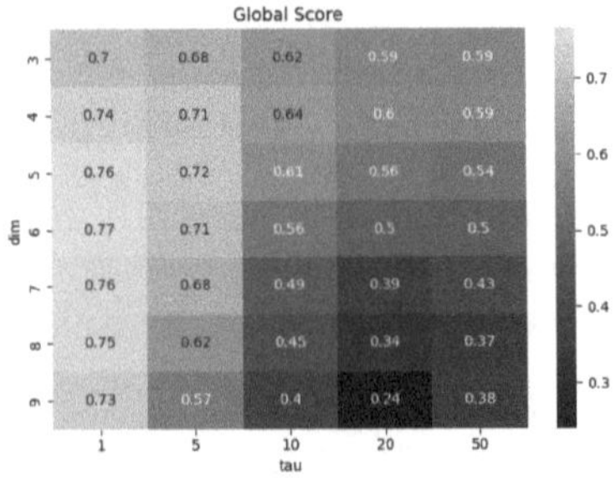

Fig. 5. Global Score as a function of dimension m and delay τ.

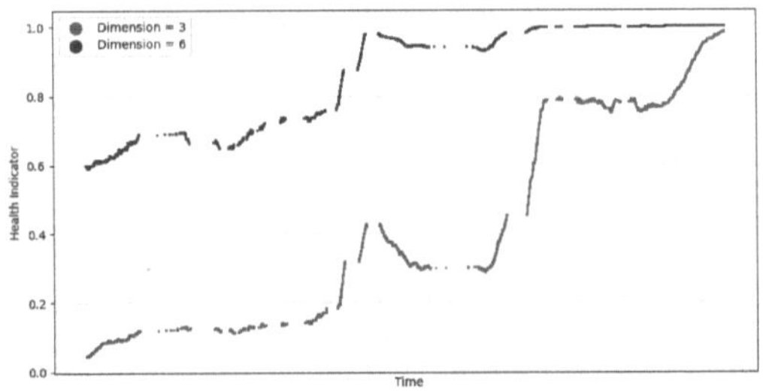

Fig. 6. Comparison of indicator calculated with dimension equal to 3 and 6.

7 Discussion and Conclusion

This paper presented a frugal and scalable geometric framework for the predictive maintenance of large-scale robotic fleets. By shifting the anomaly detection paradigm from temporal reconstruction to Phase Space Reconstruction, the Discrete Support Estimation (DSE) method isolates diverse kinematic regimes into discrete geometric regions without averaging them. Empirically, DSE outperforms deep architectures that suffer from an over-smoothing bottleneck on multi-modal cycles, while its geometric alerts remain directly traceable to a physical reality by maintenance engineers.

While more complex architectures might mitigate this bottleneck, maintaining such bespoke models per asset violates the frugality constraint of fleet-scale deployment; the geometric framework thus offers a pragmatic compromise. A primary limitation of the current DSE approach is its rigid reliance on a static nominal trajectory; if a robot is reprogrammed to perform a new operational task, the historical support becomes obsolete. Future work will focus on integrating continual learning mechanisms to dynamically update the discrete support, enabling the framework to autonomously adapt to industrial trajectory reprogramming without requiring full recalibration.

Additionally, ongoing research evaluates this geometric representation on other manufacturing assets subject to similar multi-modal characteristics, such as stamping presses, to further validate the generalizability of the proposed framework.

Disclosure of LLM Usage. During the preparation of this manuscript, the authors used a large language model to assist with language editing, text condensation, and LaTeX formatting. All scientific content, experimental design, and conclusions are the authors' own, and the authors take full responsibility for the final manuscript.

References

1. Buzug, T., Pfister, G.: Optimal delay time and embedding dimension for delay-time coordinates by analysis of the global static and local dynamical behavior of strange attractors. Phys. Rev. A **45**(10), 7073 (1992)
2. Chen, Z., Zhou, D., Zio, E., Xia, T., Pan, E.: A deep learning feature fusion based health index construction method for prognostics using multiobjective optimization. IEEE Trans. Reliab. **72**(3), 1038–1052 (2022)
3. González-Muñiz, A., Diaz, I., Cuadrado, A.A., Garcia-Perez, D.: Health indicator for machine condition monitoring built in the latent space of a deep autoencoder. Reliab. Eng. Syst. Saf. **224**, 108482 (2022)
4. Guo, L., Yu, Y., Duan, A., Gao, H., Zhang, J.: An unsupervised feature learning based health indicator construction method for performance assessment of machines. Mech. Syst. Signal Process. **167**, 108573 (2022)
5. Huang, C., Bu, S., Lee, H.H., Chan, C.H., Kong, S.W., Yung, W.K.: Prognostics and health management for predictive maintenance: a review. J. Manuf. Syst. **75**, 78–101 (2024)
6. Kennel, M.B., Brown, R., Abarbanel, H.D.: Determining embedding dimension for phase-space reconstruction using a geometrical construction. Phys. Rev. A **45**(6), 3403 (1992)
7. Li, B., Tang, B., Deng, L., Zhao, M.: Self-attention convlstm and its application in RUL prediction of rolling bearings. IEEE Trans. Instrum. Meas. **70**, 1–11 (2021)
8. Li, S., Zhang, C., Zhang, X.: A novel spatiotemporal enhanced convolutional autoencoder network for unsupervised health indicator construction. IEEE Trans. Instrum. Meas. **73**, 1–10 (2024)
9. Li, Z., Wu, J., Yue, X.: A shape-constrained neural data fusion network for health index construction and residual life prediction. IEEE Trans. Neural Netw. Learn. Syst. **32**(11), 5022–5033 (2020)
10. Liu, C., Sun, J., Liu, H., Lei, S., Hu, X.: Complex engineered system health indexes extraction using low frequency raw time-series data based on deep learning methods. Measurement **161**, 107890 (2020)
11. Liu, H., Yuan, R., Lv, Y., Yang, X., Li, H., Song, G.: Degradation tracking of rolling bearings based on local polynomial phase space warping. IEEE Trans. Reliab. **73**(2), 1380–1392 (2023)
12. Luo, P., Hu, N., Zhang, L., Shen, J., Cheng, Z.: Improved phase space warping method for degradation tracking of rotating machinery under variable working conditions. Mech. Syst. Signal Process. **157**, 107696 (2021)

13. Mao, W., Wang, Y., Kou, L., Liang, X.: A new deep tensor autoencoder network for unsupervised health indicator construction and degradation state evaluation of metro wheel. IEEE Trans. Instrum. Meas. **72**, 1–15 (2023)
14. Qin, Y., Zhou, J., Chen, D.: Unsupervised health indicator construction by a novel degradation-trend-constrained variational autoencoder and its applications. IEEE/ASME Trans. Mechatron. **27**(3), 1447–1456 (2021)
15. Takens, F.: Detecting strange attractors in turbulence. In: Dynamical Systems and Turbulence, Warwick 1980: Proceedings of a Symposium held at the University of Warwick 1979/80, pp. 366–381. Springer (2006)
16. Wagner, C., Hellingrath, B.: Implementing predictive maintenance in a company: industry insights with expert interviews. In: 2019 IEEE International Conference on Prognostics and Health Management (ICPHM), pp. 1–8. IEEE (2019)
17. Wallot, S., Mønster, D.: Calculation of average mutual information (AMI) and false-nearest neighbors (FNN) for the estimation of embedding parameters of multidimensional time series in matlab. Front. Psychol. **9**, 1679 (2018)
18. Xia, T., Shu, J., Xu, Y., Zheng, Y., Wang, D.: Multiscale similarity ensemble framework for remaining useful life prediction. Measurement **188**, 110565 (2022)
19. Xiang, S., Zhou, J., Luo, J., Liu, F., Qin, Y.: Cocktail LSTM and its application into machine remaining useful life prediction. IEEE/ASME Trans. Mechatron. **28**(5), 2425–2436 (2023)
20. Yang, Z., et al.: A novel fault detection method for rotating machinery based on self-supervised contrastive representations. Comput. Ind. **147**, 103878 (2023)
21. Ye, Z., Yu, J.: Health condition monitoring of machines based on long short-term memory convolutional autoencoder. Appl. Soft Comput. **107**, 107379 (2021)
22. Zhou, J., Yang, J., Qin, Y.: A systematic overview of health indicator construction methods for rotating machinery. Eng. Appl. Artif. Intell. **138**, 109356 (2024)
23. Zhou, J., Yang, J., Xiang, S., Qin, Y.: Remaining useful life prediction methodologies with health indicator dependence for rotating machinery: a comprehensive review. IEEE Trans. Instrum. Meas. (2025)

Interval Estimation in Water Distribution Systems Using Physics-Informed Graph Neural Networks

Inaam Ashraf(✉), André Artelt, David P. Leins, and Barbara Hammer

Faculty of Technology, Bielefeld University, Inspiration 1, 33619 Bielefeld, Germany
{mashraf,aartelt,dleins,bhammer}@techfak.uni-bielefeld.de

Abstract. Artificial Intelligence in general and Machine Learning (ML) in particular has the potential to play a key role in critical infrastructure such as Water Distribution Systems (WDSs). In the face of urban population growth, ML can pave the way towards smart cities by not only solving various tasks in WDSs but also dealing with emerging uncertainties in WDSs. For instance, demands can be subject to uncertainty intervals and pipe attributes may vary over time. This study presents a novel physics-informed Graph Neural Network (GNN) based model for WDSs that predicts output feature intervals, given the input feature intervals. A comprehensive training scheme is developed to map multiple input intervals to the corresponding multiple output intervals. To address the varying ranges and magnitudes of state variables in WDSs, we introduce a theoretically grounded, reversible, and physics-preserving data normalization method. The proposed model demonstrates strong performance across five WDS datasets, achieving results comparable to those of the computationally intensive Monte Carlo sampling method.

Keywords: Interval Estimation · Physics-Informed Graph Neural Networks · Water Distribution Systems

1 Introduction

Artificial Intelligence, particularly Machine Learning (ML), have the potential to play a key role in critical infrastructure such as Water Distribution Systems (WDSs). Rapid urbanization increases both operational complexity and uncertainty in WDSs, making robust data-driven methods increasingly important. In this context, ML can support core WDS tasks while addressing uncertainties in system inputs. For instance, input demands in a WDS can be subject to uncertainty intervals and pipe roughness coefficients may vary over time. In WDS domain, some of the important tasks solved using ML include event diagnosis

Supplementary Information The online version contains supplementary material available at https://doi.org/10.1007/978-3-032-37682-4_13.

M. Baratchi et al. (Eds.): ECML PKDD 2026, LNAI 16949, pp. 215–231, 2027.
https://doi.org/10.1007/978-3-032-37682-4_13

[12,32,33], sensor placement [9,23], state estimation [3,15,23,31,38], state simulation [2,4,19,38], and demand prediction [37]. Dealing with uncertainties in WDSs using ML is an unexplored area, which we address in this work.

A WDS is characterized by water sources (reservoirs, tanks) and consumer junctions that are connected through links (pipes, pumps, valves) (see Fig. 1). Each consumer junction is characterized by its water demand and pressure head, each water source by its pressure head, and each link by flow and pressure head loss. One of the important tasks in the WDSs is to simulate the steady state that estimates pressure heads at consumer junctions and flows through links, given consumer demands, pressure heads at water sources, link attributes, and the WDS structure. This is highly useful for WDS planning, monitoring, and event diagnosis. EPANET [27] is the current state-of-the-art (SOTA) hydraulic simulator that solves this problem using a system of non-linear equations. Since the computational complexity of the solver increases with the size of the WDS, recent works [2,4,19,38] have explored Graph Neural Networks (GNNs) to reduce this complexity and thus solve it efficiently (i.e., surrogate modeling).

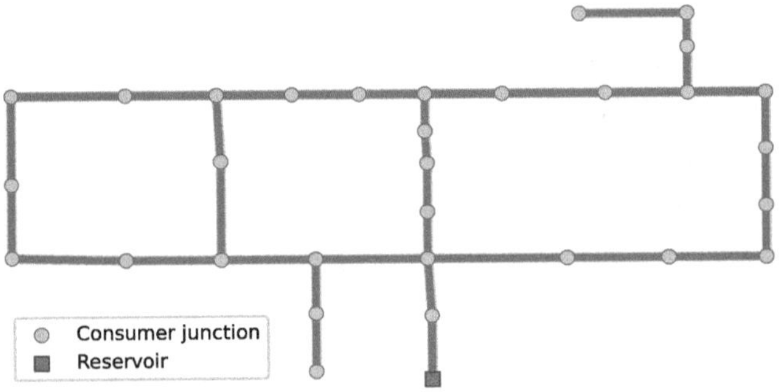

Fig. 1. Figure shows the structure of the Hanoi WDS benchmark, which consists of one reservoir, 31 consumer junctions and 34 pipes.

Both the hydraulic simulators and the ML-based surrogate models assume complete certainty in the input features such as water demands. However, in real-world WDSs, demands are not known exactly but typically subject to uncertainty intervals, and system parameters such as pipe roughness coefficients vary over time due to material degradation. Hence, uncertainty-based simulations can be highly useful in WDS planning and monitoring. One popular method to model such uncertainties is to consider the input demands lying within an interval [36]. Hence, the task is to find the corresponding intervals of the outputs (heads, flows) such that any demand sampled from the input interval yields outputs belonging to the predicted intervals. Monte Carlo sampling remains a fundamental baseline for interval estimation, providing empirically accurate estimates of output intervals given input intervals, though at high computational cost. Our proposed approach amortizes this cost by training a GNN-based model that can predict single-shot output intervals at inference, given the input intervals.

We extend the Physics-Informed GNN (PI-GNN) based model of [2,4] to map the input feature intervals to the corresponding physically plausible output feature intervals. Since the PI-GNN can only map input feature intervals to their corresponding physically correct states, we pass on the outputs of the PI-GNN to a GNN-based Calibration Network that maps those to the output feature intervals. Due to non-linear hydraulic laws governing the state of a WDS, the output state features are not guaranteed to be normally distributed. Hence, we consider all input features to be uniformly distributed and aim to estimate output feature quantiles instead of standard deviations. We expect that these quantiles are practically more useful since they can help predict output interval bounds, which is an important task in the WDS domain [36].

Main Contributions

- We propose a novel methodology for interval estimation in WDSs that extends a physics-informed GNN based surrogate model to predict output feature quantiles, given the uncertainty intervals on the input features.
- We develop a comprehensive training scheme to map multiple input intervals to the corresponding multiple output intervals.
- To address the varying ranges and magnitudes of state variables in WDSs, we propose a theoretically grounded, reversible, and physics-preserving data normalization method.
- Our proposed methodology could be used to enhance other physics-informed surrogate models to incorporate interval estimation.

To the best of our knowledge, this is the first work to integrate physics-informed GNNs with interval estimation for WDSs, thereby enabling more robust and efficient state simulation.

2 Preliminaries

Water Distribution System as a Graph: A Water Distribution System (WDS) is a heterogeneous graph $\mathcal{G} := (V, E)$ with certain node types such as consumer junctions V_c and water sources/reservoirs (lakes, rivers, etc.) V_r, where $V = V_c \cup V_r$, and certain edge types such as pipes E_{pipe}, pumps E_{pump}, and valves E_w, where $E = E_{pipe} \cup E_{pump} \cup E_w = \{e_{vu} \mid \forall v \in V; u \in \mathcal{N}(v)\}$ with cardinality $|V| = N_n$ and $|E| = N_e$ respectively.

Water Hydraulics: A set of *hydraulic principles* govern the state of a WDS that are defined for the true WDS state $(\boldsymbol{d}^*, \boldsymbol{q}^*, \boldsymbol{h}^*)$ as follows [2]:

1. For two neighboring nodes $v, u \in V$, the flow $q_{e_{vu}}$ from node v to u is equal to the negative of the flow $q_{e_{uv}}$ from u to v:

$$q^*_{e_{vu}} := -q^*_{e_{uv}} \tag{1}$$

2. The law of conservation of mass postulates that the sum of all flows at a node is equal to the negative of the demand at that node i.e.

$$\textstyle\sum_{u \in \mathcal{N}(v)} q^*_{e_{vu}} = -d^*_v \tag{2}$$

3. The law of conservation of energy states that the loss of pressure head between two neighboring nodes is related to the flow as follows:

$$\text{For pipes:} \qquad h_v^* - h_u^* = r_{e_{vu}} sgn(q_{e_{vu}}^*)|q_{e_{vu}}^*|^x, \tag{3}$$

where $r_{e_{vu}} = 10.667\, l_{e_{vu}} \psi_{e_{vu}}^{-4.871} c_{e_{vu}}^{-1.852}$, $x = 1.852$ and $l_{e_{vu}}$, $\psi_{e_{vu}}$ and $c_{e_{vu}}$ are length, diameter and roughness coefficient of the pipe [27].

$$\text{For pumps:} \qquad h_v^* - h_u^* = \omega^2 \left(\iota - \kappa \left(-q_{e_{vu}}^*/\omega\right)^\nu\right), \tag{4}$$

where ι is the pump shutoff head, ω is the relative speed of the pump, and κ and ν are pump curve coefficients [27].

State Simulation in WDSs. One of the important tasks in the WDSs is to simulate the steady state that estimates pressure heads at nodes and flows through links uniquely [29,30], given demands at consumer nodes, pressure heads at water sources, link attributes, and the WDS structure. EPANET [27] is the current SOTA hydraulic simulator that solves this problem of steady-state simulation:

Definition 1. *Given a WDS graph $\mathcal{G} := (V, E)$, the task of hydraulic steady state simulation involves estimating the pressure head at every node $(h_v)_{v \in V}$ and water flow through every link $(q_e)_{e \in E}$ given demands at every consumer node $(d_v^*)_{v \in V_c}$, pressure heads at the reservoirs $(h_v^*)_{v \in V_r}$, and edge attributes (e.g., $(r_e)_{e \in E_{pipe}}$, $(\omega_e, \iota_e, \kappa_e, \nu_e)_{e \in E_{pump}}$) [2].*

3 Related Work

ML has a lot of potential in improving and enhancing existing methods in WDSs. Some of the tasks in WDSs already addressed with ML include event diagnosis [12,32,33], demand prediction [37], and sensor placement [9,23]. The task of estimating the complete state of a WDS from sparse sensor readings from a few nodes/links has seen application of Deep Learning (DL) by [3,15,23,31,38]. This task is ill-posed since multiple physically correct states can correspond to the same sparse sensor readings, which was addressed by [5].

Since WDSs are heteregeneous graphs by nature, GNNs are a widely used DL method. The broad classes of GNNs include spectral graph convolutional neural networks (GCNs) [8,11,21], spatial GCNs [14,16,34], and recursive graph and tree models [17,28]. Our proposed approach employs an edge-based message-passing GNN architecture, which is a type of spatial GCNs.

One of the important tasks in the WDSs is to simulate the steady state as defined in Definition 1. Here, EPANET [27] is the current SOTA hydraulic simulator, which suffers from high computational cost, non-differentiability and the inability to deal with uncertainties. Some mechanistic alternatives include a method based on edge diffusion on graphs [20] and a model combining WDS hydraulics with an Extended Kalman Filter [6]. DL methods employing GNNs have lead to efficient surrogate models as demonstrated by [2,4,19,38]. Here, physics-informed neural networks (PINNs) represent a recent paradigm for incorporating physical constraints into learned models [26]. However, all those existing surrogates fail to deal with uncertainties, that occur in real-world applications. In this work, we extend the physics-informed GNNs by [2,4] to deal with uncertainty intervals [36].

Notably, there exist some work on dealing with uncertainties in WDSs using classical/mechanistic methods. For instance, [25] attempt to propagate input uncertainties through WDS hydraulic models to estimate output uncertainty bounds. Bayesian optimization is used to handle uncertainties in simulation-based optimization for WDS by [9]. One way to model uncertainties in WDSs is to consider the inputs (demands, diameters, etc.) belonging to an interval. Hence, the task is to find the corresponding intervals of the outputs (heads, flows) such that any input sampled from the input interval yields outputs belonging to the predicted intervals [36]. All of these classical approaches use Monte Carlo sampling using EPANET as ground truth for comparison and therefore suffer from high computational complexity.

Besides Bayesian neural network methods [13,18] for uncertainty quantification, that rely on the Gaussian assumption, the method proposed by [7] aims at reducing uncertainty in the output of the model by estimating the sharpest output intervals. Interval neural networks proposed by [24] use interval arithmetic to propagate input intervals to the output intervals for one-dimensional data. It is important to note that the aforementioned methods cannot be directly applied to our proposed approach due to the physics-informed and constrained GNN-based architecture. Moreover, our proposed approach differs from the aforementioned ML methods since we do not assume any specific distributional form and aim to propagate multiple high-dimensional input intervals to physics-based multiple high-dimensional output intervals. Furthermore, the use of quantile regression [10,22], allows us to compute asymmetric output interval bounds.

4 Methodology

The task of interval estimation in WDSs can be defined as follows:

Definition 2. *For a WDS graph $\mathcal{G} := (V, E)$, given interval bounds on demands at every consumer node $(d_v^*)_{v\in V_c} \in [a_{d_v}, b_{d_v}]$, pressure heads at the reservoirs $(h_v^*)_{v\in V_r}$, edge attributes (e.g., $(r_e)_{e\in E_{pipe}}$, $(\omega_e, \iota_e, \kappa_e, \nu_e)_{e\in E_{pump}}$), the task is to estimate the corresponding non-trivial interval bounds on pressure head at every node $(h_v)_{v\in V} \in [a_{h_v}, b_{h_v}]$ and water flow through every link $(q_e)_{e\in E} \in [a_{q_e}, b_{q_e}]$, such that any set of demands $(s_{d_v^*})_{v\in V_c}$ sampled from the intervals $[a_{d_v}, b_{d_v}]_{v\in V_c}$ yields pressure heads $(s_{h_v^*})_{v\in V_c}$ and flows $(s_{q_e^*})_{e\in E}$ belonging to the predicted head intervals $[a_{h_v}, b_{h_v}]_{v\in V_c}$ and flow intervals $[a_{q_e}, b_{q_e}]_{v\in V_c}$ respectively.*

One way to solve this task would be to model the demand interval as a Gaussian with mean $\mu_v = (a_{d_v} + b_{d_v})/2$ and standard deviation $\sigma_v \approx (b_{d_v} - a_{d_v})/6$. This approach will only be useful if one can propagate these uncertainties through the WDS hydraulics and can guarantee that the corresponding heads and flows will also be Gaussians. Section 2 reveals that the WDS hydraulics encompass high-dimensional non-linear relationships between the demands, heads and flows. Therefore, the Gaussian assumption is not likely to hold for both heads and flows, which we also show empirically in Appendix A. Hence, we treat demand at every node d_v^* as a random variable coming from a Uniform distribution i.e. $d_v^* \sim \mathcal{U}(a_{d_v}, b_{d_v})$ with bounds a_{d_v} and b_{d_v} and variance $\sigma_v^2 = \text{Var}(d_v^*) = \frac{(b_{d_v} - a_{d_v})^2}{12}$. Since demands at nodes are independent of each other, the diagonal covariance matrix is $\boldsymbol{\Sigma}_d = \text{diag}\left(\frac{(b_{d_1} - a_{d_1})^2}{12}, \ldots, \frac{(b_{d_{N_n}} - a_{d_{N_n}})^2}{12}\right)$. Given the hydraulic functions $\boldsymbol{h}^* = f_h(\boldsymbol{d}^*)$ and $\boldsymbol{q}^* = f_q(\boldsymbol{d}^*)$ mapping input demands $\boldsymbol{d}^*$ to physically correct heads $\boldsymbol{h}^*$ and flows $\boldsymbol{q}^*$ respectively, the propagated covariance matrices can be defined using Taylor approximation as:

$$\text{Cov}(\boldsymbol{h}) \approx \mathbf{J}_h \cdot \boldsymbol{\Sigma}_d \cdot \mathbf{J}_h^T,\ \mathbf{J}_h := \frac{\partial \boldsymbol{h}^*}{\partial \boldsymbol{d}^*}, \quad \text{Cov}(\boldsymbol{q}) \approx \mathbf{J}_q \cdot \boldsymbol{\Sigma}_d \cdot \mathbf{J}_q^T,\ \mathbf{J}_q := \frac{\partial \boldsymbol{q}^*}{\partial \boldsymbol{d}^*} \tag{5}$$

Due to the nature of WDS hydraulics, pressures and flows depend on demands at every node. Hence, these Jacobian matrices are dense. A trained ML model that simulates the hydraulic state of the WDS such as [2,4] has learned the functions $\boldsymbol{h}^* = f_h(\boldsymbol{d}^*)$ and $\boldsymbol{q}^* = f_q(\boldsymbol{d}^*)$ and thus gives us direct access to both of the Jacobian matrices $\mathbf{J}_h$ and $\mathbf{J}_q$, which were also utilized for downstream tasks by [5]. However, due to non-linear hydraulics, the Jacobians change with the change in input demands. This means that accessing the Jacobians once and using them as a measure of sensitivity/uncertainty will not be enough. Hence, we modify the surrogate model of [2,4] to estimate interval descriptors (mean, bounds) directly and train an additional GNN module end-to-end with it that maps these descriptors to output interval bounds in terms of quantiles.

Monte Carlo sampling is the SOTA approach for output interval estimation, where demands are sampled as $d_v^* \sim \mathcal{U}(a_{d_v}, b_{d_v})$ to estimate the output bounds $[a_{h_v}, b_{h_v}]$, $[a_{q_e}, b_{q_e}]$, which is computationally expensive even when using a trained ML surrogate model. Our proposed approach amortizes this cost by simultaneously training the surrogate model and using its predictions to train a GNN module (Sect. 4.6) that can predict single-shot output intervals (in terms of quantiles) at inference, given the input interval descriptors.

4.1 Model Architecture Overview

Our proposed approach (i) models input demand intervals as Uniform distributions with descriptors mean $\boldsymbol{\mu}_d$ and bounds $(\boldsymbol{a}_d, \boldsymbol{b}_d)$, (ii) extends the surrogate model of [2,4] to estimate physically correct interval descriptors for flows $\boldsymbol{\mu}_q, \boldsymbol{a}_q, \boldsymbol{b}_q$ and heads $\boldsymbol{\mu}_h, \boldsymbol{a}_h, \boldsymbol{b}_h$, and (iii) adds a Calibration Network to map these output interval descriptors to flow quantiles $\boldsymbol{q}^{(0.01)}, \boldsymbol{q}^{(0.99)}$, and head quantiles $\boldsymbol{h}^{(0.01)}, \boldsymbol{h}^{(0.99)}$. At the same time, the surrogate model estimates physically correct flows $\boldsymbol{s}_q$ and heads $\boldsymbol{s}_h$ from individual samples $\boldsymbol{s}_d$ from the input demand distributions. These samples are used to train the Calibration Network end-to-end with the surrogate model to amortize the cost of Monte Carlo sampling and estimate output interval quantiles.

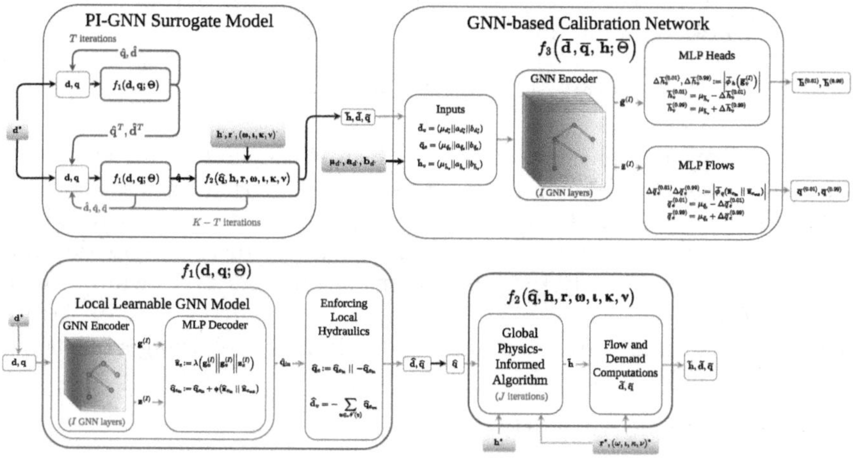

Fig. 2. Overall architecture of the proposed IPI-GNN model. The upper part shows the concise version of the PI-GNN surrogate model along with the Calibration Network f_3. The lower part shows the detailed architecture of the individual components (f_1, f_2) of the PI-GNN surrogate model.

A high-level architecture of the proposed physics-informed GNN based interval estimation (IPI-GNN) model is given in Fig. 2. We define demands $\boldsymbol{d}$ as a tuple $(\boldsymbol{s}_d, \boldsymbol{\mu}_d, \boldsymbol{a}_d, \boldsymbol{b}_d)$ and analogously $\boldsymbol{q}$ and $\boldsymbol{h}$. The overall learned function f estimates output quantiles as:

$$f(\boldsymbol{d}, \boldsymbol{q}, \boldsymbol{h}, \boldsymbol{l}; \boldsymbol{\Theta}, \bar{\boldsymbol{\Theta}}), : \longmapsto (\bar{\boldsymbol{q}}^{(0.01)}, \bar{\boldsymbol{q}}^{(0.99)}, \bar{\boldsymbol{h}}^{(0.01)}, \bar{\boldsymbol{h}}^{(0.99)}) \tag{6}$$

where $\boldsymbol{l} = (\boldsymbol{r}, \boldsymbol{\omega}, \boldsymbol{\iota}, \boldsymbol{\kappa}, \boldsymbol{\nu})$ are link attributes (Eq. 3, 4) and $(\boldsymbol{\Theta}, \bar{\boldsymbol{\Theta}})$ are learnable neural network parameters. f consists of three functions f_1, f_2, and f_3. The first function f_1 uses the input demand tuple $\boldsymbol{d}$ to estimate corresponding output flow tuple $\hat{\boldsymbol{q}}$ that is used to compute the reconstructed demand tuple $\hat{\boldsymbol{d}}$ (Eq. 2). It comprises an edge-based GNN architecture with learnable parameters $\boldsymbol{\Theta}$:

$$f_1(\boldsymbol{d}, \boldsymbol{q}; \boldsymbol{\Theta}) : \longmapsto (\hat{\boldsymbol{d}}, \hat{\boldsymbol{q}}) \tag{7}$$

As highlighted by [4], these flows may not conform to all hydraulic principles. Hence, the second function f_2 uses the physics-informed algorithm from [4] to compute the tuples $\tilde{\boldsymbol{d}}, \tilde{\boldsymbol{q}}$, and $\tilde{\boldsymbol{h}}$ using Eq. 3:

$$f_2(\hat{\boldsymbol{q}}, \boldsymbol{h}, \boldsymbol{l}) : \longmapsto (\tilde{\boldsymbol{d}}, \tilde{\boldsymbol{q}}, \tilde{\boldsymbol{h}}) \tag{8}$$

Since both f_1 and f_2 enforce physics on the distribution descriptors, they do not ensure that the corresponding outputs are the actual 1st and 99th percentiles of the output distributions. To learn the correct quantiles, we employ a learnable parametrized function f_3 that takes only the distribution descriptor tuples of input demands $\bar{\boldsymbol{d}} := (\boldsymbol{\mu}_d, \boldsymbol{a}_d, \boldsymbol{b}_d)$, estimated flows $\bar{\boldsymbol{q}} := (\boldsymbol{\mu}_{\tilde{q}}, \boldsymbol{a}_{\tilde{q}}, \boldsymbol{b}_{\tilde{q}})$ and estimated heads $\bar{\boldsymbol{h}} := (\boldsymbol{\mu}_{\tilde{h}}, \boldsymbol{a}_{\tilde{h}}, \boldsymbol{b}_{\tilde{h}})$, and predicts the output quantiles:

$$f_3(\bar{\boldsymbol{d}}, \bar{\boldsymbol{q}}, \bar{\boldsymbol{h}}; \bar{\boldsymbol{\Theta}}), : \longmapsto (\bar{\boldsymbol{q}}^{(0.01)}, \bar{\boldsymbol{q}}^{(0.99)}, \bar{\boldsymbol{h}}^{(0.01)}, \bar{\boldsymbol{h}}^{(0.99)}) \tag{9}$$

where $\bar{\boldsymbol{\Theta}}$ are learnable parameters of f_3, which is a Calibration Network based on the same edge-based GNN as f_1. It is important that f_3 does not depend on individual samples since it is aimed at mapping multiple input distributions to multiple output distributions based on the input distributions descriptors. Therefore, at inference, only the input distribution descriptors will be sufficient to estimate the output quantiles.

We elaborate on all three functions in detail in the following sections.

4.2 Graph Neural Network Based f_1

Edge-Based GNN Encoder: First, the encoder embeds the node and edge tuples using linear layers Ω and β as $\boldsymbol{g}_v := \Omega(\boldsymbol{d}_v), \boldsymbol{z}_e := \beta(\boldsymbol{q}_e)$, $\forall\ v \in V$ and $\forall\ e \in E$ respectively. Next, in each GNN layer, messages are generated and passed through an MLP γ with residual connection as:

$$\boldsymbol{m}_e^{(i)} := \mathrm{ReLU}(\boldsymbol{z}_e^{(i)} + \gamma^{(i)}(\boldsymbol{g}_u^{(i)} \parallel \boldsymbol{g}_v^{(i)} \parallel \boldsymbol{z}_e^{(i)})) \text{ with } u \in \mathcal{N}(v).$$

Finally, the messages are aggregated using max aggregation as $\boldsymbol{g}_v^{(i+1)} := \boldsymbol{m}_v^{(i)} := \max_{u \in \mathcal{N}(v)} \boldsymbol{m}_{e_{vu}}^{(i)}$, $\forall\ v \in V$. This is also the update part of the three-step message passing process since we do not use any node-level MLP. Eliminating this MLP achieved faster convergence and lower errors compared to the architecture of [4].

MLP Decoder: The decoder estimates the flow tuple $\hat{\boldsymbol{q}}$ iteratively using the linear layer ϕ as $\hat{\boldsymbol{q}}_{e_{in}} := \hat{\boldsymbol{q}}_{e_{in}} + \phi(\boldsymbol{z}_{e_{in}} \parallel \boldsymbol{z}_{e_{out}}), \forall\ e_{in}, e_{out} \in E$. Here $\boldsymbol{z}_{e_{in}}$ and $\boldsymbol{z}_{e_{out}}$ are the directional flow embeddings generated after concatenating both node and edge features from the last GNN layer I and passing through a linear layer λ, i.e., $\boldsymbol{z}_e := \lambda(\boldsymbol{g}_u^{(I)} \parallel \boldsymbol{g}_v^{(I)} \parallel \boldsymbol{z}_e^{(I)})$ with $u \in \mathcal{N}(v)$, $\forall\ e \in E$.

Enforcing Local Hydraulics: Since the decoder predicts directional flows, using Eq. 1, we compute the flows in the other direction as $\hat{\boldsymbol{q}}_{e_{out}} := -\hat{\boldsymbol{q}}_{e_{in}}$. Next, using Eq. 2, we compute the reconstructed demand tuple as $\hat{\boldsymbol{d}}_v := -\sum_{u \in \mathcal{N}(v)} \hat{\boldsymbol{q}}_{e_{vu}}$.

4.3 Physics-Informed f_2

Global Physics-Informed Algorithm: The second function f_2 includes a physics-informed algorithm (PI-Algo) that enforces the global hydraulics [2,4].

For every element of the output flow tuple from f_1, i.e. for the samples $\boldsymbol{s}_{\hat{q}}$ and the interval descriptors $\boldsymbol{\mu}_{\hat{q}}, \boldsymbol{a}_{\hat{q}}, \boldsymbol{b}_{\hat{q}}$, the PI-Algo computes physically correct pressure head tuple $\tilde{\boldsymbol{h}}$. Similar to GNN's three-step message passing process, it uses reservoir heads $\boldsymbol{h}^*_{v\in V_r}$, Eq. 3, 4 and link attributes $\boldsymbol{l}$ to *construct* and *aggregate messages* and *update* pressure heads iteratively as:

$$
\begin{aligned}
&\text{message construction:} && \boldsymbol{m}_e^{(j)} := \tilde{\boldsymbol{h}}_u^{(j)} - f_{ql}(\boldsymbol{q}_e, \boldsymbol{l}_e), \\
&\text{message aggregation:} && \boldsymbol{m}_v^{(j)} := \max\nolimits_{u\in\mathcal{N}(v)} \boldsymbol{m}_{e_{vu}}^{(j)}, \quad \forall\, v \in V \setminus V_r, \\
&\text{update:} && \tilde{\boldsymbol{h}}_v^{(j+1)} := \max\{\tilde{\boldsymbol{h}}_v^{(j)}, \boldsymbol{m}_v^{(j)}\}, \quad \forall\, v \in V \setminus V_r,
\end{aligned}
$$

where f_{ql} is a link-dependent computable function (Appendix B) and J is the number of iterations required by the algorithm to converge for all tuple elements.

Flow and Demand Computations: After convergence, flow and demand tuples are computed using hydraulic principles as $\tilde{\boldsymbol{q}}_{e_{vu}} := f_{hl}(\tilde{\boldsymbol{h}}_v, \tilde{\boldsymbol{h}}_u, \boldsymbol{l}_{e_{vu}})$ and $\tilde{\boldsymbol{d}}_v := -\sum_{u\in\mathcal{N}(v)} \tilde{\boldsymbol{q}}_{e_{vu}}, \forall\, v \in V$ respectively. Here f_{hl} is a link-dependent computable function. There are no trainable parameters in f_2. Further details about the algorithm are given in Appendix B.

4.4 Graph Neural Network Based Calibration Network f_3

Edge-Based GNN Encoder: The encoder is similar to the encoder in f_1 (Sect. 4.2), except for the inputs. Here, the node and edge features are the input distribution descriptors $\bar{\boldsymbol{d}}_v = (\mu_{d_v}, a_{d_v}, b_{d_v})$ and their corresponding estimated output descriptors $\bar{\boldsymbol{h}}_v = (\mu_{\tilde{h}_v}, a_{\tilde{h}_v}, b_{\tilde{h}_v})$, $\bar{\boldsymbol{q}}_e = (\mu_{\tilde{q}_e}, a_{\tilde{q}_e}, b_{\tilde{q}_e})$, which are embedded using linear layers $\bar{\Omega}$ and $\bar{\beta}$ as:

$$\bar{\boldsymbol{g}}_v := \bar{\Omega}(\bar{\boldsymbol{d}}_v \parallel \bar{\boldsymbol{h}}_v), \ \forall\, v \in V \qquad \boldsymbol{z}_e := \bar{\beta}(\bar{\boldsymbol{q}}_e), \ \forall\, e \in E$$

These are then processed by similar GNN layers as in f_1 using the MLPs $\bar{\gamma}$. The output node and edge embeddings $(\bar{\boldsymbol{g}}_v^{(I)}, \bar{\boldsymbol{z}}_e^{(I)})$ are then passed to the decoder.

Double-Headed Quantile Decoder: The decoder consists of two heads, one for flows and the other for pressures. The flow head first concatenates the node and edge embeddings $\bar{\boldsymbol{g}}_v^{(I)}$ and $\bar{\boldsymbol{z}}_e^{(I)}$, and passes these through the linear layer $\bar{\lambda}$:

$$\bar{\boldsymbol{z}}_e := \bar{\lambda}(\bar{\boldsymbol{g}}_u^{(I)} \parallel \bar{\boldsymbol{g}}_v^{(I)} \parallel \bar{\boldsymbol{z}}_e^{(I)}) \text{ with } u \in \mathcal{N}(v), \ \forall\, e \in E$$

Then it predicts two asymmetric distances from the mean $\boldsymbol{\mu}_{\tilde{q}}$ to the 1st and 99th percentiles using a linear layer $\bar{\phi}_q$ as follows:

$$(\Delta\bar{q}_e^{(0.01)}, \Delta\bar{q}_e^{(0.99)}) := \left|\bar{\phi}_q(\bar{\boldsymbol{z}}_e)\right|, \qquad \forall\, e \in E$$

The second head predicts the asymmetric distances from the mean $\boldsymbol{\mu}_{\tilde{h}}$ to the 1st and 99th percentiles using the node embedding $\bar{\boldsymbol{g}}_v^{(I)}$ and a linear layer $\bar{\phi}_h$:

$$(\Delta\bar{h}_v^{(0.01)}, \Delta\bar{h}_v^{(0.99)}) := \left|\bar{\phi}_h(\bar{\boldsymbol{g}}_v)\right|, \qquad \forall\, v \in V$$

Finally, the output quantiles are computed as

$$\bar{q}_e^{(0.01)} := \mu_{\tilde{q}_e} - \Delta\bar{q}_e^{(0.01)}, \qquad \bar{q}_e^{(0.99)} := \mu_{\tilde{q}_e} + \Delta\bar{q}_e^{(0.99)}, \qquad \forall\, e \in E$$
$$\bar{h}_v^{(0.01)} := \mu_{\tilde{h}_v} - \Delta\bar{h}_v^{(0.01)}, \qquad \bar{h}_v^{(0.99)} := \mu_{\tilde{h}_v} + \Delta\bar{h}_v^{(0.99)}, \qquad \forall\, v \in V$$

Instead of predicting the quantiles directly, we predict the asymmetric distances from the mean to the quantiles since these distances are more likely to be smooth and learnable compared to the actual quantiles. Moreover, this way we can ensure that the 1st percentile is always less than the mean and the 99th percentile is always greater than the mean, which is not guaranteed otherwise.

4.5 Objective Function

We use the same physics-based objective function as in [2,4] for f_1 and f_2::

$$\mathcal{L}_{12} = \mathcal{L}_1(\boldsymbol{d}^*, \hat{\boldsymbol{d}}^{(K)}) + \rho_1 \mathcal{L}_1(\boldsymbol{d}^*, \tilde{\boldsymbol{d}}^{(K)}) + \rho_2 \mathcal{L}_1(\hat{\boldsymbol{q}}^{(K)}, \tilde{\boldsymbol{q}}^{(K)}), \tag{10}$$

where $\mathcal{L}_1$ denotes the L1 loss and ρ_1 and ρ_2 are hyperparameters. For f_3, we use the pinball objective function for quantile regression [10,22] given by:

$$\mathcal{L}_{\text{pinball}}(y^*, \hat{y}, \tau) = \frac{1}{S}\frac{1}{N}\sum_{s=1}^{S}\sum_{n=1}^{N} \left[\max\{\tau(y^* - \hat{y}), (\tau - 1)(y^* - \hat{y})\}\right], \tag{11}$$

where S is the number of samples, N is the number of nodes or edges, and τ is the quantile level (0.01 or 0.99 in our case). Instead of predicting the quantiles directly, we predict the asymmetric distances from the mean to the quantiles. Hence, y^* are the distances of samples from the distribution to the mean of the distribution and $\hat{y}$ are the predicted asymmetric distances. Therefore, we can write the objective function for f_3 as follows:

$$\begin{aligned}\mathcal{L}_3 = \;& \mathcal{L}_{\text{pinball}}(\Delta\tilde{\boldsymbol{q}}, -\Delta\bar{\boldsymbol{q}}^{(0.01)}, 0.01) + \mathcal{L}_{\text{pinball}}(\Delta\tilde{\boldsymbol{q}}, \Delta\bar{\boldsymbol{q}}^{(0.99)}, 0.99)\\ & + \mathcal{L}_{\text{pinball}}(\Delta\tilde{\boldsymbol{h}}, -\Delta\bar{\boldsymbol{h}}^{(0.01)}, 0.01) + \mathcal{L}_{\text{pinball}}(\Delta\tilde{\boldsymbol{h}}, \Delta\bar{\boldsymbol{h}}^{(0.99)}, 0.99),\end{aligned} \tag{12}$$

where for each batch $s \in \{1, \ldots, S\}$, we compute $\boldsymbol{s}_{\tilde{q}}^{(s)} - \boldsymbol{\mu}_{\tilde{q}}^{(s)} \in \mathbb{R}^{N_E}$ and stack these to obtain the matrix $\Delta\tilde{\boldsymbol{q}} \in \mathbb{R}^{S \times N_E}$. We do the same for heads to get $\Delta\tilde{\boldsymbol{h}} \in \mathbb{R}^{S \times N_V}$.

Finally, the overall objective function is given by

$$\mathcal{L} = \mathcal{L}_{12} + \delta\mathcal{L}_3, \tag{13}$$

where δ is a hyperparameter.

4.6 Training Scheme

We initialize input consumer demand and reservoir head tuples as follows:

$$\boldsymbol{d}_v^{(0)} := (s_{d_v^*} \parallel \mu_{d_v^*} \parallel \mu_{d^*} - 0.98\Delta d_v{}^* \parallel \mu_{d_v^*} + 0.98\Delta d_v{}^*) \text{ if } v \in V \setminus V_r \text{ else } 0$$
$$\boldsymbol{h}_v^{(0)} := (h_v^* \parallel h_v^* \parallel h_v^* \parallel h_v^*) \text{ if } v \in V_r \text{ else } 0,$$

where $\Delta d_v{}^* = (b_{d_v{}^*} - a_{d_v{}^*})/2$. All flows are initialized to zeroes and pipe and pump attributes are just repeated four times. In our training setup, we train a surrogate model and use its outputs to train a Calibration Network. We train both the surrogate model and the Calibration Network end-to-end with both loss terms $\mathcal{L} = \mathcal{L}_{12} + \delta\mathcal{L}_3$ with the hyperparameters ρ_1, ρ_2 and δ set to 0.1. We opted for this simplest approach since other approaches like stage-wise training (first the surrogate followed by both) did not offer better convergence. For every epoch, we sample one tuple of $(\mu_{d_v}, \Delta d_v)$ per node and sample from these over all iterations of the epoch giving us 1440 samples per epoch and distribution (see Appendix D). We accumulate samples over the epoch to get ground truth samples being passed on to the quantile loss described in Eq. 12.

4.7 Physics-Preserving Data Normalization

In a WDS, demands, flows, pressure heads, and link attributes assume different ranges of values as shown in Table 2 in Appendix C. To summarize the combined effect of pipe attributes into one quantity, Table 2 lists the magnitudes for the resistance coefficient $\boldsymbol{r}$ as per Eq. 3. Since these variables can range from very big numbers to very small numbers, data normalization is critical for successfully training a physics-informed DL model. Part of the problem was addressed by [2] by proposing a physics-preserving normalization method that uses scalars, is fully reversible and supported by empirical evidence only. We provide a theoretical proof for this in the following proposition.

Proposition 1. *For a given WDS graph $\mathcal{G} = (V, E)$, any normalization of the states (demands, flows, heads, resistance coefficients, etc.) that uses only scalars per state, will preserve the physics per state and will be reversible.*

Proof. The proof is given in Appendix C.

The above proposition holds for per state scalars. However, comparing two normalized states using the above approach will be infeasible since the normalization factors are state-specific. Since we are interested in estimating uncertainty intervals for flows and heads across multiples states of the same graph, we must use the same normalization factors across all states of the graph in our training set. This way, we can ensure that the physics is preserved across all states and the normalized states can be compared to estimate uncertainty intervals:

Corollary 1. *For a given WDS graph $\mathcal{G} = (V, E)$, any normalization of the states (demands, flows, heads, resistance coefficients, etc.) that uses the same scalars per state across all states in the training set, will preserve the physics per state and will be reversible.*

5 Experiments

5.1 Experimental Setup

Datasets: WDSs are part of the critical infrastructure and are subject to strict privacy and confidentiality regulations. This prohibits publication of real-world datasets, and it is common practice to evaluate algorithms on realistic but simulated counterparts [2,4,19,38]. We conduct experiments on five WDS benchmarks listed in Table 3 in Appendix D [1]. Each of these benchmarks comes with a single set of demands except for Hanoi WDS that has around 1000 different scenarios available at [35]. However, this dataset does not account for demand uncertainties in terms of intervals or distributions. Nevertheless, we leverage the information available for Hanoi WDS to generate our own datasets centered around the single set of available demands that we denote as $d_{v_{\text{base}}}, v \in V$. For all WDS datasets, we sample the distribution parameters as $\mu_{d_v} \sim \mathcal{U}(0.5d_{v_{\text{base}}}, 2.5d_{v_{\text{base}}}), \forall\, v \in V$ and $\Delta d_v \sim \mathcal{U}(0.05d_{v_{\text{base}}}, 0.5d_{v_{\text{base}}}), \forall\, v \in V$. Next, we sample individual samples from these sampled parameters as $s_{d_v} \sim \mathcal{U}(\mu_{d_v} - \Delta d_v, \mu_{d_v} + \Delta d_v)$. We explain the choice of these parameters and the dataset generation process in Appendix D.

Data Normalization: Using Corollary 1, we normalize the datasets in two steps. First, for each dataset, for all states/samples, we choose $\alpha_d = \max_{s=1}^{S} \sum_{v \in V \setminus V_r} d_v^{*s}$ and $\alpha_r = \max_{s=1}^{S}(3 * \sigma_{r_e^{*s}})$, where s is the state/sample index and S is the total number of samples. This gives us:

$$\frac{\Delta \boldsymbol{h}^*}{\alpha_r \alpha_d^x} = \frac{\boldsymbol{r}^*}{\alpha_r}\left(\frac{\boldsymbol{q}^*}{\alpha_d}\right)^x + \boldsymbol{s}\boldsymbol{\omega}^{*2}\left(\frac{\boldsymbol{\iota}^*}{\alpha_r \alpha_d^x}\right) - \frac{\boldsymbol{s}}{\boldsymbol{\omega}^{*\boldsymbol{\nu}^*}}\left(\frac{\boldsymbol{\kappa}^*}{\alpha_r \alpha_d^{x-\boldsymbol{\nu}^*}}\right)\left(\frac{\boldsymbol{q}^*}{\alpha_d}\right)^{\boldsymbol{\nu}^*}.$$

Next, we set $\alpha_h = \max_{s=1}^{S} \frac{\Delta \boldsymbol{h}^{*s}}{\alpha_r \alpha_d^x}$ to get the final normalized state:

$$\frac{\Delta \boldsymbol{h}^*}{\alpha_h \alpha_r \alpha_d^x} = \frac{\boldsymbol{r}^*}{\alpha_h \alpha_r}\left(\frac{\boldsymbol{q}^*}{\alpha_d}\right)^x + \boldsymbol{s}\boldsymbol{\omega}^{*2}\left(\frac{\boldsymbol{\iota}^*}{\alpha_h \alpha_r \alpha_d^x}\right) - \frac{\boldsymbol{s}}{\boldsymbol{\omega}^{*\boldsymbol{\nu}^*}}\left(\frac{\boldsymbol{\kappa}^*}{\alpha_h \alpha_r \alpha_d^{x-\boldsymbol{\nu}^*}}\right)\left(\frac{\boldsymbol{q}^*}{\alpha_d}\right)^{\boldsymbol{\nu}^*}$$

This two-stage normalization is completely reversible since it involves only scalars. It ensures that pressure heads lie between 0 and 1. Moreover, in most of the cases $\sum_{v \in V \setminus V_r} d_v^* \approx \max_{e \in E} q_e^*$, hence, this normalization also ensures that both demands and flows are between 0 and 1.

Hyperparameters: All models are trained for $N_p = 6000$ epochs for all WDS datasets. The latent dimension is set to 160. The starting learning rate of 0.0001 is reduced every 300 epochs by a factor of 0.75. The norm of the gradients is clipped to 0.000001. The MLPs $\boldsymbol{\gamma}, \bar{\boldsymbol{\gamma}}$ have 2 layers each with ReLU activations. We use 5 GNN layers in both the surrogate model f_1 and the Calibration Network f_3. Rest of the PI-GNN surrogate model hyperparameters are the same as used by [2] (Appendix E).

5.2 Experimental Results

We evaluate our IPI-GNN models using the same sampling approach as used during the training. For comparison, we perform Monte Carlo sampling for every tuple of sampled $(\mu_{d_v}, \Delta d_v)$ using the simulator. We sample 5000 samples per tuple and display the results averaged over 100 different sampled tuples $(\mu_{d_v}, \Delta d_v)$. We normalize the results with min-max normalization using min and

Table 1. nMAE and MAE_{PICP} (Eq. 14) results on five WDS datasets for our IPI-GNN compared to the simulator, which acts as the ground truth. The results are averaged over 100 different sampled tuples $(\mu_{d_v}, \Delta d_v)$ and 5000 samples per tuple. All results are multiplied by 10^2 for better readability.

IPI-GNN vs Simulator	Anytown	Hanoi	Fossolo	Pescara	Balerma
	nMAE ($\times 10^{-2}$) for Demands $\boldsymbol{d}$, Heads $\boldsymbol{h}$, and Flows $\boldsymbol{q}$				
nMAE $\boldsymbol{d}$	0.23 ± 0.19	0.11 ± 0.05	0.13 ± 0.04	0.21 ± 0.05	0.17 ± 0.03
nMAE $\boldsymbol{h}$	0.12 ± 0.03	0.11 ± 0.03	0.09 ± 0.03	0.17 ± 0.03	0.02 ± 0.01
nMAE $\boldsymbol{q}$	0.16 ± 0.04	0.02 ± 0.00	0.01 ± 0.00	0.04 ± 0.01	0.00 ± 0.00
	nMAE and MAE_{PICP} ($\times 10^{-2}$) for Heads $\boldsymbol{h}$				
nMAE $\boldsymbol{h}^{(0.01)}$	0.14 ± 0.24	0.27 ± 0.25	0.21 ± 0.33	0.37 ± 0.40	0.09 ± 0.14
nMAE $\boldsymbol{h}^{(0.99)}$	0.13 ± 0.20	0.31 ± 0.27	0.28 ± 0.46	0.35 ± 0.44	0.09 ± 0.14
MAE_{PICP} $\boldsymbol{h}$	2.10 ± 1.14	0.30 ± 0.39	0.51 ± 0.47	0.57 ± 0.48	0.26 ± 0.15
	nMAE and MAE_{PICP} ($\times 10^{-2}$) for Flows $\boldsymbol{q}$				
nMAE $\boldsymbol{q}^{(0.01)}$	0.27 ± 0.34	0.09 ± 0.11	0.04 ± 0.07	0.11 ± 0.15	0.02 ± 0.03
nMAE $\boldsymbol{q}^{(0.99)}$	0.26 ± 0.37	0.10 ± 0.12	0.04 ± 0.07	0.13 ± 0.20	0.02 ± 0.03
MAE_{PICP} $\boldsymbol{q}$	2.46 ± 1.27	0.33 ± 0.33	0.65 ± 0.53	0.38 ± 0.42	0.15 ± 0.13
	Inference Time (in seconds)				
IPI-GNN	0.09	0.09	0.09	0.13	0.44
Simulator	127.42	142.17	201.43	5771.97	1762.99

max from the ground truth simulator results. We compute normalized mean absolute error (nMAE) and Prediction Interval Coverage Probability (PICP) as follows:

$$\begin{aligned} \text{nMAE} &= \frac{1}{N_t S N_n} \sum_{i=0}^{N_t S N_n} |y_i - \hat{y}_i|, \\ \text{PICP} &= \frac{1}{N_t S N_n} \sum_{i=0}^{N_t S N_n} \mathbb{I}(\hat{y}_i^{0.01} \leq y_i \leq \hat{y}_i^{0.99}) \end{aligned} \tag{14}$$

For our $(0.01, 0.99)$ intervals, the nominal target coverage is 0.98 and we report $\text{MAE}_{\text{PICP}} = |\text{PICP} - 0.98|$. Table 1 shows the nMAE, MAE_{PICP} and inference time for our IPI-GNN compared to the simulator on five WDS datasets. The results show that IPI-GNN can achieve very low nMAE for demands, heads and flows and great coverage as shown by MAE_{PICP}, all at a very low computational cost. However, the quantile estimation error (nMAE $\bar{\boldsymbol{h}}^{(0.01)}, \bar{\boldsymbol{h}}^{(0.99)}, \bar{\boldsymbol{q}}^{(0.01)}, \bar{\boldsymbol{q}}^{(0.99)}$) is somewhat higher than the state estimation error (nMAE $\tilde{\boldsymbol{h}}, \tilde{\boldsymbol{q}}$), which is a result of the noise inherent to Monte Carlo sampling process. Figure 3 shows a comparison of quantile intervals for pressure heads at selected nodes for Pescara WDS, where the estimated quantile intervals closely match the corresponding quantile intervals from the ground truth simulator, which is consistent with the results in Table 1.

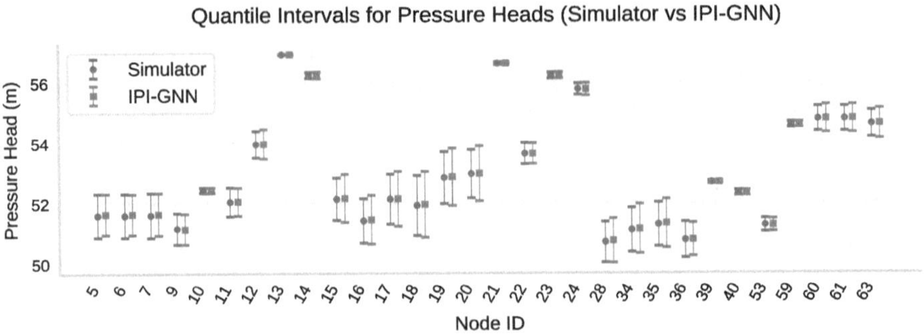

Fig. 3. Quantile intervals for pressure heads at selected nodes (Simulator vs Our Model IPI-GNN) for Pescara WDS.

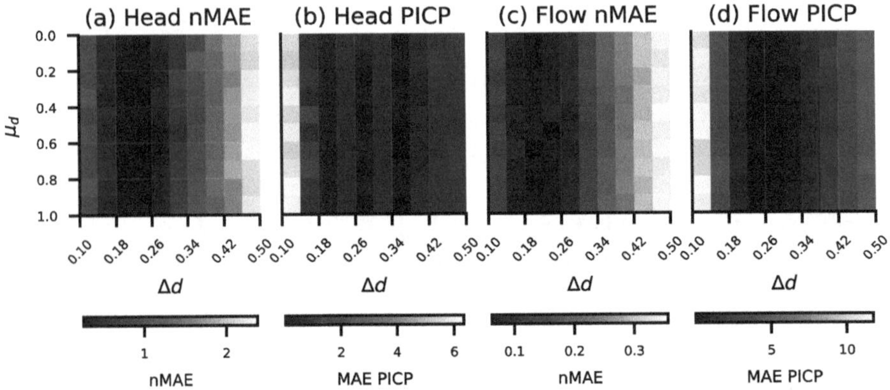

Fig. 4. nMAE and MAE$_{\text{PICP}}$ (Simulator vs Our Model IPI-GNN) for equally spaced bounds for Fossolo WDS.

In order to further understand the capabilities and limitations of the trained models, we sample (10×10) combinations of $(\mu_{d_v}, \Delta d_v)$ not from the original distributions $\mu_{d_v} \sim \mathcal{U}(0.5 d_{v_{\text{base}}}, 2.5 d_{v_{\text{base}}})$ and $\Delta d_v \sim \mathcal{U}(0.05 d_{v_{\text{base}}}, 0.5 d_{v_{\text{base}}})$ but rather over a grid with equally spaced bounds. We use a 10×10 grid of parameter pairs $\{(\mu^{(i)}, \Delta^{(j)})\}_{i=1,j=1}^{10,10}$, where each pair is sampled from uniform distributions with bounds equally spaced between $[1.0, 2.0] d_{v_{\text{base}}}$ for means and $[0.1, 0.5] d_{v_{\text{base}}}$ for spreads. Figure 4 shows nMAE and MAE$_{\text{PICP}}$ results for IPI-GNN compared to the simulator for Fossolo WDS, which demonstrate that IPI-GNN can achieve good performance across the grid of parameter pairs but the performance on the tails of the distributions (lower/higher means and spreads, Fig. 10 in Appendix D) needs improvement.

6 Limitations and Future Work

Our proposed model shows good performance on five WDS datasets but has a few limitations. For instance, despite using enough samples (i.e., 1440) there is still some noise inherent to the Monte Carlo sampling method that prevents perfect convergence as reflected in higher quantile prediction errors (nMAE $\bar{\boldsymbol{h}}^{(0.01)}$, $\bar{\boldsymbol{h}}^{(0.99)}$, $\bar{\boldsymbol{q}}^{(0.01)}$, $\bar{\boldsymbol{q}}^{(0.99)}$) compared to the state prediction errors (nMAE $\tilde{\boldsymbol{h}}$, $\tilde{\boldsymbol{q}}$), which we aim to address in the future. Moreover, we plan to experiment with more complex and large-scale WDSs along with more sources of uncertainties such as pipe roughness, pump parameters, etc. Finally, we plan to investigate the use of our model for real-time monitoring and event diagnosis in WDSs.

7 Conclusion

We propose a novel physics-informed GNN based surrogate model for interval estimation in WDSs that can map multiple input demand intervals to corresponding multiple output pressure head and flow intervals. To the best of our knowledge, this is the first work to integrate physics-informed GNNs with interval estimation for WDSs. We empirically show that our model achieves good performance on five WDS datasets and could potentially be used for various applications such as WDS planning, real-time monitoring, event diagnosis, and more. We believe that our work is a step towards robust and reliable modeling of WDSs under uncertainty. Moreover, our proposed methodology could be applied to enhance other physics-informed surrogate models to incorporate interval estimation. The code and information about dataset generation are publicly available at GitHub.

Acknowledgments. This research was supported by the Ministry of Culture and Science (NRW, Germany) as part of the Lamarr Fellow Network. We also gratefully acknowledge funding from the European Research Council (ERC) under the ERC Synergy Grant Water-Futures (Grant agreement No. 951424). This publication reflects the views of the authors only.

Disclosure of Interests. The authors have no competing interests to declare that are relevant to the content of this article.

References

1. Artelt, A., Giese, K., Vrachimis, S.G., Eliades, D.G., Polycarpou, M.M., Hammer, B.: The waterbenchmarkhub: a platform for benchmarks in water distribution networks (2025)
2. Ashraf, I., Artelt, A., Hammer, B.: Scalable and robust physics-informed graph neural networks for water distribution systems. In: 2025 IJCNN (2025)
3. Ashraf, I., Hermes, L., Artelt, A., Hammer, B.: Spatial graph convolution neural networks for water distribution systems. In: Intelligent Data Analysis (2023)
4. Ashraf, I., Strotherm, J., Hermes, L., Hammer, B.: Physics-informed graph neural networks for water distribution systems. In: AAAI Conference, p. 38 (2024)
5. Ashraf, I., Strotherm, J., Hermes, L., Hammer, B.: Go with the flow: leveraging physics-informed gradients to solve real-world problems in water distribution systems. In: ECML/PKDD, pp. 41–59. Springer (2025)

6. Bartos, M., Thomas, M., Kim, M.G., Frankel, M., Sela, L.: Online state estimation in water distribution systems via extended kalman filtering. Water Res. (2024)
7. Betancourt, D., Muhanna, R.L.: Interval deep learning for computational mechanics problems under input uncertainty. PEM **70** (2022)
8. Bruna, J., Zaremba, W., Szlam, A.D., LeCun, Y.: Spectral networks and locally connected networks on graphs. CoRR (2014)
9. Candelieri, A., Ponti, A., Giordani, I., Archetti, F.: Lost in optimization of water distribution systems: better call bayes. Water (2022)
10. Cannon, A.J.: Quantile regression neural networks: implementation in R and application to precipitation downscaling. Adv. SCMO **4** (2018)
11. Defferrard, M., Bresson, X., Vandergheynst, P.: Convolutional neural networks on graphs with fast localized spectral filtering. NIPS (2016)
12. Fan, X., Zhang, X., Yu, X.B.: Machine learning model and strategy for fast and accurate detection of leaks in water supply network. J. Infrastruct. Preserv. Resil. **2**(1), 1–21 (2021). https://doi.org/10.1186/s43065-021-00021-6
13. Gal, Y., Ghahramani, Z.: Dropout as a Bayesian approximation: representing model uncertainty in deep learning. In: ICML (2016)
14. Gao, H., Wang, Z., Ji, S.: Large-scale learnable graph convolutional networks. In: SIGKDD, pp. 1416–1424 (2018)
15. Hajgató, G., Gyires-Tóth, B., Paál, G.: Reconstructing nodal pressures in water distribution systems with graph neural networks. arXiv:2104.13619 (2021)
16. Hamilton, W.L., Ying, R., Leskovec, J.: Inductive representation learning on large graphs. In: NIPS, pp. 1025–1035 (2017)
17. Hammer, B.: Learning with Recurrent Neural Networks. Lecture Notes in Control and Information Sciences, vol. 254. Springer (2000)
18. Hernández-Lobato, J.M., Adams, R.: Probabilistic backpropagation for scalable learning of Bayesian neural networks. In: ICML (2015)
19. Kerimov, B., Taormina, R., Tscheikner-Gratl, F.: Towards transferable metamodels for water distribution systems with edge-based graph neural networks. Water Res. (2024)
20. Kerimov, B., Yang, M., Taormina, R., Tscheikner-Gratl, F.: State estimation in water distribution system via diffusion on the edge space. Water Res. (2025)
21. Kipf, T.N., Welling, M.: Semi-supervised classification with graph convolutional networks. In: ICLR (2017)
22. Koenker, R., Bassett, G., Jr.: Regression quantiles. Econometrica **46**, 33–50 (1978)
23. Magini, R., Moretti, M., Boniforti, M.A., Guercio, R.: A machine-learning approach for monitoring water distribution networks (WDNs). Sustainability **15**(4) (2023)
24. Oala, L., Heiß, C., Macdonald, J., März, M., Samek, W., Kutyniok, G.: Interval Neural Networks: Uncertainty Scores. arXiv e-prints (2020)
25. Pérez, R., Sanz, G., Àngel Cugueró, M., Blesa, J., Cugueró, J.: Parameter uncertainty modelling in water distribution network models. Procedia Eng. (2015)
26. Raissi, M., Perdikaris, P., Karniadakis, G.: Physics-informed neural networks: a deep learning framework for solving forward and inverse problems involving nonlinear partial differential equations. J. Comput. Phys. (2019)
27. Rossman, L., Woo, H., Tryby, M., Shang, F., Janke, R., Haxton, T.: Epanet 2.2 user's manual, water infrastructure division. CESER (2020)
28. Scarselli, F., Gori, M., Tsoi, A.C., Hagenbuchner, M., Monfardini, G.: The graph neural network model. IEEE Trans. Neural Networks **20**(1), 61–80 (2009)
29. Strotherm, J., Rolfes, J., Hammer, B.: Existence and uniqueness of physically correct hydraulic states in water distribution systems (2025)

30. Todini, E.: A gradient method for the analysis of pipe networks. In: International Conference on Computer Applications for Water Supply and Distribution (1987)
31. Truong, H., Tello, A., Lazovik, A., Degeler, V.: Graph neural networks for pressure estimation in water distribution systems. Water Resour. Res. (2024)
32. Vaquet, V., Artelt, A., Brinkrolf, J., Hammer, B.: Taking care of our drinking water: dealing with sensor faults in water distribution networks. In: ICANN (2022)
33. Vaquet, V., Hinder, F., Hammer, B.: Investigating the suitability of concept drift detection for detecting leakages in water distribution networks. In: ICPRAM (2024)
34. Veličković, P., Cucurull, G., Casanova, A., Romero, A., Liò, P., Bengio, Y.: Graph attention networks. In: ICLR (2018). Accepted as poster
35. Vrachimis, S., Kyriakou, M., Eliades, D., Polycarpou, M.: Leakdb: a benchmark dataset for leakage diagnosis in water distribution networks description of benchmark. In: Proceedings of WDSA/CCWI Joint Conference, vol. 1 (2018)
36. Vrachimis, S.G., Timotheou, S., Eliades, D.G., Polycarpou, M.M.: Interval state estimation of hydraulics in water distribution networks. In: ECC (2018)
37. Wu, Y., Wang, X., Liu, S., Yu, X., Wu, X.: A weighting strategy to improve water demand forecasting performance based on spatial correlation between multiple sensors (2023)
38. Xing, L., Sela, L.: Graph neural networks for state estimation in water distribution systems: application of supervised and semisupervised learning. JWRPM (2022)

Local Intrinsic Dimensionality of Ground Motion for Early Detection of Catastrophic Slope Failure

Yuansan Liu[1(✉)], James Bailey[2], and Antoinette Tordesillas[1]

[1] The University of Melbourne, Melbourne, VIC 3053, Australia
{yuansan.liu1,atordesi}@unimelb.edu.au
[2] Monash University, Clayton, VIC 3800, Australia
james.a.bailey@monash.edu

Abstract. Local Intrinsic Dimensionality (LID) has shown strong potential for anomaly detection in high-dimensional data, including landslide failure detection in granular media, where early and accurate identification of failure zones is crucial for effective geohazard mitigation. However, this task is still challenging due to the spatial correlations and temporal dynamics that are inherently present in surface displacement data. To address this gap, we propose a novel unsupervised framework called spatiotemporal LID (*st*-LID) that generalizes the LID for robust failure detection in landslide monitoring networks. Our approach introduces three key innovations: (1) Kinematic enhancement, incorporating velocity into the LID computation to capture instantaneous deformation rates and short-term temporal dynamics; (2) Bayesian spatial fusion, which aggregates LID values across spatial neighborhoods via Bayesian estimation, to embed spatial correlations and account for localized noise; and (3) Temporal modeling (*t*-LID), a new variant that characterizes long-term dynamics of displacement data, providing a robust temporal representation of displacement behavior. By unifying these components, *st*-LID identifies complex, multi-stage failure zones often overlooked by existing methods. Extensive experiments show that *st*-LID consistently outperforms state-of-the-art unsupervised baselines in detection precision and lead-time, providing a robust foundation for landslide early warning systems and targeted risk intervention to enhance community resilience and preparedness strategies.

Keywords: Local intrinsic dimensionality · Early anomaly detection · Unsupervised learning · Spatiotemporal data analysis · Landslide early warning systems

Supplementary Information The online version contains supplementary material available at https://doi.org/10.1007/978-3-032-37682-4_14.

M. Baratchi et al. (Eds.): ECML PKDD 2026, LNAI 16949, pp. 232–249, 2027.
https://doi.org/10.1007/978-3-032-37682-4_14

1 Introduction

Local Intrinsic Dimensionality (LID) has recently emerged as a robust geometric tool for characterizing anomalous behavior in high-dimensional datasets. By quantifying the expansion rate of a sample's neighborhood, LID has demonstrated significant successes across various scenarios such as intrusion detection for IoT networks [6], identifying adversarial attacks on neural networks [12], and outlier detection for high-dimensional data [1]. Recent advances in granular media mechanics have further demonstrated that LID can detect impending failures in small scale laboratory tests by identifying shifts in the latent dimensionality of deformation [20,25].

At larger scales, such failures manifest as some of the most devastating natural hazards. Among these, catastrophic landslides are becoming increasingly frequent and severe due to climate change, seismic activity, and human intervention [7,14,16]. They can occur suddenly with little warning, often resulting in significant infrastructure damage, loss of life, and long-term economic disruption [3,11,16]. Identifying anomalies in such systems is particularly challenging because they involve multi-regime transitions driven by distinct physical processes. It is rare for a single metric to track the evolution of a multi-event process across spatial and temporal scales. This underscores the importance of timely and accurate identification of high-risk areas to enable early intervention, save lives, and reduce property loss.

Existing works commonly apply traditional machine learning and statistical techniques, such as K-means clustering [18] and Empirical Dynamic Quantiles (EDQs) [15,19], to monitoring data on surface displacement in the precursory failure regime, which has been proved to be one of the most direct indicators for identifying the location and timing of slope collapses [9,24]. However, the high dimensionality and inherent spatiotemporal characteristics of such data often challenge the traditional detection methods which are built upon uni-variate time series analysis. As a result, the original informative, multidimensional data is frequently reduced to single dimensional data, leading to significant information loss and potentially inaccurate detection, in both spatial and temporal aspects. Therefore, these existing works (1) *fail to fully exploit both spatial and temporal dependencies inherited in the spatiotemporal displacement data*, (2) *fail to identify the sudden changes or accelerations in displacement over time*, (3) *fail to capture the coherent pathways of regime transitions*. Subsequently, these limitations result in an inability to distinguish between steady-state motion and the subtle precursors of a dynamical regime shift toward catastrophic failure, leading to inaccurate detection, missing opportunities for timely intervention.

To address the challenge in learning with spatiotemporal data, we extend earlier studies of LID [25] to establish a LID-based framework for dynamic detection of high-risk areas most prone to slope failure at large field scales, by accounting for the outlyingness of kinematic behavior across multiple **spatial and time scales**. We first add the velocity (v_t) at each time stamp into target sample, allowing the algorithm to leverage the variability of the displacement and learn the short-term temporal dependence. Incorporating velocity is crucial, as many landslide early warning frameworks rely on velocity thresholds to trigger alerts and guide response actions [2,23]. Secondly, we apply Bayesian estimation to aggregate LID results in a small neighborhood, accounting for spatial dynamics of the query points. Thirdly, we propose t-LID to measure the outlyingness of a target sample with respect to its t nearest temporal neighbors (historical records), enabling it to capture the long-term dynamics from the entire time series data. Finally, we integrate two LID-based scores to highlight the points that are outlying with respect to both spatial and temporal neighborhoods (Fig. 1).

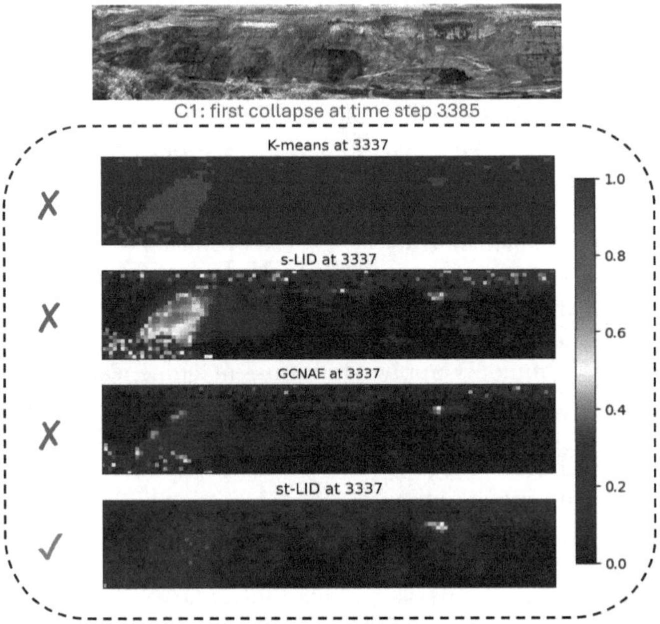

Fig. 1. Detection of location and order of successive failures in distinct sites of a slope. Top: The first failure event $C1$ (red frame) occurred at $t = 3385$. Bottom: Four methods detect impending failure locations at an earlier time step $t = 3337$ (2 h before collapse $C1$). Each monitoring point is colored based on the likelihood of failure at its location from 0 to 1. K-means produce binary results, 0 or 1. EDQs highlight points representative of the dynamics against the lower bound 0 for background. s-LID correctly identifies area of potential collapse but with extra noise. ***Only the proposed st-LID can detect and isolate the location of the first failure event*** $C1$ ***that is relevant at this time step.*** (Color figure online)

Specifically, we apply a sigmoid function to normalize both scores into probabilistic values and integrate them via multiplication to emphasize samples where both scores are high. This integration not only reduces false positives but also enables earlier detection of hazardous shifts, providing actionable insights well before visible damage occurs. We name the final score spatiotemporal **LID** (*st*-LID). Unlike traditional metrics that struggle to describe transitions across different physical processes, st-LID serves as a unified geometric measure which is able to track the evolution of multi-dynamical-regime processes. By combining spatial outlyingness with temporal shifts into a calibrated $[0, 1]$ anomaly score, the method produces interpretable visions of coherent failure pathways. This allows for the early identification of regime transitions in a strictly unsupervised manner, without the need for labels or prior model fitting. Experimental results demonstrate that the proposed *st*-LID can identify the actual landslide location in both single and multiple-failure cases with accuracy and efficiency. This highlights the practical value of *st*-LID in real-world landslide early warning systems, with the potential to save lives and protect critical infrastructures.

Our contributions can be summarized as:

- We propose a novel latent geometry-based method called *st*-LID for spatiotemporal outlier detection. This approach integrates three key components to capture both spatial correlations and temporal dynamics, enabling effective and efficient detection of landslide failures.
- We validate the proposed *st*-LID through extensive experiments on real-world datasets, demonstrating its competitive performance with respect to precision and lead-time of failure detection, and the computation efficiency of the algorithm.
- We propose a systematic failure detection procedure based on *st*-LID, showcasing its performance in early prediction of precise failure locations. This highlights the practicability of the *st*-LID in real-world landslide early warning systems, enabling timely interventions and enhanced risk management.

2 Background and Related Works

2.1 Landslide Monitoring and Statistical Solutions

Surface displacement is a primary indicator of impending slope failure. [5,9]. Figure 2 shows a typical example of the displacement time series corresponding to a catastrophic slope collapse. Notably, the displacement of points in the failure region manifest three stages of landslide creep (initial, steady-state and accelerated). In the lead-up to collapse, ground motion exhibits a distinct spatiotemporal clustering dynamics, with high-risk zones increasingly differentiating themselves from more stable areas of the slope. These patterns highlight the potential for using machine learning and data mining techniques to enable the automatic early detection of slope failure based on surface displacement data. Traditional detection relies on statistical clustering (e.g., K-means, LOF), which identifies high-risk regions but often yields noisy, binary results that ignore temporal dynamics [18,24]. Alternatively, Empirical Dynamic Quantiles (EDQs) detects failure locations by analyzing high-percentile displacement behaviors [19]. However, EDQs process sensors independently, lacking the spatial regularization necessary to handle measurement noise, leading to sparse and disjointed detections.

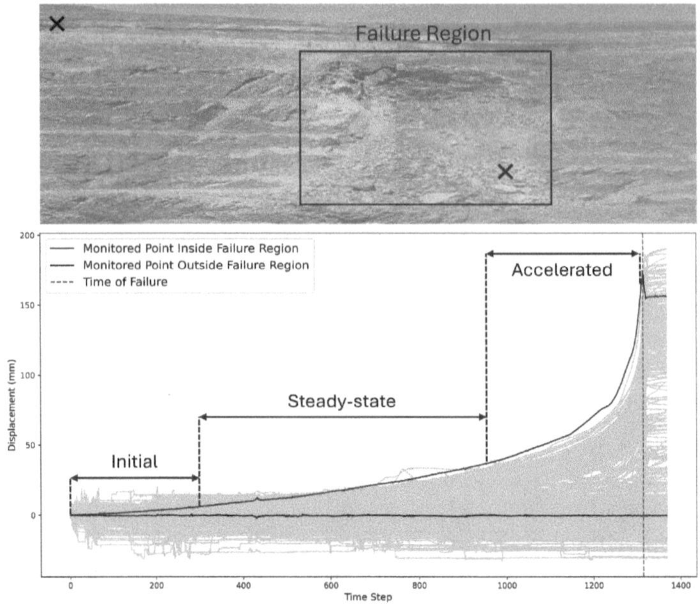

Fig. 2. Example of a real-world slope Failure (Top) and the displacement time series of each monitored point (Bottom). The failure (a collapse advised by domain expert) is located inside the blue frame. Each time series at the bottom represents the displacements of a monitored point along with the time. Two monitored points (inside and outside the failure region) are marked via '×' with different colors in the site map (their corresponding time series are highlighted with the same colors). The red dashed line indicates the time of failure (ToF). (Color figure online)

2.2 Local Intrinsic Dimensionality

Rather than analyzing raw values, Local Intrinsic Dimensionality (LID) exploits latent data properties to identify outliers [1,8,25]. LID measures the expansion rate of a sample's neighborhood, where a high value indicates the sample is outlying relative to its neighbors. For a sample x and its cumulative distance distribution $\mathcal{F}(r)$ to its neighbors, LID is defined as:

$$\text{LID}(x) = \lim_{r \to 0} \text{LID}_{\mathcal{F}(r)} = r \frac{\mathcal{F}'(r)}{\mathcal{F}(r)}. \tag{1}$$

In practice, the Maximum Likelihood Estimator (MLE) is used to approximate LID over s nearest neighbors. For landslide detection, the baseline s-LID computes this at fixed time steps based on displacement values [25]:

$$s\text{-LID}(\boldsymbol{x}_t) = -\left(\frac{1}{s} \sum_{i=1}^{s} \log \frac{dist_i(\boldsymbol{x}_t)}{dist_s(\boldsymbol{x}_t)} \right)^{-1}, \tag{2}$$

where $dist_i(\boldsymbol{x}_t)$ is the Euclidean distance of $\boldsymbol{x}_t$ to its ith nearest neighbor with displacement value of x_t^i: $dist_i(\boldsymbol{x}_t) = |x_t^p - x_t^i|$. While s-LID provides more granularity than K-means, it fails to leverage temporal dynamics and remains susceptible to sparsely distributed high-risk noise.

2.3 Deep Learning Models on Spatiotemporal Analysis

The advancements in deep learning have introduced powerful tools for learning spatial information in sensor networks. State-of-the-art models like Graph Convolution Networks (GCNs) or Graph Attention Networks (GATs) are used to extract the spatial topology between monitored points, identifying anomalies through reconstruction error. Recent works also combine these spatial models with the temporal modules such as LSTM or Transformer to jointly learn the spatial and temporal dynamics for environmental forecasting tasks [4,17,21,22].

While these deep learning approaches are able to achieve state-of-the-art performance, they typically require extensive labeled datasets for **supervised or semi-supervised** training which are extremely sparse in real-world. On the other hand, our proposed *st*-LID offers a **strictly unsupervised** solution, enabling online detection with a stream of incoming data without any training or tuning. Additionally, in contrast to these "black-box" models, *st*-LID maintains the mathematical interpretability of the LID expansion model while explicitly incorporating physical kinematics and Bayesian uncertainty to achieve state-of-the-art performance without the need for prior failure labels.

3 Methodology

To address the limitation of existing methods on learning with spatiotemporal data and improve its practicability in landslide application, we propose a novel spatiotemporal measurement to leverage both spatial correlation and temporal dynamics inherent in the displacement data.

3.1 Leveraging Velocity in LID Calculation

Firstly, to introduce short-term temporal dependency, we extend the data sample into a vector consists both displacement value and velocity $v_t^p = x_t^p - x_{t-1}^p$ at monitored point p and time step t, $\boldsymbol{x}_t = \langle x_t^p, v_t^p \rangle$. And the distance of a queried sample $\boldsymbol{x}_t$ to its ith nearest neighbor at monitored point i becomes:

$$dist_i(\boldsymbol{x}_t) = \sqrt{(x_t^p - x_t^i)^2 + (v_t^p - v_t^i)^2}. \tag{3}$$

Applying this new distance calculation to Eq. (2), we get the s-LID($\boldsymbol{x}_t$) that incorporates both displacement value and velocity at given time step. This inclusion allows the metric to perceive the instantaneous shift in dynamical behavior, identifying the transition between different motion regimes. Consequently, it effectively mitigates the bias introduced by samples exhibiting high displacement values but remain relatively stable.

Figure 3 depicts the effect of adding velocity with an real-world example: In the site map at top, different monitored points are selected as high-risk candidates ($\star$ and $\star$) according to the largest s-LID values at the last time point ($t = 4983$) when queried samples with or without the velocity. The corresponding time series at bottom illustrates the different temporal dynamics between these two monitored points, reflecting the aforementioned bias when using only displacement values for s-LID computation. Note that the actual failure region is around the monitored point $\star$. This fact justifies our enhancement of incorporating the velocity component.

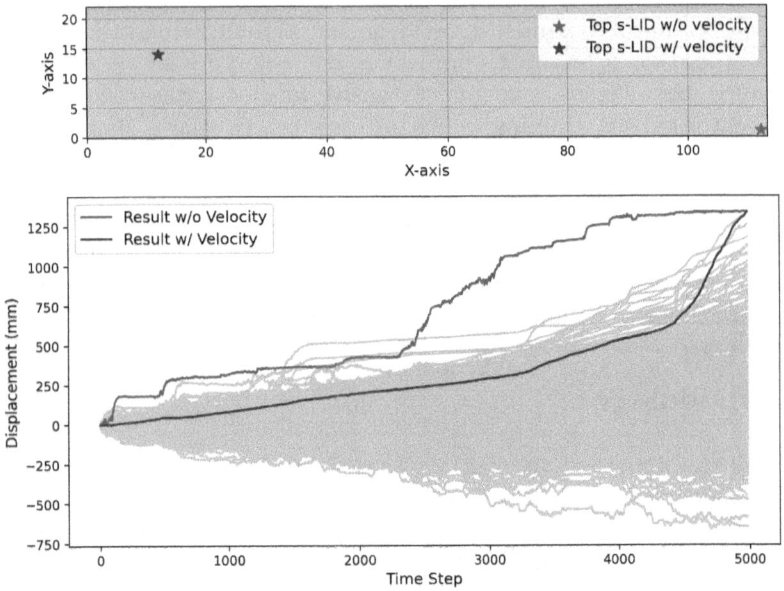

Fig. 3. Example high-risk areas and corresponding time series with & without velocity in s-LID computation. Top: Site map at last time step ($t = 4983$), with two monitored points highlighted by top s-LID values, representing the high-risk locations. $\star$ is the s-LID without velocity, $\star$ is the s-LID with velocity. Bottom: Displacement time series for each monitored point, with the same color. (Color figure online)

3.2 Spatial Fusion of LID

Although s-LID measures the query point's characteristic against its spatial neighbors, it finds the nearest neighbors in the kinematic space, without involving the spatial dependencies in physical space. To leverage the spatial relationships of all monitored points during the LID calculation, inspired by Bayesian LID algorithm [10], we integrate the s-LID results in a small neighborhood of the query point, enhancing the LID score with actual spatial dynamics. Figure 4

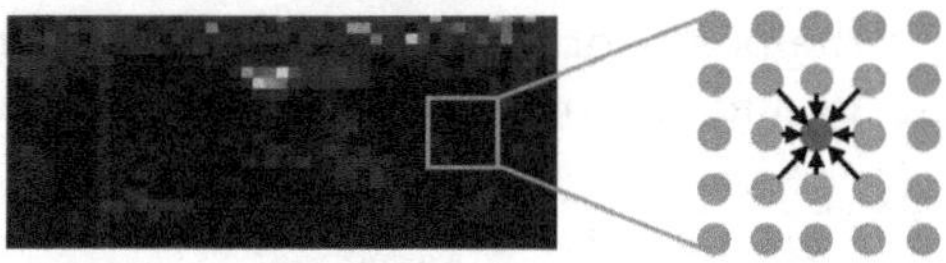

Fig. 4. Spatial fusion of s-LID. Red dot in the middle is the query point and its neighbors are colored with green. The final LID value of the query point is calculated based on its own observation and the pre-calculated s-LID of these neighbors at last time step. (Color figure online)

depicts the underlying idea, where the query point (red) is updated based on its neighbors (green).

Given a region with pre-calculated s-LID values at time step $t-1$. For each query point $\boldsymbol{x}_t$, let $\{f_{t-1}^i(l)\}_{i=1}^k$ be the k neighbors' prior densities that are built from last time step s-LID values. With a set of weights $\boldsymbol{w} = \{w_1, \cdots, w_k\}$ summing up to 1, we can combine these priors with logarithmic pooling:

$$f_t^{pool}(l|\boldsymbol{x}_t) := \left(\int_0^\infty \prod_{i=1}^k (f_{t-1}^i(l))^{w_i} dl \right) \prod_{i=1}^k (f_{t-1}^i(l))^{w_i}. \tag{4}$$

To simplify the calculation, we can assume Gamma densities $f^i = Ga(\alpha_i, \beta_i), i = 1, \cdots, k$, and Eq. (4) becomes a Gamma density as well:

$$f^{pool} = Ga(\alpha_p = \sum_{i=1}^k w_i \alpha_i, \beta_p = \sum_{i=1}^k w_i \beta_i). \tag{5}$$

Here, we apply Gaussian kernel to create weights that account for the physical proximity of the query point and its neighbors:

$$w_i = \frac{\exp\left(-\frac{d_e(p,i)^2}{2\sigma^2}\right)}{\sum_{j\in k} \exp\left(-\frac{d_e(p,j)^2}{2\sigma^2}\right)}.$$

Where $d_e(p, i(j))$ is the Euclidean distance between query point p and its $i(j)^{th}$ neighbor. This weight ensures closer neighbors have higher influences of the pooling results. Then, the parameters of the Gamma density can be derived from the weighted mean and variance of the neighbors' s-LID values:

$$\mu = \sum_{i=1}^k w_i s\text{-LID}(\boldsymbol{x}_{t-1}^i), \quad \sigma^2 = \sum_{i=1}^k w_i \left(s\text{-LID}(\boldsymbol{x}_{t-1}^i) - \mu \right)^2, \quad \alpha_p = \frac{\mu^2}{\sigma^2}, \quad \beta_p = \frac{\mu}{\sigma^2}. \tag{6}$$

Where s-LID$(\boldsymbol{x}_{t-1}^i)$ is the s-LID value of the ith neighbor of query point at $t-1$.

Once we get the current observation of query point, we can estimate its likelihood contribution via the density ratio within the k-neighborhood:

$$\alpha_o = k, \quad \beta_o = -\sum_{i=1}^k \log \frac{dist_i(\boldsymbol{x}_t)}{dist_k(\boldsymbol{x}_t)}. \tag{7}$$

Finally, we can get the posterior estimation of the query point's s-LID with parameters from Eqs. (6) and (7) following Gamma conjugacy:

$$s\text{-LID}^* = \frac{\alpha_p + \alpha_o}{\beta_p + \beta_o}.$$

This approach can effectively leverage spatial correlation in geophysical monitoring data to produce more robust LID estimates, ensuring geometric coherency and spatial continuity in LID calculation.

3.3 Temporally Informed LID

Thirdly, to learn the long-term dynamics of the time series data, we propose a temporal version of LID namely t-LID. Same as s-LID, t-LID is also estimated based on the distance expansion rate. Rather than spatial neighborhood, t-LID focuses on temporal neighborhood of the target sample, on another word, the historical values of the given sample until the analyzing time step t. Notice that, the raw displacement values are highly non-stationary across the temporal dimension. To mitigate the outlyingness contributed by such non-stationarity, we compute t-LID solely on the velocity values. This method also aligns with the common practice for de-trending non-stationary time series [13]. Hence, given a time series of samples at a fixed monitored point l: $\boldsymbol{x}_{1:t} = \{\boldsymbol{x}_1, \boldsymbol{x}_2, \cdots, \boldsymbol{x}_t\}, \boldsymbol{x}_t = \langle v_t^l \rangle$, we can write t-LID of the queried sample at current time step $\boldsymbol{x}_t$ as:

$$t\text{-LID}(\boldsymbol{x}_t) = -\left(\frac{1}{t}\sum_{i=1}^{t} \log \frac{dist_i(\boldsymbol{x}_t)}{dist_t(\boldsymbol{x}_t)}\right)^{-1}, \tag{8}$$

where $t \geq 2$ and $dist_i(\boldsymbol{x}_t) = |v_t^l - v_i^l|$ is the distance of the queried sample $\boldsymbol{x}_t$ at current time step t to its ith nearest neighbor at a historical time step i.

Similar to s-LID, which evaluates the outlyingness of a queried sample based on its spatial neighbors, t-LID measures the outlyingness of the queried samples against its own past records, enabling effective outlier detection within time series data. This temporal perspective allows t-LID to capture the dynamic changes along with the time, identifying the significant temporal deviations that may relate to the instability and emerging risks in a landslide process.

3.4 Spatiotemporal LID

Until now, we get two LID measurements: s-LID that quantifies the spatial outlyingness, and t-LID that captures the temporal deviations. At the final step, we propose a novel approach that integrates them into a unified spatiotemporal outlier detection framework. This integration aims to leverage the strengths of both methods on spatial and temporal outlier detection, addressing the limitations of traditional methods that consider these aspects in isolation.

To achieve an appropriate integration, we begin with the scale unification. Since spatial and temporal LID operate on different feature spaces and exhibit different score distributions, they are not directly comparable. We apply a scaling function: $\sigma(x) = \frac{1}{1+x}$ to map raw LID values into a normalized range $[0, 1]$. This step acts as a baseline calibration, mapping the local intrinsic dimensionality into a consistent outlier likelihood across varied monitoring sites. To ensure that only points exhibiting significant outlyingness in both spatial and temporal perspectives are highlighted, a multiplicative fusion is applied:

$$st\text{-LID}(\boldsymbol{x}_t) = \sigma(s\text{-LID}(\boldsymbol{x}_t)) \times \sigma(t\text{-LID}(\boldsymbol{x}_t)). \tag{9}$$

This multiplicative approach functions as a soft "AND" gate, effectively suppressing independent noise, such as localized sensor errors or transient temporal fluctuations, by amplifying signals where spatial clustering and temporal acceleration converge. Additionally, it also functions as a unified geometric measure designed to track multi-regime transitions. With s-LID captures the spatial outlyingness and t-LID identifies temporal shifts, the multiplication amplifies the signal only when these two distinct physical signatures align. This alignment marks the critical transition from a steady-state creep regime to an accelerated failure regime. While more complex fusion methods (e.g., rank-aggregation) could model specific dependencies, the multiplicative strategy provides a computationally efficient and interpretable precursor signal for real-time early warning.

3.5 Real-World Failure Detection via *st*-LID

The proposed st-LID is designed to identify the outliers in displacements data with precision and efficiency. However, it remains an open question to apply it in real-world scenario. In this section, we propose a systematic failure detection procedure to enable the practical deployment of st-LID.

Assuming a continuous monitoring system based on st-LID scores at each monitoring time step, we detect a potential failure region around the monitored point $\boldsymbol{x}^* \in \mathbb{R}^2$ at time step t if for n consecutive time steps $\{t-n+1, t-n+2\cdots, t\}$ the following conditions stand:

$$arg \max_{\boldsymbol{x}_t \in MP} st\text{-LID}(\boldsymbol{x}_t) = \mathcal{B}_\epsilon(\boldsymbol{x}_t^*); \quad st\text{-LID}(\boldsymbol{x}_t^*) \geq 0.5 \ . \tag{10}$$

Where MP is the set of all monitored points, and $\mathcal{B}_\epsilon(\boldsymbol{x}_t^*) = \{\boldsymbol{y} \in \mathbb{R}^2 \mid \|\boldsymbol{y}-\boldsymbol{x}_t^*\| < \epsilon\}$, $\epsilon > 0 \in \mathbb{R}$ is a small open ball around $\boldsymbol{x}_t^*$ to allow noise related fluctuation.

This procedure follows the thresholding of the failure (≥ 0.5) and ensures the convergence of the detection (small open ball). The choice of n can be decided by the domain experts, acting as a trade off between sensitivity and fidelity.

4 Experiments

4.1 Datasets

The datasets consist surface displacement measurements data from three real-world operating mine sites which experienced fatal collapses (failures). Due to confidential policy, we name these datasets as M_1, M_2, and M_3 respectively, without revealing their actual locations and names.

- M_1: Contains 2622 monitored points with displacement recorded in 8000 time steps, and there are two ground truth collapses happened at two different locations at $t = 3385, 7320$ respectively, we refer to them as $C1$ and $C2$.
- M_2: Contains 5844 monitored points with displacement recorded in 6000 time steps, and the single ground truth collapse happened at $t = 5264$.
- M_3: Contains 6624 monitored points with displacement recorded in 6500 time steps, and the single ground truth collapse happened at $t = 5806$.

The actual time interval between two consecutive time steps is 2.5 min in M_1, and 6 min in M_2 and M_3. More details of these datasets including the visualization of the displacement time series are provided in the Appendix.

4.2 Experimental Setup

The target of this work is to pinpoint the real failure locations at early time step, therefore, we evaluate the methods using two metrics:

- *Precision* (*Prec.*) measures the proportion of correct detection results (failure/collapse actually happened at the detected locations) relative to all detections from the method: $Prec. = \frac{\text{Correct Detections}}{\text{All Failure Detections}}$. Higher precision reflects less false alarms, indicating trustworthy detection.
- *Lead-time* (Δt) measures the difference between the model detection time and the actual failure time, quantifying efficiency of the method: $\Delta t = t_{failure} - t_{detection}$. Longer lead-time represents earlier detection of failure, enabling timely invention and reactions.

We compare the proposed *st*-LID with existing failure detection methods in industry including K-means and *s*-LID. We also include a cluster method: Density-based spatial clustering of applications with noise (DBSCAN), and a deep learning based SOTA anomaly detection model Graph Convolution Network Autoencoder (GCNAE). Due to the differences in output types across these methods, we unify the detection threshold for fair comparison. Specifically, in K-means and DBSCAN, all monitored points from high-risk class are regarded as failure detections. For GCNAE, we follow their original paper to get the anomaly score from the reconstruction error. The hyperparameters in all models are fixed across different dataset, detailed setup for these models is provided in the Appendix. The raw outputs of both GCNAE and *s*-LID are linearly converted to the range $[0, 1]$, and the failure detections are those with a final score ≥ 0.5. The precision score *Prec.* are computed using the detection results at the actual time of failures (collapses).

Regarding the lead-time Δt computation, to avoid the impact of noisy results in baselines, we use the top 5 results from each method, because it is the minimum detection numbers across all methods on all datasets. To be specific, these are the monitored points with: 5 shortest distance to outlying cluster's centroid in K-means and DBSCAN and top 5 scores for other methods. We record the first time when the selected points consistently fall within the actual failure regions (until the time of failure), and use it to compute Δt. We assign $\Delta t = 0$ for those methods cannot pinpoint the actual failure ahead of time.

Note that we do not include the commonly used metrics *Recall* because it requires a reliable count of all actual failures which is typically unavailable for real-world landslide scenarios. Moreover, the objective of this work is to develop manageable and high-confident early warnings for landslide failures, rather than to maximize the number of detected events at any false alarm burden. Thus, we focus on the *Precision* and *Lead-time* only.

4.3 Experimental Results

We provide both the qualitative and quantitative results in this section via the visual analysis and the aforementioned numeric metrics. The former provides intuitive insights into failure patterns, while the latter offers rigorous evaluation of performance.

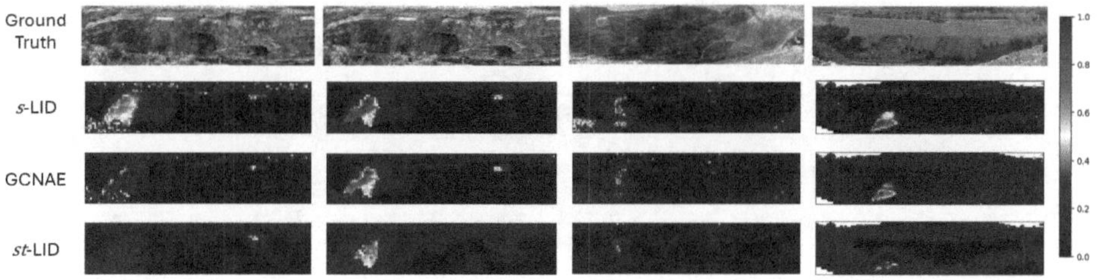

Fig. 5. Visualization of the ground truth in 4 datasets (columns) and corresponding detection results from top 3 methods (rows). Detection results are colored based on the likelihood of the failure (see color-bar for detailed range and order)

Figure 5 shows the ground truth collapse locations (red rectangle frame, advised by the domain experts) along with the detection results from top 3 methods (according to *Prec.*, visualizations of other methods are provided in Appendix). The proposed *st*-LID can precisely pinpoint the actual collapse locations in all four cases while other methods picking up both collapsed locations and the noisy results in most cases.

The detailed precision scores and lead-time are listed in Table 1, from which we can observe that the proposed *st*-LID consistently achieves perfect precision score, indicating its ability to pinpoint the failure region in a large area, which is valuable for landslide warning system. Furthermore, *st*-LID can also produce timely predictions well before the actual time of failure in all these cases, demonstrating its effectiveness and efficiency in landslide early warning tasks.

4.4 Sensitivity Analysis

A sensitivity analysis is conducted using M_2 to evaluate the impact from the nearest-neighbor parameter s. We report the precision score under different

Table 1. Precision Score *Prec.* (↑) & Lead-time Δt (↑) results from all methods. ↑ means higher values are better. Best performance are in bold format. Lead-time are shown in both raw time steps and their equivalent durations in days (d).

Metrics	Methods	M_1 ($C1$)	M_1 ($C2$)	M_2	M_3
Prec.	K-means	0.044	0.940	0.128	0.999
	DBSCAN	0.047	0.557	0.298	0.705
	s-LID	0.045	0.945	0.725	0.896
	GCNAE	0.333	0.947	0.857	0.975
	st-LID (ours)	**1.000**	**1.000**	**1.000**	**1.000**
Δt	K-means	0	220 (0.4 d)	0	427 (1.8 d)
	DBSCAN	0	1351 (2.4 d)	214 (0.9 d)	1096 (4.6 d)
	s-LID	0	1489 (2.6 d)	1383 (5.8 d)	1142 (4.8 d)
	GCNAE	0	1516 (2.6 d)	1473 (6.1 d)	1184 (4.9 d)
	st-LID (ours)	**80** (0.1 d)	**1726** (3.0 d)	**1760** (7.3 d)	**1214** (5.1 d)

Table 2. Sensitivity Analysis on parameter s.

Parameter	$s = 500$	$s = 1000$	$s = 2000$	$s = 5000$	$s = N - 1$
Prec.	0.500	0.583	0.667	0.800	1.000

parameters to compare how the performance changes with corresponding parameter. Table 2 shows the precision score with different parameters. It is clear that performance improves as s increases, with $s = N - 1$ giving the best precision for all three cases. This suggests that, for these field-scale displacement datasets, using a broader neighborhood is more robust than using a small local neighborhood. Smaller values can be too local and may respond more strongly to noise, local artifacts, or small deformation fluctuations rather than the coherent failure-region signal.

4.5 Ablation Study

To quantify the contribution of each proposed enhancement, we conduct an ablation study on dataset M_3, systematically removing individual components and evaluating the impact on *Prec.* and Δt (Table 3). The results indicate that velocity and spatial fusion primarily contribute on the *Prec.*, which aligns with their design to mitigate the impact of certain noise. The t-LID serves as the most critical part in this framework, enhancing both metrics significantly. By capturing long-term temporal dependencies, t-LID enables the framework to differentiate subtle pre-failure signals from steady-state motion, directly leading to the superior lead times observed in our primary results.

Table 3. Ablation Study on M_1 ($C1$) and M_3

Components		s-LID w./o. v	s-LID w. v	Spatial Fusion	st-LID
M_1 ($C1$)	*Prec.*	0.045	0.149	0.273	**1.000**
	Δt	0	0	0	**80**
M_3	*Prec.*	0.795	0.896	0.927	**1.000**
	Δt	1141	1142	1142	**1214**

4.6 Multi-failure Analysis

To further analyze the behavior of st-LID across multi-event processes, we demonstrate the evolution of the score for the two distinct failures in M_1. Figure 6 shows the detailed results of this analysis, with red and blue series represent one location in the $C1$ and $C2$ respectively (red and blue stars). From the figure, we can see st-LID successfully identifies the transition into the accelerated failure regime for both events, as evidenced by the clear peaks at their respective failure times (dashed lines). This underscores its ability to track dynamical regime shifts without the interference of background noise or stationary displacement signals.

Notably, the red curve exhibits a secondary surge around $t = 4500$. While this specific interval was not initially identified as a standalone failure in the ground truth labels, subsequent geotechnical analysis of the corresponding deformation and coherence confirms it as a secondary sequence of collapses. This highlights a significant ability of st-LID to track these sub-critical regime transitions and successive physical failures with high fidelity.

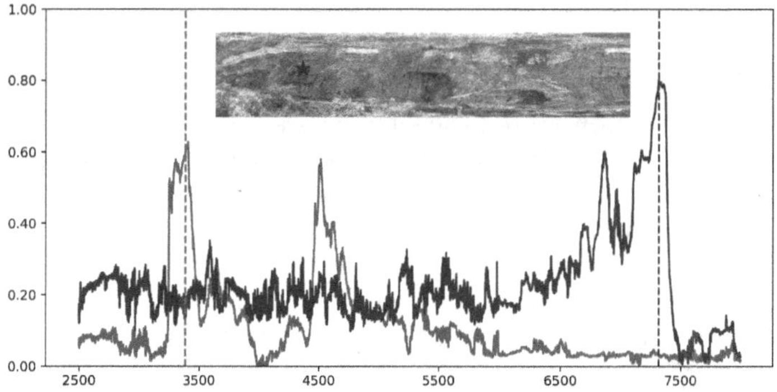

Fig. 6. Evolution of st-LID scores across multiple dynamical regimes in M_1. The red and blue curves represent the scores for distinct regions on the slope (red and blue stars). The ToF of $C1$ and $C2$ are highlighted with dashed lines. (Color figure online)

4.7 Computation Time

Efficiency is one of the important factors in evaluation of landslide warning systems. A method loses its practical values if it requires excessive computation time, especially in real-time monitoring scenarios where timely alert are crucial for risk management. In this section, we compare the computation time of all methods.

Table 4. Computation time of each failure detection methods.

Methods	Computation Time
K-means	0.192 s
DBSCAN	0.162 s
s-LID	0.649 s
GCNAE	3 h (training) + 0.645 s
st-LID (sequential)	5.342 s
st-LID (parallel)	0.721 s

The results are listed in Table 4. Here, we record the computation time of each method detecting the potential failures at a single step. We provide two versions of *st*-LID because the *s*-LID integration and *t*-LID computation happens at each monitored point (each time series), thus, one can choose to sequentially compute it or parallel the computation. From the table, we can see except GCNAE, which takes significant time to train, all the other methods are efficient and only take seconds to finish. This fact further justify the practicability of *st*-LID in real-time monitoring and analysis of the landslide-prone area.

4.8 Real-World Failure Detection Simulation

Until now, we have demonstrated the effectiveness and efficiency of the proposed *st*-LID conceptually via multiple experiments. In this section, we simulate a real-time monitoring using M_1 dataset and demonstrate a practical failure detection procedure on $C1$ collapse.

Applying the proposed detection procedure on M_1 ($C1$), we demonstrate a simulation of the failure detection, the details are shown in Fig. 7. Here, we use $n = 10$ for higher fidelity considering the real-world impact of a failure detection. From the figure, we can see the target $\boldsymbol{x}_t^*$ is fluctuating between two monitored points within a small region, following the small ball condition in Eq. (10). The target point $\boldsymbol{x}_t^*$ does not meet the detection threshold at initial steps ($t \in [3290, 3294]$), but starts to consistently exceeds such threshold $st\text{-LID}(\boldsymbol{x}_t^*) \geq 0.5$ from $t = 3295$. Finally, following to the detection procedure, the failure is detected at $t = 3305$ with $n = 10$. Note that, given the actual time interval of the dataset (2.5 min), this detection is about 3.3 hours ahead of the actual collapse at this region, allowing a timely intervention for this failure.

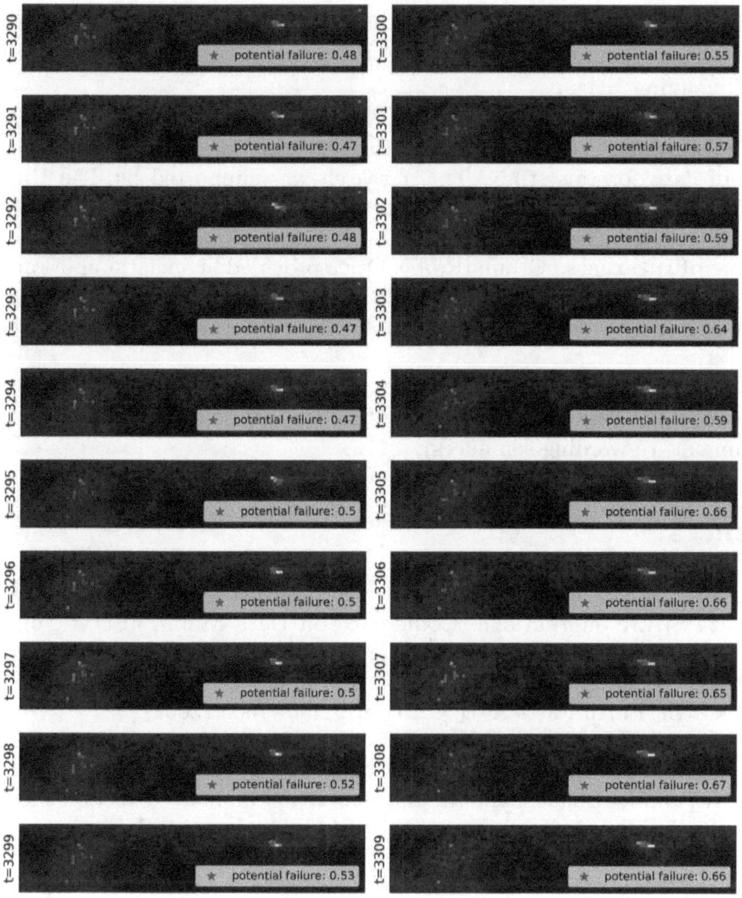

Fig. 7. Simulation of real-world failure detection using *st*-LID. The monitored point with the highest *st*-LID is marked by $\star$.

5 Conclusion

In this study, we introduce *st*-LID, a novel method designed to improve the early and accurate detection of failures in landslide-prone areas. Unlike existing approaches that typically focus on either spatial or temporal aspects of displacement data, *st*-LID effectively incorporate both the spatial correlations and temporal dynamics inherent in the displacement data. By extending the traditional LID framework with a short-term kinematic feature, Bayesian spatial fusion, and long-term temporal modeling, our unified framework robustly identifies the complex spatiotemporal outliers across highly diverse environmental and operational contexts without requiring site-specific tuning. Comprehensive experiments on three distinct real-world datasets demonstrate that *st*-LID provides a robust, interpretable, and computationally efficient foundation for early warning systems. These findings highlight the practical value of *st*-LID in real-world landslide early warning systems, paving the way for timely risk management and potentially saving lives.

Acknowledgments. We thank GroundProbe, Orica for their financial support and provision of data for this study. This research was supported by The University of Melbourne's Research Computing Services and the Petascale Campus Initiative.

Disclosure of Interests. GroundProbe, Orica provided financial support and data for this study. GroundProbe, Orica had no role in the study design, analysis, interpretation of results, or preparation of the manuscript. The authors declare no other competing interests.

Generative AI Usage Disclosure. The LLM is used at the sentence level (e.g., fixing grammar, re-wording sentences).

References

1. Anderberg, A., et al.: Dimensionality-aware outlier detection. In: Proceedings of the 2024 SIAM International Conference on Data Mining (SDM), pp. 652–660. SIAM (2024)
2. Crosta, G., Agliardi, F.: How to obtain alert velocity thresholds for large rockslides. Phys. Chem. Earth Parts A/B/C **27**(36), 1557–1565 (2002)
3. Dai, F., Lee, C.F., Ngai, Y.Y.: Landslide risk assessment and management: an overview. Eng. Geol. **64**(1), 65–87 (2002)
4. Ding, K., Li, J., Bhanushali, R., Liu, H.: Deep anomaly detection on attributed networks. In: Proceedings of the 2019 SIAM International Conference on Data Mining, pp. 594–602. SIAM (2019)
5. Finnegan, N.J., Saffer, D.M.: Seasonal slow slip in landslides as a window into the frictional rheology of creeping shear zones. Sci. Adv. **10**(42), eadq9399 (2024)
6. Gorbett, M., Shirazi, H., Ray, I.: Local intrinsic dimensionality of IoT networks for unsupervised intrusion detection. In: IFIP Annual Conference on Data and Applications Security and Privacy, pp. 143–161. Springer (2022)
7. Haque, U., et al.: The human cost of global warming: Deadly landslides and their triggers (1995–2014). Sci. Total Environ. **682**, 673–684 (2019)
8. Houle, M.E.: Local intrinsic dimensionality i: an extreme-value-theoretic foundation for similarity applications. In: Similarity Search and Applications: 10th International Conference, SISAP 2017, Munich, Germany, 4–6 October 2017, Proceedings 10, pp. 64–79. Springer (2017)
9. Intrieri, E., et al.: The maoxian landslide as seen from space: detecting precursors of failure with sentinel-1 data. Landslides **15**, 123–133 (2018)
10. Joukhadar, Z., Huang, H., Erfani, S.M., Campello, R.J., Houle, M.E., Bailey, J.: Bayesian estimation approaches for local intrinsic dimensionality. In: International Conference on Similarity Search and Applications, pp. 111–125. Springer (2024)
11. Lacroix, P., Handwerger, A.L., Bièvre, G.: Life and death of slow-moving landslides. Nat. Rev. Earth Environ. **1**(8), 404–419 (2020)
12. Ma, X., et al.: Characterizing adversarial subspaces using local intrinsic dimensionality. arXiv preprint arXiv:1801.02613 (2018)

13. Mills, T.C.: Unit roots, difference and trend stationarity, and fractional differencing. In: Mills, T.C. (ed.) Applied Time Series Analysis, pp. 71–101. Academic Press, USA (2019)
14. Ozturk, U., Bozzolan, E., Holcombe, E., Shukla, R., Pianosi, F., Wagener, T.: How climate change and unplanned urban sprawl bring more landslides. Nature **608**(7922), 262–265 (2022)
15. Peña, D., Tsay, R.S., Zamar, R.: Empirical dynamic quantiles for visualization of high-dimensional time series. Technometrics **61**(4), 429–444 (2019)
16. Sim, K.B., Lee, M.L., Wong, S.Y.: A review of landslide acceptable risk and tolerable risk. Geoenvironmental Disasters **9**(1), 1–17 (2022). https://doi.org/10.1186/s40677-022-00205-6
17. Sun, F., Chang, Y., Tanin, E., Karunasekera, S., Qi, J.: Flexireg: flexible urban region representation learning. In: Proceedings of the 31st ACM SIGKDD Conference on Knowledge Discovery and Data Mining V. 2, pp. 2702–2713 (2025)
18. Tordesillas, A., Kahagalage, S., Campbell, L., Bellett, P., Intrieri, E., Batterham, R.: Spatiotemporal slope stability analytics for failure estimation (sssafe): linking radar data to the fundamental dynamics of granular failure. Sci. Rep. **11**(1), 9729 (2021)
19. Tordesillas, A., Zheng, H., Qian, G., Bellett, P., Saunders, P.: Augmented intelligence forecasting and what-if-scenario analytics with quantified uncertainty for big real-time slope monitoring data. IEEE Trans. Geosci. Remote Sens. **62**, 1–29 (2024)
20. Tordesillas, A., Zhou, S., Bailey, J., Bondell, H.: A representation learning framework for detection and characterization of dead versus strain localization zones from pre- to post-failure. Granular Matter **24**(3), 75 (2022)
21. Veličković, P., Cucurull, G., Casanova, A., Romero, A., Liò, P., Bengio, Y.: Graph attention networks. In: International Conference on Learning Representations (2018). https://openreview.net/forum?id=rJXMpikCZ
22. Wang, J., Liu, K., Li, H.: LSTM-based graph attention network for vehicle trajectory prediction. Comput. Netw. **248**, 110477 (2024)
23. Yu, L., Huang, H., Yan, C., Yan, C., Guo, S.: Early warning system for landslide of gentle piedmont slope based on displacement velocity, factor of safety, and effective rainfall threshold. Int. J. Disaster Risk Reduction **118**, 105232 (2025)
24. Zhou, S., Tordesillas, A., Intrieri, E., Di Traglia, F., Qian, G., Catani, F.: Pinpointing early signs of impending slope failures from space. J. Geophys. Res. Solid Earth **127**(2), e2021JB022957 (2022)
25. Zhou, S., Tordesillas, A., Pouragha, M., Bailey, J., Bondell, H.: On local intrinsic dimensionality of deformation in complex materials. Sci. Rep. **11**(1), 10216 (2021)

SQC-Guard: A Statistical Quality Control Based Monitoring Framework for NLP Pipelines

Jaskaran Kawatra[1(✉)], Sanjana Rajamani[1], Sebin Sabu[1], Ewart Jonathan Sheldon[1], Nick James[1], John Booth[1], Alex Eze[1], Daniel Key[1], Shiren Patel[1], Alexandros Zenonos[2], Rebecca Pope[2], Neil Sebire[1], and Pavithra Rajendran[1]

[1] Great Ormond Street Hospital for Children NHS Foundation Trust, London, UK
Jaskaran.Kawatra@gosh.nhs.uk

[2] Roche Products Ltd., Welwyn Garden City, UK

Abstract. Deploying NLP pipelines in clinical settings introduces unique monitoring challenges including heterogeneous free-text data, multi-stage model dependencies, and rare disease terminology. In this paper, we propose to address these issues with a novel approach grounded in Statistical Quality Control theory that treats a deployed NLP pipeline as a measurable industrial process, capturing cross metric relationships while reducing the volume of false alerts that can undermine confidence in scaling NLP systems to production. Our proposed framework, **SQC-Guard** (Code available at https://github.com/gosh-dre/sqc-guard) constructs a multivariate process state vector spanning input characteristics, per-stage model confidence and generation quality signals, output class proportions and cross-stage consistency signals, monitored jointly via a Mahalanobis-distance-based Adaptive Baseline Reference Statistic with Ledoit-Wolf shrinkage estimation to handle the high-dimensional, limited-sample regime typical of clinical deployments. This framework incorporates automated iterative stability analysis to exclude anomalous historical batches before control limits are finalised. When instability is detected, a MYT-inspired decomposition quantifies each metric's contribution to the observed deviation, providing actionable root-cause information enabling manual investigation. A rule-based triage layer stratifies flagged reports by severity using NLI-derived consistency scores, directing reviewer effort to the highest-risk cases. We evaluate **SQC-Guard** on an in-house NLP pipeline for paediatric histopathology report analysis, a domain characterised by rare diagnoses and multiple interdependent models, demonstrating that the multivariate statistic detects coordinated metric shifts and that the triage layer concentrates oversight on batches with actionable pipeline inconsistencies.

Keywords: Statistical Quality Control (SQC) · Drift Detection · NLP Monitoring · Multivariate Control Charts · Clinical NLP · Paediatric Histopathology

M. Baratchi et al. (Eds.): ECML PKDD 2026, LNAI 16949, pp. 250–267, 2027.
https://doi.org/10.1007/978-3-032-37682-4_15

1 Introduction

Electronic Patient Record (EPR) systems within real-world healthcare settings provide significant advantages by capturing a diverse range of structured and unstructured information, including lab results, clinical reports, discharge summaries and other data sources [8,22]. Leveraging the capabilities of Natural Language Processing (NLP) [10,21] within healthcare domain can enhance accessibility to pertinent information within unstructured data that would otherwise remain inaccessible. Despite promising advancements in research, a significant gap remains between the development and deployment of robust, scalable NLP pipelines within a real-world healthcare environment. To overcome this gap, operational performance of the deployed pipelines requires continuous post-deployment monitoring to ensure transparency, auditability and consistency that extends beyond testing the pipelines in a controlled environment. In this paper, we present the **SQC-Guard** framework designed to overcome current limitations of drift detection methods by grounding NLP pipeline monitoring in Statistical Quality Control (SQC) principles. Our contributions are as follows:

1. We introduce **SQC-Guard**, a three-phase framework (Fig. 1) that validates statistical assumptions, constructs a stable baseline via iterative multivariate outlier removal and ensures rigorous operational monitoring using a locked baseline achieved using a held-out validation dataset.
2. Our proposed framework requires no groundtruth labels, instead monitors statistical behaviours of multistage NLP pipelines by assessing its components using proxy signals based on metrics such as confidence score distributions, entity counts, prediction proportions, text characteristics and LLM-generation based metrics. This unsupervised approach is necessary in clinical NLP, where expert annotation is difficult to obtain at the batch-level frequency required for continuous monitoring.
3. Our evaluation of **SQC-Guard** on an in-house developed multistage NLP pipeline for extracting information from complex unstructured texts present in paediatric histopathology cancer reports [9] demonstrates promising performance and highlights its potential for real-world deployment.

2 Background

2.1 Drift Detection Methods

Machine learning models are developed under the assumption that inference data will resemble training data. Due to *dataset shift* and *drift*, this assumption is routinely violated, with downstream consequences on deployed ML system reliability [15]. In clinical settings, where model outputs inform diagnostic and therapeutic decisions, undetected drift carries direct patient safety implications [5]. This problem is compounded in multi-component pipelines, where drift may originate in input data, propagate through intermediate steps, or emerge only in

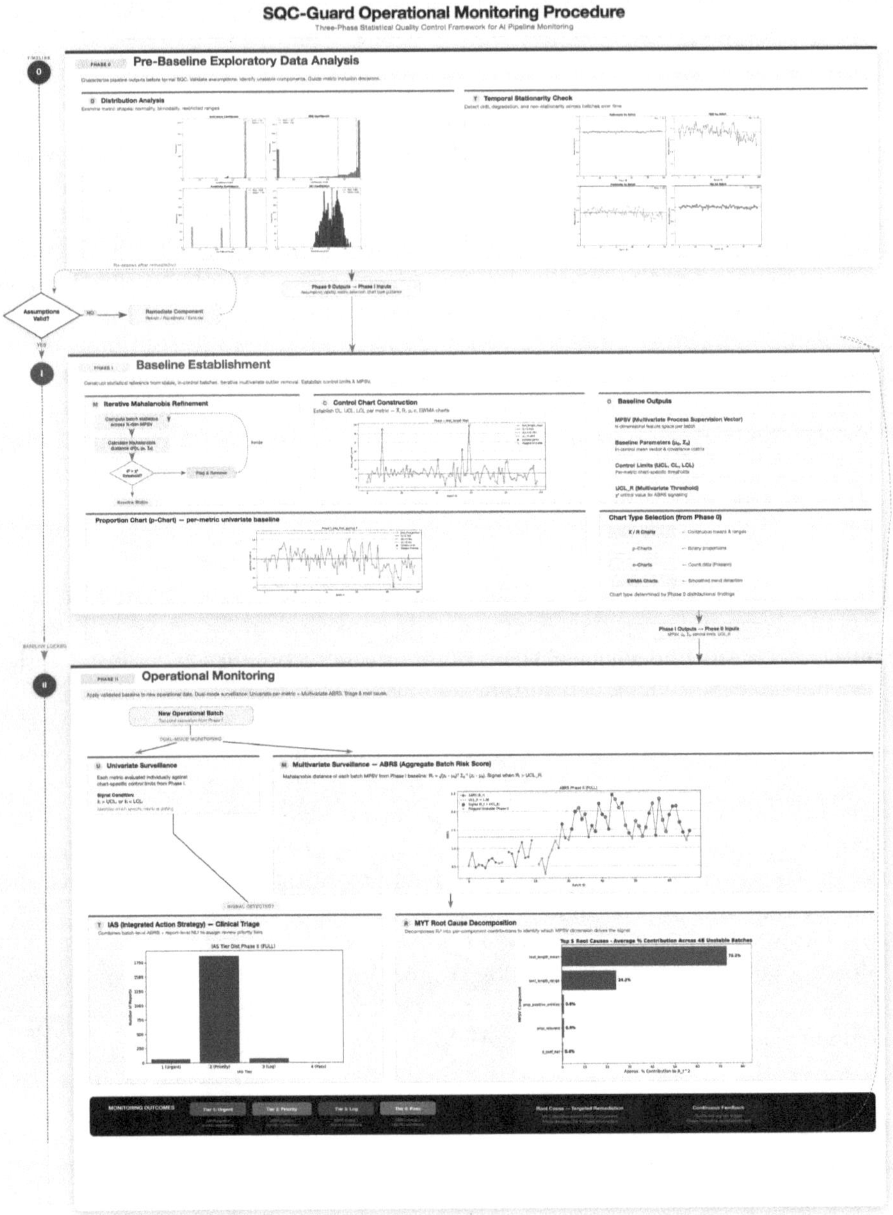

Fig. 1. SQC-Guard operational monitoring procedure. Phase 0 validates distributional assumptions and temporal stationarity; Phase I constructs the in-control baseline through iterative Mahalanobis refinement; Phase II applies the locked baseline via dual-mode univariate and multivariate (ABRS) surveillance, with IAS clinical triage and MYT root cause decomposition.

component interactions. Drift manifests in several forms: *covariate shift* ($P(X)$ changes while $P(Y|X)$ remains stable), *concept drift* (changes in $P(Y|X)$), and *prior probability shift* (changes in $P(Y)$). A clinical monitoring framework must account for all three, as each demands different detection strategies. The earliest drift detectors monitor classifier error rates over time. DDM [6] performs well for abrupt shifts but poorly for gradual drift; EDDM [2] improves gradual drift sensitivity at the cost of false alarms; ADWIN [3] dynamically adjusts sliding windows; and CUSUM variants [13] offer theoretical grounding but require careful tuning [14]. A fundamental limitation shared by all supervised detectors is their dependence on ground truth labels impractical in clinical NLP, where expert annotation cannot be obtained at the frequency required for continuous monitoring. Unsupervised methods circumvent label dependency by comparing reference and incoming distributions directly. The KS test and chi-square test provide formal statistical guarantees but are inherently univariate, missing changes in feature correlations [16]. Information-theoretic measures such as KL divergence, JS divergence, and PSI similarly operate feature-by-feature. Some multivariate approaches address this gap: MMD compares distributions in a reproducing kernel Hilbert space [7], and autoencoder-based methods monitor reconstruction error, but both lack formal statistical guarantees and require empirical threshold calibration.

Limitations for Multi-component Clinical NLP Pipelines. Structural limitations emerge when existing methods are applied to multi component clinical NLP pipelines. Standard detectors monitor individual signals in isolation with no mechanism for reasoning about joint component behaviour. A batch may exhibit normal individual metrics yet be statistically anomalous in combination. Adaptive drift detectors assume continuously evolving streams, an inadequate stance for clinical AI where regulatory requirements demand an explicitly validated and locked baseline; Phase-I/Phase-II separation from manufacturing SQC [12] addresses this directly. Furthermore, when DDM, ADWIN, or PSI signals drift, the operator receives no guidance on which component caused the signal, its severity, or what clinical action is warranted. SQC chart selection depends critically on distributional properties, and applying charts without verifying assumptions produces limits that are too tight or too wide.

Statistical Quality Control as a Monitoring Framework. Statistical quality control (SQC), originating with Shewhart [17], has been applied extensively in healthcare quality improvement [19]. Feng et al. [4] argued that SQC tools are directly applicable to deployed AI algorithm monitoring. The Mason-Young-Tracy (MYT) decomposition [11] attributes deviations to individual variables providing root cause identification absent from standard drift detection. Recent work demonstrates the applicability of this approach: Zhu et al. [25] applied SPC charts to monitor deep learning auto-segmentation across 464 radiotherapy cases, and a scoping review [1] identified SQC as an underutilised approach with significant potential for clinical AI monitoring. **SQC-Guard** addresses the limitations above by adapting a phased SQC framework to multi-component clinical NLP pipeline monitoring. The Multivariate Process State Vector (MPSV) encodes batch-level statistics from all monitored components into a joint vector, and the Aggregate Batch Risk Score (ABRS) computes the Mahalanobis distance of each new batch from the Phase I baseline, detecting correlated deviations that univariate methods miss. The Integrated Action Strategy (IAS) maps signals onto four clinical triage tiers, and MYT decomposition transforms alarms into diagnostic instruments that direct remediation to the responsible pipeline stage. While standard drift detection identifies distributional shifts in isolated streams, **SQC-Guard** provides the phased, multivariate, and action-oriented structure required for clinically regulated AI pipelines.

3 Proposed Approach

SQC-Guard operates on batches of clinical documents, reflecting how clinical NLP pipelines process data in real-world hospital settings. Rather than focusing on individual metrics in isolation, the framework combines batch-level statistics from across all pipeline stages using a phased approach. This section describes the NLP pipeline and formalises the monitoring framework.

3.1 The Monitored Pipeline and Its Monitoring Challenges

SQC-Guard monitors a deployed four-stage clinical NLP pipeline which extracts a structured final diagnosis from free-text paediatric histopathology reports [9]. The stages run in series (Fig. 2): a SetFit [20] relevance classifier retains tumour-relevant text; a fine-tuned GLiNER [23] model extracts the final-diagnosis span, *e.g. "Wilms' tumour", "mixed type", "intermediate risk", "local pathological stage 3"*; a confirmed-diagnosis SetFit classifier separates positive from negative findings, *e.g. "no evidence of residual tumour"*; and an NLI verifier [18] checks the extracted diagnosis against TinyLlama [24] generated zero shot response to the prompt, "What is the final diagnosis in the given report?". **SQC-Guard** instruments each stage with the batch-level signals, together with cross-cutting input characteristics.

Paediatric histopathology reports have long-tail tumour subtypes when present and could include regional anatomical diagnostic variability that could lead to diverse statistical correlations. Because the stages are coupled in series, an upstream error (a relevance miss at F1 0.897, an NER miss at F1 0.956) does not stay local. It shifts the downstream input distribution, so a single fault induces correlated deviations across several signals at once. Such correlated shifts can keep each component within its own univariate control band while the pipeline's joint state moves far from the baseline. The failure lives in the covariance between signals, which a per-component monitor cannot observe by construction.

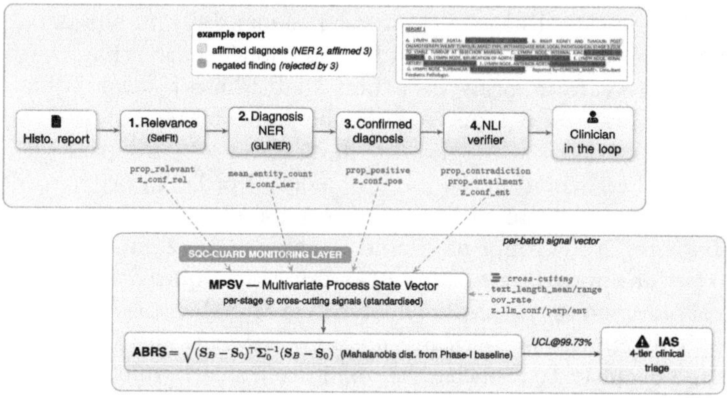

Fig. 2. End-to-end view of **SQC-Guard**. **Top band:** the monitored four-stage clinical-NLP pipeline—relevance classification → diagnosis NER → confirmed-diagnosis → NLI verification, with a clinician in the loop. **Bottom band:** the **SQC-Guard** monitoring layer.

3.2 Monitoring Setup

Monitoring Design Specifications. While we test our approach on the histopathology pipeline introduced above, in its general form an NLP pipeline $\mathcal{P}$ deployed over a corpus of retrospective documents $\mathcal{D} = \{d_1, d_2, \ldots, d_m\}$, can be said to produce a set of observable outputs $\mathbf{o}_i$ for each document d_i comprising component confidence scores, classification predictions, entity counts, text characteristics, and generative model diagnostics depending on the specific architectures used. We group these document-level outputs into sequential batches $\mathcal{B} = \{b_1, b_2, \ldots, b_n\}$, and for each batch b_k, a set of monitoring metrics $\mathcal{M} = \{M_1, M_2, \ldots, M_p\}$ is derived by computing appropriate batch-level statistics from the constituent document outputs means for continuous quantities, proportions for categorical predictions, and ranges for within-batch variability measures. The resulting summary statistics vector $\mathbf{z}_k = (z_{k,1}, \ldots, z_{k,p})^\top \in \mathbb{R}^p$ constitutes the batch-level representation used throughout the monitoring framework. The ordered sequence $\{\mathbf{z}_1, \ldots, \mathbf{z}_n\}$ forms the input to the three-phase monitoring procedure described below.

Batch Preparation Workflow. Batch size selection balances statistical reliability with detection timeliness. Following established SQC principles and the Central Limit Theorem, we adopted a minimum batch size of 30 reports. This threshold ensures sufficient stability in batch-level statistics (means, proportions, variances) to support reliable statistical inference, adequate approximation to normality for sampling distributions, enabling valid application of parametric control chart methods, and reasonable detection latency.
The corpus $\mathcal{D}$ is partitioned chronologically into a baseline period (earliest 60%) used for Phase-0 and Phase-I, and a monitoring period (remaining 40%)

reserved exclusively for Phase-II, processed sequentially to simulate real-world deployment conditions. This temporal separation ensures that the baseline is established entirely from prior data and that Phase-II evaluation is strictly prospective. Phases-0 and I operate on the same baseline-period reports but employ distinct batching strategies. In Phase-0, reports are grouped into fixed-size batches of approximately 30 in chronological order in order to detect progressive model degradation. In Phase-I, the same reports are randomly shuffled before re-batching into groups of around 30 reports, breaking temporal autocorrelation to better approximate the i.i.d. assumption required for valid estimation of in-control parameters ($\boldsymbol{\mu}_0, \boldsymbol{\Sigma}_0$). The iterative Mahalanobis distance refinement procedure then removes statistically unstable batches, ensuring the final baseline is derived exclusively from batches exhibiting stable multivariate behaviour. Phase-II batches are constructed in strict chronological order to enable detection of time-evolving drift patterns under realistic operational conditions.

3.3 Methodology

Phase 0: Pre-baseline Exploratory Analysis. Phase-0 examines pipeline outputs across four domains. **Confidence score distributions** are assessed via histogram analysis and calibration evaluation, flagging components exhibiting extreme concentration ($\sigma < 0.1$) or severe bimodality. **Prediction proportions** are evaluated for categorical imbalance, where single-class dominance ($> 95\%$) indicates insufficient monitoring sensitivity. **Text characteristics** capture input feature distributions including length statistics and vocabulary composition. **Generation quality metrics** quantify LLM output fluency and uncertainty through token-level analysis. Temporal stationarity is assessed at the batch level using Mann-Kendall trend tests, Levene's variance homogeneity test, autocorrelation analysis, and CUSUM change-point detection. Components violating stationarity are excluded before baseline reconstruction. A further screening step removes components exhibiting distributional anomalies (e.g., empty predictions or implausible confidence ranges), cross-component logical contradictions, or insufficient discriminative power as assessed by effect size analysis. Only components passing all checks proceed to Phase-I.

Phase I: Statistical Baseline Establishment. Phase I establishes control baselines for subsequent monitoring. For each batch, four categories of statistics are computed: prediction proportions, model confidence scores, text characteristics, and event counts. For the subset relying on batch-level estimators, we define:

$$\hat{p}_B = \frac{1}{n_B} \sum_{i=1}^{n_B} \mathbb{1}\{\text{pred}_i = \text{target class}\}, \qquad \bar{c}_B = \frac{1}{n_B} \sum_{i=1}^{n_B} c_i \tag{1}$$

$$\bar{L}_B = \frac{1}{n_B} \sum_{i=1}^{n_B} L_i, \qquad \text{OOV}_B = \frac{\sum_{i=1}^{n_B} |T_i \setminus V|}{\sum_{i=1}^{n_B} |T_i|} \tag{2}$$

where n_B is the batch size, c_i the confidence and L_i the length of observation i, T_i its set of tokens, V the vocabulary, $T_i \setminus V$ the out-of-vocabulary tokens, and k_B the batch event count (e.g. total entities extracted), which feeds the c-chart. Initial limits assume Phase I batches are in-control: $\bar{X}$-R charts use grand means and average ranges; p-charts the pooled proportion $\bar{p} = \sum_i x_i / \sum_i n_i$; c-charts the mean count $\bar{k} = \frac{1}{m}\sum_B k_B$; and EWMA charts baseline means and standard deviations. Batches violating 3-sigma limits are removed iteratively (max 5 iterations) until stable. Before finalising, the 3-sigma assumptions are checked: p-charts require $n_B\bar{p} \geq 5$ and $n_B(1-\bar{p}) \geq 5$, and c-charts $\bar{k} \geq 5$, so the binomial and Poisson normal approximations hold; temporal stationarity is then confirmed across retained metrics. Metrics failing these checks are excluded from the MPSV state vector but retained as univariate diagnostics.

Phase II: Operational Monitoring. Phase II applies the locked Phase I baseline to sequential batches, providing continuous multivariate surveillance with root cause analysis and clinical action prioritisation. The MPSV metrics are selected based on sensitivity to distinct failure modes, statistical stability in Phase I, and pairwise correlation below $|r| < 0.85$ to avoid multicollinearity. Each metric x_t is smoothed via an exponentially weighted moving average $z_t = \lambda x_t + (1-\lambda)z_{t-1}$, with initial state $z_0 = \mu_0$ (the Phase I baseline mean per component) and $\lambda = 0.1$, enhancing sensitivity to gradual shifts. The smoothed components are assembled into the batch state vector $\mathbf{S}_B$. The Aggregate Batch Risk Score (ABRS) summarises multivariate deviation as a Mahalanobis distance from the Phase I baseline:

$$R_B = \sqrt{(\mathbf{S}_B - \mathbf{S}_0)^\top \boldsymbol{\Sigma}_0^{-1}(\mathbf{S}_B - \mathbf{S}_0)} \tag{3}$$

where $\mathbf{S}_0$ is the Phase I baseline mean vector and $\boldsymbol{\Sigma}_0^{-1}$ is the inverse of the Phase I covariance matrix. The upper control limit UCL_R is set at the 99.73rd percentile of stable Phase I R_B values, providing an empirical 3σ equivalent. Each batch is simultaneously evaluated against per-metric univariate charts ($\bar{X}$-R, p, c/u, EWMA, T^2) and the multivariate ABRS, and is flagged if any chart signals out-of-control or $R_B > \text{UCL}_R$. When a batch triggers a multivariate signal, MYT decomposition attributes the deviation to individual MPSV components. The contribution of component j is computed as:

$$\text{Contrib}_j = (S_{B,j} - S_{0,j}) \cdot [\boldsymbol{\Sigma}_0^{-1}(\mathbf{S}_B - \mathbf{S}_0)]_j \tag{4}$$

where $S_{B,j}$ and $S_{0,j}$ are the jth elements of the batch and baseline vectors respectively. Contributions are normalised to sum to 100%, identifying whether deviation is driven by input changes, prediction shifts, or confidence degradation. Report-level triage (IAS) combines a task-specific risk quantification metric with the batch-level ABRS to estimate a composite clinical review priority score for each report:

$$\text{IAS}(d_i, b_k) = f(R_{b_k},\ q(d_i)) \tag{5}$$

where R_{b_k} is the ABRS for the batch containing report d_i and $q(d_i)$ is a report-level semantic risk quantification metric.

4 Data and Experiments

Our evaluation utilizes 5000 de-identified pathology reports collected from routine clinical operations over a six-month period. Reports underwent standard preprocessing including removal of protected health information and whitespace normalization. The dataset comprises diverse specimen types from histopathology cancer reports, representative of real-world pathology laboratory workflows.

4.1 Experimental Setup

The corpus is partitioned chronologically into a 60% Phase I baseline set (99 initial batches of 30 reports) and a 40% Phase II monitoring holdout (64 batches), with strict temporal separation to ensure prospective evaluation. Following iterative stability analysis, 52 batches were retained as the final Phase I baseline. The NLP components, each contribute monitoring signals to the MPSV: (1) the cancer relevance classifier is monitored via `prop_relevant` and `z_conf_rel`; (2) the diagnosis extraction model is monitored via `mean_entity_count` and `z_conf_ner`; (3) the confirmed diagnosis classifier is monitored via `prop_positive_entities` and `z_conf_pos`; and (4) the NLI model is monitored via `prop_contradiction`, `prop_entailment`, and `z_conf_ent`. Input text characteristics (`text_length_mean`, `text_length_range`, `oov_rate`) and LLM generation quality metrics (`z_llm_conf`, `z_llm_perp`, `z_llm_ent`) serve as cross-cutting signals. Out of all the metrics we computed, some were left out of the MPSV either because of high dimensionality, not meeting chart assumptions, or high correlation with another metric (Fig. 3).

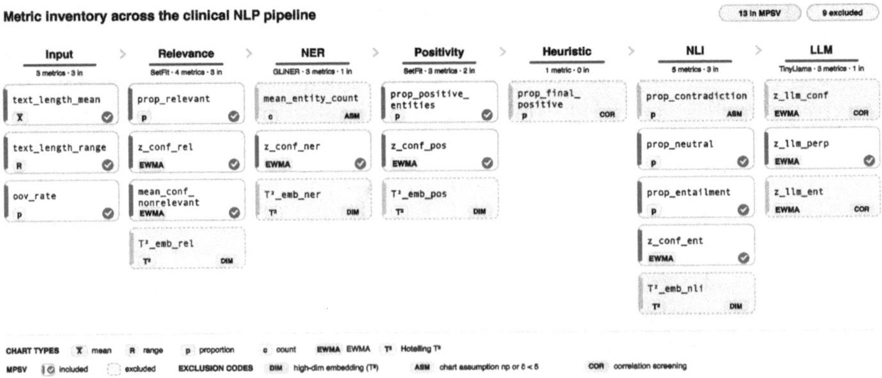

Fig. 3. Metric inventory: pipeline stage, chart type, and MPSV inclusion decision. Green shading indicates MPSV inclusion; red indicates exclusion. (Color figure online)

Further, in accordance with the IAS report-level risk tiering strategy, we combine the report level risk quantification metric (in our case, the NLI component) along with batch level ABRS to assign each report to one of four tiers:
Tier 1 (Urgent): High-risk batch ($R_B > \mathrm{UCL}_R$) with NLI contradiction or neutral, requiring immediate expert review. **Tier 2 (Priority):** High-risk batch with NLI entailment, or low-risk batch with NLI contradiction. **Tier 3 (Monitoring):** Low-risk batch with NLI neutral, tracked without immediate action. **Tier 4 (Pass):** Low-risk batch with high-confidence NLI entailment, cleared for automated processing.

4.2 Experimental Results

We present results in reverse operational order: Phase-II prospective monitoring (what the framework detects), Phase-I baseline construction (how the underlying statistical reference was built), and Phase-0 exploratory analysis (why preparatory validation was needed). This mirrors an operator's path from first observing an outlier and then determining the root cause for the behaviour.

Phase-II: Operational Monitoring. Multivariate Surveillance: ABRS Trajectory: (Fig. 4a) shows batches 0 through 25 display stable below-threshold behaviour, with R_t values ranging from approximately 0.30 to 1.25, consistent with in-control multivariate operation relative to the Phase-I baseline. Beginning at approximately batch 26, a sharp and sustained upward shift occurs: from this point onward, R_t values consistently exceed $\mathrm{UCL}_R = 1.30$, with the signal persisting through the remainder of the monitoring window. Of the 64 monitoring batches, 48 (75%) generated out-of-control signals.
IAS Tier Distribution: Tier-2 accounts for the overwhelming majority with approximately 1,850 assignments, followed by Tier-1 then Tier-3, each contributing approximately 75 reports (Fig. 4b). The complete absence of Tier-4 classifications is operationally significant. Tier-4 assignment requires both $R_t < \mathrm{UCL}_R$ and high-confidence NLI entailment at the report level, conditions not jointly satisfied for any report during the monitoring period.
MYT Decomposition: The MYT Decomposition (Fig. 4c) presents the average percentage contributions of each MPSV component to R_t^2 across the 48 signal-generating batches. The decomposition reveals extreme concentration of explanatory variance in the text input metrics: `text_length_mean` accounts for 73.2% of R_t^2 on average, with `text_length_range` contributing a further 24.3%. Together, these two input-characterisation metrics explain 97.5% of the multivariate signal, with all model-level components contributing negligibly. This suggests that the sustained ABRS signals are attributable almost entirely to systematic deviation in the distributional properties of incoming report text, not to degradation in any pipeline model component, directing remediation effort upstream to data ingestion and preprocessing rather than triggering unnecessary model retraining. Moreover, after further qualitative inspection, we found that the input data source had undergone a structural change confirming our results.

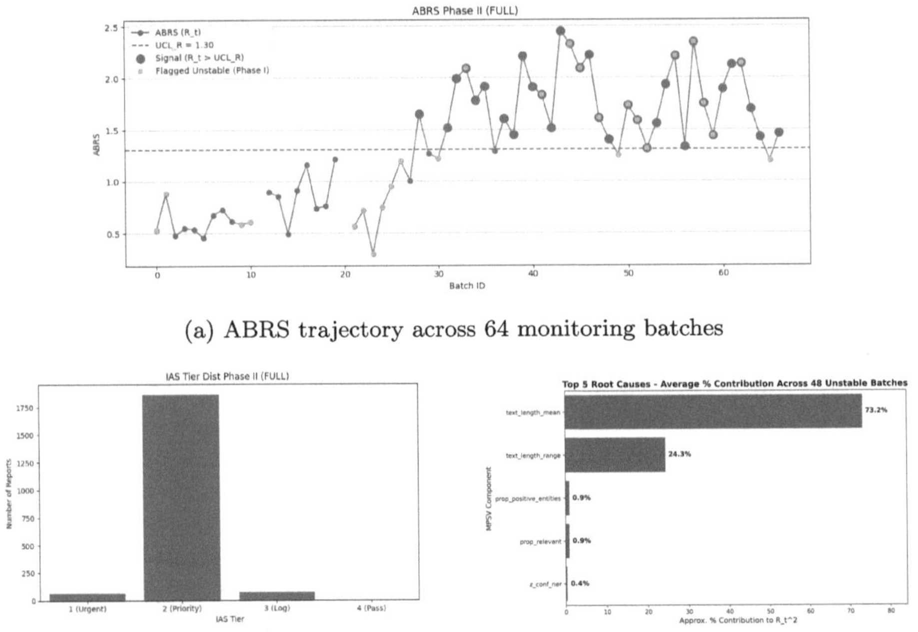

(a) ABRS trajectory across 64 monitoring batches

(b) IAS tier distribution

(c) MYT component attribution

Fig. 4. Phase II monitoring outputs: multivariate surveillance, clinical triage, and root cause decomposition. Red circles indicate ABRS signals ($R_t > \text{UCL}_R = 1.30$), orange squares denote Phase I-flagged batches. (Color figure online)

Cross-Validation Against Phase-I Patterns: To validate MYT interpretability further, the root cause signatures of the first five Phase-II signal batches were matched against the 47 Phase-I removed batches using a composite similarity score combining Jaccard (40%), cosine (40%), and directional agreement (20%).

Figure 5 reveals two distinct instability signatures. Batches 1, 13, and 15 are dominated by `text_length_range` (96.6%, 96.9%, 66.0%), indicating within-batch heterogeneity as the primary driver. Batch 12 shifts to `text_length_mean` dominance (70.5%), reflecting a systematic length shift rather than increased variability. Batch 16 presents the most distributed signal across `text_length_range` (39.3%), `prop_positive_entities` (33.9%), and `z_conf_ner` (11.7%) the only early signal batch where model-level components register non-negligible contributions.

Cross-validation of the five earliest Phase-II signal batches against the 47 Phase-I removed batches reveals a consistent root cause pattern. Batches 1, 13, and 15 are dominated by `text_length_range` (>66% contribution), achieving partial matches (similarity >0.5) with multiple Phase-I removed batches exhibiting the same signature, confirming that within-batch text length heterogeneity was a recurring instability present in the baseline period. Batch 12 shifts

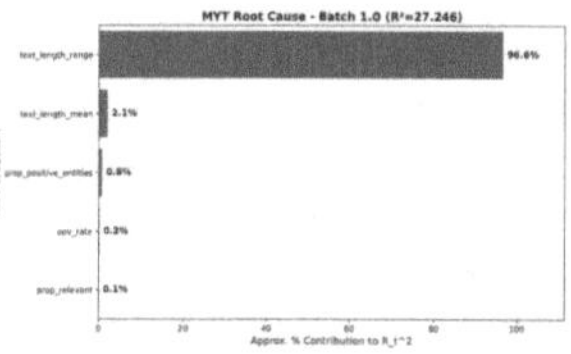

(a) Batch 1

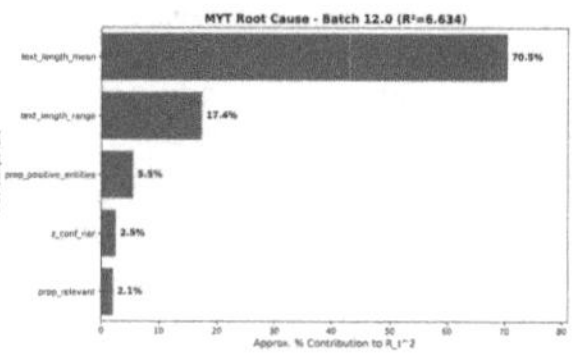

(b) Batch 12

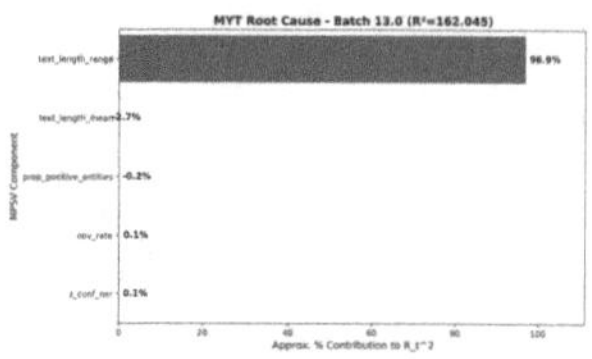

(c) Batch 13

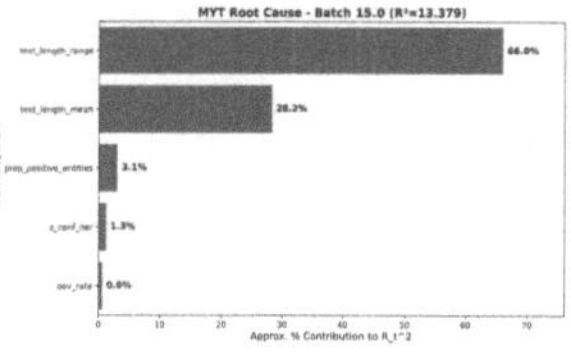

(d) Batch 15

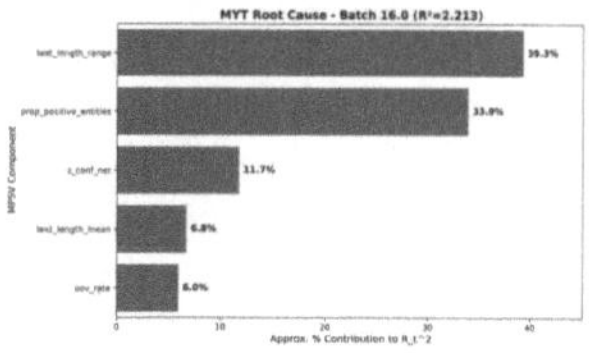

(e) Batch 16

Fig. 5. MYT root cause decompositions for the five earliest Phase II signal batches. Two distinct instability signatures emerge: `text_length_range`-dominated profiles indicating within-batch heterogeneity, and a more distributed multi-component signal where model-level metrics contribute alongside text characteristics.

toward `text_length_mean` dominance (70.5%), yet yields only weak matches (<0.25) against Phase-I batches, suggesting a subtly different instability profile. Batch 16 presents the most distributed signal, with `text_length_range` (39.3%), `prop_positive_entities` (33.9%), and `z_conf_ner` (11.7%) all contributing, and achieves only weak matches, indicating a novel multi-component deviation not strongly represented in the Phase-I removed set.

This cross-validation demonstrates two operationally valuable properties of the framework. First, the MYT decomposition produces consistent, reproducible root cause signatures across batches exhibiting the same instability type, confirming its reliability as a diagnostic instrument. Second, the similarity scoring correctly distinguishes between recurring instability patterns linked to known Phase-I anomalies and genuinely novel drift. Batch 16's weak match score and distributed multi-component signal would correctly direct an operator to investigate a broader range of pipeline components rather than focusing exclusively on data preprocessing.

Phase I: Baseline Establishment. The Phase II detections above were possible because Phase I established a valid statistical reference against which the deviations could be measured. Phase I processes 99 batches through iterative multivariate outlier removal. Of the metrics monitored, three are most relevant to the Phase II results (Fig. 6):

Text Length Mean: The $\bar{X}$ chart (Fig. 6a) establishes CL = 8.903, UCL = 11.977, LCL = 5.829 words respectively. Three batches breach the UCL, each coinciding with multivariate outlier flags and reflecting occasional full-format

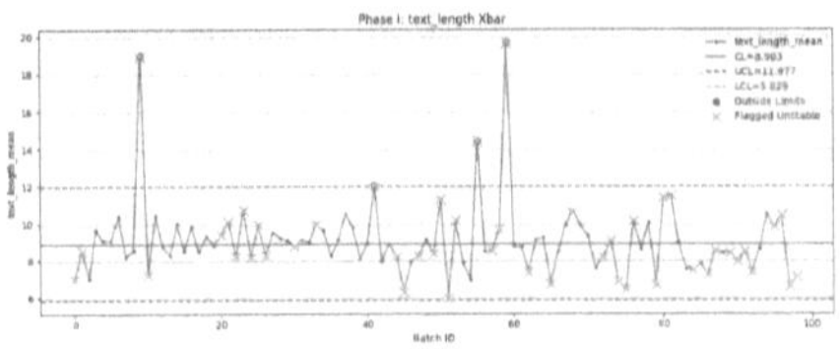

(a) $\bar{X}$ chart for `text_length_mean`

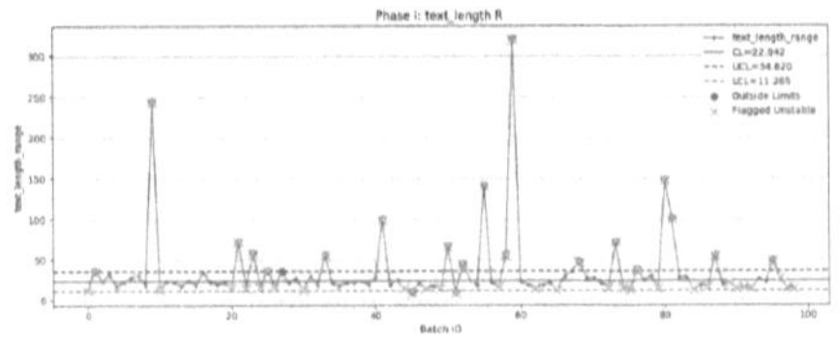

(b) R chart for `text_length_range`

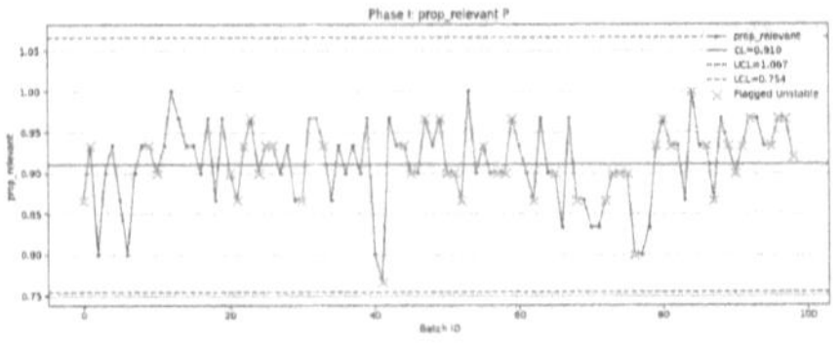

(c) p-chart for `prop_relevant`

Fig. 6. Representative Phase I control charts with baseline parameters and control limits. Orange crosses denote batches flagged during multivariate stability refinement; red circles indicate control limit violations. (Color figure online)

reports entering a pipeline otherwise processing abbreviated extracts. These batches were correctly isolated by iterative refinement. Deviation from this locked baseline drives the 73.2% MYT contribution to Phase II signals.

Text Length Variability: The R chart (Fig. 6b) shows CL = 22.942, UCL = 34.620, LCL = 11.265. Episodic spikes indicate batches containing mixed short and long reports, consistent with heterogeneous documentation practices. All spike-producing batches were excluded during refinement, and deviation from this baseline contributes 24.3% of the Phase II ABRS signal together with text length mean accounting for 97.5% of the total multivariate signal.

Relevance Proportion: The relevance proportion p-chart (Fig. 6c) shows a stable centreline at CL = 0.910 with no formal limit violations across all 99 batches. This stability is operationally significant in the context of Phase II because `prop_relevant` remained consistent throughout and contributed only 0.9% to Phase II ABRS signals per MYT decomposition, it confirms that the sustained Phase II signal is not attributable to changes in upstream classification.

Other Monitored Metrics: Two further metrics warrant brief mention. NER confidence exhibited a systematic 40-percentage-point decline from batch 0 to batch 99, violating the stationarity assumption required for valid EWMA baseline establishment. It should be noted that the MPSV framework monitors a broader set of metrics beyond those reported here. A fully deployed implementation would monitor all available metrics simultaneously, with chart type and inclusion decisions guided by the assumption validation conducted in Phase 0.

Phase 0: Pre-baseline Exploratory Analysis. Phase 0 examines the raw pipeline outputs before any baseline construction occurs. This is done to validate distributional assumptions and guide chart selection before monitoring begins. Phase 0 examined 5,000 reports across 99 batches, assessing four domains: text characteristics, model confidence scores, classification prediction distributions, and LLM generation metrics. For each, it asked two questions: does the metric's distribution satisfy the statistical assumptions required for its proposed control chart, and does the metric's temporal behaviour satisfy the stationarity assumption required for a valid Phase I baseline? The answers to these questions directly determined which metrics entered Phase I, which chart types were applied, and which components were flagged for remediation before deployment.

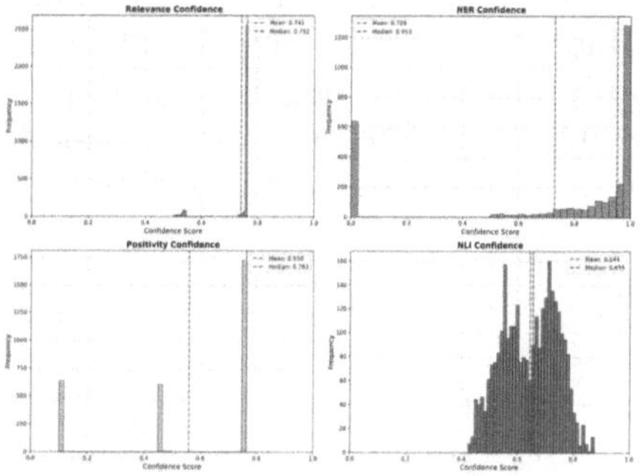

(a) Confidence score distributions

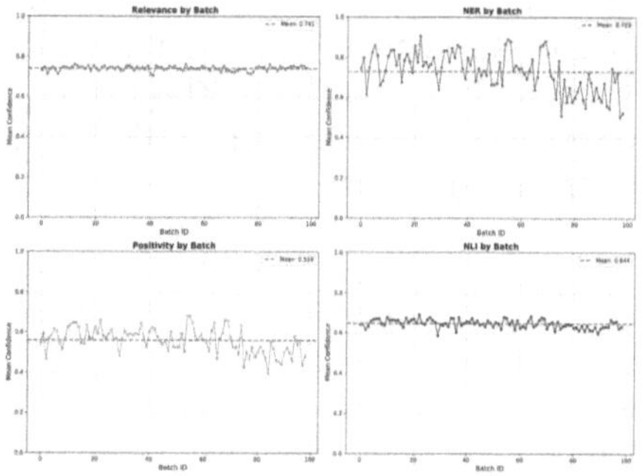

(b) Confidence temporal trends

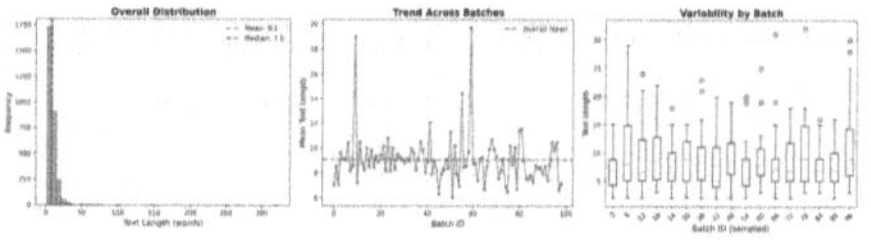

(c) Text length distribution

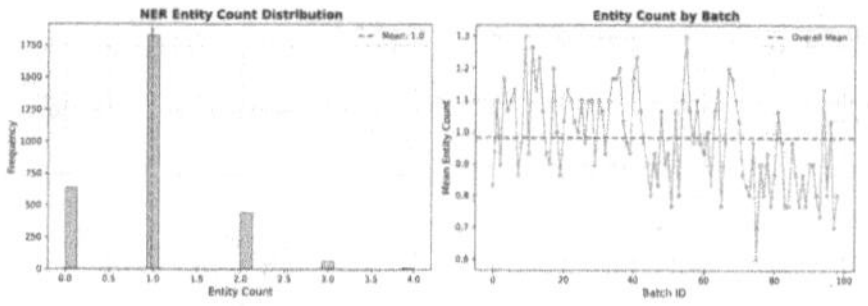

(d) NER entity count distribution

Fig. 7. Phase 0 exploratory diagnostics. Relevance and positivity show restricted variance while NLI shows the broadest spread (a). NER confidence degrades 44% across 99 batches while other components remain stable (b). Mean text length of 9.1 words with episodic batch spikes suggests heterogeneous report composition (c). Entity counts concentrate at 1.0 per report with 13% complete extraction failures, violating c-chart assumptions ($\bar{c} \geq 5$) (d).

Assumption Violations: Three critical assumption violations were identified: NER entity counts ($\bar{c} = 1.0$) and NLI contradiction proportions ($np = 1.26$) both fell below their respective chart validity thresholds, and text length exhibited temporal instability irresolvable through statistical methods alone. The remaining metrics passed all distributional checks.

Temporal Instability: Beyond distributional assumptions, Phase 0 examined whether metrics were temporally stable enough to serve as Phase I baselines. Existing drift detectors do not validate stationarity before constructing reference parameters. If a degrading metric is incorporated into the baseline, the centroid

shifts with the degradation, rendering the resulting control limits invalid. NER confidence (Fig. 7b) exhibited the most severe temporal violation: a systematic three-phase degradation from approximately 0.90 at batch 0 to 0.50 by batch 99, representing a 44% decline. Phase 0's identification of this trend directly informed Phase I's iterative refinement procedure, which targeted and removed these batches. In contrast, LLM generation metrics confidence (mean 0.901), perplexity (mean 1.118), and entropy (mean 0.339) demonstrated strong temporal stability across all 99 batches with no systematic trend. This confirmed stationarity and validated their inclusion in the Phase I MPSV baseline.
The value of Phase 0 is perhaps best illustrated by what Phase II ultimately found: 97.5% of the ABRS signal attributed to text length deviation, with model-level components contributing negligibly. Had Phase 0 not flagged text length as anomalous, and had Phase I not carefully locked the baseline from stable batches only, the Phase II ABRS signals could have been misattributed to model degradation rather than correctly identified as an input data quality issue.

5 Limitations and Future Work

Several limitations merit honest acknowledgment, particularly for applied deployment contexts. By construction, **SQC-Guard** is not specific to histopathology: its three-phase structure, MPSV construction, ABRS monitoring, and IAS triage are agnostic to clinical domain, report type, and underlying model architecture, and any multi-component NLP or Computer Vision pipeline producing scalar confidence scores, classification proportions, or generation-quality metrics across sequential batches of documents is in principle a candidate for this monitoring architecture, provided that Phase 0 assumption validation and Phase I baseline construction are conducted on representative in-control data from the target deployment. In practice, however, the framework has so far been applied to a single use case. While that deployment has shown real value, establishing generalisability empirically across tasks, institutions, and pipeline architectures remains an important next step. Extending **SQC-Guard** to other clinical NLP pipelines such as radiology report extraction and to multi-site deployments with heterogeneous data distributions and publicly available benchmark corpora would test whether its behaviour transfers across domains with different drift characteristics across both language and vision tasks.
Relatedly, benchmarking **SQC-Guard** against univariate-only monitoring and against distribution-shift detectors would quantify the incremental benefit of the multivariate SQC formulation. Moreover, a fuller ablation over key design choices including the EWMA smoothing parameter, control-limit configuration, and the composition of the MPSV would help characterise robustness and move towards more principled selection of the monitored metrics. We also note that the thresholds reported here were derived for this dataset and should be expected to adapt as batch frequency and corpus size change.
The NER component's poor performance extracting a mean of one entity per report against a clinical expectation of three to five meant a key pipeline stage

could not contribute to the multivariate baseline, reducing monitoring coverage in this evaluation. This is not a limitation of the framework itself but of the underlying model, and a fully operational NER component would be expected to enrich the MPSV with additional discriminative signal. Therefore, the results presented here represent a conservative lower bound on detection capability. Furthermore, we did not incorporate a dedicated high-dimensional embedding-based (T^2) drift component into the state vector, primarily because at present report volume its dimensionality would inflate the covariance estimate and leave too few in-control batches to satisfy the Phase I minimum-sample requirement. Integrating such a component would likely be feasible at larger report volumes, and exploring richer learned representations would extend the framework's sensitivity to semantic shifts that manually selected scalar indicators may not fully capture. Finally, the IAS triage layer's reliance on NLI entailment scores introduces a dependency on the NLI model's own calibration quality, which was not independently validated here and warrants attention in future deployments.

6 Conclusion

In this paper, we demonstrate the use of **SQC-Guard** monitoring framework on real-world paediatric histopathology reports. This type of monitoring offers meaningful advantages over standard drift detection approaches, with direct implications for how healthcare institutions can operationalise continuous AI oversight in practice. Our results showcase the framework's ability to detect a sustained multivariate shift from batch 26 onward and precisely attribute 97.5% of that signal to text input characteristics via MYT decomposition correctly directing remediation upstream to data preprocessing rather than triggering unnecessary model retraining. In a deployed clinical setting, this distinction is operationally significant as EPR systems and databases are prone to changes. This level of actionable attribution is something univariate or single-signal drift detectors cannot reliably provide. The three-phase structure was essential to achieving valid detections. The IAS triage layer translated statistical signals into a structured clinical response hierarchy, concentrating 95.5% of Phase II reports in priority review categories during the instability window and providing a direct mechanism for directing reviewer effort proportionally to evidenced risk.

Acknowledgments. This project has been completed by Great Ormond Street Hospital NHS Foundation Trust and Roche Products Ltd. M-GB-00026957 | June 2026 as part of a collaborative working agreement. We thank Dr. Jonathan Kennedy for his clinical expertise in this project. We also thank the reviewers for their valuable and constructive comments, which have improved this paper.

References

1. Andersen, E.S., et al.: Monitoring performance of clinical artificial intelligence in health care: a scoping review. JBI Evid. Synth. **22**(12), 2423–2446 (2024)

2. Baena-García, M., del Campo-Ávila, J., Fidalgo, R., Bifet, A., Gavaldà, R., Morales-Bueno, R.: Early drift detection method. In: Fourth International Workshop on Knowledge Discovery from Data Streams (2006)
3. Bifet, A., Gavaldà, R.: Learning from time-changing data with adaptive windowing. In: Proceedings of the 2007 SIAM International Conference on Data Mining, pp. 443–448 (2007)
4. Feng, J., et al.: Clinical artificial intelligence quality improvement: towards continual monitoring and updating of AI algorithms in healthcare. NPJ Digit. Med. **5**(66) (2022)
5. Finlayson, S.G., et al.: The clinician and dataset shift in artificial intelligence. N. Engl. J. Med. **385**, 283–286 (2021)
6. Gama, J., Medas, P., Castillo, G., Rodrigues, P.: Learning with drift detection. In: Bazzan, A.L.C., Labidi, S. (eds.) SBIA 2004. LNCS (LNAI), vol. 3171, pp. 286–295. Springer, Heidelberg (2004). https://doi.org/10.1007/978-3-540-28645-5_29
7. Gretton, A., Borgwardt, K.M., Rasch, M.J., Schölkopf, B., Smola, A.: A kernel two-sample test. J. Mach. Learn. Res. **13**, 723–773 (2012)
8. Hossain, E., Rana, R., Higgins, N., Soar, J., Barua, P.D., Pisani, A.R., Turner, K.: Natural language processing in electronic health records in relation to healthcare decision-making: a systematic review. Comput. Biol. Med. **155**, 106649 (2023)
9. Kawatra, J.S., et al.: Minimal data maximum impact: lessons learned from real-world unstructured data in paediatric care. In: Wu, J., Zhu, J., Xu, M., Jin, Y. (eds.) Proceedings of The First AAAI Bridge Program on AI for Medicine and Healthcare. Proceedings of Machine Learning Research, vol. 281, pp. 70–78. PMLR (2025). https://proceedings.mlr.press/v281/kawatra25a.html
10. Li, I., et al.: Neural natural language processing for unstructured data in electronic health records: a review. Comput. Sci. Rev. 46, 100511 (2022). https://doi.org/10.1016/j.cosrev.2022.100511
11. Mason, R.L., Tracy, N.D., Young, J.C.: Decomposition of T^2 for multivariate control chart interpretation. J. Qual. Technol. **27**(2), 99–108 (1995)
12. Montgomery, D.C.: Introduction to Statistical Quality Control, 8th edn. Wiley (2020)
13. Page, E.S.: Continuous inspection schemes. Biometrika **41**(1–2), 100–115 (1954)
14. Pesaranghader, A., Viktor, H.L., Paquet, E.: McDiarmid drift detection methods for evolving data streams. In: International Joint Conference on Neural Networks (IJCNN). IEEE (2018)
15. Quiñonero-Candela, J., Sugiyama, M., Schwaighofer, A., Lawrence, N.D.: Dataset Shift in Machine Learning. MIT Press (2009)
16. Rabanser, S., Günnemann, S., Lipton, Z.: Failing loudly: an empirical study of methods for detecting dataset shift. In: Advances in Neural Information Processing Systems, vol. 32 (2019)
17. Shewhart, W.A.: Economic Control of Quality of Manufactured Product. Van Nostrand (1931)
18. Sileo, D.: Tasksource: a large collection of NLP tasks with a structured dataset preprocessing framework. In: Calzolari, N., Kan, M.Y., Hoste, V., Lenci, A., Sakti, S., Xue, N. (eds.) Proceedings of the 2024 Joint International Conference on Computational Linguistics, Language Resources and Evaluation (LREC-COLING 2024), pp. 15655–15684. ELRA and ICCL, Torino (2024). https://aclanthology.org/2024.lrec-main.1361
19. Thor, J., et al.: Application of statistical process control in healthcare improvement: systematic review. Qual. Saf. Health Care **16**(5), 387–399 (2007)

20. Tunstall, L., et al.: Efficient few-shot learning without prompts (2022). arXiv:2209.11055
21. Wu, S., et al.: Deep learning in clinical natural language processing: a methodical review. J. Am. Med. Inform. Assoc. **27**(3), 457–470 (2020)
22. Yang, X., Chen, A., Poczos, B., Bian, J., Hogan, W.R., Wu, Y.: A large language model for electronic health records. NPJ Digit. Med. **5**(194) (2022)
23. Zaratiana, U., Tomeh, N., Holat, P., Charnois, T.: GLiNER: generalist model for named entity recognition using bidirectional transformer. In: Proceedings of the 2024 Conference of the North American Chapter of the Association for Computational Linguistics: Human Language Technologies (Volume 1: Long Papers). Association for Computational Linguistics, Stroudsburg (2024)
24. Zhang, P., Zeng, G., Wang, T., Lu, W.: TinyLlama: an open-source small language model (2024). arXiv:2401.02385
25. Zhu, L., Rong, Y., Yu, N.Y., Holmes, J.M., Vargas, C.E.: Establishing prospective performance monitoring for real-world implementation of deep learning-based auto-segmentation in prostate cancer radiotherapy. Radiother. Oncol. **202**, 110588 (2025)

Watt's Your Range? An AI-Powered Digital Twin for EV Energy Consumption Estimation

Lazaros Adaloglou[1], Markus Englberger[1], Nikos Avramis[2], Camiel Beckers[2], Thanasis Trantas[2], and Devendra Singh Dhami[1,3](✉)

[1] Eindhoven University of Technology, Eindhoven, The Netherlands
{adaloglouIazaros,m.englberger,d.s.dhami}@tue.nl
[2] Netherlands Organisation for Applied Scientific Research, The Hague, The Netherlands
{nikos.avramis,camiel.beckers,thanasis.trantas}@tno.nl
[3] Eindhoven Artificial Intelligence Systems Institute, Eindhoven, The Netherlands

Abstract. Electric vehicles are crucial in the transition to sustainable transportation. Specifically, in the coming years, the number of electric trucks is expected to increase significantly due to regulations and an anticipated lower total cost of ownership (TCO). As a result, electric truck adoption is growing, bringing challenges to fleet managers due to range limits and uncertain energy usage. This work introduces an AI-powered Digital Twin (DT) framework, TwinERGY, to predict the energy consumption for battery-electric trucks at the pre- and intra-trip stages. Three sequence-to-sequence models are compared for the pre-trip scenario to determine trip-level energy consumption. We utilize a conditional diffusion model for real-time probabilistic estimation of power and time elapsed, initialized on the pre-trip model's output and conditioned on historical intra-trip inputs. Combined with the pre-trip model's output using Bayesian fusion, it aims to reduce end-trip energy consumption estimation uncertainty with every lapsing segment. The results show that the framework can aid in reducing uncertainty and contribute to more confident decision making during fleet management. Going a step ahead, we also provide explanations of the obtained results, uncovering the important features affecting energy consumption.

Keywords: AI · Digital Twin · Operational Decision-Making

1 Introduction

Electric vehicles (EVs) are an important component of the transition to sustainable transportation, contributing to the reduction of greenhouse gas emissions

---

Supplementary Information The online version contains supplementary material available at https://doi.org/10.1007/978-3-032-37682-4_16.

M. Baratchi et al. (Eds.): ECML PKDD 2026, LNAI 16949, pp. 268–285, 2027.
https://doi.org/10.1007/978-3-032-37682-4_16

and dependence on fossil fuels. Specifically, in the coming years, driven by regulation and an expected lower total cost of ownership (TCO), the number of electric trucks (ETs) is anticipated to increase substantially [13]. However, their adoption also introduces operational complexity, particularly concerning energy planning. Due to the current electricity grid, their adoption can also result in grid balancing and capacity problems, as well as congestion, due to inaccurate energy consumption predictions, impeding the electrification of mobility and the logistics sector and extending the challenge of managing fleets of electric trucks. To avoid potential disruptions and enable more efficient planning, there is a clear need for accurate energy consumption estimation, which can support decisions such as re-routing a truck, stopping at a charging station, or assigning a different vehicle altogether. From a societal perspective, reliable EV deployment contributes to cleaner cities and more efficient supply chains [15]. Thus, predictive models can address this complexity by estimating energy needs in advance, enabling better management strategies.

Estimating the end-operation energy consumption of electric trucks both at prior (pre-) and during (intra-) stages of an operation would make decisions more efficient. Real-time energy consumption estimation can ensure that estimations remain reliable under changing external route conditions, such as road blockages and weather, as well as internal changes such as the driver's behavior or vehicle load. Traditional offline models often fail to capture these short-term variations because they rely on static assumptions about the future. Moreover, limitations due to the innate nature of predictive models not being able to provide an exact point-estimated output consistently because of modeling and random uncertainties, as well as real-world data measurement deviations, are addressed by incorporating uncertainty quantification. Successful real-time energy consumption estimation can aid in ensuring or reducing the uncertainty interval of the end-trip consumption during trips, contributing to more confident decision making.

Furthermore, the ability to provide explanations about energy estimations is crucial for user trust and operational decision-making. Beyond legal or ethical motivations, explainable AI (XAI) enhances user confidence and enables model validation by clarifying what the model has learned, how current decisions are made, and what drives future estimations [8]. This capability allows practitioners to confirm or challenge existing domain knowledge and fosters the generation of new scientific insights, which is particularly valuable for critical applications such as energy estimation.

Overall, this work explores models for pre-trip estimation, as well as intra-trip estimation, and designs a framework that can facilitate real time uncertainty interval reduction, as well as explanations. Specifically, a digital twin (DT) framework, TwinERGY[1], is defined to include the above, enabling continuous synchronization between physical assets, sensors and digital models. This

[1] We make our code publicly available at https://anonymous.4open.science/r/TwinERGY-XAI-Powered-Digital-Twin-3DF3/.

allows the models to update their state and estimations dynamically as new data become available, leading to more context-aware energy estimation.

2 Related Work

A truck logistics operation, in this work, is defined as a trip where the truck departs from the start and arrives at a destination. Current approaches to energy estimation at the pre- or intra-trip stage are grouped into physics-based and data-driven methods. Data-driven methods include both classical statistical modeling and modern Machine Learning (ML). Early academic efforts in this field were dominated by physics-based approaches, but over the last decade there has been a surge in adopting data-driven models, which constitute the majority of new research [12]. Most works still focus on energy modeling for passenger cars, underscoring the need for new investigations in electric trucks. This work addresses that gap by focusing on battery-electric truck energy consumption.

Sequence-to-sequence modeling has become a cornerstone in time series forecasting. Transformer-based models such as the Temporal Fusion Transformer (TFT), in particular, stand out by delivering interpretable multi-horizon forecasts that leverage static information and known future inputs, a feature advantageous when such exogenous variables are available [6]. The TFT is suited for time-series tasks due to its ability to capture short-term, instead of commonly long-term dependencies. While transformer-based models have recently emerged in time series tasks, no study has yet applied the Temporal Fusion Transformer (TFT) to the context of end-trip electric truck energy consumption estimation.

Long Short-Term Memory (LSTM) networks have shown promising performance in pre-trip energy consumption estimation [5]. Additionally, the extended LSTM model (xLSTM) has shown promising results in time series estimation and possesses an improved capacity for multivariate temporal mixing and sequence modeling [10]. Among other notable approaches, Foundation Models (FMs) have recently gained attention for their ability to leverage large-scale pretraining on diverse time series, facilitating zero-shot and few-shot generalization across domains [7]. Finetuning methods such as LoRA and VeRA add light-weight wrappers around FMs and offer fast model adaptation to downstream tasks, avoiding retraining their core parameters [9].

Works on estimating end-trip energy consumption during a trip in real time are limited. A form of digital twin technology has gained traction as a framework by creating a virtual replica of the physical system to facilitate continuous, real-time simulation that bridges the gap between model-based and data-driven approaches [18]. The use of a Digital Twin (DT) that can simulate and update end-trip energy estimations in real time has not yet been explored for our particular problem [16]. Overall, the most advanced ML models tend to sacrifice transparency since their prediction mechanisms can be opaque, limiting interpretability and practical trust [1]. The application of Explainable AI (XAI) has gained significant attention recently, driven by the need to better understand and trust complex ML models [4]. Techniques such as TimeSHAP enable the explanation of recurrent and transformer models by analyzing the influence of sequence perturbations on predictions [14].

3 TwinERGY: The AI- Powered Digital Twin Framework

We introduce TwinERGY, the digital twin for estimating electric truck end-trip energy consumption. The framework produces an initial estimate before departure (pre-trip) and progressively refines it during the trip (intra-trip) as new data become available. The objective is to reduce uncertainty over time while maintaining accurate predictions. The Digital Twin integrates route planning inputs, vehicle sensor data, preprocessing pipelines, and predictive models to continuously estimate power consumption, segment travel time, and cumulative trip energy. These estimates are updated whenever new observations become available, allowing the system to refine the predicted end-trip energy consumption. An overview of the TwinERGY architecture is shown in Fig. 1.

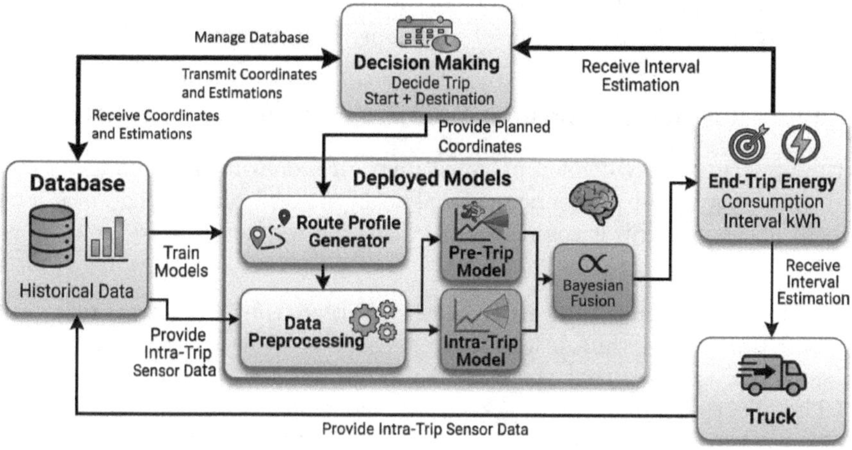

Fig. 1. TwinERGY architecture. Deployed models communicate with the truck, cloud, database and decision-making side, to train, receive input and transmit estimations.

3.1 Data Preprocessing

The available historical data consist of truck trips measured at a 1 Hz frequency and derive from sensors of three electric trucks operating primarily in the Amsterdam region between 2019 and 2021. Features include battery voltage and current, truck load, and speed. To enrich the data, planned route information is obtained through APIs, combined with a custom Route Profile Generator (RPG). These sources provide additional contextual features such as road types, elevation, tunnels, traffic lights, and date and time information.

For more stable and efficient training, the inputs are normalized, eliminating sensitivity to large differences in order-of-magnitude between inputs. Continuous real-valued features are standardized at zero mean and unit variance, and categorical features are embedded and mapped to a normalized, learnable space. To avoid data leakage, the normalization parameters are computed only on the training set, and data are chronologically sorted. Across the entire pipeline, data are converted from time to distance domain, as the truck's speed is a sensor-measured feature and not known at estimation time. The new positions are points along the trip, one every 10 m, since that is the minimum measured distance difference in the historical data. To estimate the truck's energy consumption (in kWh) and transparently attribute estimation errors, we estimate power expenditure (kW) and elapsed time (s) between the current and previous positions at each position in the trip. The energy consumption is derived by

$$E = \frac{1}{3600} \sum_{i=1}^{N} P_i \cdot \Delta t_i \tag{1}$$

where P_i is the power at position i, Δt_i is the time interval between positions $i-1$ and i, and N is the number of positions. Full dataset is in Appendix 1.1.

3.2 Pre-trip Energy Consumption Estimation

For the pre-trip energy consumption estimation scenario three models are compared, in a sequence-to-sequence task. The input and output sequence lengths are fixed and every trip is segmented to form the sequences.

Fixed Trip Segmentation. At the pre-trip stage, the estimations rely entirely on planned or known values, which are subject to time and route information. It is generally assumed that there are no long-term temporal dependencies in a trip. The effect of input features, such as road angle, max speed limit or ambient temperature, at early trip positions, is weak or non-existent on the energy consumption of far-future positions. For this reason, every trip is segmented into fixed position sequences.

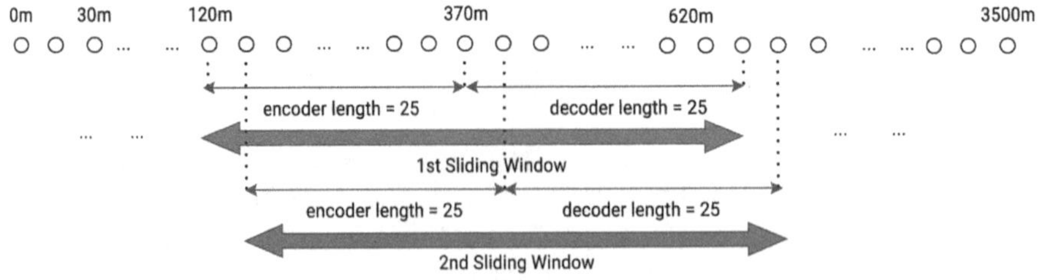

Fig. 2. Sliding window segmentation along the trip. Every segment (sliding window) is a sequence with an encoder and decoder length of 25 positions each.

To create more training samples for model training, we created sliding windows of the fixed position sequences. In Fig. 2 an example of trip coverage by segmenting in sliding windows is shown. Every sequence consists of look-back and prediction horizons, namely the encoder and decoder sequence. Normally, the encoder contains the inputs and the decoder contains the outputs. We investigate and compare three cases for encoder and decoder placements, as shown in Fig. 3. We implement this to investigate where the strongest temporal dependencies lie, to identify the temporal regions upon which energy consumption depends most significantly, whether it is past inputs, current inputs, or a combination of both. Hyperparameter tuning for the models showed they perform best when the encoder and decoder sequence length is 25 positions each.

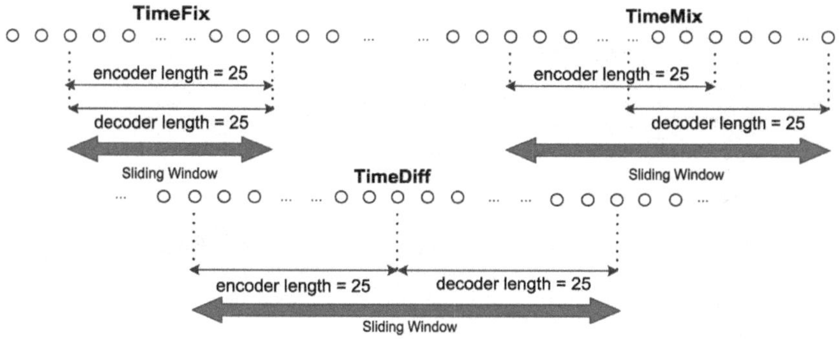

Fig. 3. Encoder-decoder configurations for sequence-to-sequence prediction. *TimeFix* (Full overlap), *TimeMix* (Partial overlap) and *TimeDiff* (No overlap).

Model Selection. We hypothesize that the TFT can improve pre-trip estimation performance by differentiating between static variables and considering inputs for future target values in the decoder sequence. Static variables are features that don't change over a trip, such as truck ID or year. The TFT combines attention mechanisms from transformer models with the sequential feature handling of Recurrent Neural Networks (RNNs), allowing for both short- and long-term dependency capture. Use of TFT is novel in using transformers for pre-trip estimation, as they previously had worse performance on capturing short-term dependencies [11].

In our context, the xLSTM is a promising candidate. It addresses limitations of conventional LSTMs, providing improved memory capacity, better scaling laws, and competitive long-range learning performance with respect to Transformer models [3]. It combines the strengths of traditional LSTM cell gating with novel exponential gating mechanisms and matrix-based memory states, enabling robust sequence modeling over both short and long forecast horizons [2].

TimeGPT is a state-of-the-art foundation model tailored for complex time series forecasting tasks [7]. It has a multi-layer transformer encoder-decoder, where the encoder captures the historical data context, and the decoder generates future predictions in a probabilistic manner. Its extension with the Vector-based Random matrix Adaptation (VeRA) method, enables efficient parameter adaptation through low-rank matrix approximations and reduces the number of trainable parameters during domain-specific fine-tuning. In Fig. 4 the model comparison and pipeline scheme is shown, as well as the difference in their input data subsets.

3.3 Intra-trip Energy Consumption Estimation

During intra-trip estimation of the truck's end-trip energy consumption, the sensor-measured data from trip start until the current position are known. Thus, extra inputs in the encoder sequence can help improve the decoder estimations.

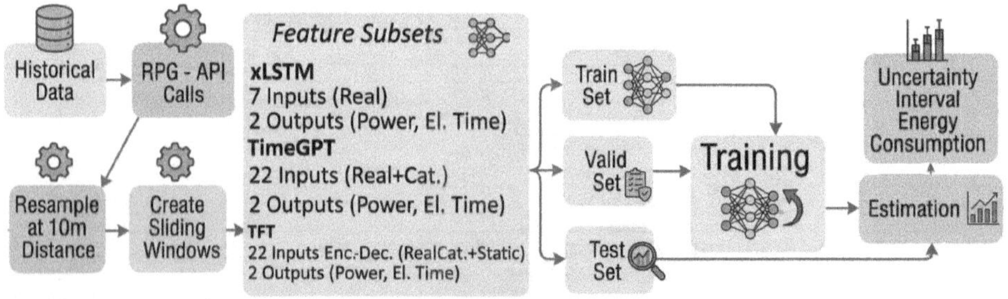

Fig. 4. Pre-trip model comparison and pipeline overview. The three compared models have different input configuration capabilities.

Trip Dynamic Segmentation. For estimation during a trip, fixed input and output lengths would only benefit the next few steps from updated contextual information. Thus, we segment the trips in a dynamic manner, where the encoder consists of all previous points in the trip and the decoder of all remaining points. Hence, the point of split in the trip changes depending on the truck's position. As new sensor observations become available at each position, the intra-trip model conditions on them to estimate the remainder trip.

Model Selection. For intra-trip energy consumption estimation, we adopt a diffusion-based generative approach, namely DiffLoad, capable of probabilistically modeling stochastic temporal trajectories conditioned on both historical and contextual features [17]. The model learns the data distribution $p(x_0)$ of the true time-series samples by progressively denoising a Gaussian noise sequence $x_T \sim \mathcal{N}(0, I)$ through a series of parameterized transformations.

DiffLoad is using the pre-trip model's estimated power and elapsed time uncertainty intervals as priors for the diffusion initialization. This initialization allows the diffusion model to leverage the pre-trip estimation while flexibly adjusting to actual trip behavior as new data accumulate. More on Diffload is given in Appendix Sect. 1.2.

3.4 Digital Twin States

After the models are trained on all available historical trips, the best performing models are deployed. In real-world use, the DT workflow depends on two states, shown in Fig. 5. To quantify uncertainty, the models' estimations are intervals created from quantiles and specifically, we use the 0.1 (lower bound), 0.5 (median), and 0.9 (upper bound) quantiles. More discussion about quantiles is in Appendix 1.3.

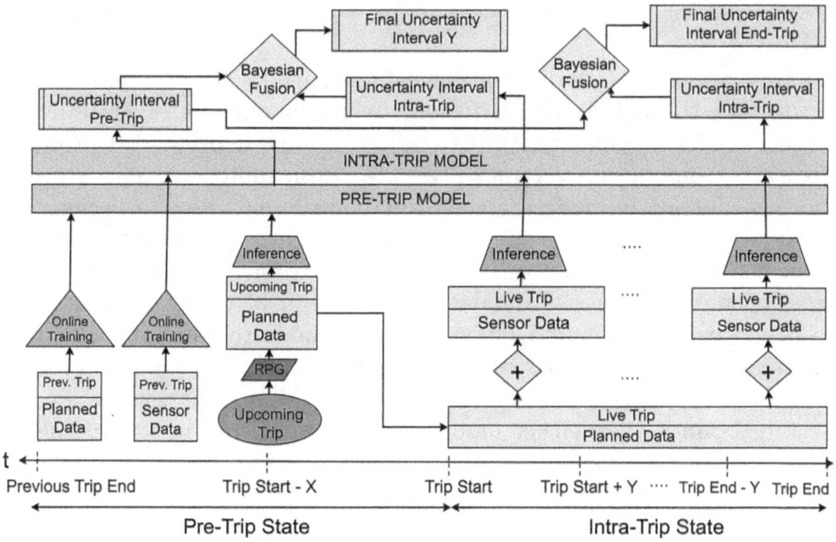

Fig. 5. Architecture of the two deployed models in TwinERGY and the communication throughout the pre-trip and intra-trip states.

Pre-trip State. In the pre-trip state, the framework does not monitor any ongoing trips, but there is an upcoming future trip. The two deployed models are being updated through online training on the latest past trip. The new planned trip is inserted in the DT through data preprocessing pipelines, including RPG feature enrichment and conversion to the distance domain. The pre-trip model estimates the final energy consumption interval and broadcasts it, at a predefined time horizon before the upcoming trip starts, depending on the user's preference.

Intra-trip State. During the intra-trip state, every X seconds, the Diffload model uses additional sensor data in past inputs to estimate the power and time elapsed for the rest of the trip. Since the past inputs up to current position are measured in time, they are preprocessed and converted to distance domain, enriched with RPG planned features.

As the trip progresses and more measured data is fed into the framework, the unknowns shrink, and DiffLoad's prediction intervals for the remaining trip get sharper. Errors and drifts that would have gone undetected in a pre-trip forecast are caught and used by the intra-trip model. The goal is, except for improving the uncertainty, to find dependencies between the planned and actual driver behavior, since DiffLoad's estimations can be influenced by dependencies that the model discovered from past inputs, which not only have the planned speed, but also the actual speed, influenced by traffic or driver behavior. Thus, trips with same planned features can differ, if differences in driver behavior or traffic exist.

Finally, the uncertainty distributions of the outputs of both models are combined together through Bayesian fusion, to produce a final uncertainty interval estimation for the energy. Bayesian fusion offers a principled probabilistic framework to combine uncertainty estimates from multiple predictive models. The pre- and intra-trip models' estimation quantiles can be interpreted as credible intervals containing the true value with a given probability. To perform Bayesian fusion, each predictive interval is approximated by a Gaussian distribution. The median forecast is taken as the mean of the Gaussian, while the distance between the 0.1 and 0.9 quantiles is used to estimate the standard deviation, assuming symmetry and normality. From the fused Gaussian parameters, new credible intervals are reconstructed, providing tighter and more reliable uncertainty bounds than either model alone, demonstrating steadily shrinking estimation intervals while maintaining calibration to the true observed outcomes. More details about Bayesian fusion are given in Appendix Sect. 1.3.

4 Results

We evaluate TwinERGY across two levels, the pre- and intra-trip estimation, using mean absolute error (MAE), root mean square error (RMSE), mean absolute percentage error (MAPE) and median absolute percentage error (MdAPE) metrics. More results and further discussion on the results presented here are given in Appendix Sect. 2.

4.1 Pre-trip Estimation

Point estimations are evaluated first at the segment level across the three temporal scenarios per model, followed by trip-level evaluation and uncertainty analysis. Energy targets integrate elapsed time and power, yielding single values per segment/trip.

Segment-Level Evaluation. In Table 1 the segment-level estimations are evaluated per temporal scenario. The dataset contains 629k training segments, 215k validation segments and 106k test segments. All trucks are used for training, so that models witness more than one instance of the truck ID, to mitigate overfitting.

Table 1. Segment-level evaluation metrics across TFT, TimeGPT, and xLSTM variants on the test set.

Var.		TFT			TimeGPT			xLSTM		
	Metric	Pow.	Time	Energy	Pow.	Time	Energy	Pow.	Time	Energy
Fix	MdAPE (%)	9.32	4.73	**11.21**	10.01	5.87	**12.32**	10.85	6.10	**14.75**
	MAPE (%)	46.64	5.25	**115.32**	50.12	5.38	**120.53**	55.25	7.02	**130.14**
	MAE	25.38	2.94	**0.148**	27.58	3.96	**0.163**	30.61	4.60	**0.258**
	RMSE	33.25	4.67	**0.272**	35.14	4.83	**0.221**	40.02	5.94	**0.310**
Mix	MdAPE (%)	8.05	5.03	**10.04**	8.82	5.13	**10.13**	14.97	7.05	**13.03**
	MAPE (%)	42.56	5.44	**103.49**	44.73	5.98	**113.57**	58.01	8.08	**124.02**
	MAE	22.72	3.24	**0.119**	24.43	3.33	**0.143**	9.96	5.99	**0.223**
	RMSE	29.16	4.83	**0.176**	32.06	4.78	**0.207**	124.05	7.94	**0.324**
Diff	MdAPE (%)	8.28	5.63	**10.85**	8.59	7.78	**11.59**	10.90	6.90	**15.90**
	MAPE (%)	43.82	6.22	**110.80**	44.83	7.57	**115.97**	57.40	8.20	**140.00**
	MAE	23.27	4.41	**0.132**	23.88	5.47	**0.168**	33.75	5.30	**0.285**
	RMSE	29.72	5.75	**0.197**	31.23	7.97	**0.232**	42.25	6.80	**0.345**

The TFT *TempFix* scenario has superior metrics for power expenditure and elapsed time, compared to energy consumption. This implies that integrating the two targets, their errors are multiplied and are increasing the energy error. In trip-level evaluation, the energy errors are expected to decrease, since while a few Whs of error in the segment are a large fraction of the energy for the segment, in the trip's scope it will be a less important error. The median MAPE (MdAPE) is smaller, hinting that estimation is accurate, and only outlier segments increase the MAPE.

In the *TempMix* scenario, TFT achieves the best overall energy performance (MAPE $\sim$ 103%), suggesting that combining past and near-future context improves estimations. In contrast, *TempDiff* performs worse, indicating weaker dependencies when encoder and decoder are temporally separated.

The elapsed time target, especially in *TempDiff*, shows the greatest deviation and error sensitivity, both a model and data artifact, as trip segment timing can be highly variable due to externalities such as traffic or driver-specific events, which are less predictable and less directly related to the physical state variables that TimeGPT specializes in modeling.

In Fig. 6 the predictions of the models for TimeMix on a segment are shown. In Fig. 7 the energy predictions for 20 consecutive segments are shown, compared for all models and scenarios against truths. The closer fits seem to hold for TFT's TimeFix and TimeMix scenarios, while TimeGPT's TimeFix seemingly tracks the curve direction very well, with some minor vertical shifts. It is evident from the results that TempMix is performing the best, therefore, the rest of the analysis uses this temporal placement scenario.

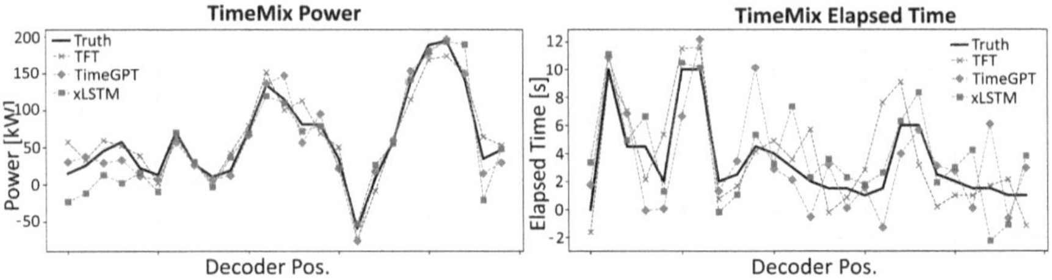

Fig. 6. Segment estimation plot of the three models and the ground truth for the *TimeMix* scenario for the two estimation targets.

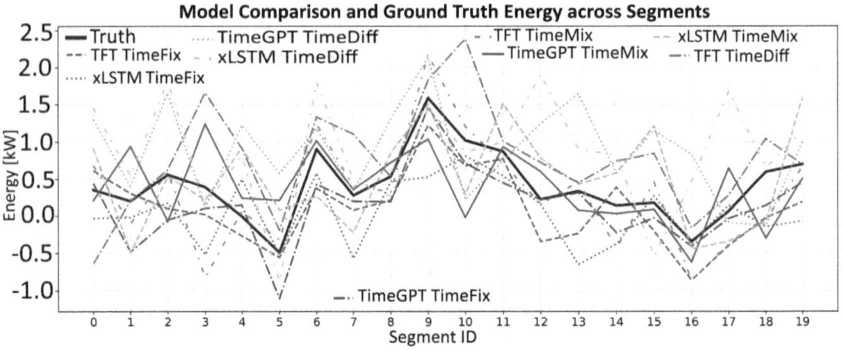

Fig. 7. Estimation plot for 20 consecutive segments for all models, scenarios and true values for the energy target.

Trip-Level Evaluation. To select a model between the three, we combine segment-level with trip-level analysis. Due to sliding windows, multiple estimations exist per trip position. We compare three aggregation methods, *averaging* all overlapping window's estimations for the position, *first-decoder* (position from first window), and *last-decoder* (position from last window). The three model's performance for the energy consumption on the test set for each method are shown in Table 2. The results are calculated on a subset of the total trips.

The *First* method performs best for TFT and xLSTM, hinting that the models capture immediate short term temporal dependencies better. This can

Table 2. Trip Reconstruction Method Comparison on 500 trips.

Trip-Rec.	Trip-Level								
Metric	TFT			TimeGPT			xLSTM		
	Avg.	First	Last	Avg.	First	Last	Avg.	First	Last
MdAPE	6.80%	6.00%	7.50%	6.70%	6.10%	6.12%	7.63%	7.25%	7.80%
MAPE	10.20%	9.70%	10.35%	10.60%	10.15%	10.12%	11.10%	10.85%	11.18%
MAE (kWh)	4.49	4.10	4.83	4.77	4.44	4.41	5.03	4.92	5.11
RMSE (kWh)	6.01	5.55	6.27	6.14	5.94	5.93	6.29	6.06	6.47

be further reinforced, as TimeGPT has slightly better performance for the *last* method, indicating better capture of longer-term dependencies.

The trip-level results for the three models and their best performing trip-reconstruction methods are demonstrated in Table 3 (Train - 4k, Valid. - 1,4k, Test - 0,6k trips). TFT achieves the lowest energy errors, with MdAPE of 8.38% and MAPE of 8.87%. Power estimation errors are notably low, with MAPE at 4.32% and RMSE at 11.14 kW. For elapsed time, the model maintains a MdAPE of 1.40%, with a RMSE of 1.59. Results indicate that TimeGPT generalizes well but may lose marginal accuracy compared to TFT, possibly reflecting more flexible temporal modeling but less deterministic structure.

Table 3. Trip-level test evaluation metrics across TFT, TimeGPT, and xLSTM.

Model	TFT			TGPT			xLSTM		
Metric	Power	Time	Energy	Power	Time	Energy	Power	Time	Energy
MdAPE	2.23%	1.40%	**8.38%**	2.55%	1.51%	9.02%	2.62%	1.72%	9.49%
MAPE	4.32%	2.01%	**8.87%**	4.71%	2.19%	9.92%	5.42%	2.33%	10.52%
MAE	8.01	1.20	**1.264**	8.76	1.26	1.315	9.89	1.37	1.456
RMSE	11.14	1.59	**2.115**	11.79	1.65	2.104	12.65	1.89	2.014

In Fig. 8, the models' predictions for energy consumption on 20 trips are shown, compared with each other and the true end-trip energy consumption. TFT fits the true energies at the trip-level best, with some exceptions where TimeGPT also performs well. From the intra-trip analysis, TFT is the best performing model and therefore, we select TFT for TwinERGY's pre-trip modeling.

Uncertainty Performance. The results in Table 4 showcase TFT performance with uncertainty quantification (UQ) on trip-level, where TFT outputs three values per target. Here, α defines the tail probability excluded from the prediction interval (e.g., $\alpha = 0.05$ targets 95% coverage). Calibration reports empirical coverage rate, improving with smaller α (wider intervals), while median sharpness

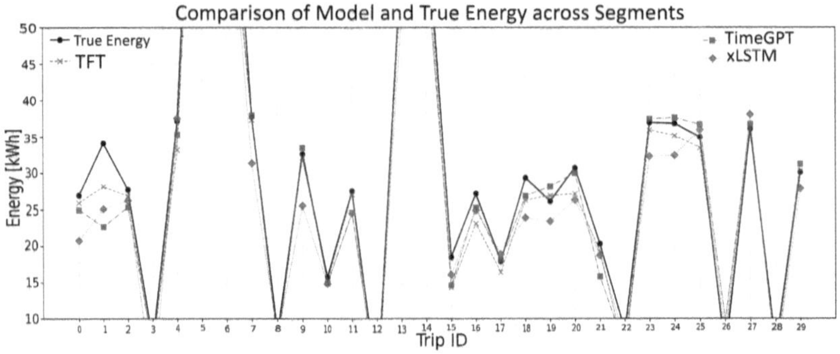

Fig. 8. Energy consumption estimation for the three models is plotted, for 20 trips, compared with true end-trip energy consumption.

measures typical relative interval width (normalized by median prediction). For our global case, $\alpha = 0.05$, calibration is strong (~82% across splits), with minor train-test decay. Sharpness is low (~13%), indicating narrow, precise intervals.

Table 4. TFT uncertainty quantification metrics across trip-level energy consumption splits.

TFT-UQ	Trip-Level Energy					
Alpha	Calibration (%)			Md Sharpness (%)		
	Train	Valid.	Test	Train	Valid.	Test
0.05	82.3	82.1	81.6	13.5	13.0	12.7
0.01	91.2	90.1	89.2	21.8	22.9	23.4

4.2 Intra-trip Estimation

The intra-trip model's performance with uncertainty quantification follows. In this stage, the model is not included in the DT simulation yet, so it inadvertently performs poorly, without fusion with TFT output. At the first trip marks, the model is largely uncertain about the end-trip estimation interval, compared to when close to the end of the trip, where almost the entire trip has been sensor-measured. Thus, uncertainty metrics such as calibration are trivial for this evaluation (~50%). A trip is visualized in Fig. 9, where in the cumulative energy figure, the uncertainty bound is wide enough, as this is the estimation of the intra-trip model at the trip's start.

TwinERGY is evaluated on dynamic trip traversal, at position X, $2X$ $\ldots MX$, simulated offline on real world trips with uncertainty reduction. In Fig. 10, an example of a trip estimation in real-time is shown, reducing the

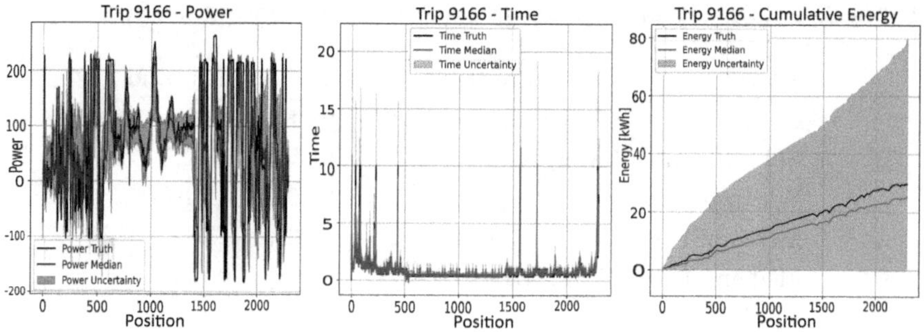

Fig. 9. A trip case of DiffLoad target estimations with uncertainty bounds. Estimating at the start of the trip, the end-trip energy consumption interval is wide.

uncertainty interval of the end-trip energy consumption estimation as the trip lapses. The figure demonstrates how the interval shrinks with time in the DT, compared to how it would shrink by only pre-trip, or only intra trip estimation.

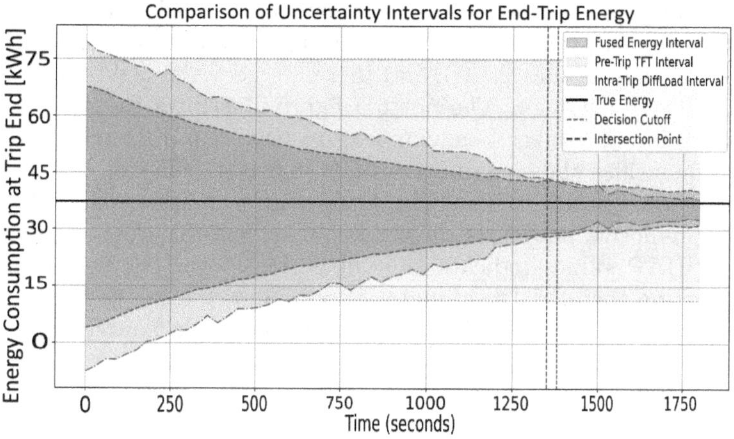

Fig. 10. An example of uncertainty reduction, evaluating TwinERGY on a trip, simulating real time estimation.

The DT is successfully reducing the uncertainty of the pre-trip estimation by combining the intervals from TFT and Diffload, through bayesian fusion. After a certain point later in the trip, termed the *intersection* point, the DT and intra-trip intervals are very similar, since the intra-trip model has witnessed most of the trip. The *decision cutoff* is the position where decision-making stops, hence the estimation after this position does not influence decisions. The all-trip results are shown in Table 5. Overall, calibration is better than the pre-trip TFT alone, proving the effect the DT has in improving the pre-trip estimation.

Table 5. TwinERGY uncertainty quantification for energy at key trip stages.

Metric	Pre-trip	1/3 Trip	2/3 Trip	Trip End
Calibration ($\alpha = 0.05$)	89.1%	95.4%	98.1%	99.3%
Md. Sharpness (kWh)	8.7%	9.1%	9.6%	10.1%
Width Reduction	–	19.5%	35.6%	51.4%
Median MAPE	11.42%	7.42%	4.03%	2.0%
Median MAE [kWh]	1.175	0.543	0.258	0.114

Explainability. Methods on explainability across the entire pipeline are applied. In Fig. 11, on top left the local TimeShap contribution of positions in the segment is shown. The input features of the positions in the decoder sequence have great positive importance for the output, together with two positions in the encoder. On the top right, the TFT's interpretable attention decoder weights are shown, showing high importance for speed limit, elevation, trip distance and ambient temperature.

Another feature we explain is driver behavior, being the difference between actual truck speed and planned speed. It is one of few 'leads' the intra-trip model has to estimate energy long-term. If in an arbitrary position, the actual speed is 70, while the speed limit is 100, and there are no traffic lights, the model can derive slow driver behavior. The bottom figure illustrates the average absolute SHAP values for the driver behavior feature over 20 min of trips' progression. The curve quantifies the contribution of past driver behavior to the intra-trip estimation at each position. The SHAP values at each minute directly represent how much predictive power the driver behavior feature provides. Early in the trip, large SHAP values indicate that deviations from planned speed have a strong impact on the model's estimate of speed and energy consumption. As the horizon extends, the influence drops, reflecting the model's increased perception of the true energy values.

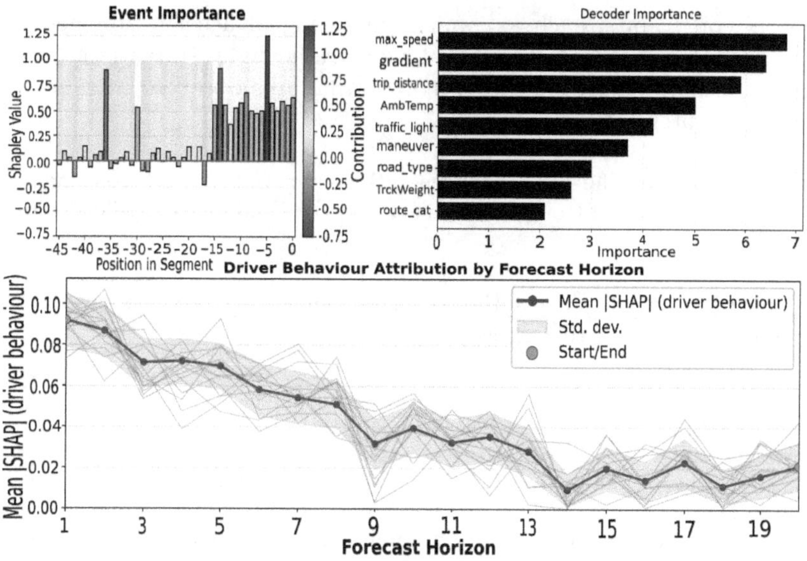

Fig. 11. Top left: local TimeShap to explain the importance of positions. Top right: interpretable attention weights. Bottom: Global driver behavior SHAP.

5 Conclusion

We presented TwinERGY, a comprehensive digital twin framework, for end-trip energy consumption estimation of electric trucks by integrating AI/ML models and uncertainty quantification. By systematically separating the energy estimation pipeline into the pre-trip and intra-trip states, our work demonstrates the value of context-aware modeling over, initially, a pre-trip approach. The most salient outcome is the clear superiority of employing both the pre-trip and intra-trip models at the same time. The pre-trip model provides essential baseline estimations using available route and planned features, but the most significant improvements are realized when the intra-trip, real-time corrections are introduced. The intra-trip model, which is updated as trip data becomes available, captures dynamic driving behaviors and route changes not observable beforehand. Results consistently show improved accuracy, reduced error propagation, and tighter uncertainty intervals with this combined approach. Finally, our quantile-based uncertainty quantification enables models to communicate their estimation confidence, supporting more robust decision-making for fleet operators. We also highlight the critical role of input features and real-time data in model performance. Empirical results indicate that accuracy gains are tightly linked to the richness and correctness of the available signals.

In the future, there is considerable potential in exploring alternative probabilistic modeling approaches for uncertainty, such as Markov models or Bayesian networks, which may offer additional insights into the temporal and structural uncertainty present in predictive energy systems. Additionally, the integration of physical constraints, such as explicit modeling of acceleration pedal input, dynamic energy recuperation, or real-time traffic light states (e.g., red-green cycles), could help resolve abrupt prediction failures observed at trip extremes or in complex intersections.

Acknowledgments. The TU Eindhoven authors received support from their Department of Mathematics and Computer Science and the Eindhoven Artificial Intelligence Systems Institute.

Disclosure of Interests. The authors have no competing interests to declare that are relevant to the content of this article.

References

1. Aksu, T., Liu, C., Saha, A., Tan, S., Xiong, C., Sahoo, D.: Xforecast: evaluating natural language explanations for time series forecasting (2024)
2. Alharthi, M., Mahmood, A.: xLSTMTime: long-term time series forecasting with xLSTM. arXiv preprint arXiv:2407.10240 (2024)
3. Beck, M., Pöppel, K.: xLSTM: extended long short-term memory. arXiv preprint arXiv:2405.04517 (2024)
4. Bento, J., Saleiro, P., Cruz, A.F., Figueiredo, M.A.T., Bizarro, P.: TimeShap: explaining recurrent models through sequence perturbations. CoRR abs/2012.00073 (2020)
5. Chen, Y., Zhang, Y., Sun, R.: Data-driven estimation of energy consumption for electric bus under real-world driving conditions. Transp. Res. Part D: Transp. Environ. **98**, 102969 (2021)
6. Ferreira, A.B., Leite, J.B., Salvadeo, D.H.: Power substation load forecasting using interpretable transformer-based temporal fusion neural networks. Electr. Power Syst. Res. (2025)
7. Garza, A., Challu, C., Mergenthaler-Canseco, M.: TimeGPT-1: foundation model for time series forecasting. arXiv preprint arXiv:2310.03589 (2023)
8. Kalasampath, K., Spoorthi, K.N., Sajeev, S., Kuppa, S.S., Ajay, K., Maruthamuthu, A.: A literature review on applications of explainable artificial intelligence (XAI). IEEE Access (2025)
9. Kopiczko, D.J., Blankevoort, T., Asano, Y.M.: VeRA: vector-based random matrix adaptation (2024). https://arxiv.org/abs/2310.11454
10. Kraus, M., Divo, F., Dhami, D.S., Kersting, K.: xLSTM-mixer: multivariate time series forecasting by mixing via scalar memories. In: NeurIPS (2025)
11. Lim, B., Arık, S., Loeff, N., Pfister, T.: Temporal fusion transformers for interpretable multi-horizon time series forecasting. Int. J. Forecast. (2021)
12. Lim, H., Lee, J.W., Boyack, J., Choi, J.B.: EV-PINN: a physics-informed neural network for predicting electric vehicle dynamics (2024)
13. Litjens, R., Medina, R., Avramis, N., Beckers, C., Wilkins, S., Pechenizkiy, M.: Energy consumption prediction with uncertainty quantification for electric truck operations: a data-driven approach (2025)
14. Masampally, V.S., Verma, R., Mitra, K.: Application of TimeSHAP, an eXplainable AI tool, for interpreting time-series model of wind turbines (2025)

15. Razmjoo, A., Gandomi, A.H., Pazhoohesh, M., Mirjalili, S., Rezaei, M.: The key role of clean energy and technology in smart cities development. Energ. Strat. Rev. **44**, 100943 (2022)
16. Thelen, A., et al.: A comprehensive review of digital twin – part 1: modeling and twinning enabling technologies (2022)
17. Wang, Z., Wen, Q., Zhang, C., Sun, L., Wang, Y.: DiffLoad: uncertainty quantification in electrical load forecasting with the diffusion model (2024)
18. Zhang, Z., Zou, Y., Zhou, T., Zhang, X., Xu, Z.: Energy consumption prediction of electric vehicles based on digital twin technology. World Electr. Veh. J. (2021)

Large Language Models, Agents and Reasoning

ARENA: A Cognitive Multi-agent Framework for Modeling Conflict-Driven Multi-party Conversation

Xu Sun[1,2], Lu Zuo[1,3], Ziyang Zeng[4], Trung Hieu Ngo[5], Kai Liu[6], Alexis Lechervy[2(✉)], Frédéric Jurie[2], Julien Hatin[1], and Emmanuel Bertin[1]

[1] Orange Research, Issy-les-Moulineaux, France
{xu.sun,lu.zuo,julien.hatin,emmanuel.bertin}@orange.com
[2] Université Caen Normandie, ENSICAEN, CNRS, Normandie Univ, GREYC UMR6072, 14000 Caen, France
{alexis.lechervy,frederic.jurie}@unicaen.fr
[3] Laboratoire d'Informatique de l'Université du Mans (LIUM – EA 4023), Avenue Olivier Messiaen, 72085 Le Mans Cedex 9, France
[4] Beijing University of Posts and Telecommunications, Beijing, China
ziyang1060@bupt.edu.cn
[5] Nantes Université, École Centrale Nantes, CNRS, LS2N, UMR 6004, 44000 Nantes, France
trung-hieu.ngo@univ-nantes.fr
[6] School of Computer Science, Wuhan University, Wuhan, China
zerkvii@whu.edu.cn

Abstract. Multi-party conversational AI is bottlenecked by data that is narrow in domain, lacks speaker-level differentiation, and provides no annotation of the cognitive processes underlying utterances. We present ARENA (https://huggingface.co/datasets/Orange/ecml_arena_dataset), a cognitive multi-agent framework addressing these gaps through three components: a *cognitive layer* in which each agent maintains Theory-of-Mind belief states and selects from eight rhetorical strategies conditioned on perceived stances; a *structural layer* governing participation balance and topical coverage via urgency-based turn management and subtopic progression; and a *quality-control layer* comprising a facilitator agent and a three-dimensional judge system that ensures naturalness, argument novelty, and discourse coherence.

On 110 evaluated conversations, ARENA outperforms CAMEL by up to 1.31 points across all quality dimensions, with the largest gains in naturalness and interaction dynamics—precisely the aspects stateless role-playing frameworks fail to model. Ablation over 592 conversations confirms that cognitive modules are the primary quality driver, improving *how* agents engage rather than *what* they say. Fine-tuning on ARENA data closes 39–60% of the gap to in-domain training on speaker-aware dialogue summarization, with consistent gains on domain classification

Supplementary Information The online version contains supplementary material available at https://doi.org/10.1007/978-3-032-37682-4_17.

M. Baratchi et al. (Eds.): ECML PKDD 2026, LNAI 16949, pp. 289–305, 2027.
https://doi.org/10.1007/978-3-032-37682-4_17

and argument relation identification. We provide an anonymized review subset of the 1,100-conversation dataset for review and will release the full dataset and framework code upon acceptance.

Keywords: Multi-agent systems · Synthetic Data Generation · Dialogue generation · Theory of Mind · Cognitive Architecture · Large language models

1 Introduction

Downstream NLP tasks such as meeting summarization, argumentation mining, stance detection require multi-party conversational understanding, yet face a fundamental data bottleneck. Real multi-party dialogue corpora are expensive to collect, limited in scale, and lack annotations of the internal reasoning that drives utterances. Existing synthetic generators address volume but not depth: participants lack persistent cognitive states and speaker-level differentiation [27].

Current approaches to multi-party dialogue generation face three fundamental limitations. First, *cognitive flatness*: participants lack internal mental models, producing utterances that respond to surface content without tracking others' evolving positions or strategic intentions [23,25]. Second, *strategic poverty*: generated turns follow simple reactive patterns (agree/disagree) rather than the rich repertoire humans employ, such as probing for weaknesses, building coalitions, and timing concessions [18]. Third, *dynamic rigidity*: conversations follow predictable paths rather than exhibiting emergent phenomena such as unexpected alliances, cascade concessions, and natural saturation.

Addressing these limitations is non-trivial because they are interdependent. In real group discussions, a speaker's choice of what to say depends on their mental model of the audience; their decision of when to speak depends on the conversational dynamics; and the other participants' reactions reshape those mental models in return. This creates a feedback loop that single-turn generation cannot capture: each utterance is simultaneously a product of accumulated social inference and an input to everyone else's. Reproducing this loop at scale while maintaining controllability and annotation quality remains an open challenge.

To this end, we present Arena, a multi-agent framework in which each participant agent is equipped with cognitive module, including: Theory of Mind, strategic reasoning, position tracking, and urgency-based turn management. A dual-model architecture separates quality-critical orchestration from high-throughput agent generation, enabling scalable production of cognitively rich conversations. Our contributions are:

1. A multi-agent dialogue generation framework that integrates five cognitive modules—Theory of Mind, strategic reasoning, stance tracking, urgency management, and subtopic progression—with a real-time judge system and facilitator agent, producing conversations with full cognitive provenance;

2. Systematic evaluation through controlled ablation across five domains, demonstrating that cognitive modeling is the primary driver of interaction quality, and downstream validation on three NLU tasks showing that ARENA-generated data closes 39–60% of the gap to in-domain human data;
3. A framework and corpus of 1,100 conversations across 11 professional domains with per-turn cognitive annotations.

2 Related Work

2.1 Multi-party Dialogue and Synthetic Data Generation

Multi-party dialogue generation has received increasing attention with the advent of large language models. Early work extended two-party systems to handle multiple speakers through speaker-conditioned generation [1,11]. More recent approaches leverage LLMs directly: CAMEL [12] introduces role-playing frameworks for cooperative agent communication, and Social Simulacra [16] and Generative Agents [17] demonstrate emergent social behaviours when agents are equipped with memory and reflection.

On the data side, SODA [7] produces social dialogues grounded in commonsense knowledge, and Meeting Bank [5] provides real meeting transcripts with limited annotations. Despite this progress, existing systems share two limitations. First, agents are *stateless responders*: each turn is generated from conversation history alone, without persistent cognitive models of other participants' goals, vulnerabilities, or evolving stances, producing conversations that are topically coherent but interpersonally flat. Second, synthetic conversations lack *contextual provenance*: there is no record of the persona demographics, or the internal logic that drove a particular argument—metadata critical for downstream tasks like argumentation mining and social bias analysis.

2.2 Theory of Mind in Language Models

Theory of Mind(ToM), the cognitive ability to attribute mental states to others has been extensively studied as an evaluation target for LLMs [8,20,21]. Recent work suggests that LLMs exhibit emergent ToM-like capabilities, though their robustness remains debated [19,23,25]. Several systems have explored using ToM mechanisms to improve agent behavior: Kwon et al. [9] augment negotiation agents with opponent modeling and show that ToM is crucial for successful negotiation, and Li et al. [13] show that explicit ToM prompting improves cooperative task performance and accuracy.

However, these approaches implement ToM as either a one-shot inference or a static prompt injection, rather than a *persistent, evolving* belief system. In real group discussions, mental models accumulate evidence across many exchanges: a participant's assessment of an opponent's flexibility changes gradually as concessions are made or resisted.

2.3 Argumentation and Stance in Dialogue

Computational argumentation has a rich history [10], with recent work applying LLMs to argument mining [2], stance detection [15], and persuasion modelling [14]. In dialogue systems, Keizer et al. [6] model persuasion strategies, while Hadoux and Hunter [3] formalise argumentation-based persuasion. These systems typically operate in two-party settings and treat strategy as a classification problem applied post-hoc to existing dialogue. In multi-party settings, the strategic landscape is richer: agents must decide not only *what* to argue but *whom* to address, when to form alliances, and when to concede. Existing multi-agent dialogue systems lack this targeting capability—they generate responses to the conversation as a whole rather than to specific participants.

The preceding analysis identifies three open problems: persistent multi-turn mental modeling, targeted multi-party strategy conditioned on social inference, and dynamic participation management beyond rigid scheduling. In the following section, we present the ARENA architecture, designed to address these gaps through an integrated cognitive architecture.

3 ARENA Architecture

ARENA generates multi-party conversations through three phases: *world generation*, where an orchestrator model creates the scenario, personas, and knowledge resources; *simulation*, where cognitive agents engage in turn-by-turn discussion; and *termination*, where saturation detection triggers natural closure. Figure 1 illustrates the complete architecture.

The system employs a **dual-model architecture**: an *orchestrator* (Qwen2.5-72B) for world generation, strategy selection, and quality judgment, and an *agent model* (Qwen3-8B) for utterance production. This separation is motivated by asymmetric computational demands—the agent model is invoked N times per turn and dominates throughput cost, while the orchestrator handles constraint-heavy structured reasoning. The framework is model-agnostic, communicating with any OpenAI-compatible endpoint. Each agent maintains a **private knowledge bank** injected by the decision router, and all agents share a **conversation memory** storing compressed representations of points, agreements, and disagreements. When ToM is active, memory retrieval is strategically reranked to surface opponent weaknesses first. Parametric model selection experiments and all prompt templates are detailed in appendix C and F.

3.1 World Generation

The meta-agent creates N participants with differentiated stances along a five-point scale (*strongly support* to *strongly oppose*), professional roles, personality traits, and per-persona speech styles verified for cross-persona distinctiveness. A knowledge bank provides pro/con arguments, complications, and reserve facts for stagnation recovery, all of which are scaled linearly with `max_turns`. Generated subtopics define the expected discussion space for coverage tracking and saturation detection. Details of the multi-pass refinement pipeline are in Appendix section F.1

3.2 Per-Agent Cognitive Modules

Real conversations are shaped by participants' internal states: their beliefs about others, their evolving positions, and their choice of rhetorical approach. Without these, generated agents respond to transcript history alone, producing utterances that are topically relevant but interpersonally generic. We model these through three per-agent modules, described below in terms of function, formalism, and inter-module interface.

Theory of Mind (ToM). In multi-party discussion, speakers tailor arguments based on what they believe others think—adjusting tone toward a receptive

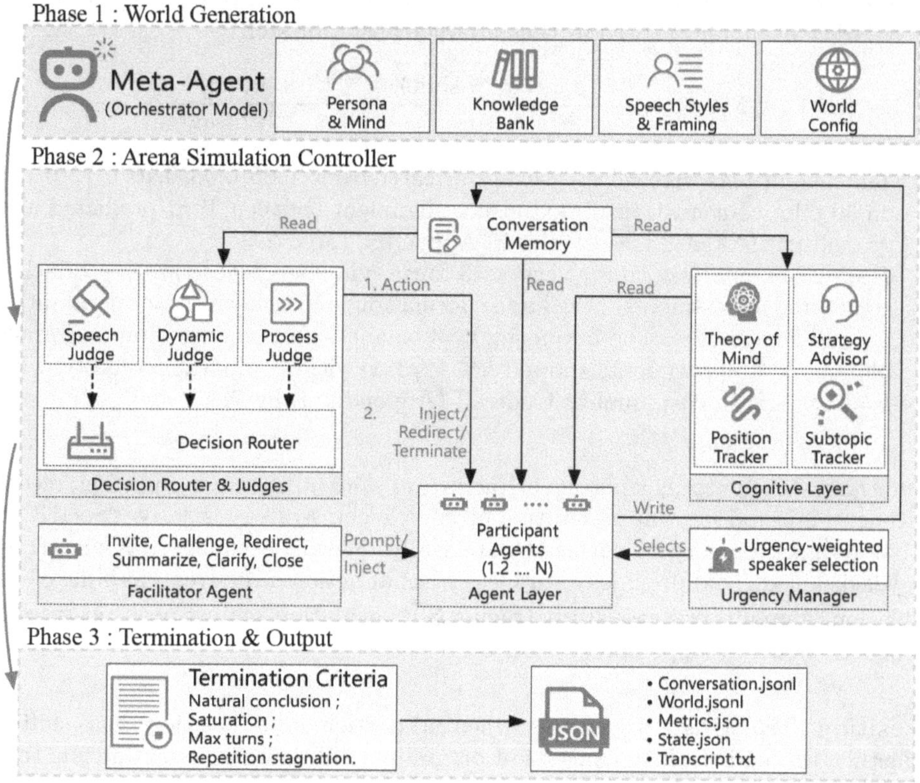

Fig. 1. Overview of the ARENA architecture. *Per-agent cognitive modules* (ToM, Strategy, Position Tracker) shape utterance generation; *conversation-level control modules* (Urgency Manager, Subtopic Tracker, Facilitator) govern turn flow and topic progression. Arrows indicate information dependencies.

listener, pressing a wavering opponent, or avoiding provocation of a hostile one. We operationalise this through per-pair belief states: each agent maintains a belief state for every ordered pair $(\text{observer}_i, \text{target}_j)$, $i \neq j$, where t denotes the conversation turn index:

$$\mathcal{B}_{i\to j}^{(t)} = \langle s, c, o, \tau, e, \mathbf{a}, \mathbf{v}, m \rangle \quad (1)$$

where $s \in \mathcal{S}$ is perceived stance (one of five categories: *supporting, opposing, softening, aligned, neutral*), $c \in [0,1]$ conviction, $o \in [0,1]$ openness, $\tau \in [0,1]$ trust, $e \in \mathcal{E}$ emotional state (seven categories), $\mathbf{a}$ key arguments, $\mathbf{v}$ vulnerabilities, and m predicted next move.

Update mechanisms. Two complementary updates maintain beliefs:

- *Fast heuristic updates* run every turn with intentionally asymmetric magnitudes: $\Delta^- = -0.12$ for concessions, $\Delta^+ = +0.08$ for continued disagreement. The asymmetry follows from a Bayesian argument: since the prior probability of concession is low ($P(\text{concede}_j) \ll P(\text{disagree}_j)$), observing one yields a larger likelihood ratio and thus a larger posterior shift:

$$|\Delta^-| > |\Delta^+| \quad \Longleftarrow \quad \frac{P(\text{concede}_j \mid \text{shift})}{P(\text{concede}_j)} \gg \frac{P(\text{disagree}_j \mid \text{no-shift})}{P(\text{disagree}_j)} \quad (2)$$

  The magnitudes were selected via grid search over $\{0.05, 0.08, 0.10, 0.12, 0.15\}$ on 50 pilot conversations, maximising alignment between ToM-predicted and ground-truth stance trajectories in Appendix Table 7.
- *Deep LLM analysis* runs every k=3 turns via the orchestrator, producing structured assessments of alliance formation and emergent vulnerabilities beyond lexical cues. The frequency k=3 balances cost against temporal granularity: pilot experiments showed $k \in \{2,3,4\}$ yield comparable quality, with k=3 optimal in cost–quality trade-off (Appendix Table 7).

Interface. ToM outputs a per-agent *room-read summary* (stance, emotion, receptiveness) injected into the generation prompt. when strategy is active (Sect. 3.2), ToM reranks memory to surface strategically relevant exchanges. When strategy is disabled, ToM provides awareness without action directives, enabling clean ablation. A qualitative case study tracing $\mathcal{B}_{i\to j}^{(t)}$ evolution against position-tracker labels is shown in Appendix section G.

Position Tracking. Detecting when a participant's position has shifted whether through explicit concession or gradual softening is essential for ToM updates and for producing the annotated stance trajectories that downstream tasks such as argumentation mining require. The position tracker maintains per-participant stance trajectories: $\mathbf{p}_i^{(t)} = \langle l_i^{(t)}, c_i^{(t)} \rangle$, where $l \in \{-2,-1,0,1,2\}$ is the discrete stance label and $c \in [0,1]$ conviction strength, updated via rule-based keyword detection plus periodic LLM analysis (every 2 turns). Concessions

Table 1. Strategy repertoire, conditioned on ToM state, position, subtopic coverage, and diversity constraints.

Strategy	Description
Attack	Challenge a weakness in an opponent's argument
Defend	Reinforce own position against criticism
Probe	Ask a targeted clarifying question
Concede	Acknowledge a valid point, then pivot
Propose	Offer a solution or compromise
Evidence	Introduce new facts or data
Redirect	Shift focus to an unexplored subtopic
Build	Extend another participant's point

reduce $c_i^{(t)}$ without automatically shifting $l_i^{(t)}$, preserving the wavering/genuine-shift distinction. An independent **stance judge** detects implicit movement (softening, hardening, tacit concession) through utterance-level LLM analysis. Position state feeds into ToM updates, strategy selection, and termination (Sect. 3.4).

Under cognitive ablation (`enable_tom=False`, `enable_strategy=False`), the tracker runs internally for metrics but withholds context from agents, preventing stance-awareness leakage while providing consistent inputs to controller-level modules (Table 1).

Strategic Argumentation. Human argumentation employs targeted moves that depend on the speaker's perception of the audience: probing an uncertain opponent differs from defending against a strong critic, and timing a concession requires awareness of the group dynamic. We formalise this as a selection over eight move types (Appendix Table 15). The `StrategyAdvisor` selects:

$$\sigma_i^{(t)} = f_{\text{strat}}\big(\{\mathcal{B}_{i\to j}^{(t)}\}_{j\neq i},\ \mathbf{p}_i^{(t)},\ \mathbf{h}^{(t-w:t)},\ \mathbf{c}^{(t)},\ \mathbf{d}_i^{(t)}\big) \tag{3}$$

where $\mathbf{h}^{(t-w:t)}$ is a sliding window of the w=4 most recent turns, $\mathbf{c}^{(t)}$ subtopic coverage, and $\mathbf{d}_i^{(t)}$ diversity constraints. The selected strategy is injected as a structured directive (e.g., *"challenge a weakness in [target]'s argument"*). A two-level diversity controller caps per-agent consecutive reuse at two turns and globally forces tension-adding moves (ATTACK, PROBE) when harmony dominates, or acknowledgment moves (CONCEDE, BUILD) when absent.

3.3 Conversation-Level Control Modules

Beyond individual cognition, group conversations require structural management: who speaks next, whether the discussion has covered sufficient ground, and when to intervene. Three modules govern these conversation-level dynamics without influencing utterance content, remaining active across all ablation conditions to ensure controlled comparison.

Urgency Manager. Natural conversations exhibit uneven but balanced participation: speakers intervene based on relevance and social pressure, not fixed order. Both one-by-one and random scheduling fail to capture this, producing either artificially uniform or chaotically imbalanced turn distributions. We replace fixed scheduling with dynamic urgency scores:

$$u_i^{(t)} = \text{clamp}\Big(\alpha_i + \beta_{\text{cd}}^{(t)} + \beta_{\text{sil}}^{(t)} + \beta_{\text{tom}}^{(t)} + \beta_{\text{freq}}^{(t)} + \beta_{\text{new}}^{(t)} + \beta_{\text{quiet}}^{(t)},\ 0,\ 10\Big) \tag{4}$$

where α_i is persona-driven activation; $\beta_{\text{cd}}^{(t)}$, $\beta_{\text{sil}}^{(t)}$ are cooldown penalty and silence bonus; $\beta_{\text{tom}}^{(t)}$ captures ToM threat/opportunity signals (decaying $0.7\times$/turn); $\beta_{\text{freq}}^{(t)}$ penalises over-speaking; $\beta_{\text{new}}^{(t)}$, $\beta_{\text{quiet}}^{(t)}$ bonus never-spoken and recently-quiet agents. The highest-urgency agent speaks next, subject to stochastic perturbation (p=0.2). Full component specifications are in the Appendix section A.

Subtopic Tracker. Without explicit topic management, generated conversations tend to either circle on a single point or jump unpredictably, reducing both the depth and coverage of the resulting data. To prevent this, the tracker monitors coverage via sentence-transformer cosine similarity (keyword-overlap fallback), progressing subtopics through UNEXPLORED → TOUCHED → EXPLORED → EXHAUSTED based on cumulative turn counts. A depth score tracks argument quality per subtopic (evidence, counterpoints, proposals). Outputs: pivot recommendations to the facilitator, reserve knowledge routing, and the weighted coverage ratio for termination (Sect. 3.4).

Facilitator. The facilitator serves as a *meta-controller with observable interventions*: it delivers guidance as visible conversational turns (not hidden prompt injections), allowing participants to react naturally. It selects from six types (REDIRECT, INVITE, CHALLENGE, CLARIFY, SUMMARIZE, CLOSE) based on recent turns and subtopic coverage.

Because the facilitator operates at the meta-level rather than as a substantive discussant, its turns are *excluded from downstream evaluation* (naturalness, stance tracking, argument quality) to avoid metric distortion. This is empirically supported by the homogeneity analysis (Sect. 4.4), where the facilitator exhibits the lowest BERTScore similarity to any participant, confirming its structurally distinct role. Full transcripts including facilitator turns are recoverable via metadata flags (`is_facilitator=true`). When the facilitator is ablated, the Decision Router suppresses redirects and saturation triggers immediate termination.

3.4 Quality Assurance and Termination

Judge System. Three judges evaluate quality continuously: *Speech Judge* (naturalness), *Progress Judge* (embedding-based[1] novelty and repetition detection),

[1] `all-MiniLM-L6-v2` [26]; https://huggingface.co/sentence-transformers/all-MiniLM-L6-v2.

and *Dynamics Judge* (speaker balance, conflict–agreement patterns). All use the orchestrator for LLM-based scoring. The circular evaluation concern is addressed in Sect. 4 via the cross-model judge experiment described in Sect. 3.

Decision Router. Judge signals feed a Decision Router with fixed priority: safety > turn limits > naturalness > progress > dynamics, producing CONTINUE, INJECT_KNOWLEDGE, REDIRECT, or TERMINATE. Response validation enforces semantic repetition checks and facilitator-compliance verification with up to three retries.

Saturation and Termination. ARENA concludes when subtopic coverage peaks, novelty plateaus, or exhaustion is detected. Each session is tagged with a termination reason (SATURATION, CONSENSUS, MAX_TURNS) for downstream analysis. All architecture hyperparameters, their empirical provenance, and sensitivity analysis under ±20% perturbation are consolidated in Appendix section B.

4 Evaluation

We evaluate ARENA at three levels of increasing external validity: (i) intrinsic conversation quality, assessing whether the cognitive architecture improves generated output; (ii) controlled ablation, isolating the contribution of selected modules; and (iii) downstream task transfer, testing whether structural properties of the data are learnable by external models [24]. This progression ensures that observed quality gains are not artifacts of the generation process but reflect properties transferable to independent tasks.

4.1 Dataset Generation

To generate a diverse conversation corpus, we adopt the industry category system from BAAI/IndustryCorpus2 [22], which defines 30 domain categories spanning programming, biomedicine, and 28 other sectors. For each category, we design 5 discussion topics using the meta-agent's topic generation pipeline, yielding 150 seed topics. Each topic produces one full ARENA conversation with $N = 4$ participants and a target range of 20–50 turns. For the experiments reported in this article, we generate 1,100 conversations in 11 domains, selected to maximize topical diversity in the category taxonomy.

For evaluation, we construct two subsets: (i) a *judge subset* of 110 conversations (sampled to ensure balanced domain coverage) were used for LLM-as-judge scoring, human annotation, and a controlled comparison with CAMEL [12] using identical world configurations; and (ii) an *ablation set* of 600 conversations (5 domains × 4 conditions × 30 repeats) with a shared world configuration per domain to isolate the contribution of individual modules (Sect. 4.3).

4.2 Conversation Quality Evaluation

We assess ARENA-generated conversations using GPT-4o as an LLM judge and three independent human annotators, both scoring on an identical four-dimension rubric (1–5 scale): *Naturalness*, *Argumentation Quality*, *Persona Consistency*, and *Interaction Dynamics*. Full protocol details, prompts, and annotation guidelines are provided in Appendix section D.

Results. Figure 2 reports LLM and human scores. Both protocols agree on dimension ranking: *Argumentation Quality* and *Persona Consistency* receive the highest scores while *Naturalness* is consistently weakest. This convergence validates that ARENA's cognitive architecture produces substantive, identity-consistent debates. The uniformly moderate Naturalness scores (GPT-4o: 3.91; human mean: 3.37) reflect a known limitation of instruction-tuned models: generated turns are overly polished and lack the hesitations of spontaneous speech.

Human–LLM Alignment. GPT-4o shows upward bias on *Naturalness* (+0.54) and *Persona Consistency* (+0.62), while bias on *Argumentation Quality* and *Interaction Dynamics* is small (+0.09 and +0.11; MAE 0.37 and 0.25). All three human annotators and GPT-4o converge on the same dimension ranking (Persona > Argumentation > Dynamics > Naturalness), and annotator pairs agree within ±1 point on 84–100% of conversations across all four dimensions, confirming reliable quality signals despite the inherent subjectivity of holistic dialogue assessment [4]. Full agreement analysis is in Appendix section D.4.

Comparison with CAMEL. We compare against CAMEL [12] using the same 110 world configurations, adapted to its native two-agent setting, and scored by the identical GPT-4o pipeline. ARENA outperforms CAMEL across all dimensions (Fig. 3), with the largest gaps in Naturalness ($\Delta = 1.30$) and Interaction Dynamics ($\Delta = 1.31$), and markedly lower variance (std: 0.09–0.42 vs. 0.56–0.80). Qualitative inspection reveals two structural failure modes in CAMEL: (i) *repetitive argumentation loops* caused by a 20-message context window that drops earlier history, and (ii) *dyadic constraint* preventing the coalition and conflict dynamics of multi-party discussion. Conversation samples are in Appendix section H.

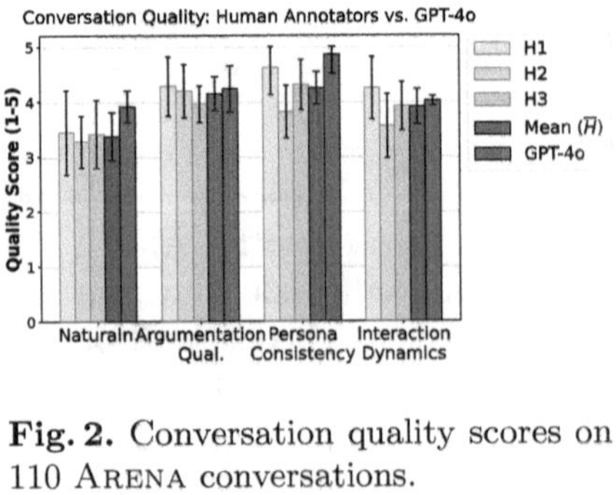

Fig. 2. Conversation quality scores on 110 ARENA conversations.

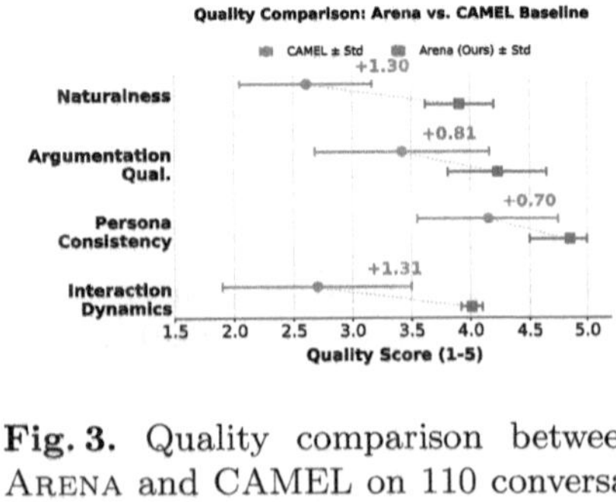

Fig. 3. Quality comparison between ARENA and CAMEL on 110 conversations.

4.3 Ablation Study

We evaluate each architectural subsystem by comparing four conditions across five randomly sampled domains ($N = 592$ conversations total; see Appendix I for full protocol, metric definitions, and per-domain breakdowns): **Full, No Cognition, No Facilitator**, and **Baseline** (single-model, no cognitive modules, no judges). The headline Overall score is the geometric mean of Content, (1 − RepRate), Engagement, and Naturalness, rewarding balanced quality across dimensions. Figure 4 reports headline metrics and Table 2 pairwise effect sizes.

Cognitive Modules are the Primary Quality Driver. Removing cognitive modules produces the largest degradation among non-baseline conditions ($d = 1.51$ overall), consistent across all five domains (per-domain d: 1.67–2.26). The effect concentrates in engagement ($d = 1.62$) and naturalness ($d = 0.85$);

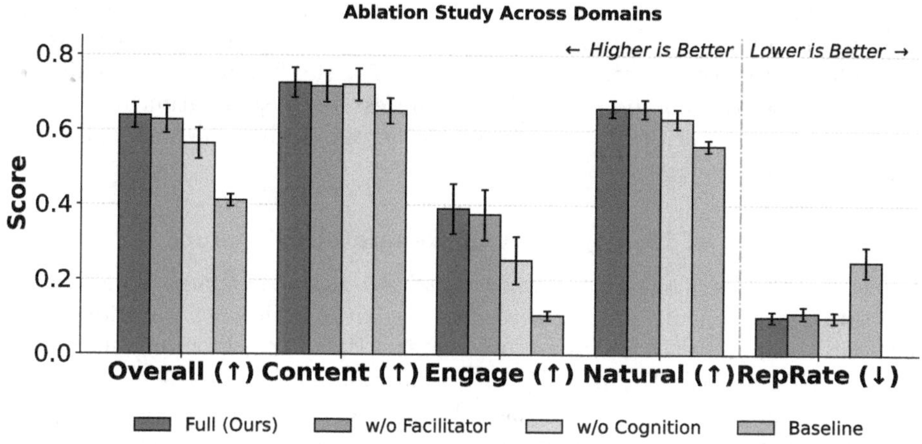

Fig. 4. Ablation results pooled across 5 domains (mean ± std). The full ARENA model consistently outperforms the ablated variants. Note that for RepRate (Repetition Rate), a lower score indicates better performance (fewer repetitions), whereas all other metrics represent higher-is-better.

Table 2. Effect sizes (Full vs. each condition), pooled across 5 domains. Δ: mean difference; d: Cohen's d. *: Wilcoxon $p < 0.05$.

Metric	vs. No Cognition			vs. No Facilitator			vs. Baseline		
	Δ	d		Δ	d		Δ	d	
Overall	+.073	+1.51	*	+.011	+0.27	*	+.226	+5.81	*
Content	+.003	+0.06		+.010	+0.21	*	+.076	+1.66	*
RepRate	+.000	+0.01		−.011	-0.51	*	−.147	-3.29	*
Engage	+.135	+1.62	*	+.016	+0.19	*	+.283	+4.09	*
Natural	+.028	+0.85	*	+.001	+0.04		+.100	+3.25	*

content is unaffected ($d = 0.06$). Cognitive modules do not generate content—they enable agents to engage with *specific people about specific claims.* Without them, agents produce topically relevant but interpersonally generic turns: they talk *about* the topic rather than *to* each other. We note that the Engagement metric partly captures behaviours cognitive modules are designed to produce (targeted addressing, substantive references); the effect size should be read as confirming intended function rather than as an independent quality signal.

The Facilitator Acts as a Conversation-Level Controller. Removing the facilitator has no significant effect on naturalness ($d = 0.04$) but reliably increases repetition ($d = -0.51$) and extends conversations from 21.1 to 24.2 mean turns. Without it, conversations stagnate or hit the turn limit rather than reaching natural closure. Its value is structural—guiding termination—not per-turn quality enhancement.

Architecture Collectively Prevents LLM Degeneration. Against the bare baseline, all metrics show very large effects (overall $d = 5.81$; engagement $d = 4.09$; naturalness $d = 3.25$; repetition $d = -3.29$). Baseline conversations accumulate a repetition rate of 0.248, nearly $2.5\times$ the full system's, confirming that the framework components jointly suppress the degeneration inherent in unconstrained generation. Effects are stable across all five domains, ruling out domain-specific artefacts.

4.4 Evaluation of Homogeneity of Generated Dialogues

We evaluate diversity along two axes: *intrinsic homogeneity* (persona distinctiveness within a dialogue) and *extrinsic homogeneity* (structural variation across dialogues), using BLEU for lexical overlap and BERTScore for semantic alignment (Fig. 5). Intrinsically, mean BLEU scores remain low across all speaker pairs (e.g., S1 vs. S2: 0.069 ± 0.028) while BERTScore values are consistently high, indicating that agents use differentiated surface forms while preserving topical coherence—a desirable property. Scores also reflect role structure: the supporting speaker (S3) is most similar to the anchor, opposing and neutral speakers are marginally lower, and the facilitator is consistently least similar, consistent with its meta-conversational role. Extrinsically, low BERTScore across dialogues (0.213 ± 0.071) and modest BLEU (0.090 ± 0.030) confirm that conversations are strongly conditioned on their topics rather than produced from fixed templates. Together, these results show that Arena generates diverse, role-differentiated dialogues without sacrificing semantic coherence.

4.5 Downstream Validation

We assess Arena's practical utility by fine-tuning small language models on Arena-generated data and evaluating on established real-world benchmarks. Three complementary tasks are selected: *topic classification* (domain-level semantics), *speaker-aware meeting summarization* (multi-party interaction structure), and *argument mining* (argumentation dynamics). All fine-tuning protocols and hyperparameters are detailed in Appendix section J.

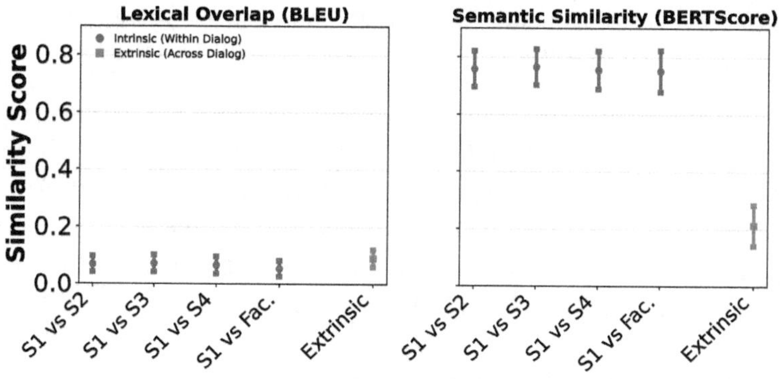

Fig. 5. Homogeneity analysis of generated dialogues. Left: Lexical overlap (BLEU) shows minimal lexical repetition across all pairs and extrinsic baselines. Right: Semantic similarity (BERTScore) demonstrates strong semantic alignment within dialogues (intrinsic) compared to the low similarity across different topics (extrinsic).

Table 3. Transfer performance on *IndustryCorpus* before and after fine-tuning on ARENA. ΔF1 denotes the absolute improvement.

Model	Before FT			After FT			
	Prec.	Rec.	F1	Prec.	Rec.	F1	Δ F1
Bert-Base-Uncased	0.0164	0.1000	0.0258	0.6563	0.5909	0.5709	+0.5451
Qwen2-0.5B-Instruct	0.1429	0.1000	0.0723	0.2516	0.2091	0.1891	+0.1168
Llama-3.2-1B-Instruct	0.0304	0.0636	0.0402	**0.6637**	**0.6273**	**0.6199**	+0.5797
gemma-2-2B-it	0.0384	0.0818	0.0391	0.5827	0.5909	0.5649	+0.5258

Topic Classification. We frame topic classification as an 11-way task across diverse professional domains (e.g., *Aerospace, Finance, Biomedicine*). Models are fine-tuned on synthetic ARENA dialogues and evaluated on a balanced subset of *BAAI/IndustryCorpus2* [22] (100 samples per class), introducing a deliberate distribution shift: conversational data → news reports and technical documents. Table 3 shows that all models gain substantially from ARENA fine-tuning, with `Llama-3.2-1B-Instruct` reaching a transfer F1 of 0.6199 (ΔF1 = +0.58). In-domain evaluation further confirms that ARENA labels are consistent and learnable, with best F1 scores exceeding 0.93 (see Appendix section K).

Speaker-Aware Conversation Summarization. We evaluate on QMSum [28] (281 test pairs from real meetings with speaker-specific queries). For training, we generate ~8,800 query-summary pairs from 1,100 ARENA conversations using Qwen2.5-72B, targeting five aspects of multi-party interaction. Cognitive metadata guides generation but is discarded from training pairs. Quality control details and query templates are in Appendix section J.1.

Table 4. Query-focused summarization on QMSum test set (scores ×100). Best synthetic result per model in **bold**. A-M: size-matched subset (1,257 pairs).

Model	Zero-shot			ARENA FT			A-M FT			QMSum FT		
	R-1	R-L	BS	R-1	R-L	BS	R-1	R-L	BS	R-1	R-L	BS
Llama-3.2-1B	26.2	17.1	85.0	30.4	19.4	86.3	**31.1**	**20.0**	**86.5**	30.5	21.9	86.5
Gemma-2-2B	26.2	16.9	84.5	**30.7**	**19.7**	86.5	30.0	19.3	**86.6**	31.2	22.2	86.7
Qwen2.5-3B	28.9	17.7	85.5	30.7	19.3	**86.6**	**30.7**	**19.6**	86.5	31.1	21.8	86.9
Llama-3.2-3B	28.1	17.6	85.4	31.7	20.1	86.6	**31.8**	**20.1**	**86.6**	31.7	22.5	86.5

Table 5. Argument Relation Identification performance before and after fine-tuning. ΔF1 denotes the absolute gain in macro-averaged F1-score.

Model	Before FT			After FT			
	Prec.	Rec.	F1	Prec.	Rec.	F1	**ΔF1**
Qwen2-0.5B-Instruct	0.1413	0.3663	0.2039	0.5616	0.5966	0.5786	+0.3747
Llama-3.2-1B-Instruct	0.2524	0.2867	0.2685	0.5321	0.5854	0.5575	+0.2890
Gemma-2-2B-it	0.2556	0.3075	0.2792	0.5113	0.5513	0.5305	+0.2513

Table 4 compares four conditions: zero-shot, full ARENA FT (8,800 pairs), size-matched ARENA-M FT (1,257 pairs), and in-domain QMSum FT (1,257 pairs). Three key findings emerge: (i) ARENA fine-tuning improves ROUGE-L by +1.6 to +2.9 points over zero-shot, closing 39–60% of the gap to in-domain training; (ii) the size-matched subset performs comparably to the full set (3/4 models achieve equal or higher ROUGE-L), isolating structural dialogue quality over data volume as the operative factor; and (iii) on BERTScore F1, ARENA-trained models essentially match QMSum-trained ones (86.5 vs. 86.7), with the remaining ROUGE gap attributable to domain-specific vocabulary rather than interaction understanding deficits.

Argument Relation Identification. Argument Relation Identification (ARI) classifies relations between argument units as Inference, Conflict, or Neutral. We construct a dataset of 14,551 samples from ARENA's cognitive annotations, deriving labels from speaker stance toward discussion topics (details in Appendix section L). Table 5 shows that all models exhibit substantial gains after fine-tuning, with macro-F1 improvements of +0.25 to +0.37. `Qwen2-0.5B-Instruct` achieves the highest post-FT F1 of 0.5786, confirming ARENA's utility as a source of structured argumentative training data.

5 Conclusion

We presented ARENA, a cognitive multi-agent framework that equips LLM-based agents with Theory of Mind, strategic argumentation, and position tracking to generate realistic multi-party conversations. Evaluation across 592 ablation conversations, downstream task transfer, and controlled comparison with CAMEL confirms that the cognitive architecture is the primary driver of conversation quality, with the largest gains in naturalness and interaction dynamics. Fine-tuning on ARENA-generated data closes 39–60% of the gap to in-domain training on meeting summarization. The anonymized review subset is provided, and the framework code and full data will be released upon acceptance. Future work includes multilingual extension, retrieval-augmented knowledge grounding, and richer stance transition modeling.

6 Limitations

Factual grounding relies on parametric memory rather than external verification, risking hallucinated evidence; evaluating modular knowledge injection remains future work. **Generation constraints** restrict ARENA to a controlled professional register, lacking the colloquialisms, humor, and spontaneity of natural speech. **Experimental scope** excludes an exhaustive evaluation of all model families, though we identify Qwen2.5-72B and Qwen3-8B as an optimal pairing. **Multilingual extensions** requiring culturally adapted personas are left for future research, as ARENA is currently English-only. **Stance dynamics** capture changes in conviction strength during concessions but omit categorical label updates, limiting observed trajectory granularity. Generated conversations may contain fabricated factual claims, and users should not treat them as factually verified.

Acknowledgments. Part of this work was performed using computing resources of CRIANN (Centre Régional Informatique et d'Applications Numériques de Normandie, France). We thank Dr. Xiaofan Lu for valuable discussions.

GenAI Usage Statement. We acknowledge the use of Claude and ChatGPT for code refactoring and polishing to ensure the reproducibility and readability of our implementation. All core algorithms and experimental designs were conceptualized and developed by the authors, who retain full accountability for the final code.

References

1. Gu, J.C., et al.: MPC-BERT: a pre-trained language model for multi-party conversation understanding. In: Proceedings of ACL-IJCNLP, pp. 3682–3692 (2021). https://aclanthology.org/2021.acl-long.285/
2. Guida, M., et al.: LLMs for argument mining: detection, extraction, and relationship classification. In: Proceedings of ALTA (2025). https://aclanthology.org/2025.alta-main.12/
3. Hadoux, E., Hunter, A., Polberg, S.: Strategic argumentation dialogues for persuasion: framework and experiments based on modelling the beliefs and concerns of the persuadee. Argument Comput. **14**(2), 109–161 (2023). https://doi.org/10.3233/AAC-210005

4. Howcroft, D.M.: Twenty years of confusion in human evaluation: NLG needs evaluation sheets and standardised definitions. In: Proceedings INLG, pp. 169–182 (2020)
5. Hu, Y.: MeetingBank: a benchmark dataset for meeting summarization. In: Proceedings of ACL, pp. 16409–16423 (2023)
6. Keizer, S., et al.: Evaluating persuasion strategies and deep reinforcement learning methods for negotiation dialogue agents. In: Proceedings of EACL, pp. 480–484 (2017). https://aclanthology.org/E17-2077/
7. Kim, H., et al.: SODA: million-scale dialogue distillation with social commonsense contextualization. In: Proceedings of EMNLP. pp. 12930–12949 (2023). https://aclanthology.org/2023.emnlp-main.799/
8. Kosinski, M.: Theory of mind may have spontaneously emerged in large language models. ArXiv abs/2302.02083 (2023)
9. Kwon, D., et al.: Are LLMs effective negotiators? Systematic evaluation of the multifaceted capabilities of LLMs in negotiation dialogues. In: Findings of EMNLP, pp. 5391–5413 (2024). https://aclanthology.org/2024.findings-emnlp.310/
10. Lawrence, J., Reed, C.: Argument mining: a survey. Comput. Linguist. **45**(4), 765–818 (2019). https://aclanthology.org/J19-4006/
11. Le, R., et al.: Who is speaking to whom? Learning to identify utterance addressee in multi-party conversations. In: Proceedings of EMNLP-IJCNLP, pp. 1909–1919 (2019). https://aclanthology.org/D19-1199/
12. Li, G., et al.: CAMEL: communicative agents for "mind" exploration of large language model society. In: Proceedings of NeurIPS, NIPS 2023. Curran Associates Inc., Red Hook (2023)
13. Li, H., et al.: Theory of mind for multi-agent collaboration via large language models. In: Proceedings of EMNLP, pp. 180–192 (2023). https://aclanthology.org/2023.emnlp-main.13/
14. Li, J., Durmus, E., Cardie, C.: Exploring the role of argument structure in online debate persuasion. In: Proceedings of EMNLP, pp. 8905–8912 (2020)
15. Ma, J., et al.: Chain of stance: stance detection with large language models. In: Proceedings of NLPCC, p. 82–94 (2024)
16. Park, J.: Social simulacra: creating populated prototypes for social computing systems. In: Proceedings of UIST (2022)
17. Park, J., et al.: Generative agents: interactive simulacra of human behavior. In: Proceedings of UIST (2023). https://doi.org/10.1145/3586183.3606763
18. Penzo, N., et al.: Don't stop the multi-party! On generating synthetic multi-party conversations with constraints (2025). https://arxiv.org/abs/2502.13592
19. Sapkota, S., et al.: Multi-party conversational agents: a survey (2025). https://arxiv.org/abs/2505.18845
20. Sclar, M., et al.: Minding language models' (lack of) theory of mind: a plug-and-play multi-character belief tracker. In: Proceedings of ACL, pp. 13960–13980 (2023). https://aclanthology.org/2023.acl-long.780/
21. Shapira, N.: Clever hans or neural theory of mind? Stress testing social reasoning in large language models. In: Proceedings of EACL, pp. 2257–2273 (2024)
22. Shi, X., et al.: Industrycorpus2 (2024). https://doi.org/10.57967/hf/3488
23. Strachan, J.W.A., et al.: Testing theory of mind in large language models and humans. Nat. Hum. Behav. **8**, 1285–1295 (2024)
24. Suresh, S.K.: DiaSynth: synthetic dialogue generation framework for low resource dialogue applications. In: Findings of the Association for Computational Linguistics: NAACL 2025, pp. 673–690 (2025)

25. Ullman, T.: Large language models fail on trivial alterations to theory-of-mind tasks (2023). https://arxiv.org/abs/2302.08399
26. Wang, W., et al.: MiniLMv2: multi-head self-attention relation distillation for compressing pretrained transformers. In: Findings of ACL-IJCNLP, pp. 2140–2151 (2021). https://aclanthology.org/2021.findings-acl.188/
27. Wang, X., et al.: Multi-party supervised fine-tuning of language models for multi-party dialogue generation (2024). https://arxiv.org/abs/2412.05342
28. Zhong, M.: QMSum: a new benchmark for query-based multi-domain meeting summarization. In: Proceedings of NAACL, pp. 5905–5921 (2021)

ASDA: Automated Skill Distillation and Adaptation for Financial Reasoning

Tik Yu Yim(✉), Wenting Tan, Sum Yee Chan, Tak-Wah Lam, and Siu Ming Yiu

The University of Hong Kong, Pokfulam, Hong Kong SAR, China
{tyyim,wt212796}@connect.hku.hk, sumychan@hku.hk, {twlam,smyiu}@cs.hku.hk

Abstract. Adapting large language models (LLMs) to specialized financial reasoning typically requires expensive fine-tuning that produces model-locked expertise. Training-free alternatives have emerged, yet our experiments show that leading methods (GEPA and ACE) achieve only marginal gains on the FAMMA financial reasoning benchmark, exposing the limits of unstructured text optimization for complex, multi-step domain reasoning. We introduce Automated Skill Distillation and Adaptation (ASDA), a framework that automatically generates structured skill artifacts through iterative error-corrective learning without modifying model weights. A teacher model analyzes a student model's failures on financial reasoning tasks, clusters errors by subfield and error type, and synthesizes skill files containing reasoning procedures, code templates, and worked examples, which are dynamically injected during inference. Evaluated on FAMMA, ASDA achieves up to +17.33 pp improvement on arithmetic reasoning and +5.95 pp on non-arithmetic reasoning, substantially outperforming all training-free baselines. The resulting skill artifacts are human-readable, version-controlled, and compatible with the Agent Skills open standard, offering any organization with a labeled domain dataset a practical and auditable path to domain adaptation without weight access or retraining (Code and skill libraries are available at https://github.com/SallyTan13/ASDA-skill).

Keywords: LLM Adaptation · Financial Reasoning · Skill Distillation · Training-Free Adaptation · Agent Skills

1 Introduction

Financial reasoning poses a distinctive challenge for general-purpose LLMs: it demands simultaneous mastery of multi-step quantitative calculation and deep domain-specific judgment—a combination that pure math or pure knowledge benchmarks do not jointly test [15,16]. Evaluations across multiple financial benchmarks confirm a persistent performance ceiling: FAMMA reveals that standard, non-reasoning frontier models achieve only 38–45% overall accuracy across

M. Baratchi et al. (Eds.): ECML PKDD 2026, LNAI 16949, pp. 306–323, 2027.
https://doi.org/10.1007/978-3-032-37682-4_18

eight financial subfields [16][1]; and FinBen finds that while LLMs handle information extraction well, they consistently struggle with advanced reasoning and complex financial QA [15]. FAMMA's error analysis finds that *domain-knowledge gaps* dominate model errors [16]—models misapply financial concepts to the wrong context or lack the expertise to select the correct procedure. These are not failures that more parameters alone will fix—they require targeted advances in domain reasoning. The standard remedy—domain-specific fine-tuning—is costly, produces *model-locked expertise* that becomes obsolete with each model release, and depends on supervision resources that many organizations lack [13,17]. This is especially problematic in regulated industries such as financial services, legal, and healthcare, where organizations deploy commercial LLMs via black-box API without weight access. Automated prompt optimization offers a training-free alternative, but methods like GEPA [1] and ACE [19] optimize *flat text strings* that cannot capture the structured, multi-step procedural knowledge financial reasoning demands—a limitation our FAMMA experiments confirm, where both methods achieve only marginal gains (Sect. 5). The missing abstraction is not a better prompt, but an *executable skill*: a modular, self-contained reasoning procedure that can be independently composed, tested, and updated for each target domain.

We introduce **Automated Skill Distillation and Adaptation (ASDA)**, a framework that automatically generates executable agent skills from error analysis without modifying model weights. A teacher model diagnoses a student's failures on financial tasks and clusters them by subfield and error type to identify the root causes of *domain-knowledge gaps*. From these clusters, it synthesizes skill files containing domain-specific reasoning procedures and code templates, which a selector injects at inference time. Evaluated on FAMMA, ASDA achieves up to **+17.33 pp on arithmetic** and **+5.95 pp on non-arithmetic reasoning** after iterative refinement, significantly outperforming all training-free baselines. The resulting skill library is not a better prompt—it is a new representational layer between the model and its deployment context that can be version-controlled, audited, and regenerated for any successor model.

Our contributions are as follows:

(1) ASDA framework. We introduce the first system to automatically generate executable agent skills for domain-specific reasoning using only black-box LLM access—no weight updates or gradient computation—substantially outperforming all training-free baselines on FAMMA.

(2) Self-sufficient adaptation from questions and answers alone. A self-teaching ablation shows that ASDA can improve a model using only the questions and ground-truth answers in the training set—no superior teacher model required—achieving +6.33 pp (73% of the full gain). This means any organization with a labeled domain dataset can run ASDA on their deployed

[1] Extended-thinking models (GPT-o1, DeepSeek-R1, Qwen-QwQ-32B) score 67–76% on FAMMA, and PoT-augmented variants reach 78–86%. We exclude these as thinking budget introduces a confound orthogonal to domain adaptation; our evaluation targets standard non-reasoning models under fixed inference budgets.

model directly, without access to a stronger or more expensive model, making the framework practical for real-world enterprise deployment.

2 Related Work

2.1 Financial LLM Adaptation

Domain-specific fine-tuning has been the dominant approach to adapting LLMs for financial tasks. BloombergGPT [13] demonstrated the potential of finance-specific pretraining but required approximately 1.3 million GPU hours on a proprietary 363B-token corpus—resources beyond most organizations. FinGPT [17] offered a more accessible alternative through LoRA-based fine-tuning on open financial data. More recently, Xue et al. [16] explored distillation from DeepSeek-R1 to smaller models for financial reasoning. Despite these advances, all fine-tuning approaches share a fundamental limitation: they produce model-locked expertise that requires re-training when the base model is updated or replaced, and many are incompatible with black-box API access to commercial LLMs.

2.2 Training-Free Adaptation

Automated prompt optimization offers a weight-free alternative. Prior work formalizes this as automatic differentiation over text [18] or optimizable module compositions [6]. GEPA [1] achieves state-of-the-art results on several benchmarks through reflective prompt evolution. ACE [19] takes a test-time knowledge accumulation approach, building contextual expertise during inference. While these methods avoid fine-tuning costs, their output remains a flat text string—a monolithic instruction block applied uniformly to all questions—that cannot represent distinct reasoning procedures for different financial subdomains or error types.

A complementary line of work treats failure analysis as the primary learning signal. LEMMA [11] synthesizes error-type-grounded training data for mathematical reasoning and consistently outperforms correction-agnostic data augmentation baselines. This establishes that failure-driven analysis yields richer adaptation signal—a principle ASDA extends to training-free, executable skill generation. At the other end of the adaptation spectrum, test-time training (TTT) methods temporarily update model weights at inference, requiring gradient access incompatible with black-box API deployments; ASDA occupies the gap between these approaches.

2.3 Skill-Based Agent Architectures

Recent agent work has established skills as reusable, first-class knowledge artifacts. Voyager [12] demonstrated that composable executable skills—stored as JavaScript code—enable continual capability growth in open-ended Minecraft environments without parameter updates. The Agent Skills open standard [3] formalized portable Markdown skill files with routing metadata, progressive disclosure, and embedded code templates; ASDA generates skill artifacts compatible with this standard.

Recent benchmarking work quantifies when skills help or hurt. SkillsBench [7] finds that curated skills raise average pass rate by +16.2 *pp* across 11 domains, while self-generated skills provide no benefit on average—models cannot reliably author the procedural knowledge they benefit from consuming. SWE-Skills-Bench [5] reports that 39 of 49 public SWE skills produce no measurable improvement (average gain: +1.2%), with three actively degrading performance due to context-mismatched guidance. Together, these results establish that skill–task alignment is a precondition for benefit—the gap ASDA's error-driven distillation addresses by generating skills calibrated to a specific model's failure distribution on a target domain.

Several concurrent systems also explore automated skill generation from failure signals. EvoSkill [2] iteratively diagnoses execution failures in coding agents, using ground-truth-supervised feedback in an online interactive loop to propose and validate new skill folders. Trace2Skill [10] collects execution logs across many tasks and analyzes them in parallel to extract recurring patterns into reusable skills, reporting strong cross-model and out-of-distribution transfer. SkillRL [14] co-evolves skills with a reinforcement learning policy, requiring SFT and weight updates. Each of these systems depends on execution traces, trajectory logs, or gradient access. ASDA requires none of these: it distills skills from static question–answer pairs alone, introduces a dual-phase refinement that explicitly balances coverage gains against regression risk, and operates entirely through black-box API access. To our knowledge, no prior work generates executable skills for domain-specific reasoning in a fully training-free setting from static question–answer pairs alone.

3 Method: ASDA Framework

ASDA follows a teacher–student architecture with two main phases: (1) a *warm-up* that establishes an initial skill library from systematic failure analysis, and (2) an *iterative refinement* loop that automatically refines the skill library through repeated evidence collection, skill revision, and validation. Figure 1 provides an overview of the full framework.

Before describing each phase, we introduce three terms used throughout the paper. An **error type** is one of ten categories from a predefined taxonomy.[2] A **pattern** is a single, named failure scenario within a skill file, one specific knowledge gap or recurring mistake the model makes. A **skill file** groups all patterns that share the same financial subfield and error type; for example,

[2] Error types are: visual evidence, wrong method selection, concept confusion, missed multi-step computation, unit/currency mistakes, missed constraints, wrong targets, wrong output format, code execution errors (PoT-specific), and other. The taxonomy was generated by prompting an LLM to categorize recurring failure patterns from the student's errors on the training set, then refined through author review.

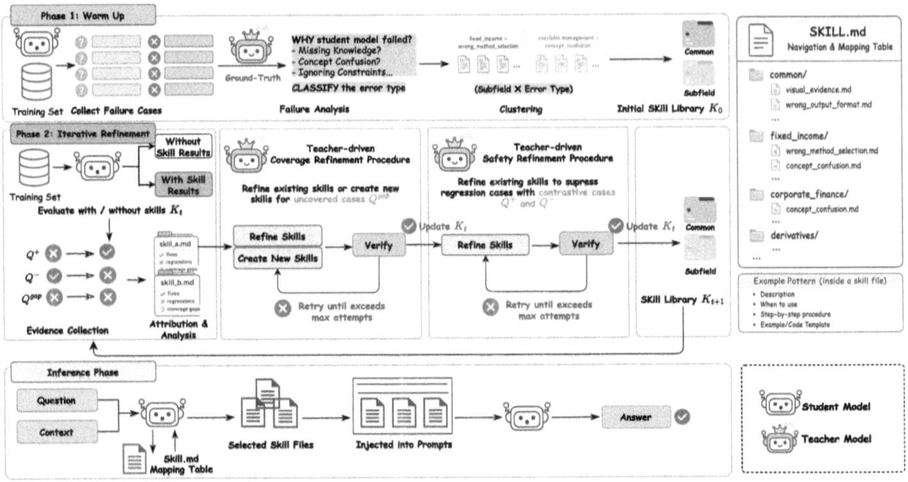

Fig. 1. Overview of the ASDA framework. **Phase 1 (warm-up):** the teacher model analyzes student failures, producing structured annotations that are clustered by subfield and error type to synthesize an initial skill library $\mathcal{K}_0$. **Phase 2 (iterative refinement):** the library is refined through three sequential procedures, evidence collection and attribution procedure, coverage refinement procedure (resolving uncovered failures in Q^{gap}) followed by safety refinement procedure (suppressing regressions in Q^-), with every skill update gated by a correctness threshold. **Inference Phase:** a selector reads `SKILL.md` and injects the relevant skill files into the student's prompt.

`fixed_income/wrong_method_selection.md` collects all wrong-method failures observed in the fixed income subfield.

3.1 Warm-Up

Failure Analysis and Structured Annotation. The warm-up phase constructs an initial skill library $\mathcal{K}_0$ from the student model's failures on the training set. For each question the student answers incorrectly, the teacher model receives the question, the student's incorrect answer and reasoning trace, and the ground-truth answer. The teacher is then prompted to perform failure analysis and output a structured annotation in the following format:

```
{
  "subfield":   "fixed_income",
  "error_type": "wrong method selection",
  "root_cause": "Lacks knowledge that forward rates must be composed
  sequentially as discount factors, not applied independently per
      period"
}
```

The `error_type` field is constrained to the taxonomy defined above. The `root_cause` field captures the underlying knowledge gap rather than a surface description of what was computed incorrectly, ensuring the diagnosis is actionable for skill synthesis.

Skill Library Organization. The annotated failures are clustered by their (subfield, error_type) pair. Each cluster becomes one skill file. The library is therefore organized as a two-level hierarchy:

```
SKILL.md                          % navigation + mapping table
common/
  visual_evidence.md              % cross-subfield patterns
  wrong_output_format.md
fixed_income/
  wrong_method_selection.md       % one file per subfield x error type
  concept_confusion.md
corporate_finance/
  concept_confusion.md
derivatives/
  ...
```

Within each skill file, the teacher synthesizes one *pattern* per distinct failure scenario identified in the cluster. Each pattern contains: a concise description of the addressed knowledge gap, explicit "when to use" conditions, step-by-step reasoning procedures, and worked examples or code templates. Figure 2 shows one pattern from `fixed_income/wrong_method_selection.md`; the full file contains five additional patterns covering other recurring failure scenarios in that subfield.

The library also includes a top-level `SKILL.md` navigation file that summarizes the scope of each skill and provides a structured mapping from subfield keywords and failed financial patterns to skill file paths. This navigation file allows the downstream selector to identify relevant skills without parsing every skill file in full.

Skill Selection and Injection. At inference time, an LLM-based selector[3] reads the question text and the `SKILL.md` mapping table to identify the relevant financial subfield and match the question's characteristics against the listed patterns. The selector may choose multiple skill files for a single question, since complex financial reasoning often requires combining guidance from several patterns (e.g., a fixed income pricing question may need both `wrong_method_selection.md` and `common/missed_constraints.md`). Selected skill files are injected into the student's prompt as domain knowledge, guiding it to follow the appropriate reasoning procedure for the question.

[3] In our experiments, we instantiate the selector using the same model as the student model. The selector is modular, and can be replaced by other LLMs.

fixed_income/wrong_method_selection.md

Sequential Discounting with Forward Rates for Coupon Bonds

When pricing coupon bonds using forward rates, each cash flow must be discounted by the cumulative product of (1 + forward_rate) for all periods from today to that cash flow's date, not by a single rate or simple average.

When to Use

Questions asking for bond price given a table/list of forward rates (labeled "Year 0 (today)", "Year 1", etc.) and bond characteristics (coupon rate, maturity, par value).

Procedure

1. Price = $\Sigma[CF_t / \Pi(1 + f_i)]$ for i=0 to $t-1$, where CF_t is cash flow at time t and f_i is forward rate for period i
2. Extract all forward rates from the given table in chronological order (f_0, f_1, f_2, ...)
3. For each cash flow date t, compute cumulative discount factor: $DF_t = (1+f_0)(1+f_1)...(1+f_{t-1})$
4. Divide each cash flow by its corresponding cumulative discount factor and sum all present values
5. Return the final sum as the bond price (expression, not print)

Correct Code

Scenario: 3-year bond, 7% annual coupon, $1,000 par. Forward rates: Year 0=4%, Year 1=5%, Year 2=6%.

```
# Bond characteristics
par_value = 1000
coupon_rate = 0.07
maturity = 3
annual_coupon = par_value * coupon_rate
# Forward rates for each period
forward_rates = [0.04, 0.05, 0.06]
# Calculate price using sequential discounting
price = 0
cumulative_discount = 1.0
for year in range(1, maturity + 1):
    cumulative_discount *= (1 + forward_rates[year - 1])
    if year == maturity:
        cash_flow = annual_coupon + par_value
    else:
        cash_flow = annual_coupon
    price += cash_flow / cumulative_discount
price  # Result: approximately 1027.51
```

Common Bugs to Avoid

- ✗ Using forward rates directly as discount rates without cumulative multiplication
- ✗ Averaging forward rates instead of compounding them sequentially
- ✗ Forgetting to include par value in final year's cash flow
- ✗ Using `print(price)` instead of returning `price` as final expression
- ✗ Off-by-one errors in indexing forward rates (Year 0 rate applies to Year 1 cash flow)

Fig. 2. One pattern from an ASDA skill file produced during warm-up from Haiku 3.5 failure analysis by Sonnet 4.5. The full file contains five additional patterns.

3.2 Iterative Refinement

The warm-up phase captures the most systematic failure patterns but leaves two residual problems. The first is *coverage gaps*: some failures remain because existing skills do not yet address the required knowledge. The second is *regressions*: skill injection causes previously correct answers to become incorrect when a skill overfits a narrow failure pattern and misleads the model on related but distinct questions. To address these issues, each refinement iteration begins with an *evidence collection and attribution procedure*, which attributes skill-induced fixes, regressions, and unresolved gaps to individual skill files. The attributed evidence then drives two refinement procedures: a *coverage refinement procedure* for expanding skill coverage and a *safety refinement procedure* for suppressing regressions. In both procedures, every candidate skill update must pass through a *verification gate*. The student re-solves the target questions with the updated skill injected, and the update is committed only if accuracy meets a predefined threshold τ. If it fails, the teacher regenerates a revised proposal, repeating up to N_{max} attempts before falling back to the previous skill version. The full process is summarized in Algorithm 1.

Evidence Collection and Attribution. At the start of each refinement iteration t, every training question is evaluated under two conditions: once with the current skill library $\mathcal{K}_t$ injected, and once without any skills. We compare the paired outcomes to derive three disjoint groups: Q_t^+ (correct with skills but incorrect without skills), Q_t^- (incorrect with skills but correct without skills, i.e., regressions introduced by the current library), and Q_t^{gap} (incorrect under both conditions, i.e., coverage failures that the library has not yet resolved).

Since multiple skill files may be loaded for each question, a naïve per-question outcome cannot be attributed to a specific file. An *attribution* step follows: for each question in Q_t^+, Q_t^-, and Q_t^{gap}, the teacher examines the student's reasoning trace alongside the loaded files and identifies the single file most responsible for the outcome. Questions are then re-grouped by their attributed file, producing per-file evidence sets that isolate each file's individual contribution to fixes, regressions, and remaining coverage gaps.

Coverage Refinement Procedure. For each skill file, the teacher examines the Q_t^{gap} cases attributed to that file and diagnoses why coverage fails. Common causes include missing procedures for an edge case, trigger conditions that are too narrow to fire on relevant questions, or the absence of a worked example for a pattern the file does not yet contain. Based on this diagnosis, the teacher proposes an update, either by refining an existing pattern or by adding a new one. Each proposal is submitted to the verification gate: the student re-solves the attributed Q_t^{gap} cases with the candidate update injected, and the update is accepted only if the recovery rate exceeds τ_{cov}.

After all per-file coverage updates are committed, a post-coverage verification pass re-evaluates the entire affected set. Cases in Q_t^{gap} that are now solved are promoted into an updated positive set $\tilde{Q}_t^+$. Cases in Q_t^+ that regress under the modified skills are merged with the existing Q_t^- to form an updated regression set $\tilde{Q}_t^-$. This updated partition forms the input to the safety refinement procedure.

Safety Refinement Procedure. The safety refinement procedure resolves regressions in $\tilde{Q}_t^-$, including both pre-existing regressions and those newly introduced by the coverage refinement procedure, while preserving correct behavior on $\tilde{Q}_t^+$. For each skill file, the teacher receives both sets as contrastive evidence:

Algorithm 1. Iterative Refinement

Require: Skill library $\mathcal{K}_0$, training set $\mathcal{D}$, student M_s, teacher M_t, max iterations T
Ensure: Refined skill library $\mathcal{K}^*$

for $t = 1$ to T **do**
    // Evidence Collection and Attribution
    $Q^+, Q^-, Q^{\text{gap}} \leftarrow \textsc{EvalWithWithout}(\mathcal{D}, \mathcal{K}_t, M_s)$
    $\textsc{AttributeToFiles}(Q^+, Q^-, Q^{\text{gap}}, M_t)$

    // Coverage Refinement Procedure
    for each file f with attributed $Q_f^{\text{gap}} \neq \emptyset$ **do**
        $f' \leftarrow M_t.\textsc{ProposeExpansion}(f,\ Q_f^{\text{gap}})$
        if $\textsc{Verify}(f', Q_f^{\text{gap}}, M_s) \geq \tau_{\text{cov}}$ **then**
            $\mathcal{K}_t[f] \leftarrow f'$
        end if
    end for
    $\tilde{Q}^+, \tilde{Q}^- \leftarrow \textsc{PostCoverageVerify}(\mathcal{K}_t, Q^+, Q^{\text{gap}}, M_s)$

    // Safety Refinement Procedure
    for each file f with attributed $\tilde{Q}_f^- \neq \emptyset$ **do**
        $f' \leftarrow M_t.\textsc{ProposeRepair}(f,\ \tilde{Q}_f^+,\ \tilde{Q}_f^-)$
        if $\textsc{Verify}(f', \tilde{Q}_f^+, M_s) \geq \tau_{\text{safe}}$ **then**
            $\mathcal{K}_t[f] \leftarrow f'$
        end if
    end for
    $\mathcal{K}_{t+1} \leftarrow \mathcal{K}_t$
end for
return $\mathcal{K}_T$

the $\tilde{Q}_t^+$ cases, annotated with what the current skill gets right, serve as preservation constraints, whereas the $\tilde{Q}_t^-$ cases, annotated with what goes wrong, serve as repair targets. The teacher proposes a revised skill that removes or narrows the guidance responsible for the regressions while preserving the reasoning steps that produce correct answers on the positive set. Each proposal again passes through the verification gate with threshold τ_{safe}, which requires that accuracy on the positive cases remain above the allowed preservation threshold while improving performance on the negative cases.

After both refinement procedures complete, the updated library $\mathcal{K}_{t+1}$ becomes the input for the next iteration.

4 Experimental Setup

4.1 Benchmark: FAMMA

FAMMA-Basic [16] provides the scale, arithmetic/non-arithmetic decomposition, and self-contained textual context our pipeline requires.[4] It comprises 1,945

[4] We also considered FinMR [4], FinanceMath [20], FinanceQA [9], and FinMME [8], but these are either too small for reliable train–test splits, withhold ground-truth

questions sourced from university textbooks and professional finance exams, spanning eight financial subdomains (e.g., corporate finance, derivatives, portfolio management) across three difficulty levels. An explicit decomposition between arithmetic and non-arithmetic questions enables separate evaluation of procedural and conceptual skill effectiveness. We use the FAMMA-Basic-Txt release, which provides OCR-extracted textual context for each question, ensuring that evaluation targets reasoning ability rather than retrieval.[5]

4.2 Data Filtering and Split

We restrict the corpus to the 1,378 English-language questions to control for language variation, ensuring that observed performance differences reflect reasoning capability alone. Since FAMMA provides no official train–test split, we construct our own: separating the English corpus into arithmetic and non-arithmetic subsets and applying stratified 60/40 splits based on difficulty level (easy, medium, hard) and question type (multiple-choice vs. open-ended). This produces 448 training and 300 test questions for arithmetic, and 378 training and 252 test questions for non-arithmetic. All reported results are on these held-out test sets and are therefore not directly comparable to those reported by Xue et al. [16].

4.3 Evaluation Protocol

ASDA's distillation pipeline operates on individual question–answer pairs, so we evaluate each question independently rather than in grouped LLM calls as in the original FAMMA protocol. FAMMA stores shared context only in the first subquestion of each group, so we propagate this context to all sub-questions to preserve information completeness.[6] Arithmetic questions use Program-of-Thought (PoT) code execution, with an additional selection step that maps numeric outputs to the closest multiple-choice option where applicable. For evaluation, we adopt a hybrid approach: rule-based exact matching for multiple-choice questions and LLM-based judging for open-ended questions, replacing the original protocol's use of LLM judging for all question types. Table 1 summarizes these modifications.

We adopt Qwen-Max rather than GPT-4o as the open-ended judge for cost[7]. Validation confirms these modifications do not inflate gains: swapping Qwen-Max for GPT-4o yields 99.3% agreement across 1,104 judgments (delta: 0.00 pp arithmetic, −0.39 pp non-arithmetic); adopting the full FAMMA LLM-judge strategy confirms the same shift.

answers for their primary test sets, yield baseline results that differ substantially from published figures, or focus on visual and retrieval-based reasoning rather than procedural financial reasoning.

[5] FAMMA also includes a LivePro subset of 103 expert-curated questions, but only 35 are English-language and most are open-ended, making it too small for our pipeline.

[6] Additional preprocessing: we enforce expression-based PoT outputs rather than `print()` statements to prevent execution failures.

[7] Qwen-Max via DashScope: $1.60 / $6.40 per M tokens in/out; GPT-4o: $2.50 / $10.00 per M tokens in/out.

Table 1. Evaluation protocol modifications.

	Original FAMMA	Ours
Question handling	Grouped sub-questions	Independent
MC evaluation	LLM judge	Rule-based exact match
Open-ended evaluation	LLM judge (GPT-4o)	LLM judge (Qwen-Max)
Arithmetic execution	PoT	PoT + MC mapping step

4.4 Baselines

We compare ASDA against two leading training-free adaptation methods that operate under the same deployment constraint—black-box API access without weight modifications: GEPA [1] and ACE [19]. Both methods optimize a single monolithic text applied uniformly to all questions. The baseline condition uses the student model with a standard task prompt and no injected skills or optimized prompts. Neither GEPA nor ACE has previously been evaluated on FAMMA; the results reported here are, to our knowledge, the first published evaluations of both methods on this benchmark.

To ensure a fair comparison, we adapt training conditions to each method's architectural requirements.[8]

4.5 Implementation Details

Two components are fixed across all experimental conditions: Qwen-Max serves as the LLM evaluation judge for open-ended questions, and Qwen-Turbo performs the MC selection step that maps numeric PoT outputs to answer choices. All inference is run at temperature 0 for reproducibility.[9]

Table 2 reports token usage and estimated cost for both the warm-up pipeline and iterative refinement through two epochs (the paper's best operating point). Warm-up cost is dominated by skill-augmented evaluation; refinement is substantially more expensive due to repeated train-and-test evaluation and teacher-driven analysis at each epoch.

[8] GEPA follows its original 3-way split protocol, training on 50% of our training pool (222 arithmetic, 188 non-arithmetic) and selecting the best prompt on the remaining 50%. ACE and ASDA use the full training pool (448 arithmetic, 378 non-arithmetic).

[9] All models are accessed via the Anthropic API, with two exceptions: Haiku 3.5 via OpenRouter (no longer available on the Anthropic API directly) and Qwen models via DashScope.

Table 2. ASDA pipeline cost (Haiku 3.5 student, Sonnet 4.5 teacher). Teacher priced at Sonnet 4.5 rates ($3 / $15 per M tokens in/out); student at Haiku 3.5 rates ($0.80 / $4 per M tokens in/out). Qwen-based judging and MC selection tokens are included in student-phase totals and conservatively priced at Haiku 3.5 rates; actual DashScope costs are approximately 10× lower. Rates as of March 2026.

Config	Stage	Teacher (S4.5)		Student (H3.5)		Cost
		In	Out	In	Out	
Arith	Warm-up	545K	121K	8.07M	331K	$11
	Refine (E1–E2)	16.1M	2.1M	65.4M	741K	$135
Non-Arith	Warm-up	485K	94K	5.80M	194K	$8
	Refine (E1–E2)	9.2M	1.2M	51.2M	598K	$89

5 Results and Analysis

5.1 Main Results

We evaluate ASDA across two student models on both arithmetic and non-arithmetic tasks. For Haiku 3.5, we additionally include GEPA and ACE as training-free reference points; both achieve only marginal gains on FAMMA, which suggests the structural limitations of flat-text optimization.

ASDA consistently improves performance for Claude-family student models. On arithmetic, Haiku 3.5 gains +8.67 pp at warm-up and +17.33 pp after two refinement epochs. Haiku 4.5, despite its stronger 64.67% baseline, achieves +5.99 pp—showing that ASDA adds value even for more capable models. Non-arithmetic gains are smaller but consistent for Haiku 3.5 (+2.78 pp warm-up, +5.95 pp at E2); Haiku 4.5 sees modest non-arithmetic improvement only after refinement (+1.60 pp at E2).

Effect of Iterative Refinement. The warm-up phase targets the most frequent failure patterns and delivers the first large wave of gains. Iterative refinement then addresses residual failures that remain after initial skill injection. For arithmetic, accuracy improves from 49.67% at warm-up to 54.67% at epoch 1 and reaches 58.33% at epoch 2. A smaller but consistent trend holds for non-arithmetic, where epoch 2 peaks at 55.16%. Both domains regress at epoch 3 (arithmetic: 54.33%; non-arithmetic: 51.98%), indicating overfitting to residual training-set patterns after two refinement passes. In practice, two refinement epochs represent the optimal operating point.

Gains by Question Type. Skills consistently produce larger gains on multiple-choice questions than on open-ended ones. For Haiku 3.5 arithmetic at warm-up, MC accuracy rises by +14.39 pp compared to +3.73 pp for open-ended; Haiku 4.5 shows the same pattern (MC +7.91 pp, open-ended +2.48 pp). A skill that narrows the solution procedure is most useful when the answer space is already constrained to a few options. For open-ended generation, where the model must

Table 3. ASDA results across student models on FAMMA. For Haiku 3.5, GEPA and ACE are shown as reference baselines. All experiments use Sonnet 4.5 as the teacher model. WU = Warm-Up; E2 = best refinement epoch. Δ denotes absolute improvement in percentage points over each model's own baseline.

Student	Method	Arithmetic		Non-Arithmetic	
		Acc. (%)	Δ	Acc. (%)	Δ
Haiku 3.5	Baseline	41.00	–	49.21	–
	GEPA [1]	42.33	+1.33	50.79	+1.58
	ACE [19]	44.30	+3.30	49.60	+0.39
	ASDA WU **(ours)**	49.67	+8.67	51.98	+2.78
	ASDA E2 **(ours)**	**58.33**	**+17.33**	**55.16**	**+5.95**
Haiku 4.5	Baseline	64.67	–	57.14	–
	ASDA WU **(ours)**	69.67	+5.00	56.35	−0.79
	ASDA E2 **(ours)**	**70.66**	**+5.99**	**58.74**	**+1.60**

produce a free-form numerical or textual response, the guidance is less precise and the room for regression is higher (Table 3).

Regressions. In sampled regression cases, the most common failure mode is skill-induced over-reasoning: the model follows the injected procedural guidance even when the question does not require it, elaborating beyond what is needed and revising an already-correct judgment. This occurs because the selector loads all skill files for a matched subfield as a bundle, so every question in that subfield receives guidance regardless of whether it needs it.

5.2 Qualitative Analysis

To illustrate how skill artifacts operate at inference time, Fig. 3 presents an arithmetic case from the Haiku 3.5 warm-up evaluation where the baseline fails and skill injection succeeds. The same skill file was credited with 7 additional fixes on related fixed income questions, illustrating the reusability of subfield-specific skill artifacts.

5.3 Where Does the Improvement Come From? Self-teaching Ablation

ASDA's gains could come from two sources: knowledge contributed by a superior teacher model, or knowledge drawn from the training data itself. To separate these, we run a self-teaching configuration where the student model acts as its own teacher—it analyzes its own failures, builds the skill library, and then uses those skills at inference. No stronger model is involved.

For Haiku 3.5 arithmetic, self-teaching achieves +6.33 pp—73% of the +8.67 pp gain from using a Sonnet 4.5 teacher. This shows that most of the

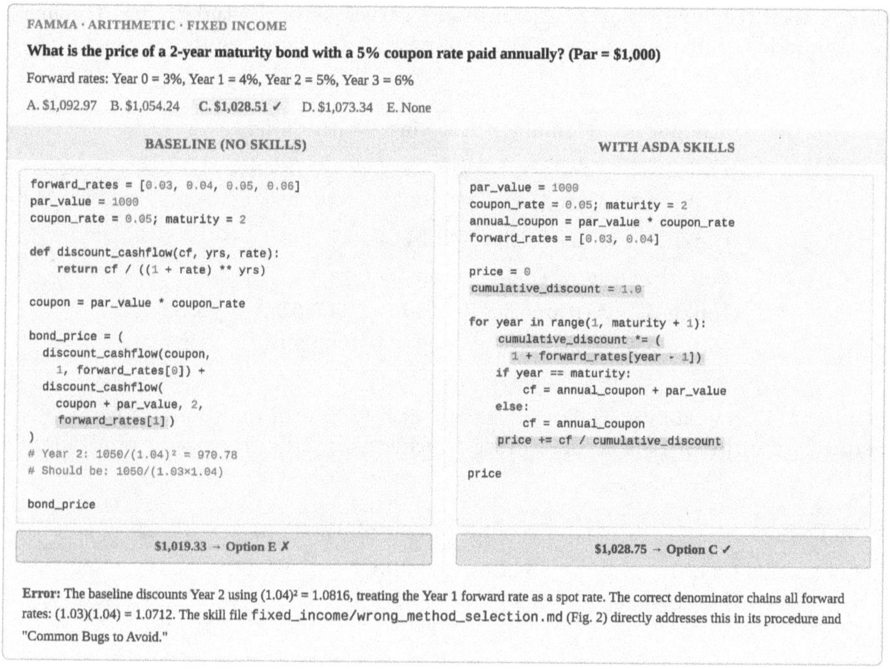

Fig. 3. Baseline vs. skill-augmented output on a FAMMA fixed income question (Haiku 3.5, warm-up). The skill file in Fig. 2 provides the domain-specific procedure that corrects the baseline error. The same skill file was credited with 7 additional fixes on related fixed income questions.

benefit comes from the training data, not from the teacher's superior knowledge. The training questions provide only the question text and the correct answer—no worked solutions or step-by-step reasoning—yet seeing where it consistently goes wrong is enough for the model to identify its recurring failure patterns and synthesize skills to address them. The model already possesses much of the relevant domain knowledge; the distillation process gives it the structure to apply that knowledge reliably. The remaining 2.34 pp gap reflects the teacher's contribution—a stronger model produces sharper failure diagnoses and more precise skill formulations. The same pattern holds for non-arithmetic (+1.58 pp self-teaching vs. +2.78 pp with a Sonnet teacher).

5.4 Are Skills Student-Specific? Cross-Transfer Experiment

The self-teaching results raise a natural follow-on question: once skills are distilled for one model, can they benefit another? We apply skills generated from Haiku 3.5's failures to Haiku 4.5 (a stronger model in the same family) and compare against skills derived from Haiku 4.5's own failures (Tables 4 and 5).

Cross-model transfer produces a net regression of −2.33 pp, driven by a sharp open-ended decline (−6.21 pp) that overwhelms modest MC gains (+2.16 pp). In

Table 4. Self-teaching ablation. Each model serves as both student and teacher; no superior model is involved. Full ASDA (Sonnet 4.5 teacher) results are shown for reference.

Student	Domain	Baseline	With Skills	Δ
Full ASDA (Sonnet 4.5 teacher), for reference				
Haiku 3.5	Arithmetic	41.00	49.67	+8.67
Haiku 3.5	Non-Arith	49.21	51.98	+2.78
Self-Teaching (student = teacher)				
Haiku 3.5	Arithmetic	41.00	**47.33**	**+6.33**
Haiku 3.5	Non-Arith	49.21	50.79	+1.58

Table 5. Skill portability: Haiku 4.5 arithmetic (300 eval questions). Own skills are generated from Haiku 4.5's failures; cross-transfer uses skills generated from Haiku 3.5's failures.

Skills Source	Baseline	With Skills	Δ	MC Δ	Open Δ
Own skills (H4.5)	64.67	**69.67**	**+5.00**	+7.91	+2.48
H3.5 skills (cross-transfer)	64.67	62.33	−2.33	+2.16	−6.21

contrast, Haiku 4.5 with its own ASDA skills gains a consistent +5.00 pp across both question types.

The practical implication is direct: skills should be generated for each deployed model independently. Reusing skills across model generations is unlikely to yield positive returns and can actively harm the stronger model. As shown in Table 2, student-specific warm-up distillation costs under \$12, with two refinement epochs adding \$89–135, making per-model regeneration operationally feasible at deployment scale.

6 Discussion and Conclusion

Discussion. Two experimental findings reveal the underlying mechanism of ASDA. The self-teaching result—where a model acting as its own teacher recovers 73% of the full arithmetic gain—shows that the primary source of improvement is not the teacher's superior knowledge but the structure imposed by the distillation process itself. Enumerating failure patterns across a training set forces the model to externalize domain knowledge it already implicitly holds but cannot reliably apply during single-pass inference. The cross-transfer failure reinforces this from the opposite direction: skills are not generic domain knowledge that transfers across models, but artifacts of a specific model's failure distribution. Applying one model's skills to a stronger model constrains it by the weaker model's blind spots. Together, these results characterize skills as *model-specific failure remedies*—a distinction with direct consequences for how skill libraries should be managed in practice.

For organizations that rely on commercial LLMs through black-box APIs, ASDA offers a concrete operational path, and credit analysis is a representative case. Drafting a credit assessment requires spreading financial statements, computing coverage and leverage ratios, testing covenant headroom, and applying the institution's own credit policy and regulatory criteria before arriving at a rating. This reasoning is procedural and quantitative, backed by a labeled history of completed assessments to distill from, and the recurring errors—an incorrect ratio definition, a misapplied policy threshold, an overlooked covenant—cluster cleanly by type. Distilling skills from that history yields a library that encodes the correct procedure for each failure mode—one that credit-risk officers can review, compliance can certify against policy, and engineering can version-control and regenerate when the base model is upgraded, without re-validating opaque fine-tuned weights. The approach suits workflows whose expertise is codified in policy and procedure more than those resting on tacit, case-specific judgment such as fraud investigation. For any regulated workflow with similar structure, the skill library provides an adaptation path that remains fully auditable—an assurance that fine-tuning cannot offer.

ASDA's gains are largest when failure patterns are clustered and the task has well-defined procedural structure, as with arithmetic reasoning via Program-of-Thought. When errors are more dispersed—as in non-arithmetic tasks—the signal available for distillation is weaker and regression risk increases. This boundary condition suggests that diagnostic quality (how cleanly errors cluster by type and subfield) predicts adaptation success alongside raw model capability.

Limitations. All experiments use a single benchmark (FAMMA) and a single model family (Anthropic's Claude). While the consistency of gains across two student models and two task types provides some evidence of robustness, it does not establish whether the error taxonomy, skill format, or refinement dynamics transfer to other domains or model architectures. FAMMA's reliance on OCR-extracted text introduces an additional confound: skills distilled from noisy transcriptions may encode artifact-specific heuristics, meaning the regression rates we report may overestimate what would be observed on cleaner datasets. More broadly, all evaluation is benchmark-based; whether the observed accuracy gains translate to practical value in production financial workflows remains an open question.

Future Work. Cross-domain transfer. Evaluating on healthcare and legal reasoning benchmarks would address the single-benchmark limitation and test whether skills transfer across domains. These domains are procedural, knowledge-intensive, and carry auditability requirements that align with the skill library's inspectable format.

Cross-Model Generalization. Our results are limited to Anthropic's Claude family in both student and teacher roles. Evaluating with models from other families (e.g., GPT, DeepSeek) would clarify whether the framework's gains depend on family-specific instruction-following behavior or generalize more broadly.

Finer-Grained Skill Selection. The current pipeline generates 10–30 skill files per configuration, and the selector loads all files for a matched subfield as a bundle. A finer-grained approach that selects at the pattern level, combined with pruning of low-value skills, could reduce the regressions caused by unnecessary procedural guidance while sharpening routing precision.

Preliminary experiments on cross-domain and cross-model evaluation are underway.

Conclusion. We have shown that failure-driven distillation can externalize latent domain knowledge into an explicit, inspectable form that single-pass inference cannot access—without modifying model weights. Our ablations further reveal that the resulting skills function as *model-specific failure remedies*: artifacts of a particular model's failure distribution that cannot be transferred across model generations, but can be cheaply regenerated for any deployed model given only a labeled domain dataset. Warm-up distillation costs under $12, with optional iterative refinement adding $89–135 (Table 2). The skill library is not a better prompt: it is a new representational layer between the raw model and its deployment context, one that can be version-controlled, audited, and regenerated for successor models. Whether this layer generalizes to other knowledge-intensive domains, and how far self-teaching can substitute for stronger supervision, remain the central open questions.

Generative AI Disclosure. The authors used generative AI tools to assist with manuscript editing and experimental pipeline development. All scientific content—hypotheses, experimental designs, and conclusions—is entirely the work of the human authors.

Disclosure of Interests. The authors have no competing interests to declare that are relevant to the content of this article.

References

1. Agrawal, L.A., et al.: GEPA: reflective prompt evolution can outperform reinforcement learning. In: The Fourteenth International Conference on Learning Representations (2026)
2. Alzubi, S., Provenzano, N., Bingham, J., Chen, W., Vu, T.: EvoSkill: automated skill discovery for multi-agent systems. arXiv preprint arXiv:2603.02766 (2026)
3. Anthropic: Agent Skills: an open standard for executable agent knowledge (2025). https://agentskills.io
4. Deng, S., Peng, H., Xu, J., Mao, R., Giurcăneanu, C.D., Liu, J.: FinMR: A knowledge-intensive multimodal benchmark for advanced financial reasoning. In: Proceedings of the 6th ACM International Conference on AI in Finance, pp. 168–176 (2025). https://doi.org/10.1145/3768292.3770365
5. Han, T., et al.: SWE-skills-bench: do agent skills actually help in real-world software engineering? arXiv preprint arXiv:2603.15401 (2026)
6. Khattab, O., et al.: DSPy: compiling declarative language model calls into state-of-the-art pipelines. In: The Twelfth International Conference on Learning Representations (2024)

7. Li, X.: SkillsBench: benchmarking how well agent skills work across diverse tasks. arXiv preprint arXiv:2602.12670 (2026)
8. Luo, J., et al.: FinMME: Benchmark dataset for financial multi-modal reasoning evaluation. In: Proceedings of the 63rd Annual Meeting of the Association for Computational Linguistics (Volume 1: Long Papers), pp. 29465–29489 (2025). https://doi.org/10.18653/v1/2025.acl-long.1426
9. Mateega, S., Georgescu, C., Tang, D.: FinanceQA: a benchmark for evaluating financial analysis capabilities of large language models. arXiv preprint arXiv:2501.18062 (2025)
10. Ni, J., et al.: Trace2Skill: distill trajectory-local lessons into transferable agent skills. arXiv preprint arXiv:2603.25158 (2026)
11. Pan, Z.: LEMMA: learning from errors for mathematical advancement in LLMs. In: Findings of ACL 2025. arXiv preprint arXiv:2503.17439 (2025)
12. Wang, G., et al.: Voyager: an open-ended embodied agent with large language models. Transactions on Machine Learning Research (2024)
13. Wu, S., et al.: BloombergGPT: a large language model for finance. arXiv preprint arXiv:2303.17564 (2023)
14. Xia, P.: SkillRL: evolving agents via recursive skill-augmented reinforcement learning. arXiv preprint arXiv:2602.08234 (2026)
15. Xie, Q.: FinBen: A holistic financial benchmark for large language models. In: NeurIPS 2024. arXiv preprint arXiv:2402.12659 (2024)
16. Xue, Z.: FAMMA: a benchmark for financial domain multilingual multimodal question answering. arXiv preprint arXiv:2410.04526 (2024)
17. Yang, H., Liu, X., Wang, C.: FinGPT: open-source financial large language models. arXiv preprint arXiv:2306.06031 (2023)
18. Yüksekgönül, M., et al.: Optimizing generative AI by backpropagating language model feedback. Nature **639**, 609–616 (2025). https://doi.org/10.1038/s41586-025-08661-4
19. Zhang, Q., et al.: Agentic context engineering: evolving contexts for self-improving language models. In: The Fourteenth International Conference on Learning Representations (2026)
20. Zhao, Y., Liu, H., Long, Y., Zhang, R., Zhao, C., Cohan, A.: FinanceMATH: knowledge-intensive math reasoning in finance domains. In: Proceedings of the 62nd Annual Meeting of the Association for Computational Linguistics (Volume 1: Long Papers), pp. 12841–12858 (2024). https://doi.org/10.18653/v1/2024.acl-long.693

Application of LLM Agents for Long-Form Question Answering in Systems Biology

Charvi Jain[1(✉)], Sahar Vahdati[1,2,7], Pauline Porschitz[8], Mounir El Hankouri[6], Nandu Gopan[1,3,5], Ivo F. Sbalzarini[1,2,3,5,6], and Jens Lehmann[1,2,4]

[1] Faculty of Computer Science, Dresden University of Technology, Nöthnitzer Str. 46, 01187 Dresden, Germany
{charvi.jain,sahar.vahdati,nandu.gopan, ivo.sbalzarini,jens.lehmann}@tu-dresden.de
[2] Center for Scalable Data Analytics and Artificial Intelligence ScaDS.AI, Dresden/Leipzig, Germany
[3] Center for Systems Biology Dresden, Pfotenhauerstr. 108, 01307 Dresden, Germany
[4] Amazon, Dresden, Germany
[5] Max Planck Institute of Molecular Cell Biology and Genetics, Pfotenhauerstr. 108, 01307 Dresden, Germany
[6] Cluster of Excellence, Physics of Life, TU Dresden, Dresden, Germany
mounir.el_hankouri@tu-dresden.de
[7] Leibniz University Hanover, Welfengarten 1, 30167 Hannover, Germany
[8] Center for Regenerative Therapies Dresden (CRTD), Technische Universität (TU) Dresden, 01307 Dresden, Germany
pauline.porschitz@tu-dresden.de

Abstract. AI-based research assistants for domains with cross disciplinary and multi-resource demands, such as systems biology, require deep reasoning and integration across diverse knowledge sources. In this work, we study the application of large language model (LLM) agents for long-form scientific question answering that requires multi-source reasoning across heterogeneous biological knowledge resources. To achieve our aim, we first introduce a high-quality, human-curated dataset, ThinkSysBio, that offers a structured testbed for long-form question answering (LFQA) with multi-source, tool-augmented scientific reasoning in systems biology. Second, we devise an adaptation of the ReAct framework, namely ReAct-LF, for inference tokens efficient LFQA. In addition, we evaluate both ReAct and ReAct-LF using four state-of-the-art open-source and closed-source LLMs. Third, we perform a systematic evaluation of agentic workflows by analyzing both the intermediate reasoning traces and the generated scholarly reports. Our results reveal a practical trade-off between report quality and computational efficiency in agent-based scientific workflows, demonstrating

J. Lehmann—Work done outside of Amazon.

Supplementary Information The online version contains supplementary material available at https://doi.org/10.1007/978-3-032-37682-4_19.

M. Baratchi et al. (Eds.): ECML PKDD 2026, LNAI 16949, pp. 324–341, 2027.
https://doi.org/10.1007/978-3-032-37682-4_19

that relevance-aware evidence filtering can substantially reduce inference token usage by an average of 61.3% across datasets while maintaining comparable report quality. **Code and dataset available at:** https://github.com/Charvijain16/LFQA_SB.

Keywords: LLMs · Long-Form Question Answering · AI for Science

1 Introduction

Systems biology is an interdisciplinary field that combines biology, mathematics, computation, and physics to understand how biological function emerges from interactions among components such as genes, proteins, pathways, cells, and tissues [3]. Research-oriented questions in systems biology are inherently cross-resource, mechanism-centered, and synthesis-heavy, and hence answering these questions rarely reduces to a single fact lookup. Instead, it often requires integrating evidence from heterogeneous resources, including biological databases, pathway repositories, and scientific literature, and synthesizing it into an expert-style scholarly report that provides mechanistic and evidence-backed explanations. In practice, this workflow is both time-consuming and cognitively demanding: researchers must reformulate searches, inspect partially overlapping evidence, reconcile different sources and assemble them into a valuable article.

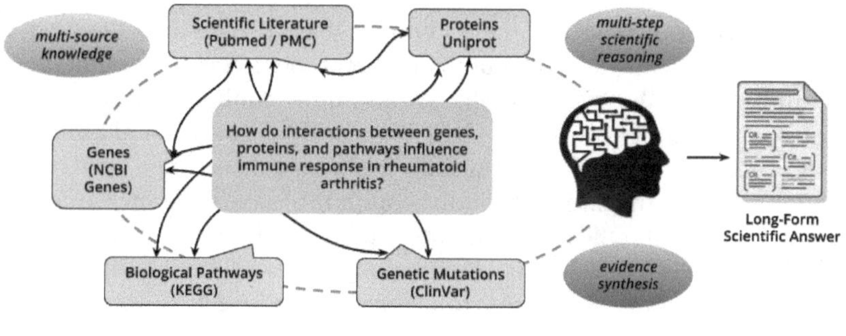

Fig. 1. Illustration of research workflow for systems biology researchers

Recent advances in AI-driven biological research have supported important but relatively isolated tasks such as protein and drug design [7] or DNA/RNA effect prediction [11]. While these efforts demonstrate the growing utility of AI in biology, they do not directly address the broader problem of multi-source scientific synthesis. Real systems biology workflows require not only retrieving information but also deciding what is relevant, connecting evidence across modalities, and producing coherent explanations. Furthermore, existing tools such as Undermind [6], Aurora [9] are valuable for literature exploration, but they focus mainly on publications and follow traditional literature-extraction processes involving a static sequence of title filtering, abstract filtering, or/and full-text filtering. For systems biology, however, literature alone is often insufficient. Relevant information must often be gathered from iterating back and forth across different biological sources as shown in Fig. 1, rather than following a static, step-by-step pipeline. To enable such dynamic exploration, AI assistants require the ability to reason. ReAct [19] is a widely known approach for interleaving reasoning and tool use, but it has mainly been studied in short-form multi-hop question answering (QA) [14]. This is a limited fit for systems biology. Short-form QA is typically focused and specific, whereas long-form, research-like questions are broad and open-ended. While short-form QA often retrieves answers directly from readily available information, LFQA requires the selection of relevant sources and conceptual entities, because the answer should be grounded in evidence drawn from diverse and credible sources. In this work, we study the application of LLM-based agents for LFQA in systems biology and provide practical insights into how such agents should be studied and evaluated under expert-domain constraints.

First, we extend ReAct with a relevance-filtering step tailored to long-form answer generation, ReAct-LF. The motivation is to remove uninformative data from retrieved evidences before answer generation to improve efficiency and reduce noise. Hence, we compare ReAct and ReAct-LF across several state-of-the-art LLMs. To enable the assessment of this application, we curated ThinkSys-Bio, an evaluation dataset for LFQA in systems biology with the help of domain experts. The dataset consists of 60 doctoral-level, high-quality scholarly questions with domain-expert reasoning steps and scholarly reports. Each sample required substantial expert effort, high cognitive load, and manual evidence verification across multiple resources. Our goal is to have a controlled testbed for depth and realism, and for analyzing agent behavior in a difficult expert-domain application. We evaluate the agents along multiple axes, consisting of generated report quality, reasoning behavior, and computational efficiency. Our results show that ReAct-LF substantially reduces token usage relative to standard ReAct while maintaining broadly comparable performance quality, highlighting an important efficiency–quality trade-off for long-form scientific QA. Through this work, we provide an application framework for studying how agentic systems can support multi-source scientific reasoning and scholarly report generation in systems biology.

Problem Formulation. We formulate the problem as a multi-source, multi-step reasoning and long-form synthesis task. Given a research-style question from the field of systems biology and access to a set of external biological knowledge sources, the LLM agent must iteratively gather relevant information and integrate into a coherent scholarly report. The task requires producing (i) a step-by-step sequence of tool-augmented reasoning steps, (ii) a final synthesized report conditioned on the original question and the information collected via tool calls. The central challenge lies in orchestrating multi-step retrieval across heterogeneous sources and modalities with well-structured final synthesis.

2 Related Work

Scientific Question Answering. Scientific and biomedical QA has been shaped by benchmarks such as PubMedQA [10] and BioASQ [18], and later extended to broader scholarly settings such as SciQA [1] and literature-centric benchmarks like LitQA/LitQA2 [17]. These resources have advanced scientific QA, but they mainly emphasize short-form answers, literature-only evidence, or scholarly knowledge. In contrast, our setting targets long-form systems biology questions that require synthesis across literature, genes, proteins, pathways, and variants.

LLM Agents and Tool Use. Agentic tool use builds on ReAct, which interleaves reasoning and acting. In science, PaperQA2 [17] iteratively retrieves and synthesizes evidence from scientific papers. Biomedical agents such as Biomni [8] and STELLA [12], which extend tool use to broader biomedical workflows, are evaluated on settings such as HLE-Biomed [16] and LAB-Bench [13]. These works show the promise of tool-augmented LLMs in science, but most focus on literature workflows or short-form evaluation. Our work instead studies domain-specific, long-form systems biology QA with explicit reasoning traces and report generation.

Long-Form Scientific Reasoning. Recent work has begun to study long-context and long-form reasoning in research settings. LongBench-v2 [2] evaluates deep reasoning over realistic long-context tasks, while CURIE [4] focuses on scientific long-context understanding across disciplines. Benchmarks such as DeepResearch Bench [5] and DeepScholar-Bench [15] move closer to open-ended, citation-rich report generation and research synthesis, and related work has also emerged on long-form medical QA with expert annotations. However, these benchmarks are largely cross-domain, web-based, or literature-centered and do not target systems biology as a multi-modal scientific workflow. Our work differs in focusing on domain-specific long-form scientific reasoning grounded in structured biological resources and expert reasoning traces.

3 Methodology

The methodology is illustrated in Fig. 2. For the curation of the evaluation dataset ThinkSysBio and for inference on the systems biology research questions, the methodology remains consistent. During the dataset curation procedure, domain experts interact with a custom user interface to record their thought process and scholarly report for a given question. In case of inference, the domain expert is replaced by an LLM agent that simulates the thought process and generates a scholarly report for the question. For uniformity, we use the term *agent* to refer to either the human domain expert or the LLM, depending on context. In both cases, the agent interacts with an external environment to gather relevant information for the question and frames a scholarly report with proper references.

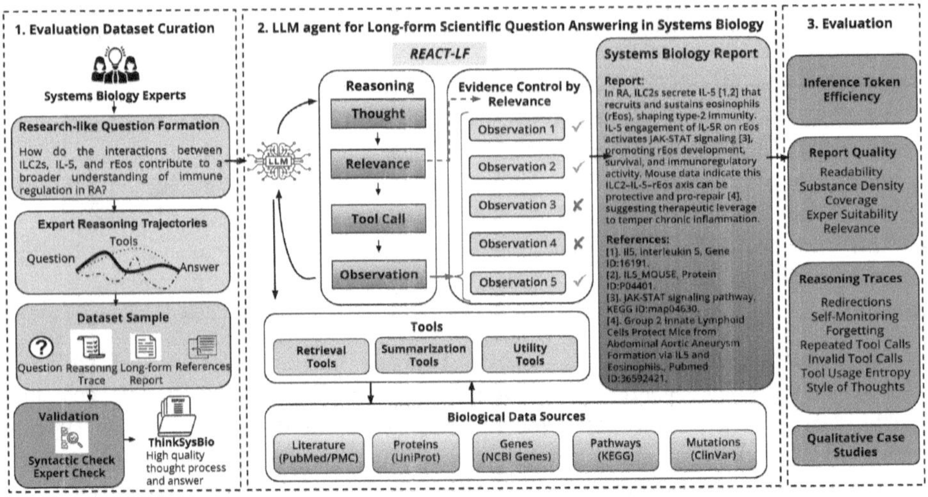

Fig. 2. End-to-End Application Framework for Systems Biology Scholarly Report.

The external environment consists of the tools listed in Table 1. For each data repository, Python tools (or functions) were created for retrieval and summarization. These tools were the only way an agent could interact with the environment to gather information. For a scholarly question Q, the tools can be categorized as retrieval or summarization tools; $\{f_{R_1}, f_{R_2}, \ldots, f_{R_m}, f_{S_1}, f_{S_2}, \ldots, f_{S_m}\} \in F$, where R stands for retrieval, S for summarization, m for data repositories, and F is the tool set.

Retrieval Tools. Given a search string q, the retrieval tool selects a ranked subset of documents from a collection $\mathcal{D} = \{d_1, d_2, \ldots, d_N\}$. Formally, the tool returns the top-k elements $f_R(q, \mathcal{D}) = \{d_{i_1}, d_{i_2}, \ldots, d_{i_k}\}\, where \quad k \ll N$, and the indices $\{i_1, \ldots, i_k\}$ are ordered according to a relevance function $\rho(d, Q)$. This is similar to performing title or abstract-based filtering for literature review.

Summarization Tools. For any subset of retrieved documents $G \subseteq f_R(q, \mathcal{D})$, the summarization tool generates succinct information w.r.t the given question Q as $f_S(G, Q) = \{g_1, g_2, \ldots, g_{|G|}\}$ where each g_j is a summary/gist of the corresponding document $d_j \in G$. This process is similar to full-text filtering for literature review.

Agent–Environment Interaction. For a given question Q, the agent dynamically alternates between using its internal knowledge and interacting with the external environment to gather relevant information for answering the question. We denote the internal knowledge of the agent by B and external knowledge by E. The agent's goal is to produce a final report $\mathcal{L}$ for question Q

$$\mathcal{L} = agent(Q, B, E)\,. \tag{1}$$

Table 1. Tools available to agents and their descriptions.

Tool	Description
Retrieve PubMed	Retrieve papers from PubMed using a search string
Summarize PMC	Summarize information from PubMed Central paper w.r.t question
Retrieve UniProt	Retrieve proteins from UniProt using a search string
Summarize UniProt	Summarize information on UniProt page for an ID and question
Retrieve KEGG	Retrieve pathways from KEGG using a search string
Summarize KEGG	Summarize information on KEGG page for an ID and question
Retrieve Genes	Retrieve genes from NCBI Genes using a search string
Summarize Genes	Summarize information on Gene page for an ID and question
Retrieve ClinVar	Retrieve mutations from NCBI ClinVar using a search string
Summarize ClinVar	Summarize information on ClinVar page for an ID and question
Exch-PMC-PMID	Map PubMed Central IDs to PubMed IDs and vice versa
Fetch Info Any	Gather information for a thought from any of the sources

For the original ReAct approach, the agent yields a trajectory of thoughts T, actions A, and observations O, and generates the final report from the collected thoughts and observations. In ReAct, external knowledge is defined as:

$$E = [\{T_1, A_1, O_1\}, \ldots, \{T_p, A_p, O_p\}] \,, \tag{2}$$

where p is the number of reasoning steps.

When dealing with biological data in LFQA, titles or names are often not enough to understand the underlying concepts. For instance, only on the basis of the names of proteins, like DLG1_DANRE or DLG1L_DANRE, it is difficult to understand their biological function. This is exacerbated by the same protein in different species often having different names. Understanding this requires going through the abstract or description to decide the relevance of a search result. When an agent invokes a retrieval tool f_R, the top-k entries are fetched, out of which only a fraction are typically relevant to the question. Similarly, for a summarization tool f_S, not all possible summaries are equally relevant to the question. Hence, in line with the "garbage in, garbage out" principle, we hypothesize that inclusion of irrelevant documents obtained during the reasoning process introduces noise while generating the scholarly report, whereas filtering such information will improve token efficiency and report quality by focusing on relevant data.

The central methodological contribution of ReAct-LF is the relevance-aware filtering mechanism. Unlike standard ReAct, which carries forward the full observation history regardless of how useful it is, ReAct-LF explicitly separates observation generation from evidence retention. At each reasoning step, the agent identifies the retrieved or summarized items that are relevant to the question and records their identifiers in a relevance field. Only judged-relevant observations are retained for final report generation.

Formally, ReAct-LF introduces a relevance field I in the reasoning and a post-filtering step $O \rightarrow O'$. This extends the ReAct approach for LFQA by modifying the $\{T, A, O\}$ reasoning step to $\{T, I, A, O'\}$. External knowledge for ReAct-LF then is:

$$E' = [\{T_1, I_1, A_1, O'_1\}, .., \{T_p, I_p, A_p, O'_p\}] \tag{3}$$

After an action yields an observation, the next ReAct-LF step combines relevance and thought into a single *structured thought.* We group these together to make explicit the connection to the thought step in standard ReAct and because the agent has to jointly reason about them. Since each entry of a tool output comes with a unique identifier from the source data repository, we directly define the relevance field I over those identifiers.

To illustrate O'_t at a certain iteration t, let

$$O_t = [\, o_1, o_2, \ldots, o_k \,] \tag{4}$$

be a list of dictionaries, where each dictionary o_i has a unique identifier $\mathrm{id}(o_i)$, and let

$$I_{t+1} = [\, i_1, i_2, \ldots, i_m \,] \tag{5}$$

be a list of relevant identifiers such that

$$I_{t+1} \subseteq \{\, \mathrm{id}(o_1), \mathrm{id}(o_2), \ldots, \mathrm{id}(o_k) \,\}\,. \tag{6}$$

Then, the filtered list O' is defined as:

$$O'_t = [\, o \in O_t \mid \mathrm{id}(o) \in I_{t+1} \,]\,. \tag{7}$$

This ensures that the report is grounded in structured reasoning and distilled external information. Relevant identifiers are selected by experts during dataset generation and by LLM agent at inference time, with trajectory filtering retaining only relevant observations for final answer generation.

4 Dataset Construction

We constructed the ThinkSysBio in a collaborative, expert-driven process involving 15 researchers from a world-renowned systems biology research institute. Four lead contributors, comprising doctoral researchers and principal investigators, served as co-authors and domain experts, involved in the formulation of scholarly questions, documenting reasoning processes, and authoring detailed answers. To ensure high quality and accuracy, we conducted three group workshops and multiple one-on-one sessions with all systems biology researchers, focusing on data creation, curation, and validation. The resulting dataset represents a rigorously curated, high-quality resource that reflects substantial expert effort, deep domain reasoning, and a strong commitment to quality.

Question Formation. The questions in the ThinkSysBio dataset are formulated by doctoral researchers in systems biology. They are equally distributed across six major categories: Definition, Mechanism, Reasoning, Comparison, Application, and Review. Table 2 details the question types for each of the categories. The categories ensure diversity and coverage of question types.

Repository Selection. To integrate multiple sources across distinct data modalities, we selected one repository per modality to build a proof of concept. The types of modalities commonly used in systems biology include: research articles, proteins, genes, biological pathways, and genetic mutations. The selected repositories (Table 3) were chosen for their practical usefulness, widespread recognition in the research community, and regular use by the contributing experts.

Table 2. Definitions of six question categories.

Category	Questions that ask for	Question format
Definition	clear definition or basic description	What is/are ...?
Mechanism	a step-by-step explanation	How does/What is the role of..?
Reasoning	the cause of a phenomenon	Why does ...?/What causes ...?
Comparison	comparison between alternatives	Which approach is better for ...?
Application	implications or practical use	How can it be applied in practice?
Review	high-level synthesis of findings/trends.	What are current trends in ...?

Validation. Two levels of quality checks were implemented to validate the constructed dataset. Syntactic validation, ensuring proper categorization of questions and the correct structure of entries, and expert validation, where domain experts evaluated the scientific correctness and usefulness of the final answer and the references.

Dataset Characteristics. The resulting dataset contained a total of 60 questions, 10 per category, each with an average of 8 structured-thought iterations. The answers are designed to be bounded by the knowledge accessible via the five sources listed in Table 3, recognizing that the complete systems biology domain may contain additional relevant data. Summary statistics are reported in Table 4.

5 Evaluation Framework

Datasets. To examine whether our analysis extends beyond the curated corpus, we also conduct evaluation on BioASQ, an established biomedical QA benchmark. For this study, we focus on the BioASQ dataset's summary questions, as they best align with our task formulation and provide reference summary answers derived from multiple sources such as PubMed and UniProt.

Models. We evaluate four strong LLMs spanning both closed-source and open-source model families: GPT-4.1, Claude 3.5 Sonnet, Gemini 2.5 Pro, and Llama

Table 3. Data modalities and their selected repositories.

Modality	Data Repo
Paper's metadata	PubMed
Paper's full text	PubMed Central
Biological pathways	KEGG
Proteins	UniProt
Genes	NCBI Gene
Mutations	NCBI ClinVar

Table 4. Summary statistics of the ThinkSysBio corpus.

Statistic	Value
Total questions	60
Question categories	6
Questions per category	10
Avg. reasoning traces	8
Evidence modalities	5

3.3 70B. All models support function calling for tool invocation, structured output generation, and context lengths of at least 128k tokens. To keep the comparison controlled, all models are prompted with the same system-level instructions, and no model-specific *deep research* mode is enabled.

Framework. We evaluate base LLMs, ReAct, and ReAct-LF. Base LLMs do not produce a reasoning chain and only a scholarly report. To ensure a fair comparison, ReAct and ReAct-LF use the same reasoning trajectories for each question, rather than independently sampling separate trajectories. This is important because LLM outputs are probabilistic, and multiple runs on the same question may produce different but valid reasoning paths. Using the same trajectory ensures that differences in the final reports are not affected by differences in sampled reasoning. While ReAct generates the final report using all observations, ReAct-LF filters observations based on the Relevance field before report generation. This setup isolates the effect of relevance-based filtering while keeping the underlying reasoning trajectory fixed.

Our evaluation centers on four research questions that focus on (i) how does evidence control impact efficiency, (ii) which agents produce high-quality scholarly reports, (iii) how do reasoning behaviors differ across models, and (iv) what do qualitative cases reveal beyond the aggregate metrics.

5.1 RQ1: How Does Evidence Control Impact Efficiency?

To examine the use of inference tokens in ReAct-LF and ReAct, we measured tokens with and without post-processing the observations. The Fig. 3a for BioASQ and Fig. 3b for ThinkSysBio clearly illustrate the significant drop of 63% (on average) and 59.6% (on average) in tokens, respectively, when ReAct-LF is chosen over ReAct.

5.2 RQ2: Which Agents Produce High Quality Scholarly Reports?

The scholarly report is the long-form answer produced after gathering information during the reasoning process. To qualitatively evaluate scholarly reports, we use an LLM as a judge on five different criteria: readability, substance density, coverage, expert suitability, and relevance. Their definitions are given in Table 5. For LLM judges, we use two state-of-the-art models, namely GPT-OSS 120B and QWEN3 30B, and prompt them to evaluate each report for each criterion on a Likert scale of 1–5, with 5 being the best. We perform this evaluation on the complete datasets, with each report scored using a single inference run for each judge model and criterion. The scores obtained using GPT-OSS-120B as a judge for BioASQ are shown in Fig. 4a and for ThinkSysBio in Fig. 4b.

Overall, Gemini and GPT perform best across all criteria, followed by Claude with moderate performance, while Llama performs the weakest. This consistent ranking in both figures suggests that model choice influences the quality of the final report. Across agents, score patterns are largely consistent: relevance and coverage are highest, substance density and readability are mid-range, and expert suitability is lowest. The base LLM shows the lowest expert suitability, suggest-

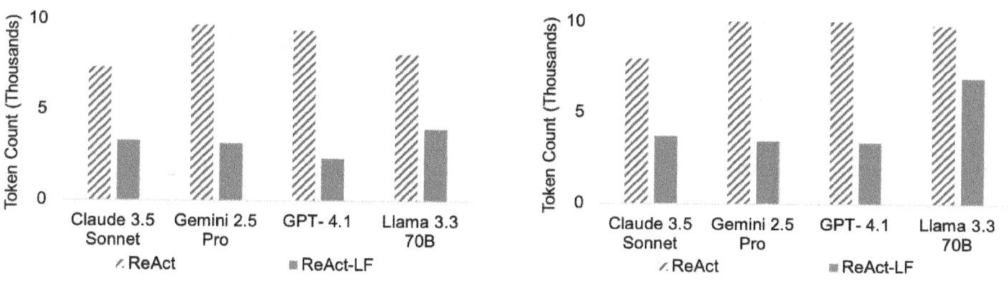

(a) BioASQ (b) ThinkSysBio

Fig. 3. Comparison of token usage for ReAct and ReAct-LF agents

Table 5. Report evaluation criteria and corresponding definitions used for qualitative LLM-as-judge evaluation.

Criterion	Judge prompt
Readability	Assess how easily the report can be followed at the sentence and paragraph level based on linguistic clarity, coherence, transitions, and grammatical flow, independent of content correctness
Substance-Density	Assess whether the report prioritizes precision, concrete claims rather than filler content or loosely related information
Coverage	Assess how well the report addresses the major aspects required to answer the question, regardless of verbosity or brevity
Expert-Suitability	Assess whether the report targets a domain expert audience, assuming prior knowledge and emphasizing insights rather than basic explanations
Relevance	Assess how well the response aligns with the core intent of the question, accounting for off-topic material without evaluating writing quality

ing a trade-off toward layman-friendly explanations over technical depth. Expert suitability increases in ReAct and ReAct-LF in comparison to the base LLM.

Comparing ReAct and ReAct-LF, we observe a slight drop in scores for ReAct-LF. A plausible explanation is that ReAct-LF restricts content to strictly relevant information, excluding background and contextual details. Although the core facts remain similar across ReAct and ReAct-LF, the additional contextual information in ReAct may support clearer explanations and conceptual links, resulting in slightly higher scores. Additionally, we measure the alignment between the two judges using quadratic weighted kappa (46%) and Krippendorff's alpha (44%), indicating moderate reliability; while exact agreement is about 50%, the very high within-one agreement (94%) and low MAE (0.56) indicate that most disagreements are minor (±1 point), which are potentially due to the open-ended and subjective nature of doctoral-level responses.

5.3 RQ3: How Do Reasoning Behaviors Differ Across Models?

The reasoning trajectories are generated by the agents before producing the final report. Analyzing these sequences helps us understand how reasoning influences the final output. We examine reasoning behaviors, tool-use distributions, and the style of generated thoughts. For ThinkSysBio, we compare the reasoning trajectories of ReAct-LF with expert-driven trajectories. The baseline LLM is excluded because it does not generate reasoning traces. For BioASQ, reasoning trajectories for ReAct-LF cannot be compared with expert or ground-truth trajectories, as the dataset lacks them.

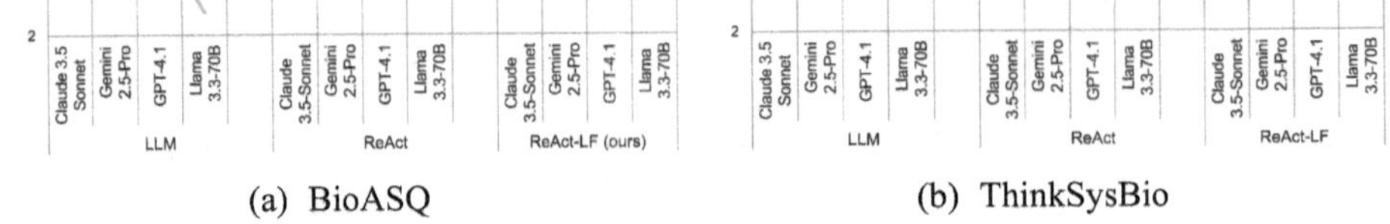

Fig. 4. Qualitative evaluation of model-generated scholarly reports using GPT-OSS-120B as judge, with GPT and Gemini leading, Claude mid-tier, and Llama weakest. ReAct and ReAct-LF show similar performance overall, confirming comparable result quality.

Table 6. Reasoning behaviors of models on BioASQ and ThinkSysBio, evaluated by GPT-OSS. Values indicate the average percentage of intermediate steps associated with each behavior. ↓ Green = lower/↑ Orange = higher within each agent block. Forgetting and Invalid Tool Calls: lower is better.

	Agent	Model	Redirections	Self Monitoring	Forgetting	Repeated Tool Calls	Invalid Tool Calls
BioASQ	ReAct-LF	Claude 3.5 Sonnet	30.79%	26.88%	2.15%	6.49%	5.01%
		Gemini 2.5 Pro	27.81%	21.58%	0%	0.30%	1.36%
		GPT 4.1	35%	25.02%	0.22%	0.50%	1.76%
		Llama 3.3 70B	31.14%	21.61%	1.16%	1.15%	1.65%
ThinkSysBio	ReAct-LF	Claude 3.5 Sonnet	37.9%	36.39%	6.91%	14.4%	1.54%
		Gemini 2.5 Pro	28.57%	23.88%	0.65%	1.32%	1.25%
		GPT 4.1	40.85%	33.9%	0%	0%	1.05%
		Llama 3.3 70B	31.71%	23.56%	1.49%	1.38%	0.79%
		Domain Expert	9.77%	7.41%	0%	0.19%	1.83%

Reasoning Behaviors. We evaluate the reasoning behaviors with the help of the same LLM judges as earlier, GPT-OSS 120B and QWEN3 30B on the complete datasets, along five dimensions: (1) thought redirections, defined as explicit strategic pivots after dead ends, ambiguity, or missing information (e.g., "this approach failed; I'll try X instead"); (2) self-monitoring, capturing meta-reasoning where the agent verifies or reflects on its own inferences (e.g., "let me double-check" or "this seems inconsistent"); (3) forgetting incidents, where previously observed information is not used later, such as repeating searches or ignoring constraints it found earlier; (4) invalid tool invocations, including incorrect tool names, malformed queries, or using a tool in a way that shows a misunderstanding of how it works; and (5) repeated tool calls, where the agent reissues the same query without modification, reflecting a failure to learn from prior results. The judges were given clear definitions and examples for each category and asked to respond with integer counts for each dimension and for every solution process. These checks show how often agents change their strategy, think about their own reasoning, or lose important context, and quantify weaknesses in how agents execute their plans. This helps measure how consistent their planning is and how well they manage their thought process, beyond the scholarly report.

The scores for all five phenomena using GPT-OSS-120B for both datasets are shown in Table 6. Domain experts exhibit fewer redirections and self-monitoring and almost no forgetting or repeated tool calls, indicating that human reasoning is more targeted and implicit. Gemini 2.5 Pro features minimal forgetting, few repeated tool calls, and comparatively stable reasoning behavior, representing the most balanced model across both datasets. GPT-4.1 shows high redirections and self-monitoring but almost no forgetting, suggesting strong retention despite a broader and more exploratory strategy. Llama is typically in the middle, but

Claude shows weak memory retention and poor understanding of tool use as demonstrated by forgetting and repetitive or invalid tool calls, respectively.

Tool-Use Behavior. To understand how different models, across different agents, use tools, we compute the Shannon entropy of the distribution of tool calls. The entropies are shown in Table 7. Across datasets, LLMs exhibit higher tool entropy than humans, indicating more diverse and exploratory tool usage patterns. GPT consistently shows the highest entropy, while Claude demonstrates low entropy.

Table 7. Tool entropies across models. Lower is better.

Dataset	Agent	Claude 3.5 Sonnet	Gemini 2.5 Pro	GPT 4.1	Llama 3.3 70B	Expert
BioASQ	ReAct-LF	1.65	2.14	**2.46**	2.33	NA
ThinkSysBio	ReAct-LF	1.58	2.05	**2.45**	2.33	1.46

Stylometric Analysis of Thoughts. In the reasoning process, thoughts are the foundation from which actions and observations emerge, so we examine how humans and different models structure them. We sample three randomly selected thoughts from the reasoning trajectory of each data sample. In total, we thus collect 150 thoughts for each model and original dataset (human-written). For each thought, we extract a suite of stylometric features designed to capture linguistic and narrative structure: token and bigram counts, stopword usage, part-of-speech ratios (nouns, adjectives, verbs), presence of discourse markers indicative of reasoning flow (e.g., "first", "next", "finally"), sentence complexity, and information density. The resulting feature vectors were standardized and projected into two-dimensional space via principal component analysis (PCA) to visualize aggregate differences and overlaps between human and model reasoning.

The PC1-PC2 scatter plot for both datasets for ReAct/ReAct-LF is shown in Fig. 5. The plots exhibit similar overall patterns across the two datasets. The BioASQ plot does not include red dots, as this dataset does not contain original or human-written reasoning traces. Overall, it is evident from the figures how human and model-generated thinking differ. Model-generated traces go toward longer, more structured, and denser reasoning, whereas human traces tend to cluster around shorter, simpler, and less explicit concepts. This implies that LLMs are more likely than humans to overtly externalize their reasoning. GPT and Llama are the models that produce the longest and most complicated ideas, Gemini is comparatively long but less complex, and Claude is yet more succinct and more human-like.

5.4 What Do Qualitative Cases Reveal Beyond Aggregate Metrics?

Aggregate metrics summarize overall performance but often hide important differences in how models gather evidence and construct reports. To better understand these dynamics, we conducted qualitative case studies with domain experts

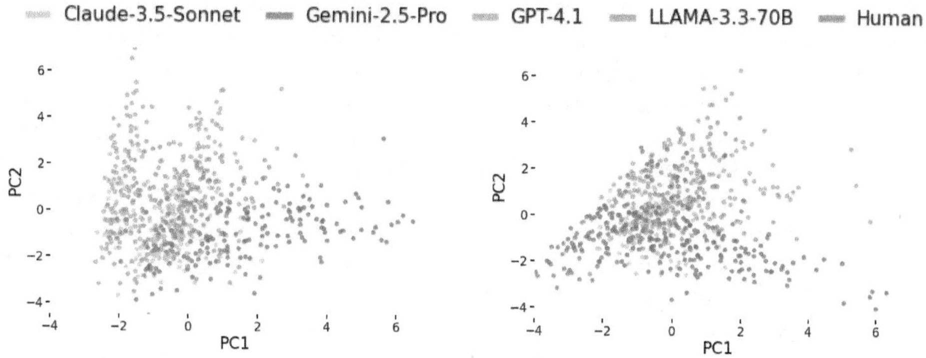

(a) BioASQ (b) ThinkSysBio

Fig. 5. Stylometric PCA of randomly sampled thoughts from BioASQ and ThinkSysBio. PC1 captures length and lexical-structural variety, while PC2 reflects sentence-level complexity and information density.

on two representative doctoral-level questions from the ThinkSysBio for all four models under both ReAct and ReAct-LF settings. For one of them, a detailed transcript is provided in the Supplementary Material, while Tables 8 and 9 summarize the observations from all case studies, based on reasoning trajectories and final reports.

Table 8. Qualitative comparison of reasoning behavior across models

Aspect	Claude3.5 Sonnet	Gemini2.5 Pro	GPT 4.1	Llama3.3 70B
Reasoning Pattern	Degradation in longer chains	Methodical	Exploratory, Coherent	Exploratory, Inconsistent
Memory	Forgetful	Strong	Strong	Weak
Tool use	Incorrect, unnecessary	Correct and coherent	Broad tool exploration	Weakly justified
Evidence	Weak	Particular	Effective	Weak

Reasoning. Domain expert's reasoning is strong and implicit rather than step-by-step articulation. This affirms the observation in reasoning behavior in Sect. 5.3 and Table 6 where experts show fewer redirections and self-monitoring and almost no forgetting or repeated tool calls. LLM agents, on the other hand, externalize their reasoning to varying degrees. GPT models exhibit coherent reasoning behavior, strong memory retention, and effectively selecting relevant evidence. Their strategy tends to be breadthwise, they explore multiple sources before converging on the most relevant evidence. Gemini shows similar powerful reasoning, but it does it in a more organized and thorough way, going over previous steps in the reasoning process and explicitly ruling out evidences that are not relevant. Although this increases focus, it sometimes results in an unnecessarily narrow selection of evidences, discarding information that is vaguely related yet possibly helpful. Claude starts with rational paths, but they get worse over longer chains, which leads to repeated or unnecessary tool calls. This indicates poor retention of prior reasoning context. Llama shows the least stable behavior, with exploratory reasoning behaviors and inconsistent relevance selection that often result in incomplete evidence collection.

Scholarly Reports. The quality of the reports produced is directly influenced by the reasoning processes used. Under the standard ReAct setting, GPT and Gemini produce detailed and comprehensive answers that closely follow the question structure, although GPT sometimes supplements retrieved information with internal model knowledge and hallucinations. Claude and Llama, by contrast, rely heavily on the completeness of retrieved evidence, which often leads to fragmented or incomplete reports when reasoning trajectories degrade. Under ReAct-LF, since the final synthesis stage only uses filtered observations, all models produce reports that are more structured and straightforward. This filtering gets rid of noise in the reasoning trace and makes the reports more factually grounded. However, the reduced evidence set can also remove contextual scaffolding that sometimes contributes to richer explanations, resulting in focused but occasionally less broad reports.

Table 9. Qualitative comparison of reports under ReAct and ReAct-LF

Aspect	Claude3.5 Sonnet	Gemini2.5 Pro	GPT 4.1	Llama3.3 70B
ReAct report	Rely only on reasoning trace for information	Verbose, mechanistic, and well-structured; minor factual issues	Well-structured; uses internal knowledge; few hallucinations	Weakly structured, limited mechanistic explanation
ReAct-LF report	Improved focus and structured; internal knowledge presents ideas	Precise and straightforward; retains key points with improved references	More direct and better grounded, with fewer inconsistencies	Slightly better organized, but still incomplete due to dependence on reasoning trace

Overall, the qualitative cases reveal that differences in reasoning style, memory retention, tool use, and relevance selection play an important role in determining the quality of long-form scientific answers. These distinctions are not always captured by aggregate report metrics alone, highlighting the importance of qualitative evaluation when evaluating agentic systems for open-ended tasks in domain-specific fields.

6 Discussion

Our results provide several practical insights for building AI systems that support long-form scientific question answering in systems biology and require navigating heterogeneous biological resources, performing multi-step reasoning, and synthesizing evidence into coherent reports.

1. **LFQA Reasoning:** Agent-based frameworks greatly enhance the capacity of LLMs to address research-oriented inquiries in systems biology by facilitating the integration and reasoning of information from external biological sources, such as genes, proteins, literature, biological pathways, and genetic variants, instead of solely depending on the model's internal knowledge. We also saw how unchecked observations during ReAct reasoning might raise the cost of tokens without making the answers any better.
2. **Evidence Control:** In systems biology procedures, the evidence that is collected can often be too wide, redundant, or only vaguely relevant to the topic. ReAct-LF is a valuable adaptation since it filters observations by relevance before producing the report. This makes the final synthesis more focused and much cheaper, even if some redundant context is lost.
3. **Model Architectures:** The efficacy of agentic systems relies not solely on the reasoning methodology but also on the model's capacity to manage long context and structured reasoning without losing track of earlier evidence. This matters in systems biology because multi-source questions often require following biological relationships over several steps before a coherent explanation can be formed.

7 Conclusion

We presented an application of LLM-based agents to long-form question answering in systems biology, where useful answers require integrating evidence across literature, genes, proteins, pathways, and variants to form mechanistic, expert-style explanations. To study this setting, we introduced ThinkSysBio, an expert-curated dataset designed to capture not only challenging research-style questions but also the reasoning processes that underlie scientific synthesis. We proposed ReAct-LF, a relevance-aware variant of ReAct for LFQA that filters intermediate observations before report generation. Across models and datasets, ReAct-LF yields token savings of 61.3% on average while maintaining comparable report quality. Overall, our findings highlight the promise of agentic systems for supporting multi-source reasoning and long-form scientific synthesis in systems biology.

Limitations: Our work has a few limitations. The ThinkSysBio contains 60 curated samples. While this limits the dataset size, it reflects a deliberate emphasis on high-quality expert reasoning traces rather than large-scale automatic generation. The primary intellectual value of the dataset lies in exposing domain expert's thought processes, rather than providing static final answers that may evolve as scientific knowledge progresses. We did not compute aggregate false-positive/false-negative rates of the relevance field in ReAct-LF over the full dataset, since this would require expert annotations for all intermediate observations. Instead, we provided a qualitative analysis through two representative case studies in Sect. 5.4 and in the Supplementary Material. Our current setup uses only one representative repository for each biological modality. This choice keeps the environment controlled and interpretable for studying multi-source reasoning. Similarly, each question is associated with a single expert reasoning trajectory. In open-ended scientific discovery, there may be multiple valid reasoning paths, but capturing all such alternatives would require extensive additional expert effort.

Acknowledgments. This work was supported by BMFTR (Federal Ministry of Research, Technology and Space) in DAAD project 57616814 (SECAI, School of Embedded Composite AI) as part of the program Konrad Zuse Schools of Excellence in Artificial Intelligence. We thank all participants of the workshop at the Center for Systems Biology Dresden for their inputs during discussions.

References

1. Auer, S., et al.: The SciQA scientific question answering benchmark for scholarly knowledge. **13**(1), 7240. https://doi.org/10.1038/s41598-023-33607-z, https://www.nature.com/articles/s41598-023-33607-z
2. Bai, Y., et al.: LongBench v2: towards deeper understanding and reasoning on realistic long-context multitasks (2025). https://arxiv.org/abs/2412.15204
3. Bruggeman, F.J., Westerhoff, H.V.: The nature of systems biology. Trends Microbiol. **15**(1), 45–50 (2007)
4. Cui, H., Shamsi, Z., Cheon, G., et al: Curie: evaluating LLMs on multitask scientific long context understanding and reasoning (2025). https://arxiv.org/abs/2503.13517
5. Du, M., Xu, B., Zhu, C., Wang, X., Mao, Z.: DeepResearch bench: a comprehensive benchmark for deep research agents (2025). https://arxiv.org/abs/2506.11763
6. Hartke, T., Ramette, J.: Benchmarking the undermind search assistant (2024)
7. Hayes, T., et al.: Simulating 500 million years of evolution with a language model. Science **387**(6736), 850–858 (2025)
8. Huang, K., et al.: Biomni: a general-purpose biomedical AI agent. biorxiv (2025)
9. Jain, C., Vahdati, S., Gopan, N., Sbalzarini, I.F., Lehmann, J.: Evaluating large language model literature reviews in interdisciplinary science: a systems biology perspective (2024). https://ceur-ws.org/Vol-3967/PD_paper_173.pdf
10. Jin, Q., Dhingra, B., Liu, Z., Cohen, W.W., Lu, X.: PubMedQA: a dataset for biomedical research question answering (2019). https://arxiv.org/abs/1909.06146
11. Jin, Q., Yang, Y., Chen, Q., Lu, Z.: GeneGPT: augmenting large language models with domain tools for improved access to biomedical information. Bioinformatics **40**(2) (2024). https://doi.org/10.1093/bioinformatics/btae075
12. Jin, R., Zhang, Z., Wang, M., Cong, L.: Stella: self-evolving LLM agent for biomedical research. arXiv preprint arXiv:2507.02004 (2025)

13. Laurent, J.M., et al.: Lab-bench: measuring capabilities of language models for biology research (2024). https://arxiv.org/abs/2407.10362
14. Lehmann, J., Bhandiwad, D., Gattogi, P., Vahdati, S.: Beyond boundaries: a human-like approach for question answering over structured and unstructured information sources. Trans. Assoc. Comput. Linguist. **12**, 786–802 (2024). https://doi.org/10.1162/tacl_a_00671, https://doi.org/10.1162/tacl_a_00671
15. Patel, L., et al.: Deepscholar-bench: a live benchmark and automated evaluation for generative research synthesis (2026). https://arxiv.org/abs/2508.20033
16. Phan, L., et al.: A benchmark of expert-level academic questions to assess AI capabilities. Nature **649**(8099), 1139–1146 (2026). https://doi.org/10.1038/s41586-025-09962-4
17. Skarlinski, M.D., et al.: Language agents achieve superhuman synthesis of scientific knowledge (2024). https://arxiv.org/abs/2409.13740
18. Tsatsaronis, G., et al.: An overview of the BIOASQ large-scale biomedical semantic indexing and question answering competition. BMC Bioinform. **16**(1), 138 (2015)
19. Yao, S., et al.: React: synergizing reasoning and acting in language models (2023). https://arxiv.org/abs/2210.03629

AutoQA-MAS: An LLM-Based Multi-agent System for Autonomous Website End-to-End Testing

Adriana-Simona Mihaita(✉) and Kai Sor

University of Technology Sydney, 61 Broadway Street, Ultimo, NSW 2007, Australia
adriana-simona.mihaita@uts.edu.au, kai.p.sor@student.uts.edu.au

Abstract. Manual execution of website end-to-end (E2E) test cases is a repetitive, labour-intensive process that creates bottlenecks in modern software development workflows. We investigate the feasibility of automating this process using AutoQA-MAS, a large language model (LLM)-based multi-agent system (MAS) comprising four specialised agents coordinated through a shared data pool: a Web Agent that interprets natural language test cases and interacts with the browser via Document Object Model (DOM) analysis; a Vision Agent that inspects screenshots and agent context for visual defects; an Accessibility Agent that audits Web Content Accessibility Guidelines (WCAG) 2.1 Level AA compliance; and a Report Agent that semantically deduplicates findings into a consolidated quality assurance (QA) report. The system was evaluated across 90 test case executions on a controlled e-commerce environment, 89 of which produced valid reports, comparing OpenAI GPT-5-mini, Google Gemini 2.5 Flash, and Anthropic Claude Sonnet 4.6. The system achieved an overall goal completion rate of 85.4%, bug recall of 76.9%, and accessibility issue precision of 76.0% (GPT-5-mini and Gemini only), with Claude Sonnet 4.6 achieving the highest bug detection performance (91.5% precision, 84.3% recall, 87.9% F1) while consuming 28% fewer tokens than GPT-5-mini. We observe that well-defined detection criteria, such as WCAG standards, yield significantly higher precision than loosely scoped bug detection (76.0% vs. 65.9%), motivating richer contextual prompting as a key direction for improvement. These results demonstrate the viability of LLM-based MAS for autonomous web QA, offering a scalable pathway to reduce manual testing effort, lower quality assurance costs, and accelerate software delivery cycles without proportional increases in engineering headcount.

Keywords: Multi-Agent Systems · Large Language Models · Web Testing · End-to-End Testing · Accessibility · Browser Automation

---

Supplementary Information The online version contains supplementary material available at https://doi.org/10.1007/978-3-032-37682-4_20.

M. Baratchi et al. (Eds.): ECML PKDD 2026, LNAI 16949, pp. 342–359, 2027.
https://doi.org/10.1007/978-3-032-37682-4_20

1 Introduction

Recent advancements in Large Language Models (LLMs) have demonstrated significant progress in natural language reasoning, problem-solving, and general intelligence [13]. In particular, LLM-based autonomous Artificial Intelligence (AI) agents have gained attention by extending these capabilities with context-aware memory, tool use, and inter-agent collaboration in the form of a Multi-Agent System (MAS). These generalist qualities allow for applications across diverse domains [5].

One such application is the automation of web browser tasks, which involves interacting with user interface (UI) elements on a website to achieve a defined outcome. While single-agent web browsing systems have been explored, their task completion rates are constrained by hallucination, inefficient exploration strategies, and looping behaviour [15]. Implementing an MAS design helps address these limitations via improved task planning and enhanced exploration strategies. The Monte Carlo Tree Search (MCTS) algorithm is one such strategy gaining traction, closely mimicking human web interaction patterns [14]. Systems such as WebPilot [14] and STEWARD [11] have adopted this design, achieving task completion rates of 37.2% and 40% respectively on the WebArena benchmark [15]. As of 2025, the top-performing agents on the WebArena leaderboard—including IBM CUGA (61.7%), OpenAI Operator (58.1%), and Jace.AI (57.1%)—remain below 62%, underscoring the persistent difficulty of general-purpose web task completion [12].

Website End-to-End (E2E) testing is a quality control process in web development that involves executing behavioural test cases simulating real user interaction. Each test case is documented with steps taken, expected versus actual outcomes, screenshots, and defect categorisation according to a predefined risk matrix. The workflow is characterised by high repetition, low cognitive demand, and a reliance on natural language specification—qualities that make it a strong candidate for LLM-based MAS automation. The automated testing market was valued at USD 17 billion in 2025 [2], underscoring the scale of commercial investment in this space and the demand for more efficient testing approaches.

In this paper, we investigate the feasibility of this approach through *AutoQA-MAS*, an LLM-based MAS designed to autonomously execute and document website E2E test cases. The system comprises four specialised agents—a Web Agent, a Vision Agent, an Accessibility Agent, and a Report Agent—coordinated through a shared data pool, achieving a Bug F1 score of up to 87.9% and an Accessibility Issue Precision of 72.7% when evaluated against a controlled e-commerce benchmark with 25 planted defects across three LLM providers. The remainder of this paper is structured as follows: Sect. 2 states the research aims and questions; Sect. 3 reviews related work on MAS, automated testing, and autonomous web agents; Sect. 4 describes the AutoQA-MAS architecture and agent design; Sect. 5 presents the experimental setup and results; Sect. 6 discusses findings, limitations, and ethical considerations; and Sect. 7 concludes with directions for future work.

2 Research Aims and Objectives

The primary aim of this research is to investigate the feasibility of implementing an LLM-based Multi-Agent System (MAS) to automate the execution and documentation of End-to-End website test cases, without hard-coded scripts or prior knowledge of the target website's internal structure.

The system is designed around four specialised agents communicating through a shared data pool—a central store of browser state, screenshots, HTML, agent outputs, and the original test prompt—rather than direct agent-to-agent messaging. This design aims to decouple agent responsibilities while enabling all agents to access the full context of each test session.

Based on this design, the research sets out five feasibility criteria, framed as Research Questions:

RQ1 [Natural language comprehension]: How effectively can the system interpret high-level natural language test case instructions and decompose them into actionable, structured browser goals?

RQ2 [Autonomous browser interaction]: Can the Web Agent interact with a live web browser, perceive page content and Document Object Model (DOM) structure, and execute browser actions to carry out each test case?

RQ3 [Bug detection and reporting]: What categories of functional and visual web page defects can the system detect and document, using both DOM-level inspection and screenshot-based visual analysis?

RQ4 [Accessibility evaluation]: To what extent does the Accessibility Agent correctly identify and classify web accessibility violations against WCAG 2.1 Level AA criteria [6]?

RQ5 [Semantic consolidation]: How accurately does the Report Agent deduplicate and semantically consolidate overlapping findings from multiple agents into a single coherent report?

3 Related Work

3.1 Multi-agent Systems

The principal advantage of a Multi-Agent approach in LLM-based systems is enhanced problem-solving capacity and task completion. By orchestrating multiple specialised agents, complex tasks can be decomposed into manageable subtasks [5]. Guided inter-agent communication can prevent hallucination by encouraging agents to review their output against structured feedback [9]. The modular nature of MAS allows scalability and flexibility across both generalised and specialised domains [1,5,10]. These domains are typically categorised as either World Simulation, such as gaming and economy, and Problem Solving, such as software development and embodied agents [5,9]. There is an ongoing effort to develop evaluation methodologies and datasets to facilitate research progress on LLM-based MAS; however, due to the wide domain potential and the complexity of typical scenarios, identifying a general evaluation methodology remains challenging [9]. There is nonetheless a general consensus on the vast application potential of LLM-based MAS across multiple fields, from transport and smart infrastructure management to finance and healthcare.

3.2 Automated Software Testing

Web browser automation has traditionally been achieved via scripting tools such as Selenium and Playwright, enabling developers to write hard-coded action scripts. This approach requires an understanding of the internal structure of target websites and carries well-documented challenges, including the difficulty of maintaining scripts as website code is updated, flaky execution arising from variable element behaviours such as differing page load times, and the overhead of designing a test execution and documentation framework [4].

3.3 MAS-Empowered Autonomous Web Browsing

STEWARD. [11] is a natural language web automation system employing multiple LLM-based components, including *HTML Element Proposal*, which identifies the most suitable element to interact with, and *Double Checking*, which verifies the proposed element. The architecture incorporates a planning component, multi-modal element detection from screenshots and HTML, a proposal system, and program synthesis to translate action verbs into pre-mapped browser operations. Tang & Shin observe that via this design they were able to achieve a task completion rate of 40%.

WebPilot. [14] is an LLM-based MAS for web task execution with strategic exploration, rooted in the MCTS algorithm. It employs a *Global Optimisation* process with a task ledger for plan generation and continual state assessment, alongside a *Local Optimisation* process using MCTS for page-level exploration and a variety of evaluation mechanisms fed back to perform Global Optimisation. WebPilot achieved a task completion rate of 37.2% on the WebArena leaderboard, representing a 93% relative increase in success rate over concurrent tree-based methods. While STEWARD and WebPilot differ architecturally, both employ MAS frameworks to exchange outputs between agents and enhance group decision-making, yielding greater task completion rates than single-agent baselines.

WebWatcher. [3] is a more recent vision-language deep research agent for the web, employing cross-validation and multi-modal reasoning to handle complex web research tasks. Its design reflects a broader trend towards agents that combine visual perception with structured reasoning pipelines, extending beyond task execution into deeper information synthesis.

BrowseMaster. [8] proposes a tool-augmented programmatic agent pair designed for scalable web browsing. Pang et al. observe that general improvements in LLM capability are progressively reducing the performance advantage previously held by specialised agent-pair architectures, suggesting that the field is converging towards simpler designs underpinned by stronger base models. This observation directly informed the architectural decisions in the present work, as discussed in Sect. 4.

4 Methodology

We propose *AutoQA-MAS*, a multi-agent architecture comprising four specialised agents that execute sequentially and communicate through a shared data pool, mirroring the structured workflow of established human quality assurance (QA) processes. Each agent consumes and extends the data artefacts produced by its predecessor, which are stored in a central shared data store $\mathcal{D}$ accessible to all agents. A purpose-built evaluation tool is used to assess report accuracy against human-annotated ground truth. An initial design explored a planner agent and MCTS-based exploration strategy, following the approaches of WebPilot and STEWARD. However, advances in base model reasoning capability at the time of development rendered a dedicated planner agent unnecessary; the architecture was consequently simplified to the current four-agent shared-pool design, consistent with the trend identified by Pang et al. [8].

4.1 Design

The **Web Agent** is responsible for interfacing with web browsers to perform page navigation and task execution. It is implemented using Browser-use, which is a multi-modal framework wrapped around Playwright. It receives natural language test case prompts and performs the web interaction and navigation. A callback hook is implemented to capture agent output and the web browser state data at each step, including HyperText Markup Language (HTML) DOM snapshots, screenshots, and agent reasoning and context. A session video is also produced by compiling the per-step screenshots into a frame-by-frame recording, providing a visual trace of the agent's browsing behaviour to assist with later evaluation. The agent is also provided with a bug-recording tool to report instances of bugs that it encounters during DOM analysis in web navigation.

The **Vision Agent** analyses browser screenshots and the Web Agent's recorded content and output, retrieved from the shared data store $\mathcal{D}$, to detect visual bugs not identifiable via DOM analysis alone. It leverages vision-language models to identify visual defects such as spacing and margin errors, broken layouts, and formatting issues. Identified bugs are reported using the same severity classification matrix as the Web Agent (see supplementary material, Appendix C).

The **Accessibility Agent** analyses screenshots and HTML code to identify accessibility issues as defined by the Web Content Accessibility Guidelines (WCAG) 2.1 Level AA standard [6], such as missing image alternative text, low visual contrast elements, and absent form labels. Each issue is linked to the relevant WCAG criterion, with agent suggestions on improving the issues. Issues are also assigned a severity score based on the issue's impact on restricting accessibility (see supplementary material, Appendix C).

The **Report Agent** is responsible for consolidating the artefacts produced by the above three agents and synthesising them into a structured report. It combines the bug lists produced by the Web Agent and Vision Agent, semantically deduplicating overlapping entries into a single consolidated list. It also analyses the Web Agent's step-by-step output and transforms it into a natural language narrative of the test steps taken, including steps to reproduce each bug. To illustrate the scale of consolidation: in a representative test case execution, the Web Agent reported 1 bug, the Vision Agent reported 5 bugs, and the Accessibility Agent reported 11 issues—a total of 17 raw findings that the Report Agent reduces to a deduplicated structured report.

Process Flow: We decompose the system process flow into three phases: Web Task Execution, Review, and Human Evaluation. The system can be expressed as a sequence of agents $\mathcal{A}$ acting as functions that operate over a shared data store $\mathcal{D}$, as illustrated in Fig. 1.

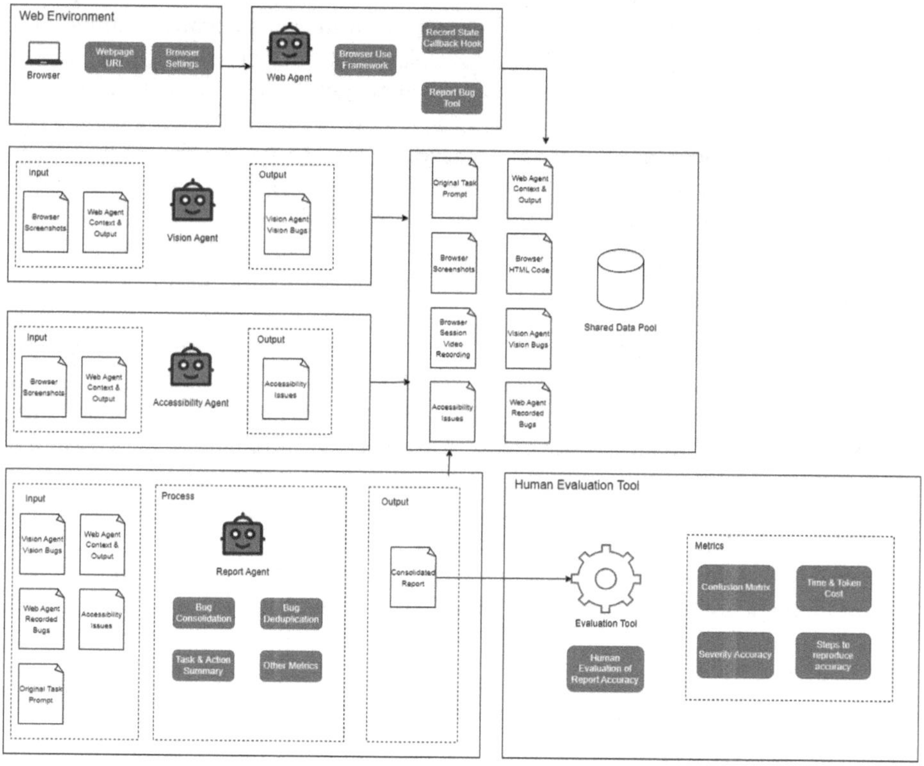

Fig. 1. System architecture overview: four specialised agents (Web, Vision, Accessibility, Report) communicating through a shared data pool

During the *Web Task Execution Phase*, the Web Agent $\mathcal{A}_{\text{web}} : (\mathcal{E}, \mathcal{T}) \rightarrow B_{\text{dom}}, \mathcal{D}$ interacts with the web browser environment $\mathcal{E}$ to perform the given test case $\mathcal{T}$ via a series of action steps S_{action}. At each step, the agent records the current page HTML D_{html}, captures a screenshot $D_{\text{screenshot}}$, and logs the model reasoning output D_{thought}. If the agent encounters a bug via DOM analysis, it reports the bug B_{dom} via the bug-reporting tool. The data and bugs are then stored in a JavaScript Object Notation (JSON) report $\mathcal{R} = (B_{\text{dom}}, \mathcal{D})$.

After completing the test case, the browser environment is no longer needed and the system enters the *Review Phase.* The Vision Agent $\mathcal{A}_{\text{vision}} : (D_{\text{screenshot}}) \rightarrow B_{\text{vision}}$ analyses the captured screenshots to identify visual bugs B_{vision} and stores them in the report. Similarly, the Accessibility Agent $\mathcal{A}_{\text{access}} : (D_{\text{html}}, D_{\text{screenshot}}) \rightarrow B_{\text{access}}$ reviews both the screenshots and HTML snapshots to identify accessibility issues B_{access}, and also stores these in the report.

At this stage, the report $\mathcal{R} = (S_{\text{action}}, B_{\text{dom}}, B_{\text{vision}}, B_{\text{access}})$ consists of the steps taken, Web Agent-reported bugs, Vision Agent-reported bugs, and accessibility issues. Due to the nature of bug reporting, there is a high likelihood of similar bugs being reported multiple times. The Report Agent $\mathcal{A}_{\text{report}} : (\mathcal{R}) \rightarrow B_{\text{deduplicated}}$ analyses the current JSON report and semantically groups similar bugs into a de-duplicated bug list $B_{\text{deduplicated}} = \text{merge}(B_{\text{dom}}, B_{\text{vision}})$. It then reads the agent output and steps taken to generate a steps-to-reproduce narrative for each de-duplicated bug.

Finally, the report accuracy is assessed in the *Human Evaluation Phase*, where an evaluation tool is used to validate bug-reporting correctness and accuracy. This is further explained in the Evaluation section below.

4.2 Implementation

The system is implemented in Python 3. The source code is publicly available at https://tinyurl.com/2w3r8rxu. The Web Agent uses Browser-use to interface with Playwright, providing multi-modal web element identification and natural language browser control. Internally, Browser-use implements an action and goal ledger that continually updates based on current browser state, and accepts any LangChain-compatible chat model as its underlying LLM. GPT-5-mini was selected as the primary model for its cost-effectiveness, multi-modal input capacity, and support for structured output via Pydantic schemas. As a comparative baseline, Google's Gemini 2.5 Flash model was evaluated via the Gemini SDK, which offers equivalent multi-modal input and structured output via Pydantic JSON schemas.

4.3 Evaluation Methodology

AcademyBugs is an interactive platform designed for QA training, providing a simulated e-commerce website with 25 planted and documented bugs spanning a range of defect categories: Functional, Visual, Content, Performance, and Crash (see Fig. 2). The platform's *Find Bugs* page presents a product listing environment in which all planted defects are embedded (see Fig. 3). Due to its controlled, ground-truth-verified nature, AcademyBugs was selected as the evaluation environment for this study.

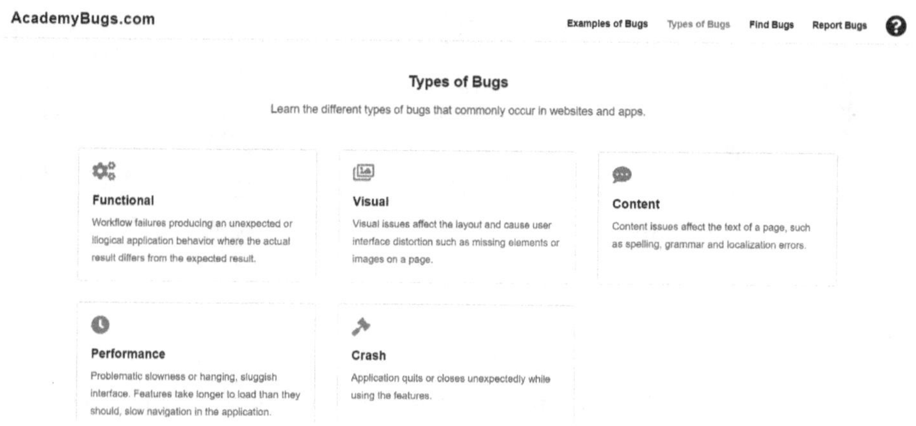

Fig. 2. AcademyBugs bug category taxonomy: Functional, Visual, Content, Performance, and Crash.

A purpose-built evaluation tool was created to assess the accuracy of generated reports against human-annotated ground truth. After the test execution, the evaluation tool was used to record the following fields for each test case report:

- Goal Completion: Whether the Web Agent was able to complete the specified test case (boolean).
- Main Bug Discovered: Whether the system was able to correctly identify and report the primary bug (boolean).
- Bug Reported Correctly: Whether the bugs reported by the system were accurate (boolean)
- Bug Severity Correctness: Whether the bugs reported had an appropriate severity score (boolean).
- Bug Duplicated: Indicates whether the bug had already been previously reported (boolean).
- Bugs Missed: The number of bugs that were present but not reported by the system (integer).
- Accessibility Issue Correctness: Indicates whether the reported accessibility issue is valid (boolean).
- Accessibility Issue Severity Correctness: Indicates whether the severity of the accessibility issue is appropriate (boolean).
- Accessibility Issue WCAG Criterion Correctness: Indicates whether the WCAG criterion used to report the issue was assigned appropriately (boolean).

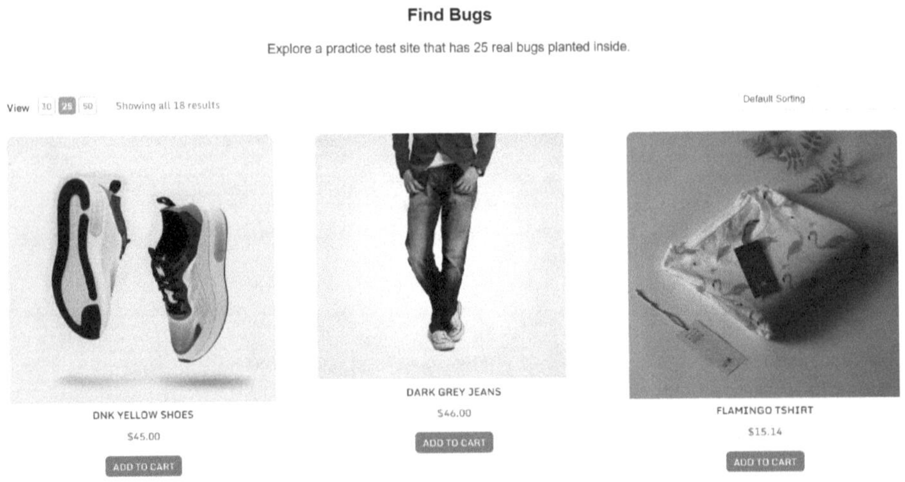

Fig. 3. AcademyBugs *Find Bugs* page—the simulated e-commerce environment used for evaluation, containing 25 planted bugs

Other metrics collected by the system include:

- Token Usage: The total number of tokens used by each agent to perform the test case (integer)
- Test Case Duration: The total time, in seconds, taken to perform the test case and produce a report (integer)

5 Experiment

The system was evaluated on 10 distinct test cases, each targeting different modalities of bugs (listed in supplementary material, Appendix B). Each test case was repeated 3 times to ensure stability of output. For this experiment, OpenAI's GPT-5-mini model was used as the primary model, Google's Gemini 2.5 Flash as a comparative baseline, and Anthropic's Claude Sonnet 4.6 as an additional provider, leading to a total of 90 test case executions. All 90 test cases were evaluated via the evaluation tool. GPT-5-mini and Gemini executions were assessed using the full evaluation tool against human-annotated ground truth; Claude Sonnet 4.6 bug metrics were estimated using the same ground-truth definitions applied directly to the raw JSON output. Aggregate metrics reported are: **Goal Accuracy** (goals completed/total); **Primary Bug** (fraction of runs identifying the primary targeted defect); **Bug Precision** (True Positives/Total Reported); **Bug Recall** (True Positives/(True Positives + False Negatives)); **Bug F1** (harmonic mean of Precision and Recall); **Bug Severity Accuracy** (fraction of reported bugs with a correct severity rating per supplementary material, Appendix C); **A11y Precision** (True Positives/total reported accessibility issues); and **A11y Severity Accuracy**.

Table 1 summarises the aggregate results from all 90 executions. Of these, one Gemini execution (the *crash* test case, third run) failed to generate a valid report, yielding 89 usable results. GPT-5-mini completed executions in an average of 188.0 s per test case, compared to 76.4 s for Gemini 2.5 Flash and 177.5 s for Claude Sonnet 4.6. Token usage was near-identical between GPT-5-mini and Gemini (174,391 vs. 176,583), while Claude consumed substantially fewer tokens (125,566 on average, 28% less than GPT-5-mini).

Table 1. Aggregate results across 90 test case executions (89 valid). *Top*: bug detection quality. *Bottom*: accessibility and efficiency. †A11y metrics for GPT-5-mini and Gemini only; Claude's Accessibility Agent encountered a JSON parsing error across all 30 runs (see Limitations).

LLM	Goal Acc. (%)	Bug Prec. (%)	Bug Rec. (%)	Bug F1 (%)	Bug S. A. (%)	Pri.Bug
OpenAI GPT-5-mini	86.7	62.5	81.7	68.7	80.5	20/30
Gemini 2.5 Flash	72.4	42.9	64.4	50.3	64.1	15/29
Claude Sonnet 4.6	**96.7**	**91.5**	**84.3**	**87.9**	**95.7**	**29/30**
Overall	85.4	65.9	76.9	69.2	80.3	64/89

LLM	A11y P. (%)	A11y S. Acc. (%)	Avg Time (s)	Avg Tokens
OpenAI GPT-5-mini	80.9	85.2	188.0	174,391
Gemini 2.5 Flash	70.9	85.2	76.4	176,583
Claude Sonnet 4.6	—†	—†	177.5	**125,566**
Overall	76.0†	85.2†	148.1	158,647

6 Discussion

6.1 Experiment Results Discussion

In addition to the results presented in Table 1, several recurring patterns were identified during manual evaluation of the generated reports.

Accessibility Issue Precision Greater Than Bug Reporting Precision. We observe that accessibility issues achieved substantially higher precision than general bug reporting across GPT-5-mini and Gemini (76.0% vs. 52.9% for those two providers). We attribute this to two complementary factors. First, the WCAG criteria provide clear, unambiguous definitions for each class of accessibility violation, compared to the bug-reporting agents where the description of a defect is more loosely scoped, affording greater room for ambiguity in the agents' reasoning. Second, and more concretely, a curated set of common WCAG violation examples—including missing interactive element labels, absent form labels, insufficient colour contrast, and missing landmark roles—was explicitly embedded into the Accessibility Agent's prompt. This richer contextual grounding enabled the agent to apply structured, criterion-level reasoning to each issue, a strategy that directly informed the precision gap observed. This finding motivates the use of similarly specific bug definition examples within the Web Agent and Vision Agent prompts as a primary improvement direction.

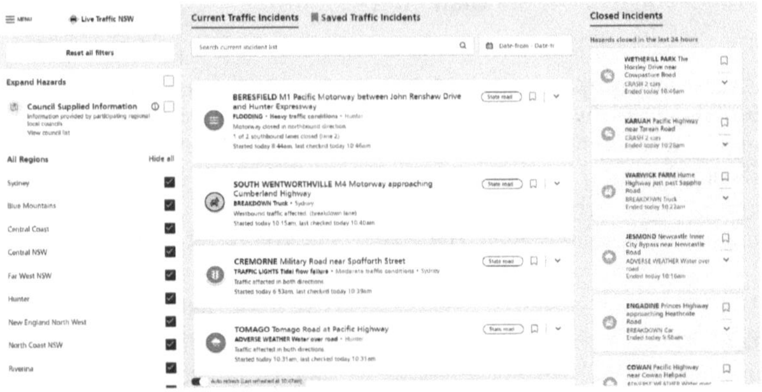

Fig. 4. Page load state incorrectly reported as a bug by the system.

Inaccurately Reported Bugs. Three categories of false positive were identified. First, *browser loading artefacts*: the system captured browser state snapshots whilst the page was still loading, resulting in empty or partially rendered sections being erroneously reported as defects (see Fig. 4).

Fig. 5. Cookie consent pop-up incorrectly reported as a layout defect by the system

Second, *cookie consent overlays*: cookie banners obscuring page content were misclassified as layout defects, as the agents lacked explicit instruction to disregard standard consent UI patterns (see Fig. 5).

Fig. 6. Sale price with strikethrough formatting incorrectly reported as a visual defect

Third, *web page styling conventions*: legitimate design patterns such as sale price displays with strikethrough formatting and sidebar UI elements were reported as visual defects, as the agents had no contextual knowledge of the website's intended design or any sale (see Fig. 6). We attribute all three failure modes to the absence of sufficiently specific bug definition context and site-specific design knowledge within the prompts provided to the generalist models.

Bug Parroting: A further pattern we observed is what we term *bug parroting*: the Vision Agent systematically repeated defects already identified and reported by the Web Agent during DOM analysis. In the current implementation, the Web Agent's recorded bug reports are included in the shared data store $\mathcal{D}$ and passed to the Vision Agent as contextual input alongside the screenshots. Despite this, the Vision Agent consistently re-identifies the same defects independently through visual analysis of the screenshots, producing near-duplicate entries. This suggests that providing the prior bug list as context is insufficient on its own to suppress redundant visual re-identification, and that a more explicit suppression mechanism—such as instructing the Vision Agent to exclude any defect already present in the Web Agent's report—is required. While the Report Agent's semantic deduplication step consolidates such duplicates in the final output, the parroting behaviour inflates the raw bug count and places a higher burden on the deduplication stage. We identify this as a structural limitation of the current shared-pool design and propose explicit cross-agent deduplication as a first-order improvement.

Notwithstanding the parroting issue, the Vision Agent does contribute unique findings that the Web Agent cannot surface via DOM analysis alone. In the representative example cited above, the Vision Agent reported five bugs against the Web Agent's one—a ratio that reflects the Vision Agent's ability to detect purely visual defects (e.g. spacing errors, broken layouts, misaligned elements) that have no DOM-level signature. A formal ablation study isolating Vision Agent-only true positives is identified as an important direction for future work to quantify this net contribution precisely.

Model Comparison: Quality Versus Speed. GPT-5-mini outperformed Gemini 2.5 Flash across all quality metrics (Table 1): goal accuracy (86.7% vs. 72.4%), bug precision (62.5% vs. 42.9%), bug recall (81.7% vs. 64.4%), bug F1 (68.7% vs. 50.3%), bug severity accuracy (80.5% vs. 64.1%), and accessibility issue precision (80.9% vs. 70.9%). However, Gemini completed executions in substantially less time (76.4 s vs. 188.0 s on average), representing a 2.5× speed advantage. Notably, token usage was near-identical (174,391 vs. 176,583), indicating that the execution time gap is attributable to inference latency rather than output length.

A notable exception to the GPT-5-mini advantage is accessibility severity accuracy, where both models achieved an identical score of 85.2%. This indicates that, once an accessibility issue is identified, both models are equally capable of assigning the correct severity level; the performance gap between models lies entirely in detection, not in severity judgement. This finding further supports the interpretation that structured criteria (WCAG) equalise model behaviour at the classification stage. By contrast, bug severity accuracy is both lower and model-dependent (80.5% GPT-5-mini vs. 64.1% Gemini 2.5 Flash), because assigning functional-impact severity to arbitrary web defects requires contextual judgement that lacks analogous structured grounding, making it more sensitive to the underlying model's reasoning capability.

This presents a quality–speed trade-off for GPT-5-mini and Gemini: GPT-5-mini is the stronger performer for high-assurance testing scenarios, while Gemini 2.5 Flash may be preferable where throughput and cost efficiency are prioritised over detection accuracy.

Claude Sonnet 4.6 achieved the strongest results across all bug detection metrics: goal accuracy of 96.7% (29/30), bug precision of 91.5%, bug recall of 84.3%, bug F1 of 87.9%, and bug severity accuracy of 95.7%. These results are particularly notable given that Claude consumed 28% fewer tokens than GPT-5-mini (125,566 vs. 174,391 on average), suggesting that a more capable model can achieve both higher detection accuracy and greater token efficiency simultaneously. Execution time (177.5 s) was comparable to GPT-5-mini, indicating that Claude's lower token count does not translate to reduced latency on this task. The high primary bug detection rate of 29/30 (96.7%), matching the goal accuracy, suggests that when Claude successfully completed a test case, it reliably identified the targeted defect. Accessibility metrics are not available for Claude due to a known parsing error in the Accessibility Agent when used with this model (see Limitations).

Test Case Difficulty Variance. Aggregating goal accuracy by test case type reveals substantial variance in web task difficulty (Table 2). Four test cases achieved 100% goal completion across all six GPT-5-mini and Gemini runs (*simple, cart, image, empty_cart*), while the *quantity* test case achieved only 17% (one successful run out of six). The quantity task requires the agent to locate a cart item, modify a form quantity field, and confirm the update—a multi-step interaction pattern that proved consistently difficult for both models. This suggests that form interaction and state-confirmation tasks represent a harder class of web automation challenge than navigation-and-observation tasks, independent of the underlying model. The *signin* and *hot_items* test cases also showed reduced goal accuracy (67%), reflecting the challenge of navigating nested menus and secondary page flows. Claude Sonnet 4.6 achieved 100% goal completion on nine of the ten test case types, with only the *hot_items* second run failing to load the linked product page—suggesting that more capable models can largely overcome the structural challenges observed with GPT-5-mini and Gemini. These findings highlight that test case complexity is a significant confounding variable in the evaluation and motivate per-task difficulty stratification in future benchmarking.

Table 2. Goal accuracy aggregated by test case type across all 89 valid executions.

Test Case	Goal Accuracy (%)
simple, cart, image, empty_cart	100
crash	80
description, manufacturer	83
signin, hot_items	67
quantity	17

Feasibility and Further Work. The overall results demonstrate the feasibility of the proposed AutoQA-MAS prototype for autonomous website quality assurance. The overall goal completion rate of 85.4% across all three providers indicates that the system successfully executed more than four out of every five test cases without human intervention, rising to 96.7% for Claude Sonnet 4.6 specifically. The overall bug recall of 76.9% confirms that the system identified the majority of valid defects present in the test environment, while the primary bug detection rate of 64/89 (71.9%) reflects the additional challenge of reliably surfacing the specific defect targeted by each test case. As discussed above, reducing false positives through more specific bug definition context in agent prompts remains the most direct path to improving overall precision.

6.2 Security and Sustainability Considerations

Wide-spread adoption of AutoQA-MAS could reduce demand for manual QA roles, though human oversight remains necessary for ambiguous or high-stakes defect triage. From a security perspective, a recently identified vulnerability in Browser-use allows agent hijacking via prompt-context overwriting [7]; mitigations include domain allowlisting, session sandboxing, and disabling high-risk actions such as external form submission. Uncontrolled parallelism in web agent deployments can generate traffic loads comparable to a DoS attack on the target server, making rate limits and session quotas a production requirement. Finally, at approximately 175,000 tokens per run, inference energy costs are non-trivial at scale and should be treated as a first-class design constraint when deploying LLM-based testing pipelines.

6.3 Limitations

Several limitations should be considered. The performance of this system is critically dependent on the capability of the Web Agent; the ceiling of system performance is therefore bounded by the prevailing state of the art in LLM-based web automation. More advanced LLMs will be able to complete more complex tasks more reliably, but at greater inference cost. The goal completion rate is also directly influenced by the structural complexity of the target webpage and the specificity of the test case instructions, both of which affect the quality of contextual memory accumulated during agent traversal.

Evaluation Scope. The evaluation is confined to a single controlled e-commerce website (AcademyBugs) with 25 planted bugs, which does not capture the diversity of defect types, page structures, dynamic content, authentication flows, and interaction complexity present in real production websites. These results should therefore be interpreted as a proof-of-concept baseline; evaluation on real-world websites—even without complete ground truth—is an important next step to assess generalizability.

Statistical Robustness. With only three repetitions per test case per model and no statistical significance tests applied, observed differences between models should be treated as indicative rather than statistically conclusive. Some metric gaps between providers may fall within noise at this sample size; broader sampling across more test cases and runs would be required to support stronger inferential claims.

Evaluation Asymmetry. Claude Sonnet 4.6 was assessed by applying ground-truth definitions directly to raw JSON output rather than through the interactive evaluation tool used for GPT-5-mini and Gemini. While the evaluation criteria were consistent, this methodological difference introduces a potential annotation confound, and the reported Claude metrics should be interpreted with this caveat in mind. A fully comparable replication using the same tool and annotator for all three models is needed before definitive cross-provider conclusions can be drawn.

Architectural Contribution vs. Model Capability. The system's effectiveness is clearly influenced by the capability of the underlying LLMs—more capable models achieve higher performance ceilings, as demonstrated by Claude's results. The architectural contribution lies in the decomposition of the testing workflow into specialised agents operating over distinct modalities (DOM analysis, visual inspection, accessibility auditing, semantic consolidation): tasks that a single monolithic prompt cannot accomplish within context and output constraints. Nevertheless, disentangling the contribution of the architecture from that of the base model requires controlled ablation experiments in the future.

Comparison with Scripted Baselines. The system has not been compared against conventional scripted testing tools such as Selenium or Playwright. A head-to-head comparison on a shared task suite would provide a clearer picture of where LLM-based automation offers genuine advantages over rule-based automation and represents an important empirical target for future evaluation.

Enriching the system with domain-specific contextual memory presents an avenue for incorporating business logic and software requirements, enabling more precise detection of application-specific defects. This could be introduced in the form of a Subject Matter Expert (SME) agent with in-depth knowledge of the website under test, to guide the Web Agent through complex interaction flows and provide application-specific context to the QA agents.

We identify the introduction of such an SME agent as a priority future direction. Real-world QA workflows involve considerably more specialised work, including website preconditions (data setup and state management required prior to test execution), post-test cleanup procedures, integration into software development pipelines (automated bug-reporting tickets, requirements traceability, and escalation workflows), and defect triage strategies.

During the Claude Sonnet 4.6 evaluation, a parsing error was identified in the Accessibility Agent due to a limitation in the API as of March 2026. As a consequence, accessibility metrics are unavailable for Claude Sonnet 4.6 and are excluded from Table 1. This issue is specific to the Claude integration and does not affect the web agent or vision agent outputs reported elsewhere in the results.

7 Conclusion

We have investigated the feasibility of implementing an LLM-based Multi-Agent System for automating website End-to-End test execution and documentation. The proposed four-agent prototype demonstrated goal-driven browser interaction, autonomous defect identification, and structured report generation, achieving an overall bug recall of 76.9% across three LLM providers and establishing a viable baseline for further development. Claude Sonnet 4.6 achieved the highest individual performance (87.9% Bug F1, 96.7% goal accuracy) while consuming 28% fewer tokens than GPT-5-mini. The observed precision gap between structured (WCAG-guided) and unstructured (general bug) detection further motivates richer contextual prompting as a first-order improvement direction.

If deployed at scale, a system achieving 85% goal completion and 77% bug recall—and up to 97% goal completion and 88% Bug F1 with more capable models—could reduce per-sprint manual QA effort by an order of magnitude, enabling continuous regression testing across large test suites without proportional increases in engineering headcount—a meaningful proposition in an automated testing market valued at USD 17 billion [2]. Future work should prioritise improved bug definition specificity through richer contextual prompting, explicit inter-agent deduplication to mitigate bug parroting, integration of domain-aware SME agents for application-specific reasoning, and improved snapshot timing to reduce browser loading artefacts.

Disclosure of Interests. The authors have no competing interests to declare that are relevant to the content of this article.

A Supplementary Material

Full supplementary material is provided in the accompanying document *Appendix_ECML.pdf* submitted alongside this paper. It contains agent and test case prompts and the severity classification matrix. The source code is available at https://tinyurl.com/2w3r8rxu.

References

1. Aratchige, R.M., Ilmini, W.M.K.S.: LLMs working in harmony: a survey on the technological aspects of building effective LLM-based multi agent systems (2025). https://arxiv.org/abs/2504.01963
2. Fortune Business Insights: Automation testing market size, share & industry analysis (2025). https://www.fortunebusinessinsights.com/automation-testing-market-107180
3. Geng, X., et al.: WebWatcher: breaking new frontiers of vision-language deep research agent (2025). https://arxiv.org/abs/2508.05748
4. Gojare, S., Joshi, R., Gaigaware, D.: Analysis and design of selenium WebDriver automation testing framework. Procedia Comput. Sci. **50**, 341–346 (2015). https://doi.org/10.1016/j.procs.2015.04.038, https://www.sciencedirect.com/science/article/pii/S1877050915005396. big Data, Cloud and Computing Challenges
5. Guo, T., et al.: Large language model based multi-agents: a survey of progress and challenges (2024). https://arxiv.org/abs/2402.01680
6. Kirkpatrick, A., O Connor, J., Campbell, A., Cooper, M.: Web content accessibility guidelines (WCAG) 2.1. W3C recommendation, World Wide Web Consortium (W3C) (2018). https://www.w3.org/TR/WCAG21/
7. Mudryi, M., Chaklosh, M., Wójcik, G.: The hidden dangers of browsing ai agents (2025). https://arxiv.org/abs/2505.13076
8. Pang, X., Tang, S., Ye, R., Du, Y., Du, Y., Chen, S.: BrowseMaster: towards scalable web browsing via tool-augmented programmatic agent pair (2025). https://arxiv.org/abs/2508.09129
9. Qian, C., et al.: ChatDev: communicative agents for software development. In: Proceedings of the 62nd Annual Meeting of the Association for Computational Linguistics (Volume 1: Long Papers), pp. 15174–15186. Association for Computational Linguistics, Bangkok (2024). https://doi.org/10.18653/v1/2024.acl-long.810

10. Talebirad, Y., Nadiri, A.: Multi-agent collaboration: harnessing the power of intelligent LLM agents (2023). https://arxiv.org/abs/2306.03314
11. Tang, B., Shin, K.G.: Steward: natural language web automation (2024). https://arxiv.org/abs/2409.15441
12. WebArena Team: WebArena leaderboard (2025). https://webarena.dev/
13. Yang, Z., et al.: The dawn of LMMs: preliminary explorations with GPT-4V(ision) (2023). https://arxiv.org/abs/2309.17421
14. Zhang, Y., Ma, Z., Ma, Y., Han, Z., Wu, Y., Tresp, V.: WebPilot: a versatile and autonomous multi-agent system for web task execution with strategic exploration (2024). https://arxiv.org/abs/2408.15978
15. Zhou, S., et al.: WebArena: a realistic web environment for building autonomous agents (2024). https://arxiv.org/abs/2307.13854

DynaPitch: A Two-Stage Framework for Dynamic Script Generation in Agent-Assisted Sales Conversations

Swapnil Parekh(✉), Sonia Sharma, Pooja Voladoddi, Ramakrishnan Sathyavageeswaran, Andrew Mattarella-Micke, and Jiayao Liu

Intuit Inc., Mountain View, CA, USA
swapnil_parekh@intuit.com

Abstract. Real-time product recommendations during live customer conversations require both precise *timing* (knowing when to pitch) and faithful *content* (generating text grounded in approved product information). Existing approaches either rely on static scripts that cannot adapt to conversational dynamics, or prompt general-purpose LLMs that hallucinate prices and mistime suggestions. We present DYNAPITCH, a two-stage framework trained exclusively on transcripts from successfully-converting calls that decomposes the problem into (1) a ModernBERT classifier operating over sliding windows of the live transcript to predict the current conversation phase, and (2) a QLoRA-fine-tuned Llama-3.1-8B generator conditioned on the predicted phase, customer context, and a product knowledge base. This decomposition yields a natural latency-cost trade-off: the lightweight classifier runs at every turn while the generator is invoked only when a pitch opportunity is detected, reducing LLM inference cost by 70–80%. The phase classifier achieves weighted F1 of **79.3%**; the 8B generator attains the highest precision of any evaluated model (**1.96**/3.0, GPT-4.1 judge), surpassing GPT-5 zero-shot despite being orders of magnitude smaller, while also achieving top helpfulness among all comparable-scale models. A trie-based constrained decoding layer eliminates **94%** of price fabrications with zero quality regression. We distill practical lessons on two-stage decomposition, LLM-based annotation at scale, class-imbalance handling, and knowledge-grounded generation that transfer to any domain with distinct conversational phases and authoritative reference content.

Keywords: Applied conversational AI · Agent assist systems · Dynamic script generation · Sales pitch classification · Conditional text generation · LLM fine-tuning

1 Introduction

1.1 Motivation

At a major financial software company, product and sales agents staff a global contact center handling millions of inbound support calls per year. After resolving a customer's issue, agents can recommend complementary products from

M. Baratchi et al. (Eds.): ECML PKDD 2026, LNAI 16949, pp. 360–377, 2027.
https://doi.org/10.1007/978-3-032-37682-4_21

the company's ecosystem: accounting software, payroll, payments, bill payment, and more. Internal analyses reveal a stark performance disparity: top-performing agents achieve conversion rates several times higher than the median by naturally sensing when to transition from support to sales, asking targeted probing questions, and handling objections with confidence. Most agents, while skilled at support, miss these opportunities or deliver pitches that feel forced and poorly timed, resulting in lost revenue and agent frustration.

Existing static scripts fail because they cannot adapt to the dynamic structure of real conversations [8]. A better approach must (a) *recognize* the current conversation phase in real time (the way a top performer intuitively does), and (b) *generate* pitch text appropriate to that phase, grounded in the customer's context and approved product information. Simply prompting a general-purpose LLM falls short: unconditioned generation is poorly timed [1,19], prone to hallucinating prices or features, and too slow for real-time turn-by-turn assistance.

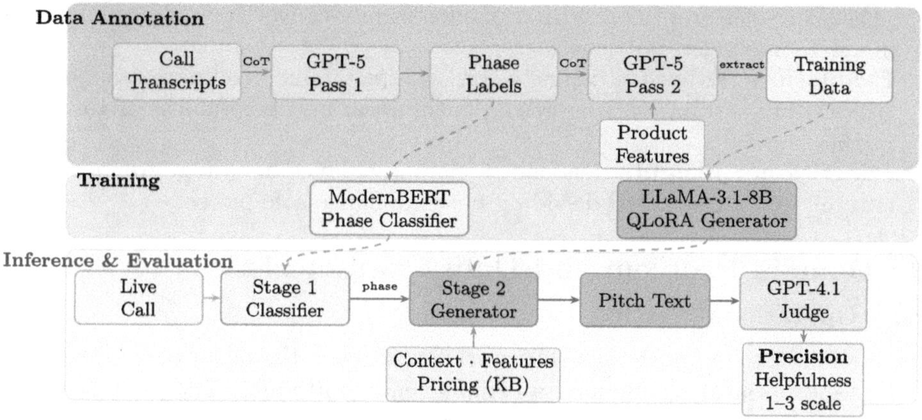

Fig. 1. DYNAPITCH system overview. *Top*: annotation pipeline. GPT-5 labels transcripts in two passes: Pass 1 produces utterance-level phase labels; Pass 2 extracts structured pitch content to form training data. *Middle*: ModernBERT trains on Phase Labels (Pass 1); LLaMA-3.1-8B QLoRA trains on the full Training Data (Pass 2). Dashed arrows = training-time flow. *Bottom*: inference pipeline and LLM-as-judge evaluation; Stage 2 is conditioned on the predicted phase, customer context, product features, and pricing from the knowledge base. Solid arrows = inference-time flow.

1.2 DynaPitch: Two-Stage Dynamic Scripting

We present DYNAPITCH (Fig. 1), a two-stage framework that decomposes dynamic script generation into a lightweight classification step and a conditional generation step. As a conversation unfolds, Stage 1 extracts a sliding window of the most recent utterances and classifies the current conversation phase using a fine-tuned ModernBERT [18] encoder. The predicted phase label is then passed to Stage 2, where a Llama-3.1-8B [7] model, fine-tuned with QLoRA [3], generates structured pitch text tailored to the specific phase. This two-stage decomposition provides a natural latency optimization: the fast classifier runs at every step, while the expensive generator is invoked only when a pitch opportunity is detected.

A key practical contribution is our LLM-based annotation pipeline, which uses frontier models, such as GPT-5, to label real-world call transcripts with utterance-level pitch categories and extract structured pitch content. This approach yields training data at a fraction of the cost and time of manual annotation [6], enabling rapid iteration as the product portfolio evolves.

Contributions.

1. **System design**: A production two-stage framework decoupling phase classification from grounded pitch generation, with a gating mechanism that reduces average LLM inference cost by 70–80%.
2. **Data pipeline**: An LLM-based annotation pipeline that labels conversation phases at scale from transcripts of successfully-converting calls, eliminating manual annotation bottlenecks.
3. **Evaluation**: Extensive window-size sweeps, model comparisons, and an LLM-as-judge framework assessing faithfulness and helpfulness of generated pitches.
4. **Practitioner insights**: Lessons on class-imbalance handling, grounded generation, and constrained decoding for compliance-safe prices.

2 Domain Problem and Data Characteristics

2.1 Operational Setting

Agents follow a "support-then-sell" workflow: resolve the customer's issue, then (when appropriate) recommend a complementary product. The pitch opportunity arises naturally after the support phase, when trust is established. Each product is backed by a *product knowledge base* (features, pricing, objection responses) maintained by product marketing. A separate upstream recommendation engine selects *which* product to pitch based on account profile; DynaPitch handles the *when* and *how*. Training data is drawn exclusively from calls by high-performing agents that resulted in successful conversions, ensuring the model learns from expert-validated pitch patterns.

2.2 Data Characteristics

Our corpus contains **3,390** transcribed conversations (**825,937** utterances, 20–200 turns each) from successfully-converting calls. Key challenges: (a) **class imbalance**: 70–80% of utterances are *no pitch*, while *objection response* and *pricing discussion* are the rarest pitch phases; (b) **label ambiguity**: phase boundaries are fuzzy, addressed through contiguity constraints and priority-based overlap resolution (Sect. 4.2); (c) **proprietary constraints**: raw transcripts cannot be released; all configurations and annotation schemas are fully specified.

2.3 Conversation Phase Taxonomy

We define five phases capturing the support-to-sales arc: **No Pitch** (support and greetings), **Probing Question** (needs discovery), **Feature Explanation** (benefit explanation), **Pricing Discussion** (price and discount), and **Objection Response** (objection handling). When phases overlap, resolution follows the priority order: Objection Response > Pricing Discussion > Feature Explanation > Probing Question > No Pitch.

Figure 2 shows representative system-generated pitches for each pitch-active phase, illustrating how the output varies in style and content across the taxonomy.

Probing Question

Ctx: Customer migrated from desktop to cloud accounting; agent resolved questions about banking transfers and budgets.

"How do you usually pay your vendors right now—are you sending checks, using online bill pay, or something else?"

Product Feature

Ctx: Customer pays vendors outside the platform; no bill-management add-on active.

"[Bill Add-on] lets you pay vendors inside [Platform]—no monthly fee; payments and records in one place."

Pricing Discussion

Ctx: Customer evaluating payroll; agent confirmed promotional discount eligibility.

"[Payroll Core] is $45/mo plus $6 per employee. Right now I can get you 50% off for your first 3 months—so you'd start at just $22.50/mo, then $45/mo after."

Objection Response

Ctx: Customer concerned about long-term commitment when agent introduced a bookkeeping add-on.

"I get that—[Live Bookkeeping] has no contract, so you can cancel anytime once your books are cleaned up."

Fig. 2. Representative DynaPitch outputs for each pitch-active phase (top-scoring by GPT-4.1 judge, held-out test set). Product names anonymized; *italics* = generated pitch.

3 Related Work

Agent Assist and Dynamic Scripting. AI-powered agent assistance has moved toward context-aware, proactive systems. AI-Salesman [19] uses reinforcement learning with a dynamic outline agent for telemarketing guidance. Fischer et al. [8] propose proactive guidance design principles; Minerva CQ [1] demonstrates goal-driven agentic AI for real-time intent triggering; OlaBench [5] benchmarks intelligent customer service systems. Our work explicitly decomposes the task into phase classification and conditional generation, enabling independent optimization and a natural latency-cost trade-off.

Dialogue Act Recognition. Classifying utterances by their communicative function is a long-standing NLP task [15]. Recent transformer-based approaches include context-aware self-attention [14] and Dual Process Masking [10], which improves both performance and interpretability. We adapt dialogue act recognition to a domain-specific taxonomy of sales phases, where the classification output directly conditions a downstream generation model.

Pre-trained Encoders and ModernBERT. BERT [4] and RoBERTa [11] have been standard for text classification, but are limited to 512 tokens. ModernBERT [18] supports 8,192-token sequences via rotary positional embeddings [16], uses FlashAttention [2] for efficiency, and alternates local/global attention. These properties are critical for our use case, where conversation windows can span 50+ turns and exceed 1,500 tokens.

Parameter-Efficient LLM Fine-Tuning. LoRA [9] reduces trainable parameters by 10,000× through low-rank adapter matrices. QLoRA [3] adds 4-bit quantization, enabling fine-tuning of 8B-parameter models on a single GPU. We use QLoRA to adapt Llama-3.1-8B [7] for domain-specific pitch generation, a practical necessity given enterprise compute constraints.

LLM-Based Annotation and Evaluation. LLMs have been shown to match or exceed crowd-worker quality on annotation tasks [6], though error propagation when training downstream models on synthetic labels remains a concern [12]. Automated extraction of structured content from large document corpora (e.g., keyphrase identification from long scientific papers [13]) informs our approach of extracting pitch sections from call transcripts at scale. For evaluation, the LLM-as-judge paradigm [20] provides scalable assessment of open-ended generation, with benchmarks like JudgeBench [17] and JETTS [21] characterizing judge reliability. We use LLMs for both annotation and evaluation, and discuss the implications of this choice in Sect. 8.

4 Methodology

4.1 System Overview

Given a live conversation transcript up to turn t, represented as a sequence of utterances $\mathcal{U} = (u_1, \ldots, u_t)$ where each $u_i = (s_i, c_i)$ has a speaker role s_i and content c_i, along with contextual metadata including the customer's products $\mathcal{P}$, recommended product p^*, and product features $\mathcal{F}(p^*)$, our system:

$$\hat{y}_t = f_\theta(\text{Window}(u_{t-W+1}, \ldots, u_t),\ p^*,\ y_{t-K}) \tag{1}$$

$$\hat{x}_t = g_\phi(\hat{y}_t,\ \mathcal{H}_t,\ \mathcal{F}(p^*),\ \mathcal{P}) \tag{2}$$

where f_θ (Stage 1) classifies the conversation phase from the last W utterances, and g_ϕ (Stage 2) generates pitch text conditioned on the predicted phase and context. Stage 2 is invoked only when a pitch-active phase is detected ($\hat{y}_t \neq$ `no_pitch`), keeping the system silent during support-only turns.

4.2 Data Annotation Pipeline

Our training corpus consists of transcripts from successfully-converting calls handled by top-performing agents. Because these calls resulted in customer conversion, pitch quality is implicitly validated by outcome; we do not require additional domain-expert quality review. The role of our annotation pipeline is thus more focused: assign utterance-level phase labels to these expert transcripts and extract structured pitch content at scale. Manual labeling of this volume would require weeks of analyst time; instead we developed a two-pass LLM-based annotation pipeline.

Pass 1: Utterance-Level Phase Labeling. We prompt GPT-5 with the full transcript and a detailed categorization schema defining the five phases with examples and boundary cases. The model outputs contiguous utterance spans per category:

$$\text{Pass}_1(\mathcal{U}) \rightarrow \{(y_j, [a_j, b_j])\}_{j=1}^{M} \tag{3}$$

The schema enforces contiguity (no single-utterance alternation), labels both agent and customer utterances within a span, and resolves overlaps by the priority ordering defined in Sect. 2.3. The model also identifies the pitched product and rates pitch signal strength (strong/moderate/weak) with chain-of-thought reasoning to improve annotation consistency.

Pass 2: Section-Level Pitch Extraction. For each pitch-active section, a second pass extracts structured pitch content including coherent pitch text rewritten in a specified conversational voice (grade 5–7 reading level, 8–16 words per sentence), customer context summary, and pitch timing rationale. For no-pitch sections, a separate prompt extracts customer context to support downstream generation.

Quality Controls. To manage annotation quality: (a) we used chain-of-thought prompting to make the model's reasoning transparent and auditable; (b) we enforced structured JSON output with validation checks for span consistency; (c) Pass 2 served as an independent verification step, cross-checking the phase assignments from Pass 1 against the extracted pitch content; (d) the annotation prompts included curated few-shot examples of correctly labeled spans to calibrate GPT-5's output distribution. Disagreements primarily occurred at phase boundaries, consistent with the inherent ambiguity noted in Sect. 2.2.

Contact-Level Splitting. All splits are performed at the contact level; no conversation appears in multiple splits, preventing data leakage from sequential utterances.

4.3 Stage 1: Conversation Phase Classifier

Sliding Window Construction. We create training samples using a sliding window parameterized by window size W and step size K. At each anchor position $i \in \{0, K, 2K, \ldots\}$, we extract the W most recent utterances:

$$\mathbf{x}_i = \text{Concat}\big(u_{\max(0, i-W+1)}, \ldots, u_i\big) \tag{4}$$

The label y_i is the phase of the anchor utterance. Each sample also carries the previous window's label y_{i-K} (or `start`), providing sequential context about the conversation trajectory.

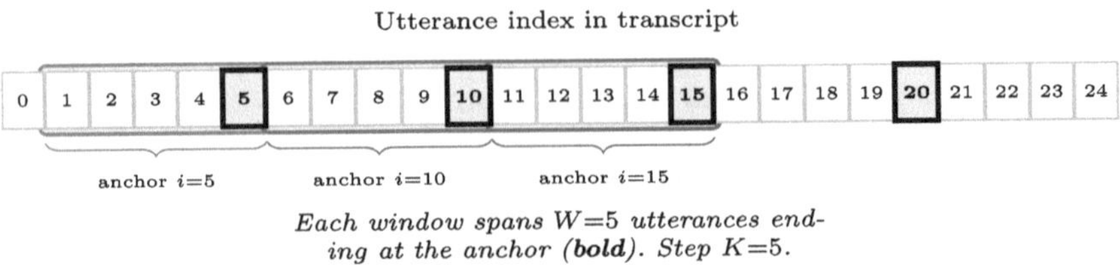

Fig. 3. Sliding window construction (simplified, $W = 5$, $K = 5$; in practice $W \in \{20, 30, 50\}$). At each anchor position (step of K), the W most recent utterances form the classifier input; the anchor's phase label is the prediction target.

Figure 3 illustrates the mechanism. The bounded-window design is driven by a live-call constraint: the system only has access to the conversation so far, and the anchor utterance's label becomes the prediction target. When a phase transition falls within a window, the anchor utterance's label is assigned as the target; the model learns to handle mixed-phase context, and the transition will be fully captured at the next anchor step. We investigate window sizes of $W \in \{20, 30, 50\}$ to understand the trade-off between context breadth and computational cost.

Input Representation. Each sample is formatted as structured text for ModernBERT:

```
Product: {pitched_product} [SEP]
Previous label: {prev_label} [SEP]
[TURN_{n}] {speaker}: {content}
...
[CURRENT_TURN] {speaker}: {content}
```

The product prefix grounds the classifier in the active recommendation. The previous label provides a lightweight autoregressive signal, cheaper than a full sequence model but sufficient to capture that, for example, *pricing discussion* rarely follows directly from *no pitch*. The `[CURRENT_TURN]` marker identifies the anchor utterance.

Model and Training. We use ModernBERT-base [18] with a 5-class sequence classification head. The model is trained with class-weighted cross-entropy:

$$\mathcal{L}_{\text{cls}} = -\sum_{i=1}^{N} w_{y_i} \log \frac{\exp(z_{y_i})}{\sum_{c \in \mathcal{Y}} \exp(z_c)} \tag{5}$$

where w_{y_i} is the inverse-frequency weight for class y_i. We additionally downsample the no-pitch class by a keep ratio ρ during data loading, as even with class weights the dominant class can overwhelm gradient signals for rare phases. Training uses early stopping on validation weighted F1.

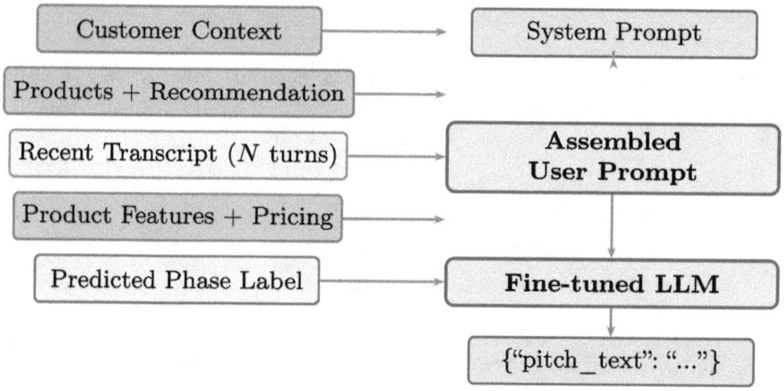

Fig. 4. Stage 2 prompt assembly. Five signals (customer context, product metadata, recent transcript, product features/pricing from the knowledge base, and the Stage 1 phase label) are combined into a structured prompt for the fine-tuned LLM.

4.4 Stage 2: Conditional Pitch Generation

Prompt Construction. The generation prompt (Fig. 4) assembles five components: (1) *customer context*, a summary of the customer's situation and needs; (2) *product information*, the customer's existing products and the recommended product; (3) *recent transcript*, the last N utterances for immediate conversational context; (4) *product features and pricing*, drawn from the product knowledge base to ground generation in approved content; and (5) *predicted phase label*, from Stage 1, constraining the type of pitch text to generate.

The system prompt specifies the generation task, voice guidelines (conversational, grade 5–7 reading level), and the JSON output format (`{''pitch_text'': ''...''}`). This structured output enables programmatic integration with the agent-assist UI.

Model and Fine-Tuning. We fine-tune Llama-3.1-8B-Instruct [7] with QLoRA [3] (4-bit NF4, r=16, α=32) on all attention and MLP projections. Loss is computed only on assistant tokens; no-pitch samples are excluded.

Table 2 lists full hyperparameters.

4.5 End-to-End Inference Pipeline

At inference time, the two stages form a gated pipeline. Stage 1 runs at every turn with sub-second latency; only when a pitch-active phase is detected does the system invoke Stage 2, which assembles the prompt and generates structured pitch text. Because roughly 70–80% of turns are classified as *no pitch*, this gating reduces average LLM inference cost proportionally. The modular design supports independent retraining: the classifier can be updated without touching the generator, and the generator adapts to new products via knowledge base updates alone.

Table 1. Dataset statistics. All splits are at the contact level. Stage 1 windows use W=20, K=5; Stage 2 examples are pitch sections extracted per the annotation pipeline.

	Train	Valid	Test
Corpus overview			
Total contacts	3,390		
Total utterances	825,937		
Products covered	8		
Stage 1: Sliding-window classification samples			
No Pitch	46,052	5,058	13,380
Probing Question	1,072	194	304
Feature Explanation	4,941	509	1,374
Pricing Discussion	4,632	422	1,166
Objection Response	1,240	132	300
Total windows	**57,937**	**6,315**	**16,524**
Stage 2: Pitch generation examples			
Probing Question	1,589	–	415
Feature Explanation	1,936	–	492
Pricing Discussion	1,495	–	373
Objection Response	1,372	–	343
Total examples	**6,392**	–	**1,623**

5 Experimental Setup

5.1 Dataset

Table 1 summarizes the dataset. Transcripts were annotated using the pipeline in Sect. 4.2. The dataset spans **8** distinct products, with conversations ranging from purely support-focused to containing extended multi-phase pitches. Splits are at the contact level to prevent leakage.

5.2 Stage 1 Configuration

Window Sweep. We investigate window sizes $W \in \{20, 30, 50\}$ with corresponding max token lengths $\{1024, 1152, 1536\}$, step size $K = 5$, and no-pitch keep ratio $\rho = 0.2$.

Hyperparameters. ModernBERT-base [18]: learning rate 2×10^{-5}, batch size 16 (effective 64 via gradient accumulation), warmup ratio 0.1, weight decay 0.01, up to 4 epochs, early stopping (patience 10 steps) on validation weighted F1. Class weights use the balanced (inverse-frequency) strategy.

Ablations. We vary: (1) utterance ordering (forward vs. reverse); (2) task prompt prefix (present vs. absent); (3) window size.

Table 2. Stage 2 QLoRA fine-tuning configurations.

Parameter	Llama-3.1-8B
Max sequence length	3072
LoRA rank (r)/alpha (α)	16/32
LoRA dropout	0.0
Quantization	4-bit NF4
Per-device batch/grad. accum.	16/1
Effective batch size	16
Learning rate	2×10^{-4}
Epochs	3
Scheduler/Optimizer	Cosine/Paged AdamW

5.3 Stage 2 Configuration

Table 2 details the fine-tuning configuration. Baselines include GPT-5 full and GPT-5-Mini (zero-shot, identical prompts) and a retrieval baseline returning the nearest training-set pitch.

5.4 Evaluation Metrics

Stage 1. Accuracy, weighted F1 (accounting for class imbalance), and per-class precision/recall/F1.

Stage 2. Following the LLM-as-judge paradigm [20], GPT-4.1 evaluates each generated pitch against its ground-truth on a 1–3 scale across two dimensions:

- **Precision** (1–3): Faithfulness to the ground-truth pitch, with no fabrications or unnecessary padding. 3 = faithful; 2 = some verbosity; 1 = mostly fabricated.
- **Helpfulness** (1–3): Usefulness to the recipient; clear, actionable, and contextually appropriate. 3 = helpful and clear; 2 = somewhat helpful; 1 = unhelpful or confusing.

6 Results

6.1 Stage 1: Conversation Phase Classification

Window Size Sweep. Table 3 reports per-class and macro F1 for all sweep configurations. The test set contains n=27,698 windows because the sweep evaluates all three window sizes ($W \in \{20, 30, 50\}$) over the same held-out contacts, generating more windows per conversation than the W=20 figures in Table 1. While the $W20/L1024$ reverse-order configuration achieves the best overall macro F1 (0.541), we select $W50/L1536$ (reverse, no-prompt) for deployment because it achieves superior recall on the operationally critical pitch-active classes: probing question recall 0.567, feature explanation recall 0.615, and the best objection response F1 (0.510). Since Stage 1's primary role is to detect pitch opportunities, missed pitches (false negatives) are more costly than spurious triggers (false positives), making recall on pitch-active classes the more appropriate optimization target than macro F1. Shorter windows ($W20$) dilute the pitch-phase signal across more no-pitch context.

Table 3. Per-class and macro metrics (Precision/Recall/F1) for all ModernBERT window-size sweep configurations on the test set (n=27,698; larger than Table 1 because all $W \in \{20, 30, 50\}$ windows are evaluated over held-out contacts). *Sweep 1*: varied window width W and max-length L, reverse-order unless marked **fwd**. *Sweep 2*: fixed W=20–50, no-prompt ablations. Bold = best per column. The deployed configuration ($W50/L1536$ rev) achieves weighted F1 of **79.3%**; the best macro-F1 configuration ($W20/L1024$ rev) achieves weighted F1 of 78.8%.

		No Pitch			Probing			Feat. Expl.			Pricing			Obj. Resp.			
Sweep	Config	P	R	F1	P	R	F1	P	R	F1	P	R	F1	P	R	F1	$\overline{F1}$
1	$W20/L1024$	.963	.831	.892	.239	.387	.295	.357	.548	.432	.300	.781	.434	.487	.456	.471	.505
	$W20/L1024$ fwd	.970	.810	.883	.192	.494	.276	.396	.584	.472	.417	.682	.518	.424	.608	.500	.530
	$W20/L1024$ rev	.969	.827	**.893**	.227	.490	.310	.433	.563	.489	.354	.781	.487	.469	.597	.525	.541
	$W30/L1200$ fwd	.968	.829	.893	.208	.518	.297	.459	.486	.472	.430	.537	.477	.363	.698	.478	.524
	$W30/L1200$ rev	.972	.814	.886	.216	.489	.300	.427	.553	.482	.330	**.819**	.470	.468	.596	.524	.532
	$W30/L1536$	.975	.801	.879	.210	.503	.296	.375	.599	.461	.399	.692	.506	.407	.628	.494	.527
	$W50/L1400$ rev	.973	.817	.888	.231	.486	**.313**	.421	.559	.480	.336	.803	.474	.451	.610	.518	.535
	$W50/L2048$	.972	.801	.878	.219	.438	.292	.317	.623	.420	.412	.568	.477	.417	.634	.503	.514
2	$W20/L1024$ fwd	.973	.806	.882	.199	.534	.290	.387	.578	.464	.376	.762	.504	.482	.584	.528	.534
	$W20/L1024$ rev	.973	.804	.880	.193	.539	.284	.381	.579	.459	.378	.764	.506	.474	.540	.505	.527
	$W20/L1024$ rev+prompt	.973	.811	.885	.200	**.541**	.292	.398	.589	.475	.369	.772	.499	.493	.534	.513	.533
	$W30/L1152$ rev	.974	.802	.880	.198	.523	.287	.379	.586	.460	.380	.750	.504	.452	.570	.504	.527
	$W50/L1536$ rev	.974	.794	.875	.187	**.567**	.281	.363	**.615**	.456	.387	.739	.508	**.506**	.514	.510	.526
Best		**.975**	**.831**	**.893**	**.239**	**.567**	**.313**	**.459**	**.615**	**.489**	**.430**	**.819**	**.518**	**.506**	**.698**	**.528**	**.541**

Per-Class Performance. From Table 3, *Probing question* is the hardest class: precision never exceeds 0.239 despite recall reaching 0.567, yielding best F1 of 0.313. This reflects the semantic overlap between probing turns and ordinary support dialogue; the distinction lies in the agent's intent, which is subtle. *Feature* *explanation* has strong recall (up to 0.615) but low precision ($\leq$0.459), indicating frequent confusion with adjacent phases. *Pricing discussion* benefits from distinctive lexical cues (dollar amounts, discount terms), achieving the highest pitch-class recall (0.819). *Objection response* shows balanced but modest performance (best F1 0.528).

Effect of No-Pitch Downsampling. Without downsampling, the no-pitch class dominates training (roughly 70–80% of windows). A keep ratio of $\rho = 0.2$ retains enough negative examples for calibration while freeing capacity for rarer pitch-active phases, consistently outperforming both the unsampled baseline and upsampling of rare classes.

6.2 Stage 2: Conditional Pitch Generation

Model Comparison. The fine-tuned Llama-3.1-8B achieves the highest precision of any evaluated model (1.957), outperforming even GPT-5 full zero-shot (1.838) despite being orders of magnitude smaller, and leads all comparable-scale models on helpfulness (2.046). Only GPT-5 full edges it on helpfulness (2.143 vs. 2.046), at the cost of lower precision, an important compliance distinction. The 3B variant is within 0.05 on both dimensions, making it viable for lower-latency deployments. The retrieval baseline underperforms on both dimensions, confirming that verbatim retrieval cannot substitute for contextual adaptation (Table 4).

Table 4. GPT-4.1-judge scores (1–3 scale) for all evaluated models on the test set.

Model	Precision	Helpfulness
Llama 3.1 8B Instruct (fine-tuned)	**1.957**	**2.046**
Llama 3.2 3B Instruct (fine-tuned)	1.911	2.038
GPT-5 (zero-shot)	1.838	2.143
GPT-5-Mini (zero-shot)	1.723	2.042
Retrieval baseline	1.581	1.877

Human Evaluation. To complement the LLM-as-judge scores and address potential evaluator bias, a domain expert independently scored a stratified sample of fine-tuned Llama-3.1-8B outputs on a 1–5 scale across three dimensions: **Relevancy** (appropriate to the customer's context and conversation phase), **Accuracy** (factually grounded in the product knowledge base), and **Conversational Quality** (deliverable by an agent without interpretation). For each phase, both the first generated candidate (*Initial*) and the highest-ranked candidate (*Optimal*) were evaluated. Table 5 reports means over n=10 samples per

Table 5. Human evaluation scores (1–5 scale, n=10 per phase) for the fine-tuned Llama-3.1-8B, comparing the first generated candidate (Initial) and the highest-ranked candidate (Optimal). Evaluated by a domain expert.

Phase	Candidate	Relevancy	Accuracy	Conv. Quality
Probing Question	Initial	4.40	4.40	5.00
	Optimal	**5.00**	**4.60**	**5.00**
Feature Explanation	Initial	5.00	3.60	5.00
	Optimal	**5.00**	**4.60**	**5.00**
Objection Response	Initial	4.80	**5.00**	5.00
	Optimal	**5.00**	4.60	**5.00**

phase. We note that this is a small-scale validation study intended to complement, not replace, the large-scale LLM-judge evaluation.

The Optimal candidate achieves near-perfect scores on Relevancy (5.0/5) and Conversational Quality (5.0/5) across all phases. The largest accuracy improvement from Initial to Optimal occurs in Feature Explanation (+1.0, from 3.60 to 4.60), consistent with the LLM-judge finding that this phase benefits most from candidate selection. Objection Response Initial accuracy (5.0) edges the Optimal (4.6), suggesting that for this phase the first candidate is already highly grounded and reranking does not further improve factual faithfulness. These human scores corroborate the LLM-as-judge precision rankings and confirm that the fine-tuned model produces relevant, accurate, and agent-ready pitch text.

Quality by Pitch Type. *Pricing discussion* achieves the highest scores (precision 2.102, helpfulness 2.118), reflecting its formulaic structure; the model learns to state prices cleanly from the knowledge base. *Objection response* is hardest (1.344, 1.516): objections are contextually diverse and require nuanced reframing. *Feature explanation* scores well on helpfulness (1.831), consistent with the model mapping features to customer needs (Table 6).

Table 6. LLM-judge scores (1–3) by pitch phase for the fine-tuned Llama-3.1-8B (GPT-5 judge; GPT-4.1 per-phase breakdown unavailable).

Pitch Type	Precision	Helpfulness
Probing Question	1.522	1.604
Feature Explanation	1.687	1.831
Pricing Discussion	**2.102**	**2.118**
Objection Response	1.344	1.516

Per-phase qualitative examples appear in Fig. 2; the variation from open-ended probing questions to precise pricing statements illustrates how the phase label steers generation style.

7 Constrained Decoding for Price Hallucination Prevention

7.1 Motivation

A persistent failure mode is *price fabrication*: the model generates dollar amounts absent from the pricing card, most commonly via arithmetic extrapolation (e.g., computing a discounted price as $[X/2] from $[X]). While numerically consistent, these derived prices constitute fabrications that could create compliance risk. We evaluated our model across all 1,623 test samples under a *forced pricing discussion* setting (every call prompted to generate a pricing pitch regardless of true phase). The baseline produced fabrications in 17/1,623 samples (1.0%), all unlisted amounts derived from arithmetic on card prices.

7.2 Approach: Trie-Based Constrained Decoding

We implemented a token-level logits processor that enforces a hard constraint: after any $ token is generated, only token sequences that spell out a price present in the customer's pricing card are permitted. All other digit-like tokens are masked to $-\infty$ in the logits.

Concretely, allowed prices are extracted from the pricing card, tokenized, and inserted into a prefix trie over token IDs. A finite-state cursor tracks progress through the trie: upon generating a $ token, the cursor enters price mode and permits only tokens that advance it; once a terminal node is reached, the cursor resets. When no pricing card is available for a sample, the constraint is lifted entirely. The approach is model-agnostic, adds negligible latency, and requires no retraining (Table 7).

Table 7. Baseline vs. constrained decoding on 1,623 forced pricing-discussion samples. Price fabrication is detected via regex matching of generated dollar amounts against the pricing card.

Metric	Baseline	Constrained	Δ
Price fabrication count	17/1623	1/1623	−16
Price fabrication rate	1.05%	0.06%	−0.99pp
Off-product rate	0.06%	0.06%	±0
Fabrications fixed	–	16	–
Regressions introduced	–	0	–

7.3 Results

Constrained decoding eliminates 94% of price fabrications (16 of 17) with zero quality regressions: the off-product rate is unchanged and no new fabrications are introduced. The single remaining violation occurs on a sample with an empty pricing card, where the constraint is intentionally lifted; by design, the model is unconstrained when no card is available. When a card is present, the fix rate is 100% (16 of 16).

7.4 Qualitative Examples

Figure 5 illustrates all three fabrication patterns observed across the 16 fixed samples. Underlined prices in the baseline are the fabricated values that the constraint eliminates.

8 Lessons Learned

Decompose for Latency and Modularity. Our first prototype attempted end-to-end generation at every turn without phase awareness, producing poorly-timed outputs and unacceptable latency. Splitting into a fast classifier gating expensive generation resolved both issues. Since ~70–80% of steps are no-pitch, Stage 2 is invoked for only 20–30% of events.

Pattern 1: Arithmetic Extrapolation

× **Baseline:** "[Plan A] is $[X]/mo. 50% off, so you'll pay **$[X/2]** each month plus taxes."

✓ **Constrained:** "[Plan A] is $[X]/mo. 50% off, so you'll pay **$[X]** today and $[X] each month for 3 months."

Pattern 2: Wrong Plan Price

× **Baseline:** "[Plan A] is **$[Y]** a month—move billing to [Co.] for a discount." *($[Y] ≠ $[X])*

✓ **Constrained:** "[Plan A] is normally **$[X]** a month—move billing to [Co.] and we can add a discount."

Pattern 3: Discount Savings Fabrication

× **Baseline:** "...you'll pay $[X/2]/mo for 3 months, so you'll save **$[computed]** a month."

✓ **Constrained:** "...you'll pay $[X/2]/mo for 3 months, so you'll save **$[X/2]** a month."

Fig. 5. Fabrication-correction patterns. × = baseline (fabricated price underlined); ✓ = constrained (anchored to pricing card).

Ground Truth Quality via Data Selection. Training on transcripts from *successfully-converting calls* means pitch quality is implicitly validated by conversion outcome; the LLM pipeline's role is structural labeling only. Annotation failure modes (granular span splits, boundary sensitivity) are mitigated through contiguity constraints, priority-based overlap resolution, and chain-of-thought prompting [12].

Treat Class Imbalance as A First-Class Hyperparameter. With 70–80% no-pitch windows, standard class weighting was insufficient. Aggressive downsampling ($\rho = 0.2$) combined with inverse-frequency weights outperformed upsampling (which risks overfitting); the keep ratio should be swept systematically.

Ground Generation in the Knowledge Base. Including product features and pricing in the Stage 2 prompt constrains the generator to approved content, preventing hallucination. For compliance-critical applications, trie-based constrained decoding adds a hard guarantee on price fidelity.

8.1 Broader Impact

DYNAPITCH democratizes expertise by distilling top-agent pitch patterns into real-time suggestions. Pitches are generated only post-resolution, and agents can accept, modify, or ignore them, preserving human agency. All content is grounded in approved product information, and the no-pitch class models when *not* to pitch. An A/B test against a manually scripted baseline is currently in progress; exact conversion figures cannot be shared due to business confidentiality constraints, but results will inform the production deployment decision.

9 Conclusion

We presented DYNAPITCH, a two-stage framework that distills pitch patterns of top-converting agents into a real-time assist system. The phase classifier achieves weighted F1 of **79.3%**; the fine-tuned 8B generator scores **2.00**/3.0 on overall quality (GPT-4.1 judge), outperforming frontier baselines on precision and corroborated by human evaluation. A trie-based constrained decoding layer eliminates 94% of price fabrications with zero regression. All hyperparameters, annotation schemas, and evaluation rubrics are fully specified to support reimplementation. The methodology is domain-agnostic: any setting with distinct conversational phases and authoritative reference content, such as technical support triage, healthcare intake, or financial advising, can adopt this architecture by redefining the phase taxonomy and knowledge base.

Future directions include reinforcement learning from conversion outcomes to optimize pitch effectiveness beyond text quality, online adaptation to individual agent communication styles, and extending to multi-turn pitch dialogues where the system adapts across several exchanges. A further direction is incorporating transcripts from unsuccessful calls. Training exclusively on successful conversions is an operational necessity: without knowing whether the pitch or other factors caused a failed outcome, failed-call pitches cannot be reliably validated as correct training signal. Future work could explore contrastive or reward-based approaches that leverage negative examples without this ambiguity.

Acknowledgments. The authors thank the product and sales agent teams whose conversations form the training corpus.

Disclosure of Interests. The authors have no competing interests to declare that are relevant to the content of this article.

Generative AI Disclosure. Generative AI tools were used during this work for two purposes: (1) assisting with software development (code generation and debugging), and (2) editing and revising the manuscript text. All AI-generated content was reviewed, verified, and approved by the authors, who take full responsibility for the final manuscript.

References

1. Agrawal, G., et al.: Redefining CX with agentic AI: Minerva CQ case study. arXiv preprint: arXiv:2509.12589 (2025)
2. Dao, T., Fu, D.Y., Ermon, S., Rudra, A., Ré, C.: FlashAttention: fast and memory-efficient exact attention with IO-awareness. In: Advances in Neural Information Processing Systems, vol. 35 (2022)
3. Dettmers, T., Pagnoni, A., Holtzman, A., Zettlemoyer, L.: QLoRA: efficient fine-tuning of quantized LLMs. In: Advances in Neural Information Processing Systems, vol. 36 (2023)
4. Devlin, J., Chang, M.W., Lee, K., Toutanova, K.: BERT: pre-training of deep bidirectional transformers for language understanding. In: Proceedings of the 2019 Conference of the North American Chapter of the Association for Computational Linguistics: Human Language Technologies, pp. 4171–4186 (2019)
5. Gao, T., et al.: Benchmarking and learning real-world customer service dialogue. arXiv preprint: arXiv:2510.22143 (2025)
6. Gilardi, F., Alizadeh, M., Kubli, M.: ChatGPT outperforms crowd workers for text-annotation tasks. Proc. Natl. Acad. Sci. **120**(30) (2023)
7. Grattafiori, A., Dubey, A., Jauhri, A., Pandey, A., Kadian, A., Al-Dahle, A.: The Llama 3 herd of models. arXiv preprint: arXiv:2407.21783 (2024)
8. Grau, M.C., Blohm, I.: Real-time guidance design: principles for AI-augmented proactive guidance systems supporting human dialogue in customer service. In: International Conference on Information Systems (ICIS) (2025)
9. Hu, E.J., et al.: LoRA: low-rank adaptation of large language models. In: International Conference on Learning Representations (2022)
10. Kim, Y.J., et al.: Dual process masking for dialogue act recognition. In: Findings of the Association for Computational Linguistics: EMNLP 2024, pp. 15270–15283 (2024)
11. Liu, Y., et al.: RoBERTa: a robustly optimized BERT pretraining approach. arXiv preprint: arXiv:1907.11692 (2019)
12. Lu, Y., Smith, K.: Feeding LLM annotations to BERT classifiers at your own risk. arXiv preprint: arXiv:2504.15432 (2025)
13. Mahata, D., et al.: LDKP: a dataset for identifying keyphrases from long scientific documents. arXiv preprint: arXiv:2203.15349 (2022)
14. Raheja, V., Tetreault, J.: Dialogue act classification with context-aware self-attention. In: Proceedings of the 2019 Conference of the North American Chapter of the Association for Computational Linguistics: Human Language Technologies, pp. 3727–3733 (2019)
15. Stolcke, A., et al.: Dialogue act modeling for automatic tagging and recognition of conversational speech. Comput. Linguist. **26**(3), 339–373 (2000)

16. Su, J., Ahmed, M., Lu, Y., Pan, S., Bo, W., Liu, Y.: RoFormer: enhanced transformer with rotary position embedding. Neurocomputing **568**, 127063 (2024)
17. Tan, S., et al.: JudgeBench: a benchmark for evaluating LLM-based judges. arXiv preprint: arXiv:2410.12784 (2024)
18. Warner, B., et al.: Smarter, better, faster, longer: a modern bidirectional encoder for fast, memory efficient, and long context finetuning and inference. arXiv preprint: arXiv:2412.13663 (2024)
19. Zhang, Q., et al.: AI-Salesman: towards reliable large language model driven telemarketing. arXiv preprint: arXiv:2511.12133 (2025)
20. Zheng, L., et al.: Judging LLM-as-a-judge with MT-Bench and chatbot arena. In: Advances in Neural Information Processing Systems, vol. 36 (2024)
21. Zhou, Y., Xu, A., Wang, P., Xiong, C., Joty, S.: Evaluating judges as evaluators: the JETTS benchmark of LLM-as-judges as test-time scaling evaluators. arXiv preprint: arXiv:2504.15253 (2025)

From Semantic Matching to Factual Pattern Mining: Fact-Anchored Iterative Reasoning for Government Hotline Dispatching

Shun Chen[1], Xiuwen Yi[1(✉)], Chengjie Guo[2], Yanyong Huang[3], Tianrui Li[1], and Yu Zheng[1,2]

[1] Southwest Jiaotong University, Chengdu, China
xiuwenyi@swjtu.edu.cn
[2] Xidian University, Xi'an, China
[3] Joint Laboratory of Data Science and Business Intelligence, Southwestern University of Finance and Economics, Chengdu, China

Abstract. Government service hotlines route citizen requests to corresponding departments, but mis-dispatches often lead to repeated departmental rejections, wasting administrative resources and delaying resolutions. Achieving precise automated dispatching is challenging because responsibilities often overlap across departments, and work order descriptions are highly unstructured. Existing methods relying on surface semantic matching frequently fail, as subtle factual differences in requests can completely shift jurisdictional boundaries. We argue that complex requests must be deconstructed into fine-grained atomic facts to uncover consistent historical adjudication patterns. To this end, we propose the Fine-grained fact-Anchored Iterative Reasoning (FAIR) approach. FAIR first employs a Fine-Grained Fact Reformulation module to distill noisy requests into standardized atomic facts, which drive the construction of a dynamic jurisdictional activation graph that aggregates historical records along factual dimensions to capture implicit consensus. Subsequently, an Evidence-Driven Iterative Reasoning module maps the facts of a new query to this graph to leverage relevant historical patterns, which a large language model then jointly evaluates with official regulations through iterative reasoning, progressively eliminating candidates to deduce the responsible department. Extensive experiments on real-world datasets from two major cities demonstrate that FAIR significantly outperforms existing baselines, particularly on easily misclassified cases. Furthermore, our approach has been deployed into an online hotline system, significantly improving hotline dispatching accuracy and efficiency.

Keywords: Government Hotline · Work Order Dispatch · Factual Pattern Mining · Iterative Reasoning · Urban Computing

M. Baratchi et al. (Eds.): ECML PKDD 2026, LNAI 16949, pp. 378–394, 2027.
https://doi.org/10.1007/978-3-032-37682-4_22

1 Introduction

In contemporary cities, residents frequently encounter diverse daily issues, ranging from construction noise to childhood education, all requiring governmental intervention. To facilitate service delivery and public engagement, many governments have established centralized service hotlines (e.g. 12345 in China, and 311 in the U.S.). These platforms receive a wide range of non-emergency requests across domains such as market supervision, public services and environmental protection. According to the public report, the Beijing service hotline processed approximately 24 million cases in 2025, marking a 12.9% year-over-year increase. As request volumes surge, processing efficiency has become a key metric for evaluating government service capacity.

However, this centralization shifts significant operational pressure to the hotline backend. Upon receiving a request, operators must assess its nature and dispatch it to the appropriate department based on jurisdictional responsibilities. The sheer scale of this task makes manual processing unsustainable. With millions of cases processed annually, even a modest mis-dispatch rate translates into thousands of errors, compounding the administrative burden. Dispatch accuracy critically depends on operators' understanding of complex and often overlapping departmental boundaries. Struggling to distinguish these subtle limits, operators frequently mis-dispatch, triggering repeated departmental rejections that delay resolution and waste administrative resources.

To alleviate this operational burden, various automated dispatching methods have been proposed. Conventional semantic models treat requests as indivisible texts, relying on global embedding similarity to retrieve historical work orders [6,20,31]. More recently, Retrieval-Augmented Generation (RAG) frameworks powered by large language models have been used to incorporate external knowledge into generation and reasoning [2,15,22]. However, both approaches share a fundamental limitation: they operate on surface-level semantic matching, failing to isolate the core factual details that determine jurisdictional boundaries. Due to the highly diverse and noisy nature of real-world incidents, these methods often retrieve conflicting regulations or superficially similar historical cases. Such misleading references disrupt reasoning, leading to dispatch decisions based on keyword overlap rather than rigorous administrative logic.

Given these limitations, transitioning from surface-level semantic matching to rigorous jurisdictional reasoning is essential yet challenging, due to the misalignment between citizen narratives and formal administrative structures. The primary obstacle lies in the extreme signal-to-noise ratio of raw requests: crucial jurisdictional triggers are consistently obscured by colloquial language and subjective venting, making it difficult for models to isolate objective facts. Furthermore, a granularity gap exists between specific real-world incidents and explicit official regulations. Administrative rules provide abstract guidelines that frequently fail to offer deterministic boundaries for complex daily events, inevitably leading to overlapping jurisdictions. Finally, true administrative boundaries are implicitly embedded in historical consensus and pivot on subtle factual variations. For instance, whether a noise complaint involves a commercial storefront or a public square can completely alter the final dispatching outcome.

To address these challenges, we propose the Fine-grained fact-Anchored Iterative Reasoning (FAIR) approach for government hotline dispatching. Our approach transforms work order dispatching from an unreliable surface-level semantic matching task into a robust, verifiable, and evidence-based reasoning process. The main contributions are summarized as follows:

- We identify the fundamental limitations of surface-level semantic matching in complex urban governance. To address this, we propose FAIR, a novel paradigm that shifts the dispatching focus from superficial text similarity to fine-grained factual deconstruction and historical pattern alignment.
- We design the Fine-Grained Fact Reformulation module to distill noisy appeals into objective atomic facts for constructing a dynamic jurisdictional activation graph. Additionally, we design the Evidence-Driven Iterative Reasoning module to empower LLMs with fact-anchored historical consensus for rigorous reasoning.
- Extensive experiments on real-world datasets from two major cities demonstrate that FAIR consistently achieves state-of-the-art performance, particularly on boundary cases easily misclassified by traditional methods.
- The successful deployment of FAIR in a real-world municipal event linkage system validates its practical effectiveness. The approach significantly improves actual dispatching accuracy and efficiency while providing verifiable evidence chains for human operators.

2 Related Work

2.1 Government Hotline

The government service hotline constitutes a vital public platform, established by governments across the globe, designed to manage the service requests of residents. Notable examples include the 12345 hotline in China and the 311 hotline in the U.S. [30]. Research pertaining to government hotlines is primarily concentrated on two pivotal categories. Firstly, researchers aim to leverage the vast amount of valuable information contained within work orders [13] and analyze various social events [21], such as urban noise [21], the COVID-19 [1] and crime [3]. Secondly, researchers have made significant contributions towards automating the work order dispatch process, streamlining efficiency and response times [9] [14], which is important to improve the government's proficiency in providing public services. Following the second category, we augment the effectiveness and efficiency of the work order dispatch process.

2.2 Work Order Dispatch

Dispatching is a pivotal step in the processing of hotline work orders [17]. When receiving a high volume of requests, the efficacy of subsequent work order management is contingent upon the precision of dispatch [28]. Traditional approaches frequently depend on manual assignments or rule-based mechanisms [20], potentially leading to time consumption and susceptibility to errors. Recent developments have concentrated on utilizing natural language processing to automate and refine the dispatch process [7,18]. Furthermore, some researchers have recognized the importance of responsibilities in the task and have made improvements to the methods [29]. Following the demonstration of powerful capabilities by large models, recent developments have focused on using LLMs for reasoning [5,25] and obtaining information via RAG [16]. Meanwhile, some researchers [12,27] are designing domain-specific approaches with LLMs, focusing on diverse dataset features to boost efficiency. Compared to these methods, our proposed approach first understands the responsibilities and their constituent affairs, especially when dealing with events related to multiple departments.

3 Overview

3.1 Preliminaries

Definition 1 (Raw Work Order). A raw hotline work order is defined as a tuple $o = (e, q)$, where e represents the unstructured, often noisy, event description (e.g., subjective narratives containing latent details about time, location, and behaviors), and q denotes the specific request proposed by the residents.

Definition 2 (Department). Departments, denoted as a set $\mathcal{D} = \{d_1, d_2, ..., d_m\}$, refer to government agencies authorized to process work orders. The dispatching boundary of each department $d \in \mathcal{D}$ is practically determined by two sources: 1) a set of explicit responsibilities $\mathcal{R}_d$, encompassing its macroscopic official duties; and 2) a set of historical precedents $\mathcal{H}_d$, consisting of past work orders correctly resolved by d, which reflects the statistical consensus of its actual jurisdiction.

Problem Statement. Given a newly arrived work order $o = (e, q)$ and a set of candidate departments $\mathcal{D}$ alongside their explicit responsibilities $\mathcal{R}$ and historical precedents $\mathcal{H}$, the objective is to learn a dispatching function $g(o, \mathcal{D}, \mathcal{R}, \mathcal{H})$. This function utilizes the available textual and historical evidence to predict the optimal department $d^* \in \mathcal{D}$. The ultimate goal is to find the department that maximizes the dispatching probability.

3.2 Framework

Figure 1 illustrates the proposed FAIR approach, featuring two modules: Fine-Grained Fact Reformulation and Evidence-Driven Iterative Reasoning. Given a noisy and colloquial raw request, the first module distills the unstructured text into aligned atomic facts, including specific subjects, behaviors, and locations. Instead of relying on macroscopic text similarity, the module utilizes these extracted facts to drive the construction of a dynamic jurisdictional activation graph. By mapping the atomic facts onto this graph, the system aggregates massive historical records to estimate the empirical distribution of past dispatch results. This process effectively translates implicit jurisdictional boundaries and historical consensus into a structured evidence set. Subsequently, taking these atomic facts and the evidence set as input, the second module executes a rigorous deductive reasoning process to resolve jurisdictional overlaps and mitigate LLM hallucinations. It guides the language model to jointly evaluate the retrieved historical consensus and explicit official regulations. By systematically verifying the factual triggers against the comprehensive evidence, the reasoning engine iteratively prunes incorrect candidate departments. Ultimately, it outputs a robust dispatch decision accompanied by a verifiable reasoning chain.

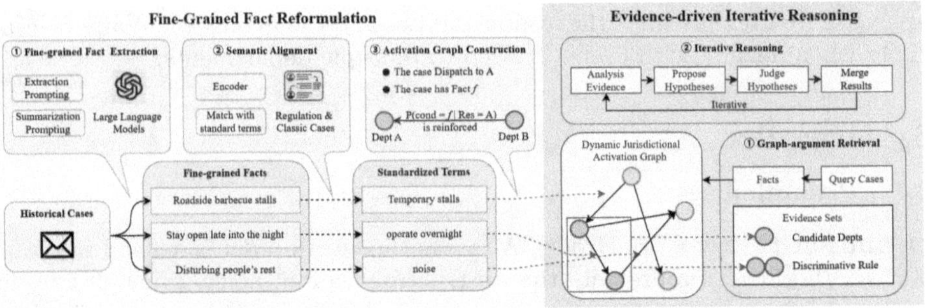

Fig. 1. The framework of proposed FAIR.

4 Methodology

4.1 Fine-Grained Fact Reformulation

The primary obstacle in government hotline dispatching lies in the high variance of informal citizen narratives, which are often too idiosyncratic to exhibit direct jurisdictional patterns. While macroscopic event descriptions frequently obscure key facts, their underlying fine-grained factual components provide a stable and objective basis for statistical modeling. To bridge this gap, we propose the Fine-Grained Fact Reformulation module to transform unstructured requests into a structured fact sequence. By decomposing holistic narratives into atomic facts, the module can reveal recurring historical patterns that are otherwise submerged in noisy macroscopic texts. To implement this, the module executes three sequential steps: Fine-Grained Fact Extraction, Semantic Fact Alignment, and Dynamic Jurisdictional Activation Graph Construction.

Fine-Grained Fact Extraction. The first step of the module is to extract fine-grained facts from the raw event description e using an LLM. To ensure precision, we provide the model with explicit departmental responsibilities $\mathcal{R}$ to guide its focus and utilize a structured prompt to force the output into a strict format. We use both fields because the event description usually contains factual triggers, while the request field may indicate the expected handling target. This process extracts a set of discrete atomic facts $F = \{f_1, f_2, ..., f_n\}$, where each fact captures a specific subject, a primary behavior, and a spatio-temporal context. This structural constraint prevents the model from generating irrelevant information and ensures that the extraction is anchored on administrative logic.

Specifically, instead of generating a generic summary, the LLM is prompted to identify specific jurisdictional triggers that align with the administrative duties defined in $\mathcal{R}$. For each raw order o, the model isolates core factual elements including: 1) the subject (e.g., specific commercial entities or public facilities); 2) the behavior (e.g., illegal construction or service complaints); and 3) the context (e.g., specific temporal or spatial constraints). If a field is not supported by the input text, the model is instructed to leave it empty rather than infer additional information. By stripping away subjective sentiments and conversational noise, this knowledge-guided approach transforms the high-variance macroscopic narrative into a collection of purified, objective facts. This transformation effectively converts a sparse event-level matching problem into a dense factual analysis task, providing the fundamental building blocks for retrieving historical patterns from the historical repository $\mathcal{H}$.

Semantic Fact Alignment. The atomic facts F extracted in the previous stage, while structurally simplified, still exhibit significant linguistic variance due to the diverse vocabulary used in citizen narratives. To ensure that these facts can be effectively matched against the historical repository $\mathcal{H}$ and explicit rules $\mathcal{R}$, it is necessary to perform semantic normalization. This step aligns colloquial expressions with a standardized jurisdictional feature space, thereby eliminating the vocabulary gap that would otherwise lead to fragmented historical patterns.

Specifically, we employ a semantic encoder to map each atomic fact $f_i \in F$ into a high-dimensional dense vector $\mathbf{v}_i \in \mathbb{R}^d$:

$$\mathbf{v}_i = \text{Encoder}(f_i) \tag{1}$$

To achieve normalization, we maintain a predefined taxonomy of standardized administrative terms $\mathcal{V}$, derived from the official responsibilities $\mathcal{R}$ and high-frequency factual keywords in $\mathcal{H}$. We first collect administrative terms from $\mathcal{R}$, including regulated objects, service categories, behaviors, and handling conditions. We then extract frequent factual phrases from anonymized historical records in $\mathcal{H}$. Colloquial expressions and synonyms are merged into the same standardized term based on embedding similarity and manual review by domain operators. The vocabulary is updated when newly audited work orders contain frequent expressions that are not covered by the current version, or when responsibility documents are revised.

Each f_i is then aligned to its closest standardized counterpart $v^* \in \mathcal{V}$ based on cosine similarity:

$$v^* = \arg\max_{v \in \mathcal{V}} \frac{\mathbf{v}_i \cdot \mathbf{v}_v}{\|\mathbf{v}_i\| \|\mathbf{v}_v\|} \tag{2}$$

This normalization process ensures that the subsequent pattern mining is invariant to linguistic surface variations. By consolidating diverse synonymous expressions into unified semantic anchors, we significantly increase the density of factual features, providing a robust foundation for identifying historical patterns from the dynamic jurisdictional activation graph.

Dynamic Jurisdictional Activation Graph Construction. The final stage of the module synthesizes jurisdictional evidence by mapping the extracted facts onto a dynamic jurisdictional activation graph. We define the jurisdictional space as a graph $\mathcal{G} = (\mathcal{D}, \mathcal{E})$, where nodes $d \in \mathcal{D}$ represent departments. An edge $e_{i,j} \in \mathcal{E}$ encapsulates the jurisdictional boundary between d_i and d_j identified from historical conflicts. Each edge $e_{i,j}$ stores a set of pattern vectors $\mathcal{P}_{i,j}$. These vectors represent factual patterns observed in historical cases involving d_i and d_j. For a pair of departments, work orders finally confirmed by the target department are used as positive examples, while rejected or reassigned cases involving the competing department provide contrastive examples when such logs are available.

To capture the dynamic influence of fine-grained facts, each edge maintains a set of pattern vectors $\mathcal{P}_{i,j}$ serving as historical tie-breaking rules. We optimize these vectors on dispatch logs using a triplet loss function. A specific pattern vector $p \in \mathcal{P}_{i,j}$ acts as the anchor. We exclusively sample from historical events associated with both conflicting departments i and j. The standardized fact embeddings of atomic events correctly dispatched to department j are selected as positive samples $\mathbf{v}^+$. The standardized fact embeddings of atomic events that should belong to department j but were incorrectly dispatched to department i serve as negative samples $\mathbf{v}^-$. The loss function is formally defined as:

$$\mathcal{L} = \max(0, \text{sim}(p, \mathbf{v}^-) - \text{sim}(p, \mathbf{v}^+) + \gamma) \tag{3}$$

where $\text{sim}(\cdot, \cdot)$ denotes the cosine similarity function and γ represents the margin hyperparameter. This optimization ensures that the learned pattern vectors accurately encode explicit historical boundaries for overlapping jurisdictions.

When an event falls into the jurisdictional overlap of two departments, these vectors dictate which department should process the case based on the presence of specific atomic facts. To evaluate a new work order, we utilize both the original fact embedding $\mathbf{v}_i$ and its standardized counterpart embedding $\mathbf{v}^*$. The $\mathbf{v}^*$ provides a stable semantic anchor to retrieve the most relevant historical pattern $p_{i,j}$ from $\mathcal{P}_{i,j}$. Subsequently, to preserve the subtle linguistic nuances of the specific citizen request, the activation score $a_{i,j}$ is calculated using the original fact embedding $\mathbf{v}_i$:

$$p_{i,j} = \arg\max_{p \in \mathcal{P}_{i,j}} sim(\mathbf{v}^*, p) \tag{4}$$

$$a_{i,j}(\mathbf{v}_i) = \sigma(\kappa \cdot sim(\mathbf{v}_i, p_{i,j})) \tag{5}$$

where $sim(\cdot, \cdot)$ denotes cosine similarity and κ controls the activation sensitivity.

These pattern vectors are optimized through contrastive learning on historical dispatch logs to maximize the margin between correct and incorrect assignments. By aggregating these activations across the graph, we translate the atomic facts into a prioritized list of explicit decision signals. This process ensures that the subsequent iterative reasoning phase is driven by verifiable factual triggers rather than opaque semantic matching, utilizing refined historical patterns for interpretable retrieval.

4.2 Evidence-Driven Iterative Reasoning

The Evidence-Driven Iterative Reasoning module is designed to resolve the inherent ambiguity found in macroscopic departmental responsibilities. While surface-level semantic matching often identifies a broad set of candidate departments, it fundamentally fails to distinguish between those with overlapping jurisdictions. To address this limitation, the module utilizes the atomic facts and historical patterns retrieved from the dynamic jurisdictional activation graph as explicit decision evidence. This mechanism transforms the work order dispatching task from an unreliable similarity search into a rigorous and verifiable deductive process. By jointly evaluating official regulations and historical consensus, the module executes an iterative reasoning process to systematically eliminate incorrect candidates and deduce the optimal responsible department.

Graph-Enhanced Evidence Retrieval. The reasoning process initiates by establishing a jurisdictional conflict set $\mathcal{D}^*$. Recognizing that macroscopic event descriptions are frequently too sparse to yield a definitive match, we utilize the extracted atomic facts F to perform an initial semantic retrieval across all departmental responsibilities. Departments exhibiting high semantic overlap regarding the current case are aggregated to form the conflict set $\mathcal{D}^*$. This step isolates the overlapping agencies, ensuring that the subsequent reasoning focuses specifically on instances where administrative boundaries are highly blurred.

To distinguish between the candidates in $\mathcal{D}^*$, the module retrieves explicit discriminative rules from the dynamic jurisdictional activation graph rather than relying solely on raw textual duties. For each pair of conflicting departments, we query the graph using the current atomic facts to retrieve the historical patterns that successfully resolved similar disputes. These retrieved patterns provide high-density discriminative evidence, illustrating how specific factual triggers, such as the involvement of underground drainage in property issues, historically dictate the assignment between departments handling similar broad domains.

By presenting these synthesized historical patterns alongside the raw responsibilities, the system provides the specific decision triggers necessary to resolve jurisdictional ambiguity. The final evidence set E is thus a structured combination of official administrative mandates and historical consensus, ensuring that the dispatch decision is both legally authorized and practically grounded.

Iterative Reasoning. The final stage of the module is an iterative reasoning process to resolve conflicts within the candidate set $\mathcal{D}^*$. The large language model executes a deductive chain that systematically tests candidate departments against the synthesized evidence set E. Instead of a single-step classification, the model performs a pairwise comparison among candidates. For any two conflicting departments d_i and d_j in $\mathcal{D}^*$, the model evaluates the current atomic facts F against their respective official rules and the retrieved historical patterns. The reasoning follows a continuous verification and pruning logic. The model first performs factual verification to check if the specific attributes of an atomic fact satisfy the jurisdictional triggers defined in the official rules. If the macroscopic rules for both departments overlap, the model then applies the historical patterns to break the deadlock, prioritizing the department whose learned boundaries align more closely with the micro-level factual signals.

This comparative process is repeated iteratively, pruning the department that fails the discriminative test from the candidate set in each turn. By decomposing the complex dispatching decision into a series of minimal-unit logical judgments, the module mitigates the risk of model hallucination and ensures that the final choice is grounded in explicit evidence. The adjudication concludes when a single optimal department remains. In cases where macroscopic rules and historical patterns for multiple departments remain indistinguishable after the iterative elimination, the module instructs the large language model to perform a final comprehensive evaluation. The model directly outputs the most probable department from the remaining candidates based on the holistic context of the synthesized evidence. The module ultimately outputs the optimal department alongside a verifiable reasoning chain that traces the factual triggers and rule segments used during the pruning process.

5 Experiments

5.1 Settings

Datasets. We evaluate the proposed approach on a real-world dual-city dataset sourced from 12345 government service hotlines. To assess temporal robustness and spatial transferability, the corpus comprises a comprehensive longitudinal three-year dataset from City A, and a single-year dataset from City B. Both datasets exhibit a severe long-tail label distribution with extreme class imbalance, where a small fraction of departments process the vast majority of work orders, leaving nearly half of the administrative categories with extremely scarce training samples. To simulate realistic deployment and prevent data leakage, all meticulously anonymized records are chronologically partitioned into training, validation, and test sets at an 8:1:1 ratio.

The input to FAIR is the textual work order record stored in the hotline platform. We do not process raw audio, spectrograms, voiceprints, or other audio-derived biometric information. For telephone requests, the existing hotline workflow converts the call content into textual work order fields before our method is applied. All experiments and deployment results reported in this paper are based on anonymized text records (Table 1).

Table 1. Statistics of the 12345 government service hotline datasets.

Statistical Metric	City A			City B
	2020	2021	2022	2022
Total Work Orders	28,499	36,210	48,450	42,100
Number of Departments	45	48	52	55
Average Text Length	154.2	162.8	175.4	148.6
Top 10% Dept. Load	78.5%	72.1%	76.4%	79.2%
Depts. with < 50 Cases	12	14	15	18

Baselines

- **TextCNN** [10]: This model utilizes convolutional filters of varying window sizes to capture local n-gram features.
- **BERT** [4]: A pre-trained bidirectional transformer that learns deep contextual representations, used for semantic-level classification.
- **LEAM** [24]: The Label-Embedding Attentive Model jointly learns word and label embeddings, utilizing the label's semantic information to guide the attention mechanism for better discriminative power.
- **Qwen-3** [26]: An LLM-based baseline that uses pre-training and instruction tuning to perform zero-shot reasoning. We utilize surface-level semantic similarity to retrieve relevant historical work orders as external knowledge.
- **Self-RAG** [2]: This framework enhances traditional retrieval-augmented generation by enabling the model to critique its own retrieval and generation through self-reflection tokens.
- **RankZephyr** [19]: An advanced listwise reranking model designed to optimize the relevance of retrieved documents, focusing on improving the selection of historical cases for the LLM.
- **RAVA** [11]: A specialized baseline designed for administrative tasks that integrates retrieval-augmented techniques with domain-specific analysis.
- **KG-LLM** [8]: This model integrates Large Language Models with Knowledge Graphs to ground administrative reasoning in structured domain knowledge, aiming to resolve jurisdictional overlaps.

Model Details

- **Privacy Preprocessing.** Considering the data contain substantial personal information, it is crucial to protect the privacy of residents. To this end, we employed the anonymization and placeholder replacement [23] to replace potential names, contact details, and addresses with corresponding tokens. The anonymization is performed before the records enter the modeling pipeline. Training and inference are conducted in a private government computing environment, and raw work order content is not sent to external

services. Due to privacy regulations and government data governance requirements, the original records and the deployed system link cannot be publicly released.
- **Implementation Details.** In the Fine-Grained Fact Reformulation module, we use a BERT structure for semantic normalization that utilizes a dropout rate of 0.1 and outputs 768-dimensional factual embeddings. The activation temperature κ in the dynamic jurisdictional activation graph is set to 0.5 to regulate the sensitivity of historical tendency signals. During the Evidence-Driven Iterative Reasoning stage, we use the Qwen-3 for reasoning. The temperature is set to 0.1 in order to reduce output variance. The fact extraction output is parsed against the predefined schema. If the output cannot be parsed, the system reissues the same prompt with an explicit formatting instruction for up to three retries.
- **Experimental Environment.** We train the models on a GPU server with dual RTX 4090D GPUs and 4x32 GB of RAM, using PyTorch as the programming environment.

Evaluation Metrics. To rigorously evaluate the dispatching performance on our highly imbalanced dataset, we employ Accuracy (Acc.), Macro-F1, and Matthews Correlation Coefficient (MCC). **Accuracy** measures the overall proportion of correctly dispatched work orders, providing an intuitive baseline for global performance. **Macro-F1** calculates the unweighted mean of F1-scores across all departments, explicitly assessing the approach's ability to retrieve correct jurisdictional boundaries for minority classes within the severe long-tail distribution. Finally, **MCC** provides a balanced evaluation of the full confusion matrix, serving as the most reliable indicator of genuine discriminative power for highly skewed administrative data.

5.2 Comparison with Baselines

Experimental results in Table 2 show that the proposed approach consistently outperforms all evaluated baselines. To ensure the reliability of performance improvements, we conduct three independent runs with different random seeds for all models and report the averaged metrics.

A key observation is the large discrepancy between overall accuracy and Macro-F1 score, especially in embedding-based models. This gap directly reflects majority-class bias caused by the severe long-tail distribution of administrative data. Standard models optimize for global text popularity and naturally favor "head" departments when processing ambiguous requests. By querying the dynamic jurisdictional activation graph with atomic facts, our approach retrieves precise historical tie-breaking rules for "tail" departments and ensures fair evaluation of minority categories based on explicit historical consensus.

Furthermore, comparisons with advanced LLM-driven baselines reveal the inherent limitations of standard retrieval-augmented generation (RAG) for jurisdictional disambiguation. Although these baselines use external knowledge, feed-

Table 2. Performance comparison of the proposed FAIR and baseline models on two city datasets. The best results are highlighted in **bold**.

Category	Methods	City A			City B		
		Acc. (%)	Macro-F1 (%)	MCC	Acc. (%)	Macro-F1 (%)	MCC
Embedding-based	TextCNN	74.12	60.35	0.572	73.58	59.42	0.565
	BERT	78.42	65.12	0.584	77.15	63.84	0.572
	LEAM	80.15	68.85	0.635	79.34	70.12	0.621
LLM-driven	Qwen-3	84.68	77.24	0.721	83.92	76.45	0.714
	Self-RAG	86.54	79.12	0.748	85.81	78.34	0.732
	RankZephyr	86.23	82.45	0.782	86.42	81.15	0.771
Domain-specific	RAVA	82.56	76.42	0.678	81.68	75.24	0.665
	KG-LLM	87.41	80.56	0.761	86.72	79.24	0.753
	Ours (FAIR)	**91.34**	**85.78**	**0.814**	**90.56**	**84.34**	**0.802**

ing entire and overlapping official mandates into an LLM inevitably causes context overload and logical hallucination. Our Evidence-Driven Iterative Reasoning (EDIR) module overcomes this bottleneck via fact-anchored rule slicing. By retaining only rule segments that strictly match activated micro-facts, we supply the LLM with a high-density, contrastive evidence set, converting open-ended semantic guesses into constrained deductive adjudication.

Finally, comparisons with domain-adapted methods highlight the unique requirements of urban governance dispatching. Approaches derived from general legal retrieval or standard knowledge reasoning usually rely on static, prescriptive ontology. Our approach outperforms these methods by moving from static knowledge querying to dynamic, conflict-aware reasoning. By modeling the historical activation of specific factual boundaries rather than only topological relations between departments, our method captures the implicit pragmatic logic of administrative dispatching and thus achieves stronger adaptability and precision.

5.3 Ablation Study

We conduct an ablation study to validate that reliable jurisdictional resolution requires capturing historical patterns at a fine-grained factual level. The results in Table 3 show that bypassing micro-level analysis inevitably leads to the failure of macroscopic dispatching. The removal of the Fine-Grained Fact Reformulation module causes the most severe performance degradation. Feeding raw text directly yields the lowest metrics, proving that conversational noise overwhelms the reasoning process. Replacing the raw text with a generic summary only marginally improves the performance. This critical comparison demonstrates that macroscopic summaries still obscure the precise triggers of jurisdictional boundaries. Deconstructing complex events into atomic facts is the absolute prerequisite for exposing the hidden patterns buried in the long-tail data.

Table 3. Ablation study of FAIR on the City A dataset.

Model Variants	Acc. (%)	Macro-F1 (%)	MCC
w/o Fact Reformulation (Generic Summary)	86.50	78.10	0.748
w/o Fact Reformulation (Raw Text)	85.42	76.85	0.738
w/o Iterative Reasoning (One-Shot Prompting)	89.85	83.21	0.795
w/o Iterative Reasoning (Full Context)	89.12	81.65	0.784
FAIR (Full)	**91.34**	**85.78**	**0.814**

The remaining variants demonstrate that fine-grained signals must be rigorously protected during the final reasoning phase. Retaining the full context of departmental manuals dilutes the extracted micro-level facts, causing the language model to lose focus amidst generic administrative clauses. Fact-anchored slicing ensures the retrieved evidence remains strictly at the same fine-grained level as the input facts. Furthermore, substituting iterative pruning with one-shot prompting leads to a noticeable decline in logical stability. Complex administrative adjudication cannot rely on a single generative guess. Iterative pruning forces the model to evaluate the retrieved historical patterns step by step, ensuring the final decision is a direct and reliable deduction from historical laws.

5.4 Robustness and Effectiveness Analysis

We evaluate performance across different department groups to analyze the impact of data imbalance. As shown in Fig. 2(a), under the long-tail distribution, baseline models suffer severe performance degradation in the torso and tail groups. This stems from their reliance on macroscopic text popularity, which inherently suppresses minority departments in global semantic matching. Our approach maintains high prediction accuracy even in the extreme tail group. Decomposing inputs into atomic facts allows the system to avoid statistical frequency bias, and the reasoning engine judges rare departments based on precise historical consensus instead of text similarity. This confirms that mapping fine-grained facts to historical patterns is the only reliable way to handle minority categories in administrative dispatching.

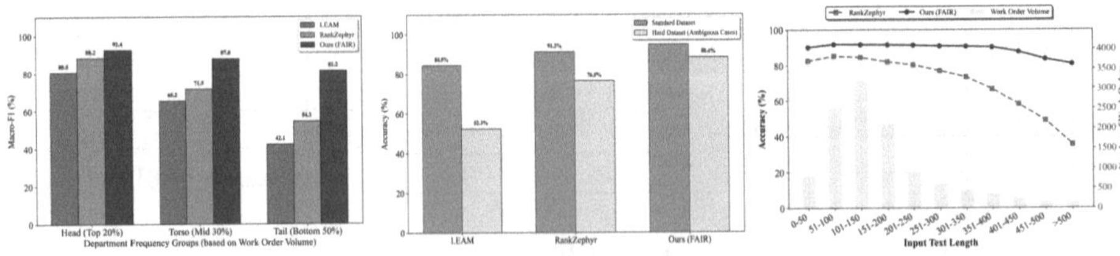

(a) The impact of data imbalance (b) The impact of ambiguous work orders (c) The impact of input text lengths

Fig. 2. Robustness and effectiveness across different scenarios.

We construct a hard subset comprising only highly ambiguous work orders to test jurisdiction disambiguation in overlapping cases. This subset features candidate departments with nearly identical textual responsibilities. Comparative results in Fig. 2(b) show that standard semantic models fail catastrophically on this dataset, as macroscopic language models cannot distinguish boundaries that are textually similar but historically distinct. Our approach substantially outperforms all baselines on these ambiguous instances. Extracting fine-grained facts provides explicit triggers within the reasoning pipeline and activates dedicated historical tie-breaking rules from the graph, effectively resolving boundary disputes that cannot be settled by broad text definitions alone.

We measure prediction accuracy across increasing input lengths to evaluate robustness to unstructured colloquial noise, as shown in Fig. 2(c). Baseline models display a steady and sharp accuracy drop as input word count rises, indicating that verbose citizen complaints conceal true jurisdictional triggers under irrelevant emotional descriptions. Our model maintains a stable performance curve regardless of input length. The input reformulation module explicitly extracts fine-grained facts from raw narratives, and the reasoning engine only processes core event semantics. This isolation ensures that historical pattern extraction and matching are robust to varying levels of macroscopic text noise.

5.5 Case Study

We present a specific case study in Table 4 to visualize the resolution process of our approach against traditional baselines. The selected work order involves a lengthy citizen complaint where overlapping jurisdictional triggers are buried in emotional language. Traditional methods rely on macroscopic keyword matching, which inevitably leads to an incorrect assignment based on secondary descriptive issues. Our approach fundamentally avoids this ambiguity. The input reformulation module strips away the emotional noise to extract the core atomic facts. By querying the discriminative graph with these facts, the reasoning engine retrieves the precise historical consensus to override superficial textual similarity. This intuitively demonstrates that deconstructing complex narratives into factual anchors is essential for resolving administrative ambiguity.

Table 4. Case study of work order dispatching across different approaches

Comparison Dimension	Traditional Baselines	Proposed Approach
Raw Narrative	Lengthy emotional complaint about a night market stall generating thick smoke and loud noises	
Extracted Features	Smoke, Noise	Street vendor, night
Decision Evidence	Superficial textual similarity	Historical consensus rules
Predicted Department	Environmental Protection	Urban Management

6 System Deployment

We deployed the proposed approach into a municipal event linkage system, where the system web interface is depicted in Fig. 3, providing operators with interpretable insights to support informed manual decisions. After deployment, we have observed significant improvements in dispatching speed and a clear reduction in operators' workload. The event dispatch rate increased from 51.62% to 73.83%, and the dispatch accuracy improved from 71.02% to 85.5%. In addition, the average event processing time was reduced by 16%, and the number of pending events handled per operator decreased by approximately 60%. These results demonstrate the practical value of our approach in reducing manual intervention and lowering personnel training costs.

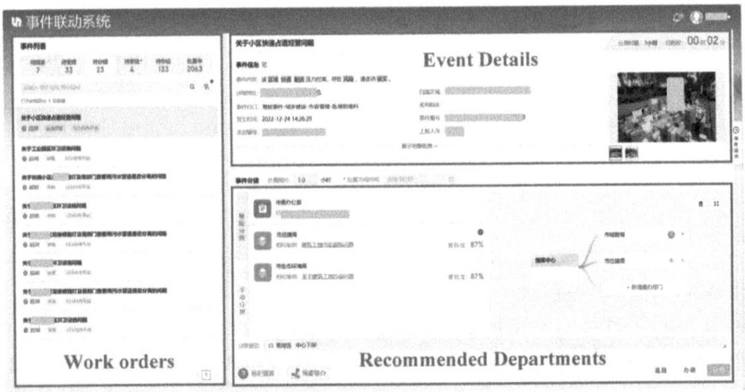

Fig. 3. The web interface of the system.

7 Conclusion

This paper introduces a novel paradigm for work order dispatching that transitions from macroscopic semantic matching to micro-level factual deduction. By deconstructing complex requests into atomic facts, the system retrieves precise historical tie-breaking rules from a dynamic jurisdictional activation graph. This ensures the reasoning process is firmly anchored on historical consensus rather than superficial text similarity. Extensive evaluations on real-world datasets confirm that this approach consistently outperforms existing baselines, effectively mitigating majority class bias and resolving boundary disputes. The successful online deployment further demonstrates its capacity to enhance both the accuracy and efficiency of urban governance. Ultimately, this work provides a robust and verifiable approach for automating complex administrative decisions.

Acknowledgments. This work is supported by the National Natural Science Foundation of China (Grant Nos. 62502028 and 72495122), and the Natural Science Foundation Project of Sichuan Province (No. 2024NSFSC0504). The author Yanyong Huang gratefully acknowledges the support of K. C. Wong Education Foundation and DAAD.

References

1. Arendt, F., Markiewitz, A., Mestas, M., Scherr, S.: COVID-19 pandemic, government responses, and public mental health: investigating consequences through crisis hotline calls in two countries. Soc. Sci. Med. **265**, 113532 (2020)
2. Asai, A., Wu, Z., Wang, Y., Sil, A., Hajishirzi, H.: Self-RAG: learning to retrieve, generate, and critique through self-reflection. In: The Twelfth International Conference on Learning Representations (2024). https://openreview.net/forum?id=hSyW5go0v8
3. Bennett, L., Riger, S., Schewe, P., Howard, A., Wasco, S.: Effectiveness of hotline, advocacy, counseling, and shelter services for victims of domestic violence: a statewide evaluation. J. Interpers. Violence **19**(7), 815–829 (2004)
4. Devlin, J.: BERT: pre-training of deep bidirectional transformers for language understanding. arXiv preprint arXiv:1810.04805 (2018)
5. Donabauer, G., Kruschwitz, U.: A reproducibility study of graph-based legal case retrieval. In: Proceedings of the 48th International ACM SIGIR Conference on Research and Development in Information Retrieval, pp. 3135–3144 (2025)
6. Gang, C.: Government hotline work-order classification fusing RoBERTa and feature extraction. Comput. Modernization (06), 21 (2022)
7. Gasparetto, A., Marcuzzo, M., Zangari, A., Albarelli, A.: A survey on text classification algorithms: from text to predictions. Information **13**(2), 83 (2022)
8. Gong, Q., Bai, Z., Gao, X., Luo, D., Ai, S.: Collaborative enhancement method of knowledge graph and large language model for dispatch of government citizen hotline. In: Proceedings of the 2025 8th International Conference on Computer Information Science and Artificial Intelligence, pp. 813–817 (2025)
9. Huang, W., Su, C., Wang, Y.: An intelligent work order classification model for government service based on multi-label neural network. Comput. Commun. **172**, 19–24 (2021)
10. Kim, Y.: Convolutional neural networks for sentence classification. In: Proceedings of the 2014 Conference on Empirical Methods in Natural Language Processing, pp. 1746–1751 (2014)
11. Li, R., Ou, R., Wang, D.: An innovative similar complaint recommendation model integrating semantic and graph embeddings. In: 2023 4th International Conference on Information Science, Parallel and Distributed Systems (ISPDS), pp. 107–111. IEEE (2023)
12. Liu, B., et al.: Structure-aware conversational legal case retrieval. ACM Trans. Inf. Syst. **43**(3), 1–28 (2025)
13. Liu, J., Chang, W.C., Wu, Y., Yang, Y.: Deep learning for extreme multi-label text classification. In: Proceedings of the 40th international ACM SIGIR Conference on Research and Development in Information Retrieval, pp. 115–124 (2017)
14. Liu, M., Liu, L., Cao, J., Du, Q.: Co-attention network with label embedding for text classification. Neurocomputing **471**, 61–69 (2022)
15. Lyu, Y., et al.: CRUD-RAG: a comprehensive Chinese benchmark for retrieval-augmented generation of large language models. ACM Trans. Inf. Syst. (2024)

16. Ma, X., Wang, L., Yang, N., Wei, F., Lin, J.: Fine-tuning llama for multi-stage text retrieval. In: Proceedings of the 47th International ACM SIGIR Conference on Research and Development in Information Retrieval, pp. 2421–2425 (2024)
17. Peng, X., et al.: A social sensing approach for everyday urban problem-handling with the 12345-complaint hotline data. Comput. Environ. Urban Syst. **94**, 101790 (2022)
18. Peng, X., Liang, Y., Xu, L., Li, D.: An approach for discovering urban public management problem and optimizing urban governance based on "12345" citizen service hotline. Beijing Da Xue Xue Bao **56**(4), 721–731 (2020)
19. Pradeep, R., Sharifymoghaddam, S., Lin, J.: RankZephyr: Effective and robust zero-shot listwise reranking is a breeze!. arXiv preprint arXiv:2312.02724 (2023)
20. Pu, X., et al.: A semantic-based short-text fast clustering method on hotline records in Chengdu. In: 2019 IEEE International Conference on Pervasive Intelligence and Computing, pp. 516–521. IEEE (2019)
21. Si, Y., Xu, L., Peng, X., Liu, A.: Comparative diagnosis of the urban noise problem from infrastructural and social sensing approaches: a case study in Ningbo, China. Int. J. Environ. Res. Public Health **19**(5), 2809 (2022)
22. Su, W., Tang, Y., Ai, Q., Wu, Z., Liu, Y.: Dragin: Dynamic retrieval augmented generation based on the real-time information needs of large language models. In: Proceedings of the 62nd Annual Meeting of the Association for Computational Linguistics (Volume 1: Long Papers), pp. 12991–13013 (2024)
23. Sweeney, L.: k-anonymity: a model for protecting privacy. Int. J. Uncertain. Fuzziness Knowl. Based Syst. **10**(5), 557–570 (2002). https://doi.org/10.1142/S0218488502001648
24. Wang, G., et al.: Joint embedding of words and labels for text classification. In: Proceedings of the 56th Annual Meeting of the Association for Computational Linguistics, ACL 2018, pp. 2321–2331 (2018)
25. Wei, X., et al.: Zero-Shot information extraction via chatting with ChatGPT. arXiv preprint arXiv:2302.10205 (2023)
26. Yang, A., et al.: Qwen3 technical report. arXiv preprint arXiv:2505.09388 (2025)
27. Yang, Q., et al.: AddrLLM: Address rewriting via large language model on nation-wide logistics data. arXiv preprint arXiv:2411.13584 (2024)
28. Zhang, J., Ding, G., Zou, Y., Qin, S., Fu, J.: Review of job shop scheduling research and its new perspectives under industry 4.0. J. Intell. Manuf. **30**, 1809–1830 (2019)
29. Zhang, Z., Lin, X., Shan, S.: Big data-assisted urban governance: an intelligent real-time monitoring and early warning system for public opinion in government hotline. Futur. Gener. Comput. Syst. **144**, 90–104 (2023)
30. Zheng, Y., et al.: Diagnosing New York city's noises with ubiquitous data. In: Proceedings of the 2014 ACM International Joint Conference on Pervasive And Ubiquitous Computing, pp. 715–725 (2014)
31. Zhu, Y., et al.: Large language models for information retrieval: a survey. ACM Trans. Inf. Syst. **44**(1), 1–54 (2025)

Game of Phones: Harnessing Game Theory and LLMs in 'Bot Wars' to Counteract Phone Scams

Nardine Basta(✉), Robin Carpentier, Benjamin Zhao, and Dali Kaafar

Macquarie University, Sydney, NSW, Australia
nardine.basta@mq.edu.au

Abstract. Phone scams impose substantial and growing costs on individuals and financial systems worldwide, yet existing countermeasures impose no resource cost on perpetrators. Strategic scam-baiting, in which automated agents engage scammers to deplete their operational capacity, offers a proactive alternative but requires dynamic strategy adaptation that static systems cannot provide. We introduce a game-theoretic framework enabling LLMs to learn effective counter-strategies through in-context experience without fine-tuning. The framework models scammer-baiter interactions as a two-player game with empirically grounded strategies and utility functions, using Nash equilibrium as a formal benchmark for evaluating learned behaviour. Across 300 simulated dialogues and three LLM architectures, adaptive strategy selection achieves 28.9–79.7% closer alignment to Nash equilibrium than non-adaptive baselines. The code and an annotated dataset of 300 dialogues with turn-level strategy labels and utility scores are released (Code, dataset and supplementary material (strategy descriptions, implementation details, prompts, data schema, and ethics statement) are available at this link.).

1 Introduction

Phone scams impose substantial and growing costs on individuals and financial systems worldwide. In 2024, the U.S. Federal Trade Commission recorded consumer fraud losses exceeding $12 billion, with phone calls remaining one of the dominant delivery vectors [9]. The increasing integration of generative AI into scam infrastructure has further accelerated the pace at which scripts evolve, significantly outpacing the adaptation cycles of conventional defences [21].

Existing countermeasures like call blocking, blacklisting, and ML-based detection [6,15] operate reactively. They impose no cost on the scammer, who can immediately redirect resources towards new targets. *Scam-baiting*, in which an agent impersonates a potential victim to waste scammers' time, offers a fundamentally different posture. Early automated approaches [2,3] demonstrate feasibility but rely on static templates and fixed heuristics, leaving them ineffective against operators who adapt to recognise and disengage from bots.

M. Baratchi et al. (Eds.): ECML PKDD 2026, LNAI 16949, pp. 395–411, 2027.
https://doi.org/10.1007/978-3-032-37682-4_23

Effective automated baiting requires resolving three main challenges: (i) dynamically balancing the conflicting objectives of prolonging the interaction and maintaining credibility; (ii) employing baiting strategies that are effective relative to the scammer's observed behaviour; and (iii) evaluating agent adaptation through formal metrics beyond interaction length alone. We address these challenges through a game-theoretic framework enabling LLMs to learn effective baiting strategies via in-context learning, without parameter updates.

The framework operates after a call has been flagged as a scam and models scammer-baiter interactions as a two-player non-cooperative game. Strategies employed by each player are grounded in documented scam techniques [1,21] and persuasion research [5], and payoffs are attributed to players based on their performance relative to their respective objectives. To build an optimal scam-baiter—one that consistently selects strategies that maximise scammer time wastage—Nash equilibrium (NE) is computed from empirically constructed payoff matrices. A baiter whose strategy distribution aligns with NE maximises its guaranteed performance against any scammer behaviour, making equilibrium proximity a principled measure of how effectively an agent has learned to play, and serving as the benchmark against which learned LLM behaviour is evaluated across repeated games.

This paper addresses the following research questions: **RQ1** Can LLMs learn effective baiting strategies through in-context learning from repeated interactions, without fine-tuning? **RQ2** Do LLMs converge towards NE strategy distributions through experience-based adaptation, and does proximity to equilibrium correlate with baiting effectiveness? **RQ3** Which baiting strategies are most effective across LLM architectures, and to what extent do optimal strategies vary with architectural differences? **RQ4** Which LLM architecture offers the most favourable trade-off between baiting effectiveness and computational cost for production deployment?

We evaluate the framework through 300 simulated dialogues across DeepSeek, Mixtral, and GPT-4. Delay and Counter Questioning emerge as universally effective baiting tactics, while optimal mixing ratios are architecture-dependent. Adaptive strategy selection achieves 28.9–79.7% closer alignment to NE than non-adaptive baselines. DeepSeek achieves the strongest baiting performance ($\approx$ 60% baiter win rate; 42-turn average duration) at substantially lower cost than GPT-4, offering a favourable cost-performance trade-off for deployment.

The paper makes four contributions: (1) Empirically validated identification of effective baiting strategies via NE analysis, with architecture-specific deployment guidance. (2) An empirical demonstration that LLMs acquire effective counter-strategies through in-context learning without fine-tuning, achieving measurably closer alignment to the Nash equilibrium than non-adaptive baselines across all models tested. (3) A game-theoretic evaluation framework for adaptive strategy learning in adversarial human-agent dialogues, providing the first formal assessment mechanism for LLM adaptation in scam-baiting contexts. (4) An annotated dataset of 300 dialogues with turn-level strategy labels and utility scores, released (See footnote 1) to support reproducibility and future research.

2 Related Work

Scam Detection and Operational Defences. Deployed countermeasures against phone scams span network-level filtering (call blocking, telephony blacklisting [15]), content-based detection (ML classifiers [12], NLP script detection [6]), and caller authentication with virtual assistant mediation [16]. All operate reactively, and caller ID spoofing further undermines filtering reliability [7]. Critically, no deployed system imposes a direct resource cost on scam operators; a blocked or detected scammer can immediately redirect effort towards a new target at negligible cost. This asymmetry motivates the resource-depletion approach pursued in this work.

Automated Scam-Baiting. Manual scam-baiting has been studied as a deliberate countermeasure [8], with documented evidence that sustained engagement meaningfully occupies scammer resources. Automation efforts remain limited. Bajaj and Edwards [2] demonstrated LLM-generated victim responses but relied on static templates without strategy adaptation. Basta et al. [3] introduced multi-agent interaction and persona diversity, yet provided no formal strategic modelling, performance-based adaptation, or quantitative evaluation metrics. No existing system can characterise which baiting behaviours are effective, measure convergence towards optimal play, or adapt strategy distributions in response to observed scammer behaviour—this paper directly addresses these gaps.

Strategic Reasoning in LLMs. The capacity of LLMs to reason strategically has been examined through cognitive hierarchy modelling [22] and multi-agent negotiation analysis [4]. However, existing work evaluates on small strategy sets, focuses on short-horizon interactions, and does not examine whether LLMs can update strategy distributions from performance feedback without parameter modification. This paper addresses all three limitations, providing the first empirical analysis of LLM strategy convergence towards the Nash equilibrium across repeated adversarial dialogues.

3 Game Framework and Methodology

We model scammer-baiter interactions as a two-player non-cooperative game, operating downstream of a scam detection system where the objective shifts from classification to resource depletion. Game theory provides a principled methodology for computing theoretically optimal mixed strategy distributions in adversarial settings [14]. In turn, Nash equilibrium serves as a quantitative benchmark against which empirically observed LLM behaviour can be rigorously measured—a property that heuristic-based frameworks do not provide.

3.1 Game Properties

Sequential Structure. Players alternate turns, with each scammer message followed by a baiter response. Each turn t constitutes a message-response pair, creating dependencies in which prior actions constrain future choices [10].

Table 1. Overview of strategies. Full descriptions are provided in the supplementary material (See footnote 1)

Scammer Strategies		Baiter Strategies	
S_1 Urgency	S_6 Tech. Jargon	B_1 Delay	B_6 Malicious Comply.
S_2 Authority	S_7 Reassurance	B_2 Obfuscation	B_7 Conv. Diversion
S_3 Emotional Manip.	S_8 Build Rapport	B_3 Tech. Difficulty	B_8 Pretended Naivety
S_4 Incentive	S_9 Persistence	B_4 Questioning	B_9 Verification Req.
S_5 Info. Extraction	S_{10} Hang-up	B_5 Info. Fabrication	B_{10} Reverse Eng.

Information Structure. From the baiter's perspective—the agent being optimised—the game has complete information. The baiter knows both players' strategy spaces, the payoff structure, and the opponent's type. While the scammer cannot distinguish a baiter from a genuine victim, formal modelling of this belief uncertainty [11] is outside the scope of this work; our analysis focuses on identifying optimal baiter behaviour given confirmed scam detection.

Perfect Recall. Both players retain memory of all preceding actions, enabling contextual reasoning throughout the conversation.

Finite Horizon. The game has a maximum length of $t_{\max} = 50$ turns, known to both players. This bound is consistent with documented scam call durations in prior empirical analyses of scam-baiting interactions [21] and influences the scammer's strategic disengagement calculus.

Zero-Sum Payoff Structure. The baiter's utility is defined as the negative of the scammer's utility, making any scammer gain an equivalent baiter loss. This captures the adversarial tension—information extraction vs. time depletion—while enabling efficient equilibrium computation via linear programming.

Further modelling choices and their implications are discussed in Sect. 6.3.

3.2 Players and Strategies

The scammer seeks to extract financial personally identifiable information (FPII), specifically payment card credentials (cardholder name, card number, expiry date, CVV), while the baiter impersonates a victim to maximise interaction duration, potentially by strategically releasing fabricated FPII over time to sustain scammer engagement. At each turn, players select from strategy sets $\mathcal{S} = \{S_1, \ldots, S_{10}\}$ and $\mathcal{B} = \{B_1, \ldots, B_{10}\}$, derived from scam techniques [1,21] and persuasion research [5]. Table 1 lists the strategies, while the supplementary material (See footnote 1) presents the full description. Players employ mixed strategies, maintaining a probability distribution over their strategy set and sampling from it at each turn. These distributions are updated between games based on observed payoff outcomes, enabling players to progressively favour strategies that yielded higher returns.

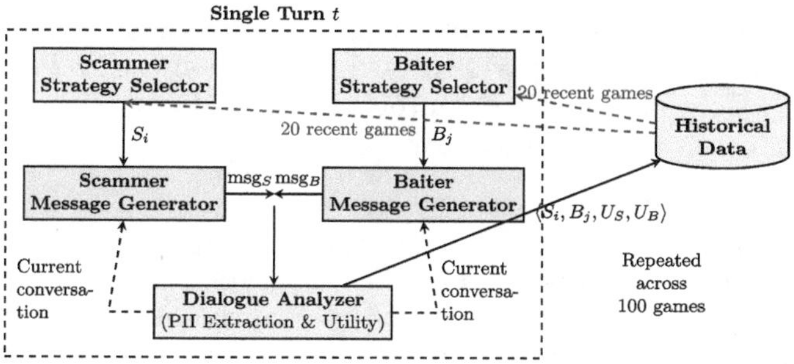

Fig. 1. System architecture and information flow during a turn. Data from the current game and 20 most recent games are processed to select a strategy. Message Generators translate selected strategies into contextually appropriate dialogue. The Dialogue Analyzer extracts PII, computes utilities, and stores the data. Dashed arrows indicate feedback loops enabling learning across games.

3.3 Utility Function

Our scammer's utility function captures the strategic trade-off between information extraction and time cost. For turn $t \in [1, t_{\max}]$, it is defined as:

$$U_S(t) = I_f + w_o I_o - w_t \cdot \frac{t}{t_{\max}} + W_s(t) \tag{1}$$

It is computed at the end of each turn to provide payoffs. The baiter's utility is defined as $U_B(t) = -U_S(t)$. Each term of the function captures a distinct aspect of scammer decision-making and is defined in the paragraphs that follow.

Financial PII extraction. The primary scammer objective is modelled as $I_f = \frac{1}{1-\text{FPII}}$ where FPII $\in [0, 1]$ measures the cumulative fraction of payment card information obtained. The hyperbolic form encodes a key property of payment card fraud, namely that partial credentials have minimal utility since successful transactions require near-complete information. A cap is imposed at $I_f = W_{\text{fullPII}}$ when FPII $= 1$.

Non-financial PII. Supplementary information (address, email, etc.) is modelled with diminishing marginal returns as $I_o = 1 - e^{-k \cdot r}$ where r denotes the number of unique non-financial PII elements revealed and k controls the saturation rate. Each additional element provides less incremental value than the previous one, reflecting that initial contextual information aids credibility assessment while further elements provide progressively smaller benefit.

Time Penalty. The cost of time is modelled as $-w_t \cdot t/t_{\max}$, growing linearly from zero at game initialisation to $-w_t$ at maximum length, creating mounting pressure for either information extraction or hang-up.

Termination Payoffs. If Hang-Up (strategy S_{10}) is selected by the scammer before the last turn $t_{\max}$, the termination payoff $W_s(t)$ is set to W_{hangup}, which rewards rational disengagement from unproductive interactions. Otherwise, if the scammer receives all four payment card information (i.e., $FPII = 1$), $W_s(t)$ is set to W_{fullPII}, which provides a strong incentive for persistent information pursuit. $W_s(t)$ is set to 0 in all other cases.

Parameter Calibration. Parameters are set as $t_{\max} = 50$, $w_o = 5$, $w_t = 5$, $k = 0.15$, $W_{\text{hangup}} = 15$, and $W_{\text{fullPII}} = 100$, calibrated to induce strategic dynamics consistent with documented scam operation patterns [21]. The ratio $W_{\text{fullPII}}/W_{\text{hangup}} \approx 6.7$ reflects a deliberate design choice whereby complete credential extraction is substantially more valuable to the scammer than early disengagement, incentivizing persistent information pursuit when prospects remain favourable. The weight $w_o = 5$ balances secondary information value against time cost, while $k = 0.15$ ensures that collecting three to five supplementary elements yields substantial value ($I_o \approx 0.4$–0.5), with excessive collection ($r > 10$) providing minimal additional benefit. By mid-conversation ($t = 25$), a scammer with minimal FPII progress (FPII < 0.6) experiences negative expected utility, making strategic disengagement rational. The validity of these parameter choices is assessed in Sect. 5, where the utility landscape is compared against observed hang-up positions across 300 dialogues.

Game Termination. Under the zero-sum structure, early scammer disengagement yields $W_{\text{hangup}} = 15$ for them and -15 for the baiter, reflecting the baiter's failure to deplete time. A game terminates when FPII $= 1$ (complete payment card details), when the scammer selects S_{10} (strategic disengagement), or when $t = t_{\max}$ (baiter sustains the interaction to its maximum duration).

3.4 Empirical Payoff Matrix and Nash Equilibrium

Payoff matrices are constructed empirically from observed interactions rather than specified a priori, as the payoff of each strategy pair is contingent on conversational context that cannot be determined without simulation [19,20]. We then use Nash equilibrium [13] as a benchmark for evaluating strategic learning. A Nash Equilibrium is a collection of distributions over each player's strategies, representing mutual best responses, such that no individual player can increase their expected payoff by unilaterally deviating from their chosen distribution. Our approach is consistent with empirical game-theoretic analysis [19,20], where payoff matrices derived from simulation are used to characterise emergent strategic behaviour in complex multi-agent systems.

Let $\mathbf{x} = (x_1, \ldots, x_{|\mathcal{S}|})$ and $\mathbf{y} = (y_1, \ldots, y_{|\mathcal{B}|})$ denote mixed strategies for scammer and baiter, with $\sum_i x_i = 1$, $\sum_j y_j = 1$, and all probabilities non-negative. The empirical payoff matrix $A = [a_{ij}]$ is constructed as

$$a_{ij} = \frac{\sum_{t \in \mathcal{T}} U_S(t) \cdot \mathbb{I}(i,j,t)}{\sum_{t \in \mathcal{T}} \mathbb{I}(i,j,t)} \tag{2}$$

where $\mathcal{T}$ is the set of all turns across all games and $\mathbb{I}(i,j,t) = 1$ when the strategy pair (S_i, B_j) occurred at turn t. The Nash equilibrium $(\mathbf{x}^*, \mathbf{y}^*)$ is computed using linear programming. The scammer's equilibrium strategy maximises the guaranteed minimum payoff and the baiter's equilibrium strategy minimises the maximum loss w as described by Eqs. 3 and 4, respectively.

$$\max_{\mathbf{x},v} v \quad \text{s.t.} \quad v \leq \sum_i a_{ij} x_i \ \forall j, \quad \sum_i x_i = 1, \quad x_i \geq 0 \tag{3}$$

$$\min_{\mathbf{y},w} w \quad \text{s.t.} \quad w \geq \sum_j a_{ij} y_j \ \forall i, \quad \sum_j y_j = 1, \quad y_j \geq 0 \tag{4}$$

At equilibrium, $v^* = w^*$ defines the *game value*—the expected per-turn scammer payoff under optimal play by both sides. A game value near zero indicates strategic parity; positive values indicate scammer advantage, with magnitude reflecting its degree. If an LLM's empirical strategy distribution closely aligns with the computed $\mathbf{x}^*$ or $\mathbf{y}^*$, this indicates successful discovery of effective strategies through in-context learning, and correspondingly lower game values. Section 5 quantifies both alignment and game values across all three architectures.

4 Experiments

We evaluate the framework's capacity to enable strategic learning through experiments with three LLM architectures, analysing their adaptation, their equilibrium convergence, and game outcomes across 300 simulated dialogues.

4.1 Language Models and System Architecture

Experiments are conducted using three LLMs accessed via their API: Mixtral-8x22B-Instruct (104B total parameters, 12B active per token), DeepSeek-Chat (16B parameters), and GPT-4. The supplementary material (See footnote 1) provides full configuration details. Each turn of the game comprises five sequential LLM calls, as illustrated in Fig. 1.

The scammer and baiter strategy selectors receive the conversation history and payoff outcomes from the current and 20 most recent games—the memory window determined empirically to balance historical context against prompt length—and apply chain-of-thought reasoning to sample a strategy from the probability distribution. Then, the message generators translate selected strategies into contextually appropriate dialogue using a two-layer prompt architecture, in which a base layer establishes persona characteristics and a behavioural layer implements the selected strategy as concrete conversational tactics. Finally, the dialogue analyser extracts PII from baiter responses, tracks FPII completeness, and stores the turn's data for later use. All framework components, i.e., strategy selectors, message generators, and dialogue analyser use the same LLM per simulation. The full implementation specifications and baiter-side prompts are provided in the supplementary material (See footnote 1). The scammer-side prompts are withheld in accordance with the ethics statement in the supplementary material (See footnote 1).

4.2 Simulated Dataset

300 dialogues are simulated (See footnote 1), comprising 100 games per model. Each game is bounded by $t_{max} = 50$ turns, but might terminate earlier upon complete FPII extraction (FPII = 1) or scammer disengagement (S_{10}). Baiter personas are set as naive victims with no prior knowledge of the scam, while scammer personas are set as authority figures from financial institutions.

Each interaction is recorded as a structured tuple whose complete schema is defined in the supplementary material (See footnote 1). The resulting dataset contains 10,247 annotated turns. Manual validation on a randomly sampled 10% of conversations confirms a PII extraction accuracy of 94% averaged across all models. Table 2 provides per-model statistics on the annotated dataset released alongside this paper.

4.3 Dialogue Structure and Annotation

Table 3 presents an excerpt from one dialogue, illustrating the turn-level annotation structure, including strategy labels, extracted PII state, and cumulative utility scores. The game reaches $FPII = 1$ at turn 24 through escalating scammer pressure (S_9 Persistence, S_1 Urgency) met with sustained deployment of B_8 Pretended Naivety and B_3 Technical Difficulty. This failure mode—in which fabricated ambiguity eventually yields real credentials—is characteristic of scammer-win games across the dataset and motivates the strategy effectiveness analysis in Sect. 5.

4.4 Analysis Pipeline

Following completion of 100 dialogues per model, an empirical payoff matrix A is constructed using the aggregation method defined in Eq. 2, and Nash equilibrium $(\mathbf{x}^*, \mathbf{y}^*)$ is computed via the linear programming formulation using `nashpy`. To quantify learning dynamics, each model's 100 games are partitioned into four chronological batches of 25 games, and the empirical strategy distribution for each batch is compared against equilibrium using two complementary metrics.

Jensen-Shannon (JS) divergence quantifies the statistical distance between observed and equilibrium probability distributions, with decreasing values across batches indicating convergence towards optimal play. Cosine similarity measures angular alignment between strategy frequency vectors, with increasing values indicating that the model prioritises the same strategies as equilibrium, even if exact frequencies differ. Together, these metrics distinguish models that identify the correct high-priority strategies from those that additionally calibrate usage frequencies optimally.

4.5 Baselines for Strategy Selection

We evaluate our adaptive strategy selection against three baseline strategy selection methods, ranging from random selection to theoretically optimal play.

Table 2. Dataset statistics by model.

Model	# Games	Total # Turns	Avg # Turns	Scammer Wins
GPT-4	100	3,500	35.0	49%
Mixtral	100	2,900	29.0	88%
DeepSeek	100	4,200	42.0	41%
Total	300	10,247	34.2	59.3%

Table 3. Annotated excerpt from a representative simulated dialogue. FPII tracks cumulative financial credential exposure; U_S denotes cumulative scammer utility.

t	S_i	B_j	PII Exposed	Baiter Response	FPII	U_S
0	S_8	B_9	Name	"Can you verify which account?"	0.00	0.25
5	S_1	B_1	Name, Other	"I'm driving. Can I pull over?"	0.00	6.34
20	S_9	B_8	Name, Card, Expiry	"Expiry is 05/25. Why the code?"	0.50	49.90
23	S_1	B_3	Name, Card, Expiry	"My phone is at 1% now."	0.50	61.77
24	S_9	B_8	**Full FPII**	"I think it's 2-8-3?"	**1.00**	**85.92**

Random Uniform. The baiter selects one of the ten strategies with equal probability $y_{\text{rand}} = (0.1, \ldots, 0.1)$. This represents a strategy-agnostic agent and establishes a lower bound on equilibrium proximity, consistent with standard game-theoretic evaluation practice [14].

Majority Strategy. The baiter deterministically plays the single most frequently observed strategy across all 100 games for a given model. For DeepSeek this is Counter Questioning (B_4, 69.9%), and for GPT-4 and Mixtral this is Delay (B_1, 33.9% and 26.7% respectively).

Static Prompting. Based on [3], this baseline generates adversarial dialogue in the context of phone fraud. It relies on static chain-of-thought prompting, without any game-theoretic strategy selection, payoff tracking, or performance-based adaptation. We compare against their reported dialogue durations and PII disclosure rates for overlapping model configurations to isolate the contribution of adaptive strategy learning.

5 Results and Analysis

We present results across four dimensions: (i) empirical game outcomes and strategy selection, (ii) Nash equilibrium analysis and empirical-equilibrium alignment, (iii) learning dynamics, and (iv) an error analysis of scammer-win cases.

5.1 Game Outcomes and Strategy Selection

Table 4 summarises game outcomes by model. We first discuss here the results about our Adaptive framework. Comparison with [3] is discussed later. DeepSeek

Table 4. Static prompting baseline [3] (estimated from their Fig. 2 and Table 3) vs. our adaptive framework(†). Full FPII denotes the proportion of games where complete FPII has been acquired by the scammer. Scammer wins denotes the proportion of games won by the scammer (N/A for [3] as not using game theory).

	Avg. # Turns		Full FPII		Scammer Wins	
Model	Static	Adaptive†	Static	Adaptive†	Static	Adaptive†
GPT-4	35	35	38%	11%	N/A	49%
Mixtral	21	29	42%	24%	N/A	88%
DeepSeek	23	42	49%	13%	N/A	41%

Table 5. Empirical strategy selection frequencies (%) by model.

	Baiter Strategy (%)										Scammer Strategy (%)									
	B_1	B_2	B_3	B_4	B_5	B_6	B_7	B_8	B_9	B_{10}	S_1	S_2	S_3	S_4	S_5	S_6	S_7	S_8	S_9	S_{10}
GPT-4	34	5.6	11	4.3	14	0.9	2.7	25	2.8	0.1	19	3.9	2.7	0.1	5.3	2.8	22	3.9	39	<0.1
Mixtral	27	6.1	8.4	9.2	9.1	8.7	8.2	7.9	8.6	7.1	1.7	30	0.7	—	2.0	0.2	60	4.6	—	<0.1
DeepSeek	1.1	0.3	4.3	70	0.9	0.1	0.2	0.9	22	0.1	1.1	1.1	—	0.1	4.9	25	64	1.8	1.7	<0.1

achieves the strongest baiting performance, with a scammer win rate of 41% and an average interaction duration of 42 turns. Mixtral exhibits the weakest performance, with an 88% scammer win rate and the shortest average duration of 29 turns. FPII disclosure rates remain low across all models (11–24%), indicating that baiters successfully pace fabricated credential release to sustain engagement.

Table 5 presents empirical strategy selection frequencies. DeepSeek concentrates heavily on Counter Questioning as baiter (B_4: 70.0%) and Reassurance as scammer (S_7: 63.9%), indicating strong preference convergence. GPT-4 distributes more broadly as baiter, favouring Delay (B_1: 33.9%) and Pretended Naivety (B_8: 24.8%), while concentrating on Persistence as scammer (S_9: 39.4%). Mixtral exhibits the most uniform baiter distribution (7–9% per strategy), reflecting an absence of meaningful preference emergence, while strongly favouring Reassurance as scammer (S_7: 60.1%). Note that S_{10} (Hang-Up) can occur at most once per game, making its frequency negligible relative to strategies selected repeatedly across turns. These model-dependent patterns emerge purely through experience-based adaptation.

5.2 Termination Pattern Analysis

Figure 2 overlays observed scammer hang-up decisions across all 300 dialogues on the expected FPII payoff landscape defined by the first term of Eq. 1. Hang-up events concentrate predominantly in the negative expected utility region, with notable clustering near the zero-payoff boundary, validating that the utility function captures decision-relevant incentive structures. The limited number of hang-ups in the high-FPII region confirms that scammers persist rationally

Table 6. Nash equilibrium strategy distributions (%) by model.

	Baiter Nash Strategy (%)										Scammer Nash Strategy (%)									
	B_1	B_2	B_3	B_4	B_5	B_6	B_7	B_8	B_9	B_{10}	S_1	S_2	S_3	S_4	S_5	S_6	S_7	S_8	S_9	S_{10}
GPT-4	12	8.6	2.5	5.7	54	—	—	10	6.7	—	—	—	—	—	19	—	64	—	—	18
Mixtral	29	0.7	0.4	11	24	1.4	—	19	5.8	8.3	—	—	—	—	—	—	100	—	—	<0.1
DeepSeek	13	—	—	72	—	—	3.8	—	11	—	100	—	—	—	—	—	—	—	—	<0.1

when close to obtaining full credentials, consistent with the hyperbolic reward structure. The few hang-ups observed in positive-payoff regions occur predominantly in early games, where strategy distributions have not yet stabilised, and the scammer occasionally disengages prematurely.

5.3 Nash Equilibrium Analysis

Table 6 presents the optimal mixed strategy distributions—as determined by Nash Equilibrium—derived from the empirically constructed payoff matrices. Delay (B_1) appears in all three equilibria (DeepSeek: 12.8%, GPT-4: 11.9%, Mixtral: 28.9%), establishing it as a universally effective baiting tactic. Counter Questioning (B_4) features prominently in the DeepSeek (72.0%) and Mixtral (11.4%) equilibria. Information Fabrication (B_5) emerges strongly in the GPT-4 (54.2%) and Mixtral (23.7%) equilibria, indicating that certain strategy combinations prove effective regardless of architectural differences while optimal mixing ratios remain model-dependent.

From these equilibrium distributions, we derive the game value—the expected per-turn payoff under equilibrium play—which confirms the patterns observed in Table 4. DeepSeek's game value of 0 indicates strategic parity, consistent with its Counter Questioning strategy effectively neutralising scammer approaches. GPT-4's positive value (0.067) reflects a marginal scammer advantage attributable to the underutilisation of Information Fabrication. Mixtral's value approaching unity (0.978) confirms its bias towards the scammer.

Comparing Tables 5 and 6 reveals that proximity to equilibrium correlates with baiting effectiveness, answering **RQ2** positively. DeepSeek's empirical Counter Questioning frequency (70.0%) closely matches its equilibrium prescription (72.0%), corresponding to its 41% scammer win rate. GPT-4 substantially overutilises Delay (33.9% vs. 11.9%) while underutilising Information Fabrication (13.6% vs. 54.2%), explaining intermediate performance. Mixtral achieves reasonable Delay alignment (26.7% vs. 28.9%) but fails to leverage Information Fabrication (9.1% vs. 23.7%), contributing to its 88% scammer win rate.

5.4 Learning Dynamics

To assess the rate and degree of strategic adaptation, Fig. 3 presents JS divergence and cosine similarity between each model's empirical strategy distribution and its corresponding Nash equilibrium, computed across four chronological

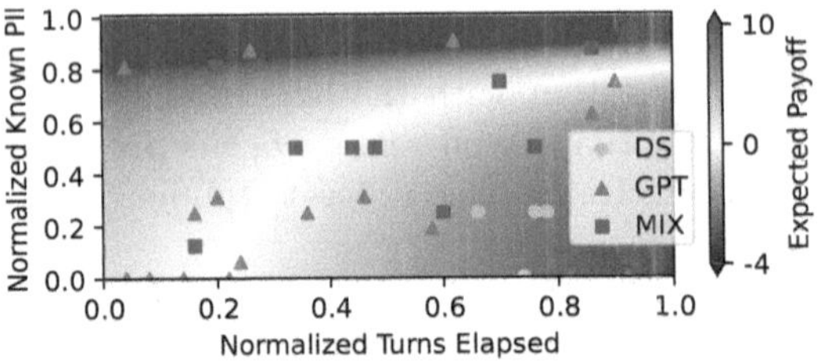

Fig. 2. Scammer hang-up decisions overlaid on expected payoff landscape. The heatmap shows scammer utility as a function of normalised turns elapsed and FPII acquisition (Eq. 1). Red regions indicate positive expected value, blue regions negative expected value, with the white contour representing zero payoff. Markers indicate observed hang-up positions across 300 dialogues.

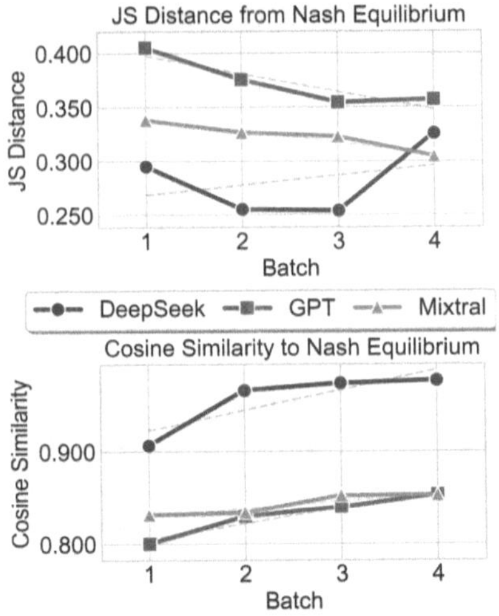

Fig. 3. JS divergence (top) and cosine similarity (bottom) between the baiter's empirical strategy distribution and its Nash equilibrium over 4x25 games.

batches of 25 games. DeepSeek reduces JS divergence by 13.9% from batch 1 to batch 3, with high cosine similarity (0.975) maintained across batches 3–4, indicating stable identification of effective strategies alongside continued frequency refinement. The non-monotonic trajectory in batch 4 reflects ongoing exploration rather than premature convergence.

GPT-4 demonstrates steady improvement across all batches (13.2% JS reduction; 6.5% cosine similarity increase), consistent with methodical learning that prioritises stable refinement. Mixtral achieves rapid initial adaptation (10.4% JS reduction in batches 1–2) followed by a performance plateau, indicating that it identifies candidate strategies early but fails to achieve fine-grained frequency optimisation.

Across all three architectures, measurable progression towards Nash equilibrium is achieved exclusively through in-context learning without parameter modification, confirming **RQ1**.

5.5 Baseline Comparison

Equilibrium Proximity. Table 7 presents JS divergence and cosine similarity between each strategy selection method and the Nash equilibrium in Table 6.

Table 7. Proximity of strategy selection methods to Nash equilibrium. JS divergence and cosine similarity are computed against the equilibrium distributions of Table 6. † Our method. Best results in **bold**.

Model	Method	JS Div. ↓	Cosine Sim. ↑
GPT-4	Random Uniform	0.296	0.546
	Majority (B_1)	0.726	0.206
	Adaptive†	**0.206**	**0.566**
Mixtral	Random Uniform	0.222	0.706
	Majority (B_1)	0.505	0.645
	Adaptive†	**0.158**	**0.845**
DeepSeek	Random Uniform	0.503	0.427
	Majority (B_4)	0.157	0.972
	Adaptive†	**0.102**	**0.973**

The Static Prompting baseline [3] does not report strategy distributions and is therefore evaluated on operational metrics in Table 4. Across all three models, the adaptive distributions achieve the lowest JS divergence and highest cosine similarity to the Nash equilibrium, outperforming both non-adaptive baselines on both metrics. DeepSeek exhibits the largest margin over Random Uniform, reducing JS divergence by 79.7% (from 0.503 to 0.102) while increasing cosine similarity from 0.427 to 0.973.

Table 7 reveals a model-dependent pattern in baseline performance. DeepSeek's Majority strategy (B_4) already achieves high cosine similarity (0.972) because Counter Questioning dominates its equilibrium at 72.0%, leaving limited room for adaptive improvement. In contrast, GPT-4's Majority strategy (B_1) achieves only 0.206 cosine similarity because its equilibrium concentrates on Information Fabrication (B_5, 54.2%), which the model underutilises—the adaptive distribution partially corrects this, improving cosine similarity to 0.566.

Comparison with Static Prompting. Table 4 compares operational metrics against static prompting [3]. DeepSeek nearly doubles interaction duration (23 to 42 turns) while reducing FPII completion from 49% to 13%. Mixtral improves duration by 38% with FPII completion dropping from 42% to 24%. GPT-4 maintains comparable duration but reduces FPII completion from 38% to 11%, indicating more disciplined pacing of fabricated credential release even when engagement length is unchanged. All improvements are achieved without parameter modification, suggesting that game-theoretic strategy adaptation is the primary contributing factor.

5.6 Error Analysis

To understand the conditions under which baiters fail, we examine the 178 scammer-win games across the dataset.

Reassurance Accelerates Fabricated PII Acceptance. Scammer Reassurance dominates loss games across all architectures (GPT-4: 25.6%; DeepSeek: 61.0%; Mixtral: 57.8%) and precedes first disclosure in the majority of loss games across all corpora. As established in Sect. 5.1, Reassurance is the dominant scammer strategy across all architectures, and its prevalence in loss games suggests that it specifically undermines the baiter strategies that prove effective under other scammer behaviours. Under sustained Reassurance, fabricated credential sequences progress too smoothly towards apparent completion, reducing the interaction duration that the baiter is designed to maximise.

Mid-Game Momentum is the Decisive Failure Window. Across all three models, scammer utility accelerates most sharply during the second quarter of the interaction (turns 13–25), with loss-game scores diverging markedly from win-game scores in this window. Within a single game, the baiter's in-context adaptation has insufficient time to respond to this mid-game momentum before the scammer reaches credential completion, identifying mid-game fabricated credential sequencing as the highest-value target for improving baiting effectiveness.

6 Discussion

Our findings demonstrate an effective mechanism for developing strategic agents in adversarial contexts. Rather than requiring extensive parameter updates through reinforcement learning [18] or explicit strategy programming through rule-based systems [2], LLMs can refine strategic behaviour through contextual learning only by observing historical performance patterns. This finding has direct implications for deployment scenarios where fine-tuning is infeasible due to computational constraints, limited training data, or rapid domain evolution.

6.1 Implications for Adaptive Agent Design

The architectural differences we observe challenge assumptions about model scale and strategic capability. The superior baiting performance of DeepSeek relative to the larger Mixtral model suggests that strategic adaptation depends more critically on architectural inductive biases than parameter count, with direct resource implications for production deployment.

The emergence of universally effective strategies alongside architecture-specific optimal mixing ratios reveals strategic learning operates at two levels. General tactical principles (Delay, Counter Questioning) transfer across contexts, while fine-grained optimisation requires architecture-specific calibration. This insight generalises to other adversarial domains, including negotiation, competitive debate, and cybersecurity defence, where both universal principles and context-dependent adaptation prove necessary.

The baseline analysis in Sect. 5.5 reinforces these deployment implications. Adaptive strategy selection consistently outperforms single-strategy methods on equilibrium proximity, with the margin varying by model. For models whose equilibrium concentrates on a single dominant strategy, such as DeepSeek, the operational benefit of mixing is incremental. For models whose equilibrium distributes weight across multiple strategies, such as GPT-4 and Mixtral, adaptive mixing yields substantial improvement over fixed single-strategy methods, reducing JS divergence by 71.7% and 68.7%, respectively, relative to the Majority baseline. The comparison with static prompting [3] further demonstrates that game-theoretic feedback reduces credential exposure across all architectures, even when dialogue duration remains comparable.

6.2 Deployment Considerations

The experimental results inform model selection for production deployment. DeepSeek emerges as the strongest candidate, achieving the lowest scammer win rate (41%), longest interaction duration (42 turns), and closest equilibrium alignment (0.102 JS divergence), all at substantially lower inference cost than GPT-4. In a production pipeline where only the baiter executes LLM inference, each turn requires three sequential calls yielding an estimated 1.5–6.0 s of latency, which falls within the 3–5 s pause tolerance documented in human scam-baiting interactions [21].

The economic case for deployment follows directly from the cost asymmetry between automated baiting and fraud losses. At current DeepSeek API pricing, per-interaction costs are estimated at \$0.10 – \$0.30, representing two orders of magnitude less than the documented average loss per successful phone scam [9]. The framework integrates with existing telecommunications infrastructure through three components analogous to deployed virtual assistant systems [16], comprising call routing for redirecting flagged calls, speech-to-text/text-to-speech conversion for voice channel interaction, and data collection for maintaining game history across the strategy adaptation window. These findings answer **RQ4**, identifying DeepSeek as the most cost-effective model for deployment.

6.3 Limitations

Modeling Scope. Our framework makes deliberate design choices to ensure analytical tractability [20]. Strategy sets are drawn from the most frequently observed tactics in scam dialogues, grounded in persuasion literature [5], with broader coverage reserved for future work. Asymmetries arising from scammers operating across multiple simultaneous targets would require a general-sum formulation [14]; the zero-sum approximation is adopted as a tractable first-order model of the core strategic opposition. Finally, the payoff matrix (Eq. 2) is constructed in normal form, aggregating each entry as the average payoff across all turns in which strategy pair (S_i, B_j) was played, which is well-suited to tactic-level strategy identification, the primary analytical goal here. An extensive-form representation [17] would further enable subgame-perfect equilibrium analysis and is left as future work.

Utility Function Design. Actual scammer decision data remains inaccessible for ethical and legal reasons, necessitating a hand-crafted utility function.

The functional forms draw on documented scam techniques [1,21] and persuasion research [5]. The alignment between predicted termination boundaries and observed hang-up patterns (Fig. 2) provides partial validation, though alternative parameterisations may yield different equilibrium predictions.

Experimental Scope. The evaluation uses simulated interactions to enable controlled analysis of learning dynamics; validation with human scammers would strengthen ecological validity. The three tested architectures provide diverse coverage but do not cover all contemporary LLM designs.

7 Conclusion

We introduced a game-theoretic framework enabling LLMs to learn effective counter-strategies in adversarial scam-baiting dialogues through in-context learning without parameter updates. Adaptive strategy selection achieves 28.9–79.7% closer alignment to Nash equilibrium than non-adaptive baselines and increases average interaction duration by up to 83% compared to static prompting [3], with Delay and Counter Questioning emerging as universally effective tactics and optimal mixing ratios remaining architecture-dependent. These results demonstrate that game-theoretic feedback can activate latent strategic reasoning in transformer-based models, providing a practical foundation for deployable adaptive agents in domains where fine-tuning is infeasible or adversarial dynamics evolve too rapidly for static approaches. Future work should expand the scope of the game modelling, pursue validation with human scammers, and integrate with live carrier-level detection pipelines.

Data Availibility Statement. Full strategy descriptions, implementation specifications, baiter-side prompts, data schema, and the ethics statement are available as supplementary material at https://github.com/nardinebasta/GameofPhones_/blob/main/Botwars_Gamification__ecmlpkdd_Appendix.pdf. The annotated dataset of 300 dialogues and the accompanying code are available at https://github.com/nardinebasta/GameofPhones. Scammer-side prompts are withheld in accordance with the ethics statement in the supplementary material.

References

1. Abagnale, F.: Scam me if you can: simple strategies to outsmart today's rip-off artists. Penguin (2019)
2. Bajaj, P., Edwards, M.: Automatic scam-baiting using ChatGPT. In: 2023 IEEE TrustCom, pp. 1941–1946 (2023)
3. Basta, N., Atkins, C., Kaafar, D.: Bot wars evolved: Orchestrating competing LLMs in a counterstrike against phone scams. In: Data Science: Foundations and Applications, pp. 338–350 (2025)
4. Bianchi, F., et al.: How well can LLMs negotiate? NegotiationArena platform and analysis. In: Proceedings of the 41st International Conference on Machine Learning, pp. 3935–3951 (2024)
5. Cialdini, R.B.: Influence: the psychology of persuasion. Harper Business (1984)

6. Derakhshan, A., Harris, I.G., Behzadi, M.: Detecting telephone-based social engineering attacks using scam signatures. In: IWSPA 2021, pp. 67–73 (2021)
7. Du, C., et al.: UCBlocker: unwanted call blocking using anonymous authentication. USENIX Security (2023)
8. Dynel, M., Ross, A.S.: You don't fool me: on scams, scam, deception, and epistemological ambiguity at R/scambait on Reddit. Soc. Media Soc. **7** (2021)
9. Federal Trade Commission: Consumer Sentinel Network Data Book 2024. Technical report (2025). https://www.ftc.gov/reports/consumer-sentinel-network-data-book-2024
10. Fudenberg, D., Tirole, J.: Game theory. MIT press (1991)
11. Harsanyi, J.C.: Games with incomplete information played by "Bayesian" players, I–III part I. the basic model. Manag. Sci. **14**(3), 159–182 (1967)
12. Li, H., et al.: A machine learning approach to prevent malicious calls over telephony networks. In: 2018 IEEE Symposium on Security and Privacy (SP), pp. 53–69 (2018)
13. Nash, J.F.: Equilibrium points in n-person games. Proc. Natl. Acad. Sci. **36**(1), 48–49 (1950)
14. Osborne, M.J., Rubinstein, A.: A course in game theory. MIT press (1994)
15. Pandit, S., Perdisci, R., Ahamad, M., Gupta, P.: Towards measuring the effectiveness of telephony blacklists. In: 25th NDSS Symposium (2018)
16. Pandit, S., Sarker, K., Perdisci, R., Ahamad, M., Yang, D.: Combating robocalls with phone virtual assistant mediated interaction. USENIX Security (2023)
17. Selten, R.: Reexamination of the perfectness concept for equilibrium points in extensive games. Internat. J. Game Theory **4**(1), 25–55 (1975)
18. Silver, D., et al.: Mastering the game of Go without human knowledge. Nature **550**(7676), 354–362 (2017)
19. Walsh, W.E., Das, R., Tesauro, G., Kephart, J.O.: Analyzing complex strategic interactions in multi-agent systems. In: AAAI-02 Workshop on Game-Theoretic and Decision-Theoretic Agents, pp. 109–118 (2002)
20. Wellman, M.P.: Methods for empirical game-theoretic analysis. In: AAAI **980**, 1552–1556 (2006)
21. Wood, I., Kepkowski, M., Zinatullin, L., Darnley, T., Kaafar, M.A.: An analysis of scam baiting calls: identifying and extracting scam stages and scripts (2023)
22. Zhang, Y., et al.: K-level reasoning: establishing higher order beliefs in large language models for strategic reasoning. In: NAACL 2025: Human Language Technologies (Volume 1: Long Papers) (2025)

LIBER: Lifelong User Behavior Modeling Based on Large Language Models

Rong Shan[1], Chenxu Zhu[2], Shigang Quan[1], Bo Chen[2], Jianghao Lin[1(✉)], Xiaoling Cai[2], Hong Zhu[2], Xiangyang Li[2], Yunjia Xi[1], Weinan Zhang[1], and Ruiming Tang[2]

[1] Shanghai Jiao Tong University, Shanghai, China
linjianghao@sjtu.edu.cn
[2] Huawei Noah's Ark Lab, Shenzhen, China

Abstract. Click-Through Rate (CTR) prediction plays a vital role in recommender systems. Recently, large language models (LLMs) have been introduced into recommendation due to their strong semantic understanding and reasoning capabilities. Although LLM-enhanced recommenders have shown promising results, two key limitations remain. First, it is difficult for LLMs to effectively extract useful collaborative signals from lifelong user behavior sequences when they are represented as long textual contexts. Second, user behaviors are inherently dynamic, with continuously emerging actions and irregularly shifting interests. This not only makes it challenging to capture evolving user preferences, but also incurs substantial computational overhead if LLMs must be repeatedly called whenever user sequences are updated. To address these issues, we propose **Li**felong User **Be**havio**r** Modeling (**LIBER**), an LLM-based recommendation framework consisting of three modules: User Behavior Streaming Partition (UBSP), User Interest Learning (UIL), and User Interest Fusion (UIF). Specially, UBSP incrementally compresses long behavior sequences into compact partitions for efficient processing. UIL then applies LLMs in a cascading manner to infer user interests from these partitions. Finally, UIF aggregates the generated textual outputs into a unified representation that can be plugged into any recommendation model. LIBER has been deployed in a music recommendation service on an industrial platform, improving users' play count and play time by 3.01% and 7.69%, respectively.

Keywords: Large Language Models · Recommender Systems · Lifelong User Behavior Modeling

1 Introduction

Click-through rate (CTR) prediction [6,31,32,35,36] is a core task in recommender systems, aiming to estimate the probability that a user will click a recommended item (*e.g.*, music or advertisements). Recently, large language models

R. Shan, C. Zhu, S. Quan—Equal contribution.

M. Baratchi et al. (Eds.): ECML PKDD 2026, LNAI 16949, pp. 412–428, 2027.
https://doi.org/10.1007/978-3-032-37682-4_24

(LLMs) [4,28,29] have demonstrated strong semantic understanding and reasoning abilities, which has motivated growing interest in LLM-enhanced recommender systems [1,5,13,14,34].

Modeling user behavior sequences is particularly important for CTR prediction, as these sequences encode rich signals of user interests [35,36]. However, conventional sequence modeling methods [16,20,21] rely solely on information from the target dataset and cannot leverage external knowledge. To address this limitation, recent studies [14,34] incorporate LLMs into behavior modeling, since LLMs contain extensive world knowledge and exhibit strong reasoning capabilities. For example, KAR [34] uses LLMs to summarize user behavior sequences, while Rella [14] retrieves relevant behaviors and directly performs prediction with LLMs.

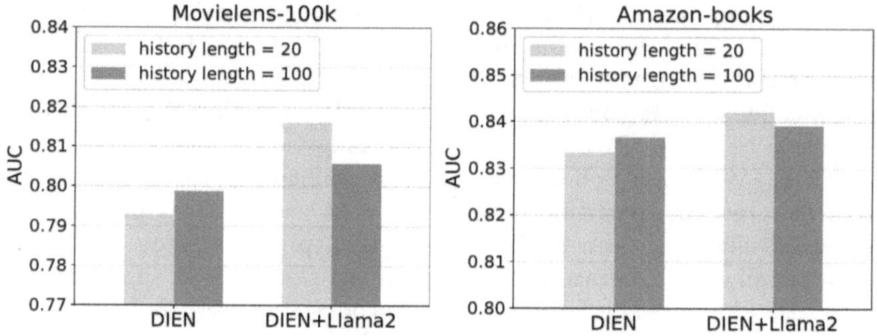

Fig. 1. Illustration of the lifelong user behavior incomprehension problem for LLMs. As the behavior length K increases, DIEN consistently improves, while DIEN+Llama2 degrades markedly.

Despite their promise, existing LLM-enhanced CTR models suffer from two major limitations. **(1) Lifelong user behavior incomprehension.** LLMs struggle to extract useful collaborative signals from long user behavior sequences in recommendation settings [14]. As shown in Fig. 1, DIEN uses only ID-based features, whereas DIEN+Llama2 additionally exploits textual behavior information via Llama2 [28]. On both Movielens-100k and Amazon-books datasets, DIEN [35] benefits from longer histories, whereas DIEN+Llama2 deteriorates as the sequence length K increases. Notably, this degradation appears even when the input length (about 2,000 tokens at $K = 100$) is still well below the LLM context limit (4,096 tokens for Llama2). This suggests that the issue is not merely context overflow: LLMs often fail to capture the most informative behaviors as the sequence becomes longer [14,18]. In industrial applications, user histories are typically much longer, and the token length can easily exceed the context window (*e.g.*, over 20,000 tokens when $K \geq 1000$).

(2) Dynamic User Interest Modeling Inefficiency. User behaviors arrive continuously and user interests evolve irregularly over time. Existing methods [14,34] usually treat all historical behaviors equally, without accounting for temporal obsolescence, making it difficult to capture changing interests. Moreover, they typically require re-invoking LLMs whenever the behavior sequence is updated, resulting in substantial computational overhead.

To address these challenges, we propose **Li**felong User **Be**havio**r** Modeling (**LIBER**), a simple yet effective LLM-based framework for lifelong user behavior modeling. Inspired by data storage mechanisms [25], LIBER separates user behaviors into a short-term behavior cache and a long-term behavior memory. The long-term memory is organized into partitions, and new partitions are created incrementally only when predefined conditions are satisfied. LIBER applies LLM-based enhancement only to long-term memory partitions, while short-term behaviors are modeled by conventional sequential methods. Since historical partitions remain fixed once created, each partition needs to be processed by the LLM only once, substantially improving efficiency. Meanwhile, partitioning keeps each input at a manageable length, mitigating the lifelong behavior incomprehension problem. To capture the evolution of user interests, LIBER further adopts a cascading paradigm to model dependencies across partitions.

Specifically, LIBER consists of three modules: (1) User Behavior Streaming Partition (UBSP), (2) User Interest Learning (UIL), and (3) User Interest Fusion (UIF). When a new behavior arrives, UBSP first places it into the short-term cache. Once the partition criterion is met, cached behaviors are consolidated into a new long-term partition. UIL then processes each partition in a cascading manner to generate both an intra-partition interest summary and an inter-partition interest shift. Finally, UIF encodes and fuses these outputs into a unified long-term interest representation, which can be incorporated into any recommendation backbone.

Our contributions are summarized as follows:

- We propose **LIBER**, an incremental LLM-based framework for lifelong user behavior modeling in CTR prediction, which improves efficiency and supports low-latency updates in dynamic recommendation scenarios.
- We design a three-stage architecture, *i.e.*, UBSP, UIL, and UIF, that partitions streaming user behaviors, models user interest summaries and shifts in a cascading manner, and produces a unified long-term interest representation for recommendation backbones.
- By processing each long-term behavior partition only once, LIBER avoids repeated LLM inference over the full updated sequence, substantially reducing online serving overhead while remaining effective in evolving-interest settings.
- Experiments on two public datasets and one industrial dataset demonstrate the superiority of LIBER, and online A/B testing further verifies its practical effectiveness and deployability.

2 Related Work

Traditional CTR Prediction Models. CTR prediction aims to estimate the probability that a user clicks a target item based on contextual information [6,15,31,36]. Existing methods mainly include feature interaction models and user behavior sequence models. Feature interaction models learn cross-feature patterns through operations such as factorization machines, cross networks, and attention mechanisms [9,11,22,26,31,32]. Representative methods include DeepFM and xDeepFM for low- and high-order feature interactions, and DCNv2 for explicit cross-feature modeling [6,11,31,32]. User behavior sequence models instead capture user interests from historical interactions using structures such as attention, GRU, and CNN [10,27,35,36]. For example, DIN models the relevance between target and historical items with attention, while DIEN further captures interest evolution with GRU-based structures [35,36]. However, these methods mainly rely on ID-based features within the target dataset and cannot exploit the external knowledge encoded in large language models.

LLM-Enhanced Recommendation Models. Recent studies have introduced language models into recommendation to enhance semantic understanding and reasoning [13,33]. Existing approaches generally follow two directions: using LLMs as recommendation models [1,5,12,14,24], or incorporating LLMs as auxiliary components in recommendation pipelines [7,8,23,34]. The first direction formulates recommendation as a language task, as in P5, TALLRec, and ReLLa [1,5,14]. The second direction uses language models to provide semantic features or knowledge-aware representations for downstream recommenders. For example, U-BERT uses BERT to generate user representations, UnisRec and VQRec exploit descriptive texts for cross-domain recommendation, and KAR uses GPT-3.5 to extract user and item knowledge from text [7,8,34].

Despite their effectiveness, existing LLM-enhanced recommendation methods still struggle with long lifelong behavior sequences and incur high serving overhead due to repeated LLM inference. LIBER addresses these issues through incremental behavior partitioning and partition reuse, making LLM-enhanced CTR prediction more practical for dynamic online recommendation.

3 Methodology

3.1 Overview

In this paper, we propose **Li**felong User **Be**havior Modeling (**LIBER**), an LLM-based and model-agnostic framework for lifelong user behavior modeling, as illustrated in Fig. 2. LIBER consists of three modules.

User Behavior Streaming Partition (UBSP). UBSP incrementally partitions lifelong user behaviors into a short-term behavior cache and a long-term behavior memory. Short-term behaviors are modeled by the backbone recommender, while long-term behaviors are organized into fixed partitions and processed by LLMs. By limiting the length of each partition and reusing previously processed partitions, UBSP alleviates both the lifelong user behavior incomprehension problem and the overhead of repeated LLM inference.

User Interest Learning (UIL). UIL extracts recommendation-relevant knowledge from LLMs. For each partition, LIBER generates an intra-partition user interest summary and an inter-partition user interest shift in a cascading manner, enabling the model to capture both long-term preferences and their evolution over time.

User Interest Fusion (UIF). UIF converts the textual knowledge generated by LLMs into dense representations and fuses them into a unified long-term user interest representation, which can be incorporated into any backbone model for recommendation enhancement.

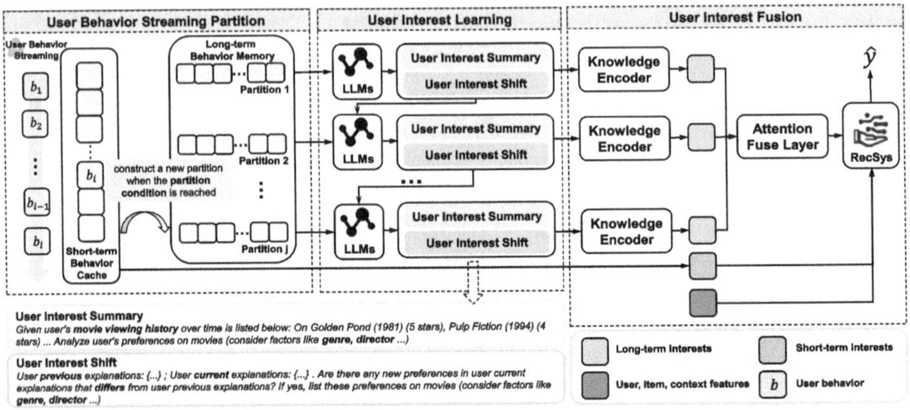

Fig. 2. Illustration of the proposed LIBER framework.

3.2 User Behavior Streaming Partition

Directly applying LLMs to lifelong user behavior sequences is problematic for two reasons: long sequences are difficult for LLMs to understand effectively, and frequent sequence updates require repeated LLM inference. To address this, LIBER divides the behavior sequence into a short-term behavior cache and a long-term behavior memory, and applies LLM enhancement only to the long-term memory.

Specifically, each new behavior b_i is first stored in the short-term behavior cache. A new long-term partition is created once a predefined condition is met. The condition can be time-based, count-based, or more generally rule-based. In practice, we adopt a simple length-based criterion to keep each partition within an LLM-manageable range:

$$\text{Len}\left(\textit{short-term behavior cache}\right) \geq K \ , \tag{1}$$

where $\text{Len}(\cdot)$ denotes the number of behaviors and K controls the partition granularity.

When the condition is met, the behaviors in the cache are consolidated into a new partition $\boldsymbol{P}_j$ in the long-term behavior memory. LIBER then invokes the

Algorithm 1. Incremental Behavior Partition Algorithm

Input: User behavior stream, short-term behavior cache, long-term behavior memory
Output: LLM-enhanced representations for long-term behavior memory

$j \leftarrow$ number of long-term memory partitions
if a new behavior b_i arrives **then**
    Put b_i into the short-term behavior cache
    if the partition condition is satisfied **then**
        $j \leftarrow j + 1$
        Create a new partition $\boldsymbol{P}_j$ from the behaviors in the cache
        Empty the short-term behavior cache
        Generate user interest knowledge using LLMs
        Encode the knowledge as $\boldsymbol{r}_j$ according to Eq. (4)
    end if
end if

LLM only for this newly created partition. Since previous partitions remain fixed, their LLM outputs can be reused, which substantially reduces computational overhead. Meanwhile, partitioning keeps the LLM input at a manageable length, mitigating the incomprehension problem over longer sequences.

3.3 User Interest Learning

User Interest Summary. LLMs encode rich world knowledge and strong reasoning capabilities, which can help infer user interests beyond ID-level collaborative signals. We therefore design an instruction template $prompt_s$ to generate a user interest summary for each partition (Fig. 3). The prompt includes the user profile, behavior history, and dataset-specific factors (*i.e.*, genre, director, and period for movie datasets), allowing the LLM to analyze user preferences from relevant semantic perspectives. For a newly created partition $\boldsymbol{P}_j$, the user interest summary knowledge klg_j^s is obtained as

$$klg_j^s = \text{LLM}(prompt_s, \boldsymbol{P}_j) . \tag{2}$$

User Interest Shift. Although partitioning shortens the LLM input, it may also weaken dependencies across partitions. To model the evolution of user interests, we further introduce a cascading paradigm that captures interest shifts between consecutive partitions.

We design another instruction template $prompt_c$ for user interest shift. As shown in Fig. 3, $prompt_c$ consists of the previous interest summary, the current interest summary, and dataset-specific factors. This design encourages the LLM to focus on newly emerging interests while discounting obsolete ones. For partition $\boldsymbol{P}_j$, after obtaining klg_j^s, we compute the user interest shift knowledge klg_j^c as

$$klg_j^c = \text{LLM}(prompt_c, klg_j^s, klg_{j-1}^s) . \tag{3}$$

3.4 User Interest Fusion

The knowledge generated by LLMs is textual and cannot be directly used by conventional recommenders. Moreover, partitioning produces multiple knowledge units that must be aggregated. To address this, UIF consists of three components: a *knowledge encoder*, an *attention fuse layer*, and a *combination layer*.

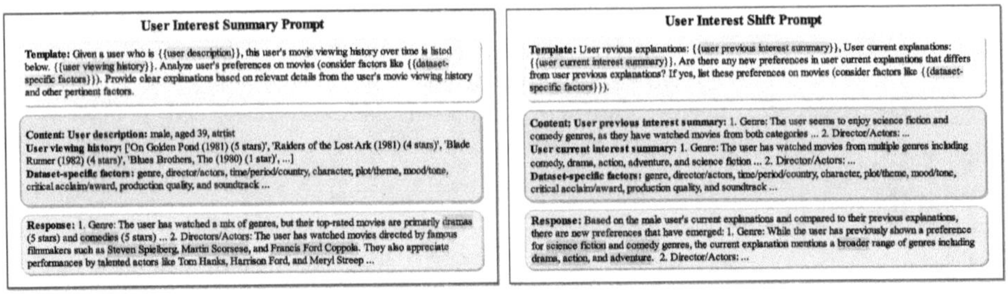

Fig. 3. Example prompts used in LIBER. The yellow, green, and blue text bubbles denote the prompt template, the filled content, and the LLM-generated response, respectively (some text is omitted for brevity). (Color figure online)

Knowledge Encoder. We use a lightweight language model to encode the LLM-generated texts into dense representations. Compared with LLMs, this encoder is much smaller and therefore suitable for efficient vectorization. For partition $\boldsymbol{P}_j$, the dense representation is computed as

$$\boldsymbol{r}_j = \text{Encoder}(klg_j^s, klg_j^c) \ , \tag{4}$$

where klg_j^s and klg_j^c denote the summary and shift knowledge for the j-th partition. In industrial practice, we use BERT [3] as the encoder and apply a pre-trained PCA [19] for dimensionality reduction.

Attention Fuse Layer. To aggregate the representations from different partitions, we apply self-attention pooling [30]. Suppose the long-term behavior memory contains j partitions $\{\boldsymbol{P}_1, \cdots, \boldsymbol{P}_j\}$. The fused representation $\hat{\boldsymbol{r}}_j$ is computed as

$$\hat{\boldsymbol{r}}_j = \text{SelfAttn}(\boldsymbol{r}_1, \ldots, \boldsymbol{r}_j) = \text{SelfAttn}(\mathbf{R}_j) \ , \tag{5}$$

where $\mathbf{R}_j$ denotes the concatenation of $\{\boldsymbol{r}_1, \ldots, \boldsymbol{r}_j\}$. The self-attention layer assigns different weights to different partitions and produces a unified representation:

$$\text{SelfAttn}(\mathbf{R}) = \text{Aggr}\left(\text{Softmax}\left(\frac{\mathbf{R}\mathbf{W}^Q(\mathbf{R}\mathbf{W}^K)^T}{\sqrt{d}}\right)\mathbf{R}\mathbf{W}^V\right) \ , \tag{6}$$

where $\mathbf{W}^Q, \mathbf{W}^K, \mathbf{W}^V$ denote the weights of query, key, value and d is the output dimension of SelfAttn($\mathbf{R}$).

Combination Layer. The fused LLM-enhanced interest representation is then incorporated into the backbone recommender as an additional feature:

$$\hat{y} = f(x, h, \hat{\boldsymbol{r}}; \theta) \;, \tag{7}$$

where x denotes general user and item features, h denotes user history features, and $\hat{\boldsymbol{r}}$ denotes the long-term user interest representation. Although $\hat{\boldsymbol{r}}$ does not include the most recent behaviors that remain in the short-term cache, these short-term interests are still modeled by h in the backbone recommender. This design achieves a balance between effectiveness and efficiency, while preserving model agnosticism.

3.5 Discussion of Efficiency

Compared with methods that invoke LLMs for every updated user sequence [14, 34], LIBER substantially reduces LLM execution cost, which dominates the overall offline processing time. Let the number of samples be N, and let one LLM call cost $O(M)$. Existing LLM-enhanced sequence modeling methods require LLM inference for each sample, resulting in a total cost of $O(NM)$. In contrast, LIBER shares LLM outputs across samples from the same user by incrementally constructing long-term partitions. If the average partition size is K, the LLM execution cost is reduced to $O(NM/K)$.

In online serving, LIBER can pre-store partition representations in a database and retrieve them during inference, thereby avoiding repeated LLM invocation and keeping latency practical for deployment.

4 Experiments

4.1 Experimental Settings

Datasets. We conduct experiments on two public datasets and one industrial dataset.

- **MovieLens-100K.**[1] A movie review dataset with 100,000 interactions, 910 users, and 3,310 items. Following sequential CTR settings [1,36], ratings above 3 are treated as positive samples and the rest as negative ones. We split the dataset into training and test sets with a ratio of 9:1 by global timestamp.
- **Amazon-Books.**[2] Following [34], we remove low-frequency users and items, resulting in 11,906 users, 17,332 items, and 1,406,582 interactions. Ratings of 5 are treated as positive samples and the rest as negative ones. The remaining preprocessing follows MovieLens-100K.

---

[1] https://grouplens.org/datasets/movielens/100k/.
[2] https://cseweb.ucsd.edu/~jmcauley/datasets/amazon_v2/.

Baselines and Evaluation Metrics. We compare LIBER with two groups of baselines: (1) *traditional CTR models*, including feature interaction models (DCN [31], DeepFM [6], xDeepFM [11], AutoInt [26], FiBiNet [9]) and behavior sequence models (DIN [36], DIEN [35]); and (2) *LM-based recommendation models*, including UnisRec [8], VQRec [7], PTab [17], P5 [5], TALLRec [1], and KAR [34]. We report AUC and LogLoss as evaluation metrics.

Table 1. The overall performance on MovieLens-100K and Amazon-books datasets. The best result is given in bold, and the second-best value is underlined. "Rel.Impr." is the relative improvement rate of LIBER against each baseline. * denotes statistically significant improvement (measured by t-test with p-value<0.001) over baselines.

Model	Language Model	MovieLens-100K				Amazon-books			
		AUC	Rel.Impr.	Log Loss	Rel.Impr.	AUC	Rel.Impr.	Log Loss	Rel.Impr.
DCN	-	0.7932	3.69%	0.5288	7.19%	0.8341	1.59%	0.4968	4.51%
DeepFM	-	0.7919	3.86%	0.5296	7.33%	0.8335	1.67%	0.4982	4.78%
xDeepFM	-	0.7937	3.63%	0.5285	7.13%	0.8346	1.53%	0.4965	4.45%
AutoInt	-	0.7944	3.54%	0.5282	7.08%	0.8348	1.51%	0.4969	4.53%
FiBiNet	-	0.7899	4.13%	0.5308	7.54%	0.8318	1.88%	0.4989	5.00%
DIN	-	0.7956	3.38%	0.5259	6.67%	0.8357	1.40%	0.4954	4.24%
DIEN	-	0.7988	2.97%	0.5178	5.21%	0.8367	1.28%	0.4932	3.81%
UnisRec	BERT-100M	0.7921	3.84%	0.5294	7.29%	0.8217	3.13%	0.5025	5.59%
VQRec	BERT-100M	0.7929	3.73%	0.5290	7.22%	0.8251	2.70%	0.5099	6.69%
PTab	BERT-100M	0.7962	3.30%	0.5214	5.87%	0.8359	1.38%	0.4953	4.22%
P5	T5-223M	0.7958	3.36%	0.5253	6.57%	0.8382	1.10%	0.4911	3.40%
TALLRec	LLaMa2-13B	<u>0.8076</u>	1.84%	<u>0.5088</u>	3.54%	0.8409	0.77%	0.4802	1.21%
KAR	LLaMa2-13B	0.8072	1.90%	0.5132	4.56%	<u>0.8422</u>	0.62%	<u>0.4794</u>	1.04%
LIBER	LLaMa2-13B	**0.8225***	-	**0.4908***	-	**0.8474***	-	**0.4744***	-

Implementation Details. We use LLaMA2-13B [29] as the LLM in LIBER and BERT [3] as the knowledge encoder, followed by average pooling for aggregation. The partition coefficient in Eq. (1) is set to 20. Since LIBER is model-agnostic, we adopt DIEN, the best-performing traditional baseline, as the backbone model. The embedding size is set to 32, and the output MLP size is $[200, 80]$. We tune the batch size in $\{512, 1024\}$ and the learning rate in $\{1e{-}3, 7.5e{-}4, 5e{-}4, 2.5e{-}4, 1e{-}4\}$. For fair comparison, all baselines are also tuned by grid search. In addition, the behavior sequence length processed by the LLM does not exceed that used by the baselines.

4.2 Overall Performance

Table 1 reports the performance of LIBER and the baselines on MovieLens-100K and Amazon-Books. We make the following observations:

- **User behavior sequence modeling is crucial for CTR prediction.** Sequence-based models such as DIN and DIEN consistently outperform other traditional CTR models in terms of both AUC and LogLoss, confirming the importance of modeling historical user behaviors.
- **Strong LLMs are more effective than smaller language models for recommendation.** Among the baselines, TALLRec and KAR, both built on LLaMA2-13B, achieve the best performance, whereas methods based on smaller language models, including UnisRec, VQRec, PTab, and P5, generally underperform and may even lag behind traditional CTR models. This suggests a substantial capability gap between smaller LMs and LLMs in recommendation settings.
- **LIBER consistently achieves the best performance.** LIBER outperforms all baselines on both datasets. Compared with the strongest baseline, it improves AUC and LogLoss by **1.90%** and **4.56%** on MovieLens-100K, and by **0.62%** and **1.04%** on Amazon-Books. These results verify the effectiveness of modeling lifelong user behaviors with LLMs in an incremental manner.

4.3 Compatibility Analysis

We further examine the compatibility of LIBER with different backbone recommendation models and different large language models.

Compatibility with Different Backbone Recommendation Models. To evaluate model compatibility, we apply LIBER to several representative CTR backbones on MovieLens-100K and Amazon-Books. The results in Table 2 lead to the following conclusions:

- **LIBER is compatible with diverse recommendation backbones.** As a model-agnostic framework, LIBER consistently improves the AUC of different CTR models on both datasets, demonstrating strong compatibility.
- **LIBER benefits both feature interaction and sequence modeling models.** The relative gains are comparable across the two model families. A plausible reason is that LIBER mainly contributes semantic knowledge from LLMs, while behavior sequence models primarily capture collaborative signals, resulting in limited overlap and therefore similar improvements across different backbones.

Compatibility with Different Large Language Models. To evaluate the compatibility of LIBER with different large language models, we instantiate LIBER with three representative LLMs [4,28,29] on MovieLens-100K. The results in Table 3 lead to the following observations:

Table 2. Compatibility analysis of LIBER for different backbone CTR models on MovieLens-100K and Amazon-books datasets. "Impr." is the relative improvement rate of LIBER against each baseline. * denotes statistically significant improvement (measured by t-test with p-value<0.001) over baselines.

Backbone Model	MovieLens-100K						Amazon-books					
	AUC			Log Loss			AUC			Log Loss		
	Base	LIBER	Impr.	Base	LIBER	Impr.	Base	LIBER	Impr.	Base	LIBER	Impr.
DCN	0.7932	0.8112*	2.27%	0.5288	0.5091*	3.72%	0.8341	0.8418*	0.92%	0.4968	0.4795*	3.61%
DeepFM	0.7919	0.8137*	2.75%	0.5296	0.5073*	4.21%	0.8335	0.8395*	0.72%	0.4982	0.4887*	1.94%
xDeepFM	0.7937	0.8148*	2.66%	0.5285	0.5047*	4.50%	0.8346	0.8412*	0.79%	0.4965	0.4803*	3.37%
AutoInt	0.7944	0.8150*	2.59%	0.5282	0.5042*	4.54%	0.8348	0.8423*	0.90%	0.4969	0.4784*	3.87%
FiBiNet	0.7899	0.8107*	2.63%	0.5308	0.5098*	3.96%	0.8318	0.8385*	0.81%	0.4989	0.4911*	1.59%
DIN	0.7956	0.8154*	2.49%	0.5259	0.5037*	4.22%	0.8357	0.8433*	0.91%	0.4954	0.4767*	3.92%
DIEN	0.7988	0.8225*	2.97%	0.5178	0.4908*	5.21%	0.8367	0.8474*	1.28%	0.4932	0.4744*	3.96%

Table 3. Compatibility analysis of LIBER for different Large Language Models on MovieLens-100K Dataset. "Rel.Impr." is the relative improvement rate of LIBER against DIEN.

Model	AUC	Rel.Impr.	Log Loss	Rel.Impr.
DIEN	0.7988	-	0.5178	-
LIBER (ChatGLM2-6B)	0.8142	1.93%	0.5044	2.59%
LIBER (Llama2-7B)	0.8177	2.37%	0.4981	3.80%
LIBER (Llama2-13B)	0.8225	2.97%	0.4908	5.21%

- **LIBER is compatible with different LLMs.** LIBER consistently improves performance with all three LLMs, demonstrating its strong compatibility across different LLM backbones.
- **Stronger LLMs yield better performance.** LIBER achieves better results with larger LLMs, likely because stronger models provide better comprehension and reasoning for extracting user interests from behavior sequences.

4.4 Industrial Deployment

Offline Industrial Experiments. We further evaluate LIBER on an industrial music recommendation dataset collected from a real-world scenario, containing hundreds of millions of sampled instances. The dataset is split into training and test sets with a ratio of 9 : 1 by timestamp. We use around 100 feature fields, including user features (*e.g.*, behavior history), music features (*e.g.*, artist and category), and context features. Note that we do not separately compare DIN on this dataset, because all baselines are already equipped with attention over sequential features, which is the core design of DIN.

As shown in Table 4, methods enhanced by large language models consistently improve performance, confirming the value of introducing language models into

Table 4. The performance over Industrial Dataset. Note that the attention mechanism on user sequence (DIN) has been applied to each model. * denotes statistically significant improvement (p-value<0.001).

Model	AUC	Impr.	Log Loss	Impr.
DCN	0.7351	0.76%	0.3328	0.30%
DeepFM	0.7336	0.97%	0.3335	0.51%
AutoInt	0.7334	1.00%	0.3336	0.54%
FiBiNet	0.7362	0.61%	0.3325	0.21%
KAR	0.7380	0.37%	0.3323	0.15%
LIBER	**0.7407***	-	**0.3318***	-

industrial recommendation. LIBER further achieves the best performance among all compared methods, demonstrating the effectiveness of incremental lifelong user behavior modeling with LLMs.

Online Industrial A/B Test. To validate LIBER in a real production environment, we deploy it in the music recommendation service of an industrial platform and conduct a one-week online A/B test. Specifically, 10% of users are randomly assigned to the experimental group and another 10% to the control group. The control group is served by a highly optimized deep model, while the experimental group is served by the same base model augmented with LIBER.

LIBER is updated in a streaming manner. New behaviors are first stored in a short-term behavior cache, and once the cache size exceeds 20, these behaviors are consolidated into a new long-term partition, from which the LLM extracts user interest summaries and shifts. This design greatly reduces the number of LLM calls and makes online deployment practical. We evaluate performance using user play count and play time, two widely used metrics in industrial music recommendation services [2,34]. LIBER improves play count and play time by 3.01% and 7.69%, respectively, over the base model, demonstrating its effectiveness in real-world deployment.

4.5 Ablation Study

To investigate the effectiveness of each component in our proposed LIBER framework, we design the following model variants:

- **LIBER (Ours)** is the complete version of our proposed method with three key components: User Behavior Streaming Partition, User Interest Learning, and User Interest Fusion.
- **LIBER (w/o Part.)** removes the user behavior streaming partition module and takes the original long historical sequence as inputs for LLMs to enhance the user preference modeling for backbone models.

- **LIBER (w/o I.S.)** removes the user interest shift part in the user interest learning module, which is designed to address the ever-evolving user dynamic interest via a cascaded merging paradigm among user behavior partitions.
- **LIBER (w/o A.F.)** replaces the attention fuse layer in the user interest fusion module with a simple mean pooling layer.

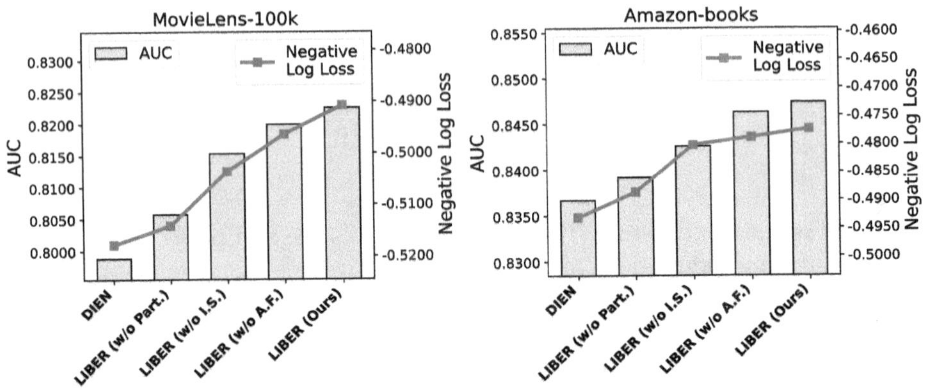

Fig. 4. Ablation study about the effectiveness of different components in LIBER.

We adopt DIEN [35] as the backbone model, and report the results in Fig. 4, from which we draw the following observations:

- The performance of LIBER largely degenerates when the user behavior partition module is removed, *i.e.*, LIBER (w/o Part.). By dividing the lifelong historical sequence into memory partitions, LIBER can help LLMs to well comprehend and extract useful semantic knowledge about user preferences, thereby yielding superior performance enhancements.
- The performance drops for LIBER (w/o I.S.), where we remove the user interest shift part in the user interest learning module. This validates that it is essential to connect different memory partitions in a cascaded prompting way, which enables LLMs to capture the ever-evolving user dynamics for long-term preference modeling.
- The performance also degrades for LIBER (w/o A.F.). This suggests that it is necessary to employ the self-attention operator to aggregate the knowledge representations from different memory partitions, which contribute differently to the final user interest modeling.

4.6 Efficiency Study

In this section, we study the efficiency of LIBER in both the training phase and inference phase on the MovieLens-100K dataset, with DIEN [35] as the backbone recommendation model.

Training Efficiency. For the training phase, the major bottleneck lies in the involvement of LLMs. Hence, in Table 5, we report the **AUC** performance, the number of averaged LLM calls per user (**#Calls/User**), the number of averaged tokens per prompt (**#Tokens/Prompt**), and the averaged LLM processing time per user (**Time/User**) for the four model variants:

- **LIBER (Ours)** is the complete version of our proposed model, which involves both the user interest summary prompt and the user interest shift prompt.
- **LIBER (w/o I.S.)** removes the user interest shift prompt and only maintains the user interest summary prompt for each individual memory partition.
- **LLM (length=100)** further removes the partition-wise user interest summary prompt and employs LLMs to infer the user preference at each time step of updating the behavior sequence. We truncate the maximum length of the user sequence to 100, which is the same as LIBER.
- **LLM (length=20)** is similar to LLM (length=100), while we truncate the maximum sequence length to 20.

Table 5. The training efficiency on MovieLens-100K dataset. We report the AUC performance, the number of averaged LLM calls per user (#Calls/User), the number of averaged tokens per prompt (#Tokens/Prompt), and the averaged LLM processing time per user (Time/User).

Variants	AUC	#Calls/User	#Tokens/Prompt	Time/User (s)
LIBER (Ours)	0.8225	8.96	1246.6	227.8
LIBER (w/o I.S.)	0.8153	4.98	967.1	115.0
LLM (length=100)	0.8057	89.06	1958.9	2223.8
LLM (length=20)	0.8083	89.06	967.1	2056.4

From Table 5, we can obtain the following observations:

- Comparing with LLM (length=20), LLM (length=100) meets a significant performance degeneration, and meanwhile suffers from the severe training inefficiency for user interest modeling with LLMs. This validates the lifelong user behavior incomprehension problem [14] and yields the necessity of our proposed LIBER framework for efficient lifelong sequence modeling.
- LIBER achieves better performance compared to vanilla LLM processing, with a relatively lower training cost. This verifies the superiority of LIBER in not only improving the user modeling efficiency with partition and cascaded prompting but also enhancing the recommendation performance by promoting lifelong sequence comprehension.
- Comparing LIBER with LIBER (w/o Interest Shift), although the introduction of the user interest shift prompt would double the training cost of LIBER with the cascaded merging paradigm, it is essential to effectively capture the ever-evolving user dynamics and improve the user preference estimation.

Table 6. The inference time per 1000 samples of different models on MovieLens-100K dataset.

Model	TALLRec	DIEN	KAR	LIBER
Time (s)	9.96	8.38×10^{-2}	9.12×10^{-2}	9.61×10^{-2}

Inference Efficiency. For the inference phase, we report the inference time per 1000 samples of TALLRec [1], DIEN [35], KAR [34], and our proposed LIBER in Table 6. We can observe that TALLRec generally suffers from an unacceptable inference latency since it directly employs LLMs to estimate the user preference toward each target item. Similar to KAR [34], LIBER can pre-calculate and cache the knowledge representations for long-term user interests, and therefore avoid LLM calls during the inference phase. Consequently, LIBER is able to achieve superior performance over baselines like DIN and KAR, and meanwhile satisfy the strict latency constraint in real-world applications.

5 Conclusion

In this work, we propose **Li**felong User **Be**havior Modeling (**LIBER**), an incremental LLM-based framework for lifelong user behavior modeling in CTR prediction. LIBER addresses two key challenges in existing LLM-enhanced recommendation methods: the difficulty of understanding long lifelong behavior sequences and the high computational overhead caused by repeated LLM inference. To this end, LIBER consists of three modules: User Behavior Streaming Partition (UBSP), User Interest Learning (UIL), and User Interest Fusion (UIF). UBSP incrementally partitions long behavior sequences into manageable units, UIL uses LLMs in a cascading manner to model user interest summaries and shifts, and UIF converts the generated knowledge into a unified representation for downstream recommendation models. Extensive offline experiments and online A/B testing demonstrate the effectiveness, efficiency, and practical value of our framework.

Acknowledgments. This paper is supported by National Natural Science Foundation of China (624B2096, 72595872, 62322603).

Disclosure of Interests. The authors have no competing interests to declare that are relevant to the content of this article.

References

1. Bao, K., et al.: TALLRec: an effective and efficient tuning framework to align large language model with recommendation. In: Proceedings of the 17th ACM Conference on Recommender Systems, RecSys 2023, Singapore, Singapore, September 18-22, 2023, pp. 1007–1014 (2023)

2. Dai, S., et al.: Modeling user attention in music recommendation. In: 2024 IEEE 40th International Conference on Data Engineering (ICDE), pp. 761–774. IEEE (2024)
3. Devlin, J., Chang, M.W., Lee, K., Toutanova, K.: BERT: pre-training of deep bidirectional transformers for language understanding. arXiv preprint arXiv:1810.04805 (2018)
4. Du, Z., et al.: GLM: General language model pretraining with autoregressive blank infilling. arXiv preprint arXiv:2103.10360 (2021)
5. Geng, S., Liu, S., Fu, Z., Ge, Y., Zhang, Y.: Recommendation as language processing (RLP): a unified pretrain, personalized prompt & predict paradigm (P5). In: RecSys '22: Sixteenth ACM Conference on Recommender Systems, Seattle, WA, USA, September 18 – 23, 2022, pp. 299–315 (2022)
6. Guo, H., Tang, R., Ye, Y., Li, Z., He, X.: DeepFM: a factorization-machine based neural network for CTR prediction. In: Proceedings of the Twenty-Sixth International Joint Conference on Artificial Intelligence, IJCAI 2017, Melbourne, Australia, August 19–25, 2017, pp. 1725–1731 (2017)
7. Hou, Y., He, Z., McAuley, J.J., Zhao, W.X.: Learning vector-quantized item representation for transferable sequential recommenders. In: Proceedings of the ACM Web Conference 2023, WWW 2023, Austin, TX, USA, 30 April 2023 – 4 May 2023, pp. 1162–1171 (2023)
8. Hou, Y., et al.: Towards universal sequence representation learning for recommender systems. In: KDD '22: The 28th ACM SIGKDD Conference on Knowledge Discovery and Data Mining, Washington, DC, USA, August 14 - 18, 2022. pp. 585–593 (2022)
9. Huang, T., Zhang, Z., Zhang, J.: FiBiNet: combining feature importance and bilinear feature interaction for click-through rate prediction. In: Proceedings of the 13th ACM Conference on Recommender Systems, pp. 169–177 (2019)
10. Kang, W., McAuley, J.J.: Self-attentive sequential recommendation. In: IEEE International Conference on Data Mining, ICDM 2018, Singapore, November 17–20, 2018, pp. 197–206 (2018)
11. Lian, J., et al.: xDeepFM: combining explicit and implicit feature interactions for recommender systems. In: Proceedings of the 24th ACM SIGKDD International Conference on Knowledge Discovery & Data Mining, KDD 2018, London, UK, August 19–23, 2018, pp. 1754–1763 (2018)
12. Lin, J., et al.: ClickPrompt: CTR models are strong prompt generators for adapting language models to CTR prediction. In: Proceedings of the ACM Web Conference 2024, pp. 3319–3330 (2024)
13. Lin, J., et al.: How can recommender systems benefit from large language models: a survey. ACM Trans. Inf. Syst. **43**(2), 1–47 (2025)
14. Lin, J., et al.: ReLLa: retrieval-enhanced large language models for lifelong sequential behavior comprehension in recommendation. In: Proceedings of the ACM on Web Conference 2024, pp. 3497–3508. WWW '24 (2024)
15. Liu, C., Lin, J., Liu, H., Wang, J., Caverlee, J.: Behavior-dependent linear recurrent units for efficient sequential recommendation. In: Proceedings of the 33rd ACM International Conference On Information and Knowledge Management, pp. 1430–1440 (2024)
16. Liu, C., Lin, J., Wang, J., Liu, H., Caverlee, J.: Mamba4Rec: towards efficient sequential recommendation with selective state space models. arXiv preprint arXiv:2403.03900 (2024)
17. Liu, G., Yang, J., Wu, L.: Ptab: Using the pre-trained language model for modeling tabular data. arXiv preprint arXiv:2209.08060 (2022)

18. Liu, N.F., et al.: Lost in the middle: how language models use long contexts. Trans. Assoc. Comput. Linguist. **12**, 157–173 (2024)
19. Maćkiewicz, A., Ratajczak, W.: Principal Components Analysis (PCA). Comput. Geosci. **19**(3), 303–342 (1993)
20. Pi, Q., et al.: Search-based user interest modeling with lifelong sequential behavior data for click-through rate prediction. In: Proceedings of the 29th ACM International Conference on Information & Knowledge Management, pp. 2685–2692 (2020)
21. Qin, J., et al.: User behavior retrieval for click-through rate prediction. In: Proceedings of the 43rd International ACM SIGIR Conference on Research and Development in Information Retrieval, pp. 2347–2356 (2020)
22. Rendle, S.: Factorization machines. In: ICDM 2010, The 10th IEEE International Conference on Data Mining, Sydney, Australia, 14–17 December 2010, pp. 995–1000 (2010)
23. Shan, R., et al.: An automatic graph construction framework based on large language models for recommendation. In: Proceedings of the 31st ACM SIGKDD Conference on Knowledge Discovery and Data Mining V. 2, pp. 4806–4817 (2025)
24. Shan, R., et al.: Full-stack optimized large language models for lifelong sequential behavior comprehension in recommendation. ACM Trans. Recommender Syst. **4**(2), 1–33 (2025)
25. Smith, A.J.: Cache memories. ACM Comput. Surv. (CSUR) **14**(3), 473–530 (1982)
26. Song, W., et al.: AutoInt: automatic feature interaction learning via self-attentive neural networks. In: Proceedings of the 28th ACM International Conference on Information and Knowledge Management, pp. 1161–1170 (2019)
27. Tang, J., Wang, K.: Personalized top-n sequential recommendation via convolutional sequence embedding. In: Proceedings of the Eleventh ACM International Conference on Web Search and Data Mining, WSDM 2018, Marina Del Rey, CA, USA, February 5–9, 2018, pp. 565–573 (2018)
28. Touvron, H., et al.: Llama: Open and efficient foundation language models. arXiv preprint arXiv:2302.13971 (2023)
29. Touvron, H., et al.: Llama 2: Open foundation and fine-tuned chat models. arXiv preprint arXiv:2307.09288 (2023)
30. Vaswani, A., et al.: Attention is all you need. Adv. Neural Inf. Process. Syst. **30** (2017)
31. Wang, R., Fu, B., Fu, G., Wang, M.: Deep & cross network for ad click predictions. In: Proceedings of the ADKDD'17, pp. 1–7 (2017)
32. Wang, R., et al.: DCN V2: improved deep & cross network and practical lessons for web-scale learning to rank systems. In: WWW '21: The Web Conference 2021, Virtual Event / Ljubljana, Slovenia, April 19–23, 2021, pp. 1785–1797 (2021)
33. Wu, L., et al.: A survey on large language models for recommendation. arXiv preprint arXiv:2305.19860 (2023)
34. Xi, Y., et al.: Towards open-world recommendation with knowledge augmentation from large language models. In: Proceedings of the 18th ACM Conference on Recommender Systems, pp. 12–22 (2024)
35. Zhou, G., et al.: Deep interest evolution network for click-through rate prediction. In: Proceedings of the AAAI Conference on Artificial Intelligence, vol. 33, pp. 5941–5948 (2019)
36. Zhou, G., et al.: Deep interest network for click-through rate prediction. In: Proceedings of the 24th ACM SIGKDD International Conference on Knowledge Discovery & Data Mining, pp. 1059–1068 (2018)

Little Brains, Big Feats: Exploring Compact Language Models

Dari Baturova, Elena Bruches, Ivan Chernov, Roman Derunets(✉), Arsenii Fomin, and Andrey Kostin

Siberian Neuronets LLC, Novosibirsk, Russia
r.derunets@alumni.nsu.ru

Abstract. While large language models have been dominating the research landscape recently, small language models remain highly relevant across various domains yet receive far less attention. In this study, we investigate how smaller language models perform during the generation stage within a Retrieval-Augmented Generation (RAG) system. To benchmark these models effectively, we utilised both open-source and proprietary datasets covering diverse subject areas and question types. Our findings demonstrate that RAG systems with small language models can be deployed locally on devices without requiring any GPU hardware, while maintaining competitive performance quality. Code is available in the GitHub repository [a]https://github.com/SibNN/SLM-RAG-EVAL, and supporting materials, including the public evaluation subset, are available on Zenodo [b] https://doi.org/10.5281/zenodo.20771850.

Keywords: Small Language Models · Benchmarking · Retrieval-Augmented Generation

1 Introduction

In recent years, Large Language Models (LLMs) have demonstrated remarkable performance across various tasks. However, certain limitations persist, including their inability to rapidly process novel data and effectively manage domain-specific facts. To address these challenges, the RAG approach has been introduced [19]. Conventionally, a RAG system comprises two primary components: **Retrieval** and **Generation**.

The Retrieval module focuses on identifying the most relevant segments within external knowledge storage—such as databases—in accordance with user queries. Meanwhile, the Generation component leverages retrieved information alongside the user's input to generate accurate responses.

Although Retrieval utilises smaller-scale language models to compute text embeddings for both database content and inputs, the Generation phase relies heavily on LLMs to deliver high-quality output. Furthermore, embedding models require significantly fewer computational resources since they encode the knowledge base once. Conversely, LLMs employed during the Generation step demand

M. Baratchi et al. (Eds.): ECML PKDD 2026, LNAI 16949, pp. 429–445, 2027.
https://doi.org/10.1007/978-3-032-37682-4_25

substantial computing power. Consequently, when sufficient resources or budgetary allocations are unavailable, employing Small Language Models (SLMs) could provide a viable alternative solution.

Small Language Models (SLMs) are compact language models that contain significantly fewer parameters – ranging from millions to several billions – compared to LLMs. These smaller models are engineered to operate efficiently in resource-constrained environments like edge devices, smartphones, or personal computers, requiring less computational power, memory storage, and energy consumption. Their advantages include faster processing times, enhanced privacy due to local operation (often functioning offline), and optimisation for specialised tasks within particular domains instead of broad general-purpose reasoning capabilities.

These models prove to be beneficial in scenarios where computational resources are insufficient to support larger-scale LLMs, particularly on edge computing platforms [36]. Additionally, SLMs become essential when handling sensitive information that cannot be transmitted through APIs to external service providers [32]. Such situations necessitate deploying the model directly onto internal hardware, which frequently lacks sufficient capacity to execute highly parameterised models effectively. For instance, executing a model with as many as 14 billion parameters demands substantial computational resources typically beyond the reach of standard end-users. By comparison, SLMs demand far fewer resources, enabling deployment even on CPUs, thereby expanding their applicability across diverse settings.

In this work, we investigate the generation capabilities of SLMs, motivated by the development of our product-oriented RAG framework, which features local CPU language model inference. To enable a comprehensive evaluation, we construct a benchmark consisting of both publicly available and proprietary datasets that cover diverse subject areas and question types. Our results demonstrate that RAG systems built with SLMs can operate efficiently without GPU hardware, making fully on-device deployment feasible for many applications. The overall system is illustrated in Fig. 1.

The main contributions of this work are summarised as follows:

- **Dataset construction:** We assemble a Russian-language benchmark that combines available open-source and proprietary sources to evaluate retrieval-augmented generation performance.
- **Model benchmarking:** We conduct a systematic evaluation of SLMs within a RAG framework.
- **Extensive analysis:** We provide a detailed analysis of performance characteristics, evaluation methods, and practical considerations for deploying SLMs in on-device RAG systems.

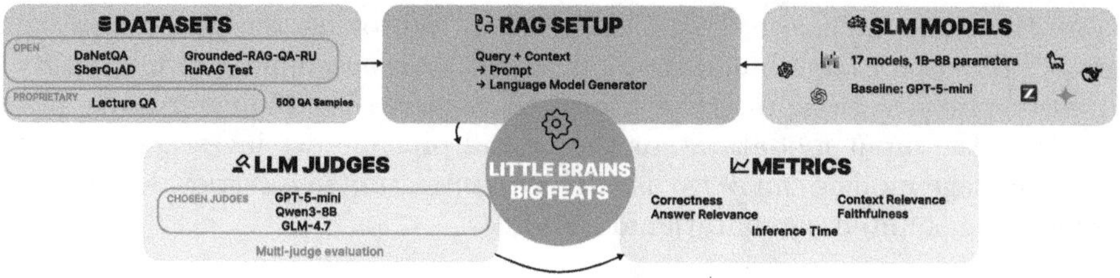

Fig. 1. Overview of the evaluation pipeline. The benchmark combines five Russian-language QA datasets. Small language models generate answers in a RAG setting, and responses are evaluated using a multi-judge LLM-as-a-Judge framework across several quality metrics.

2 Related Work

2.1 Retrieval-Augmented Generation

Retrieval-Augmented Generation (RAG) combines information retrieval techniques with neural text generation to improve factual accuracy and access to external knowledge. Early open-domain question answering systems adopted a retrieve-and-read paradigm, where relevant documents were first retrieved and then processed by a neural reader model to extract answers [5].

Traditional retrieval methods relied on lexical matching approaches such as TF-IDF [25] and BM25 [26]. While computationally efficient, these techniques are limited in their ability to capture semantic similarity between queries and documents. To address this limitation, neural retrieval models based on dense representations were introduced. Dense Passage Retrieval (DPR) [16] demonstrated that dual-encoder architectures trained with contrastive objectives significantly outperform classical sparse retrieval methods on open-domain QA tasks. Other approaches, such as ColBERT [18], further improved retrieval quality by enabling late interaction between contextual token embeddings.

Building on these developments, retrieval-augmented models integrate retrieval directly into the generation process. The RAG framework proposed by Lewis et al. [19] combines a neural retriever with a sequence-to-sequence generator, allowing the model to condition its outputs on external documents retrieved at inference time. Similar ideas were explored in REALM [12], which incorporates retrieval during language model pretraining to enable models to access large external knowledge sources.

Recent work has also extended RAG beyond purely textual question answering. For example, multimodal retrieval-augmented generation can be used to convert a text-based language model into a multimodal system by retrieving external knowledge from text, image, and audio inputs, without requiring additional resource-intensive multimodal training [7]. This line of work demonstrates that retrieval can expand model capabilities in complex settings while reducing the need for heavyweight end-to-end training.

At the same time, other studies focus on improving the generation stage through the use of large language models and their ensembles [3]. Our study is complementary to these directions: instead of increasing the complexity of the generator, the input modalities, or the overall pipeline, we investigate whether small language models can serve as effective generators in a retrieval-augmented setting under limited computational resources.

2.2 Small Language Models

Small Language Models (SLMs) are compact neural language models (hundreds of millions to a few billion parameters) designed for low-latency, low-memory inference on CPUs, mobile devices, and edge devices; they trade scale for efficiency while preserving practical NLP performance.

Compression and knowledge transfer remain the dominant training patterns: knowledge-distillation and task-aware distillation have produced widely used SLMs such as DistilBERT [27] and MobileBERT [30], which demonstrate large teacher-small student gains in latency and size.

More recent families show end-to-end SLM pretraining and strong-to-weak distillation (examples: TinyLlama [40], industry-driven smaller variants in the Qwen [38] family, and purpose-optimized models such as Shakti [28]). These models target on-device assistants, privacy-preserving analytics, and industrial automation.

In science and industry, SLMs are widely used for domain-specific chatbots, on-device document processing, real-time IoT and predictive-maintenance analytics, and privacy-preserving biomedical or legal question answering systems [15,32]. Such deployments typically combine model compression techniques such as quantisation [14], parameter-efficient fine-tuning methods including LoRA [13] and adapter-based approaches, synthetic data generated by larger teacher models, and inference optimisations designed to meet strict latency and energy constraints [34]. Frameworks and empirical studies focused on edge-oriented language models, such as TinyLLM, provide practical guidelines and evaluation pipelines for training and deploying SLMs in real-world production environments [15].

2.3 Benchmarks

There exists a variety of datasets tailored for evaluating Retrieval-Augmented Generation (RAG) systems. Among these, one of the most extensively utilised benchmarks is RAGBench [10], comprising 100,000 examples spread across five distinct industrial domains and encompassing diverse RAG task types. Another prominent framework is CRAG [39], which serves as a factual question-answering benchmark featuring 4,409 question-answer pairs along with mock APIs for web searches and knowledge graph retrievals.

Moreover, several specialised datasets have been proposed for evaluating specific RAG scenarios, including LegalBench-RAG [24], which focuses on legal retrieval-augmented generation; REAL-MM-RAG [37], which addresses multi-modal RAG challenges; DRAGOn [6], which targets periodically updated RAG settings; MultiHop-RAG [31], which evaluates complex multi-hop reasoning tasks; and MTRAG [17], which is designed for multi-turn conversational benchmarking.

However, Small Language Models (SLMs) possess unique characteristics (such as domain specificity and the ability to run under limited computational resources) that distinguish them from their larger counterparts, Large Language Models (LLMs). As such, their evaluation process should diverge accordingly. While traditional benchmarking procedures remain applicable, efforts have been made to create specialised frameworks more aligned with SLMs' inherent properties.

One illustrative example is SLM-Bench [23], a benchmark explicitly designed to evaluate SLMs across multiple dimensions, including accuracy, computational efficiency, and environmental sustainability. Comprising nine Natural Language Processing (NLP) tasks – such as classification, question answering, and sentiment analysis – and utilising 23 datasets spanning 14 diverse domains (from common sense to physics, video gaming, and news), this benchmark offers a holistic assessment of SLMs' strengths and limitations. Similarly, HealthSLM-Bench [35] focuses on health prediction tasks across three real-world mobile and wearable datasets, showcasing SLMs' utility in biomedical contexts. SLMQuant [33] introduces a systematic methodology for assessing compression techniques applied to SLMs, employing rigorous multi-dimensional evaluations across varied architectures and tasks to analyse state-of-the-art quantisation methods.

In summary, contemporary trends in benchmark development emphasise coverage across a broad spectrum of domains and tasks. However, to the best of our knowledge, there remains a significant gap regarding Russian-language RAG benchmarks capable of comprehensively covering diverse linguistic nuances and application scenarios.

2.4 LLM-as-A-Judge Evaluation

Evaluating generative systems such as LLM-based question answering or RAG pipelines remains a challenging task. Traditional automatic metrics including BLEU [22], ROUGE [20], and METEOR [1] rely on lexical overlap between generated outputs and reference texts. While these metrics are effective for machine translation or summarisation, they often fail to capture semantic correctness, factual grounding, and reasoning quality in open-ended generation tasks.

To address these limitations, recent work explores the use of large language models themselves as automated evaluators, a paradigm commonly referred to as *LLM-as-a-Judge*. One of the most influential approaches is G-Eval [21], which leverages a strong LLM (e.g., GPT-4) to assess generated responses according to predefined evaluation criteria such as coherence, factuality, and relevance. The method formulates evaluation as a structured reasoning process where the model first produces intermediate evaluation steps before assigning a final score.

Experimental results demonstrate a strong correlation between G-Eval scores and human judgments.

Similarly, frameworks such as MT-Bench and Chatbot Arena [41] evaluate conversational systems through pairwise comparisons judged by LLMs. In this setup, the evaluator model compares responses from different systems and determines which one better satisfies the user query. This pairwise ranking approach reduces bias associated with absolute scoring and has been widely used for benchmarking modern chat models.

Several studies also explore specialised evaluation pipelines for RAG systems. For instance, RAGAS [9] introduces a reference-free evaluation framework that uses LLMs to assess dimensions such as answer relevance, faithfulness to retrieved documents, and context precision. By leveraging LLM reasoning capabilities, these approaches can detect hallucinations and grounding errors that traditional string-based metrics fail to capture.

Overall, LLM-as-a-Judge methodologies provide a scalable alternative to human evaluation and enable more nuanced assessment of generative systems, particularly for complex tasks such as retrieval-augmented question answering and conversational reasoning. However, challenges remain regarding evaluator bias, reproducibility, and sensitivity to prompt design, which continue to be active research directions.

3 Data Description

To evaluate the performance of small language models in the generation stage of a RAG pipeline, we constructed a benchmark consisting of multiple Russian-language question answering datasets. The benchmark includes both publicly available datasets and one proprietary dataset in order to cover a diverse range of domains and question types.

3.1 Open-Source Datasets

Below we briefly describe the publicly available datasets used in the benchmark.

DaNetQA. DaNetQA [11] is a Russian dataset consisting of yes/no questions paired with supporting text passages. Each example is represented as a triplet containing a question, a text fragment that potentially contains the answer, and a binary label indicating whether the statement is true or false. The dataset focuses on natural language inference, commonsense reasoning, and world knowledge.

SberQuAD. SberQuAD [8] is a Russian reading comprehension dataset. The dataset contains questions written by crowdworkers based on Wikipedia articles. Each question is associated with a passage where the answer appears as a text span, although some questions may be unanswerable.

RuRAG Test Dataset. The RuRAG Test Dataset [29] was specifically designed for evaluating Russian-language RAG systems. It consists of questions, ground-truth answers, and contextual passages extracted from Russian Wikipedia articles.

Grounded-RAG-QA-RU. Grounded-RAG-QA-RU [4] is a dataset designed to evaluate the ability of language models to answer questions using information grounded in provided documents. The dataset was generated using clusters of Russian Wikipedia articles and synthetic question-answer pairs produced with GPT-4. Questions may require reasoning across multiple documents, and some examples intentionally contain out-of-distribution queries that cannot be answered using the provided context. This setup encourages models to rely strictly on retrieved documents.

3.2 Proprietary Dataset

In addition to the open-source datasets described above, we included a proprietary dataset containing domain-specific question answering samples. Due to licensing restrictions, this dataset cannot be publicly released, but it follows the same structure as the other datasets, consisting of question, context, and reference answer fields.

The dataset consists of conference presentation texts and hand-crafted questions. The knowledge base contains 5,000 lecture presentations, each around 4,500 words long. It was created to evaluate the performance of a RAG system developed for an industrial application and deployed in production. Using these data, we evaluate the robustness of RAG systems in real-world scenarios where domain-specific knowledge is required.

3.3 RAG Evaluation Dataset Construction

In total, five datasets were used for evaluation. Before inclusion in the benchmark, each dataset underwent a preprocessing stage. First, all samples containing empty or incomplete fields were removed. Then, to ensure balanced evaluation across datasets, we randomly sampled 100 examples from each dataset, resulting in a final evaluation set of 500 samples.

To analyse model performance across different reasoning patterns, we further categorised the questions by type following [2]. Question classification was performed using the Qwen3-8B model, which assigned each question to one of several categories. The categories of questions include:

- **Factoid**—questions requiring the retrieval of a specific factual piece of information;
- **Reasoning**—questions requiring logical inference or multi-step reasoning;
- **Evidence-based**—questions where the answer must be directly grounded in the provided context;
- **Comparison**—questions requiring a comparison between entities or concepts;
- **Experience-based**—questions involving subjective or experiential interpretation;
- **Instruction**—questions where the answer is supposed to be an instruction.

The distribution of these classes is shown in Table 1.

3.4 LLM-as-Judge Evaluation Dataset

In addition to evaluating the RAG pipeline itself, we constructed a separate dataset to assess the reliability of an LLM-as-Judge evaluation approach. The goal of this dataset is to test whether an evaluator model can correctly distinguish between valid and invalid answers.

To create negative examples, we intentionally mismatched elements from different samples in the RAG evaluation dataset. For example, a question from one dataset is paired with an answer from a second dataset, a golden answer from a third, and context from a fourth. These artificially constructed combinations represent incorrect responses and were assigned a score of 0.

Positive examples were created by keeping the original pairs of context, question, and correct answer from the evaluation datasets. These samples represent valid responses and were assigned a score of 1.

Finally, positive and negative samples were combined into a single benchmark dataset. This mixed dataset exposes the evaluator model to both correct and clearly incorrect answers, enabling a more robust assessment of its ability to judge response quality.

Table 1. Overview of datasets used in the RAG evaluation benchmark. For each dataset, we report the number of sampled examples and distribution of question types.

Dataset	Samples	Fact	Evidence	Reason	Comparison	Exp	Instruct
DaNetQA	100	79	2	16	1	2	0
Grounded-RAG-QA-RU	100	36	18	4	25	17	0
SberQuAD	100	60	24	8	6	2	0
ru-rag-test	100	99	0	1	0	0	0
Proprietary	100	4	33	16	8	36	3
Total	500	278	77	45	40	57	3

3.5 Dataset Analysis

As outlined earlier, our benchmark comprises 500 samples sourced from various datasets and distributed across different question types.

The mean question length amounts to 8.72 tokens (ranging from a minimum of 3 tokens to a maximum of 27 tokens), whereas the mean length for golden answers stands at 41.62 tokens (spanning from 1 token up to 364 tokens).

Additionally, we quantified the similarity among distinct data sources. Our findings revealed substantial diversity, indicating broad topic coverage and lexical variety within the final benchmark. Pairwise cosine similarities between these datasets ranged from 0.06 to 0.12, underscoring their heterogeneous nature.

Furthermore, an analysis of question complexity was conducted using the Qwen3-8B model. Questions were rated on a scale from 1 to 10. We obtained an overall average rating of 4.94, indicating that the questions are moderately challenging rather than overly simplistic.

Lastly, we evaluated the alignment between each question and its respective golden answer. Again employing the same LLM, we scored this correspondence on a scale of 1–10, achieving an average score of 7.012. This suggests high relevance and minimisation of potential errors in responses.

4 Experiments

4.1 Models

Candidate models were selected based on their parameter size, coverage of diverse model families, open-source availability, support for the GGUF format, and the ability to run within a 16 GB RAM constraint for local inference.

To ensure practical applicability, all candidate models were tested in a CPU-only environment. This preliminary evaluation allowed us to verify their compatibility with our system and confirm that inference could be executed correctly without GPU acceleration.

As a result, we identified 17 models that were suitable for further experiments. Additionally, GPT-5-mini was included as a strong proprietary reference model for comparison.

4.2 Generation Modes

At the answer generation stage, we considered two modes:

- **Context mode**: The model receives the query together with the reference documents used as contextual information for answer generation.
- **No-context mode**: The model receives only the query without any additional context.

In this setup, we focus exclusively on the generation stage, assuming that the retrieval component has already produced the most relevant documents.

All candidate models were evaluated in the context mode. Additionally, one of the modern proprietary models (GPT-5-mini) was evaluated in both modes. This allows us to compare the performance of the candidate models against a strong baseline and to analyse the impact of contextual information on answer quality.

4.3 Evaluation Setup

We conducted the evaluation in two stages. First, we assessed multiple LLM-as-Judge models and selected the most reliable ones. Second, we evaluated language models used in the generation stage of the RAG pipeline.

The following LLM-as-Judge metrics were used to evaluate the RAG systems:

- **Correctness** - whether the answer is factually correct.

- **Answer Relevance** - whether the answer addresses the user query.
- **Context Relevance** - whether the retrieved context is relevant to the user query.
- **Faithfulness** - whether the answer is supported by the provided context.

All judges provide scores in the continuous range $[0, 1]$ for each metric.

Regarding traditional metrics such as ROUGE, BLEU, or BERTScore, we deliberately opted against them as primary evaluation metrics. These metrics measure surface-level lexical or embedding similarity, which is poorly suited for open-ended RAG evaluation, where correct answers may be phrased in many valid ways. In our preliminary experiments, these metrics produced near-zero variance across candidate models, rendering them uninformative for distinguishing system quality. This is consistent with the well-documented limitations of such metrics for generative evaluation tasks.

When evaluating candidate generation models, Context Relevance was excluded from the comparison. Since all models were evaluated in context mode using the same retrieved documents for each query, this metric was independent of the generated answer and therefore identical across candidates by construction. As a result, it was uninformative for model selection. However, Context Relevance was retained at the judge selection stage, where it served as one of the criteria for assessing judge reliability.

4.4 Judge Evaluation

To assess the performance of judges for RAG evaluation, we conducted a systematic benchmarking of multiple judges on the *LLM-as-Judge Evaluation Dataset* as described in Sect. 3.4. The main goal of this evaluation was to identify a subset of judges whose assessments are both reliable and well aligned with the overall consensus.

Judge Performance Metrics. For each judge and evaluation metric, we computed several metrics.

First, we measured the **F1 score** for distinguishing correct and incorrect answers. Continuous judge scores were binarised using a threshold of 0.5.

Second, we computed the **Average Bad Score**, which reflects how strongly a judge penalises clearly incorrect answers. For judge j:

$$AvgBadScore_j = \frac{1}{|B|}\frac{1}{|M|}\sum_{i \in B}\sum_{m \in M} s_{i,j,m},$$

where B denotes the set of incorrect answers, M denotes the set of evaluation metrics, and $s_{i,j,m}$ is the score assigned by judge j to sample i for metric m.

Lower values indicate that a judge assigns lower scores to incorrect responses and therefore better identifies errors.

Third, we measured the correlation between the judges on each metric using the Pearson correlation coefficient:

$$\rho_{j,m} = \text{corr}(s_{j,m}, \overline{s_m}),$$

where $s_{j,m}$ denotes the score for judge j on metric m, and $\overline{s_m}$ denotes the average score across all judges on the same examples for metric m.

Table 2. Judge evaluation results. The table reports the Average Bad Score (ABS), indicating how highly a judge scores incorrect responses; the F1 score for classifying correct vs. incorrect responses; and correlations between each judge metric and the consensus: Correctness correlation (C Corr), Answer Relevance correlation (AR Corr), Context Relevance correlation (CR Corr), and Faithfulness correlation (F Corr). Judges selected for final evaluation are underlined.

Model Name	F1↑	C Corr↑	AR Corr↑	CR Corr↑	F Corr↑	ABS↓
DeepSeek-v3.2-alt	1.00	1.00	0.90	0.97	0.86	0.02
Gemma-3-4B-it	0.94	0.94	0.81	0.88	0.37	0.22
Gemma-3-27B-it	0.99	0.94	0.97	0.97	0.87	0.03
<u>GLM-4.7</u>	1.00	1.00	0.93	0.97	0.82	0.02
GPT-oss-120B	1.00	1.00	0.91	0.84	0.90	0.00
GPT-4o-mini	1.00	0.99	0.90	0.96	0.90	0.02
<u>GPT-5-mini</u>	1.00	0.99	0.92	0.96	0.93	0.03
GPT-5	1.00	1.00	0.84	0.86	0.86	0.01
Qwen3-4B	0.97	0.96	0.92	0.97	0.86	0.05
<u>Qwen3-8B</u>	0.97	0.96	0.91	0.97	0.88	0.02
Qwen3-32B	1.00	1.00	0.92	0.97	0.89	0.01
Qwen3-235B-A22B	1.00	1.00	0.92	0.98	0.91	0.02

Final Judge Selection. Based on the analysis above, we selected three judges for the final evaluation setup: *GPT-5-mini*, *Qwen3-8B*, and *GLM-4.7*. The selected judges are underlined in Table 2.

The selection was based on a combination of criteria:

- High F1 scores in distinguishing correct and incorrect samples.
- Strong correlation with the consensus of all judges.
- Low average bad scores on negative samples.
- Diversification: selected models should represent different families to reduce the risk of systemic bias.

For the selected judges we computed the **Intraclass Correlation Coefficient**, ICC = 0.96. This shows that the selected judges give consistent scores, which allows them to be used as a reliable multi-judge evaluation system for subsequent experiments.

A natural question is whether the judge validation dataset, which relies on artificially mismatched negative samples, is sufficient to evaluate judge reliability for nuanced RAG evaluation. We argue that it serves a deliberately scoped purpose: it functions as a baseline sanity check to filter out judges that fail on noticeably poor samples, rather than as a comprehensive benchmark of subtle judgement. A judge unable to distinguish obviously incorrect answers from correct ones is unlikely to produce meaningful scores on realistic RAG outputs. Additionally, rather than relying on a single judge, we aggregate scores across three judges from distinct model families, which reduces the influence of any individual model's outlier behaviour on the final score. The high inter-judge consistency (ICC = 0.96) suggests that the selected judges tend to agree in their assessments, making the aggregated signal more stable than any individual score alone.

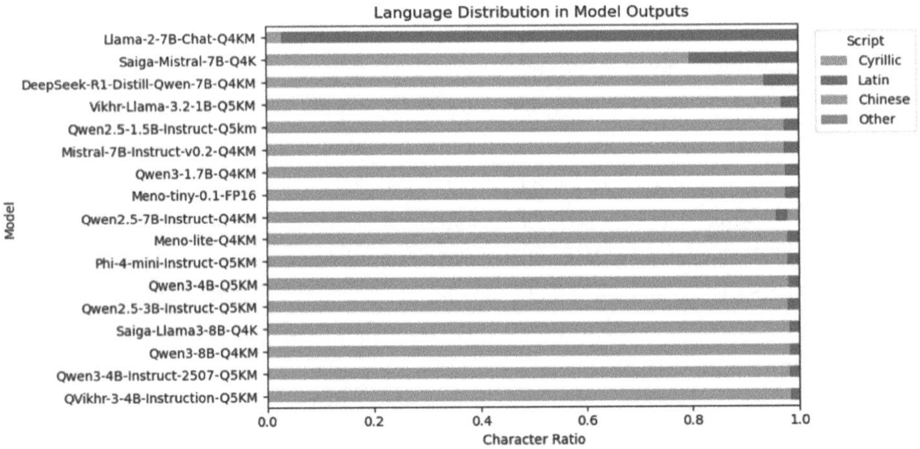

Fig. 2. Distribution of response languages across evaluated models.

5 Discussion

Results presented in Table 3 show that even small models are capable of producing results comparable to those of larger models. Although answer quality depends on model size, some sufficiently compact models still provide adequate generation quality for RAG systems. For our production system, we selected *Qwen3-4B-Instruct-2507-Q5KM* due to its favourable trade-off between response quality and CPU inference latency.

From the results produced by the baseline model *GPT-5-mini*, it becomes evident that the presence of contextual information significantly influences the accuracy of generated answers. This observation underscores a crucial characteristic of the dataset: generating correct responses requires reliance on external context rather than merely leveraging inherent model knowledge.

Table 3. Average evaluation metrics for different models. The best result is highlighted in bold, and the second-best result is underlined.

Model	Correct.	AnswerRelev.	Faithful.	Latency (s)
DeepSeek-R1-Distill-Qwen-7B-Q4KM	0.40	0.54	0.58	297.4
Llama-2-7B-Chat-Q4KM	0.32	0.46	0.42	115.0
Meno-tiny-1.5B-0.1-FP16	0.41	0.57	0.60	**27.8**
Meno-lite-7B-Q4KM	0.56	0.75	0.74	<u>31.4</u>
Mistral-7B-Instruct-v0.2-Q4KM	0.47	0.61	0.63	115.5
Phi-4-mini-Instruct-Q5KM	0.48	0.68	0.67	44.2
Qwen2.5-1.5B-Instruct-Q5KM	0.46	0.61	0.63	49.1
Qwen2.5-3B-Instruct-Q5KM	0.54	0.73	0.72	31.8
Qwen2.5-7B-Instruct-Q4KM	0.64	0.85	0.77	66.5
Qwen3-1.7B-Q4KM	0.58	0.78	0.74	55.0
Qwen3-4B-Instruct-2507-Q5KM	0.71	**0.89**	0.80	70.9
Qwen3-4B-Q5KM	0.69	0.85	0.81	205.1
Qwen3-8B-Q4KM	<u>0.72</u>	0.87	<u>0.83</u>	339.3
QVikhr-3-4B-Instruction-Q5KM	0.59	0.64	0.71	254.4
Saiga-Llama3-8B-Q4K	0.60	0.79	0.72	92.2
Saiga-Mistral-7B-Q4K	0.44	0.53	0.54	257.1
Vikhr-Llama-3.2-1B-Q5KM	0.42	0.52	0.58	34.3
GPT-5-mini	**0.73**	<u>0.88</u>	**0.89**	–
GPT-5-mini, No context	0.47	0.86	–	–

Since the dataset consists of queries written in Russian, we also analysed the language of the generated responses. Importantly, the models were not explicitly instructed to answer in Russian; only the input queries were provided in Russian. This setup allows us to observe the language preference of the models during generation.

Figure 2 shows the distribution of response languages across the evaluated models. The analysis highlights which models consistently produce answers in Russian and which tend to switch to English or generate mixed-language outputs.

To estimate the generation time, the models were run on a reduced subset of 50 samples. The evaluation was performed in a CPU-only environment without GPU acceleration to approximate typical local deployment conditions. The average generation time per answer for each model is presented in Table 3. The results demonstrate noticeable differences in inference speed across models. These measurements provide additional insights that can support model selection in practical deployment scenarios.

6 Limitations

This study provides extensive research and evaluation of SLMs specifically focusing on their performance as generative models. While this study provides valuable insights, several notable limitations constrain its scope:

1. **Evaluation Focus**: The investigation focuses exclusively on SLMs' ability to generate text, disregarding their importance in determining optimal embedding techniques, retrieval, and ranking strategies within RAG systems. In addition, the analysis of how varying quantisation levels affect model performance was beyond the scope of this study.
2. **Prompt standardisation**: A uniform prompt was applied across all models and configurations, although a single prompt may not suit every architecture equally well. Therefore, customising prompts for individual models could result in improved performance.
3. **Task Restrictions**: Our experiments focus solely on RAG-oriented tasks, omitting broader applications beyond text generation. Incorporating diverse tasks would provide greater clarity on SLM applications.
4. **Language Bias**: Results reflect performance in the Russian language alone, making generalisation to other languages uncertain without additional validation efforts.
5. **Human Evaluation**: Collecting reliable human judgements for RAG evaluation is resource-intensive and requires domain expertise, particularly for knowledge-intensive queries. That said, we performed a limited manual sanity check of the judges, verifying that assigned scores were accompanied by plausible reasoning in a handful of examples. This inspection was conducted by a single annotator and cannot substitute for a systematic human evaluation. Validating the judges against human annotations at a larger scale remains an important direction for future work.
6. **Resource Consumption**: While this paper reports the inference times of the various models, it would be valuable to additionally track memory usage and battery power draw. These factors may also play a substantial role in model selection for a particular device.

Addressing these shortcomings in subsequent studies promises to offer deeper insights into SLMs' true capabilities.

7 Conclusion

Although LLMs currently dominate the research landscape, SLMs continue to demonstrate considerable relevance across multiple domains while receiving considerably less attention. This study aims to bridge this gap by examining SLMs as generators for Russian-language RAG systems.

We introduce a curated benchmark compiled from diverse source datasets, ensuring a broad spectrum of topics to facilitate equitable comparisons among SLMs.

Subsequently, we systematically evaluated SLMs against this dataset, discovering that selected SLMs achieved competitive performance compared with the proprietary GPT-5-mini baseline, with some models outperforming it on individual metrics while remaining deployable in the tested CPU-only setting. These findings suggest promising prospects for incorporating SLMs into practical applications.

We provide an extensive analysis of the SLMs' performance to show their advantages and trade-offs between quality and latency.

For future research, we recommend exploring improvements in embedding and reranking methodologies, along with expanding the scope of SLMs to address other tasks.

Disclosure of Interests. The authors have no competing interests to declare that are relevant to the content of this article.

References

1. Banerjee, S.: Meteor: an automatic metric for mt evaluation with improved correlation with human judgments. In: Proceedings of the ACL Workshop on Intrinsic and Extrinsic Evaluation Measures for Machine Translation and/or Summarization, pp. 65–72 (2005)
2. Bolotova, V., et al.: A non-factoid question-answering taxonomy. In: Proceedings of the 45th International ACM SIGIR Conference on Research and Development in Information Retrieval. p. 1196–1207. SIGIR '22, Association for Computing Machinery, New York, NY, USA (2022). https://doi.org/10.1145/3477495.3531926
3. Bondarenko, I., Derunets, R., Sedukhin, O., Komarov, M., Chernov, I., Kulakov, M.: Raguteam at semeval-2026 task 8: meno and friends in a judge-orchestrated LLM ensemble for faithful multi-turn response generation (2026). https://arxiv.org/abs/2605.04523
4. Bratchikov, S.: Grounded-rag-qa-ru (2024). https://huggingface.co/datasets/Vikhrmodels/Grounded-RAG-QA-RU, dataset hosted on Hugging Face
5. Chen, D., et al.: Reading wikipedia to answer open-domain questions. In: Proceedings of the 55th Annual Meeting of the Association for Computational Linguistics (Volume 1: Long Papers), pp. 1870–1879 (2017)
6. Chernogorskii, F., et al.: Dragon: designing rag on periodically updated corpus (2026). https://arxiv.org/abs/2507.05713
7. Derunets, R., Bondarenko, I., Kulakov, M., Prokopenko, V., Tikhunov, F.: Knowledge as recollection: advancing multimodal retrieval-augmented generation. Investigations on applied mathematics and informatics. Part V, Zap. Nauchn. Sem. POMI **546**, 174–192 (2025)
8. Efimov, P., Chertok, A., Boytsov, L., Braslavski, P.: SberQuAD – Russian Reading Comprehension Dataset: Description and Analysis. In: Arampatzis, A., et al. (eds.) CLEF 2020. LNCS, vol. 12260, pp. 3–15. Springer, Cham (2020). https://doi.org/10.1007/978-3-030-58219-7_1
9. Es, S.: Ragas: automated evaluation of retrieval augmented generation. In: Proceedings of the 18th Conference of the European Chapter of the Association for Computational Linguistics: System Demonstrations, pp. 150–158 (2024)

10. Frie, R., et al.: Ragbench: explainable benchmark for retrieval-augmented generation systems (2025). https://arxiv.org/abs/2407.11005
11. Glushkova, T., et al.: Danetqa: a yes/no question answering dataset for the russian language. In: Analysis of Images, Social Networks and Texts, pp. 57–68. Springer-Verlag, Berlin, Heidelberg (2020). https://doi.org/10.1007/978-3-030-72610-2_4
12. Guu, K.: Retrieval augmented language model pre-training. In: International conference on machine learning, pp. 3929–3938. (2020) PMLR
13. Hu, E.J., et al.: Lora: low-rank adaptation of large language models. arXiv preprint arXiv:2106.09685 (2021). https://arxiv.org/abs/2106.09685
14. Jin, R., et al.: A comprehensive evaluation of quantization strategies for large language models. In: Findings of the Association for Computational Linguistics: ACL 2024. pp. 12186–12215. Association for Computational Linguistics, Bangkok, Thailand (2024). https://aclanthology.org
15. Kandala, S.V.: Tinyllm: a framework for training and deploying language models at the edge computers (2024). arXiv:2412.15304 arXiv preprint
16. Karpukhin, V.: Dense passage retrieval for open-domain question answering. In: Proceedings of the 2020 Conference on Empirical Methods in Natural Language Processing (EMNLP), pp. 6769–6781. (2020)
17. Katsis, Y., et al.: Mtrag: a multi-turn conversational benchmark for evaluating retrieval-augmented generation systems (2025). https://arxiv.org/abs/2501.03468
18. Khattab, O.: Colbert: efficient and effective passage search via contextualized late interaction over BERT. In: Proceedings of the 43rd International ACM SIGIR Conference on Research and Development in Information Retrieval, pp. 39–48 (2020)
19. Lewis, P., et al.: Retrieval-augmented generation for knowledge-intensive NLP tasks. In: Proceedings of the 34th International Conference on Neural Information Processing Systems. pp. 9459–9474. NIPS '20, Curran Associates Inc., Red Hook, NY, USA (2020)
20. Lin, C.Y.: Rouge: a package for automatic evaluation of summaries. In: Text Summarization Branches Out, pp. 74–81 (2004)
21. Liu, Y.: G-eval: NLG evaluation using GPT-4 with better human alignment. In: Proceedings of the 2023 Conference on Empirical Methods in Natural Language Processing, pp. 2511–2522 (2023)
22. Papineni, K.: Bleu: a method for automatic evaluation of machine translation. In: Proceedings of the 40th annual meeting of the Association for Computational Linguistics, pp. 311–318 (2002)
23. Pham, N.T., et al.: SLM-bench: A comprehensive benchmark of small language models on environmental impacts. In: Christodoulopoulos, C., Chakraborty, T., Rose, C., Peng, V. (eds.) Findings of the Association for Computational Linguistics: EMNLP 2025, pp. 21369–21392. Association for Computational Linguistics, Suzhou, China (2025). https://doi.org/10.18653/v1/2025.findings-emnlp.1165
24. Pipitone, N., et al.: Legalbench-rag: a benchmark for retrieval-augmented generation in the legal domain (2024). https://arxiv.org/abs/2408.10343
25. Ramos, J.: Using TF-IDF to determine word relevance in document queries. In: Proceedings of the First Instructional Conference on Machine Learning, vol. 242, pp. 29–48. Citeseer (2003)
26. Robertson, S.: The probabilistic relevance framework: BM25 and beyond, vol. 4, Now Publishers Inc (2009)
27. Sanh, V.: Distilbert, a distilled version of BERT: smaller, faster, cheaper and lighter (2019). arXiv:1910.01108 arXiv preprint

28. Shakhadri, S.A.G., et al.: Shakti: a 2.5 billion parameter small language model optimized for edge ai and low-resource environments (2025). https://arxiv.org/abs/2410.11331
29. slivka83: rurag test dataset (2025). https://github.com/slivka83/ru_rag_test_dataset, dataset hosted on GitHub
30. Sun, Z., et al.: Mobilebert: a compact task-agnostic bert for resource-limited devices (2020). https://arxiv.org/abs/2004.02984
31. Tang, Y., Yang, Y.: Multihop-rag: benchmarking retrieval-augmented generation for multi-hop queries (2024). https://arxiv.org/abs/2401.15391
32. Wang, F.: A comprehensive survey of small language models in the era of large language models: techniques, enhancements, applications, collaboration with LLMs, and trustworthiness. ACM Trans. Intell. Syst. Technol **16**(6), (2025). https://doi.org/10.1145/3768165
33. Wang, J., et al.: Slmquant: benchmarking small language model quantization for practical deployment. In: Proceedings of the 3rd International Workshop on Rich Media With Generative AI. p. 2–10. RichMediaGAI '25, Association for Computing Machinery, New York, NY, USA (2025). https://doi.org/10.1145/3746262.3761973
34. Wang, L., et al.: Parameter-efficient fine-tuning in large models: a survey of methodologies (2025). https://arxiv.org/abs/2410.19878
35. Wang, X., et al.: Healthslm-bench: benchmarking small language models for mobile and wearable healthcare monitoring (2025). https://arxiv.org/abs/2509.07260
36. Wang, X.: Empowering edge intelligence: a comprehensive survey on on-device ai models. ACM Comput. Surv. **57**(9) (2025). https://doi.org/10.1145/3724420
37. Wasserman, N., et al.: REAL-MM-RAG: a real-world multi-modal retrieval benchmark. In: Che, W., Nabende, J., Shutova, E., Pilehvar, M.T. (eds.) Proceedings of the 63rd Annual Meeting of the Association for Computational Linguistics (Volume 1: Long Papers). pp. 31660–31683. Association for Computational Linguistics, Vienna, Austria (2025). https://doi.org/10.18653/v1/2025.acl-long.1528
38. Yang, A., et al.: Qwen3 technical report (2025). https://arxiv.org/abs/2505.09388
39. Yang, X., et al.: Crag – comprehensive rag benchmark (2024). https://arxiv.org/abs/2406.04744
40. Zhang, P., et al.: Tinyllama: an open-source small language model (2024). https://arxiv.org/abs/2401.02385
41. Zheng, L., et al.: Judging LLM-as-a-judge with mt-bench and chatbot arena. Adv. Neural. Inf. Process. Syst. **36**, 46595–46623 (2023)

MURENA, a MUlti-agent LLM Pipeline for Large-Scale Real Estate MaNAgement

Marco De Luca[1], Simone Monaco[1(✉)], Claudiu Tcaciuc[1], Alice Gorrino[2], Giovanna De Luca[2], Daniele Apiletti[1], and Tania Cerquitelli[1]

[1] Department of Control and Computer Engineering (DAUIN), Politecnico di Torino, Turin, Italy
simone.monaco@polito.it

[2] Edilclima S.r.l., Borgomanero, Italy

Abstract. Managing large-scale public real estate portfolios requires screening thousands of buildings against technical, energy, spatial, and regulatory constraints; a process that currently takes domain experts weeks of manual cross-referencing across fragmented data sources. We present MURENA, a multi-agent Human-in-the-Loop platform where the LLM acts as a semantic controller, translating user intent into structured constraints and orchestrating execution across SQL and geospatial engines, while the final decision remains with a domain expert. Role-specialised agents (energy performance, zoning compliance, spatial accessibility, regulatory constraints) operate over a unified registry of 90,000 Italian Energy Performance Certificates enriched with geocoded proximity indicators and an expert-curated regulatory knowledge base, through three phases: requirements extraction, SQL query composition, and multi-criteria scoring, with full intermediate traceability. Evaluation combining automatic benchmarking on 486 queries and expert validation on 10 institutional change-of-use scenarios shows 90.3% perfect agent routing, 90% top-5 retrieval of expert-preferred buildings, and end-to-end execution in tens of seconds, reducing manual screening from weeks to minutes. The platform, developed with institutional stakeholders and running on locally hosted open-weight models, has attracted interest from regional and national bodies for operationalising building decarbonisation under EPBD IV.

Keywords: agentic AI · multi-agent systems · large language models · real estate · text-to-sql

1 Introduction

Managing large-scale real estate portfolios is a significant data science challenge. Policymakers must identify assets for repurposing or renovation within fragmented, heterogeneous datasets while satisfying technical, spatial, economic, and

Supplementary Information The online version contains supplementary material available at https://doi.org/10.1007/978-3-032-37682-4_26.

M. Baratchi et al. (Eds.): ECML PKDD 2026, LNAI 16949, pp. 446–462, 2027.
https://doi.org/10.1007/978-3-032-37682-4_26

regulatory constraints across multi-level governance structures. These decisions must also balance decarbonisation goals with social equity.

This challenge is becoming increasingly urgent in the context of the revised European Energy Performance of Buildings Directive (EPBD IV), which requires Member States to implement large-scale building decarbonisation policies while addressing energy poverty and ensuring a "just transition". As a result, decision-makers must operate on large building registries derived from multiple sources, often characterised by inconsistent formats, missing data, variable quality, and unit-level fragmentation that does not align directly with building-level policy actions.

For example, a municipal or regional asset manager tasked with identifying buildings suitable for social housing conversion must today cross-reference EPC registries, cadastral databases, zoning maps, and regulatory texts, often using spreadsheets and manual GIS overlays. A single screening cycle for a medium-sized city portfolio can take weeks of expert time. MURENA was developed in collaboration with institutional stakeholders to automate this workflow while maintaining full expert oversight.

MURENA (MUlti-Agent LLM pipeline for large-scale Real Estate maN-Agement) is a Human-in-the-Loop decision-support platform that suggests and decomposes complex portfolio queries while keeping the final decision with a domain expert. Real estate portfolio data are inherently sensitive: detailed building characteristics, ownership information, cadastral identifiers, and energy performance metrics may be subject to confidentiality obligations or competitive disclosure constraints in public procurement and urban planning contexts. To this end, MURENA operates on locally-hosted open-weight LLMs, ensuring data sovereignty and privacy without transmitting sensitive information to third-party APIs. For organisations that do not operate local inference infrastructure, the architecture is designed to be easily extended to remote API-based LLMs, trading on-premises privacy guarantees for deployment convenience. The system also relies on an expert-curated regulatory knowledge base to produce consistent and auditable output.

Related Work. Supporting interactive exploration across heterogeneous repositories spanning structured databases, semi-structured stores, and unstructured regulatory corpora introduces retrieval challenges that no single paradigm fully addresses. In relational settings, this problem is typically framed as text-to-SQL or semantic parsing. Recent LLM-based frameworks such as TriSQL [13] and Think2sql [9] advance this direction by analysing question complexity and applying dynamic strategies to generate accurate, executable SQL, improving schema linking and compositional generalisation on standard benchmarks such as Spider [16]. However, text-to-SQL alone is insufficient when queries must simultaneously satisfy geospatial constraints, domain-specific regulatory thresholds, and multi-criteria ranking objectives drawn from heterogeneous sources—none of which can be directly expressed as a single relational query. Tool-augmented frameworks such as ReAct [15] and Toolformer [11] demonstrate how LLMs can interleave reasoning with external actions, and multi-agent architectures extend this idea to general-purpose orchestration through graph-based and role-specialized designs [14]. Retrieval-Augmented Generation (RAG) [7] complements action-based approaches by grounding LLM outputs in domain corpora at inference time. However, in compliance-heavy domains, long, hierarchical, and frequently updated regulations make retrieval quality critical for extracting legally valid constraints [10]. Recent work on LLMs in urban planning focuses mainly on generative planning and document understanding [18], while Automated Valuation Models (AVMs) target price prediction [5] and real estate recommender systems address multi-criteria evaluation [1–3]. Geospatial reasoning has been studied in LLM-based systems like GeoGPT [17], which supports natural-language geoprocessing but lacks structured, constraint-based retrieval or aggregation with other data, such as regulatory information. Approaches including text-to-SQL, agentic orchestration, RAG, and urban decision-support have largely evolved in isolation, each with structural limitations: text-to-SQL struggles with geospatial and multi-criteria ranking, RAG risks threshold hallucination in compliance settings [10], and generic agent frameworks lack domain-specific scoring across energy, spatial, and regulatory dimensions. MURENA unifies these paradigms under a complementary division of responsibilities: the LLM acts as a semantic orchestrator that handles intent decomposition and linguistic ambiguity, while SQL and geospatial layers enforce strict filtering, and specialised agents apply domain-aware scoring calibrated against the empirical data distribution—structurally preventing each component's failure mode from propagating to the final output. Rather than claiming a full benchmark-style reimplementation of each paradigm in isolation, we validate this design empirically in Sect. 4 through a leave-one-out per-agent ablation, quantifying each module's marginal contribution when combined, and a direct structural comparison against monolithic single-prompt baselines.

Contributions. Our contributions can be summarized as follows.

- MURENA, a **multi-agent pipeline** that decomposes user intent into parallel domain-specialised agents (energy, location, proximity, regulatory, building), composes SQL queries over a structured dataset, and produces a weighted multi-criteria ranking with full intermediate traceability.
- A **data aggregation pipeline** integrating ∼90,000 of Italian Energy Performance Certificate (EPC) records into a unified structured registry, including cadastral-based meta-building construction, geocoded proximity indicators, market-zone benchmarks, and an expert-curated regulatory knowledge base, thereby establishing a reproducible benchmark for constraint-based real estate retrieval.
- A **two-tier evaluation protocol** that combines (i) automatic benchmarking on hundreds of combinatorially generated queries, measuring agent routing accuracy, retrieval diversity, ranking consistency, and qualitative output quality, with (ii) expert validation across 10 real change-of-use scenarios, demonstrating strong alignment between system recommendations and professional judgement.

2 Dataset and Materials

MURENA is evaluated on a dataset built from Italian EPCs, the *Attestato di Prestazione Energetica* (APE) [4], which is published as open datasets through Regional platforms. Compared to large-scale geographic datasets (e.g., OpenStreetMap), EPC records offer richer technical attributes for evaluating buildings, particularly for decarbonization strategies. The proposed pipeline, however, remains data-agnostic and can be applied to any structured building registry with similar attribute dimensions. EPCs do not cover the entire building stock, as they are issued only during transactions (sales and rentals) or major renovations. This study considers certificates from the last 10 years because a 2015 methodological revision limits comparability with earlier records. Despite these constraints, EPCs provide detailed information on geometry, envelope and system properties, and energy performance indicators (e.g., energy class A4–G, $EP_{gl,nren}$, and emissions). EPC records contain building address and cadastral identifiers (*foglio*/*particella*), geographic coordinates, gross floor area (e.g., 320 m^2), construction year (e.g., 1962), energy class (e.g., E), global non-renewable primary energy index $EP_{gl,nren}$ (e.g., 187 kWh/m^2year), heating system type (e.g., centralised gas boiler), and CO_2 emissions (e.g., 43 kg/m^2year). This combination of geometric, technical, energetic, and locational attributes enables the multidimensional constraint queries that MURENA is designed to support. This data model is extensible at the European scale, as the Italian EPC scheme aligns with the EPBD framework and shares common attributes with EPC systems across Member States.

2.1 Pre-Processing, Aggregation, and Enrichment

The raw EPC dataset requires preprocessing before integration into the pipeline.

First, Certificates may appear multiple times due to reissuance. Therefore, we opted for always retaining the most recent record.

Second, they are recorded at the unit level despite the need for building-scale decisions. We therefore construct *meta-buildings* (e.g., for whole-building reuse or cohousing): units sharing cadastral identifiers (*foglio*, *particella*) are merged by summing total floor area, aggregating categorical attributes via surface-weighted majority voting, and taking the minimum across sub-units for continuous energy indices (e.g., $EP_{gl,nren}$, CO_2 emissions). In the remainder of this paper, *building* denotes either an individual unit or an aggregated meta-building.

Third, EPCs lack proximity and market-zone indicators, which are required for comprehensive estates scoring. Starting from geographic coordinates, we linked corresponding OMI zones (*Osservatorio del Mercato Immobiliare*), which represent district-level market benchmarks.

Finally, EPCs also present data-quality errors from manual certification (e.g., incorrect surfaces or coordinates) that cannot be fully corrected and are discussed in Sect. 5.

The *Proximity agent* and *Regulatory agent* require inputs that are absent from the raw EPC registry—respectively, urban accessibility indicators and structured compliance rules; so we enrich the core data model with the following two resources.

Geocoding and Proximity Indicators. Computing real-time geospatial distances from all buildings to their surrounding POIs at query time would be computationally prohibitive for an interactive tool. Furthermore, the *proximity agent* must emit SQL-compatible numerical predicates; raw geospatial lookups cannot be expressed as standard relational filters. We therefore pre-compute a fixed set of accessibility scores at ingestion time and materialise them as additional columns in the unified registry, enabling the *proximity agent* to apply them directly in both *Filtering mode* and *Ranking mode* without any runtime geospatial computation. Concretely, we augment each building with these indicators summarising access to nearby urban services. We extract Points of Interest (POIs) from OpenStreetMap and associate them to macro-categories commonly used in accessibility studies [12]: *health*, *mobility*, *greenery*, *sport*, *commerce*, and *education*. The mapping covers over 230 OSM tags; nodes, ways, and relations are all considered, with ways and relations represented by their geometry centroid and a deduplication step preventing double-counting. Category-level scores are derived via an exponential decay model $f(x) = e^{-(x/(S \cdot U))^3}$, where S encodes service-specific walkability thresholds (340 m, 680 m, and 1360 m, corresponding to approximately 5-, 10-, and 20-minute walking catchments following the "15-minute city" paradigm) and U is a context-aware urban multiplier ranging from 1.0 (city centre) to 4.0 (suburban areas). Scores are then normalized to a [0, 100] scale using percentiles to improve robustness across different urban densities. The full tag-to-category mapping and scoring implementation are available in the project repository[1].

For user queries referencing explicit locations (e.g., landmarks or transit stops), the system also relies on external geocoding services (e.g., OpenStreetMap-based APIs) to resolve names to coordinates, enabling fine-grained distance constraints beyond aggregated POI indicators.

For more details, please see Appendix C.

Regulatory Corpora. To support regulatory and normative compliance in this proof-of-concept, we build a static repository of structured rules (e.g., minimum surface thresholds, capacity limits) distilled from official public repositories. Although this demonstrates feasibility in a reproducible setup, a production-grade system could improve coverage and update reliability by integrating one of the many specialised regulatory intelligence platforms that aggregate and structure normative texts across jurisdictions.

3 Methodology

The decision-support process is formalized as a multi-phase semantic transformation of the user query. The architecture comprises three distinct phases: requirements extraction, query composition, and multi-dimensional scoring (Fig. 1).

[1] https://github.com/dbdmg/murena.

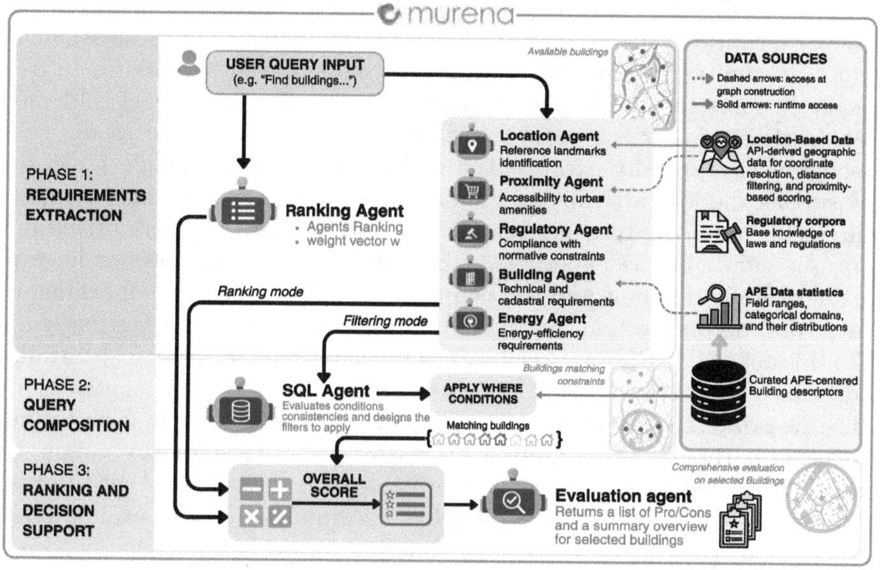

Fig. 1. Architectural overview of the decision-support pipeline: (1) requirements extraction via parallel technical agents, (2) SQL-based query composition, and (3) multi-dimensional scoring and executive synthesis for final decision-making.

3.1 Phase 1: Requirements Extraction

The process begins with the *Ranking Agent*, which acts as an orchestrator and is instructed to serve as an expert real estate analyst. Its objective is to determine, from the user query alone, which assessment dimensions are *explicitly* required, which are merely implied or secondary, and which are irrelevant—information that is then used to weight each technical agent's contribution to the final multi-criteria score. Concretely, the agent reads the full query and, for each *Technical Agent*, reasons about whether that dimension is a stated hard requirement (e.g., "I need a building near a metro station"), a soft preference (e.g., "ideally close to green areas"), or not mentioned at all; it then assigns a rank reflecting that importance order. This priority ranking S distinguishes between "core" non-negotiable needs and accessory preferences, so that agents handling explicitly stated requirements receive higher weight in the final aggregation than agents handling implicit or secondary ones. To formalize the input processed by the pipeline, we represent a user query as a structured tuple of potentially optional components:

$$Q = (I, D, L, C_b, C_e, C_p), \tag{1}$$

where I denotes the property typology or search intent (e.g., "search for a building"), D represents the intended project use or destination (e.g., co-housing, clinic), L encodes location preferences and reference landmarks (e.g., specific districts or POIs), C_b captures structural building constraints (e.g., minimum surface), C_e captures energy performance constraints (e.g., energy class), and C_p specifies proximity requirements with respect to ancillary services (e.g., public transport, sports facilities). This formulation provides a compact and modular abstraction of user requests. While not exhaustive, it captures the principal components typically expressed in real-world queries. A single LLM, especially smaller models, attempting to jointly resolve these potentially competing requirements would reduce interpretability and increase the risk of reasoning errors. As shown in the experiments, monolithic single-prompt baselines produce structurally different and less comprehensive SQL queries, confirming that architectural decomposition, not merely prompt enrichment, drives query quality. To this aim, MURENA is specifically designed to provide atomic, controllable evaluations of user requests, enabling Human-in-the-Loop refinements.

The *Ranking Agent* assigns relative importance weights w_i to each technical agent using harmonic ranking: an agent with rank r_i receives raw weight $1/r_i$, then normalized to have active agents' weights sum to 1. Agents with the same rank receive identical weights, enabling balanced multi-objective evaluation. For example, in a query like"find a large building for co-housing that is close to public transport and has good energy performance", the requirements specify size, proximity, and energy efficiency without any preference. The ranking agent assigns equal rank to the relevant agents, ensuring that their scores contribute equally and that there is no arbitrary bias in the results.

In parallel, five *Technical agents* are activated to evaluate the available buildings according to the user's query. These agents were selected to cover the primary assessment dimensions that domain experts typically consider when analyzing properties. They include (i) *location agent*, (ii) *proximity agent*, (iii) *regulatory agent*, (iv) *building agent*, and (v) *energy agent*. Each agent's prompt is further enhanced with data-driven context injection, including quartile statistics (P25, P50, P75) for the relevant dataset columns. This enables the LLM to operate as a context-aware analyst rather than a blind extractor. The proposed pipeline is designed to be modular and extensible. Additional *Technical Agents* can be easily integrated into the workflow by updating the *Ranking Agent* to account for their outputs and functional roles. Each *Technical Agent* accesses specific data and tools according to its assessment dimension. They operate in two modes: (i) *Filtering mode*, generating atomic conditions that translate into SQL `WHERE` clauses; and (ii) *Ranking mode*, assigning a score to each building based on its performance against those conditions.

Location Agent. The agent differentiates between primary search entities and contextual references (e.g., cities, districts, landmarks, or monuments) using external geocoding services, converting distance specifications to kilometre ranges with a default limiting radius R_{lim} set to 3 km. Unlike traditional Named Entity Recognition (NER) [6], the LLM-driven design handles negations, implicit constraints, and domain-specific linguistic variations without annotated training data.

Proximity Agent. It assesses buildings based on their proximity and accessibility to urban items (amenities, services, infrastructure) in the surrounding urban environment. This information is captured through pre-aggregate features that represent the macro-categories commonly used in urban accessibility analyses, as described in Sect. 2. Representing each amenity macro-category with a single pre-aggregated score simplifies the classification of buildings according to the needs associated with different intended uses.

Regulatory Agent. It is responsible for identifying regulatory and normative constraints implied by the user query, such as accessibility standards or typology-specific technical provisions. It draws on the expert-curated JSON repository described in Sect. 2, which pre-formalises compliance rules distilled from authoritative public sources. When the query matches an existing rule, the corresponding constraint is directly retrieved and translated into SQL filtering conditions, ensuring full auditability without probabilistic retrieval at inference time. In a production environment, this component can be seamlessly extended with dynamic regulatory intelligence platforms that provide up-to-date semantic legal research across jurisdictions.

Building Agent. First, it identifies the relevant building typology (e.g., "residential dwelling", "school building") and the associated technical or cadastral requirements. Then, it processes structural constraints, such as the minimum surface area or the capacity. Qualitative descriptors (e.g., "large" or "small") are mapped to quantitative thresholds derived from the empirical distribution of the corresponding attribute in the database. Specifically, terms such as "large" and "small" are translated into values above the 75th percentile and below the 25th percentile, respectively.

Energy Agent. It translates energy-efficiency requirements into structured constraints, taking EPC data as input. Attributes including the energy class label (A4–G) and $EP_{gl,nren}$ are standardised and assigned to database-based numerical thresholds to allow consistent filtering and scoring (as detailed in Sect. 2). Beyond the core EPC indicators, the agent incorporates additional energy-related attributes from the integrated dataset, including the heating system typology, energy source, and other technical specifications. To ensure robustness and prevent unrealistic or overly restrictive constraints, the derived efficiency filters are calibrated against the empirical statistical distribution of the corresponding attributes in the database. This data-driven normalisation mitigates the risk of misleading threshold selections and preserves coherence between user requirements and the actual distribution of available buildings.

3.2 Phase 2: SQL Query Composition

The requirements extracted in Phase 1 are synthesized by the *SQL agent* into an optimized relational database query. This phase is primarily a *filtering* step, intended to narrow the search space and exclude irrelevant records before any ranking is applied. To ensure auditability and prevent hallucinations, the agent follows a strict zero-addition policy: it only processes parameters explicitly provided by the technical agents, ignoring any latent intent in the original user text that was not formalized during extraction. The query generation logic includes a semantic consolidation layer that merges redundant or overlapping conditions into the most restrictive valid clause (e.g., combining `surface >= 1000` and `surface >= 3000` into `surface >= 3000`). Geospatial preferences are translated into functions using a distance metric, while qualitative textual filters employ flexible matching operators.

3.3 Phase 3: Multi-Dimensional Scoring

Retrieved assets undergo an evaluation pass where candidate properties are ranked based on their alignment with both explicit constraints and implicit preferences. *Technical Agents* are re-invoked in *Ranking mode*, using extracted filters as scoring guidance. Namely, each *Technical Agent* score is calculated as follows.

Location agent uses an exponential decay model $\propto e^{-(dist/r)^3}$, where $dist$ is the distance to the identified landmark. The parameter r is calibrated so that the score reaches the 20th percentile at the search radius limit $R_{\lim}$, after which the score exponentially goes to 0.

Proximity agent computes a weighted average of the pre-aggregated category-level scores (see Sect. 2) over the service categories *explicitly mentioned in the query*; categories not referenced by the user are excluded from this agent's score. Weights follow an inverse-ranking scheme $w_c = 1/\mathcal{R}_c$, where $\mathcal{R}_c$ denotes the LLM-derived importance rank of category c among the requested categories.

Regulatory agent computes the average adherence to the extracted requirements. Categorical requirements (e.g., intended use) are first prioritized by the LLM, and their scores are computed using an inverse-ranking weighting scheme based on this ordering. Numerical constraints (e.g., minimum surface) are instead evaluated using threshold-based logic.

Building agent evaluates typology compatibility by generating an ordered list of relevant categories and computing the score using the same inverse-ranking weighting scheme.

Energy agent evaluates energy performance directionally based on the user intent extracted by the Ranking agent. Energy classes are mapped to a linear scale (A4-G), with inversion applied when lower performance is explicitly requested. In the absence of a clear preference, the default decreasing mapping is used. Numerical indicators (e.g., $\mathrm{EP}_{gl,nren}$) follow a normalized linear scheme calibrated to query intent and dataset distribution.

The final score is computed as a weighted average of the normalized scores provided by the individual agents with weights defined in Sect. 3.1 by the *Ranking Agent* from the user query context (e.g., prioritizing locations if the user specifies "near the metro"). To prevent score dilution when an agent finds no relevant requirements, we implement a weight redistribution algorithm. If an agent k is inactive, its weight w_k is redistributed among active agents j proportionally to their initial weights.

Finally, an *Evaluation Agent* analyzes the top results, complementing quantitative scores with a qualitative assessment of repurposing and strategic potential. For each candidate, it highlights the main score drivers and provides three pros and three cons. A final executive summary compares the top-ranked options and recommends the most coherent strategic compromise.

3.4 Visual Analytics

To mitigate automation bias and fully support the Human-in-the-Loop paradigm, MURENA presents its outputs through a visually-rich web interface.

The raw numerical scores are translated into actionable Explainable AI (XAI) components, including textual justifications and multi-dimensional Radar Charts. Specifically, the Energy Radar maps raw EPC XML tags into four normalized axes (Energy Class, System Efficiency, Envelope Performance, and Renewables), while the Proximity Radar visualizes the six 15-minute city pillars. This allows human operators to visually inspect and override the LLM's multi-criteria evaluations. Screenshots of the web interface are in Appendix A.

4 Results

4.1 Experimental Setup

We evaluated MURENA on a real-world dataset of nearly 90,000 buildings in a major Italian city (Sect. 2), chosen for its representative urban structure, with distinct central and peripheral zones.

The evaluation comprises complementary tasks targeting key pipeline properties: (i) agent routing correctness (i.e., whether the correct agents are activated); (ii) ranking behaviour, including differentiation, determinism, and priority alignment; (iii) SQL synthesis structure compared to monolithic baselines; (iv) data awareness and calibration via knowledge ablations; (v) qualitative usefulness of generated pros/cons using an LLM-as-a-judge protocol; and (vi) human-centred validation with domain experts in realistic change-of-use scenarios.

The experiments were carried out on an NVIDIA RTX PRO 6000 GPU. All models used within the MURENA pipeline are open-weight and deployed locally: `gpt-oss-120b`, `gemma3-27b`, and `qwen3-8b`. These models were selected to represent three distinct scale tiers of state-of-the-art models known for their strong reasoning and instruction-following capabilities. This selection allows us to evaluate the trade-off between computational cost (e.g., `qwen3-8b`and `gemma3-27b`can be easily deployed on a single consumer-grade GPU) and multi-agent orchestration performance, while strictly satisfying the data sovereignty and local-hosting constraints required by real estate applications. The closed-weight model `gpt-5.4` is used exclusively outside the pipeline, as an external baseline and as the LLM-as-a-judge evaluator. We selected `gpt-5.4` to establish a state-of-the-art upper bound for single-prompt capabilities and to provide robust zero-shot assessments for qualitative metrics. The pipeline uses LangGraph for orchestration, DuckDB for data persistence and in-memory analytics, and scikit-learn's `BallTree` for spatial operations. Geocoding and geographic knowledge are obtained from OpenStreetMap via the Overpass API. The tracing and evaluation of the system is handled with Langfuse. The code is openly available in the project repository; a live demo is available at https://murena.vercel.app/.

Taking inspiration from state-of-the-art benchmarking schemas [8], we generated 486 combinatorial queries ($\mathcal{Q}_{\text{comb}}$; details in the Appendix B.1), of which 64 activate all five technical agents ($\mathcal{Q}_{\text{full}}$). Routing is evaluated in $\mathcal{Q}_{\text{comb}}$to assess activation correctness across optional components, while ablations are performed in $\mathcal{Q}_{\text{full}}$to ensure comparability when all agents are active.

The components were mapped to natural language queries, using the following template, eventually ignoring fields when optional:

Search a I [near L] [with C_b] [for a D] [close to C_p] [in energy class C_e].

where the square brackets indicate whether a component is optional.

4.2 Quantitative and Qualitative Performance

Agent Routing Evaluation. We evaluate the routing capability of MURENA on the full combinatorial query set $\mathcal{Q}_{\text{comb}}$, assessing whether the orchestration layer activates the correct subset of specialised agents for each query. Ground-truth activations are deterministically derived from the structured query template (Eq. 1), where components map to agents as follows: $L \rightarrow$ *location agent*, $D \rightarrow$ *regulatory agent*, $C_p \rightarrow$ *proximity agent*, $C_e \rightarrow$ *Energy agent*, and both I and $C_b \rightarrow$ ***Building Agent***. Observed activations are compared against this mapping using global and per-agent metrics, including Perfect Mapping Rate (PMR, exact activation match), Mean Jaccard Score (set overlap), and per-agent F1-scores.

Results for all three models are shown in Table 1. All achieve near-perfect per-agent F1 and high Jaccard scores, indicating that identifying individual conditions is relatively straightforward, especially when few are combined. Differences emerge in joint activation accuracy: PMR reveals that smaller models struggle to fully align with the expected agent set, and rather tend to over-activate or drop marginal secondary agents. In practice, this means smaller models remain highly usable, as the downstream SQL and scoring layers naturally filter out irrelevant agent outputs.

Ranking Dynamics and Qualitative Evaluation. The middle block of Table 1 reports ranking differentiation, determinism, and rank-effectiveness alignment on $\mathcal{Q}_{\text{full}}$. Cross-query IoU assesses ranking differentiation and remains consistently low across models, indicating that rankings adapt to query-specific constraints rather than converging to a fixed ordering. Self-IoU across three independent trials is high, confirming stable, auditable behavior despite LLM

Table 1. Routing, ranking, and qualitative evaluation results. Top: agent routing on $\mathcal{Q}_{\text{comb}}$. Middle: ranking differentiation, consistency, and weight–discovery alignment on $\mathcal{Q}_{\text{full}}$. Bottom: LLM-as-a-judge assessment of pros/cons quality. Up and down arrows indicate whether the higher or lower value is preferred for each metric.

Metric	`gpt-oss-120b`	`gemma3-27b`	`qwen3-8b`
Agent routing ($\mathcal{Q}_{\text{comb}}$)			
PMR (%) (↑)	**90.3**	54.5	54.9
Mean Jaccard score (↑)	**0.972**	0.863	0.861
F1: *Energy agent* (↑)	0.989	**0.998**	0.984
F1: *location agent* (↑)	**1.000**	**1.000**	0.995
F1: *regulatory agent* (↑)	**1.000**	0.800	0.807
F1: *proximity agent* (↑)	**0.998**	0.982	0.997
F1: *building agent* (↑)	**0.949**	0.909	0.899
Ranking consistency ($\mathcal{Q}_{\text{full}}$)			
Ranking differentiation (cross-query IoU) (↓)	0.024	0.018	**0.017**
Model consistency (self-query IoU, 3 trials) (↑)	0.705	**0.820**	0.720
Discovery rate @ Rank 1 (%) (↑)	96.3	66.7	**97.1**
Discovery rate @ Rank 5 (%) (↓)	**25.7**	69.1	42.6
LLM-as-a-judge qualitative evaluation ($\mathcal{Q}_{\text{full}}$)			
Accuracy (Pros) (↑)	69.8%	**79.5%**	63.5%
Accuracy (Cons) (↑)	52.8%	**68.9%**	50.4%
Relevance (Pros)(↑)	80.3%	79.7%	**80.8%**
Relevance (Cons) (↑)	**46.9%**	44.9%	36.4%

involvement. Discovery rates at Rank 1 and Rank 5 measure how often top- and lower-ranked agents successfully extract requirements. As expected, higher-ranked agents contribute more frequently than lower-ranked ones, supporting the effectiveness of the ranking mechanism. Without the *Ranking Agent* dynamically assigning weights based on intent, the final multi-criteria score would be uniformly diluted across all technical agents. By correctly prioritizing active agents, the ranking mechanism ensures that properties strictly matching the user's primary requirements are not outranked by properties that only excel in secondary or unrequested dimensions.

The bottom block reports LLM-as-a-judge evaluation of generated pros and cons. Accuracy scores are consistently higher for Pros than Cons, suggesting that positive evidence is easier to ground in structured attributes, while critical assessments require more interpretative synthesis. Relevance scores remain comparatively stable across models, indicating that even weaker models maintain topical alignment despite differences in factual precision.

Expert Evaluation. MURENA was validated by two senior domain experts on 10 realistic change-of-use scenarios derived from institutional cases in a major

Italian city. The task was to identify buildings suitable for co-housing conversion (10 apartments, 40–70 m^2 each) in three city areas, targeting both low-energy-class buildings (renovation candidates) and high-energy-class buildings (low-effort conversion). For each scenario, experts first defined their ideal top-5 shortlist via manual search, then compared it blindly against MURENA's ranked output. MURENA retrieved at least one expert-preferred building in the top-5 in 9 of 10 scenarios. Among the remaining system-proposed buildings, 80% were rated relevant by both experts. Human overrides were needed in only 1 of 10 cases (weight adjustment), confirming the Human-in-the-Loop design's value. A concrete example is a co-housing scenario in which MURENAcorrectly identified and aggregated 10 distinct cadastral units (ranging from 23 to 124 m^2) into a single 642 m^2 meta-building near the requested landmark. Experts confirmed that the generated "Cons" appropriately highlighted renovation constraints implied by the 1850 construction year and Class E rating, while correctly recognising the excellent mobility proximity score of 98/100. The system also surfaced dataset-based information not explicitly requested, such as the presence of green areas and sports facilities, enriching the building selection process. The experts particularly appreciated the transparency of the weighted scoring breakdown, the radar charts, and the clarity of the executive synthesis.

4.3 Ablation Study

We perform a leave-one-out ablation over the $\mathcal{Q}_{\text{full}}$to quantify each component's contribution. Removing each agent determines a ranking IoU between the ablated system and the full pipeline which is on average 0.276. For more details, see the Appendix B.2.

To assess the benefit of multi-agent modularization, we compare MURENA against two monolithic text-to-SQL baselines powered by `gpt-5.4`: (i) a schema-only prompt containing column names, and (ii) a schema+statistics prompt enriched with column quartile statistics, both generating the full query in a single pass. By deliberately selecting one of the most capable closed-weight frontier models for these baselines, we aim to demonstrate that the challenge of multi-dimensional query extraction cannot be solved merely by raw model scale.

We evaluate the architectures along two complementary dimensions. First, the domain coverage F1 score measures whether the generated SQL captures all the thematic dimensions implied by the query. Each dimension (energy, location, proximity, regulatory, structural) maps to a predefined set of schema columns and is considered "covered" if at least one corresponding column appears in the query. Second, column-set IoU on the `SELECT`/`WHERE` clauses quantifies structural divergence between multi-agent and monolithic queries, independent of output equivalence. Retrieval behaviour is evaluated separately through ranking metrics, diversity analysis, and expert validation.

As shown in Table 2, both monolithic baseline configurations achieve a domain coverage F1 of around 0.75, regardless of whether column statistics are injected into the prompt, meaning that for roughly 3 out of 4 queries the baseline entirely omits at least one thematic dimension that the query implicitly requires. The IoU analysis on the top 10 results further confirms that this gap is structural: the two baseline configurations are mutually consistent across models (ranking IoU ≈ 0.515), whereas their divergence from the multi-agent architecture (the result MURENA with the same LLM) is substantial. Architectural modularisation, rather than prompt enrichment alone, is therefore the primary driver of both domain coverage and structural differences in generated SQL.

Table 2. SQL structural comparison between multi-agent and monolithic baselines (`gpt-5.4`), evaluated on $\mathcal{Q}_{\text{full}}$.

Model	Domain F1 (↑)	column-set IoU (↑)		
		`gpt-oss-120b`	`gemma3-27b`	`qwen3-8b`
Columns only	0.757	0.126	0.125	0.191
Columns + stats	0.757	0.121	0.183	0.229
MURENA	1	1	1	1

5 Discussion and Conclusion

Impact and Deployment Perspective. MURENA demonstrates that multi-agent LLM architectures can deliver highly scalable and robust decision support for large-scale real estate management, a domain where manual workflows currently dominate. Expert validation confirms that the system reduces the portfolio screening effort from weeks to minutes, with an average end-to-end query execution time of 55 s, while maintaining alignment with professional judgement (90% top-5 retrieval, 80% of additional recommendations rated useful).

Based on our evaluation, we recommend Gemma3-27B for real-world deployments. It offers the optimal trade-off: it achieves reasoning and qualitative performance comparable to massive 120B models, yet it can be hosted on a single enterprise GPU, satisfying both operational cost constraints and strict public-sector data privacy requirements.

Crucially, the platform has attracted strong institutional interest at both regional and national level: public bodies responsible for managing large property portfolios have identified MURENA as a candidate tool to support the building decarbonisation obligations mandated by EPBD IV and the planning of just transition at scale. This institutional traction validates the system's practical relevance beyond academic evaluation and positions it as a concrete instrument for evidence-based urban policy.

Lessons Learned. Three architectural choices proved essential and generalise beyond real estate.

(i) Confining the LLM to semantic orchestration while delegating filtering and scoring to deterministic SQL and geospatial layers eliminates hallucination risk in the constraint enforcement path—a prerequisite for any regulatory application.
(ii) Locally-hosted open-weight models (Qwen3-8B, Gemma3-27B) achieve near-closed-model routing performance at a fraction of the computational cost, enabling full data sovereignty without sacrificing orchestration quality—a critical requirement for public institutions processing sensitive cadastral and ownership data.
(iii) The Human-in-the-Loop visual analytics layer (radar charts, scoring breakdowns, pros/cons) proved non-negotiable for expert trust and adoption: in our evaluation, domain experts used the interface to audit, adjust, and override the system's output, confirming that transparent scoring is what distinguishes a decision-support tool from a black-box recommendation engine.

Limitations. Several limitations should guide interpretation and future deployment.

(i) The absence of a standardised ground truth for multi-dimensional urban queries requires reliance on expert evaluation; while our 10-scenario protocol demonstrates alignment, larger-scale user studies across multiple cities would strengthen external validity.
(ii) The system assumes sufficiently specified initial queries; ambiguous or underspecified input may activate suboptimal agent configurations, a limitation we plan to address through conversational query refinement.
(iii) Spatial modelling aggregates amenities into broad macro-categories without distinguishing hierarchical service levels (e.g., metro vs. local bus), limiting accessibility granularity.
(iv) EPC data quality is inherently noisy due to manual entry and modelling assumptions, and the registry skews heavily residential (90% of records), which may bias analyses on specialised assets.

Future Work. Near-term priorities include: (a) extending the architecture to a conversational framework that dynamically solicits missing constraints, directly mitigating limitation (ii); (b) integrating finer-grained spatial taxonomies from multi-source cadastral and BIM data; and (c) conducting cross-regional deployment studies to validate scalability on national-level portfolios.

Longer-term, we envision MURENA as a reusable blueprint for compliance-heavy public-sector domains, urban planning, public procurement, ESG reporting, where the same pattern of LLM-driven orchestration over deterministic execution layers can deliver auditable, privacy-preserving, and expert-validated decision support.

Acknowledgments. This study was partially supported by the "WEBFARE" (Nr. FISA2022-00908), funded by the Italian Ministry of University and Research under the FISA 2022 programme (D.D. No. 1405 of 13/09/2022, Fondo Italiano per le Scienze

Applicate – FISA). This manuscript reflects only the authors' views and opinions; the Ministry cannot be held responsible for them.

Ethical considerations. The system processes only publicly available EPC data and aggregated OpenStreetMap indicators; no personal or sensitive ownership information is used for inference. Locally-hosted models guarantee data sovereignty. The architecture has no military or surveillance applications. All experiments comply with the European Code of Conduct for Research Integrity.

Disclosure of Interests. The authors have no competing interests to declare

Reproducibility Statement. The data derive from multiple open-access sources (Sect. 2). The full code, preprocessing scripts, experiment prompts, and reproducibility specifications are available at https://github.com/dbdmg/murena

References

1. De, O.: Recommender systems in real estate: a systematic review. Bull. Electr. Eng.Inf. (2025)
2. Gharahighehi, A., et al.: Recommender systems in the real estate market—a survey. Appl. Sci. **11**(9) (2021)
3. Ginevičius, R., Podvezko, V., Raslanas, S.: Recommender system for real estate management. Bus. Theor. Pract. **12**(4) (2011)
4. Italy: Decreto-legge 4 giugno 2013, n. 63: Disposizioni urgenti per il recepimento della direttiva 2010/31/ue sulla prestazione energetica nell'edilizia. Gazzetta Ufficiale, Serie Generale n. 130 (2013) (2013), decreto-Legge
5. Jafary, P., Shojaei, D., Rajabifard, A., Ngo, T.: Automated land valuation models: a comparative study of four machine learning and deep learning methods based on a comprehensive range of influential factors. Cities 151 (2024)
6. Jehangir, B., Radhakrishnan, S., Agarwal, R.: A survey on named entity recognition — datasets, tools, and methodologies. Natural Lang. Process. J. (2023)
7. Lewis, P., et al.: Retrieval-augmented generation for knowledge-intensive NLP tasks. In: Advances in Neural Information Processing Systems (2020)
8. Papicchio, S., Papotti, P., Cagliero, L.: Qatch: benchmarking SQL-centric tasks with table representation learning models on your data. Adv. Neural. Inf. Process. Syst. **36**, 30898–30917 (2023)
9. Papicchio, S., Rossi, S., Cagliero, L., Papotti, P.: Think2sql: Reinforce LLM reasoning capabilities for text2sql (2025). arXiv:2504.15077 arXiv preprint
10. Reuter, M., et al.: Towards reliable retrieval in RAG systems for large legal datasets. In: Spanakis, G. (ed.) Proceedings of the Natural Legal Language Processing Workshop, Association for Computational Linguistics, Suzhou, China (2025)
11. Schick, T., et al.: Toolformer: Language models can teach themselves to use tools. In: Advances in Neural Information Processing Systems, vol. 36 (2023)
12. Shi, Z.: Impacts of point of interest (poi) data selection on 15-minute city (15-mc) accessibility scores and inequality assessments. Trans. Res. Part A Policy Pract. **195** (2025)
13. Su, X., Gu, Y., Wang, P., Gu, W., Qi, L., He, J.: A robust natural language textâĂŘtoâĂŘSQL generation framework with dynamic strategies based on LLMs. Sci. Rep. **16** (2026)

14. Wang, L., et al.: A survey on large language model based autonomous agents. Front. Comput. Sci. **18**(6) (2024)
15. Yao, S., et al.: React: synergizing reasoning and acting in language models (2022). arXiv preprint
16. Yu, T., et al.: Spider: a large-scale human-labeled dataset for complex and cross-domain semantic parsing and text-to-SQL task. In: Proceedings of the 2018 Conference on Empirical Methods in Natural Language Processing (EMNLP). Association for Computational Linguistics, Brussels, Belgium (2018)
17. Zhang, Y., Wei, C., He, Z., Yu, W.: GeoGPT: an assistant for understanding and processing geospatial tasks. Int. J. Appl. Earth Obs. Geoinf. **131** (2024)
18. Zhou, Z., Lin, Y., Li, Y.: Large language model empowered participatory urban planning (2024). arXiv:2402.01698 arXiv preprint

NRITYAM: Language Models Meet Art and Heritage of Dance

Punit Kumar Singh[1,5], Niladri Ghosh[2], Advait Joshi[3], Shailee Choudhary[4], Michael Färber[6], and Haiqin Yang[1,7](✉)

[1] Shenzhen Technology University, 518118 Shenzhen, China
[2] Ramakrishna Mission Vivekananda Educational and Research Institute, Howrah, India
[3] Swami Vivekananda Institute of Technology, Secunderabad, India
[4] New Delhi Institute of Management, New Delhi, India
[5] Indian Institute of Technology, Patna, India
[6] Technische Universität Dresden, 01069 Dresden, Germany
[7] GuangDong Engineering Technology Research Center of Edge Intelligence, Shenzhen, China

yanghaiqin@sztu.edu.cn

Abstract. Language models have become essential tools in shaping modern workflows. However, their global effectiveness hinges on a nuanced understanding of local socio-cultural contexts. To address this gap, we present NRITYAM, a comprehensive benchmark for evaluating the cultural comprehension capabilities of language models in the context of global dance traditions. NRITYAM comprises 9,260 carefully curated question-answer pairs spanning 12 languages, making it the largest dataset dedicated to evaluating cultural knowledge in dance. The dataset has been developed from the ground up through close collaboration with native dance artists and native speakers of the languages, who authored and validated culturally relevant questions specific to their regions. We evaluate a broad set of models, including large language models, small language models, multimodal large language models, and small multimodal language models. As a multilingual and multicultural benchmark, NRITYAM sets a new standard for evaluating the ability of AI systems to understand and reason about traditional performing arts. Detailed dataset samples are available at https://github.com/niladrighosh03/NRITYAM.

Keywords: Large Language Model · Multimodal and Multilingual Dataset

1 Introduction

Dance serves as a powerful medium for cultural and emotional expression, bringing together individuals from varied backgrounds and traditions [8]. Exploring different traditional dance forms offers meaningful perspectives on the values,

M. Baratchi et al. (Eds.): ECML PKDD 2026, LNAI 16949, pp. 463–478, 2027.
https://doi.org/10.1007/978-3-032-37682-4_27

historical experiences, and social frameworks of the communities that create and uphold them [36]. Moreover, dance holds significant societal importance, serving as a medium for preserving cultural knowledge and shaping collective identity [3]. The language, rituals, and evolving forms of dance serve as rich expressions of a community's historical experiences, cultural transformations, and collective identity encompassing elements such as traditional attire, religious associations, embodied movement, and social heritage [14] (Fig. 1).

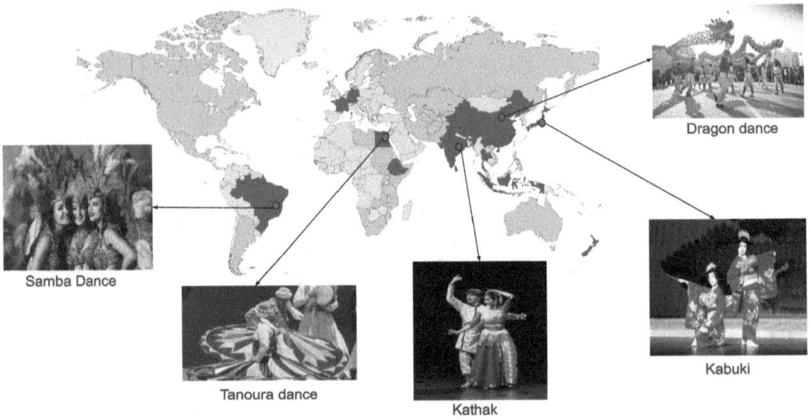

Fig. 1. NRITYAM is a diverse benchmark featuring 12 languages, with questions manually created and verified by native language speakers and dance experts. It spans 8 key aspects of traditional dance across two modalities, text and image, emphasizing mid- to low-resource languages. The benchmark features dances originating from 12 countries across 5 continents that are now performed in 100 countries across 6 continents, which are visualized with dark blue for their origins and light blue for their current reach. NRITYAM offers a wide range of question formats, including multiple-choice questions (MCQs) and both short and long visual question-answering (VQA) tasks. (Color figure online)

Researchers have increasingly turned to traditional dance as a rich lens for analyzing cultural dynamics, providing a robust framework for understanding how embodied practices evolve across regional and societal boundaries [29]. Although many traditional dance forms share foundational elements such as expressive movement, symbolic gestures, and rhythmic structure, they manifest uniquely within different cultural contexts. These divergences are evident in variations in movement style, facial expression, ritual significance, performance settings, and the terminology used to describe them. For instance, Bharatanatyam, a classical Indian dance rooted in Tamil Nadu, has been adapted in Sri Lanka through a distinctive fusion with Kandyan dance aesthetics, reflecting localized narratives and performance traditions. Such adaptations highlight how traditional dance not only preserves the heritage but also evolves through intercultural exchange and regional reinterpretation. Language Models (LMs) have revolutionized natural language understanding, content generation, and decision-making, becoming indispensable across industries such as education, governance, and entertainment [11]. From Large Language Models (LLMs) to Multimodal Language Models (MLMs) and Small Language Models (SLMs)[1], these advancements have enabled seamless communication and efficient problem-solving [35]. However, a persistent challenge remains: ensuring that these models effectively recognize and reason about diverse linguistic and cultural contexts, particularly in underrepresented domains such as traditional dance [9].

Traditional and indigenous dance forms are deeply embedded in local histories, societal values, and cultural identities [20]. Despite their significance, current language models are predominantly trained and evaluated on global popular culture and mainstream dance styles, such as hip-hop, often neglecting heritage dance traditions and culturally distinctive practices. This bias can perpetuate inaccuracies, stereotypes, and the marginalization of underrepresented communities. Conversely, models capable of understanding and respecting cultural nuances can enhance performance while promoting greater inclusivity and equity in AI applications.

Motivation for NRITYAM[2] Dataset. Existing dance-related benchmarks are largely monolingual, English-centric [5, 31], and focused primarily on motion recognition [19]. For example, PopDanceSet [30] is a monolingual dataset. To date, no comprehensive benchmark captures the rich cultural nuances of traditional dance reasoning across multiple languages, diverse cultural contexts, and visual question answering (VQA). To address this gap, we introduce NRITYAM, the **largest multicultural and multilingual traditional dance benchmark** to date. It consists of approximately 9,260 dance-related questions covering traditional dances originating from 12 countries across 5 continents, which are now performed in over 100 countries spanning 6 continents. The benchmark evaluates the capabilities of LLMs, SLMs, and MLMs across twelve languages. Questions are organized into two modalities, text-based and image-based, and systematically categorized into three key types: history-based, rule-based, scenario-based.[3]

This work is guided by the following research questions:

(1) How do different categories of models, i.e., LLMs, SLMs, MLMs, and Small Multimodal Language Models (SMLMs), perform on the NRITYAM dataset?
(2) What trends and patterns emerge in model performance across the various question types, including history-based, rule-based, scenario-based, and image-based questions, in the NRITYAM dataset?
(3) What are the performance trends of language models across different countries or languages in Asia, Africa, South America, Oceania, and Europe?

Key Contributions. Our main contributions are as follows:

[1] Any model with 7B parameters or fewer is considered a Small Language Model (SLM) in this work.
[2] The Sanskrit term "NRITYAM" holds profound significance in classical Indian dance.
[3] MLMs are used exclusively for evaluating the image-based questions.

1. The NRITYAM Dataset: We present the first and the most comprehensive QA dataset on traditional dance, covering 12 countries across 5 continents (with global reach across 100+ countries on 6 continents). The dataset is available in 12 native languages as well as in English.

2. Diverse Question Types: The dataset includes 9,260 questions spanning two modalities (text and image) and three categories, challenging AI models to reason over textual, visual, multilingual, and culturally grounded inputs.

3. Comprehensive Benchmarking: We rigorously evaluate 13 state-of-the-art language models, including LLMs, SLMs, MLMs, and SMLMs, uncovering critical gaps in their cultural and contextual reasoning abilities regarding traditional dance.

By addressing cultural under-representation in AI, **NRITYAM** establishes a robust benchmark for evaluating and improving AI systems. This research advances the intersection of NLP and culturally rich domains, contributing to greater inclusivity and equity in AI applications worldwide.

2 Related Work

Prior Cultural VQA Benchmarks. Pioneering efforts in culturally aware Vision-Question Answering (VQA) have led to datasets spanning various regional and thematic dimensions, including FM-IQA [17], MCVQA [21], xGQA [37], MaXM [12], MTVQA [40], MABL [23], MAPS [26], and MaRVL [27]. Parallel lines of work, such as CVQA [33], CulturalVQA [34], ALM-bench [43], and CultSportQA [39], offer broader resources covering distinct cultural themes, with CVQA introducing multilingual queries paired with English translations. Other benchmarks adopt granular geographic or thematic scopes; for instance, SEA-VQA [42] focuses strictly on Southeast Asia, while FoodieQA [25], World Wide Dishes [32], and WORLDCUISINES [45] focus on specific culinary traditions. While NRITYAM shares the foundational objective of using a specific cultural lens, i.e., traditional dance, it distinctly expands upon prior art through a substantially larger dataset and broader multilingual coverage.

Sociocultural Reasoning in LLMs. Complementing visual benchmarks, recent NLP research scrutinizes the behavioral and alignment gaps of LLMs through established sociological frameworks like the World Values Survey and Hofstede's cultural dimensions [4]. These studies frequently reveal critical alignment deficiencies when adapting systems to user-specific or non-Western contexts [22]. Although interventions like synthetic personas and targeted fine-tuning show promise in elevating cultural adaptability and safe text moderation (e.g., cross-lingual hate speech detection), regional and low-resource language performance persistently lags behind English baselines [13,16,24]. These systemic limitations underscore the critical necessity for robust, multilingual evaluation suites to genuinely foster and measure the cultural competence of large foundation models (Table 1).

3 Construction of NRITYAM

3.1 Manual Data Collection

The creation of NRITYAM follows a carefully structured, multi-phase process to ensure comprehensive coverage and high-quality standards. Domain experts and country-specific annotators contribute at every stage, from data collection to question formulation and manual translation across multiple languages, incorporating their cultural knowledge and expertise

Data Sources: The dataset is built by sourcing information from multiple diverse and reliable platforms, including Wikipedia, government culture websites, local culture dance blogs, dance culture journals, and news outlets. These sources are carefully selected to authentically capture the essence of traditional dance from 12 countries: Brazil, China, Egypt, Ethiopia, France, Germany, India, Indonesia, Japan, New Zealand, Sri Lanka, Thailand, with emphasis on their cultural and regional significance. The questions are designed to focus on historical, rule-based, and image-based aspects of the dance.

1. Wikipedia: As a foundational resource, Wikipedia offers well-documented, detailed insights into the history, origins, and rules of traditional dance, serving as a cornerstone for verified information across diverse dance traditions.

2. Government Culture Website: The government culture websites of each country contribute unique perspectives on the historical and cultural relevance of traditional dance forms, ensuring authenticity and depth.

3. Local Culture Dance Blogs: Dedicated blogs and websites focusing on indigenous and traditional dance offer community-driven perspectives, unique insights, and region-specific practices associated with each dance form.

4. Dance Cultural Journals: Scholarly journals and publications specializing in cultural studies enrich the dataset with detailed articles on the evolution and societal impact of traditional dance across different regions.

5. News outlets: Renowned news outlets from each country provide contemporary coverage, including recent trends, key events, and ongoing efforts to preserve or revive traditional dances.

Table 1. Comparison of our dataset with other dance-related datasets. The metadata compared includes the number of samples (questions), the number of dances, whether cultural aspects are considered, the number of languages, modalities (i.e., whether the data includes multimodal questions), and question type. "—" indicates the value is not specified.

Dataset	#Samples	#Dances	Cultural Aspects	#Languages	Modalities	Question Type
CULTURALVQA [34]	2,378	—	No	20	Image	MCQ
CVQA [33]	10,000	—	No	31	Text + Image	MCQ
NRITYAM (ours)	**9,260**	**30**	**Yes**	**12**	Text + Image	**MCQ**

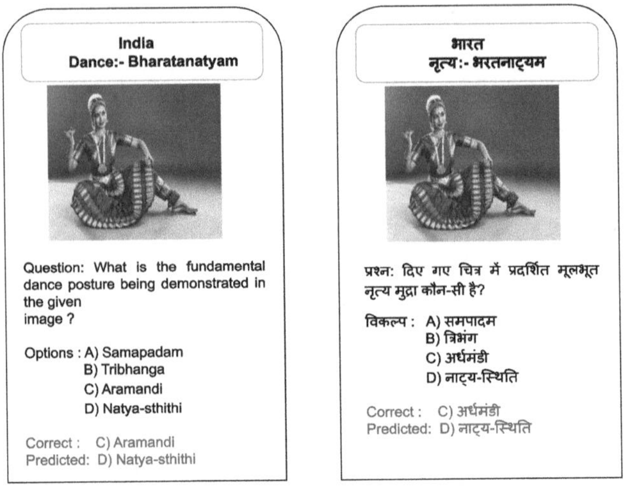

Fig. 2. Example illustration of Indian traditional dance wrong prediction by language model (in Hindi and English).

Fig. 3. Example illustration of Ethiopia's traditional dance correct prediction by language model (in Amharic and English)

Dataset Organization. The NRITYAM dataset is divided into two categories: text-based and image-based. Each category is further organized into three question types: history-based, rule-based, and scenario-based questions.

The dataset follows a multiple-choice question (MCQ) format with four options (A, B, C, D), out of which only one is correct. Each question-answer (QA) pair includes metadata such as continent, country, posture, religion, and other question types.

The text-based questions are evaluated using LLMs and SLMs, while the image-based questions are assessed using MLMs and SMLMs.

History-based questions test the model's knowledge of a dance's origins and cultural significance. Scenario-based questions assess the model's ability to determine the most appropriate move in a given dance situation for a good performance. Rule-based questions evaluate the model's understanding of the fundamental rules of the dance depicted in the text or image. Religion-based questions assess the model's understanding of dances associated with particular religions, and so on. Examples from the NRITYAM dataset are illustrated in Figs. 2 and 3.

3.2 Annotation Process

We outline the main steps in the annotation below:

1. Team Structure and Annotators Background. We hire 36 expert workers from 12 countries, with 3 representatives from each country, based on the following eligibility criteria: (1) The individual must be a native speaker. (2) They must have lived in the country for at least 10 years. (3) They must possess a strong understanding of local culture and traditional dance. (4) Their parents must also be from the country and currently reside there. (5) They must hold at least a degree from a nationally accredited dance institution. Two-thirds of the annotators are responsible for creating questions based on the provided guidelines, leveraging their knowledge of traditional dance. The remaining annotator was tasked with validating and filtering out questions that fail to meet quality standards (Fig. 4).

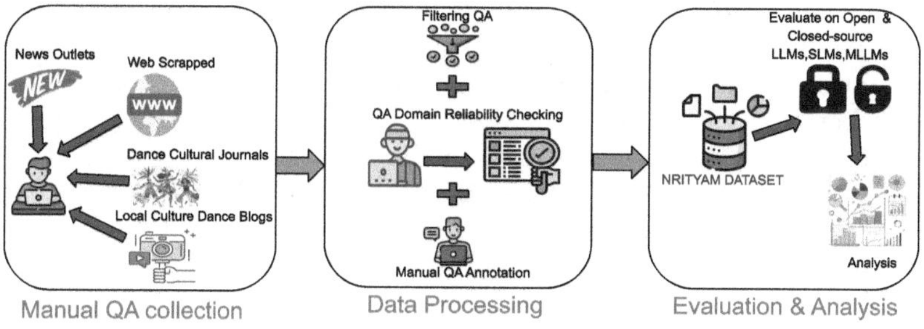

Fig. 4. Manual dataset construction pipeline for NRITYAM: The data collection process involved two key stages: (1) annotators gather data sources and generate questions, drawing from their respective cultural backgrounds and languages; (2) annotators review and verify the questions to ensure cultural authenticity and maintain high translation quality.

2. Question Formation. For each selected textual passage or image, the annotator's first task is to verify whether the content aligned with the traditional dance associated with the country. Content unrelated to the traditional dance is immediately rejected. If the content is relevant, the annotator creates questions focusing on rules, history, location, attire, religion, scenario, artist, and posture. Each question has to be complete, self-contained, and understandable without additional context. The questions follow a multiple-choice format, consisting of four options, with only one correct answer. The final annotated format includes the source passage, a relationship attribute indicating the question's context, the type of question (e.g., history-based, rule-based, scenario-based), and the four answer options. After a question is constructed, it is translated into the regional language that the annotator is familiar with. The annotators are paid at a rate between \$0.10 and \$0.50 per example, depending on the country exchange rate and difficulty of annotation.

3. Training and Guidelines. Annotators are receiving comprehensive training that covers the objectives of the NRITYAM dataset, clear definitions and examples of various question types, and best practices for ensuring consistency and cultural sensitivity. Detailed guideline documents are being provided, including templates, metadata tagging standards, and examples of culturally appropriate representations. Additional sessions focus on language and cultural training, emphasizing the correct use of local terminologies and traditions. Each participant is required to attend a live one-hour online workshop or watch a recorded version. These sessions offer an overview of the project, explaining the task instructions in detail and addressing any potential questions. To ensure a thorough understanding of the assignment, a pilot study is being conducted before the main annotation phase.

4. Quality Assurance and Cross-Validation. A rigorous quality assurance process is being conducted through multi-step validations. Each question-answer pair is undergoing cross-validation by at least one annotator, who understands the basic requirements to be qualified for inclusion in the dataset, as well as the translation quality. Image-based questions are being reviewed for proper alignment between visual elements and textual prompts. Spot checks and random sampling are being performed by quality analysts to maintain clarity and consistency. Bias mitigation measures are ensuring a balanced representation of dance across regions and question types, while cultural sensitivity reviews are eliminating stereotypes or offensive content.

4 Statistical Analysis of NRITYAM

The NRITYAM dataset shows a balanced mix of text-based and image-based questions, with a slight dominance of text-based ones comprising 5,110 questions over the visual ones, which comprise of 4,150. Image-based questions mainly focuses on dance rules, scenarios, and history. Figures 5 and 6 show the distribution of text and image-based questions across languages.

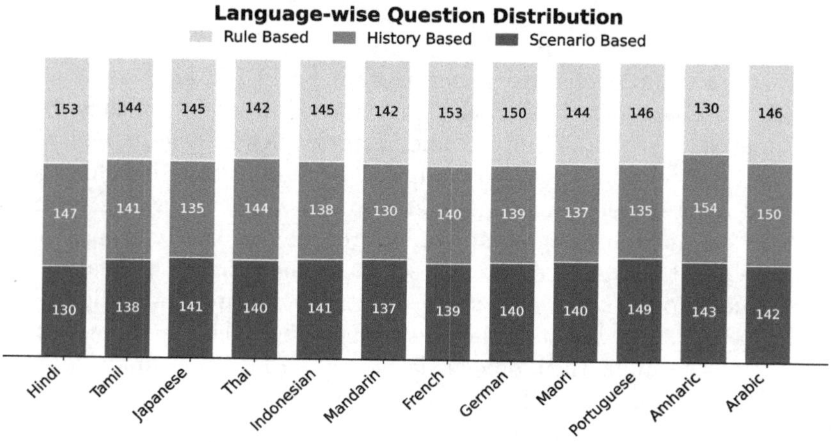

Fig. 5. Distribution of text-based questions across language.

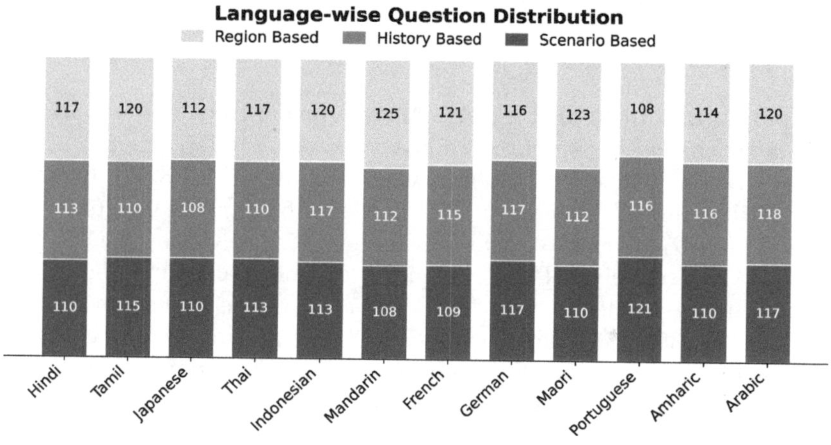

Fig. 6. Distribution of image-based questions across language.

5 Experiments

5.1 Models

To comprehensively evaluate our proposed benchmark, NRITYAM, we conduct an extensive assessment across a diverse suite of foundation models spanning both textual and visual modalities. For text-based evaluation, our suite encompasses leading LLMs, including Llama-3.1 [15], GPT-4 [2], GPT-5 [38], Gemma-7B [41], Phi-4 [1], Qwen-3 [6], and Claude-4.5. Beyond text-based models, we evaluate a wide range of MLMs to assess dance reasoning capabilities in multilingual settings. Specifically, this visual category includes mBLIP (a BLIP-2-based model) [18], PaliGemma-2 [10], LLaVA [28], Qwen3-VL [7], and DeepSeek-OCR [44].

5.2 Evaluation Setup

We conducted a comprehensive evaluation of the NRITYAM dataset, which comprises text and image-based Multiple Choice Questions (MCQs) categorized into three distinct dimensions: 1. Cultural and Historical Knowledge, 2. Rule Comprehension, and 3. Scenario-Based Reasoning. To systematically benchmark model performance across diverse languages and modalities, all evaluations are executed under a **zero-shot** prompting paradigm. For reproducibility and consistency, the temperature is set to 0, and **accuracy** serves as the primary evaluation metric. For deployment, open-source models are initialized using 16-bit floating-point precision (FP16) and evaluated via greedy decoding, whereas proprietary models are queried through their official developer APIs. Final model predictions are extracted based on the highest output token probability, establishing a standardized and deterministic evaluation pipeline.

6 Discussion on Results

6.1 Main Results

Performance of LLMs and SLMs. Across our multilingual evaluation, frontier LLMs consistently outperform compact models. GPT-5 emerges as the top performer (61.73%), closely followed by Claude Opus 4.5 (61.32%). Both display robust stability across categories: GPT-5 scores 62.51% (Rule), 62.18% (History), and 60.51% (Scenario), while Claude-4.5 Opus yields 62.21%, 61.29%, and 60.46%, respectively. GPT-4 occupies a distinct secondary tier at 53.08%. Among mid-range models, Qwen-3 32B (43.76%) outperforms Phi-4 (40.36%), LLaMA-3.1-8B (36.99%), and Gemma-7B (35.32%). Universally, models excel in European and East Asian languages (e.g., German, French, Mandarin) but degrade on low-resource languages (e.g., Māori, Amharic, Arabic). This highlights a persistent cross-lingual disparity, demonstrating that model scale correlates with better generalization on cultural QA tasks. Granular breakdowns are provided in Figs. 7, 8, and 9.

Performance of MLMs and SMLMs. Across the multilingual multimodal evaluation, DeepSeek-OCR emerges as the top-performing system with 68.64% overall average, consistently leading across Scenario-based (69.80%), History (69.32%), and Rule-based (66.30%) categories. Qwen3-VL forms a distinct secondary tier, achieving a solid overall average of 55.77% (Scenario: 57.32%, History: 56.02%, Rules: 54.47%). Among smaller and mid-range architectures, Gemma-3-12B performs competitively at 50.73%, outperforming LLaVA (40.95%), PaliGemma-2 (40.26%), and mBLIP (35.83%). Universally, models excel on scenario-based reasoning but encounter performance degradation on historical and rule-oriented cultural tasks, particularly under low-resource language settings. A shared cross-lingual bottleneck is observed: while architectures generalize effectively in high-resource languages (e.g., German, French, Mandarin, Japanese, and Thai), low-resource targets like Māori, Amharic,

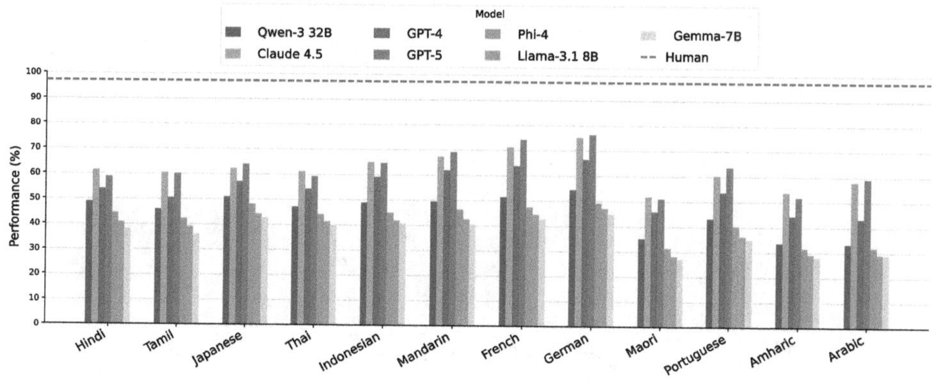

Fig. 7. Results of LLMs and SLMs on rule-based questions across languages (text modality).

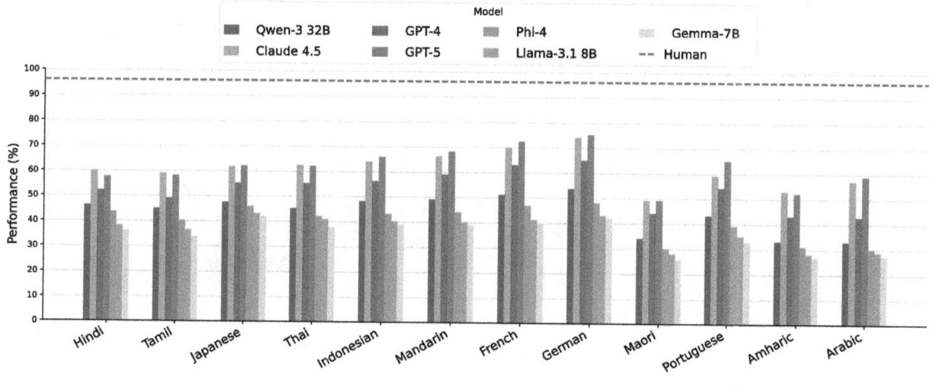

Fig. 8. Results of LLMs and SLMs on history-based questions across languages (text modality).

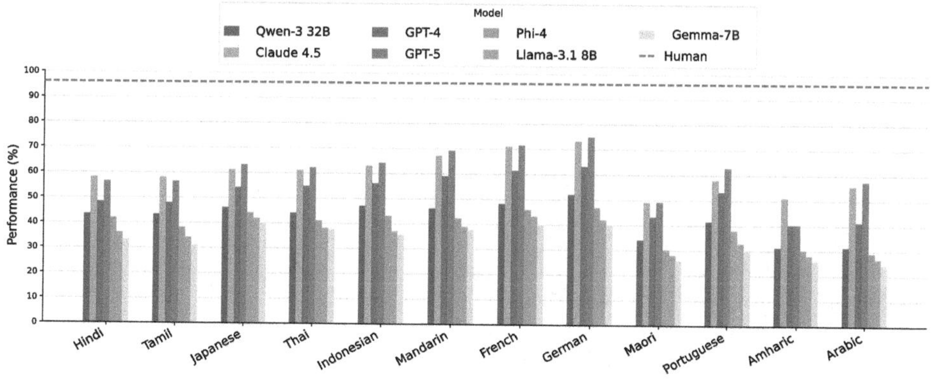

Fig. 9. Results of LLMs and SLMs on scenario-based questions across languages (text modality).

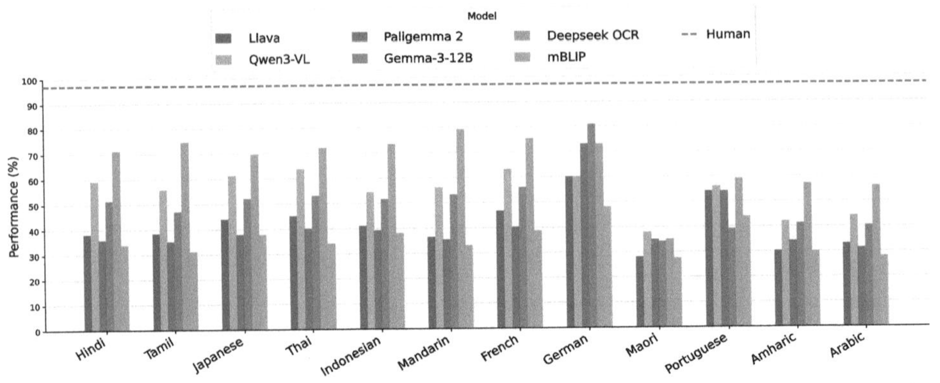

Fig. 10. Results of MLMs and SMLMs on rule-based questions across languages (image modality).

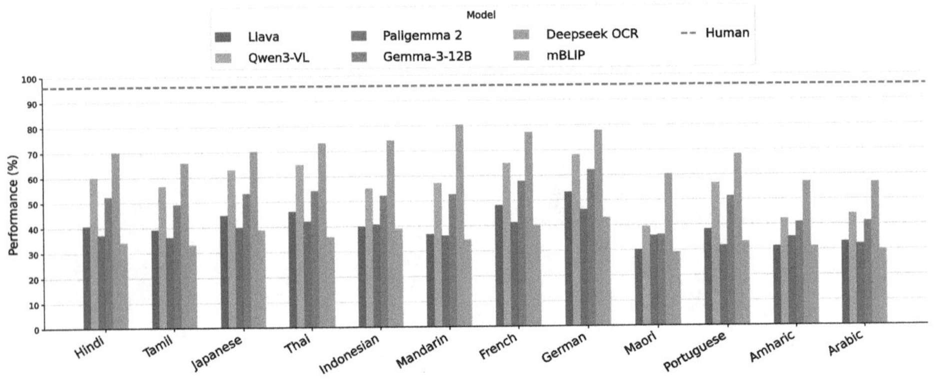

Fig. 11. Results of MLMs and SMLMs on history-based questions across languages (image modality).

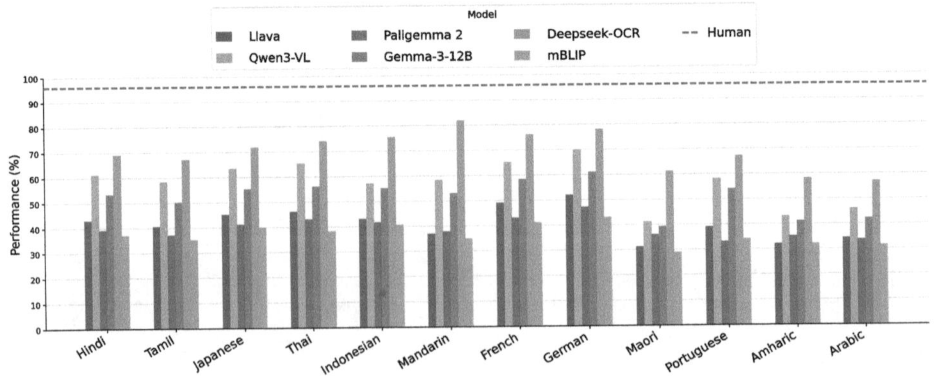

Fig. 12. Results of MLMs and SMLMs on scenario-based questions across languages (image modality).

and Arabic present persistent challenges. These results confirm that advanced vision-language scales substantially improve multimodal cultural comprehension, whereas compact architectures continue to struggle with historically grounded and rule-driven reasoning. Figures 10, 11, and 12 provide granular performance breakdowns.

6.2 Human Evaluation

Human raters evaluated the rule-based, history-based, and scenario-based categories to assess cultural reasoning. In the text modality, accuracies were 97%, 96%, and 96%, while in the image modality, they were 97%, 96%, and 96%, respectively. Despite strong human consistency, a partial misalignment with model predictions highlights that language models still fall short of replicating human-level cultural interpretation and contextual reasoning.

7 Conclusion

In this work, we construct NRITYAM, a comprehensive benchmark designed to evaluate language models' understanding of Asian, African, South American, Oceania, and European traditional dance. The dataset, consisting of 9,260 curated question-answer pairs from 12 countries, covers eight key aspects such as rules, history, location, attire, and other cultural significance. Evaluations with leading models reveal notable gaps in answering traditional dance-specific questions, highlighting biases likely caused by training data limitations. NRITYAM, built for quality and cultural sensitivity, advances inclusive AI research. Future expansions will add more languages and traditional dance to enhance its impact.

Limitations

Despite being one of the most comprehensive evaluations of language models on traditional dance and cultural knowledge, this study has several limitations:

(1) **Limited Geographic, Language, and Cultural Scope:** The NRITYAM dataset currently covers 12 languages from 12 countries across 5 continents. While valuable, its scope remains limited. Expanding to include more countries, especially those with underrepresented regions and low-resource languages, would improve cultural diversity and inclusivity, enabling fairer and broader assessments of language models.

(2) **Limited Representation of Traditional Dances:** Although the dataset covers 30 traditional dances—the largest multilingual and multimodal cultural dance dataset—it may still not fully capture the diversity of traditional dances across continents. Future versions could include more dance forms and additional question types, such as True/False, adversarial, and scenario-based reasoning tasks.

Ethics Statement

Data Collection and Bias Mitigation. Data for NRITYAM are collected from publicly accessible platforms (see Sect. 3.1), carefully selected to ensure authenticity. NRITYAM thus represents a significant step toward a standardized, inclusive benchmark for traditional dances from Asia, Europe, South America, Oceania, and Africa. All sources are verified by annotators through multiple group discussions, and irrelevant metadata was discarded

Human Annotation. A diverse team of 36 annotators—experts in Asian, Oceanian, African, South American, and European dance, linguistics, and related fields—crafted, verified, and translated questions. The team included native and bilingual speakers from 12 countries, all with deep regional and dance knowledge. Annotators underwent comprehensive training on dataset objectives, question categories, and dance-specific guidelines. Nearly all were native speakers with approximately 15 years of experience in dance, ensuring linguistic and cultural accuracy. The team, aged 28–50, provided a balanced generational perspective. Annotation was collaborative, with cross-validation by a separate subteam to ensure consistency and address biases. Ethical considerations—avoiding stereotypes and promoting inclusivity—remained central, ensuring the dataset fairly reflects diverse cultural values.

Acknowledgments. This work was supported by the Stable Support Program of Universities in Shenzhen (20231129211559001). We further acknowledge financial support from BMFTR and SMWK within the Center of Excellence for AI Research "ScaDS.AI Dresden/Leipzig".

Disclosure of Interests. The authors have no competing interests to declare that are relevant to the content of this article.

References

1. Abdin, M., et al.: Phi-3 technical report: a highly capable language model locally on your phone. arXiv preprint arXiv:2404.14219 (2024)
2. Achiam, J., et al.: GPT-4 technical report (2023). arXiv:2303.08774 arXiv preprint
3. Afolaranmi, V.B., Afolaranmi, A.O.: Cultural revitalization through dance as a panacea for peacebuilding. Adv. J. Theat. Film Stud. **2**(1), 39–45 (2024)
4. AlKhamissi, B., ElNokrashy, M.N., Alkhamissi, M., Diab, M.T.: Investigating cultural alignment of large language models. In: ACL, pp. 12404–12422 (2024)
5. Aristidou, A., et al.: Safeguarding our dance cultural heritage. In: Eurographics 2022-43nd Annual Conference of the European Association for Computer Graphics, pp. 1–6 (2022)
6. Bai, J., et al.: Qwen technical report. arXiv preprint arXiv:2309.16609 (2023)
7. Bai, S., et al.: Qwen3-vl technical report. arXiv preprint arXiv:2511.21631 (2025)
8. Bannerman, H.: Is dance a language? movement, meaning and communication. Dance Res. **32**(1), 65–80 (2014)
9. Bender, E.M., Gebru, T., McMillan-Major, A., Shmitchell, S.: On the dangers of stochastic parrots: Can language models be too big? In: Proceedings of the 2021 ACM Conference on Fairness, Accountability, and Transparency, pp. 610–623 (2021)

10. Beyer, L., et al.: Paligemma: a versatile 3b VLM for transfer (2024). arXiv:2407.07726 arXiv preprint
11. Brown, T., Mann, B., Ryder, N., et al.: Language models are few-shot learners. Adv. Neural. Inf. Process. Syst. **33**, 1877–1901 (2020)
12. Changpinyo, S., et al.: Maxm: towards multilingual visual question answering. In: Findings of the Association for Computational Linguistics: EMNLP 2023, pp. 2667–2682. (2023)
13. Deng, Y., Zhang, W., Pan, S.J., Bing, L.: Multilingual jailbreak challenges in large language models. In: International Conference on Learning Representations, vol. 2024, pp. 24634–24651 (2024)
14. Desmond, J.C.: Embodying difference: issues in dance and cultural studies. Cult. Crit. **26**, 33–63 (1993)
15. Dubey, A., et al.: The llama 3 herd of models (2024). arXiv:2407.21783 arXiv preprint
16. Dwivedi, S.K., Patel, R.: Exploring the intersections: anthropological insights into studying language and culture. State Instit. Educ. Allahabad **30**, 171–182 (2024)
17. Gao, H., Mao, J., Zhou, J., Huang, Z., Wang, L., Xu, W.: Are you talking to a machine? dataset and methods for multilingual image question. Adv. Neural. Inf. Process. Syst. **28** (2015)
18. Geigle, G., Jain, A., Timofte, R., Glavaš, G.: MBLIP: efficient bootstrapping of multilingual vision-LLMs (2023). arXiv:2307.06930 arXiv preprint
19. Grammalidis, N., et al.: The i-treasures intangible cultural heritage dataset. In: Proceedings of the 3rd International Symposium on Movement and Computing, pp. 1–8 (2016)
20. Guo, C., Li, Z.: The impact of dance culture learning on students' cultural values. Cultura: Int. J. Phil. Culture Axiology **22**(2), 422–440 (2025)
21. Gupta, D., Lenka, P., Ekbal, A., Bhattacharyya, P.: A unified framework for multilingual and code-mixed visual question answering. In: Proceedings of the 1st Conference of the Asia-Pacific Chapter of the Association for Computational Linguistics and the 10th International Joint Conference on Natural Language Processing, pp. 900–913 (2020)
22. Johnson, R.L., et al.: The ghost in the machine has an american accent: value conflict in GPT-3 (2022). arXiv:2203.07785 arXiv preprint
23. Kabra, A., et al.: Multi-lingual and multi-cultural figurative language understanding. In: Findings of the Association for Computational Linguistics: ACL 2023, pp. 8269–8284 (2023)
24. Kwok, L., Bravansky, M., Griffin, L.: Evaluating cultural adaptability of a large language model via simulation of synthetic personas. In: The First Conference on Language Modeling (2024)
25. Li, W., et al.: Foodieqa: a multimodal dataset for fine-grained understanding of chinese food culture. In: Proceedings of the 2024 Conference on Empirical Methods in Natural Language Processing, pp. 19077–19095 (2024)
26. Liu, C., Koto, F., Baldwin, T., Gurevych, I.: Are multilingual LLMs culturally-diverse reasoners? an investigation into multicultural proverbs and sayings. In: NAACL, pp. 2016–2039 (2024)
27. Liu, F., Bugliarello, E., Ponti, E.M., Reddy, S., Collier, N., Elliott, D.: Visually grounded reasoning across languages and cultures. In: Proceedings of the 2021 Conference on Empirical Methods in Natural Language Processing, pp. 10467–10485 (2021)
28. Liu, H., Li, C., Wu, Q., Lee, Y.J.: Visual instruction tuning. Adv. Neural. Inf. Process. Syst. **36** (2023)

29. Lucchi Basili, L., Sacco, P.L.: Dance and the embodied social cognition of mating: carlos saura's tango in the perspective of the tie-up theory. Integr. Psychol. Behav. Sci. **59**(1), 31 (2025)
30. Luo, Z., Ren, M., Hu, X.: Popdg: popular 3d dance generation with popdanceset (2024). arXiv:2405.03178 arXiv preprint
31. Ma, T., et al.: Vimva: innovative multimodal recognition in vietnamese folk dance video analysis. In: International Conference on Future Data and Security Engineering, pp. 283–298. Springer (2024)
32. Magomere, J., et al.: You are what you eat? feeding foundation models a regionally diverse food dataset of world wide dishes (2024). arXiv:2406.09496 arXiv preprint
33. Mogrovejo, D.O.R., et al.: CVQA: culturally-diverse multilingual visual question answering benchmark. In: The Thirty-eight Conference on Neural Information Processing Systems Datasets and Benchmarks Track (2024)
34. Nayak, S., et al.: Benchmarking vision language models for cultural understanding. In: Proceedings of the 2024 Conference on Empirical Methods in Natural Language Processing, pp. 5769–5790 (2024)
35. Ouyang, L.: Training language models to follow instructions with human feedback. Adv. Neural. Inf. Process. Syst. **35**, 27730–27744 (2022)
36. Peng, X.: Historical development and cross-cultural influence of dance creation: Evolution of body language. Herança **7**(1), 88–99 (2024)
37. Pfeiffer, J., Geigle, G., Kamath, A., Steitz, J.M.O., Roth, S., Vulić, I., Gurevych, I.: xgqa: Cross-lingual visual question answering. In: Findings of the Association for Computational Linguistics: ACL 2022, pp. 2497–2511 (2022)
38. Singh, A., et al.: Openai GPT-5 system card. arXiv preprint arXiv:2601.03267 (2025)
39. Singh, P.K., et al.: Let's play across cultures: a large multilingual, multicultural benchmark for assessing language models' understanding of sports. In: Proceedings of the 2025 Conference on Empirical Methods in Natural Language Processing, pp. 15205–15252 (2025)
40. Tang, J., et al.: MTVQA: benchmarking multilingual text-centric visual question answering. In: Findings of the Association for Computational Linguistics: ACL 2025, pp. 7748–7763 (2025)
41. Team, G., et al.: Gemma: open models based on gemini research and technology, (2024). arXiv:2403.08295 arXiv preprint
42. Urailertprasert, N., Limkonchotiwat, P., Suwajanakorn, S., Nutanong, S.: Sea-vqa: Southeast asian cultural context dataset for visual question answering. In: Proceedings of the 3rd Workshop on Advances in Language and Vision Research (ALVR), pp. 173–185 (2024)
43. Vayani, A., et al.: All languages matter: Evaluating lmms on culturally diverse 100 languages (2024). arXiv:2411.16508 arXiv preprint
44. Wei, H., Sun, Y., Li, Y.: Deepseek-ocr: contexts optical compression,] (2025). arXiv:2510.18234 arXiv preprint
45. Winata, G.I., et al.: Worldcuisines: a massive-scale benchmark for multilingual and multicultural visual question answering on global cuisines. In: Proceedings of the 2025 Conference of the Nations of the Americas Chapter of the Association for Computational Linguistics: Human Language Technologies (Volume 1: Long Papers), pp. 3242–3264 (2025)

Taxonomic and Functional Augmentation of Ecological Networks Using Large Language Models

Aleksandra Grzelik[1,2(✉)], Karol Opara[1,2], Aniket Thakur[2], Jahnavi Persadh[3], Ursula Scharler[3], and Ulf Dieckmann[2,4,5]

[1] Systems Research Institute, Polish Academy of Sciences, Newelska 6, 01-447 Warsaw, Poland
{agrzelik,karol.opara}@ibspan.waw.pl

[2] Complexity Science and Evolution Unit, Okinawa Institute of Science and Technology Graduate University (OIST), 1919-1 Tancha, Onna, Kunigami, Okinawa 904-0495, Japan
{aleksandra.grzelik,ulf.dieckmann}@oist.jp

[3] School of Life Sciences, University of KwaZulu-Natal, Durban, South Africa
214528400@stu.ukzn.ac.za, Scharler@ukzn.ac.za

[4] Advancing Systems Analysis Program, International Institute for Applied Systems Analysis (IIASA), Schlossplatz 1, 2361 Laxenburg, Austria

[5] Research Center for Integrative Evolutionary Science, The Graduate University for Advanced Studies (Sokendai), Hayama, Kanagawa 240-0193, Japan

Abstract. Ecological networks quantify the strength of interactions between taxa, typically represented by species, genera, or families. While the common names of such nodes are useful in the context of individual networks, they lack the uniformity necessary for meta-analyses. The emergence of Large Language Models (LLMs) presents the possibility to standardise and augment node data based on the common names and contextual information about the network. Here, we compare the resultant performance of four LLMs – ChatGPT 5 Mini, Claude Haiku 4.5, Gemini 2.5 Flash, and Qwen Plus – in conjunction with various prompting strategies. We evaluate the LLMs' node-augmentation results against annotations curated by marine biologists, who also interpret LLM errors. We report the following findings. First, state-of-the-art LLMs achieve an accuracy of over 80% for augmenting taxonomic ranks. Second, augmentation at the intermediate levels of order and class remains particularly prone to errors. Third, querying a domain-specific database, the World Register of Marine Species, using LLMs as translators for scientific Latin names reduces these errors. Fourth, a separate taxonomic pruning prompt curtails the tendency of LLMs to over-specify taxonomic ranks. Fifth, LLM ensembles modestly improve taxonomic accuracy. Sixth, LLMs can augment a rich set of categorical and numerical node characteristics beyond taxonomic information (such as skin covering, buoyancy, and fecundity), which subsequently improves performance in downstream prediction tasks. Finally, we discuss key considerations for achieving reliable and useful data augmentation in ecological research and conservation practice.

M. Baratchi et al. (Eds.): ECML PKDD 2026, LNAI 16949, pp. 479–495, 2027.
https://doi.org/10.1007/978-3-032-37682-4_28

Keywords: Data augmentation · Tabular data · Food webs · Taxonomic resolution

1 Introduction

Food webs represent feeding relationships in ecosystems. They are modelled as directed weighted graphs, with nodes denoting species or higher taxonomic groups as exemplified in Fig. 1. In recent years, considerable effort has been put towards standardisation of aquatic food webs. Development of dedicated software [4] led to the establishment of a unified collection, called EcoBase [5], currently containing 230 downloadable aquatic networks, with an average of 35 nodes, created by different teams of scholars. This opens possibilities to run meta-analyses and derive general conclusions about ecosystem properties, including responses to overexploitation, climate change, or pollution.

Food webs consist of numerical data, namely biomass stocks and consumption flows, as well as unstructured, categorical information about common names. Typically, nodes represent taxonomic aggregations of species, e.g., toothed whales, sharks, or copepoda.

Common names are very useful for understanding the data and case-by-case inspection but lack the unification necessary for data mining and integration with reference databases. Taxonomic resolution addresses this issue by identifying the node within the taxonomic tree. When performed through manual curation, this time-consuming activity involves searching databases or, more often, the literature for specific physiological and ecological characteristics of the node.

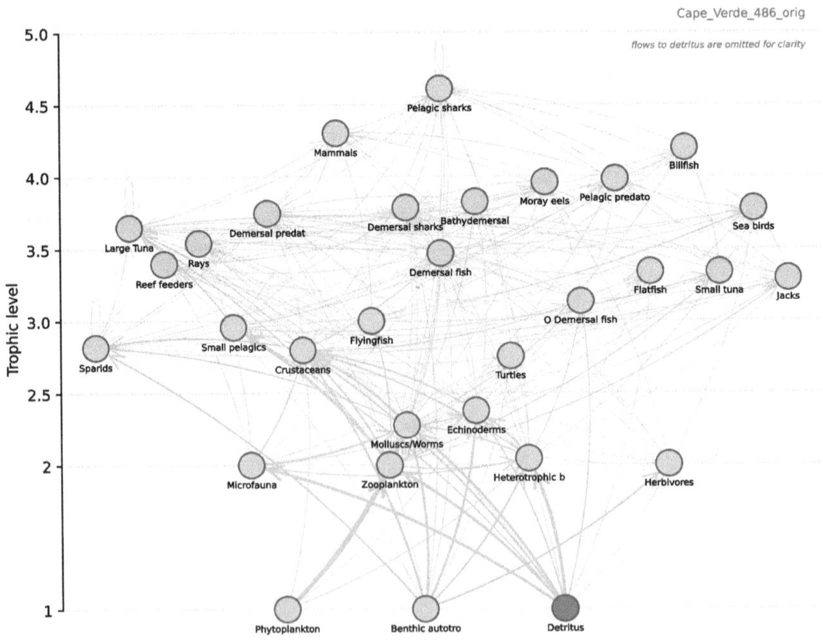

Fig. 1. A food-web example: Cape Verde coastal ecosystem [21]

Assigning species-specific information requires a confident taxonomic identification. In practice, this involves verifying the species name in a trusted taxonomic database, in our case the World Register of Marine Species (WoRMS) [6,24]. Species names in binomial nomenclature (in Latin) can be readily assigned taxonomically, whereas common names that vary geographically for the same species, or node names referring to groups of species, require additional effort to resolve. Successful scientific name resolution enables the adaptation of food-web models for different research and application goals, facilitates interpretation of network modeling outcomes in their ecological context, and allows functional traits to be retrieved from reference databases.

The advent of Large Language Models (LLMs) opens the possibility to support or even automate taxonomic name resolution. Moreover, LLMs can enrich node data with functional traits, including lifespan, fecundity, body size, and activity patterns. This capability could be useful for prediction tasks, the derivation of higher-level aggregates such as ecosystem services, or the exploration of individual nodes, provided the generated data quality is sufficient.

1.1 Contribution

In this paper, we compare four LLMs and various prompting strategies in the well-defined and verifiable task of taxonomic resolution.

To validate our approach and its potential relevance to the ecological community, we worked with marine biologists to annotate a sample of the database, which allowed us to verify the results and to fine-tune our prompting strategies.

This study examines the use of LLMs for extracting domain knowledge in marine ecology in a structured, tabular form. The following findings summarize the main insights:

- Biological data augmentation lies within the practical scope of LLMs reaching relatively high accuracy in taxonomic resolution.
- Integration of LLMs with a domain database improves the quality of taxonomic resolution at the intermediate levels of order and class.
- LLMs tend to over-specify their answers making the performance measures sensitive to the treatment of missing or non-applicable values.
- LLM ensembles provide mild improvements over zero-shot baselines, yet remain prone to propagating over-specified taxonomic ranks.
- Running a separate prompt to prune taxonomy alleviates over-specification.
- LLMs demonstrate a reassuring degree of self-consistency and cross-model consistency among several independent generations obtained with the same prompt.
- LLMs can generate dozens of categorical functional features with relevant information content, which improve node-level prediction tasks.

We outline preliminary steps for evaluating LLM-generated taxonomic and functional tabular data. Finally, a biologist-led discussion identifies the current limitations of LLMs by examining the types of common errors and proposes refinements to maximize the utility of the augmented data for researchers and practitioners in ecology and ecosystem conservation.

2 Related Work

Recent advances in the development of LLMs have positioned them as powerful tools for generating and enriching datasets, with the capability to capture complex data distributions [23], facilitate controllable sampling, and support the synthesis of both numerical and categorical features [11,22]. LLMs possess the semantic reasoning capabilities necessary to interpret structured prompts, learn table schemes, and preserve relational constraints. Consequently, LLMs are able to generate row-level data that is coherent and contextually relevant [7]. Employing multi-model LLM ensembles can enhance the efficiency and reliability of these generation processes [3].

LLMs offer flexible, prompt-driven control over augmentation for different purposes, significantly reducing the reliance on hand-engineered transformations [13]. However, critical hurdles remain, particularly regarding the evaluation of generated data and the mitigation of hallucinations or implausible patterns [15].

The use of LLMs for collation and augmentation of ecological information on species in food webs is gaining momentum among ecologists. Recent efforts investigate their role in network construction [14,17,19], modelling population dynamics [18], and taxonomic verification if species diagnostic features are available [16]. LLMs are also utilized for crowd-sourcing information about species interactions [25], predicting species presence, generating range maps, and estimating numerical traits such as mass, body part size or longevity [8]. Results outperform random guessing, but domain-specific fine-tuning may be necessary.

3 Methodology

3.1 Taxonomic Resolution Task

To create a reliable baseline for the evaluation of augmentation approaches, we downloaded taxonomic lineages from the authoritative database, WoRMS. We randomly selected a subsample of 27 networks (out of 230 available in EcoBase [5]) containing 930 nodes representing taxonomic groups. The input data, consisting of node names and associated metadata, were annotated by a marine biologist using literature resources attached to each network and iteratively checked to ensure quality. We focused on a taxonomic hierarchy consisting of the following levels: kingdom, phylum, class, order, family, genus, and species.

3.2 Data Augmentation Strategies

Given the rapid pace of research [7], we selected a flexible software architecture composed of multiple LLMs detailed in Table 1: ChatGPT, Claude, Gemini, and Qwen. This configuration provides architectural flexibility, allowing the rapid inclusion and evaluation of new LLMs as they appear, facilitates cross-model consistency checks, and enables the application of ensemble methods to support collective decision-making.

We compare four data augmentation strategies illustrated in Fig. 2.

Table 1. The table lists the models' versions and parameters.

Model	Version	Temperature	Output token limit
ChatGPT	5 Mini	not supported	variable
Claude	Haiku 4.5	0.7	4096
Gemini	2.5 Flash	0.7	8000
Qwen	Plus	0.7	8000

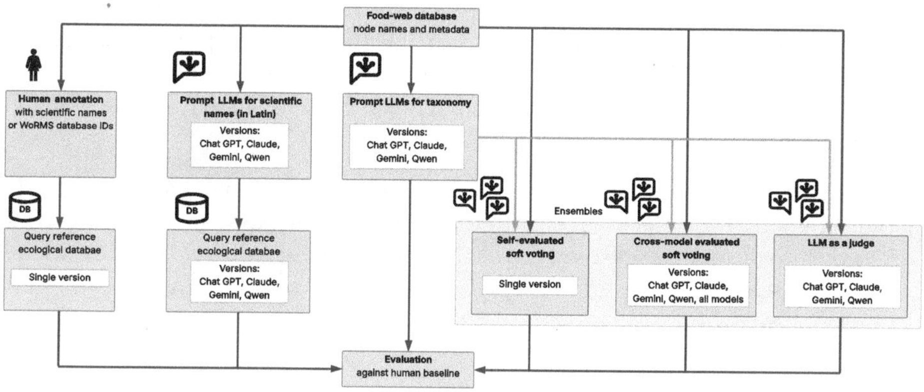

Fig. 2. Taxonomic data augmentation workflow diagram

1. *Human Annotation.* The baseline data are retrieved from the WoRMS database using human-provided Latin names or IDs as keys.
2. *Prompt for Scientific Names.* LLMs standardize and translate common names into scientific names (in Latin), which we use to query WoRMS database for taxonomic lineages.
3. *Prompt for Taxonomy.* We generate taxonomic data by directly prompting an LLM.
4. *Ensembles of LLMs.* We use three types of ensembles, all of which reason from individual responses of constituent LLMs and the network metadata:
   (a) *Self-evaluated Soft Voting.* We ask each LLM to score the confidence of its own answer and apply soft voting to choose the best answer.
   (b) *Cross-Model Evaluated Soft Voting.* Each LLM is prompted to evaluate the remaining responses and assign confidence scores to their answers. The final decision is then obtained through soft voting.
   (c) *LLM-as-a-Judge.* Each LLM acts as a meta-aggregator, producing the most consistent answer based on all model responses. This process is performed independently of confidence scores.

3.3 Prompt Composition

We prompt each LLM to generate taxonomic data, including scientific names, to provide confidence scores for self- or cross-review of the generated results, and to select the best answer. The core part of the prompt is the following:

> You are a senior marine ecologist with over 10 years of experience studying trophic networks, ecological interactions, and environmental drivers of species distribution. I have ecological food web data from marine environments that needs biological and ecological enrichment. Data Source Instructions: [...], Taxonomic & Aggregation Instructions: [...] Provide the taxonomic hierarchy in 7 separate columns: Kingdom, Phylum, Class, Order, Family, Genus, Species, if possible, otherwise insert 'N/A', Current Data: [...], Final Instructions: [...]

The user prompt provides batches of individual node names alongside the metadata about their network of origin. All system and user prompts are standardised across models and available in the code repository. Specific model parameters, selected to leverage the models' full generative capacity, are summarized in Table 1.

3.4 Taxonomic Prunning

Most nodes in our food webs correspond to taxonomic ranks higher than species. For instance, 'pelagic fish' can contain both mackerels and herrings. These fishes share only kingdom, phylum, and class. Hence, during human-expert annotation we left narrower, non-unique ranks (order, family, genus, and species) empty. Similarly, such missing, or not applicable, values can be generated by LLMs. Table 2 details the possible combinations of human baseline and LLM responses.

To mitigate the tendency of LLMs to over-specify by hallucinating overly detailed taxonomic ranks we employ a separate prompt with the following key instruction:

> Provide the most appropriate taxonomic level for the given node, choose from: Kingdom, Phylum, Class, Order, Family, Genus, Species.

Table 2. The presence of missing (not applicable) values in both the human baseline and the LLM-generated taxonomic ranks yields two concordant outcomes (correct matching and true missingness) and three discordant ones (incorrect, over-specified, and under-specified).

	LLM rank		
Human baseline rank	Same as baseline	Different from baseline	Missing
Provided	Correct	Incorrect	Under-specified
Missing	Over-specified		True missing

Taxonomic pruning replaces any ranks in the main prompt's output that fall below this identified level with a missing value.

3.5 Evaluation

To evaluate the taxonomic resolution of LLMs we use two metrics, the overall accuracy, and non-missing accuracy. The former treats missing values as if they were a separate category, while the latter excludes cases lacking a baseline:

$$\text{Accuracy}_{\text{overall}} = \frac{\text{Correct} + \text{True missing}}{\text{Number of nodes}}, \tag{1}$$

$$\text{Accuracy}_{\text{non-missing}} = \frac{\text{Correct}}{\text{Correct} + \text{Incorrect} + \text{Under-specified}}. \tag{2}$$

We calculate the accuracy of LLM-derived taxonomies on each taxonomic lineage level. To estimate the stability, we run 7,000 bootstrap iterations and compute 95% confidence intervals.

As a supplementary task, we investigate LLMs' consistency in generating taxonomic features. We conduct pairwise comparisons, and assess cross-model consistency over multiple independent generations with the same prompt. The consistency evaluation is based on the proportion of exact matches. .

3.6 Functional Traits

To verify the potential of LLMs in augmenting data beyond taxonomy, we prompted Gemini to generate 43 detailed functional traits whose list and levels allowed for categorical variables were initially suggested by an LLM. Responses underwent validation to ensure the tabular structure of the data. Below, we list the first dozen traits requested in the prompt:

1. Life Span: Typical lifespan range in years
2. Activity Patterns: diurnal, nocturnal, crepuscular, continuous
3. Typical Length: Choose from ('0-1','1-5','5-30','30-50','50-80','80-110','110-200','200+') cm
4. Sexual Dimorphism: NO, YES (Male smaller), YES (Female smaller)
5. Fecundity: low, moderate, high, extremely high
6. Water Depth: shallow coastal waters, deep waters (continental slope), benthic (seafloor), coastal benthic zone, epipelagic, mesopelagic, bathypelagic
7. Skin Covering: rough, smooth, mucous, spiny, scaly, smooth with chromatophores
8. Feeding Strategy: filter feeder, carnivore, apex predator, decomposer
9. Reproductive Strategy: oviparous, viviparous, ovoviviparous, broadcast spawning, asexual reproduction
10. Social Behavior: solitary, schooling, solitary or schooling
11. Body Form: fusiform, anguilliform, flattened, globiform, laterally compressed
12. Locomotion Mode: undulatory swimming, oscillatory fins, jet propulsion, drifting

Table 3. Comparison of the prediction tasks

Prediction task	Response levels	Source
Trophic level category	primary producer, herbivore, omnivore plant-preference, omnivore animal-preference, carnivore, top predator	Food web
Feeding guild	benthivore, carnivore, detritivore, filter feeder, herbivore, invertivore, omnivore, piscivore, planktivore, producer, scavenger, other	LLM

3.7 Evaluation of Functional Traits with Predictive Power

In principle, each of the generated traits requires separate evaluation, which exceeds the scope of this study. However, we offer a proxy approach to establish the informativeness of these features by investigating their predictive power.

We analyze two prediction tasks detailed in Table 3, for all 230 networks available in EcoBase [5]. The first concerns trophic levels, discretised into the intervals proposed in paper [20]. This node-level statistic can be exactly computed from the known flow magnitudes within a food web. Additionally, we select a corresponding LLM-generated functional trait describing the node's trophic role. Importantly, the second task may implicitly encode information correlated with the predictor features, which could inflate the resulting performance metrics.

Predictors consist of the node-level features (biomass, import, export and respiration values, in- and out-degree, betweenness, clustering coefficient, along with mean in- and out- degrees of the node neighbors) alone or combined with the LLM-generated functional traits. We used a random forest classifier with 200 trees and balanced class weights. We use grouped five-fold cross-validation, ensuring that all variants from a single ecosystem remain in the same fold, and report accuracy as the performance metric.

4 Results

4.1 Evaluation Is Sensitive to Missing and over-Specified Ranks

We excluded 37 out of 1007 nodes selected for human-expert annotation, as non-living, and an additional 40 as purely functional. The latter group mostly comprised phytoplankton, whose constituent species belong to different kingdoms. Table 4 shows the decreasing counts and percentages of human-expert annotations available for different trophic ranks due to node aggregation in the source food webs.

Despite instructions to omit non-unique taxonomic ranks, most LLMs continued to provide excessive detail. The prevalence of such over-specified responses is indicated by bold percentages in Table 5. Gemini exhibited the greatest restraint. Conversely, nearly half of ChatGPT's answers were below the lowest human-annotated rank. Large fractions of over-specification make results highly sen-

Table 4. The availability of reference annotations decreases with taxonomic rank

	Kingdom	Phylum	Class	Order	Family	Genus	Species
Number	930	707	663	550	472	316	262
Percentage	92%	70%	66%	55%	47%	31%	26%

Table 5. LLMs provide too detailed ranks, bold values denote over-specification

Human annotation	ChatGPT		Claude		Gemini		Qwen	
	Rank	Missing	Rank	Missing	Rank	Missing	Rank	Missing
Rank	26%	2%	26%	1%	26%	2%	26%	2%
Missing	**48%**	24%	**35%**	37%	**11%**	61%	**38%**	34%

sitive to the treatment of missing values and the choice between overall and non-missing accuracy as the evaluation criterion.

4.2 LLMs Provide Promising Taxonomic Resolutions

The heatmaps in Fig. 3 present the overall accuracy, defined by equation (1), for different augmentation strategies without taxonomic pruning. Subpanels decompose the errors according to categories detailed in Table 2. Corresponding results evaluated using the non-missing accuracy (2) are presented in Fig. 4.

Figure 3 (D) shows a pronounced over-specification tendency, especially for narrower ranks. Constraining to non-missing baseline in Fig. 4 provides a clear, complementary view. Directly prompting LLMs to generate the entire taxonomy follows a uniform pattern across different variants and yields similar accuracies. All evaluated methods perform well for the higher-level taxonomic ranks (kingdom, phylum), with accuracies reaching 0.98 in most cases. More specific ranks, such as family, genus, and species, are augmented with overall accuracies of 0.4–0.7 and non-missing accuracies 0.7–0.9. Unexpectedly, the augmentation performance for classes, 0.3–0.35, and orders, 0.4–0.6, are lower than for both broader and narrower ranks due to incorrect responses as shown in Figs. 3 (B) and 4 (B). This drop in accuracy is associated with taxonomy changes as well as assigning terrestrial categories to aquatic species.

Near-zero accuracy for Claude at the species rank reflects its nonadherence to prompt formatting requirements: responding with a string 'multiple', providing numerous names instead of one, and, most commonly, generating only the latter part of the scientific binomial.

4.3 Integration with Domain-Specific Database Regularizes LLM Responses Improving Predictions for Intermediate Ranks

The comparison between purely LLM-based taxonomy generation and the fusion of LLM with domain database highlights the uniformity provided by the hybrid

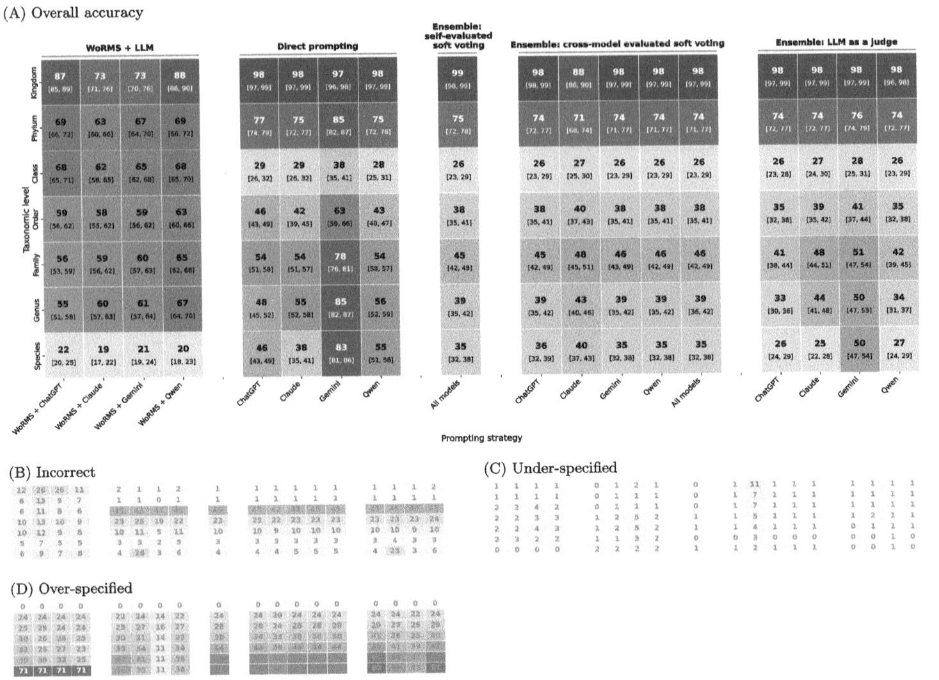

Fig. 3. Overall accuracy (A) is primarily limited by over-specification (B), whereas errors occur mostly at the intermediate ranks of class and order. Cells show percentages for different prompting methods without taxonomic pruning.

approach. Purely generative strategies produce plausible but structurally inconsistent lineages, especially at intermediate ranks (class, order). In contrast, hybridization regularizes the taxonomic data augmentation, ensuring coherence.

The accuracy of a hybrid approach depends on the quality of translation of the node name into its scientific counterpart. If it fails, the taxonomic information cannot be retrieved from WoRMS, which is the main reason behind the weaker accuracy for the lowest and highest ranks than direct prompting. This issue can be addressed by supplementing such missing values with the results of direct prompting for taxonomy. Nevertheless, integration with the domain database makes the intermediate levels of class and order much more reliable.

4.4 Ensembles of LLMs Improve Taxonomic Resolution

Aggregating responses across various LLMs provides consistent improvements in non-missing accuracy and increases the robustness across models. The performance improvements are noticeable at more detailed taxonomic levels, namely: family, genus, and species. The exact way of aggregating a common answer within an ensemble is of secondary importance. The top-performing ensemble strategies are self-evaluated soft voting and LLM-as-a-judge with stronger models (Gemini,

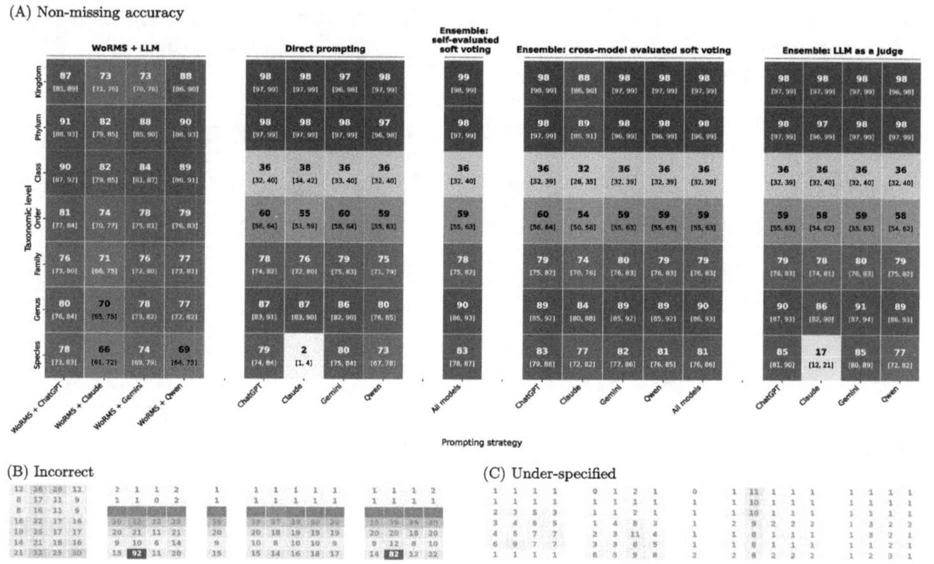

Fig. 4. Taxonomic resolution reaches a promising accuracy (A) of over 80% for direct LLM prompting. Higher errors at intermediate taxonomic ranks (class, order) can be mitigated by integration with domain-specific database. For most categories, ensemble-based methods provide limited improvements over direct prompting.

ChatGPT). Conversely, ensembles tend to vote for over-specified answers rather than retaining missing values, which degrades overall accuracy. Consequently, collective decision-making by LLMs is beneficial only after these hallucinations are mitigated.

4.5 Taxonomic Pruning Reduces over-Specification

Figure 5 presents the preliminary results of taxonomic pruning. The left columns in panels (A) and (B) show the overall and non-missing accuracies of ChatGPT, extracted from the "Direct prompting" sections of Figs. 3 and 4. The right columns display the results filtered by removing ranks below the threshold obtained in a separate prompt. The overall accuracy increases noticeably, demonstrating the utility of this approach. By design, non-missing accuracy (panel B) can only decrease under taxonomic pruning; however, this reduction exceeds 2% points only at the genus level. Finally, panel (C) reports the correctness of the pruning process across different trophic ranks.

4.6 LLM Demonstrate Self and Cross-Consistency

Repeatability of the LLMs' responses is a prerequisite for their high accuracy. On the contrary, discrepancies between independent runs signal less reliable aug-

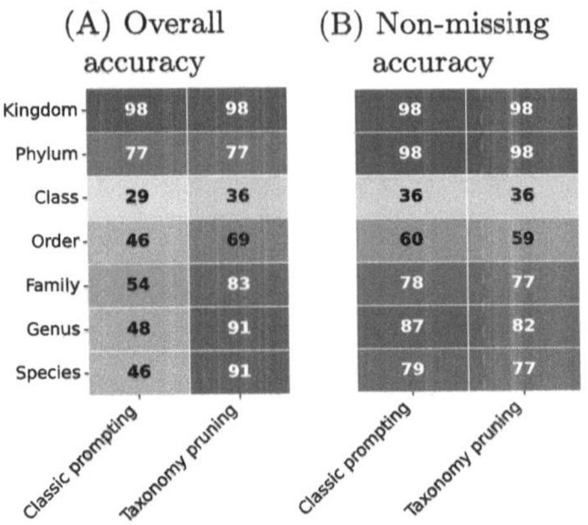

(C) Correctness of pruning across taxonomic ranks

	Under pruning	Correct pruning	Over pruning
Kingdom	203 (91%)	20 (9%)	–
Phylum	18 (50%)	18 (50%)	0 (0%)
Class	21 (17%)	100 (83%)	0 (0%)
Order	17 (22%)	58 (74%)	3 (4%)
Family	15 (10%)	92 (59%)	49 (31%)
Genus	13 (24%)	26 (48%)	15 (28%)
Species	–	227 (87%)	35 (13%)
Total	287 (31%)	541 (58%)	102 (11%)

Fig. 5. Over-specification is reduced by constraining the generated results to the resolution set by a separate prompt. Panels (A) and (B) compare the accuracy of direct ChatGPT prompting with its pruned counterpart, and panel (C) decomposes the pruning correctness across taxonomic ranks.

mentation. With multiple LLMs we can also cross-check the consistency of their answers. We present the self- and cross-model consistency in Fig. 6.

All four LLMs show similar self-consistency for a given taxonomic level, with highest scores for the most general ranks, i.e., kingdom, phylum, and class. For all of the analysed taxonomic ranks, Gemini steadily scores the best with respect to internal consistency. The differences in models' accuracies are not substantial, with the exception of Claude misformatting species names.

The inter-model accuracy is lower than self-consistency, with pairwise comparisons exceeding 80% for all ranks except for order and species. The highest agreement over different taxonomic ranks is observed for the most general taxonomic levels. Overall, the models do not differ from each other substantially.

4.7 LLM-Generated Functional Traits Improve Predictive Power

Figure 7 shows the performance for two tasks, predicting the trophic level categories (computed using food-web data only) and predicting their LLM-generated counterpart, feeding guilds. In both cases, node-level flow values and centralities outperform the majority-classifier baseline. Adding the functional traits generated by LLMs as predictors leads to further, substantially and statistically significant gains of 7 to 23 percentage points. The former result is more likely to generalize to external datasets, whereas the latter improvement may be partially due to the internal consistency of the LLM, which generated both the predictors and the target variables.

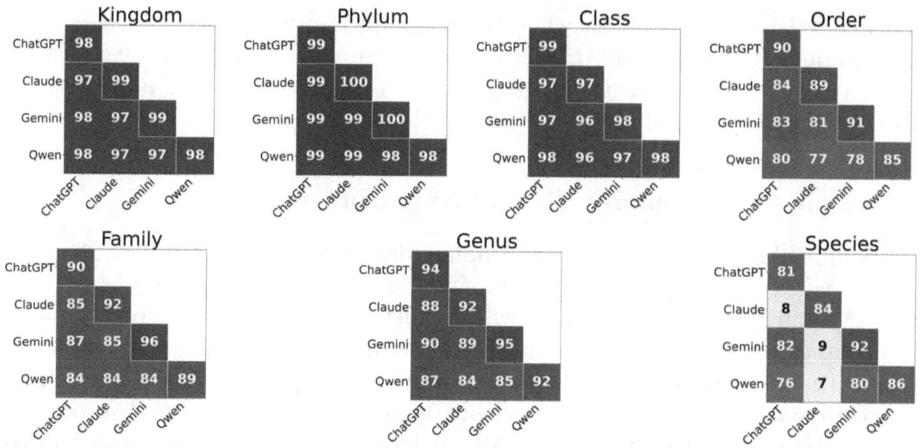

Fig. 6. High self- and cross-model consistencies of LLMs gradually decrease with the taxonomic level. Numerical values present the percentage of exact matches between independent generations from the same or different LLMs.

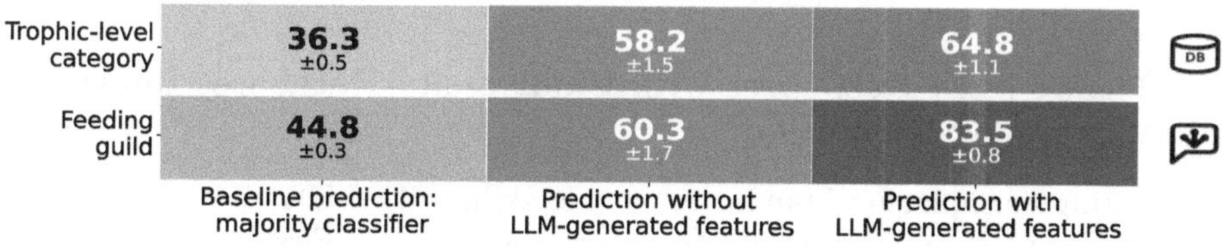

Fig. 7. Inclusion of LLM-generated functional features improves predictive power for node-level classification tasks. The heatmap reports mean classification accuracy (%), with standard deviations reported in percentage points.

5 Discussion

In this paper, we demonstrate that LLMs are capable of large-scale augmentation of food-web nodes. Taxonomic resolution is achievable with over 80% accuracy down to the species level and can be further boosted by taxonomic pruning and using ensembles of LLMs. Challenging cases at intermediate trophic ranks are amendable by integration with reference databases, in which LLMs act as a mapping layer translating natural language inputs into structured taxonomic representations, while the database enforces structural and nomenclatural correctness. We also investigate the self- and cross-model consistency and demonstrate that a rich set of functional features improves node-level prediction tasks.

5.1 Taxonomic Pruning Mitigates over-Specification

Most nodes are defined at intermediate taxonomic ranks, resulting in empty annotations for narrower ranks. However, LLMs tend to over-specify (hallucinate) complete lineages, even when the common name indicates a broader taxonomic rank. Consequently, the evaluated accuracy is highly sensitive to the treatment of missing (not applicable) values. Taxonomic pruning appears to be a straightforward and effective method for limiting this over-specification.

5.2 Evolving Taxonomy Hinders Augmentation

A common challenge is evolving taxonomic databases as new biodiversity information is generated [10]. The taxonomic classification tree is not static, but instead changes over time with new information. For instance, species names may change, or they are placed into new or different higher taxonomic levels. Part of the misclassification of nodes from this study is due to such amendments in the taxonomic tree. For instance, one genus may be split into two or more genera placed in different families. Alternatively, families may be placed in the same order, but warrant another classification layer between family and order, which may result in the addition of new suborders over time. An LLM, therefore, needs to be prompted specifically on a node's old and new classification, which is, e.g., available in WoRMS [24].

5.3 Fusing LLM Responses with Biodiversity Databases Improves Taxonomic Resolution

Augmenting or replacing human taxonomic skills with LLMs has proven to be promising, yet requires further refinement for two reasons. Firstly, the LLMs have difficulty retrieving correct taxonomic information on common species names. This could be improved by querying databases that specifically house information on common names, such as FishBase [9]. Secondly, aggregated network nodes often represent species from different genera, families, or orders, which makes the placement of such nodes in the taxonomic tree nearly impossible. In such cases, additional information on functional groups should be sought from literature or other databases, for instance, OBIS [2], GBIF [1], or FishBase [9] to complement the aggregated node name.

Our study focused on estuarine and marine food webs. Excluding species from other biomes, i.e., terrestrial species, could further limit incorrect responses. Integrating with species distribution databases, e.g. GBIF, or occurrence records from the literature would offer en even stronger solution. However, these datasets are constrained by global taxonomic gaps and regional biases, particularly regarding deep sea and the Global South.

5.4 Elaboration of Functional Traits Requires Domain Expertise

Various functional traits can be ascribed to species, depending on the main focus of the study, which can be behavioural, physiological, ecological, or organism-related. Some functional traits may be useful for several foci. For instance, diurnal migration of zooplankton up and down the water column in the ocean may be classified as predator avoidance behaviour (migrate downwards during the day), or as a trophic necessity (migrate upwards during the night to feed), and the trait could therefore be classified as an activity pattern or a feeding time. The 43 functional traits generated through LLMs in this study are consequently partially repetitive. A hierarchical classification of traits would promote their higher independence. However, the ecological literature already classifies accepted functional trait groups, for instance, in paper [12], and it is advisable to consult domain-specific knowledge instead of gathering general information.

Not all functional traits are of importance for all types of networks, and therefore could be retrieved selectively. For instance, water depth, feeding strategy, or prey capture strategy are important for trophic relationships, whereas for energy flows, knowledge on reproductive strategy, spawning strategy, or parental investment is useful information.

Lastly, the verification of matching nodes with their functional traits would require some level of human intervention. In addition, human expertise may be useful to assign certain functional traits to nodes if information can not be retrieved. An evaluation of the types of traits that are matched to the different levels of the taxonomic tree might provide insight into how accuracy changes with taxonomic level and trait type.

We have also tried prompting LLMs for links to the source data to facilitate human verification. However, most links were missing, not detailed enough (containing just the host) or incorrect.

6 Conclusions

This paper establishes that LLMs available in early 2026 serve as a relatively robust tool for ecological data standardization and augmentation, complementing expert knowledge and facilitating metaanalyses of food webs.

We show that LLMs can standardize informative yet inconsistent node labels, enabling the integration with reference ecological databases. This combined approach complements approaches based solely on LLM prompting and bolsters confidence in the quality of the results. While language models exhibit a strong tendency to over-specify results by providing overly detailed ranks, this issue can be mitigated through taxonomic pruning – using a separate prompt to establish the appropriate resolution. Ensemble methods further improve accuracy and robustness, but are also prone to propagating these over-specified solutions.

LLMs are capable of generating a rich set of data reflecting detailed functional traits in an analytically convenient tabular form. While a detailed evaluation of their quality is left for further studies, we demonstrate the practical value of such augmentation via significant improvements in various prediction tasks.

Finally, we outline steps needed to realize the full promise of the augmentation, namely: including careful selection of the functional traits and their levels, balancing between the detailed and synthetic information, fusion with reference databases, the introduction of partially and fully automated quality assurance, and carefully designing evaluation criteria.

Acknowledgments. UD gratefully acknowledges funding from the National Member Organizations that support IIASA, from the European Union's Horizon 2020 research and innovation funding programme for the projects Plant-FATE (grant no. 841283) and COMFORT (grant no. 820989; the work reflects only the authors' view, and the European Commission and their executive agency are not responsible for any use that may be made of the information the work contains), from the Japanese Society for the Promotion of Science for a KAKENHI Start-up project (grant no. 22K21333) and a KAKENHI C project (grant no. 23K11510), and from the OIST COI-NEXT Global Bioconvergence Center of Innovation supported by the Japan Science and Technology Agency (grant no. JPMJPF2205). AG and AT gratefully acknowledge the institutional support and research environment provided during their internship at the Okinawa Institute of Science and Technology (OIST). We used AI for grammatical and stylistic correction of the text.

Data Availibility Statement. Source code and data used within this study are available at https://github.com/agrzelik/Evaluating-LLMs-for-taxonomic-and-trait-augmentation-in-food-webs.

Disclosure of Interests. The authors have no competing interests to declare that are relevant to the content of this article.

References

1. GBIF: The global biodiversity information facility (2026). https://www.gbif.org
2. OBIS: Ocean biodiversity information systems (2026). https://obis.org
3. Chen, Z., et al.: Harnessing multiple large language models: A survey on LLM ensemble (2026). https://arxiv.org/abs/2502.18036
4. Christensen, V., Pauly, D.: Ecopath II–a software for balancing steady-state ecosystem models and calculating network characteristics. Ecol. Model. **61**(3–4), 169–185 (1992)
5. Colléter, M., et al.: Ecobase: a repository solution to gather and communicate information from EWE models (2013). https://doi.org/10.14288/1.0354309
6. Costello, M.J., May, R.M., Stork, N.E.: Can we name Earth's species before they go extinct? Science **339**(6118), 413–416 (2013). https://doi.org/10.1126/science.1230318
7. Ding, B., et al.: Data augmentation using large language models: Data perspectives, learning paradigms and challenges (2024). https://arxiv.org/abs/2403.02990
8. Dorm, F., Millard, J., Purves, D., Harfoot, M., Mac Aodha, O.: Large language models possess some ecological knowledge, but how much? (2025). https://doi.org/10.1101/2025.02.10.637097
9. Froese, R.: Fishbase. World-wide web electronic publication (2025). http://www.fishbase.org
10. Horton, T., et al.: Tackling temporary names: interim solutions for the taxonomic impediment. Mar. Biodivers. **55**(5) (2025). https://doi.org/10.1007/s12526-025-01559-4
11. Long, L., et al.: On LLMs-driven synthetic data generation, curation, and evaluation: a survey (2024). https://arxiv.org/abs/2406.15126
12. Martini, S., et al.: Functional trait-based approaches as a common framework for aquatic ecologists. Limnol. Oceanogr. **66**(3), 965–994 (2020). https://doi.org/10.1002/lno.11655

13. Nadă, M., Dioan, L., Tomescu, A.: Synthetic data generation using large language models: advances in text and code. IEEE Access **13**, 134615–134633 (2025). https://doi.org/10.1109/access.2025.3589503. http://dx.doi.org/10.1109/ACCESS.2025.3589503
14. Filho, E.N., et al.: Foodwebai: creating and augmenting food webs with natural language models. Preprint (2024). https://foodwebai.shinyapps.io/foodweb
15. Peng, J.L., et al.: A survey of useful LLM evaluation (2024). https://arxiv.org/abs/2406.00936
16. Sahu, N., Baburajan, R., Saravanane, N.: Taxobot: a chatbot for the taxonomy of marine organisms. Expert Syst. Appl. **315**, 131785 (2026).https://doi.org/10.1016/j.eswa.2026.131785
17. Spillias, S., et al.: AI-driven knowledge synthesis for food web parameterisation. Environ. Model. Softw. **197**, 106865 (2026). https://doi.org/10.1016/j.envsoft.2026.106865
18. Spillias, S., et al.: Data-driven discovery of mechanistic ecosystem models with LLMs. Methods Ecol. Evol. (2026). https://doi.org/10.1111/2041-210x.70244
19. Spillias, S., et al.: The future of artificial intelligence in ecosystem modeling. Bioscience **76**(1), 57–70 (2025). https://doi.org/10.1093/biosci/biaf169
20. Stergiou, K.I., Karpouzi, V.S.: Feeding habits and trophic levels of Mediterranean fish. Rev. Fish Biol. Fisheries **11**(3), 217–254 (2002). https://doi.org/10.1023/a:1020556722822
21. Stobberup, K., Ramos, V., Coelho, M.: Ecopath model of the Cape Verde coastal ecosystem. West Afr. Mar. Ecosyst. Models Fish. Impacts Fish. Cent. Res. Rep. **12**(7), 39–56 (2004)
22. Tan, Z., et al.: Large language models for data annotation and synthesis: A survey. In: Al-Onaizan, Y., Bansal, M., Chen, Y.N. (eds.) Proceedings of the 2024 Conference on Empirical Methods in Natural Language Processing. pp. 930–957. Association for Computational Linguistics, Miami, Florida, USA (2024). https://doi.org/10.18653/v1/2024.emnlp-main.54
23. Wang, P., et al.: LLM-AutoDA: large language model-driven automatic data augmentation for long-tailed problems. In: Globerson, A., et al., (eds.) Advances in Neural Information Processing Systems, vol. 37, pp. 64915–64941. Curran Associates, Inc. (2024). https://doi.org/10.52202/079017-2072
24. WoRMS Editorial Board: World register of marine species. Online database (2026). https://www.marinespecies.org. Accessed Mar 2026
25. Zou, H.X., et al.: Large language models unlock the ecology of species interactions (2026). https://doi.org/10.64898/2026.02.06.704115

The Illusion of Success: Procedure-Aware Evaluation is Critical for LLM Agents

Hongliu Cao(✉), Ilias Driouich, and Eoin Thomas

Amadeus, Nice, France
caohongliu@gmail.com

Abstract. Large Language Model (LLM)-based agents are increasingly adopted in high-stakes settings, but current benchmarks evaluate mainly *whether* a task was completed, not *how*. We introduce Procedure-Aware Evaluation (PAE), a framework that formalizes agent procedures as structured observations and exposes consistency relationships between what agents observe, communicate, and execute. PAE evaluates agents along complementary axes (Utility, Efficiency, Interaction Quality, Procedural Integrity) and applies multi-dimensional gating that categorically disqualifies corrupt outcomes. Evaluating state-of-the-art LLM agents on τ-bench yields findings at the axis, compliance, and benchmark levels. At the axis level, the dimensions capture non-redundant failure modes: utility masks reliability gaps, speed does not imply precision, and conciseness does not predict intent adherence. At the *procedural compliance* level, 27–78% of benchmark reported successes are *corrupt successes* concealing violations across interaction and integrity. Furthermore, gating substantially collapses Pass^4 rate and affects model rankings. The analysis of corrupt success cases reveals distinctive per-model failure signatures: GPT-5 spreads errors across policy, execution, and intent dimensions; Kimi-K2-Thinking concentrates 78% of violations in policy faithfulness and compliance; and Mistral-Large-3 is dominated by faithfulness failures. At the benchmark level, our analysis exposes structural flaws in the benchmark design, including task scope gaps, contradictory reward signals, and simulator artifacts that produce accidental successes.

Keywords: LLM agents · Evaluation framework · Procedural integrity · Corrupt success

1 Introduction

LLM-based agents have evolved from single-turn text generators into autonomous systems that coordinate multi-step reasoning, maintain shared state, and invoke external tools for complex real-world tasks [39]. This transition from text generation to task execution marks a fundamental shift in AI system design. It also exposes a critical gap in evaluation methodology [34,37,44]. Current benchmarks assess agents primarily through outcome metrics (binary success rates, terminal-state matching, or tool-call accuracy) [24], while ignoring

M. Baratchi et al. (Eds.): ECML PKDD 2026, LNAI 16949, pp. 496–511, 2027.
https://doi.org/10.1007/978-3-032-37682-4_29

the *procedures* by which outcomes are achieved. This creates a dangerous blind spot: an agent that completes a task by bypassing authorization, fabricating confirmations, or communicating incorrect policy is scored identically to one that follows every required step. Existing evaluation frameworks cannot distinguish these cases because they conflate *what* is achieved with *how* it is achieved.

As agents move into production deployments involving payments, personal data, and policy enforcement, this blind spot becomes a deployment risk. We address it with Procedure-Aware Evaluation (PAE), a framework that formalizes agent procedures as structured observations and evaluates them along four axes (Sect. 3): *what* was achieved (Utility), *at what cost* (Efficiency), *whether the user was correctly informed and well served* (Interaction Quality), and *whether agent actions complied with policies and agent statements were grounded in observed data* (Procedural Integrity). Six-dimension gating across interaction and integrity metrics exposes *corrupt successes*, i.e., task completions achieved through violations that production systems must categorically reject. Applying PAE to τ-bench yields three key findings:

1. **Multi-axis Evaluation.** Evaluating GPT-5, Kimi-K2-Thinking, and Mistral shows the four axes capture complementary, non-redundant failure modes: success rates do not reflect true reliability, speed does not imply precision, conciseness does not predict intent adherence, and integrity is orthogonal to all three (Sect. 4).
2. **Corrupt Success Exposure.** Gating reveals 27–78% of successes are procedurally corrupt, collapsing gated Pass^4 to 2–24%, reversing model rankings, and leaving no model above 24% procedurally compliant reliability. Manual analysis of 131 cases confirms distinctive per-model failure signatures: GPT-5 spreads errors broadly, Kimi concentrates 78% in policy faithfulness and compliance, and Mistral is dominated by faithfulness failures (data and policy faithfulness combined) (Sect. 5).
3. **Benchmark Scrutiny.** The same manual analysis exposes structural flaws in the benchmark itself: task definitions that omit legitimate agent paths, contradictory reward signals, and simulator artifacts that produce accidental successes (Sect. 5.2).

2 Related Work

2.1 Evaluation of LLM Agents

There is a growing body of work on the evaluation of LLM based agents. Recent surveys [24,39] propose multiple dimensions for organizing this space, reflecting the increasing complexity of agent behavior and deployment contexts. Building on these frameworks, we structure the literature around three evaluation objectives: agent behavior, agent capability, and reliability (robustness, safety, fairness) inspired by a recent survey [24].

Agent behavior evaluation examines how well an agent meets end-user expectations through metrics such as task completion and output quality, both of which emphasize outcome oriented aspects [24]. The dominant metrics assess task completion with Success Rate or Overall Success Rate [6,8,41]. Benchmarks such as SWE-bench [17] (resolving GitHub issues), WebArena [44] (web navigation), GAIA [23] (general assistance), and τ-bench [38] (customer service) all prioritize whether the agent reached the correct end state. Output quality metrics (fluency, coherence, factual correctness [11,12,30,42]) extend this to response characteristics. **Procedure-relevant metrics** in this category remain sparse. Latency and cost metrics (Time-to-First-Token, token usage) implicitly measure interaction efficiency (a procedural concern) but are rarely integrated into benchmark scoring [24]. More critically, *how* an agent achieves success (e.g., turns required, clarification burden) is typically unreported.

Capability evaluation targets specific capabilities of LLM based agents, including tool use, planning and reasoning, memory and context retention, and multi agent collaboration [15,32,39]. Tool use evaluation (e.g. ToolBench [27], APIBench [26]) checks whether agents invoke correct functions with valid parameters. Planning metrics (Node F1, Edge F1, Progress Rate) assess whether agents select and sequence tools appropriately [6,7,32]. These metrics are inherently **procedure-focused**: they audit the trajectory, not just the terminal state. However, these trajectory checks assess *functional correctness* (did the agent execute the right tool calls with right parameters?) rather than *procedural conformance* (did the agent communicate right information and respect constraints: authorization, data minimization, escalation protocols?).

Reliability metrics assess consistency across repetitions [21] with metrics such as pass@k and pass^k in [38], and robustness to input perturbations (HELM [20]) as well as to failures handling [31]. Safety benchmarks (Agent-safetybench [43], AgentHarm [1], ST-WebAgentBench [19], CoSafe [40]) evaluate toxicity, bias, adversarial resistance etc. Several works also highlight fairness concerns in agentic systems [3,5,28]. These remain largely **outcome-focused**: reliability tests whether outputs remain stable; safety tests whether agents refuse harmful instructions or produce toxic content. Procedural gaps span several dimensions. Existing evaluations rarely test whether an agent's task-solving procedure is stable, recoverable, or robust; they overlook whether different users experience equitable clarification load or consistent rule enforcement; and they focus on final safety outcomes while ignoring unsafe intermediate actions and privacy risks.

2.2 The Imperative for Procedure Auditing

Despite progress toward interactive and safety-aware benchmarks, existing metrics focus on task success while ignoring whether the agent followed proper procedure. Three structural risks motivate procedure auditing. First, *corrupt success*: an agent may reach the correct terminal state while violating mandatory constraints. Second, *hidden cognitive tax*: a 20-turn success is scored identically to a 3-turn success, obscuring user burden that predicts abandonment [10,35]. Third, *procedural inequity*: agents may apply inconsistent procedures across user populations, demanding additional verification from certain user groups [2,36].

Related work offers partial insights (hallucination detection [14,16], dialogue evaluation [22], task-oriented benchmarks [29]), but four gaps remain. **(1) Fragmented consistency checking**: no framework exposes the full consistency matrix (data read vs. communicated, policy retrieved vs. stated, claims vs. writes, stated vs. executed). **(2) Communication correctness**: agent statements in procedural contexts are *verifiable claims*, not just style preferences. **(3) Missing user-centric dimension**: correct database state paired with user misinformation is invisible to task-centric metrics. **(4) No rejection of corrupt outcomes**: existing frameworks treat all metrics as compensable: violations spanning interaction quality (intent, question fulfilment) and procedural integrity (policy compliance, data faithfulness) can silently coexist with a reported success. PAE addresses these gaps through procedure formalization for auditability, dual task-centric and user-centric evaluation, and integrity gates.

3 Procedure-Aware Evaluation (PAE)

We begin by distinguishing two concepts: procedure and trajectory. A *trajectory* is a sequential log of these events. Conventional trajectories are structurally complete but semantically lossy: they record which tools were called with which parameters, but do not encode whether communications were grounded in observed data, actions conformed to policies, or users received accurate accounts of what occurred [18,33]. Existing trajectory audits therefore verify *action structure* (right tools, right order, right parameters) but cannot verify *action content* (correct data communicated, correct policies applied). A *procedure* is the complete method by which an agent resolves a task: all actions, observations, policies, states, communications, and the consistency relationships among them. We formalize this through a tripartite action model and structured observation space (Sect. 3.1), then define a four-axis evaluation schema (Sect. 3.2).

3.1 Procedure Formulation

Inspired by Decentralized Partially Observable Markov Decision Process (Dec-POMDP) formalizations [25,38], we define the procedure formalization $\mathcal{F}$ as:

$$\mathcal{F} = (\mathcal{E}, \mathcal{A}, \mathcal{O}, \mathcal{T}, \Omega) \tag{1}$$

where $\mathcal{E}$ is the environment state space, $\mathcal{A}$ the action space, $\mathcal{O}$ the observation space (including policy specifications in O^{ctx}), $\mathcal{T}$ the state transition function, and Ω the system observation function (mapping environment state and read actions to system responses).

Environment State. Let $t \in \{0, \ldots, T\}$ denote the time step. We decompose $E_t \in \mathcal{E}$ as $E_t = (E_t^{db}, E_t^{session})$, where E_t^{db} represents persistent stores (databases, payment records) and $E_t^{session}$ captures ephemeral state (authentication status, conversation context). Read actions consult $E_t^{session}$ as a precondition (e.g., verifying authentication) but do not mutate it; only write actions induce state transitions. This enables fine-grained auditing: E_t^{db} changes trigger compliance checks; $E_t^{session}$ provides authorization context for access control verification.

Tripartite Action Model. Agent actions $A_t^{agent} = (A_t^R, A_t^W, A_t^C)$ decompose into: **Read** (A^R), information retrieval (audit: privacy, authorization); **Write** (A^W), state mutations $E_t \to E_{t+1}$ (audit: policy compliance, reversibility); **Communicate** (A^C), messages to users (audit: grounding, hallucination).

Dual-Control Model. User actions $A_t^{user} = (A_{user,t}^R, A_{user,t}^W, A_{user,t}^C)$ use the same tripartite structure: reading (checking status), writing (updating preferences), and communicating (requests, confirmations). The joint space $\mathcal{A} = \mathcal{A}^{agent} \times \mathcal{A}^{user}$ enables *user burden* auditing.

Structured Observations. The observation space $\mathcal{O} = (O^{ctx}, O^{sys}, O^{comm})$ comprises: **Context** (O^{ctx}), static policy specifications and tool schemas (enables: compliance audits); **System** (O^{sys}), dynamic tool responses and API results (enables: grounding audits); **Communication** (O^{comm}), dialogue history (enables: intent adherence audits).

Dynamics. Agents have partial observability: $\Omega : \mathcal{E} \times \mathcal{A}^R \to \mathcal{O}^{sys}$ yields $O_t^{sys} = \Omega(E_t, A_t^R)$. Write actions induce environment transitions $E_{t+1} = \mathcal{T}(E_t, A_t^W)$; read and communicate actions leave E_t unchanged but update observations: read actions produce O_t^{sys}, and communication history accumulates: $O_{t+1}^{comm} = O_t^{comm} \oplus (A_t^C, A_{user,t}^C)$.

Procedure-Complete Trajectory. Given $\mathcal{F}$, the complete agent-user interaction for resolving a task instance produces a procedural trace:

$$\tau = \langle (E_t, O_t, A_t^{agent}, A_t^{user}) \rangle_{t=0}^{T} \tag{2}$$

Unlike conventional trajectory logs that record only tool invocations and returns, τ preserves the tripartite action decomposition and structured observations at every step, making it *procedure-complete*: all consistency relationships needed for integrity auditing are recoverable. This enables **content validation** across four consistency pairs: $O^{sys} \leftrightarrow A^C$ (data grounding), $O^{ctx} \leftrightarrow A^C$ (policy faithfulness), $O^{ctx} \leftrightarrow A^W$ (policy compliance), and $A^C \leftrightarrow (A^R, A^W)$ (execution consistency), operationalized as integrity invariants in Sect. 3.2. A running example illustrating these audits is provided in the supplementary material[1].

3.2 Four Evaluation Axes

PAE organizes evaluation into four complementary axes. Each axis targets a distinct aspect of agent behavior: *what* was achieved (Utility), *at what cost* (Efficiency), *whether the user was well served* (Interaction), and *whether it was proper* (Integrity).

[1] Supplementary material available at https://arxiv.org/abs/2603.03116.

Utility. Utility measures task completion: whether the agent achieves predefined goals [24,39]. How success is measured varies across benchmarks. The simplest approach uses binary terminal-state matching; SWE-bench [17] runs patches against test suites; ScienceAgentBench [8] uses task-specific evaluation programs; AgentBoard [6] adds a continuous *Progress Rate* $\in [0, 1]$ capturing partial advancement. Richer benchmarks like τ-bench [38] support multiple criteria: database checks, status assertions, natural language assertions, and action checks. Metrics such as pass@k and pass^k extend binary success by measuring consistency over multiple trials. Due to the diversity of benchmark ground truths, PAE adopts the success criterion defined by each benchmark.

Efficiency. Efficiency quantifies resources consumed per task: latency, token usage, and monetary cost [24,39]. Latency manifests differently across contexts: Time To First Token (TTFT) matters for streaming interactions, whereas end-to-end latency is more relevant for asynchronous pipelines [39]. Cost, estimated from token counts under usage-based pricing, governs deployment feasibility at scale [8]. Mobile-Bench [9] quantifies efficiency via the number of API calls required. We propose five metrics:

- *Avg #Turns:* total interaction turns (reads, writes, and communications),
- *Avg Duration:* wall-clock time per task,
- *Avg #Tokens:* total token consumption,
- *Avg #Tool Calls:* total read and write actions invoked,
- *Agent Efficiency* (I_{eff})*:* absence of redundant calls, post-completion queries, and irrelevant tool invocations.

The first four are computed automatically. I_{eff} requires nuanced judgment as tasks grow complex and user communication styles diversify. We therefore use LLM-as-judge [4,13] evaluation for this metric.

Interaction Quality. Interaction quality measures user experience during task execution, independent of whether the task ultimately succeeds [10,35]. This axis shifts evaluation from a task-centric to a user-centric perspective: an agent that completes a task while demanding redundant clarifications, overwhelming with verbose responses, or ignoring stated preferences may satisfy a benchmark predicate yet fail in deployment. We define two automated metrics:

$$B(\tau) = |\{t : A^C_{user,t} \neq \emptyset\}| \qquad \text{(user communication burden)} \tag{3}$$

$$V(\tau) = \frac{\sum_t |A^C_t|_{tok}}{|\{t : A^C_t \neq \emptyset\}|} \qquad \text{(agent verbosity)} \tag{4}$$

where $|\cdot|_{tok}$ denotes token count. $B(\tau)$ counts all user turns, indicating clarification effort. Semantic dimensions that require LLM-as-judge evaluation include:

- *Tone appropriateness* (I_{tone})*:* whether all agent messages use professional, non-dismissive language.

- *User intent adherence (I_{intent}):* whether the agent respects explicit user preferences and correctly interprets user-provided information.
- *Question fulfillment (I_{qf}):* whether every direct user question is answered or its omission explained.
- *Identity accuracy (I_{id}):* whether account references match the authenticated session (applicable when agents access user accounts).
- *Personally Identifiable Information (PII) safety (I_{pii}):* whether the agent avoids exposing personal data (applicable in personal-data domains).

Procedural Integrity. Integrity measures whether the agent followed mandatory constraints throughout task execution. We identify four core dimensions, each corresponding to a consistency pair from Sect. 3.1. *Policy Compliance* ($O^{ctx} \leftrightarrow A^{agent}$): did agent actions respect domain rules (eligibility criteria, approval workflows)? *Policy Faithfulness* ($O^{ctx} \leftrightarrow A^C$): did agent statements about policy accurately reflect the actual rules, or did the agent hallucinate non-existent policies? *Execution Consistency* ($A^C \leftrightarrow (A^R, A^W)$): do agent claims match actual tool executions, or does the agent claim to have performed actions it did not execute? *Data Faithfulness* ($O^{sys} \leftrightarrow A^C$): does the agent accurately report data retrieved from system observations, or does it fabricate details such as prices, dates, or confirmation numbers? We formalize these as integrity invariants $\mathcal{I} = \{I_{pc}, I_{pf}, I_{ec}, I_{df}\}$, each yielding $I_j(\tau) \in \{0, 1\}$:

$$I_{pc}(\tau) = \mathbb{K}[\forall t : A_t^{agent} \text{ satisfies } O^{ctx}] \quad \text{(policy compliance)} \tag{5}$$

$$I_{pf}(\tau) = \mathbb{K}[\forall t : \text{policy claims in } A_t^C \subseteq O^{ctx}] \quad \text{(policy faithfulness)} \tag{6}$$

$$I_{ec}(\tau) = \mathbb{K}[\forall t : \text{action claims in } A_t^C \leftrightarrow (A_t^R, A_t^W)] \quad \text{(execution consistency)} \tag{7}$$

$$I_{df}(\tau) = \mathbb{K}[\forall t : \text{data in } A_t^C \subseteq O_{\leq t}^{sys}] \quad \text{(data faithfulness)} \tag{8}$$

When explicit policies are unavailable, agent instructions serve as the auditable specification O^{ctx}. These invariants can be evaluated via programmatic checks for deterministic constraints or LLM-as-judge for semantic consistency.

4 Implementation with τ-Bench

4.1 Experimental Setup

Domains and Models. We instantiate the PAE framework on τ-Bench [38], a widely adopted benchmark for evaluating LLM agents in Tool–Agent–User interaction across realistic task settings. Our experiments focus on two representative domains. In Airline, the agent assists users with booking, modifying, or canceling flight reservations, as well as handling refund requests. In Retail, the agent supports users in managing e-commerce tasks such as canceling or modifying pending orders, returning or exchanging delivered items, updating account addresses, and retrieving product or order information. Each domain includes detailed policy specifications (provided to agents via O^{ctx}) defining authorization requirements, fare/pricing rules, and escalation protocols. We evaluate three diverse frontier LLMs as agents: GPT-5, Kimi-K2-Thinking (hereafter Kimi), and Mistral-Large-3 (hereafter Mistral). Following the τ-Bench protocol, GPT-4.1 is used for user simulators across all experiments. Each task is executed across 4 independent trials ($k = 4$) with different random seeds.

Evaluation Protocol. Automated metrics (turns, tokens, tool calls) are computed directly from trajectory logs. Semantic metrics requiring judgment (I_{eff}, I_{tone}, I_{intent}, I_{qf}, I_{pc}, I_{pf}, I_{ec}, I_{df}) use LLM-as-judge evaluation with GPT-5. The judge takes the policy, task groudtruth information and the entire procedure transcripts, then provides turn-level attribution for failures and outputs structured JSON with schema validation. Crucially, we separate *actions* from *statements*: I_{pc} audits what the agent *did*; I_{pf} audits what the agent *said* about the policy. The full evaluation code will be open-sourced.

Metrics. We instantiate all universal metrics from Sect. 3.2 on τ-bench. Utility adopts τ-bench's success rate definition, with Pass@k and Pass^k at k=4 trials. Where τ-bench provides additional ground-truth signals, we add one benchmark-specific metric: *#Missing Actions* (ground-truth actions the agent failed to perform) under Integrity.

4.2 Experimental Results

Table 1 presents the full PAE evaluation across all four axes. All models achieve perfect I_{id}, I_{pii}, and I_{tone} (1.00) across both domains, confirming baseline deployment requirements; these are omitted from the table.

Utility. GPT-5 leads in success rate across both domains (0.79 Retail, 0.60 Airline). Kimi and Mistral swap ranks across domains: Mistral outperforms Kimi in Retail (0.68 vs. 0.61) but underperforms in Airline (0.40 vs. 0.48), suggesting domain-dependent strengths. The gap between Pass@4 (solvability) and Pass^4 (reliability) exposes a structural concern across all models. These gaps indicate that high single-trial success rates overstate deployment readiness, motivating the procedural analysis below.

Efficiency. Three findings emerge from the efficiency metrics. First, *speed and precision dissociate*: GPT-5 is 4–5× slower than the others (123.6–146.7 s vs. 25.6–50.2 s) yet achieves the highest I_{eff} (0.94-0.98), while Mistral finishes fastest (25.6-29.3 s) but scores the lowest I_{eff} in Retail (0.86). Second, *resource leanness varies by dimension*: Kimi uses the fewest tool calls (6.6-7.0) and fewest tokens in Retail (69.6K); GPT-5 consumes the fewest tokens in Airline (67.0K); Mistral is the most resource-intensive in Retail (27.6 turns, 89.2K tokens). Turn

Table 1. Full PAE results across Retail and Airline domains (k=4 trials). ↑/↓ indicates preferred direction; best per metric in **bold**. All models achieve $I_{id} = I_{pii} = I_{tone} =$ 1.00 (omitted).

Metric	Retail			Airline		
	GPT-5	Kimi-K2	Mistral	GPT-5	Kimi-K2	Mistral
Utility						
Success Rate ↑	**0.79**	0.61	0.68	**0.60**	0.48	0.40
Pass^4 ↑	**0.58**	0.31	0.46	**0.44**	0.28	0.18
Pass@4 ↑	**0.92**	0.83	0.84	**0.74**	0.62	0.62
Efficiency						
Avg #Turns ↓	23.9	**23.8**	27.6	**23.1**	23.2	23.2
Avg Duration (s) ↓	123.6	29.4	**29.3**	146.7	50.2	**25.6**
Avg #Tool Calls ↓	7.8	**6.6**	7.9	8.7	**7.0**	7.6
Avg #Tokens (K) ↓	71.2	**69.6**	89.2	**67.0**	73.1	69.3
Efficiency I_{eff} ↑	**0.98**	0.89	0.86	**0.94**	0.76	0.89
Interaction Quality						
Burden $B(\tau)$ ↓	5.36	**5.23**	7.05	5.27	**4.58**	5.76
Verbosity $V(\tau)$ ↓	119	**67**	80	131	**63**	91
Intent Adher. I_{intent} ↑	**0.98**	0.91	0.85	**0.97**	0.91	0.74
Quest. Fulfill. I_{qf} ↑	**0.98**	0.94	**0.98**	0.96	0.92	**0.99**
Procedural Integrity						
Policy Compl. I_{pc} ↑	**0.91**	0.73	0.50	**0.84**	0.77	0.36
Policy Faith. I_{pf} ↑	**0.83**	0.80	0.66	**0.88**	0.81	0.49
Exec. Consist. I_{ec} ↑	**0.99**	0.97	0.93	0.93	**0.96**	0.79
Data Faith. I_{df} ↑	**0.97**	0.91	0.59	**0.99**	0.91	0.45
#Missing Actions ↓	**0.23**	0.67	**0.23**	0.30	0.70	**0.28**

counts are otherwise comparable (∼23). Third, *judged efficiency is domain-sensitive*: Kimi's I_{eff} drops from 0.89 (Retail) to 0.76 (Airline) due to repeated identical calls, while Mistral's improves from 0.86 to 0.89. These patterns confirm that **no single efficiency metric captures deployment cost**; multi-dimensional assessment is necessary.

Interaction Quality. Kimi imposes the lowest user burden (B: 4.58-5.23) and is the most concise (V: 63-67 tokens/turn); GPT-5 is the most verbose (119-131) yet keeps user burden comparable (5.27-5.36), suggesting its longer responses reduce follow-up turns; Mistral demands the highest burden in Retail (7.05). All models achieve perfect I_{id}, I_{pii}, and I_{tone} (1.00), and I_{qf} is uniformly high (0.92-0.99). The key differentiator is I_{intent}: Mistral scores 0.74 in Airline and 0.85 in Retail, frequently misreading user constraints, while the more concise Kimi maintains 0.91 and the more verbose GPT-5 achieves 0.97-0.98. This confirms that **conciseness does not predict intent adherence**: verbosity, burden, and semantic accuracy each capture a distinct facet of user experience.

Procedural Integrity. Integrity produces the sharpest model differentiation. GPT-5 leads on policy compliance I_{pc} (0.84-0.91), policy faithfulness I_{pf} (0.83-0.88), and data faithfulness I_{df} (0.97-0.99); Kimi occupies the middle ground (I_{pc}: 0.73-0.77, I_{df}: 0.91) and is the only model to surpass GPT-5 on execution consistency I_{ec} in Airline (0.96 vs. 0.93); Mistral is consistently weakest, with I_{df} as low as 0.45 in Airline, fabricating prices, confirmation numbers, and flight details. Missing expected actions (on average) reveal a complementary pattern: Kimi omits more ground-truth actions (0.67-0.70), while GPT-5 and Mistral are comparable (0.23-0.30). Critically, **integrity is orthogonal to the other three axes**: Mistral's efficiency and question fulfillment are reasonable, yet its integrity is the poorest, confirming that no other axis proxies procedural correctness. We analyze *corrupt success* in Sect. 5.

4.3 LLM-as-Judge Validation

LLM-as-judge evaluation introduces potential biases that must be validated. We employ two complementary mechanisms (Table 2).

Table 2. LLM judge validation. *Top*: automatic proxy via action set comparison (excess actions confirm execution-related errors). *Bottom*: human spot-check on 150 randomly sampled assessments. Accuracy = confirmed/total.

Validated Error Type	Total	Confirmed	Accuracy
Automatic proxy (action set comparison)			
`UNNECESSARY_CALL`	67	60	89.6%
`HARMFUL_DISALLOWED_EXECUTION`	171	155	90.6%
Human spot-check (random sample)			
All other error types	150	134	89.3%

Automatic Proxy Validation. Errors such as UNNECESSARY CALL and HARMFUL DISALLOWED EXECUTION require the agent to have invoked an action the scenario did not require. For scenarios specifying ground-truth expected actions ($\mathcal{A}^{exp}$), we compute excess action $\mathcal{A}^{perf} \setminus \mathcal{A}^{exp}$ independently of the LLM judge: a non-empty excess set confirms the agent performed an unauthorized/unnecessary action. This achieves >89% confirmation for both error types (Table 2).

Human Spot-Check Validation. Semantic errors such as POLICY HALLUCINATION lack such automatic proxies because correctness depends on information content rather than action presence. To validate LLM judge reliability on these

Table 3. Standard utility versus gated utility requiring six-dimension compliance. Δ shows the absolute drop; largest drop per metric group in **bold**.

	Retail			Airline		
Metric	GPT-5	Kimi-K2	Mistral	GPT-5	Kimi-K2	Mistral
Success Rate (Original)	0.79	0.61	0.68	0.60	0.48	0.40
Success Rate (Gated)	0.58	0.27	0.16	0.44	0.30	0.09
Δ	−0.21	−0.34	**−0.52**	−0.16	−0.18	**−0.31**
Pass^4 (Original)	0.58	0.31	0.46	0.44	0.28	0.18
Pass^4 (Gated)	0.24	0.04	0.03	0.18	0.06	0.02
Δ	−0.34	−0.27	**−0.43**	**−0.26**	−0.22	−0.16
Pass@4 (Original)	0.92	0.83	0.84	0.74	0.62	0.62
Pass@4 (Gated)	0.87	0.56	0.36	0.68	0.52	0.22
Δ	−0.05	−0.27	**−0.48**	−0.06	−0.10	**−0.40**

and other error types, we randomly sampled 150 judge assessments and verified them manually, confirming 89.3% accuracy. Section 5.2 provides additional human verification through exhaustive manual analysis of all 131 corrupt success cases, achieving 92-95% confirmed judge precision (Table 4).

5 Unveiling the Real Performance Gap

5.1 Corrupt Success: When High Utility Masks Violations

Corrupt success occurs when an agent achieves the correct terminal state through procedural violations. Such a trajectory would be credited as a success by outcome-only evaluation, but PAE identifies it as unsafe (i.e., $U(\tau) = 1$ yet at least one semantic metric equals zero). We capture this through *gated utility* $U'(\tau)$ that requires both task success and full compliance across all six semantic dimensions: four procedural integrity metrics and two interaction quality metrics (User intent adherence and Question fulfillment):

$$U'(\tau) = U(\tau) \cdot I_{pc}(\tau) \cdot I_{pf}(\tau) \cdot I_{ec}(\tau) \cdot I_{df}(\tau) \cdot I_{intent}(\tau) \cdot I_{qf}(\tau) \qquad (9)$$

The remaining interaction quality metrics (I_{id}, I_{pii}, I_{tone}) are omitted from gating because all models achieve perfect scores (1.00) on them across both domains. Table 3 compares standard utility metrics with their gated counterparts.

Analysis. Gated metrics reveal the extent of corrupt success across all three utility metrics: Mistral exhibits the highest corruption rates: 76% of its Retail successes and 78% of its Airline successes involved at least one gating violation. Even GPT-5 shows ~27% corrupt success, indicating that outcome-only evaluation inflates its apparent reliability.

Ranking Reversal. Under standard utility, Mistral outperforms Kimi-K2-Thinking in Retail (0.68 vs. 0.61). Under gated utility, this ranking changes: Kimi-K2-Thinking achieves 0.27 versus Mistral's 0.16. This demonstrates that outcome-only evaluation can produce *misleading model rankings* by crediting procedurally unsafe completions.

Reliability Collapse. Gated Pass^4 drops dramatically: GPT-5 falls from 0.58 to 0.24 (Retail), Kimi-K2-Thinking from 0.31 to 0.04, and Mistral from 0.46 to 0.03. No model reliably completes tasks with full procedural compliance more than 24% of the time, revealing a significant gap between benchmark performance and deployment readiness.

5.2 Manual Validation and Error Profile Comparison

To validate LLM judge reliability beyond the automatic proxies of Sect. 4.3 and to understand the root causes of corrupt success, we manually analyzed all 131 corrupt success cases in the Airline domain across all three models (GPT-5: 32 cases; Kimi-K2-Thinking: 36 cases; Mistral-Large-3: 63 cases). Detailed per-case breakdowns are provided in the supplementary material.

Judge Reliability. Across all 131 manually analyzed cases, manual inspection confirms 93.8–95.2% as genuine corrupt successes (judge precision), with 4.8–6.2% false positives stemming from semantic equivalence mismatches (e.g., "forfeited" vs. "non-refundable") or simulation termination artifacts (Table 4).

Error Profiles Differ Across Architectures. While corrupt success is universal, each model exhibits a distinctive error signature (Table 4). Policy faithfulness (I_{pf}) is a substantial contributor across all models (26–48%), but each model's dominant error type differs: I_{pc} leads for GPT-5, I_{pf} for Kimi, and I_{df} for Mistral. The profiles diverge markedly:

Table 4. Manual validation and error distribution across models (Airline domain). Each model's dominant error type in **bold**. Intent/Question combines I_{intent} (user intent adherence) and I_{qf} (question fulfillment).

	GPT-5	Kimi-K2-Think.	Mistral
Judge Precision	93.8%	94.4%	95.2%
Policy Faith. I_{pf}	29.7%	**47.8%**	26.3%
Data Faith. I_{df}	5.4%	17.4%	**28.4%**
Policy Compl. I_{pc}	**35.1%**	30.4%	24.2%
Exec. Consist. I_{ec}	18.9%	2.2%	14.7%
Intent/Question	10.8%	2.2%	6.3%

- **GPT-5** is the only model where policy *compliance* (I_{pc}, 35.1%) outranks policy *faithfulness* (I_{pf}, 29.7%), indicating that GPT-5 not only misstates rules but executes disallowed actions. It also leads all models in execution consistency failures (18.9% vs. 2–15%) and intent/question errors (10.8% vs. 2–6%), both tied to a recurring pattern of verbally committing to an action after user confirmation without issuing the corresponding tool call.
- **Kimi-K2-Thinking** is dominated by policy-related failures: I_{pf} (47.8%) and I_{pc} (30.4%) together account for 78% of violations, while execution and intent errors are negligible (2.2% each). I_{pf} alone exceeds the other models by 18–22 percentage points.
- **Mistral-Large-3** is dominated by faithfulness failures: data faithfulness (I_{df}, 28.4%) and policy faithfulness (I_{pf}, 26.3%) together account for 55% of violations. I_{df} alone is 1.6–5× that of other two models, manifesting as arithmetic errors in refund calculations and fabrication of flight details.

These model-specific signatures imply that effective LLM-based agent design should be model-specific. Procedural safeguards should be calibrated to the known failure profile of the underlying model.

Benchmark Limitations. Although few in number, a subset of corrupt success cases and false positive cases (in the supplementary material) reveal systematic flaws in the benchmark design itself rather than in the agents being evaluated. Three issues emerge: (1) task definitions omit legitimate alternatives, creating evaluation blind spots; (2) fine-grained natural-language assertions correctly accept the alternative path while coarse-grained database-match checks penalize any state mutation, producing contradictory reward signals; and (3) the user simulator occasionally embeds the termination token in the same message as an action confirmation, preventing execution and producing accidental successes. These findings suggest that benchmark design deserves the same scrutiny as model behavior.

6 Conclusion and Future Works

As LLM agents move into production settings involving payments, personal data, and policy enforcement, evaluation must go beyond asking whether the task was completed to asking whether it was completed properly. We address this gap with Procedure-Aware Evaluation (PAE), a framework that formalizes agent procedures as structured observations and evaluates them along four complementary axes (Utility, Efficiency, Interaction Quality, and Procedural Integrity), with six-dimension gating that categorically disqualifies corrupt outcomes.

Our evaluation of GPT-5, Kimi-K2-Thinking, and Mistral-Large-3 on τ-bench yields some important findings. The multi-axis analysis shows the four PAE axes are genuinely non-redundant: success rates do not reflect true reliability, speed does not imply precision, and conciseness does not predict intent adherence. Taken together, the key implication is that even a model performing well with existing metrics can still fail procedurally. Corrupt success is not a rare edge case but the dominant failure mode, and it is invisible to any single metric. The analysis of corrupt success cases sharpens this picture: failure is not uniform but model-specific (GPT-5 spreads violations broadly; Kimi-K2-Thinking concentrates 78% of violations in policy faithfulness and compliance; Mistral-Large-3 is dominated by faithfulness failures in data and policy faithfulness combined), suggesting that different LLMs produce structurally different procedural weaknesses and that effective agent design should be model-specific. Finally, the same procedural lens that audits agents must also audit benchmarks: the task scope gaps, contradictory reward signals, and simulator artifacts we expose imply that: not only agents but also benchmarks require procedural scrutiny.

Limitations and Future Work. There are several limitations of the proposed PAE. First, the policy dimensions (I_{pc}, I_{pf}) presuppose an explicit O^{ctx}: in domains without formal procedures, these dimensions cannot be evaluated and gating reduces to four dimensions. Even where policies exist, violations of tacit expert norms that resist formal specification remain outside the scope. Learning implicit norms from expert demonstrations or preference annotations would extend policy-aware evaluation to settings where O^{ctx} cannot be directly specified. Second, PAE is a behavioral audit and cannot surface reasoning-level errors in agents that happen to produce correct outputs through flawed inference; logging reasoning traces ϕ_t as part of the procedure-complete trajectory would address this at the cost of increased latency and tokens. Third, the binary gate treats all violations as equally disqualifying regardless of severity; graded gating weighted by operational risk is a natural extension.

Disclosure of Generative AI. Generative AI tools were used to assist with grammar correction and proofreading. The authors take full responsibility for the content and integrity of the submitted work.

References

1. Andriushchenko, M., et al.: Agentharm: A benchmark for measuring harmfulness of LLM agents. arXiv preprint arXiv:2410.09024 (2024)
2. Blodgett, S.L., Barocas, S., Daumé Iii, H., Wallach, H.: Language (technology) is power: a critical survey of "bias" in NLP. In: Proceedings of the 58th Annual Meeting of the Association for Computational Linguistics, pp. 5454–5476 (2020)
3. Cao, H.: Writing style matters: An examination of bias and fairness in information retrieval systems. In: Proceedings of the Eighteenth ACM International Conference on Web Search and Data Mining, pp. 336–344 (2025)
4. Cao, H., Driouich, I., Singh, R., Thomas, E.: Multi-agent LLM judge: automatic personalized LLM judge design for evaluating natural language generation applications. arXiv preprint arXiv:2504.02867 (2025)
5. Cao, H., Thomas, E., Agost, R.A.: When LLMs imagine people: a human-centered persona brainstorm audit for bias and fairness in creative applications. arXiv preprint arXiv:2602.00044 (2026)

6. Chang, M., et al.: Agentboard: an analytical evaluation board of multi-turn LLM agents. In: Advances in Neural Information Processing System, vol. 37, pp. 74325–74362 (2024)
7. Chen, Z., et al.: T-eval: evaluating the tool utilization capability of large language models step by step. In: Proceedings of the 62nd Annual Meeting of the Association for Computational Linguistics (Volume 1: Long Papers), pp. 9510–9529 (2024)
8. Chen, Z., et al.: Scienceagentbench: toward rigorous assessment of language agents for data-driven scientific discovery. arXiv preprint arXiv:2410.05080 (2024)
9. Deng, S., et al.: Mobile-bench: an evaluation benchmark for LLM-based mobile agents. In: Proceedings of the 62nd Annual Meeting of the Association for Computational Linguistics (Volume 1: Long Papers), pp. 8813–8831 (2024)
10. Dixon, M., et al.: Stop trying to delight your customers. Harv. Bus. Rev. **88**(7/8), 116–122 (2010)
11. Driouich, I., Cao, H., Thomas, E.: Diverse and private synthetic datasets generation for rag evaluation: A multi-agent framework. arXiv preprint arXiv:2508.18929 (2025)
12. Es, S., James, J., Anke, L.E., Schockaert, S.: Ragas: automated evaluation of retrieval augmented generation. In: Proceedings of the 18th Conference of the European Chapter of the Association for Computational Linguistics: System Demonstrations, pp. 150–158 (2024)
13. Gu, J., et al.: A survey on LLM-as-a-judge. The Innovation (2024)
14. Huang, L., et al.: A survey on hallucination in large language models: Principles, taxonomy, challenges, and open questions. ACM Trans. Inf. Syst. **43**(2), 1–55 (2025)
15. Huang, Y., et al.: Metatool benchmark for large language models: Deciding whether to use tools and which to use. arXiv preprint arXiv:2310.03128 (2023)
16. Ji, Z., et al.: Survey of hallucination in natural language generation. ACM Comput. Surv. **55**(12), 1–38 (2023)
17. Jimenez, C.E., et al.: Swe-bench: can language models resolve real-world github issues? arXiv preprint. arXiv:2310.06770 (2023)
18. LangChain AI: AgentEvals: Evaluators for LLM agent trajectories. https://github.com/langchain-ai/agentevals (2024), gitHub repository
19. Levy, I., Wiesel, B., Marreed, S., Oved, A., Yaeli, A., Shlomov, S.: St-webagentbench: A benchmark for evaluating safety and trustworthiness in web agents. arXiv preprint arXiv:2410.06703 (2024)
20. Liang, P., et al.: Holistic evaluation of language models. arXiv preprint arXiv:2211.09110 (2022)
21. Liu, B., et al.: Advances and challenges in foundation agents: from brain-inspired intelligence to evolutionary, collaborative, and safe systems. arXiv preprint arXiv:2504.01990 (2025)
22. Mehri, S., Eskenazi, M.: USR: an unsupervised and reference free evaluation metric for dialog generation. In: Proceedings of the 58th Annual Meeting of the Association for Computational Linguistics, pp. 681–707 (2020)
23. Mialon, G., Fourrier, C., Wolf, T., LeCun, Y., Scialom, T.: Gaia: a benchmark for general ai assistants. In: The Twelfth International Conference on Learning Representations (2023)
24. Mohammadi, M., Li, Y., Lo, J., Yip, W.: Evaluation and benchmarking of LLM agents: a survey. In: Proceedings of the 31st ACM SIGKDD Conference on Knowledge Discovery and Data Mining V. 2, pp. 6129–6139 (2025)
25. Oliehoek, F.A., Amato, C.: A concise introduction to decentralized POMDPs 1. Springer (2016)

26. Patil, S.G., Zhang, T., Wang, X., Gonzalez, J.E.: Gorilla: large language model connected with massive APIs. In: Advances in Neural Information Processing System. vol. 37, pp. 126544–126565 (2024)
27. Qin, Y., et al.: ToolLLM: facilitating large language models to master 16000+ real-world APIs. arXiv preprint arXiv:2307.16789 (2023)
28. Qiu, H., et al.: Evaluating cultural and social awareness of LLM web agents. In: Findings of the Association for Computational Linguistics: NAACL 2025, pp. 3978–4005 (2025)
29. Rastogi, A., Zang, X., Sber, S., Guber, L., Khaitan, P.: Towards scalable multi-domain conversational agents: the schema-guided dialogue dataset. In: Proceedings of the AAAI Conference on Artificial Intelligence, vol. 34, pp. 8689–8696 (2020)
30. Reimann, M.M., Oertel, C., Kunneman, F.A., Hindriks, K.V.: Predicting interaction quality aspects using level-based scores for conversational agents. In: Proceedings of the 23rd ACM International Conference on Intelligent Virtual Agents, pp. 1–8 (2023)
31. Ruan, Y., et al.: Identifying the risks of LM agents with an LM-emulated sandbox. arXiv preprint arXiv:2309.15817 (2023)
32. Shen, Y., et al.: Taskbench: benchmarking large language models for task automation. In: Advances in Neural Information Processing System, vol. 37, pp. 4540–4574 (2024)
33. Sigler, I., Nardini, I.: Introducing agent evaluation in Vertex AI Gen AI evaluation service. https://cloud.google.com/blog/products/ai-machine-learning/introducing-agent-evaluation-in-vertex-ai-gen-ai-evaluation-service (2025), google Cloud Blog
34. South, T., Marro, S., Hardjono, T., Mahari, R., Whitney, C.D., Chan, A., Pentland, A.: Position: AI agents need authenticated delegation. In: Forty-second International Conference on Machine Learning Position Paper Track (2025)
35. Sweller, J.: Cognitive load during problem solving: Effects on learning. Cogn. Sci. **12**(2), 257–285 (1988)
36. Thibaut, J.W., Walker, L.: Procedural justice: A psychological analysis. (No Title) (1975)
37. Wang, G., et al.: Voyager: an open-ended embodied agent with large language models. arXiv preprint arXiv:2305.16291 (2023)
38. Yao, S., Shinn, N., Razavi, P., Narasimhan, K.: τ-bench: A benchmark for tool-agent-user interaction in real-world domains (2024). https://arxiv.org/abs/2406.12045
39. Yehudai, A., et al.: Survey on evaluation of LLM-based agents. arXiv preprint arXiv:2503.16416 (2025)
40. Yu, E., et al.: Cosafe: evaluating large language model safety in multi-turn dialogue coreference. In: Proceedings of the 2024 Conference on Empirical Methods in Natural Language Processing, pp. 17494–17508 (2024)
41. Zhang, C., et al.: Large language model-brained GUI agents: a survey. arXiv preprint arXiv:2411.18279 (2024)
42. Zhang, Y., et al.: Llmeval: a preliminary study on how to evaluate large language models. In: Proceedings of the AAAI Conference on Artificial Intelligence, vol. 38, pp. 19615–19622 (2024)
43. Zhang, Z., et al.: Agent-safetybench: evaluating the safety of LLM agents. arXiv preprint arXiv:2412.14470 (2024)
44. Zhou, S., et al.: Webarena: a realistic web environment for building autonomous agents. arXiv preprint arXiv:2307.13854 (2023)

Natural Language Processing and Information Retrieval

From Clickbait to Answers: Spoiler Generation for Multimodal Chinese News Feeds

Haoqian Song[2], Fuwen Zhao[2], Haoran Yin[2], Yiran Du[1], Xuan Luo[1], Xindi Ma[3], and Chaoyuan Zuo[1(✉)]

[1] School of Information and Communication, Nankai University, Tianjin, China
zuocy@nankai.edu.cn
[2] College of Cryptology and Cyber Science, Nankai University, Tianjin, China
[3] School of Literature, Nankai University, Tianjin, China

Abstract. Clickbait headlines on Chinese social media platforms affect hundreds of millions of daily users, yet existing countermeasures stop at detection, flagging content as clickbait without resolving the artificially created curiosity gap. We address clickbait *spoiling*, the task of automatically generating concise answers that satisfy users' information needs without requiring a click-through. To the best of our knowledge, we present CN-Spoil, the first large-scale Chinese multimodal dataset for clickbait spoiling, comprising 9,373 news samples from major platforms such as Toutiao, with human-verified spoiler annotations and internally annotated visual-dependency labels. Our task analysis reveals that while clickbait detection is achievable with text alone, nearly 29% of spoilers can only be resolved through visual inference, as the answer is absent from the text and grounded in the cover image. To meet the strict latency constraints of real-time content moderation, we propose a lightweight Gated Dual-Encoder framework (230M parameters, 27ms latency) that selectively incorporates visual information when the textual context is insufficient. Our approach achieves a ROUGE-L score of 64.55 overall and 74.97 on the visual-dependent subset, compared with only 8.34 for the text-only model, while running up to 45× faster than the evaluated large-model baselines. These results suggest that for clickbait spoiling, task-specific lightweight models with adaptive multimodal fusion offer a more practical path than scaling up general-purpose models.

Keywords: Clickbait spoiling · Content moderation · Multimodal text generation · Chinese social media · Dataset construction

1 Introduction

In the attention economy of digital media, manipulative headline strategies known as "clickbait" are widely employed to maximize user engagement. On

H. Song, F. Zhao, H. Yin and Y. Du—Equal Contribution.

M. Baratchi et al. (Eds.): ECML PKDD 2026, LNAI 16949, pp. 515–532, 2027.
https://doi.org/10.1007/978-3-032-37682-4_30

major Chinese news platforms such as Toutiao, which serves over 120 million daily active users [16], clickbait headlines account for a substantial proportion of content in algorithmic news feeds. These headlines exploit the *curiosity gap* [13] by deliberately withholding key information, compelling users to click through to satisfy their curiosity. While existing systems can accurately *detect* clickbait [1,2], they serve merely as warning labels without resolving the underlying ambiguity. From a user's perspective, the fundamental need is not a warning, but the actual answer.

This limitation motivated the *clickbait spoiling* task, formally introduced in SemEval-2023 Task 5 [5], which reframes the problem as a text generation challenge: producing a concise answer that directly resolves the headline's curiosity gap. Recent efforts have made progress in English clickbait spoiling [7,15], but these works are exclusively text-only. Meanwhile, Chinese clickbait detection has received growing attention [21,23], yet Chinese clickbait *spoiling* remains entirely unexplored.

A key reason this gap matters is that Chinese clickbait exhibits severe visual dependency. In many cases, the headline offers no textual clues whatsoever, and the answer is grounded entirely in the cover image. As illustrated in Fig. 1, when a headline asks "Who is the mysterious guest?" but the article text lacks any specific name, text-only models can only hallucinate. At the same time, not all cover images are informative; many are purely decorative, and naively fusing them into the generation process degrades output quality. This creates a tension: the model must leverage visual information when it is essential, while ignoring it when it is not.

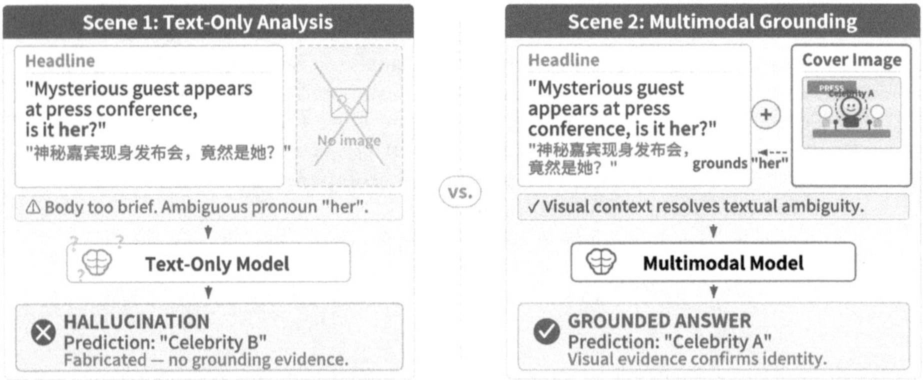

Fig. 1. The core challenge in visual-dependent clickbait spoiling. Given the headline "Who is the mysterious guest?", the text-only model (left) hallucinates an incorrect identity due to missing visual context, while the multimodal model (right) grounds the answer in the cover image.

While Large Multimodal Models such as Qwen-VL [22] can in principle handle this challenge, their computational cost (e.g., over 1,200ms per inference for a 14B model) makes them impractical for real-time content moderation on platforms processing millions of posts daily [8]. To address this, we present the first study on Chinese multimodal clickbait spoiling. We introduce CN-Spoil (Chinese News Spoiler Dataset), a large-scale dataset of 9,373 news samples from three major platforms with human-verified spoilers and internal visual-dependency annotations. We propose a lightweight Gated Dual-Encoder framework that fuses a frozen Chinese-CLIP encoder [25] with a BART-based generator [10] through a learnable gate, incorporating visual information only when the textual context is insufficient. Our main contributions are:

- We construct **CN-Spoil**, the first Chinese multimodal clickbait spoiling dataset, comprising 9,373 instances with internally annotated visual dependency.
- We propose a lightweight **Gated Dual-Encoder** framework (230M parameters, 27ms latency) that adaptively controls visual information flow, achieving strong performance while remaining deployable in real-time content moderation settings.
- We provide an in-depth empirical analysis showing that clickbait detection and spoiling have fundamentally different requirements for visual information, with direct implications for system design.
- We release spoiler annotations, splits, code, and training scripts, excluding internal dependency labels and third-party images.

2 Related Work

Clickbait Spoiling. The study of clickbait has evolved from binary classification using handcrafted features [1] and neural networks [9] toward content resolution. Early detection methods focused on identifying stylistic patterns in headlines, achieving high accuracy but offering no actionable information to users beyond a warning label. Hagen et al. [7] introduced clickbait spoiling as a question-answering task, reframing the problem from classification to generation. This was formalized in SemEval-2023 Task 5 [5], which challenged participants to both classify spoiler types and generate exact answers. Subsequent work explored multitask learning for jointly predicting spoiler types and generating answers [15]. However, all existing spoiling methods are limited to English text corpora, and none incorporate visual information.

Multimodal Text Generation. Clickbait spoiling can be viewed as a form of multimodal text generation, where visual and textual inputs are combined to produce coherent outputs [18]. A common strategy is to extract visual features from pre-trained encoders such as CLIP [17] and feed them into autoregressive decoders. The key challenge lies in fusion: how to combine visual and textual representations effectively. Approaches range from simple feature concatenation, which treats both modalities equally, to cross-attention mechanisms that allow fine-grained interaction but add substantial computational overhead. Gating mechanisms offer a middle ground by learning a scalar or vector weight that controls the flow of visual information. Large Multimodal Models such as Qwen-VL [22] and InternVL [3] unify these capabilities into single generative frameworks, but their computational cost and tendency toward hallucination in open-domain settings [6,19] limit their use in latency-sensitive scenarios.

Chinese Clickbait Analysis. For Chinese social media specifically, research has focused on fake news detection [12,27] and multimodal misinformation identification [26]. Chinese clickbait detection has seen dedicated datasets [21] and multimodal prompt-tuning methods [23]. Recent work has also explored efficient compression techniques for real-time multimodal detection [20]. However, all existing work remains in the detection paradigm. The gap between detection and resolution is particularly consequential for Chinese platforms, where the high volume of content and the prominence of visual elements in news feeds make manual fact-checking impractical.

3 The CN-Spoil Dataset

This section describes CN-Spoil, a large-scale multimodal dataset with human-verified spoilers and internal dependency annotations.

3.1 Dataset Construction

We targeted three major Chinese news aggregation platforms representing diverse content styles: Jiemian News (formal reporting), Toutiao (algorithmic feed with high clickbait density), and Baidu News (comprehensive aggregation). We crawled over 20,000 raw entries from August to November 2025, capturing headlines, article bodies, and corresponding cover images. The three platforms differ noticeably in layout format, image quality, and article length, introducing data heterogeneity that challenges model generalization but better reflects the conditions of real deployment scenarios.

To obtain high-quality annotations at scale without the prohibitive cost of fully manual labeling, we designed a three-stage model-assisted pipeline. In the first stage, we applied linguistic heuristics to detect potential curiosity gaps, retaining headlines containing forward-referencing pronouns or interrogative structures, which narrowed the pool to approximately 15,000 entries. In the second stage, we used Large Multimodal Models to filter and generate candidates: DeepSeek classified each entry as clickbait or non-clickbait based on the headline and article structure, and entries classified as non-clickbait were discarded. For the remaining entries, Qwen-VL [22] generated a candidate spoiler from the full article text and cover image. In the final stage, three trained graduate annotators, all native Chinese speakers with backgrounds in journalism and NLP reviewed each candidate against the original article and image, correcting or rewriting spoilers that were inaccurate, incomplete, or overly verbose. Annotators were explicitly instructed to freely rewrite candidate spoilers whenever necessary, rather than merely editing the generated output. This procedure was designed to minimize potential stylistic bias introduced by the teacher model. To distinguish text-based from visually inferred answers, we computed the Character Overlap Ratio (COR) between the spoiler and the article text, defined as the proportion of spoiler characters that appear in the article body. We set the threshold at 0.65 after iterative manual inspection of boundary cases around multiple candidate thresholds, finding that this value provided the best agreement with annotator judgments regarding visual dependency. The COR threshold was used only to initialize dependency categories; these internal labels were subsequently verified and corrected by human annotators when necessary.

Table 1. Statistics of the CN-Spoil dataset.

Scale and Split		Avg. Length		Modality	
Total Samples	9,373	Headline	25.8 chars	With Image	87.5%
Training Set	7,620	Article Body	3,159 chars	Text-Sufficient	71.0%
Validation Set	847	Spoiler	50.0 chars	Visual-Dependent	29.0%
Test Set	906				
Sources: Jiemian News (52.3%), Toutiao (38.9%), Baidu News (8.7%)					

We assessed annotation reliability on a random subset of 200 samples. A second annotator independently re-annotated these entries in a blind setting. Because exact string matching is overly strict for generative tasks, we evaluated agreement based on semantic equivalence, verifying whether both annotations captured the same core entity or reason. A third annotator adjudicated disagreements. This yielded a raw agreement rate of 82%, comparable to existing English spoiling datasets. Following prior clickbait spoiling work, we report raw semantic agreement because exact span matching is not appropriate for abstractive spoiler generation. Because candidate spoilers were initially generated by Qwen-VL before human verification, the resulting annotations may partially reflect stylistic preferences of the teacher model. Although annotators were instructed to freely revise or rewrite incorrect candidates, future work could further quantify potential teacher-induced biases through fully independent annotation.

3.2 Dataset Statistics and Analysis

Table 1 summarizes the key characteristics of CN-Spoil. The dataset comprises 9,373 verified samples randomly split into training, validation, and test sets. The split was performed at the article level after data collection and annotation, using a random 81/9/10 partition ratio. Duplicate headlines and duplicate article URLs were removed before splitting. Although exact event-level deduplication is difficult for large-scale news data, manual inspection did not reveal obvious near-duplicate event clusters across different splits. Future work may adopt semantic event clustering to enforce stricter event-level separation. The distribution across three platforms ensures broad coverage, and the high visual availability (87.5%) reflects the image-heavy nature of Chinese news feeds. From a generation perspective, the dataset presents a compression challenge: the average article body spans 3,159 characters, yet the target spoiler averages just 50.0 characters. The spoiler length distribution is right-skewed, with most spoilers peaking around 10–20 characters, though a long tail reflects cases where resolving the curiosity gap requires more detailed explanations.

Based on our internal annotations, 2,719 of the 9,373 samples (29.0%) require visual inference, with the answer absent from the article text. This proportion is computed over the entire CN-Spoil dataset and serves as the basis for our visual-dependency analysis. This suggests that text-only approaches face an inherent information limitation on nearly one-third of CN-Spoil instances, since the required evidence is unavailable in the provided text. The dataset covers 11 news domains, with "Finance & Business" (22.0%) and "Society & Livelihood" (19.7%) being the most prevalent. A closer look reveals a notable domain shift between text-sufficient and visual-dependent clickbait (Fig. 2): "Finance & Business" dominates the text-sufficient subset (25.0%) but drops to 14.5% among visual-dependent samples, while "Entertainment" nearly doubles from 9.7% to 17.8%. This suggests that soft news domains rely more on visual curiosity gaps, whereas hard news tends toward textual ambiguity.

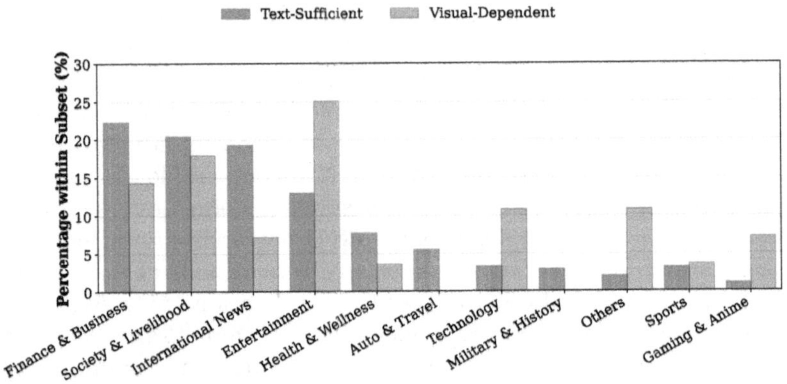

Fig. 2. Domain shift across dependency types. Hard news (e.g., Finance) dominates text-only spoilers, whereas soft news (e.g., Entertainment, Society) shows stronger reliance on visual cues.

Compared with the primary English benchmark Webis-Clickbait-22 [5], CN-Spoil is nearly twice the scale (9,373 vs. 5,000 samples), covers full-length news articles rather than short social media posts, and supports internal visual-dependency analysis with multimodal inputs, whereas Webis-Clickbait-22 is text-only and annotates spoiler types.

3.3 Visual Dependency Analysis

Not all clickbait requires visual information to resolve. Based on our internal annotations, 71% of CN-Spoil samples are text-sufficient, while the remaining 29% rely primarily on evidence from the cover image. In these cases, the spoiler depends on visual evidence that is not explicitly available in the accompanying article content. Consequently, text-only models relying solely on the provided article text are unlikely to recover the correct spoiler reliably, regardless of model scale. This pattern is rooted in how Chinese news platforms operate. Platforms like Toutiao display cover images prominently in the algorithmic feed, occupying more visual space than the headline itself. Publishers exploit this layout by keeping the headline vague while embedding key information in the image, which attracts visual attention but remains difficult to interpret at thumbnail resolution in a fast-scrolling feed.

To obtain a manageable yet representative subset for qualitative analysis, we randomly sampled 369 visual-dependent instances from the full CN-Spoil dataset (approximately 13.6% of all visual-dependent samples). Two independent annotators examined these samples and categorized them into four primary types, while disagreements were resolved by a third annotator. The resulting distribution consists of **Entity Recognition** (47.96%), requiring identification of a specific person or object; **Text Recognition/OCR** (23.85%), where the answer is explicitly written within the image; **Scene Recognition** (20.60%), requiring inference from locations, landmarks, or environmental cues; and **State Description** (7.59%), involving actions, events, or visual states depicted in the image.

These types place different demands on visual understanding. Entity Recognition and Scene Recognition require semantic alignment between visual and textual concepts, a strength of contrastive vision-language models like CLIP. OCR-heavy samples, however, require pixel-level text reading that falls outside CLIP's training objective. We revisit these differences in Sect. 5.

4 Methodology

4.1 Model Architecture

Given a multimodal clickbait instance $\mathcal{X} = \{T, I\}$, where T denotes the textual content (the concatenation of the headline and the article body) and I denotes the cover image, the task of multimodal clickbait spoiling aims to generate a concise textual answer $S = \{y_1, y_2, \dots, y_M\}$ that resolves the curiosity gap. Formally, our goal is to learn a model with parameters θ that models the conditional probability $P(S|T, I; \theta)$ over a multimodal dataset $\mathcal{D} = \{(T_i, I_i, S_i)\}_{i=1}^{N}$. In a real-time content moderation setting, two practical constraints shape the design: (1) the model must operate within tens of milliseconds to avoid becoming a pipeline bottleneck, and (2) it must handle the heterogeneous utility of cover images, since naively incorporating decorative images degrades generation quality (as we demonstrate in Sect. 5).

The core challenge lies in the adaptive utilization of visual information: while some clickbait relies heavily on visual grounding, others are text-sufficient, meaning that naive visual fusion may introduce noise. We address this via a dual-encoder architecture equipped with a learnable gating mechanism.

Text Encoder. The textual input T is formatted using a fixed task prompt, followed by the headline and article body separated by explicit field markers. We employ a pre-trained BART-base-Chinese [10][1] as the backbone. The input is tokenized into a sequence $X = \{x_1, x_2, \ldots, x_L\}$. Rather than encoding X directly into hidden states, we retain the token-level embeddings for subsequent multimodal fusion.

Visual Encoder. For visual representation, we adopt Chinese-CLIP [25], which employs a Vision Transformer (ViT-Base/16) [4] as the visual backbone, pre-trained on large-scale Chinese image-text pairs, ensuring better semantic alignment than the original English CLIP. The visual backbone remains frozen to preserve pre-trained representations and reduce computational overhead. Given an image I, the encoder outputs a global pooled feature $\mathbf{v}_{\text{raw}} \in \mathbb{R}^{d_v}$ ($d_v = 768$). To bridge the modality gap, a trainable linear projection maps the visual features into the textual embedding space:

$$\mathbf{v} = \mathbf{W}_p \cdot \mathbf{v}_{\text{raw}} + \mathbf{b}_p \tag{1}$$

where $\mathbf{v} \in \mathbb{R}^d$ is the aligned visual token, and $\mathbf{W}_p, \mathbf{b}_p$ are learnable parameters.

4.2 Gated Multimodal Fusion

Having obtained the projected visual token $\mathbf{v}$, a straightforward approach would be to directly concatenate it with the textual embeddings. However, as shown in our dataset analysis (Sect. 3.2), only 29% of samples are visually dependent; for the remaining 71%, the cover image is either decorative or redundant. Forcing visual inclusion for all samples introduces noise that degrades generation quality. At the same time, complex cross-attention fusion, while expressive, adds substantial parameters and latency that conflict with real-time deployment requirements.

We therefore introduce a context-aware gating mechanism as a lightweight, dynamic relevance filter. First, we obtain the textual token embeddings $\mathbf{H}_{\text{text}} \in \mathbb{R}^{L \times d}$ from the BART embedding layer. We derive a summary vector $\mathbf{h}_{\text{text}}$ by performing mean pooling over these embeddings to capture the global textual context. We then concatenate this summary with the aligned visual token $\mathbf{v}$ to compute the gating coefficient $g \in (0, 1)$:

$$g = \sigma(\mathbf{W}_g \cdot [\mathbf{v}; \mathbf{h}_{\text{text}}] + b_g) \tag{2}$$

where $\mathbf{W}_g \in \mathbb{R}^{1 \times 2d}$ and b_g are learnable parameters. The coefficient g acts as a relevance filter, scaling the visual token: $\tilde{\mathbf{v}} = g \cdot \mathbf{v}$.

[1] https://huggingface.co/fnlp/bart-base-chinese, a Chinese-adapted version of BART pre-trained on large-scale Chinese corpora.

Table 2. Performance comparison on the CN-Spoil test set. Fusion types: †Concatenation, ‡Cross-Attention, ⋆Gated. **Bold** indicates best in each section. For the visual-dependent subset, we report a representative subset of metrics for conciseness.

Model	Param.	Lat.	R-1	R-L	BLEU	MET.	ChrF	BS
Traditional & Text-Only Baselines								
Lead-3	–	–	22.24	16.04	7.68	27.14	12.75	40.60
BART (Text-Only)	0.14B	<20ms	53.23	49.10	34.34	50.33	32.65	67.23
Large Language and Multimodal Models (Zero-shot)								
Qwen2-VL-7B	8.3B	459ms	33.35	27.68	15.72	36.32	18.08	50.95
Qwen2.5-14B (Text)	14.8B	1210ms	38.25	32.29	22.25	38.19	19.48	55.05
Qwen-VL-Max	–	–	46.10	39.34	28.96	47.02	26.79	60.16
Fine-tuned Multimodal Methods								
mT5 + CLIP†	0.66B	28ms	41.33	37.46	23.75	39.12	21.68	60.13
BART + CLIP†	0.23B	24ms	61.20	58.28	41.57	58.73	41.19	73.03
BART + CN-CLIP†	0.23B	24ms	61.83	58.84	42.41	59.08	41.41	73.55
BART + CN-CLIP‡	0.25B	35ms	50.35	46.33	33.62	49.32	30.95	65.15
Ours⋆	**0.23B**	**27ms**	**66.97**	**64.55**	**50.50**	**64.75**	**49.45**	**77.44**
Visual-Dependent Subset Only (29% of test set)								
BART (Text-Only)	0.14B	–	8.83	8.34	3.72	11.04	11.08	44.34
BART + CLIP†	0.23B	–	72.58	72.36	42.65	69.12	39.04	84.57
BART + CN-CLIP†	0.23B	–	74.35	74.23	47.91	70.57	45.04	85.74
Ours⋆	**0.23B**	–	**75.19**	**74.97**	**50.54**	**71.51**	**48.58**	**86.49**

The modulated visual token is prepended to the textual embeddings, analogous to continuous prefix tokens in prefix-tuning [11], serving as a visual conditioning signal. The fused sequence $\mathbf{H}_{\text{fused}} = [\tilde{\mathbf{v}}; \mathbf{H}_{\text{text}}] \in \mathbb{R}^{(1+L)\times d}$ is fed into the BART encoder, which transforms it into contextualized hidden states. The decoder then generates the spoiler sequence S autoregressively, minimizing the standard cross-entropy loss:

$$\mathcal{L} = -\sum_{t=1}^{M} \log P(y_t | y_{<t}, \mathbf{H}_{\text{fused}}; \theta) \quad (3)$$

Training is conducted on a single RTX 5090 using AdamW [14] ($lr = 3e^{-5}$, 10% warmup, weight decay $1e^{-2}$) for 10 epochs. All experiments were conducted with a fixed random seed of 42.

Deployment Considerations. Our framework operates as a real-time post-processor: an upstream clickbait detection module flags potential clickbait, while efficient multimodal detection has also been explored in prior work [20]. Our model then processes only the flagged subset. Freezing CLIP, using a single visual token, and adding only $2d + 1$ gating parameters limit computational overhead and support low-latency deployment.

5 Experiments and Analysis

We evaluate our method on the CN-Spoil test set (906 samples) against three categories of baselines:

Traditional and Text-Only Baselines. (1) *Lead-3*, which extracts the first three sentences of the article body as the spoiler; (2) *BART (Text-Only)*, a fine-tuned BART-base-Chinese model using only textual input.

Zero-Shot Large Language and Multimodal Models. (1) *Qwen2-VL-7B* [22], a 7B multimodal model prompted with both headline and image; (2) *Qwen2.5-14B*, a text-only 14B model prompted with headline and article body; (3) *Qwen-VL-Max*, a commercial vision-language model accessed via API. All zero-shot models use the same task instruction to generate a concise spoiler from the headline and available context.

Fine-Tuned Multimodal Methods. (1) *mT5+CLIP*, concatenating English CLIP [17] features with mT5-base [24] text representations; (2) *BART+CLIP*, the same strategy with BART-base-Chinese and English CLIP; (3) *BART+CN-CLIP (Concat)*, a controlled baseline using Chinese-CLIP with simple concatenation to isolate the impact of the visual encoder choice; (4) *BART+CN-CLIP (Cross-Attn)*, replacing concatenation with a two-layer cross-attention module between BART hidden states and Chinese-CLIP patch-level features.

Evaluation Metrics. We report ROUGE-1/L, BLEU, METEOR, ChrF++, and BERTScore, all computed at the *character level* following standard Chinese text generation practice.

Latency Measurement. Inference latency is measured as average wall-clock time per sample on a single RTX 5090 with batch size 1, including both encoding and decoding stages.

Table 3. Subtype-level performance on the manually categorized subset of 369 visual-dependent samples.

	Entity	OCR	Scene	State/Action
Ratio (%)	47.96	23.85	20.60	7.59
R-L	50.99	51.37	42.23	45.30

5.1 Main Results

Table 2 presents the results across all models and metrics. Three findings stand out. First, task-specific fine-tuning outweighs model scale: our BART-based models (0.14–0.23B) consistently outperform zero-shot LLMs/LMMs up to 14.8B parameters, as clickbait spoilers require short, precisely grounded answers rather than open-ended generation. Second, gated fusion achieves the best efficiency-quality trade-off, yielding the highest ROUGE-L (64.55) at only 27ms latency. Third, backbone choice matters: the mT5+CLIP variant (ROUGE-L: 37.46) substantially underperforms BART+CLIP (58.28) despite more parameters (0.66B vs. 0.23B), because mT5 distributes capacity across 101 languages whereas BART is Chinese-specific—a gap compounded by English CLIP's cross-lingual alignment overhead. We further break down performance by visual dependency type in Sect. 5.3, where Table 3 reveals that the model's effectiveness varies substantially across entity recognition, OCR, scene recognition, and state description tasks. These subtype results are reported on a separate manually analyzed subset and are intended for comparison across visual dependency types rather than direct comparison with the aggregate score on the visual-dependent test subset.

A natural question is whether the gating mechanism genuinely learns to assess visual dependency, or simply converges to a fixed fusion weight. As shown in Fig. 3(a), the model exhibits a clear adaptive separation: for text-sufficient samples, the gate suppresses visual input with a median g of 0.152, while for visual-dependent samples the median rises to 0.483. This three-fold difference confirms that the gate has learned a meaningful decision boundary rather than settling on a fixed weight. Figure 3(b) further shows that this separation holds consistently across news domains, with soft-news categories like *Entertainment* and *Gaming* exhibiting higher overall gate values and text-heavy domains like *Finance* and *Tech* showing compressed low values—directly mirroring the domain shift identified in Sect. 3.2. This correspondence between data characteristics and model behavior suggests that the gate captures genuine modality relevance signals rather than superficial shortcuts.

To complement the automatic metrics, we conducted a manual evaluation on 105 randomly sampled test instances. Two independent annotators assessed each generated spoiler and categorized it as *correct*, *partially correct*, or *incorrect* based on whether it accurately resolved the curiosity gap. Disagreements were resolved by a third annotator. Of the 105 samples, 90 (85.7%) were judged fully correct, 11 (10.5%) partially correct (capturing the right topic but omitting key details), and 4 (3.8%) entirely incorrect. The incorrect cases predominantly involved misidentified entities in low-resolution cover images, consistent with the visual encoding limitations discussed in Sect. 5.4.

5.2 Ablation Study: Fusion Strategy and Visual Modality

We compare three multimodal fusion strategies in Table 2: concatenation (†), cross-attention (‡), and our gated approach (⋆). The cleanest comparison is

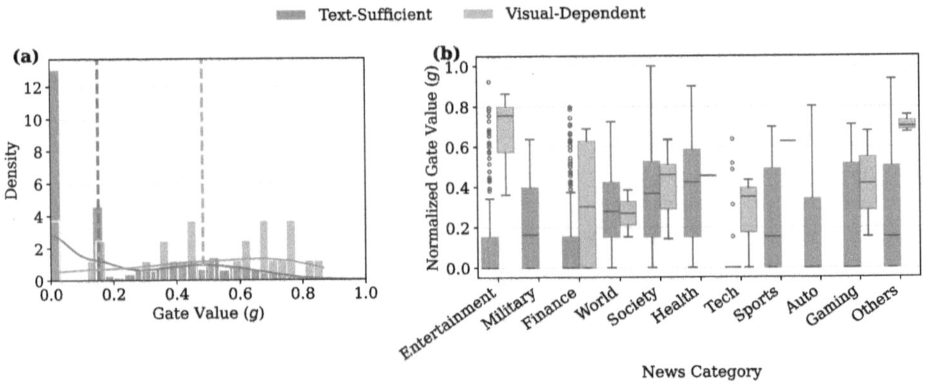

Fig. 3. Gate behavior analysis. (a) The model assigns significantly higher visual weights for visual-dependent samples (median g=0.483) compared to text-sufficient ones (median g=0.152). (b) This separation holds consistently across all news categories.

between our gated model and the cross-attention variant, as both use Chinese-CLIP as the visual encoder. The cross-attention variant (ROUGE-L: 46.33) falls below even the text-only baseline (49.10). We hypothesize that the additional randomly initialized cross-attention parameters are difficult to optimize on a moderately sized dataset, leading to representation drift and reduced utilization of the pretrained BART encoder. Unlike concatenation, which preserves the original input format by simply extending the embedding sequence, cross-attention introduces randomly initialized parameterized interactions at every encoder layer, fundamentally altering the information flow through the pre-trained network. On a moderately-sized dataset (7,620 training samples), these parameters cannot be adequately trained, resulting in representation degradation. To isolate the contribution of the gating mechanism, both BART+CN-CLIP (Concat) and our model use the same Chinese-CLIP visual backbone. The concatenation baseline (BART+CN-CLIP†, 58.84) uses the same visual encoder as our cross-attention and gated variants. The large gap between our gated approach (64.55) and both concatenation (58.84) and cross-attention (46.33) confirms that fusion strategy is the dominant factor. Our gated approach achieves the best ROUGE-L of 64.55 by operating at the input level, preserving the pre-trained encoder while adding only $2d+1$ parameters for adaptive visual filtering.

The visual-dependent subset further confirms the necessity of the visual modality. The text-only model collapses to a ROUGE-L of 8.34, as the required information is entirely absent from the textual input. Our gated model recovers to 74.97 on this subset, exceeding even its overall test set performance (64.55), because the gate assigns substantially higher visual weights to these samples to allow full visual information flow.

The high score on the visual-dependent subset should be interpreted in the context of the benchmark design, where many visual-dependent samples involve concise factual targets such as names, locations, dates, or short textual content grounded in the image.

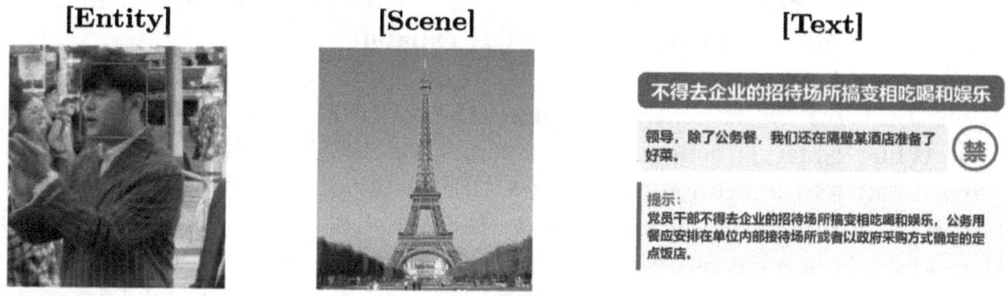

Headline: "The superstar finally shows up..."
✗ *Baseline:* A male celebrity.
✓ *Ours:* Jay Chou.

Headline: "Once called a pile of scrap iron..."
✗ *Baseline:* A building in Paris.
✓ *Ours:* Eiffel Tower.

Headline: "Off-duty officials playing cards or mahjong with friends—a violation?"
✗ *Baseline:* See the image above for details.
✓ *Ours:* Not necessarily, but there are strict boundaries.

Fig. 4. Qualitative examples of visual-dependent clickbait spoiling. (Left) *Entity Recognition*: The model grounds the celebrity's identity from facial features. (Middle) *Scene Recognition*: The model identifies the architectural landmark. (Right) *Text Recognition (OCR)*: The model extracts rules from an infographic when the article body contains only a placeholder. Green indicates successful multimodal extraction. *Image credits:* All panels are author-processed or redrawn versions based on the corresponding news cases; the original third-party cover images are not reproduced.

5.3 Qualitative Analysis

We examined cases where our multimodal model succeeds but text-only baselines fail. As shown in Fig. 4,[2] for *Entity Recognition* (Left), given the headline "The superstar finally shows up...", text-only models hallucinate generic identities while our model correctly generates "Jay Chou" by grounding the answer in facial features from the cover image. For *Scene Recognition* (Middle), our model identifies "Eiffel Tower" from visual features where the article provides only vague historical clues. For *OCR* cases (Right), where the article text redirects with "See the image above for details", our model extracts key information from the infographic and generates the correct answer.

To quantify these patterns, we examined all 22 cases in the test set where ΔROUGE-L > 40 between our model and the text-only baseline. Among the

[2] All three qualitative cases are real news articles from Toutiao: https://www.toutiao.com/article/7615855315276956223/, https://www.toutiao.com/article/7615854869122990634/, and https://www.toutiao.com/article/7533143633587946030/ (accessed Aug.–Nov. 2025).

22 high-gain cases (ΔROUGE-L > 40), Entity Recognition accounts for the largest share (50.0%), followed by OCR (31.8%) and Scene Recognition (18.2%). Notably, most OCR gains were associated with short lexical targets rather than long-form textual extraction, suggesting that the observed improvements should not be interpreted as evidence of full OCR capability.

A finer-grained breakdown by visual dependency type shows that the model performs best on OCR-heavy samples (R-L: 51.37) and Entity Recognition (50.99). While Entity Recognition naturally benefits from the semantic image-text alignment learned during Chinese-CLIP pre-training, the strong OCR performance is more surprising given that the model does not contain an explicit OCR module. Scene Recognition (42.23) and State/Action (45.30) remain more challenging, as they require holistic visual reasoning beyond object-level matching.

Interestingly, OCR achieves the highest subtype score despite the absence of an explicit OCR module and despite OCR falling outside the primary training objective of CLIP-style models. Manual inspection suggests that many OCR-dependent samples involve short and visually salient lexical outputs, such as names, dates, prices, or policy rules, with limited lexical variation. Such targets are comparatively easy to evaluate under overlap-based metrics such as ROUGE once the relevant visual region is aligned with the textual context. By contrast, Scene Recognition and State/Action categories often require richer semantic reasoning and broader contextual interpretation. Nevertheless, our model is not a dedicated OCR system, and performance may degrade substantially on images containing dense text, small fonts, or complex document layouts.

5.4 Error Analysis

Despite the overall improvements, several recurring failure modes remain.

Focus Misalignment occurs in compound clickbait containing multiple questions. When a headline asks both "who" and "why", the model occasionally addresses the secondary clause rather than the primary curiosity gap, producing factually correct but off-target answers. This suggests the need for explicit interrogative focus identification in multi-clause headlines.

Tautological Generation appears in long-context scenarios requiring multi-hop coreference resolution. Given "Who was using a mobile phone to live-stream?", the ground truth is "Congressmen", but the model outputs "Someone was live-streaming"—rephrasing the question rather than resolving it. This failure is more prevalent in articles exceeding 4,000 characters, where relevant evidence is scattered across distant paragraphs.

Visual Detail Loss arises in OCR-heavy and fine-grained entity recognition cases. Because Chinese-CLIP processes images at a fixed resolution of 224×224 and produces a single global representation, small textual content or subtle visual cues may be lost during encoding. In these cases, the model may correctly identify the overall topic while failing to recover the exact entity name, date, number, or phrase required by the spoiler.

6 Discussion

6.1 A Practical Pipeline for Combating Clickbait

Based on our findings, we propose a three-stage pipeline for real-world content governance, as illustrated in Fig. 5. The pipeline is designed around two practical constraints of large-scale news platforms: high throughput and low per-item latency.

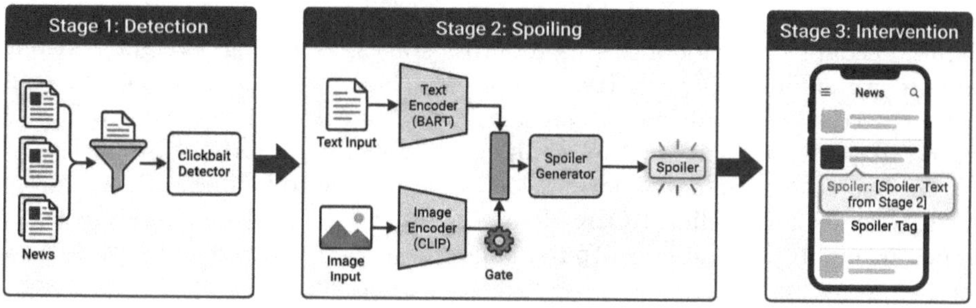

Fig. 5. The End-to-End Deployment Pipeline for Real-Time Clickbait Spoiling. The system operates in three stages: (1) **Detection**: An upstream text-only classifier screens incoming news streams; (2) **Spoiling**: Flagged instances are processed by our Gated Dual-Encoder, which dynamically regulates visual information flow to generate a spoiler; (3) **Intervention**: The spoiler is injected into the user's feed as a visual tag.

In Stage 1, existing text-only clickbait classifiers screen incoming posts at sub-millisecond latency with accuracy above 95%. On a platform like Toutiao, this coarse filter reduces the volume entering the spoiling stage by roughly an order of magnitude, confining the more expensive multimodal computation to flagged posts only. Stage 2 is where our Gated Dual-Encoder operates. At 27ms per item, a single GPU instance can process approximately 37 items per second, or over 130,000 items per hour. For platforms processing millions of new posts daily, horizontal scaling with a small number of GPU instances is sufficient to maintain real-time coverage. The frozen CLIP encoder further simplifies deployment: visual features can be pre-computed and cached during content ingestion, reducing online inference to text encoding and gated fusion only. Stage 3 presents the generated spoiler alongside the original headline, shifting the platform UI paradigm from passive warnings (e.g., "this may be clickbait") to active resolution that neutralizes the curiosity gap directly.

A useful property of this pipeline is its asymmetric failure behavior. Because the spoiling model assumes its input is clickbait, false negatives from Stage 1 (missed clickbait) simply pass through unspoiled, while false positives (non-clickbait flagged incorrectly) receive a spoiler that typically summarizes the article's main point—a degradation that is noticeable but not harmful. This makes the overall system robust to imperfect upstream detection.

6.2 Lessons Learned

Beyond the technical contributions, several practical observations from this work may be useful for practitioners building content moderation systems. During dataset construction, we found that current LMMs serve much better as candidate generators than autonomous labelers. The "generate-then-verify" paradigm significantly reduces human cognitive load—shifting the annotator's task from open-ended writing to targeted verification and correction—and may generalize to other moderation tasks where ground truth requires domain expertise.

At the system architecture level, a key lesson is that moderation pipelines should decouple the modalities used across stages. While lightweight text-only models are sufficient for upstream filtering, the downstream resolution stage strictly necessitates multimodal fusion to cover the visual-dependency tail. Scaling up text-only capacity cannot compensate for missing sensory input.

We also encountered evaluation challenges specific to Chinese spoilers. Standard overlap metrics like ROUGE sometimes fail to capture semantic equivalence in highly condensed outputs, where a single character substitution can preserve meaning entirely. We observed cases where human-judged correct spoilers received low ROUGE scores due to lexical variation, suggesting that future work on Chinese text generation evaluation should incorporate semantic similarity metrics alongside surface-level overlap.

6.3 Limitations and Future Work

The framework is primarily constrained by the frozen Chinese-CLIP encoder, which processes images at a fixed resolution of 224 $\times$ 224. This may lead to information loss for fine-grained visual details, particularly when the relevant evidence occupies only a small region of the image. Although OCR-oriented samples achieve relatively strong aggregate performance in our benchmark, manual inspection reveals that the model still struggles with dense text, small fonts, and complex document layouts, where critical information can become unreadable after resizing. Integrating a dedicated OCR module as a preprocessing step could alleviate these limitations without increasing the complexity of the generative model itself.

A related limitation is the closed-world entity assumption: the model's recognition ability is bounded by what Chinese-CLIP encountered during pre-training, and it struggles with niche or recently emerged public figures. Multimodal retrieval-augmented generation, where the model retrieves relevant entity information from an external knowledge base at inference time, offers a promising direction.

Finally, our current formulation generates a single spoiler per headline, but compound clickbait (e.g., "Who did X and why?") may require structured, multi-part answers. Extending the framework to handle multi-focus spoiling would improve coverage on these cases, which account for a notable share of our observed errors (Sect. 5.4).

7 Conclusion

We presented the first study on multimodal clickbait spoiling for Chinese social media. Our work makes two main contributions: the CN-Spoil dataset, analyzed with internal visual-dependency annotations, and a lightweight Gated Dual-Encoder framework that adaptively incorporates visual information when textual context is insufficient. Through extensive experiments, we revealed a fundamental asymmetry between clickbait detection and spoiling: the former is achievable with text alone, while the latter requires visual grounding for a substantial fraction of real-world cases. Our gating mechanism captures this distinction effectively, achieving strong performance at a latency suitable for real-time content moderation. We release textual fields, spoiler annotations, splits, and code at https://github.com/shq3526/CN-Spoil, excluding internal dependency labels and third-party images. We hope that this benchmark will facilitate future research on multimodal clickbait spoiling, visual grounding, and content moderation for Chinese news platforms.

Acknowledgment. This work was supported by the National Natural Science Foundation of China (Grant No. 62406150) and the National Undergraduate Training Program for Innovation and Entrepreneurship.

Ethics Statement. The CN-Spoil dataset was constructed from publicly available news articles. The release excludes internal dependency labels and third-party images, and contains no intentionally included private or sensitive information. Human annotators participated voluntarily and were appropriately compensated.

Use of AI Writing Tools and Competing Interests. The authors used Claude (Anthropic) for English language editing and proofreading. All outputs were reviewed and revised by the authors, who take full responsibility for the content of this publication. The authors have no competing interests to declare.

References

1. Biyani, P., Tsioutsiouliklis, K., Blackmer, J.: 8 amazing secrets for getting more clicks: detecting clickbaits in news streams using article informality. In: AAAI, vol. 30, pp. 94–100 (2016)
2. Chen, Y., Conroy, N.J., Rubin, V.L.: Misleading online content: Recognizing clickbait as false news. In: ACM WMDD, pp. 15–19 (2015)
3. Chen, Z., et al.: InternVL: scaling up vision foundation models and aligning for generic visual-linguistic tasks. In: CVPR, pp. 24185–24198. IEEE (2024)
4. Dosovitskiy, A., Beyer, L., Kolesnikov, A.: An image is worth 16 × 16 words: transformers for image recognition at scale. In: ICLR (2021)
5. Fröbe, M., Stein, B., Gollub, T., Hagen, M., Potthast, M.: The SemEval-2023 task 5: Clickbait spoiling. In: SemEval, pp. 2275–2286 (2023)
6. Guan, T., Liu, F., Wu, X.: HallusionBench: an image-context reasoning benchmark challenging alignment and hallucination. In: CVPR, pp. 14375–14385 (2024)
7. Hagen, M., Fröbe, M., Jurk, A., Potthast, M.: Clickbait spoiling via question answering and passage retrieval. In: ACL, pp. 7025–7036. ACL (2022)

8. Jin, Y., et al.: Efficient multimodal large language models: a survey. Vis. Intell. **3**(1), 27 (2025)
9. Kumar, V., Khattar, D., Gairola, S., Lal, Y.K., Varma, V.: Identifying clickbait: a multi-strategy approach using neural networks. In: SIGIR, pp. 1225–1228 (2018)
10. Lewis, M., et al.: BART: denoising sequence-to-sequence pre-training for natural language generation, translation, and comprehension. In: ACL, pp. 7871–7880 (2020)
11. Li, X.L., Liang, P.: Prefix-tuning: optimizing continuous prompts for generation. In: ACL, pp. 4582–4597 (2021)
12. Li, X., et al.: A survey of multimodal fake news detection: a cross-modal interaction perspective. IEEE Trans. Emerg. Top. Comput. Intell. **9**(4), 2658–2675 (2025)
13. Loewenstein, G.: The psychology of curiosity: a review and reinterpretation. Psychol. Bull. **116**(1), 75 (1994)
14. Loshchilov, I., Hutter, F.: Decoupled weight decay regularization. In: ICLR (2019)
15. Pal, S., Das, S., Srihari, R.K.: Mitigating clickbait: an approach to spoiler generation using multitask learning. In: ICON 2023, pp. 486–490 (2023)
16. Perdana, A., Bharathi, S.V.: Bytedance's global rise: an exemplar of strategic adaptability and digital innovation in a global context. J. Inf. Technol. Teach. Cases **16**(1), 181–190 (2026)
17. Radford, A., Kim, J.W., Hallacy, C.: Learning transferable visual models from natural language supervision. In: ICML, vol. 139, pp. 8748–8763 (2021)
18. Raffel, C., et al.: Exploring the limits of transfer learning with a unified text-to-text transformer. J. Mach. Learn. Res. **21**, 140:1–140:67 (2020)
19. Sahoo, P., et al.: A comprehensive survey of hallucination in large language, image, video and audio foundation models. In: Findings of EMNLP, pp. 11709–11724. ACL (2024)
20. Song, H., et al.: Dual-path compression for real-time multimodal clickbait detection: quantization and distillation. In: ICASSP. pp, 20526–20530 (2026)
21. Wang, H., Maslim, M., Liu, H.: CA-CD: context-aware clickbait detection using new Chinese clickbait dataset with transfer learning method. Data Technol. Appl. **58**(2), 243–266 (2024)
22. Wang, P., Bai, S., Tan, S.: Qwen-VL: a frontier large vision-language model with versatile abilities. arXiv preprint arXiv:2308.12966 (2023)
23. Wang, Y., et al.: Multi-modal soft prompt-tuning for Chinese clickbait detection. Neurocomputing **614**, 128829 (2025)
24. Xue, L., et al.: MT5: a massively multilingual pre-trained text-to-text transformer. In: NAACL, pp. 483–498 (2021)
25. Yang, A., et al.: Chinese CLIP: contrastive vision-language pretraining in Chinese. arXiv preprint arXiv:2211.01335 (2023)
26. Yu, J., et al.: Multimodal clickbait detection by de-confounding biases using causal representation inference. In: EMNLP, pp, 10300–10317 (2024)
27. Zhang, L., et al.: Early detection of multimodal fake news via reinforced propagation path generation. IEEE Trans. Knowl. Data Eng. **37**(2), 613–625 (2025)

From Rules to Neural Graphs: Scalable Structured Prediction for Patent Prior Art Search

Nikolai Zenovkin(✉) and Sebastian Björkqvist

IPRally Technologies Oy, Helsinki, Finland
{nikolai.zenovkin,sebastian}@iprally.com

Abstract. Patent search requires processing documents routinely exceeding tens of thousands of tokens. Most neural retrieval approaches operate on truncated inputs, limiting their effectiveness. Graph-based retrieval addresses this by representing each patent as a structured *invention graph*, but constructing these graphs relies on brittle rule-based parsers. We present the *neural parser*, which adapts biaffine attention from dependency parsing to predict invention graphs directly from patent text. Our *local biaffine attention* restricts pairwise scoring to a sliding window, reducing complexity from $O(n^2)$ to $O(n \cdot w)$. Since local and global scoring share the same weights, the model trains on short sequences and deploys on documents exceeding 40,000 tokens without retraining. Distilled from 1 million rule-parsed documents, it surpasses its teacher at 3× lower inference cost: neural graphs improve citation recall by 0.5% on short queries and 1.1% on full documents in a downstream Graph Transformer retrieval system.

Keywords: Patent search · Prior art search · Information retrieval · Dense retrieval · Structured prediction · Long document processing · Biaffine attention · Knowledge distillation · Natural language processing

1 Introduction

Patent prior art search—identifying existing publications that may anticipate or render obvious a patent application's claims—is essential in intellectual property law. Traditional Boolean keyword search [4,6] requires substantial domain expertise and multiple iterations, as similar concepts may use entirely different terminology across patent documents.

Dense Retrieval for Patents. Neural dense retrieval models overcome terminology variation by learning semantic representations [1,9,11], but face a fundamental length constraint: patent documents are extremely long. In our training corpus of 1 million patent documents, descriptions average 55,000 characters (median: 40,000), with the 90th percentile at 104,000 characters. Current models process only truncated inputs—typically titles and abstracts [1,9,11]—sacrificing coverage of claim-relevant content in the full text.

M. Baratchi et al. (Eds.): ECML PKDD 2026, LNAI 16949, pp. 533–549, 2027.
https://doi.org/10.1007/978-3-032-37682-4_31

Graph-Based Compression. Invention graphs address this by extracting core technical features and organizing them hierarchically [3], compressing patents into structured representations suitable for neural processing. Graph Transformers [5] process these structures via sparse attention over graph edges, enabling effective handling of documents exceeding 40,000 tokens—far beyond what standard dense retrieval supports [22] (Fig. 1).

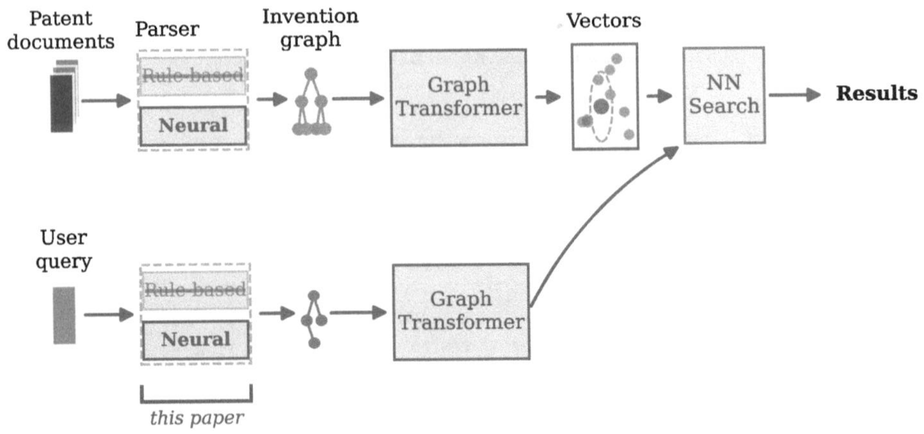

Fig. 1. End-to-end patent prior art search pipeline. Patent documents and user queries are parsed into invention graphs, encoded by a Graph Transformer [5] into dense vectors, and matched via nearest neighbor search. This work replaces the rule-based parser with a neural alternative (highlighted).

The Rule-Based Bottleneck. Existing graph-based patent search systems [3,5] rely entirely on rule-based parsers with extensive hand-crafted patterns. While achieving high precision on matched patterns, these parsers suffer from brittleness: they fail silently on novel linguistic constructions and require continuous manual curation as patent language evolves. A natural alternative is a learned graph induction model, but standard neural structured prediction methods—such as biaffine dependency parsers [7]—require scoring all $O(n^2)$ token pairs, making them intractable for documents with tens of thousands of tokens. Obtaining labeled training data at corpus scale is a further obstacle: manually annotating graph structures across millions of documents is impractical.

We address both challenges with the following contributions:

- **Scalable structured prediction**: We extend sliding-window biaffine attention [17] from flat span extraction to structured prediction (tree/DAG induction) over full-length patent documents. Crucially, local and global scoring share the same weight matrix, so the model trains on short sequences with global attention and deploys on long documents with local attention—no retraining required.

- **Student surpasses teacher**: Via knowledge distillation on 1 million rule-parsed documents, our neural parser generalizes beyond hand-crafted patterns, improving downstream prior art search over its teacher while offering 3× lower inference cost and flexibility for diverse data sources (human annotation, LLM-generated labels).

To support reproducibility, we release: (1) the evaluation set of 5,000 annotated patent documents used for intrinsic evaluation, (2) a 5,000-document sample from the training set, and (3) the evaluation framework for computing the graph quality metrics reported in this paper.[1]

2 Related Work

2.1 Patent Retrieval and Graph Representations

Dense retrieval is the leading neural approach to patent search. Patent-tuned transformers [1,9], including PaECTER [11], outperform general-purpose models [15], yet recent benchmarks support only 4,096 tokens [14]—far short of typical patent descriptions. LongEmbed [22] confirms that embedding models degrade substantially beyond 2,048 tokens.

Graph-based retrieval addresses this. Invention graphs encoded with Tree-LSTMs [3,16] significantly improve retrieval over bag-of-words baselines, and a Graph Transformer approach [5,8,18] achieves further gains via sparse attention over graph edges. Both systems rely on rule-based parsers—the bottleneck this work addresses. Open relation extraction from patent claims [10] produces flat triples rather than the hierarchical representations required for structured retrieval.

2.2 Neural Structured Prediction for Long Documents

Our formulation adapts biaffine attention from dependency parsing [7], where separate MLPs project words into head and dependent roles and a biaffine function scores pairwise arcs. While biaffine parsing remains the dominant paradigm for syntactic and semantic dependency parsing, existing methods operate at sentence level. DocBAN [17] recently applied sliding-window biaffine attention to document-level NER, reducing quadratic complexity to linear for span extraction. Our work addresses the harder problem of structured prediction—inducing tree and DAG structures via per-word parent selection rather than identifying flat spans—at much longer document scales (40,000+ vs. thousands of tokens).

Processing such long sequences requires efficient attention. Longformer [2] and BigBird [19] introduced sparse attention combining local windows with global tokens in the transformer encoder. We use Longformer as our encoder but introduce sparsity in the biaffine scoring layer—the computational bottleneck for structured prediction. A key distinction from DocBAN, which adds a

[1] Available at https://github.com/iprally/invention_graph_eval.

U-Net module for cross-window context, is that our local biaffine mechanism uses exactly the same weight matrix as global scoring. This weight-sharing property enables training with global attention on short sequences and deploying with local attention on long documents without retraining (Sect. 3.3).

We train via knowledge distillation [12] from a rule-based teacher. Combined with loss weighting (Sect. 3.3), this provides sufficient signal for the model to generalize beyond hand-crafted patterns without manual annotation at corpus scale.

3 Methodology

3.1 Invention Graphs

An **invention graph** represents a patent's technical content as two complementary structures (Fig. 2). The *feature hierarchy* is a tree of technical components organized by part-of and example-of relationships, signaled by terms such as *comprising* and *including. Functional relations* capture cross-cutting dependencies between features via verbal constructions (e.g., "ENGINE *configured to rotate* WHEELS"). Features have a single hierarchical parent but may participate in multiple relations, yielding a directed acyclic graph (DAG). In the neural parser, both structures are modeled as per-word parent predictions forming tree-like hierarchies.

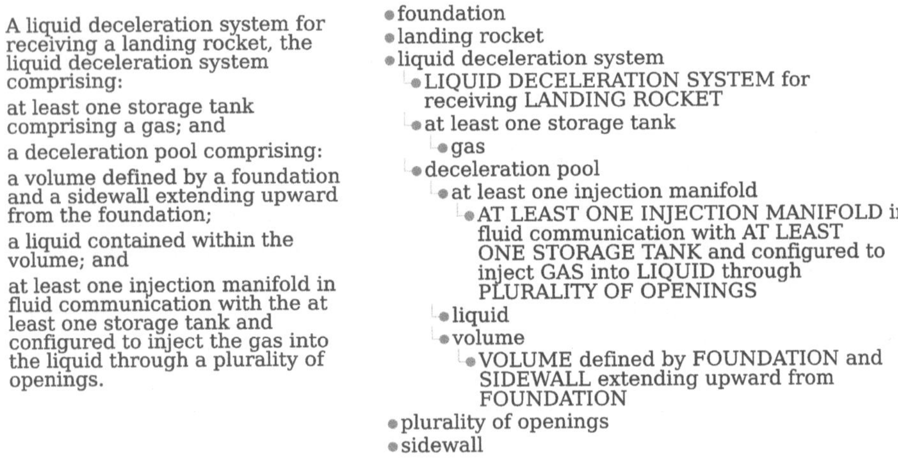

Fig. 2. A patent claim (US20250197034A1) and the corresponding invention graph. Blue bullets denote feature nodes; purple bullets denote functional relations. Indentation reflects hierarchical (part-of) edges. Features referenced inside relations are shown in uppercase. (Color figure online)

Task Definition. The model operates at the word level, predicting for each word: (1) a *parent* in the feature hierarchy (or a pseudo-node for non-graph words), (2) an *edge label* distinguishing within-phrase (syntactic) from between-feature (semantic) edges, and (3) a parent in the relation hierarchy. Syntactic edges are used in postprocessing to assemble multi-word feature spans from individual word predictions. A lightweight regular-expression post-filter then removes boilerplate patent phrasing (e.g., "according to claim 1") that should not surface as feature text.

Architecture Choice. A deployment constraint shapes the architecture: the neural parser must produce graphs structurally identical to rule-based output—same node types, edge labels, and relation format—for backward compatibility and controlled A/B testing in the search pipeline of [5]. This rules out alternative approaches (e.g., NER with heuristic tree assembly, sequence-to-sequence generation) that would produce different graph formats. The per-word parent prediction formulation directly mirrors the rule-based system's output, making biaffine structured prediction [7] the natural choice. Operating at the word level—rather than over entities or sentences—is inherited from this dependency-parsing formulation and keeps the output granularity identical to the teacher's; multi-word feature spans are reassembled from word-level predictions in postprocessing, so a separate segmentation stage is unnecessary. LLM-based extraction is prohibitively expensive at corpus scale—parsing 150 million documents costs over $80,000 in input tokens alone[2] while output tokens at least double this vs. under $10,000 on spot GPU instances (Sect. 5.3)—and introduces rate-limit and schema-consistency risks. LLM-generated labels nonetheless remain promising for augmenting training data beyond the rule-based teacher ceiling.

3.2 Model Architecture

Our architecture extends the biaffine dependency parser of Dozat and Manning [7] for invention graph induction. As shown in Fig. 3, the model has three components: a contextual encoder and two parallel prediction heads.

Encoder. We define *words* as whitespace-delimited units of the input text. The pretrained XLM-RoBERTa tokenizer is a SentencePiece model that splits each word into a *variable* number of subword tokens; we pad or truncate this to a fixed $k=3$ subword tokens per word, which suffices for almost all words (only rare strings such as long chemical or mathematical expressions tokenize into more). The resulting subword sequence is processed by XLM-RoBERTa-Longformer [2], and a learned scalar mix over the last 4 hidden layers is followed by mean pooling over each word's subword tokens, producing one representation per word. All subsequent scoring operates at this word level. To extend the encoder beyond its native 16,384-subword limit, we tile the learned position embedding matrix to support sequences up to 65,536 subwords. This requires no retraining: sequences

[2] Estimated using Gemini 2 Flash Lite batch API ($0.0375 per million input tokens).

within the original range use pretrained positions unchanged; longer sequences receive repeated embeddings that are suboptimal but sufficient under local attention.

Biaffine Scoring. Each prediction head projects encoder outputs through separate MLPs for dependent and head roles, then scores pairs using biaffine attention [7]:

$$s(i, j) = \mathbf{h}_i^{\text{dep}\top} \mathbf{W} \mathbf{h}_j^{\text{head}} + \mathbf{b}^\top \mathbf{h}_i^{\text{dep}} \quad (1)$$

The **Feature Head** uses two parallel biaffine scorers: one for parent prediction ($\mathbf{S}^{\text{arc}} \in \mathbb{R}^{n \times n}$) and one for edge label classification ($\mathbf{S}^{\text{label}} \in \mathbb{R}^{n \times n \times K}$), distinguishing syntactic edges (within-phrase) from semantic edges (between features). The **Relation Head** uses a single biaffine scorer ($\mathbf{S}^{\text{rel}} \in \mathbb{R}^{n \times n}$) for functional relationships. Unlike dependency parsing, where every word belongs to a single-rooted tree, invention graphs admit multiple roots and exclude most document words. Two pseudo-nodes—NONE (index 0) and ROOT (index 1)—model these decisions, allowing each word to be classified as a non-feature, a root feature, or attached to a parent within the graph.

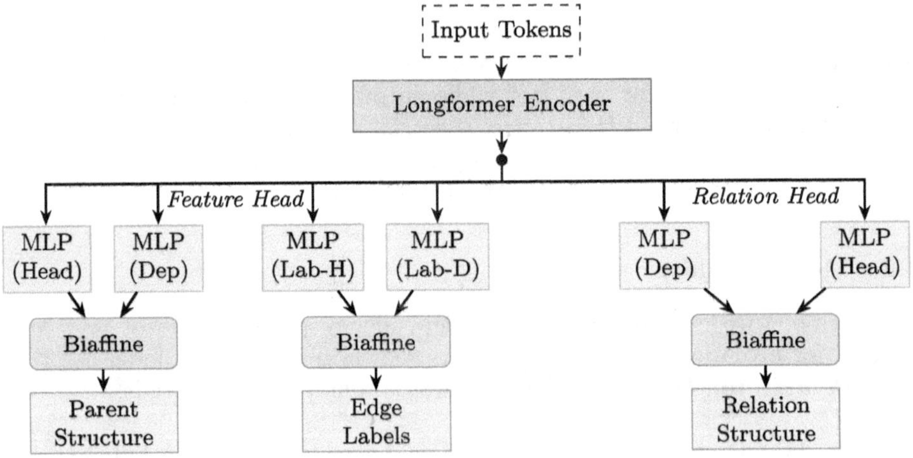

Fig. 3. Model architecture. The Feature Head predicts parent structure and edge labels (syntactic vs. semantic); the Relation Head predicts functional relationships.

3.3 Local Biaffine Attention

Standard biaffine attention computes all $O(n^2)$ pairwise scores, which is prohibitive for documents exceeding 40,000 words. Following the sliding-window principle of [17], our *local biaffine attention* reduces complexity to $O(n \cdot w)$ by restricting each word to score only positions within a window of size w, plus two pseudo-nodes. For word i, the candidate set is:

$$\mathcal{N}(i) = \{\text{None}, \text{Root}\} \cup \{j : |i - j| \leq w/2\} \quad (2)$$

This produces a score tensor of shape $[n, w+2]$ instead of $[n, n]$, as illustrated in Fig. 4.

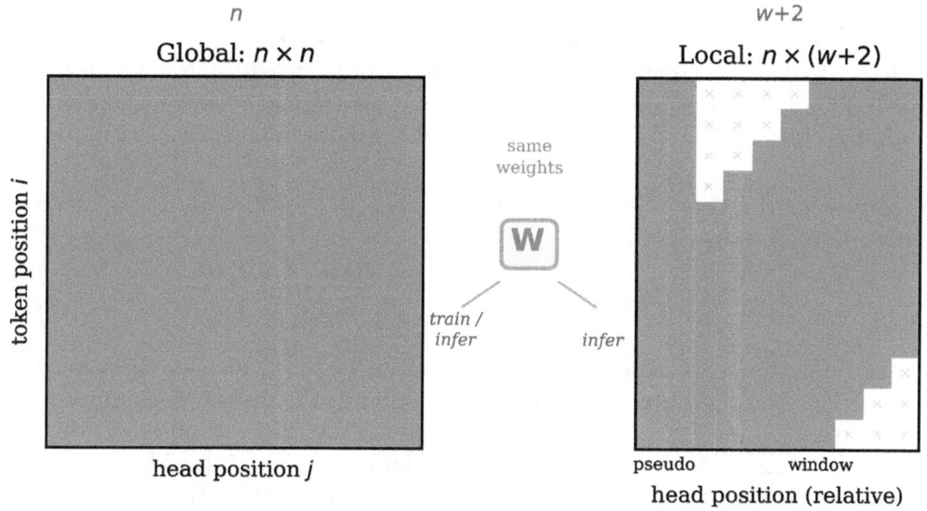

Fig. 4. Global vs. local biaffine score matrices. Global attention computes all n^2 scores; local attention computes only $n(w+2)$ scores within a sliding window plus two pseudo-node columns. Both modes share the same weight matrix $\mathbf{W}$, enabling training with global attention on short sequences and inference with local attention on long sequences.

Weight Sharing. A key property of our local attention is that it uses *exactly the same weight matrix* $\mathbf{W}$ as global biaffine attention—only the set of positions scored differs. This enables training with global attention on short sequences (600 words) and deploying with local attention on long documents (40,000+ words), or switching window sizes at inference time without retraining.

Implementation. We compute local scores efficiently using a chunking strategy adapted from Longformer [2]: the sequence is divided into overlapping chunks of size $2w$ with stride w, biaffine scores are computed within each chunk, and diagonal bands are extracted via a skew operation to produce the sliding window format. Pseudo-node scores are computed globally (as each word may be None or Root regardless of position) and concatenated with the window scores. Words near sequence boundaries have their windows masked to prevent attending to invalid positions.

Locality Justification. Patent text exhibits strong locality in hierarchical relationships: a component is typically described near its parent in the claim structure. Analysis of rule-parsed training graphs confirms that the vast majority of parent-child edges fall within a small window (Sect. 5.2); the relation head similarly benefits, as functional relationships are usually expressed in contiguous text spans.

Inference-Time Window Selection. Because local and global scoring share weights, the window is a free inference-time parameter chosen per document. In production we select the largest window fitting NVIDIA L4 memory (24 GB): global attention for documents under 5,000 words, w=2048 for 5,000–15,000 words, and w=1024 beyond 15,000. Documents shorter than $2w$ use global attention directly, avoiding the padding overhead a window would otherwise incur.

Training Objective. Both the feature parent and relation heads are trained with weighted cross-entropy:

$$\mathcal{L}_{\text{head}} = -\sum_{i \in \mathcal{M}} \alpha_{y_i} \log \frac{\exp(S_{i,y_i})}{\sum_j \exp(S_{i,j})} \tag{3}$$

where $\mathcal{M}$ is the set of non-padded word positions and α_k are per-class weights. Since most words do not participate in the graph, the NONE class dominates; we set $\alpha_{\text{NONE}} = 0.05$ for the feature head and 0.1 for the relation head, with all other positions receiving weight 1.0 (see ablation in Sect. 5.2). The edge label head uses standard cross-entropy at the gold parent position [7]. The total loss is $\mathcal{L} = \mathcal{L}_{\text{parent}} + \mathcal{L}_{\text{label}} + \mathcal{L}_{\text{rel}}$.

3.4 Training Data and Setup

Dataset Construction. The training dataset is constructed using invention graphs generated by the rule-based system of [3], which has been deployed in production for over 5 years and has processed more than 150 million patent documents. This system uses spaCy [13] for linguistic analysis combined with regular expression patterns for relation extraction.

Training Set. We sample 1 million patent documents from the full patent corpus, stratified by jurisdiction: 60% US patents, 20% Chinese patents (translated to English), and 20% from other jurisdictions.

To prevent data leakage and near-duplicate contamination, we deduplicate by patent family ID: the same invention may appear under different document identifiers across jurisdictions (e.g., US, EP, CN) with near-identical text, so only one document per family is retained across all splits. All families appearing in either the intrinsic evaluation set (5,000 documents) or the downstream search evaluation set (90,082 queries) are excluded from training entirely.

To enable efficient training with global attention, we apply a maximum sequence length of 600 words. Documents are truncated to this limit, but we require a minimum coverage threshold of 70%—documents where truncation would retain less than 70% of the original graph structure are excluded.

Test Set. We hold out 5,000 documents randomly sampled from the patent corpus for evaluation. Unlike training, test documents are processed at full length using local attention, enabling assessment of generalization to long documents not seen during training.

Training Configuration. Table 1 summarizes our training hyperparameters.

Table 1. Training hyperparameters. Architecture and regularization details in Sects. 3.2–3.3.

Parameter	Value
MLP dimensions (parent/label/relation)	256/128/256
Max subword tokens per word	3
Optimizer	AdamW (lr $= 10^{-4}$)
LR ratio (encoder vs. task layers)	1:10
Warmup	10% of total steps, then linear decay
Batch size (tokens per worker) × accumulation	1,200 × 16
GPUs (NVIDIA L4, data-parallel)	8
Feature NONE weight/Relation NONE weight	0.05/0.1
Encoder dropout/MLP shared dropout	0.1/0.33
Gradient clipping (max norm)	2.0
Precision	bfloat16 mixed

Training runs for 100 epochs distributed across 8 NVIDIA L4 GPUs using Ray data-parallel, taking approximately 60 h. We select the best checkpoint by whole graph IoU (Sect. 4.1) on the validation set.

4 Experimental Setup

4.1 Evaluation Metrics

Intrinsic Graph Quality Metrics. We compare predicted graphs against rule-based teacher graphs by representing each graph as a set of *(parent string, child string)* edge tuples and computing set-based precision, recall, and IoU (Intersection over Union). **Whole Graph IoU**, our primary metric, pools feature hierarchy and functional relation edges into a single set. We also report IoU at finer granularities (feature edges only, nodes, words), **IoU@k** (percentage of documents with IoU $\geq k/100$), and **coverage**—the fraction of document words participating in the graph, reported as total word coverage and separately for features and relations. A systematic bias affects string matching: the rule-based parser normalizes extracted text (e.g., lemmatization), while the neural parser is purely extractive, so semantically correct predictions may count as mismatches. Since no human-annotated corpus exists, intrinsic metrics measure teacher agreement; the extrinsic search evaluation serves as the primary quality signal.

Extrinsic Search Evaluation. To evaluate the impact of graph quality on downstream search, the neural parser is integrated into the Graph Transformer retrieval system of [5], which is trained on examiner-cited prior art to rank candidate patents by relevance. On the evaluation set, this system with the rule-based parser (Recall@3 = 0.416) substantially outperforms strong dense retrievers chosen to span patent-specialized and general-purpose models: PaECTER [11] (patent-tuned) achieves 0.280, while Stella [20] and GTE-ModernBERT [21]—among the top general-purpose embedding models—reach 0.273 and 0.200, despite using up to 4,096 tokens per chunk. The rule-based parser thus represents a strong baseline rather than a straw man, making it a meaningful target to surpass.

Citation-Based Ground Truth. We evaluate using examiner-cited references as relevance labels, considering both X citations (documents particularly relevant to novelty of the claimed invention) and Y citations (documents relevant when combined with other references, challenging inventive step). Citations give *binary* relevance—a candidate is either cited prior art or not, with no graded ranking among the relevant documents—so the question is simply whether the cited references appear within the top k results. We therefore report citation-averaged Recall@k rather than graded ranking metrics (e.g., NDCG), which require relevance grades we do not have:

$$\text{Recall@}k = \frac{1}{|Q|} \sum_{q \in Q} \frac{|\text{Retrieved}_k(q) \cap \text{Citations}(q)|}{|\text{Citations}(q)|} \tag{4}$$

where Q is the query set and $\text{Retrieved}_k(q)$ the top-k candidates. We focus on small k because patent novelty search is top-heavy: a single piece of prior art can be enough to challenge a claim's novelty or inventive step, and because a search may surface thousands of candidates that users have little time to review, getting a relevant document into the top few results is what saves time in practice. Production search over the full 150-million-document corpus operates at top-50; on the much smaller validation pool of 168,809 documents, larger cutoffs become easy and weakly discriminative, so we report the analogous demanding regime at small k, taking $k{=}3$ as the primary operating point and confirming the same trends at $k{=}5$ and $k{=}10$ (Sect. 5.1). Results are reported on three subsets: all 90,082 queries, the 11,698 chemical patent queries (identified by CPC classification classes C01, C05, C07, C08, C09, C10, C11, and C13), and the remaining 78,384 non-chemical queries.

Intrinsic Evaluation. We evaluate graph quality on the held-out test set of 5,000 documents described in Sect. 3.4, processed at full length.

5 Results

5.1 Main Results

Intrinsic Graph Quality. Table 2 compares the best neural parser against the rule-based teacher on the test set of 5,000 documents.

Table 2. Intrinsic graph quality on the test set (5,000 documents). The rule-based teacher achieves IoU=1.0 by definition since it generates the training labels.

Model	IoU	IoU@90	Precision	Recall	Coverage
Rule-based (teacher)	1.000	1.000	1.000	1.000	0.847
Neural	**0.653**	**0.142**	**0.761**	**0.780**	**0.861**

The neural parser achieves 0.653 IoU with the rule-based teacher, measuring distillation fidelity rather than absolute quality. Word coverage exceeds the teacher (0.861 vs 0.847), indicating richer graph structures; whether this translates to search improvement is answered below (training details in Sect. 5.2).

Search Recall. Table 3 presents extrinsic evaluation on the downstream search task using 90,082 queries, each paired with a known relevant reference retrieved from 168,809 documents. We evaluate two configurations: (1) *Claims*—only query graphs are re-parsed with the neural parser; (2) *Descriptions*—both query and corpus document graphs are re-parsed, using a 3-million-document neural-parsed subset (see Sect. 5.3).

Table 3. Search recall (Recall@3). *Claims*: queries re-parsed, corpus rule-based. *Descriptions*: both re-parsed on a corpus subset. Significance via McNemar's paired test (one-sided): $^{*}p < 0.05$, $^{**}p < 0.01$.

Configuration	Parser	All	Chemical	Non-Chemical
Claims	Rule-based	0.4163	0.3790	0.4218
	Neural	**0.4183***	**0.3799**	**0.4240***
Desc.	Rule-based	0.3336	0.3060	0.3377
	Neural	**0.3373****	**0.3095**	**0.3414****

Both overall improvements are statistically significant (McNemar's paired test, 90,082 queries; $p = 0.04$ claims, $p < 0.001$ descriptions). Re-parsing both queries and corpus documents yields the larger gain (+1.1% vs +0.5%), confirming that consistent neural graphs on both sides of retrieval—rather than query-side improvements alone—are the key driver.

The chemical subset does not reach significance ($p = 0.42$ claims, $p = 0.14$ descriptions), despite showing the largest qualitative improvements in graph structure (Fig. 5). This suggests the chemical validation set may be too small to capture observed gains; domain-specific evaluation protocols remain future work.

Recall at Other Cutoffs. Table 4 reports the full-pipeline (*Descriptions*) configuration at k=3, 5, 10: the neural parser's advantage is consistent and *widens* with k (+0.4, +0.5, +0.8 points). On the query-only (*Claims*) configuration the gain instead concentrates at the operating point, consistent with both-side re-parsing being the driver of the larger *Descriptions* gains.

Table 4. Search recall at k=3, 5, 10 for the *Descriptions* configuration (all 90,082 queries, X citations). The neural advantage holds and grows with k.

Parser	Recall@3	Recall@5	Recall@10
Rule-based	0.3336	0.4247	0.5396
Neural	**0.3373**	**0.4300**	**0.5472**

Generalization to Long Documents. The parser trains on documents truncated to 600 words yet is deployed on full patents exceeding 40,000 words. Intrinsic agreement with the teacher does decrease on longer inputs, but this largely reflects the rule-based teacher's own reduced reliability there (Sect. 5.2) rather than degraded prediction quality, so it is not a clean quality signal. The extrinsic evidence is more informative and is a direct neural-versus-rule-based comparison on identical inputs: re-parsing full descriptions—the longest inputs, far beyond the training truncation—yields the *largest* and most significant search gain (+1.1%, $p < 0.001$; Table 3), and the neural parser's coverage advantage over the teacher holds on full-length documents (Table 5). We thus find no evidence of quality collapse on long documents—if anything, the full-pipeline gains concentrate there.

Graph Structure Analysis. Table 5 compares structural properties of graphs generated by each parser.

The neural parser produces slightly shallower graphs (depth 2.057 vs 2.157) while achieving higher coverage across all metrics, suggesting a more balanced representation. Figure 5 illustrates this on a chemical patent: the neural parser extracts 13 chemical constituents as individual features where the rule-based parser captures only 3 top-level features, directly benefiting downstream search for specific alloy compositions.

Table 5. Graph structure comparison between rule-based and neural parsers.

Metric	Rule-based	Neural
Graph Depth	2.157	2.057
Word Coverage	0.847	0.862
Feature Coverage	0.514	0.521
Relation Coverage	0.369	0.376

5.2 Ablation Studies

Training Configuration Ablation. Table 6 summarizes the effect of key training decisions. We vary training set size, document length filtering, loss weights, and root penalization. All models are evaluated at the best checkpoint (maximum IoU over 100 epochs) on the same 5,000-document test set.

Table 6. Ablation of training configuration. All models use 100 training epochs; metrics reported at best checkpoint (max IoU). Coverage: fraction of document words assigned to graph features.

Configuration	IoU	P	R	Cov.
100 K dataset	0.614	0.727	0.753	0.797
1M dataset	0.651	0.766	0.772	0.846
+ short-doc filter, loss tuning	**0.653**	**0.761**	**0.780**	0.861
+ root penalization	0.637	0.748	0.768	**0.866**

Data Scale. Scaling from 100K to 1M training examples yields the largest single improvement: IoU rises from 0.614 to 0.651, with coverage increasing from 0.797 to 0.846 as the model generalizes to a wider vocabulary of feature expressions.

Document Length Filtering. Training exclusively on documents with ≤600 words (combined with the 70% coverage filter from Sect. 3.4) improves recall from 0.772 to 0.780 while maintaining IoU, even though inference uses full-length documents. The rule-based teacher produces higher-quality labels on shorter patents, and the model learns structural patterns that generalize beyond the training length distribution.

Loss Weights and Root Penalization. Down-weighting the NONE class is essential: asymmetric weights (feature 0.05, relation 0.10) outperform symmetric alternatives. Increasing the root loss weight to encourage deeper structures does not improve IoU (0.637 vs 0.653) and decreases precision; we use the default equal root weight.

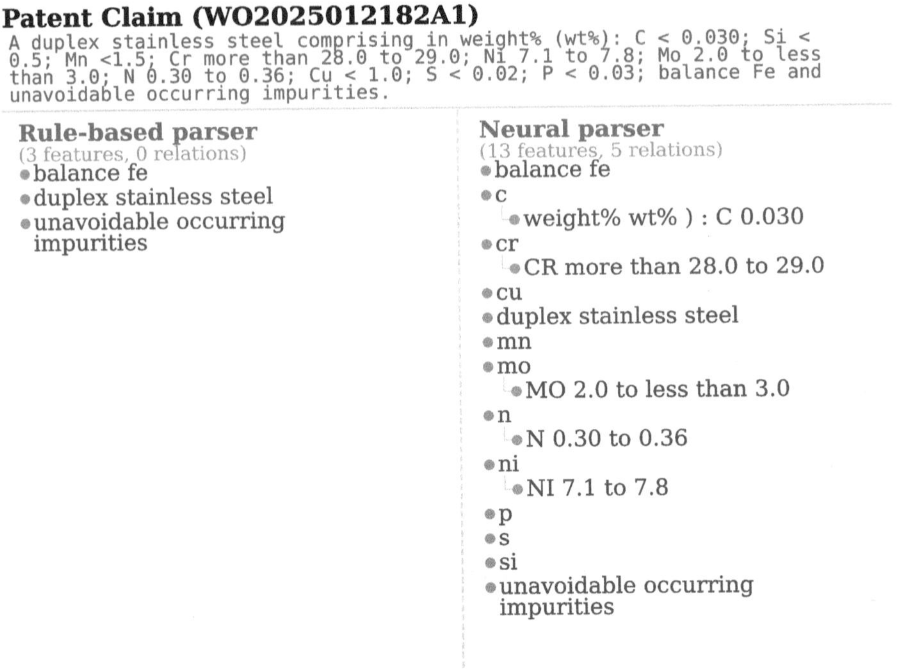

Fig. 5. Rule-based vs. neural parser output for a chemical patent claim (WO2025012182A1). The rule-based parser extracts only 3 features, while the neural parser identifies 13 features and 5 relations capturing element compositions. This domain—chemical compositions with numerical ranges—is particularly challenging for hand-crafted rules.

Window Size and Document Length. Analysis of the training data confirms that 98% of parent-child relationships occur within 2048 words, justifying local attention. Evaluating the effect of window size requires queries long enough to span more than one window: the single-claim queries used above (a few hundred words) fit inside even the smallest window, so window size would not affect them, while full corpus descriptions exceed GPU memory under global attention. We therefore use *all-claims queries*—all claims of a patent concatenated. For reference, the rule-based teacher reaches Recall@3 $\approx$ 0.47 on the same all-claims queries; the neural parser matches it across window sizes (Table 7), so the recall here is on par with the production teacher and the window-size trend is an internal property of the neural model, not a neural-versus-rule-based gap.

Larger windows consistently improve recall (Table 7), with global attention as the upper bound—motivating the inference-time adaptive selection described in Sect. 3.3.

Table 7. Effect of attention window size on search recall (Recall@3), measured using all-claims queries. The production adaptive strategy (Sect. 3.3) assigns each document the largest window that fits GPU memory; the Doc. Range column shows the resulting assignment.

Window Size	Recall@3	Doc. Range
512	0.4658	–
1024	0.4676	>15 K words
2048	0.4690	5 K–15 K words
Global	0.4714	<5 K words

5.3 Deployment Experience

The search pipeline has two parsing stages: *query parsing* at search time and *corpus indexing* of full patent descriptions offline. The neural parser is deployed in production for query parsing, replacing the rule-based parser with no user-facing disruptions. As a qualitative check—no human-annotated ground truth exists for invention graphs—domain experts with patent-search backgrounds reviewed neural and rule-based graphs side by side and confirmed structural equivalence on most documents, with the neural parser capturing additional features in challenging domains such as chemical compositions (Fig. 5). We therefore treat downstream search recall, rather than this review or the intrinsic teacher-agreement metrics, as the primary measure of graph quality. This corresponds to the Claims configuration (+0.5% recall). For corpus indexing, we have validated inference quality and cost on a 3-million-document subset (the Descriptions configuration, +1.1% recall); scaling to the full 150 million documents remains in progress.

Online Query Inference. The biaffine model runs on fourth-generation Intel Xeon Scalable processors with native `bfloat16` support, eliminating the need for GPUs in online serving. Throughput increases from 2 to 10 queries per second per CPU instance, and average latency drops from 2–3 s to under 1 s. Long queries that previously timed out after 60+ s (common for chemical patents with complex formulas) complete in under 5 s; inputs are truncated at 40,000 characters as a safety bound.

Batch Corpus Parsing. We parsed 3 million documents as a single distributed Ray Data job on 10 NVIDIA L4 spot GPU instances, with CPUs on the same nodes handling pre- and post-processing. The job completed in two days without out-of-memory errors. GPU utilization exceeded 70%, though variable-size tree outputs create packing challenges in Ray Data workers that limit further utilization. At current utilization, batch parsing cost is estimated at 3× lower than the rule-based system; improving GPU utilization to 90%+ would bring this to 5×. Scaling beyond 3 million documents will require a full orchestration framework with improved observability and error recovery.

Edge Cases and Lessons Learned. The neural parser largely reproduces the rule-based system's strengths and weaknesses: domains where rules worked well remain strong, and challenging cases (e.g., Markush structures) remain difficult. One unexpected issue arose from training on short documents: the model preserved patent jargon such as "according to claim 1" that the rule-based parser had filtered out, especially in longer inputs combining claims and descriptions. Rather than retraining on longer sequences—which risked degrading metrics (Sect. 5.2)—we relied on the regex post-filter introduced in Sect. 3.1.

6 Conclusion and Future Work

We showed that biaffine structured prediction, made tractable for long documents via local attention with shared weights, can replace brittle rule-based patent graph extraction. Knowledge distillation from 1 million rule-parsed examples produces a model that surpasses its teacher on downstream citation recall across both query-only and full-pipeline configurations, while reducing inference cost. The architecture itself was fixed by a deployment constraint—output-format compatibility with the rule-based system—so exploring alternative encoders, window/compute trade-offs, and moderate-scale LLM-based label generation is now a promising direction. Further work includes expert-annotated data to move beyond the teacher ceiling, joint training with the search model, and multilingual extension.

Use of Generative AI. Generative AI tools (Claude, Anthropic) were used to assist with proofreading and improving readability of the manuscript, and to generate code for producing figures. All scientific content, experimental design, and conclusions are solely the work of the authors.

References

1. Acikalin, U.U., Kutlu, M.: Patent search using triplet networks based fine-tuned SciBERT. arXiv preprint: arXiv:2207.11497 (2022)
2. Beltagy, I., Peters, M.E., Cohan, A.: LongFormer: the long-document transformer. arXiv preprint: arXiv:2004.05150 (2020)
3. Björkqvist, S., Kallio, J.: Building a graph-based patent search engine. In: Proceedings of the 46th International ACM SIGIR Conference on Research and Development in Information Retrieval, pp. 3300–3304 (2023). https://doi.org/10.1145/3539618.3591842
4. Clarke, N.S.: The basics of patent searching. World Patent Inf. **54**, S4–S10 (2018). https://doi.org/10.1016/j.wpi.2017.02.006
5. Daniell, K., Buzhinsky, I., Björkqvist, S.: Efficient patent searching using graph transformers. In: PatentSemTech'25: 6th Workshop on Patent Text Mining and Semantic Technologies (2025)
6. D'hondt, E., Verberne, S.: CLEF-IP 2010: prior art retrieval using the different sections in patent documents. In: Proceedings of CLEF 2010 (2010)

7. Dozat, T., Manning, C.D.: Deep biaffine attention for neural dependency parsing. In: Proceedings of the 5th International Conference on Learning Representations (ICLR) (2017)
8. Dwivedi, V.P., Bresson, X.: A generalization of transformer networks to graphs. arXiv preprint: arXiv:2012.09699 (2021)
9. Freunek, M., Bodmer, A.: BERT based patent novelty search by training claims to their own description. arXiv preprint: arXiv:2103.01126 (2021)
10. Geng, Z., Chen, G., Han, Y., Lu, G., Li, F.: Open relation extraction from patent claims using hybrid neural networks. Expert Syst. Appl. **170**, 114482 (2021)
11. Ghosh, M., Erhardt, S., Rose, M.E., Buunk, E., Harhoff, D.: PaECTER: patent-level representation learning using citation-informed transformers. arXiv preprint: arXiv:2402.19411 (2024)
12. Hinton, G., Vinyals, O., Dean, J.: Distilling the knowledge in a neural network. arXiv preprint: arXiv:1503.02531 (2015)
13. Honnibal, M., Montani, I., Van Landeghem, S., Boyd, A.: spaCy: industrial-strength natural language processing in Python (2020). https://spacy.io
14. Merrouni, I.A., Belkadi, A., Nehar, A., Boumhidi, I.: PatenTEB: a comprehensive benchmark and model family for patent text embedding. arXiv preprint: arXiv:2510.22264 (2025)
15. Reimers, N., Gurevych, I.: Sentence-BERT: sentence embeddings using Siamese BERT-networks. In: Proceedings of the 2019 Conference on Empirical Methods in Natural Language Processing and the 9th International Joint Conference on Natural Language Processing, pp. 3982–3992 (2019)
16. Tai, K.S., Socher, R., Manning, C.D.: Improved semantic representations from tree-structured long short-term memory networks. In: Proceedings of the 53rd Annual Meeting of the Association for Computational Linguistics and the 7th International Joint Conference on Natural Language Processing (Volume 1: Long Papers), pp. 1556–1566 (2015). https://doi.org/10.3115/v1/P15-1150
17. Wang, X., Shen, J., Li, J., Liu, Y.: DocBAN: an efficient biaffine attention network for document-level named entity recognition. In: Advanced Intelligent Computing Technology and Applications (ICIC 2024), pp. 65–76. Springer (2024). https://doi.org/10.1007/978-981-97-5669-8_6
18. Ying, C., et al.: Do transformers really perform bad for graph representation? arXiv preprint: arXiv:2106.05234 (2021)
19. Zaheer, M., et al.: Big Bird: transformers for longer sequences. In: Advances in Neural Information Processing Systems, vol. 33, pp. 17283–17297 (2020)
20. Zhang, D.: Jasper and stella: distillation of SOTA embedding models. Technical report, NovaSearch (2024). https://huggingface.co/NovaSearch/stella_en_400M_v5
21. Zhang, X., Li, Y., Zhang, W., Long, D., Xie, P.: GTE-ModernBERT: modernized bi-directional encoder for general text embeddings. arXiv preprint: arXiv:2412.13663 (2024)
22. Zhu, D., et al.: LongEmbed: extending embedding models for long context retrieval. In: Proceedings of the 2024 Conference on Empirical Methods in Natural Language Processing, pp. 802–816 (2024). https://aclanthology.org/2024.emnlp-main.47/

From Speech to Subtitles: Evaluating ASR Models in Subtitling Italian Television Programs

Alessandro Lucca, Francesco Corso, and Francesco Pierri(✉)

DEIB, Politecnico di Milano, Milano, Italy
{alessandro.lucca,francesco.corso,francesco.pierri}@polimi.it

Abstract. Subtitles are essential for video accessibility and audience engagement. Modern Automatic Speech Recognition (ASR) systems, built upon Encoder-Decoder neural network architectures and trained on massive amounts of data, have progressively reduced transcription errors on standard benchmark datasets. However, their performance in real-world production environments, particularly for non-English content like long-form Italian videos, remains largely unexplored. This paper presents a case study on developing a professional subtitling system for an Italian media company. To inform our system design, we evaluated four state-of-the-art ASR models (Whisper Large v2, AssemblyAI Universal, Parakeet TDT v3 0.6b, and WhisperX) on a 50-hour dataset of Italian television programs. The study highlights their strengths and limitations, benchmarking their performance against the work of professional human subtitlers. The findings indicate that, while current models cannot meet the media industry's accuracy needs for full autonomy, they can serve as highly effective tools for enhancing human productivity. We conclude that a human-in-the-loop (HITL) approach is crucial and present the production-grade, cloud-based infrastructure we designed to support this workflow.

Keywords: Subtitles · ASR Models · Television

1 Introduction

The production of accurate subtitles has become increasingly important across a wide range of video content, from social media to broadcast television [5]. High-quality subtitles not only enhance accessibility for individuals with hearing impairments but also support viewer engagement more broadly [16]. Yet subtitle creation remains a demanding task for human operators, especially in long-form television content where reliability, timing precision, and consistency are critical.

On the technological side, advances in large-scale datasets and End-to-End Neural Network architectures have substantially improved Automatic Speech Recognition (ASR) performance in speech-to-text transcription tasks [9]. However, ASR research typically evaluates systems using only Word Error Rate

M. Baratchi et al. (Eds.): ECML PKDD 2026, LNAI 16949, pp. 550–564, 2027.
https://doi.org/10.1007/978-3-032-37682-4_32

(WER), which, while being an important metric for transcription accuracy, it neglects temporal alignment, an essential aspect of subtitle production. In addition, most benchmarks target English and short audio segments, limiting their applicability to real-world subtitling workflows.
These gaps are particularly relevant in industrial media contexts, where ASR systems must operate on long-form, noisy, and linguistically diverse broadcast material. To address these challenges, we articulate our contributions through three primary research questions:

RQ1: **How do state-of-the-art ASR models perform across different television genres when evaluated on long-form content?** We addressed this by benchmarking four state-of-the-art models–Whisper Large V2 [10], NVIDIA Parakeet TDT 0.6b V3 [14], WhisperX [1], and AssemblyAI Universal [12]–across diverse program formats, including Talk Shows, Investigative Journalism, and Scientific Communication. Our findings indicate that performance is highly genre-dependent; for instance, "Scientific Communication" achieved consistent, high accuracy with a Word Error Rate (WER) as low as 0.2, while more spontaneous formats like Talk Shows showed significant variability. Our evaluation extends beyond WER to include semantic metrics (BLEURT [15]), subtitle-oriented metrics (Subtitle Edit Rate, SubER [18]), and entity-level accuracy (Entity Error Rate, EER). We also compute WER on one-minute segments to identify characteristics of video clips that induce higher error rates.

RQ2: **Can general-purpose LLMs effectively serve as zero-shot reviewers?** We investigated the efficacy of Gemini-2.5-Flash and Gemma3-12b-it as zero-shot reviewers for punctuation restoration and entity correction. The analysis revealed that Gemini-2.5-Flash provided a statistically significant improvement in entity accuracy, reducing the EER by an average of 2.3%, whereas the smaller Gemma model did not yield significant gains.

RQ3: **What are the primary technical and economic trade-offs when deploying an in-house subtitling pipeline versus using proprietary API services?** We addressed the practicalities of deployment by designing a cloud-based infrastructure and conducting a comparative cost-benefit analysis between proprietary APIs and in-house GPU solutions. Our findings suggest that while API-based services offer convenience, an internal pipeline utilizing WhisperX on NVIDIA T4/L4 GPUs is more cost-effective for large-scale production, reducing estimated hourly costs from \$7.50 to approximately \$2.56.

2 The ASR Systems

The current Automatic Speech Recognition (ASR) systems are all based on a End To End architecture with two main blocks, an Encoder and a Decoder [9]. The Encoder takes in input the acoustic representation of the audio, typically in log-mel features, and projects it in a very high dimensional space to capture all the information. The Decoder is responsible for the temporal alignment between the acoustic features in the input and the shorter sequence of output labels. Whisper Large v2 [10] is designed with a Transformer Encoder-Decoder architecture, trained as a sequence-to-sequence system on 680k hours of weakly supervised and labelled audio data. WhisperX [1] is a variation of Whisper designed for efficient long-form transcription processing, employing an intelligent preprocessing using Voice Activity Detector (VAD) and Cut&Merge strategy, and a postprocessing with a phoneme alignment model to ensure maximum temporal alignment. AssemblyAI Universal [12] is a 600-million-parameter Conformer Encoder coupled with an RNN-T Decoder, trained on a dataset composed of 12.5M hours of unsupervised data, 188k hours of supervised data, and 1.6M hours of pseudo-labelled data. To handle long-form transcriptions, it uses a divide and conquer strategy, with intelligent segmentation of the input to allow for parallel inference. NVIDIA Parakeet TDT 0.6b v3 [14] is a FastConformer Encoder paired with a TDT (Token and Duration Transducer) Decoder, a combination specifically designed to achieve a balance between transcription accuracy and computational efficiency. The model has been trained on a 660k-hour subset of the Granary dataset.

3 Related Work

Assessing the quality of out-of-the-box ASR transcription is a field of research explored in various dimensions. Kuhn et al. [6] assessed the performance of multiple open-source and commercial ASR systems using a dataset composed of higher education lectures in English and German, employing the Word Error Rate as the sole evaluation metric. Their findings reveal that the quality promised by vendors is only partially confirmed in practice, with significant variability observed across systems, speakers, and languages. Similarly, Ferraro et al. [4] conducted a comparative analysis of a broad range of ASR systems across heterogeneous datasets. Their results demonstrate that ASR performance, again measured through WER, is strongly dependent on the nature and composition of the dataset under examination. In the specific domain of automatic subtitling for professional broadcasting, Davitti et al. [2] investigated the readability and quality of subtitles produced by two professional ASR systems, using a semantic metric (NER) for evaluation. Their experiments, conducted on two distinct audiovisual contents, a British talk show and a U.S. film dubbed into Italian, demonstrated that the ASR-generated subtitles consistently fell short of the 98% accuracy threshold required in the broadcasting industry. In contrast, Romero-Fresco et al. [13] evaluated the Lexi ASR system using the same NER metric and provided the first certification demonstrating that an ASR system can exceed the 98% accuracy benchmark on specific types of videos, such as single-speech videos. However, previous studies do not provide a comprehensive evaluation of multiple ASR systems within the specific context of Italian-language subtitling. Most existing work focuses on either a single model, on short and controlled audio samples, or on English-language benchmarks, thus overlooking the challenges posed by real-world audiovisual productions. This research aims to bridge

Table 1. Descriptive statistics of the reference dataset considered in the research.

Typology	Number of Episodes	Total Duration (min)
Talk Show	10	664.66
Investigative Journalism	10	1084.66
Scientific Communication	10	1,255.53

these gaps by systematically benchmarking several ASR systems on a medium-scale dataset of real Italian television content. The evaluation covers a wide range of program types and acoustic conditions, providing a more realistic assessment of ASR performance in professional subtitling scenarios.

Several studies have investigated the use of Large Language Models as reviewers within ASR correction pipelines. Ma et al. [8] show that a zero-shot corrector (GPT-3.5) struggles to enhance transcription accuracy when limited to the 1-best hypothesis, while Fedorchenko et al. [3] report improvements in the same setting for Estonian language subtitles by using GPT-4o. Li et al. [7] demonstrate that a multilingual LLM, when fine-tuned for error correction (Qwen1.5-7b), can substantially enhance ASR output relative to a general-purpose model. Wei et al. [17] focus on LLM correction for ASR transcripts in Chinese language: their extensive experiments reveal that prompting is not effective for ASR error correction, finetuning is effective only for a portion of LLMs, while Multi-modal augmentation is the most effective method for error correction, achieving state-of-the-art performance. In any case, these studies do not focus on the Italian language, nor do they consider metrics such as Entity Error Rate to assess the specific improvements that LLMs can bring to entity recognition (Table 1).

4 Data and Methods

4.1 Dataset

The dataset consists of 50 h of audio taken from 30 episodes across 5 programs broadcast on Italian public television, each paired with its professional, human-produced SubRip Text subtitle file. All episodes were collected from the official website of Radiotelevisione Italiana (RAI), which makes this content publicly available. The programs were selected to cover a broad range of television formats and to capture different linguistic and acoustic conditions encountered in real subtitling workflows. They fall into three categories: two Talk Shows, two Investigative Journalism programs, and one Scientific Communication program. An overview of the dataset characteristics is provided in Tables 5 and 6.

4.2 Evaluation Metrics

The primary evaluation metric used in this study is Word Error Rate (WER), computed over the entire transcript. Since the reference subtitles are human-edited rather than verbatim transcriptions, WER should be interpreted with caution: professional captioners often rephrase content to meet readability and timing constraints, introducing a systematic deviation between the audio and the reference text. To identify segments where the ASR systems struggle most, WER is also computed on one-minute windows.

In addition to WER, we include SubER [18], a syntactic metric specifically designed for subtitling. SubER provides insight into segmentation and timestamp accuracy, both of which are essential for broadcast-quality subtitles.

To assess semantic coherence between reference and hypothesis, we compute AS-BLEURT scores. Sentence alignment is performed using the Levenshtein algorithm, ensuring that semantically comparable units are evaluated consistently.

Following the guidelines of major Italian broadcasters [11], the study also evaluates three key readability metrics. The Number of Characters per Segment (NCS) should fall between 30 and 74; the Mean Segment Duration (MSD) ideally ranges from 1 to 6 s; and the Characters per Second (CPS) should remain within the acceptable range of 9 to 15. These metrics allow us to assess how well automatically generated subtitles conform to industry-standard readability constraints.

Entity recognition capabilities are evaluated through a dedicated pipeline. Named entities are extracted from the reference transcript using the spaCy library and categorized into *Person*, *Organization*, and *Location*. For each reference entity, we search for the most semantically similar token in the ASR-generated transcript within a temporal window of ± 5 s, mitigating alignment mismatches between the two transcripts. This mapping enables the computation of the Entity Error Rate (EER).

Finally, we investigate the extent to which large language models can improve ASR outputs through post-editing. Two LLMs are evaluated in a zero-shot setting for punctuation restoration and entity correction. The first is a commercial general-purpose model (Gemini-2.5-Flash), which processes batches of up to 40 subtitles at a time and returns a structured output with the same number of segments. The second is a smaller open-source model (Gemma3-12b-it), which does not support structured outputs; therefore, each subtitle is processed individually. This analysis provides insight into the potential of LLM-assisted post-processing to enhance subtitle quality.

4.3 Experimental Settings

Whisper Large V2, WhisperX, and NVIDIA Parakeet TDT 0.6b V3 are open-source models and are executed in a Google Cloud environment equipped with an NVIDIA T4 GPU. AssemblyAI Universal, being a proprietary system, is accessed via API calls. Outputs from all systems are then standardized into a unified JSON structure organized at the segment level. For each segment, the JSON file records the transcribed text, start and end timestamps, and the word-level information, including both token text and precise timing. We plan to publicly release the code used to run and evaluate the models.

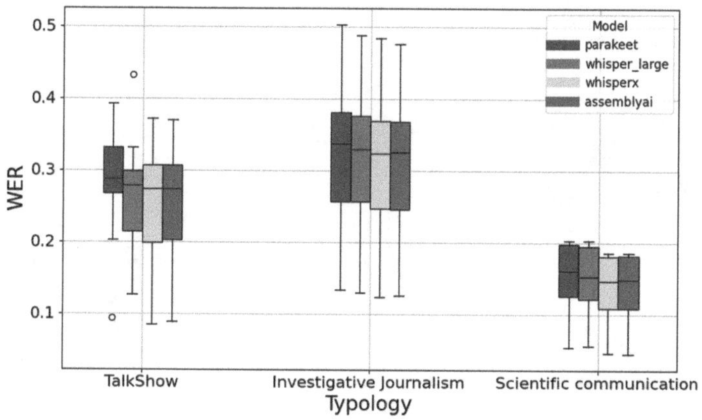

Fig. 1. Word Error Rate distribution across different types of TV programs and ASR Models (lower is better).

5 Experimental Results

The result of the Word Error Rate evaluation is reported in Fig. 1. The transcription quality of the "Scientific Communication" program is the most consistent and closely aligned with the ground truth, with a maximum WER of 0.2, a remarkably low error rate, especially considering the potential noise introduced by human post-editing. In contrast, "Investigative Journalism" and "Talk Show" formats exhibit a much wider range of WER values, strongly dependent on the specific episode, thus indicating a higher degree of variability. Across models, all four ASR systems demonstrate comparable overall performance, though WhisperX and AssemblyAI achieve the most accurate results.

The computation of WER by segmenting the audio in one minute long clips reveals that the ASR struggle in the distinction between speech and singing, trying to transcribe songs, clearly something not desired. The SubER (Fig. 2) and AS-BLEURT results show a strong correlation with WER, indicating that these metrics do not provide additional insights beyond those already captured by WER. However, they confirm the strong dependence of transcription performance on the specific type of program, with the "Scientific Communication" program emerging as the most accurately transcribed program. Concerning the Entity Error Rate (EER), the analysis is conducted on 13,463 extracted entities. Observing Fig. 3, a difference emerges among the evaluated models in their ability to recognize entities. Even if all ASR systems achieve a mean EER between 10% and 15%, WhisperX consistently achieves the lowest EER in nearly all episodes, establishing itself as the leading model in this task.

When prompted for entity correction in a zero-shot approach, Gemini-2.5-Flash leads to a statistically significant improvement in EER performance (p-value 0.006), with a mean gain of 2.3% overall (Fig. 4). An example with the differences between the ground-truth, the raw transcription made with WhisperX

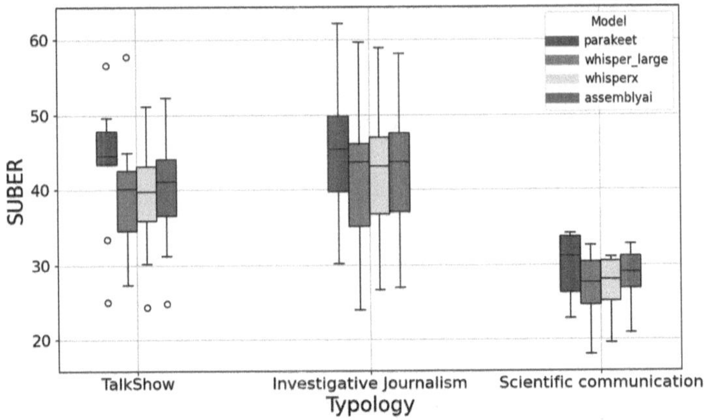

Fig. 2. Subtitle Edit Rate distribution across different types of TV programs and ASR Models (lower is better).

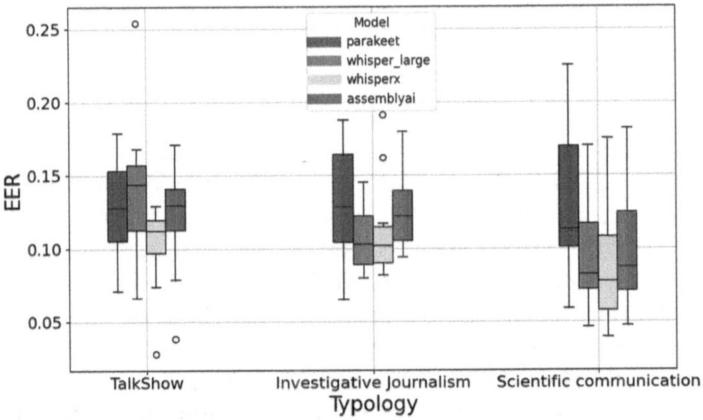

Fig. 3. Entity Error Rate distribution across different types of TV programs and ASR Models (lower is better).

and the transcription after the revision with Gemini-2.5-Flash can be found in Table 2 Using Gemma3-12b-it as a reviewer does not lead to a significant improvement in the entity correction task (p-value 0.542), with a mean gain of 0.4%.

The analysis related to the readability metrics shows that the output of the ASR transcription can not be used "as is", because it fails to respect the necessary compliance guidelines, especially exceeding frequently the NCS metric. However, an intelligent segmentation algorithm that leverages the word timestamp information is sufficient to rebuild a SubRip Text file that is compliant with all the guidelines. Specifically, the segmentation algorithm ensures that each subtitle segment respects the readability constraints. When these are not met, the

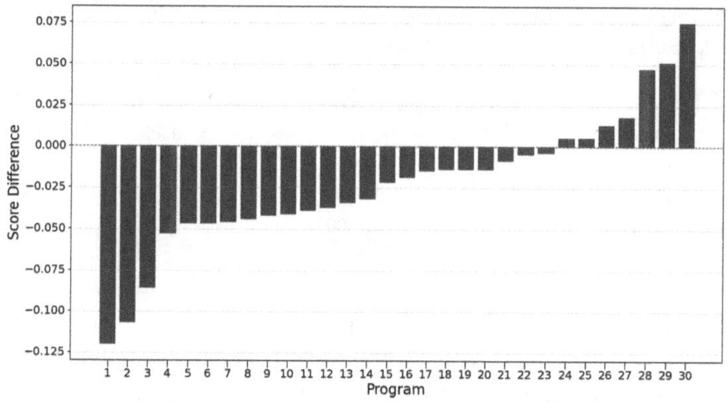

Fig. 4. Performance variation after the application of Gemini-2.5-Flash as Reviewer (negative values indicate improvement). Videos are sorted in increasing order by score difference.

Table 2. Comparison of Entity Recognition capabilities for a clip. Reference, transcription and review are shown in Italian; colors indicate correct (green) and incorrect (red) entities. The reference is human-edited and may differ from a verbatim transcript.

Reference	WhisperX Transcription	Gemini-2.5-Flash Review
E' sicuramente una grandissima operazione, sicuramente abbiamo azzerato i vertici della **'ndrangheta** della provincia di **Vibo Valentia**, oltre 13 locali in provincia di **Vibo Valentia** che erano ramificati in tutta **Italia**.	Sicuramente è una grandissima operazione, sicuramente abbiamo azzerato i vertici dell'Andrangheta della provincia di Vibo-Valenzia. Oltre 12-13 locali di Andrangheta in provincia di Vibo-Valenzia che avevano ramificazioni in tutta Italia.	Sicuramente è una grandissima operazione, sicuramente abbiamo azzerato i vertici dell''ndrangheta della provincia di Vibo Valentia. Oltre 12-13 locali di ndrangheta in provincia di Vibo Valentia che avevano ramificazioni in tutta Italia.

algorithm automatically splits the text into two lines or multiple segments, prioritizing breaks at punctuation marks. With this strategy, the resulting subtitles comply fully with the main readability metrics considered.

6 Times and Costs

The Inverse Real Time Factor (RTFx) has been computed for all four ASR models. Across the 30 programs, Whisper Large V2 achieves a mean Inverse RTFx of 4.873 (±0.596), WhisperX reaches 14.081 (±1.102), and AssemblyAI attains 26.035 (±4.690). For certain samples, Parakeet TDT v3 was executed on

Table 3. Performance Comparison and Cost-Efficiency Analysis of ASR Models. For Inverse RTFx metric, the higher is better.

ASR Model	Estimated Total Inference Cost	Inverse RTFx (Mean)	Std.Dev. (±)	Hardware Platform
Whisper Large V2	$7.04	4.873	0.596	NVIDIA T4
WhisperX	$2.56	14.081	1.102	NVIDIA T4
AssemblyAI	$7.50	26.035	4.690	Cloud API
Parakeet TDT v3	Variable	32.890	16.903	NVIDIA T4/L4

a different hardware configuration (NVIDIA L4 GPU instead of T4), resulting in greater variability in its Inverse RTFx values, with a mean of 32.89 and a standard deviation of 16.903; it is included here for completeness. Considering the estimated cost of $0.64 per hour for using a T4 GPU in the Google Cloud environment, the inference cost for Whisper Large and WhisperX amounts to approximately $7.04 and $2.56, respectively. The cost for Parakeet inference varies depending on the L4 GPU usage, while the total cost for AssemblyAI API calls is estimated at $7.50 ($0.15 per hour of audio in input). Taken together, the runtime and cost values suggest that in a production environment handling a large volume of videos, it may be preferable to accept longer processing times in exchange for lower operational costs, favoring an internal solution like WhisperX over faster but more expensive external API-based alternatives, thereby optimizing cost-efficiency at scale (Table 3).

7 Discussion

This study demonstrates that integrating an Automatic Speech Recognition system as the central component of a carefully designed subtitling pipeline can significantly streamline the production process. However, achieving fully automated subtitling that meets professional quality standards and industry compliance requirements remains beyond the current technological frontier, as performance varies considerably across program types and contexts.

Programs with a single speaker, clear articulation, and limited background noise, such as the selected "Scientific Communication" one, can be transcribed with minimal human intervention. In these cases, the application of an appropriate segmentation algorithm ensures compliance with readability and timing guidelines. In contrast, other programs (e.g., the ones of "Investigative Journalism" or "Talk Show") require greater human involvement to preserve the semantic coherence of dialogues and prevent confusion in the transcription, with varying performance between episodes due to differences in linguistic and acoustic conditions. Special attention is also required in cases involving songs or foreign languages, where ASR systems tend to diverge from expected behaviour and produce low-quality transcriptions.

Although all evaluated ASR systems exhibit broadly comparable performance, WhisperX, specifically optimized for long-form transcription, emerges as the most effective model in this benchmarking, particularly for its superior entity recognition capabilities. Moreover, the inclusion of Gemini-2.5-Flash as a reviewer, even in a zero-shot configuration and without "thinking" capabilities, demonstrates a measurable improvement in the correction of misrecognized or misspelled entities. This finding is particularly significant, as in the context of building a production-grade subtitling pipeline for a media company, minimizing entity recognition errors is crucial. Nevertheless, a human-in-the-loop review will remain essential to ensure the highest level of accuracy.

8 Conclusion and Impact

This research highlights several key aspects for the industrial development of an infrastructure dedicated to subtitle production in the media industry. Our findings suggest that because the various ASR models evaluated exhibit comparable performance, the selection of a system in an industrial setting should move beyond pure accuracy considerations. Instead, deployment strategy should be guided by practical trade-offs, such as balancing the operational costs of an in-house GPU-based solution against the convenience of proprietary APIs. For instance, handling a large volume of videos favors internal solutions like WhisperX, which optimized cost-efficiency at approximately \$2.56 per hour compared to \$7.50 for external alternatives.

A primary lesson for practitioners is the "Genre Gap" in ASR reliability. While programs with clear articulation, such as Scientific Communication, can be transcribed with minimal intervention (WER of 0.2), formats like Talk Shows or Investigative Journalism require significantly greater human involvement to preserve semantic coherence. Furthermore, we found that raw ASR output is rarely "broadcast-ready". Proper engineering–specifically utilizing word-level timestamps and intelligent segmentation algorithms–is critical to ensure that SubRip files strictly adhere to readability guidelines like the Number of Characters per Segment and Characters per Second.

The integration of a Large Language Model as a zero-shot reviewer represents a significant step forward in automation. Specifically, Gemini-2.5-Flash provided a statistically significant improvement (a 2.3% mean gain) in the correction of misrecognized named entities while preserving the original subtitle structure. To support these computationally intensive tasks at scale, we developed a decoupled cloud infrastructure that separates the user interface from the processing logic, utilizing NVIDIA L4 GPUs only when required to minimize idle hardware consumption.

While the current system provides a robust foundation, several avenues for future work have been identified to further bridge the gap to full automation. Following recent research in other languages, we plan to investigate multimodal augmentation for the LLM reviewer, providing the model with acoustic features or visual context (e.g., speaker faces or on-screen text) to improve transcription in noisy environments. Moreover, leveraging the existing infrastructure, we aim to extend the pipeline to generate interlingual subtitles and high-quality AI-driven voice dubbing using translation-oriented LLMs and text-to-speech modalities.

Future iterations could incorporate structured evaluations with professional subtitlers to measure the concrete productivity gains and reduced manual effort provided by the HITL pipeline. In conclusion, hybrid workflows that combine ASR with targeted human review represent the most effective strategy for production environments. This human-in-the-loop paradigm could enable scalable automation while maintaining the linguistic and editorial precision required for professional broadcasting.

Consequently, ensuring that end-users have the ability to monitor and edit subtitles in real-time through an intuitive interface remains a crucial component of any successful industrial deployment.

9 Limitations

This study presents several limitations that should be considered when interpreting the results.

First, the use of human-made subtitles as reference material introduces an inherent source of evaluation noise. These subtitles are not verbatim transcriptions but professionally edited outputs designed for readability and timing. As a consequence, the evaluation captures the "distance to industry-compliant output" rather than pure transcription accuracy, and may penalize acceptable paraphrases or differences in segmentation.

Second, the dataset is limited to a small set of television programs from a single Italian broadcaster. While this provides a realistic industrial scenario, it restricts generalization to other forms of audiovisual content, such as films or scripted series, which may involve distinct linguistic registers, acoustic environments, and editing styles.

Finally, the study does not incorporate collaborative assessments with professional subtitlers. Such evaluations would be crucial for two reasons: (i) they enable a more semantically grounded assessment of ASR errors beyond surface-form mismatches, and (ii) they provide a concrete measure of productivity gains achievable in real production environments.

Disclosure of Interests. The authors have no competing interests to declare that are relevant to the content of this article.

A Appendix

The high level schema of the infrastructure currently in production and developed following the results of the research is reported in Fig. 5. The subtitle processing pipeline runs on a Google Cloud Run Job, while the user interface is hosted on a Google Cloud Run Service Container. The authentication is handled via Identity-Aware Proxy identification, mantaining an allow-list of authorized users. When a user initiates processing through the UI, the Job is triggered via a dedicated Cloud Run Service Function that listens to messages on a specific Pub/Sub topic. The separation of responsibilities between the components offers two key advantages: first, it enables broader accessibility to the subtitling service, allowing it to be invoked from external entry points without relying solely on the front-end interface; second, it ensures continuous service availability for users while minimizing hardware resource consumption. This is achieved by delegating computationally intensive tasks to the Job instance, which is equipped with an NVIDIA L4 GPU to ensure optimal performance and is automatically activated only when required, shutting down once the processing is complete. Google Cloud Storage and BigQuery are used to manage the data and metadata generated during the workflow (Table 4).

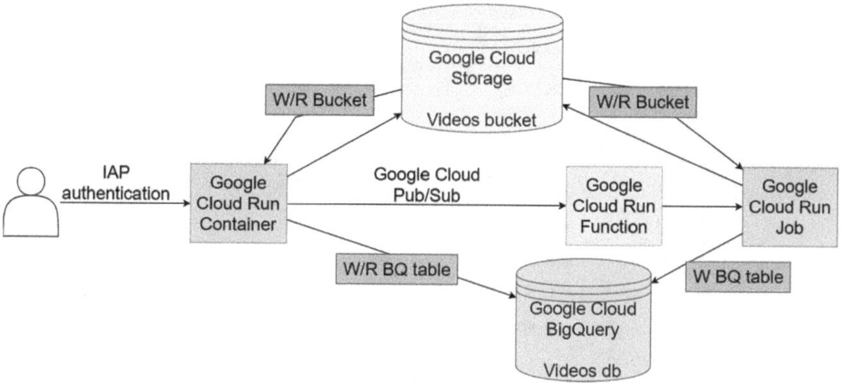

Fig. 5. High-level overview of the developed infrastructure.

Table 4. System prompt and requested structured output for the reviewer LLM.

System Prompt
You are a professional subtitle proofreader, specialized in Italian multimedia content. You will receive a series of subtitles from a video segment produced by Italian Media company (e.g. journalism, interviews, sports, etc.). Each subtitle includes an "index" field and a "subtitle" field (in Italian), extracted from an SubRip Text file. These subtitles were automatically generated with Whisper and may contain typos, formatting issues, or transcription errors. Your task is to correct evident mistakes such as typos, mis-transcribed proper names, or minor grammatical errors. Do not alter the structure or content that is already correct. IMPORTANT: return only a JSON array with the same number of elements as the input. Each element must be an object with "index" and "correct_sub".
Requested Structured Output
class CorrectSubs(BaseModel): index: int = Field(..., description="The index of the subtitled sentence") correct_sub: str = Field(..., description="The corrected sub")

Table 5. Descriptive statistics of the reference dataset considered in the research.

Program	Number of Episodes	Typology	Total Duration (min)
Mezz'ora in più	5	Talk Show	149.93
Porta a Porta	5	Talk Show	514.73
Presa Diretta	5	Investigative Journalism	540.86
Report	5	Investigative Journalism	543.80
Ulisse	10	Scientific Communication	1,255.53

Table 6. Descriptive statistics of the reference dataset considered in the research.

Program	Date	Typology	Duration (min)	Reference Number
Mezz'ora in più	14/03/2021	Talk Show	30.2	462
Mezz'ora in più	23/05/2021	Talk Show	28.83	442
Mezz'ora in più	10/10/2021	Talk Show	35.25	540
Mezz'ora in più	24/10/2021	Talk Show	27.65	435
Mezz'ora in più	27/03/2022	Talk Show	28.00	460
Porta a Porta	09/06/2021	Talk Show	86.93	1169
Porta a Porta	15/06/2022	Talk Show	104.21	1561
Porta a Porta	22/06/2022	Talk Show	118.64	1824
Porta a Porta	23/06/2022	Talk Show	96.25	1497
Porta a Porta	28/06/2022	Talk Show	108.70	1639
Presa Diretta	15/03/2021	Investigative Journalism	106.29	1394
Presa Diretta	07/02/2022	Investigative Journalism	105.76	1505
Presa Diretta	14/02/2022	Investigative Journalism	109.61	1766
Presa Diretta	14/03/2022	Investigative Journalism	109.67	1773
Presa Diretta	13/03/2023	Investigative Journalism	109.53	1610
Report	12/04/2021	Investigative Journalism	110.93	1471
Report	10/05/2021	Investigative Journalism	106.97	1363
Report	20/12/2021	Investigative Journalism	112.27	1635
Report	11/04/2022	Investigative Journalism	107.64	1659
Report	13/06/2022	Investigative Journalism	105.99	1571
Ulisse	21/04/2021	Scientific Communication	126.74	1702
Ulisse	28/04/2021	Scientific Communication	127.22	1670
Ulisse	05/05/2021	Scientific Communication	125.93	1709
Ulisse	27/05/2021	Scientific Communication	122.00	1482
Ulisse	03/06/2021	Scientific Communication	124.15	1514
Ulisse	25/01/2022	Scientific Communication	128.90	1586
Ulisse	09/04/2022	Scientific Communication	123.96	1664
Ulisse	16/04/2022	Scientific Communication	127.13	1666
Ulisse	23/04/2022	Scientific Communication	127.13	1853
Ulisse	30/04/2022	Scientific Communication	122.37	1555

References

1. Bain, M., Huh, J., Han, T., Zisserman, A.: Whisperx: time-accurate speech transcription of long-form audio (2023). https://arxiv.org/abs/2303.00747
2. Davitti, E., Sandrelli, A., Korybski, T., Zou, Y., Orasan, C., Braun, S.: Using ASR tools to produce automatic subtitles for TV broadcasting: a cross-linguistic comparative analysis. J. Audiov. Transl. **7**(2), 1–35 (2024). https://doi.org/10.47476/jat.v7i2.2024.305
3. Fedorchenko, A., Alumäe, T.: Optimizing estonian TV subtitles with semi-supervised learning and LLMs (2025). https://arxiv.org/abs/2501.05234
4. Ferraro, A., Galli, A., La Gatta, V., Postiglione, M.: Benchmarking open source and paid services for speech to text: an analysis of quality and input variety. Front. Big Data **6**, 1210559 (2023). https://doi.org/10.3389/fdata.2023.1210559
5. Gernsbacher, M.A.: Video captions benefit everyone. Policy Insights Behav. Brain Sci. **2**(1), 195–202 (2015). https://doi.org/10.1177/2372732215602130
6. Kuhn, K., Kersken, V., Reuter, B., Egger, N., Zimmermann, G.: Measuring the accuracy of automatic speech recognition solutions. ACM Trans. Accessible Comput. **16**(4), 1–23 (2023). https://doi.org/10.1145/3636513
7. Li, S., Chen, C., Kwok, C.Y., Chu, C., Chng, E.S., Kawai, H.: Investigating ASR error correction with large language model and multilingual 1-best hypotheses (2024). https://www.isca-archive.org/interspeech_2024/li24h_interspeech.pdf
8. Ma, R., Qian, M., Gales, M., Knill, K.: ASR error correction using large language models (2025). https://arxiv.org/abs/2409.09554
9. Prabhavalkar, R., Hori, T., Sainath, T.N., Schlüter, R., Watanabe, S.: End-to-end speech recognition: a survey (2023). https://arxiv.org/abs/2303.03329
10. Radford, A., Kim, J.W., Xu, T., Brockman, G., McLeavey, C., Sutskever, I.: Robust speech recognition via large-scale weak supervision. In: International Conference on Machine Learning, pp. 28492–28518. PMLR (2023)
11. RAI - Radiotelevisione Italiana: Norme e convenzioni editoriali essenziali sottotitoli televisivi per spettatori sordi e con difficoltà uditive a cura di rai (2021). https://www.rai.it/dl/doc/2020/10/19/1603121663902_PREREGISTR_22_feb_2016.pdf
12. Ramirez, F.M., et al.: Anatomy of industrial scale multilingual ASR (2024). https://arxiv.org/abs/2404.09841
13. Romero-Fresco, P., Gauwbergen, Y.: Fit for what purpose? NER certification of automatic captions in English and Spanish. Appl. Sci. **15** (2025). https://doi.org/10.3390/app15031387
14. Sekoyan, M., et al.: Canary-1b-v2 & parakeet-tdt-0.6b-v3: efficient and high-performance models for multilingual ASR and AST (2025). https://arxiv.org/abs/2509.14128
15. Sellam, T., Das, D., Parikh, A.P.: Bleurt: learning robust metrics for text generation (2020). https://arxiv.org/abs/2004.04696
16. Walker, K., Lezic, A., Bačić, D.: Unveiling the impact of subtitles: insights into recall and viewer visual engagement on streaming video content. In: Proceedings of MIPRO 2025 - Human-Computer Interaction (HCI), pp. 1540–1545. MIPRO, Ohrid, North Macedonia (2025)

17. Wei, V.J., Wang, W., Jiang, D., Song, Y., Wang, L.: ASR-EC benchmark: evaluating large language models on Chinese ASR error correction. In: Potdar, S., Rojas-Barahona, L., Montella, S. (eds.) Proceedings of the 2025 Conference on Empirical Methods in Natural Language Processing: Industry Track, pp. 1567–1575. Association for Computational Linguistics, Suzhou (China) (2025). https://doi.org/10.18653/v1/2025.emnlp-industry.110. https://aclanthology.org/2025.emnlp-industry.110/
18. Wilken, P., Georgakopoulou, P., Matusov, E.: Suber: a metric for automatic evaluation of subtitle quality (2022). https://arxiv.org/abs/2205.05805

Gradient-Scale Collapse in Additive Text-CF Fusion: Early Diagnosis and Minimal Repair

Yunan Zhang, Jingjing Fan(✉), and Yanxiao Liu

Hebei University of Architecture, Zhangjiakou, China
{fjj1960,lyx2025229119}@hebiace.edu.cn

Abstract. Additive fusion—combining CF and text embeddings as $\mathbf{e}_i = \mathbf{e}_i^{\text{CF}} + \lambda_i \mathbf{e}_i^{\text{text}}$—is a simple way to inject pre-trained text features into collaborative-filtering recommenders. We show that this fusion family has a systematic failure mode: large text-branch scale can dominate additive training and, in learned-gate variants, dominate the gate gradient. Recommendation quality collapses by up to 54% on three of six evaluated datasets. We call this *gradient-scale collapse* and demonstrate, via a concatenation-fusion control that avoids collapse on all three affected datasets (up to 76%-point gap), that the failure is architecture-specific rather than caused by text quality.

Across six datasets under a unified full-ranking protocol, we characterize three behavioral modes of additive fusion: *beneficial* (Amazon Fine Food, +19.2%), *collapse* (Yelp −54.2%, Amazon Books −28.3%, Amazon CDs −25.6%), and *no-value* (MIND, all variants below CF-only). A conservative early-diagnosis protocol based on first-K-epoch gradient-ratio dynamics identifies high-confidence collapse risk before full training (at $K = 5$: precision = 1.0, recall = 0.37 in leave-one-dataset-out cross-validation on 30 cases). Branch-wise gradient normalization is the only tested minimal repair that recovers performance across all three collapse datasets; PCGrad-style projection is not a reliable substitute and degrades Yelp and MIND. These findings yield a low-overhead *diagnose-then-act* workflow for teams with existing CF pipelines.

Keywords: Recommendation Systems · Additive Fusion · Gradient Imbalance · Early Diagnosis · Practical Workflow

1 Introduction

Additive fusion—combining CF and text embeddings as $\mathbf{e}_i = \mathbf{e}_i^{\text{CF}} + \lambda_i \mathbf{e}_i^{\text{text}}$—is a common lightweight approach to injecting pre-trained text features into collaborative-filtering (CF) recommenders. Despite its simplicity, we observe that

Supplementary Information The online version contains supplementary material available at https://doi.org/10.1007/978-3-032-37682-4_33.

M. Baratchi et al. (Eds.): ECML PKDD 2026, LNAI 16949, pp. 565–581, 2027.
https://doi.org/10.1007/978-3-032-37682-4_33

this architecture exhibits a systematic failure mode on datasets with large item catalogs and sparse interactions. Large text-branch scale can dominate additive training and, when λ_i is learned, can dominate the gate update. In our experiments, recommendation quality drops by up to 54%.

We identify the root cause as *gradient-scale collapse*: in the additive formulation, the gate gradient $\partial\mathcal{L}/\partial\lambda_i = (\partial\mathcal{L}/\partial\mathbf{e}_i)^\top \mathbf{e}_i^{\text{text}}$ contains the text embedding directly. Its magnitude is bounded by the product of the upstream-gradient norm and $\|\mathbf{e}_i^{\text{text}}\|_2$, so a large text scale can amplify gate updates when the two vectors are aligned. This structural bias does not arise in non-gated architectures such as concatenation fusion, where both branches flow through a shared MLP without a scalar gate. We confirm this distinction empirically: concatenation fusion avoids collapse on the same datasets where additive fusion fails.

Across six datasets under a unified full-ranking protocol, we characterize three behavioral modes of additive fusion: text is *beneficial*, text causes *gradient-scale collapse*, or text adds *no value*. This motivates a strategy-selection problem: **which action should a practitioner take—keep fixed fusion, apply minimal repair, or abandon text—and can this decision be made *before* full training?**

1.1 Research Questions

- **RQ1:** Under what conditions does additive text-CF fusion suffer gradient-scale collapse, and is this pattern consistent across multiple datasets?
- **RQ2:** Is collapse specific to the additive architecture, or does it also affect concatenation fusion? (Architecture contrast)
- **RQ3:** Can first-K-epoch signals ($K \in \{3, 5, 10\}$) reliably identify collapse risk before full training?
- **RQ4:** What is the minimal effective repair for collapse-prone datasets, and when should text be abandoned entirely?

1.2 Key Contributions

- **Phenomenon Identification with Architecture Contrast:** We identify gradient-scale collapse as a systematic failure mode of additive text-CF fusion, confirmed on three independent datasets (Yelp, Amazon Books, Amazon CDs). Through a concatenation-fusion control, we demonstrate that the failure is architecture-specific—caused by the gate gradient's structural dependence on text-branch magnitude—rather than a problem with text quality.
- **Theoretical Characterization:** We formally derive the scale-sensitive gate gradient in additive fusion and show how branch-wise gradient normalization controls the accompanying branch-update imbalance. We contrast this with concatenation fusion, where no scalar gate creates the same bottleneck.
- **Early Diagnostic Protocol and Minimal Repair:** Using first-K-epoch gradient-ratio dynamics, we construct a transparent early-warning rule evaluated via leave-one-dataset-out cross-validation on 30 dataset-seed cases.

Branch gradient normalization is the only tested minimal repair that succeeds on every collapse dataset. These findings yield a low-overhead *diagnose-then-act* workflow with quantified compute savings.

2 The Practitioner's Problem

Recommendation teams with an existing CF baseline face a recurring question: is it worth adding text features via additive fusion for a specific dataset? In current practice, this decision requires full-length trial runs, which is expensive when fusion collapses—as we observe on three of six datasets.

The problem is compounded by the fact that additive fusion ($\mathbf{e}_i = \mathbf{e}_i^{\mathrm{CF}} + \lambda_i \mathbf{e}_i^{\mathrm{text}}$) introduces a structural vulnerability: the gate gradient depends on pre-trained text embedding magnitude, creating a failure mode absent from non-gated alternatives. Practitioners need to know not only *whether* text helps, but *whether their chosen architecture is safe.*

Our objective is operational: provide an early-warning protocol for additive fusion that (1) detects gradient-scale collapse risk within $K = 5$ pilot epochs, and (2) routes to the appropriate strategy—keep fusion, apply gradient-balanced repair, or fall back to CF-only—before committing full training budgets.

Applied Readiness. The workflow is an empirically validated prototype for teams with an existing CF training loop. It covers pilot training, gradient-ratio extraction, threshold-based routing, and optional GradNorm repair on six real-world datasets with up to 2.2M interactions. The validation uses realistic offline constraints: a single-GPU budget and full-ranking evaluation. The diagnostic protocol requires no framework changes—it monitors standard gradient norms already available in PyTorch—and the GradNorm repair adds <1% per-epoch overhead.

3 Related Work

Text Encoders for Recommendation. BERT [3] and Sentence-BERT [14] provide rich features; P5 [6], TALLRec [1], and UniSRec [9] advance *what* to fuse. We address *when* additive fusion fails. End-to-end multi-modal models (BM3 [23], LATTICE [20], FREEDOM [22]) achieve strong absolute performance through dedicated architectures; we position our work as a complementary diagnostic layer for teams with existing CF pipelines.

Multi-task Gradient Methods. GradNorm [2], PCGrad [19], MGDA [16], and CAGrad [11] balance gradients across *loss heads*. Our setting differs: imbalance arises between *input branches* sharing a single BPR loss. We therefore test a GradNorm-inspired branch normalization and use PCGrad as a conflict-oriented comparator.

Multi-modal Fusion and Modality Competition. OGM-GE [13] and PMR [5] rebalance gradients from *separate modality-specific losses.* Our mechanism is different: in additive fusion with a single shared loss, the gate gradient is structurally biased by text embedding magnitude. We provide the first formal analysis of this architecture-specific bias.

Early Stopping. Learning-curve extrapolation [4,10] terminates weak runs. We differ in target: rather than early-stopping one model, we use branch-level signals to *select the best strategy* before committing to full training.

4 Study Design

4.1 Problem Setting

Given users $\mathcal{U}$, items $\mathcal{I}$ with binary interactions and item text descriptions, we learn a scoring function $\hat{y}_{ui} = f(u,i)$ optimized with BPR loss [15]: $\mathcal{L}_{\text{rec}} = -\sum_{(u,i^+,i^-)} \log \sigma(\hat{y}_{ui^+} - \hat{y}_{ui^-}) + \beta\|\Theta\|_2^2$. The CF branch uses a latent-factor collaborative-filtering model trained end-to-end with the BPR objective (BPR-MF), with $\mathbf{e}_i^{\text{CF}} \in \mathbb{R}^d$. The text branch uses frozen Sentence-BERT (all-MiniLM-L6-v2) [14]; its 384-dimensional output is linearly projected to $\mathbb{R}^d$.

4.2 Fusion Architectures Under Study

We study two fusion architectures that represent fundamentally different design choices:

Additive Fusion (Gated). The item representation is $\mathbf{e}_i = \mathbf{e}_i^{\text{CF}} + \lambda_i \mathbf{e}_i^{\text{text}}$, where λ_i is a learned scalar gate controlling text injection. This is the dominant lightweight fusion approach in practice.

Concatenation Fusion (Non-gated). The item representation is produced by an MLP over the concatenated CF/text vector. Both branches therefore pass through a shared nonlinear layer without a scalar gate. This serves as our architecture control.

4.3 Theoretical Motivation: Gate Gradient Bias

We identify a structural property of additive fusion that makes it vulnerable to gradient-scale collapse.

Proposition 1 (Gate Gradient Bias). In additive fusion $\mathbf{e}_i = \mathbf{e}_i^{\text{CF}} + \lambda_i \mathbf{e}_i^{\text{text}}$, the gate gradient is

$$\frac{\partial \mathcal{L}}{\partial \lambda_i} = \left(\frac{\partial \mathcal{L}}{\partial \mathbf{e}_i}\right)^\top \mathbf{e}_i^{\text{text}}. \tag{1}$$

By Cauchy–Schwarz, the gate-gradient magnitude satisfies

$$\left|\frac{\partial \mathcal{L}}{\partial \lambda_i}\right| \leq \left\|\frac{\partial \mathcal{L}}{\partial \mathbf{e}_i}\right\|_2 \left\|\mathbf{e}_i^{\text{text}}\right\|_2.$$

Thus, when the text and upstream gradients are sufficiently aligned, a large text-embedding scale can amplify the gate update and contribute to saturation.

Proof Sketch. By the chain rule, $\partial \mathbf{e}_i / \partial \lambda_i = \mathbf{e}_i^{\text{text}}$, yielding Eq. (1) directly. In the gate MLP $\lambda_i = \sigma(\mathbf{w}^\top \mathbf{h} + b)$, the update also depends on the gate Jacobian and feature alignment; the text norm therefore acts as a scale factor rather than determining the update alone. Further derivation is in the Supplementary Material.

Why Concatenation Fusion Avoids this Bias. In concatenation fusion $\hat{y}_{ui} = f_{\text{MLP}}([\mathbf{e}_u; \mathbf{e}_i^{\text{CF}}; \mathbf{e}_i^{\text{text}}])$, there is no scalar gate λ_i. Both branches contribute to a joint representation through the MLP weight matrix, which can absorb magnitude differences without a single-parameter bottleneck. The gradient with respect to any MLP parameter depends on both branches jointly, preventing one branch from monopolizing the update direction.

4.4 Minimal Repair: Branch Gradient Normalization

Motivated by Proposition 1, our primary repair is branch-wise gradient normalization:

$$\hat{g}_{\text{CF}} = \frac{g_{\text{CF}}}{\|g_{\text{CF}}\|_2 + \epsilon}, \quad \hat{g}_{\text{text}} = \frac{g_{\text{text}}}{\|g_{\text{text}}\|_2 + \epsilon}, \tag{2}$$

with $\epsilon = 10^{-8}$ and negligible computational overhead. In our implementation, these are the gradients of the CF embedding parameters and text-projection parameters; gate-network gradients are left unchanged. The intervention equalizes branch update norms and empirically stabilizes additive optimization. We call the full variant with additional gating and regularization **Gradient-Balanced Adaptive Fusion (GBAF)**; component details and the PCGrad-style comparator are in the Supplementary Material.

5 Experiments

5.1 Datasets

We evaluate on six datasets spanning distinct sparsity, text quality, and domain regimes:

- **MovieLens-1M** [7]: Structured and concise movie metadata.
- **Amazon Fine Food** [12]: Rich product text with moderate sparsity.
- **Yelp** [18]: Large-scale local business recommendation with diverse text.
- **MIND** [17]: News recommendation with short titles and strong popularity skew.

- **Amazon Books**: Book titles and descriptions; subsampled to 12K users with 10-core filtering from the Amazon review corpus [8].
- **Amazon CDs**: CD/vinyl album metadata; 10-core filtered from the Amazon review corpus [8].

Table 1 summarizes the dataset statistics. The six datasets cover a range of densities (4×10^{-4} to 4×10^{-2}), item counts (1.7K to 57K), and text types (short titles, structured metadata, long descriptions).

Table 1. Dataset statistics (train split).

Dataset	Users	Items	Train Int.	Density
MovieLens-1M	6,040	3,416	797,275	0.0386
Amazon Fine Food	6,690	1,769	43,112	0.0036
Amazon Books	12,129	14,710	291,042	0.0016
Amazon CDs	15,592	16,184	414,228	0.0016
Yelp	99,165	56,696	2,173,523	0.00039
MIND	50,000	7,713	185,581	0.00048

5.2 Compared Methods

We compare methods spanning CF-only, two fusion architectures (additive and concatenation), and gradient-balanced repair variants:

- **CF-only (BPR-MF):** Latent-factor collaborative filtering trained with BPR, without text fusion.
- **Fixed Fusion:** Additive fusion with a constant $\lambda = 0.5$ (no learned gate). This is the operational default used for short pilot runs.
- **Concat-MLP:** Concatenation fusion through an MLP, serving as the *architecture control* (non-gated, no scalar λ).
- **GradNorm-only:** Additive fusion with branch-level gradient normalization (no confidence gate or regularization).
- **GBAF:** Full gradient-balanced additive fusion with an item-level learned gate, gradient normalization, and regularization.
- **BM3** [23] / **LATTICE** [20] / **FREEDOM** [22]: End-to-end multi-modal recommenders from MMRec [21], evaluated on four datasets (ML-1M, Amazon FF, Yelp, MIND) with identical splits and seeds to provide absolute performance context.

PCGrad-style [19] (gradient conflict projection) is tested in ablations as an alternative repair strategy.

5.3 Evaluation Metrics

We report **Recall@10** and **NDCG@10** as the evaluation metrics. Following common protocol for top-K recommendation benchmarks, all main results use **full-ranking evaluation** (rank over all candidate items after masking training interactions). We report mean and standard deviation across 5 random seeds.

5.4 Implementation Details

All models are implemented in PyTorch 2.0.1 and trained on a single NVIDIA RTX 4080 GPU (16GB VRAM). The BPR-MF backbone uses 64-dimensional user and item embeddings. The text encoder is a frozen Sentence-BERT (all-MiniLM-L6-v2, 384-dim); pre-computed embeddings are shared across all methods. For additive fixed fusion, we set $\lambda = 0.5$ as an equal-weight pilot. This baseline tests whether adding text is safe before spending budget on adaptive gates or larger fusion modules; it is not itself a learned-gate experiment. For Concat-MLP, we use a two-layer MLP ([32, 16], ReLU, dropout = 0.1) with LayerNorm and residual connection. For GBAF, the quadratic gate coefficient is $\alpha = 0.1$ on MovieLens and the Amazon datasets and $\alpha = 0.05$ on Yelp/MIND; Yelp/MIND additionally use a small entropy term ($\beta = 0.001$). GBAF gate hidden sizes are [32, 16], except [64, 16] on Yelp/MIND. We use Adam with learning rate 0.003 and batch size 1024, for up to 60 epochs on Yelp/MIND (50 on others) with early stopping (patience = 10). Concat-MLP uses batch size 2048, 30 epochs, and patience 3 on Yelp/MIND; its other settings follow the released configs. Validation/testing use full ranking with train-item masking. Seeds are 42, 123, 999, 2024, and 2025. All datasets use leave-one-out splitting (last interaction for test, second-last for validation). Amazon Books and CDs use 10-core filtering; Amazon Books is subsampled to at most 30K users before a final 10-core pass. Code, final configs, and result tables are available at https://github.com/niyaobuyaochibl/gradient-scale-collapse-ecml2026.

5.5 Early Diagnosis Protocol

To evaluate whether collapse risk can be identified before full training, we construct an early-diagnosis dataset from logs of fixed-fusion and CF-only pilots across all six datasets. The fixed-fusion pilot is the practical decision point: it asks whether a team should continue with additive text fusion, repair it, or abandon text. For each dataset-seed pair, we extract first-K-epoch features ($K \in \{3, 5, 10\}$): mean/variance/slope of r_t, mean deviation $\mathbb{E}_{t \le K}|r_t - 1|$, and early validation gap $\Delta_{\text{val}}^{(K)} = \text{R@10}_{\text{fixed}} - \text{R@10}_{\text{CF}}$.

The signal r_t is computed at epoch granularity: we accumulate branch gradient ℓ_2 norms over all mini-batches on trainable branch parameters in epoch t, then take the ratio $r_t = \left(\sum_b \|g_{\text{text}}^{(b)}\|_2\right) / \left(\sum_b \|g_{\text{CF}}^{(b)}\|_2 + \epsilon\right)$.

We define collapse labels from final performance:

$$y = \mathbb{1}\left[\frac{\text{R@10}_{\text{fixed}} - \text{R@10}_{\text{CF}}}{\text{R@10}_{\text{CF}}} < -0.1\right].$$

A transparent threshold rule is evaluated: predict collapse if $\Delta_{\text{val}}^{(K)} < 0$ and $\mathbb{E}_{t \le K}|r_t - 1|$ exceeds the median. To avoid data leakage, we evaluate via **leave-one-dataset-out cross-validation**: the median threshold is computed on all datasets except the held-out one, and prediction quality is measured on the held-out dataset's seeds. This yields 30 dataset-seed cases (6 datasets × 5 seeds) with proper out-of-sample evaluation.

6 Results

We present results in three parts: overall performance with architecture contrast (RQ1–2), early diagnosis effectiveness (RQ3), and repair ablation (RQ4).

6.1 Overall Performance and Architecture Contrast

Table 2 summarizes results across all six datasets with 5-seed evaluations. Paired t-tests evaluate selected key comparisons; full statistics and non-significant cases are reported in the Supplementary Material.

Table 2 reveals three distinct behavioral modes of additive fusion:

Mode A – Beneficial (Amazon Fine Food): Fixed fusion achieves .6272 (+19.2%), outperforming repair variants and external SOTA models (FREEDOM .5401, LATTICE .5535). Small item catalog (1,769) limits gate bias impact. *Strategy: use fixed fusion.*

Mode B – Collapse (Yelp, Amazon Books, Amazon CDs): Fixed fusion collapses (−54.2%, −28.3%, −25.6%). GradNorm recovers above CF-only on all three (+35.6%, +40.9%, +57.4%). Shared characteristic: large catalogs (>14K items) with sparse interactions. *Strategy: apply GradNorm repair.*

Mode C – No Value (MIND): CF-only (.0658) beats all fusion variants and even BM3 (.0662) and FREEDOM (.0648) are at parity—text adds no signal (Sect. 7.2). *Strategy: skip text.*

Architecture Contrast (RQ2): On all Mode B datasets, Concat-MLP *avoids collapse*: Yelp +22.2%, Books +2.9%, CDs +17.4%—while additive fusion collapses by −28% to −54% with identical text features. This confirms collapse is gate-specific (Proposition 1). On MIND, both architectures underperform CF-only, confirming uninformative text. MovieLens is borderline (−2.3%), illustrating the need for quantitative diagnosis.

6.2 Early Diagnosis Effectiveness

Table 3 reports early-collapse prediction quality using only first-K-epoch features, evaluated via leave-one-dataset-out cross-validation on 30 dataset-seed cases (6 datasets × 5 seeds). The collapse label threshold (−10%) identifies 19 positive (collapse) and 11 negative cases. Figure 1 shows that collapse-prone runs exhibit distinct early r_t trajectories.

Table 2. Overall Recall@10 and NDCG@10 under full-ranking evaluation (mean, 5 seeds), shown in two dataset panels. **Bold** = best per dataset; underline = best among our methods. External SOTA (BM3, LATTICE, FREEDOM) are evaluated on four datasets using MMRec [21] with identical splits and seeds.

Method	ML-1M		Amazon FF		Amazon Books	
	R@10	N@10	R@10	N@10	R@10	N@10
CF baseline						
CF-only (BPR-MF)	.0525	.0739	.5262	.4714	.0243	.0116
Additive fusion (gated — vulnerable to gradient-scale collapse)						
Fixed (λ=0.5)	.0513	.0688	**.6272**	**.5963**	.0174	.0084
GradNorm-only	—	—	.6166	.5788	<u>.0342</u>	<u>.0168</u>
GBAF (full)	<u>.0528</u>	<u>.0668</u>	<u>.6178</u>	<u>.5766</u>	.0328	.0160
Concatenation fusion (non-gated — architecture control)						
Concat-MLP	.0494	.0636	.5504	.5061	.0250	.0122
External multi-modal SOTA (end-to-end, dedicated frameworks)						
BM3 [23]	.0418	.0623	.4340	.3583	—	—
LATTICE [20]	.0510	.0708	.5535	.5145	—	—
FREEDOM [22]	**.0593**	**.0784**	.5401	.4589	—	—

Method	Amazon CDs		Yelp		MIND	
	R@10	N@10	R@10	N@10	R@10	N@10
CF baseline						
CF-only (BPR-MF)	.0317	.0165	.0179	.0125	<u>.0658</u>	<u>.0309</u>
Additive fusion (gated — vulnerable to gradient-scale collapse)						
Fixed (λ=0.5)	.0236	.0119	.0082	.0058	.0563	.0278
GradNorm-only	<u>.0500</u>	<u>.0253</u>	<u>.0242</u>	<u>.0165</u>	.0534	.0274
GBAF (full)	.0496	.0251	.0245	.0167	.0591	.0303
Concatenation fusion (non-gated — architecture control)						
Concat-MLP	.0372	.0185	.0219	.0143	.0555	.0271
External multi-modal SOTA (end-to-end, dedicated frameworks)						
BM3 [23]	—	—	.0310	.0211	**.0662**	**.0320**
LATTICE [20]	—	—	.0306	.0206	.0482	.0235
FREEDOM [22]	—	—	**.0356**	**.0239**	.0648	.0291

ML-1M additive repair omitted: borderline (−2.3%). Standard deviations are all below 0.003; the full table is in the supplementary material. Amazon Books/CDs were not evaluated with MMRec baselines because their data conversion was pending.

The rule is deliberately conservative. It never incorrectly flags a beneficial dataset as collapse-prone (precision = 1.0 across all K), but it misses some true collapse cases (recall 0.11–0.37). We therefore use it as a high-confidence alert, not as a complete safety certificate. If the alert does not fire, the practitioner should still compare pilot validation performance before committing to full training. Recall improves from $K = 3$ to $K = 5$; beyond $K = 5$, returns diminish.

For three-way routing (Sect. 7.3), the same features partition the space: $\Delta_{\text{val}}^{(K)} > 0$ signals Mode A; $\Delta_{\text{val}}^{(K)} < 0$ with high vs. low $|r_t - 1|$ distinguishes Mode B from C. This routing is meant to reduce failed full runs, not to replace final validation on the selected strategy.

The practical metric is *per-run* compute savings: for each correctly identified high-risk run, the difference between the full training horizon and K epochs is avoided. With $K = 5$, this saves an average of 55 epochs per correctly flagged collapse run under the dataset-specific 50/60-epoch schedules (Fig. 2).

Table 3. Early-collapse diagnosis quality (leave-one-dataset-out CV, 30 dataset-seed cases).

K	Accuracy	Precision	Recall	F1	Saved Ep./run
3	0.433	1.000	0.105	0.190	57
5	0.600	1.000	0.368	0.538	55
10	0.567	1.000	0.316	0.480	48.3

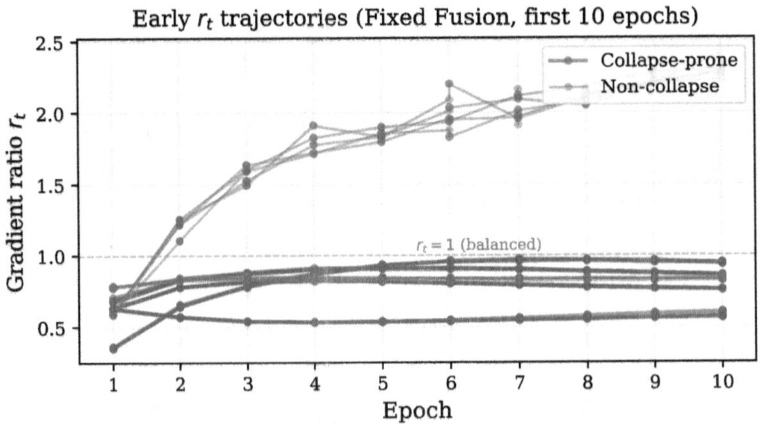

Fig. 1. Fixed-fusion early gradient-ratio trajectories ($K = 10$): collapse-prone runs (red) diverge from $r_t = 1$ more than non-collapse runs (blue). (Color figure online)

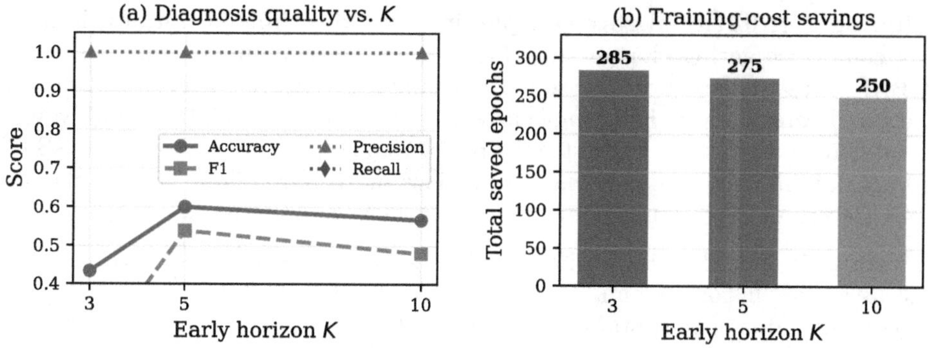

Fig. 2. Early diagnosis quality and training-cost savings across K: $K = 5$ provides the best trade-off between predictive quality and saved epochs per flagged collapse run.

6.3 Ablation: Which Repair Component Matters?

Table 4 reports ablation results on the three original datasets (Yelp: severe collapse; Amazon Fine Food: no collapse; MIND: mild collapse); Table 5 extends the comparison to the two newly added collapse datasets (Amazon Books, Amazon CDs). MovieLens-1M is omitted because its borderline status (−2.3%) yields no significant ablation differences. Together, these tables cover five of six datasets.

Finding 1: Repair necessity is dataset-dependent. On Yelp, Amazon Books, and Amazon CDs, fixed fusion collapses (−54.2%, −28.3%, −25.6% vs CF), and gradient repair is essential. On Amazon Fine Food, fixed fusion *already outperforms* CF (+19.2%), and repair is unnecessary. MIND falls in between: fixed fusion loses −14.4%, and GBAF partially recovers but does not surpass CF-only. This *dataset-dependent* pattern motivates early diagnosis: practitioners need to know *before training* whether repair is needed.

Finding 2: Branch gradient normalization is the essential repair on collapse-prone data. On Yelp, removing GradNorm from GBAF drops R@10 from 0.0245 to 0.0183 (−25.6%, $p < 0.05$), nearly erasing the recovery. GradNorm-only achieves 0.0242, capturing 96% of GBAF's gain. This pattern is consistent across all three collapse datasets. On MIND, the pattern reverses: removing GradNorm *improves* R@10 to 0.0603, suggesting that normalizing a mildly imbalanced gradient can be counterproductive. Table 5 confirms the same repair pattern on Amazon Books/CDs: fixed fusion collapses, while GradNorm-only and GBAF recover substantially above CF-only.

Finding 3: PCGrad is not a reliable magnitude repair. On Yelp, PCGrad degrades to 0.0148 (−16.9% below CF, $p < 10^{-4}$), and it also underperforms CF on MIND. PCGrad [19] targets conflicting task gradients, whereas our branches share one BPR loss and exhibit magnitude imbalance. On Amazon Fine Food, however, PCGrad remains competitive (+19.0% vs CF). The evidence therefore supports a narrower conclusion: conflict projection is not a dependable repair for this failure mode.

Finding 4: Additional gate complexity provides limited benefit. Removing confidence gating changes Recall@10 by at most about 3% relative to full GBAF across the ablation datasets. Removing regularization is also marginal on Yelp and Amazon Fine Food, but hurts MIND (0.0539 vs. 0.0591). Notably, w/o Conf-Gate achieves the highest Yelp R@10 (0.0252), slightly above full GBAF (0.0245), reinforcing the *minimal-repair* view: branch-level GradNorm is the primary lever, and the simplest effective repair may be preferred.

Finding 5: Fixed λ is a pilot, not a gate-dynamics test. We use $\lambda = 0.5$ as a fixed-fusion baseline because it is a simple equal-weight pilot for text injection. It does not contain a learnable gate and therefore does not by itself validate gate saturation. Instead, it exposes whether additive text injection is already harmful under a common lightweight setting. The learned-gate evidence comes from GBAF and its component removals: without branch normalization, adaptive gating loses much of the collapse recovery; with GradNorm, it preserves item-level modulation while controlling scale-driven updates.

Table 4. Multi-dataset ablation (Recall@10, mean ± std). Yelp uses 5 seeds; Amazon and MIND use 5 seeds for core variants, 3 for component-removal variants. † Significantly *below* CF-only ($p < 0.05$). Bold = best per dataset (including component variants).

Method	Yelp	Amazon	MIND
Baselines			
CF-only (BPR-MF)	.0179 ± .0003	.5262 ± .0028	.0658 ± .0012
Fixed ($\lambda = 0.5$)	.0082 ± .0004	**.6272** ± .0014	.0563 ± .0028
Gradient repair strategies			
GradNorm-only	.0242 ± .0005	.6166 ± .0025	.0534 ± .0018
PCGrad-style	.0148 ± .0004†	.6259 ± .0026	.0523 ± .0032†
GBAF (full)	.0245 ± .0005	.6178 ± .0009	.0591 ± .0020
GBAF component removal			
w/o Grad-Norm	.0183 ± .0003	.6228 ± .0019	**.0603** ± .0014
w/o Conf-Gate	**.0252** ± .0002	.6174 ± .0011	.0577 ± .0016
w/o Regulariz.	.0246 ± .0002	.6187 ± .0023	.0539 ± .0025

6.4 Gradient-Ratio Dynamics

Figure 3 shows branch-level dynamics via $r_t = \|g_{\text{text}}\|_2/(\|g_{\text{CF}}\|_2 + \epsilon)$: gradient-balanced training keeps r_t controlled and avoids the unstable spikes observed in fixed fusion. On MIND, epochs with higher $|r_t{-}1|$ are associated with lower recall ($\rho = -0.55$, $p < 10^{-4}$), consistent with the gate gradient bias mechanism from Proposition 1. Additional analyses (fusion weight histograms, hyperparameter

Table 5. Repair effectiveness on newly added collapse datasets (Recall@10, mean ± std, 5 seeds).

Method	Amazon Books	Amazon CDs
CF-only (BPR-MF)	.0243 ± .0004	.0317 ± .0011
Fixed ($\lambda = 0.5$)	.0174 ± .0005	.0236 ± .0019
GradNorm-only	**.0342** ± .0008	**.0500** ± .0012
GBAF (full)	.0328 ± .0012	.0496 ± .0025

sensitivity, stratified item-popularity evaluation, r_t-vs-risk scatter) are in the Appendix.

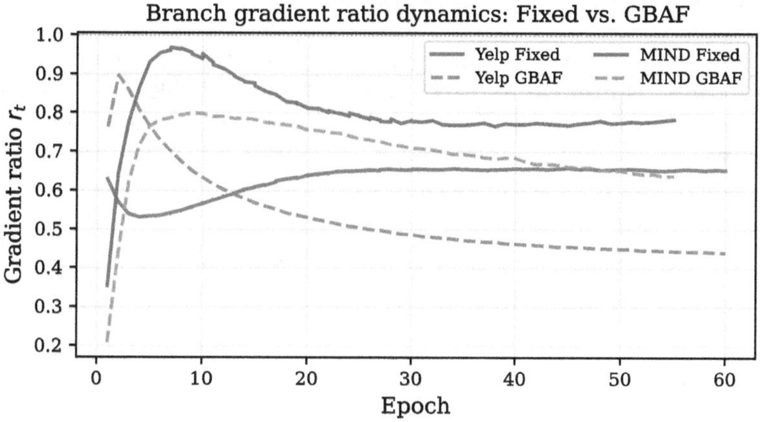

Fig. 3. Branch gradient ratio dynamics: GBAF (dashed) keeps r_t closer to 1 than fixed fusion (solid) on both Yelp and MIND.

7 Analysis and Practical Guidelines

7.1 Three Behavioral Modes and Architecture Contrast

Our results characterize three behavioral modes *specific to additive gated fusion*: **(A) Beneficial** (Amazon Fine Food)—use fixed additive fusion; **(B) Gradient-Scale Collapse** (Yelp, Amazon Books, Amazon CDs)—apply GradNorm repair; **(C) No-value** (MIND)—skip text fusion entirely.

The architecture contrast is decisive: on all three Mode B datasets, concatenation avoids collapse while additive fusion fails (Yelp: 76 pp gap; Books: 31 pp; CDs: 43 pp). The same text features are safely consumed through a non-gated architecture, localizing the failure to the gate gradient bias (Proposition 1). Mode C (MIND) confirms that uninformative text hurts regardless of architecture (−14.4% additive, −15.7% concat).

Positioning Against External SOTA. Table 2 includes BM3, LATTICE, and FREEDOM only for absolute performance context: they use dedicated end-to-end multi-modal architectures, whereas our workflow assumes frozen text embeddings and an existing CF pipeline. The results clarify the trade-off. On Mode A (Amazon FF), fixed additive fusion (R@10 = .6272) exceeds FREEDOM (.5401), LATTICE (.5535), and BM3 (.4340), so lightweight fusion is sufficient when text is informative. On Mode B (Yelp), FREEDOM (.0356) exceeds GBAF (.0245), but GBAF still recovers the collapsed additive baseline from −54% to +37% over CF-only without replacing the stack. On MIND, even FREEDOM (.0648) remains below CF-only (.0658), confirming Mode C. Thus teams should choose between GradNorm/concat repairs and full multi-modal models based on accuracy needs and infrastructure cost.

7.2 Why Does Text Hurt on MIND?

MIND uses title, abstract, category, and subcategory text. The preprocessed descriptions average 48.24 whitespace-delimited tokens. Under the evaluated frozen MiniLM representation, neither additive nor concatenation fusion improves over CF-only. Its moderate gradient ratios differ from the severe scale-imbalance pattern on Yelp, Books, and CDs, so we label it Mode C rather than attributing the result to the same collapse mechanism.

7.3 Practical Decision Framework

Based on the three modes, we recommend a short-pilot workflow (Fig. 4). Run CF-only and fixed additive-fusion pilots for $K = 5$ epochs, compute $\Delta_{\text{val}}^{(K)}$ and $\mathbb{E}_{t \le K}|r_t - 1|$, and route as follows:

- **Mode A** ($\Delta_{\text{val}}^{(K)} > 0$, low $|r_t - 1|$): text is beneficial → keep **Fixed Additive Fusion.**
- **Mode B** ($\Delta_{\text{val}}^{(K)} < 0$, high $|r_t - 1|$): gradient-scale collapse detected → switch to **GradNorm repair** or consider **concatenation fusion.**
- **Mode C** ($\Delta_{\text{val}}^{(K)} < 0$, low $|r_t - 1|$): text adds no value → fall back to **CF-only.**

7.4 Why Does Gradient Normalization Work?

Proposition 1 shows that the gate update contains the text embedding and is therefore scale-sensitive. Branch-wise normalization does not directly rescale gate parameters; it equalizes CF-embedding and text-projection update norms, which empirically prevents branch imbalance from compounding during additive training. The balance regularizer has local stationary point $\lambda^\star = \frac{1}{2} - g/(2\alpha)$ (Supplementary Material). Per-epoch cost is 1.1 min (ML-1M) to 3.0 min (Yelp) on RTX 4080. A $K = 5$ pilot avoids 55 scheduled epochs for each correctly flagged run under the corresponding 60-epoch configurations.

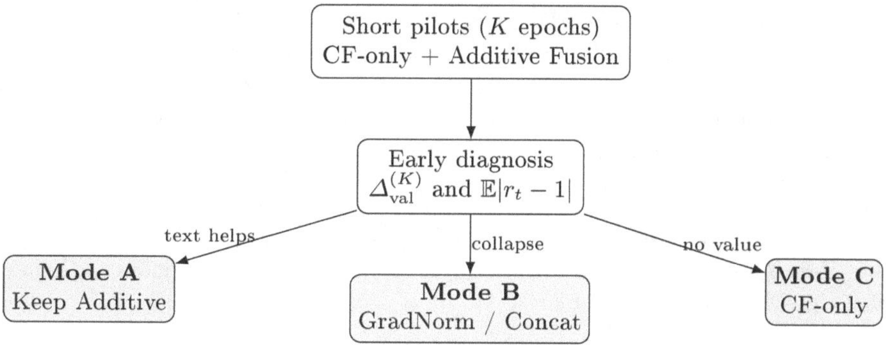

Fig. 4. Diagnose-then-act workflow for additive fusion: short pilots identify the behavioral mode, then route to the preferred lightweight strategy. For Mode B, either GradNorm repair or switching to concatenation fusion are effective responses.

7.5 Deployment Implications

The workflow fits existing ML pipelines: the r_t monitor is an epoch-level callback ($\sim$10 PyTorch lines), thresholding runs after the pilot, and GradNorm is one gradient-scaling hook before `optimizer.step()`. The offline prototype requires about 50 lines and no framework replacement.

8 Lessons Learned for Practitioners

The practitioner lessons are: (i) run 5-epoch pilots and monitor $|r_t{-}1|$ before full additive-fusion training on sparse, large-catalog datasets; (ii) treat collapse as architecture-specific, since concatenation can consume the same text safely; (iii) use GradNorm for magnitude imbalance and avoid conflict-only repairs such as PCGrad; and (iv) skip repair when fixed fusion already helps (Mode A) or when text adds no value (Mode C).

9 Conclusion

This work identifies *gradient-scale collapse*, a systematic failure mode in additive text-CF fusion caused by the gate gradient's dependence on pre-trained text embedding magnitude. Across six datasets, additive fusion exhibits three modes—beneficial, collapse, and no-value—with collapse confirmed on Yelp, Amazon Books, and Amazon CDs. A concatenation-fusion control localizes the risk to scalar additive weighting, and first-K-epoch gradient-ratio dynamics provide a conservative early warning signal. The resulting contribution is a reproducible diagnostic and decision layer for adding text to existing CF pipelines.

Scope and Limitations. The evidence is limited to additive text-CF fusion with frozen encoders and six public datasets, three Amazon-derived. End-to-end text fine-tuning, other CF backbones, and non-e-commerce domains may change the dynamics. The diagnosis rule is conservative (high precision, low recall), and the workflow is validated offline as a prototype; production deployments should recalibrate thresholds under their training schedule.

Acknowledgments. The authors thank the anonymous reviewers for their constructive comments. This work was supported by the 2025 Graduate Innovation Fund of Hebei University of Architecture (Grant No. XY2025094).

Declaration of Generative AI Usage. During the preparation of this manuscript, generative AI tools were used for drafting assistance and code debugging. All scientific content, experimental design, and analysis were conducted and verified by the authors. The authors take full responsibility for the content.

References

1. Bao, K., Zhang, J., Zhang, Y., Wang, W., Feng, F., He, X.: TALLRec: an effective and efficient tuning framework to align large language model with recommendation. In: Proceedings of the 17th ACM Conference on Recommender Systems (RecSys), pp. 1007–1014. ACM (2023)
2. Chen, Z., Badrinarayanan, V., Lee, C.Y., Rabinovich, A.: Gradnorm: gradient normalization for adaptive loss balancing in deep multitask networks. In: International Conference on Machine Learning, pp. 794–803 (2018)
3. Devlin, J., Chang, M.W., Lee, K., Toutanova, K.: BERT: pre-training of deep bidirectional transformers for language understanding. In: Proceedings of the 2019 Conference of NAACL: Human Language Technologies, pp. 4171–4186. ACL (2019)
4. Domhan, T., Springenberg, J.T., Hutter, F.: Speeding up automatic hyperparameter optimization of deep neural networks by extrapolation of learning curves. In: Proceedings of the 24th International Joint Conference on Artificial Intelligence, pp. 3460–3468 (2015)
5. Fan, Y., Xu, W., Wang, H., Wang, J., Guo, S.: PMR: prototypical modal rebalance for multimodal learning. In: Proceedings of the IEEE/CVF Conference on Computer Vision and Pattern Recognition, pp. 20029–20038 (2023)
6. Geng, S., Liu, S., Fu, Z., Ge, Y., Zhang, Y.: Recommendation as language processing (RLP): a unified pretrain, personalized prompt & predict paradigm (P5). In: Proceedings of the 16th ACM Conference on Recommender Systems, pp. 299–315. ACM (2022)
7. Harper, F.M., Konstan, J.A.: The MovieLens datasets: history and context. ACM Trans. Interact. Intell. Syst. (TiiS) **5**(4), 1–19 (2015)
8. He, R., McAuley, J.: Ups and downs: modeling the visual evolution of fashion trends with one-class collaborative filtering. In: Proceedings of the 25th International Conference on World Wide Web, pp. 507–517. ACM (2016)
9. Hou, Y., Mu, S., Zhao, W.X., Li, Y., Ding, B., Wen, J.R.: Towards universal sequence representation learning for recommender systems. In: Proceedings of the 28th ACM SIGKDD Conference on Knowledge Discovery and Data Mining, pp. 585–593. ACM (2022)

10. Klein, A., Falkner, S., Bartels, S., Hennig, P., Hutter, F.: Learning curve prediction with Bayesian neural networks. In: International Conference on Learning Representations (2017)
11. Liu, B., Liu, X., Jin, X., Stone, P., Liu, Q.: Conflict-averse gradient descent for multi-task learning. In: Advances in Neural Information Processing Systems, vol. 34, pp. 18878–18890 (2021)
12. McAuley, J., Leskovec, J.: Hidden factors and hidden topics: understanding rating dimensions with review text. In: Proceedings of the 7th ACM Conference on Recommender Systems, pp. 165–172. ACM (2013)
13. Peng, X., Wei, Y., Deng, A., Wang, D., Hu, D.: Balanced multimodal learning via on-the-fly gradient modulation. In: Proceedings of the IEEE/CVF Conference on Computer Vision and Pattern Recognition, pp. 8238–8247 (2022)
14. Reimers, N., Gurevych, I.: Sentence-BERT: sentence embeddings using siamese BERT-networks. In: Proceedings of the 2019 Conference on EMNLP-IJCNLP, pp. 3982–3992. ACL (2019)
15. Rendle, S., Freudenthaler, C., Gantner, Z., Schmidt-Thieme, L.: BPR: Bayesian personalized ranking from implicit feedback. In: Proceedings of the 25th Conference on Uncertainty in Artificial Intelligence, pp. 452–461. AUAI Press (2009)
16. Sener, O., Koltun, V.: Multi-task learning as multi-objective optimization. In: Advances in Neural Information Processing Systems, vol. 31, pp. 527–538 (2018)
17. Wu, F., et al.: MIND: a large-scale dataset for news recommendation. In: Proceedings of the 58th Annual Meeting of the Association for Computational Linguistics (ACL), pp. 3597–3606. ACL (2020)
18. Yelp Inc.: Yelp open dataset (2023). https://business.yelp.com/data/resources/open-dataset/. Accessed 01 Dec 2025
19. Yu, T., Kumar, S., Gupta, A., Hausman, K., Levine, S., Finn, C.: Gradient surgery for multi-task learning. In: Advances in Neural Information Processing Systems, vol. 33, pp. 5824–5836 (2020)
20. Zhang, J., Zhu, Y., Liu, Q., Wu, S., Wang, S., Wang, L.: Mining latent structures for multimedia recommendation. In: Proceedings of the ACM International Conference on Multimedia, pp. 3872–3880 (2021)
21. Zhou, X.: MMRec: simplifying multimodal recommendation. In: Proceedings of the 5th ACM International Conference on Multimedia in Asia Workshops, pp. 1–2 (2023)
22. Zhou, X., Shen, Z.: A tale of two graphs: freezing and denoising graph structures for multimodal recommendation. In: Proceedings of the ACM International Conference on Multimedia, pp. 935–943 (2023)
23. Zhou, X., et al.: Bootstrap latent representations for multi-modal recommendation. In: Proceedings of the ACM Web Conference, pp. 845–854 (2023)

Offline Metathesaurus Translation for Cross-Lingual Medical Entity Linking

Amaury Fierens(✉), Théodore Cousin, François Roucoux, and Sébastien Jodogne

Institute of Information and Communication Technologies, Electronics and Applied Mathematics (ICTEAM), UCLouvain, Louvain-la-Neuve, Belgium
amaury.fierens@uclouvain.be

Abstract. Cross-lingual medical entity linking (MEL) is essential for extracting structured information from clinical text. Yet, progress remains largely English-centric because biomedical terminologies and annotated corpora are far more abundant in English. To address this resource gap, we investigate a translation-based supervised MEL setting for SNOMED CT code retrieval. English UMLS concepts are translated offline to construct positive synonym pairs used to train SapBERT-style bi-encoders, without requiring online translation, reranking, or ensembling at inference time. We evaluate the approach on French, Spanish, and German using public benchmarks, and quantify how the choice of machine translation model affects downstream entity linking performance. Rank-1 metrics (F_1@1 and P@1) are reported for each benchmark, as well as top-100 candidate recall (R@100) to disentangle candidate coverage from ranking errors. We further introduce an ontology-aware metric, MGD@100, which summarises how far retrieved candidates lie from the ground-truth concept in the SNOMED CT graph, enabling the analysis of semantically close concepts when the exact concept is not retrieved. In macro-averaged comparisons across languages, the Helsinki-NLP OPUS-MT translation models provide the best average candidate coverage (mean R@100 = 0.880) while maintaining competitive ontology proximity (mean MGD@100 = 7.016, where lower values indicate that candidates are closer to the ground-truth concept). Compared with prior systems, the proposed retrieval-only approach remains competitive across languages despite the absence of reranking or ensembling, establishes new best results on all Spanish benchmarks and on several French and German ones. It is also shown that biomedical encoder backbones yield consistent but modest gains on rank-1 metrics over general-purpose encoders. Finally, correlation and information-theoretic analyses show that MGD@100 is not a surrogate for standard quality metrics, but a complementary ontology-aware evaluation signal.

Keywords: Medical Entity Linking · Entity Normalisation · Cross-lingual Methods · Ontology Graph Distance

---

Supplementary Information The online version contains supplementary material available at https://doi.org/10.1007/978-3-032-37682-4_34.

M. Baratchi et al. (Eds.): ECML PKDD 2026, LNAI 16949, pp. 582–599, 2027.
https://doi.org/10.1007/978-3-032-37682-4_34

1 Introduction

Hospitals and healthcare centres generate large amounts of textual data that are difficult to process at scale. Unstructured text is still the dominant form of medical data and takes the form of documents such as clinical notes, discharge summaries, radiology reports, and pathology reports. The free-text nature of these records necessitates normalisation to facilitate large-scale computational analysis. End-to-end entity linking addresses this challenge by grounding spans of text to standardised identifiers. In the context of healthcare, these identifiers are part of large, curated terminologies such as the Unified Medical Language System (UMLS) [1], SNOMED CT [3], or the International Classification of Diseases (ICD) [30]. By mapping heterogeneous textual mentions to normalised medical concepts, end-to-end entity linking enables the systematic, structured reuse of clinical information and is therefore a key step in many clinical natural language processing (NLP) pipelines.

End-to-end entity linking typically involves two main steps. The first step consists of identifying text spans that are likely to correspond to entities in the target ontology. This task is commonly referred to as named-entity recognition (NER). The second step, known as named-entity linking (NEL) or entity normalisation, aims to map the mentions detected by the NER step to their corresponding identifiers in the medical terminology of interest. In the context of biomedical applications, NEL is often referred to as medical entity linking (MEL). Like many other NLP tasks, MEL has recently benefited from major advances driven by transformer-based models [28], which represent the current state of the art. These encoders transform textual mentions and ontology terms into vector representations whose similarity can be exploited for concept retrieval. Such advances have been enabled by the increasing availability of large biomedical corpora, structured medical knowledge bases, and increased computational resources. Despite this progress, MEL has been predominantly studied in English, with performance in other languages hindered by the scarcity of annotated clinical corpora and domain-specific language models.

MEL approaches such as SapBERT-XLMR [15] exploit the inherent cross-language coverage of UMLS through the training of cross-lingual bi-encoders. These models project medical concepts expressed in any language covered by UMLS into a shared semantic space that can be used for concept retrieval. This approach requires little upstream effort in preprocessing the input data. However, UMLS exhibits a strong language imbalance, with approximately 70% of its entries available in English only. As a result, multilingual bi-encoders trained on these resources are predominantly trained on English data, with limited coverage of other languages. We hypothesise that this imbalance fundamentally limits the performance of such approaches on non-English clinical texts.

To address the limitations of multilingual bi-encoders trained directly on UMLS, this paper investigates an alternative strategy based on translating the English-language entries of the ontology and training monolingual bi-encoders in the target language of interest. The proposed pipeline confines machine translation (MT) to an offline supervision step: MT is used only to generate target-language training pairs from UMLS, while inference proceeds purely by encoding the input mention and retrieving the nearest SNOMED CT concept, without online translation, reranking, or ensembling. We instantiate this pipeline for French (FR), Spanish (ES), and German (DE), and investigate the impact of its two main design choices: the MT model and the encoder backbone. We further introduce MGD@100, an ontology-aware metric that measures how far retrieved candidates lie from the ground-truth concept in the SNOMED CT graph.

2 Related Work

2.1 Medical Entity Linking

Medical entity linking has received growing attention as medical knowledge resources become larger and more detailed, making entity normalisation an extreme multi-class classification problem. Retrieval-based linking is the dominant approach: mentions and ontology concepts are embedded into a shared space and top-k candidates are retrieved under a vector metric, sometimes with reranking [17]. Representative retrieval-based models include SapBERT [14], CODER [31], and NeighBERT [24]. Another line of work frames normalisation as constrained generation, where the model takes the entity mention together with its context and generates a canonical concept name or identifier, instead of retrieving nearest neighbours in an embedding space. During decoding, the output is restricted to valid entries from the target medical knowledge base, so the generated concept directly determines the final normalisation, as in mGENRE [8]. Finally, many practical systems combine lexical candidate generation, retrieval based on neural networks, and reranking in hybrid pipelines, as in xMEN [2], Con2GEN [33], MLNorm [29], VICOMTECH [34], and FUSION [13]. These hybrid systems differ mainly in how they generate candidates and in whether reranking relies on cross-encoders, ensembles, or knowledge-base features. However, they share a common pattern: stacking multiple components to compensate for the limitations of any single retrieval stage. In contrast, our work deliberately isolates the bi-encoder retrieval stage to study how translation-derived supervision affects it in the absence of reranking or ensembling.

2.2 Ontology-Aware Learning and Error Structure

Beyond lexical matching, several approaches use ontology structure or concept neighbourhood to help with disambiguation. NeighBERT [24], for example, injects relation-based neighbourhood information into transformer representations, exploiting the fact that relational context can help resolve ambiguities that text alone cannot. Recent SNOMED CT-centred evaluations also highlight the inherent difficulty of linking a single concept in large terminologies, as well as the importance of separating retrieval from ranking effects. In particular, the SNOMED CT Entity Linking Challenge [7] provides a large-scale reference resource for SNOMED CT-based evaluation and shows that candidate retrieval can be a major bottleneck in the overall linking pipeline, since the correct concept must first be surfaced among the retrieved candidates before any downstream ranking or disambiguation step can recover it. More broadly, in the context of hierarchical label spaces and ontology-derived embeddings, not all errors are equally severe and concept proximity can provide qualitative information even if the exact concept is not retrieved [18,32]. In this view, the terminology is treated as a graph in which concepts are nodes and ontology relations define the edges, so that proximity refers to structural distance in the ontology rather than to distance in the shared embedding space. Taken together, these studies motivate ontology-aware scores that complement exact matching and coverage metrics by assessing how close predicted concepts are to the ground-truth concept in the terminology graph. However, no prior work has proposed such a score for retrieval-based MEL evaluation or systematically examined its relation to standard rank-based metrics. We address this gap with the MGD@100 metric introduced in Sect. 4.2.

2.3 Cross-Lingual Transfer for Biomedical and Clinical NLP

Cross-lingual transfer in biomedical and clinical NLP mainly follows two directions. The first direction relies on multilingual bi-encoders, which provide shared semantic spaces across languages. In particular, SapBERT-XLMR self-aligns UMLS synonyms across languages on top of XLM-R [15]. Such multilingual bi-encoders are often trained mostly on general-domain corpora, which can limit their handling of fine-grained biomedical terminology, while domain-specialised bi-encoders generally provide stronger concept representations, although they are not equally available across languages [14,31]. The second direction relies on translation-based transfer to reuse English biomedical resources in other languages, for instance by translating mentions, ontology strings, or generating pseudo-labelled data [2,14,33]. In these pipelines, translation is typically entangled with reranking, ensembling, or auxiliary supervision, so its specific contribution is rarely isolated. In contrast, we study ontology translation as a standalone transfer mechanism and isolate its effect on the bi-encoder retrieval component by varying both the machine translation model and the encoder backbone in a controlled setting.

3 Methods

3.1 Overview

Our approach relies on an asymmetry between training and inference. During training, ontology strings are translated offline into the target language and used to construct positive pairs of semantically equivalent terms associated with the same concept. These pairs are used to fine-tune a SapBERT-style bi-encoder with a metric-learning objective, after which the target terminology is embedded using the backbone encoder and indexed for retrieval. At inference time, a mention in the target language is directly converted as an embedding vector by the backbone encoder. This embedding is matched against the indexed terminology through nearest-neighbour retrieval, with no online translation or reranking. This design isolates the bi-encoder retrieval component, allowing us to directly measure the effect of translation-derived supervision on the learned representations.

3.2 Translation-Derived Training Data Construction

To create supervision in the target language of interest, we translate UMLS terminology strings (labels and synonyms) using several off-the-shelf machine translation models, generating one translated resource per language-translator combination. We use UMLS release 2023AA and retain 9,710,796 non-suppressed English MRCONSO term entries, covering 4,495,569 concept unique identifiers (CUIs), as input to the translation step. In this work, we consider MT models for the French, Spanish, and German languages. Positive training pairs are built for each translated terminology by grouping strings that share the same UMLS concept identifier. These pairs provide scalable concept-level supervision without manual annotation and are used to train the bi-encoder. The strings used for training are lowercased and deduplicated.

To estimate intrinsic translation quality, BLEU score [23] is computed on the UMLS concepts shared between English and the target language, that is, concepts for which UMLS provides at least one English term and at least one target-language term in French, Spanish, or German. English strings are translated with each MT model and compared against the UMLS terms associated with the same concept in the target language.

3.3 Cross-Lingual Bi-Encoder Training

We adopt a SapBERT self-alignment pretraining paradigm [14], which brings embeddings of synonymous terms closer together via a contrastive objective with hard negative mining, while pushing apart terms corresponding to different concepts. For each target language, we vary both the machine translation model and the encoder backbone while keeping all other training hyperparameters fixed. This allows us to isolate the effect of translation-derived supervision from the choice of the encoder backbone. Cross-encoder distillation and downstream reranking are excluded from the main pipeline, as our objective is to evaluate the quality of the directly learned representations. Tokenisation and string preprocessing follow the same case-insensitive normalisation as applied to the translated resources, ensuring consistency between training supervision and encoder inputs.

3.4 Target Terminology and Retrieval

All predictions are computed against the US extension of SNOMED CT provided through UMLS 2023AA. When a benchmark uses another coding scheme, reference concepts are mapped to SNOMED CT through UMLS 2023AA concept correspondences (e.g., MRCONSO) to maintain a consistent target space. The candidate index is built from active SNOMED CT concepts and their descriptions, with duplicated terms removed and target-language descriptions prioritised over English fallbacks. Concept strings are encoded using the trained bi-encoder and efficiently indexed using FAISS [11]. Retrieval is performed via nearest-neighbour search on ℓ_2-normalised embeddings, which is equivalent to cosine similarity.

4 Experimental Setup

4.1 Benchmarks and Data Splits

The proposed approach is evaluated on biomedical and clinical entity linking public benchmarks that are available in French, Spanish, and German: Quaero FrenchMed [21], DisTEMIST [20], MedProcNER [13], MANTRA GSC [12], and XL-BEL [15]. These benchmarks differ in annotation guidelines, mention boundaries, concept granularity, and coding schemes, as well as in the number of gold-annotated mentions per split. Detailed per-benchmark statistics are released alongside the source code (cf. Sect. 4.4). For comparability, ground-truth annotations are mapped to a common SNOMED CT target space through UMLS if needed. Results are reported on the test split for all benchmarks. For MANTRA, we evaluate the three splits separately: EMEA, Medline, and Patents. The translated UMLS terminology is used only for training, while benchmark mentions are used only for evaluation.

4.2 Evaluation Metrics

Experimental results are primarily reported using the $F_1@1$ metric, which refers to the F_1 score computed using only the top-ranked prediction, and the $P@1$ metric, which denotes the proportion of examples where the top-ranked prediction is correct. These metrics are used to enable direct comparison with prior work, where the official evaluation for each benchmark is generally reported using rank-1 prediction. In addition, the $R@100$ metric is reported, which corresponds to the proportion of examples for which the correct concept appears among the top-100 retrieved candidates. Additional metrics are described in the supplementary material available in the source code repository (cf. Sect. 4.4).

This study also introduces the MGD@k metric (*Median Graph Distance at* k), which measures the ontological quality of the retrieved neighbourhood after cutting the SNOMED CT graph to keep only the "`has_ingredient`", "`has_active_ingredient`", and "`is_a`" relations. Formally:

$$\text{MGD@}k = \frac{1}{|\mathcal{M}|} \sum_{m \in \mathcal{M}} \text{median}_{c \in \mathcal{R}_k(m)} \left(\min_{g \in \mathcal{G}(m)} \text{dist}_{\text{sct}}(c, g) \right) \tag{1}$$

Here, $\mathcal{M}$ is the set of evaluable mentions, $\mathcal{R}_k(m)$ the top-k retrieved candidates for mention m, and $\mathcal{G}(m)$ the set of ground-truth concepts for m. The function $\text{dist}_{\text{sct}}(c, g)$ denotes the shortest-path distance between candidate c and ground-truth concept g in the restricted SNOMED CT graph. By construction, MGD@k is non-negative, with lower values indicating that retrieved candidates remain, on average, closer to the target concept, and is upper-bounded by the diameter of the restricted SNOMED CT graph. In this work, we set $k = 100$ and report MGD@100.

4.3 Models and Comparison Settings

This work evaluates whether lightweight, off-the-shelf machine translation models can provide useful training data for cross-lingual MEL. To this end, five families of medium-sized MT systems are considered: OPUS-MT [26], NLLB-600M and NLLB-1.3B [22], mBART [16], and M2M100 [9]. Medium-sized models are used throughout the experiments to keep the offline translation of large-scale terminologies efficient. As will be shown in the results, these medium-sized models are sufficient to achieve competitive performance compared to SapBERT-XLMR.

For each target language, SapBERT-style bi-encoders are trained with multiple backbone encoders, which may be either general-purpose or specialised on the biomedical domain. PubMedBERT [10], the original SapBERT backbone focused on the biomedical domain, is evaluated for all languages. The language-specific general domain backbones are BETO [5] for Spanish, GBERT [6] for German, and CamemBERT [19] for French, while the corresponding domain-specialised backbones are RigoBERTa-clinical [25], GerMedBERT [4], and CamemBERT-bio [27].

4.4 Implementation and Reproducibility Details

Unless stated otherwise, all models are trained under the same optimisation setup for fairness. We use the same contrastive training objective, hard negative mining strategy, batch size, learning rate, and number of epochs across experiments, and we retain the last checkpoint for evaluation. For retrieval, we use a FAISS `IndexHNSWFlat` index built over ℓ_2-normalised CLS embeddings [11]. The HNSW graph degree is set to 16, with both parameters `efConstruction` and `efSearch` set to 100. Retrieval is performed at depths $k \in \{1, 5, 100\}$. Target ontology entries are indexed as concept-term pairs derived from SNOMED CT. No reranker or cross-encoder is used in the main evaluation pipeline.

To promote reproducibility, we publicly release both the translated training datasets and the trained model checkpoints used in our experiments[1]. All source code, including preprocessing scripts, training pipelines, and evaluation routines, is made available alongside these resources[2].

[1] Data is available at: https://doi.org/10.14428/DVN/MHYOVM.

[2] Source code is available at: https://forge.uclouvain.be/AmauryFierens/cross-lingual-medical-entity-linking.

Table 1. Translation quality and macro-average retrieval performance across languages for different families of machine translation models. BLEU scores are computed on UMLS terminology strings for each target language. $R@100$ is the mean recall at rank-100, which indicates how often the ground-truth mention appears among the top-100 concepts retrieved downstream. MGD@100 captures the ontological quality of the retrieved neighbourhood.

Family of MT models	BLEU on UMLS strings			Mean $R@100$	Mean MGD@100
	FR	DE	ES		
OPUS	7.039	**7.485**	13.692	**0.880**	**7.016**
nllb-1.3B	**7.724**	7.451	**13.809**	0.873	7.042
nllb-600M	6.863	6.695	12.858	0.873	7.078
m2m	5.037	5.281	8.899	0.867	7.207
mbart	5.930	5.759	0.551	0.865	7.223

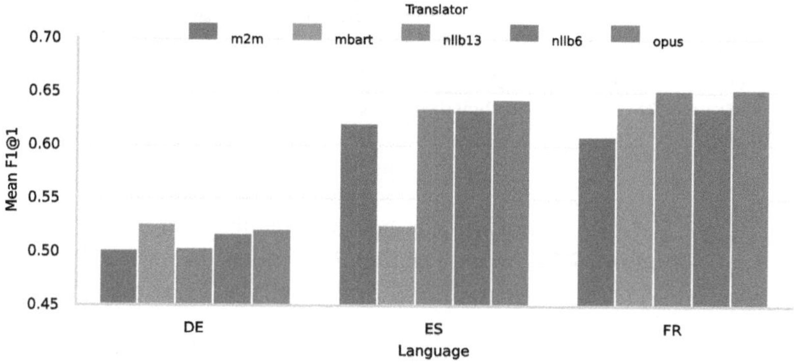

Fig. 1. Mean $F_1@1$ across translation strategies for German (DE), Spanish (ES), and French (FR), with scores macro-averaged over benchmarks within each language. These measures highlight cross-lingual variations in translation effectiveness.

5 Results

5.1 Impact of Translation Strategies

This section analyses the impact of the translation strategies on the performance of the monolingual bi-encoders. We investigate the pipeline capabilities using a *macro-over-languages* aggregation, in which each language contributes equally to the investigated scores. Table 1 summarises the performance of the different families of MT models considered in this work. Figure 1 illustrates mean $F_1@1$ across translation approaches, averaged across benchmarks. As shown in Table 1, the OPUS models outperform the other families of models across French, Spanish, and German, achieving both a higher $R@100$ and a lower MGD@100, although `nllb-1.3B` obtains slightly higher BLEU scores for French and Spanish.

This overall advantage of OPUS is more nuanced in Fig. 1, which shows that the gap remains small and varies across languages. OPUS is consistently

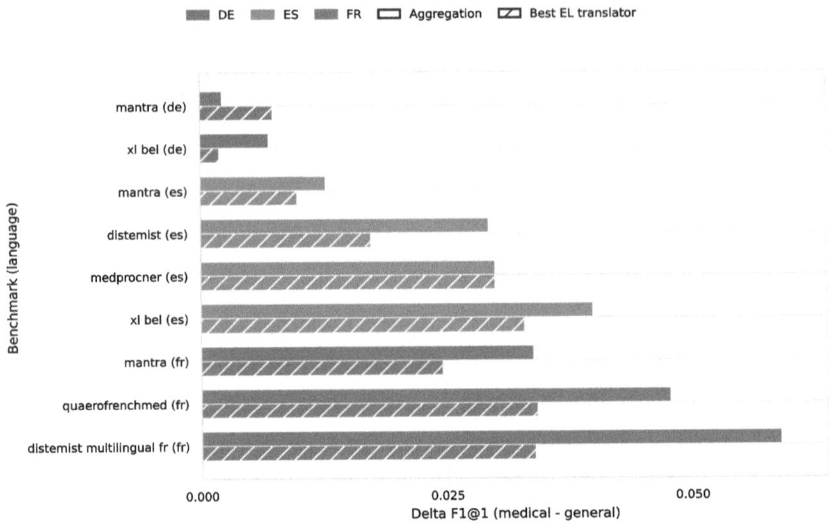

Fig. 2. Differences in $F_1@1$ between the best domain-specialised and best general-domain backbones for different benchmarks. Best-performing model and aggregation over MT models are reported.

competitive, but it is not uniformly the best-performing family in every setting. Yet, in some configurations, other families of models become competitive. In German for example, MBART performs better with a mean Metric@1 = 0.532 against 0.529 for OPUS.

5.2 General-Purpose vs. Biomedical Backbones

Figure 2 reports, for each pair of language and benchmark, the difference in $F_1@1$ between the best domain-specialised backbone encoder and the best general-domain backbone encoder, both aggregated over all MT models and restricted to the best-performing MT model for that pair. All the differences are positive under both views, indicating a systematic advantage for medical or biomedical backbones over general-purpose backbones, although the magnitude of the gain varies across benchmarks and languages.

The largest gains are observed for French and Spanish. In French, the $F_1@1$ improvement reaches about 0.06 on multilingual DisTEMIST and remains substantial on QuaeroFrenchMed and MANTRA-FR. In Spanish, the largest gain is observed on XL-BEL, followed by MedProcNER and DisTEMIST. By contrast, improvements are much smaller in German, where both MANTRA-DE and XL-BEL show only limited gains compared to the general-domain backbone.

This benchmark-level pattern should, however, be distinguished from the language-level comparison. To this end, Fig. 2 reports average benchmark-level deltas across all model configurations within each language, whereas Table 2 identifies the single best pair of translation model and backbone encoder per

Table 2. Best translation-backbone configuration selected per language using multi-benchmark comparison. Scores are averaged across benchmarks in each language.

Lang.	MT	Backbone	Benchmarks	Mean F_1@1	Mean R@100	Mean MGD@100
DE	mbart	GBERT	MANTRA-DE, XL-BEL	0.532	0.761	7.650
ES	OPUS	RigoBERTa-clinical	DisTEMIST, MANTRA-ES, MedProcNER, XL-BEL	0.655	0.906	6.314
FR	nllb13	PubMedBERT	DisTEMIST (FR), MANTRA-FR, QUAERO-FR	0.681	0.947	7.031

language after aggregation across benchmarks. Consequently, the best overall configuration for a given language may still rely on a general-domain backbone, as in German.

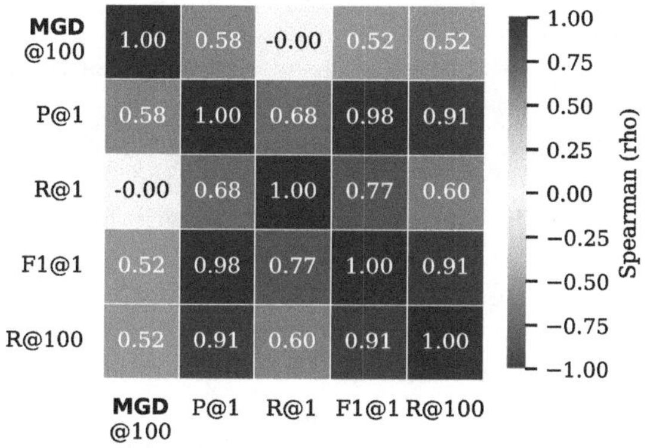

Fig. 3. Spearman correlations between MGD@100 and standard retrieval metrics (i.e., P@1, R@1, F_1@1, and R@100).

5.3 Interest of the Distance Metric

Figure 3 reports the Spearman correlation coefficients between MGD@100 and the standard quality metric. The strongest association is observed with P@1, with $\rho = 0.58$, while correlations with F_1@1 and R@100 are slightly lower but remain of similar magnitude. Conversely, the correlation with R@1 is close to zero. As a result, MGD@100 is related to standard retrieval and rank-based metrics, but it is not perfectly aligned with any of them and instead provides a complementary perspective on performance in the NEL task.

In addition to this pairwise view, we also assess whether MGD@100 can be reconstructed from the standard evaluation metrics jointly. To this end, several regression models (k-nearest neighbours, linear regression, ridge regression, gradient boosting, random forest, and extra trees) were trained and evaluated using cross-validation with grouped splits by benchmark-language pair whenever possible. The possibility of reconstructing MGD@100 was then assessed using the coefficient of determination, R^2. Values of R^2 close to 1 indicate that the target

Table 3. Continuous mutual information between MGD@100 and standard evaluation metrics, computed on $n = 135$ aggregated configurations.

Outcome metric	Mutual information (continuous)
$P@1$	1.070
$R@1$	0.586
$F_1@1$	0.827
$R@100$	1.441

can be well reconstructed from the input metrics, whereas values near 0 indicate little explanatory power. In cross-validation, R^2 may also become negative, which means that the model performs worse than a trivial baseline that always predicts the mean target value. In our case, the best cross-validated R^2 obtained when predicting MGD@100 from the other metrics was -10.3, using a k-nearest neighbour model. This analysis confirms that individual metrics alone cannot reliably reconstruct MGD@100, thereby underscoring its analytical value.

Finally, Table 3 provides an information-theoretic perspective through continuous mutual information. The mutual information values are non-zero for all metrics, with the highest value observed for $R@100$, followed by $P@1$, $F_1@1$, and finally $R@1$. Most notably, $R@100$ shares substantially more information with MGD@100 than the other standard metrics. This indicates that candidate coverage at depth 100 is the standard measure most closely related to the proposed distance metric MGD@100, although the latter still provides complementary information.

5.4 Model Comparison Across Languages

At the language level, Sect. 5.2 reported that the optimal choice of MT model and backbone encoder for the monolingual SapBERT-like bi-encoders varies by target language. The best-performing configurations were mBART with GBERT for German, OPUS with RigoBERTa-clinical for Spanish, and NLLB-1.3B with PubMedBERT for French. This section compares our best-performing configurations to systems previously reported in the literature.

In German (cf. Table 4), the combination of mBART with GBERT improves upon the strongest reported baseline by 7.2% on MANTRA-Patents and 12.3% on XL-BEL, while remaining slightly below the best reported results on MANTRA-Emea and MANTRA-Medline. In Spanish (cf. Table 5), the combination of OPUS with RigoBERTa-clinical achieves the best score on all reported benchmarks, with relative gains of 14.8% on DisTEMIST, 5.5% on MANTRA-Emea, 6.7% on MANTRA-Medline, 15.6% on MedProcNER, and 4.4% on XL-BEL. In French (cf. Table 6), the combination of NLLB-1.3B with PubMedBERT obtains the best results on MANTRA-Medline and MANTRA-Patents, with relative gains of 14.0% and 4.5%, respectively, while remaining competitive on the other French benchmarks. Table 6 also includes results on DisTEMIST-Fr as a

Table 4. Comparison with previously reported MEL pipelines on German benchmarks. In our approach, the MT model is mBART and the backbone encoder is GBERT. Scores correspond to the primary metric of the benchmark at rank-1. xMEN includes cross-encoder reranking and is therefore not directly comparable to our retrieval-only setup, so the Ensemble model of that paper is reported instead.

Model	MANTRA-DE			XL-BEL
	EMEA (F_1@1)	MED (F_1@1)	Patents (F_1@1)	(P@1)
mBART with GBERT	0.641	0.729	**0.749**	**0.357**
xMEN (Ensemble)	**0.669**	**0.731**	0.699	–
CODER	0.653	0.690	0.690	–
CON2GEN	0.555	–	0.661	0.308
mGENRE	0.541	–	0.557	0.313
SapBERT-XLMR	–	–	–	0.318

Table 5. Comparison with previously reported MEL pipelines on Spanish benchmarks. In our approach, the MT model is OPUS-es and the backbone encoder is RigoBERTa-clinical. Scores correspond to the primary metric of the benchmark at rank-1. As in Table 4, the xMEN Ensemble model is reported.

Model	DisTEMIST	MANTRA-ES		MedProc NER	XL-BEL
	(F_1@1)	EMEA (F_1@1)	MED (F_1@1)	(F_1@1)	(P@1)
OPUS-es with RigoBERTa-clinical	**0.650**	**0.695**	**0.748**	**0.660**	**0.589**
xMEN (Ensemble)	0.426	0.659	0.699	–	–
CODER	–	0.681	0.701	–	0.514
CON2GEN	–	0.639	–	–	0.527
mGENRE	–	0.620	–	–	0.498
SapBERT-XLMR	–	–	–	–	0.564
HPI-DHC	0.566	–	–	–	–
VICOMTECH	–	–	–	0.571	–
FUSION	–	–	–	0.537	–

reference for future work, since, to the best of our knowledge, no prior results are available for this benchmark.

Overall, these results indicate that the proposed retrieval-only pipeline remains competitive with previously reported systems across all three languages, while the optimal MT-backbone combination varies. The practical implications of this variation are discussed in Sect. 6.1.

Table 6. Comparison with previously reported MEL pipelines on French benchmarks. In our approach, the MT model is nllb13 and the backbone encoder is PubMedBERT. Scores correspond to the primary metric of the benchmark at rank-1. MLNorm results are reported for reference only, as its hybrid design makes it not directly comparable to our retrieval-only setup. As in Table 4, the xMEN Ensemble model is reported.

Model	DisTEMIST-FR	MANTRA-FR			QUAERO	
	(F_1@1)	EMEA (F_1@1)	MED (F_1@1)	Patents (F_1@1)	EMEA (F_1@1)	MED (F_1@1)
nllb13 with PubMedBERT	0.626	0.662	**0.690**	**0.772**	0.721	0.698
xMEN (Ensemble)	–	**0.705**	0.605	0.739	0.573	0.583
CODER	–	0.629	0.586	0.708	–	–
CON2GEN	–	0.571	–	0.640	–	–
mGENRE	–	0.564	–	0.612	–	–
MLNorm$_{DS}$	–	–	–	–	0.727	0.754
MLNorm$_{FS}$	–	–	–	–	**0.743**	**0.795**

6 Discussion

6.1 Translation Quality

Translation quality clearly affects downstream MEL performance. Figure 1 revealed that the best rank-1 performance varies by language: mBART performs better for German, while OPUS and NLLB-1.3B are more effective for Spanish and French. Therefore, translation quality should be interpreted in task-specific terms, specifically by how well the translated terminology supports contrastive training and concept retrieval. This suggests that the translated ontology is a major source of supervision for the retrieval model.

These observations have practical implications for extending the pipeline to new languages, though with an important caveat. Translation quality can, in principle, be characterised independently of downstream MEL training, for instance through BLEU on UMLS terminology strings (cf. Table 1). However, this is a necessary but not sufficient condition: BLEU correlates strongly with downstream performance for French (Pearson 0.908, Spearman 0.800) and Spanish (Pearson 0.975, Spearman 0.900), but only weakly for German (Pearson 0.084, Spearman 0.300), suggesting that lexical overlap may fail to capture medically relevant normalisation quality in morphologically richer languages. Within these limits, a suitable MT model can still be selected up front, before training the bi-encoder, with OPUS providing a strong default for the languages considered here.

6.2 Backbone Specialisation

The systematic advantage of domain-specialised backbones observed in Sect. 5.2 should be interpreted cautiously, as the varying magnitude of the gains across benchmark-language pairs may reflect differences in benchmark difficulty and evaluation conditions, not only in backbone specialisation. Moreover, this benchmark-level advantage does not always translate to the best overall configuration once the family of translation models and benchmark aggregation are taken into account. Indeed, as shown in Table 2, while the best configurations for Spanish and French rely on specialised backbones, the selected German configuration uses the general-domain backbone GBERT combined with mBART. In practice, specialisation helps on average, but some translation-backbone combinations still favour general-domain encoders.

6.3 Median Graph Distance Metric

The MGD@100 metric captures aspects of model behaviour that are not fully reflected by standard rank-based metrics. It correlates partially with existing measures, and recoverability analysis further confirms that MGD@100 cannot be reliably predicted from standard metrics, even when combined. In particular, the R@100 standard metric shares information with MGD@100, which is consistent with the fact that both evaluate the retrieved neighbourhood at depth 100. They however capture different properties: R@100 checks whether the ground-truth concept is present in the retrieved set, while MGD@100 measures the ontological proximity of retrieved candidates to the target concept.

This distinction is useful for analysing retrieval behaviour beyond exact normalisation, as illustrated in Fig. 4. Two models may achieve a similar R@100 while differing in MGD@100, as shown by the rows with median graph distance 6, where retrieved candidates are clinically related to the gold concept (sibling drugs, sibling procedures) without being exact matches. A model may also miss the rank-1 concept while keeping a low median graph distance if the retrieved neighbourhood stays ontologically close. Conversely, the rows with MGD@100 = 9 show cases where lexical similarity drives retrieval toward graph-distant, semantically unrelated concepts. Rank-based metrics flag such failures but not their severity, which MGD@100 supplies as a complementary score rather than a replacement.

6.4 Comparison with Prior Work and Limitations

Our comparison with prior work in Sect. 5.4 suggests that translation-derived supervision is a strong building block for cross-lingual MEL at the retrieval stage, even without reranking or ensembling. While offline ontology translation provides a clear benefit, remaining gaps on some benchmarks indicate that it is not sufficient on its own. It should therefore be viewed as valuable addition to cross-lingual MEL pipelines rather than a replacement for more elaborate components.

This study has several limitations. First, we focus entirely on the bi-encoder retrieval component, excluding reranking, cross-encoders, or other downstream refinement strategies. Although this isolates the effect of transition-derived supervision, it does not reflect the full complexity of end-to-end MEL systems. Second, the experiments are limited to three target languages and a fixed set

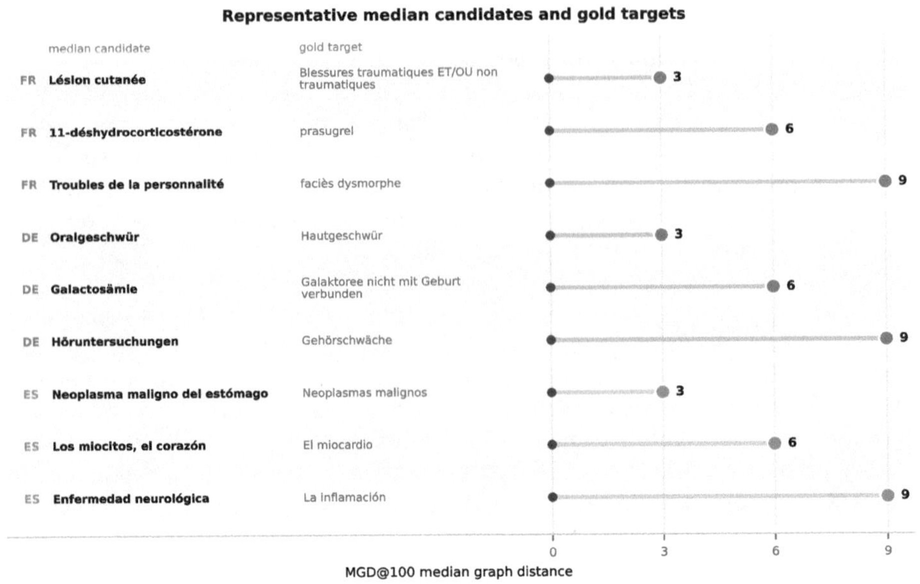

Fig. 4. Median graph distance to the gold concept for nine representative mentions, three per language. Each row illustrates a concept situated at the reported MGD@100 median graph distance from the gold target in the SNOMED CT graph.

of benchmarks, which restricts the generality of the conclusions. Third, evaluation in a unified SNOMED CT target space improves comparability but may introduce mismatches with benchmarks annotated using other coding schemes. Finally, MGD@100 depends on the SNOMED CT graph and the relations used to define concept proximity. The linguistic quality of the translated terminology is therefore not directly assessed.

7 Conclusion

Most biomedical knowledge bases, including UMLS, are largely English-centric, making cross-lingual MEL particularly challenging. In this study, we demonstrated that machine translation can serve as an effective transfer mechanism for a target language of interest. Concretely, we proposed to use medium-size machine translation models to translate the English part of the UMLS ontology to generate pairs of synonyms. These automatically generated translations were used to train monolingual SapBERT-style bi-encoders that were shown to be competitive with state-of-the-art MEL models.

Experiments across multiple benchmarks and machine translation models revealed that translation quality strongly affects downstream linking performance. Although the optimal translation model varies by language, we identified Helsinki-NLP OPUS-MT as one of the best-performing family of models overall. We also observed that biomedical-specific encoders provide consistent but modest improvements in rank-1 performance compared to general-purpose encoders. In addition, we introduced a new ontology-aware distance metric, MGD@100, designed to assess the ontological quality of retrieved concept neighbourhood. Unlike standard metrics such as F_1@1, P@1, and R@100, which focus on rank-based retrieval performance, MGD@100 measures how close retrieved candidates are to the ground-truth concept in the ontology graph. Our analysis demonstrates that this metric captures aspects of retrieval behaviour that are not reflected by standard metrics. It therefore provides complementary source of information for analysing the structure and quality of the retrieved neighbourhood, beyond exact-match evaluation. Our results show that simple offline translation can effectively transfer supervision for non-English MEL by generating training data that enables competitive cross-lingual retrieval models without requiring manual annotations.

Since our goal was to prioritise the quality of the shared concept space rather than downstream retrieval optimisation, sophisticated reranking methods were not considered. Integrating more effective downstream reranking strategies remains an important direction for future work. The results on the German language also point to an open question: translation quality, as measured by BLEU on UMLS terminology strings, correlates strongly with downstream performance in French and Spanish, but only weakly in German. One possible explanation is that a sizeable share of German medical vocabulary derives from Greek and Latin roots, which may decouple lexical translation quality from the kind of terminological alignment that drives medical entity linking. A systematic investigation of this hypothesis is left to future work. The present evaluation focuses on French, Spanish, and German because they offer multiple public benchmarks for direct comparison with prior systems. Extending the approach to lower-resource languages, where such comparison points are scarcer, is a natural next step. Future work will also involve evaluating the approach in real-world clinical settings to assess its practical utility.

Acknowledgments. François Roucoux is supported by the CLINOM-X project, cofinanced by Wallonia and the European Union through the European Regional Development Fund (ERDF). Computing infrastructure was provided by the ARC Project BiDiTwins of the Fédération Wallonie-Bruxelles (Belgium) under Grant 23/28-129. The authors would like to thank Alexandre Englebert for initial discussions that led to the definition of the MGD@k metrics.

Disclosure of Inter. The authors have no competing interests to declare.

References

1. Bodenreider, O.: The unified medical language system (UMLS): integrating biomedical terminology. Nucl. Acids Res. **32**(suppl_1), D267–D270 (2004)
2. Borchert, F., Llorca, I., Roller, R., et al.: xMEN: a modular toolkit for cross-lingual medical entity normalization. JAMIA Open **8**(1), ooae147 (2024)
3. Bos, L., Donnelly, K.: SNOMED-CT: the advanced terminology and coding system for eHealth. Stud. Health Technol. Inform. **121**, 279–290 (2006)

4. Bressem, K.K., Papaioannou, J.M., Grundmann, P.: medBERT.de: a comprehensive German BERT model for the medical domain. Expert Syst. Appl. **237**, 121598 (2024)
5. Cañete, J., Chaperon, G., Fuentes, R.: Spanish pre-trained BERT model and evaluation data. In: PML4DC at ICLR 2020 (2020)
6. Chan, B., Schweter, S., Möller, T.: German's next language model. In: Proceedings of the 28th International Conference on Computational Linguistics, pp. 6788–6796 (2020)
7. Davidson, R., Hardman, W., Amit, G., et al.: SNOMED CT entity linking challenge. J. Am. Med. Inform. Assoc. **32**(9), 1397–1406 (2025)
8. De Cao, N., Wu, L., Popat, K., et al.: Multilingual autoregressive entity linking. Trans. Assoc. Comput. Linguist. **10**, 274–290 (2022)
9. Fan, A., Bhosale, S., Schwenk, H., et al.: Beyond English-centric multilingual machine translation. J. Mach. Learn. Res. **22**(107), 1–48 (2021)
10. Gu, Y., Tinn, R., Cheng, H., et al.: Domain-specific language model pretraining for biomedical natural language processing. ACM Trans. Comput. Healthc. (HEALTH) **3**(1), 1–23 (2021)
11. Johnson, J., Douze, M., Jégou, H.: Billion-scale similarity search with GPUs. IEEE Trans. Big Data **7**(3), 535–547 (2019)
12. Kors, J.A., Clematide, S., Akhondi, S.A., et al.: A multilingual gold-standard corpus for biomedical concept recognition: the Mantra GSC. J. Am. Med. Inform. Assoc. **22**(5), 948–956 (2015)
13. Lima-López, S., Farré-Maduell, E., Gasco, L.: Overview of MedProcNER task on medical procedure detection and entity linking at BioASQ 2023. In: Conference and Labs of the Evaluation Forum (2023)
14. Liu, F., Shareghi, E., Meng, Z.: Self-alignment pretraining for biomedical entity representations. In: Proceedings of the 2021 Conference of the North American chapter of the Association for Computational Linguistics: Human Language Technologies, pp. 4228–4238 (2021)
15. Liu, F., Vulić, I., Korhonen, A., Collier, N.: Learning domain-specialised representations for cross-lingual biomedical entity linking. In: Zong, C., Xia, F., Li, W., Navigli, R. (eds.) Proceedings of the 59th Annual Meeting of the Association for Computational Linguistics and the 11th International Joint Conference on Natural Language Processing (Volume 2: Short Papers), pp. 565–574. Association for Computational Linguistics, Online (2021)
16. Liu, Y., Gu, J., Goyal, N., et al.: Multilingual denoising pre-training for neural machine translation. Trans. Assoc. Comput. Linguist. **8**, 726–742 (2020)
17. Logeswaran, L., Chang, M.W., Lee, K., Toutanova, K., Devlin, J., Lee, H.: Zero-shot entity linking by reading entity descriptions. In: Korhonen, A., Traum, D., Màrquez, L. (eds.) Proceedings of the 57th Annual Meeting of the Association for Computational Linguistics, pp. 3449–3460. Association for Computational Linguistics (2019)
18. Marcou, Q., Berti-Equille, L., Novelli, N.: Creating a computer assisted ICD coding system: performance metric choice and use of the ICD hierarchy (2024)
19. Martin, L., Muller, B., Suárez, P.J.O.: CamemBERT: a tasty French language model. In: Proceedings of the 58th Annual Meeting of the Association for Computational Linguistics (2020)
20. Nentidis, A., Katsimpras, G., Vandorou, E., et al.: Overview of BioASQ 2022: the tenth BioASQ challenge on large-scale biomedical semantic indexing and question answering. In: Experimental IR Meets Multilinguality. Multimodality, and Interaction, vol. 13390, pp. 337–361. Springer, Cham (2022)

21. Névéol, A., Grouin, C., Leixa, J., Rosset, S., Zweigenbaum, P.: The Quaero French medical corpus: a ressource for medical entity recognition and normalization. In: Proceedings of the Fourth Workshop on Building and Evaluating Resources for Health and Biomedical Text Processing - BioTxtM, pp. 24–30 (2014)
22. NLLB Team, Costa-jussà, M.R., Cross, J., et al.: No language left behind: Scaling human-centered machine translation. arXiv preprint arXiv:2207.04672 (2022)
23. Papineni, K., Roukos, S., Ward, T., Zhu, W.J.: BLEU: a method for automatic evaluation of machine translation. In: Proceedings of the 40th Annual Meeting of the Association for Computational Linguistics, pp. 311–318. Association for Computational Linguistics (2002). https://doi.org/10.3115/1073083.1073135
24. Singh, A., Krishnamoorthy, S., Ortega, J.E.: NeighBERT: medical entity linking using relation-induced dense retrieval. J. Healthc. Inform. Res. **8**(2), 353–369 (2024)
25. Subies, G.G., Álvaro Barbero Jiménez, Fernández, P.M.: ClinText-SP and RigoBERTa Clinical: a new set of open resources for Spanish clinical NLP (2025)
26. Tiedemann, J., Thottingal, S.: OPUS-MT - building open translation services for the world. In: Proceedings of the 22nd Annual Conference of the European Association for Machine Translation, pp. 479–480 (2020)
27. Touchent, R., de la Clergerie, É.: CamemBERT-bio: leveraging continual pretraining for cost-effective models on French biomedical data. In: Calzolari, N., Kan, M.Y., Hoste, V., Lenci, A., Sakti, S., Xue, N. (eds.) Proceedings of the 2024 Joint International Conference on Computational Linguistics, Language Resources and Evaluation (LREC-COLING 2024), pp. 2692–2701. ELRA and ICCL, Torino, Italia (2024)
28. Vaswani, A., Shazeer, N., Parmar, N.: Attention is all you need. In: Advances in Neural Information Processing Systems, vol. 30. Curran Associates, Inc. (2017)
29. Wajsbürt, P., Sarfati, A., Tannier, X.: Medical concept normalization in French using multilingual terminologies and contextual embeddings. J. Biomed. Inform. **114**, 103684 (2021)
30. World Health Organization: International Statistical Classification of Diseases and Related Health Problems, 10th Revision, Fifth Edition, 2016. World Health Organization, Geneva (2015)
31. Yuan, Z., Zhao, Z., Sun, H., et al.: CODER: knowledge-infused cross-lingual medical term embedding for term normalization. J. Biomed. Inform. **126**, 103983 (2022)
32. Zahra, F.A., Kate, R.J.: Obtaining clinical term embeddings from SNOMED CT ontology. J. Biomed. Inform. **149**, 104560 (2024)
33. Zhu, T., Qin, Y., Chen, Q.: Controllable contrastive generation for multilingual biomedical entity linking. In: Proceedings of the 2023 Conference on Empirical Methods in Natural Language Processing, pp. 5742–5753 (2023)
34. Zotova, E., García-Pablos, A., Cuadros, M., Rigau, G.: VICOMTECH at MedProcNER 2023: transformers-based sequence-labelling and cross-encoding for entity detection and normalisation in Spanish clinical texts. In: Conference and Labs of the Evaluation Forum (2023)

RAPT: Retrieval-Augmented Post-hoc Thresholding for Multi-label Classification

Lasal Jayawardena[1(✉)], Nirmalie Wiratunga[1], Ikechukwu Nkisi-Orji[1], and Darren Nicol[2]

[1] Robert Gordon University, Aberdeen, UK
{l.jayawardena,n.wiratunga,i.o.nkisi-orji}@rgu.ac.uk
[2] William Nicol (Aberdeen) Limited, Aberdeen, UK
darren.nicol@williamnicol.co.uk

Abstract. Industrial multi-label document understanding pipelines score candidate labels and threshold or rank them to form a label set per document. This early selection step directly affects the accuracy of downstream information extraction from the document, as well as the associated verification effort. In practice, OCR noise, label imbalance, instance-dependent label cardinality, and asymmetric error costs make global score thresholds brittle and hard to maintain as document formats evolve. We present RAPT, a deployment-oriented retrieval-augmented score thresholding wrapper, applied post-hoc to improve label set selection without retraining the underlying classifier. RAPT is a model-agnostic wrapper: any predictor that provides document representations for similarity search and per label confidence scores can be used, including metric learning encoders and fine-tuned transformer classifiers. For each query document, given a classifier's score vector, RAPT retrieves similar document thresholding situations (cases) and adapts the query's label set selection threshold using their outcomes. The adaptation selects the final label set by locally aggregating neighbour solutions (e.g. average label count, cutoff calibration). Evaluation compared multi-label classifiers (metric learners and transformers) combined with RAPT against global and label-wise thresholding baselines, and against few-shot LLMs. Across an industrial dataset and six public benchmarks, RAPT consistently outperformed global and label-wise static thresholding baselines. In the industrial setting, RAPT achieved its best predictive performance with metric learners, reaching 0.87 Macro-F1, while fine-tuned transformer variants on average achieved 0.775 Macro-F1, outperforming few-shot LLM baselines ($K = 5$) by 2× and requiring at least 115× less inference time and 13.5× less GPU memory.

Keywords: Multi-label classification · Retrieval augmentation · Case-based reasoning · Dynamic thresholding · Transformers

---

Supplementary Information The online version contains supplementary material available at https://doi.org/10.1007/978-3-032-37682-4_35.

M. Baratchi et al. (Eds.): ECML PKDD 2026, LNAI 16949, pp. 600–616, 2027.
https://doi.org/10.1007/978-3-032-37682-4_35

1 Introduction

Unlike traditional single-label classification, multi-label classification requires predicting a set of labels for each instance. This capability has become central to many high-impact applications in text, vision, recommendation, and decision support [27,35]. The practical difficulty of multi-label classification is not only learning good label rankings, but deciding which labels to actually assign at test time when label cardinality varies across instances, and label co-occurrence patterns vary across the instance space. Typically, models output per label activations that imply a label ranking, but deployment requires a cutoff rule that maps activation scores to a variable size label set, often with unequal penalties for false positives (FPs, suprious labels) and false negatives (FNs, missed labels). Global decision rules, such as fixed score thresholds, are attractive for simplicity. Still, they can be hard to specify in skewed spaces where the semantics of a given score value can differ across regions of the instance space and across labels.

In document understanding pipelines, multi-label predictions often determine pre-processing pathways. A typical workflow, shown in Fig. 1, converts raw documents to PDF, applies OCR, performs document categorisation, identifies areas of interest, and then runs document type and class specific attribute extraction. In Fig. 1, the predicted label set triggers downstream tasks, so selection errors can propagate through subsequent stages before human verification. Omitted labels (FNs) may prevent appropriate tasks from running, while spurious labels (FPs) can trigger inappropriate processes, yielding irrelevant or misleading fields and increasing verification effort and operational risk.

This challenge is particularly evident in industrial settings, where organisations maintain large collections of legacy documents in heterogeneous formats, including scanned paper records, reports, and correspondence containing operational and customer information. In collaboration with WM Nicol, an industry partner operating in the transportation and waste management domain, we consider document processing pipelines that must handle diverse document types whose content may correspond to multiple operational categories simultaneously. Accurate prediction of the label set is therefore critical to routing each document correctly to downstream extraction, review, and case handling workflows.

To address this multi-label classification challenge, we introduce RAPT, a lightweight retrieval-augmented wrapper employing case-based reasoning (CBR). It can be applied post-hoc to any multi-label classifier producing embeddings and label-wise scores, enabling instance-specific thresholding and label set selection. In addition to benchmark data, the dataset used in this study is derived from WM Nicol's operational documents which provides a realistic setting where thresholding decisions directly influence downstream processing. The contributions of this work are outlined as follows:

- propose a framework for constructing a case base from the training set, in which each case consists of a multi-label classification instance and threshold values inferred from the ground truth labels associated with its score vector, eliminating the need for additional data or human annotation;

- introduce neighbourhood-driven dynamic thresholding strategies for variable cardinality set prediction, including AvgCount and Rank Calibration, and show how residual error information from retrieved cases can be used to adapt the multi-label score vector prior to thresholding; and
- evaluate RAPT on an industrial document workflow dataset, and six public benchmarks showing consistent gains over global and label-wise thresholding baselines, with zero-shot and few-shot LLM comparators also reported.

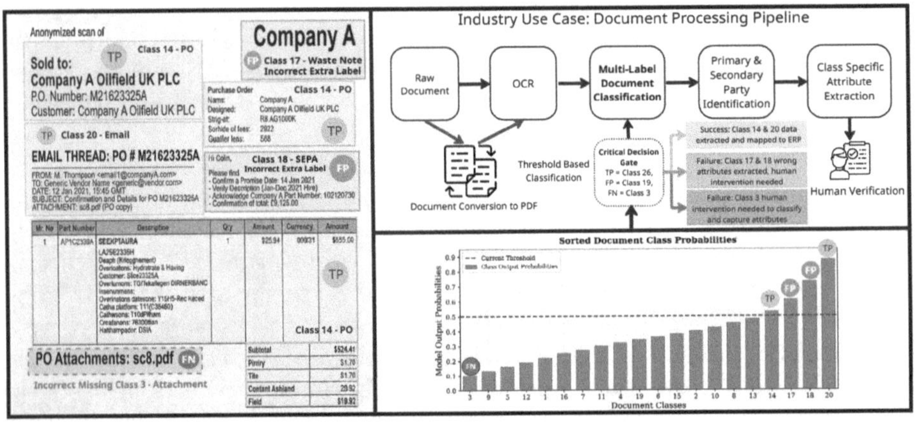

Fig. 1. Industry use case pipeline for document processing and information extraction. Left: a typical document with areas indicated for class label assignment. Top: multi-label predictions act as routing decisions for downstream extraction tasks. Bottom: typical prediction scores from a backbone model on y-axis, shown relative to class specific optimal thresholds, with x-axis showing the label set. This illustrates how a global threshold (set at 0.5 for instance) can misclassify labels, omitting required classes (class label 3) and including spurious ones (class label 17 and 18).

2 Related Work

Multi-label classification methods are commonly divided into problem transformation and algorithm adaptation approaches [27,35]. Methods such as Binary Relevance, Classifier Chains [19], RAkEL [28], and Calibrated Label Ranking [7] differ in how they model label dependence, but they still typically produce label-wise scores or rankings that must be converted into a final predicted label set. A central but often underemphasised part of this conversion is therefore thresholding: deciding where the relevance boundary should lie for a given instance. Prior work has studied **global and label-specific** thresholding strategies, including SCut [33], MCut [14], MetaLabeler [25], MALTOR [12], and more recent neighbourhood-aware approaches [20]. However, most methods either learn global thresholding rules or rely on additional predictive models, leaving open the question of how thresholding decisions might instead be derived directly from local evidence in similar labelled instances.

Case-based reasoning solves a new problem by **retrieving** similar prior cases and **adapting** their solutions to the current query [1]. This distinguishes CBR from neighbourhood-based methods that primarily aggregate local evidence, such as ML-kNN [34] or Deep k-Nearest Neighbours [18]. In this sense, useful retrieval is not only about finding similar neighbours, but about whether their solutions can be revised for the new instance [5,22]. Our work adopts this adaptation perspective, but applies it to a different target: rather than using retrieved cases for direct label voting, we use them to adapt the score-to-set conversion step in multi-label prediction.

Episodic metric meta-learning provides a natural backbone for our framework because it jointly supports retrieval and prediction. **Matching Networks** [30] condition predictions on a labelled support set, **Prototypical Networks** [23] summarise classes by embedding prototypes, **Relation Networks** [24] learn a comparison function, and **SNAIL** [16] combines temporal convolutions with attention for few-shot adaptation. These models are especially attractive here because they produce embeddings suitable for similarity return (neighbour retrieval) while also yielding per-label scores that can be post-processed by our case-based adaptation rules. Multi-label meta-learning remains comparatively underexplored. Simon et al. [21] introduced a few-shot multi-label meta-learning framework with an explicit label-counting component, which is directly relevant to dynamic thresholding. Wu et al. [31] studied learning policies for multi-label heterogeneity. Our framework is intentionally broader than any single meta-learning architecture: any backbone that provides an embedding space and per-label confidence scores can be paired with our retrieval-based adaptation layer.

Fine-tuned Transformers are a practically important family of backbones formed by transformer encoders fine-tuned for multi-label classification. Representative models include **BERT-base** and **BERT-large** [6], **DeBERTa-v3-base** and **DeBERTa-v3-large** [9], as well as domain-specialised encoders such as LegalBERT [4], ClinicalBERT [2], and PubMedBERT [8]. In these models, the `[CLS]` representation provides a compact retrieval embedding, while sigmoid-activated logits provide per-label scores for downstream thresholding and adaptation. This combination makes **fine-tuned transformers** especially convenient for our framework: they are strong discriminative classifiers, but they also expose an embedding for case representation on which case retrieval can be built.

Large language models broaden the space of possible backbones and teachers. Open-weight LLM families such as Llama [26], OpenAI's gpt-oss models [17] and Qwen [32] make it increasingly feasible to use larger generative models for classification, retrieval, synthetic data generation, or weak supervision. However, LLMs also introduce practical complications for our setting. Compared with compact fine-tuned encoders, they typically incur higher inference latency, larger memory footprints, and greater serving cost; retrieval behaviour may also depend more strongly on prompt format, instruction tuning, and context budget [36]. For a framework that performs case retrieval at prediction time, these considerations are not incidental: they affect whether retrieval remains lightweight enough to be useful in practice. For this reason, we view LLMs primarily as powerful comparative baselines, whereas compact fine-tuned encoders and meta-learners remain especially well matched to case-based test-time adaptation and in our work as the basis for the thresholding CBR wrapper.

3 CBR Wrapper Methodology for Thresholding

We formulate multi-label thresholding as a CBR problem implemented as a wrapper around an existing classifier. Rather than modifying the base model, the wrapper reuses the model's score outputs and internal representations to construct a case base from labelled instances. Given a query instance, the method retrieves similar prior cases (forming a neighbourhood) and adapts their thresholding evidence to produce instance-specific label set predictions for the query. This forms a CBR cycle in which the query defines the problem, retrieved labelled instances provide prior cases, with weighted aggregations forming case reuse and threshold adaptation corresponds to the revise step. If desired, newly verified

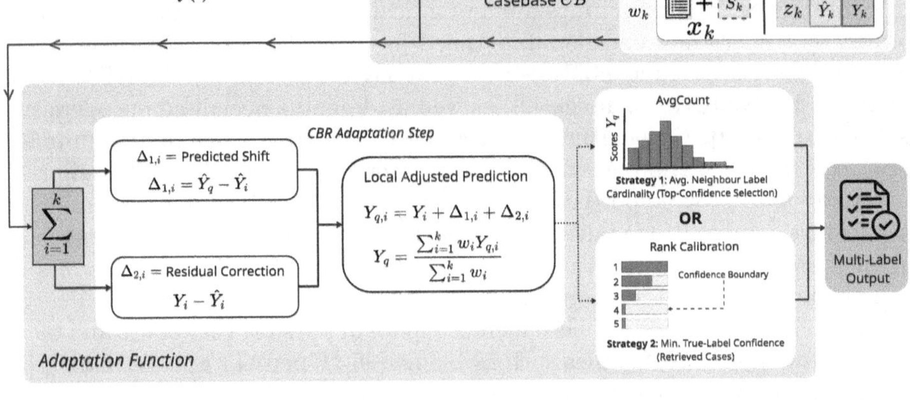

Fig. 2. CBR wrapper components, illustrated against a grey background. Given a query document, the backbone model, f, produces label scores and an embedding, which are used to retrieve similar cases from the casebase. Retrieved predictions and labels are then combined in an adaptation step to produce a locally adjusted prediction, followed by threshold calibration to obtain the final multi label output.

instances may be retained as new cases, allowing the case base to expand over time, although this retain step is not the focus of the present paper.

3.1 Thresholding Case Base Construction

The case base is constructed from existing training (and if available any validation data), requiring no additional data collection or annotation. It can be updated incrementally as newly verified documents become available, making the approach easy to integrate into existing document workflows without retraining.

Let f denote a trained multi-label classification model over a label space of size L that produces label-wise scores. For an input instance x, optionally accompanied by additional context S, the model produces a score vector $\hat{Y} \in \mathbb{R}^L$ and an associated representation $z \in \mathbb{R}^d$, written as $(z, \hat{Y}) = f(x, S)$. The vector $\hat{Y}$ contains the label-wise scores produced by the model's multi-label classification head, which may correspond to logits, activation values, or calibrated probabilities depending on the underlying architecture. Here S captures model-specific context when available, such as support sets in metric-based learners, and is null otherwise. We denote by $g(\cdot)$ the embedding function associated with f, such that $z = g(x, S)$. In practice, g may be instantiated by an internal representation of the model, such as a final hidden layer embedding. Using each labelled training instance (x, Y), we construct a case

$$\mathcal{C} = \langle x,\ S,\ z,\ \hat{Y},\ Y \rangle$$

where $Y \in \{0, 1\}^L$ denotes the ground truth binary label vector. Since the ground truth labels, Y, are known in the training data, and the model provides the $\hat{Y}$ prediction scores, thresholding evidence can be derived automatically without additional data or human annotation. In particular, when $Y_\ell = 0$, the case indicates that label ℓ is absent and therefore contributes no thresholding evidence for that label. The set of all such constructed cases forms the case base $\mathcal{CB}$.

3.2 Case Retrieval and Similarity Weighting

Given a query instance q with optional context S_q, we retrieve the k most similar cases from the case base $\mathcal{CB}$ as follows:

$$\text{Retrieve}(q, \mathcal{CB}) = \underset{\mathcal{C}_i \in \mathcal{CB}}{\text{TopK}} \left(w(z_q, z_i) \right) = \{\mathcal{C}_1, \ldots, \mathcal{C}_k\}$$

where $w(\cdot, \cdot)$ denotes cosine similarity. Here the query embedding is $z_q = g(q, S_q)$ and S_q is optional. The similarity score of each retrieved neighbour is also used as its importance weight, denoted w_i.

Given the retrieved cases, the goal is to reuse their label-wise thresholding evidence for the query instance. Since the query is rarely identical to any retrieved case, this reuse must be accompanied by an adaptation step that adjusts the retrieved thresholding evidence to the local characteristics of the query before final label set prediction.

3.3 Local Neighbourhood Adaptation Step

Given the retrieved neighbourhood $\{\mathcal{C}_1, \ldots, \mathcal{C}_k\}$, adaptation is performed in score space by transferring case-specific evidence from the retrieved cases to the query. The core idea is to begin from the query's own model output and then refine it using the observed prediction residuals of similar past cases. In this way, adaptation preserves the model's instance-specific prediction while incorporating corrective evidence from the local neighbourhood.

$$Y_q = \text{Adapt}(\hat{Y}_q, \{\mathcal{C}_1, \ldots, \mathcal{C}_k\}).$$

The locally adapted score vector of the query is inferred from each neighbouring case, $\mathcal{C}_i$'s predicted score vector, $\hat{Y}_i$, as follows:

$$Y_{q,i} = \hat{Y}_i + \Delta_{1,i} + \Delta_{2,i}.$$

Basically each retrieved case contributes a residual-based correction to the query's original score vector. Here the two Δ terms are derived from each retrieved case $\mathcal{C}_i$ by using: 1) a **Model Adaptation** ($\Delta_{1,i}$) term, which is the predicted score vector difference between the query and the retrieved case, $\Delta_{1,i} = \hat{Y}_q - \hat{Y}_i$. This term aligns the retrieved case with the query by shifting the neighbour's score profile toward the query's own model output; and 2) a **Residual Correction** ($\Delta_{2,i}$), which is a case-specific correction derived from the discrepancy between the retrieved case's ground truth labels and its score vector, $\Delta_{2,i} = Y_i - \hat{Y}_i$. Here $\Delta_{2,i}$ captures how the model erred on the retrieved case, and transfers that error pattern as corrective evidence for the query.

The final adapted query score vector is obtained by similarity-weighted aggregation over the retrieved neighbourhood:

$$Y_q = \frac{\sum_{i=1}^{k} w_i Y_{q,i}}{\sum_{i=1}^{k} w_i}.$$

In this manner, neighbours that are more similar to the query contribute more strongly to the final adapted score estimate. The resulting vector Y_q is a neighbourhood informed score estimate which is then converted into the final binary label set through dynamic thresholding.

3.4 Inference and Dynamic Thresholding

The final multi-label prediction is obtained from the adapted score vector Y_q via dynamic thresholding, with the indicator function applied element-wise:

$$Y_{\text{final}} = \mathbb{1}(Y_q > \tau_q)$$

The query specific threshold τ_q can then be determined via two alternative neighbourhood strategies. Under **AvgCount**, we estimate the expected number of active labels for the query by computing a similarity-weighted average of the neighbours' label cardinalities:

$$k^* = \frac{\sum_{i=1}^{k} w_i \|Y_i\|_1}{\sum_{i=1}^{k} w_i}. \tag{1}$$

We then set τ_{Count} so that thresholding Y_q yields approximately k^* positive labels (equivalently, we threshold between the $\lfloor k^* \rfloor$-th and $(\lfloor k^* \rfloor + 1)$-th largest entries of Y_q). The intuition is that the neighbourhood provides a local estimate of how many labels are typically active for instances in this region of the space. Under **Rank Calibration**, the threshold is set from the weighted average of the minimum confidence scores assigned to positive labels in the retrieved neighbourhood:

$$\tau_{RCal} = \frac{\sum w_i \cdot \min\{\hat{Y}_i^{(l)} \mid Y_i^{(l)} = 1\}}{\sum w_i} \tag{2}$$

this uses, for each neighbour, the lowest score that still corresponds to a relevant label as a proxy decision boundary. Averaging these boundaries produces a threshold that reflects how far scores typically need to rise before a label is considered positive in similar cases (i.e. locality thresholding knowledge).

4 Evaluation

The evaluation assesses whether the proposed RAPT thresholding wrapper improves label set selection in realistic document understanding settings. We compare five thresholding strategies:

- **Base$_{0.5}$**: a fixed global threshold where $\tau = 0.5$ applied in $Y_{\text{final}} = \mathbb{1}(Y_q > \tau)$;
- **Base***: a globally optimised threshold selected on the validation set using a greedy search procedure to maximise F1;
- **Base$_l^*$**: a label-wise optimised threshold, τ_ℓ optimised, on the validation set, where each label receives its own threshold through greedy tuning;
- **RAPT$_{\#}$**: CBR wrapper thresholding methods using dynamic τ from Avg-Count, (see Eq. 1); and
- **RAPT$_{\geq}$**: CBR wrapper using τ from rank calibration (RankCal), (see Eq. 2).

The validation tuned baselines, Base*and Base$_l^*$, provide stronger comparisons than the naive baseline Base$_{0.5}$, as they optimise thresholds to each dataset. This allows us to test whether wrappers improve not only naive thresholding, but also competitive static thresholding procedures derived from held-out validation data. For the proposed CBR thresholding wrapper, we set the retrieval neighbourhood size to $k = 10$ by default. We also control the number of unique retrieved query situations retained during adaptation, denoted n, and set this to 3 by default. Both parameters can be varied, and ablation studies examining sensitivity to these choices are reported in the supplementary material.

4.1 Backbone Models for Multi-label Classification

We evaluate all thresholding methods with two main backbone families instantiating the scoring function $f(\cdot)$ in Fig. 2: episodic metric learners and transformer encoders. For metric learners, we consider Matching Networks, Prototypical Networks, Relation Networks, and SNAIL. For transformers, we evaluate the pre-trained, head-only fine-tuned, and fully fine-tuned variants including domain-specialised encoders where appropriate. We additionally report large language model (LLM) baselines using Qwen3-32B as a comparative reference, given their growing popularity as prompt-based alternatives for document understanding. While not part of the proposed deployment pipeline, they serve as important industrial comparators for assessing predictive effectiveness, inference efficiency, and serving cost relative to the proposed wrapper. For episodic metric learners, evaluation is restricted to the labels present in the support set for a given episode, since these models only produce predictions over classes observed in support. All thresholding methods applied to metric learners are therefore compared under the same support-constrained setting. Transformer models, by contrast, output scores over the full retained label space and are evaluated across all labels. The same full-label evaluation setting is used for the LLM baselines; prompts are provided in the appendix.

4.2 Datasets

While our main focus is the WM Nicol industrial dataset, we also evaluate RAPT on six public multi-label benchmarks to assess its generalisation beyond this application setting: news (Reuters-21578 [15]), legal (EUR-Lex [3]), Event Classification [29], medical (MIMIC-III [13], OHSUMED [10]), and e-commerce (AmazonCat-13K [11]). Together, these datasets support complementary evaluation goals: WM Nicol assesses practical utility in a document workflow setting, while the public benchmarks assess robustness and transferability across broader domains and datasets (Table 1). To keep experiments computationally manageable, we restrict each dataset to its 100 most frequent labels (50 for MIMIC-III), providing a consistent setting across industrial and public data while preserving key multi-label challenges: imbalance, variable label cardinality, and threshold selection.

We report results using the original train/validation/test split for each dataset. Additional k-fold experiments examining robustness to partitioning effects are included in the supplementary material, so the main paper focuses on the standard split results, with particular attention to the industrial dataset.

4.3 Evaluation Metrics and Implementation Details

We compute standard multi-label metrics including Micro-F1, Macro-F1, Precision, Recall, and Hamming Loss. For brevity, we report only Micro-F1 and Macro-F1, which together summarise overall performance and sensitivity to label imbalance; the remaining metrics are provided in the supplementary material.

Table 1. Evaluation datasets overview. For datasets with more than 100 labels, we use the top 100 most frequent labels; MIMIC-III is restricted to the top 50 labels.

Dataset	Domain	Train	Val	Test	#Labels
WM Nicol	Resource Mngt	1,134	284	355	11
Reuters-21578	News	6,182	1,546	3,005	100
EUR-Lex	Legal	47,996	12,000	5,000	100
Event Classification	Events	2,207	552	381	29
MIMIC-III	Clinical	33,560	8,390	7,404	50
OHSUMED	Medical	43,077	10,770	289,440	100
AmazonCat-13K	E-commerce	932,636	233,159	301,377	100

We also assess deployment-oriented efficiency on the WM Nicol test set by measuring per-document inference latency and peak GPU memory usage, from which we derive hardware-normalised cost estimates (see Sect. 5.2).

All experiments were trained and evaluated on a single NVIDIA A100 80 GB GPU. This setup reflects the deployment-oriented framing of the work: the thresholding wrapper operates as a lightweight post-hoc layer on top of existing classifiers without requiring additional large-scale infrastructure. All runs use a fixed random seed of 42 for reproducibility.

All 4 **metric learners** share the same episodic training protocol, sharing the same backbone encoder `sentence-transformers/all-mpnet-base-v2`. Each episode samples $N = 10$ classes, and $K = 5$ support examples per class. Strict document-level separation is enforced: the query document is never included in its own support set, preventing information leakage between query and support. Training runs for up to 50 epochs with early stopping, using optimiser Adam (learning rate 10^{-4}, weight decay 10^{-5}) and batch size of 32. All 4 models are trained per split under identical hyperparameters, ensuring a fair intra-family comparison. To ensure fair comparison across thresholding methods and with transformer baselines, the candidate label space at evaluation time is restricted to labels present in the support set of the current episode.

We evaluated 3 **Transformer** fine-tuning training regimes: (i) *pretrained*, where the model is used frozen without any task-specific training; (ii) *head-only*, where only a randomly initialised classification head is trained on top of the frozen encoder; and (iii) *fully fine-tuned*, where all parameters are updated end-to-end. For regimes (ii) and (iii), we train for up to 25 epochs with early stopping (patience 5, improvement threshold 10^{-3}). The learning rate is 2×10^{-5} for base-sized models and 1×10^{-5} for large models, with linear warmup over the first 10% of training steps and weight decay of 0.01, with batch size 32.

5 Results

Our evaluation pursues three goals: assessing RAPT in its primary industrial application setting, examining whether its thresholding behaviour transfers to public multi-label classification dataset benchmarks, and comparing deployment efficiency against LLM baselines on the industrial task.

5.1 WM Nicol Industry Domain Effectiveness Analysis

Table 2 reports Micro-F1 and Macro-F1 across the 4 metric learners and 4 transformer models on the baselines and RAPT thresholding strategies. Among the metric learners, RAPT performs best when combined with ProtoNet: $\text{RAPT}_{\#}$ achieves a Macro-F1 of 0.8704, corresponding to relative gains of 10.8% over $\text{Base}_{0.5}$, 11.1% over Base^*, and 2.8% over Base^*_l. This is especially relevant in the presence of label imbalance, since Macro-F1 gives equal weight to each class and is therefore more sensitive to performance on rarer labels.

Table 2. Micro & Macro F1 across Model Configurations and Thresholding Methodologies. Method abbreviations: $\text{Base}_{0.5}$ = Base ($\tau = 0.5$), Base^* = Base ($\tau = opt$), Base^*_l = Base ($\tau = local$), $\text{RAPT}_{\#}$ = CBR + AvgCount, $\text{RAPT}_{\geq}$ = CBR + RankCal.

Models f	$\text{Base}_{0.5}$		Base^*		Base^*_l		$\text{RAPT}_{\#}$		$\text{RAPT}_{\geq}$	
	Micro	Macro	Micro	Macro	Micro	Macro	Micro	Macro	Micro	Macro
Metric Learners										
MatchingNet	0.9324	0.8441	0.9321	0.8111	0.9222	0.8354	0.9411	**0.8607**	0.9378	0.8502
ProtoNet	0.9283	0.7853	0.9301	0.7833	0.9378	0.8467	0.9467	**0.8704**	0.9426	0.8648
RelationNet	0.9332	0.8334	0.9147	0.7391	0.9357	0.8600	0.9424	**0.8636**	0.9416	0.8587
SNAIL	0.8853	0.4696	0.8853	0.4696	0.7977	0.4583	0.9470	**0.8694**	0.9047	0.8146
Pretrained Models										
bert-base	0.2166	0.0963	0.2419	0.1853	0.2226	0.1941	0.7868	**0.6312**	0.7894	0.6273
bert-large	0.2438	0.1510	0.2506	0.1293	0.2562	0.2132	0.7664	**0.5999**	0.7740	0.5625
deberta-v3-base	0.2414	0.1437	0.2414	0.1437	0.2274	0.1885	0.7714	**0.6149**	0.7692	0.5987
deberta-v3-large	0.2304	0.1013	0.2304	0.1013	0.2093	0.1902	0.7456	**0.5578**	0.7411	0.5413
Head-Only Fine-tuned Models										
bert-base	0.0000	0.0000	0.4000	0.0571	0.3575	0.1802	0.8018	0.6312	0.7533	**0.6596**
bert-large	0.0043	0.0011	0.3995	0.0570	0.3374	0.1592	0.7834	**0.5900**	0.7297	0.5889
deberta-v3-base	0.0000	0.0000	0.3995	0.0570	0.2091	0.1901	0.7827	0.6287	0.7842	**0.6387**
deberta-v3-large	0.0000	0.0000	0.3995	0.0570	0.2159	0.2071	0.7285	0.5497	0.7333	**0.5795**
Fully Fine-tuned Models										
bert-base	0.8166	0.5944	0.8382	0.6950	0.8412	0.7688	0.8410	**0.7753**	0.8346	0.7639
bert-large	0.8154	0.6531	0.8318	0.7440	0.8342	0.7508	0.8357	**0.7655**	0.8215	0.7192
deberta-v3-base	0.8301	0.6973	0.8379	0.7076	0.8364	0.7492	0.8163	**0.7628**	0.8032	0.7433
deberta-v3-large	0.8418	0.7514	0.8515	0.7694	0.8565	0.7886	0.8512	**0.7957**	0.8404	0.7409

Transformer backbones are overall less effective than metric learners on this task, as none reach the Macro-F1 levels above 0.85 achieved by the strongest metric models. Within the transformer family, however, the effect of RAPT depends strongly on the training regime. Fully fine-tuned transformers show only modest gains over the strongest baseline, consistent with stronger score calibration; for example, DeBERTa-v3-large improves from 0.7886 (Base_l^*) to 0.7957 ($\text{RAPT}_{\#}$) in Macro-F1, a relative gain of 0.9%. However, pretrained and head-only models benefit substantially: pretrained BERT-base increases from Macro-F1 = 0.0963 ($\text{Base}_{0.5}$) to 0.6312 ($\text{RAPT}_{\#}$), while head-only DeBERTa-v3-base increases from 0 to 0.6287. These results suggest that RAPT is useful with transformers when applied to backbones with poorly calibrated scores, where it can recover useful multi-label performance without further fine-tuning. On the WM Nicol data, RAPT configurations achieved approximately 2× the Macro-F1 of the best few-shot LLM baseline (Qwen3-32B, $K = 5$) as seen in Table 3.

Table 3. LLM (Qwen3-32B) on WM Nicol dataset. Relative scores (%) computed against the best ML and Transformer baselines. Relative improvements are computed against the
†best ML baseline (ProtoNet+$\text{RAPT}_{\#}$, Micro-F1=0.9467, Macro-F1= 0.8704); and
‡Best transformer baseline: DeBERTa-v3-large (fully fine-tuned) + $\text{RAPT}_{\#}$(Micro-F1 = 0.8512, Macro-F1 = 0.7957).
* Semantic labels were provided and represent an upper-bound reference.

Prompting Strategy	F1 Score		Rel. Best ML†		Rel. Best Trans.‡	
	Micro	Macro	Micro	Macro	Micro	Macro
Zero-shot (Semantic)*	0.6134	**0.5220**	−35.2%	−40.0%	−27.9%	−34.4%
Zero-shot (Anonymized)	0.0958	0.0845	−89.9%	−90.3%	−88.7%	−89.4%
Few-shot $K = 1$ (Anon.)	0.0996	0.1057	−89.5%	−87.9%	−88.3%	−86.7%
Few-shot $K = 3$ (Anon.)	0.4232	0.3648	−55.3%	−58.1%	−50.3%	−54.2%
Few-shot $K = 5$ (Anon.)	0.4408	0.3745	−53.4%	−57.0%	−48.2%	−52.9%

A close examination of misclassified documents in the industrial dataset revealed two recurring failure modes. The first is co-occurrence driven false positives. In 19 cases, RAPT introduced a spurious label that frequently co-occurred with the true label in the local neighbourhood. The clearest example was *Hazardous Waste Note* being added to *SEPA Note* or *Waste Transfer Note* documents, with these label pairs showing roughly 150–180 co-occurrences in training; in practice, such documents are often bundled together as part of a single case. As a result, retrieved CBR neighbours often contain both labels, inflating the spurious class score above the selection threshold. $\text{RAPT}_{\#}$was particularly susceptible in this setting, whereas $\text{RAPT}_{\geq}$partially mitigated the issue, recovering 9 of the 19 cases by applying a sufficiently conservative per-instance threshold.

The second failure mode is format–content ambiguity. In a small number of cases, Purchase Orders written in an email-like style (e.g., *"Hi Alex, please use order number DCL 417...*") retrieved neighbours that were closer in format than in semantic content. This pushed the *Purchase Order* score downward and the *Email Correspondence* score upward. More broadly, this highlights that retrieval quality depends critically on the structure of the backbone embedding space: when embeddings overemphasise superficial formatting cues, retrieval-augmented thresholding can reinforce the wrong decision.

5.2 WM Nicol Industry Domain Inference Efficiency Analysis

We profiled inference efficiency on the WM Nicol test set to assess deployment characteristics across all model families (Table 4). For each model, we measured per-document inference latency (mean and P95 via `time.perf_counter()`), throughput (documents per second), and peak GPU memory (`torch.cuda`). We additionally report GPU-hours per document as a hardware-agnostic cost proxy that practitioners can multiply by their accelerator's hourly rate.

From a deployment perspective, as expected metric-learners and transformer models combined with RAPT offer substantial advantages over LLM-based alternatives. Although GPU-time determines the deployment cost in our setup, prompt length strongly influences LLM inference latency. Average token usage

Table 4. Throughput is computed as 1000/mean latency (ms). GPU-hrs/doc converts mean latency to GPU-hrs for cost estimation.

Model	GPU (GB)	Mean (ms)	P95 (ms)	Tput (docs/s)	GPU-hrs/doc
Metric Learners					
MatchingNet	0.47	105.31	120.25	9.50	2.93×10^{-5}
ProtoNet	0.47	108.69	121.55	9.20	3.02×10^{-5}
RelationNet	0.47	110.47	125.05	9.05	3.07×10^{-5}
SNAIL	0.47	235.78	297.80	4.24	6.55×10^{-5}
Transformers					
bert-base	0.89	40.20	44.47	24.88	1.12×10^{-5}
bert-large	1.78	93.17	99.72	10.73	2.59×10^{-5}
deberta-v3-base	1.26	72.67	99.67	13.76	2.02×10^{-5}
deberta-v3-large	2.23	151.99	177.52	6.58	4.22×10^{-5}
legal-bert-base	0.92	39.86	44.89	25.09	1.11×10^{-5}
clinical-bert	0.89	37.56	42.83	26.62	1.04×10^{-5}
pubmed-bert	0.89	39.91	45.72	25.06	1.11×10^{-5}
Large Language Models (Qwen3-32B)					
Zero-shot (Semantic)*	30.10	47661.59	74174.17	0.02	1.32×10^{-2}
Zero-shot (Anon.)	30.10	28236.22	43396.21	0.04	7.84×10^{-3}
Few-shot $K=1$	30.25	28344.47	50431.93	0.04	7.87×10^{-3}
Few-shot $K=3$	30.55	27124.87	52785.33	0.04	7.53×10^{-3}
Few-shot $K=5$	30.85	30397.81	53484.44	0.03	8.44×10^{-3}

increased substantially with few-shot prompting, rising from approximately 1k tokens for zero-shot prompts to over 7.7k tokens for $K = 5$ demonstrations. This increase in prompt size explains the higher latency observed for larger few-shot versions and highlights the sensitivity of LLM inference efficiency to prompt construction. RAPT configurations are at least 115× faster (38–236 ms vs. 27–48 s per document) and required at least 13.5× less GPU memory (≤2.23 GB vs. >30 GB). These characteristics make RAPT particularly suited to higher throughput (millions of documents) industrial document workflows.

5.3 Public Benchmark Datasets Effectiveness Summary Analysis

For brevity, we summarise RAPT's effect across all seven datasets in Fig. 3, with full per-model results deferred to the Appendix. Rather than comparing only the single best configuration per family, we report how often RAPT outperforms the best static baseline for *each individual model*, along with the average F1 gain across all models. Specifically, for each model we compare its highest Macro-F1 under any static threshold ($\text{Base}_{0.5}$, Base^*, or Base^*_l) against its highest Macro-F1 under either RAPT variant ($\text{RAPT}_{\#}$or $\text{RAPT}_{\geq}$). Accordingly we have 175 model–dataset combinations, and RAPT achieves the higher Macro-F1 in 130 cases (74.3%), with an average improvement of +0.093 Macro-F1 and +0.066 Micro-F1. Among metric learners, win rates reach 75–100% on every dataset, with average Macro-F1 gains of +0.06 to +0.14.

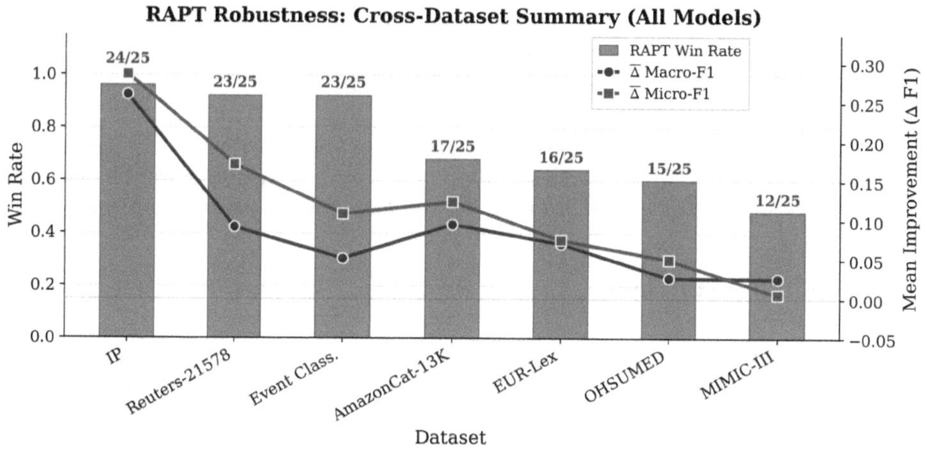

Fig. 3. Cross-dataset accuracy summary across all models. Bars show the RAPT win rate per dataset, while lines show mean improvement in Macro-F1 and Micro-F1 relative to the best static baseline. Labels above bars indicate the number of wins out of 25 model configurations (4 metric learners + 7 Transformers x 3 modes).

6 Conclusion

This paper addressed a practical problem in industrial multi-label document classification: how to convert model outputs (scores) into reliable document labels under noisy, imbalanced, heterogeneous document formats, and downstream workflow constraints. Here, the labelling decision is a critical post-processing step, as it determines downstream extraction, routing, and review actions, directly affecting operational accuracy and verification effort.

To address this challenge, we introduced RAPT, a retrieval-augmented post-hoc thresholding wrapper that adapts label set selection at inference time using case-based reasoning (CBR). Because RAPT requires only embeddings and label-wise scores, it can be paired with different backbone classifier model families, including metric learners and fine-tuned transformers, without retraining or architectural changes. This makes it attractive for applied settings where organisations already use classifiers, but need a lightweight way to improve robustness as document collections evolve. Across 175 model–dataset combinations spanning an industrial document classification pipeline and six public benchmarks from legal, biomedical, clinical, news, event, and e-commerce domains, RAPT outperformed the best static threshold approach in 130 cases (74.3%).

Looking ahead, we see two promising extensions. First, the CBR *retain* step could enable online case-base growth from newly verified documents, allowing the thresholding wrapper to adapt to distributional drift without retraining, which is valuable in settings where document templates and label distributions evolve over time. Second, evaluating RAPT on extreme multi-label tasks with the full label space (e.g. AmazonCat-13K with 13,330 labels) would test whether neighbourhood-driven thresholding remains effective when label sparsity is severe.

Acknowledgements. The authors thank William Nicol (Aberdeen) Limited for providing the proprietary industrial dataset used in this study. We also gratefully acknowledge Robert Gordon University for providing the research facilities that supported this work.

Data Availibility Statement. The source code used for the experiments in this study is available at https://github.com/LasalJayawardena/RAPT.

Generative AI Statement. Uring the preparation of this manuscript, the authors used generative AI tools for assistance with writing refinements and formatting. All intellectual content, research design, methodology, experiments, data analysis, and interpretation were conducted solely by the authors, who reviewed and approved the final manuscript. The authors take full responsibility for the content of this publication.

References

1. Aamodt, A., Plaza, E.: Case-based reasoning: foundational issues, methodological variations, and system approaches. AI Commun. **7**(1), 39–59 (1994)

2. Alsentzer, E., Murphy, J., Boag, W., et al.: Publicly available clinical BERT embeddings. In: Proceedings of the 2nd Clinical Natural Language Processing Workshop, pp. 72–78. ACL (2019)
3. Chalkidis, I., Fergadiotis, E., Malakasiotis, P., et al.: Large-scale multi-label text classification on EU legislation. In: Proceedings of the 57th Annual Meeting of the Association for Computational Linguistics, pp. 6314–6322. ACL (2019)
4. Chalkidis, I., Fergadiotis, M., Malakasiotis, P., et al.: LEGAL-BERT: the muppets straight out of law school. In: Findings of the Association for Computational Linguistics: EMNLP 2020, pp. 2898–2904. ACL (2020)
5. Craw, S., Wiratunga, N., Rowe, R.C.: Learning adaptation knowledge to improve case-based reasoning. Artif. Intell. **170**(16), 1175–1192 (2006)
6. Devlin, J., Chang, M.W., Lee, K., et al.: BERT: pre-training of deep bidirectional transformers for language understanding. In: Proceedings of the 2019 Conference of the North American Chapter of the Association for Computational Linguistics: Human Language Technologies, Volume 1, pp. 4171–4186. ACL (2019)
7. Fürnkranz, J., Hüllermeier, E., Loza Mencía, E., et al.: Multilabel classification via calibrated label ranking. Mach. Learn. **73**(2), 133–153 (2008)
8. Gu, Y., Tinn, R., Cheng, H., et al.: Domain-specific language model pretraining for biomedical natural language processing. ACM Trans. Comput. Healthc. **3**(1), 1–23 (2022)
9. He, P., Gao, J., Chen, W.: DeBERTaV3: improving DeBERTa using ELECTRA-style pre-training with gradient-disentangled embedding sharing. In: Proceedings of the 11th International Conference on Learning Representations (2023)
10. Hersh, W., Buckley, C., Leone, T.J.: OHSUMED: an interactive retrieval evaluation and new large test collection for research. In: SIGIR 1994, pp. 192–201. Springer, London (1994)
11. Jain, H., Prabhu, Y., Varma, M.: Extreme multi-label loss functions for recommendation, tagging, ranking & other missing label applications. In: Proceedings of the 22nd ACM SIGKDD International Conference on Knowledge Discovery and Data Mining, pp. 935–944. ACM (2016)
12. Jiang, J.Y., Chang, W.C., Zhang, J., et al.: Relevance under the Iceberg: reasonable prediction for extreme multi-label classification. In: Proceedings of the 45th International ACM SIGIR Conference on Research and Development in Information Retrieval, SIGIR 2022, pp. 1870–1874. ACM (2022)
13. Johnson, A.E.W., Pollard, T.J., Shen, L., et al.: MIMIC-III, a freely accessible critical care database. Sci. Data **3**, 160035 (2016)
14. Largeron, C., Moulin, C., Géry, M.: MCut: a thresholding strategy for multi-label classification. In: Hollmén, J., Klawonn, F., Tucker, A. (eds.) IDA 2012. LNCS, vol. 7619, pp. 172–183. Springer, Heidelberg (2012). https://doi.org/10.1007/978-3-642-34156-4_17
15. Lewis, D.D.: Reuters-21578 Text Categorization Test Collection, Distribution 1.0 (1997). https://kdd.ics.uci.edu/databases/reuters21578/reuters21578.html
16. Mishra, N., Rohaninejad, M., Chen, X., et al.: A simple neural attentive meta-learner. In: International Conference on Learning Representations (2018)
17. OpenAI, Agarwal, S., Ahmad, L., et al.: gpt-oss-120b & gpt-oss-20b Model Card (2025). https://doi.org/10.48550/arXiv.2508.10925
18. Papernot, N., McDaniel, P.: Deep k-Nearest Neighbors: Towards Confident, Interpretable and Robust Deep Learning (2018). https://doi.org/10.48550/arXiv.1803.04765
19. Read, J., Pfahringer, B., Holmes, G., et al.: Classifier chains for multi-label classification. Mach. Learn. **85**(3), 333–359 (2011)

20. Shamatrin, D.: Adaptive Thresholding for Multi-Label Classification via Global-Local Signal Fusion (2025). https://doi.org/10.48550/arXiv.2505.03118
21. Simon, C., Koniusz, P., Harandi, M.: Meta-learning for multi-label few-shot classification. In: Proceedings of the IEEE/CVF Winter Conference on Applications of Computer Vision, pp. 346–355 (2022)
22. Smyth, B., Keane, M.T.: Adaptation-guided retrieval: questioning the similarity assumption in reasoning. Artif. Intell. **102**(2), 249–293 (1998)
23. Snell, J., Swersky, K., Zemel, R.S.: Prototypical networks for few-shot learning. In: Advances in Neural Information Processing Systems, vol. 30, Curran Associates, Inc. (2017)
24. Sung, F., Yang, Y., Zhang, L.: Learning to compare: relation network for few-shot learning. In: Proceedings of the IEEE Conference on Computer Vision and Pattern Recognition, pp. 1199–1208 (2018)
25. Tang, L., Rajan, S., Narayanan, V.K.: Large scale multi-label classification via metalabeler. In: Proceedings of the 18th International Conference on World Wide Web, WWW 2009, pp. 211–220. ACM (2009)
26. Touvron, H., Martin, L., Stone, K., et al.: Llama 2: Open Foundation and Fine-Tuned Chat Models (2023). https://doi.org/10.48550/arXiv.2307.09288
27. Tsoumakas, G., Katakis, I.: Multi-label classification: an overview. Int. J. Data Warehous. Mining (IJDWM) **3**(3), 1–13 (2007)
28. Tsoumakas, G., Vlahavas, I.: Random *k*-Labelsets: an ensemble method for multilabel classification. In: Kok, J.N., Koronacki, J., Mantaras, R.L., Matwin, S., Mladenič, D., Skowron, A. (eds.) ECML 2007. LNCS (LNAI), vol. 4701, pp. 406–417. Springer, Heidelberg (2007). https://doi.org/10.1007/978-3-540-74958-5_38
29. Vasylevskyi, V.: events_classification_biotech (2025). https://huggingface.co/datasets/knowledgator/events_classification_biotech, huggingFace dataset
30. Vinyals, O., Blundell, C., Lillicrap, T.: Matching networks for one shot learning. In: Advances in Neural Information Processing Systems, vol. 29. Curran Associates, Inc. (2016)
31. Wu, J., Xiong, W., Wang, W.Y.: Learning to learn and predict: a meta-learning approach for multi-label classification. In: Proceedings of the 2019 Conference on EMNLP-IJCNLP, pp. 4354–4364. ACL (2019)
32. Yang, A., Li, A., Yang, B., et al.: Qwen3 Technical Report (2025). https://doi.org/10.48550/arXiv.2505.09388
33. Yang, Y.: A study of thresholding strategies for text categorization. In: Proceedings of the 24th Annual International ACM SIGIR Conference on Research and Development in Information Retrieval, SIGIR 2001, pp. 137–145. ACM (2001)
34. Zhang, M.L., Zhou, Z.H.: ML-KNN: a lazy learning approach to multi-label learning. Pattern Recogn. **40**(7), 2038–2048 (2007)
35. Zhang, M.L., Zhou, Z.H.: A review on multi-label learning algorithms. IEEE Trans. Knowl. Data Eng. **26**(8), 1819–1837 (2014)
36. Zhou, Z., Ning, X., Hong, K., et al.: A Survey on Efficient Inference for Large Language Models (2024). https://doi.org/10.48550/arXiv.2404.14294

Remote Sensing, Earth Observation and Environmental Monitoring

A High-Resolution Landscape Dataset for Concept-Based XAI With Application to Species Distribution Models

Augustin de la Brosse[1,2](✉), Damien Garreau[3], Thomas Houet[1,2], and Thomas Corpetti[1]

[1] Université Rennes 2, CNRS, Nantes Université, Univ Brest, LETG, UMR 6554, 35000 Rennes, France
{augustin.de-la-brosse,thomas.houet,thomas.corpetti}@univ-rennes2.edu
[2] LTSER Zone Atelier Armorique, Rennes, France
[3] University of Würzburg, Center for Artificial Intelligence and Data Science, Würzburg, Germany
damien.garreau@uni-wuerzburg.de

Abstract. Mapping the spatial distribution of species is essential for conservation policy and invasive species management. Species distribution models (SDMs) are the primary tools for this task, serving two purposes: achieving robust predictive performance while providing ecological insights into the driving factors of distribution. However, the increasing complexity of deep learning SDMs has made extracting these insights more challenging. To reconcile these objectives, we propose the first implementation of concept-based Explainable AI (XAI) for SDMs. We leverage the Robust TCAV (Testing with Concept Activation Vectors) methodology to quantify the influence of landscape concepts on model predictions. To enable this, we provide a new open-access landscape concept dataset derived from high-resolution multispectral and LiDAR drone imagery. It includes 653 patches across 15 distinct landscape concepts and 1,450 random reference patches, designed to suit a wide range of species. We demonstrate this approach through a case study of two aquatic insects, Plecoptera and Trichoptera, using two Convolutional Neural Networks and one Vision Transformer. Results show that concept-based XAI helps validate SDMs against expert knowledge while uncovering novel associations that generate new ecological hypotheses. Robust TCAV also provides landscape-level information, useful for policy-making and land management. Code and datasets are publicly available.

Keywords: Explainable AI · Remote sensing · UAV · Aquatic insects · Landscape Ecology

1 Introduction

Species Distribution Models (SDMs) provide a framework for spatially mapping species. These models integrate field observations with a suite of environmen-

M. Baratchi et al. (Eds.): ECML PKDD 2026, LNAI 16949, pp. 619–635, 2027.
https://doi.org/10.1007/978-3-032-37682-4_36

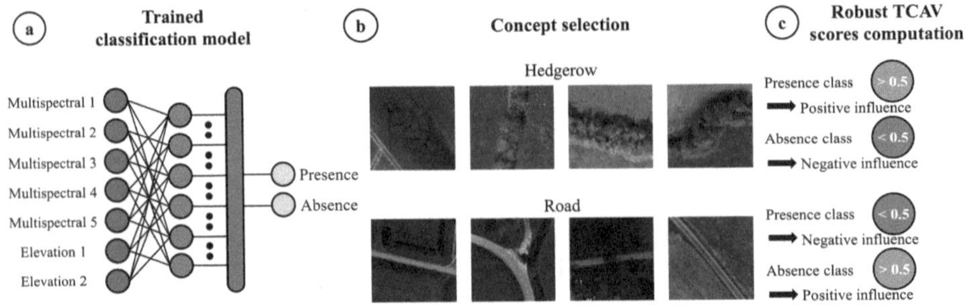

Fig. 1. Schematic overview of our implementation of Robust TCAV: After training a model to classify the classes `Presence` and `Absence` of insect ⓐ, we select concepts (*e.g.*, hedgerow) ⓑ, and quantify its importance for the chosen class by computing its Robust TCAV score ⓒ.

tal and spatial covariates to predict the presence and absence of the studied species [12]. In doing so, SDMs serve a dual purpose: achieving robust predictive performance while providing ecological insights into the drivers of distribution. Consequently, SDMs are essential for a variety of applications, ranging from conservation policy planning to risk assessment for invasive species. SDMs often rely on traditional machine learning (ML) models such as Random Forest [14] to predict species distribution and explainable artificial intelligence (XAI) techniques to extract knowledge from models [24]. Over the last decade, the adoption of complex deep learning algorithms and high-dimensional remote sensing data has improved predictive performance compared to traditional models, as shown by the GeoLifeCLEF challenge results [7,30,37]. However, unlike traditional models where feature importance can be directly assessed, deep learning models learn abstract features across millions of parameters, making it increasingly challenging for SDM developers to achieve the objective of knowledge extraction.

Fortunately, the artificial intelligence (AI) community has developed different XAI methods that can be used to interpret deep SDMs [24]. Among them, concept-based XAI methods [38] aim to align with human reasoning by explaining AI predictions through high-level, interpretable concepts (*e.g.*, colors). This facilitates interdisciplinary collaborations, as members of other scientific communities may not be ML experts, but may contribute to defining the concepts and easily understand the output. However, implementing these methods requires a dedicated concept dataset, which currently does not exist for SDMs.

In this paper, we aim to bridge the gap between predictive performance and interpretability in deep SDMs. We leverage drone data to create a unique concept dataset adapted to fine-scale SDMs. Drones have become increasingly used in ecological studies due to their flexibility in providing very-high spatial, spectral, and temporal resolution data [4]. By using multispectral and LiDAR-derived drone imagery, we extract landscape concepts that are relevant to explaining multiple ecological processes.

We apply concept-based XAI to SDMs using two taxa, Plecoptera and Trichoptera, as a case study. They are emerging aquatic insects: after a larval stage underwater, they emerge and disperse around their water body of origin. During this dispersal, they provide a number of ecosystem services, *i.e.*, the direct and indirect contributions of ecosystems to human welfare [40].

To contribute to the reconciliation of the two original objectives (interpretation and accurate predictions) of SDMs, we make the following contributions:

- We release a **new high-resolution concept dataset**. It includes 15 landscape concepts (653 patches in total) and 1,450 random patches, derived from multispectral and LiDAR drone data;
- We propose **three new SDMs for two aquatic insects**, Plecoptera and Trichoptera. These SDMs are based on distinct architectures (two convolutional neural networks and a vision transformer) adapted to leverage high-resolution multispectral and LiDAR drone imagery;
- We show that Robust TCAV [34], combined with our new dataset, provides ecologically meaningful explanations from these SDMs, constituting the **first implementation of concept-based XAI to SDMs** (Fig. 1).

The paper is structured as follows: Section 2 describes our concept (see Fig. 2) and training datasets. Section 3 details the experimental setup and presents the results for both the SDMs and the Robust TCAV implementation. Finally, Sect. 4 discusses key findings, and Sect. 5 concludes the study.

1.1 Related Work

Attribution methods such as Local Interpretable Model-agnostic Explanations (LIME) [41] and Shapley values (SHAP) [32] have been extensively applied to traditional SDMs [8,18,42] to extract insights from tabular features. However, when applied to image-based models, these methods operate at the pixel level, highlighting which individual pixels contributed most to a single prediction. This makes them both challenging to interpret for non-expert users and hinders the ability to provide the global, higher-level explanations that ecologists need to derive actionable insights [38]. Notably, they have not been used to explain deep SDMs. To date, MaskSDM [52], which is explainable by design, is the only work trying to reunite high performance with interpretability in the SDM domain.

As mentioned earlier, concept-based XAI represents a promising solution, with Testing with concept activation vectors (TCAV) [26] as a seminal work. This post-hoc approach relies on a Concept Activation Vector (CAV) which represents the direction of the concept in the latent space of the model. The TCAV score quantifies how much a prediction aligns with this concept direction. This method aims to quantify the influence of concepts in a classification result. Since its introduction, several improvements, such as Robust TCAV [34], Adversarial-TCAV [46], Concept Activation Regions [10], or pattern-based CAVs [36], have been proposed to increase its robustness. To our knowledge, only three ecological studies implement TCAV or its adaptations [2,3,22]. While none apply it to SDMs, all three indicate that the results align with expert knowledge.

2 A High-Resolution Dataset for Concept-Based XAI

In this subsection, we first describe the creation of a new and public concept dataset[1] to help SDM practitioners gain ecological insights from their models. Secondly, we describe the species distribution data.

2.1 Concept Dataset (C_i)

Concept Selection. We drew on the multidisciplinary expertise of our team to select 15 concepts inspired from land use / land cover classes. These concept are commonly used to understand ecological processes. We outline here these concepts and indicate how they are relevant to studying the distribution of Plecoptera and Trichoptera, as well as a wide range of species.

- **Hedgerows** (`Hedge`) are linear forests composed of different layers of vegetation. They contribute to the proper functioning of ecosystems by protecting crops, contributing to biological diversity and soil conservation [35];
- **Isolated trees** (`IsoTree`) are a characteristic feature of the agricultural landscape, an island of biodiversity within open and cultivated environments [39];
- **Woodlands** (`Wood`) are an essential landscape component. They are a refuge for biodiversity while also delivering several services such as pest control [49];
- **Linear bodies of water** (`LinW`) and **surface bodies of water** (`SurfW`) shelter significant biodiversity and concentrate many energy fluxes between aquatic and terrestrial ecosystems [6]. Linear bodies of water include permanent and temporary bodies: rivers, streams, stagnant and flowing ditches;
- **Wetlands** (`Wet`) represent ecosystems where water serves as the fundamental driver of environmental conditions and biological composition. These areas provide support for biodiversity and enhance water quality [53];
- **Roads** (`Road`) and **buildings** (`Build`) represent a major human-induced transformation of landscapes as they contribute to destroying and fragmenting them. Thus, they change the biotic and abiotic conditions of the landscape, often resulting in the modification of species composition [33];
- **Wheat crops** (`Wheat`), **maize crops** (`Maize`), and **other cereal crops** (`Cereal`) (millet, sorghum, durum wheat, buckwheat, and winter rye) correspond to a large proportion of agricultural landscapes. Different types of crop may have very different effects [13];
- **Permanent grasslands** (`PermG`) and **temporary grasslands** (`TempG`) are grassy expanses in a temperate climate. They have the potential to be among the most species-rich habitats globally while also delivering important ecosystem services such as pollination or pest control [51];
- **Organic crops** (`Organic`) are defined as a method of agricultural production that excludes chemical inputs, such as fertilizers or pesticides, and genetically modified organisms. As such, they are often characterized by increases in species abundance and richness compared to conventional crops [21];

[1] Access to dataset: https://zenodo.org/records/18936778.

Table 1. List of the 15 concepts as well as the number of patches.

Concept	Name	# of patches (% of total number of patches)
Hedgerow	`Hedge`	50 (7.7%)
Isolated tree	`IsoTree`	45 (6.9%)
Woodland	`Wood`	50 (7.7%)
Linear body of water	`LinW`	50 (7.7%)
Surface body of water	`SurfW`	20 (3.1%)
Wetland	`Wet`	50 (7.7%)
Road	`Road`	49 (7.5%)
Building	`Build`	50 (7.7%)
Wheat crop	`Wheat`	50 (7.7%)
Maize crop	`Maize`	50 (7.7%)
Other cereal crop	`Cereal`	20 (3.1%)
Permanent grassland	`PermG`	39 (6.0%)
Temporary grassland	`TempG`	50 (7.7%)
Organic crop	`Organic`	30 (4.6%)
Conventional crop	`Convent`	50 (7.7%)

- **Conventional crops** (`Convent`) are the most common type of crop globally. They rely on chemical input. Therefore, they are often negatively correlated with species richness and abundance [28].

Concept Patch Creation. We created the concept patches from high-resolution drone data acquired in April 2024 at five study sites in France using a Trinity F90+ drone. It was equipped with a MicaSense Dual MX sensor to acquire 5-band multispectral data, and a Qube240 sensor to acquire LiDAR data. The spectral bands are blue (475 nm ± 32), green (560 nm ± 27), red (668 nm ± 20), red-edge (717 nm ± 12), and near-infrared (842 nm ± 57). The spatial resolution is 8 cm/pixel for flight at 120 m above ground level. For each spectral band, orthophotographs (*i.e.*, photographs free from topographic distortion) were generated and radiometrically corrected. This process accounted for solar irradiance and angle using a calibrated radiometric target to provide top-of-canopy reflectance [5]. LiDAR data are characterized by a 3D point cloud (average 36.1 points per square meter) from which we derived a digital terrain model (elevation at ground level) and a digital surface model (elevation at canopy level) with a spatial resolution of 10 cm/pixel. LiDAR and multispectral data are registered using common ground control points whose positions are set using a GNSS (2-3 cm accuracy). Geometric errors are smaller than the pixel size.

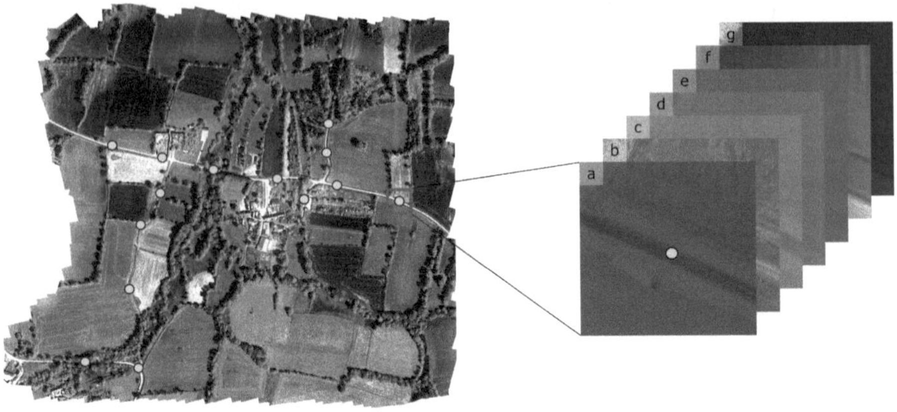

Fig. 2. *Left panel*: global overview of one of the acquisition sites. Yellow dots correspond to the locations where `Road` concept patches were extracted. *Right panel*: The patch is extracted around the point vector from the multispectral image and the digital elevation models to obtain a 7-band patch.

To create the patches, we first located concepts using point vectors in QGIS[2]. After resampling the multispectral data and the elevation models to a common spatial resolution (8 cm/pixel), we extracted from both modalities 512 × 512 pixel patches centered on the points, stacking five multispectral bands and two elevation models (respectively, bands a-e and bands f-g in Fig. 2).

In total, we created 653 concept patches (see Table 1 for the number of patches per concept). By extracting such data from five study sites, we ensured a good representation of a diversity of agricultural landscapes, ranging from extensive dairy farming systems to highly intensive cropping systems.

Creating the concept dataset was particularly challenging. Indeed, many landscape elements cannot be identified through photointerpretation [29] of the drone images. In particular, the linear and surface bodies of water are often below the canopy or too small/thin to be observed. The wetlands are also often visually covered by vegetation. Therefore, we relied on the manual mapping of the hydrographic network of the five study sites. To differentiate between the various types of crop and grassland, we used the 2024 French official agricultural land register[3]. Regarding the organic and conventional crops, we used the 2024 register of the French agency Agence Bio[4]. We conducted the identification of the hedgerows, isolated trees and woodlands through photointerpretation. We checked the digital height surface (the discrepancy between the surface and ter-

[2] QGIS is an open source geographic information system (GIS) software that allows to view, edit, print, and analyze geospatial data in various formats.

[3] https://geoservices.ign.fr/rpg.

[4] https://www.data.gouv.fr/datasets/parcelles-certifiees-en-agriculture-biologique-sur-cartobio.

rain models) to ensure that the vegetation height is over 2.5 meters. Finally, the buildings and the roads were identified by photointerpretation alone.

We also added 1,450 random patches extracted from the multispectral data and the digital elevation models by sampling random pixel coordinates and then applying the same methodology as the one employed for the concept patches.

To ensure the internal consistency and distinctiveness of our concepts, we performed a series of sanity checks (Section B of the Appendix). These checks included evaluating the separability of representative concepts against random patches and applying Robust TCAV to confirm that the Concept Activation Vector (CAV) of each concept positively influences its own classification.

2.2 Species Distribution Data

We collected distribution data for Plecoptera and Trichoptera across the same five study sites used for concept extraction.[5]

Training Labels (Y_i). The labels for our two classes are `Presence` and `Absence`, for Plecoptera and Trichoptera. This information was obtained in April 2024 from 234 sticky traps uniformly distributed at the study sites. The acquisition period coincides with the primary emergence period for Plecoptera and Trichoptera. `Presence` was recorded if at least one insect was captured during the two-week trap deployment. Otherwise, `Absence` was noted. The sample size reflects the inherent logistical constraints of field-based ecological research [14,44,47]. The trap analysis was conducted following the same protocol as in [14].

Training Patches (X_i). We generated training patches from the same drone imagery used for our concept patches. For each sampling point (*i.e.*, sticky trap), we extracted 7-band patches centered on the trap following the extraction protocol previously described (see Sect. 2.1). The patch size may be smaller than 512 × 512 if the trap is closer to the border of the multispectral images and digital elevation models than 256 pixels. These patches served as input for training both the Plecoptera and Trichoptera models.

3 Models, Experimental Setup and Results

In this section, we evaluate three SDMs with respect to the predictive performance for `Presence` and `Absence` of Plecoptera and Trichoptera before implementing Robust TCAV[6].

3.1 Model Architectures

We selected two CNNs and one Vision Transformer to train the SDMs.

CerberusCNN. This custom architecture has three parallel branches to capture spatial features at multiple scales. Each branch uses two convolutional blocks

[5] Access to distribution data: https://zenodo.org/records/18937048.
[6] Access to code: https://github.com/augustin-delabrosse/Robust-TCAV-for-SDM.

with distinct kernel sizes (3, 5, and 7) and initial max-pooling sizes (2, 4, and 8) to detect patterns across varying scales. Features are aggregated via 2D global average pooling, concatenated, and processed through a classification head consisting of two dense layers (256 and 128 neurons) with intermediate dropout (0.5 and 0.3). It has approximately 270k learnable parameters.

Adapted ResNet-50 (ARN-50). As a benchmark for deep hierarchical feature learning, we used ResNet-50 [19], an architecture commonly used in ecology [20,25,43]. The architecture was modified by replacing the initial layer to accommodate 7-channel inputs and appending a two-neuron linear layer for binary classification. It has approximately learnable 23.5M parameters.

PicoViT. In order to assess the efficacy of attention mechanisms in SDMs, we adapted the Vision Transformer (ViT) architecture [11]. We significantly reduced the model capacity to approximately 146k learnable parameters to suit our dataset scale, employing 3 layers with 3 attention heads each. The embedding and hidden MLP dimensions were set to 48 and 96, respectively, with a patch size of 16. Like the ARN-50 model, the input layer was modified to process 7-channel inputs.

An illustration of CerberusCNN is provided in the Appendix (Section D). Please refer to [19] and [11] for more details concerning the ARN-50 and the PicoViT, respectively.

3.2 Training Setup

Models were trained independently for each taxon using cross-entropy loss and AdamW optimizer [31] (learning rate: 0.001, weight decay: 0.0001, default β_1 and β_2). We set batch size to 8 and number of epochs to 50 with a 5-epoch patience with respect to validation loss as early-stopping. For pretrained ARN-50, ImageNet weights [19] were used for the RGB channels, while the four additional channels were initialized as the mean of the pretrained RGB weights before full-model fine-tuning.

Patch Preprocessing. To prevent data leakage [16] caused by overlapping of spatially close patches, we implemented a longitudinal spatial split of the drone imagery before extracting patches. We used the easternmost 20% (48 occurrences) of traps for testing, the next 20% for validation (38 occurrences), and the remainder for training (148 occurrences). Label distribution remains roughly balanced considering the small size of the dataset (Section C of the Appendix). Patches were resized via bilinear interpolation to 128 × 128 pixels, clipped at zero to remove `no data` artifacts, and Min-Max normalized per band.

Data Augmentation. We applied data augmentation to our dataset to increase the number of training samples and improve regularization. We used weak random transformations (horizontal and vertical flips, rotations). We also used MixUp [55], which linearly combines pairs of images and their labels to generate new synthetic samples.

3.3 Predictive Performance

We use the Area Under Curve (AUC) as the evaluation metric as it is frequently used by ecologists [14]. In ecology, a model is considered reliable when its AUC is over 0.7 and excellent when it is over 0.8 [17].

Table 2. Model predictive performance per taxon: mean AUC and standard deviation over three training runs. Best scores are in bold.

Taxon	CerberusCNN	ARN-50	Pretrained ARN-50	PicoViT
Plecoptera	0.88 (0.01)	0.82 (0.04)	**0.90** (0.07)	0.72 (0.02)
Trichoptera	**0.79** (0.03)	0.74 (0.04)	0.75 (0.08)	0.66 (0.06)

Table 2 shows that for all models, Plecoptera is better predicted than Trichoptera. Among models trained from scratch, CerberusCNN achieves the best results, yielding reliable AUCs for both taxa. ARN-50 also provides reliable predictions (0.82 and 0.74 AUC for Plecoptera and Trichoptera, respectively). PicoViT obtains a reliable AUC for Plecoptera (0.72 AUC), but remains unreliable for Trichoptera (0.66 AUC). When pretrained, ARN-50 outperforms all other models for Plecoptera (0.90 AUC) and improves the AUC for Trichoptera (0.75 AUC). Overall, CerberusCNN has the lowest standard deviation for both taxa. We include distribution maps in the Appendix (Section E).

3.4 Robust TCAV Configuration

To quantify concept influence for each taxon, we compute TCAV scores using the Robust TCAV methodology [34] on CerberusCNN, Pretrained ARN-50, and PicoViT (Fig. 3). While TCAV [26] defines the concept activation vector (CAV) as the normal vector to the hyperplane of the linear classifier that separates random patches from concept ones, Robust TCAV instead uses the difference between mean concept and random activations. This improves the consistency of the TCAV scores and reduces sensitivity to noise in the concept datasets [34].

Robust TCAV. Several parameters need to be specified. First, for each model, we selected a layer ℓ to extract the activation values and the gradient values. For CerberusCNN, we selected the concatenation of the three branches as it gathers information from all branches. For ARN-50, we used the last bottleneck block before the average pooling layer as deeper layers of CNNs process higher-level features than early layers [23,54,56]. For PicoViT, we used the middle layer (2nd layer) as the middle layers of Transformers allow for the extraction of high-level feature representations [9,50,57]. Secondly, we computed TCAV scores 500 times as proposed by [26]. For each iteration, we sampled 500 random patches. Finally, while Robust TCAV applies a 0.05 threshold on the sensitivity scores (see Fig. 3), we found that a zero-threshold provides more ecologically relevant insights. Conversely, applying a threshold discards low-magnitude but

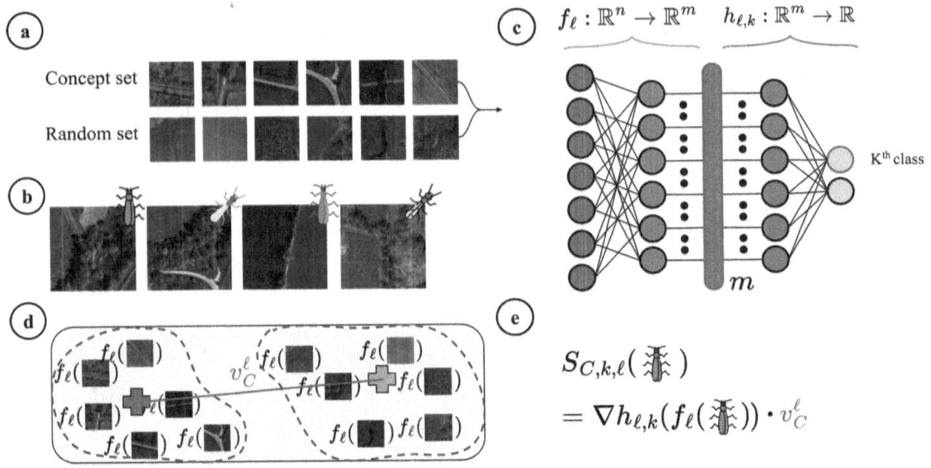

Fig. 3. Robust TCAV: Robust TCAV requires a set of examples for a concept (*e.g.*, `Road`), and random examples ⓐ, labeled test examples for the studied class (.*e.g.*, `Presence` of Plecoptera) ⓑ and a trained network ⓒ. We obtain the CAV (v_C^ℓ, orange arrow) by computing the difference between the mean activations for the concept examples and for the random examples ⓓ. We use the directional derivative to quantify the sensitivity score $S_{C,k,\ell}$ of an individual training example to concept C for the class k. Robust TCAV score for class k is the proportion of positive sensitivity scores among input examples of this class ⓔ.

biologically significant signals, which results in ambiguous results. More details about each step and the threshold are available in the Appendix (Section F).

Relative Importance. Relative TCAV was introduced by [26]. It allows the pairwise comparison of concepts. In this scenario, a linear classifier is trained to separate two concepts and the normal vector to the hyperplane is used as CAV. Although [34] do not adapt this module for Robust TCAV, we replaced the normal vector with the difference of means for consistency. In this setting, the CAV no longer represents the direction of a concept relative to a random set, but rather the direction of one concept relative to another. To obtain a concept ranking, we counted how many times each concept achieved a higher relative TCAV score compared to every other concept, separately for the `Presence` and `Absence` classes. For this step, we used the same architecture, Pretrained ARN-50, to compute relative TCAV scores for both taxa in order to enable a direct comparison of concept rankings.

3.5 Robust TCAV Results

We only show the scores for the `Presence` class, as they generally exhibit inverse behavior to those of the `Absence` class. Nonetheless, one must be aware that scores usually do not sum to 1. Full results for both the `Presence` and the `Absence` classes are available in the Appendix (Section F).

Robust TCAV. The Robust TCAV scores of the 15 landscape concepts for Plecoptera and Trichoptera classification are displayed in Table 3. Following the Robust TCAV framework, scores above or below 0.5 indicate that a concept positively or negatively influences model predictions for a specific class, respectively.

Table 3. Mean TCAV scores (with standard deviation) for the `Presence` class across all models and taxa.

Concept	CerberusCNN		ARN-50		PicoViT	
	Pleco.	Trich.	Pleco.	Trich.	Pleco.	Trich.
`Hedge`	0.30 (0.25)	0.44 (0.14)	0.90 (0.00)	0.65 (0.00)	0.85 (0.00)	0.00 (0.00)
`IsoTree`	0.85 (0.02)	0.74 (0.00)	0.90 (0.00)	0.65 (0.00)	0.85 (0.00)	0.00 (0.00)
`Wood`	0.85 (0.00)	0.74 (0.00)	0.90 (0.00)	0.65 (0.00)	0.13 (0.06)	0.01 (0.06)
`LinW`	0.84 (0.08)	0.40 (0.14)	0.79 (0.28)	0.65 (0.00)	0.84 (0.04)	0.00 (0.00)
`SurfW`	0.15 (0.00)	0.26 (0.00)	0.10 (0.00)	0.97 (0.09)	0.16 (0.03)	1.00 (0.00)
`Wet`	0.85 (0.00)	0.74 (0.00)	0.90 (0.00)	0.65 (0.00)	0.85 (0.00)	0.00 (0.00)
`Road`	0.15 (0.00)	0.79 (0.17)	0.10 (0.00)	0.65 (0.00)	0.44 (0.08)	0.00 (0.00)
`Build`	0.15 (0.00)	0.87 (0.05)	0.10 (0.00)	0.65 (0.00)	0.15 (0.00)	0.00 (0.00)
`Wheat`	0.16 (0.04)	0.26 (0.00)	0.10 (0.00)	0.35 (0.00)	0.15 (0.01)	0.00 (0.01)
`Maize`	0.15 (0.00)	0.32 (0.02)	0.10 (0.00)	0.35 (0.00)	0.34 (0.06)	0.80 (0.26)
`Cereal`	0.15 (0.00)	0.26 (0.00)	0.10 (0.00)	0.35 (0.00)	0.25 (0.01)	0.00 (0.00)
`PermG`	0.85 (0.00)	0.55 (0.08)	0.90 (0.00)	0.65 (0.00)	0.85 (0.00)	0.00 (0.00)
`TempG`	0.85 (0.00)	0.38 (0.08)	0.30 (0.37)	0.35 (0.00)	0.85 (0.00)	0.00 (0.00)
`Organic`	0.15 (0.02)	0.23 (0.09)	0.10 (0.00)	0.35 (0.00)	0.35 (0.11)	0.00 (0.00)
`Convent`	0.15 (0.00)	0.26 (0.00)	0.10 (0.00)	0.35 (0.00)	0.36 (0.15)	0.00 (0.00)

All scores are statistically significant ($p < 0.05$) against a 0.5 null hypothesis via Student's t-test.

Across all architectures, `Presence` of Plecoptera is strongly associated with natural features (isolated tree, woodland, wetland, linear body of water, permanent grassland; over 0.85 TCAV scores), while anthropogenic features (building, road, crops) consistently negatively influence this class (below 0.16 TCAV scores). Trichoptera results vary by model. CerberusCNN and ARN-50 link `Presence` to natural features (isolated tree, woodland, wetland, permanent grassland; over 0.55 TCAV scores) but also to built surfaces (road and building). In contrast, these models interpret crops and temporary grassland as negative influence. Meanwhile, PicoViT predominantly yields scores of 0.00, except for surface water (1.00) and maize (0.80). For both taxa, organic and conventional crops, despite being opposite concepts, have similar TCAV scores across all models.

With the exception of the results of PicoViT for Trichoptera, most **TCAV scores are consistent across architectures**: for both Plecoptera and Trichoptera, 12 concepts show concordant importance (all scores either above or below 0.5 across models). Nevertheless, a few discrepancies emerge between architectures for specific concepts. For Plecoptera, hedgerow strongly positively influences the `Presence` class with ARN-50 (0.90) and PicoViT (0.85), yet it shows a negative correlation with CerberusCNN (0.30). Conversely, temporary grassland has a large TCAV score for the `Presence` of Plecoptera with CerberusCNN (0.85) while it has a small TCAV score with ARN-50 (0.30).

Also, several concepts influence both `Presence` and `Absence` simultaneously (scores over 0.5 for both). This occurs for road and building with CerberusCNN, and surface body of water with ARN-50 (0.97/0.95). Finally, while most standard deviations are near zero, significant instability is observed for hedgerow in CerberusCNN and temporary grassland and linear body of water with ARN-50.

Table 4. Concept importance ranking for Plecoptera and Trichoptera `Presence` classes.

Rank	Plecoptera `Presence`	Trichoptera `Presence`
1	`Wood`	`Wet`
2	`Wet`	`Wood`
3	`PermG`	`IsoTree`
4	`IsoTree`	`PermG`
5	`Hedge`	`Hedge`
6	`LinW`	`LinW`
7	`TempG`	`Build`
8	`Wheat`	`SurfW`
9	`Organic`	`Road`
10	`Build`	`Organic`
11	`Road`	`TempG`
12	`SurfW`	`Maize`
13	`Convent`	`Convent`
14	`Maize`	`Cereal`
15	`Cereal`	`Wheat`

Relative Importance. Table 4 provides a comparative ranking of concepts based on their relative influence across all models. For the `Presence` class, a high degree of convergence is observed between the two taxa: the top 6 concepts are nearly identical, with natural features such as woodland, wetland, permanent grassland, and isolated tree consistently driving classification. The middle of the ranking diverges between Plecoptera and Trichoptera. For instance, building occupies a higher rank for Trichoptera `Presence` (Rank 7) compared to Plecoptera (Rank 10), and temporary grassland has a higher rank for Plecoptera `Presence` (Rank 7) compared to Trichoptera (Rank 11). We note that organic crops are consistently ranked higher than conventional crops. A consistent inverse relationship is observed between the `Presence` and `Absence` rankings across both taxa. Features that occupy the top three positions for `Presence` (woodland, wetland, and permanent grassland) are positioned at the bottom of the `Absence` rankings. Conversely, crop concepts occupy the highest ranks for the `Absence` class while remaining among the lowest-ranked predictors for `Presence`.

4 Discussion

As for the performance of SDMs, our study suggests that CNNs perform better than attention models, such as PicoViT, in predicting the `Presence` and `Absence` of Plecoptera and Trichoptera. While CerberusCNN and ARN-50 provided reliable results, PicoViT remained unreliable for Trichoptera. Local pixel neighborhoods likely contain more informative data regarding insect `Presence` than the long-distance relationships captured by Transformers [11,27]. Further experimentation is necessary to validate this finding. In addition, a context-adapted multiscale design allowed CerberusCNN to lead among models trained from scratch, though pretraining improved ARN-50, confirming the utility of deep CNNs even in data-limited contexts.

Regarding the interpretation, **Robust TCAV produced highly encouraging results**. First, most scores are consistent across architectures, supporting the reliability of the results. Secondly, it suggests different effects depending on land use, aligning with the literature [15]. Natural concepts (*e.g.*, woodland, wetland) appear to positively influence the prediction of Plecoptera and Trichoptera `Presence`. In contrast, crops (*e.g.*, wheat, maize) consistently indicate `Absence`, also aligning with the literature on the danger of dominant agricultural practices (pesticides and fertilizers) for large sensitive taxa such as Plecoptera and Trichoptera [40]. Moreover, the greater positive influence of permanent over temporary grasslands reinforces the importance of natural elements for the `Presence` of insects.

A few non-trivial results also emerge. While both organic and conventional crops negatively influence insect `Presence` (scores < 0.5), organic practices consistently rank higher, supporting the expectation that they better sustain biodiversity [21]. However, the negative influence of both may indicate that biodiversity-friendly practices at parcel-level may be undermined by degradation at landscape-level [1]. The road and building concepts are linked to the `Presence` class of Trichoptera for both CerberusCNN and ARN-50. As the literature is not clear on this issue [45], it might be interesting to further analyze it.

Robust TCAV also generated inconsistent scores with respect to ecological processes. The inconsistent Robust TCAV scores obtained with PicoViT, which yielded near-zero values for both `Presence` and `Absence`, demonstrate that unreliable models provide meaningless ecological insights. Moreover, while Plecoptera and Trichoptera emerge from freshwater bodies [48], linear bodies of water and more significantly surface bodies of water are not recognized as primary influences for the `Presence` of both taxa. The difficulties of LiDAR with water surfaces and the canopy interference with multispectral sensors likely explain these results. These results are a good reminder that **concept-based**

XAI techniques only explain the model and not the ecological processes. Finally, high standard deviation for TCAV scores for a few concepts (*e.g.*, temporary grassland with respect to `Presence` of Plecoptera using ARN-50) suggests less reliable Concept Activation Vectors (CAVs) for these concepts.

5 Conclusion

By leveraging our new landscape dataset, Robust TCAV successfully reunites the interpretation and prediction objectives of SDMs, validating model logic against expert knowledge. This framework offers a new pathway to generate hypotheses in cases where results are counterintuitive (*e.g.*, positive influence of buildings and roads on Trichoptera `Presence`). Finally, by providing clear, class-level explanations, our approach empowers policy-makers and land managers to make more informed, landscape-scale decisions. It is our hope that this landscape dataset will prove beneficial to the SDM community and that this work will serve as a catalyst for the adoption of concept-based XAI for SDMs.

Future work will explore additional concept-based XAI methods beyond Robust TCAV, such as Concept Activation Regions [10], to compare how different frameworks capture ecological knowledge.

Acknowledgments. This study was funded by the French National Research Agency (ANR), STRANGE project (ANR-23-CE03-0006). It has also benefited from the financial support from ANR project NIM-ML (ANR-21-CE23-0005-01) and from the international mobility grant program administered by the Doctoral College of Brittany and co-funded by the Brittany Region, as well as the logistical support of the Zone Atelier Loire, Zone Atelier Armorique, and Zone Atelier Brest-Iroise. We would like to also thank Thibaut Peres, Benjamin Bergerot and Laura Pellan for their precious contribution to the collection of field data.

Disclosure of Interests. The authors have no competing interests to declare that are relevant to the content of this article.

AI Usage Declaration. The author used LLMs to improve the readability and grammar of the manuscript, and enhance the clarity of the code (docstrings).

References

1. Allan, J.D.: Landscapes and riverscapes: the influence of land use on stream ecosystems. Annu. Rev. Ecol. Evol. Syst. **35**(1), 257–284 (2004)
2. Amara, J., König-Ries, B., Samuel, S.: Explainability of deep learning-based plant disease classifiers through automated concept identification. arXiv preprint arXiv:2412.07408 (2024)
3. Amara, J., König-Ries, B., Samuel, S.: Concept explainability for plant diseases classification. In: Proceedings of the 18th International Joint Conference on Computer Vision, Imaging and Computer Graphics Theory and Applications (VISIGRAPP 2023) - Volume 4: VISAPP, pp. 246–253. INSTICC, SciTePress (2023). https://doi.org/10.5220/0011667900003417

4. Anderson, K., Gaston, K.J.: Lightweight unmanned aerial vehicles will revolutionize spatial ecology. Front. Ecol. Environ. **11**(3), 138–146 (2013)
5. Assmann, J.J., Kerby, J.T., Cunliffe, A.M., Myers-Smith, I.H.: Vegetation monitoring using multispectral sensors–best practices and lessons learned from high latitudes. J. Unmanned Veh. Syst. **7**(1), 54–75 (2018)
6. Bergerot, B., Piscart, C., Roussel, J.: Tightly intertwined: waterscapes prompt urgent reconsideration of aquatic insects and their role in agricultural landscapes. Sci. Total Environ. **966**, 178728 (2025)
7. Botella, C., et al.: Overview of geolifeclef 2023: species composition prediction with high spatial resolution at continental scale using remote sensing. arXiv preprint arXiv:2509.25816 (2025)
8. Buebos-Esteve, D.E., Dagamac, N.H.A.: Evaluating model-agnostic post-hoc methods in explainable artificial intelligence: augmenting species distribution models. Biologia futura **76**(4), 585–595 (2025)
9. Cheng, E., et al.: Emergence of a high-dimensional abstraction phase in language transformers. In: Yue, Y., Garg, A., Peng, N., Sha, F., Yu, R. (eds.) International Conference on Learning Representations, vol. 2025, pp. 35389–35414 (2025). https://proceedings.iclr.cc/paper_files/paper/2025/file/57568e093cbe0a222de0334b36e83cf5-Paper-Conference.pdf
10. Crabbé, J., van der Schaar, M.: Concept activation regions: a generalized framework for concept-based explanations. In: Advances in Neural Information Processing System, vol. 35, pp. 2590–2607 (2022)
11. Dosovitskiy, A., et al.: An image is worth 16 × 16 words: transformers for image recognition at scale. In: International Conference on Learning Representations (2021)
12. Elith, J., Leathwick, J.R.: Species distribution models: ecological explanation and prediction across space and time. Annu. Rev. Ecol. Evol. Syst. **40**(1), 677–697 (2009)
13. Fan, S., et al.: Impact of crop type on biodiversity globally. Glob. Change Biol. **30**(12), e70005 (2024)
14. Gerber, R., et al.: Landscape models can predict the distribution of aquatic insects across agricultural areas. Landscape Ecol. **38**(11), 2917–2929 (2023)
15. Gomes, P.G.S., Lima, E.L., Silva, S.R., Juen, L., Brasil, L.S.: Does land use and land cover affect adult communities of ephemeroptera, plecoptera and trichoptera (ept)? a systematic review with meta-analysis. Environ. Monit. Assess. **194**(10), 697 (2022)
16. Guélat, J., Kéry, M.: Effects of spatial autocorrelation and imperfect detection on species distribution models. Methods Ecol. Evol. **9**(6), 1614–1625 (2018)
17. Guisan, A., Thuiller, W., Zimmermann, N.E.: Habitat suitability and distribution models: with applications in R. Cambridge University Press (2017)
18. He, B., Zhao, Y., Mao, W.: Explainable artificial intelligence reveals environmental constraints in seagrass distribution. Ecol. Ind. **144**, 109523 (2022)
19. He, K., Zhang, X., Ren, S., Sun, J.: Deep residual learning for image recognition. In: Proceedings of the IEEE Conference on Computer Vision and Pattern Recognition, pp. 770–778 (2016)
20. Hindarto, D.: Use resnet50v2 deep learning model to classify five animal species. Jurnal JTIK (Jurnal Teknologi Informasi dan Komunikasi) **7**(4), 758–768 (2023)
21. Hole, D.G., et al.: Does organic farming benefit biodiversity? Biol. Cons. **122**(1), 113–130 (2005)

22. Huang, Y., Hou, S., Horve, Z.N., Fei, S.: Barkxai: a lightweight post-hoc explainable method for tree species classification with quantifiable concepts. In: ICLR 2025 Workshop: XAI4Science: From Understanding Model Behavior to Discovering New Scientific Knowledge (2025)
23. Ilin, R., Watson, T., Kozma, R.: Abstraction hierarchy in deep learning neural networks. In: 2017 International Joint Conference on Neural Networks (IJCNN), pp. 768–774. IEEE (2017)
24. Islam, M.U., et al.: The past, present, and prospective future of XAI: a comprehensive review. Explainable Artificial Intelligence for Cyber Security: Next Generation Artificial Intelligence, pp. 1–29 (2022)
25. Kaur, J., Rani, S., Sharma, A., Dogra, A.: Enhanced bird species identification using resnet-50: a deep learning framework for high-performance classification. In: 2024 3rd International Conference on Automation, Computing and Renewable Systems (ICACRS), pp. 821–826. IEEE (2024)
26. Kim, B., et al.: Interpretability beyond feature attribution: quantitative testing with concept activation vectors (TCAV). In: Proceedings of the 35th International Conference on Machine Learning. Proceedings of Machine Learning Research, vol. 80, pp. 2668–2677. PMLR (2018)
27. LeCun, Y., Bengio, Y., Hinton, G.: Deep learning. Nature **521**(7553), 436–444 (2015)
28. Leroy, F., Jarzyna, M.A., Keil, P.: Acceleration hotspots of north American birds' decline are associated with agriculture. Science **391**(6788), 917–921 (2026)
29. Lillesand, T., Kiefer, R.W., Chipman, J.: Remote sensing and image interpretation. John Wiley & Sons (2015)
30. Lorieul, T., Cole, E., Deneu, B., Servajean, M., Bonnet, P., Joly, A.: Overview of geolifeclef 2022: predicting species presence from multi-modal remote sensing, bioclimatic and pedologic data. CLEF (Working Notes). CEUR-WS (2022)
31. Loshchilov, I., et al.: Fixing weight decay regularization in Adam. arXiv preprint arXiv:1711.05101 **5**(5), 5 (2017)
32. Lundberg, S.M., Lee, S.I.: A unified approach to interpreting model predictions. In: Advances in Neural Information Processing Systems, vol. 30 (2017)
33. Marcantonio, M., Rocchini, D., Geri, F., Bacaro, G., Amici, V.: Biodiversity, roads, & landscape fragmentation: two Mediterranean cases. Appl. Geogr. **42**, 63–72 (2013)
34. Martin, T., Weller, A.: Interpretable machine learning. M. Phil. diss., Dept. of Engineering, University of Cambridge **2**(3), 5 (2019)
35. Montgomery, I., Caruso, T., Reid, N.: Hedgerows as ecosystems: service delivery, management, and restoration. Annu. Rev. Ecol. Evol. Syst. **51**(1), 81–102 (2020)
36. Pahde, F., et al.: Navigating neural space: revisiting concept activation vectors to overcome directional divergence. In: Yue, Y., Garg, A., Peng, N., Sha, F., Yu, R. (eds.) International Conference on Learning Representations, vol. 2025, pp. 53747–53790 (2025)
37. Picek, L., et al.: Overview of geolifeclef 2024: species composition prediction with high spatial resolution at continental scale using remote sensing. In: CLEF 2024-Working Notes of the 25th Conference and Labs of the Evaluation Forum). CEUR-WS (2024)
38. Poeta, E., Ciravegna, G., Pastor, E., Cerquitelli, T., Baralis, E.: Concept-based explainable artificial intelligence: a survey, ACM computing surveys (2023)
39. Prevedello, J.A., Almeida-Gomes, M., Lindenmayer, D.B.: The importance of scattered trees for biodiversity conservation: a global meta-analysis. J. Appl. Ecol. **55**(1), 205–214 (2018)

40. Raitif, J., Plantegenest, M., Roussel, J.M.: From stream to land: ecosystem services provided by stream insects to agriculture. Agric. Ecosyst. Environ. **270**, 32–40 (2019)
41. Ribeiro, M.T., Singh, S., Guestrin, C.: "why should i trust you?" explaining the predictions of any classifier. In: Proceedings of the 22nd ACM SIGKDD International Conference on Knowledge Discovery and Data Mining, pp. 1135–1144 (2016)
42. Ryo, M., et al.: Explainable artificial intelligence enhances the ecological interpretability of black-box species distribution models. Ecography **44**(2), 199–205 (2021)
43. Sankupellay, M., Konovalov, D.: Bird call recognition using deep convolutional neural network, Resnet-50. In: Proceedings of the Acoustics, pp. 1–8 (2018)
44. Silva, D.P., et al.: Current and future ranges of an elusive north American insect using species distribution models. J. Insect Conserv. **23**(1), 175–186 (2019)
45. Smith, M.E., Kaster, J.L.: Effect of rural highway runoff on stream benthic macroinvertebrates. Environ. Pollut. Ser. A Ecol. Biol. **32**(3), 157–170 (1983)
46. Soni, R., Shah, N., Seng, C.T., Moore, J.D.: Adversarial TCAV-robust and effective interpretation of intermediate layers in neural networks. arXiv preprint arXiv:2002.03549 (2020)
47. Tognelli, M.F., Roig, S.A., Marvaldi, A., Flores, G.E., Lobo, J.M.: An evaluation of methods for modelling distribution of Patagonian insects. Rev. Chil. Hist. Nat. (2009)
48. Ulfstrand, S.: Life cycles of benthic insects in Lapland streams (ephemeroptera, plecoptera, trichoptera, diptera simuliidae). Oikos, pp. 167–190 (1968)
49. Valdés, A., et al.: High ecosystem service delivery potential of small woodlands in agricultural landscapes. J. Appl. Ecol. **57**(1), 4–16 (2020)
50. Valeriani, L., et al.: The geometry of hidden representations of large transformer models. In: Oh, A., et al.,(eds.) Advances in Neural Information Processing Systems. vol. 36, pp. 51234–51252. Curran Associates, Inc. (2023). https://proceedings.neurips.cc/paper_files/paper/2023/file/a0e66093d7168b40246af1cddc025daa-Paper-Conference.pdf
51. Wilson, J.B., Peet, R.K., Dengler, J., Pärtel, M.: Plant species richness: the world records. J. Veg. Sci. **23**(4), 796–802 (2012)
52. Zbinden, R., et al.: Masksdm with Shapley values to improve flexibility, robustness and explainability in species distribution modelling. Methods Ecol. Evol. **17**(1), 188–206 (2026)
53. Zedler, J.B., Kercher, S.: Wetland resources: status, trends, ecosystem services, and restorability. Annu. Rev. Environ. Resour. **30**, 39–74 (2005)
54. Zeiler, M.D., Fergus, R.: Visualizing and Understanding Convolutional Networks. In: Fleet, D., Pajdla, T., Schiele, B., Tuytelaars, T. (eds.) ECCV 2014. LNCS, vol. 8689, pp. 818–833. Springer, Cham (2014). https://doi.org/10.1007/978-3-319-10590-1_53
55. Zhang, H., Cisse, M., Dauphin, Y.N., Lopez-Paz, D.: Mixup: beyond empirical risk minimization. In: International Conference on Learning Representations (2018)
56. Zhong, G., Ling, X., Wang, L.N.: From shallow feature learning to deep learning: benefits from the width and depth of deep architectures. Wiley Interdisc. Rev. Data Min. Knowl. Discovery **9**(1), e1255 (2019)
57. Zou, A., et al.: Representation engineering: a top-down approach to AI transparency. arXiv preprint arXiv:2310.01405 (2023)

Assessing the Benefits of Combining Advanced Deep Learning Techniques for Post-disaster Building Damage Assessment from UAV Imagery

Huy Quang Ung[(✉)], Guillaume Habault, Roberto Legaspi, Hao Niu, Lian Cao, and Masato Taya

KDDI Research, Inc., Fujimino, Japan
{xhu-ung,xgu-habault,ha-niu,xli-cao,ma-taya}@kddi.com,
ro-legaspi@kddi-research.jp

Abstract. Rapid and accurate post-disaster building damage assessment is essential, yet remains a challenging task. Unmanned Aerial Vehicle (UAV) imagery offers a timely and high-resolution view of affected areas, but existing Computer Vision (CV) models often demand large annotated datasets, generalize poorly across geographic regions and their assessment policies, and are confined to the specific tasks they were trained for. Large Vision-Language Models (LVLMs) offer a promising alternative through their strong reasoning and generalization capabilities, but fall short on precise, low-level perception tasks such as object detection and accurate bounding box generation. Furthermore, they often require a substantial amount of data for effective fine-tuning on domain-specific tasks. In this paper, we propose a hybrid framework that decouples detection from damage assessment, combining the precision of CV models with the reasoning power of LVLMs. A CV model first detects buildings and generates bounding boxes on the image that are then passed to an LVLM for damage classification and contextual interpretation. We evaluated our framework on two real-world benchmarks: RescueNet and FloodNet. In particular, the best combination under this framework accurately counts intact, partially damaged and completely destroyed buildings, surpassing isolated baselines by up to $2.1R^2$ points, while requiring only limited annotated data for the detection stage. Beyond reporting aggregate gains, we provide a detailed analysis of failure scenarios and edge cases, offering practical insights for practitioners and concrete directions for future work. Our source code and data are publicly available to the research community via the following repository: https://github.com/ungquanghuy-kddi/VLM_GDINO.git.

Keywords: Post-disaster building damage assessment · UAV imagery · Computer Vision · Large Vision-Language Model

Supplementary Information The online version contains supplementary material available at https://doi.org/10.1007/978-3-032-37682-4_37.

M. Baratchi et al. (Eds.): ECML PKDD 2026, LNAI 16949, pp. 636–653, 2027.
https://doi.org/10.1007/978-3-032-37682-4_37

1 Introduction

Disaster management is increasingly critical as climate change drives the growing frequency and severity of extreme events worldwide. Rapid and accurate post-disaster damage assessment is essential to prioritize rescue operations, guide emergency response, and enable efficient recovery planning. However, conventional field surveys are time-consuming, labor-intensive, potentially unsafe, and might fail to prioritize the most critical areas due to the absence of preliminary damage identification.

Imagery captured from vehicle dash cameras, Unmanned Aerial Vehicles (UAVs), and satellites are valuable source of information that enables large-scale remote analysis of disaster-affected regions. Among these sources, UAVs, which can easily navigate within disaster areas, are particularly advantageous as they offer high-resolution imagery, flexible and fast deployment: making them well-suited for rapid post-disaster reconnaissance. Coupled with Computer Vision (CV) models, which have demonstrated strong performance in object detection, UAV-based imagery presents a promising pathway toward automated, timely, and cost-effective preliminary damage assessments to support disaster management efforts.

Despite this promise, several challenges remain. UAV imagery is inherently complex, often spanning large areas with significant variation in object scale, shape, and appearance, as well as partial occlusion by vegetation. These factors make accurate detection and classification of building damage particularly difficult. Beyond perception, damage level definitions vary across regions and applications (from rescue dispatch to insurance assessment) limiting the generalizability of automated systems. While recent extended CV models such as Grounding DINO [16] enable open-set object detection in both zero-shot or few shot settings, accurately assessing building damage often requires broader contextual understanding of area-wide conditions, which purely perception-based models may struggle to capture.

Lately, Large Vision-Language Models (LVLMs) have demonstrated remarkable reasoning and generalization capabilities with high-level tasks, including mathematical reasoning [1], Visual Question Answering (VQA) [15], and common sense reasoning [28]. Capabilities that are highly relevant to post-disaster building damage assessment task. Furthermore, their language-guided nature allows LVLMs more flexibility to adapt more easily to varying assessment policies and damage definitions. However, as demonstrated in [25,35], they often fall short on precise, low-level perception tasks such as object detection and accurate bounding box positioning, which are critical for identifying individual buildings in UAV imagery. Besides, fine-tuning LVLMs to address this gap is impractical, requiring substantial computational resources and large annotated datasets.

To address these limitations, we propose a hybrid framework that leverages the complementary strengths of both CV models and LVLMs for post-disaster building damage assessment from UAV imagery. This proposal decouples assessment into two stages: a CV-based detection module that identifies buildings and generates precise bounding boxes, and an LVLM-based reasoning module that classifies damage level of detected buildings as well as provides contextual interpretation. These high-level tasks span from identifying priority rescue zones, to generating descriptive damage analyses, or coordinating efficient repair of disaster areas. This design preserves the spatial accuracy and efficiency of traditional CV models while leveraging the semantic understanding and adaptability of LVLM, without requiring full fine-tuning of either component. Crucially, by requiring only limited annotated data for the detection component, our framework is practical for real-world deployment where labeled data is scarce.

Our contributions are as follows:

- We introduce a hybrid CV-LVLM framework that decouples building detection from damage assessment for post-disaster building damage assessment from UAV imagery.
- We evaluate this framework by combining Grounding DINO with two open-source and two proprietary LVLMs. The associated experiments target the identification and counting of intact, damaged or completely destroyed buildings on two real-world datasets.
- We demonstrate that our framework outperforms isolated components, particularly under limited fine-tuning data for Grounding DINO, highlighting the value of combining complementary model strengths.
- We provide a detailed analysis of our results covering failures and edge cases, offering actionable insights for practitioners and concrete directions for future research.

2 Related Work

Computer Vision-Based Damage Assessment. Computer Vision (CV) models are widely used for building detection and damage assessment in both aerial and satellite imagery. Popular detection models such as the YOLO series [21] and Mask R-CNN [9] have been applied to instance segmentation for disaster response [26] and fine-grained object-level damage assessment [23]. In addition, segmentation models such as U-Net [22] have been employed to detect damaged buildings by comparing pre- and post-disaster satellite imagery [5].

More recently, foundation open-set object detection models such as Grounding DINO [16] and YOLOE [30] have emerged, enabling flexible, text-guided detection without requiring class-specific training. This capability offers strong potential for disaster response scenarios, where damage-related targets, new or unexpected object types may need to be identified.

Pre-trained Large Vision-Language Models. Large Vision-Language Models (LVLMs) have significantly advanced multimodal understanding and reasoning across a wide range of tasks. Proprietary models such as OpenAI's GPT [17] or Google's Gemini [4], along with open-source models including InternVL [32], QwenVL [29], and LLaVA [13], have demonstrated strong capabilities in visual question answering, reasoning, and instruction following. However, these general-purpose LVLM might be primarily trained on natural images and web-scale multimodal data, which limits their effectiveness when applied directly to specialized domains such as UAV imagery and damage assessment.

Recent works adapt LVLMs to remote sensing imagery, which presents distinct challenges such as large spatial coverage and domain-specific semantics. GeoChat [12] introduces a conversational framework that integrates geospatial visual encoders with Large Language Models (LLMs) for interactive understanding of satellite images. EarthDial [27] enables multi-turn dialogue about Earth observation data through instruction tuning, while TEOChat [11] focuses on multimodal reasoning over satellite imagery using domain-specific instruction datasets. Although these approaches demonstrate the potential of LVLMs for remote sensing, they are designed for general Earth observation understanding and are not specifically tailored for post-disaster damage assessment tasks. To foster the development of LVLMs for disaster response, large scale datasets have been introduced such as DisasterM3 benchmark [31] and Incidents1M [33].

Hybrid Framework Combining LVLMs and CV Models. Hybrid framework has recently emerged as a promising direction across several CV domains. While LVLMs offer strong semantic reasoning and flexibility, they struggle with precise spatial localization and can be computationally demanding [25,35]. Conversely, dedicated CV detectors excel at localizing objects accurately but lack the contextual understanding needed for complex classification tasks. To address these complementary limitations, recent works have proposed hybrid frameworks that decouple spatial detection from semantic reasoning, assigning each task to the component best suited for it. Works such as DetGPT [18] and ContextDET [34] follow this principle by using CV detectors to localize objects and LVLMs to interpret their context or condition. A similar decoupling has been adopted in robotics, where frameworks such as SayCan [2] which separate high-level task planning, handled by language models, from low-level spatial perception, handled by vision modules. Our work extends this paradigm to the remote sensing domain, decoupling building detection (handled by a CV model) from the contextually demanding task of post-disaster damage assessment (handled by a LVLM). To the best of our knowledge, this is the first application of such a hybrid framework to UAV-based building damage assessment.

3 Methodology: Combining VLM and CV

This section presents the rationale behind our hybrid framework, details its design, and describes the experimental setup used to evaluate it.

3.1 Rationale

CV models and LVLMs each excel at fundamentally different aspects of the building damage assessment pipeline, making neither sufficient on its own. CV models achieve strong performance in spatial localization tasks: detecting objects of varying classes and generating accurate bounding boxes. However, they struggle when classification requires higher-level contextual understanding beyond object-level cues. In contrast, LVLMs are primarily designed for image understanding and reasoning rather than precise spatial detection [25,35]. Yet they

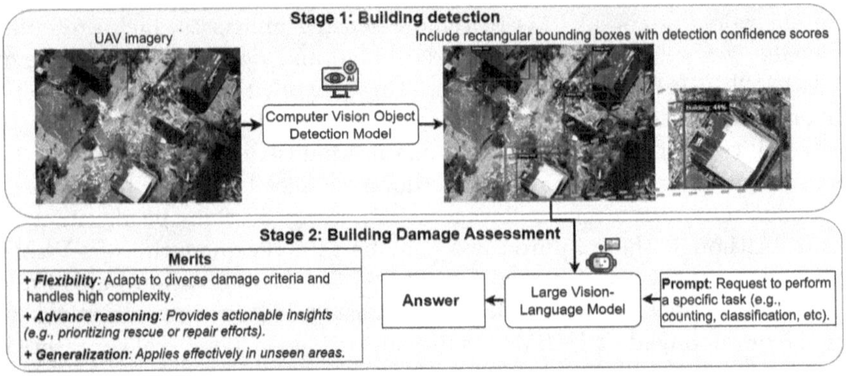

Fig. 1. Overview of our proposed hybrid framework along with its key merits: *flexibility*, *advanced reasoning*, and *generalization*. Stage 1 uses a CV model to detect buildings and generate bounding boxes with confidence scores. Stage 2 uses an LVLM, guided by a task-specific prompt, to perform damage assessment.

offer significant advantages for difficult assessment cases through semantic reasoning and contextual interpretation of scene-wide conditions. As a consequence, neither approach alone is sufficient to fully address the task. Our framework exploits their complementary strengths into a unified framework: a CV model handles building detection, while an LVLM performs damage-level assessment. Each component operates within its domain of competence.

3.2 Framework Design

To enable robust post-disaster building damage assessment from UAV imagery, we propose a two-stage pipeline that integrates a CV detector with an LVLM reasoner, as illustrated in Fig. 1.

Stage 1: Building Detection. Given an input UAV image, a CV-based object detector identifies buildings in the scene, enclosing each detected instance in a rectangular bounding box along an confidence scores. This stage leverages the strong spatial localization capability of modern CV detectors to reliably identify buildings even in cluttered, disaster-affected environments [23]. The detector can be fine-tuned on domain-specific data to further improve detection accuracy. The image, overlaid with bounding boxes, is then passed to the second stage.

Stage 2: Damage Assessment. The image enhanced with bounding boxes and confidence scores alongside a task-specific prompt are passed as input to the LVLM, which performs per-building damage classification through multi-modal reasoning. By receiving explicit spatial proposals from Stage 1, the LVLM can focus its reasoning on individual building regions as well as overall contextual information.

Interpretation. Building-level assessments produced by the LVLM are aggregated in order to generate statistics of affected and unaffected buildings in the target image. These outputs then support a range of high-level tasks: estimating the overall severity of damage across an area, prioritizing regions for urgent rescue, generating actionable situation reports, and planning how to restore critical services (e.g., electricity, water). The language-guided nature of the LVLM makes such outputs readily adaptable to different assessment policies and operational contexts

3.3 Experimental Design

Model Selection. Training CV models typically require large amount of annotated data in order to achieve strong task-specific performance. In contrast, a foundational model like Grounding DINO, which have already been pretrained, can be effectively adapted with limited labeled data. Liu et al. [16] demonstrated that fine-tuned it outperforms Mask R-CNN (pure CV model) under limited amount of annotated data. Such a finding is directly relevant to post-disaster scenarios where annotated data is scarce. Therefore, in our experiments, we adopt Grounding DINO as the detection component of our framework. We hypothesize that fine-tuning it for building detection in UAV imagery will outperform training a CV model from scratch, especially with limited data.

Task and Metrics. Our experiments target the counting of buildings across all categories (affected and unaffected by the disaster). For each image, per-class outputs are combined in order to compute different metrics. Performance on the counting task is evaluated using Root Mean Squared Error (RMSE) and Coefficient of Determination (R^2). To provide additional perspective on such performances, we report Average Precision (AP) at Intersection over Union (IoU) larger than 0.75 (denoted as AP^{75}) to evaluate the spatial accuracy of the building detection task.

Models Evaluated. In this study, we combine Grounding DINO with four LVLMs: two proprietary (GPT-5.1, Gemini 3 Pro) and two open-source (QwenVL 3 8B, InternVL 3.5 8B). Lightweight variants of the open-source models are deliberately chosen to assess the feasibility of edge deployment, such as integration directly onto UAV platforms.

Baselines. We compare our framework against the following baselines:

- *Random*: randomly guesses the number of buildings for each damage level within the observed range. It serves as a lower-bound reference.
- *Random_[class]*: simulates single-class damage detection model, designed to expose models that, under class imbalance, focus on the majority class.
- G-DINO* (Grounding DINO alone): Grounding DINO fine-tuned to perform both detection and damage assessment of all classes, followed by an algorithm counting the number of detected bounding boxes per class. This isolates the contribution of the LVLM reasoning stage.
- LVLM-alone: the LVLM performs detection, damage classification, and per-class counting of detected buildings, without spatial identification from a CV detector. This isolates the contribution of the CV detection stage.

Together, these baselines allow us to disentangle the contributions of each component and rigorously assess the value of combining them.

Fine-Tuning Subset. To validate our hypothesis that Grounding DINO can achieve satisfactory performance with limited amount of labeled data for the building damage assessment task, we define two fine-tuning subsets: "FT-100" and "FT-Full". FT-100 represents a low-data condition, comprising 100 samples drawn from the training set (80%) and the validation set (20%). These samples were randomly selected while preserving the class distribution of the full dataset as closely as possible. FT-Full uses all available training and validation samples.

To further investigate the effect of fine-tuning subset size on performance, we conduct an ablation study in which we report results across subsets of increasing size, generated using the same sampling strategy as FT-100. It is important to note that each subset is sampled independently: larger subsets do not necessarily contain all samples from smaller ones. This ablation provides a fine-grained view of how the performance of our framework scales with data availability.

LVLM Fine-Tuning. We deliberately keep all LVLMs in their original pretrained form without any fine-tuning. The available training data is relatively limited, making fine-tuning prone to both overfitting and catastrophic forgetting, causing the model to potentially lose both its broad pretrained knowledge and its visual-language alignment [14]. Moreover, Gulati et al. [8] demonstrated that parameter-efficient methods such as LoRA [10] may also introduce emergent multimodal misalignment under low-data conditions, potentially degrading multimodal reasoning performance. Given these risks, and as our main goal is to evaluate the effectiveness of the proposed framework rather than to adapt individual LVLMs, we rely on their pretrained capabilities throughout this study.

4 Dataset

We evaluate our framework on two high-resolution post-disaster UAV imagery datasets: RescueNet and FloodNet. Both were collected in the aftermath of hurricanes in the United States and provide fine-grained pixel-level annotations for semantic segmentation, covering classes representative of post-disaster environments such as water, roads, vehicles, vegetation, and buildings. Despite their shared structure, the two datasets differ in their geographic contexts, disaster type, and associated challenges, making their combination valuable for assessing

Table 1. Comparison of RescueNet and FloodNet dataset characteristics, including disaster type, image resolution, number of samples per data splits, and semantic class coverage.

Dataset	Disaster Type	Geographic Scope	Resolution (pixel)	Split Size			Annotation Methodology	Class								
				Tr	Val	Te		Background	Pool	Water	Road	Vehicle	Tree	Sand	Grass	Building
RescueNet	Hurricane	United States	3000x4000	3595	449	450	pixel-level	✓	✓	✓	✓	✓	✓	✓	✗	✓
FloodNet	Flood	Texas/Louisiana		1445	450	448	labeling	✓	✓	✓	✓	✓	✓	✗	✓	✓

the generalizability of our framework. Table 1 summarizes key information for both datasets. A key limitation of both datasets is their geographic and event-specific scope. As both were collected exclusively in the United States following a single event, models trained on them may not generalize well to other terrains or geographic contexts.

As this study focuses exclusively on building damage assessment, all non-building classes are discarded. As a result, RescueNet yields four building-related classes and FloodNet two.

4.1 RescueNet

RescueNet [19] was acquired following Hurricane Michael (2018) and defines building damage in accordance with FEMA [6] guidelines, distinguishing four levels: *no damage*, *minor damage*, *major damage*, and *total destruction*. This hierarchical taxonomy makes it particularly well-suited for structural damage assessment tasks, where differentiating degrees of destruction is critical.

Preprocessing. Distinguishing minor from major damage is inherently difficult from aerial imagery alone [7]. Therefore, we merge these two categories into a single "damaged" class, reducing the classification to three levels: *no damage*, *damaged*, and *total destruction*. Figure 2 illustrates the class distribution of RescueNet and the associated FT-100 fine-tuning subset, showing that FT-100 successfully preserves the original distribution. In addition, we observe that after merging minor and major classes, the resulting distribution is relatively balanced in terms of average building count per image.

Challenge. A key difficulty in RescueNet is the visual ambiguity between debris from totally destroyed buildings and debris transported by the hurricane. Such a distinction is particularly hard to make without pre-disaster reference imagery.

4.2 FloodNet

FloodNet [20] was acquired in the aftermath of Hurricane Harvey (2017) and defines both road and building damage along a binary dimension: *flooded* and *non-flooded*.

Preprocessing. In this study, we adopt the definition of flooded buildings from the original paper. Figure 3 illustrates the class distribution of FloodNet as well as its associated FT-100 fine-tuning subset, showing that FT-100 closely preserves the original distribution in terms of average building count per image. This figure shows that the class distribution of with a relatively balanced original distribution. However, this per-object balance masks a significant image-level imbalance with over 90% of images containing no flooded buildings, which can bias model training toward the dominant non-flooded class.

Challenges. FloodNet presents several inherent difficulties. Visually, distinguishing floodwater from natural water bodies can sometimes be challenging, as both appear similar in aerial imagery. Furthermore, the presence of dense

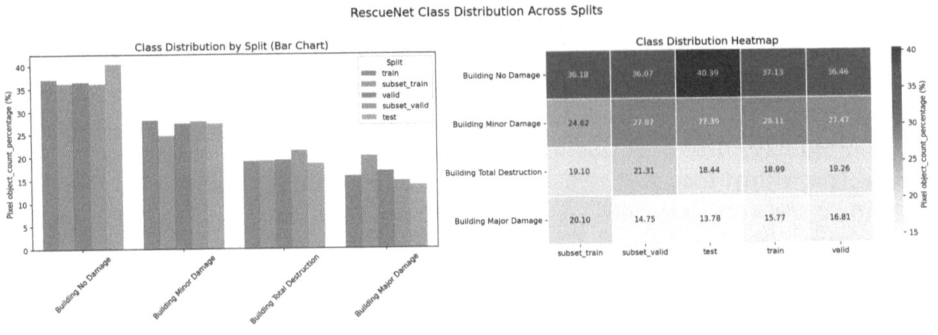

Fig. 2. Distribution of average building count per image across RescueNet data splits and the FT-100 fine-tuning subset (subset_train, subset_valid), shown as class-wise percentages. The FT-100 sampling strategy successfully preserves the original class distribution, with the *no damage* class remaining dominant across all splits.

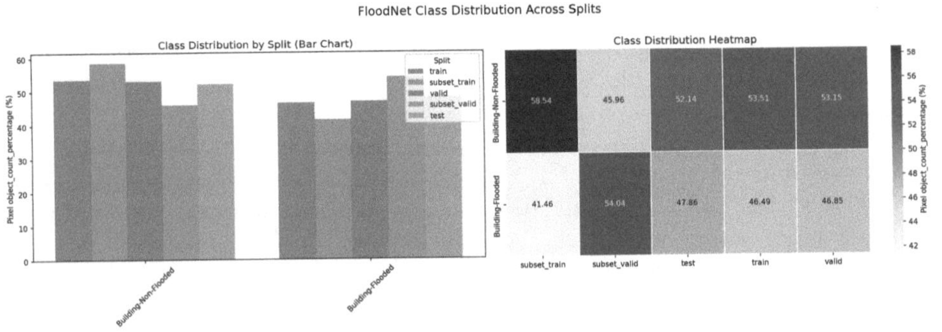

Fig. 3. Distribution of average building count per image across FloodNet data splits and the FT-100 fine-tuning subset (subset_train, subset_valid), shown as class-wise percentages. Classes are relatively balanced in terms of average building count per image and the FT-100 sampling strategy successfully preserves the original class distribution.

canopy cover, may obscure floodwater making assessment more difficult. Additionally, the lack of detailed information on the annotation process limits the ability to assess annotation reliability.

Table 2. List of our objectives for the counting task.

Task	RescueNet	FloodNet
Counting:	(1) Intact building	(1) Non-flooded building
	(2) Partially damaged building	(2) Flooded building
	(3) Totally destroyed building	

5 Results and Analysis

This section presents our experimental settings, main results, and an extensive ablation study. In addition, we report the standalone detection performance of LVLMs to motivate the need for a dedicated CV module within our framework.

5.1 Experimental Settings

We adopt the pre-trained Grounding DINO implementation from [3], configured with a Swin-T backbone. For simplicity, we refer to Grounding DINO as G-DINO in the rest of the paper. Fine-tuning hyperparameters follow the default settings in [3]. At inference, only bounding boxes with a confidence score above 0.3 are retained.

Table 2 presents the building damage classes considered in the counting task. For each LVLM query, we simply prompt the model to count buildings of a single damage class per conversation turn. The final results are computed by aggregating the per-class responses across all conversation turns.

5.2 LVLM Performance on Building Detection

Table 3 reports zero-shot detection performance on the RescueNet and FloodNet test sets for QwenVL 3 8B, InternVL 3.5 8B, GPT-5.1, Gemini 3 Pro, and G-DINO. With the exception of Gemini 3 Pro, which achieves an AP^{75} of 0.36 on RescueNet, all other LVLMs have their scores close to zero. All these scores are significantly worse than G-DINO, (1) confirming that object detection remains a key weakness of general-purpose LVLMs; and (2) providing empirical support for our framework's core design choice: decoupling detection from reasoning by delegating detection to a dedicated CV model rather than relying on LVLMs.

Table 3. Zero-shot building detection performance (AP^{75}) of LVLMs and a dedicated CV model (G-DINO) on the RescueNet and FloodNet test sets.

Dataset	QwenVL 3 8B	InternVL 3.5 8B	GPT-5.1	Gemini 3 Pro	G-DINO
RescueNet	0.0003	0.0002	0.0003	0.3625	**0.4991**
FloodNet	0.0003	0.0001	0.0002	0.0731	**0.4453**

Table 4. Main results for LVLM-alone and LVLM+G-DINO configurations on the RescueNet and FloodNet test set. "*GTBBox*" represents perfect bounding boxes extracted from ground-truth. "Not FT", "FT-100" and "FT-Full" denote G-DINO (or G-DINO*) without fine-tuning, fine-tuned with 100 samples, and fine-tuned with the full dataset, respectively.

Method	Fine-tuning	RescueNet			FloodNet		
		RMSE (↓)	R^2 (↑)	AP^{75}(↑)	RMSE (↓)	R^2 (↑)	AP^{75}(↑)
Random	✗	7.044	−23.760	–	24.117	−39.036	–
Random_intact	✗	4.221	−7.888	–	–	–	–
Random_damaged	✗	4.268	−8.089	–	–		–
Random_destroyed	✗	4.478	−9.007	–	–	–	–
Random_non_flooded	✗	–	–	–	16.885	-18.624	–
Random_flooded	✗	–	–	–	17.696	−20.556	–
G-DINO*	Not FT	2.955	-3.356	0.118	3.148	0.318	0.118
	FT-100	2.315	-1.673	0.420	3.768	0.023	0.420
	FT-Full	0.973	0.528	0.677	2.041	0.713	0.677
QwenVL 3 8B	✗	2.759	−2.798	–	2.613	0.529	–
InternVL 3.5 8B	✗	2.215	−1.447	–	1.871	0.758	–
GPT-5.1	✗	1.328	0.120	–	2.611	0.531	–
Gemini 3 Pro	✗	2.106	−1.213	–	3.790	0.011	–
QwenVL 3 8B + G-DINO	Not FT	2.957	−3.363	0.499	3.078	0.348	0.445
	FT-100	2.216	−1.450	0.710	2.781	0.467	0.772
	FT-Full	2.181	−1.374	0.839	2.832	0.448	0.840
QwenVL 3 8B + *GTBBox*	✗	1.967	−0.930	1.000	2.901	0.421	1.000
InternVL 3.5 8B + G-DINO	Not FT	2.152	−1.310	0.499	3.249	0.273	0.445
	FT-100	1.993	−0.981	0.710	2.954	0.399	0.772
	FT-Full	2.016	−1.028	0.839	2.912	0.416	0.840
InternVL 3.5 8B + *GTBBox*	✗	1.878	−0.759	1.000	2.766	0.473	1.000
GPT-5.1 + G-DINO	Not FT	1.349	0.092	0.499	2.481	0.576	0.445
	FT-100	1.181	0.304	0.710	2.538	0.557	0.772
	FT-Full	1.219	0.258	0.839	2.700	0.498	0.840
GPT-5.1 + *GTBBox*	✗	1.157	0.333	1.000	2.453	0.586	1.000
Gemini 3 Pro + G-DINO	Not FT	1.132	0.361	0.499	2.889	0.425	0.445
	FT-100	0.990	0.511	0.710	2.645	0.518	0.772
	FT-Full	1.105	0.391	0.839	2.413	0.599	0.840
Gemini 3 Pro + *GTBBox*	✗	0.918	0.579	1.000	2.838	0.445	1.000

5.3 Main Results

RescueNet. Table 4 presents the performance of the proposed framework (using G-DINO as detector) across all LVLMs and fine-tuning configurations. To establish an upper bound, we additionally report results when ground-truth bounding boxes (GTBBox) are provided directly to the LVLM component, simulating a perfect detector.

Several clear trends emerge. First, naive baselines perform poorly across all metrics, confirming that simple guessing strategies or single-class focus cannot capture the distribution of building damage levels. Second, G-DINO* (designed to perform both detection and damage classification jointly) improves with more fine-tuning data but consistently underperforms the proposed hybrid framework. Third, LVLM-alone baselines struggle to reliably detect and count buildings directly, yielding unstable performance across models compare to the proposal. These observations demonstrate that decoupling localization from reasoning is beneficial.

The proposed LVLM+G-DINO framework consistently outperforms all baselines, already achieving strong performance with limited fine-tuning data. Notably, our framework achieves the largest gains using Gemini 3 Pro and fine-tuning G-DINO with FT-100 – up to 1.6 and 2.1 R^2 points over the Gemini 3 Pro alone and G-DINO*, respectively. Such results demonstrate the effectiveness of the hybrid approach even under low-data conditions. As G-DINO is progressively fine-tuned, bounding box quality improves (AP^{75} approaching 1), which further benefits LVLM reasoning and counting, narrowing the gap toward the GTBBox upper bound.

FloodNet. Table 4 reveals a similar overall trend for proprietary LVLMs, which benefit from integration with G-DINO. However, open-source LVLMs exhibit a notably different behavior. First, combining open-source LVLMs with G-DINO occasionally degrades performance relative to the LVLM-alone baseline, suggesting that additional spatial context provided by bounding boxes alter models capabilities. Second, providing GTBBox yields only marginal improvements, and in some cases even slight degradation, as observed with Gemini 3 Pro. This behavior contrast sharply with RescueNet, where perfect localization led to significant gains. This discrepancy suggests that the primary bottleneck on FloodNet lies not in localization quality but on other visual phenomenon. We further analyze and discuss this point in the following section.

5.4 Ablation Study

Impact of Fine-Tuning Set Size. We vary the fine-tuning set size for G-DINO and G-DINO* across $[0, 100, 500, 1000, 2000, 4044]$ samples for RescueNet and $[0, 100, 500, 1000, 1895]$ samples for FloodNet. Each subset is generated using the sampling strategy described in Sect. 3.3, i.e., randomly selecting samples while approximately preserving the full dataset's class distribution.

Table 5 reports the detection performance of G-DINO and G-DINO* across fine-tuning set sizes with both datasets. Fine-tuning with as few as 100 samples already yields a substantial improvement over the zero-shot setting, and performance continues to improve steadily as more data is added. These results confirm that G-DINO adapts effectively to UAV-based building detection even under limited annotation budgets.

Figures 4a and 4b present the corresponding counting results (R^2) on RescueNet and FloodNet, respectively. As detection quality improves with more fine-tuning data, overall framework performance increases in most cases, with

Table 5. AP^{75} of G-DINO and G-DINO* on the RescueNet and FloodNet test sets, across varying fine-tuning set sizes.

	RescueNet						FloodNet				
#Fine-tuning samples	0	100	500	1000	2000	4044	0	100	500	1000	1895
G-DINO	0.499	0.71	0.76	0.793	0.813	0.839	0.445	0.772	0.822	0.827	0.840
G-DINO*	0.118	0.42	0.54	0.583	0.633	0.677	0.077	0.655	0.714	0.731	0.762

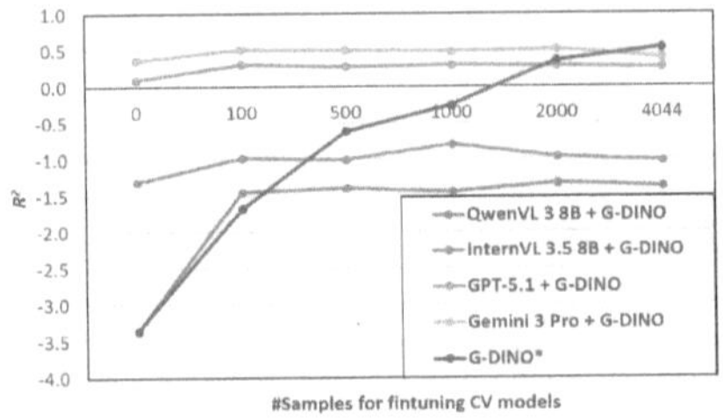

(a) RescueNet test set.

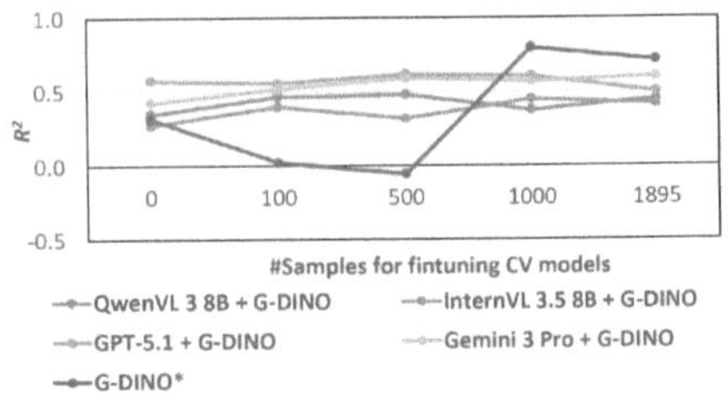

(b) FloodNet test set.

Fig. 4. Evolution of R^2 scores (y-axis) across varying fine-tuning set sizes (x-axis) of G-DINO* and our proposed LVLM+G-DINO framework on (a) RescueNet and (b) FloodNet.

particularly notable gains observed for QwenVL 3 8B. Notably, relatively small number of samples (100 and 500) already yields R^2 scores comparable to those obtained with the full fine-tuning set. This result indicates that, across different LVLMs backbones, the framework remains highly effective under limited data conditions, while consistently outperforming G-DINO*. However, when the fine-tuning set exceeds 1000 samples, G-DINO* occasionally surpasses our approach.

Interestingly, G-DINO* without any fine-tuning achieves an R^2 of approximately 0.3 despite very poor detection accuracy ($AP^{75} = 0.077$). Closer inspection reveals that while many predicted bounding boxes are poorly localized, their total count per image roughly matches the true building count. This suggests that evaluating performance only from metrics focusing on the number of bounding boxes produced by a CV model can be unreliable, as these boxes may not correspond to correctly localized objects.

Impact of Mask Representation. To investigate how the representation of areas corresponding to a detected building affects LVLM reasoning, we evaluate three types of localization mask: rectangular bounding boxes (used throughout this paper), polygonal boxes, and pixel-level segmentation masks. Figure 5a illustrates representative examples of each type. To isolate the effect of mask representation, all masks in this experiment are derived from ground-truth annotations.

As shown in Fig. 5b, mask representation has a significant impact on framework performance. Rectangular bounding boxes achieve the most stable and

(a) Illustration of the different mask types used for building detection: (1) Rectangular bounding box, (2) polygonal box, and (3) pixel-level segmentation.

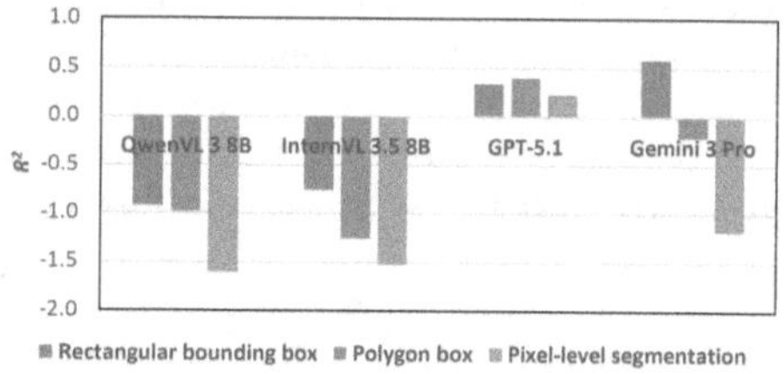

(b) R^2 performance of LVLMs on RescueNet when building identification is done with each mask type.

Fig. 5. Impact of mask representation on LVLM damage assessment performance. (a) Example of the different detection boxes considered. (b) R^2 scores on RescueNet for each LVLM when provided with each mask type.

consistently strong results across all LVLMs. Polygonal masks yield comparable performance in some cases but exhibit notable degradation in others. Pixel-level segmentation performs worst overall, and in some configurations producing negative R^2 values for Gemini 3 Pro.

We attribute this ordering to the visual information preserved by each mask type. Rectangular and polygonal masks retain the full appearance of building regions, allowing LVLMs to observe structural damage cues directly. Pixel-level segmentation, however, requires overlaying a colored mask to delineate building boundaries, which can obscure damaged surface details and hinder damage-level interpretation. These findings suggest that moderate spatial guidance (such as bounding boxes) is more effective than precise segmentation for supporting high-level reasoning in LVLMs-based damage assessment.

6 Discussion and Perspectives

6.1 Analysis of Failure Cases

We further investigate the performance degradation discovered when our framework integrates open-source LVLMs on FloodNet. A similar trend is observed in the RescueNet dataset for intact building counting (see Table 6). We hypothesize that LVLM-alone models possess sufficient internal priors to identify objects lacking disaster-related structural distortions, such as intact or flooded buildings without visible damage. In these scenarios, the introduction of bounding boxes may become redundant. By isolating the object, the bounding box may also strip essential environmental context (e.g., surrounding floodwater or blocked access routes) that the model requires for relational reasoning. This suggests that the utility of external detection boxes is non-uniform and highly dependent on the visual processing strategies inherent to the specific LVLM architecture.

6.2 Dataset Characteristics and Limitations

Both datasets are derived from UAV imagery captured along continuous flight paths, resulting in significant visual overlap between sequential frames. Our

Table 6. Performance of our framework on RescueNet for counting intact buildings, illustrating cases where combining G-DINO with LVLMs does not improve over the LVLM-alone baseline. "*GTBBox*" represents perfect bounding boxes extracted from ground-truth. "Not FT", "FT-100" and "FT-Full" denote G-DINO without fine-tuning, fine-tuned with 100 samples, and fine-tuned with the full dataset, respectively.

Method	Fine-tuning	QwenVL 3 8B		InternVL 3.5 8B		GPT-5.1		Gemini 3 Pro	
		RMSE (↓)	R^2 (↑)	RMSE (↓)	R^2 (↑)	RMSE (↓)	R^2 (↑)	RMSE (↓)	R^2 (↑)
LVLM	✗	1.109	0.494	1.317	0.287	1.255	0.352	1.555	0.007
LVLM+G-DINO	Not FT	1.449	0.137	1.432	0.152	1.225	0.383	1.148	0.458
	FT-100	1.514	0.058	1.428	0.162	1.235	0.373	1.081	0.520
	FT-Full	1.467	0.116	1.386	0.208	1.245	0.363	1.105	0.498
LVLM+*GTBBox*	✗	1.259	0.348	1.337	0.262	1.272	0.334	1.034	0.560

investigation reveals that images from the same flight sequence occasionally appear across training, validation, and test splits. This introduces the risk of spatial autocorrelation and potential data contamination, as the model may encounter visually familiar regions at test time. While we acknowledge that this is a limitation common to many aerial datasets, rigorously quantifying the impact of this sequence leakage on model performance remains an important direction for future work.

Both datasets are geographically constrained to specific regions of the United States, which may limit the cross-regional transferability of our findings. Models optimized for particular architectural styles or environmental conditions often struggle when deployed in regions with different building morphologies or disaster management infrastructures. Our framework is not exempt from this concern.

We identify a significant discrepancy between the formal definition of a flooded building in FloodNet and its ground-truth annotations. Although the dataset defines a flooded building by direct water contact (at least one side touching floodwater), many annotations appear to follow an operational logic, labeling buildings as flooded if their access routes are submerged. While pragmatically useful for emergency response, this inconsistency introduce semantic noise for prompt-based models like Grounding DINO and LVLMs, which rely on strict textual-visual alignment. This mismatch between linguistic definitions and visual labels likely undermines both zero-shot inference and the broader generalizability of the framework.

6.3 Future Directions

Finally, several constraints of the current study merit further exploration. First, while we focused on training-free integration to assess the baseline reasoning of LVLMs, future benchmarks should include comparisons with models fine-tuned on the target domain. Second, our framework is agnostic to the choice of CV detector; however, we have yet to evaluate it against fully supervised models like YOLO [24]. Given that supervised detectors require substantial high-quality annotated data to outperform open-vocabulary alternatives, future research will focus on training dedicated detectors on expanded datasets. This will provide clearer architectural guidelines for practitioners implementing automated systems for post-disaster building damage assessment.

7 Conclusion

In this paper, we propose a hybrid framework for post-disaster building damage assessment that decouples building detection from damage assessment by combining the localization capabilities of CV models with the reasoning abilities of LVLMs. A CV-based detection module identifies buildings and generates bounding boxes, while the reasoning module based on LVLM classifies damage levels and provides contextual interpretation. In this work, we use Grounding DINO as the CV model.

Evaluated on RescueNet and FloodNet, the framework consistently outperforms isolated baselines, particularly under low-data conditions. Ablation studies further show that increasing the number of fine-tuning samples for Grounding DINO improves the overall performance, and that rectangular bounding boxes perform better than polygonal boxes and pixel-level segmentation masks. Finally, we discuss failure cases, dataset limitations, and directions for future work.

References

1. Ahn, J., Verma, R., Lou, R., Liu, D., Zhang, R., Yin, W.: Large language models for mathematical reasoning: progresses and challenges (2024). https://arxiv.org/abs/2402.00157
2. Ahn, M., et al.: Do as i can, not as i say: grounding language in robotic affordances. arXiv preprint arXiv:2204.01691 (2022)
3. Chen, K., et al.: MMDetection: open mmlab detection toolbox and benchmark. arXiv preprint arXiv:1906.07155 (2019)
4. Google DeepMind: Gemini 3.1 pro (2025). https://deepmind.google/models/gemini/pro/
5. Deng, L., Wang, Y.: Post-disaster building damage assessment based on improved u-net. Sci. Rep. **12**(1) (2022)
6. FEMA: FEMA preliminary damage assessment guide (2020). https://www.fema.gov/sites/default/files/2020-07/fema_preliminary-disaster-assessment_guide.pdf
7. Gebre, T.S., Talreja, J., Hashemi-Beni, L.: Multi-Modal Attention for Automated Disaster Damage Assessment Using Remote Sensing Imagery and Deep Learning (2026)
8. Gulati, I., Raval, S.: Narrow fine-tuning erodes safety alignment in vision-language agents. arXiv preprint arXiv:2602.16931 (2026)
9. He, K., Gkioxari, G., Dollár, P., Girshick, R.: Mask R-CNN. In: Proceedings of the IEEE International Conference on Computer Vision, pp. 2961–2969 (2017)
10. Hu, E.J., et al.: Lora: low-rank adaptation of large language models. In: ICLR (2022)
11. Irvin, J.A., et al.: Teochat: a large vision-language assistant for temporal earth observation data. In: The Thirteenth International Conference on Learning Representations (2025)

12. Kuckreja, K., Danish, M.S., Naseer, M., Das, A., Khan, S., Khan, F.S.: Geochat: grounded large vision-language model for remote sensing. In: Proceedings of the IEEE/CVF Conference on Computer Vision and Pattern Recognition, pp. 27831–27840 (2024)
13. Li, B., et al.: Llava-onevision: easy visual task transfer. arXiv preprint arXiv:2408.03326 (2024)
14. Lin, Y., et al.: Lora dropout as a sparsity regularizer for overfitting control. arXiv preprint arXiv:2404.09610 (2024)
15. Liu, H., Li, C., Wu, Q., Lee, Y.J.: Visual instruction tuning. Adv. Neural. Inf. Process. Syst. **36**, 34892–34916 (2023)
16. Liu, S., et al.: Grounding DINO: marrying DINO with grounded pre-training for open-set object detection. In: European Conference on Computer Vision, pp. 38–55. Springer (2024)
17. OpenAI: Introducing GPT-5.2 (2025). https://openai.com/index/introducing-gpt-5-2/
18. Pi, R., et al.: Detgpt: detect what you need via reasoning. In: Proceedings of the 2023 Conference on Empirical Methods in Natural Language Processing, pp. 14172–14189 (2023)
19. Rahnemoonfar, M., Chowdhury, T., Murphy, R.: Rescuenet: a high resolution UAV semantic segmentation dataset for natural disaster damage assessment. Sci. Data **10**(1) (2023)
20. Rahnemoonfar, M., Chowdhury, T., Sarkar, A., Varshney, D., Yari, M., Murphy, R.R.: Floodnet: a high resolution aerial imagery dataset for post flood scene understanding. IEEE Access **9**, 89644–89654 (2021)
21. Reis, D., Kupec, J., Hong, J., Daoudi, A.: Real-time flying object detection with yolov8. arXiv preprint arXiv:2305.09972 (2023)
22. Ronneberger, O., Fischer, P., Brox, T.: U-net: convolutional networks for biomedical image segmentation. In: International Conference on Medical Image Computing and Computer-Assisted Intervention, pp. 234–241. Springer (2015)
23. Sadiq, R., et al.: Towards fine-grained object-level damage assessment during disasters. Front. Earth Sci. **11** (2023)
24. Sapkota, R., Cheppally, R.H., Sharda, A., Karkee, M.: Yolo26: key architectural enhancements and performance benchmarking for real-time object detection. arXiv preprint arXiv:2509.25164 (2025)
25. Sapkota, R., Karkee, M.: Object detection with multimodal large vision-language models: an in-depth review. Inf. Fusion **126**, 103575 (2026)
26. Sirma, A., Plastropoulos, A., Tang, G., Zolotas, A.: Drespnet: a UAV dataset and yolov8-drn model for aerial instance segmentation of building access points for post-earthquake search-and-rescue missions. arXiv preprint arXiv:2508.16016 (2025)
27. Soni, S., et al.: Earthdial: turning multi-sensory earth observations to interactive dialogues. In: Proceedings of the Computer Vision and Pattern Recognition Conference, pp. 14303–14313 (2025)
28. Suzgun, M., et al.: Challenging big-bench tasks and whether chain-of-thought can solve them. In: Findings of the Association for Computational Linguistics: ACL 2023, pp. 13003–13051. ACL Anthology, Toronto, Canada (2023)
29. Qwen Team: Qwen3 technical report (2025). https://arxiv.org/abs/2505.09388
30. Wang, A., Liu, L., Chen, H., Lin, Z., Han, J., Ding, G.: Yoloe: real-time seeing anything. In: Proceedings of the IEEE/CVF International Conference on Computer Vision, pp. 24591–24602 (2025)

31. Wang, J., et al.: Disasterm3: a remote sensing vision-language dataset for disaster damage assessment and response. In: The Thirty-Ninth Annual Conference on Neural Information Processing Systems Datasets and Benchmarks Track (2025)
32. Wang, W., et al.: Internvl3.5: advancing open-source multimodal models in versatility, reasoning, and efficiency. arXiv preprint arXiv:2508.18265 (2025)
33. Weber, E., Papadopoulos, D.P., Lapedriza, A., Ofli, F., Imran, M., Torralba, A.: Incidents1m: a large-scale dataset of images with natural disasters, damage, and incidents. IEEE Trans. Pattern Anal. Mach. Intell. **45**(4), 4768–4781 (2022)
34. Zang, Y., Li, W., Han, J., Zhou, K., Loy, C.C.: Contextual object detection with multimodal large language models. Int. J. Comput. Vision **133**(2), 825–843 (2025)
35. Zhan, Y., Zhu, Y., Chen, Z., Yang, F., Tang, M., Wang, J.: Griffon: spelling out all object locations at any granularity with large language models. In: European Conference on Computer Vision, pp. 405–422. Springer (2024)

Benchmarking Deep Learning for Agricultural Potential Estimation from Multispectral Satellite Time Series

Mohammad El Sakka[1(✉)], Lotfi Chaari[2], and Josiane Mothe[3]

[1] University of Toulouse, IRIT UMR5505 CNRS, Toulouse, France
mohammad.el-sakka@irit.fr
[2] Toulouse INP, IRIT UMR5505 CNRS, Toulouse, France
[3] INSPE, UT2J, Univ. de Toulouse, IRIT UMR5505 CNRS, Toulouse, France

Abstract. Agricultural potential estimation -assessing land suitability for crop growth- is a critical yet challenging task for food security and sustainable land use planning. While traditional approaches rely on labor-intensive field surveys or coarse-resolution data, deep learning offers a scalable alternative. In this paper, we present the first systematic benchmark of deep learning approaches for agricultural potential estimation by leveraging time series data from multispectral satellite imagery. We benchmark three prediction strategies -continuous space discretization, categorical classification, and $K-$rank ordinal classification- across four state-of-the-art deep learning architectures (2D CNN, 3D CNN, ViViT, and UTAE) on the public AgriPotential dataset. Our experiments make several key findings. Continuous space discretization consistently achieved the best performance, achieving up to 87.97% accuracy$\pm$1 and a mean absolute error below 0.7. We show that temporal modeling is essential: architectures leveraging time series data significantly outperform their static counterparts, while multi-year data improves robustness against inter-annual variability. Through spectral ablation, we show that RGB and multispectral bands provide complementary information, and error analysis confirms that regression yields the most reliable predictions, with misclassifications predominantly occurring between adjacent classes -which is critical for real-world applications. Our results establish a strong baseline for agricultural potential estimation and provide practical guidance for integrating machine learning into agricultural planning applications. Our findings highlight the importance of temporal modeling, multispectral feature fusion, and robust loss functions—key considerations for future research in remote sensing and applied machine learning. Code at https://github.com/MohammadElSakka/agripotential-benchmarks.

Keywords: Deep learning · Multispectral satellite imagery · Ordinal classification · Time series analysis · Agricultural potential

M. Baratchi et al. (Eds.): ECML PKDD 2026, LNAI 16949, pp. 654–671, 2027.
https://doi.org/10.1007/978-3-032-37682-4_38

1 Introduction

Agricultural potential estimation - the assessment of land suitability for crop growth - has traditionally relied on manual, observation-based methods, such as field surveys, soil testing, and in-situ measurements [17]. While these approaches provide detailed, localized insights, they are labor-intensive, time-consuming, and difficult to scale, limiting their applicability for large-scale agricultural planning and food security initiatives. Scalable methods are therefore necessary, especially in the context of rapid climate change.

Satellite remote sensing offers a compelling alternative to manual and in-situ measurements, enabling large-scale, up-to-date assessments. Among available sensor types, multispectral imagery has proven particularly effective in different Earth Observation tasks such as land cover and land use mapping, cloud detection, crop classification, and yield prediction due to its widespread availability [5,6,13,14,24,29,35,36]. However, agricultural potential estimation using remote sensing remains unexplored due to the challenge it presents: it requires modeling multispectral, multitemporal data and inherently ordered labels (e.g., Very Low to Very High potential), where misclassifications between adjacent classes are less costly than those between distant ones [11,12].

In this paper, we present the first systematic evaluation of deep learning approaches for agricultural potential estimation using multispectral satellite image time series (MS SITS). Concretely, we propose the following contributions:

1. A benchmark of three modeling approaches for ordinal labels (categorical classification, $K-$rank ordinal classification, and continuous space discretization) across four state-of-the-art architectures (UNet, 3D UNet, ViViT, and UTAE).
2. The introduction of ordinal variants for each architecture that enforce label ordering.
3. Extensive experiments on the public AgriPotential dataset [11], demonstrating that continuous space discretization, combined with joint spatio-temporal modeling via 3D convolutions, consistently outperforms all other modeling approaches (up to 87.97% accuracy and MAE < 0.7).

Our results establish a strong baseline for future work on agricultural potential estimation and provide practical insights for deploying machine learning in agricultural planning applications, with broader implications for remote sensing, ordinal classification, and applied machine learning.

We evaluate deep learning approaches on the AgriPotential dataset [11], which provides MS SITS and corresponding five agricultural potential levels, ranging from very low to very high. Although the dataset covers a specific region in Southern France, we suggest that the benchmarked models may be directly applied to regions with a similar climate and adapted to new geographic areas through fine-tuning or domain adaptation [15]. While there are no widely available ground-truth datasets to rigorously assess performance in these new regions, these models could nonetheless serve as useful tools to assist in generating preliminary labels for further data annotation.

2 Related Work

2.1 Deep Learning for Remote Sensing and Temporal Modeling

Deep learning, particularly Convolutional Neural Networks (CNNs), has become the dominant approach for analyzing multi and hyper-spectral images captured by satellites, UAVs, and ground-based cameras [26,41]. In smart agriculture, CNNs can process both RGB imagery for visible symptoms and multispectral/hyperspectral data that reveal crop stress before symptoms appear [8,9], consistently outperforming traditional methods like Random Forest and SVM across yield prediction, disease detection, and weed identification [12,23,25,28,31]. Their integration with UAVs, satellites, and IoT sensors creates a multi-scale observation framework for comprehensive agricultural monitoring [3,7,32].

Remote sensing inherently requires capturing temporal and spectral dynamics. Early approaches used Recurrent Neural Networks (RNNs), but recent work has shifted toward 3D convolutions and attention-based architectures [12,16,18,40]. UTAE combines a UNet encoder with temporal attention to aggregate information across time while suppressing cloudy frames [18]. For large-scale satellite time series, 3D CNNs handle spatial and temporal dimensions simultaneously in crop classification and yield prediction [16,40].

More recently, pretrained foundation models specifically designed for remote sensing have emerged [20]. Unlike general-purpose models, architectures like UTAE [18], SpectralGPT [19], and SatMAE [6] are trained on massive collections of satellite imagery, capturing the unique spectral, spatial, and temporal characteristics of Earth observation data. These models offer significant advantages for agricultural applications with limited labeled data, as they can be efficiently fine-tuned while retaining general knowledge about Earth surface patterns, spectral signatures, and seasonal dynamics [6,19,38]. Transformer-based foundation models like SpectralGPT and SatMAE learn transferable representations across time and spectral bands, though they do not process full satellite image time series as such [6,19].

2.2 Deep Learning for Ordinal Classification

Ordinal classification, also referred to as ordinal regression, is a subfield of machine learning concerned with predicting labels that follow a natural order, such as age groups, disease severity stages, agricultural potentials, or preference rankings [11,39]. Unlike nominal classification, which treats all misclassifications equally, ordinal classification exploits the inherent ordering among categories to produce predictions that are not only accurate but also meaningfully ranked [4]. This property is particularly important in domains like medical diagnosis where the cost or severity of errors increases with the distance from the true label [27].

By incorporating ordinal information, models can better reflect these real-world error costs and improve decision-making in sensitive applications.

Approaches to ordinal classification can be broadly categorized into three paradigms: (1) continuous space discretization, which transforms ordinal targets into a classification problem by dividing a continuous range into discrete values; (2) distribution ordering learning, which injects ordinal relations into model training by imposing constraints on logit or label-level distributions; and (3) ambiguous instance delving, which addresses the challenge of distinguishing samples near class boundaries through ranking-based models or generative techniques [39].

In the remote sensing domain, ordinal classification remains underexplored. A notable study applied an ordinal classification model to aerial LiDAR point clouds in forest areas, classifying points into four ordered classes: ground, low vegetation, medium vegetation, and high vegetation [30].

While ordinal classification has been explored in other domains (e.g., medical imaging [27], LiDAR point clouds [30]), its application to agricultural potential estimation from MS SITS is novel. Prior remote sensing work focuses on categorical tasks (e.g., crop mapping [36]) or standard regression (e.g., yield prediction [16]), but none address the ordinal nature of potential labels or systematically benchmark architectures for this task.

3 Methodological Design: Input Architectures and Prediction Strategies

This section describes the key design choices for modeling MS SITS in the context of ordinal classification that we apply for agricultural potential estimation using remote sensing. We structure our approach around two key dimensions:

- How features are extracted from the input data (spatial, spectral, temporal modeling).
- How the output is structured (independent, ordered, or continuous classes).

By systematically evaluating combinations of these dimensions, we aim to identify the most effective architecture for this task. Below, we detail the architectures for modeling the spatio-spectral-temporal features (Sect. 3.1) and prediction strategies (Sect. 3.2) used in our experiments.

3.1 Deep Learning Architectures for Multispectral Satellite Time Series

Agricultural potential estimation from MS SITS requires architectures capable of capturing spatial, spectral, and temporal patterns in the data. The choice of architecture directly impacts how well the model can extract meaningful features from the high-dimensional input, particularly when dealing with irregularly sampled time steps, multi-band spectral information, and fine-grained spatial details. This section introduces four deep learning paradigms that capture temporal, spectral, and spatial information differently: 2D CNNs, 3D CNNs, vision transformers, and temporal attention-based models.

2D Convolutional Neural Networks. To handle MS SITS with 2D architectures, we concatenate all timesteps along the channel dimension, creating an input tensor of size $(T \cdot B) \times H \times W$, where T is the number of timesteps, B the number of spectral bands, H and W the height and width respectively. While concatenation preserves all spectral and temporal information, it does not explicitly encode the temporal order of the timesteps. We use the standard UNet architecture [34] as our 2D CNN baseline.

3D Convolutional Neural Networks. By extending convolutions to the temporal axis, 3D CNNs jointly model spatial, spectral, and temporal dimensions, capturing patterns in the temporal evolution directly in the feature extraction stage. The input is treated as a volumetric tensor of dimensions $T \times B \times H \times W$, and 3D kernels of size $k_t \times k_h \times k_w$ slide across both space and time simultaneously, where k_t, k_h, and k_w denote the kernel size along the temporal, height, and width dimensions respectively. This enables the model to learn features that depend on temporal context, which may include vegetation growth or seasonal variations. We implement a 3D UNet that extends the standard UNet with 3D convolutions in both the encoder and decoder, followed by 3D max-pooling for temporal-spatial downsampling and transposed 3D convolutions for upsampling [33].

U-Temporal Attention Encoder (Temporal Attention CNN). UTAE combines a UNet encoder with temporal self-attention. It first extracts spatial features independently per timestep using convolutional layers, then aggregates temporal information using a lightweight attention mechanism that handles irregular sampling and cloud cover by learning to weight relevant timesteps [18]. This separation of spatial and temporal processing differs from the joint modeling of 3D CNNs.

Video Vision Transformer (ViViT). ViViT adapts the transformer architecture to spatio-temporal data by dividing the input into spatio-temporal tubelets, which are linearly embedded and processed through transformer encoders [2]. Unlike UTAE which separates spatial and temporal processing, ViViT's self-attention mechanism captures long-range dependencies across both space and time simultaneously.

In our experiments, we fine-tune a pretrained version of UTAE, initialized from weights trained on the PASTIS multispectral satellite time series dataset [18,37], while the other architectures (2D UNet, 3D UNet, and ViViT) are trained from scratch.

3.2 Output Prediction Strategies

Predicting agricultural potential involves mapping the extracted features to ordered classes. The choice of the prediction strategy significantly impacts model performance, error interpretability, and practical deployment. In this section, we compare three strategies: categorical classification (CAT), $K-$rank ordinal classification (RANK), and continuous space discretization (CSD). RANK and CSD approaches offer distinct advantages in handling the ordinal nature of the labels while CAT serves as a baseline where the classes are considered independent. We evaluate robustness to misclassifications experimentally in Sect. 5.

Categorical Classification (CAT). The baseline approach is to treat each potential level as an independent category without modeling ordinality. Models are trained with the categorical cross-entropy loss:

$$\mathcal{L}_{\text{cat}} = -\sum_{k=1}^{5} \mathbf{1}(Y = k) \log p_k$$

where p_k is the predicted probability for class k. This approach penalizes all misclassifications equally, regardless of whether the error is by one level or by multiple levels. The predicted class is the one with the highest probability among the five classes.

***K*-rank Ordinal Classification (RANK).** To model the ordering between potential classes, we adopt a K-rank method, K being the number of classes [39]. In this method, $K-1$ binary classifiers are trained to convert the ordinal regression problem into a sequence of K binary classification tasks, each designed to distinguish between neighboring classes [39]. Concretely, the features produced by the last decoder's layer are passed through $K-1$ parallel classification heads. Each head consists of a 1×1 convolution followed by sigmoid activation and is responsible of predicting the probability $p_k(i,j)$ that a pixel (i,j) exceeds a class k where class k is an agricultural potential level:

$$p_k(i,j) = P\big(Y(i,j) > k\big), \quad k = 1, \ldots, K-1$$

During training, binary cross-entropy loss is applied independently to each head. At inference, the probability maps are thresholded with τ to obtain binary indicators:

$$b_k(i,j) = \mathbf{1}[p_k(i,j) > \tau], \quad k = 1, \ldots, K-1$$

To enforce ordinal consistency, we apply a cumulative minimum operation:

$$\tilde{b}_1 = b_1, \quad \tilde{b}_k = \min(\tilde{b}_{k-1}, b_k) \text{ for } k = 2, \ldots, K-1$$

This ensures that once a threshold is not exceeded, all higher thresholds are also set to zero. The final class is recovered by summing the adjusted indicators:

$$\hat{Y}(i,j) = 1 + \sum_{k=1}^{K-1} \tilde{b}_k(i,j)$$

In our case, with $K = 5$ ordinal classes, this yields four binary heads corresponding to thresholds $k = 1, 2, 3, 4$, with $\tau = 0.5$.

Continuous Space Discretization (CSD). We also consider an approach that treats ordinal classification as a continuous ordinal representation [39]. In this approach, we treat agricultural potential as a continuous variable. This formulation preserves the natural order of the labels. We map K ordinal classes to continuous values in the range $[0, 1]$ using uniform spacing:

$$class_i \rightarrow \frac{i-1}{K-1}, i = 1, 2, ...K$$

where i represents the rank position of each class. The target values become:

$$\text{Very Low} \rightarrow 0.0, \text{Low} \rightarrow 0.25, \text{Average} \rightarrow 0.5, \text{High} \rightarrow 0.75, \text{Very High} \rightarrow 1.0$$

The model is trained with the MSE loss:

$$\mathcal{L}_{\text{MSE}} = \frac{1}{N} \sum_{n=1}^{N} \frac{1}{2} (y_n - \hat{y}_n)^2.$$

During inference, the continuous predictions are rounded to the nearest class:

$$\hat{Y} = \text{round}((K-1) \cdot \hat{y}) + 1,$$

which maps the continuous output back to the discrete classes $\{1, 2, ...K\}$.

This approach explicitly encodes the order between classes and requires only a single output neuron, making it computationally efficient. However, it assumes that intervals between consecutive classes are equal. Depending on domain knowledge, the thresholds separating classes can be revised and adapted. Despite this limitation, continuous encoding provides a useful baseline for assessing whether the ordinal structure is better captured through ranking or continuous space discretization.

4 Experimental Setup

This section describes the training configuration, loss functions, baseline models, and evaluation protocol used in our benchmark experiments.

4.1 AgriPotential Dataset

We conduct our experiments on a dataset that we recently released and which is also used in a CLEF challenge[1] [21,22], the AgriPotential dataset [11]. This dataset consists of MS SITS data covering the Hérault Department in Southern France. It provides pixel-level labels for agricultural potential across three crop types (viticulture, market gardening, field crops) on a five-level ordinal scale: Very Low, Low, Average, High, and Very High. These labels are derived from pedoclimatic factors and are independent of current land use.

[1] https://clef2026.clef-initiative.eu/labs/imageclef/.

Table 1. Combinations of input architectures and prediction strategies evaluated in this study.

Input Architecture	CAT	RANK	CSD
2D CNN (concatenated time)	UNet	RANK-UNet	CSD-UNet
3D CNN (joint spatio-temporal)	3D UNet	RANK-3D UNet	CSD-3D UNet
Self-Attention ViT (ViViT)	ViViT	RANK-ViViT	CSD-ViViT
Temporal attention + fine-tuned (UTAE)	UTAE	RANK-UTAE	CSD-UTAE

The satellite imagery has a 5 m/px resolution with 34 unevenly spaced timesteps spanning 2017–2019, capturing phenological cycles and inter-annual variability. Multispectral data includes 10 Sentinel-2 bands (B2-B8A, B11, B12). Each image patch is a 4D tensor $X \in \mathbb{R}^{34\times10\times128\times128}$ covering approximately 0.41 km^2. For each pixel and crop type c, the target label is $Y_{i,j}^{(c)} \in \{1, 2, 3, 4, 5\}$.

We use the official data split: 6,329 training image time series (65M pixels), 781 validation (7.4M pixels), and 800 test time series (7.4M pixels).

4.2 Benchmarked Models

The modeling approaches combining the axes presented in Sect. 3 are summarized in Table 1.

For each architecture, we only adapt the input and output layers of the models to match the AgriPotential dataset specifications. We modify the input layers to accept 10-band multispectral data and the output layers to match the number of target classes (five for CAT, four binary heads for RANK, one continuous output for CSD, with $K = 5$ - see Sect. 3). Each model is trained and evaluated independently per crop type, yielding separate sets of weights for viticulture, market gardening, and field crops. Joint multi-crop training was not explored in this work and is left for future work.

All models are implemented in PyTorch and trained on 2 NVIDIA RTX 2080 Ti GPUs equipped with 11 GB of memory. A consistent set of hyperparameters is used across all experiments: the AdamW optimizer with a learning rate of 1×10^{-5} and a weight decay of 1×10^{-2}. Training employed a ReduceLROnPlateau learning rate scheduler with a patience of three epochs and a reduction factor of 0.5. Models are trained for up to 100 epochs, with early stopping triggered if the validation loss does not improve for 15 consecutive epochs and a batch size of 4. No additional preprocessing or data augmentation techniques were applied.

4.3 Evaluation Metrics

Given that agricultural potentials are ordered, small deviations between predicted and true labels are less critical than large errors. In practical terms, confusing two adjacent levels (e.g., *High* vs. *Very High*) is less severe than misclassifications by several levels. For this reason, we report the accuracy with one

Table 2. Performance across methods and crop types. The best results are in **bold** and the second best are underlined.

Output Type	Method	Viticulture		Market Garden		Field Crops	
		Acc±1 ↑	MAE ↓	Acc±1 ↑	MAE ↓	Acc±1 ↑	MAE ↓
Categorical	UNet	75.34	1.06	77.66	0.97	79.06	1.02
	UTAE	72.69	0.97	79.76	0.88	77.10	0.90
	ViViT	74.03	1.05	78.78	0.94	76.32	1.06
	3D UNet	77.85	0.99	80.95	0.88	80.48	0.98
Ranking	RANK-UNet	77.04	1.05	82.62	0.89	82.18	0.97
	RANK-UTAE	80.19	0.86	81.46	0.81	80.58	0.85
	RANK-ViViT	78.90	0.97	82.59	0.86	80.69	0.96
	RANK-3D UNet	81.10	0.97	85.52	0.83	82.80	0.95
Continuous	CSD-UNet	82.81	<u>0.83</u>	<u>87.24</u>	<u>0.73</u>	<u>85.05</u>	<u>0.78</u>
	CSD-UTAE	75.25	0.98	80.28	0.88	76.27	0.95
	CSD-ViViT	<u>83.73</u>	<u>0.83</u>	86.06	0.77	82.92	0.83
	CSD-3D UNet	**85.87**	**0.78**	**87.97**	**0.69**	**85.63**	**0.76**

tolerance level [1] (Accuracy ±1) which considers a prediction correct if it differs from the ground truth by at most one class:

$$\text{Accuracy}_{\pm 1} = \frac{1}{N}\sum_{n=1}^{N} \mathbf{1}\left(\left|\hat{Y}_n - Y_n\right| \leq 1\right),$$

where N is the number of evaluated pixels, Y_n the ground-truth ordinal label, and $\hat{Y}_n$ the predicted label.

To complement this tolerance-based metric, we also report the mean absolute error [1] (MAE), which measures the average ordinal distance between predictions and ground truth:

$$\text{MAE} = \frac{1}{N}\sum_{n=1}^{N} \left|\hat{Y}_n - Y_n\right|.$$

MAE provides an interpretable measure of error magnitude, indicating how many potential levels the prediction deviates from the true class on average.

5 Results and Discussions

5.1 Quantitative Comparison

Table 2 reports the performance of all our modeling approaches across the three crop types. Overall, models that explicitly model the ordinal relationships between classes outperform standard categorical approaches. Among the categorical baselines (first block of rows), 3D UNet achieves the best performance

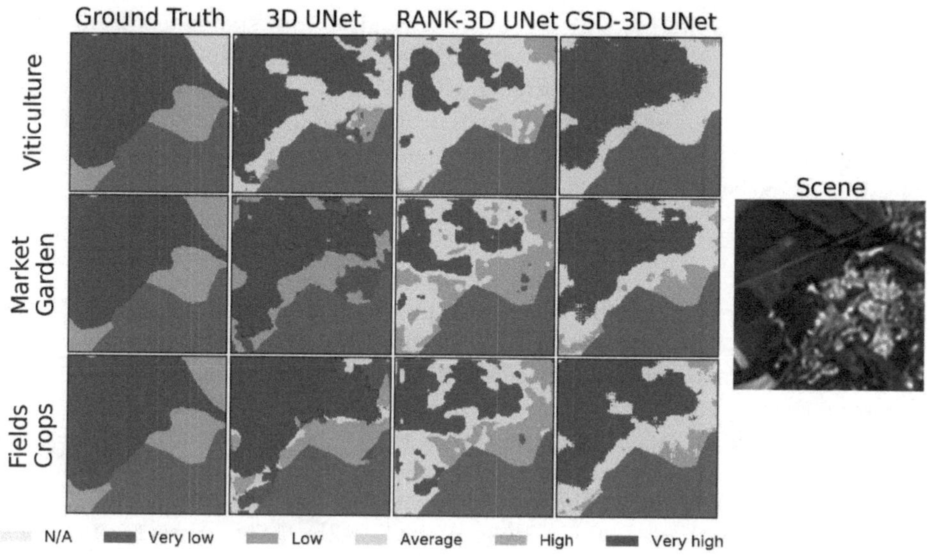

Fig. 1. Qualitative comparison of predicted agricultural potential maps.

reaching 77.85%, 80.95%, and 80.48% Acc±1 for viticulture, market garden, and field crops respectively. This highlights the benefit of jointly modeling spatial and temporal information compared to purely spatial models such as UNet. UTAE and ViViT perform competitively in some cases, particularly in market gardening, achieving 79.76% and 78.78% respectively.

Introducing ordinal encoding through RANK-based models (second block of rows) improves the performance across all crop types. In particular, RANK-3D UNet increases the Acc±1 to 81.10%, 85.52%, and 82.80%, demonstrating that incorporating ordinal constraints helps capture the ordered nature of agricultural potential classes. Similar improvements are also observed for other architectures such as RANK-UTAE and RANK-ViViT.

The CSD models (last block of rows), which treat the task as a regression problem before the discretization of the continuous domain, achieve the best overall results. In particular, CSD-3D UNet consistently outperforms all other methods across the three crop categories, reaching 85.87%, 87.97%, and 85.63% Acc±1, while also achieving the lowest MAE values (0.78, 0.69, and 0.76 respectively). However, CSD-UTAE underperforms relative to both its RANK variant and other CSD architectures: its Acc±1 drops to 75.25% for viticulture and 76.27% for field crops, worse than the categorical UTAE baseline. This suggests that UTAE's design may be less suited to regression than to classification ordinal objectives. These results suggest that modeling agricultural potential as a continuous variable better reflects the gradual transitions observed in real-world conditions.

Overall, the results indicate three main trends. First, spatio-temporal architectures outperform purely spatial approaches. Second, ordinal-aware methods outperform categorical classification, highlighting the benefit of respecting the ordered nature of potential levels. Finally, CSD-based models provide the best performance, suggesting that continuous modeling offers a more natural representation of agricultural potential.

5.2 Qualitative Analysis

Figure 1 illustrates the comparison of the predictions from the 3D UNet on the three crop types. The categorical 3D UNet produces spatially fragmented maps with salt-and-pepper artifacts and abrupt class transitions, particularly in areas of intermediate potential, which is confirmed by high MAE values in Table 2 (3D UNet). This fragmentation reflects a fundamental limitation of treating ordinal classes as independent categories because the paradigm does not impose a penalty for the severity of the misclassifications.

In contrast, both RANK-3D UNet and CSD-3D UNet generate smoother, more coherent predictions. The RANK-3D UNet reduces the salt-and-pepper noise considerably, however, it has a tendency toward underestimation. This bias is directly caused from the cumulative minimum operation presented in Sect. 3.2. For instance, in Fig. 1, a false negative from the binary head responsible for predicting the High class triggered the cumulative minimum operation, forcing all higher classes to zero regardless of their individual predictions. This explains why numerous pixels that should have been Very High were instead classified as Average.

CSD-3D UNet most closely reflects the gradual transitions expected in real agricultural landscapes, preserving smooth agricultural potential at class boundaries. The categorical model often exhibits severe discontinuities at boundaries. By learning a continuous representation before rounding to discrete levels, CSD produces realistic predictions that capture the underlying continuity of soil and climatic conditions.

5.3 Error Analysis

To better understand the types of errors made by different models, we analyze confusion matrices for CSD-3D UNet, RANK-3D UNet, and the best categorical baseline (3D UNet) across all three crop types. Table 3 presents these confusion matrices, where darker diagonal values indicate better classification performance.

Examining the confusion matrices reveals several consistent patterns. All models show highest accuracy on the extreme classes (Very Low and Very High), while the middle classes (Low, Average, High) exhibit more confusion, particularly between adjacent categories. The categorical baseline shows the highest off-diagonal dispersion, with errors spread across multiple classes, confirming that ignoring ordinal structure leads to more severe misclassifications where pixels can be off by two or more potential levels. RANK-3D UNet reduces this dispersion, concentrating errors primarily on adjacent classes, demonstrating that the ordinal formulation successfully enforces the natural ordering of potential levels.

Table 3. Confusion matrices of CSD-3D UNet, RANK-3D UNet, and 3D UNet across three crop types. Darker diagonals indicate better performance.

3D UNet — Viticulture

True \ Predicted	Very low	Low	Average	High	Very high
Very low	53%	22%	11%	4%	2%
Low	27%	46%	22%	16%	4%
Average	15%	18%	35%	26%	17%
High	4%	9%	20%	38%	12%
Very high	2%	4%	13%	16%	65%

3D UNet — Market Garden

True \ Predicted	Very low	Low	Average	High	Very high
Very low	61%	21%	18%	8%	2%
Low	27%	46%	23%	16%	3%
Average	6%	12%	38%	25%	6%
High	5%	18%	21%	45%	43%
Very high	0%	2%	0%	7%	47%

3D UNet — Field Crops

True \ Predicted	Very low	Low	Average	High	Very high
Very low	58%	25%	12%	5%	3%
Low	27%	40%	24%	16%	9%
Average	9%	16%	35%	24%	12%
High	4%	11%	21%	37%	15%
Very high	2%	8%	8%	18%	61%

RANK-3D UNet — Viticulture

True \ Predicted	Very low	Low	Average	High	Very high
Very low	55%	20%	5%	1%	0%
Low	29%	32%	16%	6%	0%
Average	12%	28%	32%	20%	5%
High	3%	14%	28%	33%	4%
Very high	2%	6%	19%	41%	90%

RANK-3D UNet — Market Garden

True \ Predicted	Very low	Low	Average	High	Very high
Very low	63%	23%	9%	4%	1%
Low	30%	40%	26%	9%	1%
Average	4%	16%	24%	24%	4%
High	3%	20%	38%	50%	48%
Very high	0%	2%	4%	12%	47%

RANK-3D UNet — Field Crops

True \ Predicted	Very low	Low	Average	High	Very high
Very low	60%	21%	8%	3%	1%
Low	29%	36%	21%	7%	3%
Average	7%	20%	28%	21%	5%
High	2%	15%	29%	37%	9%
Very high	1%	8%	15%	32%	82%

CSD-3D UNet — Viticulture

True \ Predicted	Very low	Low	Average	High	Very high
Very low	70%	36%	10%	2%	0%
Low	24%	36%	23%	7%	0%
Average	5%	19%	33%	24%	4%
High	1%	6%	22%	30%	4%
Very high	0%	3%	12%	36%	91%

CSD-3D UNet — Market Garden

True \ Predicted	Very low	Low	Average	High	Very high
Very low	72%	30%	9%	3%	1%
Low	24%	42%	24%	6%	0%
Average	3%	12%	24%	19%	3%
High	1%	14%	38%	53%	50%
Very high	0%	1%	4%	19%	47%

CSD-3D UNet — Field Crops

True \ Predicted	Very low	Low	Average	High	Very high
Very low	73%	32%	9%	3%	0%
Low	22%	39%	24%	7%	0%
Average	4%	15%	27%	20%	2%
High	1%	9%	26%	33%	6%
Very high	0%	5%	14%	38%	92%

CSD-3D UNet achieves the cleanest diagonal dominance across all crops, with confusion almost entirely confined to adjacent classes.

Crop-specific patterns emerge as well. For viticulture, the categorical baseline shows notable confusion between Low and Average, and between Average and High; RANK-3D UNet substantially reduces these errors, while CSD-3D UNet achieves near-perfect diagonal dominance. Market garden shows the cleanest confusion matrices overall, consistent with its highest Acc$\pm$1 scores in Table 2. Field crops exhibit the most challenging error patterns, with the categorical baseline showing significant confusion across multiple classes in the middle of the ordinal scale; here again, CSD-3D UNet achieves the best results with errors almost exclusively confined to adjacent classes.

These error patterns have important practical implications. For agricultural planning, confusing Very high with high is far less consequential than confusing Very High with Low. The confusion matrices demonstrate that CSD-3D UNet minimizes these severe errors, with most errors being off by only one class across all crop types. This means that when CSD-3D UNet makes a mistake, it is almost always a minor error for real-world deployment where adjacent-class errors are acceptable but large deviations are not.

Table 4. Spectral ablation study for CSD-3D UNet across all crop types.

Configuration	Viticulture		Market Garden		Field Crops	
	Acc±1	MAE	Acc±1	MAE	Acc±1	MAE
RGB only (3 bands)	67.17	1.15	68.85	1.13	65.25	1.19
Multispectral only (7 bands, no RGB)	57.77	1.42	64.99	1.20	63.14	1.31
Full model (all bands)	**85.87**	**0.78**	**87.97**	**0.69**	**85.63**	**0.76**

Table 5. Temporal ablation study for CSD-3D UNet across all crop types.

Configuration	Viticulture		Market Garden		Field Crops	
	Acc±1	MAE	Acc±1	MAE	Acc±1	MAE
2017 (13 timesteps)	75.30	1.02	79.59	0.97	74.65	1.03
2018 (10 timesteps)	63.65	1.32	66.54	1.18	65.04	1.27
2019 (11 timesteps)	53.12	1.54	60.64	1.32	58.42	1.43
2017–2018	78.99	0.94	83.80	0.91	77.81	0.97
2018–2019	55.58	1.43	64.24	1.22	60.89	1.32
Full model (all years)	**85.87**	**0.78**	**87.97**	**0.69**	**85.63**	**0.76**

5.4 Ablation Studies

To better understand the contribution of different input components to the performance of CSD-3D UNet, we conduct two ablations studies: spectral ablation and temporal ablation.

Spectral Ablation

Table 4 reports the performance of CSD-3D UNet when different spectral bands are masked during inference. When only RGB bands (B2, B3, B4) are used, performance drops substantially across all crop types, with Acc±1 falling from 85.87% to 67.17% for viticulture, from 87.97% to 68.85% for market garden, and from 85.63% to 65.25% for field crops. MAE correspondingly increases, indicating that visible spectrum alone is insufficient for accurate agricultural potential estimation.

When multispectral bands are used without RGB (bands B5–B12), the performance drop is even more pronounced: Acc±1 falls to 57.77% for viticulture, 64.99% for market garden, and 63.14% for field crops. This suggests that while non-visible bands carry valuable information, they are most effective when combined with visible spectrum data.

The full model using all ten bands significantly outperforms both ablated configurations across every metric and crop type. This demonstrates that RGB and multispectral bands provide complementary information—neither alone is sufficient, and their combination is essential for capturing the full complexity of agricultural potential.

Temporal Ablation

Single-year performance varies dramatically (Table 5): 2017 (13 timesteps) achieves the best single-year results (75.30% viticulture, 79.59% market, 74.65% field), while 2018 (10 timesteps) and 2019 (11 timesteps) perform progressively worse —despite 2019 having more timesteps than 2018, indicating that temporal coverage matters as much as quantity.

Two-year combinations show that adding data does not always help: 2017–2018 outperforms any single year (78.99%, 83.80%, 77.81%), but 2018-2019 performs worse than 2017 alone for viticulture and field crops, suggesting that poor-quality years can degrade performance.

The full three-year model achieves the best results across all crops (85.87%, 87.97%, 85.63%), confirming that sufficient temporal depth provides robustness against inter-annual variability and captures true agricultural potential.

6 Limitations and Future Work

This study establishes the first systematic benchmark for agricultural potential estimation from multispectral satellite image time series. However, many aspects remain open for future research. Despite the feasibility of applying remote sensing and deep learning for agricultural potential estimation, our evaluation remains restricted to a single geographic region (Hérault, Southern France) representing a temperate Mediterranean climate. The methodological pipeline regarding the multispectral, temporal, and ordinal modeling is transferable and not unique to this domain, but, so far, we do not have performance results on other regions with substantially different climates or phenological cycles. Future work must systematically evaluate these architectures across diverse geographic regions or simulated data in order to establish robust generalization bounds.

We also evaluated exclusively Sentinel-2 imagery given the present dataset AgriPotential. In future work, complementary sensors such as Sentinel-1, which is insensitive to cloud cover, can be considered and may yield different results. On the modeling side, more self-supervised spatio-temporal approaches such as U-BARN [10] are promising remote sensing foundation models that could be benchmarked alongside our baseline architectures.

7 Conclusion

In this paper, we presented the first systematic evaluation of deep learning approaches for agricultural potential estimation from multispectral satellite image time series. We evaluated three prediction strategies (categorical classification, $K-$rank ordinal classification, and continuous space discretization) across four state-of-the-art architectures (2D UNet, 3D UNet, ViViT, and UTAE) on the public AgriPotential dataset. Our comprehensive analysis yields several key findings.

We first demonstrate that continuous space discretization with joint spatio-temporal modeling achieves state-of-the-art performance. The CSD-3D UNet variant consistently outperformed all other approaches across all crop types. This demonstrates that treating agricultural potential as a continuous variable before discretization better captures the underlying suitability gradient than imposing discrete ordinal thresholds.

We also experimentally proved the importance of temporal modeling. Architectures leveraging temporal information outperformed their counterparts. The 3D UNet family emerged as the most robust architecture for this task, with joint spatio-temporal modeling via 3D convolutions showing the best results. Spectral and temporal ablations further confirmed that visible and infrared spectral bands provide complementary information, and multi-year depth is critical, with the full temporal coverage offering crucial insights on inter-annual variability.

Additionally, our error analysis of 3D UNet revealed that misclassifications were almost exclusively confined to adjacent classes, which is acceptable in real-world agricultural planning.

These findings establish a strong baseline for future work on agricultural potential estimation. Future work could explore extending this evaluation to other geographic regions and crop types, integrating additional data sources such as soil maps and climate variables, and investigating whether continuous suitability scoring could replace the discrete five-level scale entirely.

In conclusion, this study provides clear guidance for integrating deep learning into remote sensing and agricultural planning, demonstrating that with appropriate architectural choices and a focus on temporal and spectral richness, scalable and reliable agricultural potential estimation from satellite time series is achievable.

Acknowledgements. Experiments presented in this paper were carried out using the Grid'5000 testbed, supported by a scientific interest group hosted by Inria and including CNRS, RENATER and several Universities as well as other organizations (see https://www.grid5000.fr).

Funding Information. This work was partially funded by the European Union through the AI4AGRI project entitled "Romanian Excellence Center on Artificial Intelligence on Earth Observation Data for Agriculture", which received funding from the European Union's Horizon Europe research and innovation programme under the grant agreement no. 101079136. The Défi Région Occitanie "Observation de la Terre et Territoire en Transition" also supported this work.

Disclosure of Interests. The authors have no competing interests to declare that are relevant to the content of this article.

References

1. Amigó, E., Gonzalo, J., Mizzaro, S., de Albornoz, J.C.: An effectiveness metric for ordinal classification: formal properties and experimental results. In: Proceedings of the 58th Annual Meeting of the Association for Computational Linguistics, pp. 3938–3949 (2020)

2. Arnab, A., Dehghani, M., Heigold, G., Sun, C., Lučić, M., Schmid, C.: Vivit: a video vision transformer. In: Proceedings of the IEEE/CVF International Conference on Computer Vision, pp. 6836–6846 (2021)
3. Awad, M.M.: A new winter wheat crop segmentation method based on a new fast-unet model and multi-temporal sentinel-2 images. Agronomy **14**(10), 2337 (2024)
4. Belahcène, K., Mousseau, V., Ouerdane, W., Pirlot, M., Sobrie, O.: Multiple criteria sorting models and methods—part i: survey of the literature. 4OR **21**(1), 1–46 (2023)
5. Carlesso, H., Mothe, J., Ionescu, R.T.: Curriculum multi-task self-supervision improves lightweight architectures for onboard satellite hyperspectral image segmentation. arXiv preprint arXiv:2509.13229 (2025)
6. Cong, Y., et al.: Satmae: pre-training transformers for temporal and multi-spectral satellite imagery. Adv. Neural. Inf. Process. Syst. **35**, 197–211 (2022)
7. D'Aniello, M., et al.: Rivers' classification: integrating deep learning and statistical techniques for terrestrial and extraterrestrial drainage networks analysis. Technical report, Copernicus Meetings (2024)
8. Silva, D., Brown, M., D.: Tomato disease detection using multispectral imaging with deep learning models. In: 2024 International Conference on Artificial Intelligence, Big Data, Computing and Data Communication Systems (icABCD), pp. 1–9. IEEE (2024)
9. Duan, Z., et al.: A CNN model for early detection of pepper Phytophthora blight using multispectral imaging, integrating spectral and textural information. Plant Methods **20**(1), 115 (2024)
10. Dumeur, I., Valero, S., Inglada, J.: Self-supervised spatio-temporal representation learning of satellite image time series. IEEE J. Sel. Top. Appl. Earth Obs. Remote Sens. **17**, 4350–4367 (2024)
11. El Sakka, M., De Pourtales, C., Chaari, L., Mothe, J.: Agripotential: a novel multi-spectral and multi-temporal remote sensing dataset for agricultural potentials. In: 2025 International Conference on Content-Based Multimedia Indexing (CBMI), pp. 1–6. IEEE (2025)
12. El Sakka, M., Ivanovici, M., Chaari, L., Mothe, J.: A review of CNN applications in smart agriculture using multimodal data. Sensors **25**(2), 472 (2025)
13. El Sakka, M., Mothe, J., Ivanovici, M.: Images and CNN applications in smart agriculture. Eur. J. Remote Sens. **57**(1), 2352386 (2024)
14. ElMasry, G., Mandour, N., Al-Rejaie, S., Belin, E., Rousseau, D.: Recent applications of multispectral imaging in seed phenotyping and quality monitoring–an overview. Sensors **19**(5), 1090 (2019)
15. Farahani, A., Voghoei, S., Rasheed, K., Arabnia, H.R.: A brief review of domain adaptation. In: Advances in Data Science and Information Engineering: Proceedings from ICDATA 2020 and IKE 2020, pp. 877–894 (2021)
16. Fernandez-Beltran, R., Baidar, T., Kang, J., Pla, F.: Rice-yield prediction with multi-temporal sentinel-2 data and 3D CNN: a case study in Nepal. Remote Sens. **13**(7), 1391 (2021)
17. Food and Agriculture Organization of the United Nations: 6. Agricultural Potential (1998). https://www.fao.org/4/X5872E/x5872e08.htm. Accessed 7 May 2025
18. Garnot, V.S.F., Landrieu, L.: Panoptic segmentation of satellite image time series with convolutional temporal attention networks. In: Proceedings of the IEEE/CVF International Conference on Computer Vision, pp. 4872–4881 (2021)
19. Hong, D., et al.: Spectralgpt: spectral remote sensing foundation model. arXiv preprint arXiv:2311.07113 (2023)

20. Huo, C., et al.: When remote sensing meets foundation model: a survey and beyond. Remote Sens. **17**(2), 179 (2025)
21. Ionescu, B., et al.: Overview of imageclef 2026: multimodal challenges in medicine, science, agritech, and security. In: Experimental IR Meets Multilinguality, Multimodality, and Interaction. Proceedings of the Seventeenth International Conference of the CLEF Association (CLEF 2026), Springer Lecture Notes in Computer Science LNCS, Jena, Germany (2026)
22. Ionescu, B., et al.: Imageclef 2026: multimodal challenges in medicine, science, agritech, and security. In: Advances in Information Retrieval: 48th European Conference on Information Retrieval, ECIR 2026, Delft, The Netherlands, 29 March – 2 April 2026, Proceedings, Part IV, pp. 336–344. Springer, Heidelberg (2026). https://doi.org/10.1007/978-3-032-21321-1_44
23. Kamilaris, A., Prenafeta-Boldú, F.X.: Deep learning in agriculture: a survey. Comput. Electron. Agric. **147**, 70–90 (2018)
24. Karra, K., Kontgis, C., Statman-Weil, Z., Mazzariello, J.C., Mathis, M., Brumby, S.P.: Global land use/land cover with sentinel 2 and deep learning. In: 2021 IEEE International Geoscience and Remote Sensing Symposium IGARSS, pp. 4704–4707. IEEE (2021)
25. Kok, Z.H., Shariff, A.R.M., Alfatni, M.S.M., Khairunniza-Bejo, S.: Support vector machine in precision agriculture: a review. Comput. Electron. Agric. **191**, 106546 (2021)
26. Krichen, M.: Convolutional neural networks: a survey. Computers **12**(8), 151 (2023)
27. Lee, J.C., Byeon, K., Song, B., Kim, K., Kwak, J.T.: Dior-vit: differential ordinal learning vision transformer for cancer classification in pathology images. Med. Image Anal. **105**, 103708 (2025)
28. Liakos, K.G., Busato, P., Moshou, D., Pearson, S., Bochtis, D.: Machine learning in agriculture: a review. Sensors **18**(8), 2674 (2018)
29. Ma, F., Yuan, M., Kozak, I.: Multispectral imaging: review of current applications. Surv. Ophthalmol. **68**(5), 889–904 (2023)
30. Morales-Martín, A., Mesas-Carrascosa, F.J., Gutiérrez, P.A., Pérez-Porras, F.J., Vargas, V.M., Hervás-Martínez, C.: Deep ordinal classification in forest areas using light detection and ranging point clouds. Sensors **24**(7), 2168 (2024)
31. Neptune, N., Mothe, J.: Automatic annotation of change detection images. Sensors **21**(4), 1110 (2021)
32. Ouchra, H., Belangour, A.: Satellite image classification methods and techniques: a survey. In: 2021 IEEE International Conference on Imaging Systems and Techniques (IST), pp. 1–6. IEEE (2021)
33. Qamar, S., Jin, H., Zheng, R., Ahmad, P., Usama, M.: A variant form of 3d-unet for infant brain segmentation. Futur. Gener. Comput. Syst. **108**, 613–623 (2020)
34. Ronneberger, O., Fischer, P., Brox, T.: U-net: convolutional networks for biomedical image segmentation. In: International Conference on Medical Image Computing and Computer-Assisted Intervention, pp. 234–241. Springer (2015)
35. Segarra, J., Buchaillot, M.L., Araus, J.L., Kefauver, S.C.: Remote sensing for precision agriculture: sentinel-2 improved features and applications. Agronomy **10**(5), 641 (2020)
36. Singh, G., Singh, S., Sethi, G., Sood, V.: Deep learning in the mapping of agricultural land use using sentinel-2 satellite data. Geographies **2**(4), 691–700 (2022)
37. Vivien, S.F.G.: U-TAE pre-trained weights on pastis for semantic segmentation (2021). https://doi.org/10.5281/zenodo.5172293
38. Wang, D., et al.: Hypersigma: hyperspectral intelligence comprehension foundation model. IEEE Trans. Pattern Anal. Mach. Intell. (2025)

39. Wang, J., Chen, J., Liu, J., Tang, D., Chen, D.Z., Wu, J.: A survey on ordinal regression: applications, advances and prospects. arXiv preprint arXiv:2503.00952 (2025)
40. Yin, Q., Lin, Z., Hu, W., López-Martínez, C., Ni, J., Zhang, F.: Crop classification of multitemporal polsar based on 3-D attention module with vit. IEEE Geosci. Remote Sens. Lett. **20**, 1–5 (2023)
41. Zhao, X., Wang, L., Zhang, Y., Han, X., Deveci, M., Parmar, M.: A review of convolutional neural networks in computer vision. Artif. Intell. Rev. **57**(4), 99 (2024)

Building a Deep Temporal Emulator of an Ocean Carbon Uptake Model

Sweety Mohanty[1,2](✉), Daniyal Kazempour[1], Andrea Göhring[1], Willi Rath[2], Lavinia Patara[2], and Peer Kröger[1]

[1] University of Kiel, Kiel, Germany
{smo,dka,ang,pkr}@informatik.uni-kiel.de, agoehring@leibniz.uni-kiel.de
[2] GEOMAR Helmholtz Centre for Ocean Research Kiel, Kiel, Germany
{wrath,lpatara}@geomar.de

Abstract. The global ocean carbon sink is a critical component of the Earth's climate but current ocean models are limited in their predictive capabilities because of the high computational cost that a biogeochemical (BGC) model, required to simulate air-sea CO_2 fluxes, entails. Our research investigates the reconstruction of ocean CO_2 flux focusing on local physical oceanographic drivers, such as sea surface temperature, salinity, and sea-ice coverage, which are outputs of the simulations conducted with a global ocean BGC model. We frame the flux estimation problem as a temporal sequence problem and evaluate the efficacy of both Long Short-Term Memory (LSTM) and Temporal Convolutional Networks (TCN) architectures augmented with attention mechanisms. The models ingest eight different physical parameters over a six-month sliding window at each grid point without explicit spatial information, and are designed to identify and weigh the historical physical states that most strongly influence current ocean-atmosphere carbon fluxes. Our framework employs LSTMs to capture sequential dependencies through recurrent hidden states. Moreover, we evaluate TCNs as a distinct alternative that uses dilated convolutions to identify multi-temporal patterns. Besides, we build a probabilistic framework utilizing Gaussian Negative Log-Likelihood (NLL) loss to account for aleatoric uncertainty in the dynamical drivers of ocean CO_2 flux. To ensure credible reconstructions, we apply Conformal Prediction as a post-hoc calibration layer. This methodology yields calibrated uncertainty intervals with guaranteed 95% coverage. Our results show that for most oceanographic regimes deep temporal models can function as reliable digital twins for point-wise carbon flux estimates. The proposed framework provides a data-driven foundation for reconstruction of air-sea carbon fluxes through an AI emulator built upon dynamic physical parameters.

Keywords: ocean carbon · temporal emulator · LSTM · TCN · attention

M. Baratchi et al. (Eds.): ECML PKDD 2026, LNAI 16949, pp. 672–689, 2027.
https://doi.org/10.1007/978-3-032-37682-4_39

1 Introduction

The global ocean absorbs about 25% of anthropogenic carbon emissions each year, making it a key component of the Earth's carbon cycle and climate system [6]. Ocean CO_2 uptake is governed by interacting physical, chemical, and biological processes operating across wide spatial and temporal scales, from mesoscale circulation to multi-decadal carbon storage [9]. Assessments of the ocean carbon cycle combine observations, numerical models, and data-driven approaches, while future projections rely largely on Earth System Models. However, comprehensive biogeochemical (BGC) models that simulate air–sea CO_2 exchange and carbon storage are computationally expensive, especially at high spatial resolution or in large ensemble simulations. As higher ocean resolution becomes essential for accurate climate representation [13], BGC modules often become a major computational bottleneck. While coarsening the BGC grid relative to the physical grid [2] reduces costs, it risks oversimplifying critical bio-physical interactions. An alternative is to develop BGC emulators using deep learning. These neural emulators serve as high-speed surrogates that map physical drivers to biogeochemical outputs, approximating complex numerical simulations at a fraction of the original computational cost. For example, [25] introduced a neural emulator that predicts surface chlorophyll from physical fields with large computational speedups, while [17] demonstrated DL-based reconstruction of phytoplankton dynamics. Building on this idea, we investigate the use of BGC emulators to approximate ocean carbon uptake from physical drivers at full spatial resolution.

Related Works. In addition to the BGC ocean emulators, machine learning's footprint in environmental science has expanded rapidly, ranging from weather detection [16] to wildfire risk assessment [26], research has shifted toward deep learning architectures that can handle the high dimensionality and nonlinearity that baffle traditional geostatistics. While Convolutional Neural Networks (CNNs) excel at spatial tasks like El Niño prediction [12], they often overlook the "environmental memory" critical to the carbon cycle. Sequence models, such as LSTMs, address this by explicitly capturing temporal dependencies. Looking at the existing research landscape, [21] argue, the future of Earth system science lies in hybridizing physical insights with deep learning through neural emulation. Recent efforts include dynamic surrogates for 1D atmospheric models [22], turbulent transport in fusion reactors [3], and regional weather forecasting [20]. Others have successfully emulated Navier–Stokes simulations [5, 19], yet these remain largely restricted to pure fluid dynamics. Our work addresses the remaining gap: emulating the complex, coupled physical-chemical-biological processes of air–sea CO_2 flux while providing the statistical reliability required for climate science.

Addressing the Challenges in Ocean Carbon Reconstruction. Reconstructing global air–sea CO_2 fluxes poses conceptual and technical challenges beyond standard regression. A key difficulty is the nonlinear and non-stationary relationship between physical drivers and chemical responses. Some drivers influence air-sea CO_2 fluxes directly and approximately linearly, such as the sea surface temperature (SST) effect on CO_2 solubility, while others, such as ocean circulation and mixing affect fluxes indirectly through vertical carbon exchange [9]. These processes also regulate nutrient transport and light availability, thereby influencing blooms of CO_2-absorbing phytoplankton. Importantly, such interactions are non-stationary, as surface carbon fluxes often respond with a lag of several months to physical forcing events like vertical mixing. Consequently, accounting for this preconditioning is essential for capturing the temporal dependencies of the system. Capturing these long-term dependencies is challenging because recurrent neural networks can suffer from vanishing gradients [14], while standard convolutional layers have limited temporal receptive fields.

The goal of the proposed carbon flux emulator is therefore to reconstruct spatial (mesoscale to basin-scale) and temporal (monthly to decadal) variability in air-sea CO_2 fluxes while capturing these nonlinear and non-stationary thermal and non-thermal relationships. Two general hypotheses were identified in this context. **H1: Physical surface drivers are sufficient predictors.** Air-sea CO_2 flux variability is primarily governed by physical surface processes representing thermal and non-thermal drivers. Consequently, we select surface physical features that most closely represent these mechanisms. **H2: Lagged relationships are essential.** Air-sea CO_2 fluxes respond to physical forcing with temporal delays (e.g., mixing events influencing biological uptake months later). Therefore, the model must capture non-stationary and lagged dependencies between predictors and target fluxes.

We additionally make three simplifying assumptions that improve computational efficiency while preserving first-order dynamics: **A1: Biological variables are omitted.** Although biology mediates carbon uptake, flux variability depends primarily on physical drivers. Excluding biological predictors allows the model to operate directly on physics-only hydrodynamic simulations. **A2: Surface variables are sufficient.** Fluxes are predicted using surface variables rather than interior 3D fields. We hypothesize that relationships between surface conditions (e.g., wind, currents, temperature) and subsurface circulation can be implicitly learned. This assumption also reduces storage requirements, since surface outputs are routinely archived by ocean models. **A3: Local relationships dominate.** We assume that atmospheric forcing and vertical processes dominate over non-local horizontal interactions. Consequently, the model learns local feature–target relationships only, improving generalizability across hydrodynamic models.

We, hence, propose a temporal deep learning framework that combines sequence models with conformal calibration to ensure robustness against variations in spatio-temporal data. The model is trained using a Gaussian Negative Log-Likelihood (NLL) loss [18], enabling the prediction of both the expected CO_2 flux and a heteroscedastic uncertainty that varies across climatic conditions. To rectify the inherent miscalibration of neural networks [10], a post-hoc conformal calibration step adjusts these estimates to provide guaranteed prediction intervals. Together, this framework provides a computationally efficient and statistically reliable emulator for reconstructing global air–sea CO_2 flux variability.

Guiding Questions: While building the proposed deep temporal framework, our work was shaped by the following research questions: 1) How well can a local Deep Learning (DL) based emulator reconstruct global air-sea CO_2 fluxes and what is the relevance of including ocean memory? 2) Is the DL model capable of capturing seasonal and year-to-year variations of air-sea CO_2 fluxes distinctive of various ocean regimes? 3) Is our locally-constructed DL model capable of reconstructing both large-scale and small-scale spatial structures without relying on the location details?

2 Methods

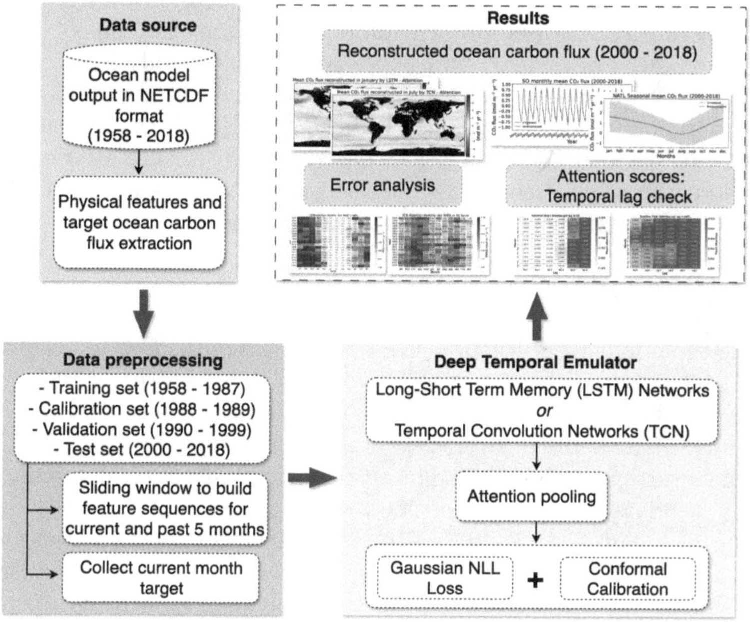

Fig. 1. A deep temporal emulator workflow for air-sea CO_2 flux reconstruction.

Our work reconstructs air–sea CO_2 flux using a deep learning framework that maps physical ocean states to biogeochemical outcomes. Using NEMO-based ocean simulations (Sect. 2.1), we replace computationally expensive biogeochemical equations with a data-driven approach capable of learning non-linear physical–flux relationships. The workflow is illustrated in Fig. 1. Physical drivers and target CO_2 flux are collected from 61 years of monthly model output and preprocessed into six-month sequential inputs for training, calibration, validation, and testing. Two models are then trained and evaluated: an LSTM-based and a TCN-based architecture, both enhanced with attention mechanisms, Gaussian NLL loss, and conformal calibration.

2.1 Data

We base our analysis on simulations from the global ocean sea-ice model NEMO-LIM2 [11], coupled with a biogeochemical model including marine carbon cycle [4]. The ocean model operates at a horizontal resolution of approximately 0.25°, corresponding to a grid of 1021 × 1442 latitude–longitude points, and includes 46 vertical ocean levels. Since air-sea CO_2 flux exchange occurs at the ocean surface, our study focuses exclusively on the uppermost model layer. The simulation is forced with atmospheric reanalysis data [23] spanning the period 1958–2018. Land points are masked during preprocessing to account for the lack of terrestrial data.

We extracted 9 metrics from the monthly ORCA025-MOPS output: sea surface temperature (SST), sea surface salinity (SSS), sea ice, mixed layer depth (MLD), downward heat flux, upward freshwater flux, wind stress curl, surface ocean current curl and preindustrial air-sea CO_2 flux whose direction is defined throughout the paper as positive into the ocean. To isolate the signal from atmospheric trends, we focused on natural CO_2 flux (FCO_2 hence after) rather than total flux. Furthermore, we omitted latitude and longitude as input features to ensure the model remained entirely location-agnostic.

2.2 Input and Target Set-Up

To include the influence of features from previous months for the reconstruction of FCO_2 for the current month, we formalize this by adopting a sliding window approach. Let $X_t \in \mathbb{R}^P$ represent a vector of P physical state variables including SST, salinity, MLD, sea-ice coverage, etc. at time t. Here, P=8, that is the total number of features considered. The input tensor $\mathbf{X}_{seq}$ for a single prediction over 6 monthly windows is defined as: $\mathbf{X}_{seq} = [X_{t-5}, X_{t-4}, X_{t-3}, X_{t-2}, X_{t-1}, X_t]$. The shape of array $\mathbf{X}_{seq}$ is (6,8) with 6 rows lagged samples for 8 different features. This 6-month temporal window allows the models to integrate the seasonal signals driving FCO_2. Unlike the input space, which incorporates a temporal history, the target space is defined as the instantaneous air-sea FCO_2 value for the current month (t). We specifically collect the FCO_2 output from the simulation to serve as the ground truth y_t. After building the input and target space, we normalize the features with mean set to zero and stand deviation set to one.

2.3 Temporal Deep Learning Framework

After building the necessary input and target arrays, we define our deep learning based models to map the temporal relationships between the physical parameters and FCO_2. We apply two sequence models to reconstruct monthly air–sea

FCO_2 from physical drivers: Long Short-Term Memory (LSTM) networks [8] and Temporal Convolutional Networks (TCN) [1]. Both architectures are augmented with a temporal attention pooling layer to identify informative temporal lags and with a heteroscedastic regression head that predicts both the conditional mean and variance of the target.

Long-Short Term Memory (LSTM) Network Augmented with Attention: Recurrent neural networks (RNNs) are commonly used to model temporal dependencies in sequential data. However, standard RNNs struggle with long-range relationships because gradients may vanish or explode during training. The Long Short-Term Memory (LSTM) architecture addresses this limitation by introducing memory cells and gating mechanisms that regulate information flow [14].

At each time step, LSTM maintains a hidden state h_t and cell state c_t. Three internal mechanisms (the input, forget, and output gates) regulate how new information is incorporated, past information is retained, and the internal state influences the output. The input gate determines how much of the candidate memory update enters the cell. The forget gate controls the proportion of the previous cell state that is preserved. The output gate regulates how much of the cell state contributes to the output. These mechanisms enable LSTMs to capture long-term temporal dependencies more effectively than standard RNNs. Given an input sequence of length T, the LSTM produces hidden states $H = (h_1, \ldots, h_T), \quad h_t \in \mathbb{R}^H$ which encode the temporal dynamics of the input features. Instead of relying solely on the final hidden state, a temporal attention pooling layer aggregates information across all time steps.

Temporal Convolution Neural Network augmented with Attention: Temporal Convolutional Networks (TCNs) provide an alternative to recurrent architectures for sequence modeling by using causal and dilated convolutions to capture temporal dependencies [1]. A dilated convolution with dilation factor d is defined as $y_t = \sum_{k=0}^{K-1} w_k x_{t-(dk)}$ where K is the kernel size. Increasing dilation exponentially across layers enables the receptive field to grow without a proportional increase in depth. Following the standard TCN formulation, our model stacks residual convolutional blocks with exponentially increasing dilation factors $d_i = 2^i$ where i is the layer index.

Each temporal block in TCN consists of weight-normalized 1D convolutions, ReLU activations, dropout regularization, and residual connections. Residual learning stabilizes training of deep convolutional networks and improves gradient flow. Given an input tensor $X \in \mathbb{R}^{B \times T \times F}$ the TCN produces temporal feature maps $Z \in \mathbb{R}^{B \times C \times T}$ where B is the batch size, $T = 6$ or the sequence length, $F = 8$ or the number of features, and C represents the number of hidden channels (filters) used in the convolutional layers. The feature maps encode hierarchical temporal patterns. Similar to LSTM, instead of global average pooling technique in TCNs, we rely on attention pooling across the temporal dimension to identify informative lags.

2.4 Temporal Attention Pooling

To explicitly identify influential temporal lags, we apply an attention mechanism [24] over the sequence representations. This allow models to dynamically weight different time steps according to their relevance to the prediction task. Given sequence representations $H = (h_1, \ldots, h_T)$, we compute attention scores $e_t = w^\top h_t$ and normalized attention weights $\alpha_t = \frac{\exp(e_t)}{\sum_{j=1}^{T} \exp(e_j)}$. The final context vector c is a weighted sum $c = \sum_{t=1}^{T} \alpha_t h_t$ where $\sum_{t=1}^{T} \alpha_t = 1$.

The attention formulation is consistent across both models but operates on architecture-specific sequence representations. In the LSTM model, attention is applied to the sequence of hidden states h_t. Each hidden state summarizes the input history through recurrent memory. Hence, the attention weights identify which time steps in the recurrent memory contribute most strongly to the prediction. In the TCN architecture, attention operates on convolutional feature maps z_t. Each z_t represents hierarchical features extracted through dilated convolutions. Attention, therefore, selects which temporal receptive field locations holds the most predictive information. As TCNs look at the past in chunks of different sizes, their attention mechanism can pinpoint specific patterns at different time intervals. In contrast, LSTM attention focuses more on the model's internal summary of the past.

2.5 Probabilistic Reconstruction Using Gaussian NLL

Standard regression models are typically trained using Mean Squared Error (MSE), which assumes all inputs are equally reliable. In complex physical systems, however, observations often contain varying levels of noise and ambiguity. Predicting only a single deterministic value therefore ignores important information about data uncertainty. To address this, we adopt a probabilistic framework that explicitly models **aleatoric uncertainty**. Thus, the aforementioned context vector c is now passed to two regression heads predicting the **mean** FCO_2 $\mu(y') = W_\mu c + b_\mu$ and **log-variance** $\log \sigma^2(y') = W_\sigma c + b_\sigma$ of the target, which enables **heteroscedastic regression**, allowing predictive uncertainty to vary across samples. By assuming the target distribution is Gaussian, we can optimize the network using the Gaussian Negative Log-Likelihood (NLL) loss over n number of observations (or data points) in the training batch is $\mathcal{L}(\theta)$ (as shown in Eq. 1) where θ represents the learnable parameters of DL models. $\mu(x_i)$ and $\sigma^2(x_i)$ are the mean and variance of the predicted CO_2 calculated for input batch x_i with n samples and $x_i \in \mathbf{X}_{seq}$.

$$\mathcal{L}(\theta) = \frac{1}{2n} \sum_{i=1}^{n} \left(\frac{(y_i - \mu(x_i))^2}{\sigma^2(x_i)} + \log \sigma^2(x_i) \right) \quad (1)$$

This approach captures heteroscedasticity, where noise varies across inputs. In the reconstruction of FCO_2 from physical drivers, some regions are inherently noisier than others, making a single global variance inadequate. Gaussian NLL allows the model to learn input-dependent uncertainty, improving the mean prediction $\mu(x_i)$ while providing a useful confidence estimate for the output.

2.6 Uncertainty Quantification

Although Gaussian NLL enables a model to estimate predictive uncertainty, these estimates are often heuristic rather than reliable guarantees. Deep learning models are frequently miscalibrated [10], producing overly narrow confidence intervals that still miss the true value. Such overconfidence makes uncertainty estimates unreliable for scientific use. To address this, we apply Conformal Prediction as a *post-hoc calibration layer*, which calibrates the model's uncertainty using a held-out calibration set and converts raw variance estimates of the model into statistically valid prediction intervals. As a result, a claimed confidence level set to 95% is supported by a distribution-free coverage guarantee, regardless of the underlying noise distribution. Using calibration set we calculate a non-conformity score S_i, representing the error of the model relative to its predicted uncertainty as shown in Algorithm 1. By approximating the $(1-\alpha)$ quantile of these scores (denoted as $\hat{q}_{1-\alpha}$), we can construct a 95% prediction interval (i.e. $\alpha = 0.05$) for any new prediction: $\hat{C}(X_{test}) = [\mu(X_{test}) \pm \hat{q}_{1-\alpha} \cdot \sigma(X_{test})]$. This ensures that the predicted intervals are statistically valid regardless of the underlying data distribution.

Algorithm 1: Conformal Calibration for Uncertainty Quantization

Input : Trained model $\mathcal{M}$ (outputting mean μ and variance σ^2);
Calibration dataset $\mathcal{D}_{cal} = \{(x_i, y_i)\}_{i=1}^{n}$;
Target error level $\alpha = 0.05$ for 95% coverage;
Small constant $\epsilon > 0$ for numerical stability.
Output: Calibrated quantile threshold $\hat{q}_{1-\alpha}$.

Initialize empty list of non-conformity scores $\mathcal{S} \leftarrow \emptyset$
foreach *batch* (X, y) *in* $\mathcal{D}_{cal}$ **do**
  $\mu, \log(\sigma^2) \leftarrow \mathcal{M}(X)$ `// Forward pass`
  $\sigma \leftarrow \exp(0.5 \cdot \log(\sigma^2))$
  foreach *sample i in batch* **do**
    Compute non-conformity score: $s_i \leftarrow \frac{|y_i - \mu_i|}{\sigma_i + \epsilon}$
    $\mathcal{S} \leftarrow \mathcal{S} \cup \{s_i\}$
  end
end
$n \leftarrow |\mathcal{S}|$ `// Total number of calibration samples`
$k \leftarrow \lceil (n+1)(1-\alpha) \rceil$
$k \leftarrow \min(\max(k, 1), n)$
$\hat{q}_{1-\alpha} \leftarrow$ the k-th smallest value in $\mathcal{S}$
return $\hat{q}_{1-\alpha}$

2.7 Experimental Setup

The dataset was partitioned chronologically to prevent temporal data leakage during training and evaluation. Data from 1958 till 1987 was used for the training set, while the model was calibrated with data from 1988 to 1989. The validation set contained samples from 1990–1999 and the test set were data from 2000–2018. After building individual $\mathbf{X}_{seq}$ we chose 2 million sequences, 100k sequences, 500k sequences (25% of the training sample size) respectively as training, calibration, and validation sets for the model training process as we had limited access to GPU computing nodes. We normalized the above sequences with mean at zero and standard deviation set to one. Then both DL models are trained for 200 epochs using the Adam optimizer [15] with a learning rate of 10^{-4} and a heteroscedastic Gaussian Negative Log-Likelihood (NLL) loss. Our LSTM model builds upon 2 hidden layers, 128 hidden units, and a dropout rate of 0.1, whereas the TCN model includes 3 convolutional blocks with 64 channels each, a kernel size of $K = 3$, and a dropout rate of 0.1 with Attention layer built on Softmax activation function [7]. To quantify the deterministic accuracy of our emulators, we evaluate their performance using Root Mean Squared Error (RMSE) and Mean Absolute Error (MAE).

3 Results and Discussion

I. Ablation Study: An analysis of the ablation study presented in Table 1 reveals an inherent trade-off between deterministic point-accuracy and probabilistic calibration within our temporal emulators. Incorporating temporal attention mechanisms without calibration (Experiments 2 and 5) yields the lowest deterministic errors, with the TCN and LSTM achieving RMSE values of 0.4826 mol m^{-2} yr^{-1} and 0.4591 mol m^{-2} yr^{-1}, respectively. While the introduction of post-hoc calibration introduces a slight penalty to point accuracy, increasing the RMSE to 0.5204 mol m^{-2} yr^{-1} for the TCN (Experiment 3) and 0.5230 mol m^{-2} yr^{-1} for the LSTM (Experiment 6), it provides essential probabilistic reliability. The differences in standard error metrics reflect stochastic variation between independent training runs, rather than an effect of conformal calibration. Ultimately, Experiments 3 and 6 were selected as our optimal configurations because they uniquely bridge the gap between physical interpretability and statistical reliability. By combining attention-driven lag detection with robust post-hoc calibration, these configurations provide trustworthy error bars ($\hat{q}_{1-\alpha}$) that are vital for physical applications like ocean carbon flux (FCO_2) modeling, fully justifying the minor increase in deterministic error.

II. Model Calibration: The scaling factor $\hat{q}_{1-\alpha}$ returned by LSTM and TCN models after training were 2.1951 and 1.9610 respectively (See Table 1). This highlights the distinct calibration behaviors between the two architectures. The $\hat{q}_{1-\alpha}$ of TCN aligned almost perfectly with the theoretical Gaussian threshold of 1.96, suggesting that its predicted variance was intrinsically well-calibrated. Conversely, the LSTM's $\hat{q}_{1-\alpha}$ indicated an initial state of model overconfidence. This required a more significant post-hoc adjustment to expand the predictive intervals of LSTM, ensuring that the rigorous 95% coverage guarantee was maintained. These results suggested that the TCN architecture was more naturally adept at quantifying the aleatoric uncertainty inherent in oceanographic drivers.

Table 1. Ablation Study. Our work details on the outcome of the two experiments highlighted (Experiment no. 3 and 6) in this table. The RMSE and MAE values (in mol m^{-2} yr^{-1}) are calculated over the test set from 2000–2018 between simulated and reconstructed FCO_2.

Exp. No.	Temporal Emulator Experiments	RMSE	MAE	Calibration	Lag Detection
1.	LSTM with NLL Loss + Calibration	0.518461	0.289833	$\hat{q}_{1-\alpha}$=2.2126	Absent
2.	LSTM with NLL Loss + No Calibration + Attention	0.459154	0.285933	Absent	Present
3.	LSTM with NLL Loss + Calibration + Attention	0.523036	0.293607	$\hat{q}_{1-\alpha}$=2.1951	Present
4.	TCN with NLL Loss + Calibration	0.531841	0.310625	$\hat{q}_{1-\alpha}$=1.9483	Absent
5.	TCN with NLL Loss + No Calibration + Attention	0.482644	0.304589	Absent	Present
6.	TCN with NLL Loss + Calibration + Attention	0.520452	0.304779	$\hat{q}_{1-\alpha}$=1.9610	Present

III. FCO_2 Reconstruction Maps: The spatial performance of the proposed models is assessed by comparing reconstructed FCO_2 with NEMO simulations for January and July (Fig. 2). Both the LSTM-Attention and TCN-Attention models capture the main large-scale patterns, including tropical outgassing, winter outgassing in the Southern Hemisphere high latitudes, and strong carbon uptake in the Northern Hemisphere mid-latitudes. Point-wise RMSE values are generally low and spatially consistent, indicating robust performance as a surrogate for the biogeochemical model. The models also maintain low errors across seasonal regimes, suggesting that the attention mechanism effectively selects relevant temporal information. In addition to large-scale structures, the models reproduce fine spatial gradients such as coastal boundary currents and mesoscale features. Higher errors occur mainly in coastal upwelling regions and sea-ice-covered areas during Northern Hemisphere winter, where non-local processes not represented by local surface features likely play a stronger role in driving FCO_2 variability.

A key result of this study is the accurate reconstruction of global spatial patterns (Fig. 2) despite the models being location-agnostic. Neither the TCN nor the LSTM received latitude or longitude as inputs, yet both captured complex FCO_2 structures, including sharp boundary current gradients and the North Atlantic sink. This indicates that the physical drivers (SST, salinity, ice coverage, MLD, etc.) act as effective proxies for geographic location. Because ocean physical properties follow distinct regional and latitudinal regimes, the models learn their characteristic signatures and implicitly infer the geographic context needed to estimate carbon flux. The success of this coordinate-free approach reflects both the physical consistency of the NEMO simulations and the models' ability to link local physical conditions to carbon flux. Because air–sea CO_2 exchange is largely governed by local solubility and circulation-driven gradients, the models can estimate the flux without explicit spatial coordinates. This suggests the models learn the underlying physical relationships rather than memorizing spatial patterns. As a result, the approach offers strong potential for transfer learning, enabling application across different grid resolutions or observational datasets without relying on fixed spatial structures that may change under climate warming.

IV. Reconstruction Error Analysis: Figure 3 provides a detailed temporal breakdown of model performance, illustrating the stability of the reconstruction tool across nearly two decades of varying climatic conditions. Monthly RMSE heatmaps for the Global Ocean (a, b), North Atlantic (c, d) between 75–0° W and 10–70° N, and Southern Ocean (e, f) between 45–77° S reveal consistently low errors under varying climatic conditions. Globally, RMSE remains stable around 0.5 mol m^{-2} yr^{-1}, demonstrating reliable large-scale reconstruction over decadal timescales. A clear seasonal pattern appears in the North Atlantic, where errors are lower in summer (June–August) than in winter (January–March). This may partly reflect larger winter flux magnitudes, but could also indicate that summer flux variability is dominated by more predictable thermal drivers such as SST, whereas winter dynamics are influenced by harder-to-model non-thermal processes like deep convective mixing. Future feature relevance analyses could help test this hypothesis. Comparing the LSTM-Attention and TCN-Attention results side-by-side across these basins shows almost identical error distributions and intensities. This confirms that the predictive skill is driven by the robust extraction of physical features rather than specific architectural biases.

V. Reconstruction of Monthly Means and Seasonality: The carbon cycle shows distinct dynamics in the Northern and Southern Hemispheres. Figure 4 demonstrates the temporal and seasonal performance of the reconstruction tool in two key basins: the North Atlantic (NATL) and the Southern Ocean (SO). Panels (a, c, e, g) show the interannual monthly mean FCO_2, where the reconstructed signal closely follows the simulated ground truth over the 19-year test period. This strong agreement indicates that the models capture year-to-year variability despite using only a 5-month memory window. Panels (b, d, f, h) further assess the seasonal climatology, evaluating the model's ability to reproduce the periodic carbon cycle. Both the LSTM-Attention and TCN-Attention models reproduce the characteristic seasonal trough–peak patterns in each basin. In the North Atlantic, winter shows the strongest uptake due to colder SSTs (thermal control), while in the Southern Ocean winter exhibits stronger CO_2 outgassing driven by wind-induced upwelling of carbon-rich deep waters (non-thermal control). The shaded variance bands indicate that the models capture not only the mean behavior but also the natural interannual variability of the NEMO simulation. Both models reconstruct FCO_2 accurately but show subtle architectural differences. The LSTM-Attention model produces smoother seasonal transitions

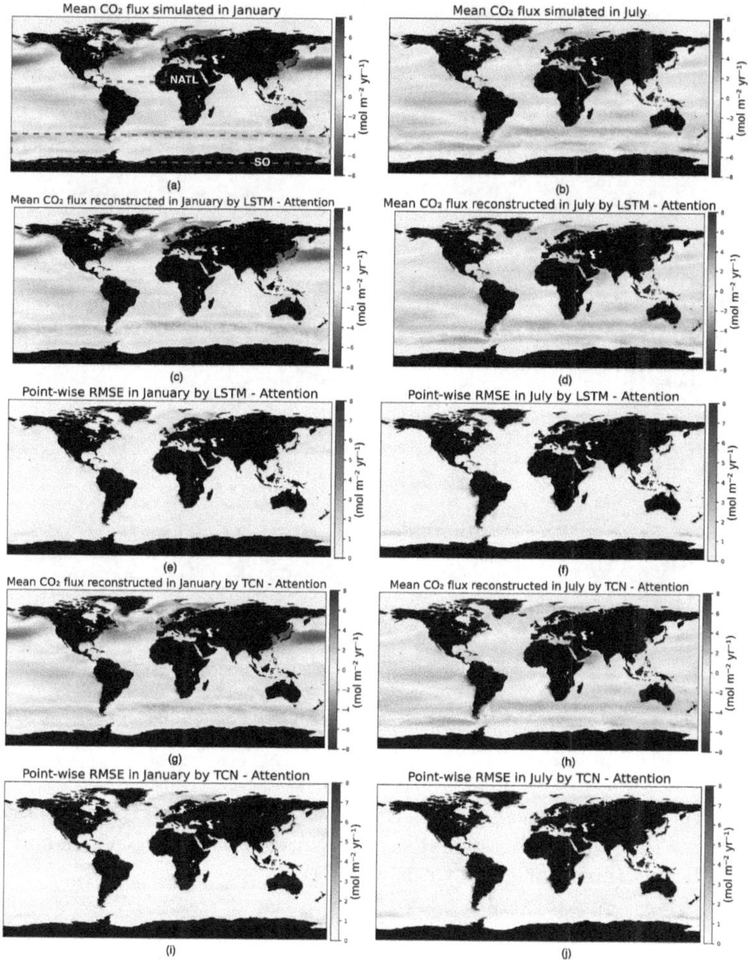

Fig. 2. LSTM-Attention and TCN-Attention test outcome: Mean reconstruction and RMSE over 19 test years (2000–2018), in January (left column) and in July (right column) a-b) Model "ground truth" with contours showing boundaries of two basins - North Atlantic (NATL) between 75–0° W and 10–70° N and Southern Ocean (SO) between 45–77° S. c-f) Mean reconstruction and RMSE by LSTM-Attention, g-j) Mean reconstruction and RMSE by TCN-Attention. **Positive values of flux imply absorption and negative values of flux imply carbon emission.**

(Fig. 4 b, d), indicating strong representation of longer temporal dependencies within the six-month window. In contrast, the TCN-Attention model (Fig. 4 f, h) responds more sharply to high-amplitude seasonal peaks, particularly in the Southern Ocean, likely due to its dilated convolutional structure. Despite these differences, the close agreement between the models provides strong cross-

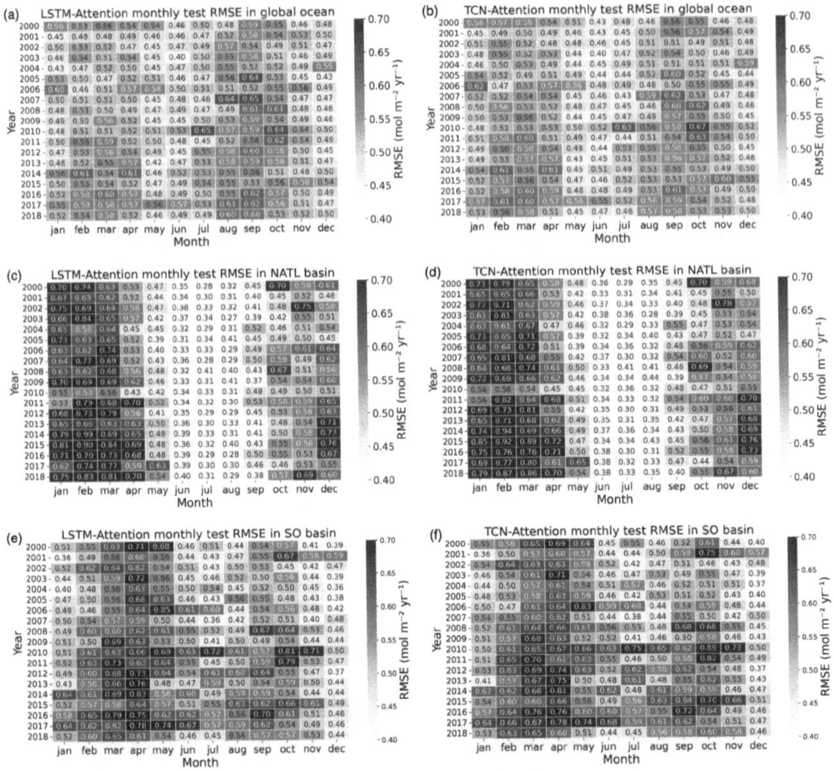

Fig. 3. Monthly RMSE Heatmaps for LSTM-Attention and TCN-Attention models over test years (2000–2018) in global ocean, North Atlantic (NATL) and Southern Ocean (SO) basins (boundaries shown in Fig. 2a).

validation, suggesting the framework captures stable physical–biogeochemical relationships rather than architecture-specific artifacts.

VI. Temporal Lag Analysis: To understand which time period influenced the CO_2 prediction the most, we relied on the attention scores. Figure 5 visualizes how the attention mechanisms distributed weight across the 6-month temporal window (lag-0 to lag-5). The heatmaps reveal a clear hierarchy in temporal importance. In both NATL and SO, the current month (lag-0) consistently receives the highest attention score. This is physically intuitive, as air-sea FCO_2 is heavily driven by instantaneous SST and stratification. Non-zero weights for lag-1 through lag-5 confirm the models utilize "ocean memory," leveraging prior physical states that dictate CO_2 absorption and release. We observe a striking difference in how the two architectures distribute this attention scores. **LSTM-Attention (Fig. 5 a, b):** The attention is extremely concentrated, with over 98–99% of the weight placed on the current month (lag-0) and the immediate previous month (lag-1). The recurrent nature of LSTM naturally carries information forward through its hidden state, which may lead the attention mechanism

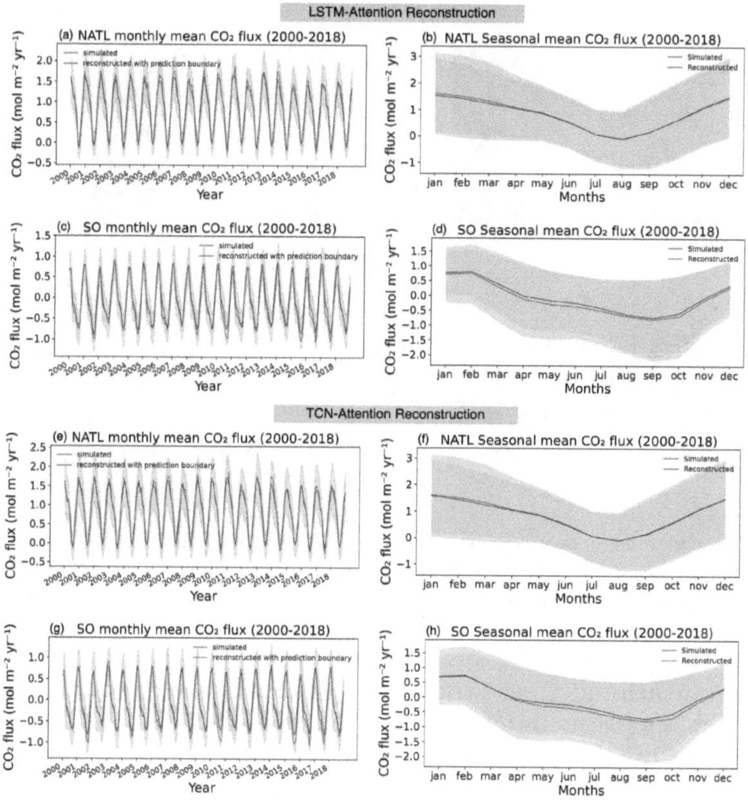

Fig. 4. Basin reconstruction results (monthly mean and seasonal mean) over test years (2000–2018) in North Atlantic (NATL) and Southern Ocean (SO) basins. Panel a, c, e, and g show the predictive boundary along with the predicted CO_2 values as returned by the models. Panel b, d, f, and h show standard deviation for both simulated and reconstructed carbon values for NATL and SO (boundaries shown in Fig. 2a).

to focus only on the end-stage refined features. **TCN-Attention (Fig. 5c, d):** The TCN exhibits a much broader receptive field. While lag-0 remains dominant (approx. 60–70%), significant weight is distributed across the entire 5-month history. In the NATL (Fig. 5 c) we see a notable increase in attention for lags 2 and 3 during the spring months (March–May), likely capturing the physical precursors to the spring bloom. We observe this difference in the distribution of attention scores because TCNs use dilated convolutions to examine the entire window simultaneously. This allows the attention head to capture the raw physical features of past months without them being filtered through several recurrent gates (as in an LSTM). While the LSTM might achieve similar accuracy, its attention maps are putting almost 100% of its focus on a single time step (usually the current month, lag-0) providing little insight into preconditioning drivers, which instead can be better learned by the broader distribution of TCN.

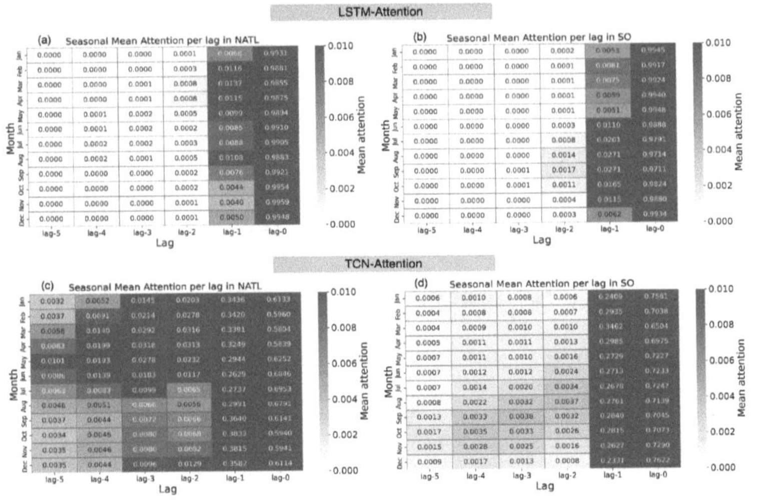

Fig. 5. Mean attention scores over test years (2000–2018) in North Atlantic (NATL) and Southern Ocean (SO) basins. Colorbar scales are tailored to highlight the subtle variations in attention scores and the basin boundaries are shown in Fig. 2a.

VII. Computational Cost Analysis: To quantify the computational advantages of our approach, we compared the inference runtime of our DL emulators against the execution time of the traditional, fully coupled physical-biogeochemical ocean model. The conventional ocean model at a horizontal resolution of 0.25°, 120 vertical levels, 4 physical prognostic variables, and 10 BGC tracers requires approximately 7 h per simulation year for 100% of the grid points, meaning a full 60-year experiment demands 420 h (7 hours/year × 60 years) of compute time across a cluster of 21 nodes (96 cores each). Crucially, 70% of this heavy computational load (5 h per simulation year) is driven purely by solving the equations for the 10 BGC tracers. In stark contrast, our DL emulators bypass this BGC bottleneck entirely by training exclusively on physical parameters. While building the DL models on a small fraction of the total 6-months windows collected over 40 years took roughly 3.5 h, the resulting model achieves an inference time of just 4 min per simulation year for 100% of the grid points. When we aim to generalize the DL model on a 60-year full experiment, the emulator completes the entire run in only 4 h on a single GPU node (4 minutes/year × 60 years = 240 minutes). Consequently, replacing the traditional model with our DL framework reduces the total execution time from extra 300 h (420 hours × $\frac{10\ \text{BGC tracers}}{14\ \text{total tracers}}$) to just 4 h, representing a massive 105-fold computational speedup ($\frac{420\ \text{hours}}{4\ \text{hours}}$) while simultaneously freeing up valuable cluster infrastructure by moving from 21 multi-CPU computing nodes to a single GPU. Furthermore, once trained, the DL approach parallelizes trivially across multiple devices, where scaling to N GPUs reduces the inference runtime to $1/N$. This stands in sharp contrast to the coupled physics-BGC model, where spatial parallelization rapidly encounters diminishing returns due to communication overhead, and strict temporal causality prevents any viable parallelization across time.

4 Conclusion, Lessons Learned, and Future Outlook

In this work, we presented a deep learning based framework for the reconstruction of air-sea CO_2 fluxes as an accurate, low-cost emulator for complex biogeochemical models. Using only physical ocean variables such as SST, salinity, and mixed layer depth, the approach avoids the high computational cost of explicitly running a biogeochemical model. Evaluation over 19 years of simulations (2000–2018) shows that both TCN and LSTM architectures with attention can reconstruct global and basin-scale fluxes with high spatial and temporal accuracy.

Some of the significant insights gained from this project are: i) Deep temporal models reconstructed global air-sea CO_2 fluxes effectively, with attention scores revealing lagged contributions. ii) The architectural differences between two DL models produced **different attention scores**. The sparse attention maps of the LSTM suggest that temporal reasoning occurs mainly in hidden states rather than in the attention layer. iii) "Ocean memory" is not uniform: different basins (e.g., North Atlantic vs. Southern Ocean) require different temporal weighting, indicating the need for **regionally aware attention mechanisms.** iv) The models captured both **seasonal and interannual variability** in air–sea CO_2 fluxes across ocean regimes. v) Locally trained models reconstructed both **large- and small-scale spatial structures** vi) Overall, the models recovered **realistic spatial air-sea CO_2 flux patterns** without explicit location information.

Several avenues remain open for future investigation. For instance, 1) an analysis of feature relevance would help to interpret the seasonality of the RMSE and would enhance explainability, 2) the generalization to other hydrodynamic models and forcing scenarios (notably, global warming) would widen the applicability of the DL model, 3) the inclusion of spatial dynamics and of the vertical dimension of the ocean could improve the reconstruction of coastal and sea ice-covered regions, and 4) validating the emulators' predictions against observational estimates of real-world ocean carbon sink dynamics.

To conclude, our results demonstrate that deep learning can capture the nonlinear, time-delayed relationships between surface ocean physical state and air-sea CO_2 fluxes. The use of multiple temporal architectures also demonstrates the flexibility and scalability of the proposed framework paving the path for reconstructing high-resolution carbon flux from physics-only ocean simulations, potentially accelerating climate monitoring while reducing the computational cost of traditional biogeochemical modeling.

Code and Data Availability. Our Python-based code is available here. Due to storage constraints associated with the large size of the dataset, a public repository is not currently maintained. Inquiries regarding access to the ocean model output should be directed to Sweety Mohanty (smo@informatik.uni-kiel.de) and Lavinia Patara (lpatara@geomar.de) via email.

Acknowledgements. The experiments were performed at the National High Performance Computing (NHR; Project shk00050). L. Patara acknowledges funding from Project PA 3075/2-1 by the German Research Foundation. AI-assisted technologies, including Gemini and Grammarly, were utilized to enhance the text structure and ensure grammatical accuracy in this document.

Disclosure of Interests. The authors have no competing interests to declare.

References

1. Bai, S., Kolter, J.Z., Koltun, V.: An empirical evaluation of generic convolutional and recurrent networks for sequence modeling (2018). https://arxiv.org/abs/1803.01271
2. Bricaud, C., et al.: Multi-grid algorithm for passive tracer transport in the nemo ocean circulation model: a case study with the nemo OGCM (version 3.6). Geosci. Model Dev. **13**(11), 5465–5483 (2020)
3. Cao, Y., et al.: TGLF-SINN: deep learning surrogate model for accelerating turbulent transport modeling in fusion. arXiv preprint arXiv:2509.07024 (2025)
4. Chien, C.T., Durgadoo, J.V.: Foci-mops v1-integration of marine biogeochemistry within the flexible ocean and climate infrastructure version 1 (foci 1) earth system model. In: Geoscientific Model Development Discussions (2022)
5. Dutta, S., Innan, N., Yahia, S.B., Shafique, M.: AQ-PINNs: attention-enhanced quantum physics-informed neural networks for carbon-efficient climate modeling. arXiv preprint arXiv:2409.01626 (2024)
6. Friedlingstein, P., et al.: Global carbon budget 2024. Earth Syst. Sci. Data Discuss. **2024**, 1–133 (2024)
7. Goodfellow, I., Bengio, Y., Courville, A., Bengio, Y.: Deep Learning, vol. 1. MIT Press, Cambridge (2016)
8. Graves, A.: Long short-term memory. Supervised sequence labelling with recurrent neural networks, pp. 37–45 (2012)
9. Gruber, N., et al.: Trends and variability in the ocean carbon sink. Nat. Rev. Earth Environ. **4**(2), 119–134 (2023)
10. Guo, C., Pleiss, G., Sun, Y., Weinberger, K.Q.: On calibration of modern neural networks. In: International Conference on Machine Learning, pp. 1321–1330. PMLR (2017)
11. Gurvan, M., Bourdallé-Badie, R., et al.: Nemo ocean engine (2022)
12. Ham, Y.G., Kim, J.H., Luo, J.J.: Deep learning for multi-year enso forecasts. Nature **573**(7775), 568–572 (2019)
13. Hewitt, H.T., et al.: Resolving and parameterising the ocean mesoscale in earth system models. Curr. Clim. Change Rep. **6**(4), 137–152 (2020)
14. Hochreiter, S., Schmidhuber, J.: Long short-term memory. Neural Comput. **9**(8), 1735–1780 (1997)
15. Kingma, D.P., Ba, J.: Adam: a method for stochastic optimization. arXiv preprint arXiv:1412.6980 (2014)
16. Lacombe, R., Grossman, H., Hendren, L.P., Ludeke, D.: Improving extreme weather events detection with light-weight neural networks. In: ICLR 2023 Workshop on Tackling Climate Change with Machine Learning (2023)

17. Lakra, M., Fablet, R., Drumetz, L., Pauthenet, E., Martinez, E.: Static and autoregressive neural emulation of phytoplankton biomass dynamics from physical predictors in the global ocean (2026). https://arxiv.org/abs/2602.04689
18. Lakshminarayanan, B., Pritzel, A., Blundell, C.: Simple and scalable predictive uncertainty estimation using deep ensembles. In: Advances in Neural Information Processing Systems, p. 30 (2017)
19. Lee, A., Mobarrat, M., Chen, X.: Periodicity-enforced neural network for designing deterministic lateral displacement devices (2025)
20. Munir, M.A., Khan, F.S., Khan, S.: Efficient localized adaptation of neural weather forecasting: a case study in the mena region. arXiv preprint arXiv:2409.07585 (2024)
21. Reichstein, M., et al.: Deep learning and process understanding for data-driven earth system science. Nature **566**(7743), 195–204 (2019)
22. Tahseen, T., Nikolaou, N., Simões, L.F., Yip, K.H., Mendonça, J.M., Waldmann, I.P.: Adaptive online emulation for accelerating complex physical simulations. arXiv preprint arXiv:2508.08012 (2025)
23. Tsujino, H., et al.: JRA-55 based surface dataset for driving ocean-sea-ice models (jra55-do). Ocean Model. **130**, 79–139 (2018)
24. Vaswani, A., et al.: Attention is all you need. In: Advances in Neural Information Processing Systems, vol. 30 (2017)
25. Wu, B., Zheng, S., Li, S., Wang, S.: Neural emulator based on physical fields for accelerating the simulation of surface chlorophyll in an earth system model. Ocean Model. **195**, 102491 (2025)
26. Xie, Y., et al.: Wildfiregpt: tailored large language model for wildfire analysis. In: NeurIPS 2024 Workshop on Tackling Climate Change with Machine Learning (2024)

HADT: A Heterogeneous Multi-agent Differential Transformer for Autonomous Earth Observation Satellite Cluster

Mohamad A. Hady[1(✉)], Muhammad Anwar Masum[1], Siyi Hu[2], Mahardhika Pratama[1], Zehong Cao[1], and Ryszard Kowalczyk[1,3]

[1] School of Computer Science and Information Technology, Adelaide University, Adelaide, SA 5095, Australia
{mohamad.hady,muhammadanwar.masum,dhika.pratama,jimmy.cao, ryszard.kowalczyk}@adelaide.edu.au

[2] School of Electrical Engineering, Computing and Mathematical Sciences (EECMS), Curtin University, Kent St, Bentley, WA 6102, Australia
siyi.hu@curtin.edu.au

[3] Systems Research Institute, Polish Academy of Sciences, Warsaw, Poland

Abstract. This work addresses the problem of autonomous resource management in heterogeneous satellite cluster conducting Earth Observation (EO) missions including optical and Synthetic Aperture Radar (SAR) satellites. In autonomous operation mode, satellites are equipped with intelligent capabilities enabling real-time decision-making based on the latest conditions, while requiring minimal interaction with ground operators. Traditional scheduling approaches typically rely on mathematical models to represent satellite mission and resource management. Then, this problem is solved by using optimization algorithms. However, such solutions become less effective when the underlying models are not available, over complex, and inaccurate due to dynamic changes and uncertainties inherent in the space mission environment. A promising alternative is to reformulate the problem as a sequential decision-making process and apply model-free reinforcement learning techniques to enable adaptive and real-time resource management. To this end, we propose a novel transformer-based architecture tailored for heterogeneous satellite cluster autonomous EO Mission with relational observations-actions tokenization and differential attention mechanism. Our experimental results demonstrate significant performance improvements compared to the available baselines. Moreover, the proposed architecture exhibits strong transferability and adaptability with respect to varying numbers of satellite clusters.

Keywords: Autonomous EO Mission · Heterogeneous Cluster · MARL · Heterogeneous MARL · Transformer-based MARL

Supplementary Information The online version contains supplementary material available at https://doi.org/10.1007/978-3-032-37682-4_40.

M. Baratchi et al. (Eds.): ECML PKDD 2026, LNAI 16949, pp. 690–705, 2027.
https://doi.org/10.1007/978-3-032-37682-4_40

1 Introduction

Coordinating and managing multiple Low Earth Orbit (LEO) satellites autonomously remains a challenge due to the dynamic, uncertain, and resource-constrained nature of satellite mission [1–4]. Unlike pre-planned mission operations, autonomous EO missions require each satellite to make real-time decisions under dynamic conditions, and resource limitations, while maintaining coordinated behaviour across the entire constellation [5,6]. These challenges stem from several interacting factors: uncertainty in observation conditions (e.g., variations in target priority and cloud coverage affecting data acquisition quality), limited onboard resources such as power, data storage, attitude control, and the intrinsic non-stationarity of multi-agent settings, where each satellite's actions continuously alter the shared environment and other agents' states [7,8]. Beyond these general coordination difficulties, EO missions increasingly employ heterogeneous satellite clusters by combining different payload types such as Synthetic Aperture Radar (SAR) and optical sensors [9–11]. The SAR sensor can operate under cloud coverage and dark condition, while the optical sensor offers high-resolution imaging under clear condition. This complementary capability substantially improves temporal coverage and observation reliability yet introduces new coordination and control complexity. The general scenario of heterogeneous cluster used in this work is illustrated in Fig. 1.

Traditional optimization techniques, such as mixed-integer linear programming (MILP), have been explored for constellation scheduling and resource allocation [12]. It is effective in static conditions, rely on predefined models and are limited in their ability to adapt to time-varying environmental and operational

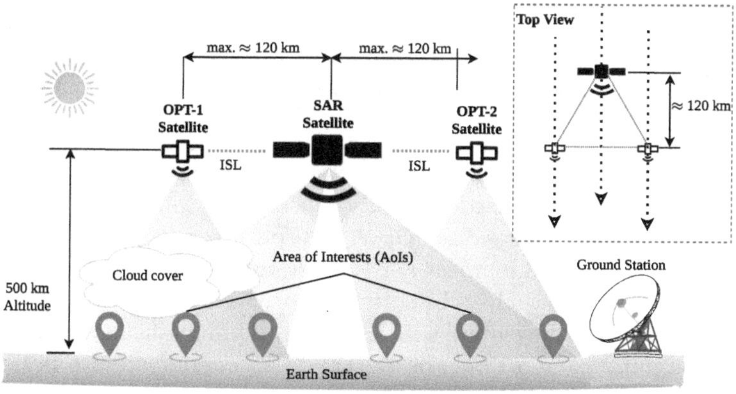

Fig. 1. Illustration of A Heterogeneous Satellite Cluster for EO Mission under different cloud condition. The satellites are deployed in three different narrow orbits forming a cooperative formation. The SAR satellite is used to cover regions with higher cloud coverage that is the burden of the Optical (OPT) satellite. Managing such a mixed constellation thus requires not only efficient resource scheduling but also adaptive policies that account for diverse capabilities.

uncertainties. A model-free Reinforcement Learning (RL) provides a promising alternative by enabling agents to learn adaptive strategies through interaction with the environment, allowing satellites to handle imaging, energy usage, and data management under uncertainty without building its mathematical model [13,14]. However, as EO missions scale from single satellites to cooperative cluster or constellations, the decision-making problem expands from isolated optimization to distributed coordination among multiple agents—a setting more naturally modelled by Multi-Agent Reinforcement Learning (MARL) [15]. The existing MARL applications in satellite operations [16,17] have shown encouraging results but often rely on fully centralized training or continuous communication assumptions, which simplifies real-world settings with limited access to the other agent information during execution. The Centralized Training with Decentralized Execution (CTDE) paradigms [18,19] achieves a practical balance by enabling satellites to learn coordinated policies during centralized training while operating independently at execution time.

Despite these advances, current MARL frameworks largely assume homogeneous agents, where all satellites share identical dynamics and observation–action structures. Recent on-policy methods such as Multi-Agent Proximal Policy Optimization (MAPPO) have demonstrated stable performance across diverse MARL environments [20] is suitable for homogenous agent assumption. This assumption limits applicability to realistic EO missions, where sensor diversity and operational asymmetry fundamentally change the learning problem. Recent progress in heterogeneous-agent MARL, such as Heterogeneous-Agent PPO (HAPPO) [21], introduces separate value estimation and policy update mechanisms to address agent heterogeneity. Although, their performance and adaptability are theoretically grounded, the improvement of the policy architecture remains unexplored. Especially under difficult task, the performance of those method still can be improved.

Therefore, we propose a transformer-based algorithm to handle autonomous and heterogeneous satellite clusters EO mission (HADT). Our contributions are listed as:

- A problem formulation of heterogeneous satellite cluster resources management based-on Decentralized Partially Observable Markov Decision Process (DecPOMDP). We proposed scenarios incorporating three different complexity levels, including randomness and uncertainty aspect.
- A new transformer-based architecture algorithm applied for heterogeneous satellite cluster. We developed a new differential multi-head attention to handle noisy inputs. In addition, the HADT is a general satellite policy model, that is adaptable to the multiple heterogeneous cluster. The code is made publicly available[1], with a demonstration video of our experimental scenario.
- A token-based agent observations which maps the observation entities to the action entities of each satellite.

[1] https://github.com/abdulhady89/HADT.

The rest of this paper is structured as follows: Sect. 2 presents the preliminary of this study from the problem formulation, motivation and review of the current state of the art. Section 3 describes the proposed method employed to solve the problem for heterogeneous satellite cluster scenarios. Section 4 discusses our experimental evaluation and results. Finally, Sect. 5 concludes the paper and discusses future directions.

2 Preliminary

2.1 Autonomous Heterogeneous Multi Satellite Cluster Problem Formulation

In this subsection, a formal model of the Autonomous Heterogeneous Multi Satellite Cluster for Earth Observation (EO) mission problem is formulated. The objective is to capture as many unique high priority target as possible during in orbits. Previous works on single-satellite EO missions have formulated the problem as a sequential decision-making task in the well-known reinforcement learning framework, specifically as a Partially Observable Markov Decision Process (POMDP) [17,22]. Building upon this, we formally define the multi-satellite EO mission as a Decentralized POMDP (Dec-POMDP) model as a tuple: $\mathcal{G} = \langle \mathcal{I}, \mathcal{S}, \mathcal{A}, \mathcal{O}, \mathcal{T}, r, \mathcal{Z}, \gamma \rangle$.

A cluster consists of three satellites (as illustrated in Fig. 1) and each satellite functions as an agent forming a set of agents ($\mathcal{I}$), making a decision at discrete time step (t) based on the current states ($\mathcal{S}$) and agent's local observations ($\mathcal{O}$). The observation is a subset of state which the agent can continuously observe, including battery level, onboard memory storage, reaction wheel speed (angular velocity), target priority, target opportunity window, cloud coverage forecast, ground station visibility windows, eclipse intervals, and simulation time. The simulation defines a finite set of possible actions ($\mathcal{A}$): *1) Charging*, which involves reorienting the satellite toward the sun to maximize solar energy absorption and recharge its battery; *2) Downlinking*, where the satellite transmits the collected EO image data whenever it has access to a ground station; *3) Desaturating*, which ensures that the Reaction Wheels (RWs), the primary actuators for attitude control, operate within safe speed limits. If the RW speed approaches saturation, the satellite must execute a desaturation manoeuver to maintain stable attitude control and prevent uncontrollable drift; *4) Capturing the i-th image target*, where the satellite must orient its optical imaging sensor toward a selected target-i among the available targets on Earth and store it in the on-board memory.

The instantaneous reward r integrates three mission objectives: data acquisition, resource utilization, and safe operation and defined as:

$$r = \begin{cases} q_i - \rho_t + c_i, & \text{if a target is successfully captured,} \\ -\rho_t + \delta_t, & \text{if any data is downlinked,} \\ -100, & \text{if a failure occurs,} \\ -\rho_t, & \text{if only power is consumed,} \\ 0, & \text{otherwise,} \end{cases} \quad (1)$$

where $q_i \in (0, 1)$ represents the priority of the target AoI at time t and promotes selecting targets with greater mission importance.

Resource usage efficiency is encouraged through three supporting terms: **1) Battery power usage** is defined as: $\rho_t = \alpha\, \Delta Q_t\, (1 - Q_t)$, and $\Delta Q_t = Q_{t-1} - Q_t$, where ρ_t penalizes excessive energy consumption (ΔQ_t) times a constant α. **2) Maximizing data downlinking** can be achieved by giving a feedback as: $\delta_t = \beta\, \Delta D_t$ and $\Delta D_t = D_t - D_{t-1}$, which rewards successful transmission of collected data. The amount of the transferred data is calculated as ΔD_t multiply by a scalar constant (β). **3) Ensuring payload correctness** either SAR or Optical (OPT) under different cloud condition:

$$c_i = \begin{cases} -1 + \sigma, & if\ \sigma < 0.5 \text{ and captured by SAR}, \\ \sigma, & if\ \sigma \geq 0.5 \text{ and captured by SAR}, \\ 1 - \sigma, & if\ \sigma < 0.5 \text{ and captured by OPT}, \\ -\sigma, & if\ \sigma \geq 0.5 \text{ and captured by OPT}, \end{cases} \tag{2}$$

where, $\sigma \in (0, 1)$ is the cloud coverage ratio, to guide SAR satellite to use only in cloudy conditions and optical payloads are used in clear conditions.

If the satellite encounters a failure, a fault condition is triggered, represented as:

$$Failure = (b_t < m_b \vee \text{any}(\hat{\Omega} \geq \Omega_{max})), \tag{3}$$

where, m_b is the minimum battery level to trigger a failure. This ensures safe and continuous satellite operation.

Satellite Resources Constraints: A single satellite has two limited resources that are considered as *constraints* in our study: battery level ($b_t \in [B_{min}, B_{max}]$) and data storage capacity ($d_t \in [D_{min}, D_{max}]$) at any time step ($t$). At each time step, the satellite consumes electrical power, denoted as $c_{b,i}$, and stores data, represented as $c_{d,i}$. The battery is rechargeable via a solar panel. To maximize battery charging, the satellite must adjust its attitude toward the sun, which may conflict with its target imaging orientation. Another constraint arises from attitude control, specifically the speed of the Reaction Wheels (RWs), denoted as $\hat{\Omega} \in [-\Omega_{max}, \Omega_{max}]$. These wheels serve as the primary actuators for satellite attitude adjustments along the three axes (x, y, z). To prevent exceeding the maximum speed threshold, the satellite must periodically desaturate the wheels. The limited resource constraints are expressed as:

$$\sum_{t=0}^{\infty} c_{b,t} \leq b_t,\ B_{min} \leq b_t \leq B_{max} \quad \text{and} \quad \sum_{t=0}^{\infty} c_{d,t} \leq d_t,\ D_{min} \leq d_t \leq D_{max}. \tag{4}$$

These constraints are incorporated into the model as *failure* (Eq. 3) triggers in the reward function, resulting in penalties or negative rewards as feedback from the environment. Some other constraints, such as the communication baud rate, have a relevant impact on the system performance. However, in this work, it is assumed as fixed in time as the transmitter specification.

2.2 Advantage of Model-Free Reinforcement Learning Solution

In traditional EO satellite mission planning, optimization problems are commonly formulated as Mixed-Integer Linear Programming (MILP) models when the system dynamics, operational constraints, and objective functions are fully known and accurately characterized [2]. Under such deterministic and well-defined conditions, MILP provides a rigorous mathematical framework capable of generating globally optimal solutions for fixed planning horizons. However, in practical on-orbit autonomous operations, model inaccuracies, environmental uncertainties, and partially observable system states may degrade the effectiveness of model-based optimization. In such cases, model-free Reinforcement Learning (RL) offers a promising alternative, as it does not require explicit knowledge of the system transition model and instead learns decision policies directly through interaction with the environment. However, as RL policy employs a model to approximate the optimal policy, the scheduling solution is not the global optimal point or it is called quasi-optimal solution.

To confirm this hypotheses, we designed a simple model of satellite cluster scheduling as initial study and comparison (detailed mathematical model provided in the Supplemental Document, Sect. 1). The cluster is homogeneous with three optical satellites and simulated under short scheduling period (400 s) with only five ground targets to be captured. The constraints used in this scenario are battery, memory storage, target opportunity windows, ground station opportunity windows, eclipse condition and unique target capturing (no duplication). The resources availability is calculated for each time step (20 s period) and the time windows opportunity information are collected by running a Basilisk simulation, then it is fed as Proximal Policy Optimization (PPO) [23] RL inputs or observation. The policy outputs or action spaces are: charging, downlinking, and i-th target capturing.

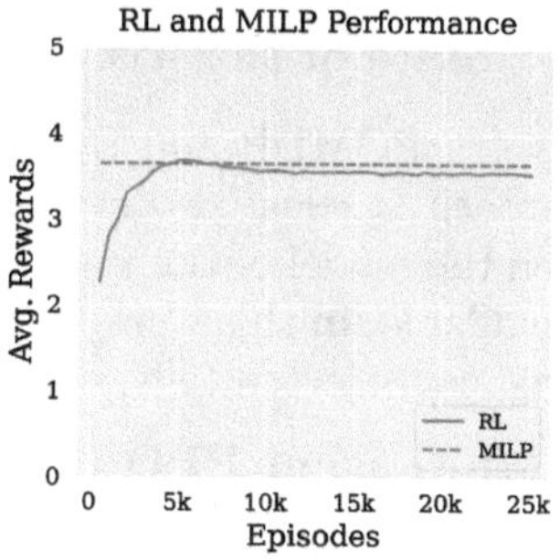

Fig. 2. RL and MILP Performance Comparison. RL can achieve comparable result to MILP under simple case study. Thus, model-free RL with PPO can be a potential solution to autonomous heterogeneous satellite cluster.

From the results as shown in Fig. 2, MILP can solve the problem and achieve the optimal scheduling solution with 3.65 rewards and 100% completion rate (5/5 targets are captured). It also confirms that RL can perform comparable to MILP in a simple EO Mission case after 5000 training episodes. By adapting this preliminary study to more complex mission with stochastic dynamics, RL can be more robust to modelling errors and unforeseen operational variations, making it suitable for autonomous and dynamic EO satellite resource management.

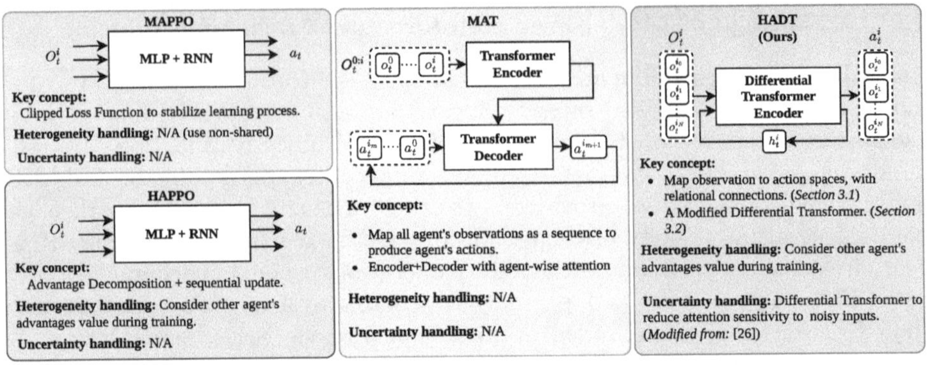

Fig. 3. HADT comparison with the baseline algorithms. Our main focus is to improve the performance under uncertainty, randomness and disturbance conditions with heterogeneous agent learning feature.

2.3 State of the Art of MARL Algorithm

To solve POMDP and Dec-POMDP of Autonomous EO Mission, a model-free approach is selected due to its flexibility to directly learn the policy, especially when the model of the system is complex and the explicit mathematical model is unavailable. In this work, three recent state-of-the-art on-policy MARL methods have been selected to be compared, which motivates us to proposed our methods:

1) Multi-agent PPO (MAPPO): MAPPO is an extension of PPO designed specifically for multi-agent systems [20]. It incorporates centralized critics and decentralized policies to improve performance in MARL tasks. MAPPO uses a single centralized critic shared by all agents, allowing the evaluation of the global state to stabilize learning and mitigate non-stationarity: $V_i^{\text{centralized}}(s) \approx \mathbb{E}\left[\sum_{t=0}^{\infty} \gamma^t r_{i,t} \mid s_0 = s\right]$, where s represents the global state, γ is the discount factor, and r_t is the reward at time step t. The loss function for the policy optimization in MAPPO is given by:
$L^{\text{MAPPO}}(\theta_i) \quad = \quad \mathbb{E}_t\left[\min\left(r_t(\theta_i)\hat{A}_t, \text{clip}(r_t(\theta_i), 1-\epsilon, 1+\epsilon)\hat{A}_t\right)\right]$, where: $r_t(\theta_i) = \frac{\pi_{\theta_i}(a_t|o_t)}{\pi_{\theta_i}^{\text{old}}(a_t|o_t)}$ is the probability ratio, $\hat{A}_t$ is the global advantage function, and ϵ is the clipping parameter.

2) Heterogeneous Agent PPO (HAPPO): This algorithm extends MAPPO by accounting for heterogeneous agents with distinct state-action spaces or roles and the sequential update scheme [21]. It uses individual advantage functions and decentralized policies while maintaining centralized critics. In HAPPO, the centralized value function is agent-specific to handle heterogeneous agents: $V_i^{\text{centralized}}(s) \approx \mathbb{E}\left[\sum_{t=0}^{\infty} \gamma^t r_{i,t} \mid s_0 = s\right]$, where i denotes the agent index and $r_{i,t}$ is the reward specific to agent i. And, the loss function for HAPPO is denoted by:

$$L_i^{\text{HAPPO}}(\theta_i) = \mathbb{E}_t\left[\min\left(r_{i,t}(\theta_i)\hat{A}_{i,t}, \text{clip}(r_{i,t}(\theta_i), 1-\epsilon, 1+\epsilon)\hat{A}_{i,t}\right)\right], \quad (5)$$

where $r_{i,t}(\theta_i) = \frac{\pi_{\theta_i}(a_{i,t}|o_{i,t})}{\pi_{\theta_i}^{\text{old}}(a_{i,t}|o_{i,t})}$ and $\hat{A}_{i,t}$ are the advantage functions of agent i. And it follows the multi agent decomposition lemma and it has sequential update mechanism denoted as: $\hat{A}_{i_{1:m},t}(o_t, a_{i_{1:m},t}) = \sum_{j=1}^{m} \hat{A}_{i_j}\left(o_t, a_{i_{1:j-1},t}, a_{i_j}\right)$.

3) Multi-Agent Transformer (MAT): This algorithm is one of the available novel architecture that reformulates cooperative multi-agent reinforcement learning (MARL) as a sequential sequence-modelling problem by mapping agents' joint observation sequences to optimal action sequences using a Transformer encoder–decoder framework [24]. Central to MAT is the application of the multi-agent advantage decomposition theorem, which decomposes the joint team advantage $A^{\pi}(o, a)$ into a sum of individual agent advantages conditioned on preceding agents' actions, enabling a sequential decision process with only linear complexity in the number of agents: $A^{\pi}(o, a) = \sum_{m=1}^{n} A_{i_m}^{\pi}\left(o,\ a_{i_{1:m-1}},\ a_{i_m}\right)$, where $A_{i_m}^{\pi}(\cdot)$ is the advantage of agent i_m's action given earlier agents' choices. MAT leverages the transformer's self-attention and autoregressive decoding to model inter-agent dependencies, enjoys monotonic performance improvement guarantees, and is trained online on-policy, outperforming strong baselines such as MAPPO and HAPPO across major benchmarks.

Although MAPPO, HAPPO, and MAT can operate effectively in the CTDE paradigm, they do not have strategy to handle randomness and uncertainty of the environment. As compared in Fig. 3, MAPPO was developed for a stable learning process, then improved by HAPPO to incorporates agent-specific advantage value update to better understanding other agent's policy in heterogeneous systems. MAT maps all agent's observation as a sequence to generate agent's action, thus in our study it is categorized as a centralized paradigm. Although, it has the decentralized variant, the complete encoder-decoder architecture is more complex and preferred to be compared with our approach, which relies on only encoder architecture. Our proposed method, HADT, is designed to solve uncertainty and randomness problem occurred under heterogeneous satellite cluster EO mission. It has a unique mapping of the satellite observations to actions entities then equipped with a differential multi-head attention.

3 Proposed Method: Heterogeneous Multi-Agent Differential Transformer (HADT)

3.1 Observation to Token Construction

Inspired by the policy decoupling mechanism in UPDeT [25], a universal policy can be designed by constructing the transformer input token based on the number of agent's observation entities. Thus, in this work, by integrating prior knowledge of the relation between the $i-th$ satellite local observation entities ($O_t = [o_t^1, o_t^2, ..., o_t^i]$) and decision (action) entities ($a_t^i = [a_t^1, a_t^2, ..., a_t^i]$) at time step t, it can construct agent's token information by mapping the observations-actions relations as shown in Fig. 4. In other words, construct the token by decoupling the observation entities into each action entities as described in Sect. 2.1.

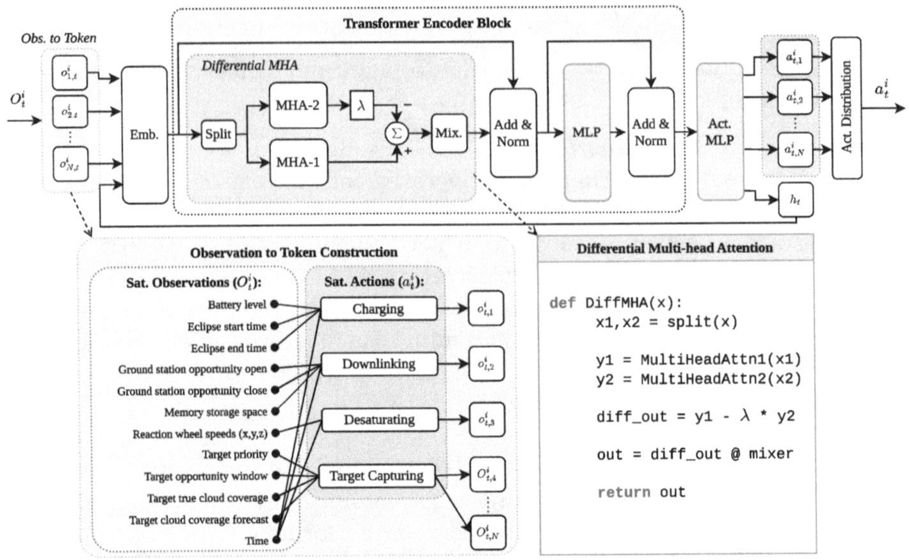

Fig. 4. HADT Policy Model. It has two main components: 1) Observation to Token Construction to map observation entities to the action entities with its relation connections; 2) Differential Multi-head Attention to reduce the sensitivity of self-attention mechanism to randomness or noisy inputs.

Since the dimensionality and semantic structure of these observations may differ across agents, a direct concatenation would be trivial for this case.

To enable structured learning, each local observation token $o^i_{t,N}$ is first projected into a shared latent space via an embedding layer $e^i_t = \text{Emb}(o^i_{t,N})$, where $\text{Emb}(\cdot)$ denotes a learnable linear or non-linear projection. The embedding layer normalizes heterogeneous feature scales and produces fixed-dimensional token representations. Consequently, the global observation is transformed into a token set: $E_t = \{e^1_t, e^2_t, \ldots, e^N_t\}$, where each token semantically represents observation-action relations. In the output side, the architecture incorporates action tokens corresponding to discrete operational modes such as charging, downlinking, target capturing, and desaturating. These action tokens allow the model to associate relational context with candidate actions and facilitate structured policy learning. The combined token representations are then processed by a Transformer encoder block composed of Differential Multi-head Attention with residual connections, layer normalization, and Multi Layer Perceptron (MLP) networks, enabling implicit inter-observations-actions and relational reasoning for each of the heterogeneous cluster satellite.

3.2 Differential Multi-head Attention

To explicitly model cooperative interactions within the heterogeneous satellite cluster under uncertainty, we propose a Differential Multi-Head Attention (Diff-

MHA) mechanism, inspired by [26]. The previous differential transformer architecture implements differential attention (Diff-Attn), where it has dual Q_1, Q_2 and K_1, K_2 parameters with multiple λ parameters. Meanwhile, our new Diff-MHA leverage a single learnable λ parameter and introduce a new mixing parameters to achieve simpler strategy yet maintain its capability. Our proposed mechanism introduces a differential MHA operations to capture contrastive dependencies among two distinct MHA that may contain noisy informations, which can degrade the overall agent's performance.

Given the input token matrix $X \in \mathbb{R}^{N \times d}$, where d is the embedding dimension, the tokens are first partitioned into two sub-representations with $X_{1,2} \in \mathbb{R}^{N \times d/2}$ and each branch is then processed by an independent Multi-head Attention (MHA) module:

$$X_1, X_2 = \text{split}(X), \quad Y_1 = \text{MHA}_1(X_1), \quad Y_2 = \text{MHA}_2(X_2). \tag{6}$$

This dual-attention modules capture the relational between observation's token, thus helps better representation to understand the current situation and decides the best action. For each MHA, we adopt standard MHA [27] with an input token matrix $X_{1,2}$, queries, keys, and values are computed as: $Q = X_{1,2}W_Q, \quad K = X_{1,2}W_K, \quad V = X_{1,2}W_V$, where $W_Q, W_K, W_V \in \mathbb{R}^{d/2 \times d_k}$ are learnable projection matrices and $d_k = \frac{d}{H}$. The scaled dot-product attention is then defined as:

$$\text{Attn}_{1,2}(Q, K, V) = \text{softmax}\left(\frac{QK^\top}{\sqrt{d_k}}\right)V. \tag{7}$$

In multi-head attention, H parallel attention heads are computed and concatenated to form the outputs:

$$Y_{1,2} = \text{MHA}_{1,2}(X) = \text{Concat}_{1,2}(\text{Attn}_{1,2}(Q, K, V)_h)_{h=1:H}W_O, \tag{8}$$

where W_O is a learnable output projection matrix. Then, a differential operation is subsequently applied into both MHA's outpus:

$$Y_{\text{diff}} = Y_1 - \lambda \, . \, Y_2, \quad Y_{\text{out}} = Y_{\text{diff}} \cdot W_{\text{mix}}, \tag{9}$$

where λ is a learnable scaling parameter controlling the influence of differential MHA. This subtraction mechanism allows the network to enhance beneficial relational signals while attenuating noisy information, thereby explicitly reduces noisy information effect. Then, the differential representation is then projected using a Mixing (Mix.) with W_{mix} parameters, where $W_{\text{mix}} \in \mathbb{R}^{d/2 \times d}$ is additional learnable projection matrix to match with the output space dimension. The output is integrated within a Transformer encoder block using residual connections and layer normalization to ensure stable training. Finally, the encoded representations are passed through an Act. (action) MLP head to produce the policy distribution $\pi(a_t \mid O_t)$, from which the action a_t is sampled or selected.

The proposed Differential Multi-Head Attention mechanism enables the HADT architecture to effectively capture structured inter observations-actions

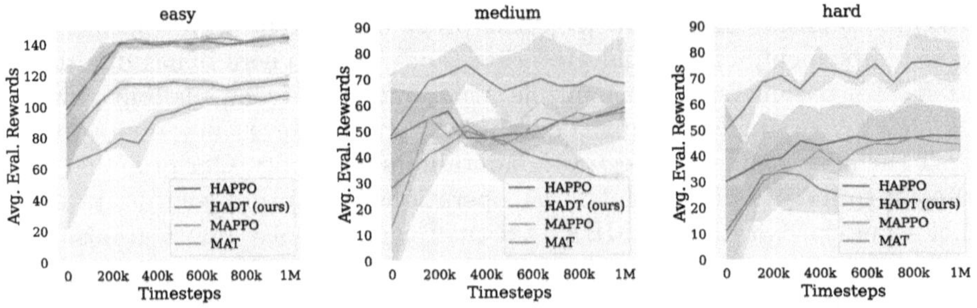

Fig. 5. Average evaluation rewards comparison across different scenarios.

dependencies, particularly it produces a suitable policy architecture for heterogeneous satellite cluster-based decision making under dynamic and constrained EO missions. This architecture eventually used as an actor encoder to approximate the policy function π with parameters ϕ (π_ϕ), where it has to be optimized following the HAPPO policy update in Eq. 5.

4 Experimental Results

4.1 Scenario Description

Our algorithm is tested under BSK-RL [14] and Basilisk simulator which contain numerous simulation parameters. Due to the page limit, some of the parameters which are adjusted to match with our scenarios (e.g. orbital parameters and satellite specifications), are listed in the Supplemental Doc., Sect. 2. Total targets to be captured are 160 targets and the location randomized within 11 different regions. We defined three different scenarios to evaluate our proposed algorithm performance incrementally from the ideal to near-realistic simulations:

Easy: This scenario is designed to study the ideal satellite parameters assumption and all of resources initial conditions are set to be fully available for executing an EO mission. The battery level is fully charged (100%), memory storage is empty (0%), there is no randomness at the attitude disturbance and reaction wheel speed initialization). It simulates the mission with less challenge of the cluster resources availability.

Medium: The *medium* scenario is designed to simulate the cluster under conditions of restricted resources condition. The downlink transmission speed (baudrate) is assumed to degrade up to 30% from its default value as in *easy* case. Additionally, the battery level is directly initialized as 85% and the memory storage is initialized as 90%. This scenario introduces more difficulties especially to balance the memory storage utilization, if too many data collected the memory will be full and can not be properly downlinked due to the issue of the transmission speed.

Hard: This scenario is our main focus in this work to have a near-realistic simulation. It integrates the *medium* scenario with additional randomness factors,

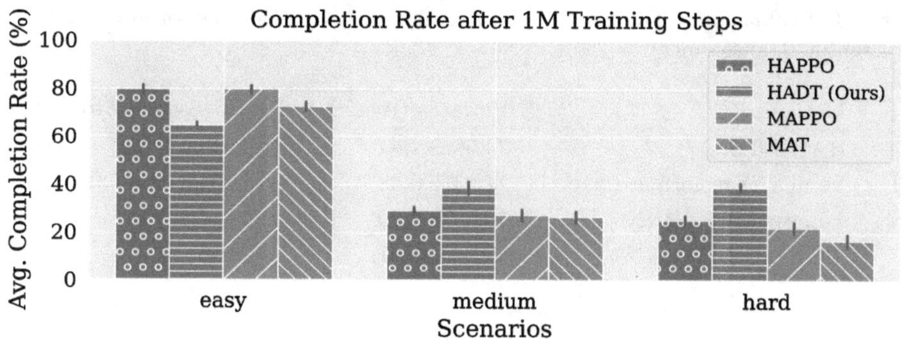

Fig. 6. Average evaluation Completion Rate (CR) in different scenarios.

including randomization of the initialization of battery, memory storage, disturbance and reaction wheels speed. This adds more challenge to the cluster to perform the EO mission and evaluate the generalization performance of the policy across different resources initial condition. It reflects more realistic case of the real satellite cluster EO mission, where the resources initial condition may vary depends on the states of its previous mission. The battery level is initialized randomly between 80–85%, the memory storage is 90–100%, disturbance is randomized with normal distribution with the scale is 10^{-4}, and the reaction wheels are uniformly randomized between -3000 to 3000 RPM. Therefore, this scenario demonstrates more realistic challenge of the resource availability as well as its uncertainty and randomness nature at the same time.

4.2 Performance Evaluation

The policies of different MARL algorithms are trained under the same machine with Intel(R) Core(TM) i9-14900K CPU, 32 GB RAM, and 24 GB GPU NVIDIA GeForce RTX 4090 in this work. The algorithm hyper-parameters are listed in Supplemental Document Sect. 3. The training is terminated at one million training time steps with 20 parallel-processing environments (rollouts). Each rollouts has its own seed with 3 different model seeds, generating 60 unique seed combinations in our training scheme. This settings achieve at least 5000 randomized target distributions and then evaluate the performance under 500 unseen target distributions with 5 episodes and 10 rollouts each to ensure the policy's generalization performance across different target locations, priorities and cloud conditions.

The averaged total rewards metric is shown in Fig. 5 and the Completion Rate (CR) is presented Fig. 6. Based on those two metrics, our proposed algorithm is not suitable for *easy* scenario. MAPPO and HAPPO with MLP+RNN based architecture achieve better performance in this scenario. However, this scenario is ideal case, where the resources constraints are neglected. Under more realistic scenarios, HADT outperforms the baselines under *medium* and *hard* scenarios.

Table 1. Evaluation of Different Model Architecture (CR: Completion Rate (%); DT: Differential Transformer)

Methods	Rewards (Avg. ± Std.)	CR (Avg. ± Std.)
HADT (ours)	74.58 ± 4.81	39.48 ± 2.29
Vanilla Transformer (w/o DT)	71.64 ± 6.48	37.94 ± 4.11
1-Layer MLP+RNN	50.39 ± 3.30	30.17 ± 1.74
2-Layer MLP+RNN	47.92 ± 2.41	28.98 ± 1.4

This can be achieved by its differential multi-head attention mechanism enabling more robust performance under uncertain observation with randomness. MAT is better than HADT in *easy* scenarios, however, it does not have uncertainty handling mechanism in the transformer architecture, thus it can not perform well under *hard* scenarios. Detailed numerical values of this experiments are presented in of Supplemental Document Sect. 4 (Table 4).

4.3 The Impact of HADT

To evaluate the significance impact of HADT, an ablation study has been performed under *hard* scenario and the results are shown in Table 1. The results clearly demonstrate the effectiveness of HADT compared with its fundamental components and architectures. HADT achieves the highest average reward (74.58 ± 4.81) and Completion Rate (CR) (39.48 ± 2.29). If the differential transformer (DT) feature is deactivated it becomes the vanilla transformer variant, which attains 71.64 ± 6.48 in reward and 37.94 ± 4.11 in CR. This performance gap highlights the contribution of the differential transformer mechanism in enhancing representation learning and stabilizing coordination among heterogeneous agents. Furthermore, the margin becomes substantially larger when compared to conventional neural architectures: 1-Layer and 2-Layer MLP+RNN models with 256 nodes, whose rewards drop to 50.39 and 47.92, respectively, with significantly lower completion rates while increasing the number of layers. This result confirms the impact of transformer-based architecture compared with MLP+RNN. The reduced variance observed in HADT also indicates more stable learning dynamics. Overall, these results validate that the proposed algorithm enables more effective decision-making under uncertainties and dynamics, leading to superior task completion performance in complex multi-agent environments.

4.4 Transferability and Adaptability

The last experiment is the extension from single to two clusters. In this study, we evaluate the HADT transferability and adaptability to the new cluster configurations under *hard* scenario. We add a new cluster separated in 45°C different orbital offset. Then, the policy is duplicated for the new cluster and then trained with 1 million time steps to adapt the policy performance to the new task. In

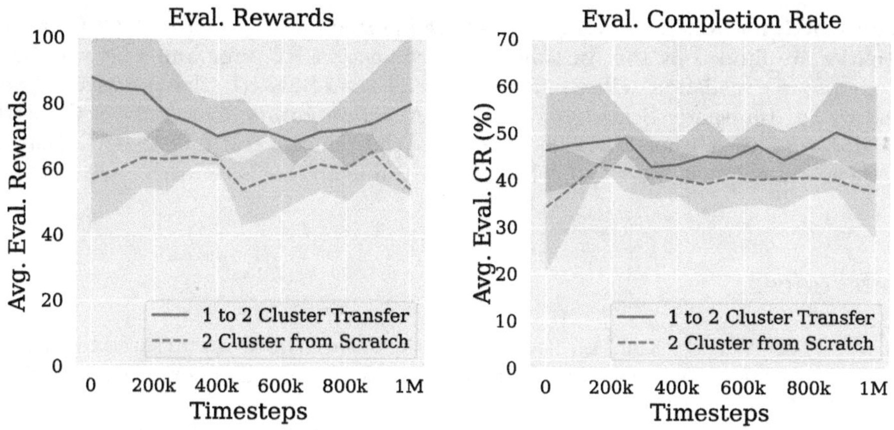

Fig. 7. HADT Policy Transfer from 1 to 2 Cluster.

other words, the pre-trained HADT policy for single cluster is transferred and adapted to the new two cluster task. The results are shown in Fig. 7. Compared with training of *2 Cluster from Scratch*, the *1 to 2 Cluster Transfer* where the HADT policy is duplicated for the new cluster, it can achieve better performance around 20 points rewards gap. This confirms the transferability and adaptability performance of our HADT algorithm. Also, by using two different cluster it can improve the completion rate (CR) around 10%.

5 Conclusion

Transformer-based architecture has a promising future to solve problems in realistic multi-agent reinforcement learning problem. From our study, we have evaluated a new differential multi-head attention can improve the vanilla transformer to help agent learn under dynamic and uncertain condition with randomness. Moreover, the observation tokenization is a key strategy to guide transformer model by constructing the relation between observations and actions spaces. Therefore, the HADT algorithm outperforms MAPPO, HAPPO, and MAT under *medium* and *hard* scenarios where it is designed to mimic near-realistic conditions in EO mission. The HADT also is a potential candidate to be used for transfer learning or fine-tuning to different cluster numbers. However, if it is considered to be implemented as onboard autonomy algorithm in the future, the model contains numerous parameters that may insufficient due to the limited computational power. One of our future research can be the integration of parameter efficient fine-tuning, where it is currently one of developing research topic especially for large model in large language modelling or image processing field and it can be adopted to online multi-agent reinforcement learning research area.

Acknowledgments. This work has been supported by the SmartSat CRC, whose activities are funded by the Australian Government's CRC Program. This work uses an open-source realistic satellite simulator (Basilisk and BSK-RL) that is actively developed by Dr. Hanspeter Schaub and team at AVS Laboratory, University of Colorado Boulder. Also, the authors would like to express their sincere gratitude to BAE Systems for their invaluable support and collaboration throughout this research.

References

1. Wang, X., Wu, G., Xing, L., Pedrycz, W.: Agile earth observation satellite scheduling over 20 years: formulations, methods, and future directions. IEEE Syst. J. **15**(3), 3881–3892 (2020)
2. Chen, X., Reinelt, G., Dai, G., Spitz, A.: A mixed integer linear programming model for multi-satellite scheduling. Eur. J. Oper. Res. **275**(2), 694–707 (2019)
3. Stephenson, M., Schaub, H.: Optimal target sequencing in the agile earth-observing satellite scheduling problem using learned dynamics. In: The AAS/AIAA Astrodynamics Specialist Conference, Big Sky, MT, USA, pp. 13–17 (2023)
4. Pan, Y., Wang, P., Hui, X., Li, J.: Dense points aggregation for efficient and collaborative earth-imaging task planning. In: Proceedings of the 2022 5th ACAI, ACAI 2022. Association for Computing Machinery, New York, NY, USA (2023)
5. Li, P., Wang, H., Zhang, Y., Pan, R.: Mission planning for distributed multiple agile earth observing satellites by attention-based deep reinforcement learning method. Adv. Space Res. (2024)
6. Yang, X., Hu, M., Huang, G.: Objective task matching strategy for multi-satellite imaging mission planning in complex heterogeneous scenarios. In: MICML 2023, New York, NY, USA, pp. 96–101. ACM (2024)
7. Araguz, C., Bou-Balust, E., Alarcón, E.: Applying autonomy to distributed satellite systems: trends, challenges, and future prospects. Syst. Eng. **21**(5), 401–416 (2018)
8. Yao, F., Li, J., Chen, Y., Chu, X., Zhao, B.: Task allocation strategies for cooperative task planning of multi-autonomous satellite constellation. Adv. Space Res. **63**(2), 1073–1084 (2019)
9. Cohen, M., Larkins, A., Semedo, P.L., Burbidge, G.: Novasar-s low cost spaceborne SAR payload design, development and deployment of a new benchmark in spaceborne radar. In: 2017 IEEE Radar Conference (RadarConf), pp. 0903–0907. IEEE (2017)
10. Dong, J., Feng, J., Tang, X.: Optisar-net: a cross-domain ship detection method for multi-source remote sensing data. IEEE Trans. Geosci. Remote Sens. (2024)
11. Alzubairi, A., Tameem, A., Kada, B.: Spacecraft formation flying orbital control for earth observation mission. Sci. Afr. **26**, e02391 (2024)
12. Kim, S.J., Kim, M., Kim, C.-H., Choi, H.: Optimal surveillance scheduling for multiple sar-eo satellite train constellation. In: AIAA Aviation Forum and Ascend 2024, p. 4851 (2024)
13. Herrmann, A., Stephenson, M.A., Schaub, H.: Single-agent reinforcement learning for scalable earth-observing satellite constellation operations. J. Spacecr. Rocket. **61**(1), 114–132 (2024)
14. Stephenson, M.A., Schaub, H.: Bsk-rl: modular, high-fidelity reinforcement learning environments for spacecraft tasking. In: 75th International Astronautical Congress, Milan, Italy, IAF (2024)

15. Tang, C., Chen, Y., Chen, G., Du, L., Liu, H.: A dynamic and collaborative spectrum sharing strategy based on multi-agent DRL in satellite-terrestrial converged networks. IEEE Trans. Veh. Technol. (2024)
16. Herrmann, A., Stephenson, M., Schaub, H.: Reinforcement learning for multi-satellite agile earth observing scheduling under various communication assumptions. In: AAS Rocky Mountain GN&C Conference (2023)
17. Stephenson, M., Schaub, H.: Reinforcement learning for earth-observing satellite autonomy with event-based task intervals. In: AAS Rocky Mountain GN&C Conference, Breckenridge, CO (2024)
18. Ning, Z., Xie, L.: A survey on multi-agent reinforcement learning and its application. J. Autom. Intell. (2024)
19. Hady, M.A., Hu, S., Pratama, M., Cao, Z., Kowalczyk, R.: Multi-agent reinforcement learning for resources allocation optimization: a survey. Artif. Intell. Rev. **58**(11), 354 (2025)
20. Yu, C., et al.: The surprising effectiveness of PPO in cooperative multi-agent games. Adv. Neur-IPS **35**, 24611–24624 (2022)
21. Zhong, Y., Kuba, J.G., Feng, X., Hu, S., Ji, J., Yang, Y.: Heterogeneous-agent reinforcement learning. JMLR **25**, 1–67 (2024)
22. Stephenson, M., Mantovani, L., Phillips, S., Schaub, H.: Using enhanced simulation environments to accelerate reinforcement learning for long-duration satellite autonomy. In: AIAA SCITECH 2024 Forum, p. 0990 (2024)
23. Schulman, J., et al.: Proximal policy optimization algorithms. arXiv preprint arXiv:1707.06347 (2017)
24. Wen, M., et al.: Multi-agent reinforcement learning is a sequence modeling problem. Adv. Neural. Inf. Process. Syst. **35**, 16509–16521 (2022)
25. Hu, S., Zhu, F., Chang, X., Liang, X.: Updet: universal multi-agent reinforcement learning via policy decoupling with transformers. arXiv preprint arXiv:2101.08001 (2021)
26. Ye, T., et al.: Differential transformer. arXiv preprint arXiv:2410.05258 (2024)
27. Vaswani, A., et al.: Attention is all you need. In: Advances in Neural Information Processing Systems, vol. 30 (2017)

Author Index

A

Abboud, Dany 198
Adaloglou, Lazaros 268
Apiletti, Daniele 446
Artelt, André 215
Ashraf, Inaam 215
Avramis, Nikos 268

B

Bader, Lukas 164
Bai, Shumeng 109
Bailey, James 232
Basta, Nardine 395
Baturova, Dari 429
Beccari, Edoardo 3
Beckers, Camiel 268
Bertin, Emmanuel 289
Björkqvist, Sebastian 533
Bonsergent-Brachet, Martin 198
Booth, John 250
Bruches, Elena 429

C

Cai, Xiaoling 412
Cao, Hongliu 496
Cao, Lian 636
Cao, Zehong 690
Carpentier, Robin 395
Cerquitelli, Tania 446
Chaari, Lotfi 654
Chan, Sum Yee 306
Chen, Bo 412
Chen, Fei 56
Chen, Shun 378
Chen, Xiaosong 147
Chernov, Ivan 429
Choudhary, Shailee 463
Chu, Chen 56
Corpetti, Thomas 619
Corso, Francesco 550
Cousin, Théodore 582
Craioveanu, Gheorghe Marian 181

D

de la Brosse, Augustin 619
De Luca, Giovanna 446
De Luca, Marco 446
Derunets, Roman 429
Dhami, Devendra Singh 268
Dieckmann, Ulf 479
Doquet, Guillaume 129
Driouich, Ilias 496
Du, Yiran 515
Duan, Changxu 91

E

El Hankouri, Mounir 324
El Sakka, Mohammad 654
Englberger, Markus 268
Eze, Alex 250

F

Fan, Jingjing 565
Färber, Michael 463
Fierens, Amaury 582
Fomin, Arsenii 429
Frey, Sebastian 3

G

Garreau, Damien 619
Ghosh, Niladri 463
Göhring, Andrea 672
Gopan, Nandu 324
Gorrino, Alice 446
Grzelik, Aleksandra 479
Guo, Chengjie 109, 378

H

Habault, Guillaume 636
Hady, Mohamad A. 690
Haji Soleimani, Behrouz 38
Hammer, Barbara 215
Han, Qiwei 3
Hatin, Julien 289
Houet, Thomas 619

M. Baratchi et al. (Eds.): ECML PKDD 2026, LNAI 16949, pp. 707–709, 2027.
https://doi.org/10.1007/978-3-032-37682-4

Hu, Siyi 690
Huang, Chuqiao 73
Huang, Qiang 73
Huang, Yanyong 378
Huang, Yihong 56
Huang, Zhichao 109

J
Jain, Charvi 324
James, Nick 250
Jayawardena, Lasal 600
Jodogne, Sébastien 582
Joshi, Advait 463
Jurie, Frédéric 289

K
Kaafar, Dali 395
Kaiser, Maximilian 3
Karaman, Ali Mete 3
Kawatra, Jaskaran 250
Kazempour, Daniyal 672
Key, Daniel 250
Kostin, Andrey 429
Kowalczyk, Ryszard 690
Kranz, Maximilian 3
Kröger, Peer 672

L
Lam, Tak-Wah 306
Lau, Wing Cheong 147
Lechervy, Alexis 289
Legaspi, Roberto 636
Lehmann, Jens 324
Leins, David P. 215
Leyli-Abadi, Milad 129
Li, Chunyang 109
Li, Pengcheng 73
Li, Ruiduan 56
Li, Tianrui 378
Li, Weisheng 73
Li, Xiangyang 412
Li, Zhihao 56
Lin, Jianghao 412
Lin, Yu 56
Liu, Jiayao 360
Liu, Kai 289
Liu, Yang 147
Liu, Yanxiao 565
Liu, Yuansan 232
Lucca, Alessandro 550
Luo, Chuanjiang 19, 73
Luo, Xuan 515

M
Ma, Xindi 515
Masum, Muhammad Anwar 690
Mattarella-Micke, Andrew 360
Matwin, Stan 38
Mihaita, Adriana-Simona 342
Mo, Zizhao 147
Mohanty, Sweety 672
Monaco, Simone 446
Mothe, Josiane 654

N
Naderi, Habibeh 38
Ngo, Trung Hieu 289
Nicol, Darren 600
Niu, Hao 636
Nkisi-Orji, Ikechukwu 600

O
Opara, Karol 479

P
Pan, Zheyi 109
Parekh, Swapnil 360
Patara, Lavinia 672
Patel, Shiren 250
Pellizzari, Nicolò Alberto 3
Peng, Zhengchao 73
Persadh, Jahnavi 479
Pierri, Francesco 550
Pope, Rebecca 250
Porschitz, Pauline 324
Pratama, Mahardhika 690

Q
Quan, Shigang 412

R
Rajamani, Sanjana 250
Rajendran, Pavithra 250
Rath, Willi 672
Razakarivony, Sébastien 129
Read, Jesse 129, 198
Roucoux, François 582

S
Sabu, Sebin 250
Sathyavageeswaran, Ramakrishnan 360
Sbalzarini, Ivo F. 324
Scharler, Ursula 479
Sebire, Neil 250
Shan, Rong 412
Sharma, Sonia 360
Sheldon, Ewart Jonathan 250
Singh, Punit Kumar 463
Song, Haoqian 515
Sor, Kai 342
Stamatescu, Grigore 181
Sun, Xu 289

T
Tan, Wenting 306
Tang, Ruiming 412
Taya, Masato 636
Tcaciuc, Claudiu 446
Terwey-Scheulen, Ina 164
Thakur, Aniket 479
Thil, Lucas 129
Thomas, Eoin 496
Tordesillas, Antoinette 232
Trantas, Thanasis 268

U
Ung, Huy Quang 636

V
Vahdati, Sahar 324
Voladoddi, Pooja 360

W
Wang, Dongjing 19
Wang, Shijia 19
Wiratunga, Nirmalie 600

X
Xi, Yunjia 412
Xiao, Liwen 19
Xiao, Qiang 19, 73
Xie, Zhongqian 73
Xu, Huanle 147

Y
Yang, Haiqin 463
Yang, Qimeng 19
Yi, Xiuwen 109, 378
Yim, Tik Yu 306
Yin, Haoran 515
Yiu, Siu Ming 306

Z
Zeng, Ziyang 289
Zenonos, Alexandros 250
Zenovkin, Nikolai 533
Zhang, Junbo 109
Zhang, Weinan 412
Zhang, Yunan 565
Zhao, Benjamin 395
Zhao, Fuwen 515
Zheng, Yu 109, 378
Zhu, Chenxu 412
Zhu, Hong 412
Zühlke, Dietlind 164
Zuo, Chaoyuan 515
Zuo, Lu 289

FSC
www.fsc.org
MIX
Papier | Fördert gute Waldnutzung
FSC® C083411

Kolibri 360 GmbH
Ferdinand-Jühlke-Straße 7
99095 Erfurt, Deutschland
produktsicherheit@kolibri360.de